Mexican Americans

A Research Bibliography

Frank Pino

University of Texas, San Antonio

Volume 2

Latin American Studies Center
Michigan State University

1974

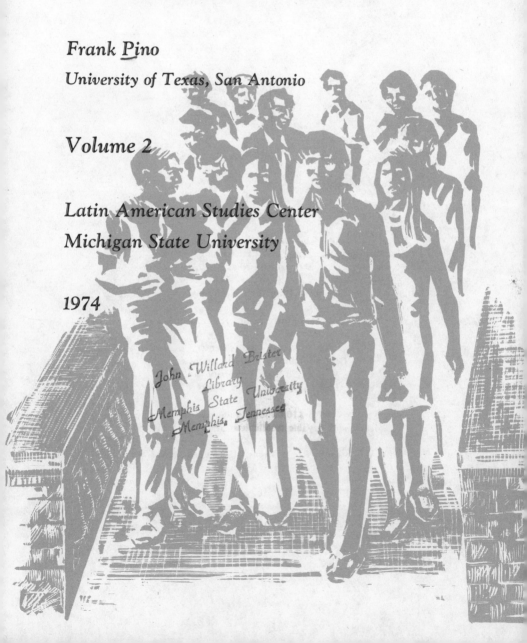

Library of Congress Catalog Card Number: 74-620088

©1974 by the Board of Trustees
Michigan State University, East Lansing, Michigan
All rights reserved

Printed in the United States of America

This publication may be ordered from the

Latin American Studies Center
Center for International Programs
Michigan State University
East Lansing, Michigan, 48824

Price   olumes
Make check paya   n State University

Cover design by Robert Brent, MSU Design Service

T A B L E   O F   C O N T E N T S

TEXAS

(HT)

ABERNETHY, FRANCIS E. J. FRANK DOBIE. AUSTIN, TEXAS:
STECK-VAUGHN COMPANY, 1967 (LI).

ACHESON, SAM AND OH CONNELL, JULIE, A.H. GEORGE WASHINTON
DIAMOND'S ACCOUNT OF THE GREAT HANGING AT GAINESVILLE,
1862. AUSTIN, TEXAS: TEXAS STATE HISTORICAL
ASSOCIAION, 1963 (TJ).

ACHESON, SAM H. 30,000 DAYS IN TEXAS. NEW YORK:
MACMILLAN, 1938 (LI).

ACHESON, SAM H., <ET AL.,EDS>. TEXIAN WHO'S WHO. DALLAS:
TEXIAN CO, 1937 (LI).

ADAIR. HEROES ALAMO: ACCOUNTS DOCUMENTS (TJ*).

ALLEN, WINNIE. THE HISTORY OF NACOGDOCHES, 1691-1830.
THE UNIVERSITY OF TEXAS, MASTER'S THESIS (1925).

ALMARAZ, FELIX, D. JR. THE HISTORICAL HERITAGE OF
THE MEXICAN AMERICAN IN 19TH CENTURY TEXAS,
AN INTERPRETATION. EDINBURG: INTER-AMERICAN
INSTITUTE OF PAN AMERICAN COLLOGE, (1969). CONFERENCE
ON THE ROLE OF THE MEXICAN AMERICAN IN THE HISTORY
OF THE SOUTHWEST (HSW).

ALMARAZ, FELIX, D. JR. "A TRIBUTE TO THE MEMORY OF A TEXAS
HISTORIAN--JOSEPH WILLIAM SCHMITZ, S.M., 1905-1966".
TEXANA, VOL. 4 NO. 2 (SUMMER 1966) (HSW).

ALMARAZ. "CARLOS EDUARDO CASTANEDA, MEXICAN-AMERICAN
(HSW*).

ALMARAZ, FELIX, D. JR. "GOVERNOR MANUEL DE SALCEDO
OF HISPANIC TEXAS, 1808-1813: A REAPPRAISAL".
TEXANA, VOL. 6 NO. 1 (SPRING 1968).

ALMARAZ, FELIX, D. JR. HISTORICAL ORIGIN OF THE MEXICAN-AMERICAN
IN TEXAS: AN INTERPRETATION. OFFICE OF BILINGUAL
AND INTERNATIONAL EDUCATION, TEXAS EDUCATION AGENCY,
JULY 15-19, 1968.

ALMARAZ, FELIX, D. JR. THE HISTORICAL HERITAGE OF
     THE MEXICAN AMERICAN IN 19TH CENTURY TEXAS, AN
     INTERPRETATION. EDINBURG: INTER-AMERICAN INSTITUTE
     OF PAN AMERICAN COLLEGE, (1969). CONFERENCE ON THE
     ROLE OF THE MEXICAN AMERICAN IN THE HISTORY OF THE
     SOUTHWONDEST.

ALMARAZ, FELIX, D. JR. A TRAGIC CAVALIER: GOVERNOR MANUEL
     SALCEDO OF TEXAS, 1808-1813. AUSTIN: UNIVERSITY OF
     TEXAS PRESS, 1970 (HSW).

AMERICAN GUIDE SERIES. TEXAS. NEW YORK: HASTINGS HOUSE,
     1940 (HSW).

AMERICAN PUBLIC WELFARE ASSOCIATICN. PUBLIC WELFARE
     SURVEY SAN ANTONIO (SO*).

ANDERSON, JOHN Q. JOHN C. DUVAL: FIRST TEXAS MAN
     OF LETTERS. AUSTIN, TEXAS:STECK-VAUGHN, 1967.

SIX FLAGS OF TEXAS. WACO, TEXAS: TEXIAN PRESS,.

TESIS ECONOMICA SOCIAL SOBREESTADO (EC*).

TEXAS, GUIDE TC LONE STAR STATE (HSW*).

RANGERS OF TEXAS. WACO, TEXAS: TEXIAN PRESS,.

"TIMELESS WAYS OF THE EARLIEST TEXANS". LIFE, VOL. 46
     (APRIL 20, 1959), PP. 84-85.

BASIC INDUSTRIES TEXAS NORTHERN (EC*).

CAPITCLS OF TEXAS. WACO, TEXAS: TEXIAN PRESS,.

HEROES OF TEXAS. WACO, TEXAS: TEXIAN PRESS,.

"MISSION CONCEPCION" (HS*).

A VISIT TO TEXAS: BEING THE JOURNAL OF A TRAVELLER. ANN
     ARBOR: UNIVERSITY MICROFILMS, 1966 (TJ).

A VISIT TO TEXAS. AUSTIN, TEXAS: STECK-VAUGHN COMPANY,
     1971 (TJ).

ARNESON, EDWARD P. "EARLY IRRIGATION IN TEXAS".
     SOUTHWESTERN HISTORICAL QUARTERLY, VOL. 25 NO.
     2 (1921), PP. 121-130 (EC).

ASHFORD. SPANISH TEXAS: YESTERDAY TODAY (HS*).

ASHFORD, GERALD. SPANISH TEXAS: YESTERDAY AND TODAY.
     AUSTIN: PEMBERTON PRESS, 1971.

ASKINS, CHARLES. TEXANS, GUNS AND HISTORY. TOTOWA, NEW
     JERSEY: WINCHESTER PRESS, 1970 (HSW HUS).

ATKINSON, MARY JOURDAN. THE TEXAS INDIANS. SAN ANTONIO:
     NAYLOR PRINTING CO., 1935 (SO).

AUDOBON. AUDUBONS AMERICA, NARRATIVES (TJ*).

AUSTIN, MATTIE ALICE. "THE MUNICIPAL GOVERNMENT OF SAN
     FERNANDO DE BEXAR, 1730-1800". QUARTERLY OF
     THE TEXAS STATE HISTORICAL ASSOCIATION, VOL. 8 NO.
     4 (1905), PP. 227-352 (LW).

AUSTIN, STEPHEN F. THE AUSTIN PAPERS. ??NO INFORMATION??,
     (WASHINGTON: UNITED STATES GOVERNMENT PRINTING
     OFFICE). 1928 (HSW).

BAKER, KARLE WILSON. "NACOGDOCHES". SOUTHWEST REVIEW,
     VOL. 21 NO. 1,2 (1935-1936), PP. 1-14, 137-154.

BANCROFT.   HISTORY NORTH MEXICAN STATESTEXAS (HSW*).

BANCROFT.   HISTORY NORTH MEXICAN STATESTEXAS (HSW*).

BANCROFT.   HISTORY NORTH MEXICAN STATESTEXAS (HSW*).

BANDELIER.   INDIANS RIO GRANDE VALLEY (HSW*).

BARKER.   TEXAS EXPEDITION TO RIO GRANDE   (HSW*).

BARKER, EUGENE C. "LAND SPECULATION AS THE CAUSE OF THE
     TEXAS REVOLUTION". QUARTERLY OF THE TEXAS STATE
     HISTORICAL ASSOCIATION, VOL. 10 (1906), PP. 76-95
     (EC   HM).

BARKER, EUGENE C. LIFE OF STEPHEN F. AUSTIN, FOUNDER OF
     TEXAS, 1793-1836. NASHVILLE: COKESBURY PRESS, 1926
     (PL).

BARKER.   MEXICO TEXAS, 1821-1835 (HM*).

BARKER.   MEXICO TEXAS, 1821-1835 (HM*).

BARKER, EUGENE C. THE AUSTIN PAPERS. (1924). REPRINT,
     NEW YORK: DA CAPO PRESS INC., 1969 (PL).

BARKER, EUGENE C. 'THE AUSTIN PAPERS.' IN EUGENE
     C. BARKER (ED), ANNUAL REPORT OF THE AMERICAN
     HISTORICAL ASSOCIATION, 1919 (PL).

BARKER, EUGENE C. THE LIFE OF STEPHEN F. AUSTIN, FOUNDER
     OF TEXAS, 1793-1836. A CHAPTER IN THE WESTWARD
     MOVEMENT OF THE ANGLO-AMERICAN PEOPLE. AUSTIN,
     TEXAS: TEXAS STATE HISTORICAL ASSOCIATION, 1949.

BARKER.   WRITINGS SAM HOUSTON, 1813-1863 (HM*).

BARRETT, THOMAS. THE GREAT HANGING AT GAINESVILLE.
     AUSTIN, TEXAS: TEXAS STATE HISTORICAL ASSOCIATION,
     1961.

BARTON, JOHN VINSON. EL PASO IN 1890. TEXAS WESTERN
     COLLEGE, MASTER'S THESIS (AUGUST 1963).

BECICHECK.   ADVENTURES WITH TEXAS NATURALIST   (AN*).

BELL.   TEXAS CONVENTION 1832 (HM*).

BELL.   NARRATIVE CAPTURE SUBSEQUENTSUFFERINGS (HM*).

BENAVIDES, ILMA MARIANA. GENERAL ADRIAN WOLL'S INVASION
     OF SAN ANTONIO IN 1842.   UNIVERSITY OF TEXAS
     AT AUSTIN, MASTER'S THESIS (1952).

BENDER, A. B. "OPENING ROUTES ACROSS WEST TEXAS, 1848-1850".
     SOUTHWESTERN HISTORICAL QUARTERLY, VOL. 36 (OCTOBER
     1933), PP. 116-135 (HSW).

BENDER, A. B. THE MARCH OF EMPIRE. LAWRENCE: UNIVERSITY
     OF KANSAS PRESS, 1952 (HSW).

BERGER.   "EDUCATION TEXAS DURING SPANISH (ED*).

BERLANDIER, JEAN LUIS. THE INDIANS CF TEXAS IN 1830.
     WASHINGTON, D. C.: SMITHSONIAN INSTITUTION PRESS, 1969.

BIERSCHWALE, MARGARET. FORT MCKAVETT, TEXAS.   SALADO,
     TEXAS: ANSON JONES PRESS,.

BINION, CHARLES H. EL PASO SCENIC AND HISTORIC LANDMARKS.
     EL PASO, TEXAS: TEXAS WESTERN PRESS, 1970.

BINKLEY, WILLIAM C. THE EXPANSIONIST MOVEMENT IN TEXAS,
     1836-1850.   BERKELEY: UNIVERSITY OF CALIFORNIA PRESS,
     1925. ALSO DA CAPO PRESS, INC., 1969 (HSW).

BIZZELL.   RURAL TEXAS (LI*).

BLAKE.   "LOCATIONS EARLY SPANISH MISSIONS (HS*).

BLAKE.   HISTORY CATHOLIC CHURCH PASO, (RE*).

BOATRIGHT.   GIB MORGAN, MINSTREL CIL FIELDS (AN*).

BOATRIGHT.   MEXICAN BORDER BALLADS CTHERLORE (AN*).

BOATRIGHT.   SKY IS MY TIPI (AN*).

BOATRIGHT.   TALL TALES TEXAS COW CAMPS (AN*).

BOLTON.   TEXAS MIDDLE EIGHTEENTH CENTURY (HS*).

BOLTON.   "NOTES CLARKS "THE BEGINNINGS (HS*).

BOLTON.   "SPANISH ACTIVITIES LOWER TRINITY (HS*).

BOLTON.   "THE NATIVE TRIBES ABOUT EAST (HS*).

BOLTON.   "THE SPANISH ABANDONMENT REOCCUPATION (HS*).

BOLTON.   "TIENCA DE CUERVOLS YNSPECION (HS*).

BOLTON.   TEXAS MIDDLE EIGHTEENTH CENTURY (HS*).

BOLTON.   TEXAS MIDDLE EIGHTEENTH CENTURY (HS*).

BRACHT.   TEXAS 1848. TEXAS IM JAHR 1848 (HS*).

BRANDENBERGER, WILLIAM SAMUEL. THE ADMINISTRATIVE SYSTEM
     OF TEXAS, 1821-1836.   UNIVERSITY OF TEXAS AT AUSTIN,
     MASTER'S THESIS (1912).

BRIDGERS.   PASO WAS WIDE OPEN BORDER TOWN (HSW*).

BRIDGES, CLARENCE ALLAN. TEXAS AND THE CRISIS OF 1850.
     UNIVERSITY OF TEXAS AT AUSTIN, MASTER'S THESIS (1925)
     (HSW).

BRISTOW, ROBERT B. INTERNAL IMPROVEMENTS IN TEXAS,
     1836-1845.   UNIVERSITY OF TEXAS AT AUSTIN, 1936.

BROOKS, CHARLES M. JR. TEXAS MISSIONS.   DALLAS: DEALEY
     AND LOWE, 1936 (HS).

BROUSSARD, RAY F. SAN ANTONIO DURING THE TEXAS REPUBLIC.
     A CITY IN TRANSITION.   EL PASO, TEXAS: TEXAS WESTERN
     PRESS, THE UNIVERSITY OF TEXAS AT EL PASO, (1967).
     SOUTHWESTERN STUDIES MONOGRAPH NUMBER 18. (HSW).

BROWN.   EXPLORATION SETTLEMENT TEXAS; (HS*).

BROWN.   HISTORY SPANISH ESTABLISHMENTS (HS*).

BROWN.   TEXAS MIDDLE EIGHTEENTH CENTURY: (HS*).

BROWN, MAURY BRIGHT. THE MILITARY DEFENSES OF TEXAS AND
     THE RIO GRANDE REGION ABOUT 1766.   UNIVERSITY
     OF TEXAS AT AUSTIN, MASTER'S THESIS (1924) (HSW).

BROWN, MRS. ALMA HOWELL. THE CONSULAR SERVICE OF THE
     REPUBLIC OF TEXAS.   UNIVERSITY OF TEXAS AT AUSTIN,
     MASTER'S THESIS (1928).

BROWN, PHILIP DALE. THE EARLY HISTORY OF FREESTONE COUNTY
     TO 1865.   UNIVERSITY OF TEXAS AT AUSTIN, MASTER'S
     THESIS (1925).

BUCKLEY.   "THE AGUAYO EXPEDITION INTO TEXAS (HS*).

BUGBEE, LESTER GLADSTONE. AUSTIN'S COLONY.   UNIVERSITY
     OF TEXAS AT AUSTIN, MASTER'S THESIS (1893).

BURNETT, ARTHUR C. YANKEES IN THE REPUBLIC OF TEXAS.
     SALADO, TEXAS: ANSON JONES PRESS,.

BURRELL.   LIFE POLITICAL IDEAS FATHER MIER   (HSW*).

CALLEROS, CLEOFAS. EL PASO'S MISSIONS AND INDIANS.   EL
     PASO: MC MATH CO., 1953.

CANEDO.   PRIMERAS EXPLORACIONES POBLAMIENTO   (HS*).

CARDONA, ING. MANUEL I. EL CHAMIZAL: ESTÚDIO PRESENTADO
     A LA VIII REUNION DEL CONGRESO MEXICANO DE HISTORIA.
     MEXICO, 1940.

CARROLL, H. ; GUTSCH, MILTON R. TEXAS HISTORY THESES.
     AUSTIN, TEXAS: TEXAS STATE HISTORICAL ASSOCIATION,
     1955.

CARROLL, H. BAILEY. THE TEXAN SANTA FE TRAIL.   CANYON,
     TEXAS: PANHANDLE-PLAINS, HISTORICAL SOCIETY, 1951.

CARROW, SISTER MARY A. THREE SIDES TO THE RIVER.   SAN
     ANTONIO, TEXAS: THE NAYLOR CO., 1963.

CARTER, JAMES DAVID. FREEMASONRY IN TEXAS: BACKGROUND,
     HISTORY AND INFLUENCE TO 1846.   UNIVERSITY OF TEXAS
     AT AUSTIN, PHD. DISSERTATION (1954).

CASEY, ROBERT J. THE TEXAS BORDER AND SOME BORDERLINERS.
     A CHRONICLE AND A GUIDE.   INDIANAPOLIS, INDIANA:
     BOBBS-MERRILL CO., 1950.

CASIS, LILIA M. "TRANSLATION OF 'LETTER OF DON DAMIAN
     MANZANET TO DON CARLOS DE SIQUENZA RELATIVE TO THE
     DISCOVERY OF THE BAY OF ESPIRITU SANTO".   QUARTERLY
     OF THE TEXAS STATE HISTORICAL ASSOCIATION, VOL. 2
     NO. 4 (1899), PP. 281-312.

CASTANEDA, CARLOS EDUARDO. "A TRIP TO TEXAS IN 1828, BY
     JOSE MARIA SANCHEZ".   SOUTHWESTERN HISTORICAL
     QUARTERLY, VOL. 29 NO. 4 (1926), PP. 249-288.

CASTANEDA, CARLOS EDUARDO. "COMMUNICATIONS BETWEEN SANTA
     FE AND SAN ANTONIO".   TEXAS GEOGRAPHICAL MAGAZINE,
     VOL. 5 NO. 1 (1941), PP. 17-38.

CASTANEDA, CARLOS EDUARCO. "EARLIEST CATHOLIC ACTIVITIES
     IN TEXAS".   PRELIMINARY STUDIES OF THE TEXAS CATHOLIC
     HISTORICAL SOCIETY, VOL. 1 NO. 8 (1931).

CASTANEDA, CARLOS EDUARDO. "SOME OF OUR EARLIEST AMERICANS
     AWAIT THE MAGIC TOUCH".   TEXAS OUTLOOK, VOL.
     37 (JANUARY 1953), PP. 22-23.

CASTANEDA, CARLOS EDUARDO. "THE MISSION ERA: THE PASSING
     OF THE MISSIONS, 1762-1782".   THE MISSION ERA, VOL.
     4 (1939).

CASTANEDA, CARLOS EDUARDO. "THE MISSION ERA: THE END OF
    THE SPANISH REGIME, 1780-1810". THE MISSION ERA,
    VOL. 5 (1942).

CASTANEDA, CARLOS EDUARDO. "THE MISSION ERA: THE FINDING
    OF TEXAS, 1579-1693". THE MISSION ERA, VOL. 1 (1936).

CASTANEDA, CARLOS EDUARDO. HISTORY OF TEXAS, 1673-1779.
    ALBUQUERQUE: QUIVIRO SOCIETY, 1935.

CASTANEDA, CARLOS EDUARDO. MORFI'S HISTORY OF TEXAS; A
    CRITICAL CHRONOLOGICAL ACCOUNT OF THE EARLY EXPLORATIONS,
    ATTEMPTS AT COLONIZATION, AND THE FINAL OCCUPATION
    OF TEXAS BY THE SPANIARDS. UNIVERSITY OF TEXAS AT
    AUSTIN, PHD. DISSERTATION (1932).

CASTANEDA, CARLOS EDUARDO. OUR CATHOLIC HERITAGE IN TEXAS,
    1519-1936. AUSTIN, TEXAS: VON BOECKMANN-JONES CO.,
    1958.

CASTANEDA, CARLOS EDUARDO. OUR CATHOLIC HERITAGE IN TEXAS,
    1519-1936. AUSTIN: VON BOECKMANN JONES COMPANY, 1936.

CASTANEDA, CARLOS EDUARDO. TRANSITION PERIOD: THE FIGHT
    FOR FREEDON, 1810-1836. AUSTIN: VON BOECKMANN JONES
    COMPANY, 1950.

CASTANEDA, CARLOS EDUARDO. THE CHURCH IN TEXAS SINCE
    INDEPENDENCE, 1836-1950. 1958,.

CASTANEDA, CARLOS EDUARDO. THE CHURCH IN TEXAS SINCE
    INDEPENDENCE, 1836-1950. AUSTIN: VON BOECKMANN JONES
    COMPANY, 1958.

CASTANEDA, CARLOS EDUARDO. THE MISSION ERA: THE FINDING
    OF TEXAS, 1579-1693. AUSTIN: VON BOECKMANN JONES
    COMPANY, 1936.

CASTANEDA, CARLOS EDUARDO. THE MISSION ERA: THE WINNING
    OF TEXAS, 1693-1731. AUSTIN: VON BOECKMANN JONES
    COMPANY, 1936.

CASTANEDA, CARLOS EDUARDO. THE MISSION ERA: THE MISSIONS
    AT WORK, 1731-1761. AUSTIN: VON BOECKMANN JONES
    COMPANY, 1938.

CASTANEDA, CARLOS EDUARDO. THE MISSION ERA: THE PASSING
    OF THE MISSIONS, 1762-1782. AUSTIN: VON BOECKMANN
    JONES COMPANY, 1939.

CASTANEDA, CARLOS EDUARDO. THE MISSION ERA: THE END OF
    THE SPANISH REGIME, 1780-1810. AUSTIN: VON BOECKMANN
    JONES COMPANY, 1942.

CASTANEDA, CARLOS EDUARDO. A REPORT ON THE SPANISH
    ARCHIVES IN SAN ANTONIO, TEXAS. UNIVERSITY OF TEXAS
    AT AUSTIN, MASTER'S THESIS (1923).

CASTANEDA, CARLOS. OUR CATHOLIC HERITAGE IN TEXAS,
    1519-36. PREPARED UNDER THE AUSPICIES OF THE KNIGHTS
    OF COLUMBUS OF TEXAS, PAUL J. FOIK, EDITOR 7 V.
    AUSTIN: VON BOECKMANN-JONES CO, 1936.

CATTERTON, CONN DE WITT. THE POLITICAL CAMPAIGNS OF THE
    REPUBLIC OF TEXAS OF 1841 AND 1844. UNIVERSITY OF
    TEXAS AT AUSTIN, MASTER'S THESIS (1935).

CAZNEAU, C. M. EAGLE PASS, LIFE IN THE BORDER. NEW YORK,
    1852.

CEZEAUX, LOUISE CATHERINE. SOCIAL LIFE IN THE REPUBLIC
    OF TEXAS, 1836-1845. UNIVERSITY OF TEXAS AT AUSTIN,
    MASTER'S THESIS (1933).

CHABOT, FREDERICK C. SAN ANTONIO AND ITS BEGINNINGS.
    SAN ANTONIO: NAYLOR PRINTING CO., 1931.

CHABOT, FREDERICK C. WITH THE MAKERS OF SAN ANTONIO;
    GENEALOGIES OF THE EARLY LATIN, ANGLO A MERICAN, AND
    GERMAN FAMILIES. SAN ANTONIO: ARTES GRAFICAS.
    REPRINTED, 1973.

CHABOT, FREDERICK C. THE ALAMO; ALTAR OF TEXAS LIBERTY.
    SAN ANTONIO, PUBLISHED BY AUTHOR, 1931. THE LEAKE
    COMPANY, 1935 (LI).

CHABOT, FREDERICK C. THE PURISSIMA CONCEPCION OF SAN
    ANTONIO. SAN ANTONIO: NAYLOR PRINTING CO, 1935.

CHAMBERS, W. T.; KENNAMER, LORRIN. TEXANS AND THEIR LAND.
    AUSTIN, TEXAS: STECK-VAUGHN COMPANY, 1963.

CHAMPMAN, BOB. HOTEL ANGELUS HISTORY. EL PASO: EL PASO
    TIMES, FEBRUARY 24,1952.

CHANDLER, CHARLES RAY. THE MEXICAN AMERICAN PROTEST
    MOVEMENT IN TEXAS. TULANE UNIVERSITY, PHD.
    DISSERTATION (1968) (SO PL).

CLARK. SPANISH REATION TO FRENCH INTRUSION (HS*).

CLARK. BEGINNINGS TEXAS, 1684-1718 (HS*).

CLARK. E BEGINNINGS TEXAS: FORT ST (HS*).

CLARK. "LOUIS JUCHEREAU DE SAINT-DENIS (HS*).

CONDRON, STUART HARKINS. THE FIRST TEXAS AGENCY AT NEW
    ORLEANS IN 1836. UNIVERSITY OF TEXAS AT AUSTIN,
    MASTER'S THESIS (1912).

CONNOR, SEYMOUR V. BATTLES OF TEXAS. WACO, TEXAS: TEXIAN
    PRESS, 1967.

CONNOR, SEYMOUR V. TEXAS: A HISTORY. NEW YORK,
    NEW YORK: THOMAS Y. CROWELL COMPANY, 1971.

CORCORAN, LILLIAN HAGUE. "HE BROUGHT THE RAILROAD TO EL
    PASO--THE STORY OF JUDGE JAMES P. HAGUE". PASSWORD,
    VOL. 1 (MAY 1956), PP. 45-54 (EC).

CORNER, WILLIAM. SAN ANTONIO DE BEXAR: A GUIDE AND
    HISTORY. SAN ANTONIO: BAINBRIDGE AND CORNER, 1890.

CORNISH, BEATRICE QUIJADA. 'THE ANCESTRY AND FAMILY OF
    JUAN DE ONATE.' IN THE PACIFIC OCEAN IN HISTORY.
    H. MORSE STEPHENS AND HERBERT E. BO LTTON, (ED).

CORTES, CARLOS E. CONCEPTS AND STRATEGIES FOR TEACHING
    THE MEXICAN-AMERICAN EXPERIENCE. RIVERSIDE,
    CALIFORNIA: SYSTEM AND EVALUATION IN EDUCATION, 1973.

COVINGTON, CAROLYN CALLAWAY. THE "RUNAWAY SCRAPE": AN
    EPISODE OF THE TEXAS REVOLUTION. UNIVERSITY OF TEXAS
    AT AUSTIN, MASTER'S THESIS (1942).

COVINGTON, NINA. THE PRESIDENTIAL CAMPAIGNS OF THE
    REPUBLIC OF TEXAS OF 1836 AND 1838. UNIVERSITY OF
    TEXAS AT AUSTIN, MASTER'S THESIS (1929).

COWLING, ANNIE. THE CIVIL WAR TRADE OF THE LOWER RIO
    GRANDE VALLEY. UNIVERSITY OF TEXAS AT AUSTIN,
    MASTER'S THESIS (1926).

COX, C. C. "FROM TEXAS TO CALIFORNIA IN 1849 (DIARY OF
    C. C. COX)". SOUTHWESTERN HISTORICAL QUARTERLY, VOL.
    29 (JULY 1925), PP. 36-50, 128-46 (HC).

COX, I. J. THE EXPLORATION OF THE LOUISIANA FRONTIER,
    1803-1806. WASHINGTON, D. C.: UNITED STATES
    GOVERNMENT PRINTING OFFICE, (1905).

COX, ISAAC J. "THE EARLY SETTLERS OF SAN FERNANDO".
    TEXAS STATE HISTORICAL ASSOCIATION QUARTERLY, VOL.
    5 (OCTOBER 1901), PP. 142-160.

COX, ISAAC J. "THE FOUNDING OF THE FIRST TEXAS MUNICIPALITY".
    QUARTERLY OF THE TEXAS STATE HISTORICAL ASSOCIATION,
    VOL. 2 NO. 3 (1899), PP. 217-226.

COX, ISAAC J. "THE LOUISIANA-TEXAS FRONTIER". QUARTERLY
    OF THE TEXAS STATE HISTORICAL ASSOCIATION, VOL. 110
    NO. 1 (1906), PP. 1-75.

COX, ISAAC J. "THE LOUISIANA-TEXAS FRONTIER". SOUTHWESTERN
    HISTORICAL QUARTERLY, VOL. 10 NO. 1 (1906), PP. 1-75.

COX, ISAAC J. THE JOURNEYS OF RENE ROBERT CAVELIER, SIEUR
DE LA SALLE, AS RELATED BY HENRI DE TONTY. REPRINT.
AUSTIN: THE PEMBERTON PRESS, 1968.

COX, ISAAC JOLIN. MONROE AND THE EARLY MEXICAN REVOLUTIONARY
AGENTS. IN ANNUAL REPORT AMERICAN HISTORIAL
ASSOCIATION. WASHINGTON, D. C.: UNITED STATES
GOVERNMENT PRINTING OFFICE, (1911) (HSW).

CRANE, OLATIA. THE GUTIERRES-MAGEE EXPEDITION. AUSTIN,
TEXAS: UNIVERSITY OF TEXAS, 1903.

CRAVENS, LUCY ELIZABETH. THE CONGRESSIONAL HISTORY OF THE
ANNEXATION OF TEXAS. UNIVERSITY OF TEXAS AT AUSTIN,
MASTER'S THESIS (1927).

CRAWFORD, POLLY PEARL. THE BEGINNINGS OF SPANISH SETTLEMENT
IN THE LOWER RIO GRANDE VALLEY. UNIVERSITY OF TEXAS
AT AUSTIN, MASTER'S THESIS (1925).

CREEL. SAM HOUSTON (LI*).

CRIMMINS, COL. MARTIN L. "COLONEL J. K. F. MANSFIELD'S
REPORT OF THE INSPECTION OF THE DEPARTMENT OF TEXAS
IN 1856.". SOUTHWESTERN HISTORICAL QUARTERLY, VOL.
42 NO. 2, 3, 4 (SEPTEMBER 1868) (TJ).

CRIMMINS, COL. MARTIN L. "THE JUMANOS INDIANS". WEST
TEXAS HISTORICAL AND SCIENTIFIC SOCIETY PUBLICATIONS,
VOL. 2 (SEPTEMBER 1868), PP. 69-71.

CRIMMINS, COL. MARTIN L. "TWO THOUSAND MILES BY BOAT IN
THE RIO GRANDE IN 1850". WEST TEXAS HISTORICAL AND
SCIENTIFIC SOCIETY PUBLICATIONS, NO. 2 (1928), PP.
69-71.

CROCKETT, DAVID. AUTOBIOGRAPHY. PHILADELPHIA: T. K. AND
P. G. COLLINS, 1836. REPRINT, NEW YORK: SCRIBNER, 1923
(TJ).

CROCKETT, DAVID. COLONEL CROCKETT'S EXPLOITS AND ADVENTURES
IN TEXAS. LONDON: R. KENNETT, 1837 (TJ).

CROFOOOT. FLYING CHIPS: LATIN-AMERICAN (RE*).

CRUZ, GILBERT R., <TRANS AND ED>. "THE CITY ORDINANCES
FOR THE INTERNAL MANAGEMENT AND ADMINISTRATION OF THE
GOVERNMENT OF SAN ANTONIO DE BEJAR, 1829". TEXANA,
VOL. 3 NO. 2 (SUMMER ISSUE) (HS HM).

CUNNINGHAM, MARY S. A HISTORY OF THE WOMAN'S CLUB
1894-1945. EL PASO: PRIVATELY PRINTED, MARCH 1945
(SO).

CUNNINGHAM, ROBERT EMMET. JAMES TREAT AND HIS MISSION TO
MEXICO. UNIVERSITY OF TEXAS AT AUSTIN, MASTER'S
THESIS (1950) (HUS).

CURL. SOUTHWEST TEXAS METHODISM (RE*).

CURLEE, ABIGAIL. THE HISTORY OF A TEXAS SLAVE PLANTATION,
1831-1863. UNIVERSITY OF TEXAS AT AUSTIN, MASTER'S
THESIS (1922).

CURRY, ORA MAE. THE TEXAN SIEGE OF SAN ANTONIO, 1853.
UNIVERSITY OF TEXAS, MASTER'S THESIS (1927).

DABBS. "LOPEZS REPORT TEXAS MISSIONS (HSW*).

DABBS. "THE TEXAS MISSIONS 1785" (HSW*).

DANIEL. "DIARY PEDRO JOSE DE FUENTE,CAPTAIN (TJ*).

DANIEL. "THE SPANISH FRONTIER WEST TEXAS (HSW*).

DAVENPORT. "GEOGRAPHIC NOTES SPANISH TEXAS (GE*).

DAVENPORT, HARBERT; WELLS, JOSEPH K. "THE FIRST EUROPEANS
IN TEXAS, 1528-1836". SOUTHWESTERN HISTORICAL
QUARTERLY, VOL. 22 NO. 2 (1918), PP. 111-142 (HSW).

DAVENPORT, HARBERT; WELLS, JOSEPH K. "THE FIRST EUROPEANS
IN TEXAS, 1528-1836". SOUTHWESTERN HISTORICAL
QUARTERLY, VOL. 22 NO. 3 (1919), PP. 205-259 (HSW).

DAVIS. DIARY WILLIAM BARRET TRAVIS (TJ*).

DAWSON, JOSEPH MARTIN. JOSE ANTONIO NAVARRO, CO-CREATOR
OF TEXAS. WACO, TEXAS: BAYLOR UNIVERSITY PRESS,
1969 (HSW).

DAY, DONALD; ULLOM, HARRY H. THE AUTOBIOGRAPHY OF
SAM HOUSTON. NORMAN, OKLAHOMA: UNIVERSITY OF
OKLAHOMA PRESS, 1954 (TJ).

DAY. BLACK BEANS GOOSE QUILLS, LITERATURE (HSW*).

DE WETTER, MARDEE. REVOLUTIONARY EL PASO, 1910-1917.
TEXAS WESTERN COLLEGE, MASTER'S THESIS (1946).

DECORDOVA, JACOB. TEXAS: HER RESOURCES AND HER PUBLIC
MEN. PHILADELPHIA: E. CROZET, 1858.

DEVEAU, AUGUSTINE FRANCIS. FRAY ANTONIO MARGIL DE JESUS,
APOSTOLIC MISSIONARY. UNIVERSITY OF TEXAS AT AUSTIN,
MASTER'S THESIS (1953).

DEVINEY, MARVIN LEE. THE HISTORY OF NUECES COUNTY TO 1850.
UNIVERSITY OF TEXAS AT AUSTIN, MASTER'S THESIS (1933).

DEWEESE. LETTERS EARLY SETTLER TEXAS (TJ*).

DIXON, HELEN MILLER. THE MIDDLE OF THE ADMINISTRATION OF
    JUAN MARIA, BARON DE RIPPERCA, GOVERNOR OF TEXAS,
    1773-1775.   UNIVERSITY OF TEXAS AT AUSTIN, MASTER'S
    THESIS (1934).

DOBKINS.   SPANISH ELEMENT TEXAS WATER LAW (HS*).

DOKEY.   SANCHEZ (LMA*).

DOLORES.   DOCUMENTOS PARA HISTORIA ECLESTIASTICA (HS*).

DOMENECH, EMMANUEL. MISSIONARY ADVENTURES IN TEXAS AND
    MEXICO. A PERSONAL NARRATIVE OF SIX YEARS' SOJOURN
    IN THOSE REGIONS.   LONDON, ENGLAND: LONGSMANS,
    BROWN, GREEN, LONGMANS AND ROBERTS, 1858 (RE).

DONAHUE.   "THE MISSIONARY ACTIVITIES FRAY (HS*).

DUNN.   "APACHE RELATIONS TEXAS, 1718-1750" (HS*).

DUNN.   "MISSIONARY ACTIVITIES AMONGEASTERN (HS*).

DUNN.   "THE APACHE MISSION SAN SABARIVER: (HS*).

DUNN.   "THE FOUNDING NUESTRA SENORAREFUGION (HS*).

DWINKLER.   CHECK LIST TEXAS IMPRINTS, 1861-1876 (B*).

EAVES, CHARLES DUDLEY; HUTCHINSON, C. A.   POST CITY, TEXAS;
    C. W. POST'S COLONIZING ACTIVITIES IN WEST TEXAS.
    AUSTIN, TEXAS: TEXAS STATE HISTORICAL ASSOCIATION,
    1952.

ECKHART.   "SPANISH MISSIONS TEXAS, 1680-1800" (HS*).

EDMAN.   COMPILATION ROYAL DECREES ARCHIVO (HS*).

EDWARDS, HERBERT ROOK. THE DIPLOMATIC RELATIONS BETWEEN
    FRANCE AND THE REPUBLIC OF TEXAS.   UNIVERSITY
    OF TEXAS AT AUSTIN, MASTER'S THESIS (1916).

EL PASO CHAMBER OF COMMERCE.   7ISSIONS PASO VALLEY
    JUAREZ,CHIHUAHUA (HS*).

EL PASO HERALD. THE GREAT SOUTHWEST, SOUVENIR EDITION OF
    THE EL PASO DAILY HEARLD, 1880-1900.   EL PASO, TEXAS:
    THE HERALD COMPANY, 1900 (HSW).

EL PASO PIONEERS ASSOCIATION. BIOGRAPHYICAL AND HISTORICAL
    SKETCHBOOK.   MANUSCRIPT, UNIVERSITY OF TEXAS AT EL
    PASO LIBRARY.

EL PASO WOMAN'S CLUB. CURRENT TOPICS CLUB YEAR BOOK, 1898.
    EL PASO WOMAN'S CLUB, 1898.

EL PASO, COUNTY OF. EL PASO AND THE MEXICAN REVOLUTION.
     TRANSCRIPT MADE FROM TAPE RECORDING OF OLD TIMERS
     NIGHT PROGRAM, APRIL 26, 1962 (TJ).

ELLIOTT.   THESES TEXAS HISTORY; CHECK LIST (B*).

ELLWELLS.   FACTORS INFLUENCING ASSIMILATION   (SO*).

ERSKINE, M. H. "A CATTLE DRIVE FROM TEXAS TO CALIFORNIA".
     SOUTHWESTERN HISTORICAL QUARTERLY, VOL. 68 (JANUARY
     1964), PP. 404-405 (EC).

ESPINOSA.   RIO ABAJO (HSW*).

ETHERIDGE.   EDUCATION REPUBLIC TEOAS (ED*).

EVANS, C. E. THE STORY OF TEXAS SCHOOLS.   AUSTIN, TEXAS:
     STECK-VAUGHN COMPANY, 1955 (ED).

EVANS, KENNETH. THE ADMINISTRATION OF MANUEL DE SANDOVAL,
     GOVERNOR OF TEXAS, 1734 TO 1736.   UNIVERSITY OF TEXAS
     AT AUSTIN, MASTER'S THESIS (1928).

FARBER, LT. COLONEL JAMES. TEXAS C. S. A..   NEW YORK AND
     TEXAS: JACKSON CO, 1947 (LI).

FARRIS, FRANCES BRAMLETTE. SOUTH OF THE ALAMO.   UNPUBLISHED
     MS IN POSSESSION OF CLS.

FAULK .   SUCCESSFUL FAILURE (HS*).

FAULK.   "A DESCRIPTION TEXAS 1803"   (HS*).

FAULK.   "RANCHING SPANISH TEXAS" (HS*).

FAULK.   LAST YEARS SPANISH TEXAS, 1778-1821 (HS*).

FEHRENBACH, T. R. LONE STAR: A HISTORY OF TEXAS AND THE
     TEXANS.   NEW YORK: MACMILLAN, 1968.

FILIZOLA, UMBERTO DANIEL. CORRESPONDENCE OF SANTA ANNA
     DURING THE TEXAS CAMPAIGN, 1835-1836 TRANSLATED, WITH
     INTRODUCTION AND NOTES.   UNIVERSITY OF TEXAS
     AT AUSTIN, MASTER'S THESIS (1939) (HM).

FOIK.   "CAPTAIN DON DOMINGO RAMON SDIARY   (TJ*).

FOLMER, HENRI. "DE BELLISLE ON THE TEXAS COAST".
     SOUTHWESTERN HISTORICAL QUARTERLY, VOL. 44   NO.
     2 (1940), PP. 204-231.

FOLMER, HENRI. "REPORT ON LOUIS DE ST DENIS' INTENDED RAID
     ON SAN ANTONIO IN 1721".   SOUTHWESTERN HISTORICAL
     QUARTERLY, VOL. 52   NO. 1 (1948), PP. 83-88.

FOLMER, HENRY. FRANCO-SPANISH RIVALRY IN NORTH AMERICA.
     1524-1763. GLENDALE, CALIFORNIA: ARTHUR H. CLARK,.

FOOTE, HENRY STUART. TEXAS AND THE TEXANS. PHILADELPHIA:
     COWPERTHWAIT AND COMPANY, 1841.

FOOTE, HENRY STUART. TEXAS AND THE TEXANS, OR ADVANCE OF
     THE ANGLO AMERICANS TO THE SOUTHWEST. PHILADELPHIA,
     PENNSYLVANIA: T. COPPERTHWAIT, 1951 (HSW).

FOREMAN. COWN TEXAS ROAD (HSW*).

FORNELL, EARL W. THE GALVESTON ERA, THE TEXAS CRESCENT
     ON THE EVE OF SECESSION. AUSTIN: UNIVERSITY OF TEXAS
     PRESS, 1961.

FRANTZ, J. B. HOUSTON: A STUDENT'S GUIDE TO LOCALIZED
     HISTORY. NEW YORK: TEACHERS COLLEGE, COLUMBIA
     UNIVERSITY PRESS9,.

FREEMAN, THOMAS ; CUSTIS, PETER. ACCOUNT OF THE RED RIVER
     IN LOUISIANA, DRAWN UP FROM THE RETURNS OF MESSRS.
     FREEMAN AND CUSTIS TO THE WAR OFFICE OF THE UNITED
     STATES, WHO EXPLORED THE SAME IN THE YEAR 1806.
     WWASHINGTON, D. C., (1806) (TJ).

FREUDENTHAL. SAMUEL J. FREUDENTHAL; PASOMERCHANT (EC*).

FRIEDRICKS, I. H. HISTORY OF GOLIAD. GOLIAD, TEXAS:
     REGAL PRINTERS, 1961.

FRIEND, LLERENA BEAUFORT. THE GREAT DESIGNER--SAM HOUSTON
     IN THE AMERICAN POLITICAL SCENE. THE UNIVERSITY OF
     TEXAS AT AUSTIN, 1951.

FRIEND, LLERENA. "W. P. WEBER'S TEXAS RANGERS".
     SOUTHWESTERN HISTORICAL QUARTERLY, VOL. 74 NO.
     3 (JANUARY 1971), PP. 293-323.

FRIEND, LLERENA. SAM HOUSTON, THE GREAT DESIGNER.
     AURSIN: UNIVERSITY OF TEXAS PRESS, 1954.

FUENTE. "DIARY PEDRO JOSE DE FUENTE,CAPTAIN (TJ*).

GAMBRELL, HERBERT AND VIRGINIA. A PICTORIAL HISTORY OF
     TEXAS. NEW YORK: DUTTON, 1960.

GAMBRELL, HERBERT P. ANSON JONES, THE LAST PRESIDENT OF
     TEXAS. NEW YORK: DOUBLEDAY, 1948 (LI).

GAMBRELL, HERBERT P. MIRABEAU B. LAMAR, TROUBADOUR AND
     CRUSADER. DALLAS: SOUTHWEST PRESS, 1934 (LI).

GAMBRELL, HERBERT, (ED.). TEXAS TODAY AND TOMMORROW.
     DALLAS: SOUTHERN METHODIST UNIVERSITY PRESS, 1962.

GAMBRELL, HERBERT, EDITOR. TEXAS TODAY AND TOMMORROW.
    DALLAS: SOUTHERN METHODIST UNIVERSITY PRESS, 1961.

GANTT, FRED, JR.; DAWSON, IRVING G.; HAGARD, LUTHER G.,
    JR. (EDITORS). GOVERNING TEXAS : DOCUMENTS AND
    READINGS. NEW YORK, NEW YORK: THOMAS Y. CROWELL
    COMPANY, 1970.

GARAZA, GEORGE J. "GOOD NEIGHBORS -- TEXAS VERSION?".
    THE TEXAS OUTLOOK, VOL. 27 (JUNE), P. 39.

GARCIA.   DOLORES, REVILLA, LAREDO: THREE   (HS*).

GARD. RAWHIDE TEXAS (HUS*).

GARNER, CLAUD. SAM HOUSTON, TEXAS GIANT.   SAN ANTONIO:
    NAYLOR, 1969.

GARRETT, JULIA KATHRYN. GREEN FLAG OVER TEXAS.   NEW YORK
    AND DALLAS: CORDOVA PRESS, 1939.

GARRETT, JULIA KATHRYN. GREEN FLAG OVER TEXAS: THE LAST
    YEARS OF SPAIN IN TEXAS.   AUSTIN, TEXAS: PEMBERTON
    PRESS, 1970.

GARRETT, JULIA KATHRYN. GREEN FLAG OVER TEXAS; A STORY
    OF THE LAST YEARS OF SPAIN IN TEXAS.   THE CORDOVA
    PRESS, NEW YORK AND DALLAS: REPRINTED BY PEMBERTON
    PRESS, AUSTIN, 1969.

GARRISON, GOERGE PIERCE. TEXAS: A CONTEST OF CIVILIZATIONS.
    BOSTON AND NEW YORK: HOUGHTON, MIFFLIN AND CO, 1903.

GARZA.   "GOOD NEIGHBORS: TEXAS VERSION?" (SO*).

GERSON, NOEL B. SAM HOUSTON.   GARDEN CITY, NEW YORK:
    DOUBLEDAY AND COMPANY, INC., 1968.

GEUE, CHESTER WILLIAM AND ETHEL HANDER. A NEW LAND
    BECKONED, GERMAN IMMIGRATION TO TEXAS, 1844-1847.
    WACO: TEXIAN PRESS, 1967.

GIBSON, LOUISE. EFFORTS OF THE TEXAS GOVERNMENT TO OBTAIN
    PEACE WITH MEXICO THROUGH SANTA ANNA; 1836-1837.
    UNIVERSITY OF TEXAS AT AUSTIN, MASTER'S THESIS.

GILLETT, JAMES B. SIX YEARS WITH THE TEXAS RANGERS:1875-1881.
    AUSTIN: VON BOECKMAN-JONES, 1921. EDITED BY M.
    M. QUAIFE, NEW HAVEN: YALE UNIVERSITY PRESS, 1963.

GRAF.   "COLONIZING PROJECTS TEXAS SOUTH (HS*).

GRAVES, J. "OVERLAP LAND, GRINGO AND MEXICAN MEET IN THE
     RIO GRANDE COUNTRY". HOLIDAY, VOL. 35 (MARCH
     1964), PP. 74-75 (HSW).

GREEN. JOURNAL EXPEDITION AGAINST MIER: (TJ*).

GREER, JAMES K., ED. TEXAS RANGER AND FRONTIERSMAN, THE
     DAYS OF BUCK BARRY IN TEXAS, 1845-1906. DALLAS:
     SOUTHWEST PRESS, 1932.

GRIFFITH, WILLIAM JOYCE. THE HASINAI INDIANS OF EAST TEXAS
     AS SEEN BY EUROPEANS, 1687-1772. NEW ORLEANS: TULANE
     UNIVERSITY, (1954). PHILOGICAL AND DOCUMENTARY
     STUDIES, VOLUMN 2, NO. 3, MIDDLE AMERICAN RESEARCH
     INSTITUTE (LI).

GRONET, R. W. W. "UNITED STATES AND THE INVASION OF TEXAS
     1810-1814". AMERICAS, VOL. 25 (JANUARY 1969), PP.
     281-306.

GUICE, C. NORMAN. "TRADE GOODS FOR TEXAS". SOUTHWESTERN
     HISTORICAL QUARTERLY, VOL. 60 NO. 4 (1957), PP. 507-519.

GUICE, C. NORMAN, <TRANSLATOR AND EDITOR>. "TEXAS
     IN 1804". SOUTHWESTERN HISTORICAL QUARTERLY, VOL.
     59 NO. 1 (1955), PP. 46-56.

HABIG, MARION A., O. F. M. "MISSION SAN JOSE". LESSER
     BROTHERS, VOL. 4 NO. 2 (1970), PP. 67-76.

HABIG, MARION A., O. F. M. "MISSION SAN JOSE Y SAN MIGUEL
     DE AGUAYO, 1720-1824". SOUTHWESTERN HISTORICAL
     QUARTERLY, VOL. 71 NO. 4 (1968), PP. 496-516.

HABIG, MARION A., O. F. M. "SPAIN IN TEXAS: THE APACHE
     AREA". EL CAMPANARIO, VOL. 3 NO. 3 (1972), PP. 1-5.

HABIG, MARION A., O. F. M. "SPAIN IN TEXAS : EAST TEXAS
     AREA -- PART 1". EL CAMPANARIO, VOL. 2 NO.
     1 (1971), PP. 4-7.

HABIG, MARION A., O. F. M. "SPAIN IN TEXAS: EAST TEXAS
     AREA -- PART 2". EL CAMPANARIO, VOL. 2 NO.
     2 (1971), PP. 1-5.

HABIG, MARION A., O. F. M. "SPAIN IN TEXAS: EL PASO
     AREA". EL CAMPANARIO, VOL. 1 NO. 2 (1970), PP. 3-4.

HABIG, MARION A., O. F. M. "SPAIN IN TEXAS: THE PRESIDIO
     AREA". EL CAMPANARIO, VOL. 1 NO. 4 (1970), PP. 2-4.

HABIG, MARION A., O. F. M. "SPAIN IN TEXAS: THE SAN
     ANTONIO AREA". EL CAMPANARIO, VOL. 2 NO. 2 (1971),
     PP. 1-6.

HABIG, MARION A., O. F. M. "SPAIN IN TEXAS: THE SAN
    XAVIER AREA". EL CAMPANARIO, VOL. 3 NO. 3 (1972),
    PP. 2-5.

HABIG, MARION A., O. F. M. "SPAIN IN TEXAS: THE SPANISH
    MISSIONS, PRESIDIOS AND VILLAS IN THE STATEOF TEXAS
    (1680-1821)". EL CAMPANARIO, VOL. 1 NO. 2 (1969),
    PP. 1-5.

HABIG, MARION A., O. F. M. HEROES OF THE CROSS.
    PATERSON, NEW JERSEY: ST. ANTHONY GUILD, 1947 (HS).

HABIG, MARION A., O. F. M. MISSION NUESTRA SENORA DE LA
    PURISIMA CONCEPCION DE ACUNA, 1731-1824. MANUSCRIPT
    ON FILE AT THE TEXAS HISTORICAL COMMISSION, AUSTIN.

HABIG, MARION A., O. F. M. SAN ANTONIO'S MISSION SAN JOSE
    STATE AND NATIONAL HISTORIC SITE, 1720-1968.
    CHICAGO: FRANCISCAN HERALD PRESS, CHICAGO; AND SAN
    ANTONIO: NAYLOR PRIINTING CO., 2 1968.

HABIG, MARION A., O. F. M. THE ALAMO CHAIN OF MISSIONS:
    A HISTORY OF SAN ANTONIO'S FIVE OLD MISSIONS.
    CHICAGO: FRANCISCAN HERALD PRESS, 1968.

HAGGARD, JUAN VILLASANA. "THE NEUTRAL GROUND BETWEEN
    LOUISIANA AND TEXAS, 1806-1821". LOUISIANA HISTORICAL
    QUARTERLY, VOL. 28 NO. 4 (1945), PP. 1001-1128.

HAGGARD, JUAN VILLASANA. THE NEUTRAL GROUND BETWEEN
    LOUISIANA AND TEXAS, 1806-1821. UNIVERSITY OF TEXAS
    AT AUSTIN, PHD. DISSERTATION (1942).

HAGGARD, JUAN VILLASANA. THE NEUTRAL GROUND BETWEEN
    LOUISIANA AND TEXAS, 1806-1821. UNIVERSITY OF TEXAS
    AT AUSTIN, PHD. DISSERTATION (1942).

HALE, WILL. TWENTY FOUR YEARS A COWBOY AND RANCHMAN IN
    SOUTHERN TEXAS AND OLD MEXICO. NORMAN OKLAHOMA:
    UNIVERSITY OF OKLAHOMA PRESS, 1959 (HM TJ).

HALEY.   "A LOG TEXAS-CALIFORNIA CATTLE (LI*).

HALEY.   CHARLES GOODNIGHT (LI*).

HALEY.   FORT CONCHO TEXAS FRONTIER (LI*).

HALEY.   GEORGE LITTLEFIELD, TEXAN (LI*).

HALEY.   JEFF MILTON: GOOD MAN WITH GUN (LI*).

HALEY.   SURVEY TEXAS CATTLE DRIVES TO (LI*).

HALEY.   XIT RANCH TEXAS EARLY DAYS LLANO (LI*).

HALL.   ENCHANTED SAND (LI*).

HAMMONS, NANCY LEE. A HISTORY OF EL PASO COUNTY, TEXAS
     TO 1900.   TEXAS WESTERN COLLEGE, MASTER'S THESIS
     (SEPTEMBER 1942).

HANEY, P. L. THE INTERNATIONAL CONTROVERSY OVER THE WATERS
     OF THE UPPER RIO GRANDE.   TEXAS WESTERN COLLEGE,
     MASTER'S THESIS (AUGUST 1948).

HARRIS.   -HE GILA TRAIL: TEXAS ARGONAUTS (HSW*).

HARRIS, HARRY. BILLY JOE AND THE RANGERS.   NEW YORK:
     HASTINGS, 1965 (LI).

HARRIS, HELEN WILLITS. THE PUBLIC LIFE OF JUAN NEPOMUCENO
     ALMONTE.   UNIVERSITY OF TEXAS AT AUSTIN, PHD.
     DISSERTATION (1935).

HATCHER, MATTIE ALICE. "TEXAS IN 1820 BY JUAN PADILLA".
     SOUTHWESTERN HISTORICAL QUARTERLY, VOL. 23 NO.
     1 (1919), PP. 47-68.

HATCHER, MATTIE ALICE. THE OPENING OF TEXAS TO FOREIGN
     SETTLEMENT, 1806-1821.   AUSTIN, 1927.

HATCHER, MATTIE AUSTIN. "CONDITIONS IN TEXAS AFFECTING
     THE COLONIZATION PROBLEM, 1795-1801".   SOUTHWESTERN
     HISTORICAL QUARTERLY, VOL. 25 NO. 2 (1921), PP. 81-97.

HATCHER, MATTIE AUSTIN. "DESCRIPTIONS OF THE TEJAS
     OR ASINAI INDIANS, 1691-1722".   SOUTHWESTERN
     HISTORICAL QUARTERLY, VOL. 30 NO. 3 (1927), PP. 206-218.

HATCHER, MATTIE AUSTIN (TRANSLATOR). "LETTERS OF AN EARLY
     AMERICAN TRAVELER--MARY AUSTIN HOLLEY, HER LIFE AND
     HER WORKS".   SOUTHWESTERN HISTORICAL QUARTERLY, VOL.
     30 NO. 4 (1927), PP. 283-304 (TJ).

HATCHER, MATTIE AUSTIN. "THE EXPEDITION OF DON DOMINGO
     TERAN DE LOS RIOS INTO TEXAS (1691-1692)".   PRELIMINARY
     STUDIES OF THE TEXAS CATHOLIC HISTORICAL SOCIETY, VOL.
     2 NO. 1 (1932), PP. 3-67.

HATCHER, MATTIE AUSTIN. MUNICIPAL GOVERNMENT OF SAN
     FERNANDO DE BEXAR.   AUSTIN, TEXAS: UNIVERSITY
     OF TEXAS, 1903.

HAYNE, COE. "STUDYING MEXICAN RELATIONS AT EL PASO".
     MISSIONARY REVIEW, VOL. 50 (FEBRUARY 1927), PP. 110-112.

HENDERSON, MARY VIRGINIA. MINOR EMPRESARIO GRANTS
     IN TEXAS, 1825-1834.   UNIVERSITY OF TEXAS AT AUSTIN,
     MASTER'S THESIS (1926).

HERTZOG, CARL; LEA, TOM. FORT BLISS: ONE HUNDREDTH
    ANNIVERSARY.   EL PASO: GUYNES PRINTING COMPANY,
    (1948). COMMEMORATIVE BROCHURE DESIGNED AND PRODUCED
    BY CARL HERTZOG AND TOM LEA..

HESTIR, BLUFORD BRADFORD. THE URGES TO A TEXAS LITERATURE,
    1526-1716.   UNIVERSITY OF TEXAS AT AUSTIN, MASTER'S
    THESIS (1947).

HILL. "EL CHAMIZAL" (GE*).

HILL, JIM DAN. THE TEXAS NAVY.   NEW YORK: A. S. BARNES,
    1962.

HINSLEY, J. C. (ED). THE HANDBOOK OF TEXAS SCHOOL LAW.
    AUSTIN, TEXAS: STECK-VAUGHN, 1968 (LW).

HOFFMAN.   DIARY ALARCON EXPEDITION INTO (TJ*).

HOFFMAN, FRITZ LEO (TRANS AND ED). FRANCISCO CELIZ. DIARY
    OF THE ALARCON EXPEDITION INTO TEXAS, 1718-1719.
    UNIVERSITY OF TEXAS AT AUSTIN, PHD. DISSERTATION (1935).

HOFFMANN, FRITZ LEO. THE FIRST THREE YEARS OF THE
    ADMINISTRATION OF JUAN MARIA, BARON DE RIPPERDA,
    GOVERNOR OF TEXAS, 1770-1778.   UNIVERSITY OF TEXAS
    AT AUSTIN, MASTER'S THESIS (1930).

HOGAN, WILLIAM RANSOM. THE LIFE AND LETTERS OF HENRY
    AUSTIN, 1782-1852.   UNIVERSITY OF TEXAS AT AUSTIN,
    MASTER'S THESIS (1932).

HOGAN, WILLIAM RANSOM. A SOCIAL AND ECONOMIC HISTORY OF
    THE REPUBLIC OF TEXAS.   UNIVERSITY OF TEXAS AT
    AUSTIN, PHD. DISSERTATION (1942).

HOGAN, WILLIAM RANSOM. THE TEXAS REPUBLIC: A SOCIAL AND
    ECONOMIC HISTORY.   NORMAN OKLAHOMA: UNIVERSITY OF
    OKLAHOMA PRESS, 1946.

HOGAN, WILLIAM RANSOM. THE TEXAS REPUBLIC.   NORMAN,
    OKLAHOMA: UNIVERSITY OF OKLAHOMA PRESS, 1946.

HOGAN, WILLIAM RANSOM. THE TEXAS REPUBLIC: A SOCIAL AND
    ECONOMIC HISTORY.   AUSTIN: UNIVERSITY OF TEXAS PRESS,
    1969.

HOLDEN, NARCISSA JANE. ARCHAEOLOGICAL INVESTIGATIONS AT
    THE BONNELL SITE, SOUTHEASTERN NEW MEXICO.   UNIVERSITY
    OF TEXAS AT AUSTIN, MASTER'S THESIS (1951).

HOLDEN, WILLIAM C. THE ESPUELA LAND AND CATTLE COMPANY:
    THE STUDY OF A FOREGIN OWNED RANCH IN TEXAS.   AUSTIN,
    TEXAS: TEXAS STATE HISTORICAL ASSOCIATION, 1970.

HOLDEN, WILLIAM CURRY. ANDER AND THE COAST OF THE SENO
     MEXICANO: WITH INTRODUCTION AND ANOTATIFRAY VICENTE
     SANTA MARIA: HISTORICAL ACCOUNT OF THE COLONY OF NUEVO
     SANTONS.   UNIVERSITY OF TEXAS AT AUSTIN, MASTER'S
     THESIS (1924) (HM).

HOLLAND, JOHN W. BROWNSVILLE, TEXAS: INTER-NATIONAL LAND,
     SEA AND AIR PORT.   IMMIGRATION AND NATURALIZATION
     SERVICE, U. S. DEPT. OF JUSTICE, (JANUARY 1952).
     MONTHLY REVIEW, VOLUME 9, NUMBER 7 (EC).

HOLLEY.   TEXAS (TJ*).

HOLMES, LT. COL. WILLIAM H. THE ACEQUIAS OF SAN ANTONIO.
     SAN ANTONIO: SAINT MARY'S UNIVERSITY, MASTER'S THESIS
     (1962).

HOLMES, WILLIAM H. "ANTIQUITY OF MAN ON THE SITE OF THE
     CITY OF MEXICO".   TRANSACTIONS OF ANTHROPOLOGICAL
     SOCIETY OF WASHINGTON, VOL. 3 (1895) (AN).

HOUSE, BOYCE. CITY OF FLAMING ADVENTURE, THE CHRONICLE
     OF SAN ANTONIO.   SAN ANTONIO: NAYLOR, 1949 (LI).

HOUSE, BOYCE. OIL BOOM: THE STORY OF SPINDLETOP,
     BURKBURNETT, MEXIA, SMACKOVER, DESDEMONA, AND RANGER.
     CALDWELL, IDAHO: CAXTON PRINTERS, 1941 (LI).

HOUSE, BOYCE. ROARING RANGER.   SAN ANTONIO: NAYLOR, 1951
     (LI).

HOUSE, BOYCE. SAN ANTONIO: CITY OF FLAMING ADVENTURE.
     SAN ANTONIO, TEXAS: THE NAYLOR COMPANY, 1968 (LI).

HOUSE, BOYCE. TEXAS RHYTHM.   DALLAS: REGIONAL PRESS, 1936
     (LI).

HOUSE, BOYCE. WERE YOU IN RANGER.   DALLAS: TARDY, 1935
     (LI).

HOUSTON, SAMUEL. PROCLAMATION BY THE PRESIDENT OF TEXAS,
     ANNOUNCING AN ARMISTICE BETWEEN TEXAS AND MEXICO, 29
     JULY 1843.   SIGNED BY ANSON JONES, SECRETARY OF STATE
     OF TEXAS. ORIGINAL DOCUMENT. SAN MARINO, CALIFORNIA.
     HENRY E. HUNTINGTON LIBRARY. <EXCERPTS QUOTED
     BY PERMISSION OF THE HUNTINGTON LIBRARY.>.

HOUSTON, SAMUEL. THE AUTOBIOGRAPHY OF SAM HOUSTON (,ED.
     DONALD DAY).   NORMAN: UNIVERSITY OF OKLAHOMA PRESS,
     1954.

HOWARD, CARL D. "A TALE OF TWO TEXAS CITIES".   THE
     NATIONAL OBSERVER, VOL. 4 NO. 15 (APRIL 12, 1965).

HUGHES. MEMOIR DESCRIPTIVE MARCH DIVISION (TJ*).

HUGHES, VERNON. CURRENCY OF THE REPUBLIC OF TEXAS.
    UNIVERSITY OF TEXAS AT AUSTIN, MASTER'S THESIS (1927).

HUNLEY, JOSEPHINE KELLER. A DOCUMENTARY HISTORY OF TEXAN
    SENTIMENT FOR ANNEXATION TO THE UNITED STATES,
    1835-1838. UNIVERSITY OF TEXAS AT AUSTIN, MASTER'S
    THESIS (1937).

HUNTER, JOHN MARVIN, ED. THE TRAIL-DRIVERS OF TEXAS.
    SAN ANTONIO: GLOBE PRINTING COMPANY, 1924: REPRINT,
    NASHVILLE: COKESBURY PRESS, 1926 (LI).

HUSER. "SAN ANTONIO EDUCATES LITTLEMEXICO" (ED*).

HUSTON, CLEBURNE. TOWERING TEXAS: BIOGRAPHY OF THOMAS
    J. RUSK. WACO, TEXAS: TEXIAN PRESS,.

JACKSON, MRS. LILLIS TISDALE. SAM HOUSTON IN THE TEXAS
    REVOLUTION. UNIVERSITY OF TEXAS AT AUSTIN, MASTER'S
    THESIS (1932).

JAMES, MARQUIS. THE RAVEN, A BIOGRAPHY OF SAM HOUSTON.
    INDIANAPOLIS: BOBBS-MERRILL COMPANY, 1929.

JAMES, WILL S. 27 YEARS A MAVRICK OR LIFE ON A TEXAS
    RANGE. AUSTIN, TEXAS: STECK-VAUGHN COMPANY, 1968.

JENKINS, JOHN H. CRACKER BARREL CHRONICLES. AUSTIN,
    TEXAS: THE PEMBERTON PRESS, 1965.

JENNINGS, NAPOLEON AUGUSTUS. A TEXAS RANGER. NEW YORK:
    SCRIBNER, 1899. REPRINT, DALLAS: SOUTHWEST PRESS, 1930.

JENNINGS, VIVIAN. HISTORY OF SAM HOUSTON'S GOVERNORSHIP
    OF TEXAS. UNIVERSITY OF TEXAS AT AUSTIN, MASTER'S
    THESIS (1934).

JOHNSON, ALVIN S. "MEXICO IN SAN ANTONIO". NEW REPUBLIC,
    VOL. 7 , PP. 190-91 (AN).

JOHNSON, ROBERTA MURIEL. HISTORY OF THE EDUCATION
    OF SPANISH-SPEAKING CHILDREN IN TEXAS. AUSTIN,
    TEXAS, MASTER'S THESIS (1932).

JOHNSON, WILLIAM WEBER. SAM HOUSTON, THE TALLEST TEXAN.
    NEW YORK: RANDOM HOUSE, 1953 (LJE).

JONES, ANSON. REPUBLIC OF TEXAS; ITS HISTORY AND ANNEXATION.
    GLORIETA, NEW MEXICO: RIO GRANDE PRESS, INC.,.

JONES, BILLY M. A SEARCH FOR MATURITY: THE SAGA OF TEXAS,
    1875-1900. AUSTIN, TEXAS: STECK-VAUGHN, 1965.

JONES. "MEANY, AT SENATE HEARING SCORES (EC*).

JORDAN, MILDRED L. RAILROADS IN THE EL PASO AREA.   TEXAS
    WESTERN COLLEGE, MASTER'S THESIS (1957).

KELLAM, FRANCES WADE. ECONOMIC AND COMMERCIAL HISTORY OF
    TEXAS, 1821-1835.   UNIVERSITY OF TEXAS AT AUSTIN,
    MASTER'S THESIS (1925).

KELLY, EDITH AND MATTIE AUSTIN HATCHER <TRANSLATORS>.
    "TADEO ORTIZ DEY AYALA AND THE COLONIZATION OF TEXAS,
    1822-1833".   SOUTHWESTERN HISTORICAL QUARTERLY, VOL.
    32 NO. 4 (1929), PP. 311-343.

KELLY, J. CHARLES. "JUAN SABEATA AND DIFFUSION IN
    ABORIGINAL TEXAS".   AMERICAN ANTHROPOLOGIST, VOL.
    57 NO. 5 (1955), PP. 981-995.

KENNEDY, WILLIAM. TEXAS.   REPRINT, NEW YORK. BENJAMIN
    AND YOUNG 1844; REPRINT FORT WORTH: MOLYNEAU, 1925.

KENNON, BOB. FROM THE PECOS TO THE POWDER.   NORMAN:
    UNIVERSITY OF OKLAHOMA PRESS, 1965.

KERBEY, MCFALL. "TEXAS DELTA OF AN AMERICAN NILE".
    NATIONAL GEOGRAPHIC MAGAZINE, VOL. 75 NO. 1 (JANUARY
    1939).

KERBOW, MRS. BLEWETT BARNES. THE EARLY HISTORY OF
    RED RIVER COUNTY, 1817-1865.   UNIVERSITY OF TEXAS
    AT AUSTIN, MASTER'S THESIS (1936).

KERR, HOMER LEE. MIGRATION INTO TEXAS 1865-1880.
    UNIVERSITY OF TEXAS AT AUSTIN, PHD. DISSERTATION (1953).

KIDDER.   INTRODUCTION TO STUDY SOUTHWESTERN (AN*).

KIDDER, ALFRED VINCENT. THE ARTIFACTS OF PECOS.
    NEW HAVEN: YALE UNIVERSITY PRESS, 1932.

KIELMAN.   UNIVERSITY TEXAS ARCHIVES: GUIDE   (B*).

KING.   PSYCHOLOGY MEXICAN COMMUNITYSAN   (PY*).

KING, NYAL C. CAPTAIN ANTONIO GIL Y'BARBO: FOUNDER OF
    MODERN NACOGCOCHES, 1729-1809.   AUSTIN STATE TEACHERS
    COLLEGE, MASTER'S THESIS (1949).

KING, RICHARD C., <ED.>.   VICTORIAN LADY ON THE TEXAS
    FRONTIER: THE JOURNAL OF ANN RANEY COLEMAN.   NORMAN,
    OKLAHOMA: UNIVERSITY OF OKLAHOMA PRESS, 1971.

KINGREA, NELLIE WARD. HISTORY OF THE FIRST TEN YEARS OF
    THE TEXAS GOOD NEIGHBORS COMMISSION, AND DISCUSSION
    OF THE MAJOR PROBLEMS.   FORT WORTH: TEXAS CHRISTIAN
    UNIVERSITY PRESS, 1954 (SO).

KNAPP, FRANK AVERILL. THE LIFE OF SEBASTIAN LERDO
DE TEJADA, 1823-1889 A STUDY OF INFLUENCE ANDBSCURITY.
UNIVERSITY OF TEXAS AT AUSTIN, PHD. DISSERTATION (1950).

KNIGHT, OLIVER. FORT WORTH: OUTPOST ON THE TRINITY.
NORMAN, OKLAHOMA: UNIVERSITY OF OKLAHOMA PRESS, 1953.

KOEMER, DR. FERDINAND. TEXAS. TRANSLATED BY OSWALD
MUELLER. REPRINT, SAN ANTONIO: STANDARD PRINTING
COMPANY, 1935.

KOHLBERG. LETTERS, 1875-1877 (TJ*).

KOHLBERG. TRANSLATION LETTERS WRITTEN BY (TJ*).

KUBELA, MARGUERITE EVELYN. HISTORY OF FORT CONCHO, TEXAS.
UNIVERSITY OF TEXAS AT AUSTIN, MASTER'S THESIS (1936).

LABADIE, N. D. "LET US ATTACK THE ENEMY AND GIVE THEM
HELL: THE BATTLE OF SAN JACINTO, AN EYEWITNESS
ACCOUNT". AMERICAN WEST, (MAY 1968), PP. 26-34.

LANIER, SIDNEY. RETROSPECTS AND PROSPECTS. NEW YORK:
CHARLES SCRIBNER'S SONS, 1899.

LASSWELL, MARY. I'LL TAKE TEXAS. BOSTON: HOUGHTON, 1958.

LATHAM, JEAN LEE. SAM HOUSTON: HERO OF TEXAS. CHAMPAIGN,
ILLINOIS: GARRARD PUBLISHING COMPANY, 1965.

LATHROP, BARNES F. MIGRATION INTO EAST TEXAS, 1835-1860.
AUSTIN, TEXAS: TEXAS STATE HISTORICAL ASSOCIATION,
1949 (SI).

LEACH, JOSEPH. "STAGECOACH THROUGH THE PASS--THE BUTTERFIELD
OVERLAND MAIL COMES TO EL PASO". PASSWORD, VOL. 3
(OCTOBER 1958), PP. 130-137.

LEACH, JOSEPH. THE TYPICAL TEXAN: BIOGRAPHY OF AN AMERICAN
MYTH. DALLAS: SOUTHERN METHODIST UNIVERSITY PRESS,
1971.

LEUTENEGGER, B. "TWO FRANCISCAN DOCUMENTS ON EARLY SAN
ANTONIO, TEXAS". AMERICAS, VOL. 25 (OCTOBER 1968),
PP. 191-206.

LEVY, ESTELLE GOODMAN. "EL PASO DEFENDS HER CULTURE--OPERA
AT THE PASS OF THE NORTH". PASSWORD, VOL. 4 (JULY
1959), PP. 90-95.

LEVY, ESTELLE GOODMAN. "THE MYAR OPERA HOUSE AND OTHER
THEATERS IN OLD EL PASO". PASSWORD, VOL. 5 (APRIL
1960), PP. 65-73.

LEWIS, EDWARD ALLEN. AN ANALYSIS OF THE RELATIONSHIPS
    BETWEEN DESEGREGATED EDUCATION AND ACHIEVEMENT
    ANXIETY, CONCEPT OF SELF AND ATTITUDES TOWARDS SCHOOL
    OF PRIMARYSCHOOL CHILDREN. RIVERSIDE: UNIVERSITY
    OF CALIFORNIA, 1970.

LISS, SHELDON B. A CENTURY OF DISAGREEMENT: THE CHAMIZAL
    CONFLICT, 1864-1964. WASHINGTON: UNIVERSITY PRESS
    OF WASHINGTON, 1965.

LITTLE. SPANISH SPEAKING CHILDREN TEXAS (SO*).

LITTLE. SPANISH SPEAKING CHILDREN TEXAS (SO*).

LONG, GRACE. THE ANGLO-AMERICAN OCCUPATION OF THE EL PASO
    DISTRICT. UNIVERSITY OF TEXAS, MASTER'S THESIS
    (1931) (ED).

LONG, W. E. STEPHEN F. AUSTIN'S LEGACIES. AUSTIN, TEXAS:
    STECK-VAUGHN COMPANY, 1970.

LOPEZ, FRAY JOSE FRANCISCO. THE TEXAS MISSIONS IN 1785.
    TRANSLATED BY J. AUTREY DABBS, (1940). PRELIMINARY
    STUDIES OF THE TEXAS CATHOLIC HISTORICAL SOCIETY,
    VOLUME 3 NUMBER 6 (HS).

LORD, WALTER
    LORD, WALTER. "MYTHS AND REALITIES OF THE ALAMO".
    THE AMERICAN WEST, VOL. 5 (MAY 1969), PP. 18-25 (LI).

LOTT, V. N. ; FENWICK, V. M. PEOPLE AND PLOTS ON THE RIO
    GRANDE. SAN ANTONIO, TEXAS: NAYLOR CO., 1957 (EC).

LOZANO, R. R. VIVA TEJAS. SAN ANTONIO: SOUTHERN LITERARY
    INSTITUTE, 1936.

LUKER, JULIA EUGENIA. UNKNOWN MEXICO. NEW YORK, 1902
    (HM).

MAC CALLUM, ESTHER DARBYSHIRE. THE HISTORY OF ST.
    CLEMENT'S CHURCH, EL &ASO, TEXAS 1870-1925
    THE HISTORY OF ST. CLEMENT'S CHURCH, EL PASO, TEXAS
    1870-1925. EL PASO: THE MCMATH COMPANY, 1925 (RE).

MADISON, VIRGINIA. THE BIG BEND COUNTRY OF TEXAS.
    ALBUQUERQUE: UNIVERSITY OF NEW MEXICO PRESS, 1955.

MADSEN. MEXICAN-AMERICANS SOUTH TEXAS (AN*).

MAISSIN. FRENCH MEXICO TEXAS, 1838-1839 (HM*).

MANGAN, FRANK. BORDERTOWN. EL PASO: CARL HERTZOG, 1964.

MARTIN, JACK. BORDER BOSS: CAPTAIN JOHN R. HUGHES. SAN
    ANTONIO: THE NAYLOR COMPANY, 1942.

MARTIN.   "CALIFORNIA EMIGRANT ROADS THROUGH   (HC*).

MARTIN, MABELLE EPPARD.   "FROM TEXAS TO CALIFORNIA IN 1849:
    DIARY OF C.C. COX".   SOUTHWESTERN HISTORICAL
    QUARTERLY, VOL. 29   (JULY 1925), PP. 36-50 (TJ).

MARTIN, MABELLE EPPARD.   "FROM TEXAS TO CALIFORNIA IN 1849:
    DIARY OF C.C. COX".   SOUTHWESTERN HISTORICAL
    QUARTERLY, VOL. 29   (OCTOBER 1925), PP. 128-146 (TJ).

MARTIN, MABELLE EPPARD.   "FROM TEXAS TO CALIFORNIA IN 1849:
    DIARY OF C.C. COX".   SOUTHWESTERN HISTORICAL
    QUARTERLY, VOL. 29   (JANUARY 1926), PP. 201-223 (TJ).

MARTIN, MARY JEAN. MAYOR OF EL PASO, 1910-1915.   HISTORY
    SEMINAR PAPER, TEXAS WESTERN COLLEGE, AUGUST, 1956.

MARTIN, ROBERT L.   THE CITY MOVES WEST, ECONOMIC AND
    INDUSTRIAL GROWTH IN CENTRAL WEST TEXAS.   AUSTIN:
    UNIVERSITY OF TEXAS PRESS, 1969.

MAUDSLAY, ROBERT.   TEXAS SHEEP MAN.   AUSTIN: UNIVERSITY
    OF TEXAS PRESS, 1951.

MAXWELL, VERA ROGERS.   THE DIARIO HISTORICO" OF CARLOS
    MARIA BUSTAMANTE FOR 1824.   UNIVERSITY OF TEXAS AT
    AUSTIN, PHD. DISSERTATION.

MAYHALL, MILDRED PICKLE.   THE INDIANS OF TEXAS: THE
    ATAKAPA, THE KARANKAWA, THE TONKAWA.   UNIVERSITY OF
    TEXAS AT AUSTIN, PHD. DISSERTATION (1939).

MC ARTHUR, D. E.   THE CATTLE INDUSTRY OF TEXAS 1685-1918.
    UNIVERSITY OF TEXAS, MASTER'S THESIS (1918).

MC CALEB, WALTER FLAVIUS.   THE SPANISH MISSIONS OF TEXAS.
    UNIVERSITY OF TEXAS AT AUSTIN, MASTER'S THESIS.

MC CALEB, WALTER FLAVIUS.   THE SPANISH MISSIONS OF TEXAS.
    SAN ANTONIO: NAYLOR PRINTING COMPANY, 1954.

MC CARY.   THESE MINORITIES OUR MIDST: WITH   (SO*).

MC CLEAN, FRANCIS H.   "PASSAGE TO TEXAS".   SURVEY,
    (NOVEMBER 19, 1910), PP. 285-94.

MC CONVILLE, JAMES EDWARD.   "EL PASO-CIUDAD JUAREZ: A FOCUS
    OF INTER-AMERICAN CULTURE".   NEW MEXICO HISTORICAL
    REVIEW, VOL. 40   (JULY 1965), PP. 233-247.

MC DONALD, JOHNNIE BELLE.   THE SOLDIERS OF SAN JACINTO.
    UNIVERSITY OF TEXAS AT AUSTIN, MASTER'S THESIS (1922).

MC GARY, MOLLIE M. THESE MINORITIES IN OUR MIDST: WITH
    EMPHASIS ON LATIN AMERICANS IN TEXAS.   UNIVERSITY
    OF TEXAS, MASTER'S THESIS (195) (SO).

MC GILL, MARGARET. THE ADMINISTRATION OF CARLOS FRANQUIS
    DE LUGO, GOVERNOR OF TEXAS, 1736-1737.   UNIVERSITY
    OF TEXAS AT AUSTIN, MASTER'S THESIS (1928).

MC KAY, SETH, AND FAULK, ODIE B. TEXAS AFTER SPINDLETOP:
    THE SAGA OF TEXAS, 1901-1965.   AUSTIN, TEXAS:
    STECK-VAUGHN, 1965.

MC KNIGHT, JOSEPH W. THE SPANISH WATERCOURSES OF TEXAS.
    INDIANAPOLIS: BOBBS-MERRILL COMPANY, 1966 (LW).

MC LEAN, MALCOLM DALLAS. THE LIFE AND WORKS OF GUILLERMO
    PRIETO, 1818-1897.   UNIVERSITY OF TEXAS AT AUSTIN,
    PHD. DISSERTATION (1951).

MC MASTER, RICHARD K. "CANBY'S CAPTAINS OF THE SOUTHWEST:
    1860-1862".   PASSWORD, VOL. 6 (FALL 1961), PP. 123-140.

MC MASTER, RICHARD K. "CANBY'S CAPTAINS OF THE SOUTHWEST:
    1860-1862".   PASSWORD, VOL. 6 (SUMMER 1961), PP.
    79-95.

MC MASTER, RICHARD K. "THE EVOLUTION OF EL PASO COUNTY".
    PASSWORD, VOL. 3 (JULY 1958), PP. 120-122.

MC MASTER, RICHARD K. "THE MANSFIELD REPORT". PASSWORD,
    VOL. 4 (JULY 1959), PP. 96-112.

MC MASTER, RICHARD K. MUSKET, SHEER, AND MISSILE:
    A HISTORY OF FORT BLISS.   EL PASO: COMPLETE PRINTING
    AND LETTER SERVICE, 1962.

METZ, LEON. "WHY OLD JOHN SELMAN DIED".   FRONTIER TIMES,
    VOL. 39 (OCTOBER-NOVEMBER 1965), PP. 30-31, 64-65.

METZ, LEON. DALLAS STOUDENMIRE: EL PASO MARSHAL.   MS..

METZ, LEON. JOHN SELMAN, TEXAS GUNFIGHTER.   NEW YORK:
    HASTINGS HOUSE, 1966.

MEXICO. GOOD NEIGHBOR POLICY MEXICANS (SO*).

MEYERS. "EMPLOYMENT RELATIVE EARNINGS (EC*).

MEYERS. SPANISH-NAME PERSONS LABOR FORCE (EC*).

MIDDAGH. PASO AFTER DARK (SO*).

MIDDLETON, ANNIE LAURA. THE FORMATION OF THE TEXAS
    CONSTITUTION OF 1845.   UNIVERSITY OF TEXAS AT AUSTIN,
    MASTER'S THESIS (1920) (PL).

MILLER.   "THE CONNECTION PENALOSA WITH (TJ*).

MILLER, EDMUND THORNTON. A FINANCIAL HISTORY OF TEXAS.
    NEW YORK, NY AND LONDON, GREAT BRITAIN: AMS PRESS,
    INC (EC).

MILLS, W. W. FORTY YEARS AT EL PASO, 1858-1898.   EL PASO:
    CARL HERTZOG, 1962.

MILLS, W. W. EL PASO. A GLANCE AT ITS MEN AND CONTESTS
    FOR THE LAST FEW YEARS: THE ELECTION FRAUD, THE
    MARSHES, WILLIAMS, PEARSON, VERNEY, STINE AND
    FOUNTAINTHE INFAMOUS.   AUSTIN: REPUBLICAN OFFICE,
    1871.

MINOR, JOSEPH E. AND STEINBERG. A BRIEF ON THE ACEQUIAS
    OF SAN ANTONIO.   SAN ANTONIO BRANCH OF THE TEXAS
    SECTION OF THE AMERICAN SOCIETY OF CIVIL ENGINEERS
    (GE).

MOORE, WILMAN HARPER. A HISTORY OF SAN FELIPE DE AUSTIN,
    1824-1836.   UNIVERSITY OF TEXAS, MASTER'S THESIS (1929).

MORFI, AUGUSTIN. HISTORY OF TEXAS, 1673-1799.   ALBUQUERQUE,
    NEW MEXICO: QUIVIRA SOCIETY, 1935.

MORFI, FRAY JUAN AGUSTIN. HISTORY OF TEXAS, 1673-1779.
    TRANSLATED WITH BIOGRAPHICAL INTRODUCTION AND
    ANNOTATIONS BY CARLOS EDUARDO CASTANEDA, ALBUQUERQUE:
    THE QUIVIRA SOCIETY, 1935.

MORFI, FRAY JUAN AGUSTIN. HISTORY OF TEXAS, 1673-1779.
    NEW YORK, NEW YORK: ARMO PRESS, 1971.

MORGAN, THOMAS B. "TEXAS GIANT AWAKENS. GREATER POLITICAL
    INFLUENCE FOR MEXICANOS".   LOOK, VOL. 27 (OCTOBER
    8, 1963), P. 71 (PL).

MORIN.   ATTITUDES TEXAS MEXICAN AMERICANS (PY*).

MORRELL.   RISE GROWTH PUBLIC EDUCATIONPASO (ED*).

MORRILL, SIBLEY S. THE TEXAS CANNIBALS.   OAKLAND,
    CALIFORNIA: THE HOLMES BOOK COMPANY, 1964.

MORSE, FREDERIC C. THE COMMERCE AND THE COMMERCIAL POLICY
    OF THE REPUBLIC OF TEXAS.   UNIVERSITY OF TEXAS AT
    AUSTIN, MASTER'S THESIS (1906) (EC).

MORTON.   LIFE GENERAL DON MANUEL DE MIER (HSW*).

MOSELEY.   DAVY CROCKETT: HERO WILD FRONTIER   (LI*).

MUCKLEROY, ANNA.   THE INDIAN POLICY OF THE REPUBLIC
      OF TEXAS.   UNIVERSITY OF TEXAS AT AUSTIN, MASTER'S
      THESIS (1919).

MULLIN.   "DAVID MERIWETHER, TERRITORIAL   (HN*).

MULLIN, ROBERT N.   "IN EL PASO, JOHN WESLEY HARDIN TRIED
      TO LIVE DOWN GUNMAN REPUTATION".   THE SOUTHWESTERNER,
      VOL. 2   (DECEMBER 1962), P. 2.

MYERS, JOHN MYERS.   ALAMO.   NEW YORK: BANTAM,.

MYERS, JOHN MYERS.   THE ALAMO.   NEW YORK: DUTTON, 1948.

NAGEL.   IRRIGATION TEXAS   (EC*).

NANCE, JOSEPH M.   AFTER SAN JACINTO: THE TEXAS-AMERICAN
      FRONTIER, 18361841.   AUSTIN: UNIVERSITY OF TEXAS
      PRESS, 1963 (LI).

NANCE, JOSEPH MILTON.   ATTACK AND COUNTERATTACK: THE
      TEXAS-MEXICAN FRONTIER 1842.   AUSTIN: UNIVERSITY OF
      TEXAS PRESS, 1964.

NEIGHBORS, KENNETH.   "THE EXPEDITION OF MAJOR ROBERT S.
      NEIGHBORS TO EL PASO IN 1849".   SOUTHWESTERN
      HISTORICAL QUARTERLY, VOL. 58   (JULY 1954), PP. 36-59.

NEIGHBOURS, KENNETH FRANKLIN.   ROBERT S. NEIGHBORS
      IN TEXAS, 1836-1859.   UNIVERSITY OF TEXAS AT AUSTIN,
      PHD. DISSERTATION (1955).

NELSON, A. B.   "CAMPAIGNING IN THE BIG BEND OF THE
      RIO GRANDE IN 1787".   SOUTHWESTERN HISTORICAL
      QUARTERLY, VOL. 39 NO. 3 (1936), PP. 200-227.

NEU, CHARLES LUIS TERNAY.   THE EASTERN BOUNDARY OF TEXAS
      FROM THE GULF OF MEXICO TO THE RED RIVER.   UNIVERSITY
      OF TEXAS AT AUSTIN, MASTER'S THESIS (1909).

NEWCOMB, WILLIAM WILMON, JR.   INDIANS OF TEXAS: FROM
      PREHISTORIC TO MODERN TIMES.   AUSTIN: UNIVERSITY OF
      TEXAS PRESS, 1961.

NICOLL, MARIAN C.   A HISTORY OF THE EL PASO SEWAGE
      TREATMENT AND PUMPING PLANT.   TEXAS WESTERN COLLEGE,
      JANUARY 1951.

NIEMEYER, EBERHARDT VICTOR, JR.   THE PUBLIC CAREER
      OF GENERAL BERNARDO REYES.   UNIVERSITY OF TEXAS AT
      AUSTIN, PHD. DISSERTATION (1958).

NIMMO, DAN.   THE TEXAS POLITICAL SYSTEM.   ENGLEWOOD
      CLIFFS, NEW JERSEY: PRENTICE-HALL, INC., 1971 (PL).

NORDYKE.   CATTLE EMPIRE   (LI*).

NORDYKE.   GREAT ROUNDUP   (LI*).

NORDYKE.   JOHN WESLEY HARDIN: TEXAS GUNMAN   (LI*).

NORDYKE.   TRUTH ABOUT TEXAS   (LI*).

NORQUEST.   RIO GRANDE WETBACKS: MEXICAN   (LI*).

O' DONNELL, WALTER J.   "LA SALLE'S OCCUPATION OF TEXAS".
    MID-AMERICA, VOL. 18   (1936).

OATES, STEPHEN B.   "LOS DIABLOS TEJANOS".   THE AMERICAN
    WEST, VOL. 2 NO. 3 (SUMMER 1965), PP. 41-50.

OATES, STEPHEN B.   THE REPUBLIC OF TEXAS.   AUSTIN, TEXAS:
    TEXAS STATE HISTORICAL ASSOCIATION, 1968.

OATES, STEPHEN B. (ED).   "SPECIAL ISSUE: THE REPUBLIC OF
    TEXAS".   THE AMERICAN WEST, VOL. 5   (MAY 1968), P.
    3.

OATES, STEPHEN B. (ED).   VISIONS OF GLORY: TEXANS ON THE
    SOUTHWESTERN FRONTIER.   NORMAN, OKLAHOMA: UNIVERSITY
    OF OKLAHOMA PRESS, 1970.

OBERSTE, WILLIAM H.   HISTORY OF REFUGIO MISSION.
    PRIVATELY PRINTED, REFUGIO, 1942.

OBERSTE, WILLIAM H.   REMEMBER GOLIAD.   AUSTIN: VON
    BOECKMANN-JONES COMPANY, 1949.

OBERSTE, WILLIAM H.   THE RESTLESS FRIAR: VENERABLE FRAY
    ANTONIO MARGIL DE JESUS, MISSIONARY TO THE AMERICAS
    -- APOSTLE OF TEXAS.   AUSTIN: VON BOECKMANN-JONES
    COMPANY, 1970.

ODELL, ARABELLA GERTRUDE.   REOPENING THE AFRICAN SLAVE
    TRADE IN TEXAS.   UNIVERSITY OF TEXAS AT AUSTIN,
    MASTER'S THESIS (1946).

ODEN, ALONZO VAN.   RANGER'S DIARY AND SCRAPBOOK.   DALLAS:
    THE KALEIDOGRAPH PRESS, 1936.

OLDER, FREMONT.   CALIFORNIA MISSIONS AND THEIR ROMANCE.
    NEW YORK: COWARD-MCCANN INC., 1938.

OLGUIN, JOSEPH.   SAM HOUSTON: FRIEND OF THE INDIANS.   NEW
    YORK: HOUGHTON, 1958.

ORNDORFF, HELEN.   HISTORY OF THE DEVELOPMENT OF AGRICULTURE
    IN THE EL PASO VALLEY.   TEXAS WESTERN COLLEGE,
    MASTER'S THESIS (MAY 1957) (EC).

ORNELAS, CHARLES. "THE DEVELOPMENT OF AGRICULTURE IN THE
    EL PASO VALLEY--THE SPANISH PERIOD". PASSWORD, VOL.
    5 (OCTOBER 1960), PP. 139-145 (EC).

ORTIZ, TADEO. "TADEO ORTIZ DEY AYALA AND THE COLONIZATION
    OF TEXAS, 1822-1833". SOUTHWESTERN HISTORICAL
    QUARTERLY, VOL. 32 NO. 4 (1929), PP. 311-343.

OWEN. SWING TURN (AN*).

OWENS. REVEREND CARLOS M. PINTO, S.J (RE*).

PADILLA, JUAN ANTONIO. "TEXAS IN 1820". SOUTHWESTERN
    HISTORICAL QUARTERLY, VOL. 23 NO. 1 (1919), PP. 47-68.

PARISOT. HISTORY CATHOLIC CHURCH DIOCESE (RE*).

PARRISH, JOE K. "HANGED BY THE NECK TILL DEAD".
    PASSWORD, VOL. 3 (APRIL 1958), PP. 68-75.

PARRISH, JOE K. MRS. MARY M. PHILLIPS LIVES AL PASO
    HISTORY. EL PASO TIMES, JANUARY 7, 1951.

PARRISH, JOE K. RANGER KILLED IN GUN BATTLE. EL PASO
    TIMES SUN DIAL, SEPTEMBER 26, 1965.

PARRISH, JOE, AND CALLEROS, CLEOFAS. HAS DAUGHTER OF EL
    PASOS FIRST SETTLER BEEN FOUND?. EL PASO TIMES,
    JANUARY 17, 1965.

PARRSIH, JOE K. COFFINS, CACTUS AND COWBOYS: THE EXCITING
    STORY OF EL PASO, 1536 TO THE PRESENT. EL PASO:
    SUPERIOR PUBLISHING COMPANY, 1964.

PATTERSON. OCCUPATIONAL CHANGE AMONG SPANISH-AMERICANS
    (EC*).

PAYNE, LEONIDAS W. A SURVEY OF TEXAS LITERATURE.
    CHICAGO: RAND MCNALLY, 1928.

PEAVY, CHARLES D. A TEXAS PICARO. AUSTIN, TEXAS:
    STECK-VAUGHN COMPANY, 1967.

PEEVY, LUCIEN ELLICT. THE FIRST TWO YEARS OF TEXAS
    STATEHOOD 1846-1847. UNIVERSITY OF TEXAS AT AUSTIN,
    PHD. DISSERTATION (1948).

PERRY, GEORGE SESSIONS. THE STORY OF TEXAS. GARDEN CITY,
    NEW YORK: GARDEN CITY BOOKS, 1956 (LJE).

PEYTON, GREEN. SAN ANTONIO, CITY IN THE SUN. NEW YORK:
    WHITTLESEY HOUSE, 1946.

PEYTON, GREEN. SAN ANTONIC: CITY IN THE SUN. NEW YORK:
    MCGRAW-HILL, 1946.

PHILLIPS, MARY. STATEMENT OF MARY M PHILLIPS OF EARLY DAYS
     IN EL PASO, TEXAS, MAY 26, 1934.   R. F. BURGES
     COLLECTION, BOOK L, 14-30.

PICHARDO, JOSE ANTONIO. PICHARDOS TREATISE ON THE LIMITS
     OF LOUISIANA AND TEXAS.   AUSTIN: UNIVERSITY OF TEXAS
     PRESS, 1931.

PIERCE, GERALD S. TEXAS UNDER ARMS: THE CAPS, POSTS, FORTS
     AND MILITARY TOWNS OF THE REPUBLIC OF TEXAS, 1836-1846.
     AUSTIN, TEXAS: THE ENCINO PRESS, 1969.

PILGRIM, THOMAS. LIVE BOYS OR CHARLEY AND NASHO IN TEXAS.
     BOSTON: LEE AND SHEPARD, 1878 (LI).

PORTER, EUGENE O. "MAP NO. TWO OF SATTERTHWAITES ADDITION
     TO EL PASO, 1884".   PASSWORD, VOL. 1 (MAY 1956),
     P. 68.

PORTER, EUGENE O. "NO DARK AND COLD AND DREARY DAYS-EL
     PASO, TEXAS, AS A HEALTH RESORT".   PASSWORD, VOL.
     4 (APRIL 1959), PP. 71-74.

PORTER, EUGENE O. "SAN ELIZARIO, A CENTURY OF HISTORY".
     PASSWORD, VOL. 9 (WINTER 1964), PP. 137-146.

PORTER, EUGENE O. "THE FOUNDING OF SAN ELIZARIO".
     PASSWORD, VOL. 9 (FALL 1964), PP. 87-98.

POTTER, MRS. W. R. TEXAS IN HISTORY-STORY-LEGEND.
     DALLAS: SOUTHWEST PRESS, 1933 (LI).

PRESTWOOD, NADINE H. SOCIAL LIFE AND CUSTOMS OF THE PEOPLE
     OF EL PASO.   TEXAS WESTERN COLLEGE, MASTER'S THESIS
     (1949).

PRIDGEN, MRS. VELMA HILL. THE ADMINISTRATION OF DON
     JACINTO DE BARRIOS Y JAUREGUI AS GOVERNOR OF TEXAS,
     1751-1759.   UNIVERSITY OF TEXAS AT AUSTIN, MASTER'S
     THESIS (1933).

PROCTER, BEN H. NOT WITHOUT HONOR, THE LIFE OF JOHN
     REAGAN.   AUSTIN: UNIVERSITY OF TEXAS PRESS, 1962.

RAMSDELL, CHARLES JR. SPANISH GOLIAD.   MANUSCRIPT,
     UNIVERSITY OF TEXAS ARCHIVES, AUSTIN.

RAMSDELL, CHARLES WILLIAM. RECONSTRUCTION IN TEXAS.   NEW
     YORK: LONGMANS, GREEN, 1910 (HS).

RAMSDELL, CHARLES. SAN ANTONIO: A HISTORICAL AND PICTORIAL
     GUIDE.   AUSTIN: UNIVERSITY OF TEXAS PRESS, 1959.

RAMSDELL, CHARLES. SAN ANTONIO: A HISTORICAL AND PICTORIAL
     GUIDE.   AUSTIN: UNIVERSITY OF TEXAS PRESS, 1960.

RANSON, NANCY R. TEXAS WILDFLOWER LEGENDS.   DALLAS:
    KALEIDOGRAPH PRESS, 1933 (AN LJE).

RAYMOND, DORA NEILL. CAPTAIN LEE HALL OF TEXAS.   NORMAN,
    OKLAHOMA: UNIVERSITY OF OKLAHOMA PRESS, 1940.

REED, S. G. A HISTORY OF THE TEXAS RAILROADS.   HOUSTON:
    ST. CLAIR PUBLISHING COMPANY, 1941 (EC).

REHN.   SAN ANTONIO MISSIONS LITERATURE (LI*).

REMY, CAROLINE. "HISPANIC-MEXICAN SAN ANTONIO: 1836-1861".
    SOUTHWESTERN HISTORICAL QUARTERLY, VOL. 71 NO.
    4 (1968), PP. 564-570 (HS).

RENDON LOZANO, RUBEN. VIVA TEJAS; THE STORY OF THE
    MEXICAN-BORDER PATRIOTS OF THE REPUBLIC OF TEXAS.
    SAN ANTONIO SOUTHERN LITERARY INSTITUTE, 1936.

RICHARDS.   ESTABLISHMENT CANDELARIA SANLORENZO   (HS*).

RICHARDS, NORMAN. THE STORY OF THE ALAMO.   CHICAGO,
    ILLINOIS: CHILDRENS PRESS, 1970.

RICHARDSON, RUPERT N. FRONTIER OF NORTHWEST TEXAS,
    1846-1876.   GLENDALE, CALIFORNIA: ARTHUR H. CLARK
    COMPANY, 1963 (HUS).

RIGLER, FRANK CLEMENT. THE HISTORY OF THE SAN ANTONIO
    EXPRESS.   UNIVERSITY OF TEXAS AT AUSTIN, MASTER'S
    THESIS (1932) (NP).

RISTER, CARL COKE. FORT GRIFFIN ON THE TEXAS FRONTIER.
    NORMAN, OKLAHOMA: UNIVERSITY OF OKLAHOMA PRESS, 1956.

ROBINSON.   "FLAG ILLUSION: TEXAS REVOLUTION (LI*).

ROBINSON, DUNCAN W. JUDGE ROBERT MCALPIN WILLIAMSON:
    TEXAS' THREELEGGED WILLIE.   AUSTIN, TEXAS: TEXAS
    STATE HISTORICAL ASSOCIATION, 1948.

ROBINSON.   MUSTANGS MUSTANGING SOUTHWEST (LI*).

RODRIGUEZ.   HENRY B. GONZALES, POLITICALPROFILE (PL*).

RODRIGUEZ.   RODRIGUEZ MOMOIRS EARLY TEXAS (TJ*).

ROY, ADDIE MAY. HISTORY OF TELEGRAPH AND TEXAS REGISTER.
    UNIVERSITY OF TEXAS AT AUSTIN, MASTER'S THESIS (1931).

ROY, MARY MARGUERITE. RELATIONS BETWEEN THE UNITED STATES
    AND MEXICO DURING THE ADMINISTRATIONOF LERDO DE
    TEJADA, 1872-1876.   UNIVERSITY OF TEXAS AT AUSTIN,
    MASTER'S THESIS (1933) (HSW HUS).

RUECKING, FREDERICK HENRY, JR. THE COAHUILTECAN INDIANS
    OF SOUTHERN TEXAS AND NORTHEASTERN MEXICO. UNIVERSITY
    OF TEXAS AT AUSTIN, MASTER'S THESIS (1955) (HM).

RYAN. ELECTION LAWS TEXAS, 1827-1875 (PL*).

SANCHEZ LAMEGO, MIGUEL A. THE SIEGE AND TAKING OF
    THE ALAMO. SANTA FE, NEW MEXICO: PRESS OF THE
    TERRITORIAN, 1968.

SANCHEZ NAVARRO. SANCHEZ NAVARRO PAPERS (1658-1895).
    VOLUME 1, NUMBER 1, SUMMER 1944. PAGES 31-32.

SANCHEZ NAVARRO. THE SANCHEZ NAVARRO COLLECTION OF
    DOCUMENTS FOR A HISTORY OF TEXAS AND COAHUILA.
    TYPEWRITTEN CALENDAR, LATIN AMERICAN COLLECTION,
    UNIVERSITY OF TEXAS, AUSTIN, TEXAS..

SANCHEZ-NAVARRO, CARLOS. LA GUERRA DE TEJAS: MEMORIAS DE
    UN SOLDADO. MEXICO: EDITORIAL JUS, S.A., 1960.

SANCHEZ. "A TRIP TO TEXAS 1828" (TJ*).

SANCHEZ. VIAJE TEXAS -- EN 1828-1829,DIARIO (TJ*).

SANDBO, ANNA IRENE. BEGINNINGS OF THE SECESSION MOVEMENT
    IN TEXAS. UNIVERSITY OF TEXAS AT AUSTIN, MASTER'S
    THESIS (1913).

SANGER, DONALD BRIDGMAN. THE STORY OF FORT BLISS. EL
    PASO: PRIVATELY PRINTED, 1933.

SANTLEBEN, AUGUST. A TEXAS PIONEER. EARLY STAGING
    AND OVERLAND FREIGHTING DAYS ON THE FRONTIERS OF TEXAS
    AND MEXICO. NEW YORK AND WASHINGTON: THE NEALE
    PUBLISHING COMPANY, 1910.

SANTOS, RICHARD G. "A PRELIMINARY SURVEY OF THE SAN
    FERNANDO ARCHIVES". TEXAS LIBRARIES, VOL. 28 NO.
    4 (1966-1967), PP. 152-172.

SANTOS, RICHARD G. "THE QUARTEL DE SAN ANTONIO DE BEXAR".
    TEXANA, VOL. 5 NO. 3 (1967), PP. 187-202.

SANTOS, RICHARD G. SANTA ANNA'S CAMPAIGN AGAINST TEXAS.
    1835-1836. WACO, TEXAS: TEXIAN PRESS, 1968.

SCARBOROUGH, FRANCES. OLD SPANISH MISSIONS IN TEXAS.
    SOUTHWEST REVIEW, VOLUME 13, NUMBER 2, 1926. PAGES
    155-177; NUMBER 3, PAGES 367-397: NUMBER 4, PAGES
    491-502., VOLUME 14, NUMBER 1, PAGES 87-105: NUMBER
    2, PAGES 237-255, 1929 (HS).

SCHMITT, EDMOND J. P. A CATALOGUE OF FRANCISCAN MISSIONARIES
    IN TEXAS, 1528-1859. AUSTIN, 1901.

SCOTT, ALAN. "TWENTY-FIVE YEARS OF OPINON ON INTEGRATION
     IN TEXAS".   SOUTHWEST SOCIAL SCIENCE QUARTERLY, VOL.
     48 NO. 2 (SEPTEMBER 1967), PP. 155-164.

SCRUGGS, O. M. "TEXAS AND THE BRACERO PROGRAM".   PACIFIC
     HISTORICAL REVIEW, VOL. 32 (AUGUST 1963), PP.
     251-264 (EC).

SCRUGGS, OTEY M. "TEXAS, GOOD NEIGHBOR?".   SOUTHWESTERN
     SOCIAL SCIENCE QUARTERLY, VOL. 43 (SEPTEMBER 1962),
     PP. 118-125 (SO).

SELMAN, JOHN, JR. JOHN SELMAN OF EL PASO.   MS.

SEYMOR, V. CONNOR. ADVENTURE IN GLORY: THE SAGA OF TEXAS,
     1836-1849.   AUSTIN, TEXAS: STECK-VAUGHN COMPANY, 1965.

SHANNON.   IDOLS CROWD (LI*).

SHELBY, CHAMION CLAIR. "ST. DENIS'S DECLARATION CONCERNING
     TEXAS IN 1717".   SOUTHWESTERN HISTORICAL QUARTERLY,
     VOL. 26 NO. 3 (1923), PP. 165-183.

SHELBY, CHAMION CLAIR. "ST. DENIS'S SECOND EXPEDITION TO
     THE RIO GRANDE, 1716-1719".   SOUTHWESTERN HISTORICAL
     QUARTERLY, VOL. 27 NO. 3 (1924), PP. 190-216.

SHELBY, CHAMION CLAIR. "THE EFFECT OF THE SPANISH
     REOCCUPATION OF EASTERN TEXAS UPON FRENCH POLICY IN
     LOUISIANA, 1715-1717".   HISPANIC AMERICAN HISTORICAL
     REVIEW, VOL. 24 NO. 4 (1944), PP. 605-613.

SHELBY, CHAMION CLAIR. INTERNATIONAL RIVALRY IN NORTHEASTERN
     NEW SPAIN, 1700-1725.   UNIVERSITY OF TEXAS AT AUSTIN,
     PHD. DISSERTATION (1935).

SHELBY, CHAMION CLAIR. ST. DENIS'S SECOND EXPEDITION FROM
     LOUISIANA TO THE RIO GRANDE, 1716-1719.   UNIVERSITY
     OF TEXAS AT AUSTIN, MASTER'S THESIS (1927).

SHERMAN, EDWARD F. A DECADE OF EXPLORATION IN THE
     SOUTHWEST.   TEXAS WESTERN COLLEGE, MASTER'S THESIS
     (1962).

SHOCKLEY.   CHICANO REVOLT TEXAS TOWN.   (PL*).

SIBLEY.   TRAVELERS TEXAS, 1761-1860 (HSW*).

SIEGEL, STANLEY. SELECTED READINGS IN TEXAS HISTORY.
     BERKELEY, CALIFORNIA: MC CUTCHAN PUBLISHING CORPORATION,
     1970.

SIMPSON, COL. HAROLD B. HOOD'S TEXAS BRIGADE IN POETRY
     AND SONG.   HILLSBORO, TEXAS: HILL JUNIOR COLLEGE
     PRESS, 1968 (LI).

SIMPSON, WILLIAM HASKELL. MICHAEL BONHAM OR THE FALL OF
    BEXAR. JNO. R. THOMPSON, 1852.

SJOBERG, ANDREE F. "LIPAN APACHE CULTURE IN HISTORICAL
    PERSPECTIVE". SOUTHWESTERN JOURNAL OF ANTHROPOLOGY,
    VOL. 9 NO. 1 (1953), PP. 76-98.

SJOBERG, ANDREE F. "THE CULTURE OF THE TONKAWA, A TEXAS
    INDIAN TRIBE". TEXAS JOURNAL OF SCIENCE, VOL. 5
    NO. 3 (1953), PP. 280-304.

SKEELS. ETHNOHISTORICAL SURVEY TEXASINDIANS (LI*).

SKRABANEK, R. L. A DECADE OF POPULATION CHANGE IN TEXAS.
    COLLEGE STATION, TEXAS: TEXAS AGRICULTURAL EXPERIMENT
    STATION, SEPTEMBER 1963.

SMITH, ERWIN E. LIFE ON THE TEXAS RANGE. AUSTIN:
    UNIVERSITY OF TEXAS PRESS, 1952.

SMITH, HARVEY. ROMANTIC SAN ANTONIO. SAN ANTONIO:
    JACKSON PRINTING COMPANY, 1918.

SMITH, JUSTIN H. THE ANNEXATION OF TEXAS. NEW YORK:
    BARNES AND NOBLE, INC., 1941.

SMITH, JUSTIN HARVEY. "LA REPUBLICA DEL RIO GRANDE.
    AMERICAN HISTORICAL REVIEW". AMERICAN HISTORICAL
    REVIEW, VOL. 5 NO. 25 (OCTOBER 1919-JULY 1920).

SMITH, JUSTIN HARVEY. THE ANNEXATION OF TEXAS. CEPRINTED
    BY NEW YORK, NEW YORK AND LONDON, GREAT BRITAIN: AMS
    PRESS, INV.,.

SMITH, RUBY CUMBY. JAMES W. FANNIN, JR., IN THE TEXAS
    REVOLUTION. UNIVERSITY OF TEXAS AT AUSTIN, MASTER'S
    THESIS (1919).

SMITH, VICTOR J. "A SURVEY OF INDIAN LIFE IN TEXAS".
    WEST TEXAS HISTORICAL AND SCIENTIFIC SOCIETY, NO.
    5 (1941).

SMITH, VICTOR J. "EARLY SPANISH EXPLORATION IN THE BIG
    BEND OF TEXAS". WEST TEXAS HISTORICAL AND SCIENTIFIC
    SOCIETY PUBLICATIONS, NO. 2 (1926), PP. 55-68.

SMITHWICK, NOAH. THE EVOLUTION OF A STATE. REPRINT,
    AUSTIN: STECK, 1935.

SMOKER, D. E. "SOUTHWESTERN COOPERATIVE EDUCATIONAL
    LABORATORY; ADULT BASIC EDUCATION PROJECT". ADULT
    LEADERSHIP, VOL. 17 (JUNE 1968), PP. 73-74.

SOLIS. "DIARY VISIT INSPECTION TEXAS (TJ*).

SOLIS.   "THE SOLIS DIARY 1767"   (TJ*).

SOUKUP, JAMES RUDOLPH: MC CLESKY, CLIFRON: HOOLOWAY, HARRY.
     PARTY ANC FACTIONAL DIVISION IN TEXAS
     THE ANNALS OF SAN FRANCISCO.   AUSTIN, TEXAS:
     UNIVERSITY OF TEXAS PRESS, 1964 (PL).

SPLAWN.   DON JOSE ANTONIO PICHARDO: INVESTIGATION   (HSW*).

SPRATT, JCHN S.   THE ROAD TO SPINDLETOP: ECONOMIC CHANGE
     IN TEXAS, 1875-1901.   AUSTIN, TEXAS: UNIVERSITY
     STATION, (EC).

STAMBAUGH, J. LEE; STAMBAUGH, LILLIAN J.   THE LOWER RIO
     GRANDE VALLEY OF TEXAS.   SAN ANTONIO, TEXAS:
     THE NAYLOR CO.,.

STAMBAUGH.   MARKETING PERISHABLE FARM PRODUCTS   (EC*).

STARNES.   SAN GABRIEL MISSIONS, 1746-1756   (HS*).

STEAKLEY, DAN LEWIS.   THE BORDER PATROL OF THE SAN ANTONIO
     COLLECTION DISTRICT.   UNIVERSITY OF TEXAS AT AUSTIN,
     MASTER'S THESIS (1936).

STECK.   "FORERUNNERS CAPTAIN CE LEONS   (HS*).

STEEN, RALPH W. (ED.).   THE TEXAS STORY.   AUSTIN, TEXAS:
     STECK-VAUGHN COMPANY, 1960.

STEEN, RALPH W.: DONECKER, FRANCES.   TEXAS: OUR HERITAGE.
     AUSTIN, TEXAS: STECK-VAUGHN, 1962.

STEPHENS, ANDREW JACKSON.   A CALENCAR OF THE WRITINGS OF
     SAM HOUSTCN IN THE VARIOUS COLLECTIONS IN AUSTIN.
     UNIVERSITY OF TEXAS AT AUSTIN, MASTER'S THESIS (1927).

STEPHENSON, NATHANIEL W.   TEXAS AND THE MEXICAN WAR:
     A CHRONICLE OF THE WINNING OF THE SOUTHWEST.   NEW
     HAVEN: YALE UNIVERSITY PRESS, 1921.

STERLING, WILLIAM WARREN.   TRAILS AND TRIALS OF A TEXAS
     RANGER.   NORMAN, OKLAHOMA: UNIVERSITY OF OKLAHOMA
     PRESS, 1969.

STEVENSON.   GOOD NEIGHBCR POLICY MEXICANS   (SO*).

STIFF, EDWARD.   THE TEXAN EMIGRANT.   (1840)9 WACO, TEXAS:
     TEXIAN PRESS, (SI).

STOES.   SMUGGLERS GAP OFFERED PROTECTION   (HSW*).

STORY, ANNA B.   THE ALAMO FROM ITS FCUNDING TO 1937.
     UNIVERSITY OF TEXAS AT AUSTIN, MASTER'S THESIS (1938).

STRATEMEYER, EDWARD. UNDER SCOTT IN MEXICO.. BOSTON,
    ESTES, 1901. BOSTON: LOTHROP, 1909.

STRATEMEYER, EDWARD. WITH TAYLCR ON THE RIO GRANDE..
    BOSTON, ESTES, 1901. BOSTON: LOTHROP, 1909.

STRATEMEYER, EDWARD. FOR THE LIBERTY OF TEXAS. BOSTON,
    ESTES, 1900. BOSTON: LOTHROP, 1909.

STRATEMEYER, EDWARD. FOR THE LIBERTY OF TEXAS. BOSTON,
    ESTES, 1902. BOSTON: LOTHROP, 1909.

STRICKLAND, REX W. SIX WHO CAME TO EL PASO: PIONEERS OF
    THE 1840'S. EL PASO, TEXAS: TEXAS WESTERN COLLEGE
    PRESS, THE UNIVERSITY OF TEXAS AT EL PASO, 1963 (HSW).

STRICKLAND. "P. T. HERBERT: ANTE BELLUM RESIDENT (HSW*).

STRICKLAND, REX W. T. W. W. MILLS, EL PASO POLITICIAN.
    PASSWORD, 7.

STRICKLAND, REX WALLACE. "MOSCOSCO'S JOURNEY THROUGH
    TEXAS". SOUTHWESTERN HISTORICAL QUARTERLY, VOL. 46
    NO. 2 (1942), PP. 109-137.

STRICKLAND, REX WALLACE. ANGLO-AMERICAN ACTIVITIES
    IN NORTHEASTERN TEXAS, 1803-1845. UNIVERSITY
    OF TEXAS AT AUSTIN, PHD. DISSERTATION (1937) (HSW).

SUMPTER. LIFE JESSE SUMPTER, OLDEST CITIZEN (TJ*).

SUTHERLAND, T. S. "TEXAS TACKLES THE RACE PROBLEM".
    SATURDAY EVENING POST, VOL. 24 (JANUARY 12, 1952),
    PP. 22-23, 64, 66 (LI).

SWEET, ALEXANDER E. AND KNOX, JOHN. ON A MEXICAN MUSTANG
    THROUGH TEXAS. HARTFORD. SCRANTON, 1883. REPRINT.
    NEW YORK: OGILVIE, 1917.

TANNER. HANDBOOK: GOOD NEIGHBOR COMMISSION (SO*).

TARSHIS, ELIZABETH. THE VILLAGE THAT LEARNED TO READ.
    NEW YORK: HOUGHTON-MIFFLIN, 1941.

TAYLOR. AMERICANIZATION HARLINGENS MEXICAN (ED*).

TAYLOR. SPANISH ARCHIVES GENERAL LAND (HS*).

TAYLOR, ROSS M. BRAZOS. INDIANAPOLIS, BOBBS.

TEXAS FOLKLORE SOCIETY. BACKWOODS TO BORDER (AN*).

TEXAS FOLKLORE SOCIETY. CORONADOS CHILDREN (AN*).

TEXAS FOLKLORE SOCIETY. COYOTE WISDOM (AN*).

TEXAS FOLKLORE SOCIETY.   FOLK TRAVELERS: BALLADS, TALES
    (AN*).

TEXAS FOLKLORE SOCIETY.   FOLLOW DE DRINKIN GOUD   (AN*).

TEXAS FOLKLORE SOCIETY.   GOLDEN LOG   (AN*).

TEXAS FOLKLORE SOCIETY.   GOOD TALE BONNIE TUNE   (AN*).

TEXAS FOLKLORE SOCIETY.   HEALER LOS OLMOS OTHER MEXICAN
    (AN*).

TEXAS FOLKLORE SOCIETY.   HELL TO BREAKFAST   (AN*).

TEXAS FOLKLORE SOCIETY.   HORNS TOADS   (AN*).

TEXAS FOLKLORE SOCIETY.   HUNTERS HEALERS   (AN*).

TEXAS FOLKLORE SOCIETY.   LEGENDS TEXAS   (AN*).

TEXAS FOLKLORE SOCIETY.   MADSTONES TWISTERS   (AN*).

TEXAS FOLKLORE SOCIETY.   MAN, BIRD BEAST   (AN*).

TEXAS FOLKLORE SOCIETY.   MESQUITE WILLOW   (AN*).

TEXAS FOLKLORE SOCIETY.   MUSTANGS COW HORSES   (AN*).

TEXAS FOLKLORE SOCIETY.   PUBLICATIONS TEXAS FOLKLORE
    SOCIETY (AN*).

TEXAS FOLKLORE SOCIETY.   PUBLICATIONS TEXAS FOLKLORE
    SOCIETY (AN*).

TEXAS FOLKLORE SOCIETY.   PUBLICATIONS TEXAS FOLKLORE
    SOCIETY (AN*).

TEXAS FOLKLORE SOCIETY.   PUBLICATIONS TEXAS FOLKLORE
    SOCIETY (AN*).

TEXAS FOLKLORE SOCIETY.   PURO MEXICANO   (AN*).

TEXAS FOLKLORE SOCIETY.   SHADOW HISTORY   (AN*).

TEXAS FOLKLORE SOCIETY.   SINGERS STORYTELLERS   (AN*).

TEXAS FOLKLORE SOCIETY.   SOUTHWESTERN LORE   (AN*).

TEXAS FOLKLORE SOCIETY.   SPUR COCK   (AN*).

TEXAS FOLKLORE SOCIETY.   STRAIGHT TEXAS   (AN*).

TEXAS FOLKLORE SOCIETY.   SUNNY SLOPES LONG AGO   (AN*).

TEXAS FOLKLORE SOCIETY.   TEXAS FOLK SONGS   (AN*).

TEXAS FOLKLORE SOCIETY.   TEXAS FOLK FOLKLORE   (AN*).

TEXAS FOLKLORE SOCIETY.   TEXAS SOUTHWEST LORE   (AN*).

TEXAS FOLKLORE SOCIETY.   TEXIAN STOMPING GROUNDS   (AN*).

TEXAS FOLKLORE SOCIETY.   TIRE SHRINKER TO DRAGSTER   (AN*).

TEXAS FOLKLORE SOCIETY.   TONE BELL EASY   (AN*).

TEXAS STATE HISTORICAL SOCIETY. SOUTHWESTERN HISTORICAL
     QUARTERLY.   AUSTIN, TEXAS, 1911-1926 (HSW NP).

TEXAS STATE HISTORICAL ASSOCIATION. THE REPUBLIC OF TEXAS.
     TEXAS STATE HISTORICAL ASSOCIATION, 1968.

TEXAS. ADJUTANT GENERAL. REPORT OF THE ADJUTANT GENERAL
     OF THE STATE OF TEXAS FOR THE FISCAL YEAR ENDING
     AUGUST 31, 1878.   GALVESTON: BOOK AND JOB OFFICE OF
     THE GALVESTON NEWS, 1878.

THE NEW TEXAS READER. THE NEW TEXAS READER: A FACSIMILE
     OF THE 1864 EDITION.   AUSTIN, TEXAS: STECK-VAUGHN
     COMPANY, 1971.

THOMLINSON, M. H. "THE DRAGOONS AND EL PASO 1848".   NEW
     MEXICO HISTORICAL REVIEW, VOL. 23 (JULY 1948), PP.
     217-224.

THOMLINSON, MATTHEW H. THE GARRISON AT FORT BLISS.   EL
     PASO: HERTZOG AND RESLER, 1945.

THOMPLKINS, WALKER A. OLD SPANISH SANTA BARBARA: FROM
     CABRILLO TO FREMONT.   SANTA BARBARA, CALIFORNIA:
     MCNALLY AND LOFTIN, 1967.

THOMPSON, DR. HOWARD. BUILDERS OF EL PASO.   TYPESCRIPT
     1945.

THOMPSON, HOLLAND (ED.). THE BOOK OF TEXAS.   DALLAS:
     GROLIER SOCIETY, 1929.

THOMPSON, STITH. ROUND THE LEVEE.   REPRINT EDITION.
     AUSTIN, TEXAS: TEXAS FOLKLORE SOCIETY, 1935 (AN).

THOROUGHGOOD.   MARY HUNTER AUSTIN, INTERPRETER (HSW*).

THRALL, H. S. A HISTORY OF TEXAS.   NEW YORK: UNIVERSITY
     PUBLISHING COMPANY, 1876.

TINKLE, LON. THE ALAMO (ORIGINAL TITLE: 13 DAYS TO
     GLORY).   NEW YORK: A SIGNET KEY BOOK PUBLISHED BY
     THE NEW AMERICAN LIBRARY, 1958.

TOLBERT, FRANK X. THE DAY OF SAN JACINTO.   NEW YORK:
     MCGRAW-HILL BOOK COMPANY, 1959.

TOLBERT, FRANK X. AN INFORMAL HISTORY OF TEXAS.
    NEW YORK: HARPER, 1961.

TOLBERT, FRANK X. THE STAKED PLAINS.   NEW YORK: HARPER,,
    1958.

TORNEL, JOSE MARIA. TEXAS AND THE UNITED STATES OF AMERICA
    IN THEIR RELATIONS WITH THE MEXICAN REPUBLIC.
    COMPILED AND TRANSLATED BY CARLOS E. CASTANEDA.
    DALLAS: P. L. TURNER COMPANY, 1928 (HSW HUS HM).

TOULOUSE.   PIONEER POSTS TEXAS (HS*).

TOWNSEND, E. E. EARLY BORDER ELECTIONS. BULLETIN 44.
    ALPINE, TEXAS, SUL ROSS STATE TEACHERS COLLEGE,
    (1932). WEST TEXAS HISTORICAL AND SCIENTIFIC SOCIETY,
    PUBLICATIONS NUMBER 4..

TOWSEND, E. E. RANGERS AND INDIANS IN THE BIG BEND REGION.
    BULLETIN 56.   ALPINE, TEXAS: SUL ROSS STATE TEACHERS
    COLLEGE, (1935). WEST TEXAS HISTORICAL AND SCIENTIFIC
    SOCIETY, PUBLICATIONS NUMBER 6..

TURNER, MARTHA ANNE. SAM HOUSTON AND HIS TWELVE WOMEN.
    AUSTIN: PEMBERTON PRESS, 1966.

TURNER.   BULLETS, BOTTLES, GARDENIAS (LI*).

TYLER, RONNIE. VISION, DESTINY—WAR.   AUSTIN, TEXAS:
    STECK—VAUGHN COMPANY, 1970.

U. S.   EXECUTIVE DOCUMENT NO. 257.DEPREDATIONS (LW*).

U. S.   EXECUTIVE DOCUMENT NO. 13. MEXICAN (LW*).

U. S.   TEXAS FRONTIER TROUBLES (LW*).

U. S.   PRELIMINARY REPORT NATIONALITY (LW*).

U. S.   HEARINGS BEFORE SUB—COMMITTEE (LW*).

VAN ZANDT, K. M. FORCE WITHOUT FANFARE.   FORT WORTH:
    TEXAS CHRISTIAN UNIVERSITY PRESS, 1968.

VIGNESS, DAVID MARTELL. THE REPUBLIC OF THE RIO GRANDE:
    AN EXAMPLE OF SEPARATISM IN NORTHERN MEXICO.
    UNIVERSITY OF TEXAS AT AUSTIN, PHD. DISSERTATION
    (1951) (HSW).

VOWELL, JACK. POLITICS IN EL PASO, 1850—1920.   TEXAS
    WESTERN COLLEGE, MASTER'S THESIS (1950) (PL).

WALLACE, ERNEST AND VIGNESS, DAVID (EDS). DOCUMENTS OF
    TEXAS HISTORY.   AUSTIN, TEXAS: STECK—VAUGHN COMPANY,
    1963.

WALLACE, ERNEST. TEXAS IN TURMOIL THE SAGA OF TEXAS
     1849-1875.   AUSTIN, TEXAS: STECK-VAUGHN COMPANY, 1965.

WALLER, J. L. "THE CIVIL WAR IN THE EL PASO AREA".   WEST
     TEXAS HISTORICAL ASSOCIATION YEAR BOOK, VOL. 22
     (OCTOBER 1946), PP. 3-14 (HUS).

WALLER, JOHN L. COLOSSAL HAMILTON OF TEXAS.   EL PASO,
     TEXAS: TEXAS WESTERN PRESS, 1968.

WALLIS.   SIXTY YEARS BRAZOS--THE LIFELETTERS   (TJ*).

WALSH, SISTER NATALIE. THE FOUNDING OF LAREDO AND
     ST. AUGUSTINE CHURCH.   UNIVERSITY OF TEXAS AT AUSTIN,
     MASTER'S THESIS (1935).

WALZ, VINA. HISTORY OF THE EL PASO AREA, 1680-1692.
     UNIVERSITY OF NEW MEXICO, PHD. DISSERTATION (1951).

WARD, MARIE ERWIN. SWIFTLY THE YEARS.   DALLAS: TRIANGLE
     PUBLISHING COMPANY, 1968.

WEBB, JESSE OWEN. THE HISTORY OF GALVESTON TO 1865.
     UNIVERSITY OF TEXAS AT AUSTIN, MASTER'S THESIS (1924).

WEBB.   TEXAS RANGERS, CENTURY FRONTIER   (HS*).

WEBB, WALTER PRESCOTT (ED). THE HANDBOOK OF TEXAS.
     AUSTIN: TEXAS STATE HISTORICAL ASSOCIATION, 1952.

WEBB, WALTER PRESCOTT. THE TEXAS RANGERS: A CENTURY OF
     FRONTIER DEFENSE.   AUSTIN, TEXAS: UNIVERSITY OF TEXAS
     PRESS, 1965.

WEBB, WALTER PRESCOTT. THE TEXAS RANGERS IN THE MEXICAN
     WAR.   UNIVERSITY OF TEXAS AT AUSTIN, MASTER'S THESIS
     (1920).

WEDDLE, ROBERT S. SAN JUAN BAUTISTA, GATEWAY TO SPANISH
     TEXAS.   AUSTIN: UNIVERSITY OF TEXAS PRESS, 1968 (HS).

WEDDLE, ROBERT S. THE SAN SABA MISSION: SPANISH PIVOT IN
     TEXAS.   AUSTIN: UNIVERSITY OF TEXAS PRESS, 1964 (HS).

WEEKS, OLIVER DOUGLAS. "THE TEXAS-MEXICAN AND THE POLITICS
     OF SOUTH TEXAS".   AMERICAN POLITICAL SCIENCE REVIEW,
     VOL. 24 (AUGUST 1930), PP. 606-27 (PL).

WEIR, E. P. "THE MEXICAN CHILD".   TEXAS OUTLOOK, VOL.
     20 (JUNE 1936), P. 23 (LI).

WHALEN, WILLIAM A. "THE WETBACK PROBLEM IN SOUTHEAST
     TEXAS".   MONTHLY REVIEW, VOL. 8 NO. 8 (FEBRUARY
     1951).

WHARTON, CLARENCE. THE ISLE OF MAL HADO AND OTHER
    SKETCHES: THREE HUNDRED AND FIFTY YEARS OF TEXAS
    HISTORY. HOUSTON, TEXAS: THE FLETCHER YOUNG
    PUBLISHING COMPANY, 1968.

WHEELER, KENNETH. TO WEAR A CITY'S CROWN, THE BEGINNINGS
    OF URBAN GROWTH IN TEXAS. CAMBRIDGE: HARVARD
    UNIVERSITY PRESS, 1968 (SO).

WHITE . "A GLANCE AT MEXICANS" (LI*).

WHITE . AUTOBIOGRAPHY CURABLE SINNER (LI*).

WHITE . MY TEXAS TIS THEE (LI*).

WHITE . MY TEXAS, TIS THEE (LI*).

WHITE . OUT DESERT: HISTORICAL ROMANCE (LI*).

WHITE . TEXAS: INFORMAL BIOGRAPHY (LI*).

WHITE . TRIGGER FINGER (LI*).

WHITE, ALICE M. HISTORY OF THE DEVELOPMENT OF IRRIGATION
    IN THE EL PASO VALLEY. TEXAS WESTERN COLLEGE,
    MASTER'S THESIS (MAY 1950).

WHITE, ZACH T. "ZACH WHITE TELLS STORY OF FAMOUS CITY
    MARSHAL". EVENING POST, (MAY 30, 1928).

WILCOX, RUTH TURNER. FIVE CENTURIES OF AMERICAN COSTUME.
    NEW YORK: SCRIBNER, 1963.

WILCOX, SEB. B. "CONVERSATIONS". SOUTHWESTERN HISTORICAL
    QUARTERLY, VOL. 42 NO. 2 (OCTOBER 1938).

WILLIAMS. ROUTE CABEZA DE VACA TEXAS:STUDY (HS*).

WILLIAMS, AMELIA. A CRITICAL STUDY OF THE SIEGE OF THE
    ALAMO AND OF THE PERSONNEL OF ITS DEFENDERS.
    UNIVERSITY OF TEXAS AT AUSTIN, PHD. DISSERTATION (1931).

WILLIAMS, AMELIA. THE SIEGE AND FALL OF THE ALAMO.
    UNIVERSITY OF TEXAS AT AUSTIN, MASTER'S THESIS (1926).

WILLIAMS, ELGIN. ANIMATING PURSUITS IN SPECULATION: LAND
    TRAFFIC IN THE ANNEXATION OF TEXAS. NEW YORK, 1949
    (EC).

WILLIAMS. ORCHESTRAS BANDS, PASO MUSIC, (MU*).

WILLIAMSON, ROBERT LEE. A HISTORY OF COMPANY E OF
    THE TEXAS FRONTIER BATTALION, 1874-1879. UNIVERSITY
    OF TEXAS AT AUSTIN, MASTER'S THESIS (1952).

WILSON.   INEZ, TALE ALAMO (LI*).

WINKLER.   CHECK LIST TEXAS IMPRINTS, 1846-1860   (B*).

WISE, CLYDE.   "THE EFFECTS OF THE RAILRCADS UPON EL PASO".
     PASSWORD, VOL. 5 (JULY 1960), PP. 91-100 (EC).

WOODWARD, ARTHUR. "GREAT WESTERN WAS EARLIEST INN-KEEPER
     IN OLD EL PASO".   THE SOUTHWESTERNER, VOL. 3 (AUGUST
     1963), P. 1, 22 (HSW).

WOOTEN, DUDLEY. A COMPREHENSIVE HISTORY OF TEXAS.
     DALLAS: SCARFF, 1898.

WORLEY, JOHN LEWIS.   THE DIPOLMATIC RELATIONS OF ENGLAND
     AND THE REPUBLIC OF TEXAS.   UNIVERSITY OF TEXAS AT
     AUSTIN, MASTER'S THESIS (1905).

WORTHAM, LOUIS J.   A HISTORY OF TEXAS FROM WILDERNESS TO
     COMMONWEALTH.   FORT WORTH, WORTHAM-MOLYNEAUX COMPANY,
     1924.

WRIGHT, GEN. MARCUS. TEXAS IN THE WAR, 1861-1865.
     HILLSBORO, TEXAS: HILL JUNIOR COLLEGE PRESS, 1965 (HUS).

YAGER, HOPE. THE ARCHIVE WAR IN TEXAS.   UNIVERSITY OF
     TEXAS AT AUSTIN, MASTER'S THESIS (1939).

YELVINGTON, RAMSEY. A CLOUD OF WITNESSES, THE DRAMA OF
     THE ALAMO.   AUSTIN: UNIVERSITY OF TEXAS PRESS, 1959.

YOAKUM, H. HISTORY OF TEXAS FROM ITS FIRST SETTLEMENT IN
     1685 TO ITS ANNEXATION TO THE UNITED STATES IN 1846.
     NEW YORK, REDFIELD, 1856. REPRINT AUSTIN-STECK, 1935
     (HS).

ZAVALA, ADINA DE. HISTORY AND LEGENDS OF THE ALAMO AND
     OTHER MISSIONS.   SAN ANTONIO: PUBLISHED BY AUTHOR,
     1917 (AN).

ZINGG.   "THE IMPORTANCE PASO AREA CONQUEST (HN*).

UNITED STATES HISTORY

(HUS)

ABEL, ANNIE LOUISE <ED.>. THE OFFICIAL CORRESPONDENCE OF
    JAMES S. CALHOUN WHILE INDIAN AGENT AT SANTA FE AND
    SUPERINTENDENT OF INDIAN AFFAIRS IN NEW MEXICO.
    WASHINGTON. GOVERNMENT PRINTING OFFICE, (1915).

ABELS, ROBERT. EARLY AMERICAN FIREARMS. CLEVELAND AND
    NEW YORK: THE WORLD PUBLISHING CO., 1950.

ADAMS. SELECTED LETTERS HENRY ADAMS (PL*).

ADAMS, JOHN, AND JOHN QUINCY. THE SELECTED WRITINGS..EDITED
    AND WITH AN INTRODUCTION BY ARDIENNE KOCH AND WILLIAM
    PEDEN=. NEW YORK: ALFRED A. KNOPF, 1946 (PL).

ALBERT, JAMES W. <ED BY JOHN GAVIN>. WESTERN AMERICA IN
    1846-1847; THE ORIGINAL TRAVEL DIARY OF LT. J.W.
    ALBERT. SAN FRANCISCO, CALIFORNIA: JOHN HOWELL
    BOOKS, 1966 (TJ).

ALLEN, HENRY EASTON. "THE PARILLA EXPEDITION TO THE RED
    RIVER IN 1759". SOUTHWESTERN HISTORICAL QUARTERLY,
    VOL. 43 NO. 1 (1939), PP. 53-71 (HSW).

AMERICAN HISTORICAL ASSOCIATION. ORIGINAL NARRATIVES OF
    EARLY AMERICAN HISTORY. NEW YORK: C. SCRIBNER'S
    SONS, 1906.

ANDERSON, JOHN Q. <ED>. CAMPAIGNING WITH PARSONS' TEXAS
    CAVALRY BRIGADE, CSA. HILLSBORO, TEXAS: BILL JUNIOR
    COLLEGE PRESS, 1967.

ANDREWS, CHARLES M. OUR EARLIEST COLONIAL SETTLEMENTS:
    THEIR DIVERSITIES OF ORIGIN AND LATER CHARACTERISTICS.
    ITHACA, NEW YORK: CORNELL UNIVERSITY PRESS, 1959 (HS).

INTERNATIONAL BOUNDARY COMMISSION (HSW*).

MINORITY GROUP ADOLESCENTS U. S. (SO*).

POPULAR TRIBUNALS. THE HISTORY COMPANY, 1887.

TRATADO DE GUADALUPE HIDALGO1848 (LW*).

TRATADO DE GUADALUPE HIDALGO1848 (LW*).

TREATY GUADALUPE HILDAGO, FEBRUARY (LW*).

THE WAR OF THE REBELLION RECORDS: A COMPILATION OF THE
    OFFICIAL RECORDSOF THE UNION AND CONFEDERATE ARMIES.
    WASHINGTON, D. C.: U. S. GOVERNMENT PRINTING OFFICE,
    (1882, 1883, 1897).

ASKINS.   TEXANS, GUNS HISTORY (HT*).

BAKELESS, JOHN. THE EYES OF DISCOVERY--THE PAGEANT
    OF NORTH AMERICA AS SEEN BY THE FIRST EXPLORERS.
    MASSACHUSETTS: PETER SMITH PUBLISHER, INC, 1961.

BAKER, RAY STANNARD. WOODROW WILSON, LIFE AND LETTERS.
    V. 6. FACING WAR, 1915-1917.   GARDEN CITY: DOUBLEDAY,
    DORAN AND CO., 1937.

BALCH.   MINES, MINERS MINING INTEREST (EC*).

BALLOU, ROBERT. EARLY KLICKITAT VALLEY DAYS.   PORTLAND,
    OREGON: BINFORDS & MORT, PUBLISHERS, 1971.

BANCROFT, CAROLINE. COLORADO'S LOST GOLD MINES AND BURIED
    TREASURE.   CHICAGO: SWALLOW, (HCO).

BANCROFT, CAROLINE. COLORFUL COLORADO: ITS DRAMATIC
    HISTORY.   CHICAGO: SWALLOW, (HCO).

BANCROFT, CAROLINE. DENVER'S LIVELY PAST.   CHICAGO:
    SWALLOW, (HCO).

BARBOUR.   JOURNALS LATE PHILIP NORBOURNE (TJ*).

BARTON.   DIPLCMATIC RELATIONS BETWEENUNITED (PL*).

BASTERT, RUSSELL H. AMERICAN FOREIGN POLICY TO 1880.
    CHICAGO: RAND MCNALLY, 1967.

BAYITCH, STOJAN A. AND SIQUIEROS, JOSE LUIS. CONFLICT OF
    LAWS: MEXICO AND THE UNITED STATES; A BILATERAL
    STUDY.   CORAL GABLES: UNIVERSITY OF MIAMI PRESS, 1968
    (HM   LW).

BEAGLEHOLE, J. C. THE EXPLORATION OF THE PACIFIC.
    STANFORD: CALIFORNIA STANFORD UNIVERSITY PRESS: 1934.
    REVISED 1947, 1966..

BEMIS, SAMUEL F. AND GRIFFIN, GRACE GARDNER. GUIDE TO THE
    DIPLOMATIC HISTORY OF THE U. S. 1775-1921.
    WASHINGTON, D. C.: U. S. GOVERNMENT PRINTING OFFICE,
    (1935) (PL).

BENNETT.   NARRATIVE WHALING VOYAGE ROUND (TJ*).

BENNETT.   FORTS FORAYS. DRAGOON NEW MEXICO (HN*).

BESHOAR, BARRON B. WESTERN TRAILS TO CALVERY.   AUSTIN:
    UNIVERSITY OF TEXAS PRESS, 1963 (LI).

BOLTON.   WIDER HORIZONS AMERICAN HISTORY   (HS*).

BOND, BEVERLEY WAUGH. THE CIVILIZATION OF THE OLD
      NORTHWEST; A STUDY OF POLITICAL, SOCIAL, ANDECONOMIC
      DEVELOPMENT, 1788-1812.   NEW YORK, 1934. NEW YORK:
      AMS PRESS, INC.,.

BOSCH, GARCIA CARLOS. HISTORIA DE LAS RELACIONES ENTRE
      MEXICO Y LOS ESTADOS UNIDOS.   MEXICO: ESCUELA
      NACIONAL DE CIENCIAS POLITICAS Y SOCIALES, 1961 (HM).

BOWLES.   ACROSS CONTINENT (TJ*).

BOYD.   CALVARY LIFE TENT FIELD   (HSW*).

BRADDY, HALDEEN. PERSHING'S MISSION IN MEXICO.   EL PASO:
      TEXAS WESTERN PRESS, 1966.

BRIGGS, HAROLD EDWARD. FRONTIERS OF THE NORTHWEST;
      A HISTORY OF THE UPPER MISSOURI VALLEY.   NEW YORK:
      D. APPLETON-CENTURY COMPANY, 1940.

BROWN, DEE. TRAIL DRIVING DAYS.   NEW YORK: CHARLES
      SCRIBNER'S SONS, 1952 (HSW).

BROWN.   ONE AMERICA: HISTORY CONTRIBUTIONS   (SO*).

BROWNING, VIVIAN ALMA. WILSON'S POLICY TOWARD HUERTA,
      1913-1914.   UNIVERSITY OF TEXAS AT AUSTIN, MASTER'S
      THESIS (1935).

BUSTAMANTE.   MEXICAN-AMERICAN UNITED STATES   (SO*).

BUTTERFIELD, ROGER. THE AMERICAN PAST, A HISTORY OF THE
      UNITED STATES FROM CONCORD TO HIROSHIMA.   NEW YORK:
      SIMON AND SCHUSTER, 1947.

CALLAHAN.   AMERICAN FOREIGN POLICY MEXICAN   (HM*).

CALLCOTT.   CARIBBEAN POLICY UNITED STATES   (HM*).

CAMPBELL, CAMILLA. A HISTORY AND ANALYSIS.   NEW YORK,
      NEW YORK: JOHN DAY COMPANY, INC., 1968.

CANTU. S. JUAREZ: CONFLICTS BETWEEN MEXICO   (HM*).

CANTU, CAESAR C. THE TERRITORIAL GROWTH OF THE UNITED
      STATES OF AMERICA.   LOS ANGELES, CALIFORNIA: MODERN
      WORLD PUBLISHING COMPANY, 1968.

CARSTENSEN, VERNON, (ED.). THE PUBLIC LANDS: STUDIES IN
      THE HISTORY OF THE PUBLIC DOMAIN.   MADISON, WINCONSIN:
      UNIVERSITY OF WISCONSIN PRESS, 1963 (EC).

CARTER, ROBERT ARTHUR, JR. ANTHONY BUTLER AND HIS MISSION
      TO MEXICO.   UNIVERSITY OF TEXAS AT AUSTIN, MASTER'S
      THESIS.

CHIDSEY, DONALD BARR.   FRENCH AND INDIAN WAR.   NEW YORK,
    NEW YORK: CROWN PUBLISHERS, INC., 1969.

CHIDSEY, DONALD BARR.   THE WAR WITH MEXICO.   NEW YORK,
    NEW YORK: CROWN PUBLISHERS, INC., 1968.

CLAWSON, MARION AND HELD, BURNELL.   THE FEDERAL LANDS:
    THEIR USE AND MANAGEMENT.   LINCOLN, NEBRASKA:
    UNIVERSITY OF NEBRASKA PRESS, 1965.

CLAWSON, MARION.   THE LAND SYSTEM OF THE UNITED STATES:
    AN INTRODUCTION TO THE HISTORY AND PRACTICE OF LAND
    USE AND LAND TENURE.   LINCOLN NEBRASKA: UNIVERSITY
    OF NEBRASKA PRESS, 1968.

CLINE.   IMPROVING LANGUAGE ARTS BILINGUALS   (HM*).

COE, MICHAEL D.   AMERICA'S FIRST CIVILIZATION.   NEW YORK
    AMERICAN HERITAGE, 1968 (HM).

COIT, MARGARET L.   THE SWEEP WESTWARD.   NEW YORK:
    TIME-LIFE BOOKS, 1963.

COLTON, RAY C.   THE CIVIL WAR IN THE WESTERN TERRITORIES:
    ARIZONA, COLORADO, NEW MEXICO, AND UTAH.   NORMAN,
    OKLAHOMA: UNIVERSITY OF OKLAHOMA PRESS, 1959.

COLTON, RAY C.   THE CIVIL WAR IN THE SOUTHWEST.   NORMAN:
    UNIVERSITY OF OKLAHOMA PRESS, 1959.

COLTON.   THREE YEARS CALIFORNIA   (HC*).

COLYER, VINCENT.   PEACE WITH THE APACHES OF NEW MEXICO AND
    ARIZONA.   REPORT OF VINCENT COLYER MEMBER OF BOARD
    OF INDIAN COMMISSIONERS, 1871.   WASHINGTON:
    GOVERNMENT PRINTING OFFICE, (1872).

COMMAGER, HENRY STEEL.   AMERICA IN PERSPECTIVE, THE UNITED
    STATES THROUGH FOREIGN EYES.   NEW YORK: RANDOM HOUSE,
    1947.

COMMISSIONER OF INDIAN AFFAIRSCOMMISSIONER-GENERAL
    OF IMMIGRATIONANONYMO.   ANNUAL REPORT.   WILLIAM
    P. DOLE, COMMISSIONER, TO HON. CALEB B. SMITH,
    SECRETARY OF THE INTERIOR, (1861).

CONKLING, ROSCOE P. AND CONKLING, MARGARET B.   THE
    BUTTERFIELD OVERLAND MAIL, 1857-1859.   GLENDALE:
    ARTHUR H. CLARK CO, 1947.

CONNELLY, WILLIAM ELSEY.   DONIPHAN'S EXPEDITION AND THE
    CONQUEST OF NEW MEXICO AND CALIFORNIA.   TOPEKA: CRANE
    AND CO., 1907.

CONNERS, C. KEIGH AND EISBERG, LEON. THE EFFECT OF TEACHER
    BEHAVIOR ON VERBAL INTELLIGENCE IN OPERATION HEADSTART
    CHILDREN.   BALTIMORE: JOHNS HOPKINS UNIVERSITY,
    SCHOOL OF MEDICINE, 1966 (TJ).

COOK.   LANE LLANO (HC*).

CORTES, CARLOS E. BEING AMERICAN IN AMERICA.   NEW YORK:
    HARCOURT BRACE JOVANOVICH, 1975 (SO AN).

CORTES, CARLOS E. BEING AMERICAN IN AMERICA.   (EW YORK:
    HARCOURT, BRACE, JOVANOVICH, 1975.

COTNER.   DIPLOMATIC RELATIONS BETWEENUNITED (HM*).

COUES, ELLIOTT <ED>. THE EXPEDITIONS OF ZEBULON MONTGOMERY
    PIKE.   3 VOLUMES. NEW YORK: FRANCIS P. HARPER, 1895.

COUES, ELLIOTT. ON THE TRAIL OF A SPANISH PIONEER.   NEW
    YORK: F. P. HARPER, 1900.

COULTER, E. MERTON. THE CONFEDERATE STATES OF AMERICA,
    1861-1865.   BATON ROUGE: LOUISIANA STATE UNIVERSITY
    PRESS; AUSTIN, UNIVERSITY OF TEXAS, 1950.

COYNER, DAVID H. THE LOST TRAPPERS: AN ACCOUNT OF THE
    FUR TRADE.   CINCINNATI, OHIO: ANDERSON GATES
    AND WRIGHT, 1859. REPRINTED BY RIO GRANDE PRESS, INC.
    GLORIETA, NEW MEXICO, (EC).

CRANDALL, SAMUEL BENJAMIN. TREATIES, THEIR MAKING
    AND ENFORCEMENT.   1904. REPRINTED BY: NEW YORK, NEW
    YORK AND LONDON, GREAT BRITAIN: AMS PRESS, INC..

CROGHAN, COLONEL GEORGE. ARMY LIFE ON THE WESTERN
    FRONTIER: SELECTIONS FROM THE OFFICIAL REPORTS MADE
    BETWEEN 1826 AND 1845.   EDITED BY FRANCIS PAUL
    PRUCHA. NORMAN, OKLAHOMA: UNIVERSITY OF OKLAHOMA
    PRESS, 1958 (TJ).

CUE CANOVAS.   LOS ESTADOS UNIDOS MEXICO OLIVIDADO (HM*).

CUNNINGHAM.   JAMES TREAT HIS MISSION TO MEXICO (HT*).

CURTI.   MAKING AMERICAN COMMUNITY: FRONTIER (HSW*).

CURTI, MERLE. THE GROWTH OF AMERICAN THOUGHT.   NEW YORK:
    HARPER AND BROTHERS, 1943.

DALE, HARRISON C. THE ASHLEY-SMITH EXPLORATIONS AND THE
    DISCOVERY OF A CENTRAL ROUTE TO THE PACIFIC.
    GLENDALE: A.H. CLARK CO., 1918,1941 (HSW).

DALLAM, SAMUEL F. "THE PUNITIVE EXPEDITION OF 1916 — SOME
    PROBLEMS AND EXPERIENCES OF A TROOP COMMANDER".
    CAVALRY JOURNAL, (JULY 1927) (TJ).

DE LUXAN. EXPEDITION INTO NEW MEXICO MADE (TJ*).

DE VOTO. ACROSS WIDE MISSOURI (HS*).

DELLENBAUGH. ROMANCE COLORADO RIVER; SECOND (TJ*).

DEPARTMENT OF INDUSTRIAL RELATIONS. CALIFORNIANS OF
    SPANISH SURNAME. SAN FRANCISCO, CALIFORNIA:
    DEPARTMENT OF INDUSTRIAL RELATIONS, DIVISION OF FAIR
    EMPLOYMENT PRACTICES, MAY, 1964 (HS SO).

DEPARTMENT OF SUPERVISORS AND DIRECTORS OF INSTRUCTION OF
    THE NATIONAL EDUCATION ASSOCIATION, THE NATIONAL
    COUNCIL OF TEACHERS OF ENGLISH, THE SOCIETY FOR
    CURRICULUM STUDY. AMERICANS ALL: STUDIES IN
    INTERCULTURAL EDUCATION. WASHINGTON, D. C.:
    DEPARTMENT OF SUPERVISORS AND DIRECTORS OF INSTRUCTION
    OF THE NATIONAL EDUCATION ASSOCIATION, 1942 (ED).

DICK. TALES FRONTIER: LEWIS CLARK TO (TJ*).

DICK. TALES FRONTIER: LEWIS CLARKTO (TJ*).

DICK. VANGUARDS FRONTIER: SOCIAL HISTORY (HS*).

DICK. VANGUARDS FRONTIER: SOCIAL HISTORY (TJ*).

DILLON, RICHARD H. A CANNONEER IN NAVAJO COUNTRY.
    DENVER, COLORADO: THE OLD WEST PUBLISHING COMPANY,
    1970.

DONNELL, GUY RENFRO. UNITED STATES INTERVENTION IN MEXICO,
    1914. UNIVERSITY OF TEXAS AT AUSTIN, PHD. DISSERTATION
    (1951) (HM).

DORIAN, EDITH M. TRAILS WEST AND MEN WHO MADE THEM. NEW
    YORK, NEW YORK: MC GRAW-HILL, 1955.

DOZER, DONALD M., EDITOR. THE MONROE DOCTRINE: ITS MODERN
    SIGNIFICANCE. NEW YORK, NEW YORK: ALFRED KNOPF,
    1965.

DU BOIS. CAMPAIGNS WEST, 1856-1861. JOURNALS (TJ*).

DULLES, FOSTER RHEA. AMERICA IN THE PACIFIC: A CENTURY
    OF EXPANSION. NEW YORK, NEW YORK: DA CAPO PRESS,
    INC., 1969.

DUNBAR, SEYMOUR. A HISTORY OF TRAVEL IN AMERICA. NEW
    YORK, NEW YORK: TUDOR PUBLISHING COMPANY, 1937.

EDWARDS.   JOURNAL MARCELLUS BALL EDWARDS   (TJ*).

EISENSTADT, ABRAHAM S.   A STUDY IN AMERICAN HISTORICAL
    WRITING.   NEW YORK, NEW YORK: AMS PRESS, INC., 1956.

ELLIS, DAVID M. <ED>.   THE FRONTIER IN AMERICAN DEVELOPMENT:
    ESSAYS IN HONOR OF PAUL WALLACE GATES.   ITHACA, NEW
    YORK: CORNELL UNIVERSITY PRESS, 1969.

EMMETT.   REPORT U. S.-MEXICAN BOUNDARY   (HSW*).

EMORY.   NOTES MILITARY RECONNOISSANCE   (TJ*).

EMORY.   REPORT WILLIAM H. EMORY, MAJOR   (TJ*).

FAULKNER, EDWARD H.   PLOWMAN'S FOLLY.   NORMAN OKLAHOMA:
    UNIVERSITY OF OKLAHOMA PRESS,.

FAULKNER, HAROLD UNDERWOOD; TYLER, KEPNER.   AMERICA, ITS
    HISTORY AND PEOPLE.   NEW YORK: HARPER AND BROTHERS,
    1942.

FITE, EMERSON D. AND FREEMAN, ARCHIBALD (EDITORS).   A BOOK
    OF OLD MAPS DELINEATING AMERICAN HISTORY.   NEW YORK,
    NEW YORK: DOVER PUBLICATIONS, INC., 1969.

FOREMAN, GRANT.   INDIANS AND PIONEERS.   NORMAN OKLAHOMA:
    UNIVERSITY OF OKLAHOMA PRESS, 1936.

FOREMAN, GRANT.   A HISTORY OF OKLAHOMA.   NORMAN OKLAHOMA:
    UNIVERSITY OF OKLAHOMA PRESS, 1942.

FREEMAN, DOUGLAS SOUTHALL.   R. E. LEE, A BIOGRAPHY.   NEW
    YORK: CHARLES SCRIBNER'S SONS, 1935.

GAMBOA, ERASMO.   CHICANOS IN THE NORTHWEST: A HISTORICAL
    PERSPECTIVE.   CHICANO STUDIES INSTITUTES, (SUMMER
    1971). PROGRAM COORDINATED BY MONTAL SYSTEMS, INC..

GARD, WAYNE.   FRONTIER JUSTICE.   NORMAN OKLAHOMA:
    UNIVERSITY OF OKLAHOMA PRESS, 1949.

GARD, WAYNE.   RAWHIDE TEXAS.   NORMAN OKLAHOMA: UNIVERSITY
    OF OKLAHOMA PRESS, 1965 (HT).

GARD, WAYNE.   THE CHISHOLM TRAIL.   NORMAN OKLAHOMA:
    UNIVERSITY OF OKLAHOMA PRESS, 1954.

GARRER.   PUERTO RICO UNSOLVED PROBLEM   (SO*).

GIBSON, DOROTHY K.   SOCIAL LIFE IN SAN ANTONIO (ON THE EVE
    OF THE CIVIL WAR).   AUSTIN: UNIVERSITY OF TEXAS, 1937
    (SO).

GOETZMANN, WILLIAM H.   ARMY EXPLORATION IN THE AMERICAN
    WEST.   NEW HAVEN, CONNECTICUT: YALE UNIVERSITY PRESS,
    1959 (HSW).

GOETZMANN, WILLIAM H. EXPLORATION AND EMPIRE: THE
    EXPLORER AND SCIENTIST IN THE WINNING OF THE AMERICAN
    WEST. NEW YORK: ALFRED A. KNOPF, 1966 (HSW).

GORDON. "LINCOLN JUAREZ; BRIEF REASSESSMENT (HM*).

GOSSETT. RACE: HISTORY IDEA AMERICA (SO*).

GRASSI, GIOVANNI ANTONIO. 'NOTIZIE VARIE SULLO STATO
    PRESENTE DELLA REPUBBLICA DEGLI STATI UNITI DELL'
    AMERICA ....' IN THIS WAS AMERICA, EDITED BY OSCAR
    HANDLIN.

GREENBERG, DAVID B. LAND THAT OUR FATHERS PLOWED:
    THE SETTLMENT OF OUR COUNTRY AS TOLD BY THE PIONEERS
    THEMSELVES AND THEIR CONTEMPORARIES. NORMAN
    OKLAHOMA: UNIVERSITY OF OKLAHOMA PRESS, 1969.

GRIFFIN. UNITED STATES DISRUPTION SPANISH (HS*).

GRIFFIN, RAMONA. PIONEERING IN CHACO CAYNON. FLAGSTAFF,
    ARIZONA: NORTHLAND PRESS, 1971.

GRISWOLD, BERT JOSEPH, <ED>. FORT WAYNE, GATEWAY OF THE
    WEST, 1802-1813. INDIANAPOLIS, 1927. REPRINTED BY:
    NEW YORK, NEW YORK AND LONDON, GREATBRITAIN: AMS
    PRESS, INC.,.

HAMILTON, HOLMAN. ZACHARY TAYLOR, SOLDIER OF THE REPUBLIC.
    INDIANAPOLIS: THE BOBBS-MERRILL CO., 1941.

HAMILTON, HOLMAN. ZACHARY TAYLOR: SOLDIER OF THE
    REPUBLIC. INDIANAPOLIS: BOBBS-MERRILL, 1941.

HANDLIN, OSCAR (ET AL). HARVARD GUIDE TO AMERICAN HISTORY.
    CAMBRIDGE: HARVARD UNIVERSITY PRESS, 1954 (SO).

HANDLIN, OSCAR. "HISTORICAL PERSPECTIVES OF THE AMERICAN
    ETHNIC GROUP". DAEDALUS, (SPRING, 1961), P. 228
    (SO).

HANDLIN, OSCAR. BOSTON'S IMMIGRANTS; A STUDY IN ACCULTURATION.
    REVISED AND ENLARGED. CAMBRIDGE, MASSACHUSETTS:
    BELKNAP PRESS OF HARVARD UNIVERSITY, 1959 (SO).

HANDLIN, OSCAR. CHILDREN OF THE UPROOTED. NEW YORK:
    BRAZILLER, 1966 (SO).

HANDLIN, OSCAR. RACE AND NATIONALITY IN AMERICAN LIFE.
    BOSTON: BROWN AND CO., 1957 (SO).

HANDLIN, OSCAR. THIS WAS AMERICA. CAMBRIDGE, MASSACHUSETTS:
    HARVARD UNIVERSITY PRESS, 1949 (SO).

HANDLIN, OSCAR. THE AMERICAN PEOPLE IN THE TWENTIETH
    CENTURAY. CAMBRIDGE: HARVARD UNIVERSITY PRESS, 1954.

HANDLIN, OSCAR. THE AMERICANS; A NEW HISTORY OF THE PEOPLE
    OF THE UNITED STATES. BOSTON: LITTLE, BROWN, 1963
    (SO).

HANDLIN, OSCAR. THE UPROOTED; THE EPIC STORY OF THE GREAT
    MIGRATIONS THAT MADE THE AMERICAN PEOPLE. BOSTON:
    LITTLE, BROWN, 1951 (SO).

HAVIGHURST, WALTER W. THE UPPER MISSISSIPPI VALLEY. NEW
    YORK: TEACHERS COLLEGE PRESS, 1966.

HERGESHEIMER, JOSEPH. SHERIDAN, A MILITARY NARRATIVE.
    BOSTON: HOUGHTON, MIFFLIN CO., 1931.

HIGHAM, JOHN. STRANGERS IN THE LAND; PATTERNS OF AMERICAN
    NATIVISM, 1860-1925. NEW YORK: ATHENEUM, 1963.

HINCKLEY, TED C. "AMERICAN ANTI-CATHOLICISM DURING THE
    MEXICAN WAR". PACIFIC HISTORICAL REVIEW, (MAY
    1962), PP. 121-137.

HINE, ROBERT V. BARTLETT'S WEST: DRAWING THE MEXICAN
    BOUNDARY. NEW HAVEN, CONNECTICUT: YALE UNIVERSITY
    PRESS, 1968 (GE).

HINE, ROBERT V. CALIFORNIA'S UTOPIAN COLONIES. NEW
    HAVEN, CONNECTICUT: YALE UNIVERSITY PRESS, 1966 (HC
    GE).

HINE, ROBERT V. EDWARD KERN AND AMERICAN EXPANSION. NEW
    HAVEN, CONNECTICUT: YALE UNIVERSITY PRESS, 1962 (GE).

HINKLE, STACY C. WINGS OVER THE BORDER. EL PASO, TEXAS:
    TEXAS WESTERN PRESS, 1970.

HODGE. ORIGINAL NARRATIVES EARLY AMERICAN (HS*).

HODGE. SPANISH EXPLORERS SOUTHWESTERN (HS*).

HODGES, CLAUDIUS BRASHIER. DIPLOMATIC RELATIONS BETWEEN
    THE UNITED STATES AND THE REPUBLIC OF PANAMA,
    1903-1918. UNIVERSITY OF TEXAS AT AUSTIN, MASTER'S
    THESIS (1935).

HOFSTADTER, RICHARD. GREAT ISSUES IN AMERICAN HISTORY.
    NEW YORK: VINTAGE BOOKS, 1958.

HUNT, AURORA. THE ARMY OF THE PACIFIC. GLENDALE: THE
    ARTHUR H. CLARK COMPANY, 1951.

HUNTINGTON, ELLSWORTH. THE RED MAN'S CHRONICLE, A
    CHRONICLE OF ABORIGINAL AMERICA. NEW HAVEN: YALE
    UNIVERSITY PRESS, 1921 (HSA).

HUTHMACHER, J. JOSEPH.   A NATION OF NEWCOMERS: ETHNIC
    MINORITY GROUPS IN AMERICAN HISTORY.   NEW YORK, NEW
    YORK: DIALDELACORTE PRESS, 1969 (SO).

JENKINS.   BORDER WAR; STUDY U. S. MEXICAN   (HM*).

JENSEN.   REGIONALISM AMERICA   (SO*).

JOHNSON, ALLEN AND NEVINS, ALLAN (EDS).   YALE CHRONICLES
    OF AMERICA.   NEW ROCHELLE, NEW YORK: UNITED STATES
    PUBLISHERS ASSOCIATION, INC.,.

JOSEPH, ALVIN.   THE INDIAN HERITAGE OF AMERICA.   BANTAM,
    1968.

KATZ, WILLIAM LOREN AND WARREN J. HALLIBURTON.   AMERICAN
    MAJORITIES AND MINORITIES: A SYLLABUS OF UNITED STATES
    HISTORY AMR SECONDARY SCHOOLS.   REPRINTED BY: NEW
    YORK, NEW YORK: ARNO PRESS, 1971.

KNAUTH.   "MC LANE INTERVENCION NORTEAMERICANA"   (HM*).

KOWNSLAR, A. O.   MANIFEST DESTINY AND EXPANSIONISM IN THE
    1840'S.   BOSTON: D. C. HEATH, 1967.

LA FEBER, WALTER.   THE NEW EMPIRE: AN INTERPRETATION OF
    AMERICAN EXPANSION, 1860-1898.   ITHACA, NEW YORK:
    CORNELL UNIVERSITY PRESS, 1963 (HSW).

LA PENA Y PENA.   MEXICO REPUBLIC. TREATIES. TREATY   (LW*).

LEVENSTEIN.   "AFL MEXICAN IMMIGRATION 1920S: (SI*).

LEWIS, MACMILLAN.   WOODROW WILSON OF PRINCETON.   NARBERTH,
    PENNASYLVANIA: LIVINGSTON PUBLISHING CO., 1952.

LOWERY.   SPANISH SETTLEMENTS WITHIN PRESENT   (HS*).

LOWRIE.   CULTURE CONFLICT TEXAS, 1821-1835   (HS*).

LOWRY.   THEY STARVE THAT WE MAY EAT   (HS*).

LOYOLA.   AMERICAN OCCUPATION NEW MEXICO   (HN*).

LYND, STAUGHTON.   NONVIOLENCE IN AMERICA: A DOCUMENTARY
    HISTORY.   INDIANAPOLIS: BOBBS-MERRILL, 1966 (SO).

MAC CORKLE, STUART ALEXANDER.   AMERICAN POLICY OF RECOGNITION
    TOWARDS MEXICO.   BALTIMORE, 1933. REPRINTED BY, NEW
    YORK, NEW YORK AND LONDON, GREAT BRITAN: AMS PRESS,
    INC.,.

MARSHALL, JAMES LESLIE.   SANTA FE, THE RAILROAD THAT BUILT
    AN EMPIRE.   NEW YORK: RANDOM HOUSE, 1945.

MASON, AUGUSTUS LYNCH. THE PIONEER HISTORY OF AMERICA.
     SAN FRANCISCO: A. L. BANCROFT AND COMPANY, 1883.

MC AVOY, THOMAS T., C. S. C. THE AMERICANIST HERISY IN
     ROMAN CATHOLICISM 1895-1900.   NOTRE DAME, INDIANA:
     UNIVERSITY OF NOTRE DAME PRESS, 1963 (RE).

MC AVOY, THOMAS T., C. S. C. A HISTORY OF THE CATHOLIC
     CHURCH IN THE UNITED STATES.   NOTRE DAME, INDIANA:
     UNIVERSITY OF NOTRE DAME PRESS, 1969 (RE).

MC CORMAC, EUGENE IRVING. JAMES K. POLK, A POLITICAL
     BIOGRAPHY.   BERKELEY, CALIFORNIA: UNIVERSITY
     OF CALIFORNIA PRESS, 1922.

MC COY, JOHN C. PAPER READ BEFORE OLD SETTLERS HISTORICAL
     SOCIETY.   JACKSON COUNTY, MISSOURI, 1871.

MC DONALD, LUCILE. SEARCH FOR THE NORTHWEST PASSAGE.
     PORTLAND, OREGON: BINFORDS AND MORT, PUBLISHERS, 1971.

MC DONALD, LUCILE. WASHINGTONS YESTERDAYS.   PORTLAND,
     OREGON: BINFORDS AND MORT, PUBLISHERS, 1971.

MERRILL.   GRINGO: AMERICAN AS SEEN BYMEXICAN   (LI*).

MILLER.   POVERTY: AMERICAN STYLE   (EC*).

MILLS, C. WRIGHT, SENIOR, CLARENCE, AND GOLDSEN, ROSE.
     THE PUERTO RICAN JOURNEY.   NEW YORK: HARPER AND
     BROTHERS, 1950.

MINOT.   TREATY WITH REPUBLIC MEXICO FEBRUARY   (LW*).

MONTLEZUN.   VOYAGE FAIT DANS LE ANNEES 1816   (TJ*).

MOORE.   "ANTONIO DE ULLCA: PROFILE FIRST   (HS*).

MOORE.   REVOLT LOUISIANA: THREAT TO FRANCO-SPANISH   (HS*).

MOORE.   HISTORY DIGEST INTERNATIONALARBITRATIONS   (HSW*).

MOREAU DE SAINT- MERY.   VOYAGE AUX ETATS-UNIS DE LAMERIQUE
     (TJ*).

MOREHEAD.   PERSONAL RECOLLECTIONS CHARLES   (TJ*).

MORGAN, H. WAYNE. WILLIAM MC KINLEY AND HIS AMERICA.
     NEW YORK; SYRACUSE UNIVERSITY PRESS, 1963.

MORIN, RAUL. AMONG THE VALIANT, MEXICAN AMERICANS IN WW
     II AND KOREA.   LOS ANGELES, BORDEN PUBLISHING CO,
     1963 (SO).

NATIONAL ARCHIVES. MEMORIALS ACCOMPANYING CLAIMS NOS.
    129C, 726, 727, 728, AND 729, MEXICANDOCKET, UNITED
    STATES AND MEXICAN CLAIMS COMMISSION OF 1868.
    MEMORIALS ACCOMPANYING CLAIMS NOS. 129C, 726, 727,
    728, AND 729, MEXICAN DOCKET, UNITED STATES AND
    MEXICAN CLAIMS COMMISSION OF 1868, RECORD GROUP NO.
    76, NATIONAL ARCHIVES, WASHINGTON, D. C. (HSW HM).

NEW YORK CITY MAYOR'S COMMITTEE ON PUERTO RICAN AFFAIRS.
    THE PUERTO RICAN PUPILS IN THE PUBLIC SCHOOLS OF NEW
    YORK CITY.   NEW YORK: THE COMMITTEE, 1951.

NOSTRAND.   PRELIMINARY LIST TOPOGRAPHICMAPS   (GE*).

NUNN, DR. W. C. (ED). TEN TEXANS IN GRAY.   HILLSBORO,
    TEXAS: HILL JUNIOR COLLEGE PRESS, 1968.

NUNN, W. C. ESCAPE FROM RECONSTRUCTION.   FORT WORTH,
    ARKANSAS: LEO POTISHMAN FOUNDATION, 1956.

OEHLERTS.   GUIDE TO WISCONSIN NEWSPAPERS (B*).

OEHLERTS.   GUIDE TO WISCONSIN NEWSPAPERS (B*).

OLIPHANT, J. ORIN. ON THE CATTLE RANGES OF THE OREGON
    COUNTRY.   SEATTLE: UNIVERSITY OF WASHINGTON PRESS,
    1968.

OLIVA, LEO E. SOLDIERS ON THE SANTA FE TRAIL.   NORMAN:
    UNIVERSITY OF OKLAHOMA PRESS, 1967.

OTTOSON, HOWARD W.; BIRCH, ELEANOR M.; HENDERSON, PHILIP
    A.; AND ANDER. LAND AND PEOPLE IN THE NORTHERN
    PLAINS TRANSITION AREA.   LINCOLN, NEBRASKA: UNIVERSITY
    OF NEBRASKA PRESS, 1966.

OTTOSON, HOWARD W., (ED). LAND USE POLICY AND PROBLEMS
    IN THE UNITED STATES.   LINCOLN, NEBRASKA: UNIVERSITY
    OF NEBRASKA PRESS, 1963.

PALMER, FREDERICK. NEWTON D. BAKER, AMERICA AT WAR.   NEW
    YORK: DODD, MEAD AND COMPANY, 1931.

PERKINS, D. A HISTORY OF THE MONROE DOCTRINE.   BOSTON:
    LITTLE, BROWN AND COMPANY, 1955.

POLK, JAMES K. POLK, THE DIARY OF A PRESIDENT, 1845-1849.
    NEW YORK: LONGMANS, GREEN, 1929.

POMEROY, EARL S. THE TERRITORIES AND THE UNITED STATES,
    1861-1890.   SEATTLE: UNIVERSITY OF WASHINGTON PRESS,
    1969.

PRESLEY.   ANGLO-SPANISH RIVALRY PACIFIC (HS*).

PRESS.   MEXICAN POPULATION LARAMIE (SI*).

PRICE.   DIPLOMACY BETWEEN UNITED STATES (HM*).

PRICE.   ORIGINS WAR WITH MEXICO; POLK-STOCKTON (HM*).

PRICE, GRADY DANIEL. THE UNITED STATES AND WEST FLORIDA,
    1803-1812.   UNIVERSITY OF TEXAS AT AUSTIN, PHD.
    DISSERTATION (1939).

PRIDA, RAMON. LA CUPLA DE LANE WILSON, EMBAJADOR DE LOS
    E.U.A. EN LA TRAGEDIA MEXICANADE 1913.   MEXICO:
    EDICIONES BOTAS, 1962.

PRINGLE, HENRY F. LIFE AND TIMES OF WILLIAM HOWARD TAFT.
    NEW YORK: FARRAR AND RINEHART, 1939.

QUINN, ARTHUR HOBSON. A HISTORY OF THE AMERICAN DRAMA FROM
    THE BEGINNING TO THE CIVIL WAR.   NEW YORK: HARPER
    AND BROTHERS, 1923.

QUIRK, ROBERT E. AFFAIR OF HONOR: WOODROW WILSON AND THE
    OCCUPATION OF VERA CRUZ.   NORTON, 1968.

QUIRK, ROBERT E. AN AFFAIR OF HONOR; WOODROW WILSON AND
    THE OCCUPATION OF VERACRUZ.   UNIVERSITY OF KENTUCKY
    PRESS, 1962.

RADEMAKER.   THESE ARE AMERICANS (SO*).

RADER, JESSE L. SOUTH OF FORTY, FROM THE MISSISSIPPI TO
    THE RIO GRANDE.   NORMAN, OKLAHOMA: UNIVERSITY
    OF OKLAHOMA PRESS, 1947.

RICHARDSON, HAROLD CHARLES. U. S. MILITARY POSTS IN
    ARIZONA FROM 1849 THROUGH 1900.   ARIZONA STATE
    UNIVERSITY, MASTER'S THESIS (1954) (HA).

RICHARDSON.   FRONTIER NORTHWEST TEXAS, 1846-1876   (HT*).

RICHARDSON, RUPERT N.; WALLACE, ERNEST AND ANDERSON,
    ADRIAN N. TEXAS , THE LONE STAR STATE.   THIRD
    EDITION, ENGLEWOOD CLIFFS, NEW JERSEY: PRENTICE-HALL,
    1970 (HSW).

RICHARDSON, RUPERT N. THE COMANCHE BARRIER TO SOUTH PLAINS
    SETTLEMENT.   GLENDALE, CALIFORNIA: ARTHUR C. CLARKE
    COMPANY, 1933.

RICHARDSON, RUPERT N. THE GREATER SOUTHWEST.   GLENDALE:
    THE ARTHUR H. CLARK COMPANY, 1934 (HSW).

RICHMOND, ROBERT W. AND MARDOCK, ROBERT W. (EDS). A NATION
    MOVING WEST: READINGS IN THE HISTORY OF THE AMERICAN
    FRONTIER.   LINCOLN, NEBRASKA: UNIVERSITY OF NEBRASKA
    PRESS, 1966.

RIEGEL, ROBERT EDGAR. THE STORY OF THE WESTERN RAILROADS.
    LINCOLN: UNIVERSITY OF NEBRASKA, 1967.

RIPPY, JAMES FRED. RIVALRY OF THE UNITED STATES AND GREAT
    BRITAIN OVER LATIN AMERICA, 1808-1830. BROOKLYN,
    NEW YORK: FARRAR, STRAUS AND GIROUX, 1964.

RIPPY.   UNITED STATES MEXICO   (HSW*).

RIPPY.   UNITED STATES MEXICO   (HSW*).

RIVES.   UNITED STATES MEXICO, 1821-1848; (HSW*).

ROBERTSON.   "TRUE RELATION HARDSHIPS SUFFERED   (HS*).

ROBERTSON.   LOUISIANA UNDER RULE SPAIN, FRANCE   (HS*).

ROMANO-V.   THE HISTORICAL INTELLECTUALPRESENCE   (AN*).

ROMANO-V.   "THE HISTORICAL INTELLECTUALPRESENCE   (AN*).

ROOT.   OVERLAND STAGE TO CALIFORNIA; (HC*).

ROSS.   DEBATABLE LAND: SKETCH ANGLO   (HS*).

ROURKE, CONSTANCE. AMERICAN HUMOR, A STUDY OF THE NATIONAL
    CHARACTER.   NEW YORK: HARCOURT, BRACE AND COMPANY,
    1931 (LI).

ROURKE, CONSTANCE. THE ROOTS OF AMERICAN CULTURE,
    AND OTHER ESSAYS.   NEW YORK: HARCOURT, BRACE
    AND COMPANY, 1942 (LI).

ROY.   RELATIONS BETWEEN UNITED STATES   (HT*).

SCHEIBER, HARRY N. (ED). THE OLD NORTHWEST: STUDIES IN
    REGIONAL HISTORY, 1787-1910.   LINCOLN, NEBRASKA:
    UNIVERSITY OF NEBRASKA PRESS, 1969.

SCHELL, HERBERT S. HISTORY OF SOUTH DAKOTA.   REVISED
    EDITION. LINCOLN, NEBRASKA: UNIVERSITY OF NEBRASKA
    PRESS, 1968.

SELIGMAN.   "AMERICAN POVERTY: RURAL URBAN"   (EC*).

SHEARER.   BORDER DIPLOMATIC RELATIONS BETWEEN   (HM*).

SOUTHWEST TEXAS STATE TEACHERS COLLEGE. U. S. EXPANSIONISM:
   THE IMPERIALIST URGE IN THE 1890S.   MADISON:
   UNIVERSITY OF WISCONSIN PRESS, 1970.

SPICER, EDWARD. "INDIGINISM IN THE UNITED STATES,
   1870-1960".   AMERICAN INDIGENA, VOL. 24 (OCTOBER
   1964), PP. 349-363 (AN).

SPRAGUE.   ORIGIN, PROGRESS, CONCLUSIONFLORIDA (HS*).

STEINFIELD.   MINORITIES, THEIR HISTORY, THEIR (SO*).

STEINFIELD.   POPULATION CHARACTERISTICS DALLAS (SO*).

STENBERG.   "THE FAILURE POLKS MEXICAN WAR (HSW*).

STENBERG.   AMERICAN IMPERIALISM SOUTHWEST (HSW*).

STENBERG.   PRESIDENT POLK ANNEXATION TEXAS (HSW*).

STEPHENSON.   LANDOWNERSHIP MAPS. CHECKLIST (GE*).

STILL.   WEST; CONTEMPORARY RECORDS AMERICAS (HSW*).

STUART.   OREGON TRAIL: ROBERT STUARTS (TJ*).

SULLIVAN, MARK. OUR TIMES; VOLUMES 4 AND 5: THE UNITED
   STATES, 1900-1925.   NEW YORK: CHARLES SCRIBNER'S
   SONS, 1933.

SUTHERLAND, STELLA H. POPULATION DISTRIBUTION IN COLONIAL
   AMERICA.   NEW YORK, 1936. REPRINTED BY NEW YORK, NEW
   YORK AND LONDON, GREAT BRITAIN: AMS PRESS, INC..

SWEETMAN, JACK. THE LANDING AT VERACRUZ: 1914.   ANNAPOLIS:
   UNITES STATES NAVAL INSTITUTE, 1968 (LI).

TAYLOR.   "SOME OBSERVATIONS MARGINAL MAN (ED*).

TEITELBAUM.   WOODROW WILSON MEXICAN REVOLUTION (HM*).

TETREAU. S. "THE IMPACT WAR SOME COMMUNITIES (SO*).

THE MINNESOTA HISTORICAL SOCIETY. INFORMATION SHEETS ON
   MINNESOTA.   ST. PAUL, MINNESOTA: THE MINNESOTA
   HISTORICAL SOCIETY, 1971.

THOBURN.   "ANCIENT IRRIGATION DITCHES PLAINS (GE*).

THOREAU. S. ANTI-SLAVERY REFORM PAPERS (LI*).

THORPE.   TOWN DIVIDED; STUDY VISALIA, (HC*).

THORPE.   OUR ARMY RIO GRANDE (HSW*).

TOCQUEVILLE, ALEXIS DE. DEMOCRACY IN AMERICA. NEW YORK:
    ALFRED A KNOPF, 1945 (LI).

TORNEL. TEXAS UNITED STATES AMERICA THEIR (HT*).

TOULMIN. WITH PERSHING MEXICO (HM*).

TRASK. BIBLIOGRAPHY UNITED STATES-LATIN (B*).

TRENNERT, ROBERT ANTHONY. THE FAR WESTERN INDIAN FRONTIER
    AND BEGINNINGS OF THE RESERVATIONS SYSTEM, 1846-1851.
    UNIVERSITY OF CALIFORNIA, SANTA BARBARA, PHD.
    DISSERTATION (1969).

TROXEL, O. C. "THE TENTH CAVALRY IN MEXICO". CAVALRY
    JOURNAL, (JULY 1927).

TUMULTY, JOSEPH P. WOODROW WILSON AS I KNOW HIM. GARDEN
    CITY: DOUBLEDAY PAGE AND COMPANY, 1921.

TURNER. AMERICAS GREAT FRONTIERS SECTIONS (HSW*).

TURNER. SIGNIFICANCE FRONTIER AMERICAN (HSW*).

TURNER. UNITED STATES: 1830-1850 (HSW*).

U. S. EXECUTIVE DOCUMENT NO. 257.DEPREDATIONS (LW*).

U. S. EXECUTIVE DOCUMENT NO. 13. MEXICAN (LW*).

U. S. HOUSE. HOUSE EXECUTIVE DOCUMENT, 36TH CONGRESS, 2ND
    SESSION, NO. 537, 129, 1848. WASHINGTON, D.C..

U. S. TEXAS FRONTIER TROUBLES (LW*).

U. S. PASSPORT ISSUED TO PARTY PRAIRIE (LW*).

UNITED STATES. CONSULAR DISPATCHES FROM CIUDAD JUAREZ.
    CONSULAR DESPATCHES (U. S.) FROM CIUDAD JUAREZ, APRIL
    10, 1850 TO DECEMBER 23, 1859; JANUARY 16, 1889 TO
    JULY 1, 1891. EL PASEO: MICROFILM, UNIVERSITY OF
    TEXAS, EL PASO LIBRARY,.

UNITED STATES. INTER-AMERICAN ACTIVITIES UNITED (SO*).

UNITED STATES. SPANISH-SPEAKING AMERICANS WAR: (SO*).

VIGIL, ANTONIO S. THE UGLY ANGLO; AN ANALYSIS OF WHITE
    EXTREMISM IN LATIN-AMERICAN RELATIONS. NEW YORK:
    EXPOSITION PRESS, 1967 (HSA).

VIGIL, ANTONIO, S. THE COMING OF THE GRINGO (AY VIENEN
    LOS GRINGOS) AND THE MEXICAN-AMERICAN REVOLT: AN
    ANALYSIS OF THE RISE AND DECLINE OF ANGLO-AMERICA,
    U.S.A.. NEW YORK: VANTAGE PRESS, 1970 (HSA).

WALLER.   "THE CIVIL WAR PASO AREA"   (HT*).

WALLING.   MEXICAN QUESTION; MEXICO AMERICAN-MEXICAN   (HM*).

WEINBERG, ALBERT K. MANIFEST DESTINY: A STUDY IN
     NATIONALIST EXPANSION. BALTIMORE: JOHNS HOPKINS,
     1935 (HSW).

WEINBERG, ALBERT K. MANIFEST DESTINY: A STUDY OF
     NATIONALIST EXPANSIONISM IN AMERICAN HISTORY.
     CHICAGO: QUADRANGLE BOOKS INC., 1963 (HSW).

WHEELER.   IMMIGRANT EXPERIENCE: ANGUISH   (SO*).

WHITFORD, WILLIAM CLARKE. COLORADO VOLUNTERRS IN THE CIVIL
     WAR; THE NEW MEXICO CAMPAIGN IN 1862.   DENVER: THE
     STATE HISTORICAL AND NATURAL HISTORY SOCIETY, 1906
     (HSW).

WILSON, THOMAS WOODROW. THE PUBLIC PAPERS OF WOODROW
     WILSON. THE NEW DEMOCRACY. PRESIDENTIAL MESSAGES,
     ADDRESSES, AND OTHER PAPERS (1913-1917).   EDITED BY
     RAY STANNARD BAKER AND WILLIAM E. DODD. NEW: HARPER
     AND BROTHERS, 1926.

WINSOR, JUSTIN. NARRATIVE AND CRITICAL HISTORY OF AMERICA.
     BOSTON: HOUGHTON-MIFFLIN, 1889 (HS).

WINTHER.   OLD OREGON COUNTRY: HISTORYFRONTIER (HSW*).

WINTHER.   VIA WESTERN EXPRESS STAGECOACH: (HC*).

WITTKE.   WE WHO BUILT AMERICA: SAGA IMMIGRANT (SI*).

WITTKE.   WE WHO BUILT AMERICA (SI*).

WOOD, BRYCE. THE MAKING OF THE GOOD NEIGHBOR POLICY.
     NEW YORK: COLUMBIAN UNIVERSITY PRESS, 1961 (HSA).

WOOD, BRYCE. THE MAKING OF THE GOOD NEIGHBOR POLICY.
     NEW YORK: W. W. NORTON AND COMPANY, INC., 1967 (HSA).

WOOFTER.   RACES ETHNIC GROUPS AMERICANLIFE (SO*).

WOOFTER.   RACES ETHNIC GROUPS AMERICANLIFE (SO*).

WRIGHT.   TEXAS WAR, 1861-1865 (HT*).

WRIGHT.   OTHER AMERICANS: MINORITIESAMERICAN (SO*).

WRIGHT, LYLE H., AND BYNUM, JOSEPHINE (ED). THE BUTTERFIELD
     OVERLAND MAIL. SAN MARINO: HENRY E. HUNTINGTON
     LIBRARY, 1954 (HSW).

YINGER.   "INTEGRATION AMERICANS MEXICAN (SI*).

YINGER.   MINORITY GROUP AMERICAN SOCIETY   (SI*).

YINGER.   MINORITY GROUPS AMERICAN SOCIETY   (SI*).

ZAVALA.   POLITICAL PHILOSOPHY CONQUEST   (HS*).

ZORILLA.   HISTORIA DE LAS RELACIONES ENTRE   (HM*).

L A N G U A G E - L I N G U I S T I C S

(LA)

AARONS. "LINGUISTIC- CULTURAL DIFFERENCES (ED*).

ADKINS, PATRICIA G. "REVERSE BORROWINGS OF ENGLISH
    CORRUPTIONS OF SPANISH". SPEECH TEACHER, (NOVEMBER
    1968), PP. 331-333.

ADKINS, PATRICIA G. THE LINGUISTIC PUZZLE OF FIGURATIVE
    LANGUAGE AND THE ESL STUDENT. EL PASO, TEXAS: THE
    UNIVERSITY OF TEXAS AT EL PASO, 1970.

AJUBITA, MARIA LUISA. LANGUAGE IN SOCIAL RELATIONS WITH
    SPECIAL REFERENCE TO THE MEXICAN-AMERICAN PROBLEM.
    TULANE UNIVERSITY, MASTER'S THESIS (1943) (ED).

ALARCOS LLORACH, EMILIO. FONOLOGIA ESPANOLA. MADRID:
    EDITORIAL GREDOS, 1959.

ALATIS, JAMES E. BILINGUALISM AND LANGUAGE CONTACT:
    ANTHROPOLOGICAL, LINGUISTIC, PSYCHOLOGICAL, AND
    SOCIOLOGICAL ASPECTS. WASHINGTON, D. C. .
    GEORGETOWN UNIVERSITY, PUBLICATIONS DEPARTMENT SCHOOL
    AND LANGUAGES AND LINGUISTICS, (1970) (ED AN PY
    SO).

ALCALA, ANTONIO WENCESLADA. VOCABULARIO ANDALUZ.
    BARCELONA, 1951 (HS).

ALEGRIA, FERNANDO. "NOMBRES ESPANOELES EN CALIFORNIA".
    ATENEA, VOL. ANO 27 NO. 50 (NOVEMBER 29, 1968), PP.
    218-287 (HS).

ALLRED, FORREST RICH. ERRORS IN ORAL ENGLISH USAGE
    OF MEXICAN-AMERICAN PUPILS WITH A SPANISH LANGUAGE
    BACKGROUND IN GRADE 3 IN THE STATE OF COLORADO.   ANN
    ARBOR, MICHIGAN: UNIVERSITY OF MICROFILMS, INC., 1971.

ALONSO, AMADO. "NOTAS BIBLIOGRAFICAS SOBRE ANITA POST".
    REVISTA DE FILOLOGIA EXPANOLA, VOL. 22.

ALONSO, AMADO. PROBLEMAS DE DIALECTOLOGIA HISPANOAMERICANA.
    BUENOS AIRES, 1930.

ALONSO, AMADO. VIDA Y OBRA DE MEDRANO, VOL. 1.   CONSEJO
    SUPERIOR DE INVESTIGACIONES CIENTIFICAS, INSTITUTO
    MIGUEL DE CRVANTES, 1,1948; 2,1958 (HS).

ALONSO, AMADO. DEL SIGLO DE ORO A ESTE SIGLO DE SIGLAS.
    MADRID: GREDOS, 1962 (HS).

ALONSO, DAMASO. VIDA Y OBRA DE MEDRANO. CONSEJO SUPERIOR
    DE INVESTIGACIONES CIENTIFICAS, INSTITUTO MIGUEL DE
    CERVANTES, 1, 1948; 2, 1958 (HS).

ALVAREZ, GEORGE R. "CALO: THE 'OTHER' SPANISH". ETC:
    A REVIEW OF GENERAL SEMANTICS, VOL. 24 (MARCH 1967),
    PP. 7-13.

ANASTASI. "LANGUAGE DEVELOPMENT NONVERBAL (ED*).

ANASTASI. "SOME EFFECTS BILINGUALISM UPON (ED*).

ANDERSON. "LANGUAGE ARTS RESEARCH, 1956: (ED*).

ANDERSON, MERLIN D. LA LENGUA EXTRANJERA EN LA ESCUELA
    PEQUENA. A REPORT OF AN EXPERIMENTAL WESTERN STATES
    SMALL SCHOOLS PROJECT STUDY DESIGNED TO PROVIDE
    FOREIGN LANGUAGE PROGRAMS IN THE SMALL ELEMENTARY
    SCHOOLS. CARSON CITY: NEVADA STATE DEPARTMENT OF
    EDUCATION, 1966 (ED).

ANDERSSON. "AATSP, PRESIDENTS CORNER: LENGUAJE (ED*).

ANDERSSON. "AATSP, PRESIDENTS CORNER: CHOQUE (ED*).

ANDERSSON. "AN FL BLUEPRINT FOCUS" (ED*).

ANDERSSON. "BILINGUAL SCHOOLING: OASIS OR (ED*).

ANDERSSON. "BILINGUAL EDUCATION EARLY CHILDHOOD" (ED*).

ANDERSSON. "EXAMPLES BILINGUAL SCHOOLING (ED*).

ANDERSSON. "LANGUAGES EDUCATION - CRITICISM" (ED*).

ANDERSSON. "NEW DIRECTIONS FOREIGN LANGUAGE (ED*).

ANDERSSON. "THE FACES LANGUAGE: TOOL-COMMUNICATION-CULTURE-STYLE"
    (ED*).

ANDERSSON. "THE OPTIMUM AGE BEGINNING STUDY (ED*).

ANDERSSON. "UNIDAD DIVERSIDAD EN LOS ESTUDIOS (ED*).

ANDERSSON. "WHAT IS IDEAL ENGLISH-SPANISH (ED*).

ANDERSSON. AGE FACTOR BILINGUAL EDUCATION (ED*).

ANDERSSON. BILINGUAL SCHOOLING UNITED STATES (ED*).

ANDERSSON. BILINGUAL EDUCATION: AMERICAN (ED*).

ANDERSSON.   BILINGUALISM EARLY CHILDHOOD   (ED*).

ANDERSSON.   BILINGUAL ELEMENTARY SCHOOLING: (ED*).

ANDERSSON.   BILINGUALISM: TEMPORARY PERMANENT?   (ED*).

ANDERSSON.   CARLOS MARIA OCANTOS, ARGENTINE   (ED*).

ANDERSSON.   CARLOS MARIA OCANTOS SU OBRA   (ED*).

ANDERSSON.   EXTENDING BILINGUAL EDUCATION   (ED*).

ANDERSSON.   FOREIGN LANGUAGES ELEMENTARYSCHOOL   (ED*).

ANDERSSON.   FOREIGN LANGUAGES ELEMENTARYSCHOOL: (ED*).

ANDERSSON.   FRENCH PLAYS   (ED*).

ANDERSSON.   INTRODUCTION TO FOREIGN LANGUAGE   (ED*).

ANDERSSON.   PHILOSOPHICAL PERSPECTIVES BILINGUAL   (ED*).

ANDERSSON.   ROLE TEACHER BILINGUAL BICULTURAL   (ED*).

ANDERSSON.   TEACHER MODERN LANGUAGES   (ED*).

ANDERSSON.   TEACHING MODERN LANGUAGES   (ED*).

ANDERSSON.   TEACHING SPANISH PORTUGUESE ELEMENTARY   (ED*).

ANDREWS.   "THE HANDICAP LIMITED VOCABULARY"   (ED*).

"PACHUCO: SECRET LANGUAGE".   SCIENCE DIGEST, VOL.
     28 (OCTOBER 1950), PP. 47-48.

ENGLISH LANGUAGE TEST FOREIGN (ED*).

"AUTHENTIC PACHUCO"   (AN*).

ARAUJO, F.   ESTUDIOS DE FONETICA CASTELLANA.   TOLEDO, 1894.

ARNOLD.   "MEXICAN-AMERICANS LANGUAGE LEARNING"   (ED*).

ARNOLD.   "SOCIAL STUDIES CULTURALLY LINGUISTICALLY   (ED*).

ATWOOD, E. BAGBY.   THE REGIONAL VOCABULARY OF TEXAS.
     AUSTIN: UNIVERSITY OF TEXAS PRESS, 1962.

AVERETT.   SOUTH NEVADA PLACE NAMES   (HS*).

AYER, GEORGE W.   LANGUAGE AND ATTITUDES OF THE SPANISH-SPEAKING
     YOUTH OF THE SOUTHWESTERN UNITED STATES.   CAMBRIDGE:
     CAMBRIDGE UNIVERSITY PRESS, 1971 (ED).

BACKUS, BERTHA RHODES. A COMMUNICATOR FOR LA CAUSA:
     A BURKEIAN ANALYSIS OF THE RHETORIC OF CESAR CHAVEZ.
     UNIVERSITY OF CALIFORNIA IN SANTA BARBARA, MASTER'S
     THESIS (1970) (EC).

BAIN, WINIFRED E. "MOTHER TONGUE OR OTHER TONGUE?".
     PARENTS' MAGAZINE, VOL. 17 NO. 40 (MARCH 1942), PP.
     26-27 (ED).

BAKER.   COMPARATIVE STUDY THOSE CULTURES (AN*).

BARKER, GEORGE CARPENTER. "GROWING UP IN A BILINGUAL
     COMMUNITY".   KIVA, VOL. 17 NO. 1-2 (NOVEMBER-DECEMBER
     1951) (SO).

BARKER, GEORGE CARPENTER. "PACHUCO: AN AMERICAN-SPANISH
     ARGOT AND ITS SOCIAL FUNCTIONS IN TUCSON, ARIZONA".
     UNIVERSITY OF ARIZONA BULLETIN, VOL. 21 NO. 1
     (JANUARY 1950) (SO).

BARKER, GEORGE CARPENTER. "SOCIAL FUNCTIONS OF LANGUAGE
     IN THE MEXICAN-AMERICAN COMMUNITY".   ACTA AMERICANA,
     VOL. 5 (1947), PP. 185-202 (SO).

BARKER, GEORGE CARPENTER. PACHUCO: AN AMERICAN-SPANISH
     ARGOT AND ITS SOCIAL FUNCTIONS IN TUCSON, ARIZONA.
     TUCSON, ARIZONA: UNIVERSITY OF ARIZONA PRESS, 1958
     (SO).

BARKER, GEORGE CARPENTER. SOCIAL FUNCTION OF LANGUAGE IN
     A MEXICAN-AMERICAN COMMUNITY.   UNIVERSITY OF CHICAGO,
     PHD. DISSERTATION (1947) (SO).

BARKER, GEORGE CARPENTER. SOCIAL FUNCTIONS OF LANGUAGE
     IN THE MEXICAN-AMERICAN COMMUNITY.   TUCSON, ARIZONA:
     UNIVERSITY OF ARIZONA PRESS, (SO).

BARNES.   ARIZONA PLACE NAMES (HA*).

BARROWS, SARH T. "SPEECH HABITS OF THE FOREIGN CHILD".
     GRADE TEACHER, VOL. 949 (FEBRUARY-APRIL 1932), PP.
     446-479; 614-650.

BATRES, ANTONIO JAUREGUI. EL CASTELLANO EN AMERICA.
     GUATEMALA, 1904.

BAUGH.   STUDY PRE-SCHOOL VOCABULARY SPANISH-SPEAKING   (ED*).

BEBERFALL, LESTER. "SOME LINGUISTIC PROBLEMS OF THE
     SPANISH-SPEAKING PEOPLE OF TEXAS".   MODERN LANGUAGE
     JOURNAL, VOL. 42 , PP. 87-90.

BEHERFALL, LESTER. "SOME LINGUISTIC PROBLEMS OF THE
    SPANISH-SPEAKING PEOPLE OF TEXAS". MODERN LANGUAGE
    JOURNAL, VOL. 42 (FEBRUARY 1958), PP. 87-90.

BENTLEY, HAROLD W. A DICTIONARY OF SPANISH TERMS IN
    ENGLISH WITH SPECIAL REFERENCE TO THE AMERICAN
    SOUTHWEST. NEW YORK: COLUMBIA UNIVERSITY PRESS, 1932.

BENTLEY, HAROLD W. AND SAVAGE, H. J. A DICTIONARY
    OF SPANISH TERMS IN ENGLISH. NEW YORK: COLUMBIA
    UNIVERSITY PRESS, 1932.

BERNEY, T. D. AND COOPER, R. L. "SEMANTIC INDEPENDENCE
    AND DEGREE OF BILINGUALISM IN TWO COMMUNITIES".
    MODERN LANGUAGE JOURNAL, VOL. 53 (MARCH 1969), PP.
    182-185.

BERREY, LESTER V. AND VANDEN BARK, MELVIN. THE AMERICAN
    THESAURUS OF SLANG. NEW YORK, 1942.

BLACKMAN, ROBERT D. THE LANGUAGE HANDICAP OF SPANISH
    AMERICAN CHILDREN. UNIVERSITY OF ARIZONA, MASTER'S
    THESIS (1939).

BLANCO S., ANTONIO. LA LENGUA ESPANOLA EN LA HISTORIA DE
    CALIFORNIA. MADRID: EDICIONES CULTURA HISPANICA,
    1971 (HS).

BLANTON, M. G. AND BLANTON, S. SPEECH TRAINING FOR
    CHILDREN. NEW YORK: APPLETON-CENTURY, 1919.

BOAS, FRANZ. "HANDBOOK OF AMERICAN INDIAN LANGUAGES".
    BUR. AMERICAN ETHNIC BULLETIN, VOL. 40 (1911).

BOAS, FRANZ. "NOTES ON MEXICAN FOLK-LORE". JOURNAL OF
    AMERICAN FOLK-LORE, VOL. 25 , PP. 204-60 (AN).

BOAS, FRANZ. RACE, LANGUAGE, AND CULTURE. NEW YORK:
    MACMILLAN, 1940 (AN).

BOLDYREFF. BY WORD MOUTH; INFORMAL ESSAYS (ED*).

BOSSARD. "THE BILINGUAL AS PERSON-- LINGUISTIC (SO*).

BOSWICK. "THEY SPEAK SAME LANGUAGE" (ED*).

BOURKE, JOHN GREGORY. "NOTES ON THE LANGUAGE AND FOLK
    USAGES OF THE RIO GRANDE VALLEY". JOURNAL OF
    AMERICAN FOLKLORE, VOL. 9 (1896), P. 81, 115 (AN).

BOVEE. NEEDED: LINGUISTIC LOCARNO (ED*).

BOWEN, JEAN DONALD. THE SPANISH OF SAN ANTONIO, NEW
    MEXICO. UNIVERSITY OF NEW MEXICO, PHD. DISSERTATION
    (1972).

BOYD-BOWMAN, PETER M. "LA PERDIDA DE VOCALES ATONAS EN
    LA ANTIPLANICIE MEXICANA". NUEVA REVISTA DE
    FILOLOGIA HISPANICA, VOL. 4 (1952), PP. 138-140.

BOYD-BOWMAN, PETER M. "REGIONAL ORIGINS OF THE EARLIEST
    SPANISH COLONIST OF AMERICA". PMLA, VOL. 121 (1956).

BOYD-BOWMAN, PETER M. A LINGUISTIC STUDY OF THE SPANISH
    OF GUANAJUATO, MEXICO. HARVARD UNIVERSITY, 1950.

BOYD-BOWMAN, PETER. EL HABLA DE GUANAJUATO. UNIVERSIDAD
    DE MEXICO, 1960.

BRADDY, H. "PACHUCOS AND THEIR ARGOT". SOUTHERN
    FOLK-LORE QUARTERLY, VOL. 24 (DECEMBER, 1960), PP.
    255-271.

BRAMBILA, ALBERTO M. PELAYO. LENGUAJE POPULAR EN JALISCO.
    GUADALAJARA, MEXICO,.

BREND, RUTH M. A TAGMEMIC ANALYSIS OF MEXICAN SPANISH
    CLAUSES. UNIVERSITY OF MICHIGAN, 1964.

BRENGELMAN, FREDERICK H. AND MANNING, JOHN C. A LINGUISTIC
    APPROACH TO THE TEACHING OF ENGLISH AS A FOREIGN
    LANGUAGE TO KINDERGARTEN PUPILS WHOSE PRIMARY
    LANGUAGE IS SPANISH. ??NO INFORMATION??, 1966.

BRIGANCE, WILLIAM N. "SPEAKING IN TWO TONGUES".
    THE FRIEND, VOL. 106 (DECEMBER 1936), P. 225.

BROOKS, NELSON. LANGUAGE AND LANGUAGE LEARNING: THEORY
    AND PRACTICE. NEW YORK: HARCOURT, BRACE AND WORLD,
    INC., 1964.

BROWN. "FOREIGN-LANGUAGE ERRORS CHICAGO (ED*).

BROWN, DOLORES. 'A TWO-SYLLABLE AFFECTIVE AFFIRMATION IN
    SPOKEN SPANISH.' IN RALPH W. EWTON, JR., AND JACOB
    ORNSTEIN, STUDIES IN LANGUAGE AND LINGUISTICS.

CABAZA, BERTA. THE SPANISH LANGUAGE IN TEXAS: CAMERON AND
    WILLACY COUNTIES, DISTRICT 1 OA. UNIVERSITY
    OF TEXAS, MASTER'S THESIS (1950).

CAMPA. INDIVIDUALISM HISPANIC SOCIETY (AN*).

CAMPA. SAYINGS RIDDLES NEW MEXICO (AN*).

CAMPBELL, ANNA L. A STUDY OF SOME FACTORS IN THE WRITTEN
    LANGUAGE OF A GROUP OF TEXAS LAN D-GRANT COLLEGE
    FRESHMEN TO SHOW HOW THE NATURE OF THE LANGUAGE
    REFLECT S THE SOCIO-ECONOMIC BACKGROUNDS OF THESE
    STUDENTS. NEW YORK UNIVERSITY, 1956.

CANELLADA DE ZAMORA, MARIA JOSEFA. "VOCALES CADUCAS DEL
    ESPANOL MEXICANO". NUEVA REVISTA DE FILOLOGIA
    HISPANICA, VOL. 14 (1960), PP. 221-241.

CANFIELD, D. LINCOLN. SPANISH LITERATURE IN MEXICAN
    LANGUAGES AS A SOURCE FOR THE STUDY OF SP ANISH
    PRONUNCIATION. COLUMBIA UNIVERSITY, 1934.

CARDENAS, DANIEL N. THE SPANISH OF JALISCO: A CONTRIBUTION
    TO SPANISH AMERICAN LINGUISTIC GEOGRAPHY. COLUMBIA
    UNIVERSITY, 1953.

CARLISLE, JEANNE. A SOUTHWESTERN DICTIONARY. UNIVERSITY
    OF NEW MEXICO, 1939.

CARLSON, HELEN S. NEVADA PLACE-NAMES: ORIGIN AND MEANING.
    UNIVERSITY OF NEW MEXICO, 1959.

CARRELL, T.; STEVENS, T. "LEAPING THE LANGUAGE BARRIER".
    TEXAS OUTLOOK, VOL. 45 (SEPTEMBER 1961), PP. 19-20.

CARROW, SISTER MARY ARTHUR. "LINGUISTIC FUNCTIONING OF
    BILINGUAL AND MONOLINGUAL CHILDREN". THE JOURNAL
    OF SPEECH AND HEARING DISORDERS, VOL. 22 (SEPTEMBER
    1957), PP. 371-380.

CARROW, SISTER MARY A. A COMPARATIVE STUDY OF THE
    LINGUISTIC FUNCTIONING OF BILINGUAL SPANISH-AMERICAN
    CHILDREN AND MONOLINGUAL ANGLO AMERICAN CHILDREN AT
    THE THIRD GRADE LEVEL. NORTHWESTERN UNIVERSITY, 1955.

CASTILLO NAJERA, FRANCISCO. BREVES CONSIDERACIONES SOBRE
    EL ESPANOL QUE SE HABLA EN MEXICO. NUEVA YORK:
    INSTITUTO DE LAS ESPANAS EN ESTADOS UNIDOS, 1936.

CENTER FOR APPLIED LINGUISTICS. AURAL AIDS IN ENGLISH FOR
    FOREIGNERS. AURAL AIDS IN ENGLISH FOR FOREIGNERS.

CENTER FOR APPLIED LINGUISTICS. UNIVERSITY RESOURCES IN
    THE UNITED STATES FOR LINGUISTICS AND TEACHER TRAINING
    IN ENGLISH AS A FOREIGN LANGUAGE. WASHINGTON, D.
    C.: CENTER FOR APPLIED LINGUISTICS, 1966 (LAE).

CERDA, GILBERTO. THE SPANISH LANGUAGE IN TEXAS, NO. 1:
    VAL VERDE, EDWARDS, AND KINNEY CO UNTIES. UNIVERSITY
    OF TEXAS AT AUSTIN, (1950).

CERDA, GILBERTO; CABAZA, BERTRAM; FARIAS, JULIETE.
    VOCABULARIO ESPANOL DE TEXAS. AUSTIN, TEXAS:
    UNIVERSITY OF TEXAS HISPANIC STUDIES,.

CHABAT, CARLOS G. DICCIONARIO DE CALO <EL LENGUAJE DEL
    HAMPA EN MEXICO>. FRANCISCO MENDEZ OTEO <EDITOR>
    MEXICO, 1964.

CHARTERS, W. W. ; PAUL, HARY G. GAMES AND OTHER DEVICES
     FOR IMPROVING PUPILS ENGLISH.   WASHINGTON, D. C.:
     UNITED STATES GOVERNMENT PRINTING OFFICE, (1923).

CHRISTIAN.   "ACCULTURATION BILINGUAL CHILD" (ED*).

CHRISTIAN, JANCE AND CHRISTIAN, CHESTER J. 'SPANISH
     LANGUAGE AND CULTURE IN THE SOUTHWEST.'   IN JOSHUA
     A. FISHMAN, <ED>. LANGUAGE LOYALTY IN THE UNITED
     STATES: THEMAINTENANCE AND PERPETUATION OF NON-ENGLISH
     MOTHER TONGUES BY AMERICAN ETHNIC AND RELIGIOUS
     GROUPS, PP. 280-317 (AN).

CLIFFORD, ROY A. 'THE RIO GRANDE FOLLD: A COMPARATIVE
     STUDY OF BORDER COMMUNITIES IN DISASTER.'   A
     RIO GRANDE FLOOD: A COMPARATIVE STUDY OF BORDER
     COMMUNITIES IN DISASTER, DISASTER STUDY NO. 7.

COLTHARP, LURLINE H. 'SOME ADDITIONS: LEXICON OF
     THE TONGUE OF THE TIRILONES.'   SOME ADDITIONS:
     LEXICON OF THE TONGUE OF THE TIRILONES, IN PALPH W.
     EWTON, JR. AND JACOB ORNSTEIN, STUDIES IN LANGUAGE
     AND LINGUISTICS,.

COLTHARP, LURLINE H. THE TONGUE OF THE TIRILONES:
     A LINGUISTIC STUDY OF A CRIMINAL ARGOT.   UNIVERSITY
     OF ALABAMA PRESS, 1965.

COLTHARP, MARY L. THE INGLUENCE OF ENGLISH ON THE LANGUAGE
     OF THE TIRILONES.   UNIVERSITY OF TEXAS, 1964.

COLVIN.   LINGUISTIC ABILITY (ED*).

CONSTANTINO, ERNESTO A. A GENERATIVE GRAMMAR OF A DIALECT
     OF ILOCANO.   INDIANA: INDIANA UNIVERSITY, 1959.

COOPER.   "WORLD FREQUENCY ESTIMATION AS   (ED*).

COOPER.   "TWO CONTEXTUALIZED MEASURE DEGREE (ED*).

CORBIN.   LANGUAGE PROGRAMS DISADVANTAGED (ED*).

COROMINAS, JUAN. DICCIONARIO CRITICO ETIMOLOGICO DE LA
     LENGUA CASTELLANA.   BERNA, 1954.

CORTICHS DE MORA, ESTRELLA. CONSTITUTIONAL LAW AND
     POLITICS: THREE ARIZONA CASE-STUDIES.   TESIS,
     MEXICO, 1951.

CUERVO, RUFINO JOSE. "EL CASTELLANC EN AMERICA".   REVUE
     HISPANIQUE, VOL. 3 (1901).

CUERVO, RUFINO JOSE. APUNTACIONES CRITICAS SOBRE EL
     LENGUAJE BOGOTANO, CON FRECUENTE REFERENCIA AL DE LOS
     PAISES DE HISPANO-AMERICA. PARIS, 1907.

CULLEN, A. J. "A NEW KIND OF SPANISH LANGUAGE AND
     INTER-AMERICAN AREA CENTER". HISPANIA, VOL.
     47 (SEPTEMBER 1964), PP. 593-596.

DAVIS. ANNOTATED BIBLIOGRAPHY AMERICAN (B*).

DAVIS. "TEACHING SPANISH BILINGUAL AREA" (ED*).

DAVIS. ANNOTATION ANALYSIS SIXTY SPANISH (ED*).

DAWSON. "SPANISH BY ACCIDENT" (HS*).

DAWSON. GUIDING LANGUAGE LEARNING (ED*).

DE VARGAS. "TEACHING MEXICANS ENGLISH VOCABULARY" (ED*).

DEBOER. "SOME SOCIOLOGICAL FACTORS LANGUAGE (SO*).

DELAGUNA, GRACE ANDRUS. SPEECH: ITS FUNCTION AND
     DEVELOPMENT. NEW HAVEN, CONNECTICUT: YALE UNIVERSITY
     PRESS, 1927.

DELK. SPANISH LANGUAGE LITERATURE PUBLICATIONS (B*).

DOCKSTADER, FREDERICK J. "SPANISH LOAN WORDS IN HOPI;
     A PRELIMINARY CHECKLIST". INTERNATIONAL JOURNAL OF
     AMERICAN LINGUISTICS, VOL. 21 (MAY 1931), PP. 157-159.

DOOB, L. W. "THE EFFECT OF LANGUAGE ON VERBAL EXPRESSION
     AND RECALL". AMERICAN ANTHROPOLOGIST, VOL. 59 (FEB
     1957), PP. 88-100.

DREHER, B. B. "LANGUAGE TRAINING IN A PRESCHOOL FOR
     SPANISH-SPEAKING MIGRANT CHILDREN". THE SPEECH
     TEACHER, VOL. 20 (JAN 1971), PP. 64-65.

EATON, HELEN S. SEMANTIC FREQUENCY LIST FOR ENGLISH,
     FRENCH, GERMAN, AND SPANISH: A CORELATION OF THE FIRST
     SIX THOUSAND WORDS IN FOUR SINGLE LANGUAGE FREQUENCYLISTS.
     CHICAGO, ILLINOIS: THE UNIVERSITY OF CHICAGO PRESS,
     1940.

ECHEVERRIA Y REYES, ANIBAL. VOCES USADAS EN CHILE.
     SANTIAGO, CHILE,.

EDWARDS. CALIFORNIANS MEXICAN DESCENT (HC*).

ELERICK, CHARLES. 'THE CONTRASTIVE SEMOLOGY OF SPANISH
     AND ENGLISH VERBS OF VISUAL PERCEPTION.' IN RALPH
     W. EWTON, JR. AND JACCB CRNSTEIN, STUDIES IN LANGUAGE
     AND LINGUISTICS,.

ELLIOTT, JAMES ALTON. THE LANGUAGE HANDICAP IN SPANISH
    AMERICAN CHILDREN IN INTELLIGENCE AND ACHIEVEMENT.
    UNIVERSITY OF ARIZONA, MASTER'S THESIS (1942).

ESPINOSA. "FOLKLORE INFANTIL DE NUEVO MEJICO" (LMA*).

ESPINOSA. "PROBLEMAS LEXICO-GRAFICOS ESPANOL (LMA*).

ESPINOSA, AURELIO M. "SPANISH FOLKLORE IN NEW MEXICO".
    NEW MEXICO HISTORICAL REVIEW, VOL. 1 (1926),
    P. 135,155 (LMA).

ESPINOSA, AURELIO M. STUDIES IN NEW MEXICAN SPANISH.
    ALBUQUERQUE, NEW MEXICO: UNIVERSITY OF NEW MEXICO
    BULLETIN, (1909). LANGUAGE SERIES, VOL. 1, NO. 2 (LMA).

ETTEN. TEACHERS SHOULD BREAK LANGUAGE (ED*).

EWTON, RALPH W. JR. AND ORNSTEIN, JACOB (EDS). STUDIES
    IN LANGUAGE AND LINGUISTICS 1969-1970. EL PASO,
    TEXAS: TEXAS WESTERN PRESS, 1970.

EYRING. "SPANISH SPANISH-SPEAKING STUDENTS (ED*).

FAIRBANKS, G. VOICE AND ARTICULATION DRILLBOOK.
    NEW YORK: HARPER AND BROTHERS, 1940.

FARIAS, MARIA J. THE SPANISH LANGUAGE IN TEXAS, NO. 3:
    DUVAL, WEBB, AND ZAPATA COUNTIES. AUSTIN: UNIVERSITY
    OF TEXAS, (1951). NUMBER 3: DUVAL, WEBB, AND ZAPATA
    COUNTIES.

FATOUT, PAUL. AMBROSE BIERCE, THE DEVEIL'S LEXICOGRAPHER.
    NORMAN: UNIVERSITY OF OKLAHOMA PRESS, 1951.

FICKINGER. STUDY CERTAIN PHOAES LANGUAGE (ED*).

FINDLING. "BILINGUAL NEED AFFILIATION FUTURE (ED*).

FISHMAN, A. A.; HERASIMCHUK, E. "MULTIPLE PREDICTION OF
    PHONOLOGICAL VARIABLES IN A BILINGUAL SPEECH COMMUNITY".
    AMERICAN ANTHROPOLOGIST, VOL. 71 (AUGUST 1969), PP.
    648-657 (ED).

FISHMAN, J. A. "SOCIOLINGUISTIC CENSUS OF A BILINGUAL
    NEIGHBORHOOD". AMERICAN JOURNAL OF SOCIOLOGY, VOL.
    75 (NOVEMBER 1969), PP. 323-339 (ED).

FISHMAN, J. A., ET AL. "BILINGUALISM IN THE BARRIO".
    MODERN LANGUAGE JOURNAL, VOL. 53 (MARCH-APRIL 1969),
    PP. 151-185, 227-258 (ED).

FISHMAN, JOSHUA A. "LANGUAGE MAINTENANCE AND LANGUAGE
    SHIFT AS A FIELD OF INQUIRY". LINGUISTICS, VOL. 9
    (NOVEMBER 1964), PP. 32-70 (SO).

FISHMAN, JOSHUA A. BILINGUAL ATTITUDES AND BEHAVIORS.
    BLOOMINGTON: INDIANA UNIVERSITY RESEARCH CENTER FOR
    THE LANGUAGE SCIENCES, 1969 (ED).

FISHMAN, JOSHUA A. LANGUAGE LOYALTY IN THE UNITED STATES;
    THE MAINTENANCE AND PERCEPTION OFNON-ENGLISH MOTHER
    TONGUES BY AMERICAN ETHNIC AND RELIGIOUS GROUPS.
    THE HAGUE: MOUTON, 1966 (SO).

FISHMAN, JOSHUA A. THE MEASUREMENT AND DESCRIPTION
    OF LANGUAGE DOMINANCE IN BILINGUALS. FINAL REPORT,
    PHASE I.. ERIC, 1967 (ED).

FISHMAN, JOSHUA A. (ED.). READINGS IN THE SOCIOLOGY OF
    LANGUAGE. THE HAGUE: MOUTON, 1968 (SO).

FISHMAN, JOSHUA. THE IMPLICATIONS OF BILINGUALISM
    FOR LANGUAGE TEACHING AND LANGUAGE LEARNING.
    IN ALBERT VALDAM (ED), TRENDS IN LANGUAGE TEACHING.
    NEW YORK: MCGRAW-HILL BOOK COMPANY, 1966 (ED).

FLOOD. TEACHING ENGLISH AS FOREIGN LANGUAGE (ED*).

FLORES, ZELLA K. JORDAN. THE RELATION OF LANGUAGE
    DIFFICULTY TO INTELLIGENCE AND SCHOOL RETARDATION IN
    A GROUP OF SPANISH-SPEAKING CHILDREN. UNIVERSITY
    OF CHICAGO, MASTER'S THESIS (1926) (ED).

FONTECHA, CARMEN. GLOSARIO DE VOCES COMENTADAS EN
    EDICIONES DE TEXTOS CLASICOS. MADRID, 1941.

FRANCIS, W. NELSON. THE STRUCTURE OF AMERICAN ENGLISH.
    NEW YORK: RONALD PRESS, 1958.

FRATTO. STUDY EFFECT HEAD START VOCABULARY (ED*).

FULLER. "THE EFFECT KINDERGARTEN SPEECH (ED*).

GAARDER, A. BRUCE. "CONSERVING OUR LINGUISTIC RESOURCES".
    PMLA, VOL. 80 NO. 2B (MAY 1965), PP. 19-23 (ED).

GAARDER, A. BRUCE. "NOTES ON SOME SPANISH TERMS IN THE
    SOUTHWEST". EN HISPANIA, VOL. 27 (1944), PP.
    330-334 (ED).

GALVAN, R. A. EL DIALECTO ESPANOL DE SAN ANTONIO, TEXAS.
    TULANE UNIVERSITY, 1955.

GALVAN, ROBERT A. UN ESTUDIO GEOGRAFICO DE ALGUNOS
     VOCABLOS USADOS POR LOS HABITANTES DEHABLA ESPANOLA
     DE SAN ANTONIO, TEXAS.   UNIVERSITY OF TEXAS AT
     AUSTIN, MASTER'S THESIS (1949).

GAMEZ, LUIS EZEQUIEL. JUSTO SIERRA: HISTORIADOR, EDUCADOR,
     Y LITERATO.   UNIVERSITY OF TEXAS AT AUSTIN, 1939.

GARCIA ICAZBALCETA. VOCABULARIO DE MEXICANISMOS.   MEXICO,
     1899.

GARCIA.   USE READINGS SPANISH-AMERICAN   (B*).

GARCIA, ERNEST FELIX. INTERFERENCE BY TEXTUAL STIMULI ON
     SELECTED ELEMENTS OF SPANISH PRONUNCIATION.
     UNIVERSITY OF CALIFORNIA-LOS ANGELES, PHD. DISSERTATION
     (1966).

GARCIA, ERNEST. "CHICANO SPANISH DIALECTS AND EDUCATION".
     CHICANO JOURNAL OF THE SOCIAL SCIENCES AND THE ARTS,
     VOL. 2 NO. 1 (SPRING 1971), PP. 67-77 (ED).

GARTH.   "THE ADMINISTRATION NON-LANGUAGE (PY*).

GRAFF, W. L. LANGUAGE AND LANGUAGES: AN INTRODUCTION TO
     LINGUISTICS.   APPLETON-CENTURY, NEW YORK INC., 1932.

GRAY, EDWARD D. MC QUEEEN. "SPANISH LANGUAGE IN NEW
     MEXICO: A NATIONAL RESOURCE".   UNIVERSITY OF
     NEW MEXICO BULLETIN, SOCIOLOGICAL SERIES, VOL. 1 NO.
     2 (1912) (HN HS SO).

GRAY, HOLLIS, ET AL. "GRINGOISMS IN ARIZONA".   AMERICAN
     SPEECH,   (OCTOBER 1949), PP. 234-236.

GRIFFITH. "THE PACHUCO PATOIS" (SO*).

GUERARD, A. L. A SHORT HISTORY OF THE INTERNATIONAL
     LANGUAGE MOVEMENT.   NEW YORK: BONI & LIVERIGHT, 1921.

GUERRA.   LANGUAGE INSTRUCTION INTERGROUP (ED*).

GUERRA.   THE MEXICAN-AMERICAN CHILD: (ED*).

GUERRA.   THE MEXICAN-AMERICAN CHILD: (ED*).

GUERRA.   THE RETENTION MEXICAN AMERICAN (ED*).

GUERRA.   WHY JUANITO DOESNT READ (ED*).

GUERRA.   "WHY JUANITO DOESNT READ" (ED*).

GURREN, LOUISE. A COMPARISON ON A PHONETIC BASIS OF THE
    TWO CHIEF LANGUAGES OF THE AMERICAS, ENGLISH AND
    SPANISH.   NEW YORK UNIVERSITY, 1955.

HALL, EDWARD T. THE SILENT LANGUAGE.   NEW YORK: DOUBLEDAY,
    1959 (AN).

HANSSEN, FRIEDRICH. ALTSPANISCHEN PRATERITA VON TYPUS
    (OVE, PUDE).   VALPARAISO, 1898.

HARRINGTON, ANN KAY. RECENT BORROWINGS FROM ENGLISH FOUND
    IN MEXICAN SPANISH.   UNIVERSITY OF TEXAS AT AUSTIN,
    MASTER'S THESIS (1956).

HARRISON, HELENE W. A METHODOLOGICAL STUDY IN ELICITING
    LINGUISTIC DATA FROM MEXICAN AMERICAN BILINGUALS.
    AUSTIN, TEXAS, (1967). DISSERTATION ABSTRACTS
    28: 4157A- 58A (ED).

HAUGHT.   "THE LANGUAGE DIFFICULTY SPANISH—AMERICAN (PY*).

HELMKE.   EFFECT ENGLISH LANGUAGE HANDICAP (PY*).

HENDRIX.   AUDITORY DISCRIMINATION DIFFERENCES (ED*).

HENRIQUES URENA.   "EL ESPANOL EN JEJICO, LOS ESTADOS (HS*).

HENRIQUES URENA.   ESPANOL EN MEXICO, LOS ESTADOS (HS*).

HENRIQUES URENA.   HENRY -- BOY BARRIO (HS*).

HENRIQUES URENA.   MUTACIONES ARTIULATORIAS EN HABLA (HS*).

HENRIQUES URENA.   OBSERVACIONES SOBRE EXPANOL DE (HS*).

HENRIQUES URENA.   SOBRE PROBLEMA ANDALUCISMO DIALECTAL
    (HS*).

HENRIQUES URENA.   STORY MEXICAN WAR (HS*).

HENRIQUES URENA. "ROMANCES EN AMERICA" (HS*).

HESS.   COMPARATIVE STUDY UNDERSTANDINGS (ED*).

HILLS, E. C. NEW MEXICAN SPANISH.   BOSTON: PUBLICATIONS
    OF THE MODERN LANGUAGE ASSOCIATION OF AMERICA, 1906.

HOBSON, ARLINE BOOTH. A COMPARISON OF THE CONTROL
    OF LINGUISTIC MANIFESTATION OF RELATIONAL THINKING
    OF MEXICAN AMERICAN CHILDREN WITH FOUR, FIVE AND SIX
    YEARS OF SCHOOLING.   UNIVERSITY OF ARIZONA AT TUCSON,
    MASTER'S THESIS (1970).

HOLLAND.   "LANUGUAGE BARRIER AS EDUCATIONAL (ED*).

HOPKINS, THOMAS R.   LANGUAGE TESTING OF NORTH AMERICAN
    INDIANS.   WASHINGTON, D. C.: DEPARTMENT OF
    THE INTERIOR, BUREAU OF INDIAN AFFAIRS, (1967).

HOYDE, MARSHA JAN. AUDITORY DISCRIMINATION OF AMERICAN
    ENGLISH SOUNDS BY NATIVE AMERICAN ENGLISH, NATIVE
    SPANISH, AND NATIVE JAPANESE SPEAKERS.   SANTA
    BARBARA-UNIVERSITY OF CALIFORNIA SANTA BARBARA,
    MASTER'S THESIS (1968) (ED).

HUGHES.   ENGLISH LANGUAGE FACILITY MEXICAN-AMERICAN (ED*).

HUSE.   PSYCHOLOGY FOREIGN LANGUAGE STUDY   (PY*).

INTERNATIONAL CENTER FOR RESEARCH ON BILINGUALSIM.
    CONFERENCE CHILD LANGUAGE   (ED*).

ISLAS, LEOVIGILDO ESCARCEGA.   DICCIONARIO RURAL DE MEXICO.
    MEXICO, 1961.

IVEY, ALFRED JOE.   A STUDY OF THE VOCABULARY OF NEWPAPERS
    PRINTED IN THE SPANISH LANGUAGE ITEXAS.   UNIVERSITY
    OF TEXAS AT AUSTIN, MASTER'S THESIS (1927).

JACOBOVITS.   "DIMENSIONALITY COMPOUND-COORDINATE (ED*).

JOHNSON, CHARLES, E. ; FLORES, JOSEPH S.; ELLISON, FRED
    P. AND RIESTRA, MIGUEL A. "THE NON-SPECIALIST TEACHER
    IN FLES".   THE MODERN LANGUAGE JOURNAL, VOL.
    51 (FEBRUARY 1967), PP. 76-79 (ED).

JOHNSTON.   COGNATE RELATIONSHIPS BETWEEN   (ED*).

JOHNSTON.   "NSPANISH SPANISH-SPEAKING PUPILS"   (ED*).

JONES.   "A VOCABULARY STUDY CHILDRENFOREIGN   (PY*).

JONES.   PROGRAM FIRST GRADE SPANISH-AMERICAN   (ED*).

JONES.   PROGRAM FIRST GRADE SPANISH AMERICAN   (ED*).

JONES, MORGAN E.   A PHONOLOGICAL STUDY OF ENGLISH AS SPOKEN
    BY PUERTO RICANS, CONTRASTED WITH PUERTO RICAN SPANISH
    AND AMERICAN ENGLISH.   UNIVERSITY OF MICHIGAN, 1962.

JOSLIN, SESYLE.   THERE IS A BULL ON MY BALCONY.   HARCOURT,
    1968.

KANY, E. CHARLES.   AMERICAN-SPANISH SYNTAX.   SECOND
    EDITION: THE UNIVERSITY OF CHICAGO PRESS, 1963.

KERCHEVILLE, F. M.   PRACTICAL SPOKEN SPANISH.   ALBUQUERQUE,
    NEW MEXICO: UNIVERSITY OF NEW MEXICO PRESS, 1969.

KERCHEVILLE, F. M.   PRELIMINARY GLOSARY OF NEW MEXICAN
    SPANISH.   THE UNIVERSITY OF NEW MEXICO, (1934).
    BULLETIN 5.

KERNAN, KEITH T., AND B. G. BLOUNT. "THE ACQUISITION OF
     SPANISH GRAMMAR BY MEXICAN CHILDREN". ANTHROPOLOGICAL
     LINGUISTICS, (1966).

KIDDLE, LAWRENCE B. "'TURKEY' IN NEW MEXICAN SPANISH".
     ROMANCE PHILOLOGY, VOL. 5 (AUGUST 1965), PP. 190—197.

KIDDLE, LAWRENCE B. SPANISH LOAN WORDS IN AMERICAN INDIAN
     LANGUAGE. HISPANIA, 35.

KIRK. ILLINOIS TEST PSYCHOLINGUISTIC (PY*).

KREAR, M. L. AND C. R. BOUCHER. "COMPARISON OF SPECIAL
     PROGRAMS OR CLASSES IN ENGLISH FOR ELEMENTARY SCHOOL
     PUPILS". MODERN LANGUAGE JOURNAL, VOL. 51 (OCTOBER
     1967), PP. 335—337 (ED).

KREAR, SERAFINA E. THE ROLE OF THE MOTHER TONGUE AT HOME
     AND AT SCHOOL. EDITED BY NATHANIEL N. WAGNER AND
     MARSHA J. HAUG. SAINT LOUIS, MISSOURI: THE C.V. MOSBY
     COMPANY, 1971 (SO).

KREIDLER, CHARLES W. A STUDY OF THE INFLUENCE OF ENGLISH
     ON THE SPANISH OF PUERTO RICANS IN JERSEY CITY, NEW
     JERSEY. UNIVERSITY OF MICHIGAN, 1958.

KURATH, WILLIAM. A BRIEF INTRODUCTION TO YAQUI, A NATIVE
     LANGUAGE OF SONORA. TUCSON: UNIVERSITY OF ARIZONA,
     1947.

LA FARGE, OLIVER. "ASSIMILATION—THE INDIAN VIEW". NEW
     MEXICO QUARTERLY, VOL. 26 (SPRING 1956), PP. 5—13
     (ED).

LADO. LINGUISTICS ACROSS CULTURES, APPLIED LINGUISTICS
     FOR LANGUAGE TEACHERS. ANN ARBOR: THE UNIVERSITY
     OF MICHIGAN PRESS, 1957.

LADO, ROBERT. 'ENGLISH PATTERN PRACTICES.' ANN ARBOR,
     MICHIGAN.

LADO, ROBERT. LANGUAGE TESTING. ANN ARBOR, MICHIGAN:
     GEORGE WAHR PUBLISHING COMPANY, 1951.

LADO, ROBERT. A STUDY OF THE USE OF MOTION PICTURES IN
     TEACHING SPANISH SPEAKING ADULTS TO READ. UNIVERSITY
     OF TEXAS AT AUSTIN, MASTER'S THESIS (1945).

LADO, ROBERT: FRIES, CHARLES C. ENGLISH LANGUAGE TEST FOR
     FOREIGN STUDENTS. ANN ARBOR, MICHIGAN: THE UNIVERSITY
     OF MICHIGAN PRESS, 1961.

LADO, ROBERT: FRIES, CHARLES C. ENGLISH PRONUNCIATION.
     ANN ARBOR, MICHIGAN: THE UNIVERSITY OF MICHIGAN PRESS,
     1960.

LADO, ROBERT: FRIES, CHARLES C. ENGLISH SENTANCE PATTERNS.
ANN ARBOR, MICHIGAN: THE UNIVERSITY OF MICHIGAN PRESS,
1960.

LADO, ROBERT: FRIES, CHARLES C. LESSONS IN VOCABULARY.
ANN ARBOR, MICHIGAN: THE UNIVERSITY OF MICHIGAN PRESS,
1960.

LAMANO Y BENEYTE. EL DIALECTO VULGAR SALMANTINO.
SALAMANCA, 1915.

LAMBERT, WALLACE; TUCKER, R. G. TU, VOUS, USTED. ROWLEY,
MASSACHUSEYTS: NEWBURY HOUSE PUBLISHERS, INC.,.

LANCASTER, LOUISE. INTROCUCING ENGLISH. BOSTON: HOUGHTON
MIFFLIN COMPANY, 1966.

LAREW, LEONOR A. A STUDY OF SPANISH ARTICULATION IN THE
ELEMENTARY SCHOOL : A PILOT STUDY. UNIVERSITY OF
MISSOURI, 1960 (ED).

LENZ, RODOLFO. "CHILENISCHE STUDIEN. PHONETISCHE
STUDIEN". MAGDEBURGO, VOL. 5 (1892), PP. 272-292.

LENZ, RODOLFO. "EL LENGUAJE VULGAR DE CHILE". HISPANICA,
VOL. 6 (1940).

LENZ, RODOLFO. DICCIONARIO ETIMOLOGICO DE VOCES CHILDENAS
DERIVADAS DE LENGUAS INDIGENAS AMERICANAS. S. DE
CHILE, 1905-1910.

LENZ, RODOLFO. ENSAYOS FILOLOGICOS AMERICANOS. ALALES
DE LA UNIVERSIDAD DE S. DE CHILE, TOMO 87, 1894.

LEONARD, WILLIAM E. SPEECH DEVELOPMENT OF A BILINGUAL
CHILD; A LINGUIST'S RECORD. REPRINTED BY NEW YORK,
NEW YORK AND LONDON, GREAT BRITAIN: AMS PRESS, INC.1939-1949.

LIEBERMAN, PHILIP. INTONATION, PERCEPTION, AND LANGUAGE.
CAMBRIDGE: MIT PRESS, 1967 (PY).

LINN, GEORGE BYRON. A STUDY OF SEVERAL LINGUISTIC
FUNCTIONS OF MEXICAN AMERICAN CHILDREN IN A TWO
LANGUAGE ENVIRONMENT. UNIVERSITY OF SOUTHERN
CALIFORNIA, PHD. DISSERTATION (1965).

LINN, GEORGE BYRON. A STUDY OF SEVERAL LINGUISTIC
FUNCTIONS OF MEXICAN AMERICAN CHILDREN IN A TWO
LANGUAGE NEVIRONMENT. SAN FRANCISCO, CALIFORNIA:
R & E RESEARCH ASSOCIATES, 1971.

LYNN, KLONDA. A PHONETIC ANALYSIS OF THE ENGLISH SPOKEN
BY MEXICAN CHILDREN IN THE ELEMENTARY SCHOOLS
OF ARIZONA. LOUISIANA STATE UNIVERSITY, 1940.

MAC CURDY, RAYMOND R. "A SPANISH WORD LIST OF THE 'BRULIS' DWELLERS OF LOUISIANA". HISPANIA, VOL. 42 (1959), PP. 547-554.

MAC CURDY, RAYMOND R. LOUISIANA-FRENCH LOAN WORDS FOR 'WATER-FOWL' IN THE SPANISH OF ST. BERNARD PARISH, LOUISIANA. ROMANCE STUDIES PRESENTED TO WILLIAM MORTON DEY, CHAPEL HILL, NORTH CAROLINA, 139-142..

MAC CURDY, RAYMOND R. THE SPANISH DIALECT IN ST BERNARD PARISH, LOUISIANA. THE UNIVERSITY OF NEW MEXICO PRESS, 1950.

MAC CURDY, RAYMOND R., JR. THE SPANISH DIALECT IN ST. BERNARD PARISH, LOUISIANA. UNIVERSITY OF NORTH CAROLINA, 1948.

MAC LEARIE, ELIZABETH G. "FOREIGN ACCENT AMONG BOYS AND GIRLS". QUARTERLY JOURNAL OF SPEECH, VOL. 18 (NOVEMBER 1932), PP. 612-21.

MAC WAB CHRISTIAN, JANE AND CHRISTIAN, CHESTER JR. SPANISH LANGUAGE AND CULTURE IN THE SOUTHWEST. A FINAL REPORT TO THE U. S. OFFICE CF EDUCATION, LANGUAGE RESEARCH SECTION, VOLUME 3, PAGE 389 (HS).

MACAULAY. "VOCABULARY PROBLEMS SPANISHLEARNERS" (ED*).

MACKEY, WILLIAM F. "BILINGUALISM". ENCYCLOPEDIA BRITANNICA, VOL. 3 (1965), PP. 610-611.

MALARET, AUGUSTO. DICCIONARIO DE AMERICANISMOS. BIBLIOTECA EMECE, BUENOS AIRES, 1878. 2 EDICION, PUERTO RICO, 1931.

MALARET, AUGUSTC. VOCABULARIO DE PUERTO RICO. LAS AMERICAS PUBLISHING COMPANY, 1955.

MALLERY, RICHARD D. OUR AMERICAN LANGUAGE. GARDEN CITY, NEW YORK, 1947.

MAMORU, STANLEY. ENGLISH INFLUENCE IN SPANISH OF DETROIT. UNIVERSITY OF MICHIGAN, MASTER'S THESIS (1963).

MANGELS, ANNA. SONDERESCHEINUNGEN DES SPANISCHEN IN AMERIKA. UNIVERSIDAD DE HAMBURGO, PHD. DISSERTATION (1926).

MANN, C. "FAILURES DUE TO LANGUAGE CEFICIENCY". PSYCHOLOGICAL CLINIC, VOL. 13 (1921), PP. 230-237.

MARDEN, C. C. LA FCNOLOGIA DEL ESPANOL EN LA CIUDAD DE MEXICO. BUENOS AIRES: UNIVERSITY DE BUENOS AIRES, 1938.

MARKLEY, JAMES G.   THE VERBAL CATERGORIES OF SUB—STANDARD
     SPANISH.   UNIVERSITY OF ILLINOIS, 1954.

MARKWARDS A., ALBERT.   AMERICAN ENGLISH.   NEW YORK: OXFORD
     UNIVERSITY PRESS, 1932.

MASSAD, CAROLYN EMRICK, ET A.   "STIMULUS MODES AND LANGUAGE
     MEDIA; A STUDY OF BILINGUALS".   ALSOIN PSYCHOLOGY
     IN THE SCHOOLS, VOL. 7   (JANUARY 1970), PP. 38—42
     (PY).

MATHEWS, MITFORD M.   A DICTIONARY OF AMERICANISMS ON
     HISTORICAL PRINCIPLES.   THE UNIVERSITY OF CHICAGO
     PRESS, 1951.

MATLUCK, JOSEPH.   LA PRONUNCIACION DEL ESPANOL EN EL VALLE
     DE MEXICO.   NUEVA REVISTA DE FIIOLOGIA HISPANICA,
     TOMO 4, 1952.

MAYS, RUTH.   "TEACHING SPANISH IN THE LOWER GRADES".
     HISPANIA, VOL. 25   (MAY   1942), PP. 141—143.

MAYS, RUTH.   "TEACHING SPANISH IN THE GRADES".   HISPANIA,
     VOL. 26   (FEBRUARY 1943), PP. 46—50.

MC CULLOUGH, GRACE A.   CORRECTING SPEECH DEFECTS AND
     FOREIGN ACCENT.   NEW YORK: CHARLES SCRIBNER'S SONS,
     1925.

MC DONALD.   "LANGUAGE DEVELOPMENT THROUGH   (ED*).

MC IVER, ZADIE RUNKLES.   LINGUISTIC BORROWINGS FROM THE
     SPANISH AS REFLECTED IN WRITINGS OF THE SOUTHWEST.
     UNIVERSITY OF TEXAS AT AUSTIN, MASTER'S THESIS (1939).

MC NEILL, DAVID.   THE DEVELOPMENT OF LANGUAGE.   ??NO
     INFORMATION??, 1967.

MENCKEN, H. L.   THE AMERICAN LANGUAGE, AN INQUIRY INTO THE
     DEVELOPMENT OF ENGLISH IN THEUNITED STATES.   NEW YORK
     ALFRED A KNOPF, 1936.

MESSINEO.   ENVIRONMENTAL UTILIZATION PSYCHOLINGUISTIC
     (PY*).

MILLS, DOROTHY A.   A DESCRIPTIVE ANALYSIS OF THE MORPHOLOGY
     OF THE DIMINUTIVES ITO, ILLO,   ICO, UELO, AND OF THEIR
     INCREMENTS <INCLUDING FEMININE AND PLURAL FORMS > AS
     USED IN SPANISH AMERICA.   UNIVERSITY OF SOUTHERN
     CALIFORNIA, 1955.

MOLINA FRAY ALONSO DE.   VOCABULARIO EN LENGUA CASTELLANA
     Y MEXICANA.   VOCABULARIO EN LENGUA CASTELLANA
     Y MEXICANA, MEXICO, 1571.

MORAN.   STUDY ORAL READING VOCABULARIES (ED*).

MORTON.   "EXPERIMENTAL APPROACH TO LANGUAGE   (ED*).

MOULTON, WILLIAM G. A LINGUISTIC GUIDE TO LANGUAGE
     LEARNING.   NEW YORK: THE MODERN LANGUAGE ASSOCIATION
     OF AMERICA, 1970.

MOWAT, OLIVE M. A SYNOPSIS OF ENGLISH SOUNDS.   NEW YORK:
     MACMILLAN CO., 1926.

MOZA, H. "LANGUAGE DIFFERENCE AND POLITICAL INTEGRATION".
     MODERN LANGUAGE JOURNAL, VOL. 41 (DECEMBER   1957),
     PP. 365-372 (PL).

MUGICA, PEDRO DE. DIALECTOS CASTELLANOS, MONTANES,
     VIZCAINO, ARAGONES.   DEALECTOS CASTELLANOS, MONTANES,
     VIZCAINO, ARAGONES, BERLIN, 1892.

MURPHY, SPENCER L. A DESCRIPTION OF NOUN SUFFIXES
     IN COLLOQUIAL MEXICAN SPANISH.   UNIVERSITY OF
     ILLINOIS, 1950.

NAVARRO TOMAS, TOMAS. CUESTIONARIO LINGUISTICO HISPANOAMERICANO.
     UNIVERSIDAD DE BUENOS AIRES, 1945.

NEWMARK, MAXIM. "SPECIAL SPANISH: A COURSE FOR SPANISH-SPEAKING
     STUDENTS".   HIGH POINTS, VOL. 40 (APRIL   1958), PP.
     70-73.

NILSEN, DON AND NILSEN, ALLEIN. PRONUNCIATION CONTRASTS
     IN ENGLISH.   NEW YORK: REGENTS PUBLISHING COMPANY,.

NINE, C. J. "EXPERIENCES IN CULTURE SHOCK;NDEA OVERSEAS
     INSTITUTES ON ENGLISH AS A FOREIGN LANGUAGE".   MODERN
     LANGUAGE JOURNAL, VOL. 51 (FEBRUARY   1967), PP. 89-92.

NORMAN, ARTHUR M. A SOUTHEAST TEXAS DIALECT STUDY.
     UNIVERSITY OF TEXAS, 1955.

NYKL, A. R. "NOTAS SOBRE EL ESPANOL DE YUCATAN, VERACRUZ
     Y TLAXCALA".   BIBLIOTECA DE DIALECTOLOGIA HISPANOAMERICANA,
     VOL. 4 (JANUARY   1967), PP. 207-225.

O' CONNOR, PATRICIA AND HADEN, ERNEST F. ORAL DRILL IN
     SPANISH.   BOSTON: HOUGHTON MIFFLEN COMPANY, 1957.

OCHOA, HERMELINDA. LINGUISTIC ERRORS MADE BY SPANISH-SPEAKING
     CHILDREN IN WRITTEN ENGLISH.   AUSTIN: UNIVERSITY OF
     TEXAS, 1942.

OLPIN.   SOME LINGUISTIC DIFFERENCES BETWEEN (ED*).

ORNSTEIN, JACOB. 'SOCIOLINGUISTICS AND NEW PERSPECTIVES
    IN THE STUDY OF SOUTHWEST SPANISH.'   EL PASO, TEXAS:
    THE UNIVERSITY OF TEXAS AT EL PASO.

ORNSTEIN, JACOB. "THE ARCHAIC AND THE MODERN IN THE
    SPANISH OF NEW MEXICO".   AZTLAN—CHICANO JOURNAL OF
    THE SOCIAL SCIENCES AND THE ARTS, VOL. 2   NO.
    1 (SPRING   1971), PP. 23-35.

OSGOOD.   PSYCHOLINGUISTICS: SURVEY THEORY (PY*).

PACIN, JOSE. "ENGLISH IN PUERTO RICO".   LA REVISTA
    ESCOLAR DE PUERTO RICO, VOL. 20 (MARCH 1935), PP.
    3-9.

PARTRIDGE, ERIC. ETYMOLOGICAL DICTIONARY OF MODERN
    ENGLISH.   LONDON, 1935.

PEARCE.   NEW MEXICO PLACE NAMES, GEORGRAPHICAL (HN*).

PEARCE, T.M. "SPANISH PLACE NAME PATTERNS IN THE SOUTHWEST".
    NAMES, VOL. 3 , PP. 201-209.

PEARCE, THOMAS M. "TRADER TERMS IN SOUTHWESTERN ENGLISH".
    AMERICAN SPEECH, VOL. 16 (1946) (LI).

PENUELAS, MARCELINO C. LO ESPANOL EN EL SUROESTE DE LOS
    ESTADOS UNIDOS.   MADRID: EDICIONES CULTURA HISPANICA,
    1964 (HS).

PERALES, ALONSO M. "THE AUDIO-LINGUAL APPROACH AND THE
    SPANISH-SPEAKING STUDENT".   HISPANIA, VOL. 48 (MARCH
    1965), PP. 99-102.

PHILLIPS, ROBERT N. JR.
    PHILIBERT, SISTER MARY.   LOS ANGELES SPANISH:
    A DESCRIPTIVE ANALYSIS
    CHRISTMAS IN NEW MEXICO.   WISCONSIN,.

PROTHEROE.   LANGUAGE USED BY CHILDREN CONTRASTING (SO*).

RAMOS, DUARTE FELI. DICCIONARIO DE MEJICANISMOS.   MEXICO,
    1898.

RAMOS, MAXIMO. LANGUAGE POLICY IN CERTAIN NEWLY INDEPENDENT
    STATES.   PASAY, PHILIPPINES, PHILIPPINE CENTER FOR
    LANGUAGE STUDY, 1961.

RANSON, H. M. "MANITOS AND THEIR LANGUAGE".   HISPANIA,
    VOL. 36 (AUGUST 1953), PP. 310-313.

RAPIER.   "EFFECTS VERBAL MEDITATION UPON (ED*).

RAUBICHECK, L. "PSYCHOLOGY OF MULTILINGUALISM".   VOLTA
    REVIEW, VOL. 36 (JANUARY 1934), PP. 17-20.

RAY.   GANDHI, INDIA WORLD (ED*).

RAYFIELD.   LANGUAGES BILINGUAL COMMUNITY (ED*).

REBOLLEDO, ANTONIO. "LA ENSENANZA DEL ESPANOL EN LAS
     ESCUELAS ELEMENTAS DE TEXAS Y DE NUEVO MMEXICO
     A TRAVES DE SUS TEXAS".   HISPANIA, VOL. 25 (DECEMBER
     1942), PP. 399-404 (ED).

REGAN, TIMOTHY F.   TEFL AND THE CULTURALLY DEPRIVED.   ??NO
     INFORMATION??, 1967 (AN).

REVILLA, M. G.   PROVINCIALISMOS DE EXPRESION Y DE FONETICA
     DE MEXICO.   WALTER V. SCHOLES (TRANS), ELLIOTT B.
     SCHEER. COLUMBIA, MISSOURI: UNIMMVERSITY OF MISSOURI
     PRESS, 1970.

RINGO, ELBERT WINFRED.   WORD ORDER IN COLLOQUIAL MEXICAN
     SPANISH.   UNIVERSITY OF ILLINOIS THESIS ABSTRACT,
     URBANA, 1950.

RINGO, ELBERT WINFRED.   THE POSITION OF THE NOUN MODIFIER
     IN COLLOQUIAL SPANISH.   URBANA, ILLINOIS,.

RINGO, ELBERT WINFRED.   THE POSITION OF THE NOUN MODIFIER
     IN COLLOQUIAL MEXICAN SPANISH.   UNIVERSITY OF
     ILLINOIS DISSERTATION.

RIVERA, HUGO H.   ASCERTAINING LANGUAGE AND COMPUTATIONAL
     CURRICULUM NEEDS FOR ECONMICALLY DISADVANTAGED MEXICAN
     AMERICAN ELEMENTARY STUDENTS.   ARIZONA STATE
     UNIVERSITY, PHD.   DISSERTATION (1971) (ED).

RIZZO, GINO L.   "LINGUA E COSTUMI SPAGNOLI IN CALIFORNIA
     AD UN SECOLO DALL'OCCUPAZIONE STATUNITENSE".
     QUADERNI IBERO-AMERICANI,   NO. 7 , PP. 23-30 (AN
     HC).

ROBE, STANLEY L.   A DIALECT AND FOLKLORISTIC STUDY OF TEXTS
     RECORDED IN LOS ALTOS OF JALISCO, MEXICO.   UNIVERSITY
     OF NORTH CAROLINA, 1950 (AN).

ROBERTS, HOLLAND D. AND KAULFERS, WALTER V.   "INTEGRATION
     IN LANGUAGE ARTS".   SCHOOL REVIEW, VOL. 43 (DECEMBER
     1935), PP. 737-44 (ED).

ROBERTS.   ERRORS ORAL ENGLISH USAGE MEXICAN-AMERICAN   (ED*).

ROMAN, MANUEL ANTONIO.   CICCIONARIO DE CHILENISMOS Y DE
     OTRAS VOCES Y LOCUCIONES VICIOSAS.   SANTIAGO
     DE CHILE, 1905-1918.

ROSALDO, RENATO.   "A LIST OF SLANG AND COLLOWUIAL EXPRESSIONS
     OF MEXICO CITY".   HISPANIA, VOL. 31 (1948), PP. 439-445.

ROSALDO, RENATO. "DE MAYORIA A MINORIA". HISPANIA, VOL.
    51 (MARCH 1968), PP. 18-28 (SO).

ROSEN, CARL L. ISSUES IN LANGUAGE AND READING INSTRUCTION
    OF SPANISH-SPEAKING CHILDREN. NEWARK, DELAWARE:
    INTERNATIONAL READING ASSOCIATION, 1969 (ED).

RUBEL. SOME CULTURAL ASPECTS LEARNING (AN*).

RUBEL. "THE MEXICAN AMERICAN PALOMILLA" (AN*).

SAAVEDRA, B. H. "APPLIED LANGUAGE RESEARCH CENTER".
    MODERN LANGUAGE JOURNAL, VOL. 53 (FEBRUARY 1969),
    P. 97 (ED).

SAMORA. "LANGUAGE USAGE AS POSSIBLE INDEX (SO*).

SAMORA. LANGUAGE FOUR-FIVE YEAR OLD BILINGUAL (SO*).

SANTAMARIAS, FRANCISCO J. DICCIONARIO DE MEJICANISMOS.
    MEXICO: ED PORRUA, 1942, 1959.

SAPIR, EDWARD. 'CULTURAL IMPLICATIONS OF SOME NAVAJO
    LINGUISTIC CATEGORIES.' IN DALE HAYNE'S (ED)
    LANGUAGE IN CULTURE AND SOCIETY.

SAPIR, EDWARD. "THE STATUS OF LINQUISTICS AS A SCIENCE".
    LANGUAGE, VOL. 5 (1929), P. 209.

SAPIR, EDWARD. SELECTED WRITINGS OF EDWARD SAPIR. LOS
    ANGELES: UNIVERSITY OF CALIFORNIA PRESS,.

SAPORTA, SOL. PSYCHOLINGUISTICS: A BOOK OF READINGS.
    NEW YORK: HOLT RINEHART AND WINSTON, 1961 (PY).

SAWYER, JANET B. M. A DIALECT STUDY OF SAN ANTONIO TEXAS:
    A BILINGUAL COMMUNITY. UNIVERSITY OF TEXAS, 1957.

SEIJAS, JUAN. DICCIONARIO DE BARBARISMOS COTIDIANOS.
    BUENOS AIRES, 1890.

SEMELEDER, F. EL ESPANOL DE LOS MEJICANOS , 1890.
    BIBLIOTECA DE DIALECTOLOGIA HISPANO-AMERICANA, PAGS.
    75-861..

SERGEANTSON, MARY S. A HISTCRY OF FOREIGN WORDS IN
    ENGLISH. NEW YORK: BARNES AND NOBLE, INC, 1962.

SERRANO. BARRIO LANGUAGE--AN ANALYSISPOCHO (ED*).

SERRANO. SOCIOCULTURAL INFLUENCES DEVELOPMENT (AN*).

SERVEY. ANALYSIS WRITTEN LANGUAGE STRUCTURE (ED*).

SEVILLA, ALBERTO. VOCABULARIO MURCIANO. MURCIA, 1919.

SHARP, JOHN M. 'THE ORIGIN OF SOME NON-STANDARD LEXICAL
    ITEMS IN THE SPANISH OF EL PASO.'   IN RALPH W. EWTON,
    JR, AND JACOB ORNSTEIN, (ECS) STUDIES IN LANGUAGE AND
    LINGUISTICS.

SHIPLEY, WILLIAM. "SPANISH ELEMENTS IN THE INDIGENOUS
    LANGUAGES OF CENTRAL CALIFORNIA".   ROMANCE PHILOLOGY,
    VOL. 16 (AUGUST 1962), PP. 1-21 (HC).

SHULMAN, DAVID. "SOME CALIFORNIAN CONTRIBUTIONS TO THE
    AMERICAN VOCABULARY".   AMERICAN SPEECH,   (DECEMBER
    1949), PP. 264-267 (HC).

SHUY, ROGER W. SOCIAL DIALECTS AND LANGUAGE LEARNING.
    NATIONAL COUNCIL OF TEACHERS OF ENGLISH, 1967 (ED).

SITJAR, B. VOCABULARY OF THE LANGUAGE OF SAN ANTONIO
    MISSION, CALIFORNIA.   REPRINTED BY NEW YORK, NEW YORK
    AND LONDON, GREAT BRITAIN: AMS PRESS, INC.,.

SLEDD, JAMES. "SLEEPY LAGCON DEFENSE COMMITTEE, LOS
    ANGELES. 1942-1945".   ENGLISH JOURNAL, VOL. 58
    (DECEMBER 1969), PP. 1307-15, 1319.

SORVIG. "SOUTHWESTERN PLANT NAMES SPANISH" (HS*).

SORVIG, RALPH. TOPICAL ANALYSIS OF SPANISH LOAN-WORDS IN
    WRITTEN AMERICAN ENGLISH OF THE AMERICAN SOUTHWEST.
    UNIVERSITY OF DENVER, 1952.

SPOLSKY. "LANGUAGE TESTING; PROBLEM VALIDATION" (ED*).

STANLEY, MEMOREE SUE OSBORN. THE SPEECH OF EAST TEXAS.
    COLUMBIA UNIVERSITY, 1936.

STEIGER, A. "FRAZADA, FREZADA".   REVISTA DE FILOLOGIA
    ESPANOLA, VOL. 7 (1920), PP. 371-372.

STEINER, MARY F. ETYMOLOGICAL STUDY OF OLD SPANISH
    PERSONAL NAMES.   NORTHWESTERN UNIVERSITY, 1953.

STODDARD, ELLWYN R. THE SOUNDS OF ENGLISH AND SPANISH.
    CHICAGO: UNIVERSITY OF CHICAGO PRESS, 1965.

THOMAS, CYRUS, AND SWANTON, JOHN R. INDIAN LANGUAGES OF
    MEXICO AND CENTRAL AMERICA.   WASHINGTON, 1911 (HM).

TORO GISBERT. REIVINDICACION DE AMERICANISMOS.   BOLETIN
    DE LA R. A..

TRUJILLO, LUIS M. DICCIONARIO DEL ESPANOL DEL VALLE DE
    SAN LUIS DE COLORADO Y DEL NORT DE NUEVO MEXICO.
    ADAMS STATE COLLEGE, MASTER'S THESIS (1961).

TSUZAKI, STANLEY M. ENGLISH INFLUENCES ON MEXICAN SPANISH
    IN DETROIT.   THE HAGUE AND PARIS: MOUTON AND COMPANY,
    1970.

UTLEY, JOHN. "A MEXICAN WORD LIST".   HISPANIA, VOL. 23
    (1940), PP. 357-361.

VELASCO, JUAN B. DE.   ARTE DE LA LENGUA CAHITA.   MEXICO,
    1890.

VELASCO, M. VALDES.   VOCABULARIC POPULAR MEXICANO.
    MEXICO, 1953.

VENEZKY, RICHARD L. "ENGLISH ORTHOGRAPHY--ITS GRAPHICAL
    STRUCTURE AND ITS RELATION TO SOUND".   READING
    RESEARCH QUARTERLY,   (SPRING 1967).

VINCENT.   STUDY PERFORMANCE SPANISH-SPEAKING   (ED*).

WAGNER, M. L. "EIN MEXIKANISH-AMERIKANISCHEN ARGOT: DAS
    PACHUCO".   ROMANISTISCHES JAHRBUCH, VOL. 4 (BAND
    1953-54).

WARDBOUGH, RONALD. READING: A LINGUISTIC PERSPECTIVE.
    NEW YORK: HARCOURT, BRACE AND WORLD, INC., 1969.

WATERS.   MEXICAN GEOGRAPHICAL NAMES OLD (HS*).

WATTHEWS FEARCE, THOMAS. "THE ENGLISH LANGUAGE IN
    THE SOUTH WEST".   NEW MEXICO HISTORICAL REVIEW, VOL.
    7-8 (1932-1933).

WEDBERG.   "TEACHING SPEECH TO MEXICAN CHILDREN"   (ED*).

WEINER, SOLOMON. MANUAL DE MODISMOS AMERICANOS MAS
    COMUNES.   NEW YORK: REGENTS PUBLISHING COMPANY,.

WEINREICH, URIEL. LANGUAGES IN CONTACT.   NEW YORK, NEW
    YORK, 1953, PUBLICATIONS OF THE LINGUISTIC CIRCLE.
    THE HAGUE: MOUTON AND COMPANY, 1967.

WELLBORNE.   "SPANISH CHILDREN HISPANO DESCENT"   (ED*).

WHORF, B. L.   THE RELATION OF HABITUAL THROUGHT AND
    BEHAVIOR TO LANGUAGE.   MANASHA: SAPIR MEMORIAL
    PUBLICATION FUND, 1941 (AN PY).

WHORF, BENJAMIN LEE. SCIENCE AND LINGUISTICS.   NEW YORK:
    HOLT, RINEHART AND WINSTON, 1966 (PY).

WILKINSON, D. H. "SELF-REALIZATION AND GROUP LIVING
    THROUGH LANGUAGE DEVELOPMENT".   ELEMENTARY ENGLISH,
    VOL. 31 (APRIL 1954), PP. 210-213 (ED).

WILLIAMS, EDWIN B. "THE PROBLEM OF BILINGUAL LEXICOGRAPHY,
    PARTICULARLY AS APPLIED TO SPANISH AND ENGLISH".
    HISPANIC REVIEW, VOL. 27 , PP. 246-253.

ZAMORA VICENTE, ALONSO. "VOCALES CADUCAS DEL ESPANOL
    MEXICANO".   HISPANICA, VOL. 14 (1960), PP. 221-241.

ZAMORA VICENTE, ALONSO. EL HABLA DE MERIDA Y SUS CERCANIAS.
MADRID, 1943.

E N G L I S H   L A N G U A G E

(LAE)

AGARD, FREDERICK, B. AND DUNKEL, HARLOD B. AN INVESTIGATION
OF SECOND LANGUAGE TEACHING. BOSTON: GINN AND CO.,
1948.

ALLEN, HAROLD B. TEACHING ENGLISH AS A SECOND LANGUAGE.
NEW YORK: MCGRAW-HILL BOOK COMPANY, 1965.

ALLEN, HAROLD B. ED. TEACHING ENGLISH AS A SECOND
LANGUAGE; A BOOK OF READINGS. NEW YORK: MCGRAW-HILL,
1965.

ALLEN, VIRGINIA FRENCH. ENGLISH AS A SECOND LANGUAGE.
NEW YORK: TEACHERS COLLEGE PRESS, 1967.

ALLEN, VIRGINIA FRENCH. ON TEACHING ENGLISH TO SPEAKERS
OF OTHER LANGUAGES. CHAMPAIGN, ILLINOIS: NATIONAL
COUNCIL OF TEACHERS OF ENGLISH, 1965.

AMSDEN.   READING PROGRAM MEXICAN-AMERICAN (ED*).

AMSDEN.   READING PROGRAM MEXICAN AMERICAN (ED*).

AMSDEN.   READING PROGRAM MEXICAN AMERICAN (ED*).

"THE ENGLISH PROFICIENCY FOREIGN (ED*).

"HARVEST NEARS CESAR CHAVEZ" (ED*).

"TEACHING ENGLISH TO CHILDREN (ED*).

"TEACHING SPANISH TO ELEMENTARY (ED*).

ACQUISITION LANGUAGE BY CHILDREN (ED*).

TEACHING ENGLISH READING TO FOREIGN (ED*).

TEACHING ENGLISH TO SPANISH-SPEAKING (ED*).

ARNOLD, R. D. "ENGLISH AS A SECOND LANGUAGE". READING
TEACHER, VOL. 21 (APRIL 1968), PP. 634-639.

ATKINS, E. "TEACHING SPECIAL ENGLISH TO SPANISH-SPEAKING
PUPILS". ILLINOIS EDUCATION, VOL. 55 (JANUARY
1967), P. 219.

BARBER, JOSEPH E. "FINDS ENGLISH GRAMMAR OF NO BENEFIT
    TO PUPILS OF FOREIGN LANGUAGE". THE NATION'S
    SCHOOLS, VOL. 17 (JANUARY 1936), P. 25 (LAF).

BARCELO, GUADALUPE CANEDO. TEACHING ENGLISH AS A SECOND
    LANGUAGE; A MANUAL FOR PRIMARY SHOOOL TEACHERS.
    UNIVERSITY OF CALIFORNIA AT LOS ANGELES, MASTER'S
    THESIS (1962).

BARROWS, SARAH. "TEACHING ENGLISH TO FOREIGN CHILDREN".
    GRADE TEACHER, VOL. 49 (APRIL 1932), PP. 614-650.

BROUSSARD. SPELLING ERRORS MEXICAN-AMERICAN (ED*).

BURRIS, QUINCY GUY
    BURRIS, QUINCY GUY. ENGLISH FOR RURAL NEW MEXICO,
    SUMMER WORKSHOP, 1945. LAS VEGAS, NEW MEXICO
    HIGHLANDS UNIVERSITY (ED).

CALEXICO UNITED SCHOOL DISTRICT. TEACHING ENGLISH
    AS SECOND LANGUAGE (ED*).

CAPONE. "TEACHING ENGLISH AS SECOND LANGUAGE" (ED*).

CENTER FOR APPLIED LINGUISTICS. ENGLISH AS A SECOND
    LANGUAGE IN ELEMENTARY SCHOOLS: BACKGROUND AND TEX
    T MATERIALS. WASHINGTON, D. C.:CENTER FOR APPLIED
    LINGUISTICS, (1967). BACKGROUND AND TEXT MATERIALS.

CENTER FOR APPLIED LINGUISTICS. UNIVERSITY RESOURCES
    UNITED STATES (LA*).

COCHRAN, ANNE. MODERN METHODS OF TEACHING ENGLISH AS A
    SECOND LANGUAGE. WASHINGTON, D. C.: EDUCATIONAL
    SERVICES, (1954).

COINDREAU. S. "TEACHING ENGLISH TO SPANISH-SPEAKING (ED*).

COLEMAN, ALGERNON AND KING, CLARE BRESLOVE. ENGLISH
    TEACHING IN THE SOUTHWEST: ORGANIZATION AND MATERIALS
    FOR INSTRUCTING SPANISH-SPEAKING CHILDREN. CHICAGO:
    UNIVERSITY OF CHICAGO PRESS, 1938 (ED).

COLEMAN. ENGLISH TEACHING SOUTHWEST:ORGANIZATION (ED*).

COLEMAN, ALGERNON. EXPERIMENTS AND STUDIES IN MODERN
    LANGUAGE TEACHING. WASHINGTON D. C.: AMERICAN
    COUNCIL ON EDUCATION, (1940).

COLEMAN. ANALYTICAL BIBLIOGRAPHY MODERN (B*).

DANN. "INTRODUCING ENGLISH TO BILINGUAL (ED*).

DAVENPORT. SPANISH-NAME CHILDRENS DIFFICULTIES (ED*).

DAVIS.   DIAGNOSTIC TEST STUDENTS ENGLISH   (ED*).

DE VARGAS.   "TEACHING MEXICANS ENGLISH VOCABULARY"   (ED*).

DECKER.   "FROM SI TO YES"   (ED*).

DEJESUS, C.   A STUDY OF LANGUAGE DEVELOPMENT AND GOODENOUGH
     1. 2. OF PUERTO RICAN PRE-SCHOOL CHILDREN IN A NEW
     YORK CITY SCHOOL.   TEACHERS COLLEGE, COLUMBIA
     UNIVERSITY, NEW YORK, MASTER'S THESIS (1935).

DEUTSCH.   DISADVANTAGED CHILD LEARNINGPROCESS: (ED*).

DIMITROFF.   "SMALL GROUP TRAINING SPANISH   (ED*).

DIXSON.   PRACTICAL GUIDE TO TEACHING ENGLISH   (ED*).

EL PASO BOARD OF EDUCATION.   FROM SPANISH TO ENGLISH THE
     NATURAL WAY.   EL PASO, TEXAS: BOARD OF EDUCATION,
     1949 (ED).

ERAZMUS.   ENGLISH AS A SECOND LANGUAGE: A READER.
     DUBUQUE, IOWA: WM. C. BROWN COMPANY PUBLISHERS, 1970.

FIFE.   TEACHING ENGLISH PUERTO RICO   (ED*).

FINOCCHIARO.   "SUGGESTED PROCEDURE TEACHING   (ED*).

FINOCCHIARO.   ENGLISH AS SECOND LANGUAGE: THEORY   (ED*).

FINOCCHIARO.   TEACHING CHILDREN FOREIGN LANGUAGES   (ED*).

FINOCCHIARO.   TEACHING ENGLISH AS SECOND LANGUAGE   (ED*).

FLOOD.   TEACHING ENGLISH AS FOREIGN LANGUAGE   (ED*).

FRIES, CHARLES C.   TEACHING AND LEARNING ENGLISH AS
     A FOREIGN LANGUAGE.   ANN ARBOR, MICHIGAN: UNIVERSITY
     OF MICHIGAN PRESS, 1945.

FRIES, CHARLES C.   AN INTENSIVE COURSE IN ENGLISH FOR LATIN
     AMERICANS.   UNIVERSITY OF MICHIGAN ENGLISH LANGUAGE
     INSTITUTE, 1943.

FRITZ.   "THE ENGLISH HANDICAP JUNIORHIGH   (ED*).

GARZA.   TEACHING ENGLISH TO SPANISH-SPEAKING   (ED*).

GOLDBERGER, HENRY H.   HOW TO TEACH ENGLISH TO FOREIGNERS.
     NEW YORK: INTERNATIONAL PRESS, 1918 (ED).

GOLDBERGER, HENRY H.   TEACHING ENGLISH TO THE FOREIGN BORN:
     A TEACHER'S HANDBOOK.   WASHINGTON, D. C: GOVERNMENT
     PRINTING OFFICE, (1920) (ED).

GORUN, JACQUELINE. "ENGLISH AS A FOREIGN LANGUAGE".
    ELEMENTARY ENGLISH, (DECEMBER 1958), PP. 513-515
    (ED).

GRAY, ROBERT F. "THE TEACHING CF ENGLISH TO THE FOREIGN-BORN".
    SCHOOL AND SOCIETY, VOL. 13 (JANUARY 15, 1921), PP.
    67-71 (ED).

HICKS. ERRORS ORAL ENGLISH USAGE MEXICAN (ED*).

HOARD, LUCY CLARIE. TEACHING ENGLISH TO THE SPANISH-SPEAKING
    CHILD IN THE PRIMARY GRADES. EL PASO, TEXAS: BOARD
    OF EDUCATION, 1936.

KAVETCHY, JOSEPH AND J. CAYCE MORRISON. ENGLISH AS
    A SECOND LANGUAGE. CHESTER W. HARRIS, EDITOR. NEW
    YORK: THE MACMILLAN CO., 1960 (EC).

LAMBERT, J. J. TEACHING ENGLISH AS A SECOND LANGUAGE.
    TUCSON: ARIZONA STATE DEPARTMENT OF PUBLIC INSTRUCTION,
    1962.

LEE, CHLOE IRENE. A STUDY OF ENGLISH INFLECTIONAL FORMS
    USED BY SPANISH-SPEAKING CHILDREN. ARIZONA STATE
    UNIVERSITY, MASTER'S THESIS (1950) (ED).

LESLEY. BILINGUAL EDUCATION CALIFORNIA (ED*).

LESPINOIS, PIERRE C. "EDUCATING FOREIGN ILLITERATES IN
    ENGLISH". MODERN LANGUAGE JOURNAL, VOL. 42 (APRIL
    1958), PP. 178-185.

LOS ANGELES CITY SCHOOLS. ENGLISH AS SECOND LANGUAGE
    (HC*).

LOS ANGELES CITY SCHOOLS. ENGLISH NON-ENGLISH SPEAKING:
    (HC*).

LOYD. EXPERIMENT TEACHING SPANISH ENGLISH (ED*).

MACAVLAY. "VOCABULARY PROBLEMS SPANISHLEARNERS" (ED*).

MALSTEAD, ROGER HENRY. MEASUREMENTS OF ETHNOCENTRISM AMONG
    TEACHERS OF MINORITY STUDENTS; A PILOT STUDY.
    UNIVERSITY OF CALIFORNIA AT LOS ANGELES, MASTER'S
    THESIS (1970).

MANNING. "A LINGUISTIC APPROACH TO TEACHING (ED*).

MARRS. COURSE ENGLISH NON-ENGLISH-SPEAKING (ED*).

MARTINEZ, PAUL G. "TEACHING ENGLISH TO SPANISH-SPEAKING
    AMERICANS IN NEW MEXICO". NEW MEXICO SCHOOL REVIEW,
    VOL. 13 (SEPTEMBER 1933), PP. 22-23 (ED).

MERIAM.   "LEARNING ENGLISH INCIDENTALLY: (ED*).

MERIAM.   "PLAY ENGLISH LANGUAGE FOREIGN   (ED*).

MERIAM.   "THE ENGLISH LANGUAGE FOREIGN   (ED*).

MIRAS.   "LANGUAGE DEVELOPMENT PROJECT"   (ED*).

MORAN.   "THE INTENSIVE VS. INCIDENTAL   (ED*).

MURDOCH.   STUDY RELATION BETWEEN INTELLIGENCE   (PY*).

MURRA, ELIZABETH.   "LEARNING ENGLISH AS A SECOND LANGUAGE".
    THE JOURNAL OF EDUCATIONAL SOCIOLOGY, VOL. 28
    (DECEMBER 1954), PP. 181-192.

PEDTKE.   REFERENCE LIST MATERIALS ENGLISH   (B*).

PERREN.   TEACHERS ENGLISH AS SECOND LANGUAGE: (ED*).

PHILLIPS, NINA.   CONVERSATIONAL ENGLISH FOR THE NON-ENGLISH-SPEAKING
    CHILD; AN AUDIO-VISUAL-LINGUAL APPROACH TO ENGLISH
    AS A SECOND LANGUAGE, WITH SPECIAL EMPHASIS ON THE
    NEEDS OF THE DISADVANTAGED CHILD.   NEW YORK: TEACHERS
    COLLEGE PRESS, 1968.

POWELL.   "FINAL CLUSTERS SPANISH-SPEAKING   (ED*).

POWELL, D. R.   "INITIAL CLUSTERS AND THE SPANISH-SPEAKING
    LEARNER".   ENGLISH LANGUAGE TEACHING, VOL. 16
    (1962), PP. 95-101 (ED).

POWERS.   SUCCESSFUL METHODS TEACHING ENGLISH   (ED*).

PUERTO RICAN STUDY, LANGUAGE GUIDE SERIES.   TEACHING
    ENGLISH TO PUERTO RICAN PUPILS.   NEW YORK: BOARD OF
    EDUCATION, THE CITY OF NEW YORK, 1956.

REINDORP.   REFERENCES TEACHERS ENGLISH AS   (B*).

ROGDE.   "LEARNING TO SPEAK ENGLISH FIRST   (ED*).

ROHR.   CORRECTING PRONUNCIATION ERRORS   (ED*).

ROJAS.   CRITICAL ANALYSIS VOCABULARYTHREE   (ED*).

ROJAS, PAULINE M.   "THE TEACHING OF ENGLISH AS A MODERN
    FOREIGN LANGUAGE".   COLLEGE ENGLISH, VOL. 9   (MARCH
    1948), PP. 322-326 (ED).

ROJAS, PAULINE M.   (DIRECTOR).   FRIES AMERICAN ENGLISH
    SERIES FOR THE STUDY OF ENGLISH AS A SECOND LANGUAGE.
    BOSTON: D. C. HEATH AND COMPANY, 1957 (ED).

ROJAS, PAULINE. "INSTRUCTIONAL MATERIALS AND AIDS
TO FACILITATE TEACHING THE BILINGUAL CHILD". THE
MODERN LANGUAGE JOURNAL, (APRIL 1965), PP. 237-239
(ED).

ROSEN, CARL L. PROBLEMS AND STRATEGIES IN TEACHING THE
LANGUAGE ARTS TO SPANISH-SPEAKING MEXICAN AMERICAN
CHILDREN. NEW MEXICO STATE UNIVERSITY, 1969 (ED).

ROSEN, CARL L. PROBLEMS AND STRATEGIES IN TEACHING THE
LANGUAGE ARTS TO SPANISH-SPEAKING MEXICAN AMERICAN
CHILDREN. NEW MEXICO STATE UNIVERSITY, 1969 (ED).

ROSEN, CARL L. AND ORTEGO, PHILIP D. "LANGUAGE AND READING
PROBLEMS OF SPANISH SPEAKING CHILDREN IN THE SOUTHWEST".
JOURNAL CF READING BEHAVIOR, (WINTER 1969), PP.
51-70 (ED).

ROSEN, CARL L. AND ORTEGO, PHILIP D. "LANGUAGE AND READING
PROBLEMS OF SPANISH SPEAKING CHILDREN IN THE SOUTHWEST".
JOURNAL CF READING BEHAVIOR, (WINTER 1969), PP.
51-70 (ED).

ROSEN, CARL L. AND ORTEGO, PHILIP D. PROBLEMS AND
STRATEGIES IN TEACHING THE LANGUAGE ARTS TO SPANISH-SPEAKING
MEXICAN-AMERICAN CHILDREN. ERIC: MICROFICHE ED 025
358 (ED).

ROSS, VICTORIA LYNN. A SURVEY OF ATTITUDES OF TEACHERS
IN INDIANA TOWARD MIGRANT CHILDREN. UNIVERSITY OF
CALIFORNIA, LOS ANGELES, MASTER'S THESIS (1970) (ED).

ROTUNDA, DOMINIC P.; SMITH, WILLARC M.; AND WRIGHT, EVALINE
UHL. ESSENTIALS OF ENGLISH FOR LATIN AMERICANS.
BERKELEY, CALIFORNIA: GILLICK, 1945.

RUSSELL, D. H. CHILDREN LEARN TO READ. BOSTON: GINN AND
COMPANY, 1949.

SAN JOSE EXPERIMENTAL SCHOOL. WE LEARN ENGLISH (ED*).

SCARTH, PETER; REGAN, TIMOTHY F. "TESOL AND THE MEXICAN
AMERICAN". LINGUISTIC REPORTER, (APRIL 1968),
PP. 1-2.

SMITH, MARGUERITE. ENGLISH AS A SECCND LANGUAGE FOR
MEXICAN AMERICANS. UNIVERSITY PARK: NEW MEXICO STATE
UNIVERSITY, 1968.

STANDERFORD, BETWY. NO HABLO INGLES, OPEN DOOR. CHICAGO,
ILLINOIS: CHILDRENS PRESS, 1970.

STREIFF, MARJORIE C. REMEDIAL ENGLISH FOR STUDENTS FROM SPANISH SPEAKING HOMES. PROCEEDINGS OF THE TUCSON CONFERENCE, MAY 1964. NATIONAL COUNCIL OF TEACHERS OF ENGLISH..

TAYLOR, JOSEPH ALEXANDER. TEACHING ENGLISH TO CHICANO STUDENTS: A RATIONAL FOR CHANGE. UNIVERSITY OF CALIFORNIA AT LOS ANGELES, MASTER'S THESIS (1971).

TEXAS STATE DEPARTMENT OF EDUCATION. COURSE ENGLISH NON-ENGLISH SPEAKING (ED*).

TEXAS. COURSE ENGLISH NON-ENGLISH-SPEAKING (ED*).

THE BOARD OF EDUCATION OF THE CITY OF NEW YORK. TEACHING ENGLISH TO PUERTO RICAN (ED*).

THOMPSON, HILDEGARD. ON TEACHING ENGLISH TO SPEAKERS OF OTHER LANGUAGES. CHAMPAIGN, ILLINOIS: NATIONAL COUNCIL OF TEACHERS OF ENGLISH, 1966 (AN).

TORRES. "SPANISH-SPEAKING STUDENTS CORRECT (ED*).

TROIKE, RUDOLPH C. INTRODUCTION TO ENGLISH LINGUISTICS FOR THE TEACHER OF ENGLISH. NEW YORK: MCGRAW-HILL, 1970.

TURNER. EDUCATION MEXICAN-AMERICAN CHILDREN (ED*).

ULIBARRI. PENSAMIENTOS SOBRE TEACHING ENGLISH (ED*).

ULIBARRI. "CHILDREN SECOND LANGUAGE" (ED*).

VALETTE. "SOME REFLECTIONS SECOND-LANGUAGE (ED*).

VARNER, CARL L. TEACHING ENGLISH AS A SECOND LANGUAGE TO PUPILS OF FOREIGN BORN, MEXICANHERITAGE. LESSON PLANS I. EL CENTRO, CALIFORNIA: IMPERIAL COUNTY SCHOOLS, 1965.

VARNER, CARL L. TEACHING ENGLISH AS A SECOND LANGUAGE TO PUPILS OF FOREIGN BORN, MEXICANHERITAGE. LESSON PLANS II.. EL CENTRO, CALIFORNIA: IMPERIAL COUNTY SCHOOLS, 1965.

VITO. TEACHING ENGLISH TO NON-ENGLISH (ED*).

WALLACE, ALBERTA. "TEACHING READING TC FOREIGN CHILDREN". EDUCATIONAL METHOD, VOL. 10 (MARCH 1931), PP. 363-367.

WALLACE, ALBERTA. "TEACHING THE MEANING OF WORDS TO FOREIGN-BORN CHILDREN". GRADE TEACHER, VOL. 48 (OCTOBER 1930), PP. 104-105.

WALLACE, BETTY J. PRONUNCIATION OF AMERICAN ENGLISH FOR
    TEACHERS OF ENGLISH AS A SECOND LANGUAGE.   ANN ARBOR,
    MICHIGAN: GEORGE WAHR PUBLISHING COMPANY, 1951.

WEST, M. P., SWENSON, E. (ET AL). A CRITICAL EXAMINATION
    OF BASIC ENGLISH.   TORONTO: THE UNIVERSITY OF TORONTO
    PRESS, (1934). BULLETIN NUMBER 2 OF THE DEPARTMENT
    OF EDUCATIONAL RESEARCH, ONTARIO COLLEGE OF EDUCATION.

WOLK.   "TEACHING ENGLISH AS SECOND LANGUAGE (ED*).

WOOD. "SPEAK ENGLISH" (ED*).

YONEMURA, MARGARET. DEVELOPING LANGUAGE PROGRAMS OFR
    DISADVANTAGED CHILDREN..   NEW YORK: TEACHER'S COLLEGE
    PRESS, 1969 (ED).

S P A N I S H   L A N G U A G E   E D U C A T I O N

(LAF)

ANDERSSON.   "FLES CONSERVATION OUR LANGUAGE   (ED*).

ANDERSSON, THEODORE. FOREIGN LANGUAGES IN THE ELEMENTARY
     SCHOOL: A STRUGGLE AGAINST MEDIOCRITY.   INCLUDES
     BIBLIOGRAPHY.

ANDERSSON.   "FL BLUEPRINT IN FOCUS"   (ED*).

BALLESTEROS.   "THE FOREIGN LANGUAGE TEACHER   (ED*).

BARBER.   "FINDS ENGLISH GRAMMAR NO BENEFIT   (LAE*).

BARKER, MARIE ESMAN.   ESPANOL PARA EL BILINGUE: A READING,
     WRITING, SPEAKING TEXT.   SKOKIE, ILLINOIS: NATIONAL
     TEXTBOCK COMPANY, 1972.

BRAULT.   "SOME MISCONCEPTIONS ABOUT TEACHING   (ED*).

BUTLER.   PRINCIPLES MODERN FOREIGN LANGUAGE   (ED*).

COON.   HISTORY TEACHING SPANISH TEXAS   (ED*).

DE SAUZE.   "NOTES SOME PHASES FOREIGN LANGUAGE   (ED*).

DUFNER.   TEACHING SPANISH ELEMENTARY GRADES   (ED*).

FINOCCHIARO.   TEACHING CHILDREN FOREIGN LANGUAGES   (ED*).

GERALE, R. C.   "FOREIGN LANGUAGE AND BASIC LEARNINGS".
     ELEMENTARY SCHOOL JOURNAL, VOL. 57   (MAY   1957), PP.
     418-419 (ED).

GINSBURG.   "A NEW PROGRAM SPANISH LCS ANGELES"   (ED*).

MICHEL, JOSEPH.   "FLES CERTIFICATICN: A LACK CF PROGRESS
     REPORT, WITH T. BRUCE FRYER,".   HISPANIA, VOL. 53
     NO. 3 (1970).

MICHEL, JOSEPH.   ACTFL ANNUAL BIBLICGRAPHY, FOREIGN
     LANGUAGE ANNALS, SECTION HEAD, DIVIDSON II, THEORY
     AND PRACTICE OF FOREIGN LANGUAGE TEACHING AND
     LEARNING: MTHODS.   NEW YORK: THE MODERN LANGUAGE
     ASSOCIATION OF AMERICA, 1967-1970.

MICHEL, JOSEPH. BEHAVIORAL OBJECTIVES FOR FLES: LISTENING
    AND SPEAKING SKILLS, AND DEVELPMENT OF CULTURAL
    AWARENESS WITH WILLIAM HEROLD, FLES: GOALS AND
    GUIDES1.   ED BY GLADYS C. LIPTON AND VIRGINIA
    SPARR-RAUCH, NEW YORK: THE FLES CMMITTEE OF THE
    AMERICAN ASSOCIATION OF TEACHERS OF FRENCH, 1971.

MICHEL, JOSEPH. BIBLIOGRAPHY OF BILINGUAL MATERIALS IN
    THE FOREIGN LANGUAGE EDUCATION CETER LIBRARY,
    MIMEOGRAPHED PAPER.   AUSTIN, TEXAS: THE FOREIGN
    LANGUAGE EDUCATION CENTER, THE UNIVERSITY OF TEXAS,
    1969.

MICHEL, JOSEPH. EPDA INSTITUTE FOR BILINGUAL TEACHERS AND
    TEACHER AIDES, SUMMER 1969: AWORKBOOK, PROJECT
    DIRECTOR.   AUSTIN, TEXAS: THE FOREIGN LANGUAGE
    EDUCATION CENTER, THE UNIVERSITY OF TEXAS, JUNE 9 -
    AUGUST 1, 1969.

MICHEL, JOSEPH. ERIC FOCUS REPORTS ON THE TEACHING
    OF FOREIGN LANGUAGES, EDITORIAL ADVIS.   NEW YORK:
    AMERICAN COUNCIL ON THE TEACHING OF FOREIGN LANGUAGES,
    1969.

MICHEL, JOSEPH. FOREIGN LANGUAGE TEACHING: AN ANTHOLOGY.
    NEW YORK: THE MACMILLAN COMPANY, 1967.

MICHEL, JOSEPH. GRADUATE EDUCATION OF THE FOREIGN LANGUAGE
    SPECIALIST.   ADFL BULLETIN, 2, NO. 2, 1970.

MICHEL.   METHODS ARTICULATION (ED*).

MICHEL.   PREPARATION FOREIGN LANGUAGETEACHER   (ED*).

MICHEL, JOSEPH. SOME TECHNIQUES FOR TEACHING VOCABULARY,
    WITH PAUL PATIN.   ERIC FOCUS REPORTS ON THE TEACHING
    OF FOREIGN LANGUAGES, NO. 27, NEW YORK: AMERICAN
    COUNCIL ON THE TEACHING OF FOREIGN LANGUAGES, 1972.

MICHEL, JOSEPH. SPANISH AIDS AND SUGGESTIONS FOR HIGH
    SCHOOL TEACHERS WITH MARIA SPENCERET AL.   SANTA FE,
    NEW MEXICO: THE MEXICO STATE BOARD OF EDUCATION,
    BULLETIN NO. 19, 1957.

MICHEL, JOSEPH. TEACHING SPANISH READING TO THE SPANISH
    DOMINANT CHILD, FOR THE TEXAS EDCATION AGENCY.
    HANDBOOK FCR THE FOREIGN LANGUAGE TEACHER, 1973.

MICHEL, JOSEPH. 1964 SUPPLEMENT FOR SPANISH AND PORTUGUESE
    TO THE MLA SELECTIVE LIST OF MATERIALS EVALUATOR FOR
    SPANISH MATERIALS.   NEW YORK: THE MODERN LANGUAGE
    ASSOCIATION OF AMERICA, 1965.

MICHEL, JOSEPH. THE EDUCATION OF THE MODERN FOREIGN
    LANGUAGE TEACHER FOR AMERICAN SCHOOL, WITH JOSEPH
    AXELROD AND OTHER MEMBERS OF THE INSTITUTE STUDY
    PROJECT.   NEW YORK: THE MODERN LANGUAGE ASSOCIATION
    OF AMERICA, 1966.

MICHEL, JOSEPH. THE GRADUATE EDUCATION OF THE FOREIGN
    LANGUAGE EDUCATION SPECIALIST IN TU.S., (ABSTRACT).
    THIRD INTERNATIONAL CONGRESS OF APPLIED LINGUISTICS:
    CONGRESS ABSTRACTS, AUGUST, 21-26, 1972. COPPENHAGEN,
    DENMARK: THE DANISH ASSOCIATIONFOR APPLIED LINGUISTICS,
    ADLA,.

MICHEL, JOSEPH. THE PREPARATION OF THE FLES TEACHER, WITH
    ALBERT JEKENTA, FLES: PATTERS OR CHANGE.   FD
    BY GLADYS C. LIPTON AND VIRGINIA SPAAR-RAUCH,
    NEW YORK: THE FLES COMMITTEE OF THE AMERICAN
    ASSOCIATION OF TEACHERS OF FRENCH, 1970.

MICHEL, JOSEPH. A SUGGESTED BIBLIOGRAPHY FOR FOREIGN
    LANGUAGE TEACHERS (ABSTRACT).   RESEARCH IN EDUCATION,
    6, NO.6, 1971.

MICHEL, JOSEPH. A SUGGESTED BIBLIOGRAPHY FOR FOREIGN
    LANGUAGE TEACHERS, MEMEOGRAPHED PAPR.   AUSTIN, TEXAS:
    THE FOREIGN LANGUAGE EDUCATION CENTER, THE UNIVERSITY
    TEXAS, 1966, 1970 REVISED,.

SPELL.   HISTORY SPANISH TEACHING UNITED   (ED*).

TEXAS STATE DEPARTMENT OF EDUCATION.   TENTATIVE COURSE
    STUDY TEACHING   (ED*).

ABBOTT, E. C. (TEDDY BLUE), AND SMITH, HELENA HUNTINGTON.
WE POINTED THEM NORTH: RECOLLECTIONS OF A COWPUNCHER.
NORMAN, OKLAHOMA: UNIVERSITY OF OKLAHOMA PRESS, 1955.

ABEL, LIONEL. "IN THE SACRED PARK". PARTISAN REVIEW,
VOL. 25 (WINTER 1958).

ABERNETHY. J. FRANK DOBIE (HT*).

ACHESON. 30,000 DAYS TEXAS (HT*).

ACHESON. TEXIAN WHOS WHO (HT*).

ACHESON. THREE SOUTHWEST PLAYS (AT*).

ADAMS, ANDY. CATTLE BRANDS. BOSTON: HOUGHTON, 1906.

ADAMS, ANDY. LOG OF A COWBOY. BOSTON: HOUGHTON, 1903,
1927.

ADAMS, ANDY. REED ANTHONY, COWMAN. BOSTON: HOUGHTON,
1907.

ADAMS, ANDY. THE OUTLET. BOSTON: HOUGHTON, 1905.

ADAMS, ANDY. THE RANCH ON THE BEAVER. BOSTON: HOUGHTON,
1927.

ADAMS, ANDY. A TEXAS MATCHMAKER. NEW YORK: HOUGHTON,
1904.

ADAMS, EMMA H. TO AND FRO IN SOUTHERN CALIFORNIA; WITH
SKETCHES IN ARIZONA AND NEW MEXICO. CINCINNATI: W.
M. B. C. PRESS, 1887.

ADAMS, RAMON F. COWBOY LINGO. BOSTON: HOUGHTON, 1936.

ADAMS, RAMON F. WESTERN WORDS. NORMAN, OKLAHOMA:
UNIVERSITY OF OKLAHOMA PRESS, 1945.

ADAMS, RAMON F. THE COWMAN SAYS IT SALTY. TUCSON,
ARIZONA: UNIVERSITY OF ARIZONA PRESS,.

ADAMS. BURRS UNDER SADDLE: SECOND LOOK (B*).

ADAMS, SAMUEL H. SANTA FE TRAIL. NEW YORK: RANDOM HOUSE,
1951 (LJE).

ADAMS, SAMUEL H. THE PONY EXPRESS.   NEW YORK: RANDOM
    HOUSE, 1950 (LJE).

AIKEN, CONRAD. A HEART FOR THE GODS OF MEXICO.   LONDON:
    MARTIN SECKER, 1939.

AIKMAN, D., <ED>. THE TAMING OF THE FRONTIER.   NEW YORK:
    MINTON, BALCH & CO., 1925.

ALEXANDER, L. "TEXAS HELPS HER LITTLE LATINS".   SATURDAY
    EVENING POST, VOL. 234 (AUGUST 5, 1961).

ALLEN, JOHN HOUGHTON. "THE LOW RIVER".   SOUTHWEST REVIEW,
    VOL. 158 NO. 1 (SUMMER 1963), PP. 29-36.

ALLEN, JOHN HOUGHTON. SOUTHWEST.   PHILADELPHIA: LIPPINCOTT,
    1952.

ALLEN, JOHN HOUGHTON. SOUTHWEST.   NEW YORK: BANTAM BOOKS,
    1953.

ALLEN, STEVE. THE GROUND IS OUR TABLE.   GARDEN CITY, NEW
    YORK: DOUBLEDAY AND COMPANY, 1966.

ALMARAZ.   PROBLEM PROMISE: TREATMENT MINORITIES (HSW*).

AMARAL, ANTHONY. WILL JAMES, THE GILT EDGED COWBOY.   LOS
    ANGELES, CALIFORNIA: WESTERNLORE PRESS, PUBLISHERS,
    1967.

ANDERSON, MAXWELL. NIGHT OVER TAOS.   NEW YORK: SAMUEL
    FRENCH, 1935.

ANDERSON.   AMERICAN MAXIMILIANS MEXICO (HM*).

ANDERSON.   AMERICAN MAXIMILIANS MEXICO, (HM*).

ANDRIST, RALPH K. THE LONG DEATH.   NEW YORK: THE
    MACMILLAN COMPANY, 1964.

ANGELO.   NINOS EASTER (LJE*).

"SUNSHINE AND ADOBE CHRISTMAS".   THE HORN BOOK MAGAZINE,
    VOL. 22 (NOVEMBER 1946), PP. 446-453.

LIFE JOAQUIN MURIETA (HC*).

SOUTHWESTERN AMERICAN LITERATURE.   DENTON, TEXAS,.

"DISAPPOINTMENT, NOT PERSONALITY ISSUE".   ALAMO MESSENGER,
    (APRIL 1971).

"PEOPLE IN PLASTIC HOUSES".   FORTUNE, VOL. 73 (APRIL
    1966), P. 170.

"TEXAS ENTRY".   LIFE, VOL. 25 (NOVEMBER 1, 1958), P.
     44 (ED).

"TIO TACO IS DEAD".   NEWSWEEK, VOL. 75 (JUNE 29, 1970),
     PP. 22-24 (SO).

THE EYE OF MEXICO.   NEW YORK, NEW YORK, 1959.

THE TEXAS MEXICAN.   NEW YORK AND SCARBOROUGH, ONTARIO:
     A MENTOR BOOK FROM NEW AMERICAN LIBRARY, 1972 (SO).

ANTHONY, EARL. PICKING UP THE GUN.   NEW YORK: DIAL, 1970.

APPLEGATE, FRANK. "NEW MEXICAN SKETCHES".   YALE REVIEW,
     VOL. 21 (1932), PP. 376-92 (AN LMA).

APPLEGATE, FRANK. NATIVE TALES OF NEW MEXICO.   PHILADELPHIA:
     LIPPINCOTT, 1932 (AN LMA).

ARMER, LANRA. WATERLESS MOUNTAIN.   NEW YORK: LONGMAN,
     1931, 1933.

ARMER, LAURA. SOUTHWEST.   NEW YORK: LONGMANS, 1931,1933.

ARNOLD, ELLIOTT. THE TIME OF THE GRINGO.   NEW YORK:
     ALFRED A. KNOPF, 1953.

ARRINGTON, ALFRED W. ('CHARLES SUMMERFIELD'). POEMS.
     CHICAGO: E. B. MYERS CO., 1869.

ARRINGTON, ALFRED W. ('CHARLES SUMMERFIELD').   THE RANGERS
     AND REGULATORS OF THE TANAHA, OR LIFE AMONG THE
     LAWLESS.   NEW YORK: ROBERT M. DE WITT, 1856.

ASHBAUGH.   NEVADAS TURBULENT YESTERDAY (HSW*).

ASTROV, MARGOT. THE WINGED SERPENT.   NEW YORK: JOHN DAY,
     1946.

ATHERTON.   CALIFRNIA: INTIMATE HISTORY (HC*).

ATHERTON, GERTRUDE. LA PERDIDA
     THE VENGEANCE OF PADRE ARROY.   IN EDWARD SIMMEN. THE
     CHICANO: FROM CARICATURE TO SELF-PORTRAIT. NEW YORK:
     NEW AMERICAN LIBRARY, 1971.

ATHERTON, GERTRUDE. THE SPLENDID IDLE FORTIES.   NEW YORK:
     MACMILLAN COMPANY, 1902.

AUSTIN, MARY. "CATHOLIC CULTURE IN OUR SOUTHWEST".
     COMMONWEALTH, VOL. 8 (1928), PP. 510-512, 544-546,
     572-575 (RE).

AUSTIN, MARY. "MEXICANS AND NEW MEXICO".   SURVEY, VOL.
     66 (MAY 1931), PP. 187-190.

AUSTIN, MARY. "TRAIL OF BLOOD; AN ACCOUNT OF THE PENITENT
    BROTHERHOOD OF NEW MEXICO".   CENTURY, VOL. 108
    (MAY), PP. 35-44 (RE).

AUSTIN, MARY. EARTH HORIZON.   BOSTON: HOUGHTON MIFFLIN
    AND COMPANY, 1932.

AUSTIN, MARY. EXPERIENCES FACING DEATH.   INDIANAPOLIS,
    INDIANA: BOBBS, 1931.

AUSTIN, MARY. LOST BORDERS.   NEW YORK: HARPER, 1909.

AUSTIN, MARY. NEW MEXICAN SPANISH.   THE SATURDAY REVIEW
    OF LITERATURE, JUNE 27, 1931 (HS).

AUSTIN, MARY. ONE SMOKE STORIES.   BOSTON: HOUGHTON
    MIFFLIN AND COMPANY, 1934.

AUSTIN, MARY. STARRY ADVENTURE.   BOSTON: HOUGHTON MIFFLIN
    AND COMPANY, 1931.

AUSTIN, MARY. WHAT THE MEXICAN CONFERENCE REALLY MEANS.
    NEW YORK, LATIN AMERICAN NEWS ASSOCIATION, NO..

AUSTIN, MARY. THE AMERICAN RHYTHM.   NEW YORK: HARCOURT,
    1923.

AUSTIN, MARY. THE CHILDREN SING IN THE FAR WEST.   BOSTON:
    HOUGHTON, MIFFLIN AND COMPANY, 1928.

AUSTIN, MARY. THE FLOCK.   BOSTON: HOGHTON, MIFFLIN AND
    COMPANY, 1906.

AUSTIN, MARY. THE LAND OF JOURNEY'S ENDING.   NEW YORK:
    THE CENTURY CO., 1924.

AUSTIN, MARY. THE LAND OF LITTLE RAIN.   BOSTON: HOUGHTON
    MIFFLIN AND COMPANY, 1903.

AZUELA.   TWO NOVELS MEXICAN REVOLUTION (HM*).

AZUELA, MARIANO. TWO NOVELS OF MEXICO; THE FLIES AND THE
    BOSSES.   BERKELEY: UNIVERSITY OF CALIFORNIA PRESS,
    1956.

BABBITT, IRVING. SPANISH CHARACTER AND OTHER ESSAYS.
    HOUGHTON MIFFLIN AND COMPANY, 1940.

BADGER, JOSEPH E. JACK RABBIT, THE PRARIE SPORT.   NEW
    YORK: BEADLE AND ADAMS, 1878.

BADGER, JOSEPH E. JOACHIM, THE SADDLE KING.   NEW YORK:
    BEADLE AND ADAMS, 1881.

BAILEY, BERNADINE. PICTURE BOOK OF ARIZONA.   CHICAGO:
    WHITMAN, 1960 (LJE).

BAILEY, BERNADINE. PICTURE BOOK OF TEXAS. CHICAGO:
    WHITMAN, 1950 (LJE).

BAILEY, HELEN MILLER. SANTA CRUZ OF THE ETLA HILLS.
    GAINESVILLE, FLORIDA: UNIVERSITY OF FLORIDA PRESS,
    1958.

BAKER, D. W. C. A TEXAS SCRAPBOOK. NEW YORK AND CHICAGO:
    A. S. BARNES, 1875.

BALL, EVE. MA'AM JONES OF THE PECOS. TUCSON, ARIZONA:
    UNIVERSITY OF ARIZONA PRESS, 1969 (TJ).

BALL, EVE. RUIDOSO: THE LAST FRONTIER. SAN ANTONIO:
    NAYLOR, 1963 (TJ).

BALL, EVE. IN THE DAYS CF VICTORIO. TUCSON: UNIVERSITY
    OF ARIZONA PRESS, 1970 (TJ).

BARD, W. E. A LITTLE FLAME BLCWN. CALLAS: SOUTHWEST
    PRESS, 1934.

BARD, WILLIAM E. THIS LANC, THIS PEOPLE. SAN ANTONIO:
    NAYLOR, 1966.

BARKER, OMAR. BUCAROO BALLADS. SANTA FE: NEW MEXICAN
    PUBLISHING COMPANY, 1928.

BARKER, OMAR. VIENTOS DE LA SIERRA. BEAULAH, NEW MEXICO,
    1924.

BARKER, RUTH LAUGHLIN. "WHERE AMERICANS ARE 'ANGLOS'".
    NORTH AMERICAN REVIEW, VOL. 228 (1929), PP. 568—73
    (SO).

BARKER, RUTH LAUGHLIN. CABALLEROS. NEW YORK: D. APPLETON
    AND COMPANY, 1931.

BARKER, S. CMAR (ED). FRONTIERS WEST. FREEPORT,
    NEW YORK: BOOKS FOR LIBRARIES, INC.,.

BARKER, S. CMAR ED. SPURS WEST. FREEPORT, NEW YORK:
    BOOKS FOR LIBRARIES, INC.,.

BARKER, S. OMAR. "SAGEBRUSH SPANISH". NEW MEXICO
    MAGAZINE, VOL. 20 (DECEMBER 1942), PP. 18—19,32—33.

BARNES, WILL C. TALES FROM THE X—BAR HORSE CAMP; THE
    BLUE—ROAN OUTLAW AND CTHER STORIES. CHICAGO:
    BREEDERS GAZETTE, 1920.

BARNEY, JAMES M. TALES OF APACHE WAREFARE. TRUE STORIES
    OF MASSACRES, FIGHTS AND RAIDS IN ARIZONA AND
    NEW MEXICO. PHOENIX, 1933.

BARR, AMELIA E. REMEMBER THE ALAMO.   REPRINT 1927 NEW
    YORK: DODD, 1888, 1927.

BARRELL, WILLIAM E. THE SHADOWS OF THE IMAGES.   DOUBLEDAY,
    GARDEN CITY, NEW YORK, 1953.

BARRETT, MONTE. THE TEMPERED BLADE.   NEW YORK: BOBBS,
    1946.

BARROWS.   "PIO PICO: BIOGRAPHICAL CHARACTER (HC*).

BARROWS.   DON ANTONIO MARIA LUGO: PICTURESQUE (HC*).

BARRY, JANE. A SHADOW OF EAGLES.   GARDEN CITY, NEW YORK:
    DOUBLEDAY AND COMPANY, 1964.

BARRY, ROBERT. THE MUSICAL PALM TREE.   NEW YORK: MCGRAW,
    1965.

BARTLETT, W. S. MY FOOT'S IN THE STIRRUP.   DALLAS: DEALEY
    AND LOWE, 1937.

BEALS, CARLETON. "MEXICAN AS HE IS".   NORTH AMERICAN
    REVIEW, VOL. 214 (OCTOBER 1921), PP. 538-46.

BEALS, CARLETCN. MEXICO: AN INTERPRETATION.   NEW YORK:
    B. W. HUEBSCH, INC., 1923.

BEALS.   DAVY CROKETT (LJE*).

BEALS.   KIT CARSON (LJE*).

BEAN.   MEMOIR COLONEL ELLIS P. BEAN, (TJ*).

BEAN.   MEMOIR. 1856 (TJ*).

BEAN.   BOSS RLEFS SAN FRANCISCO (TJ*).

BEATY, JOHN O (ET AL). TEXAS POEMS.   DALLAS: DEALEY AND
    LOWE, 1936.

BECHDOLDT, FRED R. TALES OF THE OLD TIMERS.   NEW YORK:
    CENTURY, 1924.

BECHDOLDT, FRED R. WHEN THE WEST WAS YOUNG.   NEW YORK:
    CENTURY, 1922.

BECKETT, HILARY. MY BROTHER, ANGEL.   NEW YORK: DODD, MEAD
    AND CO., 1972.

BEDFORD, ANNE N. ROY ROGERS Y EL NUEVO 'COWBOY.'   MEXICO:
    EDITORIAL NOVARO, 1969 (LJS).

BEDICHECK.   ADVENTURES WITH TEXAS NATURALIST (AN*).

BENTON, THOMAS HART. THIRTY YEARS' VIEW.   2 VOLS. NEW
     YORK: D. APPLETON & CO., 1854-1856.

BERGER, JOSEF. TRUE STORY OF A LITTLE BOY WHO IS ADOPTED
     INTO A NEW FAMILY.   NEW YORK: SIMON AND SCHUSTER,.

BESHOAR.   WESTERN TRAILS TO CALVERY   (HSW*).

BESHOAR.   WESTERN TRAILS TO CALVERY   (HUS*).

BIBERMAN, HERBERT. SALT OF THE EARTH.   BOSTON: BEACON
     PRESS, 1965.

BIERCE, AMBROSE. 'ANTEPENULTIMATA.'   IN THE COLLECTED
     WORKS OF AMBROSE BIERCE.

BINGHAM, EDWIN R. CHARLES F. LUMMIS, EDITOR OF THE
     SOUTHWEST.   SAN MARINO, CALIFORNIA: HUNTINGTON
     LIBRARY, 1955 (AN).

BIRD, ROBERT MONTGOMERY. CALAVAR; OR THE KNIGHT OF THE
     CONQUEST: A ROMANCE OF MEXICO.   PHILADELPHIA: LEA
     AND BLANCHARD, 1847.

BIRD, ROBERT MONTGOMERY. THE INFIDEL; OR THE FULL
     OF MEXICO.   2 VOLUMES. PHILADELPHIA: CAREY, LEA AND
     BLANCHARD, 1834.

BIRKINBINE, J. "OUR NEIGHBOR MEXICO".   NATIONAL GEOGRAPHIC
     MAGAZINE, VOL. 22   (SUMMER   1967).

BIZZELL, WILLIAM R. RURAL TEXAS.   NEW YORK: MACMILLAN,
     1924 (HT).

BLACKBURN, TOM W. 'PELADO.'   IN DON WARD (ED), BRANDED
     WEST: A WESTERN WRITERS OF AMERICA ANTHOLOG Y.

BLATT.   THE MEXICAN-AMERICAN CHILDRENS   (LJE*).

BLATT.   "THE MEXICAN-AMERICAN CHILDRENS   (LJE*).

BLATT.   "THE MEXICAN-AMERICAN CHILDRENS   (LJE*).

BOATRIGHT, MODY C. FOLK LAUGHTER ON THE AMERICAN FRONTIER.
     NEW YORK, NEW YORK, MACMILLAN (AN).

BOATRIGHT, MODY C. GIB MORGAN, MINSTREL OF THE OIL FIELDS.
     EL PASO, TEXAS: TEXAS FOLKLORE SOCIETY, 1945.

BOATRIGHT, MODY C. TALL TALES FROM TEXAS COW CAMPS.
     DALLAS, TEXAS: SOUTHWEST PRESS, 1934.

BOATRIGHT, MODY C. THE SKY IS MY TIPI.   DALLAS, TEXAS:
     SOUTHERN METHODIST UNIVERSITY PRESS, 1971 (AN).

BOATRIGHT.   MEXICAN BORDER BALLADS OTHERLORE   (AN*).

BOATRIGHT, MODY C. AND OWENS, W. A.   TALES FROM THE DERRICK
     FLOOR.   GARDEN CITY, NEW YORK: DOUBLEDAY, 1970 (AN).

BOATRIGHT, MODY C.; DAY, DONALD. BACKWOODS TO BORDER.
     DALLAS, TEXAS: SOUTHERN METHODIST UNIVERSITY PRESS,
     1971.

BOATRIGHT, MODY C.; HUDSON, WILSON M. AND MAXWELL, ALLEN
     (EDS). FOLK TRAVELERS: BALLADS, TALES AND TALK.
     DALLAS: SOUTHERN METHODIST UNIVERSITY PRESS, 1971
     (AN TJ).

BOATRIGHT, MODY C.; HUDSON, WILSON M. AND MAXWELL, ALLEN
     (EDS). MADSTONES AND TWISTERS.   DALLAS, TEXAS:
     SOUTHERN METHODIST UNIVERSITY PRESS, 1971.

BOATRIGHT, MODY C.; HUDSON, WILSON M. AND MAXWELL, ALLEN
     (EDS). MESQUITE AND WILLOW.   DALLAS, TEXAS: SOUTHERN
     METHODIST UNIVERSITY PRESS, 1971.

BOATRIGHT, MODY C.; HUDSON, WILSON M. AND MAXWELL, ALLEN
     (EDS). SINGERS AND STORYTELLERS.   DALLAS, TEXAS:
     SOUTHERN METHODIST UNIVERSITY PRESS, 1971 (AN).

BOATRIGHT, MODY C.; HUDSON, WILSON M. AND MAXWELL, ALLEN
     (EDS). TEXAS FOLK AND FOLKLORE.   2ND PRINTING, 1955.
     DALLAS: SOUTHERN METHODIST UNIVERSITY PRESS, 1971 (AN).

BOATRIGHT, MODY C.; HUDSON, WILSON M. AND MAXWELL, ALLEN
     (EDS). THE GOLDEN LOG.   DALLAS, TEXAS: SOUTHERN
     METHODIST UNIVERSITY PRESS, 1971.

BOATRIGHT, MODY C.; HUDSON, WILSON M. AND MAXWELL, ALLEN
     (EDS). A GOOD TALE AND A BONNIE TUNE.   DALLAS,
     TEXAS: SOUTHERN METHODIST UNIVERSITY PRESS, 1971.

BOATRIGHT, MODY C.; HUDSON, WILSON M. AND MAXWELL, ALLEN
     (EDS). FROM HELL TO BREAKFAST.   DALLAS, TEXAS:
     SOUTHERN METHODIST UNIVERSITY PRESS, 1971.

BOATRIGHT, MODY C.;HUDSON, WILSON M.; MAXWELL, ALLEN. AND
     HORNS ON THE TOADS.   DALLAS, TEXAS: SOUTHERN
     METHODIST UNIVERSITY PRESS, 1971.

BOATRIGHT.   GIB MORGAN, MINSTREL OIL FIELDS   (AN*).

BOATRIGHT.   MEXICAN BORDER BALLADS OTHERLORE   (AN*).

BOATRIGHT.   SKY IS MY TIPI (AN*).

BOATRIGHT.   TALL TALES TEXAS COW CAMPS (AN*).

BODE, ELROY. "IN THE BUS STATION".   SOUTHWEST REVIEW,
     VOL. 54   NO. 4 (AUTUMN, 1969), PP. 426-428.

BODE, WINSTON. A PORTRAIT OF PANCHO, THE LIFE OF A GREAT
     TEXAN: J. FRANK DOBIE.   AUSTIN, TEXAS: PEMBERTON
     PRESS, 1965.

BODY, ELROY. "VIEWS FROM THE BORDER (REGIONAL SKETCHBOOK)".
     SOUTHWEST REVIEW, VOL. 50 NO. 4 (AUTUMN, 1965), PP.
     404-410.

BODY, ELROY. TEXAS SKETCHBOOK.   EL PASO, TEXAS: TEXAS
     WESTERN PRESS, 1967.

BOLTON.   RIM CHRISTENDOM (HS*).

BORLAND.   WHEN LEGENDS DIE (AN*).

BOTKIN.   TREASURY AMERICAN FOLKLORE. STORIES (AN*).

BOWMAN, JAMES K. 'EL PATRON.'   IN EDWARD SIMMEN,
     THE CHICANO FROM CARICATURE TO SELF-PORTRAIT..

BOWYER, JOHN W. AND THURMAN, C. H. (EDS). THE ANNALS OF
     ELDER HORN.   NEW YORK, NEW YORK: RICHARD R. SMITH,
     1930.

BOYD, BOB. "PEDRO (REGIONAL SKETCHBOOK)".   SOUTHWEST
     REVIEW, VOL. 53 NO. 4 (AUTUMN 1968), PP. 423-437.

BOYER, MARY G. ARIZONA IN LITERATURE.   GLENDALE,
     CALIFORNIA: A. H. CLARK, 1934.

BRACHT.   TEXAS 1848. TEXAS IM JAHR 1848 (HS*).

BRADBURY, RAY. 'THE WONDERFUL ICE CREAM SUIT.'   IN EDWARD
     SIMMEN, THE CHICANO FROM CARICATURE TO SELF-PORTRAIT..

BRADDY, HALDEEN. COCK OF THE WALK.   ALBUQUERQUE,
     NEW MEXICO: UNIVERSITY OF NEW MEXICO, 1955.

BRANCH, DOUGLAS. THE COWBOY AND HIS INTERPRETERS.   NEW
     YORK, NEW YORK: APPLETON, 1926.

BRANCH, DOUGLAS. THE HUNTING OF THE BUFFALO.   LINCOLN,
     NEBRASKA: UNIVERSITY OF NEBRASKA, 1962.

BRANCH, DOUGLAS. THE ROMANCE OF THE AMERICAN FRONTIER.
     NEW YORK, NEW YORK: COOPER SQUARE PUBLISHERS, 1930.

BRECKENRIDGE, W. M. HELLDORADO.   BOSTON: HOUGHTON, 1928.

BREITHAUPT, THELMA. NO SILENCE HEARD.   DALLAS: TARDY,
     1937.

BRETT, DOROTHY. LAWRENCE AND BRETT.   PHILADELPHIA:
     LIPPINCOTT, 1933.

BREWER, J. MASON. NEGRITO. SAN ANTONIO: NAYLOR, 1933.

BRIGHT, ROBERT. THE LIFE AND DEATH OF LITTLE JO.
     DOUBLEDAY, DORAN, GARDEN CITY, NEW YORK, 1944.

BROWN, RICHARD G. 'MR. ISCARIOT.' IN EDWARD SIMMEN, THE
     CHICANO FROM CARICATURE TO SELF-PORTRAIT..

BROWNE. CRUSOES ISLAND ... WITH SKETCHES (TJ*).

BROWNE. TOUR THROUGH ARIZONA, 1864 OR (TJ*).

BROWNE. J. ROSS BROWNE, LETTERS, JOURNALS (TJ*).

BRYANT. WHAT I SAW CALIFORNIA (TJ*).

BRYANT. LIFE WORKS WILLIAM CULLEN BRYANT (TJ*).

BRYNNER, WITTER. JOURNEY WITH GENIUS: RECOLLECTIONS AND
     REFLECTIONS CONCERNING THE D. H. LAWRENCES.
     NEW YORK: THE JOHN DAY COMPANY, 1951 (TJ).

BUNKER, ROBERT MANSON. OTHER MAN'S SKIES. BLOOMINGTON,
     INDIANA: INDIANA UNIVERSITY PRESS, 1956.

BURNETT, W. R. SAINT JOHNSON. NEW YORK: DIAL PRESS, 1930.

BURR, ANNA R. THE GOLDEN QUICKSAND. NEW YORK: APPLETON,
     1936.

BUSCHLEN, JOHN P. SENOR PLUMMER. LOS ANGELES: TIMES-MIRROR
     PUBLICATION, 1942.

BUSH, DR. I. J. GRINGO DOCTOR. CALDWELL IDAHO: CAXTON
     PRINTERS, 1939.

BYNNER, WITTER. INDIAN EARTH. NEW YORK: ALFRED A KNOPF,
     1930.

BYRD, SIGMAN. 'MAY THE LAND BE BRIGHT.' IN E. N. BRANDT,
     THE SATURDAY EVENING POST READER OF WESTERN STORIES.

CABEZA DE BACA. WE FED THEM CACTUS (AN*).

CAIN, JAMES M. SERENADE. NEW YORK: ALFRED A. KNOPF,
     1937.

CALLAHAN, SISTER M. GENEROSA. THE LITERATURE OF TRAVEL
     IN TEXAS, 1803-1846: AN ANALYSIS OF IDEAS AND
     ATTITUDES. UNIVERSITY OF TEXAS AT AUSTIN, PHD.
     DISSERTATION (1945).

CALVIN, ROSS. RIVER OF THE SUN. ALBUQUERQUE: UNIVERSITY
     OF NEW MEXICO PRESS, 1946.

CALVIN, ROSS. SKY DETERMINES: AN INTERPRETATION OF THE
    SOUTHWEST.   ALBUQUERQUE, NEW MEXICO: NEW MEXICO
    UNIVERSITY PRESS, 1965.

CAMPBELL, WALTER S. BIG FOOT WALLACE.   BOSTON: HOUGHTON,
    1942.

CAMPBELL, WALTER S. DOBE WALLS. BOSTON: HOUGHTON, 1929.

CAMPBELL, WALTER S. FANDANGO. BALLADS OF THE OLD WEST.
    BOSTON: HOUGHTON, 1927.

CAMPBELL, WALTER S. KIT CARSON. BOSTON: HOUGHTON, 1928.

CAMPBELL, WALTER S. MOUNTAIN MEN.   BOSTON: HOUGHTON,
    1937.

CAMPBELL, WALTER S. REVOLT ON THE BORDER.   BOSTON:
    HOUGHTON, 1938.

CAMPBELL, WALTER S. SHORT GRASS COUNTRY.   NEW YORK:
    DUELL, 1941.

CAMPBELL, WALTER S. THE OLD SANTA FE TRAIL.   BOSTON:
    HOUGHTON, 1939.

CARB, DAVID. SUNRISE IN THE WEST.   NEW YORK: BREWER, 1931.

CARLISLE, IRENE. MUSIC BY LAMPLIGHT.   LA PORTE, IND:
    DIERKES PRESS, 1945.

CARNER, CLAUD. —HE WETBACK.   NEW YORK: HOWARD MC CANN,
    1947.

CARR, LORRAINE. MOTHER OF THE SMITHS.   NEW YORK:
    MACMILLAN, 1940.

CARR, ROBERT VAN. COWBOY LYRICS.   BOSTON: SMALL, 1912.

CARSON.   KIT CARSONS AUTOBIOGRAPHY (HSW*).

CARSON.   KIT CARSONS OWN STORY (HSW*).

CATHER, WILLA SIBERT. DEATH COMES FOR THE ARCHBISHOP.
    NEW YORK: ALFRED A. KNOPF, 1951.

CATHER, WILLA SIBERT. THE PROFESSOR'S HOUSE.   NEW YORK:
    ALFRED A. KNOPF, 1925.

CATHER, WILLA SIBERT. THE SONG OF THE LARK.   BOSTON,
    MASSACHUSETTS: HOUGHTON, MIFFLIN AND COMPANY, 1943.

CAVITCH, DAVID. D. H. LAWRENCE AND THE NEW WORLD.   NEW
    YORK: OXFORD PRESS, 1969.

CHABOT.   ALAMO; ALTAR TEXAS LIBERTY (HT*).

CHAMBERLAIN, MARY STUART. WE INHERITORS.   NEW YORK:
     FURMAN, 1937.

CHAMBERLAIN, SAMUEL E.   MY CONFESSION.   NEW YORK: HARPER
     BROTHERS, 1956.

CHANT, ELSIE RUTH; KELCHER, JULIA.   THE PADRE OF ISLETA.
     SANTA FE: RYDAL PRESS, 1940.

CHAPMAN.   RECEPTION UNITED STATES FICTION (HSA*).

CHAPMAN, ARTHUR. THE PONY EXPRESS.   NEW YORK: PUTNAM,
     1932.

CHAPMAN, WALKER. THE GOLDEN DREAM: SEEKERS OF EL DORADO.
     INDIANAPOLIS, INDIANA: BOBBS-MERRILL, INC., 1967 (HSA).

CHASE, AMANDA M. "SANTA SUSANA".   SURVEY GRAPHIC, VOL.
     66 (MAY 1, 1931), PP. 161-62, 190-93.

CHASE, AMANDA M. "SANTA SUSANA".   SURVEY, VOL. 66 (MAY
     1931), PP. 161-162.

CHAVEZ.   CLOTHED WITH SUN (HS*).

CHAVEZ.   CONQUISTADORA, AUTOBIOGRAPHYANCIENT (HS*).

CHAVEZ.   LADY TOLEDO (HS*).

CHAVEZ.   NEW MEXICO TRIPTYCH (HS*).

CHAVEZ.   SELECTED POEMS (HS*).

CHAVEZ.   SINGLE ROSE (HS*).

CHAVEZ.   VIRGIN PORT LLIGAT (HS*).

CHAY, MARIE. "FOR A WHILE THE GATE WAS STUCK".   THE
     ARIZONA QUARTERLY, VOL. 19 NO. 2 (SUMMER 1963) (SO).

CHAY.   "I LIKE IT BETTER THAT WAY" (LMA*).

CHAY.   "IN OTHER PEOPLES HOUSES" (LMA*).

CHAY.   "SOMEONES UP AT MACHADOS" (LMA*).

CHAY, MARIE. "THEN YOU'LL BE LEFT BEHIND".   ARIZONA
     QUARTERLY, VOL. 21 NO. 2 (SUMMER 1965) (SO).

CHAY.   "GRINGOS ARE FOOLS" (LMA*).

CHAY.   "ITS ALL WORLD" (LMA*).

CHAY. "MARRIAGE IS DIFFERENT" (LMA*).

CHEW, BRYON. CORRIDA AND OTHER POEMS. COLUMBUS, OHIO,
1967.

CHEW, BYRON. CORRIDA AND OTHER POEMS. TYLER, TEXAS:
MERCHANTS PRESS, 1966.

CHITTENDEN, LARRY. RANCH VERSES. NEW YORK: PUTNAM, 1893,
1925.

CHURCH, PEGGY POND. "MARIA". COMMON GROUND, VOL.
6 (SUMMER 1946), PP. 35-38.

CHURCH, PEGGY POND. FORETASTE. SANTA FE: WRITERS'
EDITIONS, 1933.

CHURCH, PEGGY POND. THE HOUSE AT OTOWI BRIDGE. ALBUQUERQUE,
NEW MEXICO: UNIVERSITY OF NEW MEXICO PRESS, 1960 (HN).

CLARK, ANN NOLAN. PACO'S MIRACLE. BROOKLYN, NEW YORK:
FARRAR, STRAUS AND GIROUX, 1962.

CLARK, ANN NOLAN. SUMMER IS FOR GROWING. NEW YORK:
FARRAR, 1968.

CLARK, ANN NOLAN. THIS FOR THAT. SAN CARLOS, CALIFORNIA:GOLDEN
GATE JUNIOR BOOKS, 1965.

CLARK, ANN NOLAN. TIA MARIAS GARDEN. NEW YORK: THE
VIKING PRESS, 1963 (LJE).

CLARK, BADGER. SUN AND SADDLE LEATHER. BOSTON. R. G.
BADGER, 1915; REPRINT, CHAPMAN & GRIMES, 1936 (LJE).

CLARK, BADGER. THESE WERE THE VALIANT. BOSTON: R. G.
BADGER, 1915 (LJE).

CLARK, H. H. THE CLIPPER SHIP ERA, 1843-1869. NEW YORK,
1910.

CLARK, LA VERNE. THEY SANG FOR HORSES. TUCSON: UNIVERSITY
OF ARIZONA PRESS, 1966.

CLARK, WALTER VAN TILBURG. THE OX-BOW INCIDENT.
NEW YORK: READERS CLUB, 1942.

CLEAVELAND, AGNES MORLEY. NO LIFE FOR A LADY. BOSTON:
HOUGHTON, 1941.

CLEMENS, JEREMIAH. BERNARD LILE, AN HISTORICAL ROMANCE.
PHILADELPHIA: J. B. LIPPINCOTT AND COMPANY, 1856.

CLEMENS, SAMUEL LANGHORNE "MARK TWAIN". ROUGHING IT.
PHILADELPHIA: J. B. LIPPINCOTT, 1858.

CLEMENS, SAMUEL LANGHORNE "MARK TWAIN". SKETCHES NEW AND
    OLD.   NEW YORK: HARPER AND BROTHERS, 1899.

CLEMENTS, HAROLD M. AN ANALYSIS OF LEVELS OF LIVING OF
    SPANISH-AMERICAN RURAL AND URBAN FAMILIES IN TWO SOUTH
    TEXAS COUNTIES.   NEW YORK: HARPER AND BROTHERS, 1905.

CLEVY, LOYD S. A LINGUISTIC STUDY OF THE JOURNALS OF THE
    CORONADO EXPEDITION.   UNIVERSITY OF COLORADO, (1958).
    A LINGUISTIC STUDY OF THE JOURNALS OF THE CORONADO
    EXPEDITION..

COBLENTZ, STANTON A. VILLAINS AND VIGILANTES.   NEW YORK:
    WILSON-ERICKSON, 1938.

CODY, WILLIAM FREDERICK "BUFFALO BILL". STORY OF THE WILD
    WEST AND CAMP-FIRE CHATS.   PHILADELPHIA, CHICAGO,
    ETC.:HISTORICAL PUBLISHING COMPANY, 1888.

COE, GEORGE W. FRONTIER FIGHTER.   BOSTON: HOUGHTON, 1934.

COE, MICHAEL D. RANCH ON THE RUIDOSO.   NEW YORK: KNOPF,
    1968.

COHEN, J. LATIN AMERICAN WRITING TODAY.   NEW YORK:
    PENGUIN, 1968.

COLE, MARY. SUMMER IN THE CITY.   NEW YORK: P. J. KENNEDY,
    1968.

COLE, MAUDE E. WIND AGAINST STONE.   LOS ANGELES: LYMAN
    HOUSE, 1941.

COLLIER, NED (ED). GREAT STORIES OF THE WEST.   GARDEN
    CITY, NEW YORK: DOUBLEDAY AND COMPANY, INC.,.

COMFIRT, WILL LEVINGTON. MANGAS COLORADAS.   LONDON:
    SLTEIN, 1931.

CONNOR, SEYMOUR V. ADVENTURE IN GLORY.   AUSTIN, TEXAS:
    STECK-VAUGHN, 1965.

CONNOR, SEYMOUR V. NORTH AMERICA DIVIDED: THE MEXICAN
    WAR, 1846-1848.   NEW YORK: OXFORD UNIVERSITY PRESS,
    1971.

CONNOR, SEYMOUR V. THE SAGA OF TEXAS SERIES.   AUSTIN:
    STECK-VAUGHN, 1965 (TJ).

COOK.   FIFTY YEARS OLD FRONTIER (HSW*).

COOLIDGE, DANE AND COOLIDGE, MARY. THE LAST OF THE SERIS
    (OF MEXICO).   GLORIETA, NEW MEXICO: RIO GRANDE PRESS,
    INC., 1971 (HC).

COOLIDGE, DANE. GRINGO GOLD.   NEW YORK, 1939.

COOPER, JAMES FENIMORE,. JACK TIER, THE WORKS OF JAMES
     FENIMORE COOPER.   NEW YORK: G. P. PUTNAM'S SONS, 1896.

COOPER.   PRAIRIE, WORKS JAMES FENIMORE (LI*).

COOPER, JAMES FENIMORE. THE PRAIRIE, THE WORKS OF JAMES
     FENIMORE COOPER.   NEW YORK: G. P. PUTNAM'S SONS, (LI).

CORLE, EDWIN. DESERT COUNTRY.   NEW YORK: DUELL, 1941.

CORLE, EDWIN. LISTEN, BRIGHT ANGEL.   NEW YORK: DUELL,
     1946.

CORLE, EDWIN. PEOPLE ON THE EARTH.   NEW YORK: RANDOM
     HOUSE, 1937.

CORLE.   ROYAL HIGHWAY (EL CAMINO REAL) (HS*).

CORNELIUS, JOHN SCOTT. THE EFFECTS OF CERTAIN CHANGES OF
     CURRICULUM AND METHODS ON THE SCHOOL ACHIEVEMENT OF
     MEXICAN CHILDREN IN A SEGREGATED SCHOOL.   UNIVERSITY
     OF SOUTHERN CALIFORNIA, MASTER'S THESIS (1941).

CORTES.   CHICANO SOCIAL BANDIT AS ROMANTIC (HSW*).

CORTES, CARLOS E.; GREEN, ALAN; JOSEPH, JAMES; AND
     GINSBERG, ARLIN. BLACKS, CHICANOS, NATIVE AMERICANS,
     PUERTO RICANS: HISTORY AND SELF-EXPRESSION.
     NEW YORK: G. P. PUTNAM'S SONS, 1974 (HSW).

COWAN, JAMES C. D. H. LAWRENCE'S AMERICAN JOURNEY, A STUDY
     IN LITERATURE AND MYTH.   CLEVELAND: CASE WESTERN
     RESERVE PRESS, 1970.

CRADY, KATE MC ALPIN. FREE STEPPIN.'   DALLAS: MATHIS,
     VAN NORT, 1938.

CRAMPTON, GREGORY C. "THE GREATER SOUTHWEST".   THE
     AMERICAN WEST, VOL. 3 NO. 3 (SUMMER 1966), PP. 4-5.

CRANE, HART. THE COLLECTED POEMS OF HART CRANE.   EDITED
     WITH INTRODUCTION BY WALDO FRANK. NEW YORK: LIVERIGHT
     PUBLISHING CORPORATION, 1933.

CRANE, HART. THE LETTERS OF HART CRANE, 1916-1932.
     EDITED BY BROWN WEBER, NEW YORK: HERMITAGE HOUSE, 1952.

CRANE, STEPHEN. MEXICAN SIGHTS AND STREET SCENES.   EDITED
     BY WILSON FOLLETT. 12 VOLUMES. NEW YORK: ALFRED A.
     KNOPF, 1926.

CRANE, STEPHEN. 'A MAN AND SOME OTHERS.'   IN THOMAS A.
     GULLASON, THE COMPLETE SHORT STIES AND SKETCHES OF
     SEPHENCRANE.

CREEL, GEORGE. SAM HOUSTON. NEW YORK: COSMOPOLITAN, 1928
     (HT).

CREEL, GEORGE. THE PEOPLE NEXT DOOR: AN INTERPRETIVE
     HISTORY OF MEXICO AND THE MEXICANS. NEW YORK: JOHN
     DAY, 1926 (HM).

CRICHTON, KYLE SAMUEL. PROUD PEOPLE. NEW YORK: SCRIBNER'S,
     1944.

CROSS, RUTH. THE BIG ROAD. NEW YORK: LONGMANS, 1931.

CROWELL, CHESTER T. LIQUOR, LOOT AND LADIES. NEW YORK:
     KNOPF, 1930.

CROWELL, GRACE NOLL. FLAME IN THE WIND. DALLAS:
     SOUTHWEST PRESS, 1930.

CROWELL, GRACE NOLL. LIGHT OF THE YEARS. NEW YORK:
     HARPER, 1936.

CROWELL, GRACE NOLL. SILVER IN THE SUN. DALLAS: P. L.
     TURNER, 1928.

CROWELL, GRACE NOLL. SOME BRIGHTER DAWN. NEW YORK:
     HARPER, 1943.

CROWELL, GRACE NOLL. SONGS OF COURAGE. DALLAS. SOUTHWEST
     PRESS, 1930. REPRINT. NEW YORK: DALLAS,.

CROWELL, GRACE NOLL. SPLENDOR AHEAD. NEW YORK: HARPER,
     1940.

CROWELL, GRACE NOLL. WIND SWEPT HARP. NEW YORK: HARPER,
     1946.

CULP, JOHN H. THE TREASURE OF THE CHISOS. NEW YORK:
     HOLT, 1971.

CUNNINGHAM, EUGENE. TEXAS SHERIFF. BOSTON, HOUGHTON,
     1934. REPRINT. NEW YORK: TRIANGLE BOOKS, 1944.

CUNNINGHAM, EUGENE. TRIGGERNOMETRY: A GALLEY OF GUNFIGHTERS.
     CALDWELL, IDAHO: CAXTON, PRINTERS, 1947.

CURRENT-GARCIA, EUGENE. O. HENRY (WILLIAM SYDNEY PORTER)..
     NEW YORK: TWAYNE, 1965.

CURTIS, EDITH ROELKER. MEXICAN ROMANCE. PHILADELPHIA,
     PENNSYLVANIA: DORRANCE & COMPANY, 1969.

DANA RICHARD HENRY. TWO YEARS BEFORE THE MAST. NEW YORK:
     NEW YORK: E.P. DUTTON, 1921 (TJ).

DASBURGH, MARINA WISTER. FANTASY AND FUGUE. NEW YORK,
     NEW YORK: MACMILLAN, 1937.

DAVIDSON.   DISCOVERY SAN FRANCISCO BAY   (HS*).

DAVIS, ANNE PENCE.   THE CUSTOMER IS ALWAYS RIGHT.   NEW
     YORK: MACMILLAN, 1940.

DAVIS, EDWARD EVERETT.   THE WHITE SCOURGE.   SAN ANTONIO,
     TEXAS: THE NAYLOR CO., 1940.

DAVIS, J. FRANK.   THE ROAD TO SAN JACINTO.   INDIANAPOLIS,
     INDIANA: BOBBS, 1936.

DAVIS.   CALIFORNIA ROMANTIC RESOURCEFUL   (HC*).

DAVIS, LORENA HOOD.   "P. E. KERN, THE PIONEER, IS EL PASO'S
     MONTE CRISTO".   EL PASO TIMES,   (JANUARY 23, 1912).

DAVIS, RICHARD HARDING.   THE WEST FROM A CAR WINDOW.   NEW
     YORK: HARPER AND BROTHERS, 1892 (TJ).

DAVIS, WILLIAM W. H.   SEVENTY-FIVE YEARS IN CALIFORNIA.
     SAN FRANCISCO, CALIFORNIA: J. HOWELL BOOKS, 1967 (HC).

DAVIS, WILLIAM W. H.   EL GRINGO, OR NEW MEXICO AND
     HER PEOPLE.   CHICAGO: RIO GRANDE PRESS, 1962 (HC).

DAVIS, WILLIAM W. H.   THE SPANISH CONQUEST OF NEW MEXICO.
     DOYLESTOWN, PENNSYLVANIA, 1869 (HN).

DAWSON, CLEO.   SHE CAME TO THE VALLEY.   NEW YORK,
     NEW YORK: MORROW, 1943.

DAWSON, JOSEPH MARTIN.   A THOUSAND MONTHS TO REMEMBER.
     WACO, TEXAS: BAYLOR UNIVERSITY PRESS, 1964.

DAY, DONALD.   BIG COUNTRY TEXAS.   NEW YORK, NEW YORK:
     DUELL, (1947). AMERICAN FOLKWAYS SERIES.

DE SHIELDS, JAMES T.   CYNTHIA ANN PARKER.   SAN ANTONIO,
     TEXAS: NAYLOR, 1934.

DE VOTO, BERNARD AUGUSTINE.   1846, THE YEAR OF DECISION.
     BOSTON, MASSACHUSETTS: LITTLE, BROWN AND COMPANY,
     1943.

DE VOTO, BERNARD AUGUSTINE.   THE YEAR OF DECISION, 1846.
     BOSTON, MASSACHUSETTS: HOUGHTON MIFFLIN COMPANY, 1961.

DEFOREST, JOHN WILLIAM.   OVERLAND.   NEW YORK, NEW YORK:
     SHELDON AND COMPANY, 1871.

DELANEY.   SPANISH GOLD   (HS*).

DELANO.   ACROSS PLAINS AMONG DIGGINS   (TJ*).

DELANO.   ACROSS PLAINS AMONG DIGGINGS   (TJ*).

DELLENBAUGH, FREDERICK S. BREAKING THE WILDERNESS. NEW
    YORK, NEW YORK: PUTNAM, 1905.

DEMARIS, OVID. POSO DEL MUNDO. NEW YORK, NEW YORK:
    LITTLE, BROWN AND CO., 1970.

DIAZ, VIRGILIC ALEJANDRO. "ARCADIO". AMERICAS, VOL. 12
    NO. 6 (JUNE 1960), PP. 24-26.

DICKERSON, GEORGE. "CHICO". PHOENIX, (SPRING 1962).

DIXON, SAM H. THE POETS AND POETRY OF TEXAS. AUSTIN,
    TEXAS: SAM H. DIXON AND COMPANY, 1885.

DOBIE, JAMES FRANK. "RANCH MEXICANS". SURVEY GRAPHIC,
    VOL. 66 (MAY 1931), PP. 167-170 (SO).

DOBIE, JAMES FRANK. "THE MEXICAN VAQUERO OF THE TEXAS
    BORDER". SOUTHWESTERN POLITICAL AND SOCIAL SCIENCE
    QUARTERLY, VOL. 8 (JUNE 1927), PP. 15-26 (SO).

DOBIE, JAMES FRANK. APACHE GOLD AND YAQUI SILVER.
    BOSTON, MASSACHUSETTS: LITTLE, BROWN AND COMPANY,
    1939.

DOBIE, JAMES FRANK. CORONADO'S CHILDREN; TALES OF LOST
    MINES AND BURIED TREASURES OF THE SOUTHWEST. DALLAS,
    TEXAS: THE SOUTHWEST PRESS, 1930.

DOBIE, JAMES FRANK. CORONADO'S CHILDREN; TALES OF LOST
    MINES AND BURIED TREASURES OF THE SOUTHWEST. NEW
    YORK, NEW YORK: LITERARY GUILD OF AMERICA, 1931.

DOBIE. GUIDE TO LIFE LITERATURE SOUTHWEST (B*).

DOBIE. GUIDE TO LIFE LITERATURE SOUTHWEST (B*).

DOBIE, JAMES FRANK. SOUTHWESTERN LORE. DALLAS, TEXAS:
    SOUTHERN METHODIST UNIVERSITY PRESS, 1965 (AN).

DOBIE, JAMES FRANK. SOUTHWESTERN LORE. HATBORO,
    PENNSYLVANIA: FOLKLORE ASSOCIATES, 1961 (AN).

DOBIE, JAMES FRANK. SPUR-OF-THE-COCK. DALLAS, TEXAS:
    SOUTHERN METHODIST UNIVERSITY PRESS, 1933.

DOBIE, JAMES FRANK. TALES OF OLD-TIME TEXAS. BOSTON,
    MASSACHUSETTS: LITTLE, BROWN AND COMPANY, 1955.

DOBIE, JAMES FRANK. TEXAS AND SOUTHESTERN LORE. DALLAS,
    TEXAS: SOUTHERN METHODIST UNIVERSITY PRESS, 1967.

DOBIE, JAMES FRANK. TEXIAN STAMPING GROUNDS. DALLAS,
    TEXAS: SOUTHERN METHODIST UNIVERSITY PRESS, 1941.

DOBIE, JAMES FRANK. TONGUES OF THE MONTE. GARDEN CITY,
     NEW YORK: DOUBLEDAY, DORAN AND COMPANY, 1935.

DOBIE, JAMES FRANK. THE LONGHORNS.   BOSTON, MASSACHUSETTS:
     LITTLE, BROWN AND COMPANY, 1952.

DOBIE, JAMES FRANK. ON THE OPEN RANGE.   DALLAS, TEXAS:
     SOUTHWEST PRESS, 1931 (LJE).

DOBIE, JAMES FRANK. A VAQUERO OF THE BRUSH COUNTRY.
     DALLAS, TEXAS: SOUTHWEST PRESS, 1929.

DOBIE, JAMES FRANK. A VAQUERO OF THE BRUSH COUNTRY.
     BOSTON, MASSACHUSETTS: LITTLE, BROWN AND COMPANY,
     1952.

DOBIE, JAMES FRANK. THE VOICE OF THE COYOTE.   LINCOLN,
     NEBRASKA: UNIVERSITY OF NEBRASKA PRESS, 1961.

DOBIE, JAMES FRANK; BOATRIGHT, MODY C.; RANSOM, HARRY H.,
     EDITORS. COYOTE WISDOM.   DALLAS, TEXAS: SOUTHERN
     METHODIST UNIVERSITY PRESS, 1971.

DOBIE, JAMES FRANK, EDITOR. COFFEE IN THE GOURD.   DALLAS,
     TEXAS: SOUTHERN METHODIST UNIVERSITY PRESS, 1971.

DOBIE. FOLLOW DE DRINKIN GOUD (B*).

DOBIE, JAMES FRANK, (ED). MAN, BIRD, AND BEAST.   DALLAS,
     TEXAS: SOUTHERN METHODIST UNIVERSITY PRESS, 1971.

DOBIE, JAMES FRANK, EDITOR. PURO MEXICANO.   DALLAS,
     TEXAS: SOUTHERN METHODIST UNIVERSITY PRESS, 1969.

DOBIE, JAMES FRANK, EDITOR. PURO MEXICANO.   AUSTIN,
     TEXAS: TEXAS FOLK-LORE SOCIETY, 1935 (LMA).

DOBIE, JAMES FRANK, EDITOR. TONE THE BELL EASY.   DALLAS,
     TEXAS: SOUTHERN METHODIST UNIVERSITY PRESS, 1971.

DODGE, DAVIS. "MY FAVORITE MEXICAN CHARACTER".   UNITED
     STATES WORLD, VOL. 4 (JUNE 1950), PP. 60-61 (AN).

DOKEY. "SANCHEZ" (LMA*).

DOKEY. SANCHEZ (LMA*).

DOS PASSOS, JOHN. U. S. A.. NEW YORK, NEW YORK: RANDOM
     HOUSE, THE MODERN LIBRARY,.

DOS PASSOS, JOHN. IN ALL COUNTRIES.   NEW YORK, NEW YORK:
     HARCOURT, BRACE AND COMPANY, 1934.

DRAGO. GREAT RANGE WARS: VIOLENCE GRASSLANDS (HSW*).

DRAGO.   NOTORIOUS LADIES FRONTIER (HSW*).

DRAGO.   ROADS TO EMPIRE: DRAMATIC CONQUEST (HSW*).

DUFFUS, ROBERT LUTHER.   SANTA FE TRAIL.   ALBUQUERQUE,
    NEW MEXICO: UNIVERSITY OF NEW MEXICO PRESS, 1971.

DUFFUS, ROBERT LUTHER. JORNADA.   NEW YORK, NEW YORK:
    COVIVI, 1935.

DUFFUS, ROBERT LUTHER. THE SANTA FE TRAIL.   NEW YORK,
    NEW YORK: LONGMANS, GREEN AND COMPANY, 1930.

DUGANNE, A. J. A. THE PEON PRINCE OR THE YANKEE KNIGHT
    ERRANT.   NEW YORK, NEW YORK: BEADLE AND COMPANY,
    1861.

DUGGER, RONNIE, EDITOR. THREE MEN IN TEXAS: BEDICHEK,
    WEBB, DOBIE.   AUSTIN, TEXAS: UNIVERSITY OF TEXAS
    PRESS, 1967.

DUVAL, JOHN C. EARLY TIMES IN TEXAS (REPRINT).   DALLAS,
    TEXAS: TARDY, 1936.

DUVAL, JOHN C. EARLY TIMES IN TEXAS.   AUSTIN, TEXAS:
    H. P. N. GAMMEL, 1892.

EAGLETON, D. F. WRITERS AND WRITINGS OF TEXAS.   NEW YORK,
    NEW YORK: BROADWAY PUBLISHING COMPANY, 1913.

EASTLAKE.   PORTRAIT ARTIST WITH 26 HORSES (AR*).

EDELL, CELESTE. A PRESENT FROM ROSITA.   NEW YORK, NEW
    YORK: WASHINGTON PRESS, 1960.

EDELSTEIN, ARTHUR. 'THAT TIME OF YEAR.'   IN WALLACE
    STEGNER AND RICHARD SCOWCROFT, EDS., TWENTY YEARS OF
    STANFORD SHORT STORIES, PALO ALTO, CALIFORNIA:
    STANFORD UNIVERSITY PRESS, 1966.

ELLSWROTH, HENRY LEAVITT. WASHINGTON IRVING ON THE
    PRAIRIE.   NEW YORK, NEW YORK: AMERICAN BOOK COMPANY,
    1937.

ELSER, FRANK B. THE KEEN DESIRE.   NEW YORK, NEW YORK:
    BONI, LIVERIGHT, 1926.

EMERY, GEORGE F. 'THE WATER WITCH.'   THE OVERLAND MONTHLY.

EMERY, M. "PILOT PROJECT IN BILINGUAL OFFICE OCCUPATINS
    COMSTOCK BONANZA: RARE WESERN AMERICANA".   AMERICAN
    VOCATIONAL JOURNAL, VOL. 45 (MAR 1970), PP. 45-62.

EMMETT.   TEXAS CAMEL TALES (AN*).

ERASMUS, CHARLES J. MAN TAKES CONTROL. MINNEAPOLIS,
    MINNESOTA: UNIVERSITY OF MINNESOTA PRESS, 1961.

ERDMAN, LOULA GRACE. THE YEARS OF THE LOCUST. NEW YORK,
    NEW YORK: DODD, 1947.

ESTERGREEN, M. MORGAN. KIT CARSON: A PORTRAIT IN COURAGE.
    NORMAN, OKLAHOMA: UNIVERSITY OF OKLAHOMA PRESS, 1962
    (HSW).

ETS. BAD BOY, GOOD BOY (LJE*).

ETS. GILBERTO WIND (LJE*).

EVANS. MEXICAN GOLD TRAIL, JOURNAL 49ER (TJ*).

EVANS, JAMES LEROY. THE INDIAN SAVAGE, THE MEXICAN BANDIT,
    THE CHINESE HEATHEN --THREE POPULLAR STEREOTYPES.
    UNIVERSITY OF TEXAS AT AUSTIN, PHD. DISSERTATION
    (1968) (SO).

EVERTS., HAL. SMUGGLERS ROAD. NEW YORK, NEW YORK:
    SCRIBNER, 1968.

FALCONER. NOTES JOURNEY THROUGH TEXAS NEW (TJ*).

FARBER. TEXAS C. S. A. (HT*).

FARQUHAR. JOAQUIN MURIETA, BRIGAND CHIEF (HC*).

FAUNCE, HILDA. DESERT WIFE. BOSTON: LITTLE, 1934.

FAY, ELIOT GILBERT. LORENZO IN SEARCH OF THE SUN; D. H.
    LAWRENCE IN ITALY, MEXICO, AND THE AMERICAN SOUTHWEST.
    REPRINTED BY: NEW YORK, NEW YORK AND LONDON, GREAT
    BRITAIN: AMS PRESS, INC., 1953.

FELLOWS, MURIEL H. LAND OF LITTLE RAIN. PHILADELPHIA:
    WINSTON, 1936 (LJE).

FELTON. COWBOY JAMBOREE, WESTERN SONGS (AN*).

FELTON, HAROLD W. PECOS BILL, TEXAS COWPUNCHER.
    NEW YORK: ALFRED A. KNOPF, 1949.

FERBER, EDNA. GIANT. GARDEN CITY, NEW YORK: DOUBLEDAY,
    1952.

FERGUSON, HARVEY. THE CONQUEST OF DON PEDRO. NEW YORK:
    WILLIAM MORROW AND COMPANY, 1954.

FERGUSON, MRS. TOM B. THEY CARRIED THE TORCH. KANSAS
    CITY, MISSOURI: BURTON PUBLISHING COMPANY, 1937.

FERGUSSEN, ERNA. OUR SOUTHWEST. NEW YORK: ALFRED
    A. KNOPF, 1940.

FERGUSSON, ERNA. "FROM REDSKINS TO RAILROADS". CENTURY
    MAGAZINE, VOL. 113 , PP. 23-31.

FERGUSSON, ERNA. "NEW MEXICO'S MEXICANS". CENTURY, VOL.
    116 (AUGUST 1928), PP. 437-44.

FERGUSSON, ERNA. "THE NEW NEW MEXICO". NEW MEXICO
    QUARTERLY REVIEW, VOL. 19 (WINTER 1949), PP. 417-426.

FERGUSSON, ERNA. ALBUQUERQUE. ALBUQUERQUE: MERLE
    ARMITAGE EDITIONS, 1947.

FERGUSSON, ERNA. DANCING GODS. NEW YORK: ALFRED
    A. KNOPF, 1931.

FERGUSSON, ERNA. MEXICAN COOKBOOK. ALBUQUERQUE,
    NEW MEXICO: UNIVERSITY OF NEW MEXICO PRESS, 1967.

FERGUSSON, ERNA. MEXICO REVISITED. NEW YORK, KNOPF, 1955.

FERGUSSON, ERNA. MURDER AND MYSTERY IN NEW MEXICO.
    ALBUQUERQUE: MERLE ARMITAGE, 1948.

FERGUSSON, ERNA. NEW MEXICO, A PAGENT OF THREE PEOPLES.
    NEW YORK: KNOPF, 1951.

FERGUSSON, HARVEY. BLOOD OF THE CONQUERORS. NEW YORK:
    ALFRED A KNOPF, 1921.

FERGUSSON, HARVEY. FOLLOWERS OF THE SUN, A TRIOLOGY OF
    THE SANTA FE TRAIL (WOLF SONG, 1927. IN THOSE DAYS,
    1929. BLOOD OF THE CONQUERORS, 1921.). NEW YORK:
    ALFRED A KNOPF, 1936.

FERGUSSON, HARVEY. FOOTLOOSE MCGARNIGAL. NEW YORK:
    KNOPF, 1930.

FERGUSSON, HARVEY. GRANT OF KINGDON. NEW YORK: WILLIAM
    MORROW AND COMPANY, 1950.

FERGUSSON, HARVEY. HOME IN THE WEST: AN INQUIRY INTO MY
    ORIGINS. NEW YORK: DUELL, 1945.

FERGUSSON, HARVEY. RIO GRANDE. NEW YORK: WILLIAM MORROW
    AND COMPANY, 1955.

FERGUSSON, MRS. C. M. CONVERSATIONS. ALBUQUERQUE, NEW
    MEXICO,.

FERLINGHETTI. MEXICAN NIGHT; TRAVEL JOURNAL (TJ*).

FERN, EUGENE. LORENZO AND ANGELINA. NEW YORK: FARRAR,
    STRAUS AND GIROUX, 1968.

FERRIL, THOMAS HORNSBY. WESTERING. NEW HAVEN: YALE
    UNIVERSITY PRESS, 1934.

FERRIS, ROBERT G. THE AMERICAN WEST: AN APPRAISAL.
    SANTA FE: MUSEUM OF NEW MEXICO PRESS, 1963.

FERRY, GABRIEL (LOUIS DE BELLEMARE). VAGABOND LIFE
    IN MEXICO. NEW YORK: HARPER, 1856.

FEY, HAROLD E. "OUR DEBTS TO MEXICO". CHRISTIAN CENTURY,
    (DECEMBER 28, 1966), PP. 1594-1595.

FICKE, ARTHUR DAVISON. MOUNTAIN AGAINST MOUNTAIN. GARDEN
    CITY, NEW YORK: DOUBLEDAY, 1929.

FINGER, CHARLES J. ADVENTURE UNDER SAPPHIRE SKIES. NEW
    YORK: MORROW, 1931.

FINGER, CHARLES J. FRONTIER BALLADS. GARDEN CITY, NEW
    YORK: DOUBLEDAY, 1927.

FINGER, CHARLES J. OZARK FANTASIA. FAYETTEVILLE,
    ARKANSAS: GOLDEN HORSEMAN PRESS, 1927.

FINNEY, JACK. PRISON LEGEND. NEW YORK: SIMON AND
    SCHUSTER, 1962.

FISHER, ANNE B. THE SALINAS. UPSIDE-DOWN RIVER. NEW
    YORK, TORONTO: FARRAR AND RINEHART, INC, 1945.

FISHER, FREDERICK VINING. THE TRANSORMATION OF A JOB; A
    TALE OF THE HIGH SIERRAS. NEW YORK: BOOKS FOR
    LIBRARIES, INC.,.

FISHER, HOWARD T; HALL, MARION (EDITORS). LIFE IN MEXICO:
    THE LETTERS OF FANNY CALDERON DE LA BARCA. NEW YORK:
    DOUBLEDAY AND COMPANY, INC., 1970 (TJ).

FLETCHER, JOHN GOULD. SELECTED POEMS. NEW YORK: FARRAR
    AND RINEHART, 1938.

FLINT, TIMOTHY. FRANCIS BERRIAN, OR THE MEXICAN PATRIOT.
    BOSTON: CUMMINGS, HILLIARD AND COMPANY, 1826.

FLINT, TIMOTHY. FRANCIS BERRIEN, OR THE MEXICAN PATRIOT.
    PHILADELPHIA: KEY, BIDDLE, 1834.

FOSTER, O'KANE. IN THE NIGHT DID I SING. NEW YORK:
    SCRIBNER, 1942.

FOWLER, JACOB. JOURNAL OF JACOB FOWLER. NEW YORK:
    FRANCIS P. HARPER, 1898.

FRANCIS, MARY E., (TRANS.). THE HERMIT OF THE CAVERN.
    SAN ANTONIO: NAYLOR, 1934.

FRANK, WALDO. OUR AMERICA. NEW YORK: BONI AND LIVERIGHT
    PUBLISHERS, 1919.

FRANTZ, JOE B. "LONE STAR MYSTIQUE".   THE AMERICAN WEST,
    VOL. 5 (MAY 1968), PP. 6-9.

FRANTZ, JOE B. AND CHOATE, J. E. JR.   THE AMERICAN COWBOY,
    THE MYTH AND THE REALITY.   NORMAN: UNIVERSITY
    OF OKLAHOMA PRESS, 1955.

FRASCONI, ANTONIO (TRANS).   THE SNOW AND THE SUN (LA NIEVE
    Y EL SOL): A SOUTH AMERICAN FOLK RHYME IN TWO
    LANGUAGES.   NEW YORK: HARCOURT, BRACE AND WORLD,
    INC., 1961.

FRASER, JAMES. LAS POSADAS.   FLAGSTAFF, ARIZONA:
    NORTHLAND PRESS, 1963.

FREMONT.   EXPLORING EXPEDITION TO ROCKY   (TJ*).

FRENCH, ALICE. KNITTERS IN THE SUN.   BOSTON: HOUGHTON,
    1887.

FUERMANN, GEORGE. HOUSTON, THE FEAST YEARS.   HOUSTON:
    PREMIER PRINTING CO, 1962.

FUERMANN, GEORGE. HOUSTON, LAND OF THE BIG RICH.   GARDEN
    CITY, NEW YORK: DOUBLEDAY, 1952.

FUERMANN, GEORGE. RELUCTANT EMPIRE, THE MIND OF TEXAS.
    GARDEN CITY, NEW YORK: DOUBLEDAY, 1957.

FUERMANN, GEORGE. THE FACE OF HOUSTON.   HOUSTON: PRESS
    OF PREMIER, 1963.

GALLEGLY, JOSEPH. THE ADVENTURES OF STEVE WATERHOUSE.
    SAN ANTONIO: NAYLOR, 1947.

GALLEN, A. A. THE WETBACK.   BOSTON: BRUCE HUMPHRIES, 1961.

GAMBRELL.   ANSON JONES, LAST PRESIDENT TEXAS   (HT*).

GAMBRELL.   MIRABEAU B. LAMAR, TROUBADOUR   (HT*).

GANILH.   MEXICO VERSUS TEXAS   (HSW*).

GANITH.   AMBROSIO DE LETINEZ   (HSW*).

GARD, WAYNE. SAM BASS.   BOSTON: HOUGHTON, 1936 (HSW).

GARDINER, DOROTHY. WEST OF THE RIVER.   NEW YORK: THOMAS
    CROWELL COMPANY, 1963 (HM).

GARLAND, HAMLIN. "DELMAR OF PIMA".   MCCLURE'S MAGAZINE,
    VOL. 18 NO. 4 (FEBRUARY 1902).

GARLAND, HAMLIN. THE CHICANO: FROM CARICATURE TO SELF-PORTRAIT.
    NEW YORK: NEW AMERICAN LIBRARY, 1971.

GARNER, CLAUD. WETBACK. NEW YORK: COWARD-MCCANN, 1947.

GARZA, CONSUELO M. WOMAN IN THE SPANISH ROMANCE.
    UNIVERSITY OF TEXAS AT AUSTIN, MASTER'S THESIS (1952).

GAST. "MINORITY AMERICANS CHILDRENS (ED*).

GASTON, EDWIN W., JR. THE EARLY NOVEL OF THE SOUTHWEST.
    ALBUQUERQUE: UNIVERSITY OF NEW MEXICO PRESS, 1961.

GASTON, EDWIN W., JR. THE EARLY NOVEL OF THE SOUTHWEST.
    ALBUQUERQUE, NEW MEXICO: UNIVERSITY OF NEW MEXICO
    PRESS, 1961.

GATES, DORIS. BLUE WILLOW. NEW YORK: VIKING, 1940.

GAULD, WILLIAM CAMPBELL. THE DREAM. NEW YORK: E.
    P. DUTTON AND COMPANY,.

GAVIN. CACTUS CROWN (HM*).

GERSON. KIT CARSON: FOLK HERO MAN (LJE*).

GERSTACKER. SCENES LIFE CALIFORNIA (HC*).

GILLIS, EVERETT A. HELLOW THE HOUSE . DALLAS: KALEIDOGRAPH
    PRESS, 1944.

GILLMOR, FRANCES. FRUIT OUT OF ROCK. NEW YORK: DUELL,
    1940.

GILLMOR, FRANCES. WINDSINGER. NEW YORK: MINTON, BALCH
    AND COMPANY, 1930.

GILSTRAP, ROBERT. TEN TEXAS TALES. AUSTIN: STECK-VAUGHN
    COMPANY, 1963.

GLASGOW. CONVERSATIONS (TJ*).

GODAY, MERCEDES. WHEN I WAS A GIRL IN MEXICO. BOSTON:
    LOTHROP, LEE AND SHEPARD COMPANY, 1919 (TJ).

GONZALEZ OBREGON. STREETS MEXICO (HM*).

GOOCH, FANNY CHAMBERS. FACE TO FACE WITH THE MEXICANS.
    EDITED WITH AN INTRODUCTION BY C. HARVEY GARDINER.
    CARBONDALE, ILLINOIS: SOUTHERN ILLINOIS UNIVERSITY
    PRESS, 1966.

GOODWYN, FRANK. THE BLACK BULL. GARDEN CITY, NEW YORK:
    DOUBLEDAY AND COMPANY, 1958.

GOODWYN, FRANK. THE DEVIL IN TEXAS. DALLAS: DEALEY AND
    LOWE, 1936.

GOODWYN, FRANK. THE MAGIC OF LIMPING JOHN, A STORY OF THE
    MEXICAN BORDER COUNTRY.   NEW YORK: FARRAR AND
    RINEHART, INC., 1944.

GORDON, ALVIN. INHERIT THE EARTH; STORIES FROM MEXICAN
    RANCH LIFE.   TUCSON: UNIVERSITY OF ARIZONA PRESS,
    1963 (LMA TJ).

GORDON, ALVIN. INHERIT THE EARTH; STORIES FROM MEXICAN
    FARM LIFE.   TUCSON: UNIVERSITY OF ARIZONA PRESS, 1963
    (LMA TJ).

GRAHAM, PHILIP. EARLY TEXAS VERSE.   AUSTIN: STECK, 1936.

GRAHAM, PHILIP. LIFE AND POEMS OF MIRIBEAU B. LAMAR.
    CHAPEL HILL: UNIVERSITY OF NORTH CAROLINA PRESS, 1938.

GRANAT, ROBERT. TO ENDURE.   GARDEN CITY, NEW YORK:
    DOUBLEDAY, 1960 (LMA).

GREEN,. MANUEL, YOUNG MEXICAN AMERICAN.   NOUNT VERMONT,
    NEW YORK: LANTERN PRESS, INC. PUBLISHERS, 1971.

GREENBERG, JOANNE. SURVIVOR.   IN SUMMERING: A BOOK OF
    SHORT STORIES. NEW YORK: HOH, RINEHART & WINSTON,
    1966.

GREER, HILTON ROSS. BEST SHORT—STORIES FROM THE SOUTHWEST.
    FIRST AND SECOND SERIES. DALLAS: SOUTHWEST PRESS,
    1928, 1931.

GREER, HILTON ROSS. TEN AND TWENTY APRILS.   DALLAS:
    TARDY, 1935.

GREER, HILTON ROSS. VOICES OF THE SOUTHWEST.   NEW YORK:
    MACMILLAN, 1923.

GREER, HILTON ROSS, AND BARNS, FLORENCE E. EDS. NEW VOICES
    OF THE SOUTHWEST.   DALLAS: TARDY, 1934.

GREGORY, JACKSON. RIDERS ACROSS THE BORDER.   NEW YORK:
    DODD, 1932.

GREGSON, PEGGY MAURINE. WESTERN POETRY.   SAN ANGELO,
    TEXAS: EDUCATOR BOOKS, INC.,.

GREY, ZANE. THE HERITAGE OF THE DESERT.   NEW YORK.
    HARPER, 1910. NEW YORK: GROSSET AND DUNLAP, 1920 (HSW).

GREY, ZANE. THE RANGER.   NEW YORK: HARPER AND ROW, 1960.

GRIFFITH.   HASINAI INDIANS EAST TEXAS AS (HT*).

GRIMM, AGNES C. LLANOS MESTENOSMUSTANG PLAINS.   WACO,
    TEXAS: TEXIAN PRESS, 1968.

GUSTAT, JENNIE B. HIS BAND MARCHES ON: THE STORY OF PETER
    GUSTAT. NEW YORK: VANTAGE PRESS, 1954.

HACKETT. "SUCCESS LINDBERGHS GOOD WILL (HSW*).

HALEY, J. EVETTS. "A LOG OF THE TEXAS-CALIFORNIA CATTLE
    TRAIL, 1854". SOUTHWESTERN HISTORICAL QUARTERLY,
    VOL. 35 (JANUARY 1932), PP. 208-237 (HT).

HALEY, J. EVETTS. CHARLES GOODNIGHT. BOSTON: HOUGHTON,
    1936 (HT).

HALEY, J. EVETTS. FORT CONCHO AND THE TEXAS FRONTIER.
    SAN ANGELO, TEXAS: SAN ANGELO STANDARD-TIMES, 1952
    (HT).

HALEY, J. EVETTS. GEORGE LITTLEFIELD, TEXAN. NORMA:
    UNIVERSITY OF OKLAHOMA PRESS, 1943 (HT).

HALEY, J. EVETTS. JEFF MILTON: A GOOD MAN WITH A GUN.
    NORMAN: UNIVERSITY OF OKLAHOMA PRESS, 1948 (HT).

HALEY, J. EVETTS. SURVEY OF TEXAS CATTLE DRIVES TO THE
    NORTH. UNIVERSITY OF TEXAS, 1920 (HT).

HALEY, J. EVETTS. THE XIT RANCH OF TEXAS AND THE EARLY
    DAYS OF THE LLANO ESTACADO. CHICAGO: LAKESIDE PRESS,
    1929. REPRINT, NORMAN, OKLAHOMA: UNIVERSITY OF
    OKLAHOMA PRESS, 1953, 1954, 1967 (HT).

HALL, D. J. ENCHANTED SAND. NEW YORK: MORROW, 1933 (HT).

HALL, MAJOR SAM. THE SERPENT OF EL PASO. NEW YORK:
    BEADLE AND ADAMS, 1882.

HAMMETT, SAMUEL A. A PINEY WOODS TAVERN; OR SAM SLICK IN
    TEXAS. PHILADELPHIA: T. B. PETERSON AND BROTHERS,
    1858.

HANNUM, ALBERTA PIERSON. PAINT THE WIND. NEW YORK:
    VIKING PRESS, 1958.

HANNUN, ALBERTA. SPIN A SILVER DOLLAR, THE STORY OF
    A DESERT TRADING POST. NEW YORK: VIKING, 1946.

HARRIS. BILLY JOE RANGERS (HT*).

HARRIS, LARRY M. MEX. ENGLEWOOD CLIFFS, NEW JERSEY:
    PRENTICE-HALL, 1960.

HARRIS, WILLIAM FOSTER. THE LOOK OF THE OLD WEST. NEW
    YORK: VIKING, 1955 (HSW).

HARRISON, HENRY (ED). TEXAS POETS. NEW YORK: HENRY
    HARRISON CO., 1936.

HART.   AMERICAN IMAGES SPANISH CALIFORNIA   (HS*).

HARTE, BRET.   "FRIAR PEDRO'S RIDE".   THE OVERLAND MONTHLY,
     VOL. 2 (APRIL 1869).

HARTE, BRET.   GABRIEL CONROY.   EDITION OF WORKS, 13 AND
     14. BOSTON: HOUGHTON, MIFFLIN AND COMPANY, 1896.

HARTE, BRET.   MARUJA, AND OTHER TALES.   FREEPORT,
     NEW YORK: HOUGHTON, MIFFLIN AND COMPANY, 1885.

HARTE, BRET.   OPENINGS IN THE OLD TRAIL.   FREEPORT, NEW
     YORK: P. F. COLLIER, 1903.

HARTE, BRET.   UNDER THE REDWOODS.   FREEPORT, NEW YORK:
     COLLIER, 1901.

HARTE, BRET.   WORKS.   NEW YORK: P. F. COLLIER AND SON,
     1896-1914.

HARTE, BRET.   THE DEVOTION OF ENRIQUEZ.   NEW YORK: PLATT
     AND MUNK, 1964.

HARTER, HELEN.   CARMELO.   CHICAGO: FOLLETT, 1962.

HARTER, HELEN.   ENGLISH IS FUN: THE RHYTHM AND SONG
     APPROACH TO THE TEACHING OF ENGLISHTO NON ENGLISH
     SPEAKING BEGINNERS.   HARTER, 1960.

HASELDEN, KYLE.   "PEACE AND PERIL AT GHOST RANCH; CONFERENCE
     CENTER AT ABIQUIU, NEW MEXICO".   CHRISTIAN CENTURY,
     VOL. 84 (AUSLST 2, 1967), PP. 988-990.

HASLAM, GERALD W.   FORGOTTEN PAGES OF AMERICAN LITERATURE.
     BOSTON: HOUGHTON MIFFLIN, 1970.

HASLAM, GERALD.   "POR LA CAUSA: MEXICAN-AMERICAN LITERATURE".
     COLLEGE ENGLISH, VOL. 31 NO. 7 (APRIL 1970), PP.
     695-709.

HASTINGS.   CLASSIFICACION ESTUDIO ESTADISTICO (TJ*).

HAWKES, JOHN.   "THE HONEYMOON HIDEAWAY".   THE TEXAS
     QUARTERLY, VOL. 6 (SUMER 1963), PP. 20-32.

HEAPS, WILLARD A.   "SIMPATICO AT COWAGIAC".   ROTARIAN,
     VOL. 68 (JANUARY 1946), PP. 28-30.

HELM, MAC KINLEY.   A MATTER OF LOVE.   NEW YORK: HARPER
     AND BROTHERS, 1945.

HEMINGWAY, ERNEST.   WINNER TAKES NOTHING.   NEW YORK:
     NORTON, 1962.

HEMINGWAY, ERNEST.   THE GAMBLER, THE NUN, AND THE RADIO.
     NEW YORK, NEW YORK AND LONDON, GREAT BRITAIN: AMS
     PRESS, INC.,.

HENDRICK, BURTON J. LIFE AND LETTERS OF WALTER H. PAGE.
    GARDEN CITY: DOUBLEDAY, PAGE AND CO., 1922.

HENRY, ROBERT SELPH. L'HEROINE DU TEXAS. TRANSLATED BY
    DONALD JOSEPH WITH INTRODUCION BY FANNIE RATCHFORD.
    DALLAS: BOOK CLUB OF TEXAS, 1937 (HSW).

HENRY, W. GHOST WOLF OF THUNDER MOUNTAIN. PHILADELPHIA:
    CHILTON BOOKS, 1966.

HERNANDEZ, LUISA JOSEFINA. LOS PALACIOS DESIERTOS.
    MEXICO: UNIDAD MEXICANA DE ESCRITORES, 1960.

HERRICK, ROBERT. WASTE. NEW YORK: HARCOURT, BRACE AND
    COMPANY, 1924.

HERRING. DON QUIXOTE NEW MEXICO (HN*).

HERZOG, PETER. THE GRINGO AND GREASER. THE TERRITORIAN
    PRESS, 1964.

HILL, DONNA. CATCH A BRASS CANARY. PHILADELPHIA:
    LIPPINCOTT, 1965.

HILL, ROBERT L. "RUNNING THE CANYONS OF THE RIO GRANDE.
    A CHAPTER OF RECENT EXPLORATION". CENTURY MAGAZINE,
    VOL. 61 NO. 3 (JANUARY 1901) (HSW).

HINGA, D. "RIO GRANDE, RIVER OF DEATH". COLLIERS, VOL.
    118 (AUGUST 17, 1946), PP. 24-26.

HINTON, RICHARD J. LAND OF GOLD. BALTIMORE, 1955.

HOLTON, PRISCILLA. CHUCK MARTINEZ. NEW YORK, 1940.

HOPE, THOMAS WELLBORN. THE GREAT RIVER AND OTHER POEMS.
    NORMAN: UNIVERSITY OF OKLAHOMA PRESS, 1970.

HORGAN, PAUL. "A TREE ON THE PLAINS". SOUTHWEST REVIEW,
    VOL. 38 NO. 4 (1943) (HS).

HORGAN, PAUL. "ABOUT THE SOUTHWEST: A PANORAMA OF NUEVA
    GRANADA". SOUTHWEST REVIEW, VOL. 18 (1933),
    P. 329,359 (HS).

HORGAN, PAUL. COLONIAL LIFE IN LATIN AMERICA, AN EXHIBITION
    OF HISTORY AND ART. ROSWELL, NEW MEXICO: ROSWELL
    MUSEUM, 1949 (HS).

HORGAN, PAUL. CONQUISTADORS IN NORTH AMERICAN HISTORY.
    NEW YORK: FARRAR, STRAUS AND COMPANY, 1963 (HS).

HORGAN, PAUL. FAR FROM CIBOLA. NEW YORK: HARPER, 1938
    (HS).

HORGAN, PAUL. FIGURES IN A LANDSCAPE. NEW YORK: HARPER
    AND BROTHERS, 1931 (HS).

HORGAN, PAUL. GREAT RIVER, THE RIO GRANDE IN NORTH
    AMERICAN HISTORY. NEW YORK: RINEHART AND COMPANY,
    1954 (HS).

HORGAN, PAUL. HIGH FEELINGS FROM LONG AGO. MOUNTAIN
    STANDARD TIME: THREE NOVELS OF THE TWENTIETH CENTURY
    WEST. (HS).

HORGAN, PAUL. HUMBLE POWERS. GARDEN CITY, NEW YORK:
    IMAGE BOOKS, 1956 (HS).

HORGAN, PAUL. HUMBLE POWERS. GARDEN CITY, NEW YORK: NEW
    YORK: DOUBLEDAY, 1954 (HS).

HORGAN, PAUL. MAIN LINE WEST. NEW YORK: HARPER AND
    BROTHERS, 1936 (HS).

HORGAN, PAUL. MEMORIES OF THE FUTURE. NEW YORK: FARRAR,
    1966 (HS).

HORGAN, PAUL. NEW MEXICO'S OWN CHRONICLE. DALLAS: B.
    UPSHAW AND COMPANY, 1937 (HS).

HORGAN, PAUL. NO QUARTER GIVEN. NEW YORK: HARPER AND
    BROTHERS, 1935 (HS).

HORGAN, PAUL. PETER HURD, A PORTRAIT SKETCH FROM LIFE.
    AUSTIN: UNIVERSITY OF TEXAS PRESS, 1965 (HS).

HORGAN, PAUL. RETURN OF THE WEED. NEW YORK: HARPER, 1936
    (HS).

HORGAN, PAUL. WHITEWATER. NEW YORK: FARRAR, 1970 (HS).

HORGAN, PAUL. THE CENTURIES OF SANTA FE. NEW YORK, NEW
    YORK: E.P. DUTTON AND COMPANY, INC., 1956 (HS).

HORGAN, PAUL. THE COMMON HEART. NEW YORK: HARPER, 1942
    (HS).

HORGAN, PAUL. A DISTANT TRUMPET. NEW YORK: FARRAR, 1960
    (HS).

HORGAN, PAUL. THE HABIT OF EMPIRE. NEW YORK: HARPER AND
    BROTHERS, 1939 (HS).

HORGAN, PAUL. THE HABIT OF EMPIRE. SANTA FE: RYDAL
    PRESS, 1938 (HS).

HORGAN, PAUL. THE HEROIC TRIAD. ESSAYS IN THE SOCIAL
      ENERGIES OF THREE SOUTHWESTERN CULTURES.   NEW YORK:
      HOLT, RINEHART AND WINSTON, 1954 (HS).

HORGAN, PAUL. A LAMP ON THE PLAINS.   NEW YORK: HARPER,
      1937 (HS).

HORGAN, PAUL. 'THE SURGEON AND THE NUN.'   IN EDWARD
      SIMMEN, THE CHICANO: FROM CARICATURE TO SELF-PORTRAIT..

HORTON, INEZ. COPPER'S CHILDREN.   JERICHO, NEW YORK:
      EXPOSITION PRESS, INC., 1968.

HOUGH, E:. THE STORY OF THE COWBOY.   NEW YORK: D.
      APPLETON AND COMPANY, 1904.

HOUSE.   CITY FLAMING ADVENTURE, CHRONICLE   (HT*).

HOUSE.   OIL BOOM: STORY SPINDLETOP,BURKBURNETT   (HT*).

HOUSE.   ROARING RANGER   (HT*).

HOUSE.   SAN ANTONIO: CITY FLAMING ADVENTURE   (HT*).

HOUSE.   TEXAS RHYTHM   (HT*).

HOUSE.   WERE YOU RANGER   (HT*).

HOUSTON, NOLL. THE GREAT PROMISE.   NEW YORK: REYNAL AND
      HICHCOCK, 1946.

HOWE, HAROLD II. COWBOYS, INDIANS, AND AMERICAN EDUCATION.
      OFFICE OF UNITED STATES COMMISSIONER OF EDUCATION,
      (JUNE 1968) (ED).

HOWE, HAROLD. "COWBOYS, INDIANS, AND AMERICAN EDUCATION".
      THE TEXAS OUTLOOK, VOL. 52 (JUNE 1968), PP. 12-13
      (ED).

HOYT, HENRY F. A FRONTIER DOCTOR.   BOSTON: HOUGHTON, 1929.

HUDSON, WILLIAM M. ANDY ADAMS: HIS LIFE AND WRITINGS.
      DALLAS: SOUTHERN METHODIST UNIVERSITY PRESS, 1971.

HUDSON, WILLIAM M. THE SUNNY SLOPES OF LONG AGO.   DALLAS:
      SOUTHERN METHODIST UNIVERSITY PRESS, 1971.

HUNTER.   TRAIL-DRIVERS TEXAS   (HT*).

IRVING, WASHINGTON. THE ADVENTURES OF CAPTAIN BONNEVILLE.
      NEW YORK: G. P. PUTNAM'S SONS, 1895.

IRVING, WASHINGTON. 'A TOUR ON THE PRAIRIES.'   1835.
      EDITED GEORGE C. WELLS. OKLAHOMA CITY.

IRVING, WASHINGTON. THE WORKS OF WASHINGTON IRVING.   THE
    KINDERHOOK EDITION. 10 VOLUMES. NEW YORK: G. P.
    PUTNAM'S SONS,.

JACKSON, HELEN, HUNT. RAMONA.   BOSTON: LITTLE, BROWN AND
    COMPANY, 1935.

JARAMILLO.   ROMANCE LITTLE VILLAGE GIRL   (LMA*).

JARRELL, RANDALL. POETRY AND THE AGE.   NEW YORK: VINTAGE
    BOOKS, 1955.

JEFFERS, ROBINSON. CAWDOR AND OTHER POEMS..   NEW YORK:
    RANDOM HOUSE, 1934.

JEFFERS, ROBINSON. FLAGONS AND APPLES.   LOS ANGELES:
    GRAFTON PUBLISHING COMPANY, 1912.

JEFFERS, ROBINSON. ROAN STALLION.   NEW YORK: THE MODERN
    LIBRARY, 1935.

JEFFERS, ROBINSON. WOMEN AT POINT SUR.   NEW YORK: RANDOM
    HOUSE, 1935.

JEFFERS, ROBINSON. THE SELECTED POETRY OF ROBINSON
    JEFFERS.   NEW YORK: RANDOM HOUSE, 1937.

JEFFERSON.   TRAVELS CALIFORNIA SCENES PACIFIC   (TJ*).

JESSEY.   TEACH ANGRY SPIRIT   (SO*).

JOHNSON, A. AND E. THE RESCUED HEART.   NEW YORK: HARPERS,
    1961.

JOHNSON, DOROTHY. INDIAN COUNTRY.   NEW YORK, NEW YORK:
    BALLANTINE BOOKS, INC.,.

JOHNSON, DOROTHY. THE HANGING TREE.   NEW YORK, NEW YORK:
    BALLANTINE BOOKS, INC.,.

JOHNSON, DOROTHY. A MAN CALLED HORSE AND OTHER STORIES.
    NEW YORK, NEW YORK: BALLANTINE BOOKS, INC.,.

JOHNSON, SPUD. HORIZONTAL YELLOW.   SANTE FE: WRITERS'
    EDITIONS, 1935.

JOHNSTON, S. M. "JOSE'S VILLAGE".   YALE REVIEW, VOL. 28
    (SEPTEMBER 1938), PP. 130-43.

JONES.   MEXICO ITS RECONSTRUCTION (HM*).

JONES, DANIEL. FORTY YEARS AMONG THE INDIANS.   LOS
    ANGELES: WESTERNLORE PRESS, 1961.

JOSEPH, DONALD. FOUR BLIND MICE.   NEW YORK: STOKES, 1932.

JOSEPH, DONALD. OCTOBER'S CHILD. NEW YORK: STOKES, 1929.

JOSEPH, DONALD. THE LONG BONDAGE. NEW YORK: STOKES, 1930.

JOUGHTON, JOHN. "ALWAYS A BRAVE RIVER". SOUTHWEST
    REVIEW, VOL. 50 (1965), PP. 345-354.

JUAREZ, NICANDRO, FRANCIS. JOSE VASCONCELOS' THEORY OF
    THE COSMIC RACE. UNIVERSITY OF CALIFORNIA, LOS
    ANGELES, MASTER'S THESIS (1965).

JURUP, H. A. "SOME ADVENTURES OF AN AMATEUR PROPAGANDIST".
    CHRISTIAN CENTURY, VOL. 43 (FALL 1969), PP. 1420-22.

KARCHMER, SYLVAN. A FISTFUL OF ALAMO HEROES. EDITED BY
    EDWARD SIMMEN. A MENTOR BOOK. NEW YORK: NEW AMERICAN
    LIBRARY, 1971.

KAUFMAN, KENNETH C. LEVEL LAND. DALLAS: KALEIDOGRAPH
    PRESS, 1935.

KELLY, FRANCIS CLEMENT. BLOOD DRENCHED ALTERS. MILWAUKEE:
    BRUCE, 1935.

KEMP, LYSANDER. THE ONLY BEAST. NEW YORK: POCKET BOOKS,
    1954.

KEROUAC, JACK. ON THE ROAD. NEW YORK: SIGNET BOOKS, 1958.

KINCAID. MEXICAN PASTOR (RE*).

KING, CHARLES. STARLIGHT RANCH AND OTHER STORIES OF ARMY
    LIFE ON THE FRONTIER. PHILADELPHIA: LIPPINCOTT,
    1890, 1905.

KING, EDITH SHATTO. "MY MEXICAN NEIGHBORS". SURVEY, VOL.
    37 (39 SEPTIEMBRE 1939), PP. 624-26.

KLINE. FORGOTTEN VILLAGE (HSW*).

KRETTEK, GERMAINE, AND EILEEN D. COOKE. "MINORITIY GROUPS
    IN TEXTS AND LIBRARY BOOKS". WILSON LIBRARY
    BULLETIN, (OCTOBER 1966), P. 235.

LANE, FERDINAND C. EARTH'S GRANDEST RIVERS. GARDEN CITY:
    DOUBLEDAY AND COMPANY, 1949.

LANGFORD, GERALD. ALIAS O. HENRY, A BIOGRAPHY OF WILLIAM
    SIDNEY PORTER. NEW YORK: MACMILLAN, 1957.

LANSFORD, WILLIAM DOUGLAS. PANCHO VILLA. LOS ANGELES:
    SHERBOURNE PRESS, 1965 (HM).

LARKIN, MARGARET. EL CRISTO. NEW YORK: FRENCH, 1926.

LARKIN, MARGARET. THE SINGING COWBOY. NEW YORK: ALFRED
    A. KNOPF, 1931.

LAUT, AGNES. PILGRIMS OF THE SANTA FE. NEW YORK:
    MCBRIDE, NAST, 1913 (HSW).

LAWRENCE, D. H. "NEW MEXICO". SURVEY, VOL. 66 (1931),
    PP. 153-55.

LAWRENCE, D. H. MORNINGS IN MEXICO. NEW YORK: KNOPF,
    1927.

LAWRENCE, D. H. THE PLUMED SERPENT. NEW YORK: KNOPF,
    1926.

LAWRENCE, FRIEDA. NOT I, BUT THE WIND. NEW YORK: VIKING,
    1934.

LEA, TOM. THE BRAVE BULLS. NEW YORK: POCKET BOOKS, 1951.

LEA, TOM. THE KING RANCE. BOSTON: LITTLE, BROWN
    AND COMPANY, 1957.

LEA, TOM. THE WONDERFUL COUNTRY. BOSTON: LITTLE, BROWN
    AND COMPANY, 1952.

LEE, ALWYN. "SOMETHING FOR BRADSHAW'S TOMBSTONE".
    PARTISAN REVIEW, VOL. 22 (SUMMER 1955).

LEE, JAMES W. (ED.). SOUTHWEST WRITERS SERIES. AUSTIN:
    STECK-VAUGH, 1967-71 (HSW).

LEE, ROBERT EDSON. FROM WEST TO EAST: STUDIES IN THE
    LITERATURE OF THE AMERICAN WEST. URBANA, ILLINOIS:
    UNIVERSITY OF ILLINOIS PRESS, 1966.

LEE, W. STORRS. COLORADO: A LITERARY CHRONICLE.
    NEW YORK, NEW YORK: FUNK AND WAGNALLS, INC., 1968.

LEWIS, ALFRED HENRY. WOLFVILLE. NEW YORK: FREDERICK A.
    STOKES COMPANY, 1897.

LEWIS, ALFRED HENRY. WOLFVILLE DAYS. NEW YORK: FREDERICK
    A. STOKES COMPANY, 1902.

LLOYD, EVERETT. LAW WEST OF THE PECOS. SAN ANTONIO:
    UNIVERSITY PRESS, 1931, REPRINT, NAYLOR.

LOMAX. ADVENTURES BALLAD HUNTER (AN*).

LONDON, JACK. THE NIGHT-BORN. NEW YORK: GROSSET
    AND DUNLAP, 1913.

LONDON, JOAN. SO SHALL YE REAP; THE STORY OF CESAR CHAVEZ
    AND THE FARM WORKERS MOVEMENT. NEW YORK: CROWELL,
    1970.

LONG, E. HUDSON. O. HENRY, THE MAN AND HIS WORK.
    PHILADELPHIA: UNIVERSITY OF PENNSYLVANIA PRESS, 1949.

LONG, HANIEL. ATLANTIDES.   SANTA FE: WRITERS' EDITIONS,
    1933.

LONG, HANIEL. INTERLINEAR TO CABEZA DE VACA.   SANTA FE.
    WRITERS EDITION. REPRINT. PITTSBURGH: FRONTIER PRESS,
    1969.

LONG, HANIEL. MALINCHE.   SANTA FE: WRITERS' EDITIONS,
    1939.

LONG, HANIEL. PINON COUNTRY.   NEW YORK: DUELL, SLOAN &
    PEARCE, 1941.

LONG, HANIEL. THE GRIST MILL.   SANTA FE: RYDAL PRESS,
    1945.

LONG, MARGARET. THE SANTA FE TRAIL.   DENVER, 1954 (HSW).

LONG, STANTON C. EARLY NINETEENTH CENTURY EL PASO.
    UNIVERSITY OF TEXAS AT AUSTIN, MASTER'S THESIS (1953).

LOOK.   REMINISCENCES (TJ*).

LOPEZ.   "HERE THEY COME AGAIN" (EC*).

LORD.   "MYTHS REALITIES ALAMO" (HT*).

LOVECRAFT.   TRANSITION JUAN ROMERO (LMA*).

LOVELACE.   WHAT CABRILLO FOUND (HSW*).

LUMMIS.   FLOWERS OUR LOST ROMANCE (AN*).

LUMMIS.   KING BRONCOS, CTHER STORIES NEW (AN*).

LUMMIS.   LAND POCO TIEMPO (AN*).

LYMAN.   SAGA COMSTOCK LODGE (HSW*).

M' COLLUM, WILLIAM S. CALIFORNIA AS I SAW IT; PENCILLINGS
    BY THE WAR OF ITS GOLD AND GOLD DIGGERS, AND INCIDENTS
    OF TRAVEL BY LAND AND WATER.   EDITED BY DALE
    L. MORGAN. LOS GATOS, CALIFORNIA: TALISMAN PRESS, 1960
    (HC).

MAC LEISH, ARCHIBALD. CONQUISTADOR.   BOSTON: HOUGHTON
    MIFFLIN COMPANY, 1932.

MACLEOD, NORMAN. THANKSGIVING BEFORE
    THANKSGIVING BEFORE NOVEMBER.   NEW YORK: PARNASSUS
    PRESS, 1936.

MACOBY.   "LOVE AUTHORITY STUCY MEXICAN   (SO*).

MACOBY.   "ON MEXICAN NATIONAL CHARACTER"   (SO*).

MAJOR, MABEL AND SMITH, REBECCA W., EDS. THE SOUTHWEST
     IN LITERATURE.   NEW YORK: MACMILLAN, 1929.

MAJOR, MABEL, AND PEARCE, T. M. (EDS).   SIGNATURE OF THE
     SUN, SOUTHWEST VERSE,1900-1950.   ALBUQUERQUE:
     UNIVERSITY OF NEW MEXICO PRESS, 1950.

MAJOR, MABEL, SMITH, REBECCA W. AND PEARCE, T. M.
     SOUTHWEST HERITAGE.   ALBUQUERQUE: UNIVERSITY OF NEW
     MEXICO PRESS, 1938.

MANSELL, MABEL JEANETTE. IGNACIO MANUEL ALTAMIRANO:
     A BIOGRAPHICAL AND CRITICAL STUDY.   UNIVERSITY OF
     TEXAS AT AUSTIN, MASTER'S THESIS (1928).

MARANON, GREGORIO.   "GRANDEUR AND MISERY OF THE COUNT OF
     VILLAMEDIANA".   PARTISAN REVIEW, VOL. 24   (SUMMER
     1957).

MARINONI, ROSA. BEHIND THE MASK.   NEW YORK: HARRISON,
     1927.

MARRIOTT, ALICE. THE POTTER OF SAN ILDEFONSO.   NORMAN:
     UNIVERSITY OF OKLAHOMA PRESS, 1948.

MARRIOTT, ALICE. THE TEN GRANDMOTHERS.   NORMAN: UNIVERSITY
     OKLAHOMA PRESS, 1945.

MARRIOTT, ALICE. THE VALLEY BELOW.   NORMAN: UNIVERSITY
     OF OKLAHOMA, 1949.

MARSH, WILLARD. 'MEXICAN HAYRIDE.'   IN P. ENGLE (ED),
     BEST AMERICAN SHORT STORIES, 1961.

MARTI, W. H. MESSENGER OF DESTINY.   SAN FRANCISCO: JOHN
     HOWELL BOOKS, 1960.

MARTIN, PERCY. MEXICO'S TREASURE-HOUSE <GUANAJUATO>.
     NEW YORK: CHELTENHEM PRESS, 1906.

MAUGHAM, W. SOMERSET. DON FERNANDO, OR VARIATIONS ON SOME
     SPANISH THEMES.   GARDEN CITY: DOUBLEDAY,DORAN AND
     CO., 1935.

MC CAMPBELL, COLEMAN. SAGA OF A FRONITER SEAPORT.
     DALLAS: SOUTHWEST PRESS, 1934 (HSW).

MC CLUNG.   SKETCHES WESTERN ADVENTURE <1832> (HSW*).

MC CLURE, JOHN. AIRS AND BALLADS.   NEW YORK: KNOPF, 1918.

MC CONNELL.   FIVE YEARS CAVALRYMAN (TJ*).

MC ELRAVY, MAY F. TORTILLA GIRL.   CHICAGO, 1946.

MC GINITY, SUE SIMMONS. THE IMAGE OF THE SPANISH—AMERICAN
    WOMAN IN RECENT SOUTHWESTERN FICTION.   EAST TEXAS
    STATE UNIVERSITY, PHD. DISSERTATION (1969).

MC MILLION, BONNER. SO LONG AT THE FAIR.   GARDEN CITY,
    NEW YORK: DOUBLEDAY, 1964.

MC RILL, ALBERT. AND SATAN CAME ALSO.   OKLAHOMA CITY:
    BURRON PUBLISHING COMPANY, 1955.

MEINE, FRANKLIN, ED. TALL TALES OF THE SOUTHWEST.   NEW
    YORK: KNOPT, 1930.

MELAS, ROXYLEA. REVIVAL.   SAN ANTONIO NAYLOR, 1934 (SO).

MELCON.   CALIFORNIA FICTION (HC*).

MELLARD.   SOUTH BY SOUTHWEST (HSW*).

MELVILLE, HERMAN. BILLY BUDD, FORETOPMAN.   NEW YORK: THE
    POPULAR LIVING CLASSICS LIBRARY, 1962.

MERRIAM, H. G., ED. WAY OUT WEST: RECOLLECTIONS AND
    TALES.   NORMAN: OKLAHOMA UNIVERSITY OF OKLAHOMA
    PRESS, 1969 (AN TJ).

MERRILL, JOHN CALHOUN. GRINGO: THE AMERICAN AS SEEN BY
    MEXICAN JOURNALISTS.   GAINESVILLE, FLORIDA: UNIVERSITY
    OF FLORIDA PRESS, 1963 (HUS).

MILLER, JOAQUIN. "EL VAQUERO".   THE OVERLAND MONTHLY,
    VOL. 10 (1873) (AN MU).

MILLER, JOAQUIN. SONGS OF THE SIERRA.   BOSTON: ROBERT
    BROTHERS, 1873 (AN MU).

MILLS, ANSON. MY STORY.   WASHINGTON: BYRON S. ADAM>, 1921.

MONTGOMERY, VAIDA STEWART, ED. LOCOED AND OTHER POEMS.
    DALLAS: KALEIDOGRAPH PRESS, 1930.

MONTGOMERY, VAIDA STEWART, ED. A CENTURY WITH TEXAS POETS
    AND POETRY.   DALLAS: KALEIDOGRAPH PRESS, 1934.

MONTGOMERY, WHITNEY. CORN SILKS AND COTTON BLOSSOMS.
    DALLAS: P. L. TURNER, 1928.

MONTGOMERY, WHITNEY. HOUNDS IN THE HILLS.   DALLAS:
    KALEIDOGRAPH PRESS, 1934.

MONTGOMERY, WHITNEY. JOSEPH'S COAT.   DALLAS: KALEIDOGRAPH
    PRESS, 1946.

MOODY, ALAN. SLEEP IN THE SUN.   BOSTON: HOUGHTON-MIFFLIN
     CO, 1945.

MOONEY, HARRY JOHN, JR. THE FICTION AND CRITICISM
     OF KATHERINE ANNE PORTER.   PITTSBURG: UNIVERSITY OF
     PITTSBURG PRESS, 1957.

MOORE, DANIEL G. LOG OF A TWENTIETH CENTURY COWBOY.
     TUCSON, ARIZONA: THE UNIVERSITY OF ARIZONA PRESS, 1965.

MOORE, HARRY T. THE INTELLIGENT HEART, THE STORY OF D.
     H. LAWRENCE.   LONDON: HEINEMANN, 1955.

MOORE, HARRY T., ED. D. H. LAWRENCE: HIS LIFE AND WORKS.
     NEW YORK: TWAYNE, 1951, REVISED EDITION, 1964.

MOORE, HARRY T., ED. THE COLLECTED LETTERS OF D. H.
     LAWRENCE.   NEW YORK: VIKING PRESS, 1962.

MOREHART, MARTHA JUNE. PORTRAYAL OF THE MEXICAN IN
     AMERICAN NON-FICTION WORKS SUITABLE FOR YOUNG ADULTS,
     1940-67.   AUSTIN: UNIVERSITY OF TEXAS AT AUSTIN, 1968
     (HSW).

MORRIS, ANN AXTELL. DIGGING IN THE SOUTHWEST.   GARDEN
     CITY NEW YORK, DOUBLEDAY, 1933 (HSW).

MORRIS, WRIGHT. LOVE AMONG THE CANNIBALS.   NEW YORK:
     HARCOURT, BRACE AND COMPANY, 1957.

MORRIS, WRIGHT. THE FIELD OF VISION.   NEW YORK: HARCOURTB
     BRACE AND COMPANY, 1956.

MOSELEY, ELIZABETH R. DAVY CROCKETT: HERO OF THE WILD
     FRONTIER.   CHAMPAIGN, ILL.: GARRARD PUBLISHING CO.,
     1967 (HT).

MOYLAN. NUNS TALE (LMA*).

MUMEY, NOLIE. NATHAN ADDISON BAKER.   DENVER, COLORADO:
     THE OLD WEST PUBLISHING COMPANY, 1965 (HSW).

MYERS, VIRGINIA. ANGELO'S WIFE.   INDIANAPOLIS: BOBBS-MERRILL,
     1948.

MYRES.   O . W. WILLIAMS STORIES BIGBEND (AN*).

NANCE, BERTA HART. CATTLE.   DALLAS: KALEIDOGRAPH PRESS,
     1932.

NANCE, BERTA HART. FLUTE IN THE DISTANCE.   DALLAS:
     KALEIDOGRAPH PRESS, 1935.

NANCE.   AFTER SAN JACINTO: TEXAS-AMERICAN (HT*).

NANCE, WILLIAM L. KATHERINE ANNE PORTER AND THE ART OF
     REJECTION.   CHAPEL HILL: UNIVERSITY OF NORTH CAROLINA
     PRESS, 1963.

NANCE, WILLIAM L. KATHERINE ANNE PORTER AND THE ART OF
     REJECTION.   CHAPEL HILL: UNIVERSITY OF NORTH CAROLINA
     PRESS, 1963.

NEAL, DOROTHY JENSEN. CAPTIVE MOUNTAIN WATERS.   EL PASO:
     TEXAS WESTERN PRESS, 1961.

NEAL, DOROTHY JENSEN. THE CLOUD CLIMBING RAILROAD.
     ALAMOGORDO, NEW MEXICO: ALAMOGORDO PRINTING COMPANY,
     1966.

NEHLS, EDWARD (ED). D. H. LAWRENCE, A COMPOSITE BIOGRAPHY.
     MADISON: UNIVERSITY OF WISCONSIN PRESS, 1957, 1958,
     1959.

NELSON, MARY CARROLL. PABLITA VELARDE.   MINNEAPOLIS,
     MINNESOTA: DILLON PRESS, INC.,.

NELSON.   MEXICAN HISTORICAL NOVEL   (HM*).

NEW YORK PUBLIC LIBRARY. BULLETIN OF THE NEW YORK PUBLIC
     LIBRARY.   NEW YORK: NEW YORK PUBLIC LIBRARY.

NEWTON, MARGARET ELIZABETH. THE TEXAS COWBOY AND THE
     ARGENTINE GAUCHO IN LITERATURE, AS FOUND IN ANDY
     ADAMS' NOVELS, BADGER CLARK'S POETRY, RICARDO
     GUIRALDES' "DON SEGUNDO SOMBRA," AND JOSE HERNANDEZ'
     "MARTIN FIERRO".   UNIVERSITY OF TEXAS AT AUSTIN,
     MASTER'S THESIS (1942).

NIEVA, RODOLFO. "VASCONCELOS HISPANISTA".   EL UNIVERSAL,
     NO. 29 (1962).

NIGGLI, JOSEPHINA. MEXICAN VILLAGE.   CHAPEL HILL: NORTH
     CAROLINA UNIVERSITY PRESS, 1945.

NIGGLI, JOSEPHINA. STEP DOWN ELDER BROTHER.   NEW YORK:
     RINEHART AND COMPANY, 1947.

NIGGLI, JOSEPHINA. SUNDAY COSTS FIVE PESOS.   MEXICAN—AMERICAN
     AUTHORS. AMERICO PAREDES AND RAYMUNDO PAREDES (EDS).
     BOSTON, MASSACHUSETTS: HOUGHTON MIFFLIN COMPANY, 1972.

NIGGLI, JOSEPHINA. THE ENGAGEMENT.   MEXICAN—AMERICAN
     AUTHORS. AMERICO PAREDES AND RAYMUNDO PAREDES (EDS).
     BOSTON, MASSACHUSETTS: HOUGHTON MIFFLIN COMPANY, 1972.

NIGGLI, JOSEPHINA. THE STREET OF THE CMEXICAN—AMERICAN
     AUTHORS. AMERICO PAREDES AND RAYMUNDO PAREDES (EDS).
     BOSTON, MASSACHUSETTS: HOUGHTON MIFFLIN COMPANY, 1972.

NIGGLI, JOSEPHINA. THE STREET OF THE THREE CROSSES.
    MEXICAN-AMERICAN AUTHORS. AMERICO PAREDES AND RAYMUNDO
    PAREDES (EDS). BOSTON, MASSACHUSETTS: HOUGHTON MIFFLIN
    COMPANY, 1972.

NORDYKE, LEWIS. CATTLE EMPIRE. NEW YORK: MORROW, 1949
    (HT).

NORDYKE, LEWIS. GREAT ROUNDUP. NEW YORK: MORROW, 1955
    (HT).

NORDYKE, LEWIS. JOHN WESLEY HARDIN: TEXAS GUNMAN. NEW
    YORK: WILLIAM MORROW AND COMPANY, 1957 (HT).

NORDYKE, LEWIS. THE TRUTH ABOUT TEXAS. NEW YORK:
    CROWELL, 1957 (HT).

NORQUEST, CARROL. RIO GRANDE WETBACKS: MEXICAN MIGRANT
    WORKERS. ALBUQUERQUE, NEW MEXICO: UNIVERSITY OF NEW
    MEXICO PRESS, 1972 (HT).

NUNN, GUY T. WHITE SHADOWS. NEW YORK: REYNAL AND
    HITCHCOCK, 1947.

O' CONNOR. BOOM TOWN. NEW YORK: HARPER, 1930.

O' CONNOR. CONQUEST: A NOVEL OF THE OLD SOUTHWEST.
    MEXICO: PRIVATELY PRINTED.

O' MEARA, WALTER. THE SPANISH BRIDE. NEW YORK: PUTNAM,
    1954.

O SHAUGHNESSY. DIPLOMATS WIFE MEXICO (HM*).

ORMSBY, VIRGINIA. TWENTY-ONE CHILDREN. LIPPINCOTT, 1958.

ORMSBY, VIRGINIA. WHAT'S WRONG WITH JULIO?. LIPPINCOTT,
    1965.

ORTEGA Y MEDINA. MEXICO EN CONCIENCA ANGLOSAJONA (HM*).

OSKISON, JOHN M. BROTHERS THREE. NEW YORK: MACMILLAN,
    1935.

OTERO Y HERRERA, ALFREDO. "OTHER TEXANS: MEXICANOS".
    LOOK, VOL. 27 (OCTOBER 8, 1963), PP. 68-70.

OTERO, NINA. FIRE IN THE NIGHT. LONDON: GOLLANCZ, 1936.

OTIS, RAYMOND. MIGUEL OF THE BRIGHT MOUNTAIN. TORONTO:
    RYERSON PRESS, 1936.

OWEN. SWING TURN (AN*).

OWENS, WILLIAM A. FEVER IN THE EARTH. NEW YORK: PUTNAM,
    1958.

OWENS, WILLIAM A. LOOK TO THE RIVER.   NEW YORK: ATHENAEUM,
    1963.

OWENS, WILLIAM A. SWING AND TURN.   DALLAS: TARDY, 1936.

OWENS, WILLIAM A. TEXAS FOLK SONGS.   AUSTIN: TEXAS
    FOLK-LORE SOCIETY, 1950.

OWENS, WILLIAM A. THIS STUBBORN SOIL.   NEW YORK:
    SCRIBNER, 1966.

OWENS, WILLIAM A. THREE FRIENDS: BEDICHEK, DOBIE, WEBB.
    GARDEN CITY, NEW YORK: DOUBLEDAY, 1969.

OWENS, WILLIAM A. WALKING ON BORROWED LAND.   NEW YORK:
    BOBBS, 1954.

PAINE, ALBERT BIGELOW. CAPTAIN BILL MCDONALD, TEXAS
    RANGER.   NEW YORK: LITTLE, IVES, 1909.

PAINE, ALBERT BIGELOW. THE ARKANSAS BEAR.   AUSTIN:
    GAMMEL, 1905.

PAINE, ALBERT BIGELOW. THE ARKANSAS BEAR.   PHILADELPHIA:
    ALTEMUS, 1902, 1929.

PARKE, JAMES H. IT RUNS IN THE FAMILY.   PHILADELPHIA:
    PENN PUBLISHING COMPANY, 1928.

PATTERSON, PAUL. PECOS TALES.   AUSTIN: ENCINO PRESS, 1967.

PAUL.   MEXICAN HACIENDA: ITS PLACE ITS   (HS*).

PAYNE, VIOLA M. 'AUTUMN EPISODE.'   IN V. M. PAYNE, SCURRY
    COUNTRY STYLE: STORIES FROM BELOW THE CAP ROCK AND
    BEYOND.

PAYNE, VIOLA M. 'THE HAND.'   IN V. M. PAYNE, SCURRY
    COUNTRY STYLE: STORIES FROM BELOW THE CAP ROCK AND
    BEYOND.

PEARCE, T. M. CARTOON GUIDE OF NEW MEXICO.   NEW YORK:
    AUGUSTIN, 1939.

PEARCE, T. M. MARY HUNTER AUSTIN.   NEW YORK: TWAYNE, 1965.

PEARCE, T. M. OLIVER LA FARGE.   NEW YORK: TWAYNE, 1971.

PEARCE, T. M. THE BELOVED HOUSE.   CALDWELL, IDAHO: CAXTON
    PRINTERS, 1940.

PEARCE.   SOUTHWEST HERITAGE: LITERARYHISTORY   (HSW*).

PEARCE.   LANE LLANO   (HSW*).

PEARCE.   SOUTHWESTERNERS WRITE (HSW*).

PEARCE.   AMERICA SOUTHWEST; REGIONAL ANTHOLOGY (HSW*).

PEARCE.   AMERICAN SOUTHWEST (HSW*).

PEARCE.   "TRADER TERMS SOUTHWESTERN ENGLISH" (LA*).

PEAVEY, JOHN R. ECHOES FROM THE RIO GRANDE, 1905 TO N-O-W.
    BROWNSVILLE, TEXAS: SPRINGMAN-KING COMPANY, 1963.

PEAVY, CHARLES D., AND SIRINGO, CHARLES A. A TEXAS PICARO.
    AUSTIN, TEXAS: STECK-VAUGHN, 1967.

PEERY, WILLIAM (ED). TEXAS SHORT STORIES.   AUSTIN:
    UNIVERSITY OF TEXAS PRESS, 1954.

PEON, MAXIMO. COMO VIVEN LOS MEXICANOS EN LOS ESTADOS
    UNIDOS.   MEXICO: COSTA AMIC EDITOR, 1966 (TJ).

PEREDA, PRUDENCIO DE. 'CONQUISTADOR.'   IN LILLIAN
    FADERMAN AND BARBARA BRADSHAW (EDS), SPEAKING
    FOR OURSELVES: AMERICAN ETHNIC WRITING..

PERELMAN, S. J. "THE MACHISMO MYSTIQUE".   MCCALL'S, VOL.
    98 NO. 5 (FEBRUARY 1971), P. 88.

PEREZ, LUIS. EL COYOTE THE REBEL.   NEW YORK, 1947.

PERRY, GEORGE S. "THE GONZALEZES OF SAN ANTONIO".
    SATURDAY EVENING POST, VOL. 221 (OCTOBER 2, 1948),
    P. 24.

PHILLIPS, JAMES. THE INHERITORS.   NEW YORK: DIAL PRESS,
    1940.

PIKE, ALBERT. PROSE POEMS AND SKETCHES.   BOSTON: LIGHT
    AND HORTON, 1834.

PILGRIM.   LIVE BOYS OR CHARLEY NASHO TEXAS (HT*).

PILLSBURY, DOROTHY L. "ADOBE ALPHABET".   COMMON GROUND,
    VOL. 7 (AUTUMN 1946), PP. 82-87.

PILLSBURY, DOROTHY L. "ADOBE CHRISTMAS".   COMMON GROUND,
    VOL. 4 (AUTUMN 1943), PP. 22-25.

PILLSBURY, DOROTHY L. "ADOBE GRACE".   COMMON GROUND, VOL.
    5 (SUMMER 1945), PP. 48-52.

PILLSBURY, DOROTHY L. "ADOBE PAY CHECKS".   COMMON GROUND,
    VOL. 5 (WINTER 1945), PP. 87-91.

PILLSBURY, DOROTHY L. "ADOBE VILLAGE".   COMMON GROUND,
    VOL. 4 (SUMMER 1944), PP. 38-43.

PILLSBURY, DOROTHY L. "ANCIENT ADOBE SOIL". COMMON
    GROUND, VOL. 3 (SUMMER 1943), PP. 44-48.

PILLSBURY, DOROTHY L. "ANCIENT ADOBE SOIL". COMMON
    GROUND, VOL. 3 (SUMMER 1943), PP. 44-48.

PILLSBURY, DOROTHY L. NO HIGH ADOBE. ALBUQUERQUE:
    UNIVERSITY OF NEW MEXICO PRESS, 1950.

PILLSBURY, DOROTHY L. ROOTS IN ADOBE. ALBUQUERQUE:
    UNIVERSITY OF NEW MEXICO PRESS, 1959.

PILLSBURY, DOROTHY L. ROOTS IN ADOBE. ALBUQUERQUE: NEW
    MEXICO PRESS, 1960.

PORTER, JENNY LIND. AZLE AND THE ATTIC ROOM. LOS
    ANGELES: WARD RITCHIE PRESS, 1957.

PORTER, KATHERINE A. "CORRIDOS". SURVEY, VOL. 52
    (WINTER 1964), PP. 157-59.

PORTER, KATHERINE ANNE. FLOWERING JUDAS AND OTHER STORIES.
    NEY YORK: HARCOURT, 1935, MODERN LIBRARY, 1940.

PORTER, KATHERINE ANNE. PALE HORSE, PALE RIDER.
    NEW YORK: HARCOURT, 1939.

PORTER, KATHERINE ANNE. SHIP OF FOOLS. BOSTON: LITTLE,
    1962.

PORTER, KATHERINE ANNE. THE COLLECTED STORIES OF KATHERINE
    ANNE PORTER. NEW YORK: HARCOURT, 1965.

PORTER, KATHERINE ANNE. THE LEANING TOWER. NEW YORK:
    HARCOURT, 1944.

PORTER, WILLIAM SIDNEY <PSEUD. O. HENRY>. HEART OF THE
    WEST. REPRINT, GARDEN CITY, NEW YORK: DOUBLEDAY,
    1918.

PORTER, WILLIAM SIDNEY <O. HENRY>. HEART OF THE WEST.
    NEW YORK: DOUBLEDAY, PAGE AND COMPANY, 1927.

PORTER, WILLIAM SIDNEY <O. HENRY>. ROLLING STONES. NEW
    YORK: P. F. COLLIER AND SON,.

PORTERFIELD, BILL. THERES AN AWAKENING IN THE VALLEY.
    EDITED WITH AN INTRODUCTION BY EDWARD SIMMEN. NEW YORK
    AND SCARBOROUGH, ONTARIO: A MENTOR BOOK FROM NEW
    AMERICAN LIBRARY, 1972.

POSEY ALEXANDER. POEMS. EDITED BY MRS. MINNIE H. POSEY,
    TOPEKA: CRANE, 1910.

POSTL, KARL (PSEUD. CHARLES SEALSFIELD). LIFE IN THE NEW
    WORLD. NEW YORK: NEW WORLD PRESS, 1842.

POTTER, DAVID. PEOPLE OF PLENTY. CHICAGO: CHICAGO
     UNIVERSITY PRESS, 1954.

POTTER. TEXAS HISTORY-STORY-LEGEND (HT*).

POURADE, RICHARD F. GLORY YEARS. SAN DIEGO: UNION-TRIBUNE,
     1964.

POURADE, RICHARD F. GOLD IN THE SUN. SAN DIEGO:
     UNION-TRIBUNE, 1964.

PROVOST, F. "NEW LIFE IN MEXICO". PAN-AMERICAN MAGAZINE,
     VOL. 25 , PP. 33-39.

RAMSEY, ROBERT. FIESTA. NEW YORK: THE JOHN DAY COMPANY,
     1955.

RAYNOLDS, ROBERT. BROTHERS IN THE WEST. NEW YORK:
     HARPER, 1931 (HSW).

REAGAN, ROCKY. ROCKY'S CHUCK WAGON STORIES. SAN ANTONIO,
     TEXAS: THE NAYLOR COMPANY, 1968.

REHN, DOROTHY. SAN ANTONIO AND THE MISSIONS IN THE
     LITERATURE OF THE SOUTHWEST. UNIVERSITY OF TEXAS
     AT AUSTIN, MASTER'S THESIS (1938) (HT).

REMINGTON, FREDERIC. AN OUTPOST OF CIVILIZATION. HARPERS
     MAGAZINE, 88.

REMINGTON, FREDERICK. PONY TRACKS, SKETCHES OF IONEER
     LIFE. NEW YORK: HARPER AND BROTHERS, 1895.

REYNOLDS, QUENTIN. "GIRLS AT CAMP: SPANISH AMERICAN GIRLS
     ARE TAUGHT A NEW WAY OF LIFE IN CAMP CAPITAN".
     COLLIERS, VOL. 103 (MARCH 4, 1937), P. 16 (SO).

RHODES, EUGENE MANLOVE. BEYOND THE DESERT. INTRODUCTION
     BY W. H. HUTCHINSON. LINCOLN, NEBRASKA: UNIVERSITY
     OF NEBRASKA PRESS, 1967 (HSW).

RHODES, EUGENE MANLOVE. CCPPER STREAK TRAIL. BOSTON:
     HOUGHTON MIFFLIN COMPANY, 1922 (HSW).

RHODES, EUGENE MANLOVE. PENDLOSA. SANTA FE: WRITERS'
     EDITIONS, 1934 (HSW).

RHODES, EUGENE MANLOVE. THE BEST NOVELS AND STORIES OF
     EUGENE MANLOVE RHODES. J. FRANK DOBIE, (ED). BOSTON:
     HOUGHTON MIFFLIN COMPANY, 1949 (HSW).

RICE, MARTIN. OLD TIMERS' POEM. MISSOURI: JACKSON
     COUNTY, 1880.

RICHTER, CONRAD. EARLY AMERICANA AND OTHER STORIES. NEW
     YORK: ALFRED A. KNOPF, 1936.

RICHTER, CONRAD. TACEY CROMWELL. NEW YORK: ALFRED A.
    KNOPF, 1942.

RICHTER, CONRAD. THE LADY. NEW YORK: KNOPF, 1957.

RICHTER, CONRAD. THE SEA OF GRASS. NEW YORK: KNOPF, 1937.

RITCHEE, R. W. "MAKING FRIENDS FOR AMERICA". SUNSET,
    VOL. 49 (NOVEMBER 1954), PP. 22-23.

ROARK, GARLAND. WAKE OF THE RED WITCH. BOSTON: LITTLE,
    1946.

ROBERTS, MARTA. TUMBLEWEED. NEW YORK: G. P. PUTNAM'S
    SONS, 1945.

ROBERTS, WARREN. A BIBLIOGRAPHY OF D. H. LAWRENCE.
    LONDON: RUPERT HART-DAVIS, 1963.

ROBINSON, CECIL. "FLAG OF ILLUSION: THE TEXAS REVOLUTION
    VIEWED AS A CONFLICT OF CULTURES". THE AMERICAN
    WEST, VOL. 5 NO. 3 (MAY 1968), PP. 10-17 (HT).

ROBINSON, CECIL. "SPRING WATER WITH A TASTE OF THE LAND;
    THE MEXICAN PRESENCE IN THE AMERICAN SOUTHWEST".
    THE AMERICAN WEST, VOL. 3 NO. 3 (SUMMER 1966), PP.
    6-15 (HSW).

ROBINSON, CECIL. WITH THE EARS OF STRANGERS: THE MEXICAN
    IN AMERICAN LITERATURE. TUCSON, ARIZONA: UNIVERSITY
    OF ARIZONA PRESS, 1963 (HSW).

ROBINSON, G. C. MUSTANGS AND MUSTANGING IN SOUTHWEST
    TEXAS, THE DALLAS MORNING NEWS. ARTICULO REPRODUCIDO
    EN EL LIBRO MUSTANGS AND COW HORSES, EDITADO POR FRANK
    DOBIE, AUSTIN: TEXAS FOLKLORE SOCIETY, 1940, PAGS.
    3-4 (HT).

ROJAS. CALIFORNIA VAQUERO (HC*).

ROJAS. LORE CALIFORNIA VAQUERO (HC*).

ROJAS. VAQUERO (HC*).

ROLLINS. "THE COWBOY: HIS EQUIPMENT HIS (HSW*).

ROLLINS. JINGLEBOB (SO*).

ROMERO, RUTH. AMIGOS. ROWLEY, MASSACHUSETTS: NEWBERRY
    HOUSE PUBLISHERS, INC, (SO).

ROOSEVELT. RANCH LIFE FAR WEST (HSW*).

ROURKE. AMERICAN HUMOR, STUDY NATIONAL (HUS*).

ROURKE.   ROOTS AMERICAN CULTURE, CTHER (HUS*).

ROWAN, HELEN. "A MINORITY NOBOCY KNOWS".   THE ATLANTIC,
     VOL. 219 (JUNE 1967), PP. 47-52.

RUBY, CARRIE LOUISE LOKEY. ATTITUDES TOWARD LATIN
     AMERICANS AS REVEALED IN SCUTHWEST LITERATURE.
     UNIVERSITY OF TEXAS AT AUSTIN, MASTER'S THESIS (1953).

RUHL, A. B. "THE HOOKED".   OUTLCCK,   (AUGUST 26, 1911),
     PP. 978-88.

RUSSELL.   TRAILS PLCWED UNDER (HSW*).

RUTHERFORD.   MEXICAN SOCIETY DURING REVOLUTION: (HM*).

RUXTON, GEORGE F. ADVENTURES IN MEXICC AND THE ROCKY
     MOUNTAINS.   NEW YORK: HARPER AND BROTHERS, 1848.

RUXTON, GEORGE FREDERICK. LIFE IN THE FAR WEST.
     BLACKWOOD, 1849. EDITED BY HORACE KEPHART AS IN THE
     OLD WEST. NEW YORK, CUTING PUBLISHING COMPANY, 1915.

RUXTON, GEORGE FREDERICK. RUXTON CF THE ROCKIES.
     COLLECTED BY CLYDE AND MAE REED PORTER, EDITED
     BY LEROY R. HAFEN. NORMAN: UNIVERSITY CF OKLAHOMA
     PRESS, 1950.

RYE.   QUIRT SPUR (HSW*).

SAGAR, KEITH. THE ART OF D. H. LAWRENCE.   CAMBRIDGE:
     CAMBRIDGE UNIVERSITY PRESS, 1966.

SANDBURG, CARL. SMOKE AND STEEL, SLABS OF THE SUNBURNT
     WEST, GOOD MCRNING, AMERICA.   NEW YORK: HARCOURT,
     BRACE AND COMPANY,.

SANTIAGO, DANNY. "THE SCMEBODY".   REDBOOK,   (FEBRUARY
     1970), P. 68.

SAROYAN, WILLIAM. 'WITH A HEY NCNNY NONNY.' IN EDWARD
     SIMMEN, THE CHICANO: FROM CARICATURE TO SELF PORTRAIT.

SCHAEFER, JACK. NEW MEXICO.   STATE OF THE NATION BOOKS.
     NEW YORK: COWARD-MCCANN, 1967.

SCHAEFER, JACK. OLD RAMON.   NEW YORK: HOUGHTON, 1960.

SCHAEFER, JACK. THE RIDERS OF SAINT NICHOLAS.   THE
     SATURDAY EVENING POST STORIES 1961: SELECTED FROM
     1960. GARDEN CITY, NEW YORK: DCUBLEDAY, 1961.

SCHMITZ, JOSEPH W. THUS THEY LIVED.   SAN ANTONIO: NAYLOR,
     1935.

SCHOCKLEY.   OLD RAMON   (AN*).

SCHOCKLEY.   SOUTHWEST WRITERS ANTHOLOGY   (AN*).

SCOBEE, BARRY. OLD FORT DAVIS.   SAN ANTONIO: NAYLOR, 1947.

SEALE, GEORGE. 'DILEMMA, MI AMIGO.'   IN EDWARD SIMMEN,
     THE CHICANO: FROM CARICATURE TO SELF PORTRAIT.

SEALE, GEORGE. "DILEMMA, MI AMIGO".   THE TEXAS QUARTERLY,
     VOL. 9 (SPRING 1966), PP. 111-124.

SEARS, PAUL B. DESERTS ON THE MARCH.   NORMAN: UNIVERSITY
     OF OKLAHOMA PRESS, 1935.

SEGALE, SISTER BLANDINA. AT THE END OF THE SANTA FE TRAIL.
     REVISED EDITION MILWAUKEE: BRUCE PUBLISHING COMPANY,
     1948 (HSW).

SENDER, RAMON. 'DESERT GUESTS.'   IN SENDER, TALES
     OF CIBOLA. TRANSLATED FLORENCE SENDER AND OTHERS.

SETON, ANYA. THE TURQUOISE.   NEW YORK: HOUGHTON, 1946.

SHANNON, MONICA. CALIFORNIA FAIRY TALES.   NEW YORK:
     FREDERICK UNGAR PUBLISHING COMPANY, INC,.

SHANNON, W. V. IDOLS OF THE CROWD.   IN SHANNON, THE
     AMERICAN IRISH. NEW YORK: MCMILLAN, 1966 (HT).

SHULMAN, IRIVING. THE SQUARE TRAP.   BOSTON: LITTLE,
     BROWN, AND COMPANY, 1935.

SIEMERING, A. THE HERMIT OF THE CAVERN.   MAY FRANCIS.
     (TRANS) SAN ANTONIO: NAYLOR, 1932.

SIMMEN, EDWARD. 'CHICANO: ORIGIN AND MEANING.'   IN EDWARD
     SIMMEN (ED), PAIN AND PROMISE: THE CHICANO TODAY (LMA).

SIMMEN, EDWARD. "THE CHICANO FROM CARICATURE TO SELF-PORTRAIT".
     PUBLISHERS' WEEKLY, VOL. 199 NO. 5 (FEBRUARY
     1, 1971), P. 73 (LMA).

SIMMEN, EDWARD. PAIN AND PROMISE: THE CHICANO TODAY.
     A MENTOR BOOK. NEW YORK: THE NEW AMERICAN LIBRARY,
     1972 (LMA).

SIMMEN, EDWARD. THE CHICANO FROM CARICATURE TO SELF-PORTRAIT.
     NEW YORK: NEW AMERICAN LIBRARY, INC., 1971 (LMA).

SIMMONS, MARC. INTRODUCTION.   EDITED BY EDWARD SIMMEN.
     A MENTOR BOOK. NEW YORK: NEW AMERICAN LIBRARY, 1971
     (LMA).

SIMPSON.   HOODS TEXAS BRIGADE POETRY SONG   (HT*).

SINCLAIR, JOHN. IN TIME OF HARVEST.   NEW YORK: MACMILLAN,
    1943.

SJOLANDER, JOHN P. SALT OF THE EARTH AND SEA.   DALLAS:
    P. L. TURNER, 1928.

SKEELS, LYDIA LOWNDES MAURY. AN ETHNOHISTORICAL SURVEY
    OF TEXAS INDIANS.   AUSTIN: TEXAS HISTORICAL SURVEY
    COMMITTEE, OFFICE OF THE STATE ARCHEOLOGIST, (1972).
    REPORT NUMBER 22. (HT).

SMALL, JOE ANSTELL (ED.). THE BEST OF TRUE WEST.   NEW
    YORK: SIMON AND SCHUSTER, 1964.

SMITH, DAMA MARGARET. I MARRIED A RANGER.   PALO ALTO,
    CALIFORNIA: STANFORD UNIVERSITY PRESS, 1930.

SMITH, GOLDIE CAPERS. DEEP IN THIS FURROW.   DALLAS:
    KALEIDOGRAPH PRESS, 1950.

SMITH, SARAH BIXBY. ADOBE DAYS.   LOS ANGELES, 1931.

SONNEBORN, RUTH. SEVEN IN BED.   VIKING, NEW YORK, 1968
    (LJE).

SONNEBORN, RUTH. THE LOLLIPOP PARTY.   VIKING, NEW YORK:
    VIKING C, 1967 (LJE).

SONNICHSEN, CHARLES LELAND. BILLY KING'S TOMBSTONE.   NEW
    YORK: THE DEVIN-ADAIR CO, 1962 (HSW).

SONNICHSEN, CHARLES LELAND. COWBOYS AND CATTLE KINGS.
    NORMAN: UNIVERSITY OF OKLAHOMA PRESS, 1950 (HSW).

SONNICHSEN, CHARLES LELAND. COWBOYS AND CATTLE KINGS:
    LIFE ON THE RANGE TODAY.   NORMAN, OKLAHOMA: UNIVERSITY
    OF OKLAHOMA PRESS, 1950 (HSW).

SONNICHSEN, CHARLES LELAND. I'LL DIE BEFORE I'LL RUN, THE
    STORY OF THE GREAT FEUDS OF TEXAS.   NEW YORK: HARPER,
    1951 (HSW).

SONNICHSEN, CHARLES LELAND. I'LL DIE BEFORE I'LL RUN.
    THE STORY OF THE GREAT FEUDS OF TEXAS.   NEW YORK:
    THE DEVIN-ADAIR COMPANY, 1962 (HSW).

SONNICHSEN, CHARLES LELAND. OUTLAW.   DENVER: SAGE BOOKS,
    1965 (HSW).

SONNICHSEN, CHARLES LELAND. PASS OF THE NORTH.   EL PASO:
    TEXAS WESTERN PRESS, 1968 (HSW).

SONNICHSEN, CHARLES LELAND. PASS OF THE NORTH. FOUR
    CENTURIES ON THE RIO GRANDE.   EL PASO, TEXAS: TEXAS
    WESTERN PRESS, 1968 (HSW).

SONNICHSEN, CHARLES LELAND. PASSWORD.   NEW YORK:
    DEVIN-ADAIR, 1960 (HSW).

SONNICHSEN, CHARLES LELAND. ROY BEAN, LAW WEST OF
    THE PECOS.   OLD GREENWICH, CONNECTICUT: DEVIN-ADAIR
    COMPANY, (HSW).

SONNICHSEN, CHARLES LELAND. TEN TEXAS FEUDS.   ALBUQUERQUE:
    UNIVERSITY OF NEW MEXICO PRESS, 1957 (HSW).

SONNICHSEN, CHARLES LELAND; MC KINNEY, M. G. TULAROSA.
    OLD GREENWICH, CONNECTICUT: DEVIN-ADAIR COMPANY, 1960
    (HSW).

SONNICHSEN, CHARLES LELAND. TULAROSA: LAST OF THE FRONTIER
    WEST.   NEW YORK: DEVIN, 1960 (HSW).

SONNICHSEN, CHARLES LELAND. THE EL PASO SALT WAR, 1877.
    CARL HERZOG, 1961 (HSW).

SONNICHSEN, CHARLES LELAND. THE MESCALERO APACHES.
    NORMAN: UNIVERSITY OKLAHOMA PRESS, 1958 (HSW).

SONNICHSEN, CHARLES LELAND. THE SOUTHWEST IN LIFE
    AND LITERATURE; A PAGEANT IN SEVEN PARTS.   NEW YORK:
    DEVIN-ADAIR, 1962 (HSW).

SONNICHSEN, CHARLES LELAND. THE SOUTHWEST: THE RECORD IN
    BOOKS.   EL PASO, TEXAS: TEXAS WESTERN COLLEGE, 1961
    (HSW).

SONNICHSEN, CHARLES LELAND. THE STATE NATIONAL SINCE 1881.
    EL PASO, TEXAS: TEXAS WESTERN PRESS, THE UNIVERSITY
    OF TEXAS AT EL PASO, 1971 (HSW).

SONQUIST, HANNE D. AND KAMII, CONSTANCE K. "APPLYING SOME
    PIAGETIAN CONCEPTS IN THE CLASSROOM FOR THE DISADVANTAGED".
    YOUNG CHILDREN,   (MARCH 1967), PP. 231-238V 246 (HSW).

SORENSEN, VIRGINIA. THE PROPER GODS.   NEW YORK: D.
    APPLETON & CO, 1855.

SOUTHWESTERN COOPERATIVE EDUCATIONAL LABORATORY. THE
    CHICANO IS COMING OUT OF TORTILLA FLATS-- ONE WAY OR
    ANOTHER.   ALBUQUERQUE, NEW MEXICO: THE LABORATORY,
    1968 (ED SO).

SPERRY.   GREAT RIVER, WIDE LAND, RIO GRANDE   (LJE*).

SPRATLING, WILLIAM PHILIP. A SMALL MEXICAN WORLD.
    BOSTON: LITTLE BROWN, 1964.

STACY, MAY H. UNCLE SAM'S CAMELS.   CAMBRIDGE: HARVARD
     UNIVERSITY PRESS, 1929.

STANTON, ROBERT BREWSTER. DOWN THE COLORADO.   NORMAN:
     UNIVERSITY OF OKLAHOMA PRESS, 1965.

STECKMESSER, KENT LADD. THE WESTERN HERO IN HISTORY AND
     LEGEND.   NORMAN, OKLAHOMA: UNIVERSITY OF OKLAHOMA
     PRESS,.

STEELE.   FRONTIER ARMY SKETCHES (TJ*).

STEELE.   OLD CALIFORNIA DAYS (TJ*).

STEGNER, WALLACE E. ONE NATION.   BOSTON: HOUGHTON
     MIFFLIN, 1945 (SO).

STEGNER, WALLACE E. ONE NATION.   BOSTON: HOUGHTON MIFFLIN
     CO., RIVERSIDE PRESS, 1945 (SO).

STEINBECK, JOHN. CANNERY ROW.   NEW YORK: THE VIKING
     PRESS, 1945.

STEINBECK, JOHN. FLIGHT.   EDITED BY EDWARD SIMMEN.
     A MENTOR BOOK. NEW YORK: NEW AMERICAN LIBRARY, 1971.

STEINBECK, JOHN. SWEET THURSDAY.   NEW YORK: THE VIKING
     PRESS, 1954.

STEINBECK, JOHN. THEIR BLOOD IS STRONG.   ANN ARBOR:
     UNIVERSITY MICROFILMS, 1970.

STEINBECK, JOHN. TORTILLA FLATT.   NEW YORK, COVICI,
     FRIEDE PUBLISHER, 1935. ALSO NEW YORK: VIKING PRESS,
     1935.

STEINBECK, JOHN. TORTILLA FLATT.   NEW YORK: THE VIKING
     PRESS, 1963.

STEINBECK, JOHN. THE FORGOTTEN VILLAGE.   NEW YORK: THE
     VIKING PRESS, 1941.

STEINBECK, JOHN. THE LOG FROM THE SEA OF CORTEZ.   NEW
     YORK: THE VIKING PRESS, 1951.

STEINBECK, JOHN. THE LONG VALLEY.   NEW YORK: THE VIKING
     PRESS, 1938.

STEINBECK, JOHN. THE PASTURES OF HEAVEN.   NEW YORK: THE
     VIKING PRESS, 1932.

STEINBECK, JOHN. THE PEARL.   NEW YORK: THE VIKING PRESS,
     1947.

STEINER, EDWARD ALFRED. ON THE TRAIL OF THE IMMIGRANT.
     NEW YORK: F. H. REVELL, 1906.

STERLING, PHILIP. THE QUIET REBELS. NEW YORK: DOUBLEDAY,
    1968.

STEVENS. HERE COMES PANCHO VILLA; ANECDOTAL (HM*).

STEVENS, WALLACE. THE COLLECTED POEMS OF WALLACE STEVENS.
    NEW YORK: ALFRED A. KNOPF, 1955.

STEWART, J. BLUES FOR PABLO. STANFORD, CALIFORNIA:
    STANFORD, UNIVERSITY PRESS, 1962.

STILWELL, HART. "PORTRAIT OF THE MAGIC VALLEY".
    NEW REPUBLIC, VOL. 116 (APRIL 1947), PP. 14-17.

STILWELL, HART. "THE WETBACK TIDE". COMMON GROUND, VOL.
    9 NO. 4 (SUMMER 1949), PP. 3-15 (SI).

STILWELL, HART. THE UNCOVERED WAGON. GARDEN CITY, NEW
    YORK: DOUBLEDAY, 1947.

STINETORF, L. A. MANUEL AND THE PEARL. NEW YORK, NEW
    YORK: JOHN DAY COMPANY, INC., 1966.

STINETORF, L. A. A CHARM FOR PACO'S MOTHER. NEW YORK,
    NEW YORK: JOHN DAY COMPANY, INC., 1965.

STONE, JOHN AUGUSTUS. MATAMORA AND OTHER PLAYS.
    PRINCETON: PRINCETON UNIVERSITY PRESS, 1941.

STONE. AT SIGN MIDNIGHT: CONCHEROS DANCES (TJ*).

SUMMERS, RICHARD. DARK MADONNA. CALDWELL, IDAHO: CASTON
    PRINTERS, 1937.

SUMMERS, RICHARD. DARK MADONNA. NEW YORK: BANTAM BOOKS,
    1952.

SUMMERS, RICHARD. THE DEVIL'S HIGHWAY. NEW YORK, 1937.

SUTHERLAND. "TEXAS TACKLES RACE PROBLEM" (HT*).

SWEETMAN. LANDING AT VERACRUZ: 1914 (HUS*).

TEBBEL. SOUTH BY SOUTHWEST: MEXICAN-AMERICAN (HSW*).

TEDLOCK, E. W. JR. THE FRIEDA LAWRENCE COLLECTION OF D.
    H. LAWRENCE MANUSCRIPTS. ALBUQUERQUE: UNIVERSITY
    OF NEW MEXICO PRESS, 1948.

TEDLOCK, W. W. JR. (ED). FREIDA LAWRENCE, THE MEMOIRS
    AND CORRESPONDENCE. NEW YORK: ALFRED A. KNOPF, 1964.

TEDLOCK, W. W. JR. D. H. LAWRENCE, ARTIST AND REBEL.
    LAWRENCE, ARTIST AND REBEL.   ALBUQUERQUE: UNIVERSITY
    OF NEW MEXICO PRESS, 1963.

TEXAS FOLKLORE SOCIETY.   BACKWOODS TO BORDER (AN*).

TEXAS FOLKLORE SOCIETY.   CORONADOS CHILDREN (AN*).

TEXAS FOLKLORE SOCIETY.   COYOTE WISDOM (AN*).

TEXAS FOLKLORE SOCIETY.   FOLK TRAVELERS: BALLADS, TALES
    (AN*).

TEXAS FOLKLORE SOCIETY.   FOLLOW DE DRINKIN GOUD (AN*).

TEXAS FOLKLORE SOCIETY.   GOLDEN LOG (AN*).

TEXAS FOLKLORE SOCIETY.   GOOD TALE BONNIE TUNE (AN*).

TEXAS FOLKLORE SOCIETY.   HEALER LOS OLMOS OTHER MEXICAN
    (AN*).

TEXAS FOLKLORE SOCIETY.   HELL TO BREAKFAST (AN*).

TEXAS FOLKLORE SOCIETY.   HORNS TOADS (AN*).

TEXAS FOLKLORE SOCIETY.   HUNTERS HEALERS (AN*).

TEXAS FOLKLORE SOCIETY.   LEGENDS TEXAS (AN*).

TEXAS FOLKLORE SOCIETY.   MADSTONES TWISTERS (AN*).

TEXAS FOLKLORE SOCIETY.   MAN, BIRD BEAST (AN*).

TEXAS FOLKLORE SOCIETY.   MESQUITE WILLOW (AN*).

TEXAS FOLKLORE SOCIETY.   MUSTANGS COW HORSES (AN*).

TEXAS FOLKLORE SOCIETY.   PUBLICATIONS TEXAS FOLKLORE
    SOCIETY (AN*).

TEXAS FOLKLORE SOCIETY.   PUBLICATIONS TEXAS FOLKLORE
    SOCIETY (AN*).

TEXAS FOLKLORE SOCIETY.   PUBLICATIONS TEXAS FOLKLORE
    SOCIETY (AN*).

TEXAS FOLKLORE SOCIETY.   PUBLICATIONS TEXAS FOLKLORE
    SOCIETY (AN*).

TEXAS FOLKLORE SOCIETY.   PURO MEXICANO (AN*).

TEXAS FOLKLORE SOCIETY.   SHADOW HISTORY (AN*).

TEXAS FOLKLORE SOCIETY.   SINGERS STORYTELLERS   (AN*).

TEXAS FOLKLORE SOCIETY.   SOUTHWESTERN LORE   (AN*).

TEXAS FOLKLORE SOCIETY.   SPUR COCK   (AN*).

TEXAS FOLKLORE SOCIETY.   STRAIGHT TEXAS   (AN*).

TEXAS FOLKLORE SOCIETY.   SUNNY SLOPES LONG AGO   (AN*).

TEXAS FOLKLORE SOCIETY.   TEXAS FOLK SONGS   (AN*).

TEXAS FOLKLORE SOCIETY.   TEXAS FOLK FOLKLORE   (AN*).

TEXAS FOLKLORE SOCIETY.   TEXAS SOUTHWEST LORE   (AN*).

TEXAS FOLKLORE SOCIETY.   TEXIAN STOMPING GROUNDS   (AN*).

TEXAS FOLKLORE SOCIETY.   TIRE SHRINKER TO DRAGSTER   (AN*).

TEXAS FOLKLORE SOCIETY.   TONE BELL EASY   (AN*).

THALER, SUSAN. ROSARIA.   MCKAY, 1967.

THOMASON, JOHN W. GONE TO TEXAS.   NEW YORK: SCRIBNER,
     1937.

THOMPSON.   PEOPLE SERPENT   (HM*).

THOMPSON.   RECOLLECTIONS MEXICO   (TJ*).

THOREAU, HENRY DAVID.   ANTI-SLAVERY AND REFORM PAPERS.
     EDITED BY H. S SALT. LONDON: SWAN SONNENSCHEIN AND
     COMPANY, 1890 (HUS).

THOREAU, HENRY DAVID.   THE WRITINGS OF HENRY DAVID THOREAU.
     S.   BOSTON: HOUGHTON MIFFLIN COMPANY, 1906 (TJ).

THORP.   SONGS COWBOYS   (AN*).

TINKER, EDWARD LAROCQUE.   THE HORSEMEN OF THE AMERICAS AND
     THE LITERATURE THEY INSPIRED.   NEW YORK: HASTINGS
     HOUSE, 1953.

TINKLE, LON.   13 DAYS TO GLORY, SIEGE OF THE ALAMO.   NEW
     YORK: MCGRAW, 1958, REPRINT TITLED THE ALAMO,
     NEW YORK: NEW AMERICAN LIBRARY, 1960 (HSW).

TINKLE, LON.   A BIOGRAPHY OF EVERETTE LEE DEGOLYER.
     BOSTON: LITTLE, 1970 (HSW).

TOCQUEVILLE.   DEMOCRACY AMERICA   (HUS*).

TODD, JOHN.   THE SUNSET LAND.   BOSTON: LEE AND SHEPARD,
     1870.

TOPPERWEIN, EMILY AND FRITZ A.   JOSE AND THE MEXICAN
    JUMPING BEAN (EL BRINCADOR MEXICANO).   BOERNE, TEXAS:
    THE HIGHLAND PRESS, 1965 (SO).

TRAVEN, B.   THE NIGHT VISITOR, AND OTHER STORIES.   NEW
    YORK: HILL AND WANG, 1966.

TREVINO, ELIZABETH BORTON DE.   MY HEART LIES SOUTH: THE
    STORY OF MY MEXICAN MARRIAGE.   NEW YORK, NEW YORK:
    THOMAS Y. CROWELL COMPANY, 1953 (SO).

TREVINO, ELIZABETH.   WHERE THE HEART IS.   NEW YORK:
    DOUBLEDAY AND COMPANY, 1962 (SO).

TULLY, JIM.   LADIES IN THE PARLOR.   NEW YORK: GREENBERG,
    1935.

TURNBULL.   "A PRONUNCIAMIENTO"   (HSW*).

TURNER, TIMOTHY G.   BULLETS, BOTTLES, AND GARDENIAS.
    DALLAS: SOUTHWEST PRESS, 1935 (HT).

UNDERWOOD, JOHN CURTIS.   TRAIL'S END, POEMS OF NEW MEXICO.
    SATA FE, NEW MEXICO: SATA FE PUBLISHING COMPANY, 1921.

VAN DYKE, JOHN C.   GRAND CANYON OF THE COLORADO.
    NEW YORK: SCRIBNER, 1920.

VAN STONE, MARY R.   SPANISH FOLK SONGS OF NEW MEXICO.
    CHICAGO: SEYMOUR, 1926 (LMA AN).

VAN STONE, MARY R., AND LOUISE MORRIS.   LOS PASTORES.
    CLEVELAND: GATES PRESS, 1933.

VANN, GERALD.   THE WATER AND THE FIRE.   NEW YORK: SHEED
    AND WARD, 1954.

VASCONCELOS, JOSE.   LA CULTURA EN HISPANOAMERICA.
    LA PLATA, ARGENTINA: UNIVERSIDAD NACIONAL, 1934 (HM).

VASCONCELOS, JOSE.   EL DESASTRE: TERCERA PARTE DE ULISES
    CRIOLLO.   MEXICO: BOTAS, 1938 (HM).

VINACUA, RODOLFO.   "PERCHANCE TO DREAM".   AMERICAS, VOL.
    12   NO. 4 (APRIL   1960), PP. 23-24.

WALKER, FRANKLIN.   LITERARY FRONTIER.   NEW YORK: ALFRED
    A. KNOPF, 1939 (HC).

WALKER, FRANKLIN.   A LITERARY HISTORY OF SOUTHERN CALIFORNIA.
    BERKELEY: UNIVERSITY OF CALIFORNIA PRESS, 1950 (HC).

WALLACE.   GENERAL WILLIAM JENKINS WORTH: (HM*).

WALLACE, SUSAN E.   "AMONG THE PUEBLOS".   ATLANTIC MONTHLY,
    VOL. 46   (AUGUST   1880) (AN).

WALLACE, SUSAN E. THE LAND OF THE PUEBLOS. NEW YORK:
    J. A. BERRY AND COMPANY, 1888 (AN).

WALTER. OLD SANTA FE VICINITY (HN*).

WARD, ELIZABETH. NO DUDES, FEW WOMEN. ALBUQUERQUE:
    UNIVERSITY OF NEW MEXICO PRESS, 1951.

WARFEL, HARRY R. G. AND ORIANS, HARRISON. AMERICAN
    LOCAL-COLOR STORIES. NEW YORK: AMERICAN BOOK
    COMPANY, 1941.

WARREN, BETSY. INDIANS WHO LIVED IN TEXAS. AUSTIN:
    STECK-VAUGHN, 1970 (LJE).

WARREN, BETSY. PAPACITO AND HIS FAMILY. AUSTIN:
    STECK-VAUGHN COMPANY, 1969 (LJE).

WARREN, ROBERT PEN. REMEMBER THE ALAMO. NEW YORK: RANDON
    HOUSE, 1958 (LJE).

WATERS, FRANK. PEOPLE OF THE VALLEY. NEW YORK: FARRAR
    AND RINEHART, 1941.

WATERS, FRANK. PEOPLE OF THE VALLEY. CHICAGO: THE
    SWALLOW PRESS, INC., 1941.

WATERS, FRANK. THE YOGI OF COCKROACH COUNT. NEW YORK:
    RINEHART, 1947.

WAUGH, JULIA. THE SILVER CRADLE. AUSTIN: UNIVERSITY OF
    TEXAS PRESS, 1955.

WEEKS, GEORGE F. SEEN IN A MEXICAN PLAZA. NEW YORK:
    FLEMING H. REVELL COMPANY, 1918.

WEIR. "THE MEXICAN CHILD" (HT*).

WELLMAN, PAUL. DEATH IN THE DESERT. NEW YORK: MACMILLAN,
    1935.

WELLMAN, PAUL. DEATH ON THE PRAIRIE. NEW YORK: MACMILLAN,
    1934.

WELLMAN, PAUL. GLORY, GOD, AND GOLD. GARDEN CITY, NEW
    YORK: DOUBLEDAY AND COMPANY, 1954.

WELLMAN, PAUL. IRON MISTRESS. GARDEN CITY, NEW YORK:
    DOUBLEDAY AND COMPANY, 1951.

WELLMAN, PAUL. MAGNIFICENT DESTINY. GARDEN CITY, NEW
    YORK: DOUBLEDAY AND COMPANY, 1962.

WEST, RAY B. KATHERINE ANNE PORTER. MINNEAPOLIS:
    UNIVERSITY OF MINNESOTA PRESS, 1963.

WESTON, JOHN. HAIL HERO.   NEW YORK: MCKAY, 1968.

WHITE ., OWEN P. "A GLANCE AT THE MEXICANS".   AMERICAN
    MERCURY, (FEBRUARY 1925) (HT).

WHITE ., OWEN P. MY TEXAS 'TIS OF THEE.   NEW YORK:
    PUTNAM, 1936 (HT).

WHITE ., OWEN P. MY TEXAS, 'TIS OF THEE.   NEW YORK: G.
    P. PUTNAM'S SONS, 1936 (HT).

WHITE ., OWEN P. OUT OF THE DESERT: THE HISTORICAL
    ROMANCE OF EL PASO.   EL PASO: THE MCMATH COMPANY,
    1924 (HT).

WHITE ., OWEN P. TEXAS: AN INFORMAL BIOGRAPHY.
    NEW YORK: G. P. PUTNAM'S SONS, 1945 (HT).

WHITE ., OWEN P. TRIGGER FINGER.   NEW YORK: PUTNAM, 1926
    (HT).

WHITE ., OWEN P. THE AUTOBIOGRAPHY OF A DURABLE SINNER.
    NEW YORK: G. P. PUTNAM'S SONS, 1942 (HT).

WHITE, STEWARD EDWARD. ARIZONA NIGHTS.   NEW YORK,
    MCCLURE, GROSSET,1907, GARDEN CITY, NEW YORK: SUN DIAL
    PRESS, 1937.

WHITE, STEWARD EDWARD. THE LONG RIFLE.   GARDEN CITY, NEW
    YORK: DOUBLEDAY, 1932.

WHITLOCK, V. H. COWBOY LIFE ON THE LLANO ESTACADO..
    NORMAN, OKLAHOMA: UNIVERSITY OF OKLAHOMA PRESS, 1970
    (HSW).

WHITMAN, WALT. LEAVES OF GRASS.   NEW YORK: HERITAGE PRESS,.

WHITMAN, WALT. PROSE WORKS.   PHILADELPHIA: DAVID MCKAY,.

WHITMAN, WALT. THE COMPLETE POETRY AND PROSE OF WALT
    WHITMAN AS PREPARED BY HIM FOR THEDEATH BED EDITION.
    NEW YORK: PELLEGRINI AND CUDAHY, 1948.

WHITMAN, WALT. THE GATHERING OF THE FORCES.   NEW YORK:
    G. P. PUTNAM'S SONS, 1920.

WHITMAN, WILLIAM. THE PUEBLO INDIANS OF SAN ILDEFONSO,
    A CHANGING CULTURE.   NEW YORK: COLUMBIA UNIVERSITY
    PRESS, 1947.

WHITNEY, PHYLLIS. A LONG TIME COMING.   MAYFLOWER BOOK,
    1954.

WILLARD.   LAST LEAVES AMERICAN HISTORY: (HC*).

WILLIAMS, MARY FLOYD.   BAJA EL SOL.   PAMPHLET. UNDATED..

WILLIAMS, O. W.   PECOS COUNTY--ITS HISTORY.   PAMPHLET.
    UNDATED..

WILLIAMS, O. W.   UNTITLED PAMPHLET IN FORM OF A LETTER,
    DATED ALPINE, TEXAS, MARCH 16TH, 1902, ADDRESSED TO
    "MY DEAR CHILDREN".   ALPINE, TEXAS, MARCH 16, 1902.

WILLIAMS, O. W.   IN OLD NEW MEXICO, 1879-1880.   PRIVATELY
    PRINTED.

WILLIAMS, OLIVER P.: PRESS, CHARLES (ED.).   DEMOCRACY IN
    URBAN AMERICA.   SECOND EDITION. CHICAGO: RAND
    MCNALLY, 1968.

WILLIAMS, STANLEY T.   THE LIFE OF WASHINGTON IRVING.
    LONDON: OXFORD UNIVERSITY PRESS, 1935.

WILLIAMS, WILLIAM C.   SELECTED ESSAYS OF WILLIAM CARLOS
    WILLIAMS.   NEW YORK: RANDOM HOUSE, 1954.

WILLIAMSON BROADWELL.   CAMINO REAL   (HS*).

WILMARTH, A. I.   MESA LAND.   BOSTON AND NEW YORK, 1933
    (HSW).

WILSON, AUGUSTA EVANS.   INEZ, A TALE OF THE ALAMO.   NEW
    YORK, HARPER 1855, NEW YORK: G. W. CARLETON, 1882 (HT).

WILSON, EDMUND.   "REPORTER IN NEW MEXICO".   THE NEW
    YORKER, VOL. 25   (APRIL   15, 1949), PP. 80-94 (HN).

WILSON, KEITH.   SKETCHES FOR A NEW MEXICO HILL TOWN.
    PORTLAND, OREGON: PORTLAND STATE UNIVERSITY, 1966 (HN).

WINSLOW, THYRA SAMTER.   MY OWN, MY NATIVE LAND.   GARDEN
    CITY, NEW YORK: DOUBLEDAY, 1935 (SO).

WINTON, GEORGE B.   "PROGRESS IN MEXICO".   METHODIST
    QUARTERLY REVIEW, VOL. 73   , PP. 424-36 (SO).

WINTON, GEORGE B.   MEXICO PAST AND PRESENT.   NASHVILLE,
    TENNESSEE: COKESBURY PRESS, 1928 (HM).

WINTON, GEORGE B.   MEXICO TODAY.   NEW YORK, 1913 (SO).

WISE, EVELYN VOSS.   THE SHEPHERD OF THE VALLEY.   MILWAUKEE:
    BRUCE, 1959.

WOJEIECHOWSKI, MAIA.   SHADOW OF A BULL.   ANTHENUM, 1969.

WOLFE, BERNARD.   CONSTANTA'S UPSET STOMACH.   GARDEN CITY,
    NEW YORK: DOUBLEDAY, 1968.

WOLFE, BERNARD. THE NEVER ENDING PENNY.   CHICAGO,
    ILLINOIS: PLAYBOY PRESS,.

WOOD, DANIEL B. SIXTEEN MONTHS AT THE GOLD DIGGINGS.
    LONDON, 1852 (HC).

WOODS.   "THE BLONDES VALLECITO"   (HN*).

WOODS, CLEO. "HE FOUND HIS GLORY HOLE IN HIS OWN FRONT
    YARD".   THE DESERT MAGAZINE, VOL. 6 (JANUARY 1943),
    PP. 11-13.

WOODWARD, ARTHUR. FEUD ON THE COLORADO.   LOS ANGELES,
    CALIFORNIA: WESTERNLORE PRESS, 1956 (HCO).

WRIGHT , BETTY. "A TALE OF MEXICO' OR 'HOW TO MARRY OFF
    A TROUBLESOME MAMACITA-IN-LAW".   THE TEXAS QUARTERLY,
    VOL. 13 NO. 2 (SUMMER 1970), PP. 52-55 (SO).

WYLLYS.   PIONEER PADRE (HSW*).

ZAVALA PAZ, JOSE. EL BAJIO.   MEXICO, 1955.

J U V E N I L E   L I T E R A T U R E

(LJE)

ACUNA. STORY MEXICAN AMERICANS (HSW*).

ADAMS. PONY EXPRESS (LI*).

ADAMS. SANTA FE TRAIL (LI*).

ALEXANDER, FRANCES. MOTHER GOOSE ON THE RIO GRANDE.
     DALLAS, TEXAS: BANKS UPSHAW AND COMPANY, 1960.

ALLEN, ALLYN. LONE STAR TOMBOY. NEW YORK: WATTS, 1951.

AMERICAN HERITAGE. DISCOVERERS OF THE NEW WORLD.
     CHICAGO: AMERICAN HERITAGE, 1960.

ANDERSON, HANS CHRISTIAN. CUATRO CUENTOS DE ANDERSEN.
     EDITORIAL TIMUN.

ANGELO, VALENTI. NINO'S EASTER. NEW YORK: CROWELL—COLLIER
     PUBLISHING COMPANY, 1962 (LI).

ARMSTRONG, RUTH. NEW MEXICO, FROM ARROWHEAD TO ATOM.
     NEW YORK: BARNES, 1969.

ARNOLD, OREN. YOUNG PEOPLE'S ARIZONA. SAN ANTONIO:
     NAYLOR, 1968.

ASTIGARRAGA, L. M. JUAN SEBASTIAN ELCANO. SPAIN:
     EDITORIAL FELICIDAD, 1963.

ATKIND, ELIZABETH H. TREASURES OF MEDRANOS. NEW YORK:
     PARNASSUS,.

BAILEY. PICTURE BOOK ARIZONA (LI*).

BAILEY. PICTURE BOOK TEXAS (LI*).

BAILEY, JANEY C. THE WOODEN BICYCLE. NEW YORK: VANTAGE
     PRESS, 1965.

BAKER, NINA B. JUAN PONCE DE LEON. NEW YORK: ALFRED
     KNOPH, 1957.

BARKER, NINA. JUAREZ, HERO OF MEXICO. WEBSTER, 1942 (HM).

BARLOW. LATIN AMERICAN TALES (LMA*).

BAUER, HELEN. CALIFORNIA GOLD DAYS.   GARDEN CITY:
    DOUBLEDAY, 1954 (HC).

BAUER, HELEN. CALIFORNIA MISSION DAYS.   GARDEN CITY, NEW
    YORK: DOUBLEDAY & COMPANY, INC., 1951 (HC).

BAUER, HELEN. CALIFORNIA RANCHO DAYS.   GARDEN CITY, NEW
    YORK: DOUBLEDAY & COMPANY, INC., 1953 (HC).

BEALS, FRANK. DAVY CROKETT.   NEW YORK: HARPER AND ROW,
    1956 (LI).

BEALS, FRANK. KIT CARSON.   NEW YORK: HARPER AND ROW, 1956
    (LI).

BEEBE, B. F. ANIMALS SOUTH OF THE BORDER.   NEW YORK:
    MCKAY, 1968.

BISHOP, CURTIS. FAST BREAK.   PHILADELPHIA, PENNSYLVANIA:
    LIPPINCOTT,.

BLATT, GLORIA T. "THE MEXICAN-AMERICAN IN CHILDREN'S
    LITERATURE".   ELEMENTARY ENGLISH, VOL. 45 (APRIL,
    1968), PP. 446-451 (LI).

BLATT, GLORIA T. "THE MEXICAN-AMERICAN IN CHILDREN'S
    LITERATURE".   ELEMENTARY ENGLISH, VOL. 45 (APRIL,
    1968), PP. 446-451 (LI).

BLATT, GLORIA T. 'THE MEXICAN-AMERICAN IN CHILDREN'S
    LITERATURE.'   IN JAMES A. BANKS AND WILLIAM W. JOYCE
    (LI).

BLEEKER, SONIA. THE MAYA; INDIANS OF CENTRAL AMERICA.
    NEW YORK: NEW YORK: MORROW, 1961.

BLEEKER, SONIA. THE MISSION INDIANS OF CALIFORNIA.   NEW
    YORK, NEW YORK: MORROW, 1956.

BOGGS, RALPH S.; DAVIS, MARY G. THREE GOLDEN ORANGES AND
    OTHER SPANISH FOLK TALES.   NEW YORK, NEW YORK: DAVID
    MC KAY, 1936 (AN).

BOLTON, IVY. FATHER JUNIPERO SERRA.   MESSNER,.

BONHAM, FRANK. VIVA CHICANO.   NEW YORK: DUTTON,.

BOSWORTH, ALLEN. SANCHO OF THE LONG, LONG HORNS.   GARDEN
    CITY, NEW YORK: DOUBLEDAY, 1947.

BRADBURY, RAY. 'EN LA NOCHE.'   IN TWICE TWENTY-TWO.

BRADBURY, RAY. 'I SEE YOU NEVER.'   IN ROGER B. GOODMAN.
    SHORT MASTERPIECES: STORIES FROM THE WORLDS LITERATURE.

BRADBURY, RAY. 'THE LITTLE MICE.'   IN TWICE TWENTY-TWO.

BRENNER, ANITA. THE BOY WHO COULD DO ANYTHING AND OTHER
    MEXICAN FOLKTALES.   NEW YORK: WILLIAM R. SCOTT, 1942
    (AN).

BROCK.   PINATAS (AN*).

BROCK, VIRGINIA. PINATAS.   ABINGDON,.

BRUENHOFF, LAURENT. EL CASTILLO DE BARBAR.   SPAIN:
    EDITORIAL AYMA, 1964.

BUCHANAN, ROSEMARY. DON DIEGO DE VARGAS.   NEW YORK:
    KENEDY, 1963.

BUEHR, WALTER. THE SPANISH CONQUISTADORES IN NORTH
    AMERICA. NEW YORK: PUTNAM, 1962.

BUFFLER, ESTER. RODRIGO AND ROSALITA.   AUSTIN, TEXAS:
    STECK-VAUGHN COMPANY, 1949.

BULLA, CLYDE. BENITO. NEW YORK: THOMAS Y. CROWELL, 1961.

BULLA, CLYDE. BENITO.   NEW YORK: CROWELL,.

BUTTS, DAVID P.; LEE, ADDISON E. THE STORY OF CHOCALATE.
    AUSTIN: STECK-VAUGN COMPANY, 1967.

CALT, TOM. VOLCANO.   NEW YORK: CHARLES SCRIBNER'S SONS,
    1946.

CAMPBELL, CAMILLA. CORONADO AND HIS CAPTAINS.   CHICAGO:
    FOLLETT, 1958.

CAMPBELL, CAMILLA. GALLEONS SAIL WESTWARD.   NEW YORK:
    WHITTLESEY HOUSE, 1946.

CANNON, CORNELIA. FIGHT FOR THE PUEBLO.   BOSTON:
    HOUGHTON, 1934.

CANNON, CORNELIA. LAZARO IN THE PUEBLO.   BOSTON:
    HOUGHTON, 1931.

CANNON, CORNELIA. PUEBLO BOY.   BOSTON: HOUGHTON, 1926.

CANNON, CORNELIA. PUEBLO GIRL.   BOSTON: HOUGHTON, 1929.

CANNON, CORNELIA. THE FIGHT FOR THE PUEBLO.   BOSTON:
    HOUGHTON, 1934.

CARPENTER, ALLAN.   ARIZONA (1966), ARKANSAS (1967), NEW
    MEXICO (1967), OKLAHOMA (1965), T EXAS <1965>.
    CHICAGO, ILLINOIS: CHILDREN'S PRESS, 1966.

CARROLL, CURT. SAN JACINTO.   AUSTIN: STECK-VAUGHN
     COMPANY, 1957.

CARTER, HENRY. THE FIRST BOOK OF THE SPANISH AMERICAN
     WEST.   NEW YORK: WATTS, 1963 (HSW).

CASTELLANOS, JANE. SOMETHING NEW FOR TACO.   SAN CARLOS,
     CALIFORNIA: GOLDEN GATE JUNIOR BOOKS, 1965.

CATHEY, WALLACE; ARAGON, CLAUDE. CAN AND HIS PETS.   NEW
     MEXICO: INDEPENDENT SCHOOL DISTRICT #22, 1968.

CERVANTES, LETICIA P. LOS GRANDES ANIMALES DE LA SELVA.
     MEXICO: EDITORIAL NOVARO, 1959.

CLARK, ANN NOLAN. PACO'S MIRACLE.   NEW YORK: FARRAR,.

CLARK.   TIA MARIAS GARDEN (LI*).

CLARK, ANN NOLAN, AND CAREY, FRANCES. A CHILD'S STORY OF
     NEW MEXICO.   LINCOLN, NEBRASKA: UNIVERSITY PUBLISHING
     CO., 1960 (HN).

CLARK.   SUN SADDLE LEATHER (LI*).

CLARK.   THESE WERE VALIANT (LI*).

CLARKE, THELMA. RUNAWAY BOY.   ALBUQUERQUE, NEW MEXICO:
     ALBUQUERQUE PRINTING AND STAMP CO, 1969.

COBLENTZ, CATHERINE. AH-JO-KA, DAUGHTER OF SEQUOYA.
     EVANSTON, ILLINOIS: ROW, 1950.

CONCHEFF, B. ED. PAN-AMERICANA: A PAGEANT OF THE
     AMERICAS.   NEW YORK: NATIONAL TEXTBOOK COMPANY,.

CONGER, MARION. EN EL PARQUE ZOOLOGIES.   MEXICO:
     EDITORIAL MOVARO, 1959.

COPE, MALENA. "FLACO, THE HERO".   HUMPTY DUMPTY'S
     MAGAZINE FOR LITTLE CHILDREN,   (SEPTEMBER U970), PP.
     23-30.

COX, BERTHA MAY. TRUE TALES OF TEXAS.   DALLAS: TURNER,
     1949 (AN).

COX, WILLIAM R. JUMP SHOT JOE.   NEW YORK: DODD, MEAD,.

COX, WILLIAM R. TROUBLE AT SECOND BASE.   NEW YORK: DODD,
     MEAD,.

CRANDALL, ELIZABETH L. SANTA FE.   CHICAGO: RAND MCNALLY,
     1965.

CRAWFORD, M. COWBOYS.   NEW YORK: GOLDEN PRESS,.

CROSBY, ALEXANDER L.   THE RIO GRANDE.   CHAMPAIGN,
     ILLINOIS: GARRARD, 1966.

CROSS, JACK LEE.   ARIZONA, ITS PEOPLE AND RESOURCES.
     TUCSON: UNIVERSITY OF ARIZONA PRESS, 1960.

CROWNFIELD, GERTRUDE.   LONE STAR RISING.   NEW YORK:
     CROWELL, 1940.

DALGLIESH, ALICE.   AMERICA BEGINS: THE STORY OF THE
     FINDING OF THE NEW WORLD.   NEW YORK: CHARLES
     SCRIBNER'S SONS, 1958 (HSA).

DIAZ, PAUL.   UP FROM EL PASO, OPEN DOOR.   CHICAGO,
     ILLINOIS: CHILDRENS' PRESS, 1970.

DOBIE.   OPEN RANGE (LI*).

DOBRIN, ARNOLD.   THE NEW LIFE: LA VIDA NEUVA--THE MEXICAN
     AMERICAN TODAY.   NEW YORK: DODD, MEAD,.

DOLCH, EDWARD W.; DOLCH, MARGUERITE P.   STORIES FROM
     MEXICO: FOLKLORE OF THE WORLD.   CHAMPAIGN, ILLINOIS:
     GERRARD PUBLISHING COMPANY, 1960.

DUQUE, CALLY.   CALIFORNIA'S FATHER SERRA.   NEW YORK:
     BINFORDS AND MORT,.

DUQUE, SALLY.   CALIFORNIA'S FATHER SERRA.   PORTLAND,
     OREGON: BINFORDS AND MORT, PUBLISHERS, 1957 (HS).

EBERLE, IRMENGARDE.   THE VERY GOOD NEIGHBORS.   PHILADELPHIA,
     PENNSYLVANIA: LIPPINCOTT, 1945.

ELTING, MARY.   THE SECRET STORY OF PUEBLO BONITO.
     IRVINGTON-ON-HUDSON, NEW YORK: HARVEY HOUSE, 1957.

EMERSON.   PEDRO AND CATALINA (HS*).

EPSTEIN, SAM AND BERYL.   THE FIRST BOOK OF MEXICO.   WATTS,
     1955 (HM).

ERDMAN, LOULA GRACE.   SEPARATE STAR.   NEW YORK, NEW YORK:
     LONGMANS, 1944.

ETS, MARIA HALL.   BAD BOY, GOOD BOY.   NEW YORK, NEW YORK:
     CROWELL, 1967 (LI).

ETS, MARIE H.   GILBERTO AND THE WIND.   NEW YORK: VIKING,.

ETS, MARIE HALL.   GILBERTO AND THE WIND.   NEW YORK, NEW
     YORK: VIKING, 1963 (LI).

ETS, MARIE HALL.   GILBERTO YEL VIENTO.   NEW YORK,
     NEW YORK: VIKING, 1967.

EVANS.   ONE GOOD DEED DESERVES ANOTHER   (SO*).

FELLOWS.   LAND LITTLE RAIN   (LI*).

FELT, SUE.   ROSA TOO LITTLE.   NEW YORK: DOUBLEDAY
        AND COMPANY, 1950.

FINGER, CHARLES J.   TALES FROM SILVER LANDS.   GARDEN CITY,
        NEW YORK: DOUBLEDAY, 1924.

FITZPATRICK.   NEW MEXICO YOUNG PEOPLE   (ED*).

FRANKLIN, GEORGE CORY.   PANCHO.   BOSTON: HOUGHTON, 1953.

FRANKLIN, GEORGE CORY.   PEDRO, THE ROADRUNNER.   NEW YORK:
        HASTINGS HOUSE, 1957.

FRANKLIN, GEORGE CORY.   PIONEER HORSE.   BOSTON: HOUGHTON,
        1960.

FRANKLIN, GEORGE CORY.   SON OF MONTE.   BOSTON: HOUGHTON,
        1956.

FRANKLIN, GEORGE CORY.   TRAILS WEST.   BOSTON: HOUGHTON,
        1960.

FRANKLIN, GEORGE CORY.   TUFFY.   BOSTON: HOUGHTON, 1954.

FRANKLIN, GEORGE CORY.   WILD ANIMALS OF THE FIVE RIVERS
        COUNTRY.   BOSTON: HOUGHTON, 1947.

FRANKLIN, GEORGE CORY.   WILD ANIMALS OF THE SOUTHWEST.
        BOSTON: HOUGHTON, 1950.

FRANKLIN, GEORGE CORY.   WILD HORSES OF THE RIO GRANDE.
        BOSTON: HOUGHTON, 1951.

FRANKLIN, GEORGE CORY.   ZORRA.   BOSTON: HOUGHTON, 1957.

FRASER, WILLIAM MCKINLEY.   A STUDY OF THE ABILITIES
        OF SPANISH-SPEAKING AND ENGLISH-SPEAKING CHILDREN OF
        KINNEY COUNTY, TEXAS.   UNIVERSITY OF TEXAS AT AUSTIN,
        MASTER'S THESIS (1946) (LJS).

FRAZER, STEVE.   FIRST THROUGH THE GRAND CANYON.   NEW YORK:
        HOLT, 1961.

FRIBOURG.   BILL RIGHTS   (LW*).

FRIBOURG.   SUPREME COURT AMERICAN HISTORY   (LW*).

FRIEDMAN.   DIGGING INTO YESTERDAY: DISCOVERY   (AN*).

GARTHWAITE, MARION.   MARIO, A MEXICAN BOY'S ADVENTURE.
        NEW YORK: DUTTON, 1958.

GATES, DORIS. BLUE WILLOW.   NEW YORK: VIKING, 1940.

GEIS, DARLENE, ED. LET'S TRAVEL IN MEXICO.   CHILDREN'S
     PRESS, 1965.

GERSON, N. B. KIT CARSON: FOLK HERO AND MAN.   GARDEN
     CITY, NEW YORK: DOUBLEDAY, 1964 (HSW LI).

GILBERT, N. 'CHRISTMAS IN CARTHAGE.'   IN VETTER, MARJORIE
     CINTA.

GOETZ, DELIA. NEIGHBORS TO THE SOUTH.   NEW YORK:
     HARCOURT, BRACE AND WORLD, 1956.

GREENE, CARLA. MANUEL, YOUNG MEXICAN AMERICAN.   LANTERN,.

HAMPTON, DORIS. JUST FOR MANUEL.   AUSTIN: STECK-VAUGHN
     COMPANY, 1971.

HARTMIRE, WAYNE C. "FARM WORKERS ON THE FRINGE".
     CHRISTIAN CENTURY,   (JULY 29, 1964), PP. 959-962.

HIGGINS, H. B. OLD TRAILS AND NEW.   NEW YORK: FRIENDSHIP
     PRESS,.

HILLYER, V. M. AND HUEY, E. G. YOUNG PEOPLE'S STORY OF
     OUR HERITAGE. CHICAGO, ILLINOIS: CHILDRENS PRESS,
     1966.

HILLYER, V. M. AND HUEY, E. G. THE AMERICAS -- CANADA,
     MEXICO, AND SOUTH AMERICA.   CHICAGO, ILLINOIS:
     CHILDRENS PRESS,.

HITTE, KATHRYN. MEXICALI SOUP.   PARENTS,.

HOFF, CAROL. HEAD TO THE WEST.   CHICAGO: FOLLETT, 1957.

HOFF, CAROL. JOHNNY TEXAS.   CHICAGO: FOLLETT, 1950.

HOFF, CAROL. JOHNNY TEXAS ON THE SAN ANTONIO ROAD.
     CHICAGO: FOLLETT, 1953.

HOFF, CAROL. WILDERNESS PIONEER, STEPHEN F. AUSTIN
     OF TEXAS.   CHICAGO: FOLLETT, 1955.

HOLLAND, RUTH. FORGOTTEN MINORITY: AMERICA'S TENANT
     FARMERS AND MIGRANT FARM WORKERS.   CROWELL COLLIER,
     1970 (EC).

HOLMAN, ROSEMARY. SPANISH NUGGETS.   SAN ANTONIO: NAYLOR,
     1968.

HOLT, STEPHEN. WE WERE THERE WITH THE CALIFORNIA RANCHEROS.
     NEW YORK: GROSSET,.

HOOD, FLORA M. ONE LUMINARIA FOR ANTONIO: A STORY OF NEW
    MEXICO. NEW YORK: PUTNAM,.

HOOD, FLORA. ONE LUMINARIA FOR ANTONIO. NEW YORK:
    PUTNAM, 1966.

HOOD, MARGARET PAGE. TEQUILA. NEW YORK: COWARD-MCCANN,
    1950.

HUBP, LORETTA BURKE. WHAT CAN IT BE? QUE SERA?. NEW
    YORK: THE JOHN DAY COMPANY, 1970.

HUNTER, VICKIE AND HAMMA, ELIZABETH. STAGECOACH DAYS.
    MENLO PARK, CALIFORNIA: LANE PUBLISHING COMPANY, 1963.

JEAN MARIE. "THE STORY OF PEDRO" (EC*).

JENKINS, MILDRED. BEFORE THE WHITE MAN CAME. PORTLAND,
    OREGON: BINFORDS AND MORT, PUBLISHERS,.

JOHNSON, SIDDLE JOE. TEXAS, THE LAND OF THE TEJAS. NEW
    YORK: RANDOM HOUSE, 1943.

JOHNSON, WILLIAM W. THE BIRTH OF TEXAS. NEW YORK:
    HOUGHTON-MIFFLIN, 1960.

JOHNSON. SAM HOUSTON, TALLEST TEXAN (HT*).

KRUMGOLD, JOSEPH. AND NOW MIGUEL. NEW YORK: CROWELL,.

KRUMGOLD, JOSEPH. AND NOW MIGUEL. NEW YORK: CROWELL,
    1953.

LADD, ILETA KERR. SEEING TEXAS. DALLAS: MATHIS VAN NORT,
    1943.

LAMPMAN, EVELYN SIBLEY. THE BANDIT OF MOK HILL. GARDEN
    CITY, NEW YORK: DOUBLEDAY AND COMPANY, INC., 1969.

LENSKI. GRANJA PEQUENA (LJS*).

LENSKI. PAPA PEQUENO: PAPA SMALL (LJS*).

LENSKI. VAQUERO PEQUENO: COWBOY SMALL (LJS*).

LENSKI, LOIS. WE LIVE IN THE SOUTHWEST. PHILADELPHIA,
    PENNSYLVANIA: LIPPINCOTT,.

LEWITON, MINA. JOSE'S CHRISTMAS SECRET. DIAL PRESS, 1963.

LEWITON, MINA. THAT BAD CARLOS. NEW YORK: HARPER, 1964.

LEXAN, JOAN. LEY DE MIGRACION DE LOS ESTADOS UNIDOS
    MEXICANOS. MEXICO: TALLERES GRAFICOS DE LA NACION,
    1926.

LEXAN, JOAN. MARIA.   DIAL PRESS, 1964.

LOCKWOOD, MYNA. UP WITH YOUR BANNER.   NEW YORK: DUTTON,
    1943.

MACLEOD, RUTH. BUENOS DIAS TEACHER.   MESSNER,.

MARSHALL, HELEN LAUGHLIN. NEW MEXICAN BOV.   NEW YORK:
    HOLIDAY HOUSE, 1940.

MARTIN, PATRICIA MILES. TINA'S BOXCAR.   NEW YORK:
    ABINGDON PRESS, 1967.

MAUZEY, MERRITT. OILFIELD BOY.   NEW YORK: ABELARD—SCHUMAN,
    1957.

MAUZEY, MERRITT. TEXAS RANCH BOY.   NEW YORK: ABELARD—SCHUMAN,
    1955.

MC CALL, EDITH. COWBOYS AND CATTLE DRIVES.   CHICAGO,
    ILLINOIS: CHILDRENS PRESS, 1964.

MC CALL, EDITH. CUMBERLAND GAP AND TRAILS WEST.   CHICAGO,
    ILLINOIS: CHILDRENS PRESS, 1961.

MC CALL, EDITH. EXPLORERS IN A NEW WORLD.   CHICAGO,
    ILLINOIS: CHILDRENS PRESS, 1960.

MC CALL, EDITH. FORTS IN THE WILDERNESS.   CHICAGO,
    ILLINOIS: CHILDRENS PRESS, 1968.

MC CALL, EDITH. HEROES OF THE WESTERN OUTPOSTS.   CHICAGO,
    ILLINOIS: CHILDRENS PRESS, 1960.

MC CALL, EDITH. HUNTERS BLAZE THE TRAILS.   CHICAGO,
    ILLINOIS: CHILDRENS PRESS, 1959.

MC CALL, EDITH. LOG FORT ADVENTURES.   CHICAGO, ILLINOIS:
    CHILDRENS PRESS, 1958.

MC CALL, EDITH. MAIL RIDERS.   CHICAGO, ILLINOIS:
    CHILDRENS PRESS, 1961.

MC CALL, EDITH. MEN ON IRON HORSES.   CHICAGO, ILLINOIS:
    CHILDRENS PRESS, 1960.

MC CALL, EDITH. PIONEER SHOW FOLK.   CHICAGO, ILLINOIS:
    CHILDRENS PRESS, 1963.

MC CALL, EDITH. PIONEER TRADERS.   CHICAGO, ILLINOIS:
    CHILDRENS PRESS, 1964.

MC CALL, EDITH. PIONEERING ON THE PLAINS.   CHICAGO,
    ILLINOIS: CHILDRENS PRESS, 1962.

MC CALL, EDITH. PIONEERS ON EARLY WATERWAYS.   CHICAGO,
    ILLINOIS: CHILDRENS PRESS, 1961.

MC CALL, EDITH. PIRATES AND PRIVATEERS.   CHICAGO,
    ILLINOIS: CHILDRENS PRESS, 1963.

MC CALL, EDITH. SETTLERS ON A STRANGE SHORE.   CHICAGO,
    ILLINOIS: CHILDRENS PRESS, 1960.

MC CALL, EDITH. STALWART MEN OF EARLY TEXAS.   CHICAGO,
    ILLINOIS: CHILDRENS PRESS, 1970.

MC CALL, EDITH. STEAMBOATS TO THE WEST.   CHICAGO,
    ILLINOIS: CHILDRENS PRESS, 1959.

MC CALL, EDITH. WAGONS OVER THE MOUNTAINS.   CHICAGO,
    ILLINOIS: CHILDRENS PRESS, 1961.

MC CLARREN, J. K. MEXICAN ASSIGNMENT.   NEW YORK,
    NEW YORK: FUNK AND WAGNALLS, INC., 1957.

MC CRACKEN.   WINNING WEST (HSW*).

MC GRIFFIN, LEE. TEN TALL TEXANS.   NEW YORK: LOTHROP,
    1956.

MC GUIRE, EDNA. A BRAVE YOUNG LAND.   NEW YORK: MACMILLAN,
    1946.

MC NEER, MARY AND WARD, LYNN. THE MEXICAN STORY.   NEW
    YORK: ARIEL BOOKS, 1953.

MC NEER, MARY. THE STORY OF CALIFORNIA.   NEW YORK: HARPER
    AND ROW, 1944.

MC NEER, MAY. WAR CHIEF OF THE SEMINOLES.   NEW YORK:
    RANDOM HOUSE, 1954.

MC NEER, MAY. THE STORY OF THE SOUTHWEST.   NEW YORK:
    HARPER AND ROW, 1948.

MEADOWCRAFT, ENID LA MONTE. TEXAS STAR.   NEW YORK:
    CROWELL, 1950.

MEANS, FLORENCE C. ADELLA MARY IN OLD NEW MEXICO.
    BOSTON, MASSACHUSETTS: HOUGHTON, 1930.

MEANS, FLORENCE C. SHADOW OVER WIDE RUIN.   BOSTON,
    MASSACHUSETTS: HOUGHTON, 1942.

MEANS, FLORENCE C. TANGLED WATERS.   BOSTON, MASSACHUSETTS:
    HOUGHTON, 1936.

MEANS, FLORENCE C. TERESITA OF THE VALLEY.   BOSTON,
    MASSACHUSETTS: HOUGHTON MIFFLIN, 1943.

MEANS, FLORENCE C. WHISPERING GIRL. BOSTON, MASSACHUSETTS: HOUGHTON, 1941.

MEANS, FLORENCE CRANNELL. BUT I AM SARA. BOSTON, MASSACHUSETTS: HOUGHTON, 1961.

MEANS, P. A. SPANISH MAIN: FOCUS OF ENVY, 1492-1700. NEW YORK: GORDIAN PRESS, 1965.

MEREDITH, ROBERT, AND SMITH, E. BROOKS, <EDS>. RIDING WITH CORONADO. BOSTON: LITTLE, 1964.

MOODY, RALPH. KIT CARSON AND THE WILD FRONTIER. NEW YORK: RANDOM HOUSE, 1955.

MOODY, RALPH. RIDERS OF THE PONY EXPRESS. NEW YORK: DELL,.

OLOEFFLER, H. W. SAN ANTONIOHS MEXICAN CHILD. NEW YORK: DUTTON, 1945.

PARISH, HELEN RAND. OUR LADY OF GUADALUPE. NEW YORK: THE VIKING PRESS, 1955.

PECK, ANNE MERRIMAN. 'LUPITA AND PEDRO OF NEW MEXICO.' IN PECK, A. M., AND JOHNSON, ENID. YOUNG AMERICANS FROM MANY LANDS.

PECK, ANNE MERRIMAN. JO ANN OF THE BORDER COUNTRY. NEW YORK: DODD, 1952.

PECK, ANNE MERRIMAN. SOUTHWEST ROUNDUP. NEW YORK: DODD, 1950.

PECK, LEIGH. DON COYOTE. BOSTON: HOUGHTON, 1942.

PECK, LEIGH. PECOS BILL AND LIGHTNING. BOSTON: HOUGHTON, 1940.

PELAEZ, JILL. DONKEY TALES. ABINGDON PRESS, 1970.

PERRY. STORY TEXAS (HT*).

PLACE, MARION T. THE FIRST BOOK OF THE SANTA FE TRAIL. NEW YORK: FRANKLIN WATTS, INC., 1966.

POLITI, LEO. JUANITA. NEW YORK: SCRIBNER, 1948.

POLITI, LEO. LITO AND THE CLOWN. SCRIBNER, 1964.

POLITI, LEO. PEDRO THE ANGEL OF OLVERA ST. NEW YORK: SCRIBNER, 1946.

POLITI, LEO. ROSA. NEW YORK: SCRIBNER, 1963.

POLITI, LEO. SONG OF THE SWALLOW. NEW YORK: SCRIBNER, 1948.

POLITI, LEO.   THE MISSION BELL.   NEW YORK: SCRIBNER,.

PRICE, JOAN.   A VERY SPECIAL BURRO.   SAN ANTONIO: NAYLOR,
     1966.

PRIETO, MARIANA.   JOHNNY LOST (JUANITO PERDIDO).
     NEW YORK, NEW YORK: JOHN DAY COMPANY, INC., 1969.

PRIETO, MARIANA.   TOMATO BOY.   NEW YORK, NEW YORK: JOHN
     DAY COMPANY, INC., 1967.

PRIETO, MARIANA.   A KITE FOR CARLOS: A STORY ABOUT A LITTLE
     SPANISH-AMERICAN BOY TOLD IN ENGLISH AND SPANISH.
     NEW YORK: THE JOHN DAY COMPANY, 1966.

PRIETO, MARIANA.   THE WISE ROOSTER.   NEW YORK, NEW YORK:
     JOHN DAY COMPANY, INC., 1962.

RANSON.   TEXAS WILDFLOWER LEGENDS (HT*).

RHOADS, DOROTHY.   THE CORN GROWS RIPE.   NEW YORK: VIKING,
     1956.

RIDLER, ALEX.   WHEN WE GO TO SCHOOL: CUANDO VAMOS A
     LA ESCUELA.   FUNK AND WAGNALLS, 1967 (LJS).

RITCHIE, BARBARA.   RAMON MAKES A TRADE.   NEW YORK:
     PARNASSUS, 1959.

ROBINSON, BENELLE H.   CITIZEN PABLO.   NEW YORK: JOHN DAY,.

ROBINSON, BENNELLE.   CITIZEN PABLO.   NEW YORK: JOHN DAY,
     1959.

RYAN, CHILI DURAN.   PAZ.   NEW YORK: MACMILLAN, 1971.

SASEK, M.   THIS IS TEXAS.   NEW YORK: MACMILLAN, 1967.

SAWYER, RUTH.   THE YEAR OF THE CHRISTMAS DRAGON.
     NEW YORK: VIKING, 1960.

SCHAEFER, JACK.   OLD RAMON.   NEW YORK: HOUGHTON MIFFLIN,.

SCHWEITZER, BYRD BAYLOR.   AMIGO.   NEW YORK: HOUGHTON, 1968.

SCHWEITZER, BYRD BAYLOR.   ONE SMALL BEAD.   NEW YORK:
     MACMILLAN, 1965.

SMITH, TERESA KALAB.   PONCHO AND THE PINK HORSE.   AUSTIN:
     STECK-VAUGHN COMPANY, 1951.

SOMMERFELT, AIMEE.   MY NAME IS PABLO.   NEW YORK, NEW YORK:
     CRITERION BOOKS, 1965.

SONNEBORN.   LOLLIPOP PARTY (LI*).

SONNEBORN.   SEVEN BED   (LI*).

SPERRY, ARMSTRONG. GREAT RIVER, WIDE LAND, THE RIO GRANDE
    THROUGH HISTORY.   NEW YORK: MACMILLAN, 1967 (LI).

SPLEVACK, YETLA. SPIDER PLANT.   ATHENAUM PRESS, 1965.

STANEK, MURIEL. ANIMALS WE KNOW.   WESTCHESTER, ILLINOIS:
    BENEFIC PRESS, 1968 (LJS).

STANEK, MURIEL. COMMUNITY FRIENDS: AMIGOS DE LA COMUNIDAD.
    WESTCHESTER, ILLINOIS: BENEFIC PRESS, 1968 (LJS).

STANEK, MURIEL. I LIVE IN THE CITY: YO VIVO EN LA CIUDAD.
    WESTCHESTER, ILLINOIS: BENEFIC PRESS, 1968 (LJS).

SYME, RONALD. ZAPATA, MEXICAN REBEL.   WEST CLADWELL, NEW
    JERSEY: MORROW JUNOIR BOOKS, 1971 (HM).

TARSHIS, ELIZABETH. THE VILLAGE THAT LEARNED TO READ.
    BOSTON: HOUGHTON MIFFLIN, 1941.

TEBBEL, JOHN AND RUIZ, RAMON R. SOUTH BY SOUTHWEST: THE
    MEXICAN AMERICAN AND HIS HERITAGE.   NEW YORK: DOUBLEDAY,.

VERNE, JULIC. LOS HIJOS DEL CAPITAN GRANT.   SPAIN: BILBAO
    EDITORIAL FELICIDAD, 1964.

VOGAN.   MERRY-GO-ROUND GAMES SPANISH   (ED*).

WARREN.   INDIANS WHO LIVED TEXAS   (LI*).

WARREN.   PAPACITO HIS FAMILY   (LI*).

WARREN, BETSY. PAPACITO AND HIS FAMILY.   AUSTIN, TEXAS:
    STECK-VAUGHN,.

WARREN.   REMEMBER ALAMO   (LI*).

WATERHOUSE, E. B.   SERRA, CALIFORNIA CONQUISTADOR.   PARKER
    AND SON, INC., 1968 (HS).

WHEAT, COLLINS G.   EL MUNDO DE LAS HERMIGAS.   MEXICO:
    EDITORIAL NOVARO, 1965.

WHITNEY,.   JUAN OF PARICUTIN.   AUSTIN: STECK-VAUGHN
    COMPANY, 1953.

WILSON.   FAIRY TALES MEXICO   (AN*).

WRIGHT, FRANCES F.   SAM HOUSTON, FIGHTER AND LEADER.
    DALLAS: COKESBURY BOOK STORE, 1953 (HSW).

YOUNG, BOB AND JAN. GOOD-BYE AMIGOS.   MESSNER, 1963.

YOUNG, BOB AND YOUNG, JAN. ACROSS THE TRACKS.   MESSNER,.

YOUNG, BOB AND YOUNG, JAN. GOOD-BYE, AMIGOS.   MESSNER,.

L I T E R A T U R A   J U V E N I L

(LJS)

ADLER, IRVING. LIBROS DE ORO DEL SABER. MATEMATICAS.
MEXICO, D.F.: ORGANIZACION EDITORIAL NOVARO, S.A.,.

ADORNO FERNANDEZ, YOLANDA. CUENTAME UN CUENTO. MEXICO,
D.F.: ORGANIZACION EDITORIAL NOVARO, S.A., 1966.

ALBA, MANUEL AND LUIS GONZALES. LOS SERVIDORES PUBLICOS.
MEXICO, D.F.: FERNANDEZ EDITORES, S.A., 1967.

ALEXANDER, FRANCES. MOTHER GOOSE ON THE RIO GRANDE.
SKOKIE, ILLINOIS: NATIONAL TEXTBOOK COMPANY, 1960.

ALLEN, JOAN. SILUETAS DE ORO. CHITTY CHITTY BANG BANG.
TRANSLATED BY YOLAND ADORNO. MEXICO, D.F.:
ORGANIZACION EDITORIAL NOVARO, S.A.,, 1969.

ALMENDROS, H., AND FRANCISCO ALVERC. ABC LEO Y ESCRIBO.
CIUDAD DE GUATEMALA, GUATEMALA: CULTURAL CENTROAMERICANA,
S.A., 1965.

LJS
WHEAT, G. COLLINS. UTILIDAD Y PRODUCTO DE LOS
ANIMALES   LIBROS
DE ORO DEL SABER. EL MUNDO DE LAS HORMIGAS.   BILBAO,
ESPANA: EDITORIAL VASCO AMERICANA, 1968.

ABC DE LA NATURALEZA. BILBAO, ESPANA: EDITORIAL VASCO
AMERICANA, S. A., 1963.

BEGINNING TO READ SPANISH BOOKS. CHICAGO, ILL.: FOLLETT
PUBLISHING COMPANY, 1960.

BIBLIOTECA CULTURAL. BILBAO, ESPANA: EDITORIAL VASCO
AMERICANA, S.A., 1968.

CANCIONES DE NAVIDAD. COMPILED AND ADAPTED BY INA RAMBOZ
AND J.C. FREMONT. SKOKIE, ILL.: NATIONAL TEXTBOOK
CO., 1955.

COLCOLECCION ANIMALES FELICES. BILBAO, ESPANA: EDITORIAL
FHER, S.A,.

COLECCION ABECEDARIO. BILBAO, ESPANA: EDTORIAL VASCO
AMERICANA, S.A,.

COLECCION ERASE UNA VEZ. BILBAO, ESPANA: EDITORIAL FHER,
1964.

COLECCION FANTASIAS EVA.   BILBAO, ESPANA: EDITORIAL VASCO
     AMERICANA, S.A.,.

COLECCION FELICIDAD EN LA GRANJA.   BILBAO, ESPANA:
     EDITORIAL FHER, 1965.

COLECCION GRANDES ALBUMES EVA.   BILBAO, ESPANA: EDITORIAL
     VASCO AMERICANA, S.A.,.

COLECCION MINI EVA.   BILBAO, ESPANA: EDITORIAL VASCO
     AMERICANA, S.A., 1966.

COLECCION MIS ANIMALITOS.   BILBAO, ESPANA: EDITORIAL
     VASCO AMERICANA, L.A,.

COLECCION PARAISO.   BILBAO, ESPANA: EDITORIAL VASCO
     AMERICANA, S.A,.

COLECCION PEQUENOS ALBUMES EVA.   BILBAO, ESPANA:
     EDITORIAL VASCO AMERICANA, S.A,.

COLECCION PRIMERAS LETRAS.   BARCELONA, ESPANA: EDITORIAL
     MOLINO, 1963.

COLEDDION OFICIOS Y ANIMALES.   BILBAO, ESPANA: EDITORIAL
     VASCO AMERICANA, S. A., 1967.

CUENTAME UN CUENTO.   MEXICO, D.F.:   ORGANIZACION EDITORIAL
     NOVARO, S.A.,.

CUENTAME UN CUENTO.   MEXICO, D.F.:   ORGANIZACION EDITORIAL
     NOVARO, S.A,.

CUENTO: ABECEDARIO.   BILBAO, ESPANA: EDITORIAL FHER,
     S.A.,.

CUENTOS DE ILUSION.   BILBAO, ESPANA: EDITORIAL VASCO
     AMERICANA, 1966.

CUENTOS INMORTALES.   BILBAO, ESPANA: EDITORIAL VASCO
     AMERICANA, S.A., 1964.

CUENTOS PARA LEER Y ESCRIBIR.   SALAMANCA, ESPANA:
     EDICIONES ANAYA, S.A., 1967.

CUENTOS PARA NINOS.   BILBAO, ESPANA. EDITORIAL CANTABRICA,
     S.A., 1963.

DIVIERTETE CON PAPEL.   MEXICO, D.F.:   EDITORA TECNICA,
     1968.

ELENA Y DANI.   CIUDAD DE GUATEMALA, GUATEMALA: CULTURAL
     CENTROAMERICANA, S.A.,.

ENCICLOPEDIA EN COLORES.   BARCELONA, ESPANA: EDITORIAL
     TIMUN MAS, 1961.

ENCICLOPEDIA DE ORO.   MEXICO, D. F.: ORGANIZACION
    EDITORIAL NOVARO, S. A.,.

ENCICLOPEDIA EN COLORES.   BARCELONA, ESPANA: EDITORIAL
    TIMUN MAS, 1961.

ETS, MARIE HALL. GILBERTO Y EL VIENTO.   TRANSLATED BY A.
    LABASTIDA. NEW YORK: VIKING PRESS, INC.,, 1967.

FAVORITE SPANISH FOLKSONGS.   COMPILED AND EDITED BY ELENA
    PAZ. NEW YORK: OAK PUBLICATIONS, 1965.

GOLDILOCKS Y LOS TRES OSOS Y OTROS CUENTROS.   RETOLD BY
    HELEN HARTER. SKOKIE, ILL.: NATIONAL TEXBOOK CORP.,,
    1955.

JOYA INFANTIL.   ESPANA: EDITORIAL CULTURA Y PROGRESO,
    S.A.,.

KENWORTHY'S LAGUNA LANGUAGE SERIES.   ADAPTED AND DEVELOPED
    BY HANNA HUTCHINSON AND JOSE ELGORRIA,.

LANGUAGE THROUGH SONGS. CANTEMOS EN ESPANOL.   ARRANGED
    AND EDITED BY BEATRICE AND MAX KRONE. PARK RIDGE,
    ILL.: NEIL A. KJOS MUSIC CO., 1961.

LANGUAGE THROUGH SONGS. CANTEMOS NONOS.   ARRANGED
    BY BEATRICE AND MAX KRONE. PARK RIDGE, ILL.: NEIL
    A. KJOS MUSIC CO., 1961.

LAS SIETE BOLAS DE CRISTAL.   NEW YORK: FRENCH AND
    EUROPEAN PUBLICATIONS, INC.,, 1961.

LENGUA ESPANOLA.   CIUDAD DE GUATEMALA, GUATEMALA:
    CULTURAL CENTROAMERICANA, S.A., 1968.

LINEA INFANTI.   ADAPTED FROM WALT DISNEY PRODUCTIONS.
    BILBAO, ESPANA: EDITORIAL FHER, 1967.

LOS DIEZ PERRITOS.   BARCELONA, ESPANA: EDITORIAL MOLINO,
    1962.

MEXICAN FOLKSONGS — CANCIONES DE MEXICO.   ARRANGED AND
    TRANSLATED BY BEATRICE AND MAX KRONE. PARK RIDGE,
    ILL.: NEIL A. KJOS MUSIC CO., 1948.

MIS PRIMEROS CONOCIMIENTOS.   NEW YORK: GROLIER, INC., 1969.

MIS PRIMERAS LETRAS.   MEXICO, D.F.: EDITORIAL F. TRILLAS,
    S.A., 1969.

NUBE ROSA Y ROSA DE MAYO.   BILBAO, ESPANA: EDITORIAL FHER,
    1965.

PEQUENO LAROUSSE ILUSTRADO.   BUENOS AIRES, ARGENTINA:
    EDITORIAL LAROUSSE, 1965.

PEQUENOS LIBROS DE ORO.   MEXICO, D.F.: ORGANIZACION
     EDITORIAL NOVARO, S.A., 1966.

PEQUENOS GRANDES CUENTOS. BLANCA NIEVES Y LOS SIETE ENANOS
     EN FELIZ CUMPEANOS.   ADAPTED BY OTTO RAUL GONZALES.
     MEXICO D.F.: ORGANIZACION EDITORIAL NOARO, S.A.,,
     1966.

POLLITOS Y PATITOS.   BARCELONA, ESPANA: EDITORIAL MOLINO,
     1961.

PREGUNTAS Y REPUESTAS SOBRE CIENCIA.   BUENOS AIRES,
     ARGENTINA: EDITORIAL SIGMAR, S.A.C.,.

PULGARCITO.   BILBAO, ESPANA: EDITORIAL FHER, 1967.

SERIE ABECEDARIOS.   BILBAO, ESPANA: EDITORIAL CANTABRICA,
     S.A., 1962.

SERIE ANIMALES TRAVIESOS.   BILBAO, ESPANA: EDITORIAL
     VASCO AMERICANA, S.A, 1964.

SERIE DE CUENTOS CHIQUI.   BARCELONA, ESPANA: EDITORIAL
     ROMA,.

SERIE NUEVA DE TEXTO. ME ESCUELA (GRADE TWO).   CIUDAD DE
     GUATEMALA, GUATEMALA: CULTURAL CENTROAMERICANA, S.A.,.

SILUETAS DE ORO. EL RATON MICKEY.   TRANSLATED BY LUIS
     GUZMAN FLORES. MEXICO, D.F.: ORGANIZACION EDITORIAL
     NOVARO, S.A.,, 1969.

SILUETAS DE ORO. LAS PELOTAS.   TRANSLATED BY MARIA LUISA
     PUGA M. MEXICO, D.F.: ORGANIZACION EDITORIAL NOVARO,
     S.A.,.

SILUETAS DE ORO. WALT DISNEY PRESENTA: EL LIBRO DE
     LA SELVA.   MEXICO, D.F.: ORGANIZACION EDITORIAL
     NOVARO, S.A.,, 1967.

SILUETAS DE ORO. LOS PECES.   TRANSLATED BY JUAN JOSE
     UTRILLA. MEXICO, D.F.: ORGANIZACION EDITORIAL NOVARO,
     S.A.,, 1967.

SILUETAS DE ORO. LOS PERROS.   TRANSLATED BY GUADALUPE
     CORDERO LEON. MEXICO, D.F.: ORGANIZACION EDITORIAL
     NOVARO, S.A., 1966.

TESORO INFANTIL.   BILBAO, ESPANA: EDITORIAL CULTURA Y
     PROGRESO, S.A, 1968.

EL CARRO VERDE.   MADRID, ESPANA: EDITORIAL MAGISTERIO
     ESPANOL, S. A.,.

EL CARRO VERDE.   MADRID, ESPANA: EDITORIAL MAGISTERIO
     ESPANOL, S.A.,.

EL GLOBO DE COLORES. LA FAMILIA.   MADRID, ESPANA:
     AGUILAR, S.A. DE EDICIONES, 1966.

EL GLOBO DE COLORES. LAS HORAS DEL DIA.   MADRID, ESPANA:
     AGUILAR, S. A. DE EDICIONES, 1967.

EL GLOBO DE COLORES. JUGAR Y CANTAR (SECOND EDITION).
     MADRID, ESPANA: AGUILAR, S.A. DE EDICIONES, 1961.

EL GLOBO DE COLORES. LA FAMILIA.   MADRID, ESPANA:
     AGUILAR, S.A. DE EDICIONES, 1966.

EL GLOBO DE COLORES. LA TIERRA.   MADRID, ESPANA: AGUILAR,
     S.A. DE ECICIONES, 1958.

EL GLOBO DE COLORES. LOS VEHICULOS.   MADRID, ESPANA:
     AGUILAR, S.A. DE EDICIONES, 1967.

EL SOLDADITO DE PLOMO.   BILBAO, ESPANA: EDITORIAL FHER,
     1967.

A WORLD IN TUNE FOLKSONGS OF OUR INTERAMERICANA SOUTHERN
     NEIGHBCRS.   ARRANGEC BY BEATRICE AND MAX KRONE. PARK
     RIDGE, ILL.: NEIL A. KJOS MUSIC CO., 1945.

ARCE, MANUEL (ED). NUEVOS CAMINOS.   GUATEMALA: ALIANZA,
     1964.

ARGUELLOS LOPEZ, JOSEFINA. EJERCICIOS DE LENGUAJE.
     MEXICO, D.F.: HERRERO HERMANOS, SUCS., S.A., 1960.

ARRECHEA RODRIGUEZ, ELIO. NUESTRO MUNDO.   CARACAS,
     VENEZUELA: EDICIONES CULTURAL VENEZOLANA, S. A., 1965.

ARROYO DEL CASTILLO, VICTORINO AND GIRON, ALBERTO FERNANDEZ.
     LECTURAS JUVENILES DE ESPANA Y AMERICA.   MADRID,
     ESPANA: EDICIONES ANAYA, S. A., 1968.

BABCOCK, EDNA E., HELEN KWAPIL, AND EDITH ANN BACH (EDS).
     CHILDREN OF THE AMERICAS SPANISH SERIES.   SAN
     FRANCISCO: HARR WAGNER PUBLISHING CO., 1959.

BABCOCK, EDNA E., HELEN KWAPIL, ANC ECITH ANN BACH (EDS).
     CHILDREN OF THE AMERICAS SPANISH SERIES.   SAN
     FRANCISCO: HARR WAGNER PUBLISHING CO., 1959.

BAEZ, SERGIO MADERO. BOMBON QUISE SER ARTISTA.   MEXICO:
     EDITORIAL NOVARO, 1962.

BAEZ, SERGIO MADERO. CANTA PAJARITC.   MEXICC: EDITORIAL
     NOVARO, 1959.

BARDASANO. LA BANDERA DE MEXICO.   MEXICO, D.F.:
     FERNANDEZ EDITORES,.

BARNETT, HARRIET, AND BETTY M. BARLOW (EDS). HOLA VAMOS
     A CANTAR.   DELAWARE WATER GAP, PA.: SHAWNEE PRESS,
     INC.,.

BASURTO, CARMEN G. ARITMETICA ILUSTRADA.   MEXICO, D.F.:
     EDITORIAL TRILLAS, S.A., 1968.

BASURTO, CARMEN G. ESCRITURA MUSCULAR ILUSTRADA.   MEXICO,
     D.F.: EDITORIAL F. TRILLAS, S.A., 1968.

BASURTO, CARMEN G. MIS PRIMERAS LETRAS.   MEXICO, D. F.:
     EDITORIAL F. TRILLAS, S. A., 1967.

BASURTO, CARMEN. LIBRO DE CONOCIMIENTOS GENERALES.
     MEXICO, D. F.: EDITORIAL PATRIA, S. A., 1958.

BEAUCHAMP, WILBUR R. (ET AL). MI PRIMER LIBRO DE CIENCIAS.
     MEDELLIN, COLOMBIA: EDITORIAL BEDOUT, 1961.

BEAUCHAMP, WILBUR R. (ET AL). MI SEGUNDO LIBRO DE
     CIENCIAS.   MEDELLIN, COLOMBIA: EDITORIAL BEDOUT, 1961.

BEDFORD.   ROY ROGERS NUEVO COWBOY (LI*).

BELPRE, PURA. PEREZ Y MARTINA (REVISED EDITION).   NEW
     YORK: FREDERICK WARNE & CO., INC.,, 1966.

BENTON, WILLIAM (ED). ENCICLOPEDIA BARSA DE CONSULTA
     FACIL.   CHICAGO, ILLINOIS: ENCYCLOPEDIA BRITANNICA,
     INC., 1964.

BERLITZ SCHOOLS OF LANGUAGES OF AMERICA. BERLITZ SPANISH
     ALPHABET AND NUMBERS FOR CHILDREN AND BERLITZ SPANISH
     ZOO ANIMALS. NEW YORK: GROSSET,.

BERLITZ, C. AND STRUMPEN-DARRIE, ROBERT (EDS). BERLITZ
     SPANISH ZOO ANIMALS FOR CHILDREN. NEW YORK: GROSSET
     AND DUNLAP, INC., 1963.

BINDER, OTTO. LIBROS DE ORO DEL SABER. LA LUNA.   DOLORES
     B. DE ROBLES (TRANS). MEXICO, D. F.: ORGANIZACION
     EDITORIAL NOVARO, S. A., 1967.

BINDER, OTTO. UN LIBRO DE ORO DE ESTAMPAS: REACTORES Y
     COHETES DEL ESPACIO.   MEXICO: EDITORIAL NOVARO, 1962.

BINDER, OTTO. LA LUNA.   MEXICO: EDITORIAL NOVARO, 1965.

BLACKWOOD, PAUL (ED). COMO Y PORQUE DE.   BARCELONA,
     ESPANA: EDITORIAL MOLINO,.

BLANCO, CAROLINA (ET AL). LOS PRIMEROS PASOS ARITMETICA.
     ILLINOIS: RIVER FOREST, 1961.

BLOUGH, GLENN O. EL ACURARIO.   EVANSTON, ILLINOIS: HARPER
     AND ROW, 1961.

BOLINAGA, JOSEFINA. SOLO PARA NINAS.   MADRID, ESPANA:
     AGUILAR, S. A. DE EDICIONES, 1959.

BONSALL, CROSBY N. EL CASO DEL FORASTERO HAMBRIENTO.
     NEW YORK: HARPER,.

BORDEN, MARION. CUENTAME UN CUENTO.   MEXICO, D.F.:
     ORGANIZACION EDITORIAL NOVARO, S.A., 1966.

BRACHO, HAYDEE. PABLO Y TAMBORIN.   VENEZUELA: ALIANXA,
     1962.

BRANLEY, FRANKLYN M. COMO ES LA LUNA?.   NEW YORK: CROWELL,.

BRANLEY, FRANKLYN. COMO ES LA LUNA?.   NEW YORK: THOMAS
     V. CROWELL, 1968.

BRANLEY, FRANKLYN. LEAMOS Y AVERICUEMOS. COMO ES LA LUNA?.
     R. J. PALMERO (TRANS). NEW YORK: THOMAS Y. CROWELL
     COMPANY, 1968.

BRIDGES, WILLIAM. UN LIBRO DE ORO DE ESTAMPAS: ANECTODAS
     DEL ZOOLOGICO.   MEXICO: NOVARO, 1963.

BRIGHT, ROBERT. MI PARAQUAS ROJO.   NEW YORK: MORROW,.

BRULAT, MARIA ALBA DELOR. LA GRANJA BLANCA.   PARAGUAY:
     MINISTERIO DE EDUCACION Y CULTO, 1961.

BRUNHOFF, JEAN DE. BARBAR Y EL PAPA NOEL.   SPAIN:
     EDITORIAL AYMA, 1965.

BRUNHOFF, JEAN DE. EL REY BABAR.   SPAIN: EDITORIAL AYMA,
     1964.

BRUNHOFF, LAURENT DE. BABAR'S SPANISH LESSONS.   NEW YORK:
     RANDOM,.

BUETTNER, CARL. PIXIE, DIXIE Y EL SR. JINX.   MEXICO:
     EDITORIAL NOVARO, 1963.

BUETTNER, CARL. EL PAJARO LOCO ENSENA A DIBUJAR.   MEXICO:
     EDITORIAL NOVARO, 1962.

BUETTNER, CARL. EL PAJARO LOCO.   MEXICO: EDITORIAL
     NOVARO, 1962.

BURNETT, JANE. CRUCIGRAMAS PARA ESTUDIANTES.   SKOKIE,
     ILLINOIS: NATIONAL TEXTBOOK COMPANY, 1965.

CABALLERO, ARQUIMEDES, LORENZO MARTINEZ, AND JESUS
     BERNARDEZ (EDS). CUADERNOS MATEMATICOS ALFA.
     EJERCICIOS DE ARITMETICA GEOMETRIA.   MEXICO, D.F.:
     EDITORIAL ESFINGE, S.A., 1965.

CAMARILLO Y ROA, VCA. DE PEREYRA, MARIA ENRIQUETA (EDS).
    ROSAS DE LA INFANCIA.   MEXICO, D.F.:   EDITORIAL
    PATRIA, S.A.,.

CAMINO, GUMERSINDA FERNANDEZ DE, AND MIREYA AVILA DE
    PIMENTAL (EDS).   CUADERNOA GADER ARITMETICA Y
    GEOMETRIA.   MEXICO, D.F.:   ENRIQUE SAINZ EDITORES,
    S.A., 1969.

CARNEIRO, ANTONIO.   CAMELLAS Y BEDUINOS.   MEXICO:EDITORIAL
    NOVARO,.

CARNEIRO, ANTONIO.   CLEOPATRA VII, REINA DE EGIPTO.
    MEXICO:EDITORIAL NOVARO,.

CARNEIRO, ANTONIO.   LOS DINOSAURIOS.   MEXICO:EDITORIAL
    NOVARO,.

CARNEIRO, ANTONIO.   PRINCIPIO Y EVOLUTION DE LA VIDA.
    MEXICO: NOVARO, 1962.

CARNEIRO, ANTONIO.   VIDA SUBMARINE: PROTOZOOS, MEDUSAS Y
    SIFONOFOROS.   MEXICO:EDITORIAL NOVARO, 1962.

CARNEIRO, ANTONIO.   DEL PEZ AL HOMBRE.   MEXICO:EDITORIAL
    NOVARO,.

CARR, ARCHIE.   COLECCION DE LA NATURALEZA DE LIFE.
    LOS REPTILES.   NEW YORK: TIME-LIFE BOOKS, 1968.

CARRANZA, F. J.   ENCICLOPEDIA ESCOLAR MEXICANA.   MEXICO,
    D. F.: EDITORIAL AVANTE S. DE R. L., 1969.

CARROLL, LEWIS.   ADVENTURAS DE ALICIA EN EL PAIS DE
    LA MARAVILLA.   BUENOS AIRES, ARGENTINA: CASA JACOBO
    PEUSER, 1960.

CARTILLA FONETICA.   BILBAO, ESPANA: EDITORIAL VASCO
    AMERICANA, 1965.

CASADO, LISARDO, AND JOSE MATA HONORIO MURO (EDS).
    AVENTURA DEL LENGUAJE.   MADRID, ESPANA: EDITORIAL
    MAGISTERIO ESPANOL, 1967.

CLEVELAND, CATHERINE CAROLINE.   THE GREAT REVIVAL IN THE
    WEST, 1797-1801.   CHICAGO, ILLINOIS: THE UNIVERSITY
    OF CHICAGO PRESS, 1916.

CONNOR, SEYMOUR V.   BUFFALO BILL.   SPAIN: EDITORIAL
    FELICIDAD, 1964.

CONTRERAS, A. RUBIO.   APRENDE I..   GUADALAJARA, JALISCO,
    MEXICO: EL ESTUDIANTE, S.A, 1952.

COOKE, DAVID.   TRANSPORTES DE AYER Y DE HOY.   MEXICO:
    NOVARO, 1958.

COOPER, LEE P. FUN WITH SPANISH. BOSTON, MASSACHUSETTS:
    LITTLE,.

COOPER, LEE P. MORE FUN WITH SPANISH.   BOSTON, MASSACHUSETTS:
    LITTLE,.

COOPER, LEE. FUN WITH SPANISH.   BOSTON, MASSACHUSETTS:
    LITTLE, BROWN AND COMPANY, 1960.

CORTEZ, HAYDEE BRACHO. ROSA Y SU GALLINA.   COLORADO:
    VENEZUELA, ALIANZA, 1967.

COSSIO, SARA SCTA DE. LA MATEMATICA MODERNA.   BILBAO,
    ESPANA: EDITORIAL VASCO AMERICANA, S.A.,.

COTS, JORGE. LA GALERA DE ORO. EL ABETO VALIENTE.
    BARCELONA, ESPANA: EDICIONES LA GALERA, 1966.

COUGHRAN, MABEL HARRIS. HORAS ENCANTADAS.   SKOKIE,
    ILLINOIS: NATIONAL TEXTBOOK COMPANY, 1963.

CRAWFORD, MEL. SILUETAS DE ORO. BAMB.   EDITED BY MARIA
    LUISA PUGA M. MEXICO, D.F.: ORGANIZACION EDITORIAL
    NOVARO, S.A.,, 1967.

CRUME, MARION. CUE DICES?.   BOWMAR,.

CURRY, NANCY. LA MANZANA ES ROJA.   BOWMAR,.

CURRY, NANCY. LA SENORA JONES ES MI AMIGA.   BOWMAR,.

CUYAS, ARTURO. NEW APPLETON-CUYAS DICTIONARY--ENGLISH-SPANISH
    AND SPANISH-ENGLISH.   ERNESTO G. DA CAL, ET EL (ED).
    NEW YORK: APPLETON CENTURY, 1964.

D'AMATO, JANET; D'AMATO, ALEX. EL CONEJITO MATO.   MEXICO,
    D.F.: EDITORIAL NOVARO, 1964.

DAROQUI, JULIA AND RODOLFO, DAN. MI PRIMER DICCIONARIO.
    BUENOS AIRES, ARGENTINA: EDITORIAL SIGMAR, S. A. C.,
    1953.

DAROQUI, JULIA. FABULAS.   BUENOS AIRES, ARGENTINA:
    EDITORIAL SIGMAR, S.A.C.,, 1963.

DAROQUI, JULIA. LEYENDAS UNIVERSALES.   BUENOS AIRES,
    ARGENTINA: EDITORIAL SIGMAR, 1961.

DAROQUI, JULIA. LEYENDAS UNIVERSALES.   BUENOS AIRES,
    ARGENTINA: EDITORIAL SIGMAR, 1961.

DAVIS, DAPHNE. SILUETAS DE ORO. EL PATO DONALD. TRANSLATED
    BY LUIS GUZMAN FLORES.   MEXICO, D.F.: ORGANIZACION
    EDITORIAL NOVARO, S.A.,, 1966.

DE BRUNHOFF, L. BARBAR EN GLOBO.   BARCELONA, ESPANA:
     AYMA, S.A. EDITORA, 1964.

DE CAMP, L. SPRAGUE. LIBROS DE ORO DEL SABER. ENERGIA Y
     POTENCIA.   MEXICO, D. F.: ORGANIZACION EDITORIAL
     NOVARO, S. A., 1967.

DE CAMP, L. SPRAGUE. LIBROS DE ORO DEL SABER. MOTORES.
     MEXICO, D. F.: ORGANIZACION EDITORIAL NOVARO, S. A.,
     1967.

DE LA ORDEN, ARTURO, AND JAIME ACEBRON. EL MUNDO DE LOS
     NUMEROS, PRIMER CURSO.   SALAMANCA, ESPANA: EDICIONES
     ANAYA, S.A., 1966.

DEDIAZ, MARIA LUZ B. EL MUCHACHO DEL CIRCO.   MEXICO:
     EDITORIAL NOVARO, 1964.

DEFOE, DANIEL. ROBINSON CARUSOE.   MADRID: EDITORIAL
     FELICIDAD, 1961.

DEL CARMEN, MARIA. ALEGRE COMIENZO (GRADE ONE).   MEXICO,
     D.F.: EDITORIAL PATRIA, S.A., 1962.

DEL REY, LESTER. LIBROS DE ORO DEL SABER. VUELOS ESPACIALES.
     MEXICO, D. F.: ORGANIZACION EDITORIAL NOVARO, S. A.,
     1967.

DELABESSE, THELMA. EL ARBOL CHICO.   MADRID, ESPANA:
     AGUILAR, S.A. DE EDICIONES, 1968.

DELABESSE, THELMA. EL ARBOL CHICO.   MADRID, ESPANA:
     AGUILAR, S.A. DE EDICIONES, 1968.

DELAGE, NATALIE. LOS BARCOS Y LA AVENTURA.   BARCELONA,
     ESPANA: EDITORIAL TIMUN MAS,.

DELGADILLO, DANIEL. LEO Y ESCRIBO.   MEXICO, D.F.:
     HERRERO HERMANOS, SUCS., S.A., 1968.

DESTUET, LUIS. COLECCION ESTRELLA. GAUCHOS Y GAUCHITOS.
     BUENOS AIRES, ARGENTINA: EDITORIAL SIGMAR, 1964.

DIANA, EDITORIAL. LOS QILANES DE LA LITERATURA INFANTILE.
     MEXICO: EDITORIAL DIANA, 1964.

DIAZ-PLAJA, AURORA. LA RUTA DEL SOL.   BARCELONA, ESPANA:
     EDICAIONES LA GALERA, 1965.

DIMNA, DEL CALILA E. AND OTHERS. ADIOS CORDERA Y OTROS
     CUENTOS ESPANOLES.   MEXICO: EDITORIAL RENACIMIENTO,
     1962.

DISNEY, WALT
     DISNEY, WALT. AVENTURAS DE LA VIDA REAL. EL DESIERTO
     VIVIENTE.   MEXICO, D. F.: FERNANDEZ EDITORES, S. A.,.

DISNEY, WALT. AVENTURAS DE LA VIDA REAL. UN SOLAR DE LA
     NATURALEZA.   MEXICO, D. F.: FERNANDEZ EDITORES, S.
     A.,.

DISNEY, WALT. BLANCA NIEVES Y LOS SIETE ENANOS..   MEXICO,
     D.F.: ORGANIZACION EDITORIAL NOVARO MEXICO, S.A.,,
     1950.

DISNEY, WALT. LA PRADERA DEL PASADO.   ADAPTED BY JANE
     WERNER WATSON. MEXICO, D.F.: FERNANDEZ EDITORES,
     S.A., 1962.

DUMAS, ALEJANDRO. LOS TRES MOSQUETEROS.   SPAIN:
     EDITORIAL FELICIDAD, 1964.

DUPLAIX, LILY. PEDRO, NINA AND PERRITO.   NEW YORK, NEW
     YORK: HARPER, 1939.

DUPLAIX, LILY. EL CONEJITO BLANCO.   MEXICO: EDITORIAL
     NOVARO, 1963.

DUPRE, RAMONA D. DEMASIADOS PERROS.   CHICAGO, ILLINOIS:
     FOLLET PUBLISHING COMPANY, 1960.

EASTMAN, P.D. SPANISH BEGINNER BOOKS. ERES TU MI MAMA?.
     TRANSLATED BY CARLOS RIVERA. NEW YORK: RANDOM HOUSE,,
     1967.

EASTMAN, PHILIP T. AND GEISEL, THEODOR S. EL GATO
     ENSOMBRERADO.   NEW YORK: RANDOM,.

EDITORIAL FELICIDAD. MARCO POLO.   SPAIN, 1964.

EDITORIAL FHER. COLECCION CUENTOS DE HADAS FANISSAS.
     SPAIN: EDITORIAL FHER, 1964.

EDITORIAL FHER. COLECCION FANTASIAS ORIENTALES.   SPAIN:
     EDITORIAL FHER, 1964.

EPSTEIN, SAM AND BERYL. ELECTRICIDAD.   MEXICO, D. F.:
     COMPANIA GENERAL DE EDICIONES, A. S., 1963.

ESPINA, ANTONIO. EL LIBRO DE LAS MONTANAS; EL LIBRO DEL
     AIRE.   MADRID, ESPANA: AGUILAR, S.A. DE EDICIONES,
     1958.

ETS, MARIE H. GILBERTO Y EL VIENTO.   NEW YORK: VIKING,.

FEDERICO, HELEN. PRIMEROS LIBROS DE ORO. LOS NUMEROS.
     MEXICO, D.F.: ORGANIZACION EDITORIAL NOVARO, S.A.,
     1966.

FEDERICO, HELEN. SILUETAS DE ORO. EL SOL.   MARIA LUISA
    PUGA M. (TRANS). MEXICO, D. F.: ORGANIZACION EDITORIAL
    NOVARO, S. A., 1967.

FERAVOLO, ROCCO V. AGUA, AIRE Y CALOR.   MEXICO, D. F.:
    EDITORA TECNICA, S. A., 1966.

FICHTER, GEORGE S. LIBROS DE ORO DEL SABER. ANIMALES QUE
    VUELAN.   MEXICO, D. F.: ORGANIZACION EDITORIAL
    NOVARO, S. A., 1967.

FICHTER, GEORGE S. LIBROS DE ORO DEL SABER. LA VIDA DE
    LOS PECES.   MEXICO, D. F.: ORGANIZACION EDITORIAL
    NOVARO, S. A., 1967.

FICHTER, GEORGE S. LIBROS DE ORO DEL SABER. LA VIDA DE
    LOS REPTILES.   MEXICO, D. F.: ORGANIZACION EDITORIAL
    NOVARO, S. A., 1967.

FLAMMARION, ERNESTO. EL LIBRO DE LOS ANIMALES ENEANTADOS.
    MEXICO: RENACIMIENTO, 1962.

FLOURNOY, F., AND OTHERS. PROGRAMA DE MATEMATICA.
    TRANSLATED BY CARMEN S. SANGUINETTI NEW YORK: HOLT,
    RINEHART AND WINSTON, ENC., 1968.

FONTANELLI, G. FALZONE. COLECCION RAFAEL. EL OSITO
    ESQUIADOR.   MEXICO, D.F.: EDITORA CULTURAL Y
    EDUCATIVA, N.D.,.

FONTENEAU, M. AND THEUREAU, S. (EDS). MI PRIMER LAROUSSE
    EN COLORES.   BUENOS AIRES ARGENTINA: EDITORIAL
    LAROUSSE, 1967.

FORTUN, ELENA. EL GLOBO DE COLORES. EL BAZAR DE TODAS LAS
    COSAS.   MADRID, ESPANA: AQUILAS, S. A. DE EDICIONES,
    1959.

FRANCOIS, AUDRE. LAS LAGRIMAS DE COCODRILO.   BARCELONA,
    ESPANA: EDITORIAL LUMEN, 1961.

FRANK, JANET. DIAS FELICES.   MEXICO: EDITORIAL NOVARO,
    1961.

FRASCONI, ANTONIO. THE SNOW AND THE SUN—LA NIEVE Y EL
    SOL.   NEW YORK: HARCOURT, BRACE AND WORLD, INC., 1961.

FRASER.   STUDY ABILITIES SPANISH-SPEAKING   (LJE*).

GALARZA, ERNESTO. ZOO-RISA.   SANTA BARBARA, CALIF.:
    MCNALLY AND LOFTIN PUBLISHERS, 1968.

GARCIA NIETO, JOSE. PIPEPACO EN LA SELVA.   MADRID,
    ESPANA: EDITORIAL MAGISTERIO ESPANOL, 1960.

GARCIA RUIZ, RAMON. ABCD LIBRO SEGUNDO DE LECTURA.
    GUADALAJARA, JALISCO, MEXICO: EDICIONES EL ESTUDIANTE,
    S.A.,.

GARCIA RUIZ, RAMON. ABCD: LIBROS DE LECTURAS.   MEXICO:
    EDICIONES EL ESTUDIANTE, S. A.,.

GARRIGA, ANGELES. LA GALERA DE ORO. LA MAS TRAVIESA DEL
    REBANO.   BARCELONA, ESPANA: EDICIONES LA GALERA, 1964.

GEISEL, T. S. AND EASTMAN, P. D.   THE CAT IN THE HAT
    BEGINNER BOOK DICTIONARY IN SPANISH.   NEW YORK:
    BEGINNER BOOKS, 1969.

GEISEL, THEODOR S.   THE CAT IN THE HAT: BEGINNER BOOK
    DICTIONARY IN SPANISH.   NEW YORK: RANDOM,.

GIL, BONIFACIO.   EL GLOBO DE COLORES. CANCIONES INFANTIL
    UNIVERSAL.   MADRID, ESPANA: AGUILAR, S.A. DE
    EDICIONES, 1964.

GOLDEN, AUGUSTA. PELO LACIO, PELO RIZO.   R.J. PALMER
    (TRANS). NEW YORK: THOMAS Y. CROWELL COMPANY, 1968.

GOMEZ CARDENAS, MATILDE. EJERCICICS PRACTICOS DE LA
    LENGUAJE (PRIMER ANO).   MEXICO, D.F.: NYL, S.
    DE R.L., 1960.

GOMEZ DEL VALLE, PABLO.   ENCICLOPEDIA DE LAS AFICIONES.
    JUEGOS DE EDUCACION FISICA.   MADRID, ESPANA:
    SANTILLANA, S. A. DE EDICIONES, 1967.

GOMEZ DEL VALLE, PABLO.   ENCICLOPEDIA DEL LAS AFICIONES.
    JUEGOS DE EDUCATION FISICA.   MADRID, ESPANA:
    SANTILLANA, S. A. DE EDICIONES, 1967.

GONZALES, L. AND ALBA M.   LA VIDA DEL NINO A TRAVES DEL
    RELOJ.   MEXICO, D. F.: FERNANDEZ EDITORES, S. A.,
    1969.

GOSSO, JUAN B., AND LUIS R. SANMARTINO (EDS).   EL BICHITO
    GUITARRERO Y OTRAS CANCIONES INFANTILES.   BUENOS
    AIRES, ARGENTINA: EDITORIAL KAPELUSZ, S.A., 1947.

GRASCONI, ANTONIO.   AGAIN, SAY AGAIN—GUARDA DE NEVO, PARLA
    DE NUEVO.   NEW YORK: HARCOURT, BRACE & WORLD INC.,,
    1964.

GREENE, CARLA. LOS CAMIONEROS: QUE HACEN?   NEW YORK:
    HARPER,.

GRIMM, ANDERSON, AND OTHERS.   LOS TITANES DE LA LITERATURA
    INFANTIL.   MEXICO, D.F.: EDITORIAL DIANA, S.A.,,
    1961.

GRISMER, RAYMOND L., AND MARGARITA MOLINOS. CONQUISTADORES
Y DEFENSORES. BOSTON, MASS.: D.C. HEATH AND CO.,
1953.

GUILLOT, RENE. LA MANSION DEL PAJARILLO. BARCELONA,
ESPANA: EDITORIAL TIMUN MAS, S.A., 1967.

GURNEY, NANCY AND ERIC. SPANISH BEGINNER BOOKS. EL REY,
LOS RATONES Y EL QUESO. TRANSLATED BY CALOS RIVERA.
NEW YORK: RANDOM HOUSE,, 1967.

HANNA Y BARBERA. CUENTAME UN CUENTO. MEXICO, D. F.:
ORGANIZACION EDITORIAL NOVARO,.

HARRIGAN, JOAN. TESORO DE ORO BOOKS FOR SPANISH SPEAKING
STUDENTS. DENVER: COLORADO STATE DEPARTMENT
OF EDUCATION, 1966.

HERGE. COLECCION LAS AVENTURAS DE TIN-TIN. EL LOTO AZUL.
BARCELONA, ESPANA: EDITORIAL JUVENTUD, 1966.

HERNANDEZ RUIZ, SANTIAGO. AMANECER EN MI JARDIN. BILBAO,
ESPANA: EDITORIAL VASCO AMERICANA, S.A.,.

HERNANDEZ RUIZ, SANTIAGO. ARITMETICA INFANTIL (GRADES ONE
AND TWO). MEXICO, D.F.: HERRERO HERMANOS SUCS.,
1969.

HERNANDEZ RUIZ, SANTIAGO. PRIMERAS LUCES. MEXICO, D.F.:
FERNANDEZ EDITORES, S.A., 1950.

HERRERA, JOSE LUIS. EL LIBRO DEL DESIERTO; EL LIBRO DE
LOS RIOS Y LAGOS; EL LIBRO DEL FUEG 3. MADRID,
ESPANA: AGUILAR, S.A. DE EDICIONES, 1958.

HERRMANNS, RALPH. LI LAN, HING Y LA COMETA DRAGON.
BARCELONA, ESPANA: EDITORIAL TIMUN MAS, 1962.

HERRMANNS, RALPH. EL NINO Y EL RIO. BARECELONA, ESPANA:
EDITORIAL TIMUN MAS, 1965.

HIGGINS, DON. PRIMEROS LIBROS DE ORO. TRANSLATED
BY MARIA LUISA PUGA M. MEXICO D.F.: ORGANIZACION
EDITORIALNOVARO, S.A.,, 1966.

HILLS, ELIJAH CLARENCE, AND JUAN CANO. CUENTOS Y LEYENDAS.
BOSTON, MASS.: HEATH AND CO., 1922.

HINOJOSA, IDA N. (ED). FOLLETT WORLD-WIDE DICTIONARIES:
SPANISH. CHICAGO, ILLINOIS: FOLLETT PUBLISHING
COMPANY, 1966.

HOFF, SYD. DANIELITO Y EL DINOSAURO. NEW YORK: HARPER,.

HOLMAN, ROSEMARY. SPANISH NUGGETS. SAN ANTONIO, TEX.:
THE NAYLOR CO., 1968.

HOLSAERT, EUNICE. LIBROS DE ORO DEL SABER. AVES DEL MUNDO.
    MEXICO, D. F.: ORGANIZACION EDITORIAL NOVARO, S. A.,
    1967.

HUERTA, DELFINA. MI PRIMERA GRAMATICA.   MEXICO, D. F.:
    EDITORIAL F. TRILLAS, S.A.,.

HUPB, LORETTA B. QUE SERA: TRADITIONAL SPANISH RIDDLES.
    NEW YORK: JOHN DAY,.

IBARBOUROU, JUANA DE. CHICO CARLO.   BUENOS AIRES,
    ARGENTINA: EDITORIAL KAPELUSZ, S.A.,, 1953.

JACOME, G. ALFREDO. RONDA DE LA PRIMAVERA Y OTRAS RONDAS
    INFANTILES (SECOND EDITION).   MUSIC BY JOSE FRANCISCO
    EDUEZ. BUENOS AIRES, ARGENTINA: EDITORIAL KAPELUSZ,
    1959.

JARNES, BENJAMIN. EL LIBRO DE ORO DE LOS NINOS.   MEXICO:
    HISPANO AMERICANA, 1961.

JAUREGUI, A. L. ADIVINANZAS INFANTILES.   MEXICO, D. F.:
    EDITORIAL AVANTE S. DE R. L., 1969.

JAUREGUI, A. L. GALLITO DE PLATA.   MEXICO, D. F.:
    EDITORIAL AVANTE S. DE R.L., 1969.

JAUREGUI, A. L. JARDIN DE NINOS.   MEXICO, D. F.:
    EDITORIAL AVANTE, S. DE R. L., 1963.

JAYNE, RUTH. AMIGOS AMIGOS AMIGOS . BOWMAR,.

JAYNE, RUTH. LOS CUATRO SOMBREROS DE BENNY.   BOWMAR,.

JAYNE, RUTH. SABES QUE?.   BOWMAR,.

JAYNES, RUTH. SERIE DE LIBROS PARA LA NINEZ DE BOWMAR.
    GLENDALE, CALIF.: BOWMAR PUBLISHING CORP.,, 1967.

JIJENA SANCHEZ, RAFAEL. DO OIR Y CONTAR.   BUENOS AIRES,
    ARGENTINA: LIBRERIA EDITORIAL HACHETTE, S. A., 1960.

JIJENA SANCHEZ, RAFAEL. DON MENIQUE.   BUENOS AIRES,
    ARGENTINA: LIBRERIA EDITORIAL HACHETTE, S. A., 1960.

JIMENEZ-LANDI ANTONIO (ALSO LISTED UNDER A.J.M. IN SOME
    SOURCES). EL GLOBO DE COLORES. EL CAMPO.   MADRID,
    ESPANA: AGUILAR, S.A. DE EDICIONES, 1967.

JIMENEZ-LANDI, ANTONIO. LIBROS PARA MIRAR. LIBROS DE LOS
    ANIMALES.   MADRID, ESPANA: AGUILAR, S. A. DE EDICIONES,.

JIMENEZ-LANDI, ANTONIO. EL GLOBO DE COLORES. ABC...XYZ..
    MADRID, ESPANA: AGUILAR, S.Z. DE EDICIONES,, 1966.

JIMENEZ—LANDI, ANTONIO. EL GLOBO CE COLORES. EL CIELO.
    MADRID, ESPANA: AGUILAR, S. A. DE EDICIONES, 1966.

JIMENEZ—LANDI, ANTONIO. EL GLOBO CE COLORES. EL MAR.
    MADRID, ESPANA: AGUILAR, S. A. DE EDICIONES, 1967.

JIMENEZ—LANDI, ANTONIO. EL LIBRO CE LOS ANIMALES.
    MADRID, ESPANA: AGUILAR, S. A. DE EDICIONES, 1958.

JIMENEZ, EMMA HCLGUIN, ANC CONCFITA MORALES PUNCEL (EDS).
    PARA CHIQUITINES.   GLENDALE, CALIF.:   BCWMAR
    PUBLISHING CORP., 1969.

JONES, EDWINA, AND OTHERS. EL CAMINO HACIA LA SALUD
    (REVISED EDITON).   RIVER FOREST, ILL.: LAIDLAW BROS,
    1970.

JOSLIN, SESYLE AND ALCORN, JOHN. THERE IS A BULL ON MY
    BALCONY.   HARCOURT,.

JOSLIN, SESYLE AND ALCORN, JCHN. LA FIESTA.   HARCOURT,.

JOSLIN, SESYLE. HAY UN TORO EN ME BALCON.   NEW YORK:
    HARCOURT, BRACE & WORLD INC.,, 1966.

JOSLIN, SESYLE, ANC LEONARD WEISGARD. SENOR BABY ELEPHANT,
    THE PIRATE.   NEW YORK; HARCOURT, BRACE & WORLD,
    INC.,, 1962.

JOSLIN, SESYLE, AND JOHN ALCORN. LA FIESTA.   NEW YORK:
    HARCOURT, BRACE & WORLD, INC.,, 1967.

KAUFMAN, JOE. SILUETAS DE ORO. LOS JUGUETES DE COLORES.
    TRANSLATED BY LUIS GUZMAN FLORES. MEXICO, D.F.:
    ORGANIZACION EDITORIAL NOVARO, S.A.8, 1966.

KAUFMAN, JOE. SILUETAS DE ORO. LOS BARCOS.   TRANSLATED
    BY MARIA LUISA PUGA M. MEXICO, D.F.: ORGANIZACION
    EDITORIANOVARO, S.A.,.

KESKOWITZ, IRVING, AND A. FARRIS STONE. LOS ANIMALES SON
    ASI.   MEXICO, D.F.: EDITORA TECNICA, 1968.

KESSLER, LEONARD. AQUI VIENE EL PONCHADO.   NEW YORK:
    HARPER,.

KIPLING, RUDYARD. PRECISAMENTE AS.   BARCELONA, ESPANA:
    EDITORIAL JUVENTUD, S.A.,, 1967.

KORN, JERRY. A'TOMAS.   MEXICO: NOVARO, 1965.

KORN, JERRY. LIBROS DE ORO DEL SABER ATOMOS.   MEXICO,
    D.F.: ORGANIZACION EDITORIAL NOVARO, S.A., 1967.

LACHMAN, RUTH MABEE. BARCCS.   MEXICO: EDITORIAL NOVARO,
    1964.

LAROUSSE. GEOGRAFIA UNIVERSAL. BARCELONA, ESPANA:
    EDITORIAL BRUGUERA, S.A., 1968.

LAYDU, CLAUDE. NUMURUS EN EL MAR. BARCELONA, ESPANA:
    EDITORIAL TIMUN MAS, 1966.

LEAF, MUNRO. EL CUENTO DE FERDINANDO. NEW YORK:
    THE VIKING PRESS, 1962.

LECHUGA, ROSAURA. ARITMETICA INFANTIL (SECOND EDITION)
    (GRADES ONE AND TWO). MEXICO, D.F.: EDITORIAL
    PATRIA, S.A., 1968.

LENSKI, LOIS. PAPA PEQUENO: PAPA SMALL. NEW YORK: HENRY
    Z. WALCK, INC., 1961 (LJE).

LENSKI, LOIS. VAQUERO PEQUENO: COUBOY SMALL. NEW YORK:
    HENRY Z. WALCK, INC., 1960 (LJE).

LENSKI, LOIS. EL AUTO PEQUENO; LA GRANJA PEQUENA; PAPA
    PEQUENO; AND VAQUERO PEQUENO. WALCK,.

LENSKI, LOIS. LA GRANJA PEQUENA. NEW YORK: HENRY
    Z. WALCK, INC., 1968 (LJE).

LEOPOLD, A. STARKER. COLECCION POPULAR EL DESIERTO. NEW
    YORK: TIME-LIFE BOOKS,, 1969.

LEVENTHAL, J. P. AYER Y HOY. MEXICO: EDITORIAL NOVARO,
    1959.

LEY, WILLY. VIAJES INTERPLANETARIOS. MEXICO: EDITORIAL
    NOVARO, 1959.

LEY, WILLY. A VENTURAS EN EL ESPACIO. ESTACIONES EN EL
    ESPACIO. MEXICO, D.F.: ORGANIZACION EDITORIAL
    NOVARO, S.A.,.

LIRA, MIGUEL N., AND ZAMORA, VALENTIN (EDS). MIS JUGUETES
    Y YO. MEXICO, D.F.: MORALES HERMANOS IMPRESORES,
    S.A.,.

LOBSENZ, NORMAN M. LIBROS DE ORO DEL SABER. EL MUNDO DE
    LOS INSECTOS. MEXICO, D.F.: ORGANIZACION EDITORIAL
    NOVARO, S.A.,.

LOPEZ LAY, ANA LUISA, AND RENEE CABRERA DE LAS CASAS (EDS).
    SERIE NUEVA DE TEXTO. BUENOS AMIGOS (GRADE ONE).
    CIUDAD DE GUATEMALA, GUATEMALA: CULTURAL CENTROAMERICANA,
    S.A.,.

LOPEZ, FRANCISCO M. VIDA MUNDIAL (SEXTO LIBRO DE LECTURA).
    MEXICO, D.F.: EDITORIAL PATRIA, S.A., 1960.

LOUVAIN, ROBERT. LIBROS DE ORO DEL SABER. ANIMALES SAVAJES
    DEL OESTE.   MEXICO, D.F.: ORGANIZACION EDITORIAL
    NOVARO, S.A., 1967.

LOW, ALICE. A TRAVES DE MI VENTANA.   MEXICO: EDITORIAL
    NOVARO, 1964.

LYNN, PATRICIA. EL PERRITO SIN DUENO.   MEXICO: EDITORIAL
    NOVARO, 1961.

MADARIAGA, SALVADOR DE. EL SOL, LA LUNA Y LAS ESTRELLAS.
    BARCELONA, ESPANA: EDITORIAL JUVENTUD S. A., 1960.

MARRERO, LEWIS. COLECCION GEOGRAFIA VISUALIZADA.
    CARACAS, VENEZUELA: EDUCIONES CULTURAL VENZOLANA,
    S.A., 1964.

MARTIN, RICHARD A. LIBROS DE ORO DEL SABER. LOS VIAJES
    DE LOS ANIMALES.   MEXICO, D.F.: ORGANIZACION
    EDITORIAL NOVARO, S.A., 1967.

MC SWAIN, E.T., AND OTHERS. BASIC MATHEMATICS SERIES.
    RIVER FOREST, ILL.: LAIDLAW BROS., 1966.

MENDEZ GARCIA, ANDRES. EL MUNDO DE LAS PALABRAS.   MADRID,
    ESPANA: EDICIONES ANAYA, 1967.

MICHEL, JOSEPH. AVENTURAS EN EL ESPACIO. PILOTOS DEL
    ESPACIO.   MEXICO, D.F.: ORGANIZACION EDITORIAL
    NOVARO, S.A.,.

MICHEL, JOSEPH. LIBROS DE ORO DEL SABER. EL ARTICO
    SALVAJE.   MEXICO, D. F.: ORGANIZACION EDITORIAL
    NOVARO, S.A., 1967.

MILNE, A.A. SILUETAS DE ORO. WALT DISNEY PRESENTA: WINNIE
    PUH.   ADAPTED BY AL WHITE. TRANSLATED BY MARIA LUISA
    PUGA M. MEXICO, D.F.: ORGANIZACION EDITORIAL NOVARO
    S.A.,, 1967.

MILOR, JOHN H. HISTORIETAS EN ESPANOL.   SKOKIE, ILLINOIS:
    NATIONAL TEXTBOOK CORP, 1965.

MINARIK, ELSE H. OSITO.   NEW YORK; HARPER,.

MIROSLAW, SASEK. ESTO ES ROMA.   BARCELONA, ESPANA:
    EDITORIAL MOLINO, 1966.

MONROY PADILLA, NATALIO. NUESTRA AMIGA NATURALEZA.
    MEXICO, D.F.: HERRERO HERMANOS, SUSCS., S.A., 1966.

MONROY. ARREGLO GEOGRAFICO DE LA REPUBLICA MEXICANA.
    MEXICO, D.F.: FERNANDEZ EDITORES, S.A.,.

MORALES, FRANCISCO C. ALMA LATINA.   MEXICO: EDICIONES
    AGUILAS, 1964.

MORALES, RAFAEL. LEYENDAS MEXICANAS.   MEXICO, D.F.:
    AGUILAR, S.A. DE EDICIONES, 1964.

MORTON, ROBERT LEE, AND OTHERS.   MATEMATICA MODERNA.
    MORRISTOWN, N. J.:   SILVER BURDETT CO., 1966.

MURGIA, THEODORE, AND ROBERT R. RANGEL.   EXPLORANDO HAWAII.
    CHICAGO, ILL.:   STONE EDUCATIONAL PUBLICATIONS, 1967.

MUSSONS ARTIGAS, MONTSERRAT.   PIO PIO.   BARCELONA, ESPANA:
    EDICIONES LA GALERA, 1967.

MYRHOJ, IVAR.   EL PINGUINO PONDUS.   BARCELONA, ESPANA:
    EDITORIAL TIMUN MAS, 1966.

NICHOLAS, CHARLES.   SILUETAS DE ORO. EL ELEFANTE.
    TRANSLATED BY GUADALUPE CORDERO LEON. MEXICO, D.F.:
    ORGAINZACION EDITORIAL NOVARO, S.A., 1966.

NORMA, CARMEN.   ROSITA Y JUANITO.   MEXICO, D.F.:
    EDITORIAL F. TRILLAS, S.A., 1969.

OLAGUE, JOSE ARDANUY.   MI PRIMER DICCIONARIO ESCOLAR.
    BILBAO, ESPANA: EDITORIAL VASCO AMERICANA, 1965.

PAHLEN, KURT, AND JUAN B. GROSSO (EDS).   MUSICA Y CANCIONES
    PARA LOS MAS PEQUENOS.   BUENOS AIRES, ARGENTINA:
    EDITORIAL KAPELUSZ, 1967.

PALMER, HELEN AND ROVERA, CARLOS.   UN PESCADO FUERA
    DE AGUA.   NEW YORK: RANDOM HOUSE, INC., 1967.

PALMER, HELEN.   SPANISH BEGINNER BOOKS. UN PEZ FUERA DEL
    AGUA.   TRANSLATED BY CARLOS RIVERA. NEW YORK: RANDOM
    HOUSE, 1967.

PAPE, DONNA LUGG.   CUENTAME UN CUENTO.   ORGANIZACION
    EDITORIAL NOVARO, S. A.,.

PARKER, BERTHA MORRIS.   SERIE EDUCATIVA DE CIENCIA
    ELEMENTAL.   NEW YORK: HARPER & ROW PUBLISHERS, INC.,.

PASTOR, ANGELE, AND OTHERS.   POR EL MUNDO DEL CUENTO Y LA
    AVENTURA.   , ILL.:   LAIDLAW BROS., 1969.

PASTOR, ANGELES.   ESTA ERA UNA VEZ BAJO LAS PALMERAS.
    RIVER FOREST, ILLINOIS: LAIDLAW BROTHERS, DIVISION
    OF DOUBLEDAY AND COMPANY, INC, 1962.

PAUL BLACKWOOD (ED).   COMO Y PORQUE DE.   BARCELONA,
    ESPANA: EDITORIAL MOLINO,.

PEERS, EDGAR A. (ED). CASSELL'S SPANISH DICTIONARY—SPANISH-ENGLISH;
ENGLISH-SPANISH. NEW YORK: FUNK AND WAGNALLS
COMPANY, 1959.

PEREZ Y SOTO, A. LIBRO 30 DE LECTURA. MEXICO, D.F.:
EDITORIAL PATRIA, S.A., 1961.

PERRAULT, CHARLES. EL GATO CON BOTAS. LIBRERIA EDITORIAL
HACHETTE, S. A., 1960.

PFLOGG, JAN. SILUETAS DE ORO. TRANSLATED BY MARIA LUISA
PUGA M. MEXICO, D.F.: ORGANIZACION EDITORIAL NOVARO,
S.A., 1967.

PHODES, DOROTHY. COMO LEER UN MAPA DE UNA CIUDAD.
TRANSLATED BY BETTY RUSSEY FULTON. LOS ANGELES,
CALIF.: ELK GROVE PRESS, INC., 1969.

PINE, T. S., AND J. LEVINE (EDS). EL MUNDO QUE NOS RODEA.
NEW YORK: ARIEL PRESS LTD., 1967.

PLANELLA, ANTONIC CARRERO (ED). DICCIONARIO INFANTIL
ILUSTRADO. MEXICO, D. F.: PLAZA AND JANES, S. A.,
1966.

POLITI, LEO. PEDRO, EL ANGEL DE LA CALLE OLVERA. NEW
YORK: CHARLES SCRIBNER'S SONS, 1961.

POTTER, BEATRIX. PEDRIN AL EONEJO TRAVIESO. WARNE,.

POTTER, BEATRIX. PEDRIN EL CONEJO TRAVIESO. NEW YORK:
FREDERICK WARNE AND COMPANY, INC, 1931.

PRIETO, MARIANA B. EL GALLO SABIO—THE WISE ROOSTER.
NEW YORK: JOHN DAY COMPANY, 1962.

PRIETO, MARIANA B. A KITE FOR CARLOS; THE WISE ROOSTER;
GALLO SABIO. NEW YORK: JOHN DAY,.

PRIETO, MARIANA. EL GALLO SABIO. NEW YORK: JOHN
DAY COMPANY, 1962.

PROBST, PIERRE. FANFAN Y EL MONITO VERDE. BARCELONA,
ESPANA: EDITORIAL TIMUN MAS, 1968.

PROBST, PIERRE. FANFAN Y EL ULTIMO LOBO. BARCELONA,
ESPANA: EDITORIAL TIMUN MAS, 1968.

QUERALTO GARRIGO, F. PRACTICAS Y EJERCICIOS DE VACACIONES.
BARCELONA, ESPANA: EDITORIAL TEIDE, S. A., 1969.

QUERALTO, F. LENGUAJE ALBORADO. BARCELONA, ESPANA:
EDITORIAL TEIDE, S.A., 1968.

RACHLIS, EUGENE. LIBROS DE ORO DEL SABER LOS PRIMEROS
AUTOMOVILES. MEXICO, D.F.: ORGANIZACION EDITORIAL
NOVARO, S.A., 1967.

RADLAUER, RUTH AND RADLAUER, ED. PAPA ES GRANDE; FATHER
    IS BIG. BOWMAR,.

RAILLON, MADELEINE. PICO, EL PATITO PRESUMIDO. BARCELONA,
    ESPANA: EDITORIAL JUVENTUD, S. A., 1958.

RAINWATER, JANETTE. LIBROS DE ORO DEL SABER. LA VISION.
    MEXICO, D.F.: ORGANIZACION EDITORIAL NOVARO, S.A.,
    1967.

RAMIREZ, PABLO. MANUELITO, EL NINO NAVAJO. BARCELONA,
    ESPANA: EDITORIAL JUVENTUD, S.A., 1963.

REID, ALASTAIR AND KERRIGAN, ANTHONY. MOTHER GOOSE
    IN SPANISH. NEW YORK: THOMAS Y. CROWELL COMPANY,
    1968.

REY, H. JORGE EL CURIOSO. MIFFLIN, 1961.

REY, HANS A. JORGE EL CURIOSO. NEW YORK: HOUGHTON MIFFLIN,.

REY, HANS A. JORGE EL CURIOSO. BOSTON, MASSACHUSETTS:
    HOUGHTON MIFFLIN COMPANY, 1961.

REYMUNDO, MANUEL SECO, AND OTHERS. IMAGENES Y PALABRAS.
    MADRID, ESPANA: EDITORIAL MAGISTERIO ESPANOL, S.A.,
    1967.

RIDER, ALEX. LEARN A LANGUAGE BOOKS. NEW YORK: FUNK AND
    WAGNALLS COMPANY, 1967.

RIDLER. WHEN WE GO TO SCHOOL: CUANDOVAMOS (LJE*).

RITCHIE, BARBARA. RAMON MAKES A TRADE. NEW YORK: PARNASSUS,.

RITCHIE, BARBARA. RAMON MAKES A TRADE--LOS CAMBIOS
    DE RAMON. KENNETH EDWARDS (TRANS). BERKELEY,
    CALIFORNIA: PARNASSUS PRESS, 1959.

RODARI, GIANNI. JIP EN EL TELEVISOR. BARCELONA, ESPANA:
    EDITORIAL LUMEN, 1964.

ROMNEY, GAY. CORALITO. BUENOS AIRES, ARGENTINA:
    EDITORIAL KAPELUSZ, S. A., 1950.

ROSS, PATRICIA E. THE HUNGRY MOON: MEXICAN NURSERY TALES.
    NEW YORK: ALFRED A. KNOPF,.

SAMANIEGO, LA FONTAINE, IRIARTE, AND OTHERS. EL LIBRO DE
    LAS FABULAS. BARCELONA, ESPANA: EDITORIAL JUVENTUD,
    S.A., 1952.

SANDI, LUIS. DO-RE-ME LECTURAS MUSICALES. MEXICO, D.F.:
    LIBRERIA ARIEL, S.A., 1967.

SASEK, M. ESTO ES CABO KENNEDY.   BARCELONA, ESPANA:
    EDITORIAL MOLINO, 1967.

SCARRY, RICHARD.   LOS MARAVILLOSOS ANIMALES.   MEXICO,
    D.F.:   ORGANIZACION EDITORIAL NOVARO, S.A., 1964.

SCARRY, RICHARD.   SILUETAS DE ORO. LAS AVES.   JUAN JOSE
    UTRILLA (TRANS). MEXICO, D. F.: ORGANIZACION EDITORIAL
    NOVARO, S. A., 1967.

SCARRY, RICHARD.   SILUETAS DE ORO. LOS CONEJOS.   MARIA
    LUISA PUGA M (TRANS). MEXICO, D. G.: ORGANIZACION
    EDITORIAL NOVARO, S. A., 1967.

SCARRY, RICHARD.   VIAJAR Y REIR.   BARCELONA, ESPANA:
    EDITORIAL BRUGUERA, S.A., 1966.

SCHULZ, CHARLES M.   ADELANTE, CHARLIE BROWN.   NEW YORK:
    HOLT, RINEHART AND WINSTON, INC., 1969.

SCHULZ, CHARLES M.   SNOOPY, VUELVE A CASA.   NEW YORK:
    HOLT, RINEHART AND WINSTON, INC., 1969.

SCHULZ, CHARLES M.   LA FELICIDAD ES UN PERRITO CALIENTITO.
    MEXICO, D. F.: EDITORIAL DIANA, S. A., 1964.

SELSAM, MILLICENT E.   I CAN READ BOOKS. TERESITA Y
    LAS ORUGAS.   TRANSLATED BY PURA BELPRE. NEW YORK:
    HARPER & ROW PUBLISHERS, INC.,.

SERRANO, MARIE LAURA.   LAS ARDILLAS MELLIZAS.   BUENOS
    AIRES, ARGENTINA: EDITORIAL SIGMAR, S.A.C., 1966.

SERRANO, MARIE LAURA.   LOS GATITOS MELLIZOS.   BUENOS
    AIRES, ARGENTINA: EDITORIAL SIGMAR, S.A.C., 1965.

SERRANO, MARIE LAURA.   LOS NINOS QUE VIVIAN EN UN ZAPATO.
    BUENOS AIRES, ARGENTINA: EDITORIAL SIGMAR, S.A.C.,
    1965.

SEUSS, DR.   SPANISH BEGINNER BOOKS. EL GATO ENSOMBRERADO.
    CARLOS RIVERA (TRANS). NEW YORK: RANDOM HOUSE, 1966.

SHAFFER, PAUL.   LIBRO DE ORO DE ESTAMPAS.   MEXICO, D. F.:
    ORGANIZACION EDITORIAL NOVARO, S. A., 1968.

SHORTALL, LEONARD.   SILUETAS DE ORO. EL SOMBRERO.   LUIS
    GUZMAN FLORES (TRANS). MEXICO, D. F.: ORGANIZACION
    EDITORIAL NOVARO, S. A., 1966.

SHOWERS, PAUL.   LEAMOS Y AVERIGUEMOS.   TRANSLATED
    BY RICHARD J. PALMER. NEW YORK: THOMAS Y. CROWELL
    COMPANY, 968.

SIMON, NORMA.   WHAT DO I SAY?.   CHICAGO, ILLINOIS: ALBERT
    WHITMAN AND COMPANY, 1967.

SIMON, NORMA. WHAT DO I SAY?. CHICAGO, ILLINOIS: ALBERT
    WHITMAN AND COMPANY, 1967.

SMITH, C. C. DAVIES, G. A. AND HALL, H. B. LANGENSCHEIDT
    STANDARD DICTIONARY OF THE ENGLISH AND SPANISH
    LANGUAGES. NOVATO, CALIFORNIA: WEBSTER DIVISION,
    MCGRAW-HILL BOOK COMPANY, 1969.

SMITH, OSWALD J. LAS AVENTURAS DE ANDRES. BARCELONA,
    ESPANA: EDITORIAL JUVENTUD, S.A., 1967.

SOLER, CAROLA. EL GLOBO DE COLORES. JUEGOS PARA TODOS.
    MADRID, WSPANA: AGUILAR, S. A. DE EDICIONES, 1958.

SOLIS, GUSTAVO. CUENTAME UN CUENTO. MEXICO, D. F.:
    ORGANIZACION EDITORIAL NOVARO, S. A.,.

SPAR, JEROME. LA RUTA DEL TIEMPO (THIRD EDITION).
    MANKATO, MINN.: CREATIVE EDUCATIONAL SOCIETY, INC.,
    1967.

STANEK. ANIMALS WE KNOW (LJE*).

STANEK, MURIEL. BILINGUAL ENRICHMENT BOOKS. AMIGOS DE LA
    COMUNIDAD; ANIMALES QUE CONOCEMS; YO VIVO EN LA
    CIUDAD. WESTCHESTER, ILL.: BENEFIC PRESS, 1969.

STANEK. COMMUNITY FRIENDS: AMIGOS DECOMUNIDAD (LJE*).

STANEK. I LIVE CITY: YO VIVO EN CIUDAD (LJE*).

STEPHENS, EDWARD C. LIBROS DE ORO DEL SABER. SUBMARINOS.
    MEXICO, D.F.: ORGANIZACION EDITORIAL NOVARO, S.A.,
    1967.

STONE, A. HARRIS, AND IRVING LESKOWITZ (EDS). ASI SON LAS
    PLANTAS. MEXICO, D.F.: EDITORA TECNICA, 1968.

STONE, A. HARRIS, AND BERTRAM M. SIEGEL (EDS). DIVIERTETE
    CON JABON. MEXICO, D.F.: EDITORA TECNICA, 1968.

SUCKSDORFF, ASTRID B. CHENDRU Y SU AMIGO EL TIGRE.
    BARCELONA, ESPANA: EDITORIAL TIMUN MAS, 1964.

SUCKSDORFF, ASTRID B. LA CABANA DESIERTA. BARCELONA,
    ESPANA: EDITORIAL TIMUN MAS, 1964.

SULLIVAN, WALTER. LIBROS DE ORO DEL SABER. LAS REGIONES
    POLARES. MEXICO, D.F.: ORGANIZACION EDITORIAL
    NOVARO, S.A., 1967.

TALLON, JOSE SEBASTIAN. LAS TORRES DE NURENBERG. BUENOS
    AIRES, ARGENTINA: EDITORIAL KAPELUSZ, S.A., 1962.

TALLON, ROBERT. ABCDEFGHIJKLMNOPQRSTUVWXYZ IN ENGLISH AND
    SPANISH. LION,.

TARDY, WILLIAM T. BEDTIME STORIES IN SPANISH.   SKOKIE,
    ILLINOIS: NATIONAL TEXTBOOK COMPANY, 1960.

UN PAPALOTE PARA CARLOS. UNPAPALOTE PARA CARLOS.   NEW
    YORK: JOHN DAY COMPANY, 1966.

URCELAY, R. FERNANDEZ. PEQUENA ENCICLOPEDIA.   BILBAO,
    ESPANA: EDITORIAL CANTABRICA, S. A., 1966.

VALDEZ GALINDO, MARIA ESTER. FELICIDAD, LIBRO DE LECTURA
    Y ESCRITURA (THIRD EDITION).   MEXICO, D.F.:
    EDITORIAL AZTECA, S.A., 1960.

VALDEZ ZAMORA, OROZCO. VERDE Y AZUL.   MEXICO, D.F.:
    MORALES HERMANOS IMPRESORES, S.A.,.

VAVRA, ROBERT. FELIPE, EL APRENDIZ DE TORERO.   BARCELONA,
    ESPANIA: EDITORIAL TIMUN MAS, 1968.

VAVRA, ROBERT. LA VUELTA AL MUNDO.   BARCELONA, ESPANA:
    AYMA, S.A. EDITORA,.

VEGA, BLANCA DE. ANTOLOGIA DE LA POESIA INFANTIL.   BUENOS
    AIRES, ARGENTINA: EDITORIAL KAPELUSZ, 1960.

VEGA, JOSE. METODO PRACTICO DE LECTURA Y ESCRITURA. AURORA
    - LER ANO.   MEXICO, D.F.: EDITORIAL PATRIA, S.A.,.

VELASQUEZ DE LA CADENA, MARIANO (ET AL). VELASQUEZ SPANISH
    AND ENGLISH DICTIONARY.   REVISED BY IDA NAVARRO
    HINOJOSA. CHICAGO, ILLINOIS: FOLLETT PUBLISHINGCOMPANY,
    1966.

VERRAL, CHARLES SPAIN. LA FLECHA ROTA.   MEXICO: EDITORIAL
    NOVARO, 1964.

VIGIL, CONSTANCIO. MANGOCHO.   BUENOS AIRES, ARGENTINA:
    LIBRERIA ATLANTIDA EDITORIAL,.

VIGIL, CONSTANCIO. LA HORMIGUITA VIAJERA.   BUENOS AIRES,
    ARGENTINA: LIBRERIA ATLANTIDA EDITORIAL, 1965.

VIGIL, CONSTANCIO. LA REINA DE LOS PAJAROS.   BUENOS
    AIRES, ARGENTINA: LIBRERIA ATLANTIDA EDITORIAL, 1967.

WADSWORTH, WALLACE C. LOS SIETE GATOS MARAVILLOSOS.
    BUENOS AIRES, ARGENTINA: EDITORIAL SIGMAR, S.A.C.,
    1966.

WATSON, JANE. NUESTRO MUNDO.   MEXICO: NOVARO, 1959.

WATTS, MABEL. ESTO PARA TI, ESTO PARA MI.   BARCELONA,
    ESPANA: EDITORIAL LUMEN, 1963.

WHITE, PETER. CON LAPIZ Y PAPEL.   MADRID, ESPANA:
    SANTILLANA, S. A. DE EDICIONES, 1967.

WILLIAMS, ECWIN B. HOLT SPANISH AND ENGLISH DICTIONARY.
    NEW YORK: HOLT, RINEHART ANC WINSTON, INC., 1963.

WILLIAMS, GARTH. ANIMALITOS EN LA GRANJA.   MEXICO:
    EDITORIAL NOVARO, 1961.

WILLIAMS, HERB AND WILLIAMS, LETTY. LA PEQUENA GALLINA
    ROJA.   DORIS CHAVES (TRANS). NEW YORK: PRENTICE-HALL,
    INC., 1969.

WILLIAMS, LETTY. LITTLE RED HEN.   ENGLEWOOD CLIFFS, NEW
    JERSEY: PRENTICE-HALL,.

WILLIAMS, LETTY. LA PEQUENA GALLINA ROJA; THE TIGER.
    ENGLEWOOD CLIFFS, NEW JERSEY: PRENTICE-HALL,.

WILLIAMS, LETTY. EL TIGRE.   ENGLEWOOD CLIFFS, NEW JERSEY:
    PRENTICE-HALL,.

YURCHENCO, HENRIETTA. A FIESTA CF FOLK SONGS FROM SPAIN
    AND LATIN AMERICA.   NEW YORK: G. P. PUTNAM'S SONS,
    1967.

ZANINI, GIUSEPPE. EL MUNDO DE LCS INSECTOS.   BARCELONA,
    ESPANA: EDITORIAL MOLINO, 1965.

ZIM, HERBERT S. LIBROS DE ORO DEL SABER. ROCAS.   MEXICO,
    D.F.: ORGANIZACION EDITORIAL NCVARO, S.A., 1967.

L I T E R A T U R E

(LMA)

ABELARDO. 25 PIECES OF A CHICANC MIND.   SANTA BARBARA:
LA CAUSA, 1971.

ACOSTA, OSCAR ZETA:. THE AUTCBIOGRAPHY OF A BROWN
BUFFALC..   SAN FRANCISCO, CALIFORNIA: STRAIGHT ARROW
BOOKS, 1972.

ADAMS.   "BOOKS NEW MEXICO, 1598-1680"   (8*).

ALEGRIA, FERNANDC. POETRY.   REVISTA CHICANO-RIQUENA, ANO
UNO, NUMERO DOS (OTONO 1973) PAGS. 22.

ALURISTA. "POESIA".   HISPAMERICA, VCL. 2 NO. 6 (1974),
PP. 95-102.

ALURISTA. "POETRY".   EL GRITO, VCL. 2 NO. 1 (FALL
1968), PP. 6-12.

ALURISTA. FLORICANTO EN AZTLAN.   LOS ANGELES: UNIVERSITY
OF CALIFORNIA, 1971.

ALURISTA. NATIONCHILD PLUMA ROJA.   SAN DIEGO: CENTRO
CULTURAL DE LA RAZA, 1972.

ALURISTA. POETRY.   OCTAVIO ROMANC, EL ESPEJO. BERKELEY,
CALIFORNIA: QUINTO SOL PUBLICATICNS, INC., 1969.

ALURISTA. POETRY.   REVISTA CHICANO-RIQUENA, ANO DOS,
NUMERO UNO (INVIERNO 1974) PAG. 24.

ALURISTA. EL OMBLIGO DE AZTLAN.   SAN DIEGO, CALIFORNIA:
SAN DIEGO STATE UNIVERISTY, 1972.

ALVA, JANVIER. "THE SACRED SPOT".   CON SAFOS, VOL. 1
NO. 3 (MARCH 1969), PP. 21-23.

ALVAREZ, JORGE. "POETRY".   EL GRITO, VOL. 3 NO.
2 (WINTER 1973), PP. 42-46.

ALVAREZ, JORGE. "POETRY".   EL GRITO, VOL. 5 NO. 1 (FALL
1971), PP. 62-66.

AMARAL, JOSE VAZQUEZ. LOS GRINGOS.   MEXICO:, 1969 (SO).

ANAYA, RODOLFC A. "BLESS ME, ULTIMA. EXCERPTS".
EL GRITO, VOL. 5 NO. 3 (SPRING 1972), PP. 4-17.

ANAYA, RODOLFO A. BLESS ME, ULTIMA. BERKELEY, CALIFORNIA
     QUINTO SOL PUBLICATIONS, 1972.

ANCHONDO, PEDRO B. "LONELY VIETNAM". EL GRITO, VOL. 3
     NO. 1 (FALL 1969), P. 3.

ANDERSON IMBERT, ENRIQUE. LITERATURA HISPANOAMERICANA;
     ANTOLOGIA E INTRODUCCION HISTORICA. NEW YORK: HOLT,
     RINEHART AND WINSTON, 1960.

ANDERSON. TALES FRONTIER TEXAS, 1830-1860 (AN*).

ANDERSON, ROBERT. A STUDY OF THE THEORY OF THE NOVEL IN
     REPRESENTATIVE SPANISH-AMERICAN AUTHORS, 1896-1956.
     BERKELEY: UNIVERSITY OF CALIFORNIA, 1957.

"A UNA MEMORIA". EL GRITO, VOL. 1 (FALL 1971), P. 25.

"ELEGIA A LA MEMORIA DE DONA MARIA IGNACIA ALVARADO
     DE PICO. AGOSTO 6, DE1855". EL GRITO, VOL. 5 NO.
     1 (FALL 1971), P. 24.

ENTRELINEAS (NP*).

JOURNAL MEXICAN AMERICAN HISTORY (HSW*).

LOS PASTORES. M. R. COLE (TRANS). BOSTON: HOUGHTON, 1907
     (AN).

APPLEGATE. NATIVE TALES NEW MEXICO (LI*).

APPLEGATE. "NEW MEXICAN SKETCHES" (LI*).

ARECHIGA, JAVIER. POETRY. REVISTA CHICANO-RIQUENA, ANO
     UNO, NUMERO DOS (OTONO 1973) PAGS. 25-28.

ARELLANO, ESTEVAN <ED>. ENTRE VERDE Y SECO. SAN ANSELMO,
     CALIFORNIA: AL ACADEMIA DE LA NUEVA RAZA, (1972).
     LA ACADEMIA DE LA NUEVA RAZA PUBLICATION SERIES.

ARIAS, RON. STOOP LABOR. REVISTA CHICANO-RIQUENA, ANO
     DOS, NUMERO UNO (INVIERNO 1974) PAGS. 7-14.

ARIAS, RON. THE INTERVIEW. REVISTA CHICANO-RIQUENA, ANO
     DOS, NUMERO UNO (INVIERNO 1974) PAGS. 2-6.

ARIAS, RONALD. "EL MAGO". EL GRITO, VOL. 3 NO.
     3 (SPRING 1970), PP. 51-55 (AN).

ARIAS. WERE SUPPOSED TO BELIEVE WERE (PY*).

ARIAS, RONALD. THE BARRIO. IN ED LUDWIG AND JAMES
     SANTIBANEZ, THE CHICANOS: MEXICAN-AMERICAN VOICES.
     BALTIMORE, MARYLAND: PENGUIN BOOKS, INC., 1971 (AN
     SO).

ARREOLA, JESUS A., JR. MY NAME IS JESUS.   IN JOSEPH A.
    FLORES, SONGS AND DREAMS. WEST HAVEN, CONNECTICUT:
    PENDULUM PRESS, INC., 1972.

ARREOLA, JESUS A., JR. MY NAME IS JESUS.   IN ED LUDWIG
    AND JAMES SANTIBANEZ. THE CHICANOS: MEXICAN-AMERICAN
    VOICES. BALTIMORE, MARYLAND: PENGUIN BOOKS, INC., 1971.

ASTROV, MARGOT <ED>. AMERICAN INDIAN PROSE AND POETRY.
    CAPRICORN (SO).

AVEDANO, FAUSTO. "LA MUJER DESNUDA".   EL GRITO, VOL. 5
    NO. 1 (FALL 1971), PP. 33-37.

AZUELA, MARIANC. THE UNDERDOGS.   MEXICO, 1916.

BAEZ, JOAN. DAYBREAK.   NEW YORK: AVON<HEARST>,.

BALLESTER, PAULA. " POETRY".   EL GRITO, VOL. 1 (FALL
    1971), P. 67.

BARAKAT. "AZTEC MOTIFS LA LLORONA" (AN*).

BARLOW, GENEVIEVE. LATIN AMERICAN TALES.   CHICAGO: RAND
    MCNALLY, 1966 (AN LJE).

BARON, VIRGINIA OLSEN, (ED). HERE I AM. AN ANTHOLOGY OF
    POETRY WRITTEN BY YOUNG PEOPLE IN SOME OF AMERICA'S
    MINORITY GROUPS.   NEW YORK, NEW YORK: DUTTON
    AND COMPANY, INC., (SO).

BARRETT, WILLIAM E. 'SENOR PAYROLL.'   IN EDWARD SIMMEN,
    THE CHICANO: FROM CARICATURE TO SELF PORTRAIT.

BARRIO, RAYMOND. THE PLUM PLUM PICKERS.   SUNNYVALE,
    CALIFORNIA: VENTURA PRESS, 1969.

BARRIO, RAYMOND. 'THE PLUM PLUM PICKERS.'   IN ED LUDWIG
    AND JAMES SANTIBANZ, (EDS), THE CHICANOS: MEXICAN-AMERICAN
    VOICES.

BARRON, BOB. "VIET NAM VETERAN".   EL GRITO, VOL. 1 NO.
    3 (SPRING 1968), PP. 18-19.

BARRON, ROBERT. "VIETNAM VETERAN".   EL GRITO, VOL. 1
    NO. 3 (SPRING 1968), PP. 18-19.

BAZIN, ROBERTC. HISTORIA DE LA LITERATURA AMERICAN
    EN LENGUA ESPANOLA.   BUENOS AIRES: EDITORIAL NOVA,
    1958.

BELTRAN, LUIS. POETRY.   REVISTA CHICANO-RIQUENA, ANO UNO,
    NUMERO DOS (OTONO 1973) PAGS. 29-30.

BONHAM, FRANK. VIVA CHICANO.   NEW YORK, NEW YORK: E. P.
    DUTTON, 1970.

BROWN, RICHARD G. "MR. ISCARIOT". THE LITERARY REVIEW,
    VOL. 6 (SUMMER U963), PP. 441-451.

BRUSHWOOD, JAMES S. "LA NCVELA MEXICANA FRENTE AL
    PORFIRISMO". HISTORIA MEXICANA, VOL. 7 NO.
    3 (1958), PP. 368-405 (HM).

BRUSHWOOD, JAMES S. THE ROMANTIC NCVEL IN MEXICO.
    COLUMBIA: UNIVERSITY OF MISSOURI PRESS, 1954.

BRUSHWOOD, JOHN S. MEXICO IN ITS NOVEL; A NATICNS SEARCH
    FOR IDENTITY. AUSTIN: UNIVERSITY OF TEXAS PRESS,
    1966.

BRUSHWOOD. MEXICO ITS NOVEL: NATIONS SEARCH (HM*).

BURNS. ROBIN HOCD DORADO: SAGA JCAQUIN (AN*).

BURRUEL, FRANCISCO O. "THE DIALOGUE OF CUCO ROCHA". EL
    GRITO, VOL. 3 NO. 4 (SUMMER 1970), PP. 37-45.

BURRUEL, FRANCISCC O. SUMMER OF MY ROSE. EL GRITO,
    (SUMMER 1970).

CABOS, GEORGIA M. "POETRY". EL GRITO, VOL. 2 NO.
    4 (SUMMER 1969), PP. 35-36.

CABOS, GEORGIA M. "POETRY". EL GRITO, VOL. 2 NO.
    3 (SUMMER 1969), PP. 36-38.

CALDERON, BERNIE. "TE LO ADVERTI". EL GRITO, VOL. 3
    NO. 2 (WINTER 1970), PP. 37-38.

CAMP, FRANK BERNARD. MEXICAN BORDER BALLADS. DOUGLAS,
    ARIZONA: F. B. CAMP, 1916 (AN).

CAMPA. SPANISH, MEXICAN, NATIVE: PROBLEM (AN*).

CAMPA. "LANGUAGE BARRIERS INTER-CULTURAL (AN*).

CAMPA. "RELIGIOUS SPANISH FOLK-DRAMA (AN*).

CAMPA. "SPAINS LINK WITH PAST" (AN*).

CAMPA. "SPANISH FOLKLORE NEW MEXICO" (AN*).

CAMPA. "THE NEW MEXICAN SPANISH FOLKTHEATER" (AN*).

CAMPA. COLORADCS YOUTH LCOKS TC SKIES (AN*).

CAMPA. FCLK POETRY NEW MEXICO: COMPARATIVE (AN*).

CAMPA. LCS COMANCHES (AN*).

CAMPA. NEW MEXICAN SPANISH FOLK TALES (AN*).

CAMPA.   SPANISH RELIGIOUS FOLK THEATRE   (AN*).

CAMPA.   SPANISH RELIGIOUS FOLK THEATRE   (AN*).

CAMPBELL.   TREASURE SANGRE DE CRISTOS; TALES   (AN*).

CAMPOS.   FOLKLORE LITERARIO CE MEXICO   (AN*).

CANDELARIA, FREDERICK H.   "POETRY: "RODEO", "TOURING TEXAS:
    TALL TALE FROM LBJ COUNTRY," "SPANISH CURRENCY",
    "BORDER INCIDENT"".   EL GRITO, VOL. 3 NO. 3 (SPRING
    1970), PP. 56-57.

CARBALLO, EMMANUEL (ED.).   EL CUENTO MEXICANO DEL SIGLO
    XX: ANTOLOGIA.   MEXICO: EMPRESAS EDITORIALES, 1964.

CARDENAS, RENE.   "POETRY".   EL GRITO, VOL. 4 NO.
    2 (WINTER 1971), PP. 78-80.

CARRANZA, ELIU. S. PENSAMIENTOS CN LOS CHICANOS: A CULTURAL
    REVOLUTION.   BERKELEY: CALIFORNIA BOOK CO., 11969.

CARRANZA, ELIU. S. PENSAMIENTOS CN LOS CHICANOS: A CULTURAL
    REVOLUTION.   SECOND EDITION. BERKELEY, CALIFORNIA:
    CALIFORNIA BOOK CO.,LTD., 1971.

CARRANZA, ELIU. S. THE GORKASE MIRROR.   BALTIMORE,
    MARYLAND: PENGUIN BOOKS, IMC., 1971.

CARRIZALES, PABLO.   CANCION DE LA RAZA.   COACHELLA,
    CALIFORNIA: IDEAL, 1970.

CASSIDY.   "CHRISTMAS NEW MEXICO" (AN*).

CASTANEDA SHULAR, ANTONIO; YBARRA-FRAUSTO, TOMAS; SOMMERS,
    JOSEPH. LITERATURA CHICANA: TEXTO Y CONTEXTO.
    ENGLEWOOD CLIFFS, NEW JERSEY: PRENTICE-HALL, 1972.

CASTANEDA, IRENE.   "CHRONICLE CF CRYSTAL CITY".   EL GRITO,
    VOL. 4 NO. 2 (WINTER 1971), PP. 48-53.

CASTANEDA, IRENE.   "CRONICA".   EL GRITO, VOL. 4 NC. 2
    (WINTER 1971), PP. 42-47.

CASTILLO, NICOLAS.   HOMENAJE GUADALUPANO.   MIMIOGRAPHED.

CASTILLO, PEDRO AND CAMARILLO, ALBERT: (EDS).   LOS BANDIDOS
    CHICANOS..   LOS ANGELES, CALIFORNIA: AZTLAN
    PUBLICATIONS, 1973 (HSW).

CERDA, EVANGELINA.   LA REVOLUCION MEXICANA EN LA NOVELA
    MEXICANA.   UNIVERSITY OF TEXAS AT AUSTIN, MASTER'S
    THESIS (1937).

CHACON, ESTELLE. "OPEN LETTER TO: WOMEN'S INTERNATIONAL
    LEAGUE FOR PEACE AND FREEDOM, LA JOLLA, CALIFORNIA".
    EL GRITO, VOL. 1 NO. 3 (SPRING 1968), PP. 46-47 (PL
    SO).

CHACON, ESTELLE. "POCHISMOS". EL GRITO, VOL. 3 NO. 1
    (FALL 1969), PP. 34-35.

CHAVES, ALBERT (ED.). YEARNING. WESTPORT, CONNECTICUT:
    PENDULUM PRESS, 1972.

CHAVEZ. ELEVEN LADY-LYRICS, OTHER POEMS (HS*).

CHAVEZ. CLOTHED WITH SUN (HS*).

CHAVEZ. CONQUISTADORA, AUTOBIOGRAPHYANCIENT (HS*).

CHAVEZ. LADY TOLEDO (HS*).

CHAVEZ. SELECTED POEMS (HS*).

CHAVEZ. SINGLE ROSE (HS*).

CHAVEZ. VIRGIN PORT LLIGAT (HS*).

CHAVEZ, MAURO. "THE LAST DAY OF CLASS". EL GRITO, VOL.
    4 NO. 3 (SPRING 1971), PP. 48-63.

CHAY, MARIE. "GRINGOS ARE FOOLS". ARIZONA QUARTERLY,
    VOL. 18 NO. 2 (SUMMER 1962) (LI SO).

CHAY, MARIE. "I LIKE IT BETTER THAT WAY". SOUTHWEST
    REVIEW, VOL. 53 NO. 1 (WINTER 1968), PP. 65-73 (LI
    SO).

CHAY, MARIE. "IN OTHER PEOPLES HOUSES". SOUTHWEST
    REVIEW, VOL. 60 NO. 1 (WINTER 1970), PP. 65-71 (LI
    SO).

CHAY, MARIE. "ITS ALL WORLD". SOUTHWEST REVIEW, VOL.
    45 NO. 1 (WINTER 1960) (LI SO).

CHAY, MARIE. "MARRIAGE IS DIFFERENT". SOUTHWEST REVIEW,
    VOL. 48 NO. 2 (SPRING 1963) (LI SO).

CHAY, MARIE. "SOMEONE'S UP AT THE MACHADOS". ARIZONA
    QUARTERLY, VOL. 24 NO. 4 (WINTER 1968) (LI SO).

CHICANO COMMENCEMENT. "CHICANO COMMENCEMENT". EL GRITO,
    VOL. 1 NO. 4 (SUMMER 1968), PP. 7-8.

CISNEROS, NATIVIDAD PEREYRA. "THE DREAM". CON SAFOS,
    VOL. 1 NO. 3 (MARCH 1969), P. 15.

CISNEROS, NATIVIDAD PEREYRA. THE DREAM. WEST HAVEN
    CONNECTICUT: PENDULUM PRESS, INC., (1972). IN JOSEPH
    A. FLORES.

CLAYTON, NORMAN DALE. "JUSTICE--WHATEVER THE COST".   CON
    SAFOS, VOL. 1 NO. 3 (MARCH 1969), P. 2.

CONTRERAS, HELEN. THE CHICANO'S SEARCH FOR IDENTITY.
    WEST HAVEN, CONNECTICUT: PENDULUM PRESS, INC., 1972.

CONTRERAS, HELES. "THE CHICANO'S SEARCH FOR IDENTITY".
    CONSAFOS, VOL. 2 NO. 5 , PP. 26-80.

CORDOVA, FERNANDO A. THE RELATIONSHIP OF ACCULTURATION,
    ACHIEVEMENT, AND ALIENATION AMONG SPANISH-AMERICAN
    SIXTH GRADE STUDENTS.   LAS CRUCES, NEW MEXICO:
    EDUCATIONAL RESOURCES INFORMATION, NEW MEXICO STATE
    UNIVERSITY, FEBRUARY 1969 (SO).

CORTES.   ALBUM MEXICAN AMERICAN   (HSW*).

CORVALAN, OCTAVIO. EL POSTMODERNISMO.   NEW YORK:
    LAS AMERICAS PUBLISHING CO., 1961.

COTERA, MARTHA. MEXICAN AMERICAN LITERATURE: A PRIMARY
    LIST--MARCH, 1970.   AUSTIN, TEXAS: SOUTHWEST
    EDUCATIONAL LABORATORY, 1970.

DAVILA, LUIS. CHICANO FANTASY THROUGH A GLASS DARKLY.
    MEMORIAS DEL XVI CONGRESO DEL INSTITUTO INTERNACIONAL
    DE LITERATURA IBEROAMERICANA. HELD AT MICHIGAN STATE
    UNIVERSITY, AUGUST 19749.

DAVILA, LUIS. HIJOS PRODIGOS.   REVISTA CHICANO-RIQUENA,
    ANO UNO, NUMERO UNO (PRIMAVERA 1973) PAG. 1.

DAVILA, LUIS. OTHERNESS IN CHICANO LITERATURE.   PAPERS
    OF IV INTERNATIONAL CONGRESS OF MEXICAN STUDIES.

DAVILA, LUIS. PUEBLO DESDENADO.   REVISTA CHICANO-RIQUENA,
    ANO DOS, NUMERO DOS (PRIMAVERA 1974).

DAVILA, LUIS. PURA LITERATURA.   REVISTA CHICANO-RIQUENA,
    ANO DOS, NUMERO UNO (INVIERNO 1974) PAG. 1.

DAVILA, LUIS. ON THE NATURE OF CHICANO LITERATURE: EN
    LOS EXTREMOS DEL LABERINTO.   PAPER DELIVERED AT THE
    MIDWEST MODERN LANGUAGE ASSOCIATION MEETING, NOVEMBER
    1971.

DAVIS, E. ADAMS. OF THE NIGHT WIND'S TELLING: LEGENDS
    FROM THE VALLEY OF MEXICO.   NORMAN, OKLAHOMA:
    UNIVERSITY OF OKLAHOMA PRESS, 1946 (AN).

DE ANDA.   "MEXICAN CULTURE MEXICAN-AMERICAN"   (AN*).

DE ANGULO, JAIME. INDIAN FIELDS. SPEAKING FOR OURSELVES:
AMERICAN ETHNIC WRITING. OAKLAND, NEW JERSEY:
SCOTT, FOREMAN AND COMPANY, 1969.

DE LA CUEVA, MARIO, ET. AL. MAJOR TRENDS IN MEXICAN
PHILOSOPHY. NOTRE DAME, INDIANA: UNIVERSITY
CF NOTRE DAME PRESS, 1966.

DE LA GUERRA. "EXCERPT HIS SPEECH" (SC*).

DE LA GUERRA. "EXTRACTO CEL DISCOURSO" (SO*).

DE LA TORRE, ALFREDO. "ILEANA". EL GRITO, VOL. 5 NO.
3 (SPRING 1972), PP. 70-73.

DE LEON, NEPHTALI. CHICANO POET. LUBBOCK, TEXAS: TRUCHA
PUBLICATIONS, INC., 1973.

DE LEON, NEPHTALI. CHICANOS: OUR BACKGROUND AND PRIDE.
DENVER, CCLORADO: AZTLAN BOOKSTORE, 1972.

DE LEON, NEPHTALI. I WILL CATCH THE SUN.. LUBBOCK,
TEXAS, TRUCHA PUBLICATIONS, INC., 1973.

DEANDA, DIANE. "Y VIENE". EL GRITO, VOL. 5 NO. 1 (FALL,
1971), PP. 38-42.

DEHUFF. SAY BELLS OLD MISSIONS: LEGENDS (AN*).

DELGADO, ABELARDO. THE CHICANO MOVEMENT: SOME NOT TOO
OBJECTIVE OBSERVATIONS. DENVER, COLORADO: TOTINEM
PUBLISHING CO., 1972 (SO PL).

DELGADO, ABELARDO; PEREZ, REYMUNDO "TIGRE"F SANCHEZ,
RICARDO; VALDEZ, JUAN (MAGDALENO AVILA). LOS CUATRO.
DENVER, CCLCRADO: BARRIO PUBLICATIONS, 1971.

DOBIE. PURO MEXICANO (LI*).

DOKEY, RICHARD. 'SANCHEZ.' EC LUDWIG AND JAMES SANTIBANEZ
(EDS) THE CHICANOS: MEXICAN-AMERICAN VOICES, BALTIMORE,
MARYLAND: PENGUIN BOOKS, INC., (HT).

DOKEY, RICHARD. 'SANCHEZ.' IN THE CHICANO: FROM
CARICATURE TO SELF-PORTRAIT, EDITED BY EDWARD SIMMEN,
NEW YORK: NEW AMERICAN LIBRARY, 1971 (LI).

DOKEY, RICHARC. "SANCHEZ". SOUTHWEST REVIEW, VOL. 42
(AUTUMN 1967), PP. 354-367 (LI).

DOMINGUEZ. OFERTA DE UNA FAMILIA: CANCIONES (MU*).

EL TEATRO CAMPESINO. CANCICNERO DE RAZA (MU*).

EL TENAZ. ORGANO DE PRENSA TEATRO NACIONAL (AT*).

ELIZONDO, PEDRO BRAVO. EL TEATRO CHICANO.   REVISTA
    CHICANO-RIQUENA, AÑO UNO, NUMERO DOS (OTOÑO 1973)
    PAGS. 36-42.

ELIZONDO, SERGIO. "ANTIPERROS".   EL GRITO, VOL. 3 NO.
    4 (SUMMER 1973), PP. 4-11.

ELIZONDO, SERGIO. PERROS Y ANTIPERROS: UNA EPICA CHICANA.
    BERKELEY, CALIFORNIA: QUINTO SOL PUBLICATIONS, INC.,
    1972.

ESPINOSA, AURELIO M. "ESTUDIOS SOBRE EL ESPAÑOL DE NUEVO
    MEJICO".   BIBLIOTECA DE DIALECTOLOGIA HISPANICA, VOL.
    1 (1930), PP. 1-313 (AN).

ESPINOSA, AURELIO M. "FOLKLORE INFANTIL DE NUEVO MEJICO".
    REVISTA DIALECTOLOGIA Y TRADICIONES POPULARES, VOL.
    10 , PP. 499-547 (LA).

ESPINOSA, AURELIO M. "LOS TEJANOS".   HISPANIA, VOL. 17
    (1944), P. 291 (AN).

ESPINOSA, AURELIO M. "NEW MEXICAN SPANISH COPLAS POPULARES".
    HISPANIA, VOL. 18 (1935), P. 136.

ESPINOSA, AURELIO M. "NEW MEXICO SPANISH FOLKLORE".
    JOURNAL OF AMERICAN FOLKLORE, VOL. 23 (1910), P. 395,
    418 (AN).

ESPINOSA, AURELIO M. "PROBLEMAS LEXICO-GRAFICOS DEL
    ESPAÑOL DEL SUDOESTE".   HISPANIA, VOL. 40 ,
    PP. 139-143 (LA).

ESPINOSA, AURELIO M. "ROMANCERO NUEVOMEJICANO".   REVUE
    HISPANIQUE, VOL. 33 (1915) (AN).

ESPINOSA, AURELIO M. "SPANISH AND SPANISH-AMERICAN FOLK
    TALES".   JOURNAL OF AMERICAN FOLKLORE,   (APRIL-JUNE
    1951), PP. 151-162 (AN).

ESPINOSA.   "SPANISH FOLKLORE NEW MEXICO" (LA*).

ESPINOSA, AURELIO M. "SPANISH FOLKTALES FROM CALIFORNIA".
    HISPANIA, VOL. 23 (1940), PP. 121-144 (AN).

ESPINOSA, AURELIO M. JR. "SPANISH-AMERICAN FOLKLORE".
    JOURNAL OF AMERICAN FOLKLORE, VOL. 60 (OCT-DEC 1947),
    PP. 373-377 (AN).

ESPINOSA, AURELIO M. "THE FIELD OF SPANISH FOLKLORE IN
    AMERICA".   SOUTHERN FOLKLORE QUARTERLY, VOL.
    5 (1941), PP. 29-35 (AN).

ESPINOSA, AURELIO M. "TRADITIONAL SPANISH BALLADS IN NEW
    MEXICO".   HISPANIA, VOL. 15 (MAR 1932).

ESPINOSA, AURELIO M. ESTUDIOS SOBRE EL ESPANOL DE NUEVO
     MEXICO.   BUENOS AIRES, 1946.

ESPINOSA, AURELIO M. ESTUDIOS SOBRE EL ESPANOL DE NUEVO
     MEJICO.   BUENOS AIRES, BRAZIL: IMPR DE LA UNIVERSIDAD
     DE BUENOS AIRES, 1930-1946 (AN).

ESPINOSA, AURELIC M. SPANISH FOLK-TALES FROM NEW MEXICO.
     NEW YORK, NEW YORK: AMERICAN FOLKLORE SOCIETY, 1937
     (AN).

ESPINOSA.   STUDIES NEW MEXICAN SPANISH (LA*).

ESPINOSA, AURELIC M. THE SPANISH LANGUAGE IN NEW MEXICO
     AND SOUTHERN COLORADO.   SANTA FE, NEW MEXICO:
     HISTORICAL SOCIETY OF NEW MEXICO, (1911). PUBLICATION
     16 (AN).

ESPINOSA, AURELIC. LOS COMANCHES.   ALBUQUERQUE, NEW
     MEXICO: UNIVERSITY OF NEW MEXICO PRESS, 1907.

ESPINOSA, AURORA M. DE. "PLATICA DE LA SENORA AURORA M.
     DE ESPINOSA EN EL ATENEO FRONTERIZO".   EL FRONTERIZO,
     (OCT 1943).

ESPINOSA.   "NEW MEXICO AS HISTORICAL LABORATORY   (HN*).

ESPINOSA.   "THE LEGEND SIERRA AZUL"   (HN*).

ESPINOSA, RUDY. 'KIKO'S TALE.'   IN OCTAVIO, ROMANO, EL
     ESPEJO.

ESPINOSA, RUDY. 'LITTLE EAGLE.'   IN OCTAVIO I. ROMANO-V.,
     EL ESPEJO.

ESPINOSA, RUDY. "LA CASITA".   EL GRITO, VOL. 4 NO. 2
     (WINTER 1971), PP. 54-55.

ESPINOSA, RUDY. "LITTLE EAGLE AND THE RAINBOW".
     EL GRITO, VOL. 2 NO. 2 (WINTER 1969), PP. 78-80.

ESPINOSA, RUDY. "MAMA".   EL GRITC, VOL. 5 NO. 3 (SPRING
     1972), PP. 57-64.

ESPINOSA, RUDY. "MI CASA ES SU CASA".   EL GRITO, VOL.
     3 NO. 2 (WINTER 1970), PP. 19-27.

ESPINOSA, RUDY. "MONO".   EL GRITO, VCL. 4 NO. 2 (WINTER
     1971), PP. 38-39.

ESTUPINIAN , RAFAEL. 'POETRY.'   IN OCTAVIO I. ROMANO-V.,
     EL ESPEJO.

ESTUPINIAN, RAFAEL. THE CULTURAL ARTS AND THEIR ROLE IN
    THE EDUCATION OF THE MEXICAN AMERICAN. PAPER
    PRESENTED AT THE CONFERENCE "TOWARD A PHILOIOPHY OF
    EDUCATION FOR THE MEXICAN-AMERICAN" ON OCTOBER 14,
    1971, AUSTIN, TEOAS.

FERNANDEZ-LOPEZ, MARIA. EL VIAJE CE DON RAMON DE LA SAGRA
    A LOS ESTADOS UNIDOS.   UNIVERSITY OF TEXAS AT AUSTIN,
    MASTER'S THESIS (1953) (TJ HS).

FIGUERO, B. G. "EL GRITO".   EL GRITO, VOL. 1 NO.
    3 (SPRING 1968), PP. 8-9.

FIGUEROA, JOHN. "ANTONIO AND THE GREAT WORLD".   CON
    SAFOS, VOL. 1 NO. 3 (MARCH 1969).

FIGUEROA, JOHN. "NIGHT VOICES".   CON SAFCS, VOL.
    7 (1971), PP. 14-16.

FLORES, JOSEPH A. 'COULD IT HAVE BEEN?.'   IN JOSEPH A.
    FLORES, SONGS AND DREAMS: MEXICAN-AMERICAN LITERATURE.

FLORES, JOSEPH A. 'FALLING OUT.'   IN JOSEPH A. FLORES,
    SONGS AND DREAMS: MEXICAN-AMERICAN LITERATURE.

FLORES, JOSEPH A. 'POETRY.'   IN JOSEPH A. FLORES, SONGS
    AND DREAMS: MEXICAN-AMERICAN LITERATURE.

FLORES, JOSEPH A. 'FOR A RICE.'   IN JOSEPH A. FLORES,
    SONGS AND DREAMS: MEXICAN-AMERICAN LITERATURE.

FLORES, JOSEPH. SONGS AND DREAMS.   WEST HAVEN, CONNECTICUT:
    PENDULUM PRESS, INC., 1972.

FRANCO, ABEL. 'POETRY.'   IN JOSEPH A. FLORES. SONGS AND
    DREAMS: MEXICAN-AMERICAN LITERATURE..

GALARZA, ERNESTO. BARRIO BOY.   NCTRE DAME, INDIANA:
    UNIVERSITY OF NOTRE DAME PRESS, 1971 (SO).

GALARZA.   SPIDERS HOUSE WORKERS FIELD (SO*).

GALLEGOS, ALBERTO. "A POET".   EL GRITO, VOL. 4 NO. 2
    (WINTER 1971), P. 72.

GALLEGOS, ALBERTO. "DREAMS".   EL GRITO, VOL. 4 NO. 2
    (WINTER 1971), P. 72.

GALLEGOS, ALBERTO. "MARKED".   EL GRITO, VOL. 4 NO. 2
    (WINTER 1971), P. 72.

GALLEGOS, ALBERTO. "RAIN ON THE RIC GRANDE".   EL GRITO,
    VOL. 4 NC. 2 (WINTER 1971), P. 73.

GALLEGOS, ALBERTO. "THE DEAD".   EL GRITO, VOL. 4 NO.
    2 (WINTER 1971), P. 73.

GARCIA, JUAN ANTONIO. "EL PADRECIDO MODERNO". EL GRITO,
    VOL. 5 NO. 1 (FALL 1971), PP. 55-56.

GARCIA, JUAN ANTONIO. "LAS PULGAS SOLTERAS". EL GRITO,
    VOL. 5 NO. 1 (FALL 1971), PP. 56-57.

GARCIA, JUAN. SUNS SOUL. BERKELEY, CALIFORNIA: QUINTO
    SOL PUBLICATIONS, INC., 1969.

GARCIA, JUAN. TIME CHANGES THINGS. BERKELEY, CALIFORNIA:
    QUINTO SOL PUBLICATIONS, INC., 1969.

GARCIA, MARIO T. "JOSE VASCONCELOS AND LA RAZA".
    EL GRITO, VOL. 2 NO. 4 (SUMMER 1969), PP. 49-51.

GARCIA, RICHARD. "IT IS ALWAYS MORNING.". EL GRITO, VOL.
    4 NO. 2 (WINTER 1971), P. 75.

GARCIA, RICHARD. "WE SIT ABOVE THE SEA". EL GRITO, VOL.
    4 NO. 2 (WINTER 1971), P. 74.

GARCIA, RICHARD. "YOU WALK THROUGH THE DEAD HOUSE". EL
    GRITO, VOL. 4 NO. 2 (WINTER 1971), P. 75.

GARCIA, RICHARD. SELECTED POETRY. BERKELEY, CALIFORNIA:
    QUINTO SOL PUBLICATIONS, 1973.

GARZA, DANIEL. "SATURDAY BELONGS TO THE PALOMILLA".
    HARPER'S MAGAZINE, VOL. 225 (JULY 1962), PP. 42-44.

GARZA, DANIEL. ACROSS THE RIVER AT RAINBOW'S END. EDITED
    BY JOSEPH A. FLORES. WEST HAVEN, CONNECTICUT: PENDULUM
    PRESS, INC., 1972.

GARZA, DANIEL. JUST LIKE UNCLE CARLTON. EDITED BY JOSEPH
    A. FLORES. WEST HAVEN, CONNECTICUT: PENDULUM PRESS,
    INC., 1972.

GARZA, DANIEL. SATURDAY BELONGS TO THE PALOMILLA. EDITED
    BY ED LUDWIG AND JAMES SANTIBANEZ. BALTIMORE,
    MARYLAND: PENGUIN BOOKS, INC., 1971.

GARZA, DANIEL. STRIPPER WHIRLWIND: THE PIZCADORES AND THE
    MACHINES. EDITED BY ED LUDWIG AND JAMES SANTIBANEZ.
    BALTIMORE, MARYLAND: PENGUIN BOOKS, INC., 1971.

GMEZ, ANTONIO. BARRIOLOGY EXAM.. EDITED BY ED LUDWIG
    AND JAMES SANTIBANEZ. BALTIMORE, MARYLAND: PENGUIN
    BOOKS, INC., 1971.

GOMEZ, RODOLFO CORTINA. JOSE GAUTIER BENITEZ, POETA
    ESENCIAL. REVISTA CHICANO-RIQUENA, ANO UNO, NUMERO
    DOS (OTONO 1973) PAGS. 43-48.

GONZALES PENA, CARLOS. HISTORY OF MEXICAN LITERATURE.
     THIRD EDITION. TRANSLATED BY GUSTA BARFIELD NANCE AND
     FLORENE JOHNSON DUNSTAN. DALLAS: SOUTHERN METHODIST
     UNIVERSITY PRESS, 1968.

GONZALES, RODOLFO. I AM JOAQUIN.   DENVER, COLORADO:
     CRUSADE FOR JUSTICE, 1967.

GONZALES, STEVE. "THE ADVERTISEMENT".   EL GRITO, VOL.
     1 NO. 1 (FALL 1967), PP. 12-14.

GONZALEZ, GENARO. UN HIJO DEL SOL.   IN EDWARD SIMMEN
     <ED>, THE CHICANO. FROM CARICATURE TO SELF-PORTRAIT.
     NEW AMERICAN LIBRARY, NEW YORK: A MENTOR BOOK, 1971.

GONZALEZ, JOSE ELIAS. "A C...V...".   EL GRITO, VOL. 5
     NO. 1 (FALL 1971), P. 26.

GONZALEZ, JOSUE M. "DEAN'S LIST".   EL GRITO, VOL. 1 NO.
     3 (SPRING 1968), PP. 43-44.

GONZALEZ. "POETRY" (HM*).

GONZALEZ. "MEXICO-LIMBO LOST WORDS" (HM*).

GONZALEZ, RAFAEL JESUS. TO AN OLD WOMAN.   IN AMERICO
     POREDES AND RAYMUND POREDES, MEXICAN AMERICAN AUTHORS.
     BOSTON, MASSACHUSETTS: HOUGHTON MIFFLIN COMPANY, 1972.

GONZALEZ. "FLOWER OF JADE" (HM*).

GONZALEZ. "NAHUATL POETRY" (HM*).

GONZALEZ, RODOLFO. I AM JOAQUINYO SCY JOAQUIN.   NEW YORK:
     A BANTAM BOOK, 1972.

GORDON.   INHERIT EARTH; STORIES MEXICAN (LI*).

GORDON.   INHERIT EARTH; STORIES MEXICAN (LI*).

GRANAT, ROBERT. "SANCHEZ AND THE VIBORA: A NEW MEXICAN
     TALE".   THE TEXAS QUARTERLY, VOL. 7 (AUTUMN 1964),
     PP. 128-138.

GRANAT, ROBERT. SANCHEZ AND THE VIBORA: A NEW MEXICAN
     TALE. EDWARD SIMMEN. THE CHICANO: FROM CARICATURE
     TO SELF PORTRAIT. NEW AMERICAN LIBRARY. NEW YORK: A
     MENTOR BOOK, 1971.

GRANAT.   TO ENDURE (LI*).

GUERRA, FERMINA. MEXICAN AND SPANISH FOLKLORE AND
     INCIDENTS IN SOUTHWEST TEXAS.   UNIVERSITY OF TEXAS
     AT AUSTIN, MASTER'S THESIS (1941) (AN).

GUERRA, FERMINA. RANCHO BUENA VISTA. IN AMERICO PAREDES
AND RAYMUND PAREDES. MEXICAN AMERICAN AUTHORS. BOSTON,
MASSACHUSETTS:HOUGHTON MIFFLIN COMPANY, 1972.

GUEVARA, JUAN G. "POETRY". EL GRITO, VOL. 4 NO.
2 (WINTER 1971), PP. 59-60.

GUEVARA, JUAN G. "POETRY". EL GRITO, VOL. 5 NO. 1 (FALL
1971), PP. 61-62.

GUTIERREZ, F. N. "POETRY". EL GRITO, VOL. 5 NO. 1 (FALL
1971), P. 32.

GUTIERREZ, JOSE ANGEL. 'MEXICANOS NEED TO CONTROL THEIR
OWN DESTINIES.' IN EDWARD SIMMEN, (ED) PAIN
& PROMISE: THE CHICANO TODAY.

GUTIERREZ, JOSE ANGEL. "POETRY". EL GRITO, VOL. 1 NO.
3 (SPRING 1968), PP. 40-42.

GUTIERREZ, JOSE E. "POETRY". EL GRITO, VOL. 5 NO. 1
(FALL 1971), P. 31.

GUZMAN. EAGLE SERPENT (HM*).

GUZMAN. EAGLE SERPENT (HM*).

GUZMAN. EAGLE SERPENT (HM*).

GUZMAN. MEMOIRS PANCHO VILLA (HM*).

HADDOX, JOHN H. ANTONIO CASO, PHILOSOPHER OF MEXICO.
AUSTIN: UNIVERSITY OF TEXAS PRESS, 1971.

HADDOX, JOHN H. LOS CHICANOS; AN AWAKENING PEOPLE. THE
UNIVERSITY OF TEXAS AT EL PASO, TEXAS WESTERN PRESS,
(1970). SOUTHWESTERN STUDIES MONOGRAPH, NO. 28.

HADDOX, JOHN H. VASCONCELOS OF MEXICO, PHILOSOPHER AND
PROPHET. AUSTIN: UNIVERSITY OF TEXAS PRESS, 1967.

HALY. "PASTORES DEL PALO DURO" (AN*).

HANSEN, TERRENCE L. "CORRIDOS IN SOUTHERN CALIFORNIA".
WESTERN FOLKLORE, VOL. 18 (FALL 1969), PP. 203-232,
295-315 (AN).

HASTINGS, D. H. WITH DONIPHAN IN MEXICO. DOCUMENTS AND
NOTES COLLECTED BY JUSTIN H. SMITH, PART 2. LATIN-AMERICAN
COLLECTION, UNIVERSITY OF TEXAS.

HAWLEY, RENEE DUNIA. LOS ANGELES AND THE DANCE 1850-1930.
UNIVERSITY OF CALIFORNIA, LOS ANGELES, MASTER'S THESIS
(1971).

HAWS, JAK. "SHORT STORY". EL GRITO, VOL. 5 NO. 1 (FALL
    1971), PP. 43-44.

HEDRICK, BASIL C.; KELLEY, J. CHARLES; AND RILEY, CARROLL
    L. (EDS). THE NOVELS OF JUAN ANTONIO MATEOS.
    UNIVERSITY OF TEXAS AT AUSTIN, MASTER'S THESIS (1947).

HERNANDEZ CRUZ, VICTOR. SNAPS. NEW YORK: VINTAGE BOOKS,
    1969.

HERNANDEZ, ALEX. POETRY. REVISTA CHICANO-RIQUENA, ANO
    UNO, NUMERO UNO (PRIMAVERA 1973) PAGS. 19-21.

HERNANDEZ, JULIA. NOVELISTAS Y CUENTISTAS DE LA REVOLUCION.
    UNIVERSITY OF ARIZONA AT TUCSON, MASTER'S THESIS (1972).

HERRA, MARIA DIAZ. THE BRACERO EXPERIENCE: IN LIFE AND
    FICTION. UNIVERSITY OF CALIFORNIA AT LOS ANGELES,
    MASTER'S THESIS (1971).

HERRERA, JUAN FELIPE. "POESIA". HISPAMERICA, VOL. 2
    NO. 6 (1974), P. 107.

HIJAR Y JARO, JUAN B. "POETRY". EL GRITO, VOL. 5 NO.
    1 (FALL 1971), PP. 28-31.

HINOJOSA-SMITH, R. R. E PLURIBUS VITAE. REVISTA
    CHICANO-RIQUENA, ANO UNO, NUMERO DOS (OTONO 1973)
    PAGS. 14-15.

HINOJOSA-SMITH, ROLANDO. "POR ESAS COSAS QUE PASAN".
    EL GRITO, VOL. 3 (SPRING 1972), PP. 26-36.

HINOJOSA-SMITH, ROLANDO. ESTAMPAS DEL VALLE. BERKELEY:
    QUINTO SOL, PUBLICATIONS, 1973.

HINOJOSA, ROLANDO R. ESTAMPAS DEL VALLE Y OTRAS OBRAS.
    BERKELEY, CALIFORNIA: QUINTO SOL PUBLICATIONS, 1973.

HUERTA, JORGE A. "CHICANO TEATRO: A BACKGROUND".
    AZTLAN--CHICANO JOURNAL OF THE SOCIAL SCIENCES AND
    THE ARTS, VOL. 2 NO. 2 (FALL 1971), PP. 63-78.

IBAQNEZ. PASTORELA (AR*).

JARAMILLO. CLEOFAS M. ROMANCE OF A LITTLE VILLAGE GIRL.
    SAN ANTONIO: NAYLOR COMPANY, 1955 (LI).

JARAMILLO. CLEOFAS M. SHADOWS OF THE PAST (SOMBRAS DEL
    PASADO). SANTA FE: SETON VILLAGE PRESS, 1941.

JIMENEZ, FRANCISCO. "CHRISTMAS GIFT". EL GRITO , VOL.
    5 NO. 3 (SPRING 1972), P. 75.

JIMENEZ, FRANCISCO. "COLD DEATH". EL GRITO, VOL. 5 NO.
    3 (SPRING 1972), PP. 78-79.

JIMENEZ, FRANCISCO. "MUERTE FRIA". EL GRITO, VOL. 5
     NO. 3 (SPRING 1972), PP. 76-77.

JIMENEZ, FRANCISCO. "UN AGUINALDO". EL GRITO, VOL. 5
     NO. 3 (SPRING 1972), P. 74.

JIMENEZ, J. PHILIP. "BUENOS DIAS, SENORA". EL GRITO,
     VOL. 1 NO. 2 (WINTER 1968), P. 31.

JIMENEZ, J. PHILIP. "THERE WAS A BABY". EL GRITO, VOL.
     1 NO. 2 (WINTER 1968), P. 31.

JIMENEZ, PHILIP J. "VIETNAM". EL GRITO, VOL. 1 NO. 3
     (SPRING 1968), PP. 31-34.

JOHNSON, HENRY SIOUX: HERNANDEZ, WILLIAM J. 'WHO AM I?
     EDUCATING THE MEXICAN AMERICAN.' IN HENRY SIOUX
     JOHNSON AND WILLIAM J. HERNANDEZ-M. EDUCATING
     THE MEXICAN AMERICAN.

JONES.   SPANISH AMERICAN LITERATURE TRANSLATION: (HSA*).

KANELLOS, NICOLAS. NUESTRO TEATRO.   REVISTA CHICANO-RIQUENA,
     ANO UNO, NUMERO DOS (OTONO 1973) PAG. 1.

KANELLOS, NICOLAS. UN RELATO DE AZTECA (BROMEANDO).
     REVISTA CHICANO-RIQUENA, ANO UNO, NUMERO UNO (PRIMAVERA
     1973) PAGS. 5-8.

LANGFORD, WALTER M. THE MEXICAN NOVEL COMES OF AGE.
     NOTRE DAME, INDIANA: UNIVERSITY OF NOTRE DAME PRESS,
     1971.

LARRALDE, CARLOS. BLESSING THE ANIMALS.   EDITED BY JOSEPH
     A. FLORES. WEST HAVEN, CONNECTICUT: PENDULUM PRESS,
     INC., 1972.

LARRALDE, CARLOS. LEGEND OF THE GREEN CROSS.   EDITED BY
     JOSEPH A. FLORES. WEST HAVEN, CONNECTICUT: PENDULUM
     PRESS, INC., 1972.

LARRALDE, CARLOS. LUCKY PERRITO.   EDITED BY JOSEPH A.
     FLORES. WEST HAVEN, CONNECTICUT: PENDULUM PRESS, INC.,
     1972.

LARRALDE, CARLOS. SANTOS Y SANTEROS.   EDITED BY JOSEPH
     A. FLORES. WEST HAVEN, CONNECTICUT: PENDULUM PRESS,
     INC., 1972.

LARRALDE, CARLOS. THE LAZY FOX.   EDITED BY JOSEPH
     A. FLORES. WEST HAVEN, CONNECTICUT: PENDULUM PRESS,
     INC., 1972.

LARRALDE, CARLOS. A RICH UNCLE'S REVENGE.   EDITED
     BY JOSEPH A. FLORES. WEST HAVEN, CONNECTICUT: PENDULUM
     PRESS, INC., 1972.

LARREY, MARTIN GERMIN. A VICERCY AND HIS CHALLENGES:
    SUPREMACY STRUGGLES DURING THE VICEREGENCY OF MARTIN
    ENRIQUEZ, 1568-1580.   UNIVERSITY OF CALIFORNIA, SANTA
    BARBARA, PHD. DISSERTATION (1965).

LE STRANGE.   SPANISH BALLADS   (AN*).

LEA, AURORA LUCERO-WHITE. "OUR TREASURY OF SPANISH
    FOLKLCRE".   NEW MEXICO FOLKLCRE RECORD, VOL. 9 ,
    PP. 15-19 (AN).

LEA, AURORA. LITERARY FCLKLORE OF THE HISPANIC SOUTHWEST.
    SAN ANTONIO: THE NAYLOR COMPANY, 1953 (AN).

LEAL, LUIS. "DISERTACIONES Y TESIS SOBRE LITERATURA
    MEXICANA EN LOS ESTADOS UNIDOS".   HISPANIA, VOL. 45
    (MAY 1962), PP. 281-283.

LEAL, LUIS. MEXICAN AMERICAN LITERATURE: A HISTORICAL
    PERSPECTIVE.   REVISTA CHICANO-RIQUENA, ANO UNO,
    NUMERO UNC (PRIMAVERA 1973) PAGS. 32-44.

LEAL, LUIS. MEXICO.   CAMBRIDGE, MASSACHUSETTS: HOUGHTON,
    MIFFLIN COMPANY, THE RIVERSIDE PRESS, 1955.

LEITMAN, SPENCER. EXILE AND UNION IN INDIANA HARBOR.
    REVISTA CHICANO-RIQUENA, ANO DOS, NUMERO UNO (INVIERNO
    1974) PAGS. 50-57.

LIPPARC, GEORGE. LEGENDS OF MEXICO.   PHILADELPHIA: T.
    B. PETERSON, 1847.

LOPEZ DE GCMARA, FRANCISCO. CORTEZ: THE LIFE OF THE
    CONQUEROR AND HIS SECRETARY.   BERKELEY: UNIVERSITY
    OF CALIFORNIA PRESS, 1966.

LOPEZ Y FUENTES, GREGORIO. HUASTECA; NOVELA MEXICANA.
    MEXICO: A. BOTAS, 1939.

LOPEZ Y FUENTES, GREGORIO. EL INDIO.   NEW YORK: BREDERICK
    UNGAR, 1961.

LOPEZ, DIANA. "LA SOCIEDAD".   EL GRITO, VOL. 3 NO. 2
    (WINTER 1970), PP. 40-41.

LOPEZ, ENRIQUE. "BACK TO BACKIMBA".   HORIZON, VOL. 9
    (WINTER 1967), PP. 80-83.

LOPEZ, ENRIQUE. "LATE, LATE LOVERS".   ATLANTIC, VOL. 220
    (4ULY 1967), P. 95.

LOPEZ, ENRIQUE. "MEXICO".   AMERICAN HERITAGE, VOL. 20
    (APRIL 29, 1969), PP. 4-39 (HM).

LOPEZ, ENRICUE. BACK TO BACKIMBA.   BALTIMORE, MARYLAND:
    PENGUIN BOOKS, INC., 1971.

LOPEZ, HECTOR. "TIBIA INCERTIDUMBRE". EL GRITO, VOL.
    3 NO. 2 (WINTER 1970), PP. 35-37.

LOPEZ, MANUEL. "NOTES FROM A DENVER JAIL". CONSAFOS,
    VOL. 1 NO. 4 (OCTOBER 1954), PP. 33-35.

LOS CUATRO. LOS CUATRO--POEMS. DENVER: BARRIO PUBLICATIONS,
    NO DATE.

LOVECRAFT, H. P. THE TRANSITION OF JUAN ROMERO. SAUK
    CITY, WISCONSIN: ARKHAM HOUSE, 1965 (LI).

LOZADA, FROBEN. PULQUE AND THE PUTOS: OR, THE CHICANO
    STRUGGLE FOR SELF-DETERMINATION. EL POCHO CHE, JULY
    1969.

LUDWIG, EDWARD; SANTIBANES, JAMES. THE CHICANOS: MEXICAN
    AMERICAN VOICES. BALTIMORE: PENGUIN BOOKS, INCORPORATED,
    1971.

MAGANA ESQUIVEL, ANTONIO. MEDIO SIGLO DE TEATRO MEXICANO
    1900-1961. MEXICO INSTITUTO NACIONAL DE BELLAS
    ARTES, DEPARTMENTO DE LITERATURA, 1964.

MAGANA ESQUIVEL, ANTONIO. TEATRO MEXICANO DEL SIGLO XX.
    MEXICO: FONDO DE CULTURA ECONOMICA AV DE LA UNIVERSIDAD,
    1970.

MAHLER, THEODOR. LIFE AND WORK OF ANGEL DE CAMPO.
    UNIVERSITY OF TEXAS AT AUSTIN, MASTER'S THESIS (1933).

MALDONADO, JESUS. "CAPRICOCITA ROJA". EL GRITO, VOL.
    3 NO. 4 (SUMMER 1970), PP. 12-16.

MALDONADO, JESUS. "POETRY". EL GRITO, VOL. 4 NO.
    2 (WINTER 1971), PP. 68-69.

MANCILLAS, STELLA. WHO AM I ?. EDITED BY JOSEPH
    A. FLORES. WEST HAVEN, CONNECTICUT; PENDULUM PRESS,
    INC., 1972.

MARIN, LUIS MUNOZ. 'PAMPHLET.' IN LILLIAN FADERMAN AND
    BARBARA BRADSHAW. AMERICAN ETHNIC WRITING.

MARIN, LUIS MUNOZ. 'QUERIES: UNBRELLAS AND A DEATH.'
    IN LILLIAN FADERMAN AND BARBARA BRADSHAW (EDS),
    SPEAKING FOR OURSELVES: AMERICAN ETHNIC WRITING..

MARIN, REYMUNDO. "TENTO". EL GRITO, VOL. 4 NO.
    2 (WINTER 1971), PP. 34-37.

MARTIN, ELEANOR JEAN. CARNAVAL AFUERA, CARNAVAL ADENTRO:
    SINTESIS DEL PENSAMIENTO SOCIAL DE RENE MARQUES.
    REVISTA CHICANO-RIQUENA, ANO DOS, NUMERO UNO (INVIERNO
    1974) PAGS. 39-49.

MARTINEZ, AL. "HORROR IS THE NAME OF THE GAME".
EL GRITO, VOL. 1 NO. 4 (SUMMER 1968), PP. 36-37.

MASILUNAS, MARGARITA BARRIOS. POETRY. REVISTA CHICANO-RIQUENA,
ANO DOS, NUMERO UNO (INVIERNO 1974) PAGS. 31-34.

MC KENNA, TERESA. "THREE NOVELS: AN ANALYSIS". AZTLAN--CHICANO
JOURNAL OF THE SOCIAL SCIENCES AND THE ARTS, VOL. 1
NO. 2 (FALL 1970), PP. 47-56.

MENA, FRANCISCO. POETRY. REVISTA CHICANO-RIQUENA, ANO
DOS, NUMERO UNO (INVIERNO 1974) PAGS. 36-37.

MENDEZ-M., MIGUEL. 'TALLER DE IMAGENES.' QUINTO
SOL PUBLICATIONS INC.

MENDEZ-M., MIGUEL. 'TATA CASEHUA.' QUINTO SOL PUBLICATIONS
INC.

MENDEZ-M., MIGUEL. 'WORKSHOP FOR IMAGES.' IN OCTAVIO
ROMANO EL ESPEJO.

MENDEZ-M., MIGUEL. "TRAGEDIAS DEL NORESTE". EL GRITO,
VOL. 2 (JULY 1955), PP. 3-16.

MENDEZ-M., MIGUEL. "TRAGEDIES OF THE NORTHWEST".
EL GRITO, VOL. 2 NO. 2 (WINTER 1969), PP. 17-31.

MENDOZA, DURANGO. SUMMER WATER AND SHIRLEY. BALTIMORE,
MARYLAND: PENGUIN BOOKS INC, 1971.

MENDOZA, DURANGO. THE PASSING. BALTIMORE, MARYLAND:
PENGUIN BOOKS INC, 1971.

MENDOZA, DURANGO. THE WOMAN IN THE GREEN HOUSE.
BALTIMORE, MARYLAND: PENGUIN BOOKS INC, 1971.

MENDOZA, JUAN JOSE. THE GIFT. WEST HAVEN, CONNECTICUT:
PENDULUM PRESS INC, 1972.

MENESES DE MARA, EL MANDO. CHILDREN PLAYING. WEST HAVEN,
CONNECTICUT: PENDULUM PRESS INC., 1972.

MEXICAN AMERICAN STUDIES CENTER. AZTLAN: JOURNAL OF THE
SOCIAL SCIENCES AND THE ARTS. LOS ANGELES, CALIFORNIA,.

MILLER. MEXICAN FOLK NARRATIVE LOS ANGELES (AN*).

MIR DE LASSALETTA, ANTONIA M. LA VIDA ES UN RUEDA HASTA
QUE SE PARA. REVISTA CHICANO-RIQUENA, ANO UNO,
NUMERO DOS (OTONO 1973) PAGS. 16-17.

MONTOYA, JOSE. POETRY. EL ESPEJO, BERKELEY, CALIFORNIA:
QUINTO SOL PUBLICATIONS INC., 1969.

MORA, RICARDO:. THE BLACK SUN.. LUBBOCK, TEXAS: TRUCHA
    PUBLICATIONS, 1973.

MORALES, DR. ARMANDO. ANDO SANGRANDO I AM BLEEDING..
    LA PUENTE, CALIFORNIA, 1972 (SO).

MORENO, BERTHA. DEFINE NOWHERE. SONGS AND DREAMS:
    MEXICAN-AMERICAN LITERATURE. WEST HAVEN, CONNECTICUT:
    PENDULUM PRESS INC., 1972.

MORENO, BERTHA. THERE WAS NO SUN TODAY. SONGS AND
    DREAMS: MEXICAN-AMERICAN LITERATURE. WEST HAVEN,
    CONNECTICUT: PENDULUM PRESS INC., 1972.

MORENO, CARLOS. INTERLUDE. SONGS AND DREAMS: MEXICAN-AMERICAN
    LITERATURE. WEST HAVEN, CONNECTICUT: PENDULUM PRESS
    INC., 1972.

MORENO, RAQUEL. "EL MILAGRUCHO". EL GRITO, VOL. 4 NO.
    3 (SPRING 1971), PP. 64-67.

MORENO, STEVE. "PROBLEMS RELATED TO PRESENT TESTING
    INSTRUMENTS". EL GRITO, VOL. 3 NO. 3 (SPRING
    1970), PP. 25-29.

MORENO, STEVE. PROBLEMS RELATED TO PRESENT TESTING
    INSTRUMENTS. VOICES: READINGS FROM EL GRITO.
    BERKELEY, CALIFORNIA: QUINTO SOL PUBLICATION, 1971.

MOYLAN, SISTER MARY PRUDENCE, B. V. M. THE NUN'S TALE.
    THE CHICANOS: MEXICAN-AMERICAN VOICES. BALTIMORE,
    MARYLAND: PENGUIN BOOKS, INC., 1971 (LI).

MURGUIA, ALEJANDRO. LAST TIME AROUND. REVISTA CHICANO-RIQUENA,
    ANO UNO, NUMERO DOS (OTONO 1973) PAGS. 18-20.

MURO, AMADO. "CECILIA, I LOVED YOU". NEW MEXICO
    QUARTERLY, VOL. 34 (WINTER 1964), PP. 353-364.

MURO, AMADO. "MALA TORRES". ARIZONA QUARTERLY,
    (SUMMER, 1968).

MURO, AMADO. "MARIA TEPACHE". ARIZONA QUARTERLY,
    (WINTER, 1969).

MURO, AMADO. "MY GRANDFATHER'S BRAVE SONGS". AMERICAS,
    VOL. 12 NO. 12 (DECEMBER 1960).

MURO, AMADO. CECILIA ROSAS. BOSTON, MASSACHUSETTS:
    HOUGHTON MIFFLIN COMPANY, 1972.

MURO, AMADO. MALA TORRES. THE CHICANOS: MEXICAN AMERICAN
    VOICES. BALTIMORE, MARYLAND: PENGUIN BOOKS, INC., 1971.

MURO, AMADO. MARIA TEPACHE. THE CHICANOS: MEXICAN-AMERICAN
    VOICES. BALTIMORE, MARYLAND: PENGUIN BOOKS, INC., 1971.

NAJERA, JOSE. "POETRY".   EL GRITO, VOL. 5   NO. 1 (FALL
    1971), P. 58.

NAVARRO GARCIA, LUIS.   DON JOSE DE GALVEZ Y LA COMANDANCIA
    GENERAL DE PROVINCIAS INTERNAS DE LANUEVA ESPANA.
    MADRID, 1964.

NAVARRO, J. L.   "CON SAFOS".   CON SAFOS, VOL. 1   NO. 3
    (MARCH   1969), PP. 32-33.

NAVARRO, J. L.   "PASSING TIME".   CON SAFOS, VOL. 1   NO.
    3 (MARCH   1969), PP. 28-31.

NAVARRO, J. L.   "TAMALE LEOPARD".   EL GRITO, VOL. 4   NO.
    4 (SUMMER   1970), PP. 46-55.

NAVARRO, J. L.   BLUE DAY ON MAIN STREET AND OTHER SHORT
    STORIES.   QUINTO SOL PUBLICATIONS,.

NAVARRO, J. L.   TO A DEAD LOWRIDER.   CON SAFOS, 1.

NERUDA, PABLO.   SPLENDOR AND DEATH OF JOAQUIN MURIETA.
    NEW YORK: FARRAR, STRAUS, AND GIROUX, 1972.

NEW MEXICO WRITERS' PROJECT.   WORKS PROGRESS ADMINISTRATION.
    "SPANISH AMERICAN WEDDING CUSTOMS".   EL PALACIO, VOL.
    49 (1942), PP. 1-6 (AN).

NEW MEXICO WRITERS' PROJECT.   WORKS PROGRESS ADMINISTRATION.
    THE SPANISH AMERICAN SONG AND GAME BOOK.   NEW YORK:
    A. S. BARNES, 1942 (AN).

NEWSWEEK.   'TIO TACO IS DEAD.'   IN EDWARD SIMMEN (ED),
    PAIN AND PROMISE: THE CHICANO TODAY.

OLVERA, JOE.   VOCES DE LA GENTE.   EL PASO: MICTLA
    PUBLICATION, 1970.

OROZCO, FLORA V.; CHAVEZ, JENNIE V.; GONZALES, CECILIA
    ABEYTA, BACALSKI,AND ROBERT: (EDS).   LA FRAGUA SIN
    FUEGO NO FIRE FOR THE FORGE..   CERRILLOS, NEW MEXICO,
    1971 (AN).

ORTEGA, JERONIMO.   BLUE BIKE BRINGS A BLUE DAY.   EDITED
    BY JOSEPH A. FLORES. WEST HAVEN, CONNECTICUT: PENDULUM
    PRESS, INC., 1972.

ORTEGO, PHILIP D.   "MONTEZUMA'S CHILDREN".   EL GRITO, VOL.
    3 NO. 3 (SPRING   1970), PP. 38-50.

ORTEGO, PHILIP D.   "MONTEZUMA'S CHILDREN".   THE CENTER
    MAGAZINE, VOL. 3   NO. 6 (NOVEMBER, DECEMBER   1970).

ORTEGO, PHILIP D.   "SOLEDAD".   PUERTO DEL SOL,   (WINTER
    1969).

ORTEGO, PHILIP D. "THE COMING OF ZAMORA". EL GRITO, VOL.
    1 NO. 3 (SPRING 1968), PP. 12-17 (ED).

ORTEGO, PHILIP D. "THE DWARF OF SAN MIGUEL". THE NEW
    ENGLAND REVIEW, (APRIL-MAY 1970).

ORTEGO, PHILIP D. MONTEZUMA'S CHILDREN. EL PASO, TEXAS:
    AMEREX PRESS, CHICANO RESEARCH INSTITUTE, 1971.

ORTEGO, PHILIP D. MONTEZUMA'S CHILDREN. EDITED BY
    OCTAVIO I. ROMANO-V. BERKELEY, CALIFORNIA: QUINTO SOL
    PUBLICATIONS, 1971.

ORTEGO, PHILIP D. WE ARE CHICANOS. NEW YORK: WASHINGTON
    PRESS, 1973.

ORTIZ, ORLANDO. "REFLECTIONS OF AN INARTICULATE CHILDHOOD".
    EL GRITO, VOL. 1 NO. 3 (SPRING 1968), PP. 36-39.

OTERO, MIGUEL ANTONIO. THE BENDING OF A TWIG. EDITED
    BY AMERICO PAREDES AND RAYMUND PAREDES. BOSTON,
    MASSACHUSETTS: HOUGHTON MIFFLIN COMPANY, 1972.

PADILLA, ERNIE. "POETRY". EL GRITO, VOL. 4 NO.
    2 (WINTER 1971), PP. 70-71.

PADILLA, ERNIE. "POETRY". EL GRITO, VOL. 3 NO. 1 (FALL
    1969), PP. 49-55.

PADILLA, RAY. "APUNTES PARA LA DOCUMENTACION DE LA CULTURA
    CHICANA". EL GRITO, VOL. 5 NO. 2 (WINTER 1971-72),
    PP. 3-46 (AN).

PADILLA, RAYMOND. "POETRY". EL GRITO, VOL. 5 NO.
    1 (FALL 1971), PP. 72-75.

PAREDES, AMERICO (ED.). FOLKTALES OF MEXICO. CHICAGO,
    ILLINOIS: UNIVERSITY OF CHICAGO PRESS, 1972 (AN).

PAREDES, AMERICO AND PAREDES, RAYMUND, EDS. CORRIDO DE
    JACINTO TREVINO. BOSTON, MASSACHUSETTS: HOUGHTON
    MIFFLIN COMPANY, 1972.

PAREDES, AMERICO AND PAREDES, RAYMUND. MEXICAN AMERICAN
    AUTHORS. HOUGHTON MIFFLIN, 1972.

PAREDES, AMERICO. "LUIS INCLAN FIRST OF THE COWBOY
    WRITERS". AMERICAN QUARTERLY, VOL. 12 (SPRING
    1960), PP. 55-70.

PAREDES. "TEXAS THIRD MAN: TEXAS-MEXICAN" (AN*).

PAREDES, AMERICO. "THE MEXICAN CORRIDO ITS RISE AND FALL".
    MADSTONES AND TWISTERS, VOL. 3 , PP. 99-105.

PAREDES.   BALLADS LOWER BORDER   (AN*).

PAREDES.   CORRIDO DE GREGORIC CORTEZ, BALLAD   (AN*).

PAREDES.   DICHOS   (AN*).

PAREDES.   FOLKTALES MEXICO   (AN*).

PAREDES, AMERICO. GUITARREROS.   EDITED BY AMERICO PAREDES
    AND RAYMUND PAREDES. BOSTON, MASSACHUSETTS: HOUGHTON
    MIFFLIN COMPANY, 1972.

PAREDES, AMERICO. WITH A PISTOL IN HIS HAND: A BORDER
    BALLAD AND ITS HERO.   AUSTIN: UNIVERSITY OF TEXAS,
    1958 (AN).

PAREDES.   WITH HIS PISTOL HIS HAND   (AN*).

PAREDES, AMERICO. 'THE HAMMON AND THE BEANS.'   IN MARTIN
    SHOCKLEY (ED), SOUTHWEST WRITER ANTHOLOGY.

PAREDES, AMERICO. 'THE LEGEND OF GREGCRIO CORTEZ.'   IN
    LILLIAN FADERMAN AND BARBARA BRADSHAW (EDS), SPEAKING
    FOR OURSELVES: AMERICAN ETHNIC WRITING..

PAREDES, AMERICO. THE LEGEND OF GREGORIO CORTEZ.   EDITED
    BY AMERICO PAREDES ANC RAYMUND PAREDES. BOSTON,
    MASSACHUSETTS: HOUGHTON MIFFLIN CCMPANY, 1972.

PAZ, OCTAVIO. ANTHOLOGY OF MEXICAN POETRY.   TRANSLATED
    BY SAMUEL BECKET. LONDON: THAMES AND HUDSON, 1958.

PAZ, OCTAVIO. CONFIGURATIONS.   NEW YORK: NEW DIRECTION
    BOOKS, 1971.

PAZ, OCTAVIO. CORRIENTE ALTERNA.   MEXICO: SIGLO VEINTIUNO
    EDITORES, 1967.

PAZ, OCTAVIO. LAS PERAS DEL OLMO.   MEXICO: IMPR.
    UNIVERSITARIA, 1957.

PAZ, OCTAVIO. LIBERTAD BAJO PALABRA: OBRA POETICA,
    1935-1958.   MEXICO: FONDO DE CULTURA ECONOMICA, 1960.

PAZ, OCTAVIC. NEW POETRY OF MEXICO.   NEW YORK: E.
    P. DUTTON AND COMPANY, 1970.

PAZ, OCTAVIC. POESIA EN MOVIMIENTO.   MEXICO: SIGLO
    VIENTIUNO EDITORES, 1966.

PAZ, OCTAVIC. PUERTAS AL CAMPO.   MEXICO: UNIVERSIDAD
    NACIONAL AUTONOMA DE MEXICO, 1967.

PAZ, OCTAVIO. SALAMANDRA 1958-1961.   MEXICO: J. MCRTIZ,
    1962.

PAZ, OCTAVIO. SELECTED POEMS. BLOOMINGTON: INDIANA
UNIVERSITY PRESS, 1963.

PAZ, OCTAVIO. SUN STONE (PIEDRA DE SOL). NEW YORK:
GROVE, 1948.

PAZ, OCTAVIO. AN ANTHOLOGY OF MEXICAN POETRY. SAMUEL
BECKELL (TRANS). BLOOMINGTON, INDIANA: INDIANA
UNIVERSITY PRESS, 1958.

PAZ, OCTAVIC. A LA ORILLA DEL MUNDO Y PRIMER DIA, BAJO
TU CLARA SOMBRA, RAIZ DE NOMBRENOCHE DE RESURRECCIONES.
MEXICO: COMPANIA EDITORIA Y LIBRERA ARS, S.A., 1962.

PAZ, OCTAVIO. THE LABYRINTH OF SOLITUDE: LIFE AND THOUGHT
IN MEXICO. NEW YORK: GROVE PRESS, 1961.

PEARCE, T. M. "THE BAD SON IN SOUTHWESTERN SPANISH
FOLKLORE". WESTERN FOLKLORE, VOL. 9 , PP. 295-301.

PEREZ DIAZ, ROBERTO. "LO NEGRO ". EL GRITO, VOL. 1 NO.
4 (SUMMER 1968), P. 41.

PEREZ DIAZ, ROBERTO. "UN INSTANTE". EL GRITO, VOL. 1
NO. 4 (SUMMER 1968), P. 41.

PEREZ, JAMES H. 'WHAT HAVE THE TIMES DONE.' IN JOSEPH
A. FLORES (ED), SONGS AND DREAMS: MEXICAN-AMERICAN
LITERATURE.

PEREZ, JAMES H. 'ON THE WALLS OF MARAVILLA.' IN JOSEPH
A. FLORES (ED), SONGS AND DREAMS: MEXICAN-AMERICAN
LITERATURE.

PEREZ, MARTHA. 'DON,T GET CLOSE.' IN JOSEPH A. FLORES
(ED), SONGS AND DREAMS: MEXICAN-AMERICAN LITERATURE.

PEREZ, RAYMUNDOCEL TIGRE. FREE, FREE AT LAST. MISSION,
TEXAS, 1970.

PEREZ. MEXICAN FOLKLORE AUSTIN (AN*).

PHILLIPS, JUANITA STROUD. THE SPANISH FOLKLORE OF TEXAS:
NO. 1, CAMERON COUNTY. UNIVERSITY OF TEXAS AT
AUSTIN, MASTER'S THESIS (1950) (AN).

PINO, FRANK. "CHICANO POETRY: A POPULAR MANIFESTO".
JOURNAL CF POPULAR CULTURE, VOL. 6 NO. 4 (SPRING
1973), PP. 718-730.

PINO, FRANK. "POESIA". HISPAMERICA, VOL. 2 NO.
6 (1974), PP. 105-106.

PINO, FRANK. HISPANIC TRADITION IN TOMAS RIVERA'S . . .
    Y NO SE LO TRAGO LA TIERRA.   IN TOMAS RIVERA Y LA
    LITERATURA CHICANA. EDITOR LUIS DAVILA, INDIANA UNIVERSITY.

PINO, FRANK. REALIDAD Y FANTASIA EN . . . Y NO SE LO TRAGO
    LA TIERRA.   MEMORIAS DEL XVI CONGRESO DEL INSTITUTO
    DE LITERATURA HISPANO-AMERICANA. HELD AT EAST LANSING
    MICHIGAN, AUGUST 1973.

PINO, FRANK. EL TEATRO.   REVISTA CHICANO-RIQUENA, ANO
    UNO, NUMERO DOS (OTONO 1973) PAGS. 11-13.

PIRULI. POETRY.   REVISTA CHICANO-RIQUENA, ANO UNO, NUMERO
    UNO (PRIMAVERA 1973) PAGS. 22-23.

PIRULI, MACIGAN. THE DEVIL AND JUAN PISTOLAS.   LUBBOCK,
    TEXAS, 1973.

POAG, GOLDSBY MAY. THE NOVELS OF MARIANO AZUELA.
    UNIVERSITY OF TEXAS AT AUSTIN, MASTER'S THESIS (1932).

PONCE, MIGUEL. "POETRY".   EL GRITO, VOL. 3 NO. 2 (WINTER
    1970), PP. 47-49.

PONCE, MIGUEL. "POETRY".   EL GRITO, VOL. 2 NO. 2 (WINTER
    1969), PP. 71-77.

PONCE, MIGUEL. POETRY.   BERKELEY, CALIFORNIA: QUINTO SOL
    PUBLICATIONS, INC., 1969.

POOLER, LOLITA H. "NEW MEXICAN FOLK TALES".   WESTERN
    FOLKLORE, VOL. 10 (JANUARY 1951), PP. 63-71 (AN).

POOLER, LOLITA H. "THREE SPANISH FOLK TALES".   NEW MEXICO
    FOLKLORE RECORD, VOL. 4 (1949-1950), PP. 20-22 (AN).

PORTILLO DE TRAMBLEY, ESTELA. "THE DAY OF THE SWALLOWS".
    EL GRITO, VOL. 4 NO. 3 (SPRING 1971), PP. 4-47.

PORTILLO, ESTELA. "THE APPLE TREES".   EL GRITO, VOL. 5
    NO. 3 (SPRING 1972), PP. 42-56.

PPAREDES.   MEXICAN-AMERICAN AUTHORS (AN*).

QUILES, EDGARDO. POETRY.   REVISTA CHICANO-RIQUENA, ANO
    UNO, NUMERO UNO (PRIMAVERA 1973) PAGS. 24-30.

RAEL, JUAN B. "CUENTOS ESPANOLES DE COLORADO Y DE NUEVO
    MEJICO, PRIMERA SERIE".   JOURNAL OF AMERICAN
    FOLKLORE, VOL. 52 (JULY-DECEMBER 1939), PP. 232-323
    (AN).

RAEL, JUAN B. "CUENTOS ESPANOLES DE COLORADO Y DE MEJICO,
SEGUNDA SERIE". JOURNAL OF AMERICAN FOLKLORE, VOL.
55 (JULY-DECEMBER 1939), PP. 3-93 (AN).

RAEL, JUAN B. "NEW MEXICAN SPANISH FEASTS". WESTERN
FOLKLORE QUARTERLY, VOL. 1 (JANUARY 1942), PP. 83-90
(AN).

RAEL, JUAN B. "NEW MEXICAN SPANISH FEASTS". CALIFORNIA
FOLKLORE QUARTERLY, VOL. 1 (JANUARY 1942), PP. 83-90
(AN).

RAEL, JUAN B. "NEW MEXICANS WEDDING SONGS". SOUTHERN
FOLKLORE QUARTELY, (MARZO 1940) (AN).

RAEL, JUAN B. CUENTOS ESPANOLES DE COLCRADO Y DE NUEVO
MEJICO. STANFORD: STANFORD UNIVERSITY PRESS, 1957
(AN).

RAEL, JUAN B. THE NEW MEXICAN ALBADO. STANFORD,
CALIFORNIA: STANFORD UNIVERSITY PRESS, (1951).
UNIVERSITY SERIES ON LANGUAGE AND LITERATURE, VOLUME
9, NUMBER 3 (AN).

RAEL, JUAN B. THE SOURCES AND DIFFUSION OF THE MEXICAN
SHEPHERDS' PLAYS. GUADALAJARA, MEXICO: LIBRERIA LA
JOYITA, 1965 (AN).

RAEL, JUAN B. A STUDY OF THE PHONOLOGY AND MORPHOLOGY OF
NEW MEXICAN SPANISH BASED ON A COLLECTION OF 410 FOLK
TALES. STANFORD UNIVERSITY, 1937 (AN).

RAMIREZ, FRANCISCO P. "POETRY". EL GRITO, VOL. 5 NO.
1 (FALL 1971), PP. 22-23.

RAMIREZ, JAVIER. "EL VIAJE". EL GRITO, VOL. 3 NO. 2
(WINTER 1970), P. 39.

RAMOS, MOISES ROSA. POETRY. REVISTA CHICANO-RIQUENA,
ANO UNO, NUMERO DOS (OTONO 1973) PAGS. 32-34.

RAMOS, SAMUEL. ASAVE FERNANCEZ CEL VALLE
SAMUEL RAMOS; TRAYECTORIA FILOSOFICA Y ANTOLOGIA DE
TEXTOS POR AUGUSTIN. MEXICO: CENTRO DE EXTUDIOS
HUMANISTICOS DE LA UNIVERSIDAD CE NUEVO LEON, 1965.

RAMOS, SAMUEL. PROFILE OF MAN AND CULTURE IN MEXICO.
TRANSLATED BY PETER G. EARLE, AUSTIN: UNIVERSITY OF
TEXAS PRESS, 1962.

RAMOS, SAMUEL. PSYCHO ANALYSIS OF THE MEXICAN. TORONTO:
UNIVERSITY OF TORONTO PRESS, 1965.

READ, JOHN LLOYD. THE MEXICAN HISTORICAL NOVEL, 1826-1910.
NEW YORK: INSTITUTO DE LAS ESPANAS IN LOS ESTADOS
UNIDOS, 1939.

RECHY, JOHN. "EL PASO DEL NORTE".   EVERGREEN REVIEW,
     (AUTUMN   1958).

RECHY, JOHN. "EL PASO DEL NORTE".   EVERGREEN REVIEW,
     (AUTUMN   1958).

REY.   "TIERRA AMARILLA IS DYING"   (SO*).

REYNA, THELMA T. "THE GRAPEVINE".   EL GRITO, VOL. 5 NO.
     3 (SPRING 1972), PP. 65-69.

RIDGE.   LIFE ADVENTURES JOAQUIN MURIETA   (HC*).

RIOS, ANTONIO JOSE. "AZTLAN: THE NATIONAL QUESTION".
     EL POCHO CHE, VOL. 1 (JULY 1969).

RIOS, FRANCISCO ARMANDO. "THE MEXICAN IN FACT, FICTION
     AND FOLKLORE".   EL GRITO, VOL. 2 NO. 4 (SUMMER
     1969), PP. 14-28 (AN).

RIOS, FRANCISCO ARMANDO. 'THE MEXICAN IN FACT, FICTION
     AND FOLKLCRE.' IN OCTAVIO I. ROMANO-V., VOICES:
     READINGS FROM EL GRITO (AN).

RIOS, FRANCISCO ARMANDO. 'THE MEXICAN IN FACT, FICTION
     AND FOLKLORE.' IN EDWARD SIMMEN, PAIN AND PROMISE:
     THE CHICANO TODAY (AN).

RIOS, HERMINIO AND CASTILLO, LUPE. "TOWARD A TRUE CHICANO
     BIBLIOGRAPHY: MEXICAN-AMERICAN NEWSPAPERS: 1848-1942".
     EL GRITO, VOL. 3 NO. 4 (SUMMER 1970), PP. 17-24.

RIOS, HERMINIO. "CHICANO".   EL GRITO, VOL. 3 NO.
     3 (SPRING 1970), PP. 67-71.

RIOS, HERMINIC. "INTRODUCTORY COMMENTS, COMPARATIVE
     LITERATURE".   EL GRITO, VOL. 5 NO. 1 (FALL 1971),
     PP. 9-12.

RIVERA, TOMAS. 'YOUNG VOICES.'   IN JOSEPH A. FLORES (ED),
     SONGS AND DREAMS: MEXICAN-AMERICAN LITERATURE.

RIVERA, TOMAS. "AND THE EARTH DID NOT PART".   EL GRITO,
     VOL. 4 NO. 2 (WINTER 1971), PP. 17-21.

RIVERA, TOMAS. "EL ANO PERDIDO".   EL GRITO, VOL. 4 NO.
     2 (WINTER 1971), P. 9.

RIVERA, TOMAS. "EL ANO PERDIDO".   EL GRITO,   (WINTER
     1970).

RIVERA, TOMAS. "EVA AND DANIEL".   EL GRITO, VOL. 5 NO.
     3 (SPRING 1972), PP. 22-25.

RIVERA, TOMAS. "EVA Y DANIEL".   EL GRITO, VOL. 5 NO.
     3 (SPRING 1972), PP. 18-21.

RIVERA, TOMAS. "EVA Y DANIEL". EL GRITO, VOL. 5 NO.
3 (1972).

RIVERA, TOMAS. "LOOKING FOR BORGES". REVISTA CHICANO-RIQUENA,
VOL. 1 NO. 1 (SPRING 1973).

RIVERA, TOMAS. "POETRY". EL GRITO, VOL. 3 NO. 1 (FALL
1969), PP. 56-63.

RIVERA, TOMAS. "THE LOST YEAR". EL GRITO, VOL. 4 NO.
2 (WINTER 1971), PP. 10-11.

RIVERA, TOMAS. "Y NO SE LO TRAGO LA TIERRA". EL GRITO,
VOL. 4 NO. 2 (WINTER 1971), PP. 12-16.

RIVERA, TOMAS. "Y NO SE LO TRAGO LA TIERRA". EL GRITO,
(WINTER 1970).

RIVERA, TOMAS. ALWAYS AND OTHER POEMS. SAN ANTONIO
TEXAS: SISTERDALE PRESS, SPRING 1973.

RIVERA, TOMAS. ANTOLOGIA DE LITERATURA CHICANA.
BERKELEY: QUINTO SOL PUBLICATION>,.

RIVERA, TOMAS. CAFE SOLO. GLENDALE, CALIFORNIA, SPRING
1974.

RIVERA, TOMAS. DEBAJO DE LA CASA. SAN ANTONIO, TEXAS,
FEBRUARY 1973.

RIVERA, TOMAS. INTO THE LABYRINTH: THE CHICANO IN
LITERATURE. PAN AMERICAN UNIVERSITY MONOGRAPH
SERIES, (SPRING 1972). SYMPOSIUM IN MEXICAN-AMERICAN
LITERATURE.

RIVERA, TOMAS. LABYRINTHS AND LITERATURE. DENTON, TEXAS,
FALL 1972.

RIVERA, TOMAS. LAS SALAMANDRAS, PUERTO DEL SOL.
LAS CRUCES: NEW MEXICO STATE UNIVERSITY, CREATIVE
WRITING CENTER, SPRING 1974.

RIVERA, TOMAS. LITERATURA CHICANA: VIDA EN BUSCA DE FORMA.
NEW YORK: ERIC, MLA, 1972.

RIVERA, TOMAS. LOOKING FOR BORGES. UNIVERSITY OF
CINCINNATI, FALL 1973.

RIVERA, TOMAS. LOOKING FOR BORGES. REVISTA CHICANO-RIQUENA,
ANO UNO, NUMERO UNO (PRIMAVERA 1973) PAGS. 2-4.

RIVERA, TOMAS. ME LO ENTERRARON. NORMAN, OKLAHOMA,
SPRING 1967.

RIVERA, TOMAS. PERSPECTIVES ON CHICANO LITERATURE. SOUTHWESTERN SOCIOLOGICAL ASSOCIATION AND SOUTHERN SOCIOLOGICAL SOCIETY SPECIAL SPRING ISSUE, 1972.

RIVERA, TOMAS. POETRY. BERKELEY, CALIFORNIA: QUINTO SOL PUBLICATIONS, 1969.

RIVERA, TOMAS. POETRY. REVISTA CHICANO-RIQUENA, ANO UNO, NUMERO UNO (PRIMAVERA 1973) PAGS. 17-18.

RIVERA, TOMAS. SEVEN POEMS. OCTAVIO ROMANO AND HERMINIO RIOS (EDS). REVISED EDITION, QUINTO SOL PUBLICATIONS, AUGUST 1972.

RIVERA, TOMAS. TEN POEMS. PHILLIP ORTEGO (ED). NEW YORK: SIMON AND SCHUSTER, FALL 1973.

RIVERA, TOMAS. WHEN LOVE TO BE. BLOOMINGTON, (SPRING 1973). REVISTA CHICANO-RIQUENA, VOLUME 1, I.

RIVERA, TOMAS. YOUNG VOICES. JOSEPH FLORES (ED). WEST HAVEN, CONNECTICUT: PENDULUM PRESS, 1972.

RIVERA, TOMAS. YOUNG VOICES. BLOOMINGTON, (SPRING 1973). REVISTA CHICANO-RIQUENA, VOLUME 1, I.

RIVERA, TOMAS. THE CHILD. BLOOMINGTON, (SPRING 1973). REVISTA CHICANO-RIQUENA, VOLUME 1, I.

RIVERA, TOMAS. EL ESPEJOTHE MIRROR. HERMINIO RIOS AND OCTAVIO ROMANO (EDS). REVISED EDITION, BERKELEY: QUINTO SOL PUBLICATIONS, AUGUST 1972.

RIVERA, TOMAS. THE NEW BREED, ANTHOLOGY OF TEXAS POETS. D. OLIPHANT (ED), DALLAS, TEXAS: PRICKLY PEAR PRESS, 1974.

RIVERA, TOMAS. Y NO SE LO TRAGO LA TIERRATHE EARTH DID NOT PART. BERKELEY, CALIFORNIA: QUINTO SOL PUBLICATIONS, 1971.

RIVERA, TOMAS. Y NO SE LO TRAGO LA TIERRA. OCTAVIO ROMANO AND HERMINIO RIOS (EDS). REVISED EDITION, BERKELEY, CALIFORNIA: QUINTO SOL PUBLICATIONS, 1972.

RIVERA, TOMAS. EL PETE FONSECA. LUIS VALDEZ AND STAN STEINER (EDS), NEW YORK: ALFRED A. KNOPF, 1972.

RIVERA, TOMAS. EL PETE FONSECA. REVISTA CHICANO-RIQUENA, ANO DOS, NUMERO UNO (INVIERNO 1974) PAGS. 15-22.

RIVERA, TOMAS. EL RECUERDO, DESCUBRIMIENTO Y LA VOLUNTAD. LUIS DAVILA (ED), BLOOMINGTON: UNIVERSITY OF INDIANA, SPRING 1974.

ROBBINS.   TALES LOVE HATE OLD SAN FRANCISCO   (AN*).

ROBE.   MEXICAN TALES LEGENDS LOS ALTOS   (AN*).

ROBE, STANLEY L. (ED). ANTOLOGIA DEL SABER POPULAR: A
    SELECTION FROM VARIOUS GENRES OF MEXICAN FOLKLORE
    ACROSS BORDERS.   LOS ANGELES: AZTLAN PUBLICATIONS,
    CHICANO STUDIES CENTER, UNIVERSITY OF CALIFORNIA, LOS
    ANGELES, (1971). MONOGRAPH NUMBER 2.

RODRIGUEZ, JOSEF. 'PRAYER.'   IN LILLIAN FADERMAN
    AND BARBARA BRADSHAW.

RODRIGUEZ, JOSEF. 'SMOKE.'   IN LILLIAN FADERMAN AND
    BARBARA BRADSHAW.

RODRIGUEZ, JUAN. POETRY.   REVISTA CHICANO-RIQUENA, ANO
    UNO, NUMERO DOS (OTONO 1973) PAGS. 23-24.

ROMANO-V.   GOODBY REVOLUTION-- HELLO SLUM   (AN*).

ROMANO-V.   THE HISTORICAL INTELLECTUALPRESENCE   (AN*).

ROMANO-V.   VOICES: READINGS GRITO   (AN*).

ROMANO-V.   VOICES: READINGS GRITO.   (AN*).

ROMANO-V., OCTAVIO IGNACIO. "EL GRITO".   EL GRITO, VOL.
    4 NO. 2 (WINTER 1971), P. 66.

ROMANO-V.   "GOODBY REVOLUTION-- HELLO SLUM"   (AN*).

ROMANO-V., OCTAVIO IGNACIO. "MUGRE DE LA CANCION".   EL
    GRITO, VOL. 3 NO. 2 (WINTER 1970), PP. 32-46.

ROMANO-V., OCTAVIO IGNACIO. "POETRY".   EL GRITO, VOL.
    4 NO. 2 (WINTER 1971), P. 66.

ROMANO-V., OCTAVIO IGNACIO. "POETRY".   EL GRITO, VOL.
    4 NO. 2 (WINTER 1971), PP. 32-46.

ROMANO-V., OCTAVIO IGNACIO. "POETRY".   EL GRITO, VOL.
    4 NO. 2 (WINTER 1971), PP. 64-65.

ROMANO-V., OCTAVIO IGNACIO. "STRINGS FOR A HOLIDAY".
    EL GRITO, VOL. 4 NO. 1 (FALL 1971), PP. 45-54 (AN).

ROMANO-V.   "THE CHOSEN ONE, ARCO IRIS; MISSIONARY   (AN*).

ROMANO-V., OCTAVIO IGNACIO. "THE CHOSEN ONE; EL ARCO IRIS;
    THE MISSIONARY JUAN; EL MESTIZO; Y EL CONS".
    EL GRITO, VOL. 4 (SPRING 1972), PP. 37-41 (AN).

ROMANO-V.   "THE HISTORICAL INTELLECTUALPRESENCE   (AN*).

ROMANO-V.   DON PEDRITO JARAMILLC EMERGENCE   (AN*).

ROMANO-V.   DON PEDRITO JARAMILLC: EMERGENCE   (AN*).

ROMANO-V.   ESPEJO: SELECTED MEXICAN AMERICAN   (AN*).

ROMANO-V.   MOSAICO MEXICANO   (AN*).

ROMANO-V., OCTAVIO IGNACIO (ED).   EL ESPEJO: SELECTED
    MEXICAN AMERICAN LITERATURE.   QUINTO SOL, BERKELEY,
    CALIFORNIA, 1969.

ROMANO-V., OCTAVIO IGNACIO.   'A ROSARY FOR DONA MARINA.'
    IN OCTAVIO I. ROMANO-V.   BERKELEY, CALIFORNIA: QUINTO
    SOL PUBLICATIO NS, INC.

ROMERO, JOSE RUBEN.   THE FUTILE LIFE CF PITO PEREZ.
    TRANSLATED FROM THE ORIGINAL SPANISH BY WILLIAM O.
    CORD. ENGLEWOOD CLIFFS, NEW JERSEY: PRENTICE-HALL,
    1967.

ROMERO, JOSE RUBEN.   LA VIDA INUTIL DE PITO PEREZ.
    MEXICO: EDITORIAL PORRUA, 1961.

ROSALDO, RENATC.   POETRY.   REVISTA CHICANO-RIQUENA, ANO
    DOS, NUMERO UNO (INVIERNO 1974) PAG. 25.

ROSALES, ARTURC.   POETRY.   REVISTA CHICANO-RIQUENA, ANO
    UNO, NUMERO DOS (OTONO 1973) PAGS. 31.

SAENZ, GERARDC.   POETRY.   REVISTA CHICANO-RIQUENA, ANO
    DOS, NUMERO UNO (INVIERNO 1974) PAG..35.

SALAZ, RUBEN DARIO.   "THE RACE".   EL GRITO, VOL. 4 NO.
    2 (WINTER 1971), PP. 22-23.

SALAZAR, RUBEN.   'AQUI NO SE HABLA ESPANOL.'   IN EDWARD
    SIMMEN (ED), PAIN AND PROMISE: THE CHICANO TODAY.

SALAZAR, RUBEN.   'LOS POBRES.'   IN EDWARD SIMMEN (ED),
    PAIN AND PROMISE: THE CHICANO TODAY.

SALAZAR, RUBEN.   'NO HAY TRABAJO.'   IN EDWARD SIMMEN (ED),
    PAIN AND PROMISE: THE CHICANO TODAY.

SALAZAR, RUBEN.   "BROWN BERETS HAIL 'LA RAZA' AND SCORN
    THE ESTABLISHMENT".   LOS ANGELES TIMES, VOL. 1 (JUNE
    16, 1969), P. 3.

SALAZAR, RUBEN.   "LATIN WARNS OF RISING ANGER TOWARD
    BLACKS".   LOS ANGELES TIMES, VOL. 2 (JUNE 17,
    1969), P. 4.

SALAZAR, RUBEN. STRANGERS IN ONE'S LAND. UNITED STATES
    COMMISSION ON CIVIL RIGHTS, (MARCH 1970). CLEARINGHOUSE
    PUBLICATION NUMBER 19.

SALINAS, LUIS OMAR AND FADERMAN, LILLIAN: (EDS). FROM THE
    BARRIO (A CHICANO ANTHOLOGY).. SAN FRANCISCO,
    CALIFORNIA: CANFIELD PRESS, 1973.

SALINAS, LUIS OMAR. CRAZY GYPSY. FRESNO: ORIGENES
    PUBLICATIONS, LA RAZA STUDIES F.S.C., 1970.

SALINAS, OMAR. 'PEDRO.' IN AMERICO PAREDES AND RAYMUND
    PAREDES (EDS).

SALINAS, OMAR. 'THIS DAY OF QUIXOTIC EXPECTATION.' IN
    LILLIAN FADERMAN AND BARBARA BRADSHAW (ED), SPEAKING
    FOR OURSELVES: AMERICAN ETHNIC WRITING.

SALINAS, OMAR. 'FROM AZTEC ANGEL.' IN LILLIAN FADERMAN
    AND BARBARA BRADSHAW (ED), SPEAKING FOR OURSELVES:
    AMERICAN ETHNIC WRITING.

SALINAS, RICARDO. "LA TORTILLA". EL GRITO, VOL. 4 NO.
    2 (WINTER 1971), PP. 67-68.

SALINAS, RODOLFO. 'CHICANO POWER.' IN JOSEPH A. FLORES
    (ED), SONGS AND DREAMS: MEXICAN-AMERICAN LITERATURE.

SALINAS, RODOLFO. "CHICANO POWER: PRIDE OR PREJUDICE".
    CON SAFOS, VOL. 1 NO. 3 (MARCH 1969), P. 14.

SAN JOSE, CALIFORNIA. SAN JOSE UNIFIED SCHOOL DISTRICT.
    MEXICAN AND MEXICAN AMERICAN LITERATURE FOR THE SENIOR
    HIGH SCHOOL: SHORT STORY, NOVEL, BIOGRAPHY. SAN
    JOSE, CALIFORNIA: SAN JOSE UNIFIED SCHOOL DISTRICT,
    1970.

SANCHEZ, RICARDO. "POETRY". EL GRITO, VOL. 3 NO.
    2 (WINTER 1970), PP. 28-34.

SANCHEZ, RICARDO. CANTO Y GRITO MI LIBERACION, Y LLORO
    MIS DESMADRAZGOS. EL PASO, TEXAS: MICTLA PUBLICATIONS,
    1971.

SANCHEZ, RICARDO:. CANTO Y GRITO MI LIBERACION..
    EL PASO, TEXAS: MICTLA PUBLICATIONS, 1970.

SANTAYANA, GEORGE. 'THE POET'S TESTAMENT.' IN LILLIAN
    FADERMAN AND BARBARA BRADSHAW, (EDS), SPEAKING FOR
    OURSELVES: AMERICAN ETHNIC WRITING.

SANTIBANEZ, JAMES. 'EL TEATRO CAMPESINO TODAY AND
    EL TEATRO URBANO.' IN ED LUDWIG AND JAMES SANTIBANEZ,
    THE CHICANOS: MEXICAN-AMERICAN VOICES. (AT).

SAUCEDA, CECILIC. 'THE FIRE ANTS.'   IN JOSEPH A. FLORES
    (ED), SONGS AND DREAMS: MEXICAN—AMERICAN LITERATURE.

SIERRA, PEDRO UGALDE. "MEDITANDO EN LA CLASE DE DON
    QUIJOTE".   EL GRITO, VOL. 4 NO. 2 (WINTER 1971),
    PP. 60-61.

SIFUENTES, FRANK. "A CRITIQUE ON GENTLE REVOLUTIONARIES:
    BROWN POWER BY PROFESSOR RALPH GUZMAN".   LA RAZA,
    VOL. 2 NO. 4 (FEBRUARY 7, 1969), PP. 6-7.

SIFUENTES.   "NOTE TO OFFICE EDUCATION" (ED*).

SIMMEN, EDWARD (ED.). WHO AM I? PAIN & PROMISE:
    THE CHICANO TODAY..   EDITED WITH AN INTRODUCTION BY
    EDWARD SIMMEN. NEW YORK AND SCARBOROUGH, ONTARIO: A
    MENTOR BOOK FROM NEW AMERICAN LIBRARY, 1972.

SIMMEN.   CHICANO: ORIGIN MEANING (LI*).

SIMMEN.   "THE CHICANO CARICATURE TO SELF—PORTRAIT" (LI*).

SIMMEN.   CHICANO CARICATURE TO SELF-PORTRAIT (LI*).

SIMMEN.   PAIN PROMISE: CHICANO TODAY (LI*).

SIMMONS.   INTRODUCTION (LI*).

SIMMONS.   MEXICAN CORRIDO AS SOURCE INTERPRETIVE (AN*).

SOL, PACO. "EN DEFENSA DE LOS TACOS".   EL GRITO, VOL.
    1 NO. 3 (SPRING 1968), PP. 20-21.

SOMMERS.   AFTER STORM: LANDMARKS MODERN (HM*).

SPRADLIN, T. RICHARD. "THE MEXICAN FARM LABOR IMPORTATION
    PROGRAM: REVIEW AND REFORM".   GEORGE WASHINGTON LAW
    REVIEW, VOL. 30   (DECEB ER 1961), PP. 84-122.

STRAND, MARK (ED.). NEW POETRY OF MEXICO: 1915-1966.
    NEW YORK, NEW YORK: E. P. DUTTON AND COMPANY, INC.,
    1970.

SUAREZ, MARIO. 'SENOR GARZA.'   IN AMERICO PAREDES AND
    RAYMUND PAREDES, (EDS) MEXICAN—AMERICAN AUTHORS.
    BOSTON, MASSACHUSETTS.

SUAREZ, MARIO. "EL HOYO".   CON SAFOS, VOL. 1 NO.
    3 (MARCH 1969), PP. 36-37.

SUAREZ, MARIO. "MEXICAN HEAVEN".   ARIZONA QUARTERLY, VOL.
    6 (WINTER 1950), PP. 310-315.

SUAREZ, MARIO. LAS COMADRES.   CON SAFOS. I, 3 (MARCH
    1969),, 36-37.

SUAREZ, MARIO. MAESTRIA.   EDITED BY AMERICO PAREDES AND
     RAYMUND PAREDES. BOSTON, MASSACHUSETTS: HOUGHTON
     MIFFLIN COMPANY, 1972.

SUAREZ, MARIO. SENOR GARZA.   EDITED BY EDWARD SIMMEN.
     A MENTOR BOOK. NEW YORK: NEW AMERICAN LIBRARY, 1971.

SUAREZ, MARIO. EL HOYO.   BOSTON, MASSACHUSETTS: HOUGHTON
     MIFFLIN COMPANY, 1972.

SUAREZ, MARIO. 'EL HOYO.'   IN JOSEPH A. FLORES. (EDS)
     SONGS AND DREAM: MEXICAN-AMERICAN LITERATU RE WEST
     HAVEN, CONNECTICUT: PENDULUM PRESS, INC..

TEATRO DESENGANO DEL PUEBLO. EL ALCALDE.   REVISTA
     CHICANO-RIQUENA, ANO UNO, NUMERO DOS (OTONO 1973)
     PAGS. 2-9.

THEATER IN THE STREETS PRESENTS MY PEOPLE. "VISTA
     VOLUNTEER" (AT*).

THOMAS. ALIEN TURF (SO*).

TIJERINA. PRISON (HN*).

TOPETE. AVENTURAS DE UN BRACERO (SI*).

TORRES RIOSECO.   ASPECTS SPANISH-AMERICAN LITERATURE (HSA*).

TORRES, JOSE ACOSTA. CACHITO MIO.   BERKELEY, CALIFORNIA:
     QUINTO SOL PUBLICATIONS, 1973.

TORRES, LUCY. POETRY.   REVISTA CHICANO-RIQUENA, ANO UNO,
     NUMERO UNO (PRIMAVERA 1973) PAGS. 15-16.

TORRES, LUIS LLORENS. 'JIBARO.'   IN LILLIAN FADERMAN AND
     BARBARA BRADSHAW (EDS), SPEAKING FOR OURSELVES:
     AMERICAN ETHNIC WRITING..

TORRES. EPIC LATIN AMERICAN LITERATURE (HSA*).

TORRES. "DAY DREAMS HOSPITAL BED" (AR*).

TORRES. "EL GRITO" (AR*).

TREJO, ARNULFO D. MAESTRO.   EDITED BY AMERICO PAREDES
     AND RAYMUND PAREDES. BOSTON, MASSACHUSETTS: HOUGHTON
     MIFFLIN COMPANY, 1972.

ULIBARRI, SABINE R. TIERRA AMARILLA. STORIES OF NEW MEXICO
     CUANTOS DE NUEVO MEXICO.   ALBUQUERQUE, NEW MEXICO:
     UNIVERSITY OF NEW MEXICO PRESS, 1971.

ULIBARRI, SABINE R. LA FRAGUA SIN FUEGO: NO FIRE FOR THE
     FORGE.   CERRILLOS, NEW MEXICO: SAN MARCOS PRESS,
     1971.

VACA, NICK C. "MARTIN". EL GRITO, VOL. I NO. I (FALL 1970), PP. 25-31.

VACA, NICK C. "THE BLACK PHASE". EL GRITO, VOL. 2 NO. 1 (FALL 1968), PP. 40-48.

VACA, NICK C. "THE NEGRO MOVEMENT AS AN ANTI-REVOLUTION". EL GRITO, VOL. 2 NO. 2 (WINTER 1969), PP. 61-69 (SO).

VACA, NICK C. "THE SOCIOLOGY OF BEING A MEXICAN-RUSSIAN". EL GRITO, VOL. 1 NO. 4 (SUMMER 1968), PP. 38-40.

VACA, NICK C. "VIVA CHICANO". EL GRITO, VOL. 3 NO. 4 (SUMMER 1970), PP. 32-33.

VACA, NICK C. MESSAGE TO THE PEOPLE. BERKELEY, CALIFORNIA: QUINTO SOL PUBLICATIONS, 1967 (SO).

VACA, NICK C. THE PURCHASE. EDITED BY AMERICO PAREDES AND RAYMUND PAREDES. BOSTON, MASSACHUSETTS,.

VACA, NICK C. THE VISIT. EDITED BY OCTAVIO I. ROMANO-V. BERKELEY, CALIFORNIA: QUINTO SOL PUBLICATIONS, INC., 1969.

VACA, NICK C. THE WEEK IN THE LIFE OF MANUEL HERNANDEZ. EDITED BY OCTAVIO I. ROMANO-V. BERKELEY, CALIFORNIA: QUINTO SOL PUBLICATIONS, INC., 1969. ALSO IN EDWARD SIMMEN, THE CHICANO: FROM CARICATURE TO SELF-PORTRAIT. A MENTOR BOOK. NEW YORK: NEW AMERICAN LIBRARY, 1971..

VALDEZ, LUIS AND STEINER, STAN (ED). AZTLAN, AN ANTHOLOGY OF MEXICAN AMERICAN LITERATURE. NEW YORK, N. Y.: ALFRED A. KNOPF, 1972.

VALDEZ, LUIS AND STEINER, STAN. AZTLAN: AN ANTHOLOGY OF MEXICAN AMERICAN LITERATURE. NEW YORK: RANDOM HOUSE, 1972.

VALDEZ, LUIS. THE TALE OF LA RAZA. EDITED BY ED LUDWIG AND JAMES SANTIBANEZ. BALTIMORE, MARYLAND: PENGUIN BOOKS, INC., 1971.

VALDEZ, LUIS. EL TEATRO CAMPESINO, ITS BEGINNINGS. EDITED BY ED LUDWIG AND JAMES SANTIBANEZ. BALTIMORE, MARYLAND: PENGUIN BOOKS, INC., 1971.

VALDEZ, LUIS, AND EL TEATRO CAMPESINO. ACTOS. FRESNO, CALIFORNIA: CUCARACHA PRESS, 1971.

VAN STONE. SPANISH FOLK SONGS NEW MEXICO (LI*).

VAN, MARY R., AND MORRIS, LOUISE. LOS PASTORES. CLEVELAND: GATES PRESS, 1933 (AN).

VARGAS, ROBERTC. REFLECTIONS. MIMEOGRAPHED. MEXICAN-AMERICAN
    CONFERENCE SPONSORED BY THE UNIVERSITY OF CALIFORNIA
    EXTENSION PROGRAMS. SAN FRANCISCO, JUNE 21-22, 1969..

VASCONCELOS, JOSE. "EDUCATIONAL ASPIRATIONS".   SURVEY,
    VOL. 52 (DECEMBER 24,   1954), PP. 167-69.

VASCONCELOS, JOSE. ASPECTS OF MEXICAN CIVILIZATION.
    UNIVERSITY OF CHICAGO PRESS, 1926 (HM).

VASCONCELOS, JOSE. INDOLOGIA.   BARCELONA: AGENCIA MUNDIAL
    DE LIBRERIA, 1927.

VASCONCELOS, JOSE. MEXICO.   CHICAGC: UNIVERSITY OF
    CHICAGO PRESS, 1928.

VASCONCELOS, JCSE. A MEXICAN ULYSSES, AN AUTOBIOGRAPHY.
    BLOOMINGTON: INDIANA UNIVERSITY PRESS, 1963.

VASCONCELOS, JCSE. EL PROCONSULACO.   MEXICO: EDICIONES
    BOTAS, 1939.

VASCONCELOS, JOSE. LA RAZA COSMICA; MISION DE LA RAZA
    IBERO-AMERICANA; ARGENTINA Y BRASIL.   MEXICO:
    ESPASA-CALPE MEXICANA, 1966.

VASCONCELOS, JOSE. LA RAZA COSMICA: MISSION DE LA RAZA
    IBERO-AMERICANA.   MEXICO: ESPASA CALPE MEXICANA, 1948.

VASCONCELOS, JOSE. LA TORMENTA.   MEXICO, EDICIONES BOTAS,
    1936.

VASQUEZ, DAVID. A HISTORY OF LATIN AMERICAN CIVILIZATION:
    SOURCES AND INTERPRETATIONS.   REVISTA CHICANO-RIQUENA,
    ANO UNO, NUMERO UNO (PRIMAVERA 1973) PAGS. 9-11.

VASQUEZ, ELFIDA. GRUPOS Y TENDENCIAS LITERARIAS EN MEXICO
    A PARTIR DE LA REVISTA "CONTEMPORANEOS": SUS ORGANOS
    DE EXPRESION.   UNIVERSITY OF TEXAS AT AUSTIN,
    MASTER'S THESIS (1949).

VASQUEZ, RICARDO. ... POETRY.   EL GRITO, 4.

VASQUEZ, RICARDC. POETRY.   REVISTA CHICANO-RIQUENA, ANO
    DOS, NUMERO UNO (INVIERNO 1974) PAGS. 26-30.

VASQUEZ, RICHARD. CHICANO.   NEW YORK: DOUBLEDAY AND
    COMPANY, 1970.

VASQUEZ, RICHARD. CHICANO STUDIES: SENSITIVITY FOR TWO
    CULTURES.   EDITED BY ED LUDWIG AND JAMES SANTIBANEZ.
    BALTIMORE, MARYLAND: PENGUIN BOOKS, INC., 1971 (AN).

VAZQUEZ, RICHARD. "CHICANO".   INTERNATICNAL MIGRATION
    REVIEW, VOL. 6 (SPRING   1972), PP. 88-89.

VELEZ-I., CARLOS G. SO FAREWELL HOPE, AND WITH HOPE,
    FAREWELL FEAR. EDITED BY OCTAVIO I. ROMANO-V.
    BERKELEY, CALIFORNIA: QUINTO SOL PUBLICATIONS, 1969.

VELEZ-I., CARLOS G. THE RAID. EDITED BY OCTAVIO
    I. ROMANO-V. BERKELEY, CALIFORNIA: QUINTO SOL
    PUBLICATIONS, INC., 1969.

VERGARA, LAUTARO. ECOS SERRANOS OR SOUTHWESTERN POEMS.
    PLACITAS, NEW MEXICO: TUMBLEWEED PRESS, 1971.

VERGARA, LAUTARO. LUZ Y SOMBRA. TRANSLATIONS, 1965.
    PLACITAS, NEW MEXICO: TUMBLEWEED PRESS, 1967.

VETANCURT. TEATRO MEXICANO, III, CRONICA (HS*).

VIGIL, J. M. "EL AMOR Y LA AMISTAD". EL GRITO, VOL. 5
    NO. 1 (FALL 1971), P. 27.

VILLA, ESTEBAN. "VIET NAM". EL GRITO, (SPRING 1968),
    PP. 22-30.

VILLAGRAN, VINCE. "THE DEATH OF MISS JONES". CON SAFOS,
    VOL. 1 NO. 3 (MARCH 1969), PP. 43-45.

VILLANUEVA, TINO. "POESIA". HISPAMERICA, VOL. 2 NO.
    6 (1974), PP. 103-105.

VILLANUEVA, TINO. "POETRY". EL GRITO, VOL. 5 NO.
    1 (FALL 1971), PP. 68-71.

VILLANUEVA, TINO. HAY OTRA VOZ POEMS. STATEN ISLAND,
    NEW YORK: MENSAJE DE NUEVA YORK, 1972.

VILLANUEVA, TINO. POETRY. REVISTA CHICANO-RIQUENA, ANO
    UNO, NUMERO UNO (PRIMAVERA 1973) PAGS. 13-14.

VILLAREAL, ALBERTO. "MAN'S HUMANITY". EL GRITO, VOL.
    1 NO. 4 (SUMMER 1968), PP. 34-35.

VILLAREAL, JOSE ANTONIO. "MEXICAN-AMERICANS IN UPHEAVAL".
    WEST, (SEPTEMBER 18, 1966), PP. 21-30 (SO).

VILLAREAL, JOSE ANTONIO. POCHO. NEW YORK: DOUBLEDAY AND
    COMPANY, 1959.

VILLARREAL, JOSE ANTONIO. "MEXICAN-AMERICANS AND THE
    LEADERSHIP CRISIS". LOS ANGELES TIMES: WEST
    MAGAZINE, (SEPTEMBER 25, 1966) (SO).

VILLASENOR, EDMUND. MACHO. NEW YORK, N. Y.: BANTAM
    BOOKS, 1973.

VILLAVICENCIO, SILVIO. "EL ESPEJO". EL GRITO, VOL. 2
    NO. 2 (WINTER 1969), PP. 47-53.

VILLAVICENCIO, SILVIO. "THE MIRROR". TRANSLATED
    BY OCTAVIO I. ROMANO-V. EL GRITO, VOL. 2 NO.
    2 (WINTER 1969), PP. 54-60.

VILLAVICENCIO, SILVIO. EL ESPEJO. EDITED BY OCTAVIO I.
    ROMANO-V. BERKELEY, CALIFORNIA: QUINTO SOL PUBLICATIONS,
    INC., 1969.

VILLAVICENCIO, SILVO. ES AQUI--DICE FELIPE. EDITED BY
    OCTAVIO I. ROMANO-V. BERKELEY, CALIFORNIA: QUINTO SOL
    PUBLICATICNS, INC., 1969.

VILLAVIVENCIO, SILVIO. " "IT IS HERE", SAYS FELIPE".
    EL GRITO, VOL. 2 NO. 1 (FALL 1968), PP. 33-39.

VILLAVIVENCIO, SILVIO. "-- ES AQUI--DICE FELIPE". EL
    GRITO, VOL. 2 NO. 1 (FALL 1968), PP. 27-32.

WALLRICH, WILLIAM J. "FIVE BRUJA TALES FROM THE SAN LUIS
    VALLEY". WESTERN FOLKLORE, VOL. 9 (DECEMBER 1921),
    PP. 359-62 (AN).

WALLRICH, WILLIAM J. "SPANISH AMERICAN DEVIL LORE
    IN SOUTHERN COLORADO". WESTERN FOLKLORE, VOL. 9
    (DECEMBER 1921), PP. 50-55 (AN).

WESLEY. RANCHERO SAYINGS BORDER (AN*).

WILSON. FAIRY TALES MEXICO (AN*).

WOMACK. "WHO ARE THE CHICANOS?" (AN*).

YANEZ, AGUSTIN. THE EDGE OF THE STORM. AUSTIN: UNIVERSITY
    OF TEXAS PRESS, 1963.

YANEZ, AGUSTIN. THE LEAN LANDS. AUSTIN: UNIVERSITY OF
    TEXAS PRESS, 1968.

ZERMENO, ANDY AND STAFF OF EL MALCRIADO. DON SOTACO.
    DELANO, CALIFORNIA: FARM WORKER PRESS, 1966.

ABRAHAM.   FREEDOM COURT; CIVIL RIGHTS LIBERTIES (SO*).

ACOSTA, OSCAR ZETA. "THE EAST L.A. 13 VS. THE L.A.
    SUPERIOR COURT".   EL GRITO, VOL. 3 NO. 2 (WINTER
    1970), PP. 12-18 (SO).

ADLER, HERMAN MORRIS; CAHN, 6RANCES; AND JOHANNES, STUART.
    THE INCIDENCE OF DELINQUENCY IN BERKELEY, 1928-1932.
    BERKELEY, CALIFORNIA: UNIVERSITY OF CALIFORNIA PRESS,
    1934.

ADLER, PATRICIA. THE 1943 ZOOT-SUIT RIOTS: BRIEF EPISODE
    IN A LONG CONFLICT.   IN MANUAL P. SERVIN: THE
    MEXICO-AMERICAN: AN AWAKENING MINORITY, 1970 (HC).

AGUILAR.   LOS METODOS CRIMINALES EN MEXICO (HM*).

ALDER, HERMAN; FRANCES CAHN AND STUART JOHANNES. THE
    INCIDENCE OF DELINQUENCY IN BERKELEY, 1929-1932.
    BERKELEY: UNIVERSITY OF CALIFORNIA PRESS, 1934.

ALMANZA, ARTURO S. MEXICAN-AMERICANS AND CIVIL RIGHTS.
    LOS ANGELES: LOS ANGELES COUNTY COMMISSION ON HUMAN
    RELATIONS, 1964.

ALVIDREZ, SAMUEL R. 'NARCOTICS AND DRUG USE TRENDS
    IN CALIFORNIA.' IN OCTAVIO ROMANO, VOICES READINGS
    FROM EL GRITO (MD SO).

ALVIDREZ, SAMUEL R. "DRUG USE TRENDS IN CALIFORNIA".
    EL GRITO, VOL. 4 NO. 1 (FALL 1970), PP. 65-81 (MD
    SO).

"SPANISH AMERICANS POLITICS" (PL*).

SPANISH NAME BOOK (SI*).

"ANOTHER CIVIL-RIGHTS HEADACHE: PLIGHT OF MEXICAN-AMERICANS,
    LOS ANGELES".   NEWS AND WORLD REPORT, VOL. 60 (JUNE
    6, 1966), PP. 46-48.

"BREAKTHROUGH AGREEMENT COACHELLA (EC*).

"BREAKTHROUGH HUELGA" (EC*).

"FORD FOUNDATION ANNOUNCES LEGAL (ED*).

"GREEN LIGHT BRACEROS: PUBLIC (EC*).

"JUDGE GERALD S. CHARGIN SPEAKS".   EL GRITO, VOL. 3 NO.
     1 (FALL 1969), PP. 4-5, 32-33.

"MEXICAN AMERICAN LEGAL DEFENSE".   THE NEW YORK TIMES,
     VOL. 1 (MAY 2, 1968), P. 38 (PL).

"STUDY SOCIO-CULTURAL FACTORS (SO*).

"UNHAPPY MEXICO--OUR DUTY" (SO*).

EX PARTE JAMES MANNING. HABEAS CORPUS PROCEEDINGS BEFORE
     JUDGE T. A. FALVEY, FEBRUARY 15, 1882.   HABEAS CORPUS
     PROCEEDINGS BEFORE JUDGE T. A. FALVEY, FEBRUARY 15,
     1882.

PARATHION RESIDUE POISONING AMONG ORCHARD WORKERS.   IN
     U. S. CONGRESS. SENATE. LABOR AND PUBLIC WELFARE
     COMMITTEE. HEARINGS. MIGRANT AND SEASONAL FARMWORKER
     POWERLESS, PART 6-C: PESTICIDES AND THE FARMWORKER
     PAGES 3124-3129. WASHINGTON, D. C.: U. S. GOVERNMENT
     PRINTING OFFICE, (AUGUST 3, 1964) (EC MD).

SUMMER PREPARATORY INSTITUTE, (ED*).

TESTIMONY IN THE TRIAL OF JUAN DOMINGUEZ DE MENDOZA
     IN ABSENTIA, SEPTEMBER 28 TO OCTOBER 6, 1685.   NEW
     MEXICO ARCHIVES NO. 35 (SO).

TREATY OF GUADALUPE HILDAGO, FEBRUARY 28 1848.
     WASHINGTON, D. C.: UNITED STATES GOVERNMENT PRINTING
     OFFICE, (1910) (HSW HM HUS).

EL PASO TROUBLES IN TEXAS.   HOUSE EXECUTIVE DOCUMENT.
     , (93).

EL TRATADO DE GUADALUPE HIDALGO 1848.   TELEFACT FOUNDATION
     IN COOPERATION WITH THE CALIFORNIA STATE DEPARTMENT
     OF EDUCATION, 1968 (HSW HM HUS).

EL TRATADO DE GUADALUPE HIDALGO 1848 TREATY OF GUADALUPE
     HIDALGO 1848.   SACRAMENTO, CALIFORNIA: TELEFACT
     FOUNDATION, 1968 (HSW HM HUS).

ARMENDARIZ.   DISCRIMINATION AGAINST MEXICAN-AMERICANS
     (EC*).

ASHTON, RICHARD PRICE. THE FOURTEENTH AMENDMENT AND THE
     EDUCATION OF LATIN-AMERICAN CHILDREN INTEXAS.
     UNIVERSITY OF TEXAS AT AUSTIN, MASTER'S THESIS (1949)
     (ED).

ASTER, RICHARD FREDERICK JR. THE TERMINATION OF THE
    BRACERO PROGRAM--ITS PROBABLE IMBACT ON WELFARE AND
    EDUCATION IN SANTA BARBARA COUNTY.   UNIVERSITY OF
    CALIFORNIA AT SANTA BARBARA, MASTER'S THESIS (1965)
    (SI SO).

AUERBACH.   LABOR LIBERTY: FOLLETT COMMITTEE (EC*).

AUSTIN.   "THE MUNICIPAL GOVERNMENT SAN (HT*).

AVINS, ALFRED. OPEN OCCUPANCY VS. FORCED HOUSING UNDER
    THE FOURTEENTH AMENDMENT; A SYMPOSIUM ON ANTIDISCRIMINATION
    LEGISLATICN, FREEDOM OF CHOICE, AND PROPERTYRIGHTS
    IN HOUSING.   NEW YORK: BOOKMAILER, 1963 (SO).

AYALA DE SIFUENTES, LORETTA. "CONSPIRACY AND THE RIGHT
    TO DISSENT".   AZTLAN--CHICANO JOURNAL OF THE SOCIAL
    SCIENES AND THE ARTS, VOL. 1 NO. 1 (SPRING 1970),
    P. 792100 (SO).

BANDURA, ALBERT, AND WALTERS, RICHARD H.   ADOLESCENT
    AGGRESSION.   NEW YORK: RONALD PRESS, 1959 (SO).

BATTEN, JAMES H. "NEW FEATURES OF MEXICAN IMMIGRATION:
    THE CASE AGAINST FUTHER RESTRICTIVE LEGISLATION".
    PACIFIC AFFAIRS, VOL. 3 (OCTOBER 1930), PP. 956-966
    (SO SI).

BAUR, EDWARD JACKSON. DELINQUENCY AMONG MEXICAN BOYS IN
    SOUTH CHICAGO.   UNIVERSITY OF CHICAGO, MASTER'S
    THESIS (1938) (SO).

BAYITCH.   CONFLICT LAWS: MEXICO UNITED (HUS*).

BERARD.   "DETENTION FACILITIES ALONG MEXICAN (SI*).

BERGER, MORROE. EQUALITY BY STATUTE; THE REVOLUTION IN
    CIVIL RIGHTS.   GARDEN CITY, NEW YORK: DOUBLEDAY, 1967.

BERNSTEIN, SAUL. ALTERNATIVES TO VIOLENCE; ALIENATED YOUTH
    AND RIOTS, RACE AND POVERTY..   (1806) NEW YORK:
    ASSOCIATION PRESS, 1967 (SO).

BLOOM.   "BEGINNINGS REPRESENTATIVE GOVERNMENT (HSW*).

BOSCH, ROBERT VAN DEN. THE INSECTICIDE CRISIS.   IN U.
    S. CONGRESS. SENATE. LABOR AND PUBLIC WELFARE
    COMMITTEE. HEARINGS. MIGRANT AND SEASONAL FARMWORKER
    POWERLESS, PART 6-C: PESTICIDES AND THE FARMWORKER
    PAGES 3239-3249. WASHINGTON, D. C.: U. S. GOVERNMENT
    PRINTING OFFICE, (EC MD).

BOWDEN.   RANCHO DE PONCE (HS*).

BOWIE, AUGUSTUS JESSE, JR. IRRIGATION IN SOUTHERN TEXAS.
    WASHINGTON, D. C.: U. S. DEPARTMENT OF AGRICULTURE,
    (1905).

BRACE.   FEDERAL PROGRAMS TO IMPROVE MEXICAN—AMERICAN   (ED*).

BRACE.   FEDERAL PROGRAMS TO IMPROVE MEXICAN—AMERICAN   (ED*).

BRANN.   "HOUSING MIGRANT AGRICULTURAL   (EC*).

BRANN, RICHARD R.   HOUSING OF MIGRANT AGRICULTURAL WORKERS.
     IN UNITED STATES CONGRESS. SENATE HEARINGS, LABOR AND
     PUBLIC WELFARE COMMITTEE. MIGRANT AND SEASONAL
     FARMWORKER POWERLESS,. WASHINGTON, D. C. U. S.
     GOVERNMENT PRINTING OFFICE, (MAY 2 1, 1969) (EC SO).

BRAYER.   PUEBLO INDIAN LAND GRANTS "RIO   (HS*).

BROADDUS.   LEGAL HERITAGE PASO (HS*).

BROWN.   CHILDREN WORKING SUGAR BEET FIELDS   (EC*).

BURMA.   "THE PUSH ELBOW; CIVIL RIGHTS   (SO*).

BURMA.   "THE PUSH ELBOW; CIVIL RIGHTS   (SO*).

CALIFORNIA ADVISORY COMMITTEE TO THE U. S. COMMISSION OF
     CIVIL RIGHTS.   REPORT OF CALIFORNIA POLICE — MINORITY
     RELATIONS.   SACRAMENTO: CALIFORNIA ADULT EDUCATION
     BUREAU, 1967 (SO HC).

CALIFORNIA CITIZENS' COMMITTEE ON CIVIL DISTURBANCES IN
     LOS ANGELES. REPORT AND RECOMMENDATIONS.   SAN
     FRANCISCO: BAY AREA COUNCIL AGAINST DISCRIMINATION,
     1943 (SO).

CALIFORNIA CORRECTIONS DEPARTMENT. CALIFORNIA PRISONERS;
     SUMMARY STATISTICS OF FELON PRISONERS AND PAROLES.
     SACRAMENTO: CALIFORNIA CORRECTIONS DEPARTMENT,
     1960—1967 (SO).

CALIFORNIA CRIMINAL STATISTICS BUREAU. S. CALIFORNIA
     PRISONERS SUMMARY STATISTICS.   SACRAMENTO: CALIFORNIA
     CRIMINAL STATISTICS BUREAU, 1952.

CALIFORNIA CRIMINAL STATISTICS BUREAU. S. CRIME AND
     DELINQUENCY IN CALIFORNIA.   SACRAMENTO: CALIFORNIA
     CRIMINAL STATISTICS BUREAU, 1965—1968.

CALIFORNIA CRIMINAL LAW AND ENFORCEMENT DIVISION. GUIDE
     TO COMMUNITY RELATIONS FOR PEACE OFFICERS.   SACRAMENTO:
     CALIFORNIA CRIMINAL LAW AND ENFORCEMENT DIVISION, 1958.

CALIFORNIA DEPARTMENT OF THE YOUTH AUTHORITY.   CHARACTERISTICS
     CALIFORNIA YOUTH   (SO*).

CALIFORNIA DEPARTMENT OF THE YOUTH AUTHORITY.   EMPLOYMENT
     TRENDS AMONG CALIFORNIA   (SO*).

CALIFORNIA DEPARTMENT OF HEALTH, BUREAU OF OCCUPATIONAL
    HEALTH. OCCUPATIONAL DISEASE IN CALIFORNIA ATTRIBUTED
    TO PESTICIDES AND OTHER AGRICULTURAL CHEMICALS. IN
    U. S. CONGRESS. SENATE. LABOR AND PUBLIC WELFARE
    COMMITTEE. HEARINGS. MIGRANT AND SEASONAL FARMWORKER
    POWERLESS, PART 6-C: PESTICIDES AND THE FARMWORKER
    PAGES 3912-3924. WASHINGTON, D. C.: U. S. GOVERNMENT
    PRINTING OFFICE, (NOVEMBER 1968) (EC MD).

CALIFORNIA STATE ADVISORY COMMITTEE ON CIVIL RIGHTS.
    EDUCATION MEXICAN AMERICAN COMMUNITY (ED*).

CALIFORNIA STATE DEPARTMENT OF CORRECTIONS. ANNUAL
    STATISTICAL REPORT (SO*).

    CALIFORNIA STATE DEPARTMENT OF JUSTICE. EQUAL RIGHTS
    UNDER THE LAW; PROVIDING FOR EQUAL TREATMENT FOR ALL
    CITIZENS REGARDLESS OF RACE, RELIGION, COLOR, NATURAL
    ORIGIN OF ANCESTRY. SACRAMENTO, CALIFORNIA:
    CALIFORNIA JUSTICE DEPARTMENT, 1960.

CALIFORNIA STATE DIVISION OF CRIMINAL LAW AND ENFORCEMENT.
    GUIDE TO COMMUNITY RELATIONS FOR PEACE OFFICERS.
    SACRAMENTO, CALIFORNIA: CALIFORNIA, DIVISION OF
    CRIMINAL LAW AND ENFORCEMENT, 1958 (SO).

CALIFORNIA STATE LAW LIBRARY. LEGAL SERVICES TO POOR:
    SELECTIVE (B*).

CALIFORNIA STATE LEGISLATURE. FOURTEENTH REPORT (EC*).

CALIFORNIA YOUTH AUTHORITY. CHARACTERISTICS CALIFORNIA
    YOUTH (SO*).

CALIFORNNIA SUPREME COURT. JUVENILE DIVISION. STATEMENTS
    OF THE COURTS. CALIFORNIA: SUPREME COURT, SEPTEMBER
    2, 1969.

CITIZENS COMMITTEE FOR THE DEFENSE OF MEXICAN AMERICAN
    YOUTH. THE SLEEPY LAGOON CASE. LOS ANGELES: THE
    COMMITTEE, 1942 (SO).

CIVIL RIGHTS DIGEST. "MEXICAN? AMERICAN?". CIVIL RIGHT
    DIGEST, VOL. 3 NO. 1 (WINTER 1970) (SO).

CLEARY, HUGH WILLIAM. RECRUITMENT OF MINORITY PROGRAMS
    FOR LAW ENFORCEMENT. ARIZONA STATE UNIVERSITY,
    MASTER'S THESIS (1970) (SO).

COHEN. DERECHO INDIGENA: CONTRIBUCION (HS*).

COHEN, IRVING J. LA HUELGA--IN STARR COUNTY TEXAS. IN
    UNITED STATES CONGRESS. SENATE HEARINGS, LABOR AND
    PUBLIC WELFARE COMMITTEE. MIGRANT AND SEASONAL
    FARMWORKER POWERLESS,. WASHINGTON, D. C. U. S.
    GOVERNMENT PRINTING OFFICE, (MAY 2 1, 1969) (EC   SO).

COHEN, JERRY AND MURPHY, WILLIAM S. BURN BABY BURN: THE
    LOS ANGELES RACE RIOT, AUGUST, 1965. NEW YORK: E.
    P. DUTTON, 1966 (SO).

COLORADO. TIME CHANGE CHALLENGE (HCO*).

COLORADO. A REPORT SPANISH-AMERICANS CORRECTIONAL (HCO*).

CONGRESSICNAL QUARTERLY SERVICE. REVOLUTION IN CIVIL
    RIGHTS.   WASHINGTON: REVOLUTICN IN CIVIL RIGHTS,
    (1968).

COOK, J. WILLIAM. PESTICIDE MULTIRESIDUE METHODOLOGY.
    IN U. S. CONGRESS. SENATE. LABOR AND PUBLIC WELFARE
    COMMITTEE. HEARINGS. MIGRANT AND SEASONAL FARMWORKER
    POWERLESS, PART 6-C: PESTICIDES AND THE FARMWORKER
    PAGES 3479-3485. WASHINGTON, D. C.: U. S. GOVERNMENT
    PRINTING OFFICE, (NOVEMBER 1968) (EC   MD).

CORMACK. "THE MEXICAN LABOR LAW" (EC*).

COX, ARCHIBALD, HOWE, MARK DE WOLFE, AND WIGGINS, J. R.
    CIVIL RIGHTS, THE CONSTITUTION, AND THE COURTS.
    CAMBRIDGE, MASSACHUSETTS: HARVARD UNIVERSITY PRESS,
    1967.

CRICHTON. LAW ORDER, LTD., LIFE ELFEGOBACA (HN*).

EATON, JOSEPH; POLK, KENNETH. MEASURING DELINQUENCY; A
    STUDY OF PROBATION DEPARTMENT REFERRALS. PITTSBURGH,
    PENNSYLVANIA: UNIVERSITY OF PITTSBURG PRESS, 1961
    (SO).

EMERSON, THOMAS IRWIN. POLITICAL AND CIVIL RIGHTS IN THE
    UNITED STATES; A COLLECTION OF LEGAL AND RELATED
    MATERIALS. BOSTON, MASSACHUSETTS: LITTLE, BROWN,
    1967.

ENDORE, GUY. JUSTICE FOR SACIDO. LOS ANGELES: CIVIL
    RIGHTS CONGRESS OF LOS ANGELES, JULY, 1948.

ENDCRE. SLEEPY LAGOON MYSTERY (SO*).

EULAU. S. "SLEEPY LAGOON CASE; CCURT APPEAL (SO*).

FARENHOLT, MARY K. THE NEW MASKED MAN IN AGRICULTURE.
    IN U. S. CONGRESS. SENATE. LABOR AND PUBLIC WELFARE
    COMMITTEE. HEARINGS. MIGRANT AND SEASONAL FARMWORKER
    POWERLESS, PART 6-C: PESTICIDES AND THE FARMWORKER
    PAGES 3486-3530. WASHINGTCN, D. C.: U. S. GOVERNMENT
    PRINTING OFFICE, (NOVEMBER 1968) (EC   MD).

FARRIS.   "1965 — FIVE YEAR ENCCUNTER WITH   (SC*).

FINNEY, FLCY C.   JUVENILE CELINQUENCY IN SAN ANTONIO TEXAS.
    UNIVERSITY OF TEXAS, MASTER'S THESIS (1932) (ED).

FISHER.   "THE PERFORMANCE MALE PRISONERS   (PY*).

FOGELSON.   LOS ANGELES RIOTS (1969)   (SO*).

FOGELSON.   FRAGMENTED METROPOLIS: LCS ANGELES   (SO*).

FOSTER.   "THE LEGAL STATUS FILIPINO INTERMARRIAGES   (SO*).

FOUNTAIN, A. J.   ANSWERS TO INTERRCGATCRIES IN CASE PENCING
    IN MCLENNAN COUNTY, GEORGE B.ZIMPELMAN PLAINTIFF,
    FRANK HOWARD ET AL DEFENDANTS, ANSWEREC BEFORE
    L. W.LENOIR, NOTARY PUBLIC, LAS CRUCES, NEW MEXICO,
    APRIL 6,1887.   MS. COPY IN THE LIBRARY OF THE
    UNIVERSITY OF TEXAS AT EL PASO.

FRIBOURG, MARJCRIE G. THE BILL OF RIGHTS.   NEW YORK:
    AVON, 1967 (LJE).

FRIBOURG, MARJCRIE.   THE SUPREME COURT IN AMERICAN HISTORY.
    PHILADELPHIA: MACRAE SMITH COMPANY, 1965 (LJE).

FUCHS.   AMERICAN ETHNIC POLICIES   (PL*).

GARFIELD.   "LOCAL GCVERNMENT SPANISH COLONIES"   (HS*).

GAVALDCN-SALAMANCA, IGNACIC.   THE MEXICAN WRIT OF APMARO.
    UNIVERSITY OF TEXAS AT AUSTIN, MASTER'S THESIS (1937).

GECRGI, PETER HUGH.   THE DELANO GRAPE STRIKE AND BOYCOTT:
    INROADS TC COLLECTIVE BARGAINING INAGRICULTURE.   IN
    UNITED STATES CONGRESS. SENATE HEARINGS, LABOR AND
    PUBLIC WELFARE COMMITTEE. MIGRANT AND SEASONAL
    FARMWORKER POWERLESS,.   WASHINGTON, D. C. U. S.
    GOVERNMENT PRINTING OFFICE, (MAY 2 1, 1969) (EC   SO).

GREENE.   "IMMIGRATION LAW RURAL PCVERTY   (EC*).

GREENE.   "OPERATICN SISYPHUS, WETBACKS   (EC*).

GREGORY, GLADYS GRACE.   THE CHAMIZAL SETTLEMENT: A VIEW
    FROM EL PASO.   EL PASO: TEXAS WESTERN PRESS, (1963).
    SOUTHWESTERN STUDIES, 1, NUMBER 2.

GREGORY, GLADYS GRACE.   EL CHAMIZAL: A BOUNDARY PROBLEM
    BETWEEN THE UNITED STATES AND MEXICO.   UNIVERSITY
    OF TEXAS AT AUSTIN, PHD. DISSERTATION (1937).

GROVER, GEORGE G., SPECIAL COUNSEL. OPENING BRIEF
    OF APPELANT, THE CITY OF LOS ANGELES, APPENDIX VOLUME.
    IN THE COURT OF APPEAL, SECOND APPELLATE DISTRIC,
    STATE O; CALIFORNIA, 2ND CIVIL 33708, CITY OF
    LOS ANGELES, A MUNICIPAL CORPORATION, PLAINTIFF AND
    APPELLANT VS CITY OF SAN FERNANDO, A MUNICIPAL
    CORPORATION, ET AL. DEFENDANTS AND RESPONDENTS. 1969.

GUADALUPE HIDALGO. THE TREATY THAT WON THE WEST.
    TRUCHAS, NEW MEXICO: TATE GALLERY PUBLICATIONS, 1848
    (PL).

HADLEY, ELEANOR M. "A CRITICAL ANALYSIS OF THE WETBACK
    PROBLEM". LAW AND CONTEMPORARY PROBLEMS, VOL. 21
    (SPRING 1956), PP. 334-357 (SO).

HALLECK, H. W. "REPORT ON THE LAWS AND REGULATIONS
    RELATIVE TO GRANTS OR SALES OF PUBLICLANDS IN
    CALIFORNIA". UNITED STATES CONGRESS, VOL. HOUSE
    EXECUTIVE DOCUMENTS NO. 31 CONGRESS, 1 SESSION (17,
    APPEXDIX 13), PP. 148-149.

HARPER, ELIZABETH J. AUERBACH, IMMIGRATION LAWS OF THE
    UNITED STATES. INDIANAPOLIS, INDIANA: BOBBS-MERRILL
    COMPANY, INC., 1971.

HIDALGO, ERNESTO. LA PROTECCION DE MEXICANOS EN LOS
    ESTADOS UNIDOS. MEXICO CITY: SECRETARIA DE RELACIONES
    EXTERIORES, 1940.

HILL, CHARLES E. LEADING AMERICAN TREATIES. REPRINTED
    BY: NEW YORK, NEW YORK AND LONDON, GREAT BRITAIN: AMS
    PRESS, INC., 1922.

HINSLEY. HANDBOOK TEXAS SCHOOL LAW (HT*).

INTER- AGENCY COMMITTEE ON MEXICAN- AMERICAN AFFAIRS. "THE
    CHAGRIN OVER JUDGE CHAGRIN". NEWSLETTER, VOL. 1
    (NOVEMBER 1969).

KAPPLER, CHARLES J. INDIAN AFFAIRS, LAWS, AND TREATIES.
    WASHINGTON: GOVERNMENT PRINTING OFFICE, (1904).

KEEFE, EDGAR S. DENIAL OF JUSTICE AS INTEPRETED AND
    APPLIED BY THE UNITED STATES-MEXICANGENERAL CLAIMS
    COMMISSION UNDER THE CONVENTION OF SEPTEMBER 8, 1923.
    UNIVERSITY OF TEXAS AT AUSTIN, MASTER'S THESIS (1933).

KRUEGER, REV. EDGAR A. M.A.Y.O. DEL CAMPO. IN UNITED
    STATES CONGRESS. SENATE HEARINGS, LABOR AND PUBLIC
    WELFARE COMMITTEE. MIGRANT AND SEASONAL FARMWORKER
    POWERLESS,. WASHINGTON, D. C. U. S. GOVERNMENT
    PRINTING OFFICE, (MAY 2 1, 1969) (EC SO).

LA PENA Y PENA. MEXICO REPUBLIC. TREATIES. THE TREATY OF
     GUADALUPE HIDALGO.   BERKELEY: FRIENDS OF THE BANCROFT
     LIBRARY, 1949 (HSW HUS HM).

LANG, MARGARET H. EARLY JUSTICE IN SONORA.   SONORA,
     CALIFORNIA: THE MOTHER LODE PRESS, 1963 (HSW).

LOS ANGELES COUNTY GRAND JURY.   FINAL REPORT LOS ANGELES
     COUNTY (HC*).

LOS ANGELES COUNTY.   SURVEY MEDICAL CARE FACILITIES (HC*).

LUCEY.   "JUSTICE MEXICANS" (SO*).

LUCEY. "MIGRATORY WORKERS" (SO*).

LYON.   LEGAL STATUS AMERICAN MEXICAN   (SI*).

MALAGON-BARCELO, JAVIER. LA LITURATURA JURIDICA ESPANOLA
     DEL SIGLO DE ORO EN LA NUEVA ESPANA.   MEXICO, D. F.:
     UNIVERSIDAD NACIONAL AUTONAMA DE MEXICO, 1959 (HS).

MALLOY, WILLIAM M. TREATIES, CONVENTIONS, INTERNATIONAL
     ACTS, PROTOCOLS AND AGREEMENTS BETWEEN THE UNITED
     STATES OF AMERICA AND OTHER POWERS, 1776-1909.
     WASHINGTON, D. C.: UNITED STATES GOVERNMENT PRINTING
     OFFICE, (1910).

MC BRIDE, GEORGE MC CUTCHEN. THE LAND SYSTEMS OF MEXICO.
     NEW YORK:1923:AMERICAN GEOGRAPHICAL SOCIETY, RESEARCH
     SERIES, NUMBER 1NEW YORK, (1923). AMERICAN GEOGRAPHICAL
     SOCIETY, RESEARCH SERIES, NUMBER 12. (HS).

MC BRIDE, GEORGE MC CUTCHEN. THE LAND SYSTEMS OF MEXICO.
     BROOKLYN, NEW YORK: FARRAR, STRAUS AND GIROUX, 1971
     (HS).

MC KNIGHT.   SPANISH WATERCOURSES TEXAS (HT*).

MICHIGAN. CIVIL RIGHTS COMMISSION. CIVIL RIGHTS COMMISSION.
     A COMMITMENT TO SOCIAL CHANGE.   A COMMITMENT
     TO SOCIAL CHANGE. REPORT OF PROGRESS. 1965-1966 (SO).

MICHIGAN. CIVIL RIGHTS COMMISSION. CIVIL RIGHTS COMMISSION.
     DIRECTIVE TO STATE CONTRACTORS AND BIDDERS.
     COMPLIANCE WITH STATE POLICY OF EQUAL EMPLOYMENT
     OPPORTUNITY, BASIS, PURPOSE, REQUIREMENT, PROCEDURE.
     (SO EC).

MICHIGAN. CIVIL RIGHTS COMMISSION. CIVIL RIGHTS COMMISSION
     RULES GOVERNING ORGANIZATION, PRACTICE, PROCEDURE AND
     GENERAL SUBSTANTIVE RULES.   MICHIGAN. CIVIL RIGHTS
     COMMISSION,.

MICHIGAN. CIVIL RIGHTS COMMISSION. EQUAL OPPORTUNITY IN
     HIGHER EDUCATION.   SUMMARY OF A SEMINAR HELD DECEMBER
     3,1968 (SO EC).

MICHIGAN. CIVIL RIGHTS COMMISSION. FAIR HOUSING GUARANTEES
IN MICHIGAN. LANSING, MICHIGAN, (SO EC).

MICHIGAN. CIVIL RIGHTS COMMISSION. FAIR HOUSING JURISDICTION
OF THE MICHIGAN CIVIL RIGHTS COMMISSION. FAIR
HOUSING JURISDICTION OF THE MICHIGAN CIVIL RIGHTS
COMMISSION (SO EC).

MICHIGAN. CIVIL RIGHTS COMMISSION. GUIDELINES FOR
INSURING EQUAL TREATMENT, EQUAL PROTECTION FOR
STUDENTS. GUIDELINES FOR PREVENTING, RESOLVING
INTER-GROUP TENSION IN MICHIGAN PUBLIC SCHOOLS (ED).

MICHIGAN. CIVIL RIGHTS COMMISSION. HOW THE BACKLOG GREW.
FOUR YEAR REPORT OF CLAIMS ACTIVITY, 1964-1967 (SO
EC PL).

MICHIGAN. CIVIL RIGHTS COMMISSION. MEMORANDUM TO
EMPLOYERS. ASSURING THE RIGHTS TO EQUAL JOB
OPPORTUNITY (EC).

MICHIGAN. CIVIL RIGHTS COMMISSION. MODEL CITIES GUIDELINES.
MODEL CITIES GUIDELINES (EC SO).

MICHIGAN. CIVIL RIGHTS COMMISSION. MODEL FAIR HOUSING
ORDINANCE FOR COUNTIES, CITIES, VILLAGES, AND TOWNSH
IPS. MICHIGAN, CIVIL RIGHTS COMMISSION, (EC SO).

MICHIGAN. CIVIL RIGHTS COMMISSION. PRE-EMPLOYMENT INQUIRY
GUIDE. PRE-EMPLOYMENT INQUIRY GUIDE (EC).

MICHIGAN. CIVIL RIGHTS COMMISSION. PROCEDURES IN
INVESTIGATING AND RESOLVING COMPLAINTS OF DISCRIMINATION.
MICHIGAN. CIVIL RIGHTS COMMISSION, (EC SO).

MICHIGAN. CIVIL RIGHTS COMMISSION. REACHING FOR EQUALITY.
A PROJECTION OF LABOR FORCE, OCCUPATIONAL LEVELS AND
DISTRIBUTION BY INDUSTRY OF WHITE AND NON-WHITE
WORKERS IN 1970 AND 1980 (EC).

MICHIGAN. CIVIL RIGHTS COMMISSION. RELOCATION, PUBLIC
HOUSING. RELOCATION, PUBLIC HOUSING, POLICIES.
GUIDELINES MEASURES FOR IMPLEMENTATION (EC SO).

MICHIGAN. CIVIL RIGHTS COMMISSION. REPORT AND RECOMMENDATIONS.
A FIELD STUDY OF MIGRANT WORKERS IN MICHIGAN, 1969
(SI EC).

MICHIGAN. CIVIL RIGHTS COMMISSION. REPORT AND RECOMMENDATIONS
INTO THE STATUS OF RACE RELATIONS IN THE CIT Y
OF KALAMAZOO, 1969. KALAMAZOO, MICHIGAN, 1969 (SO).

MICHIGAN. CIVIL RIGHTS COMMISSION. TOWARD EQUALITY.
TWO YEAR REPORT OF CLAIMS ACTIVITY, 1968-1969 (SO
EC).

MICHIGAN. CIVIL RIGHTS COMMISSION. VOCATIONAL PREPARATION
    AND RACE IN MICHIGAN HIGHER EDUCATION. VOCATIONAL
    PREPARATION AND RACE IN MICHIGAN HIGHER EDUCATION (ED
    EC).

MICHIGAN. CIVIL RIGHTS COMMISSION. RESEARCH DIVISION.
    A REPORT ON THE CHARACTERISTICS OF MICHIGAN'S
    NON—WHITE POPULATION. A REPORT ON THE CHARACTERISTICS
    OF MICHIGAN'S NON—WHITE POPULATION (SO).

MICHIGAN. STATE BOARD OF EDUCATION. OPPORTUNITIES FOR
    THE DSADVANTAGED. A REPORT TO THE STATE ON TITLE
    I OF THE ELEMENTARY AND SECONDARY EDUCATION ACT OF
    1965 IN MICHIGAN, MAY 1967 (ED).

MICHIGAN. CIVIL RIGHTS COMMISSION, COMISION DE DERECHOS
    CIVILES. GARANTIAS DE IGUALES OPORTUNIDADES EN
    MICHIGAN. MICHIGAN: COMMISSION ON CIVIL RIGHTS, (SO
    EC).

MICHIGAN. COMISICN DE DERECHOS CIVILES. INFORME Y
    RECOMENDACIONES SOBRE LA SITUATION DE LOS TRABAJADORES
    MIGRAT ORIOS EN MICHIGAN, 1968. MICHIGAN, COMISION
    DE DERECHOS CIVILES, 1968 (EC SI).

MICHIGAN. PONTIAC SCHOOL DISTRICT. EL BILINGUE, TWO
    CULTURES, TWO LANGUAGES. PONTIAC SCHOOL DISTRICT,
    MICHIGAN, (EC SO).

MIDWEST EDUCATORS CONFERENCE AGAINST DISCRIMINATION.
    "RECOMMENDATIONS MIDWEST EDUCATORS (ED*).

MINISTERIO DE RELACIONES EXTERIORES. LA PROTECCION
    DE MEXICANOS EN LOS ESTADOS UNIDOS. MEXICO:
    MINISTERIO DE RELACIONES EXTERIORES, 1940.

MINOT, GEORGE, EC. TREATY WITH THE REPUBLIC OF MEXICO
    FEBRUARY 2, 1848. IN THE STATUTES AT LARGE AND THE
    TREATIES OF THE UNITED STATES OF AMERICA FROM DECEMBER
    1, 1845 TO MARCH 3, 1851, (BOSTON: LITTLE BROWN AND
    COMPANY). 1862 (PL HM HUS).

MORALES, ARMANDO. "JUSTICE AND THE MEXICAN AMERICAN".
    EL GRITO, VOL. 1 NO. 4 (SUMMER 1968), PP. 42—48 (PY).

MORALES, ARMANDO. "POLICE DEPLOYMENT THEORIES AND
    THE MEXICAN AMERICAN COMMUNITY". EL GRITO, VOL. 4
    NO. 1 (FALL 1970), PP. 52—64 (PY SO).

MORALES, ARMANDO. POLICE DEPLOYMENT THEORIES. VOICES:
    READINGS FROM EL GRITO. BERKELEY, CALIFORNIA: QUINTO
    SOL PUBLICATIONS, 1971 (PY SO).

MORGAN, PATRICIA. SHAME OF A NATION: A DOCUMENTED STORY
    OF POLICE-STATE TERROR AGAINST MEXICAN AMERICANS IN
    THE U. S. A..   LOS ANGELES COMMITTEE FOR THE
    PROTECTION OF FOREIGN BORN 1954 (SO   SI).

MYERS.   BORDER WARDENS (HSW*).

NATHANIEL N. WAGNER AND MARSHA J. HAUG (EDS). 'JUDGE
    GERALD S. CHARGIN: A PUBLIC RECORD.'   IN NATHANIEL
    N. WAGNER AND MARSHA J. HAUG (EDS). CHICANOS: SOCIAL
    AND PSYCHOLOGICAL PERSPECTIVES.

NATIONAL COMMISSION ON LAW OBSERVANCE AND ENFORCEMENT.
    U. S. REPORT CRIME FOREIGN BORN   (SI*).

NEUMEYER, JOHN (ET AL). PESTICIDES.   IN U. S. CONGRESS.
    SENATE. LABOR AND PUBLIC WELFARE COMMITTEE. HEARINGS.
    MIGRANT AND SEASONAL FARMWORKER POWERLESS, PART 6-C:
    PESTICIDES AND THE FARMWORKER PAGES 3329-3341.
    WASHINGTON, D. C.: U. S. GOVERNMENT PRINTING OFFICE,
    (NOVEMBER 1968) (EC MD).

NEW MEXICO STATE ADVISORY COMMITTEE TO THE UNITED STATES
    COMMISSION ON CIVIL RIGHTS. THE CIVIL RIGHTS STATUS
    OF MINORITY GROUPS IN CLOVIS, NEW MEXICO.   NEW
    MEXICO, 1969.

PATTON , F. H. COURTS OF NEW MEXICO HEAR BOTH SPANISH AND
    ENGLISH.   STATE GOVERNMENT, MARZO, 1938.

PAYNE, WILLIAM. "MEXICAN AMERICAN FARMERS, VICTIMS
    OF NEGLECT".   CIVIL RIGHTS DIGEST, VOL. 2 NO.
    2 (SPRING 1969), PP. 37-38 (EC).

PENROD.   CIVIL RIGHTS PROBLEMS MEXICAN-AMERICANS (SO*).

PROCTOR, BEN H. THE MODERN TEXAS RANGERS: A LAW-ENFORCEMENT
    DILEMMA IN THE RIO GRANDE VALLEY.   EDITED BY MANUEL
    P. SERVIN. BEVERLY HILLS, CALIFORNIA: GLENCOE PRESS,
    1970.

RAMIREZ.   "REPORT U. S. COMMISSION CIVIL   (ED*).

ROEDER.   STUDY SITUATION MEXICAN AMERICANS   (SO*).

ROHRMAN, DOUGLAS F. THE LAW OF PESTICIDES; PRESENT AND
    FUTURE.   IN U. S. CONGRESS. SENATE. LABOR AND PUBLIC
    WELFARE COMMITTEE. HEARINGS. MIGRANT AND SEASONAL
    FARMWORKER POWERLESS, PART 6-C: PESTICIDES AND THE
    FARMWORKER PAGES 3634-3684. WASHINGTON, D. C.: U.
    S. GOVERNMENT PRINTING OFFICE, (FEBRUARY 1969) (EC
    MD).

ROWAN, HELEN. THE MEXICAN AMERICAN.   WASHINGTON: U.S.
    COMMISSION ON CIVIL RIGHTS, (1968) (SO   EC).

RUIZ, MANUEL. "LATIN-AMERICAN JUVENILE DELINQUENCY IN LOS
     ANGLES, BOMB OR BUBBLE".   CRIME PREVENTION DIGEST,
     VOL. 1 NO. 13 (DECEMBER 1942) (SO).

RUSK.   STUDY DELINQUENCY AMONG URBAN (SO*).

SCOTT, J. B. "SETTLEMENT OF OUTSTANDING CLAIMS BETWEEN
     MEXICO AND THE UNITED STATES".   AMERICAN JOURNAL OF
     INTERNATIONAL LAW,   (APRIL 1924) (HSW).

STEPHENSON.   RACE DISTINCTIONS AMERICAN LAW (AN*).

TEXAS EDUCATION AGENCY.   TEXAS EDUCATION CODE SUPPLEMENT
     (ED*).

U. S. NATIONAL COMMISSION OF LAW OBSERVANCE AND ENFORCEMENT.
     REPORT ON CRIME AND THE FOREIGN BORN.   WASHINGTON,
     D. C.: NATIONAL COMMISSION OF LAW OBSERVANCE AND
     ENFORCEMENT U. S. GOVERNMENT PRINTING OFFICE, (1931).

U. S. BUREAU OF AGRICULTURAL ECONOMICS. CULTURE OF
     A CONTEMPORARY RURAL COMMUNITY: EL CERRITO, NEW
     MEXICO.   U. S. BUREAU OF AGRICULTURE OF ECONOMICS,
     1941 (EC).

U. S. BUREAU OF EMPLOYMENT SECURITY. FARM PLACEMENT
     SECURITY. INFORMATION ABOUT REGISTRATION OF INTERSTATE
     FARM LABOR CONTRACTORS.   WASHINGTON, D. C.: U. S.
     GOVERNMENT PRINTING OFFICE, (1966) (EC SI).

U. S. BUREAU OF EMPLOYMENT SECURITY. INFORMATION CONCERNING
     ENTRY OF MEXICAN AGRICULTURAL WORKERS INTO THE UNITED
     STATES.   WASHINGTON, D. C.: U. S. GOVERNMENT
     PRINTING OFFICE, (1952) (SI EC).

U. S. BUREAU OF LABOR STATISTICS. JOB GAINS OF MEXICAN-AMERICAN
     MEN.   WASHINGTON, D. C.: U. S. GOVERNMENT PRINTING
     OFFICE, (1968) (EC).

U. S. BUREAU OF LABOR STATISTICS. MONEY DISBURSEMENTS OF
     WAGE EARNERS AND CLERICAL WORKERS IN FIVE CITIES IN
     THE PACIFIC COAST AND REGION, 1934-1936.   WASHINGTON,
     D. C.: U. S. GOVERNMENT PRINTING OFFICE, (1939) (EC).

U. S. BUREAU OF THE CENSUS.   UNITED STATES CENSUS OF THE
     POPULATION: 1950.   WASHINGTON, D. C.: U. S.
     GOVERNMENT PRINTING OFFICE, (1950-1952) (SO).

U. S. BUREAU OF THE CENSUS. CHARACTERISTICS OF THE SOUTH
     AND EAST LOS ANGELES AREAS: NOVEMBER, 1965.   CURRENT
     POPULATION REPORTS, SERIES P-23, NO. 18, WASHINGTON,
     D. C., 1966 (SO).

U. S. BUREAU CF THE CENSUS. FIFTEENTH CENSUS OF THE UNITED
    STATES: 1930.   WASHINGTON, D. C.: U. S. GOVERNMENT
    PRINTING OFFICE, (1933) (SC).

U. S. BUREAU OF THE CENSUS. FIFTEENTH CENSUS OF THE UNITED
    STATES: 1930.   WASHINGTON, D. C.: U. S. GOVERNMENT
    PRINTING OFFICE, (1932) (SO).

U. S. BUREAU OF THE CENSUS. FIFTEENTH CENSUS OF THE UNITED
    STATES: 1930.   WASHINGTON, D. C.: U. S. GOVERNMENT
    PRINTING OFFICE, (1931—1934) (SC).

U. S. BUREAU OF THE CENSUS. MOTHER TONGUE OF THE FOREIGN—BORN
    WHITE POPULATION IN FIFTEENTH CENSUS OF THE UNITED
    STATES=1930=.   WASHINGTON, D. C.: U. S. GOVERNMENT
    PRINTING OFFICE, (1932) (SO).

U. S. BUREAU OF THE CENSUS. PERSONS OF SPANISH SURNAME.
    WASHINGTON, D. C.: U. S. GOVERNMENT PRINTING OFFICE,
    (1961) (SC   SI).

U. S. BUREAU OF THE CENSUS. PERSONS OF SPANISH SURNAME
    (1950).   WASHINGTON, D. C.: U. S. GOVERNMENT
    PRINTING OFFICE, (1953) (SO).

U. S. BUREAU OF THE CENSUS. PERSONS OF SPANISH SURNAME
    (1963).   WASHINGTON, D. C.: U. S. GOVERNMENT
    PRINTING CFFICE, (1963) (SO).

U. S. BUREAU OF THE CENSUS. PERSONS OF SPANISH ORIGIN IN
    THE UNITED STATES: NOVEMBER 1969.   WASHINGTON, D.
    C.: U. S. GOVERNMENT PRINTING OFFICE, (1969) (SO).

U. S. BUREAU OF THE CENSUS. PERSONS OF SPANISH SURNAME:
    SOCIAL AND ECONOMIC DATA FOR WHITE PERSONS OF SPANISH
    SURNAME IN THE SOUTHWESTERN STATES.   WASHINGTON,
    D. C.: U. S. GOVERNMENT PRINTING OFFICE, (1963) (SO).

U. S. BUREAU OF THE CENSUS. POPULATICN OF SPANISH MOTHER
    TONGUE. PART OF SIXTEENTH CENSUS OF THE UNITED
    STATES: 1940 POPULATION.   WASHINGTON, D. C.: U.
    S. GOVERNMENT PRINTING OFFICE, (1942) (SO).

U. S. BUREAU OF THE CENSUS. SIXTEENTH CENSUS OF THE UNITED
    STATES: 1940 POPULATION PPOPULATION CF SPANISH MOTHER
    TONGUE: 1940.   WASHINGTON, D. C.: U. S. GOVERNMENT
    PRINTING OFFICE, (1942) (SO).

U. S. BUREAU OF THE CENSUS. SIXTEENTH CENSUS OF THE UNITED
    STATES: 1940.   WASHINGTON, D. C.: U. S. GOVERNMENT
    PRINTING OFFICE, (1942—1947) (SO).

U. S. BUREAU OF THE CENSUS. SPECIAL REPORT ON FOREIGN-BORN WHITE FAMILIES BY COUNTRY OF BIRTH OF HEAD WITH AN APPENDIX GIVING STATISTICS FOR MEXICAN, ETC., FAMILIES. PART OF FIFTEENTH CENSUS OF THE UNITED STATES: 1930 POPULATION.   WASHINGTON, D. C.: U. S. GOVERNMENT PRINTING OFFICE, (1933) (SO).

U. S. BUREAU OF THE CENSUS. U.S. CENSUS OF POPULATION: 1960, SUBJECT REPORTS, PERSONS OF SPANISH SURNAME. WASHINGTON, D. C.: U. S. GOVERNMENT PRINTING OFFICE, (1962) (SO).

U. S. BUREAU OF THE CENSUS. U.S. CENSUS OF HOUSING: 1950, VOL. 1, GENERAL CHARACTERISTICS.   WASHINGTON, D. C.: U. S. GOVERNMENT PRINTING OFFICE, (1952) (SO).

U. S. BUREAU OF THE CENSUS. U.S. CENSUS OF POPULATION: 1950.   SPECIAL REPORTS, PART 3, CHAPTER C, PERSONS OF SPANISH SURNAME (SO).

U. S. BUREAU OF THE CENSUS. U.S. CENSUS OF POPULATION: 1950. VOLUME IV. SPECIAL REPORTS. PART 3. C HAPTER C.: PERSONS OF SPANISH SURNAME.   WASHINGTON, D. C.: U. S. GOVERNMENT PRINTING OFFICE, (1962) (SO).

U. S. BUREAU OF THE CENSUS. UNITED STATES CENSUS OF THE POPULATION: 1960.   WASHINGTON, D. C.: U. S. GOVERNMENT PRINTING OFFICE, (1960) (SO).

U. S. BUREAU OF THE CENSUS. WE THE MEXICAN AMERICANS. WASHINGTON, D. C.: U. S. GOVERNMENT PRINTING OFFICE, (1970) (SO).

U. S. CABINET COMMITTEE ON OPPORTUNITY FOR THE SPANISH SPEAKING. DIRECTORY OF SPANISH SPEAKING ORGANIZATIONS IN THE UNITED STATES.   WASHINGTON, D. C.: U. S. GOVERNMENT PRINTING OFFICE, (1970) (EC).

U. S. CABINET COMMITTEE ON OPPORTUNITY FOR THE SPANISH SPEAKING. SPANISH SURNAMED AMERICAN COLLEGE GRADUATES, 1971-72.   WASHINGTON, D. C.: U. S. GOVERNMENT PRINTING OFFICE, (1971-72) (EC).

U. S. CHAMBER OF COMMERCE - IMMIGRATION COMMITTEE. MEXICAN IMMIGRATION.   WASHINGTON, D. C.: U. S. GOVERNMENT PRINTING OFFICE, (1930) (SI EC SO PL).

U. S. CHILDREN'S BUREAU. S. THE WORK AND WELFARE OF CHILDREN OF AGRICULTURAL LABORERS IN HIDALGO COUNTY, TEXAS.   WASHINGTON, D. C.: U. S. GOVERNMENT PRINTING OFFICE, (1943) (EC).

U. S. CIVIL RIGHTS COMMISSION. EDUCATION AND THE MEXICAN-AMERICAN
    COMMUNITY IN LOS ANGELES COUNTY.   WASHINGTON, D.
    C.: U. S. GOVERNMENT PRINTING OFFICE, (APRIL 1968)
    (ED).

U. S. CIVIL SERVICE COMMISSION. MEXICAN-AMERICAN AND TOTAL
    EMPLOYMENT IN SELECTED STATES AND STANDARD METROPOLITAN
    STATISTICAL AREAS.   IN STUDY OF MINORITY GROUP
    EMPLOYMENT IN THE FEDERAL GOVERNMENT. PREPRED FOR
    THE PRESIDENT'S COMMITTEE ON EQUAL EMPLOYMENT
    OPPORTUNITY, JUNE 1963 (EC).

U. S. CIVIL SERVICE COMMISSION. SPANISH AMERICANS IN THE
    FEDERAL GOVERNMENT.   , (1966) (EC).

U. S. CIVIL SERVICE COMMISSION. SPANISH-SPEAKING AND TOTAL
    EMPLOYMENT IN SELECTED AGENCIES.   IN STUDY OF
    MINORITY GROUP EMPLOYMENT IN THE FEDERAL GOVERNMENT.
    PREPARED FOR THE PRESIDENT'S COMMITTEE ON EQUAL
    EMPLOYMENT OPPORTUNITY, JUNE 1963 (EC).

U. S. CIVIL SERVICE COMMISSION. STUDY OF MINORITY GROUP
    EMPLOYMENT IN THE FEDERAL GOVERNMENT 1965, 1967.
    WASHINGTON, D. C.: U. S. GOVERNMENT PRINTING OFFICE,
    (1967) (ED EC).

U. S. CIVIL SERVICE COMMISSION. STUDY OF MINORITY GROUP
    EMPLOYMENT IN THE FEDERAL GOVERNMENT.   WASHINGTON,
    D. C.: U. S. GOVERNMENT PRINTING OFFICE, (1965 AND
    1968) (EC).

U. S. CIVIL SERVICE COMMISSION. STUDY OF MINORITY GROUP
    EMPLOYMENT IN THE FEDERAL GOVERNMENT.   WASHINGTON,
    D. C.: U. S. GOVERNMENT PRINTING OFFICE, (ANNUAL) (EC).

U. S. COMMISSION ON CIVIL RIGHTS. "CIVIL RIGHTS DIGEST".
    CIVIL RIGHTS DIGEST,   (WINTER 1970) (EC).

U. S. COMMISSICN ON CIVIL RIGHTS. "CONGRESSIONAL 'SI' ON
    BILINGUALISM".   CIVIL RIGHTS DIGEST,   (SPRING
    1968), PP. 17-18.

U. S. COMMISSION ON CIVIL RIGHTS. "HOW MUCH LONGER . .
    . THE LONG ROAD?".   CIVIL RIGHTS DIGEST,   (SUMMER
    1968), PP. 34-44.

U. S. COMMISSION ON CIVIL RIGHTS. "LA RAZA--TODAY, NOT
    MANANA".   CIVIL RIGHTS DIGEST,   (SPRING 1968), PP.
    7-17.

U. S. COMMISSION ON CIVIL RIGHTS. "SPECIAL EDUCATION
    CLASSES, BARRIER TO MEXICAN-AMERICANS".   CIVIL RIGHTS
    DIGEST,   (FALL 1968), PP. 36-39.

U. S. COMMISSION ON CIVIL RIGHTS. CIVIL RIGHTS DIRECTORY.
    WASHINGTON D. C.: CLEARINGHOUSE PUBLICATION NO 15,
    (1970) (SC).

U. S. COMMISSION ON CIVIL RIGHTS. TEXAS ADVISORY COMMITTEE.
CIVIL RIGHTS IN TEXAS: A REPORT OF THE TEXAS ADVISORY
COMMISSION.   WASHINGTON, D. C.: U. S. GOVERNMENT
PRINTING OFFICE, (1970).

U. S. COMMISSION ON CIVIL RIGHTS, TEXAS ADVISORY COMMITTEE.
CIVIL RIGHTS IN TEXAS.   WASHINGTON, D. C.: U. S.
GOVERNMENT PRINTING OFFICE, (FEBRUARY 1970).

U. S. COMMISSION ON CIVIL RIGHTS. CYCLE TO NOWHERE.
WASHINGTON, D. C.: U. S. GOVERNMENT PRINTING OFFICE,
(SPRING 1968).

U. S. COMMISSION ON CIVIL RIGHTS CALIFORNIA ADVISORY
COMMITTEE. EDUCATION AND THE MEXICAN—AMERICAN
COMMUNITY IN LOS ANGELES COUNTY: A REPORT OF AN OPEN
MEETING BY THE CALIFORNIA STATE ADVISORY COMMITTEE
TO TTHE U.S. COMMISSION ON CIVIL RIGHTS.   WASHINGTON,
D. C.: U. S. GOVERNMENT PRINTING OFFICE, (1968) (EC).

U. S. COMMISSION ON CIVIL RIGHTS. EDUCATION AND THE
MEXICAN—AMERICAN COMMUNITY IN LOS ANGELES COUNTY.
WASHINGTON, D. C.: U. S. GOVERNMENT PRINTING OFFICE,
(1968).

U. S. COMMISSION ON CIVIL RIGHTS. EDUCATION PARKS.
APPRAISALS OF PLANS TO IMPROVE EDUCATIONAL QUALITY
AND DESEGREGATE THE SCHOOLS. CLEARINGHOUSE PUBLICATION
NO 9. WASHINGTON, D. C.: U. S. GOVERNMENT P RINTING
OFFICE,.

U. S. COMMISSION ON CIVIL RIGHTS. CALIF. STATE ADVISORY
COMMITTE. EDUCATION AND THE MEXICAN AMERICAN
COMMUNITY IN LOS ANGELES COUNTY, REPORT OF THE OPEN
MEETING BY THE CALIFORNIA STATE ADVISORY COMMITTEE.
WASHINGTON, D. C.: U. S. GOVERNMENT PRINTING OFFICE,
(1968).

U. S. COMMISSION ON CIVIL RIGHTS. CALIF. STATE ADVISORY
COMM. EDUCATION AND THE MEXICAN—AMERICAN COMMUNITY
IN LOS ANGELES COUNTY. LOS ANGELES, 1968.

U. S. COMMISSION ON CIVIL RIGHTS. CALIF. STATE ADVISORY
COMM. EDUCATION AND THE MEXICAN AMERICAN COMMUNITY
IN LOS ANGELES COUNTY. LOS ANGELES, 1968.

U. S. COMMISSION ON CIVIL RIGHTS. EMPLOYMENT TESTING:
GUIDE SIGNS, NOT STOP SIGNS. CLEARINGHOUSE PUBLICATION
NO 10. WASHINGTON, D. C.: U. S. GOVERNMENT PRINTING
OFFICE,.

U. S. COMMISSION ON CIVIL RIGHTS. TEXAS ADVISORY COMMITTEE.
EMPLOYMENT PRACTICES AT KELLEY AIR FORCE BASE, SAN
ANTONIO, TEXAS.   WASHINGTON, D. C.: U. S. GOVERNMENT
PRINTING OFFICE, (1968).

U. S. COMMISSION ON CIVIL RIGHTS. EQUAL EDUCATIONAL
OPPORTUNITIES FOR THE SPANISH-SPEAKING CHILD.
CLEARINGHOUSE PUBLICATION NO 27. WASHINGTON, D. C.:
U. S. GOVERNMENT PRINTING OFFICE,.

U. S. COMMISSION ON CIVIL RIGHTS. EQUAL EMPLOYMENT
OPPORTUNITY UNDER FEDERAL LAW: A GUIDE TO FEDERAL
LAW PROHIBITING DISCRIMINATION ON ACCOUNT OF RACE,
RELIGION, SEX, OR NATIONAL ORIGIN IN PRIVATE AND
PUBLIC EMPLOYMENT. CLEARINGHOUSE PUBLICATION NO 17.
WASHINTON, D. C.: U. S. GOVERNMENT PRPRINTING OFFICE,
(1971).

U. S. COMMISSION ON CIVIL RIGHTS. ETHNIC ISOLATION
OF MEXICAN AMERICANS IN THE PUBLIC SCHOOLS OF
THE SOUTHWEST. WASHINGTON, D. C.: U. S. GOVERNMENT
PRINTING OFFICE,.

U. S. COMMISSION ON CIVIL RIGHTS. HEARING . . . HELD IN
SAN FRANCISCO, CALIFORNIA, MAY 1-3, 1967, AND OAKLAND,
CALIFORNIA, MAY 4-6, 1967.

U. S. COMMISSION ON CIVIL RIGHTS. HEARING HELD IN
SAN ANTONIO, TEXAS, DEC. 9-14, 1968. WASHINGTON,
D. C.: U. S. GOVERNMENT PRINTING OFFICE, (DECEMBER
9- 14, 1968).

U. S. COMMISSION ON CIVIL RIGHTS. HEARINGS BEFORE THE U.S.
COMMISSION ON CIVIL RIGHTS, FEB. 3, 1962, HELD
IN PHOENIX, ARIZONA. WASHINGTON, D. C.D U.
S. GOVERNMENT PRINTING OFFICE, (1962).

U. S. COMMISSION ON CIVIL RIGHTS. HEARINGS IN LOS ANGELES
AND SAN FRANCISCO BEFORE THE U.S. COMMISSION ON CIVIL
RIGHTS (JANUARY 1960). WASHINGTON, D. C.: U. S.
GOVERNMENT PRINTING OFFICE, (1960).

U. S. COMMISSION ON CIVIL RIGHTS. HEARINGS. . . HELD IN
LOS ANGELES, CALIFORNIA, JANUARY 25-26, 1960, AND SAN
FRANCISCO, CALIFORNIA, JANUARY 27-28, 1960.

U. S. COMMISSION ON CIVIL RIGHTS. HEW AND TITLE VI. A
REPORT ON THE DEVELOPMENT OF THE ORGANIZATION,
POLICIES, AND COMPLIANCE PROCEDURES OF THE DEPARTMENT
OF HEALTH, EDUCATION, AND WELFARE UNDER TITLE VI OF
THE CIVIL RIGHT ACT OF 1964. CLEARINGHOUSE PUBLICATION
NO 22. WASHINGTON, D. C.: U. S. GOVERNMENT PRINTING
OFFICE, (NOVEMBER 1969).

U. S. COMMISSION ON CIVIL RIGHTS. HOME OWNERSHIP FOR LOWER
INCOME FAMILIES. A REPORT ON THE RACIAL AND ETNIC
IMPACT OF THE SECTION 235 PROGRAM. WASHINGTON,
D. C.: U. S. GOVERNMENT PRINTING OFFICE, (JUNE 1971).

U. S. COMMISSICN ON CIVIL RIGHTS. JCBS AND CIVIL RIGHTS.
THE ROLE OF THE FEDERAL GOVERNMENT IN PROMOTING EQUAL
OPPORTUNITY IN EMPLOYMENT AND TRAINING. PREPARED BY
THE BROOKINGS INSTITUTE.   WASHINGTCN, D. C.: U.
S. GOVERNMENT PRINTING OFFICE, (SUMMER 1968).

U. S. COMMISSICN ON CIVIL RIGHTS. MEXICAN AMERICAN
EDUCATION STUDY.   WASHINGTCN, D. C.: U. S.
GOVERNMENT PRINTING OFFICE, (APRIL 1971).

U. S. COMMISSION ON CIVIL RIGHTS. MEXICAN AMERICANS AND
THE ADMINISTRATION OF JUSTICE IN THE SOUTHWEST.
WASHINGTON, D. C.: U. S. GOVERNMENT PRINTING OFFICE,
(MARCH 1970).

U. S. COMMISSION ON CIVIL RIGHTS. MEXICAN–AMERICAN
EDUCATION STUDY, REPCRT 1: ETHNIC ISOLATICN OF THE
MEXICAN–AMERICAN IN THE PUBLIC SCHOOLS OF THE
SOUTHWEST.   WASHINGTON, D. C.: U. S. GOVERNMENT
PRINTING OFFICE, (1971).

U. S. COMMISSION ON CIVIL RIGHTS. CALIF. STATE ADVISORY
COMMITTEE. POLICE MINORITY GROUP RELATIONS IN LOS
ANGELES AND THE SAN FRANCISCO BAYAREA.   WASHINGTON,
D. C.: U. S. GOVERNMENT PRINTING OFFICE, (1963).

U. S. COMMISSION ON CIVIL RIGHTS. CALIF. STATE ADVISORY
COMM. POLICE MINORITY GROUP RELATIONS IN LOS ANGELES
AND THE SAN FRANCISCO BAYAREA.   WASHINGTON, D. C.:
U. S. GOVERNMENT PRINTING OFFICE, (1963).

U. S. COMMISSICN ON CIVIL RIGHTS. PROCESS OF CHANGE.
CLEARINGHOUSE PUBLICATICN NO 7. WASHINGTON, D. C.:
U. S. GOVERNMENT PRINTING OFFICE,.

U. S. COMMISSION ON CIVIL RIGHTS. RACIAL ISOLATION IN THE
PUBLIC SCHOOLS.   CLEARINGHOUSE PUBLICATION NO 7.
WASHINGTON, D. C.: U. S. GOVERNMENT PRINTING OFFICE,
(MARCH 1967).

U. S. COMMISSICN ON CIVIL RIGHTS. REPORT OF THE U.S.
COMMISSION ON CIVIL RIGHTS: EQUAL OPPORTUNITY IN FORM
PROGRAMS, AN APPRAISAL OF SERVICES RENDERED BY
AGENCIES CF THE U.S. DEPARTMENT OF AGRICULTURE.
WASHINGTON, D. C.: U. S. GOVERNMENT PRINTING OFFICE,
(1965).

U. S. COMMISSION ON CIVIL RIGHTS. REPORT ON APPRENTICESHIP
BY THE ADVISORY COMMITTEES TO THE U.S. COMMISSION ON
CIVIL RIGHTS IN: CALIFORNIA, FLORIDA, NEW YORK,
CONNECTICUT, MARYLAND, TENNESSEE, DISTRICT OF
COLOMBIA, NEW JERSEY AND WISCONSIN.   WASHINGTON,
D. C.: U. S. GOVERNMENT PRINTING OFFICE, (1964).

U. S. COMMISSION ON CIVIL RIGHTS. SCHOOL CAN BE DESEGREGATED.
    CLEARINGHOUSE PUBLICATION NO 8. WASHINGTON, D. C.:
    U. S. GOVERNMENT PRINTING OFFICE, (JUNE 1967).

U. S. COMMISSION ON CIVIL RIGHTS. SPANISH—SPEAKING
    PEOPLES.   STAFF PAPER, FEBRUARY 5, 1964.

U. S. COMMISSION ON CIVIL RIGHTS. STRANGER IN ONE'S LAND.
    CLEARINGHOUSE PUBLICATION NO 19. WASHINGTON, D. C.:
    U. S. GOVERNMENT PRINTING OFFICE, (MAY 1970).

U. S. COMMISSION ON CIVIL RIGHTS. STUDY ON EQUAL EMPLOYMENT
    OPPORTUNITY PROGRAMS AND ACTIVITIES OF THE FEDERAL
    GOVERNMENT.   WASHINGTON, D. C.: U. S. GOVERNMENT
    PRINTING OFFICE, (1969).

U. S. COMMISSION ON CIVIL RIGHTS. SUPPLEMENT — JOBS AND
    CIVIL RIGHTS. THE ROLE OF THE FEDERAL GOVERNMEMT
    PROMOTING EQUAL OPPORTUNITY IN EMPLOYMENT TRAINING.
    WASHINGTON, D. C.: U. S. GOVERNMENT PRINTING OFFICE,
    (APRIL 1969).

U. S. COMMISSION ON CIVIL RIGHTS. WHAT STUDENTS PERCEIVE.
    CLEARINGHOUSE PUBLICATION NO 4. WASHINGTON, D. C.:
    U. S. GOVERNMENT PRINTING OFFICE, .

U. S. COMMISSION ON CIVIL RIGHTS. WHO WILL LISTEN?.
    CLEARINGHOUSE PUBLICATION NO 13. WASHINGTON, D. C.:
    U. S. GOVERNMENT PRINTING OFFICE, .

U. S. COMMISSION ON CIVIL RIGHTS. WHO WILL WEAR THE BADGE?
    A REPORT OF THE UNITED STATES COMMISSION ON CIVIL
    RIGHTS, 1971.   CLEARINGHOUSE PUBLICATION NO 25.
    WASHINGTON, D. C.: U. S. GOVERNMENT PINTING OFFICE,
    (1971).

U. S. COMMISSION ON CIVIL RIGHTS. FOR ALL THE PEOPLE BY
    ALL THE PEOPLE. A REPORT ON EQUAL OPPORTUNITY
    IN STATE AND LOCAL GOVERNMENT EMPLOYMENT.   CLEARINGHOUSE
    PUBLICATION NO 18. WASHINGTON, D. C.: U. S.
    GOVERNMENT PPRINTING OFFICE, (NOVEMBER 1969).

U. S. COMMISSION ON CIVIL RIGHTS. TEXAS ADVISORY COMMITTEE.
    THE CIVIL RIGHTS STATUS OF SPANISH—SPEAKING AMERICANS
    IN KELBERG, NUECESAND SAN PATRICO COUNTIES, TEXAS.
    WASHINGTON, D. C.: U. S. GOVERNMENT PRINTING OFFICE,
    (1967).

U. S. COMMISSION ON CIVIL RIGHTS, STAFF REPORT. THE
    COMMUTER ON THE U.S.—MEXICO BORDER.   WASHINGTON D.
    C.. ,.

U. S. COMMISSION ON CIVIL RIGHTS. THE CONCENTRATION OF
SPANISH SURNAMES IN THE FIVE SOUTHWESTERN STATES.
WASHINGTON, D. C.: U. S. GOVERNMENT PRINTING OFFICE,
(1962) (EC).

U. S. COMMISSION ON CIVIL RIGHTS. THE CONCENTRATION OF
SPANISH SURNAME PERSONS IN THE FIVE SOUTHWESTERN
STATES.   WASHINGTON, D. C.: U. S. GOVERNMENT
PRINTING OFFICE, (1962).

U. S. COMMISSION ON CIVIL RIGHTS. THE FEDERAL CIVIL RIGHTS
ENFORCEMENT SUMMARY.   CLEARINGHOUSE PUBLICATION NO
31. WASHINGTON D. C.:   U. S. GOVERNMENT PRINTING OFFICE,.

U. S. COMMISSION ON CIVIL RIGHTS, MEXICAN AMERICAN
EDUCATION IN TEXAS. A FUNCTION OF WEALTH.   WASHINGTON,
D. C., 1972.

U. S. COMMISSION ON CIVIL RIGHTS. THE MEXICAN AMERICAN.
A PAPER PREPARED FOR THE U. S. COMMISSION ON CIVIL
RIGHTS, 1968.

U. S. COMMISSION ON CIVIL RIGHTS. THE NATIONAL CONFERENCE
AND THE REPORTS OF THE STATE ADVISORY COMMITTEESTO
THE U.S. COMMISSION ON CIVIL RIGHTS, 1959.
WASHINGTON, D. C.: U. S. GOVERNMENT PRINTING OFFICE,
(1960).

U. S. COMMISSION ON CIVIL RIGHTS. A TIME TO LISTEN ...
A TIME TO ACT.   WASHINGTON, D. C.: U. S. GOVERNMENT
PRINTING OFFICE, (1967) (EC).

U. S. COMMISSION ON CIVIL RIGHTS. A TIME TO LISTEN, A TIME
TO ACT, VOICES FROM THE GHETTOS OF THE NATION'SCITIES.
WASHINGTON, D. C.: U. S. GOVERNMENT PRINTING OFFICE,
(1967).

U. S. CONGRESS. BILINGUAL EDUCATION.   90TH, 1ST SESSION.
SENATE HEARINGS BEFORE SPECIAL SUBCOMMITTEE ON
BILINGUAL EDUCATION OF THE COMMITTEE ON LABOR
AND PUBLIC WELFARE. WASHINGT ON, D.C.:   U. S.
GOVERMENT PRINTING OFFICE, (1967) (EC).

U. S. DEPARTMENT OF COMMERCE BUREAU OF CENSUSES. CENSUSES
OF 1900, 1910 AND 1920.   WASHINGTON, D. C.: U.
S. GOVERNMENT PRINTING OFFICE, (SO).

U. S. DEPARTMENT OF COMMERCE. BUREAU OF THE CENSUS.
NATIVITY AND PARENTAGE OF THE WHITE POPULATION:
MOTHER TONGUE BY NATIVITY, PARENTAGE, COUNTRY
OF ORIGIN, AND AGE FOR STATES AND LARGE CITIES, PART
OF SIXTEENTH CENSUS OF THE UNITED STATES.
WASHINGTON, D. C.: U. S. GOVERNMENT PRINTING OFFICE,
(1943) (SO).

U. S. DEPARTMENT OF AGRICULTURE. PESTICIDE REVIEW 1968.
    IN U. S. CONGRESS. SENATE. LABOR AND PUBLIC WELFARE
    COMMITTEE. HEARINGS. MIGRANT AND SEASONAL FARMWORKER
    POWERLESS, PART 6-C: PESTICIDES AND THE FARMWORKER
    PAGES 3342-3358. WASHINGTON, D. C.: U. S. GOVERNMENT
    PRINTING OFFICE, (AUGUST 3, 1964) (EC MD).

U. S. DEPARTMENT OF AGRICULTURE. PRELIMINARY REPORT ON
    CONCHO. REGIONAL BULLETIN NO. 29, CONSERVATION
    ECONOMICS SERIES NO. 2. ALBUGUERQUE, NEW MEXICO,
    (1935) (EC).

U. S. DEPARTMENT OF AGRICULTURE AND CCOPERATORS. REPORT
    ON PESTICIDES AND RELATED ACTIVITIES--1968 ABSTRACTS.
    IN U. S. CONGRESS. SENATE. LABOR AND PUBLIC WELFARE
    COMMITTEE. HEARINGS. MIGRANT AND SEASONAL FARMWORKER
    POWERLESS, PART 6-C: PESTICIDES AND THE FARMWORKER
    PAGES 3253-3265. WASHINGTON, D. C.: U. S. GOVERNMENT
    PRINTING OFFICE, (FEBRUARY 1969) (EC MD).

U. S. DEPARTMENT OF JUSTICE. UNIFORM CRIME REPORTS.
    WASHINGTON, D. C.: DEPARTMENT OF JUSTICE, (OCTOBER,
    1968).

U. S. DEPARTMENT OF AGRICULTURE. A CAMERA REPORT ON EL
    CERRITO, A TYPICAL SPANISH-AMERICAN COMMUNITY IN NEW
    MEXICO.   WASHINGTON, D. C.: U. S. GOVERNMENT
    PRINTING OFFICE, (1942) (EC).

U. S. DEPT OF AGRICULTURE. FIELD FLOOD CONTROL CO-ORDINATING
    COMMITTEE. DEPARTMENT OF AGRICULTURE. FIELD FLOOD
    CONTROL CC-ORDINATING COMMITTEE. URVEY REPORT. RUN-OFF
    AND WATER-FLOW RETARDATION AND SOIL-EROSION PREVENION
    FOR FLOOD-CONTROL PURPOSES. RIO PUERCO WATERSHED,
    TRIBUTARY OF THE UPER RIO GRANDE.   WASHINGTON, D.
    C.: U. S. GOVERNMENT PRINTING OFFICE, (1940) (EC GE).

U. S. DEPT OF AGRICULTURE, ECONOMIC RESEARCH SERVICE.
    ECONOMIC, SOCIAL AND DEMOGRAPHIC CHARACTERISTICS OF
    SPANISH-AMERICAN WAGE WORKERS ON U.S. FARMS.
    AGRICULTURE ECONOMIC REPORT, NO 27. WASHINGTON, D.
    C.: U. S. GOVERNMENT PRINTING OFFICE, (1962) (EC).

U. S. DEPT OF AGRICULTURE. ECONOMIC RESEARCH SERVICE.
    ECONOMIC, SOCIAL AND DEMOGRAPHIC CHARACTERISTICS OF
    SPANISH-AMERICAN WAGE WORKERS ON U.S. FARMS.
    WASHINGTON, D. C.: U. S. GOVERNMENT PRINTING OFFICE,
    (1962) (EC).

U. S. DEPT CF AGRICULTURE. ECONOMIC RESEARCH SERVICE.
    MEXICAN AMERICANS. ANNOTATEDANNOTATED ANNOTATED
    BIBLICGRAPHY OF THE ECONOMIC REACH SERVICE REPORTS-1965-1966.
    WASHINGTON, D. C.: U. S. GOVERNMENT PRINTING OFFIE,
    (1966) (EC B).

U. S. DEPT OF AGRICULTURE. SOIL CONSERVATION SERVICE.
VILLAGE DEPENDENCE ON MIGRATORY LABOR IN THE UPPER
RIO GRANDE AREA.   REGIONAL BULLETIN NO, 47, CONSERVATION
ECONOMICS SERIES NO 20. , (1937) (EC).

U. S. DEPT OF AGRICULTURE, ECONOMIC RESEARCH SERVICE.   THE
HIRED FARM WORKING FORCE OF 1966: A STATISTICAL
REPORT.   AGRICULTURE ECONOMIC REPORT 121. WASHINGTON,
D. C.: U. S. GOVERNMENT PRINTING OFFICE, (1964) (EC).

U. S. DEPT OF AGRICULTURE. ECONOMIC SURVEYS DIVISION, VOL.
II. THE SPANISH—AMERICAN VILLAGES.   ALBUQUERQUE,
NEW MEXICO: TEWA BASIN STUDY, 1939 (EC).

U. S. DEPT OF COMMERCE. ECONOMIC DEVELOPMENT ADMINISTRATION.
INDUSTRIAL AND EMPLOYMENT POTENTIAL OF THE U.S.—MEXICO
BORDER.   WASHINGTON, D. C.: U. S. GOVERNMENT
PRINTING OFFICE, (1966) (EC SI).

U. S. DEPT OF HEW. BILINGUAL EDUCATION: A HANDBOOK FOR
EDUCATORS.   MARYLAND: NATIONAL CASH REGISTER
(ERIC), (EC).

U. S. DEPT OF HEW. DOMESTIC AGRICULTURAL MIGRANTS IN THE
UNITED STATES.   WASHINGTON, D. C.: U. S. GOVERNMENT
PRINTING OFFICE, (1966) (EC SI).

U. S. DEPT OF HEW. CHILDREN'S BUREAU. S. THE WORK AND
WELFARE OF CHILDREN OF AGRICULTURAL LABORERS IN
HIDALGO COUNTY, TEXAS.   AMBER A. WHARBURTON, (ET AL).
WASHINGTON, D. C.: U. S. GOVERNMENT PRINTING OFFICE,
(1935) (ED EC).

U. S. DEPT OF HEW. OE. "HELP FOR SPANISH SPEAKING
YOUNSTERS".   J. STOCKER. AMERICAN EDUCATION, VOL.
4 NO. 3 (MAY 1968) (ED).

U. S. DEPT OF HEW. OE. "SPEAK UP, CHICANO, FIGHT FOR
EDUCATIONAL EQUALITY".   AMERICAN EDUCATION, VOL. 4
NO. 10 (NOVEMBER 1968), PP. 29-31 (ED).

U. S. DEPT OF HEW. OE. ANNOTATED BIBLIOGRAPHY FOR TEACHERS
OF ENGLISH AS A FOREIGN LANGUAGE.   WASHINGTON, D.
C.: U. S. GOVERNMENT PRINTING OFFICE, (B).

U. S. DEPT OF HEW. OE. AWARDS FOR MODERN FOREIGN LANGUAGE
AND AREA STUDY.   WASHINGTON, D. C.: U. S. GOVERNMENT
PRINTING OFFICE, (1971-72) (ED).

U. S. DEPT OF HEW. OE. BILINGUAL SCHOOLING IN THE U.S..
THEODORE ANDERSSON AND MILDRED BOYER. WASHINGTON,
D. C.: U. S. GOVERNMENT PRINTING OFFICE, (1970) (ED).

U. S. DEPT OF HEW. OE. EDUCATIONAL MATERIALS CENTER. BOOKS
RELATED TO ADULT EDUCATION AND TEACHING ENGLISH TO
SPEAKERS CF OTHER LANGUAGES.   WASHINGTON, D. C.:
U. S. GOVERNMENT PRINTING OFFICE, (1970) (ED).

U. S. DEPT OF HEW. OE.   BUREAU OF ELEMENTARY AND SECONDARY
EDUCATION PROGRAMS.   WASHINGTON, D. C.: U.
S. GOVERNMENT PRINTING OFFICE, (1968) (ED).

U. S. DEPT OF HEW. OE.   CATALOG OF SELECTED DOCUMENTS ON
THE DISADVANTAGED.   ERIC. WASHINGTON, D. C.: U. S.
GOVERNMENT PRINTING OFFICE, (1966) (B   ED).

U. S. DEPT OF HEW. OE.   EDUCATIONAL ACHIEVEMENT AMONG
MEXICAN-AMERICANS: A SPECIAL REPORT FROM THE EDUCATIONAL
OPPORTUNITIES SURVEY.   WASHINGTON, D. C.: U. S.
GOVERNMENT PRINTING OFFICE, (1967) (ED).

U. S. DEPT OF HEW. OE AND OEO. EDUCATION: AN ANSWER TO
POVERTY.   WASHINGTON, D. C.: U. S. GOVERNMENT
PRINTING OFFICE, (1966) (ED).

U. S. DEPT OF HEW. OE.   ELEMENTARY PROGRAM IN COMPENSATORY
ED. 2: MALABAR READING PROGRAM FOR MEXICAN-AMERICAN
CHILDREN, LOS ANGELES, CALIF.   WASHINGTON, D. C.:
U. S. GOVERNMENT PRINTING OFFICE, (1969) (ED).

U. S. DEPT OF HEW. OE.   GUIDE TO OE-ADMINISTERED PROGRAMS,
FISCAL YEAR, 1971.   REPRINTED FROM AMERICAN EDUCATION,
NOVEMBER, 1970. WASHINGTON, D. C.: U. S. GOVERNMENT
PRINTING OFFICE, (1970) (ED).

U. S. DEPT OF HEW. OFFICE OF THE SECRETARY. H.E.W. NEWS.
WASHINGTON, D. C.: U. S. GOVERNMENT PRINTING OFFICE,
(ED).

U. S. DEPT OF HEW. OFFICE FOR CIVIL RIGHTS. HEW Y DERECHOS
CIVILES.   WASHINGTON, D. C.: U. S. GOVERNMENT
PRINTING OFFICE, (1971) (ED).

U. S. DEPT OF HEW. OE.   IMPROVING EDUCATIONAL OPPORTUNITIES
FOR MEXICAN-AMERICAN HANDICAPPED CHILDREN.
WASHINGTON, D. C.: U. S. GOVERNMENT PRINTING OFFICE,
(1968) (ED).

U. S. DEPT OF HEW. OE.   LANGUAGE LOYALTY IN THE UNITED
STATES.   OFFICE OF EDUCATION. WASHINGTON, D. C.:
U. S. GOVERNMENT PRINTING OFFICE, (1963) (ED).

U. S. DEPT OF HEW. OE.   LEARNING ENGLISH INCIDENTALLY: A
STUDY OF BILINGUAL CHILDREN.   BULLETINS 1937, NUMBER
15, PROJECT IN RESEARCH UNIVERSITIES. WASHINGTON,
D. C.: U. S. GOVERNMENT PRINTING OFFICE, (1938) (ED).

U. S. DEPT OF HEW. OE. MAMA GOES TC NURSERY SCHOOL; SCHOOL
BELLS FOR MIGRANTS; LEARN A LITO ENGLISH; SE HABLA
ESPANOL. OE-20109. WASHINGTON, D. C.: U. S.
GOVERNMENT PRINTING OFFICE, (1968) (ED).

U. S. DEPT OF HEW. OE. MEXICAN-AMERICANS: A HANDBOOK FOR
EDUCATORS. JACK D. FORBES. WASHINGTON, D. C.: U.
S. GOVERNMENT PRINTING OFFICE, (1969) (ED).

U. S. DEPT OF HEW. OE. MEXICAN-AMERICAN AFFAIRS UNIT.
MEXICAN-AMERICAN EDUCATION. SPECIAL REPORT.
WASHINGTON, D. C.: U. S. GOVERNMENT PRINTING OFFICE,
(1968) (ED).

U. S. DEPT OF HEW. OE. MEXICAN-AMERICAN EDUCATION:
A SEARCH FOR IDENTITY. REPRINT FROM AMERICAN
EDUCATOR, NUMBER 1968. WASHINGTON, D. C.: U.
S. GOVERNMENT PRINTING OFFICE, (1968) (ED).

U. S. DEPT OF HEW. OE. MEXICAN-AMERICAN EDUCATION:
A SPECIAL REPORT. WASHINGTON, D. C.: U. S.
GOVERNMENT PRINTING OFFICE, (1969) (ED).

U. S. DEPT OF HEW. OE. MODEL PROGRAMS, CHILDHOOD EDUCATION;
BILINGUAL EARLY CHILDHOOD PROGRAM, SAN ANTONIO, TEXAS.
WASHINGTON, D. C.: U. S. GOVERNMENT PRINTING OFFICE,
(1970) (ED).

U. S. DEPT OF HEW. OE. MODERN FOREIGN LANGUAGES IN HIGH
SCHOOL. PATRICIA O'CONNOR. BULLETIN 1960, NO. 9.
WASHINGTON, D. C.: U. S. GOVERNMENT PRINTING OFFICE,
(1960) (ED).

U. S. DEPT OF HEW. OE. NATIONAL CONFERENCE ON BILINGUAL
EDUCATION LANGUAGE SKILLS. PAMPHLET NO. 63.
WASHINGTON, D. C.: U. S. GOVERNMENT PRINTING OFFICE,
(1935) (ED).

U. S. DEPT OF HEW. OE. NATIONAL CONFERENCE ON EDUCATIONAL
OPPORTUNITIES FOR MEXICAN AMERICANS. WASHINGTON,
D. C.: U. S. GOVERNMENT PRINTING OFFICE, (1969) (ED).

U. S. DEPT OF HEW. OE. PROGRAMS FCR THE DISADVANTAGED.
WASHINGTON, D. C.: U. S. GOVERNMENT PRINTING OFFICE,
(1969) (ED).

U. S. DEPT OF HEW. OE. RACE AND PLACE. A LEGAL HISTORY
OF THE NEIGHBORHOOD SCHOOL. WASHINGTON, D. C.:
U. S. GOVERNMENT PRINTING OFFICE, (1967) (ED).

U. S. DEPT OF HEW. OFFICE FOR SPANISH SPEAKING AFFAIRS.
REPORT FRCM OFFICE FOR SPANISH SPEAKING AMERICAN
AFFAIRS. WASHINGTON, D. C.: U. S. GOVERNMENT
PRINTING OFFICE, (1970) (ED).

U. S. DEPT OF HEW. OE.   REPORT FROM MEXICAN AMERICAN
   AFFAIRS UNIT.   WASHINGTON, D. C.: U. S. GOVERNMENT
   PRINTING OFFICE, (1969) (ED).

U. S. DEPT OF HEW. OE.   SCHOOL TRANSFER RECORD SYSTEM FOR
   FARM MIGRANT CHILDREN.   BULLETIN NO. 32.   WASHINGTON,
   D. C.: U. S. GOVERNMENT PRINTING OFFICE, (1965) (ED
   SI).

U. S. DEPT OF HEW. OE.   SE HABLA EXPANOL, HELP FOR SPANISH
   SPEAKING YOUNGSTERS.   OE 30020. WASHINGTON, D. C.:
   U. S. GOVERNMENT PRINTING OFFICE, (1967) (ED).

U. S. DEPT OF HEW. OE.   SELECTED STATE PROGRAMS IN MIGRANT
   EDUCATION.   BULLETIN NO. 35.   WASHINGTON, D. C.: U.
   S. GOVERNMENT PRINTING OFFICE, (1963) (ED).

U. S. DEPT OF HEW. OE.   SPEAK UP, CHICANO, MEXICAN-AMERICAN
   FIGHTS FOR EDUCATIONAL EQUALITY.   A. M. RODRIGUEZ.
   WASHINGTON, D.C.: U. S. GOVERNMENT PRINTING OFFICE,
   (NOVEMBER 1968) (ED).

U. S. DEPT OF HEW. OE.   STUDENT FINANCIAL ASSISTANCE
   OE-55055.   WASHINGTON, D.C.: U. S. GOVERNMENT
   PRINTING OFFICE, (SEPTEMBER 1968) (ED).

U. S. DEPT OF HEW. OE.   SUCCESSFUL PRACTICES IN THE
   TEACHING OF ENGLISH TO BILINGUAL CHILDREN IN HAWAII.
   WASHINGTON, D. C.: U. S. GOVERNMENT PRINTING OFFICE,
   (1938) (ED).

U. S. DEPT OF HEW. OE.   TEACHERS AND COUNSELORS FOR
   MEXICAN-AMERICAN CHILDREN.   MARYLAND: ERIC, (1969)
   (ED).

U. S. DEPT OF HEW. OE.   TREATING READING DIFFICULTIES. THE
   ROLE OF THE PRINCIPAL, TEACHER, SPECIALIST, ADMINISTRATION.
   CARL B. SMITH, BARBARA URTER AND GLORIA DAPPER.
   WASHINGTON, D. C.: U. S. GOVERNMENT PRINTING OFFICE,
   (1970) (ED).

U. S. DEPT OF HEW. OE.   UPRISING IN THE BARRIOS.   CHARLES
   A. ERICSEN. AMERICAN EDUCATION, (VOL. 4, NO.   10
   (NOVEMBER, 1968) PP 29-31) (ED).

U. S. DEPT OF HEW. OE.   VIVA LA RAZA: MEXICAN-AMERICAN
   EDUCATION; A SEARCH FOR IDENTITY.   REPRINTS FROM
   AMERICAN EDUCATION. WASHINGTON, D. C.: U. S.
   GOVERNMENT P

U. S. DEPT OF HEW. O E.   YOUNG SPANISH-SPEAKING CHILDREN
   IN OUR SCHOOLS.   ELEMENTARY EDUCATION SERIES NO. 30.
   WASHINGTON, D. C.: U. S. GOVERNMENT PRINTING OFFICE,
   (1951) (ED).

U. S. DEPT OF HEW. O E. THE ARTS AND THE POOR. NEW
CHALLENGE FOR EDUCATORS. JUDITH MURPHY AND RONALD
GROSS. WASHINGTON, D. C.: U. S. GOVERNMENT PRINTING
OFFICE, (1968) (ED).

U. S. DEPT OF HEW. OE. THE EDUCATION OF MIGRANT CHILDREN;
QUESTIONS AND ANSWERS.   OE—20038. WASHINGTON, D.
C.: U. S. GOVERNMENT PRINTING OFFICE, (1962) (EC ED).

U. S. DEPT OF HEW. OE. THE EDUCATION OF SPANISH-SPEAKING
CHILDREN IN FIVE SOUTHWESTERN STATES.   WASHINGTON,
D. C.: U. S. GOVERNMENT PRINTING OFFICE, (1933) (ED).

U. S. DEPT OF HEW. OE. THE MEXICAN AMERICANS.
WASHINGTON, D. C.: U. S. GOVERNMENT PRINTING OFFICE,
(ED).

U. S. DEPT OF HEW. OE. A NEW LOOK AT THE ATTRIBUTES OF
THE MEXICAN—AMERICAN.   MARYLAND: ERIC, (1969) (ED).

U. S. DEPT OF HEW. SOC SECURITY ADMIN. DIV. OF RESEARCH
AND STATISTICS. SLUMS AND SOCIAL INSECURITY.
AN APPRAISAL OF THE EFFECTIVENESS OF HOUSING POLICIES
IN HELPING TO ELIMINATE POVERTY IN THE U. S..   ALVIN
L. SCHORR. RESEARCH REPORT, NO. 1. WASHINGTON, D.
C.: U. S. GOVERNMENT PRINTING OFFICE, (ED).

U. S. DEPT OF HEW. SOCIAL AND REHABILITATION SERVICE. A
RIGHT TO A DECENT HOME....   WASHINGTON, D. C.: U.
S. GOVERNMENT PRINTING OFFICE, (ED).

U. S. DEPT OF LABOR. BUREAU OF LABOR STATISTICS. 'MEXICAN
FAMILIES IN LOS ANGELES.'   IN MONEY DISBURSEMENTS
OF WAGE EARNERS AND CLERICAL WORKERS IN FIVE CITIES
IN THE PACIFIC COAST REGION, 1934—1936, PAGES 85—109
(EC).

U. S. DEPT OF LABOR. BUREAU OF LABOR STATISTICS. "INCREASE
OF MEXICAN LABOR IN CERTAIN INDUSTRIES IN THE UNITED
STATES".   MONTHLY LABOR REVIEW, VOL. 32 (JANUARY
1931), PP. 81—83 (EC).

U. S. DEPT OF LABOR. BUREAU OF LABOR STATISTICS. "INCREASE
OF MEXICAN POPULATION IN THE UNITED STATES".   MONTHLY
LABOR REVIEW, VOL. 37 (JULY 1933), PP. 46—48 (EC).

U. S. DEPT OF LABOR. BUREAU OF LABOR STATISTICS. "LABOR
AND AGRICULTURAL MIGRATION TO CALIFORNIA, 1935-1940".
MONTHLY LABOR REVIEW, VOL. 53 (JULY 1941), P. 18
(EC).

U. S. DEPT OF LABOR. BUREAU OF LABOR STATISTICS. "LABOR
AND SOCIAL CONDITIONS OF MEXICANS IN CALIFORNIA".
MONTHLY LABOR REVIEW, VOL. 32 (JANUARY 1931), PP.
83—89 (EC).

U. S. DEPT OF LABOR. BUREAU OF LABOR STATISTICS. "MEXICAN
LABOR COLONY AT BETHLEHEM, PENNSYLVANIA". MONTHLY
LABOR REVIEW, VOL. 33 (OCTOBER 1931), PP. 74-78 (EC).

U. S. DEPT OF LABOR. BUREAU OF LABOR STATISTICS. "MEXICAN
LABOR IN THE IMPERIAL VALLEY, CALIFORNIA". MONTHLY
LABOR REVIEW, VOL. 28 (MARCH 1929), PP. 59-65 (EC).

U. S. DEPT OF LABOR. BUREAU OF LABOR STATISTICS. "MINORITY
GROUPS IN CALIFORNIA". MONTHLY LABOR REVIEW, VOL.
89 (SEPTEMBER 1966), PP. 978-983 (EC).

U. S. DEPT OF LABOR. BUREAU OF LABOR STATISTICS. "RESULTS
OF ADMISSION OF MEXICAN LABORERS UNDER DEPARTMENTAL
ORDER FOR EMPLOYMENT IN AGRICULTURAL PURSUITS".
MONTHLY LABOR REVIEW, VOL. 11 (NOVEMBER 1920), PP.
1095-1097 (EC).

U. S. DEPT OF LABOR. BUREAU OF LABOR STATISTICS. "WAGES,
EMPLOYMENT CONDITIONS, AND WELFARE OF THE SUGAR-BEET
LABORERS". MONTHLY LABOR REVIEW, VOL. 46 (FEBRUARY
1938), PP. 322-333 (EC).

U. S. DEPT OF LABOR. ANNUAL REPORTS OF THE COMMISSIONER
GENERAL OF IMMIGRATION. WASHINGTON, D. C.: U. S.
GOVERNMENT PRINTING OFFICE, (ANNUAL) (ED GE).

U. S. DEPT OF LABOR. ANNUAL REPORTS OF THE COMMISSIONER
OF NATURALIZATION. WASHINGTON, D. C.: U. S.
GOVERNMENT PRINTING OFFICE, (ANNUAL) (SI).

U. S. DEPT OF LABOR. SECRETARY OF LABOR. ANNUAL REPORT
OF THE SECRETARY OF LABOR. 1932-1933 TO 1939-1940.
WASHINGTON, D. C.: U. S. GOVERNMENT PRINTING OFFICE,
(JULY 1933) (EC).

U. S. DEPT OF LABOR. COMMISSIONER-GENERAL OF IMMIGRATION.
ANNUAL REPORTS OF THE COMMISSIONER-GENERAL OF
IMMIGRATION. 1895-1932. WASHINGTON, D. C.: U. S.
GOVERNMENT PRINTING OFFICE, (JULY 1933) (EC).

U. S. DEPT OF LABOR. MANPOWER ADMINISTRATION. CIVIL RIGHTS
IN THE URBAN CRISES. CONDENSED TRANSCRIPT.
WASHINGTON, D. C.: U. S. GOVERNMENT PRINTING OFFICE,
(1968) (EC).

U. S. DEPT OF LABOR. MANPOWER POLICY, EVALUATION AND
RESEARCH OFFICE. EDUCATION AND TRAINING OF RACIAL
MINORITIES; PROCEEDINGS. PREPARED BY THE CENTER FOR
STUDIES IN VOCATIONAL AND TECHNICAL EDUCATION.
UNIVERSITY OF WISCONSIN. 1968. (EC).

U. S. DEPT OF LABOR. MANPOWER ADMINISTRATION. EQUALITY
OF OPPORTUNITY IN MANPOWER PROGRAMS. REPORT
OF ACTIVITY UNDER TITLE 6 OF THE CIVIL RIGHTS ACT OF
1964. WASHINGTON, D. C.: U. S. GOVERNMENT PRINTING
OFFICE, (SEPTEMBER, 1968) (EC).

U. S. DEPT OF LABOR. INDUSTRIAL ACCIDENTS; MEXICAN LABOR
IN THE UNITED STATES. BULLETIN 78. WASHINGTON, D.
C.: U. S. GOVERNMENT PRINTING OFFICE, (1968) (EC).

U. S. DEPT OF LABOR. MANPOWER ADMINISTRATION. MANPOWER
SERVICES TO MINORITY GROUPS: A DESK REFERENCE FOR ES
PERSONNEL. WASHINGTON, D. C.: U. S. GOVERNMENT
PRINTING OFFICE, (1970) (EC).

U. S. DEPT OF LABOR. LIBRARY. MEXICAN–AMERICANS, SELECTED
REFERENCES. WASHINGTON, D. C.: U. S. GOVERNMENT
PRINTING OFFICE, (1967) (EC).

U. S. DEPT OF LABOR. MEXICAN–AMERICANS: BIBILIOGRAPHICS
AND LIST OF PUBLICATIONS. WASHINGTON, D. C.: U.
S. GOVERNMENT PRINTING OFFICE, (1967) (EC).

U. S. DEPT OF LABOR. RESEARCH AND STATISTICS DIV. WAGES
AND HOURS DIV. REPORT ON THE CITRUS FRUIT PACKING
INDUSTRY MADE UNDER THE FAIR LABOR STANDARDS ACT.
WASHINGTON, D. C.: U. S. GOVERNMENT PRINTING OFFICE,
(1940) (EC).

U. S. DEPT OF LABOR. SELECTED REFERENCE ON DOMESTIC
MIGRATORY AGRICULTURAL WORKERS, THEIR FAMILIES,
PROBLEMS AND PROGRAMS, 1955–1960.. BULLETIN NO. 225.
WASHINGTON, D. C.: U. S. GOVERNMENT PRINTING OFFICE,
(1961) (EC).

U. S. DEPT OF LABOR. YEAR OF TRANSITION, SEASONAL FARM
LABOR, 1965; A REPORT FROM THE SECRETARY OF LABOR.
WASHINGTON, D. C.: U. S. PRINTING OFFICE, (1965) (EC).

U. S. DEPT OF LABOR. BUREAU OF LABOR STATISTICS. THE
COMMUNITY MEETS THE MIGRANT WORKER. BULLETIN 221.
WASHINGTON, D. C.: THE BUREAU OF LABOR STANDARDS,
(1960) (EC).

U. S. DEPT OF STATE. FOREIGN SERVICE INSTITUTE. ADAPTING
AND WRITING LANGUAGE LESSONS. WASHINGTON, D. C.:
U. S. GOVERNMENT PRINTING OFFICE, (1971) (ED).

U. S. DEPT OF STATE. ARRANGEMENT FOR MIGRATION TO
THE UNITED STATES OF MEXICAN FARM LABOR. DEPARTMENT
OF STATE BULLETIN, 689–90. WASHINGTON, D. C.: U. S.
GOVERNMENT PRINTING OFFICE, (AUGUST 8, 1942) (SI).

U. S. DEPT OF STATE. CIVIL RIGHTS AND RACE RELATIONS,
    SEMINAR. DEPARTMENT, AND FOREIGN SERVICE SERIES,
    NO. 153. WASHINGTON, D. C.: U. S. GOVERNMENT PRINTING
    OFFICE, (1966).

U. S. DEPT OF STATE. OFFICE OF THE DEPUTY UNDER SECRETARY
    FOR ADMIN. CIVIL RIGHTS AND RACE RELATIONS. A
    SEMINAR, JUNE 23, 1966. DEPARTMENT OF STATE
    PUBLICATIONS 8157. DEPARTMENT AND FOREIGN SERVICE
    SERIES 135. WASHINGTON, D. C.: U. S. GOVERNMENT
    PRINTING OFFICE, (1966) (EC).

U. S. DEPT OF STATE. FOREIGN RELATIONS OF THE UNITED
    STATES 1902. WASHINGTON, D. C.: U. S. GOVERNMENT
    PRINTING OFFICE, (1903).

U. S. DEPT OF STATE. MIGRATORY WORKERS: MEXICAN AGRICULTURAL
    WORKERS. AGREEMENT BETWEEN THE UNITED STATES
    OF AMERICA AND MEXICA, DEC 20, 1963. TREATIES SERIES
    NO. 5492. WASHINGTON, D. C.: U. S. GOVERNMENT
    PRINTING OFFICE, (DECEMBER 20, 1963) (SI).

U. S. DEPT OF THE INTERIOR. NATIONAL PARK SERVICE. AZTEC
    RUINS NATIONAL MONUMENT, NEW MEXICO. JOHN M.
    CORBETT. NATIONAL PARK SERVICE HISTORICAL HANDBOOK
    SERIES NO. 36. WASHINGTON, D. C.: U. S. GOVERNMENT
    PRINTING OFFICE, (1962) (HN).

U. S. DEPT OF THE INTERIOR. NATIONAL PARK SERVICE.
    BANDELIER NATIONAL MONUMENT, NEW MEXICO. KITTRIDGE
    A. WING. NATIONAL PARK SERVICE HISTORICAL HANDBOOK
    SERIES NO. 23. WASHINGTON, D. C.: U. S. GOVERNMENT
    PRINTING OFFICE, (1955) (HN).

U. S. DEPT OF THE INTERIOR. REGION 5. BRIEF DESCRIPTIONS
    OF IRRIGATION AND MULTIPLE-PURPOSE PROJECTS PROPOSED
    FOR CONSTRUCTION IN THE POST-WAR PERIOD, JUNE 1, 1945.
    WASHINGTON, D. C.: U. S. GOVERNMENT PRINTING OFFICE,
    (1945) (GE).

U. S. DEPT OF THE INTERIOR. OE. EDUCATION OF NATIVE AND
    MINORITY GROUPS: A BIBLIOGRAPHY, 1932-34. OE-37053.
    WASHINGTON, D. C.: U. S. GOVERNMENT PRINTING OFFICE,
    (1969) (B ED).

U. S. DEPT OF THE INTERIOR. NATIONAL PARK SERVICE. FORT
    DAVIS NATIONAL HISTORIC SITE, TEXAS. ROBERT
    M. UTLEY. NATIONAL PARK SERVICE HISTORICAL HANDBOOK
    SERIES NO. 38. WASHINGTON, D. C.: U. S. GOVERNMENT
    PRINTING OFFICE, (1965) (HN).

U. S. DEPT OF THE INTERIOR. NATIONAL PARK SERVICE. FORT
    UNION NATIONAL MONUMENT, NEW MEXICO. ROBERT
    M. UTLEY. NATIONAL PARK SERVICE HISTORICAL HANDBOOK
    SERIES NO. 35. WASHINGTON, D. C.: U. S. GOVERNMENT
    PRINTING OFFICE, (1962) (HN).

U. S. DEPT OF THE INTERIOR. NATIONAL PARK SERVICE.
MONTEZUMA CASTLE NATIONAL MONUMENT, ARIZONA.   ALBERT
H. SCHOEDER AND HOMER F. HASTINGS. NATIONAL PARK
SERVICE HISTORICAL HANDBOOK SERIES NO. 27. WASHINGTON,
D. C.: U. S. GOVERNMENT PRINTING OFFICE, (1958) (HA).

U. S. DEPT OF THE INTERIOR. BUREAU OF RECLAMATION.
RECLAMATION HANDBOOK.   SUPERINTENDENT OF DOCUMENTS.
WASHINGTON, D. C., (1942) (ED).

U. S. DEPT OF THE INTERIOR. NATIONAL PARK SERVICE. SAN
BEUNAVENTURA MISSION, GRAN QUIVIRA NATIONAL MONUMENT.
SANTA FE, NEW MEXICO. SOUTHWESTERN MONUMENTS ASSOCIATION,
(ED GE).

U. S. DEPT OF THE INTERIOR. NATIONAL PARK SERVICE. SAN
BUENA VENTURA MISSION, GRAN QUIVIRA NATIONAL MONUMENT,
SOUTHWESTERN MONUMENTS ASSOCIATION, GLOBE, ARIZONA.
WASHINGTON, D. C.: U. S. GOVERNMENT PRINTING OFFICE,
(HN).

U. S. DEPT OF THE INTERIOR. OFFICE OF EDUCATION. SUCCESSFUL
METHODS OF TEACHING ENGLISH TO BILINGUAL CHILDREN IN
SEATTLE PUBLIC SCHOOLS.   FRANCIS F. POWERS AND
MARJORIE HETZLER. WASHINGTON, D. C.: U. S. GOVERNMENT
PRINTING OFFICE, (1937) (ED).

U. S. DEPT OF THE INTERIOR. NATIONAL PARK SERVICE. THE
HISTORY OF CASTILLO DE SAN MARCOS & FORT MATANZAS FROM
CONTEMPORARY NARRATIVES AND LETTERS.   WASHINGTON,
D. C.: U. S. GOVERNMENT PRINTING OFFICE, (1955) (HN).

U. S. DEPT. OF AGRICULTURE, ECONOMIC RESEARCH SERVICE,
1964. DOMESTIC AND MIGRATORY FARM WORKERS: PERSONAL
AND ECONOMIC CHARACTERISTICS.   AGRICULTURE ECONOMIC
REPORT 120. WASHINGTON, D. C.: U. S. GOVERNMENT
PRINTING OFFICE, (1967) (EC SI).

U. S. ECONOMIC RESEARCH SERVICE. DOMESTIC MIGRATORY
FARM-WORKERS; PERSONAL AND ECONOMIC CHARACTERISTICS.
AGRICULTURAL ECONOMIC REPORT NO. 14. WASHINGTON, D.
C.: U. S. GOVERNMENT PRINTING OFFICE, (1967) (EC SI).

U. S. ECONOMIC RESEARCH SERVICE. LOW-INCOME FAMILIES IN
THE SPANISH-SURNAME POPLUATION OF THE SOUTHWEST.
WASHINGTON, D. C.: U. S. GOVERNMENT PRINTING OFFICE,
(1967) (EC SI).

U. S. EMPLOYMENT SECURITY BUREAU. S. INFORMATION CONCERNING
ENTRY OF MEXICAN AGRICULTURAL WORKERS INTO THE UNITED
STATES.   WASHINGTON, D. C.: U. S. GOVERNMENT
PRINTING OFFICE, (1962) (EC SI).

U. S. EQUAL EMPLOYMENT OPPORTUNITY COMMISSION. ANNUAL
REPORT.   WASHINGTON, D. C.: U. S. GOVERNMENT
PRINTING OFFICE, (196566—196768) (EC).

U. S. EQUAL EMPLOYMENT OPPORTUNITY COMMISSION. HEARINGS
ON UTILILATION OF MINORITY AND WOMEN WORKERS IN
CERTAIN MAJOR INDUSTRIES.   HEARINGS HELD IN LOS
ANGELES, CALIFORNIA, 1969. WASHINGTON, D. C.: U. S.
GOVERNMENT PRINTING OFFICE, (1969) (EC).

U. S. EQUAL EMPLOYMENT OPPORTUNITY COMMISSION. SPANISH
SURNAMED AMERICAN EMPLOYMENT IN THE SOUTHWEST.
WASHINGTON, D. C.: U. S. GOVERNMENT PRINTING OFFICE,
(1970) (EC).

U. S. FARM SECURITY ADMINISTRATION.   DISADVANTAGED CLASSES
IN AMERICAN AGRICULTURE.   CARL C. TAYLOR. SOCIAL
RESEARCH REPORT, NO. 8. WASHINGTON, D. C.: U.
S. GOVERNMENT PRINTING OFFICE, (1938) (EC SI).

U. S. FARM SECURITY ADMINISTRATION.   MIGRANT FARM LABOR.
WASHINGTON, D. C.: U. S. GOVERNMENT PRINTING OFFICE,
(1940) (EC).

U. S. FARM SECURITY ADMINISTRATION.   SOCIAL RELATIONSHIPS
AND INSTITUTIONS IN SEVEN NEW RURAL COMMUNITIES.
SOCIAL RESEARCH REPORT, NO. 18. WASHINGTON, D. C.:
U. S. GOVERNMENT PRINTING OFFICE, (1940) (EC SI).

U. S. FARM SECURITY ADMINISTRATION.   STANDARDS OF LIVING
IN AN INDIAN—MEXICAN VILLAGE AND ON A RECLAMATION
PROJECT.   OLEN LEONARD AND CHARLES P. LOOMIS. SOCIAL
RESEARCH REPORT, NO. 14. WASHINGTON, D. C.: U. S.
GOVERNMENT PRINTING OFFICE, (1938) (EC SO).

U. S. FARM SECURITY ADMINISTRATION.   STANDARDS OF LIVING
OF RESIDENTS OF SEVEN RURAL RESETTLEMENT COMMUNITIES.
SOCIAL RESEARCH REPORT NO. 11. WASHINGTON, D. C.:
U. S. GOVERNMENT PRINTING OFFICE, (1938) (EC SI).

U. S. FARM SECURITY ADMINISTRATION.   A STUDY OF 6,655
MIGRANT HOUSEHOLDS RECEIVING EMERGENCY GRANTS.
WASHINGTON, D. C.: U. S. GOVERNMENT PRINTING OFFICE,
(1938) (EC SI).

U. S. FEDERAL INTERAGENCY COMMITTEE ON MIGRANT LABOR.
MIGRANT LABOR: A HUMAN PROBLEM; REPORT AND RECOMMENDATIONS.
WASHINGTON, D. C.: U. S. GOVERNMENT PRINTING OFFICE,
(1947) (EC SI).

U. S. FEDERAL WORKS AGENCY. DIVISION OF RESEARCH. MEXICAN
MIGRATORY WORKERS OF SOUTH TEXAS.   SELDEN C. MENEFEE.
WASHINGTON, D. C.: U. S. GOVERNMENT PRINTING OFFICE,
(1941) (EC SI).

U. S. FEDERAL WRITERS' PROJECT, WORKS PROGRESS ADMINISTRATION.
ORGANIZATION EFFORTS OF MEXICAN AGRICULTURAL WORKERS.
OAKLAND, CALIFORNIA, 1938 (SI   MD).

U. S. GOVERNMENT EXPANDS MIGRANT HEALTH PROGRAM.   "AMERICAN
JOURNAL OF NURSING".   AMERICAN JOURNAL OF NURSING,
(JULY   1968), PP. 1405, 1532—1534 (SI   MD).

U. S. HEALTH SERVICES AND MENTAL HEALTH ADMINISTRATION.
THE USE OF HEALTH AIDES IN MIGRANT HEALTH PROJECTS.
WASHINGTON, D. C.: U. S. GOVERNMENT PRINTING OFFICE,
(1970) (SI   MD).

U. S. HOUSE COMMITTEE ON AGRICULTURE.   MEXICAN FARM LABOR.
WASHINGTON, D. C.: U. S. GOVERNMENT PRINTING OFFICE,
(1952) (EC   SI).

U. S. HOUSE OF COMMITTEE ON TERRITORIES.   HEARINGS
AND STATEHOOD BILL BEFORE COMMITTEE ON TERRITORIES
ON THE HOUSEOF REPRESENTATIVES.   WASHINGTON, D.
C.: U. S. GOVERNMENT PRINTING OFFICE, (1903).

U. S. HOUSE.   CLAIMS ON THE PART OF CITIZENS OF THE UNITED
STATES AND MEXICO UNDER THECONVENTION OF JULY 4, 1868,
BETWEEN THE UNITED STATES AND MEXICO.   SENATE
EXECUTIVE DOCUMENT NO 31, 44TH CONG., 2D SESS..   33RD
CONGRESS, 1ST SESSION HOME EXECUTIVE NO 10 DOUCUMENT.
WASHINGTON, D. C.:   U. S. GOVERNMENT PRINTING OFFICE,
(1854).

U. S. HOUSE.   EXECUTIVE DOCUMENT NO. 257.   DEPREDATIONS
ON THE FRONTIERS OF TEXAS.   MESSAGE FROM THE PRESIDENT
OF THE UNITED STATES, TRANSMITTING A COMMUNICATION
FROM THE SECRETARY OF STATE, AND A COPY OF THE REPORT
OF THE COMMISSIONERS TO INQUIRE INTO DEPREDATIONS ON
THE FRONTIERS OF TEXAS.   93RD CONGRESS, 1ST SESSION.
WASHINGTON, D.C., (MAY 26,   1874) (HUS HT).

U. S. HOUSE.   EXECUTIVE DOCUMENT NO. 13.   MEXICAN BORDER
TROUBLES.   MESSAGE FROM THE PRESIDENT OF THE UNITED
STATES . . . 1877.   95TH CONGRESS. 1ST SESSION.
WASHINGTON, D.C., (1877) (HUS HT).

U. S. HOUSE.   TEXAS FRONTIER TROUBLES.   49TH CONGRESS.
1ST SESSION. WASHINGTON, D.C., (FEBRUARY 29,   1876)
(HUS HT).

U. S. HOUSE.   TREATY BETWEEN THE UNITED STATES OF AMERICA
AND THE MEXICAN REPUBLIC, CONCLUDED AT THE CITY OF
MEXICO, DECEMBER 30, 1853.   HOUSE EXECUTIVE DOCUMENT
NO. 109, 33RD CONGRESS, 1ST SESSION.   WASHINGTON, D.
C.: U. S. GOVERNMENT   PRINTING OFFICE, (1854).

U. S. HOUSE. THE NEW RACISM. CONGRESSIONAL RECORD,
PROCEEDINGS AND DEBATES OF THE 91ST CONGRESS, FRIST
SESSION. APRIL 3, 15, 28, 29, AND MAY 1, 1969,
WASHINGTON, D.C. U. S. GOVERNMENT PRINTING OFFICE.

U. S. IMMIGRATION COMMISSION. IMMIGRANTS IN AGRICULTURE.
WASHINGTON, D. C.: U. S. GOVERNMENT PRINTING OFFICE,
(1911) (SI   EC).

U. S. IMMIGRATION COMMISSION. IMMIGRANTS IN INDUSTRIES.
25 PARTS. WASHINGTON, D. C.: U. S. GOVERNMENT
PRINTING OFFICE, (1911) (EC SI).

U. S. INTER—AGENCY COMMITTEE ON MIGRANT LABOR. MIGRANT
LABOR — A HUMAN PROBLEM: REPORT AND RECOMMENDATIONS.
WASHINGTON, D. C.: U. S. GOVERNMENT PRINTING OFFICE,
(1947) (EC).

U. S. INTER—AGENCY COMMITTEE ON MIGRANT LABOR. A GUIDE
TO MATERIALS RELATING TO PERSONS OF MEXICAN HERITAGE
IN THE UNITED STATES.   WASHINGTON, D. C.: U. S.
GOVERNMENT PRINTING OFFICE, (1969) (B).

U. S. INTER—AGENCY COMMITTEE ON MEXICAN—AMERICAN AFFAIRS
EL PASO, TEXAS. A NEW FOCUS ON OPPORTUNITY. TESTIMONY
PRESENTED AT CABINET MEETING HEARINGS.   HEARINGS,
EL PASO, TEXAS OCTOBER, 1967. WASHINGTON, D. C.: U.
S. GOVERNMENT PRINTING OFFICE, (1968) (SO ED).

U. S. LABOR STANDARDS BUREAU. S. COMMUNITY MEETS THE
MIGRANT WORKER.   WASHINGTON, D. C.: U. S. GOVERNMENT
PRINTING OFFICE, (1960) (EC).

U. S. LABOR STANDARDS BUREAU. S. GUIDE TO COMMUNITY EFFORTS
TO IMPROVE CONDITIONS AGRICULTURAL MIGRANTS.
WASHINGTON, D. C.: U. S. GOVERNMENT PRINTING OFFICE,
(1964) (EC).

U. S. LABOR STANDARDS BUREAU. S. HOUSING FOR MIGRANT
AGRICULTURAL WORKERS, LABOR CAMP STANDARDS.
WASHINGTON, D. C.: U. S. GOVERNMENT PRINTING OFFICE,
(1961) (SI   EC).

U. S. LABOR STANDARDS BUREAU. S. STATE COMMITTEES ON
SEASONAL AGRICULTURAL LABOR, THEIR ORGANIZATION AND
PROGRAMS.   WASHINGTON, D. C.: U. S. GOVERNMENT
PRINTING OFFICE, (1965) (EC).

U. S. LABOR STANDARDS BUREAU. S. STATE MIGRATORY LABOR
COMMITTEES: THEIR ORGANIZATION AND PROGRAMS.
WASHINGTON, D. C.: U. S. GOVERNMENT PRINTING OFFICE,
(1960) (EC).

U. S. LIBRARY CF CONGRESS. LEGISLATIVE REFERENCE SERVICE.
MIGRANT LABOR LAW AND RELATIONS: SELECTED REFERENCES,
1960-1969.   WASHINGTON, D. C.: U. S. GOVERNMENT
PRINTING OFFICE, (1969) (B   SI).

U. S. LIBRARY OF CONGRESS. LEGISLATIVE REFERENCE SERVICE.
MIGRATORY AGRICULTURAL LABOR: REFERENCES TO BOOKS,
PERIODICALS, AND FILMS, 1959-1969.   WASHINGTON,
D. C.: U. S. GOVERNMENT PRINTING OFFICE, (1969) (B
SI).

U. S. LIBRARY OF CONGRESS. LEGISLATIVE REFERENCE SERVICE.
MIGRATORY AGRICULTURAL LABOR: REFERENCES TO FEDERAL
PUBLICATIONS, STUDIES AND REPORTS, 1959-1968.
WASHINGTON, D. C.: U. S. GOVERNMENT PRINTING OFFICE,
(1969) (B   SI).

U. S. LIBRARY OF CONGRESS. LEGISLATIVE REFERENCE SERVICE.
THE STRIKE OF THE UNITED FARM WORKERS ORGANIZING
COMMITTEE IN DELANO, CALIFORNIA: BACKGROUND AND ITS
RELATICNSHIP TO LEGISLATIVE EFFORTS TO ORGANIZE FARM
WORKERS.   WASHINGTON, D. C.: U. S. GOVERNMENT
PRINTING OFFICE, (1968) (EC).

U. S. NATIONAL ARCHIVES AND RECORDS SERVICE. RECORDS OF
THE PRESIDENT'S COMMISSION ON MIGRATORY LABOR.
WASHINGTON, D. C.: U. S. GOVERNMENT PRINTING OFFICE,
(1955) (SI   EC).

U. S. NATIONAL COMMISSION ON LAW OBSERVATION AND ENFORCEMENT.
CRIME AND THE FOREIGN-BORN: THE PROBLEM OF THE
MEXICAN.   IN REPORT CN CRIME AND THE FOREIGN-BORN.
WASHINGTON, D. C.: U. S. GOVER(MENT PRINTING OFFICE,
(1931) (B   SI).

U. S. NATIONAL COMMISSION ON LAW OBSERVATION AND ENFORCEMENT.
PRELIMINARY REPORT ON NATIONALITY AND DELINQUINEY:
THE MEXICAN IN TEXAS.   IN REPORT ON CRIME AND THE
FOREIGN-BORN. WASHINGTON, D. C.: U. S. GOVERNMENT
PRINTING OFFICE, (1931) (HT).

U. S. NATIONAL COMMISSION ON LAW OBSERVATION AND ENFORCEMENT.
REPORT ON CRIME AND THE FOREIGN BORN.   WASHINGTON,
D. C.: U. S. GOVERNMENT PRINTING OFFICE, (1931) (EC).

U. S. NATIONAL LABOR BOARD. REPORT TO THE NATIONAL LABOR
BOARD BY SPECIAL COMMISSION ON LABOR CONDITIONS IN
THE IMPERIAL VALLEY-CALIFORNIA.   RELEASE NUMBER 3325.
WASHINGTON, D. C.: U. S. GOVERNMENT PRINTING OFFICE,
(EC).

U. S. OFFICE OF ECONOMIC OPPORTUNITY. MIGRANT EDUCATION:
ADVANCED LEVEL.   WASHINGTON, D. C.: U. S. GOVERNMENT
PRINTING OFFICE, (1968) (SI   ED).

U. S. OFFICE OF ECONOMIC OPPORTUNITY. MIGRANT EDUCATION:
INTERMEDIATE LEVEL.   WASHINGTON, D. C.: U.
S. GOVERNMENT PRINTING OFFICE, (1968) (SI   ED).

U. S. OFFICE OF ECONOMIC OPPORTUNITY. MIGRANT WORKER
PROGRAMS IN RURAL COMMUNITY ACTION.   WASHINGTON,
D. C.: U. S. GOVERNMENT PRINTING OFFICE, (1966).

U. S. OFFICE OF ECONOMIC OPPORTUNITY. THE MIGRANT
FARM-WORKER AND THE ECONOMIC OPPORTUNITY ACT.
WASHINGTON, D. C.: U. S. GOVERNMENT PRINTING OFFICE,
(1966) (SI   EC).

U. S. OFFICE OF EDUCATION. LEARNING ENGLISH INCIDENTLY:
A STUDY OF BI-LINGUAL CHILDREN.   BULLETIN 1937 NO.
15. WASHINGTON, D. C., (1938) (ED).

U. S. OFFICE OF EDUCATION. OPPORTUNITIES FOR THE PREPARATION
OF TEACHERS OF CHILDREN OF NATIVE AND MINORITY GROUPS.
PAMPHLET NO. 77. WASHINGTON, D. C.: U. S. GOVERNMENT
PRINTING OFFICE, (1937) (ED).

U. S. OFFICE OF EDUCATION. RACE AND PLACE, LEGAL HISTORY
OF NEIGHBORHOOD SCHOOLS.   MYER WEINBERG. WASHINGTON,
D. C.: U. S. GOVERNMENT PRINTING OFFICE, (1968) (ED).

U. S. OFFICE OF THE SUPERINTENDENT OF INDIAN AFFAIRS.
PASSPORT ISSUED TO A PARTY OF PRAIRIE TRAVELERS;
SIGNED BY WILLIAM CLARK, SUPERINTENDENT OF INDIAN
AFFAIRS, JULY 23, 1820.   ORIGINAL DOCUMENT. SAN
MARINO, HENRY E. HUNTINGTON LIBRARY. (HUS).

U. S. PRESIDENT'S COMMISSION ON MIGRATORY LABOR. MIGRATORY
LABOR IN AMERICAN AGRICULTURE.   WASHINGTON, D. C.:
U. S. GOVERNMENT PRINTING OFFICE, (1951).

U. S. PRESIDENT'S COMMITTEE ON CIVIL RIGHTS. TO SECURE
THESE RIGHTS; THE REPORT OF THE PRESEDENT'S COMMITTEE
ON CIVIL RIGHTS.   NEW YORK: SIMON AND SCHUSTER, 1947.

U. S. SELECT COMMISSION ON WESTERN HEMISPHERE IMMIGRATION.
IMPACT OF COMMUTER ALIENS ALONG THE MEXICAN AND
CANADIAN BORDERS: HEARINGS.   WASHINGTON, D. C.:
U. S. GOVERNMENT PRINTING OFFICE, (1968) (SI).

U. S. SELECT COMMISSION ON WESTERN HEMISPHERE IMMIGRATION.
THE IMPACT OF COMMUTER ALIENS ALONG THE MEXICAN AND
CANADIAN BORDERS; HEARINGS..   WASHINGTON, D. C.:
U. S. GOVERNMENT PRINTING OFFICE, (1968).

U. S. SELECT COMMITTEE ON WESTERN HEMISPHERE IMMIGRATION.
THE IMPACT OF COMMUTER ALIENS ALONG THE MEXICAN AND
CANADIAN BORDERS.   HEARINGS PARTS 1 AND 2. JANUARY
26, FEBRUARY 10, 1968. WASHINGTON, D. CC: U.
S. GOVERNMENT PRINTING OFFICE, (1968) (SI).

U. S. SENATE. AVAILABILITY AND USEFULNESS OF FEDERAL
PROGRAMS AND SERVICES TO ELDERLY MEXICAN-AMERICANS,
PART 5.   WASHINGTON, D. C.: U. S. GOVERNMENT
PRINTING OFFICE, (NOVEMBER 20,   1969) (EC   SO).

U. S. SENATE. CLAIMS ON THE PART OF CITIZENS OF THE UNITED
STATES AND MEXICO UNDER THE CONVENTION OF JULY
4, 1868. BETWEEN THE UNITED STATES AND MEXICO.   44TH
CONGRESS, 2ND SESSION. SENATE EXECUTIVE DOCUMENT NO
31. WASHINGTON, D. C.: U. S. GOVERNMENT PRINTING
OFFICE, (1877).

U. S. SENATE. CLAIMS ON THE PART OF CITIZENS OF THE UNITED
STATES AND MEXICO UNDER THE CONVENTION OF JULY
4, 1868, BETWEEN THE UNITED STATES AND MEXICO.
SENATE EXECUTIVE DOCUMENT NO. 31, 44TH CONGRESS, 2ND
SESSION. WASHINGTON, D. C.: U. S. GOVERNMENT PRINTING
OFFICE, (1877).

U. S. SENATE. HEARINGS BEFORE SUBCOMMITTEE, ON LABOR AND
LABOR-MANAGEMENT RELATIONS OF THE COMMITTEE ON LABOR
AND PUBLIC WELFARE.   82ND CONGRESS, SECOND SESSION.
WASHINGTON, D. C.: U. S. GOVERNMENT PRINTING OFFICE,
(1952) (EC).

U. S. SENATE. MANPOWER DEVELOPMENT AND TRAINING LEGISLATION,
1970.   ALEX ZERMENO, TESTIMONY, OAKLAND CALIFORNIA.
, (APRIL   17, 1970) (EC).

U. S. SENATE. MIGRANT AND SEASONAL FARMWORKER POWERLESS,
PART 4-B: FARMWORKER LEGAL PROBLEMS.   HEARING.
WASHINGTON, D. C.: UNITED STATES GOVERNMENT PRINTING
OFFICE, (AUGUST 8,   1969) (EC   SI).

U. S. SENATE. MIGRANT AND SEASONAL FARMWORKER POWERLESS,
PART 2: THE MIGRANT SUBCULTURE.   HEARING. U. S.
GOVERNMENT PRINTING OFFICE, (AUGUST 8,   1969) (EC
SI).

U. S. SENATE. PROBLEMS OF MIGRANT WORKERS.   HEARINGS AT
WESLACO, TEXAS, LABOR CAMP. , (NOVEMBER 24,   1969)
(EC   SI).

U. S. SENATE. STUDY OF MIGRATORY LABOR.   89TH CONGRESS
SENATE REPORT 33. WASHINGTON, D. C.: U. S. GOVERNMENT
PRINTING OFFICE, (SI   EC).

U. S. SENATE. STUDY OF MIGRATORY LABOR.   89TH CONGRESS.
SENATE REPORT 991. WASHINGTON, D. C.: U. S.
GOVERNMENT PRINTING OFFICE, (SI   EC).

U. S. SENATE. STUDY OF MIGRATORY LABOR.   90TH CONGRESS.
SENATE REPORT 51. WASHINGTON, D. C.: U. S. GOVERNMENT
PRINTING OFFICE, (SI   EC).

U. S. SENATE. TREATY OF PEACE, FRIENDSHIP, LIMITS, AND
   SETTLEMENT BETWEEN THE UNITED STATES OF AMERICA AND
   THE MEXICAN REPUBLIC, CONCLUDED AT GUADALUPE HIDALGO,
   ON THE 2ND DAY OF FEBRUARY, IN THE YEAR 1848.   SENATE
   EXECUTIVE DOCUMENT NO. 52, 30TH CONGRESS, 1ST SESSION.
   WASHINGTON, D. C.: U. S. GOVERNMENT PRINTING OFFICE,
   (1847).

U. S. SENATE. THE MIGRATORY FARM LABOR PROBLEM IN
   THE UNITED STATES.   88TH CONGRESS SENATE REPORT 167.
   WASHINGTON, D. C.: U. S. GOVERNMENT PRINTING OFFICE,
   (SI   EC).

U. S. SENATE. THE MIGRATORY FARM LABOR PROBLEM IN
   THE UNITED STATES.   89TH CONGRESS. SENATE REPORT 155.
   WASHINGTON, D. C.: U. S. GOVERNMENT PRINTING OFFICE,
   (SI   EC).

U. S. SENATE. THE MIGRATORY FARM LABOR PROBLEM IN
   THE UNITED STATES.   89TH CONGRESS. SENATE REPORT
   1549. WASHINGTON, D. C.: U. S. GOVERNMENT PRINTING
   OFFICE, (SI   EC).

U. S. SENATE. THE MIGRATORY FARM LABOR PROBLEM IN
   THE UNITED STATES.   90TH CONGRESS. SENATE REPORT 71.
   WASHINGTON, D. C.: U. S. GOVERNMENT PRINTING OFFICE,
   (SI   EC).

U. S. SENATE. THE MIGRATORY FARM LABOR PROBLEM IN
   THE UNITED STATES.   90TH CONGRESS. SENATE REPORT
   1006. WASHINGTON, D. C.: U. S. GOVERNMENT PRINTING
   OFFICE, (SI   EC).

U. S. SENATE. THE MIGRATORY FARM LABOR PROBLEM IN
   THE UNITED STATES.   91ST CONGRESS. SENATE REPORT 83.
   WASHINGTON, D. C.: U. S. GOVERNMENT PRINTING OFFICE,
   (SI   EC).

U. S. SENATE. BANKING AND CURRENCY COMMITTEE.   FAIR HOUSING
   ACT OF 19679 HEARINGS.   WASHINGTON, D. C.: U. S.
   GOVERNMENT PRINTING OFFICE, (1967) (EC   SO).

U. S. SENATE. BANKING AND CURRENCY COMMITTEE.   FEDERAL
   MINORITY ENTERPRISE PROGRAM. HEARINGS.   WASHINGTON,
   D. C.: U. S. GOVERNMENT PRINTING OFFICE, (1970) (SO
   EC).

U. S. SENATE. COMMITTEE ON LABOR AND PUBLIC WELFARE.
   EDUCATIONAL ASSISTANCE TO MIGRANT AGRICULTURAL
   EMPLOYEES AND THEIR CHILDREN.   WASHINGTON, D. C.:
   U. S. GOVERNMENT PRINTING OFFICE, (1960) (ED   SI).

U. S. SENATE. COMMITTEE ON EQUAL EDUCATIONAL OPPORTUNITY.
EFFECTS OF TELEVISION ON EQUAL EDUCATIONAL OPPORTUNITY.
HEARINGS. WASHINGTON, D.C.:   U. S. GOVERNMENT
PRINTING OFFICE, (1970) (ED).

U. S. SENATE. COMMITTEE ON LABOR AND PUBLIC WELFARE.
EMERGENCY SCHOOL AID ACT OF 1970.   HEARINGS. JULY
10, 1970, PP. 286-373. WASHINGTON, D. C.: U.
S. GOVERNMENT PRINTING OFFICE, (1970) (EC).

U. S. SENATE. COMMITTEE ON LABOR AND PUBLIC WELFARE.   EQUAL
EMPLOYMENT OPPORTUNITIES ENFORCEMENT ACT.
WASHINGTON, D. C.: U. S. GOVERNMENT PRINTING OFFICE,
(1969) (EC).

U. S. SENATE. COMMITTEE ON GOVERNMENT OPERATIONS.
ESTABLISHING A CABINET COMMITTEE ON OPPORTUNITIES FOR
SPANISH-SPEAKING POPLE.   91ST CONGRESS, 1ST SESSION,
REPORT NO 422. WASHINGTON, D. C.:   U. S. GOVERNMENT
PRINTING OFFICE, (1969) (EC ED).

U. S. SENATE. COMMITTEE ON AGRICULTURE AND FORRESTRY.
EXTENSION OF MEXICAN FARM LABOR PROGRAM. HEARINGS..
87TH COMGRESS, 1ST SESSION. WASHINGTON, D. C.:   U.
S. GOVERNMENT PRINTING OFFICE, (MARCH 30,   1961) (EC).

U. S. SENATE. COMMITTEE ON LABOR AND PUBLIC WELFARE.
HEARINGS BEFORE THE SPECIAL SUBCOMMITTEE ON BILINGUAL
EDUCATION OF THE COMMITTEE ON LABOR AND PUBLIC
WELFARE.   WASHINGTON, D. C.: U. S. GOVERNMENT
PRINTING OFFICE, (1967) (ED   SI).

U. S. SENATE. COMMITTEE ON LABOR AND PUBLIC WELFARE.
HEARINGS BEFORE THE SUBCOMMITTEE ON MIGRATORY LABOR
LEGISLATION.   PART 1, 90TH CONGRESS, 1ST SESSION.
MAY 17, JULY 11, 12, 13 AND AGUST , 1967. WASHINGTON,
D.C.:   UNITED STATES GOVERNMENT PRINTING OFFICE,
(1967) (EC   SI).

U. S. SENATE. COMMITTEE ON LABOR AND PUBLIC WELFARE.
HEARINGS BEFORE THE SUB-COMMITTEE ON MIGRATORY LABOR
LEGISLATION.   PART 2, 90TH CONGRESS, 1ST SESSION.
RIO GRANDE CITY, TEXAS: JUNE 29, 1967. EDINBURG,
TEXAS: JUNE 30, 1967. WASHINGTON, D. C.:   UNITED
STATESGOVERNMENT PRINTING OFFICE, (1967) (EC   SI   HT).

U. S. SENATE. COMMITTEE ON LABOR AND PUBLIC WELFARE.
HEARINGS BEFORE THE SUBCOMMITTEE ON MIGRATORY LABOR
LEGISLATION.   PART 4, 90TH CONGRESS, 2ND SESSION,
APPENDIX 2, 1968. WASHINGTON, D. C.:   U. S. GOVERMENT
PRINTING OFFICE, (1968) (EC   SI).

U. S. SENATE. COMMITTEE ON LABOR AND PUBLIC WELFARE.
HEARINGS BEFORE THE SUBCOMMITTEE ON MIGRATORY LABOR
LEGISLATION.   PART 4, 90TH CONGRESS, 1ST SESSION,
APPENDIX 1. WASHINGTON, D.C.: UNITED STATES GOVERNMENT
PRINTING OFFICE, (1968) (EC SI).

U. S. SENATE. COMMITTEE ON LABOR AND PUBLIC WELFARE.
MANPOWER DEVELOPMENT AND TRAINING LEGISLATION.
HEARINGS, LOS ANGELES, CALIFORNIA. WASHINGTON, D.
C.: U. S. GOVERNMENT PRINTING OFFICE, (JANUARY 9,
1970) (EC ED).

U. S. SENATE. COMMITTEE ON LABOR AND PUBLIC WELFARE.
MIGRANT AND SEASONAL FARM WORKER POWERLESSNESS.
WASHINGTON, D. C.: U. S. GOVERNMENT PRINTING OFFICE,
(1969) (EC SI).

U. S. SENATE. COMMITTEE ON LABOR AND PUBLIC WELFARE.
MIGRANT AND SEASONAL FARMWORKER POWERLESS.   HEARINGS.
, (JANUARY 9, 1970) (EC SO).

U. S. SENATE. COMMITTEE ON LABOR AND PUBLIC WELFARE.
MIGRANT AND SEASONAL FARMWORKER POWERLESS. PART 5-A:
BORDER COMMUTER LABOR PROBLEM.   HEARINGS. WASHINGTON
D. C.: U. S. GOVERNMENT PRINTING OFFICE, (MAY 2 1,
1969) (EC SO).

U. S. SENATE. COMMITTEE ON LABOR AND PUBLIC WELFARE.
MIGRANT AND SEASONAL FARMWORKER POWERLESS, PART 6-C:
PESTICIDES AND THE FARMWORKER.   WASHINGTON, D. C.:
U. S. GOVERNMENT PRINTING OFFICE, (EC MD).

U. S. SENATE. COMMITTEE ON LABOR AND PUBLIC WELFARE.
MIGRANT AND SEASONAL FARMWORKER POWERLESSNESS.
HEARINGS.   91ST CONGRESS, 1S AND 2ND SESSION, PARTS
1-8C. WASHINGTON, D. C.: U. S. GOVERNMENT PRINTING
OFFICE, (SI EC).

U. S. SENATE. COMMITTEE ON LABOR AND PUBLIC WELFARE.
MIGRANT FARM WORKER IN AMERICA.   WASHINGTON, D.
C.: U. S. GOVERNMENT PRINTING OFFICE, (1960) (EC SI).

U. S. SENATE. COMMITTEE ON LABOR AND PUBLIC WELFARE.
MIGRANT HEALTH SOURCES.   WASHINGTON, D. C.: U. S.
GOVERNMENT PRINTING OFFICE, (1969) (EC SI).

U. S. SENATE. COMMITTEE ON LABOR AND PUBLIC WELFARE.
MIGRANT HEALTH PROGRAM: CURRENT OPERATIONS AND
ADDITIONAL NEEDS.   WASHINGTON, D. C.: U. S.
GOVERNMENT PRINTING OFFICE, (1967) (SI MD).

U. S. SENATE. COMMITTEE ON LABOR AND PUBLIC WELFARE.
MIGRANT HEALTH SERVICES. HEARINGS.   90 TH CONGRESS.
1ST SESSION. WASHINGTON, D. C.: U. S. GOVERNMENT
PRINTTING OFFICE, (SI MD).

U. S. SENATE. COMMITTEE ON LABOR AND PUBLIC WELFARE.
MIGRANT HEALTH SERVICES. HEARINGS. 91ST SESSION.
HEARINGS. WASHINGTON, D. C.: U. S. GOVERNMENT
PRINTING OFFICE, (SI MD).

U. S. SENATE. COMMITTEE ON LABOR AND PUBLIC WELFARE.
MIGRANT LABOR. HEARINGS. WASHINGTON, D. C.: U.
S. GOVERNMENT PRINTING OFFICE, (1961) (SI MD).

U. S. SENATE. COMMITTEE ON LABOR AND PUBLIC WELFARE.
MIGRATORY LABOR. WASHINGTON, D. C.: U. S.
GOVERNMENT PRINTING OFFICE, (1952) (EC SI).

U. S. SENATE. COMMITTEE ON LABOR AND PUBLIC WELFARE.
MIGRATORY LABOR BILLS. HEARINGS. WASHINGTON, D.
C.: U. S. GOVERNMENT PRINTING OFFICE, (1963) (EC
SI).

U. S. SENATE. COMMITTEE ON LABOR AND PUBLIC WELFARE.
MIGRATORY LABOR LEGISLATION. HEARINGS. WASHINGTON,
D. C.: U. S. GOVERNMENT PRINTING OFFICE, (1967–1968)
(EC SI).

U. S. SENATE. COMMITTEE ON LABOR AND PUBLIC WELFARE.
MIGRATORY LABOR LEGISLATION, PART II. 90TH CONGRESS,
1ST SESSION. WASHINGTON, D. C.: U. S. GOVERNMENT
PRINTING OFFICE, (1968) (EC).

U. S. SENATE. COMMITTEE ON BANKING AND CURRENCY. PROBLEMS
OF MEXICAN AMERICAN BUSINESSMEN IN THE WESTERN AREA
OF THE UNITD STATES. FEDERAL MINORITY ENTERPRISE
PROGRAM. HEARINGS, DECEMBER 10, 1969. WASHINGTON
D.C, (U. S. GOVERNMENT PRINTING OOFFICE) (SO EC).

U. S. SENATE. COMMITTEE ON LABOR AND PUBLIC WELFARE.
PROBLEMS OF MIGRANT WORKERS. HEARING. 91ST
CONGRESS, 2ND SESSION. WASHINGTON, D. C.: U.
S. GOVERNMENT PRINTING OFFICE, (SO EC).

U. S. SENATE. COMMITTEE ON THE JUDICIARY. TO CONTROL
ILLEGAL MIGRATION. HEARINGS BEFORE THE SUBCOMMITTEE
ON IMMIGRTION AND NATURALIZATION OF THE COMMITTEE ON
THE JUDICIARY.. SENATE DOCUMENTS 3660 AND 3661, 83RD
CONGRESS, SECOND SESSION, JULY 12–14, 1954 (SI).

U. S. SENATE. COMMITTEE ON LABOR AND PUBLIC WELFARE. THE
MIGRANT FARM WORKER IN AMERICA. BACKGROUND DATA ON
THE MIGRANT WORKER SITUATION IN THE UNITED STATES
TODAY. WASHINGTON, D. C.: U. S. GOVERNMENT
PRINTING OFFICE, (1960) (SI EC).

U. S. SENATE. COMMITTEE ON LABOR AND PUBLIC WELFARE. THE
MIGRATORY FARM LABOR PROBLEM IN THE UNITED STATES.
89TH CONGRESS 2ND SESSION SENATE REPORT NO 1549.
WASHINGTON, D. C.: U. GOVERNMENT PRINTING OFFICE,
(1966) (EC SI).

U. S. SENATE. COMMITTEE ON LABOR AND PUBLIC WELFARE. THE
MIGRATORY FARM LABOR PROBLEM IN THE UNITED STATES.
90TH 1ST CONGRESS SESSION SENATE REPORT NO 71.
WASHINGTON, D. C.: U. S. GOVERNMENT PRINTING OFFICE,
(1967) (EC SI).

U. S. SENATE. COMMITTEE ON LABOR AND PUBLIC WELFARE. THE
MIGRATORY FARM LABOR PROBLEM IN THE UNITED STATES.
90TH 2ND CONGRESS SESSION SENATE REPORT NO 1006.
WASHINGTON, D. C.: U. S. GOVERNMENT PRINTING OFFICE,
(1968) (EC SI).

U. S. SENATE. COMMITTEE ON LABOR AND PUBLIC WELFARE. THE
MIGRATORY FARM LABOR PROBLEM IN THE UNITED STATES.
91ST CONGRESS 1ST SESSION REPORT NUMBER 91-93.
WASHINGTON, D.C.: U. S. GOVERNMENT PRINTING OFFICE,
(FEBRUARY 19, 1969) (EC SI).

U. S. SENATE. COMMITTEE ON LABOR AND PUBLIC WELFARE. THE
MIGRATORY FARM LABOR PROBLEM IN THE UNITED STATES.
WASHINGTON, D. C.: U. S. GOVERNMENT PRINTING OFFICE,
(1967) (SI EC).

U. S. SENATE. COMMITTEE ON LABOR AND PUBLIC WELFARE. THE
MIGRATORY FARM LABOR PROBLEM IN THE UNITED STATES.
WASHINGTON, D. C.: U. S. GOVERNMENT PRINTING OFFICE,
(ANNUAL) (SI EC).

U. S. SENATE. SELECT COMMITTEE ON EQUAL EDUCATIONAL
OPPORTUNITY. HEARINGS BEFORE THE SELECT COMMITTEE
ON EQUAL EDUCATIONAL OPPORTUNITY OF THE UNITED STATES
SENATE.   91ST CONGRESS, 2ND SESSION. EQUAL EDUCATION
OPPORTUNITIES. PART 4; MEXICAN AMERICAN EDUCATION
AUGUST 18, 19, 20, 21, 1970. WASHINGTON, D. C.: U.
S. GOVERNMENT PRINTING OFFICE, (1971) (ED).

U. S. SENATE. SELECT COMM ON EQUAL EDUCATIONAL OPPORTUNITY,
PART 4. MEXICAN-AMERICAN EDUCATION.   HEARINGS.
WASHINGTON, D. C.: U. S. GOVERNMENT PRINTING OFFICE,
(AUGUST 18-21, 1970) (ED).

U. S. SENATE. SELECT SUBCOMMITTEE ON NUTRITION AND HUMAN
NEEDS. NUTRITION AND HUMAN NEEDS.   HEARINGS.
WASHINGTON, D. C.: U. S. GOVERNMENT PRINTING OFFICE,
(1969).

U. S. SENATE. SELECT COMMITTEE ON NUTRITION AND HUMAN
NEEDS. PROBLEMS AND PROSPECTS.   90TH CONGRESS 2ND
SESSION DECEMBER 18, 19, 1968. WASHINGTON, D. C.:
U. S. GOVERNMENT PRINTING OFFICE, (MD SO).

U. S. SENATE. SELECT COMM ON SMALL BUS SUBCOMM ON GOVT
PROCUREMENT. SMALL BUSINESS AND LABOR SURPLUS AREA
SET-ASIDES AND SUBCONTRACTS. HEARING. WASHINGTON,
D. C.: U. S. GOVERNMENT PRINTING OFFICE, (AUGUST 2
1, 1970) (ED).

U. S. SENATE. SELECT COMMITTEE ON NUTRITION AND HUMAN
NEEDS. THE NATIONAL NUTRITION SURVEY, PART 3.
HEARINGS, JANUARY 22, 23, 27, 28, 1969. WASHINGTON,
D. C.: U. S. GOVERNMENT PRINTING OFFICE, (1969) (MD
SO).

U. S. SENATE. SPECIAL COMMITTEE ON AGING. AVAILABILITY
AND USEFULNESS OF FEDERAL PROGRAMS AND SERVICES TO
ELDERLY MEXICAN—AMERICANS. HEARINGS.   90TH CONGRESS,
2ND SESSION, 91ST CONGRESS, 1ST SESSION PARTS 1—5.
WASHININGTON, D. C.: U. S. GOVERNMENT PRINTING
OFFICE, (MD SO).

U. S. SENATE. SPECIAL COMMITTEE ON AGING. AVAILABILITY
AND USEFULNESS OF FEDERAL PROGRAMS AND SERVICES TO
ELDERLY MEXICAN—AMERICANS. HEARINGS. 90TH CONGRESS
2ND SESSION. WASHINGTON, D. C.: U. S. GOVERNMENT
PRINTING OFFICE, (1969—69) (SC).

U. S. SOCIAL SECURITY ADMINISTRATION. NOT JUST SOME OF
US.   WASHINGTON, D. C.: U. S. GOVERNMENT PRINTING
OFFICE, (1969) (B   SO).

U. S. TREASURY DEPT. IMMIGRATION INTO THE U.S. FROM
1820—1930.   WASHINGTON, D. C.: U. S. GOVERNMENT
PRINTING OFFICE, (1930) (SI).

U. S. TREATIES. THE TREATY OF GUADALUPE HIDALGO.
BERKELEY, CALIFORNIA: FRIENDS OF THE BANCROFT LIBRARY,
1949.

U. S. TREATIES, ETC., 1845—1949. GUADALUPE HILDALGO,
TREATY OF PEACHE, 1848; AND THE GADSDEN TREATY WITH
MEXICO, 1853..   TRUCHAS, NEW MEXICO: TATE GALLERY,
1969.

U. S. WORKS PROGRESS ADMINISTRATION. MEXICAN MIGRATORY
WORKERS OF SOUTH TEXAS.   WASHINGTON, D. C.: U. S.
GOVERNMENT PRINTING OFFICE, (1941) (EC SI).

U. S. WORKS PROGRESS ADMINISTRATION. MIGRATORY COTTON
PICKERS IN ARIZONA.   WASHINGTON, D. C.: U.
S. GOVERNMENT PRINTING OFFICE, (1939) (EC SO).

U. S. WORKS PROGRESS ADMINISTRATION. SPANISH AMERICAN
SINGING GAMES OF NEW MEXICO.   NEW MEXICO: U. S. WORKS
PROJECTS ADMINISTRATION, 1940 (EC AN).

U. S. WORKS PROGRESS ADMINISTRATION. THE PECAN SHELLERS
OF SAN ANTONIO; THE PROBLEM OF UNDERPAID AND UNEMPLOYED
MEXICAN LABOR.   SELDEN C. MENEFEE AND ORIN C.
CASSMORE. WASHINGTON, D. C.: U. S. GOVERNMENT
PRINTING OFFICE, (1940) (EC SI).

UNITED STATES COMMISSION ON CIVIL RIGHTS.   MEXICAN-AMERICANS
    REPORT.   WASHINGTON, D. C.: U. S. GOVERNMENT
    PRINTING OFFICE, (1962).

UNITED STATES COMMISSION ON CIVIL RIGHTS. THE 50 STATE
    REPORT SUBMITTED TO THE COMMISSION ON CIVIL RIGHTS
    BY THE STATE ADVISORY COMMITTEES, 1961.   WASHINGTON,
    D. C.: U. S. GOVERNMENT PRINTING OFFICE, (1961).

UNITED STATES CONGRESS. SENATE. THE MIGRATORY FARM LABOR
    PROBLEM IN THE UNITED STATES.   88TH CONGRESS SENATE
    REPORT 934. WASHINGTON, D. C.: U. S. GOVERNMENT
    PRINTING OFFICE, (SI EC).

UNITED STATES DEPARTMENT OF AGRICULTURE. SOIL CONSERVATION
    SERVICE, REGION 8.   RECONNAISSANCE SURVEY OF HUMAN
    DEPENDENCY ON RESOURCES IN THE RIO GRANDE WATERSHED.
    ALBUQUERQUE, (DECEMBER 1936). REGIONAL BULLETIN NO.
    33, CONSERVATION ECONOMICS SERIES NO. 6 (EC   GE).

UNITED STATES DEPARTMENT OF AGRICULTURE. SOIL CONSERVATION
    SERVICE, REGION 8.   RIO GRANDE WATERSHED IN COLORADO
    AND NEW MEXICO. A REPORT ON THE CONDITION AND USE OF
    THE LAND AND WATER RESOURCES TOGETHER WITH A GENERAL
    PROGRAM FOR SOIL AND WATER CONSERVATION.   ALBUQUERQUE,
    AUGUST 1939 (EC   GE).

UNITED STATES DEPARTMENT OF AGRICULTURE. SOIL CONSERVATION
    SERVICE, REGION 8.   TEWA BASIN STUDY, THE INDIAN
    PUEBLOS, THE SPANISH-AMERICAN VILLAGES, PHYSICAL
    SURVEYS AND OTHER STUDIES.   MIMEOGRAPHED. ALBUQUERQUE,
    APRIL 1935 (EC   GE).

UNITED STATES DEPARTMENT OF AGRICULTURE. SOIL CONSERVATION
    SERVICE, REGION 8.   A DESCRIPTION OF THE LANDS
    CONTIGUOUS TO THE ELEPHANT BUTTE IRRIGATION DISTRICT
    OF SOUTHERN NEW MEXICO.   TYPESCRIPT. ALBUQUERQUE,
    1938 (EC GE).

UNITED STATES DEPARTMENT OF AGRICULTURE. SOIL CONSERVATION
    SERVICE, REGION 8.   A REPORT ON THE RIO GRANDE
    WATERSHED WITH SPECIAL REFERENCE TO SOIL CONSERVATION
    PROBLEMS.   PREPARED BY RIO GRANDE DISTRICT STAFF IN
    COLLABORATION WITH THE STAFF OF THE REGIONAL OFFICE.
    SIGNED E. R. SMITH, DISTRICT MANAGER, RIO GRANDE
    DISTRICT. ALBUQUERQUE, NOVEMBER 22, 1936 (EC   GE).

UNITED STATES DEPARTMENT OF AGRICULTURE. SOIL CONSERVATION
    SERVICE, REGION 8.   THE SOCIOLOGICAL SURVEY OF THE
    RIO GRANDE WATERSHED.   TYPESCRIPT. ALBUQUERQUE, 1936
    (EC   GE).

UNITED STATES. COMMISSION ON CIVIL RIGHTS. THE MEXICAN
    AMERICAN: A PAPER PRESENTED FOR THE U. S. COMMISSION
    ON CIVIL RIGHTS. WASHINGTON, D. C.. U. S.
    GOVERNMENT PRINTING OFFICE, (1968) (PL).

UNITED STATES. DISTRICT COURT, TEXAS. BASTROP INDEPENDENT
    SCHOOL DISTRICT OF BASTROP COUNTY, ET AL. FINAL
    JUDGMENT. UNITED STATES DISTRICT COURT, TEXAS,
    DELGADO, AUSTIN, 1950 (ED).

UNIVERSITY OF CALIFORNIA. CONFERENCE ON THE LAW OF THE
    POOR, 1966. THE LAW OF THE POOR. SAN FRANCISCO:
    CHANDLER PUBLISHING CO., 1966 (EC).

UNIVERSITY OF DENVER, COLLEGE OF LAW. LAW SCHOOL PREPARATORY
    PROGRAM FOR COLLEGE GRADUATES OF SPANISH-AMERICANDESCENT;
    PROGRESS REPORT TO THE FORD FOUNDATION. DENVER:
    COLLEGE OF LAW, UNIVERSITY OF DENVER, 1967 (ED).

VEGA. "POLICE PROFESSIONALIZATION" (SO*).

WARNSHIPS, PAUL L. CRIME AND CRIMINAL JUSTICE AMONG THE
    MEXICANS OF ILLINOIS. WASHINGTON, D. C.: U. S.
    GOVERNMENT PRINTING OFFICE, (1931) (SI).

WARNSHUIS, PAUL L. CRIME AND CRIMINAL JUSTICE AMONG THE
    MEXICANS OF ILLINOIS. WASHINGTON, D. C.: U. S.
    GOVERNMENT PRINTING OFFICE, (1931) (SI).

WAUGH, EVELYN. ROBBERY UNDER LAW: THE MEXICAN OBJECT
    LESSON. LONDON: CATHOLIC BOOK CLUB, 1940.

WESTPHALL. PUBLIC DOMAIN NEW MEXICO: 1854-1891 (HN*).

WITHERSPOON, JOSEPH PARKER. ADMINISTRATIVE IMPLEMENTATION
    OF CIVIL RIGHTS. AUSTIN: UNIVERSITY OF TEXAS PRESS,
    1968.

WOLFE HOMER R. (ET AL). EXPOSURE OF WORKERS TO PESTICIDES.
    IN U. S. CONGRESS. SENATE. LABOR AND PUBLIC WELFARE
    COMMITTEE. HEARINGS. MIGRANT AND SEASONAL FARMWORKER
    POWERLESS, PART 6-C: PESTICIDES AND THE FARMWORKER
    PAGES 3105-3116. WASHINGTON, D. C.: U. S. GOVERNMENT
    PRINTING OFFICE, (APRIL 1967) (EC MD).

YALE. LEGAL TITLE MINING CLAIMES WATER (HC*).

ZEIGLER, B. M. (ED.). DESEGREGATION AND THE SUPREME COURT.
    BOSTON: D. C. HEATH, 1958 (SO).

M E D I C I N E - H E A L T H

(MD)

ALDER, SOL. THE HEALTH AND EDUCATION OF THE ECONOMICALLY DEPRIVED CHILD. ST. LOUIS: W. H. GREEN, 1968 (ED EC).

ALVIDREZ. NARCOTICS DRUG USE TRENDS CALIFORNIA (LW*).

ALVIDREZ. "DRUG USE TRENDS CALIFORNIA" (LW*).

ANDERSON, DONNA L. JOHNSON. EXPERIENCE IN ATTAINING DIETARY INTAKE INFORMATION ON ARIZONA MEXICAN AMERICANS. UNIVERSITY OF ARIZONA, MASTER'S THESIS (1971).

ANDERSON. TEXAS FOLK MEDICINE (AN*).

"FEDERAL PROGRAM OF PUBLIC HEALTH AND MEDICAL SERVICES FOR MIGRATORY FARMWORKERS". PUBLIC HEALTH REPORTS, VOL. 60 NO. 9 (MARCH 1945) (SI).

E SOUTHWESTERN CONFERENCE CULTURAL (SC*).

"UNIFORM PERSONAL HEALTH RECORD (SI*).

"VITAL STATISTICS NEW MEXICO" (HN*).

CHILD'S MEDICAL RECORD. CHILD'S MEDICAL RECORD (SO).

PARATHION RESIDUE POISONING AMONG (LW*).

"MIGRATORY LABOR" (EC*).

"MIGRATORY LABOR" (EC*).

THE FORGOTTEN EGG; AN EXPLORATION INTO MENTAL HEALTH PROBLEMS AMONG URBAN MEXICAN-AMERICAN FAMILITES AND THEIR CHILDREN. TEXAS DIVISION OF MENTAL HEALTH, 1961 (SO).

BACA. "SOME HEALTH BELIEFS OF THE SPANISH-SPEAKING". AMERICAN JOURNAL OF NURSIN, VOL. 69 (OCTOBER 1696), P. 2172 (AN).

BAKER, HELEN. "SCHOOL NURSE TO MIGRANT CHILDREN". AMERICAN JOURNAL OF NURSING, (JULY, 1957), PP. 904-935 (SI).

BARFELL, LAWRENCE OTTO. A STUDY OF THE HEALTH PROGRAM
    AMONG MEXICAN CHILDREN WITH SPECIAL REFERENCE TO THE
    PREVALENCE OF TUBERCULOSIS AND ITS CAUSES. UNIVERSITY
    OF SOUTHERN CALIFORNIA, MASTER'S THESIS (1937).

BARRICS, RUTH. "NUTRITION EDUCATION IN SACRAMENTO COUNTY
    FOR THE AMERICAN OF MEXICAN DESCENT". AZTLAN:
    CHICANO JOURNAL OF THE SOCIAL SCIENCES AND THE ARTS,
    VOL. 1 NO. 2 (FALL 11970), PP. 57-7.

BEXAR COUNTY TUBERCULOSIS ASSOCIATION. ANNUAL REPORT FOR
    1939.   SAN ANTONIO, TEXAS: TEXAS COUNTY TUBERCULOSIS
    ASSOCIATION, 1940.

BEXAR COUNTY TUBERCULOSIS ASSOCIATION. LIKE A SORE THUMB.
    SAN ANTONIO, TEXAS: TEXAS COUNTY TUBERCULOSIS
    ASSOCIATION, 1945.

BEXAR COUNTY TUBERCULOSIS ASSOCIATION. TUBERCULOSIS AND
    ITS CONTROL— FACTS AND FIGURES IN SAN ANTONIO AND
    BEXAR COUNTY.   SAN ANTONIO, TEXAS: TEXAS COUNTY
    TUBERCULOSIS ASSOCIATION, 1939.

BLACK, LAURA SUE. FOOD MANAGEMENT PRACTICES OF HEAD START
    FAMILIES IN TUCSON, ARIZONA.   TUCSON, ARIZONA:
    UNIVERSITY OF ARIZONA, 1970 (SO B).

BLAZEK.   FOOD HABITS LIVING CONDITIONS (EC*).

BOOKER, MARGARET. A STUDY OF THE DIETARY HABITS OF MEXICAN
    FAMILIES IN TUSCON, ARIZONA.   TUCSON, ARIZONA:
    UNIVERSITY OF ARIZONA, MASTER'S THESIS (1937).

BOSCH.   INSECTICIDE CRISIS (LW*).

BOURKE.   FOLK-FOODS RIO GRANDE VALLEYNORTHERN (AN*).

BRITTON, GERTRUDE HOWE; CONSTABLE, KATE. OUR MEXICAN
    PATIENTS AT CENTRAL FREE DISPENSARY.   PAMPHLET.
    CHICAGO, 1925.

BRITTON, ROBERT B.; CONSTABLE, KATE. "ANALYSIS OF MEXICAN
    PATIENTS AT CHICAGO DISPENSARY".   NATION'S HEALTH,
    VOL. 7 NO. 7 (JULY 1926).

BUECHLEY, ROBERT W.; DUNN, JOHN E; LINDEN, GEORGE,
    AND BRESLOW, LESTER. "EXCESS LUNG CANCER MORTALITY
    RATES AMONG MEXICAN WOMEN IN CALIFORNIA".   CANCER,
    VOL. 10 (FEBRUARY 1957), PP. 63-66 (SO).

BULLOUGH.   POVERTY, ETHNIC IDENTITY, HEALTH (EC*).

BURT, A. L. "MORES AND NURSING CARE: THE NURSE'S
     RESPONSIBILITY FOR UNDERSTANDING RAACIAL DIFFERENCES".
     PUBLIC HEALTH NURSING, VOL. 42 (FEBRUARY 1950), PP.
     65-68 (SO).

CALIFORNIA DEPARTMENT OF PUBLIC HEALTH. "HEALTH OF
     MEXICANS IN CLAIFORNIA". WEEKLY BULLETIN, VOL. 17
     (JULY 1938), PP. 105-106.

CALIFORNIA DEPARTMENT OF HEALTH.   OCCUPATIONAL DISEASE
     CALIFORNIA (LW*).

CALIFORNIA FEDERATION FOR CIVIC UNITY.   GET OUT IF YOU
     CAN: SAGA SAL (EC*).

CALIFORNIA STATE DEPARTMENT OF SOCIAL WELFARE. 'HEALTH,
     RELIEF, AND DELINQUENCY CONDITIONS AMONG THE MEXICANS
     OF CALIFORNIA.'   IN MANUEL P. SERVIN. THE MEXICAN-AMERICANS:
     AN AWAKING MINORITY (SO).

CALIFORNIA STATE DEPARTMENT OF EDUCATION.   SCHOOL HEALTH
     RECORD TRANSFER (ED*).

CALIFORNIA.   CALIFORNIA FARM WORKERS HEALTH (EC*).

CALIFORNIA.   HEALTH HARVESTERS. DECADE HOPE (EC*).

CARMELIA F.; KRATZ, F. W. TUBERCULOSIS CONTROL IN
     LOS ANGELES CITY.   LOS ANGELES: LOS ANGELES
     DEPARTMENT OF HEALTH, 1940.

CASTRO, ESTRADA S; LANG, C. A; CHOW, B. F. "APPLICATION
     OF VITAMIN B12 TOLERANCE TEST TO AMERICAN AND MEXICAN
     SUBJE CTS".   JOURNAL OF LABORATORY AND CLINICAL
     MEDICINE, VOL. 43 (MARCH), PP. 406-410.

CHADEK, MARIAN. "NURSING SERVICE FOR MIGRANT WORKERS".
     AMERICAN JOURNAL OF NURSING, (JUNE 1965), PP. 62-65.

CHALDEK, MARIAN. "NURSING SERVICE FOR MIGRANT WORKERS".
     AMERICAN JOURNAL OF NURSING, (JUNE 1965), PP. 62-65
     (SO).

CHARLTON, M. N. "APHASIA IN BILINGUAL AND POLYGLOT
     PATIENTS, A NEUROLOGICAL AND PSYCHOLO GICAL STUDY".
     JOURNAL CF SPEECH AND HEARING DISORDERS, VOL.
     29 (AUGUST 1964), PP. 307-311 (PY).

CHILDRENS BUREAU. S. CHILD LABOR WORK MOTHERS BEET (EC*).

CLARK.   "THE SOCIAL FUNCTIONS MEXICAN-AMERICAN (SO*).

CLARK.   HEALTH MEXICAN CULTURE: COMMUNITY (SO*).

CLARK.   SICKNESS HEALTH SAL SI PUEDES: (SO*).

COOK.   PESTICIDE MULTIRESIDUE METHODOLOGY (LW*).

CRAWFORD, FRED R. THE FORGOTTEN EGG: A STUDY OF THE
     MENTAL HEALTH PROBLEMS OF THE MEXICAN—AMERICAN
     RESIDENTS IN THE NEIGHBORHOOD OF THE GOOD SAMARITAN
     CENTER, SAN ANTONIO, TEXAS.   SAN ANTONIO, TEXAS: GOOD
     SAMARITAN CENTER, 1961 (SO PY).

CRAWFORD, FRED R. THE FORGOTTEN EGG: A STUDY OF THE
     MENTAL HEALTH PROBLEMS OF MEXICAN—AMERICAN RESIDENTS
     IN THE NEIGHBORHOOD OF THE GOOD SAMARATIN CENTER, SAN
     ANTONIO, TEXAS.   AUSTIN: DIVISION OF MENTAL HEALTH,
     TEXAS STATE DEPARTMENT OF HEALTH, 1961 (SO PY).

CURRAN.   NEW APPROACH TO HEALTH PHYSICAL (SO*).

CURRIER, R. L. "HOT—COLD SYNDROME AND SYMBOLIC BALANCE
     IN MEXICAN AND SPANISH—AMERICAN FOLK MEDICINE".
     ETHNOLOGY, VOL. 5 (JULY 1966), PP. 251—263 (PY AN).

CURTIN, LEONNORA SCOTT MUSE. HEALING HERBS OF THE UPPER
     RIO GRANDE.   SANTA FE, NEW MEXICO, . LABORATORY OF
     ANTHROPOLOGY (AN).

DARRAH. "A MOBILE HEALTH SERVICE FOR MIGRANT FAMILIES".
     NURSING OUTLOOK, VOL. 10 (MARCH 1962), PP. 172—175
     (SI).

DE LA ROSE, L. "MINISTRY OF PUBLIC HEALTH AND WELFARE OF
     MEXICO ON SANITARY PROBLEMS OF MEXICANS LIVING IN THE
     UNITED STATES".   WASHINGTON, D. C.: BOLETIN DE LA
     OFICINA SANITARIO PANAMERICANA, VOL. 27 (AUGUST
     1948), PP. 752—755 (SO).

DES MARAIS, ALICE. ENVIRONMENTAL AND CULTURAL FACTORS
     ASSOCIATED WITH INFANT DIARRHEA IN SAN ANTONIO, TEXAS.
     WASHINGTON UNIVERSITY, MASTER'S THESIS (1949) (SO).

DOEGE, THEODORE C.; LEVY, PAUL S.; HEATH, CLARK W.
     "A DIPTHERIA EPIDEMIC RELATED TO COMMUNITY IMMUNIZATION
     LEVELS AND THE HEALTH PROBLEMS OF MIGRANT WORKERS".
     PUBLIC HEALTH REPORTS,   (FEB 1963), PP. 151—160 (SO).

DOUGHERTY, S. E.; UHDE, M. "SCHOOL HEALTH PROGRAM
     FOR CHILDREN OF SEASONAL AGRICULTURAL WORKERS".
     JOURNAL OF SCHOOL HEALTH, VOL. 35 (FEB 1965), PP.
     85—90.

DROLET, GODIAS J. "DISCUSSION OF PAPER PRESENTED BY
     BENJAMIN GOLDBERF, M. D., ON "TUBERCULOSIS IN RACIAL
     TYPES WITH SPECIAL REFERENCE TO MEXICANS".   AMERICAN
     JOURNAL OF PUBLIC HEALTH, VOL. 19 (MAR 1929), PP.
     285—286 (SO).

DUBLIN, LOUIS I. "THE MORTALITY FROM TUBERCULOSIS AMONG
    THE RACIAL STOCKS IN THE SOUTHWEST". AMERICAN REVIEW
    OF TUBERCULOSIS, VOL. 45 NO. JANUARY (1942), PP. 61-71.

EISNER. "HEALTH SERVICES UNDER ELEMENTARY (ED*).

ELLIOT. HEALTH RELIEF PROBLEMS GROUPNON-FAMILY (SO*).

ELLIS. "SPANISH SURNAME MORTALITY DIFFERENCES (SO*).

FANTINI, ALBINO EDWARD. ILLNESS AND CURING AMONG THE
    MEXICAN AMERICANS OF MISSION, TEXAS. AUSTIN:
    UNIVERSITY OF TEXAS, MASTER'S THESIS (1962).

FARENHOLT. NEW MASKED MAN AGRICULTURE (LW*).

FOSTER. "RELATIONSHIPS BETWEEN THEORETICAL (AN*).

FOSTER. PROBLEMS INTERCULTURAL HEALTH (AN*).

FOSTER. "RELATIONSHIPS BETWEEN SPANISH (AN*).

FREIDSON, ELLIOT. PATIENTS' VIEWS OF MEDICAL PRACTICE.
    NEW YORK: RUSSELL SAGE FOUNDATION, 1961.

GILBERT. "EFFECTS RURAL POVERTY HEALTH (EC*).

GILBERT. "HEALTH NEEDS MIGRANT CHILDREN (EC*).

GITTELSOHN, A. M., HEMPHILL, E. C., HOLLISTER, A. C. AND
    BECK, M. C. "INFLUENCE OF WATER AVILABILITY ON
    SHIGELLA PREVALENCE IN CHILDREN OF FARM LABOR
    FAMILIES". AMERICAN JOURNAL OF PUBLIC HEALTH, VOL.
    45 (MARCH 1955), PP. 354-362 (SO).

GLADNEY, VIRGINIA M. FOOD PRACTICES OF THE MEXICAN
    AMERICAN IN LOS ANGELES COUNTY. LOS ANGELES,
    CALIFORNIA: LOS ANGELES COUNTY HEALTH DEPT, 1966 (SO).

GOLDBERG, BENJAMIN. "TUBERCULOSIS IN RACIAL TYPES WITH
    SPECIAL REFERENCE TO MEXICANS". AMERICAN JOURNAL
    OF PUBLIC HEALTH, VOL. 19 (MARCH 1929), PP. 274-86
    (AN).

GOLDBERG, BENJAMIN. TUBERCULOSIS AND THE MEXICAN. CITY
    OF CHICAGO, (NOVEMBER 1930). MUNICIPAL TUBERCULOSIS
    SANATARIUM BULLETIN, MARCH-APRIL 1929, PAGE 36. (AN).

GONZALEZ. "AN OUNCE OF PREVENTION MAY BE WORTH OF NOTHING
    -- A MEXICAN AMERICAN GHETTO". BULLETIN OF THE
    NATIONAL TUBERCULOSIS AND RESPIRATORY DISEASE
    ASSOCIATION, VOL. 55 (JANUARY 1969), P. 14 (SO).

GOULD, DAVID M. "MASS X-RAY IN SAN ANTONIO". PUBLIC
    HEALTH REPORTS, VOL. 60 (FEBRUARY 2, 1945), PP. 117-126.

GREENFIELD, MYRTLE. A HISTORY OF PUBLIC HEALTH IN
    NEW MEXICO. ALBUQUERQUE, NEW MEXICO: UNIVERSITY OF
    NEW MEXICO PRESS, 1962.

GREGG, R. "MEDICAL EXAMINATION AND VACCINATION OF FARM
    LABORERS RECRUITED FROM MEXICO". PUBLIC HEALTH
    REPORTS, VOL. 65 (JUNE 23, 1950), PP. 807-809 (SI).

HANSON, ROBERT C. "COMMUNICATING HEALTH ARGUMENTS ACROSS
    CULTURES". NURSING RESEARCH, (FALL 1963), P. 12
    (SO).

HANSON, ROBERT C. "THE SYSTEMATIC LINKAGE HYPOTHESIS AND
    ROLE CONSENSUS PATTERNS IN HOSPITAL-COMMUNITY
    RELATIONS". AMERICAN SOCIOLOGICAL REVIEW, VOL. 27
    (JUNE 1962), PP. 304-313 (SO).

HANSON, ROBERT C. NURSE-PATIENT COMMUNICATION; A MANUAL
    FOR PUBLIC HEALTH NURSES IN NORTHERN NEW MEXICO.
    BOULDER: UNIVERSITY OF COLORADO. BUREAU OF SOCIOLOGICAL
    RESEARCH. INSTITUTE OF BEHAVIORAL SCIENCE, 1964 (SO).

HANSON, ROBERT C. THE STRUCTURE AND CONTENT OF HEALTH
    BELIEF SYSTEMS. NEW MEXICO RURAL HEALTH SURVEY
    FILES, UNIVERSITY OF COLORADO, 1961 (SO).

HANSON, ROBERT C. AND SAUNDERS, LYLE. NURSE-PATIENT
    COMMUNICATION: A MANUAL FOR PUBLIC HEALTH NURSES IN
    NORTHERN NEW MEXICO. SANTA FE, NEW MEXICO: NEW
    MEXICO STATE DEPARTMENT OF PUBLIC HEALTH, 1964 (SO).

HARMER, R. "POISONS, PROFITS AND POLITICS: CASES OF DEATH
    AND SEVERE ILLNESS DUE TO PESTICIDE POISONING
    IN CALIFORNIA". NATION, VOL. 209 (AUGUST 25,
    1969), PP. 134-137 (EC).

HARPER. "A COMPREHENSIVE CARE PROGRAM FOR MIGRANT
    FARMWORKERS". PUBLIC HEALTH REPORTS, VOL. 84
    (AUGUST 1969), P. 690 (SI).

HARRISON, I. A. HEALTH NEEDS AND INTERESTS OF SPANISH
    SPEAKING CHILDREN OF INTERMEDIATE GRADES. UNIVERSITY
    OF CALIFORNIA AT LOS ANGELES, MASTER'S THESIS (1957)
    (ED).

HAY, R. W. "ESCUELITA: PUBLIC HEALTH WORK IN MEXICAN LABOR
    CAMPS". PUBLIC HEALTH NURSING, VOL. 20 (1928), PP.
    185-187 (SO).

HERNANDEZ. "A CULTURALLY RELEVANT FOODSNUTRITION (AN*).

HOLLAND. "MEXICAN-AMERICAN MEDICAL BELIEFS (ED*).

HOLLINGSHEAD. SOCIAL CLASS MENTAL ILLNESS: (SO*).

HOLLISTER, ARTHUR C., JR ET AL. "INFLUENCE OF WATER
     AVAILABILITY ON SHIGELLA PREVALANCE IN CHILDREN OF
     FARM LABOR FAMILIES". AMERICAN JOURNAL OF PUBLIC
     HEALTH, VOL. 45 (MARCH 1955), PP. 354-362.

HORTON, FRANCES. FOOD HABITS AND LIVING CONDITIONS
     OF MEXICANS DWELLING IN THE RIO GRANDE VALLEY BETWEEN
     ROMA AND MERCEDES. UNIVERSITY OF TEXAS, MASTER'S
     THESIS (1936) (SO).

HORTON, FRANCES. FOOD HABITS AND LIVING CONDITIONS
     OF MEXICANS DWELLING IN THE RIO GRANDE VALLEY BETWEEN
     ROMA AND MERCEDES. AUSTIN: UNIVERSITY OF TEXAS, 1936
     (SO).

HUDDLESTON, RUTH B. "NEW MEXICO—LA TIERRA DE MANANA".
     PUBLIC HEALTH NURSING, VOL. 29 (JULY 1937),
     PP. 421-424 (AN).

JACO, E. GARTHY. PATIENTS, PHYSICIANS AND ILLNESS:
     SOURCE-BOOK IN BEHAVIORAL SCIENCE AND MEDICINE.
     GLENCOE, ILLINOIS: FREE PRESS, 1958 (SO).

JACO, E. GARTLEY. "SOCIAL FACTORS IN MENTAL DISORDERS IN
     TEXAS". SOCIAL PROBLEMS, VOL. 4 (1957), PP. 322-328
     (SO).

JACO, E. GARTLEY. "THE SOCIAL ISOLATION HYPOTHESIS AND
     SCHIZOPHRENIA". AMERICAN SOCIOLOGICAL REVIEW, VOL.
     19 (OCTOBER 1954), PP. 567-577 (SO).

JACO, E. GARTLEY. MENTAL HEALTH OF THE SPANISH AMERICAN
     IN TEXAS. IN MARVIN K. OPLER (ED). CULTURE AND
     MENTAL HEALTH. NEW YORK: THE MACMILLAN COMPANY, 1959
     (AN).

JACO, E. GARTLEY. THE SOCIAL EPIDEMIOLOGY OF MENTAL
     DISORDERS: A PSYCHIATRIC SURVEY OF TEXAS. NEW YORK:
     RUSSEL SAGE FOUNDATION, 1960 (SO).

JOHNSON, CARMEN ACOSTA. "NURSING AND MEXICAN-AMERICAN FOLK
     MEDICINE". NURSING FORUM, NO. 2 (1964), PP.
     102-112 (AN).

KARNO. A COMMUNITY MENTAL HEALTH SERVICE (SO*).

KARTMAN, L. AND BETTYE M. MAYS. "MALARIA BLOOD SURVEY OF
     MEXICAN LABORERS IN ARKANSAS COUNTY". PUBLIC HEALTH
     REPORTS, VOL. 67 NO. 6 (JUNE 1952), PP. 561-562 (SI).

KELLEY. "SEGREGATION MEXICAN AMERICAN (SO*).

KERRICK. PRELIMINARY REPORT—ATTITUDES (SO*).

LANGHAM. ASCORBIC ACID METABOLISM MEXICAN (ED*).

LELAND, R. G. "MEDICAL CARE FOR MIGRATORY WORKERS".
    JOURNAL OF THE AMERICAN MEDICAL ASSOCIATION, VOL. 114
    (JANUARY 6, 1940), PP. 45-55 (SI).

LEVY, JOHN. "THE IMPACT OF CULTURAL FORMS UPON CHILDREN'S
    BEHAVIOR". MENTAL HYGIENE, VOL. 16 (APRIL 1932),
    PP. 208-220 (AN).

LOS ANGELES CITY HEALTH DEPARTMENT. DATA MEXICANS
    COMPILED RECORDS (HC*).

LOS ANGELES COUNTY BUREAU OF INSPECTIONS. HOUSING
    SANITATION SURVEY ACTIVE (HC*).

LOS ANGELES COUNTY COMMITTEE FOR INTERRACIAL PROGRESS.
    MINORITY GROUP EMPLOYMENT PATTERNS (HC*).

LOS ANGELES COUNTY TUBERCULOSIS AND HEALTH ASSOCIATION.
    TUBERCULOSIS HIGH INCIDENCE AREA: (HC*).

LUKENS. FACTORS AFFECTING UTILIZATION (SO*).

MADSEN. STUDY CHANGE MEXICAN FOLK MEDICINE (AN*).

MADSEN. VALUE CONFLICTS FOLK PSYCHOTHERAPY (AN*).

MADSEN. "CULTURAL VARIATION CONCEPTSSICKNESS (AN*).

MADSEN. MENTAL HEALTH PROBLEMS PUBLIC (AN*).

MADSEN. SOCIETY HEALTH LOWER RIO GRANDE (AN*).

MANN, VIRGINIA R. FOOD PRACTICES OF THE MEXICAN-AMERICAN
    IN LOS ANGELES COUNTY. SAN JOSE, CALIFORNIA: HEALTH
    DEPARTMENT OF SANTA CLARA COUNTY, 1963.

MARQUEZ. "MEDWIFERY LORE IN NEW MEXICO". AMERICAN
    JOURNAL OF NURSING, VOL. 64 (SEPTEMBER 1964), P.
    81.

MARQUEZ, MARY N., AND PACHECO, CONSUELO. PARTERAS
    IN NORTHERN NEW MEXICO: A DESCRIPTIVE REVIEW
    OF SELECTED PRACTICE IN MEDWIFERY. UNITED STATES
    PUBLIC HEALTH RESEARCH PROJECT, GRANT NO. GM 05615,NO
    DATE.

MARSHALL. DIFFERENCES HEALTH BEHAVIOR MEXICAN-AMERICAN
    (ED*).

MC LEMORE. "ETHNIC ATTITUDES TOWARD HOSPITALIZATION:
    (SO*).

MEADOW, A., ET AL. "SYMPTOMATIC BEHAVIOR OF HOSPITALIZED
    PATIENTS: A STUDY OF MEXICAN-AMERI CAN AND ANGLO-AMERICAN
    PATIENTS". ARCHIVES OF GENERAL PSYCHIATRY, VOL. 12
    (MARCH 1966), PP. 267-277 (PY).

MEIER, HAROLD C. THE ORAL COMMUNICATION OF HEALTH-DISEASE
    BELIEFS IN A SERIAL REPRODUCTION EXPERIEMENT.
    UNIVERSITY OF COLORADO, PHD. DISSERTATION (1963) (AN
    SO).

MERCER. "IMPRINTS CULTURE PERSONALITIES (PY*).

MIGRANT HEALTH PROJECT. MIGRANTS: WHERE WHEN: GEOGRAPHIC
    (SI*).

MOORE, FARAONE. "HABLA USTED ESPANOL?". NURSING OUTLOOK,
    VOL. 10 (APRIL 1962), PP. 250-252 (ED).

MORALES. "MENTAL PUBLIC HEALTH ISSUES: (PY*).

MOTT, FREDERICK D. "HEALTH SERVICES FOR MIGRANT FARM
    FAMILIES". AMERICAN JOURNAL OF PUBLIC HEALTH, VOL.
    35 (APR., 1945), PP. 308-314 (SI).

MOUSTAFA, A. TAHER, AND WEISS, GERTRUDE. HEALTH STATUS
    AND PRACTICES OF MEXICAN AMERICANS. LOS ANGELES,
    MEXICAN-AMERICAN STUDY PROJECT, DIVISION OF RESEARCH,
    GRADUATE SCHOOL OF BUSINESS ADMINISTRATION, UNIVERSITY
    OF CALIFORNIA AT LOS ANGELES, 1968 (EC).

MULKY, CARL. "PROGRAM FOR TUBERCULOSIS CONTROL AMONG
    SPANISH-SPEAKING PEOPLE". NEW MEXICO HEALTH OFFICER,
    VOL. 2 (SEPT. 1943), PP. 13-16.

MULKY, CARL. "TUBERCULOSIS IN THE SPANISH POPULATION OF
    NEW MEXICO". SOUTHWESTERN MEDICINE, VOL. 25 (1941),
    PP. 165-166.

NALL. "SOCIAL CULTURAL FACTORS RESPONSES (SO*).

NEUMEYER. PESTICIDES (LW*).

NICHOLS, ANDREW W. A PROPOSED MANNER OF INTRODUCTION OF
    MORE ADEQUATE MEDICAL CARE TO A SEMI-ISOLATED
    MEXICAN-INDIAN COMMUNITY. STANFORD, CALIFORNIA:
    STANFORD UNIVERSITY, 1961.

OPLER. CULTURE MENTAL HEALTH; CROSSCULTURAL (AN*).

OWEN, ROGER CORY. THE INDIANS OF SANTA CATARINA, BAJA,
    CALIFORNIA NORTE, MEXICO: CONCEP TS OF DISEASE AND
    CURING. UNIVERSITY OF CALIFORNIA, LOS ANGELES, PHD.
    DISSERTATION (1962) (AN).

PARSONS, TALCOTT. DEFINITIONS OF HEALTH AND ILLNESS IN
    THE LIGHT OF AMERICAN VALUES AND SOCIAL STRUCTURE.
    GLENCOE: THE FREE PRESS, 1958.

PATRIC.   STUDY HOUSING SOCIAL CONDITIONS   (SO*).

PAUL, BENJAMIN DAVID. HEALTH, CULTURE AND COMMUNITY: CASE
    STUDIES OF PUBLIC REACTIONS TO HEALTH PROGRAMS EDITED
    BY BENJAMIN D. PAUL WITH THE COLLABORATION OF WALTER
    B. MILLER.   NEW YORK: RUSSELL SAGE FOUNDATION, 1955
    (SO).

PETERS. "NEW MEXICO MEDICINE" (AN*).

PIJOAN, MICHAEL. "FOOD AVAILABILITY AND SOCIAL FUNCTION".
    NEW MEXICO QUARTERLY REVIEW, VOL. 12 (NOVEMBER
    1942), PP. 419-423 (SO).

PIJOAN, MICHAEL. NUTRITION AND CERTAIN RELATED FACTORS
    OF SPANISH-AMERICANS IN NORTHERN COLORADO.   DENVER,
    COLORADO: ROCKY MOUNTAIN COUNCIL ON INTER-AMERICAN
    AFFAIRS, 1943 (SO).

PIJOAN, MICHEL. CERTAIN FACTORS INVOLVED IN THE STRUGGLE
    AGAINST MALNUTRITION AND DISEASE, WITH SPECIAL
    REFERENCE TO THE SOUTHWEST OF THE UNITED STATES AND
    LATIN AMERICA.   UNIVERSITY OF NEW MEXICO PRESS,
    ALBUQUERQUE, (1943). SCHOOL OF INTER-AMERICAN AFFAIRS,
    SHORT PAPERS, NUMBER 7 (SO).

POEK, K. "SOCIAL AND CULTURAL FACTORS IN MENTAL ILLNESS
    OF MIGRANT WORKERS".   WORLD MEDICAL JOURNAL, VOL.
    11 (MARCH 1964), PP. 75-76 (SI).

POND, M. ALLEN. "INTERRELATIONSHIP OF POVERTY AND
    DISEASE".   PUBLIC HEALTH REPORTS,   (NOVEMBER 1961),
    PP. 967-974.

RAHM, HAROLD J. AND WEBER, J. ROBERT. OFFICE IN THE ALLEY:
    REPORT ON A PROJECT WITH GANG YOUNGSTERS.   AUSTIN,
    TEXAS: HOGG FOUNDATION FOR MENTAL HEALTH, UNIVERSITY
    OF TEXAS PRINTING DIVISION, 1958.

ROBERTSON, LEON S. "ANTICIPATED ACCEPTANCE OF NEIGHBORHOOD
    HEALTH CLINICS BY THE URBAN POOR".   AMERICAN MEDICAL
    ASSOCIATION JOURNAL,   (SEPTEMBER 16, 1968),
    PP. 815-818 (SO).

ROBINSON, NORMA J. "THE PUBLIC HEALTH PROGRAM FOR MEXICAN
    MIGRANT WORKERS".   PUBLIC HEALTH REPORTS, VOL. 73
    (SEPTEMBER 1958), PP. 851-860 (SI).

ROHRMAN.   LAW PESTICIDES; PRESENT FUTURE   (LW*).

ROMANO-V.   "CHARISMATIC MEDICINE, FOLK HEALING   (AN*).

ROSENBLATT, JOAN BARBOZA SHUFRO. MEASURE OF IMPULSE
    CONTROL AS RELATED TO FIRST GRADE CHILDREN'S SOCIO—ECONMIC
    CLASS AND ETHNIC GROUP BACKGRCUND.   TUCSON, UNIVERSITY
    OF ARIZONA, PHD. DISSERTATION (1966) (AN).

RUBEL.   "A GUIDE FIELDWORKERS FOLKLORE (AN*).

RUBEL.   "ANALISIS FUNCIONAL EFECTOS NEGATIVOS (AN*).

RUBEL.   "CONCEPTS DISEASE MEXICAN—AMERICAN (AN*).

RUBEL.   "HEALTH MEXICAN—AMERICAN CULTURE: (AN*).

RUBEL.   CONCEPTS DISEASE MEXICAN—AMERICAN (AN*).

RUBEL.   MAGICAL FRIGHT ILLNESS (AN*).

RUBEL.   U. S. CO-ARRANGER, ANTHROPOLOGY (AN*).

RUBEL.   "WORKING CLASS MEXICAN PSYCHIATRIC (AN*).

SAMORA.   "EDUCATICN SOCIAL CHANGE LATIN (SO*).

SAMORA.   A MECICAL CARE PROGRAM COLORADO (SO*).

SAMORA.   MEDICAL VOCABULARY KNCWLEDGE (SO*).

SAMORA.   MEDICAL VOCABULARY KNOWLEDGE (AN*).

SAMORA.   "CONCEPTIONS HEALTH DISEASE AMONG (SO*).

SAMORA.   "THE SOCIAL SCIENTIST AS RESEARCHER (SO*).

SAMORA.   "MEDICAL VOCABULARY KNOWLEDGE (SO*).

SAMORA, JULIAN, SAUNDERS, L. AND LARSCN, R. F. "KNOWLEDGE
    ABOUT SPECIFIC DISEASES IN FOUR SELECTED SAMPLES".
    JOURNAL OF HEALTH ANC HUMAN BEHAVIOR, VOL. 3 (FALL
    1962) (SO).

SAUERWEIN, MARIA THANOPOULOU. S. SERUM PROTEIN AND
    LIPOPROTEIN COMPONENTS OF MEXICAN AMERICAN WOMEN
    LIVING IN TUCSON, ARIZONA.   TUCSON: UNIVERSITY OF
    ARIZONA, MASTER'S THESIS (1970) (SO).

SAUNDERS.   "FOLK MEDICINE MEDICAL PRACTICE" (ED*).

SAUNDERS.   HEALING WAYS SPANISH SOUTHWEST (ED*).

SAUNDERS.   ANGLOS SPANISH-SPEAKING: CONTRASTS (AN*).

SAUNDERS.   CULTURAL DIFFERENCES MEDICALCARE; (ED*).

SAUNDERS.   CULTURAL FACTORS AFFECTING PUBLIC (ED*).

SAUNDERS.   MEDICAL CARE PROGRAM COLCRADO   (ED*).

SCHAUPP, KARL L.   "MEDICAL CARE OF MIGRATORY AGRICULTURAL
     WORKERS".   CALIFORNIA AND WESTERN MEDICINE, VOL. 60
     (MAY 1944), PP. 1-12.

SCHOLES, REV. WILLIAM E.   STILL 'GRAPES OF WRATH' FOR
     MIGRANTS.   BULLETIN NATIONAL TUBERCULOSIS AND
     RESPIRATORY DISEASE ASSOCIATION.

SCHULMAN, SAM.   "RURAL HEALTH WAYS IN NEW MEXICO".   IN
     VERA RUBEN (ED), CULTURE, SOCIETY AND HEALTH, ANNALS
     OF THE NEW YORK ACADEMY OF SCIENCES, VOL. 84
     (DECEMBER 1960), PP. 950-959 (AN HN).

SCHULMAN, SAM; AND SMITH, ANNE M.   "THE CONCEPT OF 'HEALTH'
     AMONG SPANISH SPEAKING VILLAGERS OF NEW MEXICO AND
     COLORADO".   JOURNAL OF HEALTH AND HUMAN BEHAVIOR,
     VOL. A   (WINTER 1963), PP. 296-304 (AN HN).

SHAFER, JAMES, K.; HARTING, DONALD; JOHNSTON, HELEN L.
     "HEALTH NEEDS OF SEASONAL FARMWORKERS AND THEIR
     FAMILIES".   PUBLIC HEALTH REPORTS,   (JUNE 1961),
     PP. 469-474 (SI).

SHAPIRO.   "HEALTH CONDITIONS SAN ANTONIO   (SO*).

SIEGEL, EARL.   HEALTH AND DAY CARE FOR CHILDREN OF MIGRANT
     WORKERS.   PUBLIC HEALTH REPORTS,.

SILVERSTEIN.   "CULTURAL FACTORS INTELLECTUAL   (PY*).

SILVERSTEIN, A. B.; SHOTWELL, ANNA; FISHER, GARMY M.
     "CULTURAL FACTORS IN THE INTELLECTUAL FUNCTIONING OF
     THE METALLY RETARDED MEXICAN MAID".   AMERICAN JOURNAL
     OF MENTAL DEFICIENCY, VOL. 67   (1962), PP. 396-401
     (PY).

SMITH, HELEN PERRIN.   HEALTH AND NUTRITION OF THE MEXICAN
     INFANT AND PRESCHOOL CHILD.   UNIVERSITY OF TEXAS AT
     AUSTIN, MASTER'S THESIS (1930) (ED).

SMITH, HOWARD E.   PROCEEDINGS OF THE U. S. - MEXICO BORDER
     HEALTH CONFERENCE, CIUDAD JUAREZ, CHIHUAHUA, MEXICO,
     AND EL PASO, TEXAS, MAY 30-JUNE 1, 1944.   MEXICO
     BORDER HEALTH CONFERENCE, CIUDAD JUAREZ, CHIHUAHUA,
     MEXICO AND EL PASO, TEXAS, MAY 30-JUNE 1, 1944..

SMITH, R. M.   "THE PROBLEM OF TUBERCULOSIS AMONG MEXICANS
     IN THE U. S.".   TRANSACTIONS OF THE NATIONAL
     TUBERCULOSIS ASSOCIATION, VOL. 34   (1938), PP. 247-253.

SPIELBERG.   SOCIAL CULTURAL CONFIGURATIONS   (AN*).

STEINER, PAUL E. CANCER: RACE AND GEOGRAPHY; SOME
    ETIOLOGICAL, ENVIRONMENTAL, ETHNOLOGICAL, EPIDEMIOLOGICAL
    AND STATISTICAL ASPECTS IN CAUCASOIDS, MONGOLOIDS,
    NEGROIDS AND MEXICANS. BALTIMORE: WILLIAMS AND
    WILKENS, 1954 (AN).

STOKER, DAVID HERBERT. HA COMPARISON OF THE SYMPTOMATOLOGY
    OF SPANISH AMERICAN AND ANGLO AMERICAN HOSPITAL
    PATIENTS. TUCSON: UNIVERSITY OF ARIZONA, MASTER'S
    THESIS (1963) (SO).

TEXAS STATE DEPARTMENT OF HEALTH. LATIN-AMERICAN HEALTH
    PROBLEMS IN TEXAS. AUSTIN, TEXAS: TEXAS STATE
    DEPARTMENT OF HEALTH, 1940.

TEXAS STATE DEPARTMENT OF HEALTH. TEXAS STATE DEPARTMENT
    OF HEALTH MIGRANT PROJECT. AUSTIN, TEXAS: TEXAS
    STATE DEPARTMENT OF HEALTH, 1966 (SI).

TEXAS STATE DEPARTMENT OF HEALTH, DIVISION OF MATERNAL AND
    CHILD HEALTH. THE LATIN-AMERICAN HEALTH PROBLEM IN
    TEXAS. AUSTIN, TEXAS: TEXAS STATE DEPARTMENT
    OF HEALTH, AUGUST, 1940.

TEXAS STATE DEPARTMENT OF HEALTH, DIVISION OF MATERNAL AND
    CHILD HEALTH. THE LATIN-AMERICAN HEALTH PROBLEM IN
    TEXAS. AUSTIN, TEXAS: TEXAS STATE DEPARTMENT
    OF HEALTH, AUGUST, 1940 (SI).

TEXAS STATE DEPARTMENT OF HEALTH, DIVISION OF MENTAL
    HEALTH. A STUDY OF THE MENTAL HEALTH PROBLEMS
    OF MEXICAN-AMERICAN RESIDENTS. AUSTIN, TEXAS: TEXAS
    STATE DEPARTMENT OF HEALTH, 1961.

TEXAS STATE EMPLOYMENT SERVICE. ORGINS AND PROBLEMS OF
    TEXAS MIGRATORY FARM LABOR. AUSTIN, TEXAS: TEXAS
    STATE EMPLOYMENT SERVICE, 1940 (SI).

THOMPSON, EDYTH T. A STATISTICAL STUDY OF SICKNESS AMONG
    MEXICANS IN THE LAS ANGELES HOSPITAL. CALIFORNIA
    STATE BOARD OF HEALTH, 1925.

THOMPSON, EDYTHE TATE. PUBLIC HEALTH AMONG THE MEXICANS.
    CLAREMONT, CALIFORNIA: POMONA COLLEGE, 1928.

THOMPSON, EDYTHE TATE. SUMMARY OF MEXICAN CASES WHERE
    TUBERCULOSIS IS A FACTOR. IN THE LOS ANGELES
    HOSPITAL: CALIFORNIA STATE BOARD OF HEALTH, 1925.

THOMPSON, EDYTHE TATE. SURVEY OF MEXICAN CASES WHERE
    TUBERCULOSIS IS A PROBLEM. CALIFORNIA STATE BOARD
    OF HEALTH, 1926.

THOMPSON, EDYTHE, T. A STATISTICAL STUDY OF SICKNESS AMONG
    MEXICANS IN THE LOS ANGELES HOSPITAL. IN THE LOS
    ANGELES HOSITAL: CALIFORNIA STATE BOARD OF HEALTH,
    1925.

TODD. DOCTOR CALIFORNIA TRAIL (HC*).

U. S. PESTICIDE REVIEW 1968 (LW*).

U. S. REPORT PESTICIDES RELATED ACTIVITIES--1968 (LW*).

U. S. ORGANIZATION EFFORTS MEXICANAGRICULTURAL (LW*).

U. S. "AMERICAN JOURNAL NURSING" (LW*).

U. S. USE HEALTH AIDES MIGRANT HEALTH (LW*).

U. S. HEALTH SERVICES MIGRATORY SEASONAL (SI*).

U. S. HOUSE. "APPROPRIATIONS FOR DEPARTMENT OF HEALTH,
    EDUCATION AND WELFARE. MAY 27, JUNE 2-5, 8-12, 1970".
    INCLUDES SMALL HEALTH GROUP BUILDS BIG SUCCESS IN THE
    SOUTHWEST, (1970) (ED).

U. S. PUBLIC HEALTH SERVICE. PUBLIC HEALTH SURVEY OF SAN
    ANTONIO, TEXAS, WITH PARTICULAR REGARD TO TUBERCULOSIS
    AND VENEREAL DISEASE CONTROL. U. S. PUBLIC HEALTH
    SERVICE (SO).

U. S. MIGRANT HEALTH PROGRAM: CURRENT (LW*).

U. S. MIGRANT HEALTH SERVICES. HEARINGS (LW*).

U. S. MIGRANT HEALTH SERVICES. HEARINGS (LW*).

U. S. MIGRANT LABOR (LW*).

U. S. MIGRANT SEASONAL FARMWORKER POWERLESS (LW*).

U. S. NATIONAL NUTRITION SURVEY, PART (LW*).

U. S. PROBLEMS PROSPECTS (LW*).

U. S. AVAILABILITY USEFULNESS FEDERAL (LW*).

WHITE HOUSE CONFERENCE ON CHILD HEALTH AND PROTECTION.
    CHILD HEALTH PROTECTION. WHITE HOUSE CONFERENCE ON
    CHILD HEALTH AND PROTECTION, EDUCATION AND TEACHING.

WHITE HOUSE CONFERENCE ON CHILD HEALTH AND PROTECTION.
    MEXICAN CALIFORNIA (HC*).

WILLARD. STUDY DIET NUTRITIONAL STATUS (ED*).

WILLIAMS. CULTURAL DIFFERENCES MEDICALCARE (AN*).

WINTERS.   REPORT HEALTH NUTRITION MEXICANS   (SO*).

WITACRE.   DIET TEXAS SCHOOL CHILDREN   (ED*).

WOLFE HOMER R.   EXPOSURE WORKERS TO PESTICIDES   (LW*).

WOODS.   "CULTURAL CONDITIONING MENTAL   (AN*).

YANOVSKI.   FOOD PLANTS NORTH AMERICAN INDIANS   (HSW*).

M U S I C

(MU)

ALEXANDER, W. P. "HISPANIC FOLK MUSIC IN INTERCULTURAL
EDUCATION IN NEW MEXICO". DISSERTATION ABSTRACTS,
VOL. 22 (MARCH, 1962), P. 3217.

"ACTOS: TEATRO CAMPESINO, A THEATRICAL PART OF THE UNITED
FARMWORKERS ORGANIZING COMMITTEE". NEW YORKER, VOL.
43 (AUGUST 19, 1967), PP. 23-25 (AT).

"MEXICAN MUSICAL GAME". SOCIAL EDUCATION, VOL. 34
(OCTOBER 1970), PP. 648-649.

BROWN-WRINKLE, MARY HELEN. PITCH IMPROVEMENT IN ANGLO AND
LATIN AMERICAN CHILDREN. UNIVERSITY OF TEXAS
AT AUSTIN, MASTER'S THESIS (1950) (PY).

CAMPA, A. L. "SPANISH FOLKSONGS IN METROPOLITAN DENVER".
SOUTHERN FOLKLORE QUARTERLY, VOL. 24 (SEPTEMBER
1960), PP. 179-192.

DASILVA. MISSION MUSIC CALIFORNIA, COLLECTION (RE*).

DEERING, T. "MUSIC AS A WELDER OF RACES IN CALIFORNIA".
PLAYGROUND, VOL. 17 (JAN 1965), P. 234 (AN SO).

DOBIE, J. FRANK (ED). HAPPY HUNTING GROUND. HATBORO,
PENNSYLVANIA: FOLKLORE ASSOCIATES, 1966.

DOMINGUEZ, E. ZAPATA. OFERTA DE UNA FAMILIA: CANCIONES
DEL MOVIMIENTO CHICANO. DENVER, COLORADO: CENYILITZLI
DOMINGUEZ, 1970 (LMA).

DOWNES, OLIN; SIEGMEISTER, ELIE. A TREASURY OF AMERICAN
SONG. NEW YORK, NEW YORK: HOWELL, SOSKIN AND
COMPANY, 1940.

EL TEATRO CAMPESINO. CANCIONERO DE LA RAZA. FRESNO,
CALIFORNIA (LMA).

FELTON. COWBOY JAMBOREE, WESTERN SONGS (AN*).

FOSTER. "THE SONG WITHIN: MUSIC DISADVANTAGED (ED*).

FOSTER, FLORENCE P. "THE SONG WITHIN: MUSIC AND THE
DISADVANTAGED PRESCHOOL CHILD". YOUNG CHILDREN,
(SEPTEMBER 1965), PP. 373-376.

GONZALEZ, RAFAEL JESUS. "THE ROOTS OF MODERN MEXICAN
    MUSIC". ARIZONA QUARTERLY, VOL. 20 NO. 4 (WINTER
    1964), PP. 339-353.

HERZOG, GEORGE. RESEARCH IN PRIMITIVE AND FOLK MUSIC IN
    THE UNITED STATES. WASHINGTON, D. C., (APRIL 1936).
    AMERICAN COUNCIL OF LEARNED SOCIETIES, BULLETIN 424
    (AN).

HIPPLER, A. E. "POPULAR ART STYLES IN MARIACHI FESTIVALS".
    AMERICAN IMAGE, VOL. 26 (SUMMER 1969), PP. 167-181.

HYLAND, E. D. "USING MUSIC TO TEACH ENGLISH TO SPANISH-SPEAKING
    BEGINNER". TEXAS OUTLOOK, VOL. 29 (MAY 1945), P.
    30 (ED).

JOHNSON. EFFECTIVENESS SIGHT SINGING INSTRUCTION (ED*).

KING, GWENDOLYN. MUSICAL EXPERIENCE TO AID MEXICAN
    BILINGUAL CHILDREN IN CORRECTING SPEECH DEFECTS.
    UNIVERSITY OF ARIZONA, MASTER'S THESIS (1946) (PY
    ED).

KNOTT, S. G. "MANY SONGS, MANY DANCES: FOLK MUSIC OF THE
    UNITED STATES: CULTURAL IMPRINT OF FOREIGN COUNTRIES".
    AMERICAS, VOL. 17 (FEBRUARY 1965), PP. 27-33 (AT).

KUHNS, L. "MUSIC WITH MEXICAN CHILDREN". ARIZONA
    TEACHER, VOL. 27 (APRIL 1939), PP. 237-239 (ED).

LOS ANGELES COUNTY, CALIFORNIA. BOARD OF EDUCATION.
    MEXICAN MUSIC. LOS ANGELES COUNTY CALIFORNIA BOARD
    OF EDUCATION, 1940.

LOS ANGELES COUNTY. MEXICO: FOLK DANCES (AN*).

LUMMIS, CHARLES F. SPANISH SONGS OF OLD CALIFORNIA. LOS
    ANGELES, 1923 (AN HS).

MADRID, MIGUEL ANGEL. THE ATTITUDES OF THE SPANISH
    AMERICAN PEOPLE AS EXPRESSED IN THEIR COPLAS OR FOLK
    SONGS. COLUMBIA UNIVERSITY, PHD. DISSERTATION (MAY
    1970).

MANHEIM, HENRY AND CUMMINS, ALICE. "SELECTED MUSICAL
    TRAITS AMONG SPANISH, NEGRO AND ANGLO-AMERICAN GIRLS".
    SOCIOLOGY AND SOCIAL RESEARCH, (OCTOBER 1960), PP.
    56-65.

MARTIN, MARJORIE KATHRYN. A COMPARATIVE STUDY OF CLASS
    AND INDIVIDUAL INSTRUCTION IN LATIN AND ANGLO-AMERICAN
    MUSIC CLASSES. UNIVERSITY OF TEXAS AT AUSTIN,
    MASTER'S THESIS (1948).

MENDOZA, VICENTE T. EL ROMANCE ESPANOL Y EL CORRIDO
    MEJICANO. MEXICO, 1939 (AN).

MILLER.   SONGS SIERRA   (LI*).

MILLER.   "EL VAQUERO"   (LI*).

MILLER, W.   "LATIN AMERICAN CHILD AND MUSIC".   TEXAS
     OUTLOOK, VOL. 31 (OCTOBER 1947), P. 26 (PY   SO).

MOORE, ETHEL AND CHAUNCEY O.   BALLADS AND FOLK SONGS OF
     THE SOUTHWEST: MORE THAN 600 TITLES, MELODIESAND
     TEXTS COLLECTED IN OLKLAHOMA.   NORMAN OKLAHOMA:
     UNIVERSITY OF OKLAHOMA PRESS, 1964 (AN   HSW).

MOORE, MILBURN R.   "SPANISH LANGUAGE FESTIVALS IN THE LAND
     OF ENCHANTMENT".   CHURCH MUSICIAN, VOL. 12 NO. 1
     (MAY 1967).

NOLL, ARTHUR HOWARD.   "LIPPINCOTT'S MONTHLY MAGAZINE".
     LIPPINCOTT'S MONTHLY MAGAZINE, VOL. 60 , PP. 424-28
     (HM).

REUTHINGER, HORTENSE.   A COMPARATIVE STUDY OF TWO METHODS
     OF THEORY INSTRUCTION FOR SEVENTH GRADE LATIN AMERICAN
     GIRLS.   UNIVERSITY OF TEXAS AT AUSTIN, MASTER'S
     THESIS (1956) (ED).

ROBB, J. D.   "THE SOURCES OF A NEW MEXICAN FOLKSONG".
     NEW MEXICO FOLKLORE RECORD, VOL. 5 (1950-1951), PP.
     9-16 (AN   HN).

ROBB, JOHN DONALD.   HISPANIC FOLKSONGS OF NEW MEXICO.
     ALBUQUERQUE: UNIVERSITY OF NEW MEXICO PRESS, 1954 (AN
     HN).

SIMMONS, MERLE E.   THE MEXICAN CORRIDO.   BLOOMINGTON,
     INDIANA: INDIANA UNIVERSITY PRESS, 1969.

SPELL.   MUSICAL EDUCATION NORTH AMERICA   (ED*).

STEVENSON, ROBERT MURRELL.   MUSIC IN MEXICO, A HISTORICAL
     SURVEY.   NEW YORK: CORWELL, 1952 (HM).

STEVENSON, ROBERT MURRELL.   SPANISH CATHEDRAL MUSIC IN THE
     GOLDEN AGE.   BERKELEY: UNIVERSITY OF CALIFORNIA
     PRESS, 1961 (HM).

STOHL, MRS. DARTHULA DAVIS.   A STUDY TREATING THE TEACHING
     OF LANGUAGE SKILLS THROUGH MUSIC TO SPANISH-SPEAKING
     CHILDREN.   UNIVERSITY OF TEXAS AT AUSTIN, MASTER'S
     THESIS (1959) (ED).

TATA.   COMPARATIVE STUDY MEASUREMENT (PY*).

TAYLOR.   MUSICAL ABILITIES SPANISH-AMERICAN   (PY*).

TEXAS.   MUSIC ACTIVITIES LATIN AMERICAN   (ED*).

THORP.   SONGS COWBOYS   (AN*).

TINKER.   CORRIDOS CALAVERAS   (AN*).

TUCKER.   "MEXICAN FOLK-DANCING CLASS JUNIOR   (AN*).

VASCO, EUSEBIO. TREINTA MIL CANTARES POPULARES.
     VALDEPENAS, 1930 (HSA).

WILLIAMS, GLADYS. ORCHESTRAS AND BANDS, EL PASO MUSIC,
     1880-1960.   TEXAS WESTERN COLLEGE, MASTER'S THESIS
     (1960) (HT).

WILLIAMS.   PIONEER SONGSTER   (HSW*).

WORKS PROJECTS ADMINISTRATION.   SPANISH-AMERICAN SONG GAME
     BOOK   (ED*).

YURCHINCO, H. "SURVIVALS OF PRE-HISPANIC MUSIC IN
     NEW MEXICO".   JOURNAL OF THE INTERNATIONAL FOLK MUSIC
     COUNCIL, VOL. 15 (1963), PP. 15-18.

J O U R N A L I S M

(NP)

ALAMO MESSENGER. "CONSECRATION AGENDA". SAN ANTONIO:
ALAMO MESSENGER, NO. 14 (APRIL 3, 1970), P. 1.

EVENING PICAYUNE. DIARIO DE SAN FRANCISCO, 1850.

LADO. NEWSPAPER.

SOL DE AZTLAN. LANSING, MICHIGAN.

LA LUZ. NEWSPAPER.

THE VALLEY OF THE DAMNED. LAREDO, TEXAS.

ANONYAMOUS. IDEAL. COACHELLA, CALIFORNIA.

ALTA CALIFORNIA (DIARIO). SAN FRANCISCO, 1849.

AMERICAN AGRICULTURIST (EC*).

BASTA YA. SAN FRANCISCO, CALIFORNIA.

BRONCE. OAKLAND, CALIFORNIA, 1969-.

CALIFORNIA STAR. SAN FRANCISCO, CALIFORNIA: CALIFORNIA
STAR, 1847-48.

CALIFORNIAN. MONTERREY, CALIFORNIA, 1846-48.

CARTA EDITORIAL. LOS ANGELES, CALIFORNIA.

CARTA EDITORIAL. LOS ANGELES, CALIFORNIA.

ENTRELINEAS. KANSAS CITY, MISSOURI, (LMA).

HOY. PHARR, TEXAS.

INFERNO. SAN ANTONIO, TEXAS.

INSIDE EASTSIDE. LOS ANGELES, CALIFORNIA.

NEW MISSION NUEVA. NEWSPAPER.

NOSOTROS. NEWSPAPER-EL PASO, TEXAS.

NOTICIAS. NEWSPAPER-MEXICO.

NOTICIERO HISPANO.   NEWSPAPER GARY, INDIANA.

NUESTRA LUCHA.   NEWSPAPER-DEL REY BEACH, FLORIDA.

PADRES.   NEWSPAPER-SAN ANTONIO, TEXAS.

REVISTA HISPANO-AMERICANA DE LOS ANGELES.   LOS ANGELES,
     1889-1892.

SIEMPRE.   LOS ANGELES, CALIFORNIA.

TIMES OF THE AMERICAS.   CORAL GABLES, FLORIDA.

VIVA.   KANSAS CITY, KANSAS.

YA MERO.   MC ALLEN, TEXAS.

LA CAUSA.   LOS ANGELES, CALIFORNIA.

EL DIARIO.   LA PRESNA.   NEW YORK, NEW YORK.

THE FORUMEER.   SAN JOSE, CALIFORNIA.

EL GALLO.   NEWSPAPER.

EL GRITO DEL NORTE.   ESPANOLA, NEW MEXICO.

LA GUARDIA.   NEWSPAPER.

EL HISPANO.   SACRAMENTO, CALIFORNIA.

EL HISPANO.   SACRAMENTO, CALIFORNIA.

EL HISPANOAMERICANO.   SACRAMENTO, CALIFORNIA.

EL INFORMADOR.   CHICAGO, ILLINOIS.

EL INSURGENTE.   LAREDO, TEXAS.

LA JUSTICIA MAYORISTA M.A.Y.O..   SAN FELIPE DEL RIO TEJAS,.

THE MEXICAN REVIEW.   WASHINGTON, D.C., 1916-1920 (HM).

LA NUEVA RAZA.   NEWSPAPER-SAN ANTONIO, TEXAS.

LA OPINION.   NEWSPAPER-LOS ANGELES, CALIFORNIA.

EL PAISANO.   NEWSPAPER-TOLLESON, ARIZONA.

LA PALABRA.   NEWSPAPER-STEILACOOM, WASHINGTON.

EL PAPEL.   NEWSPAPER-ALBUQUERQUE, NEW MEXICO.

THE PEOPLES VOICE.   NEWSPAPER-KANSAS CITY, MISSOURI.

EL POCHO CHE.   NEWSPAPER.

EL POPO.   NEWSPAPER.

LA PRENSA.   REYNOSA, TAMAULIPAS (MEXICO).

LA PRENSA LIBRE.   BERKELEY, CALIFORNIA.

LA RAZA.   LOS ANGELES, CALIFORNIA.

LA RAZA.   LOS ANGELES, CALIFORNIA.

LA RAZA MAGAZINE.   LOS ANGELES, CALIFORNIA.

EL RENACIMIENTO.   LANSING, MICHIGAN.

EL TIEMPO.   REYNOSA, TAMAULIPAS (MEXICO).

LA VERDAD.   SAN DIEGO, CALIFORNIA.

LA VIDA NUEVA.   CHICANO PRESS ASSOCIATION, LOS ANGELES,
     CALIFORNIA.

LA VOZ.   LOS ANGELES, CALIFORNIA.

LA VOZ CHICANA.   SAN JUAN, TEXAS.

LA VOZ DE AZTLAN.   AZTLAN, CALIFORNIA.

LA VOZ DE LOS LLANOS.   LUBBOCK, TEXAS.

LA VOZ MEXICANA.   WAUTOMA, WISCONSIN.

EL YAQUI.   HOUSTON, TEXAS.

CHARNO, STEPHEN M. (COMP.).   LATIN-AMERICAN NEWSPAPERS IN
     U. S. LIBRARIES.   AUSTIN AND LONDON: UNIVERSITY OF
     TEXAS PRESS, 1969.

CHICANO DEPARTMENT, SAN DIEGO STATE COLLEGE.   EL LENO.
     SAN DIEGO, CALIFORNIA: EL LENO PUBLICATIONS.

CHICANO STUDENT MOVEMENT.   CHICANO STUDENT MOVEMENT.   NEWSPAPER.

CHICANO TIMES.   CHICANO TIMES.   SAN FRANCISCO, CALIFORNIA:
     CHICANO PRESS ASSOCIATION,.

COLEGIO DE MEXICO.   HISTORIA MEXICANA: REVISTA TRIMESTRAL
     (HM*).

CON SAFOS.   CON SAFOS: REFLECTIONS OF LIFE IN THE BARRIO.
     MAGAZINE.

CORAJE.   CORAJE.   NEWSPAPER.

CORONADO MAGAZINE. CORONADO MAGAZINE.   NEW MEXICO, 1940.

DAUGLAS A. WILLIAMS, (ED.).   THE TEXAS CATHOLIC HEARLD.
     POST OFFICE BOX 3944, BEAUMONT, TEXAS 77704.

EL AZTECA. EL AZTECA.   LINGSVILLE, TEXAS,.

EL CHICANO. EL CHICANO.   SAN BERNARDINO, CALIFORNIA,.

EL GOLPE AVIS. EL GOLPE AVIS.   NEWSPAPER.

EL GRITO: JOURNAL OF CONTEMPORARY MEXICAN AMERICAN
     THOUGHT. EL GRITO: JOURNAL OF CONTEMPORARY MEXICAN
     AMERICAN THOUGHT.   BERKELEY, CALIFORNIA,.

EL MACHETE. EL MACHETE.   NEWSPAPER.

EL MAGAZIN. EL MAGAZIN.   NEWSPAPER.

EL MALCRIADO. EL MALCRIADO.   NEWSPAPER.

EL MANANA. EL MANANA.   NEWSPAPER.

EL MESTIZO. EL MESTIZO.   SALT LAKE CITY, UTAH,.

EL PASO TIMES. "EL PASO TIMES".   MIDSUMMER TRADE EDITION,
     (AUG 1887).

EL REBOZO. EL REBOZO.   SAN ANTONIO, TEXAS.

FOLEY, DORIS. THE DIVINE ECCENTRIC, LOLA MONTEZ AND THE
     NEWSPAPERS.   LOS ANGELES, CALIFORNIA: WESTERNLORE
     PRESS, PUBLISHERS, 1969 (SO).

FRIERSON, EDWARD BERNARD. EXCELSIOR OF MEXICO CITY: STUDY
     OF A SPANISH-AMERICAN NEWSPAPER.   UNIVERSITY OF TEXAS
     AT AUSTIN, MASTER'S THESIS (1955) (HM).

GEORGE H. MONAHAN <EDITOR>. THE VOICE.   MIAMI, FLORIDA.

GRAFICA. GRAFICA.   NEWSPAPER.

HOY. M. A. Y. O..   MC ALLEN, TEXAS.

KEMBLE.   HISTORY CALIFORNIA NEWSPAPERS (B*).

KENNEDY, DIANE. "THE CHICANO PRESS".   MISSOURI LIBRARY
     QUARTERLY,   (SEPTEMBER 1969), PP. 221-224.

LA REVOLUCION. LA REVOLUCION.   UVALDE, TEXAS.

LEAVENWORTH PENITENTIARY. AZTLAN.   LEAVENWORTH, KANSAS:
     LEAVENWORTH PENITENTIARY,.

LOS ANGELES STAR.   ESTRELLA CLAMOR PUBLICO (HC*).

LOS ANGELES TIMES.   RUBEN SALAZAR: REPRINTS   (HC*).

LUTRELL, ESTELLE.   NEWSPAPER AND PERIODICALS OF ARIZONA,
     1859-1911.   NEWSPAPERS (HA).

MAC CURDY.   HISTORY BIBLIOGRAPHY SPANISH-LANGUAGE   (B*).

MAC CURDY.   HISTORY BIBLIOGRAPHY SPANISHLANGUAGE   (B*).

MATHIESEN, L. T. (ED.).   WEST TEXAS REGISTER.   AMARILLO,
     TEXAS.

MC GLOIN, PETER M. ED.   ARIZCNA REGISTER.   TUCSON, ARIZONA,.

MOUTON, REV. RICHARD(EDS.).   "SOUTHWEST LOUISIANA REGISTER".
     NEWSPAPER, VOL.
     SOUTHWEST REVIEW   NO. 14 (MARCH   1967), P. 1929.

NATION.   TENTATIVE CHECK LIST ARIZONAPERIODICALS   (B*).

NEVADA REGISTER.   NEVADA REGISTER.   NEWSPAPER.

NOSOTROS.   LA VOZ DE LA COMUNIDAD HISPANOAMERICANA
     DE DETROIT.   LA VOZ DE LA COMUNIDAD HISPANOAMERICANA
     DE DETROIT.   NEWSPAPER.

NOTICIAS.   SEMANARIO DEL MEDIO OESTE.   SPANISH AND ENGLISH
     NEWSPAPER.   SEMANARIO DEL MEDIO OESTE.   NEWSPAPER-CHICAGO,
     ILLINOIS.

PAN AMERICAN UNION.   AMERICAS.   WASHINGTON, D. C..,.

REGENERACION.   REGENERACION.   LOS ANGELES, CALIFORNIA.

REV. DAVID P. PAGE (ED.).   THE FLORIDA CATHOLIC.   ORLANDO,
     FLORIDA.

REV. DONNAN HERBE OFM, <EDITOR>.   THE VOICE OF THE
     SOUTHWEST.   LUMBERTON, NEW MEXICO.

REV. JOH L. FOS, (ED).   THE TEXAS CATHOLIC HERALD.   1700
     SAN JACINTO, HOUSTON, TEXAS 77002.

REV. MSGR. MARTIN B. MOLLOY, (ED.).   TEXAS CATHOLIC HEARLD.
     1212 GAUDALUPE, AUSTIN, TEXAS 78701.

REV. THOMAS H. SEIBT.   TEXAS CONCHO REGISTER.   116
     S. OAKES, SAN ANGELO, TEXAS 76901.

REXROAT, RUTH.   THE DIARIO DE MEXICO: FIRST DAILY OF NEW
     SPAIN: ITS LITERATURE.   UNIVERSITY OF TEXAS AT
     AUSTIN, PHD.   DISSERTATION (1956).

RICE.   EARLY HISTORY LOS ANGELES STAR (HC*).

RIGLER.   HISTORY SAN ANTONIO EXPRESS (HT*).

SERA, JAMES R. ED. THE REGISTER, DENVER EDITION.   DENVER,
    COLORADO.

SHERRY, GERARD E. (ED.).   CENTRAL CALIFORNIA REGISTER.
    FRESNO, CALIFORNIA,.

STEVE LANDREGAN (ED.).   THE TEXAS CATHOLIC.   3915 LEMMON
    AVENUE, DALLAS, TEXAS 75219.

STRATTON.   TERRITORIAL PRESS NEW MEXICO,   (HN*).

TARACENA, ALFONSO. ED TAQUE.   NEWSPAPER.

TEXAS STATE HISTORICAL SOCIETY.   SOUTHWESTERN HISTORICAL
    QUARTERLY (HT*).

P O L I T I C A L   S C I E N C E

(PL)

ACUNA.   CULTURES CONFLICT, PROBLEMS MEXICAN—AMERICANS
   (AN*).

ACUNA.   OCCUPIED AMERICA: CHICANO STRUGGLE (AN*).

ADAIR.   "CESAR CHAVEZS BIGGEST BATTLE" (EC*).

ADAMS, HENRY. SELECTED LETTERS OF HENRY ADAMS.   NEW YORK:
   FARRAR, STRAUS AND YOUNG, INC9, 1951 (HUS).

ADAMS.   SELECTED WRITINGS..EDITED WITH   (HUS*).

AGUILAR, ALONSO. PAN—AMERICANISM FROM MONROE TO THE
   PRESENT.   NEW YORK: MONTHLY REVIEW PRESS, 1968.

ALEXANDER, R. J. LATIN AMERICAN POLITICS AND GOVERNMENT.
   NEW YORK: HARPER AND ROW, 1965.

ALISKY.   "THE MEXICAN—AMERICANS MAKE THEMSELVES (SO*).

ALMAGUER.   "TOWARD STUDY CHICANO COLONIALISM" (EC*).

ALVARADO, ROGER. LA RAZA: WHY A CHICANO PARTY?.   NEW
   YORK: PATHFINDER PRESS, INC,.

AMERICAN BIBLICGRAPHICAL CENTER. POLITICAL SCIENCE,
   AMERICA: HISTORY AND LIFE AND HISTORICAL ABSTRACTS.
   SANTA BARBARA, CALIFORNIA: ABC—CLIO PRESS, INC., 1971
   (HC).

ANDERSON, CHARLES W. POLITICS AND ECONOMIC CHANGE IN LATIN
   AMERICA.   PRINCETON: D. VAN NOSTRAND, 1967.

"SPANISH SURNAME WAR DEAD —— VIETNAM".   EL GRITO, VOL.
   3 NO. 1 (FALL 1969), PP. 6—31 (SO EC).

"SPANISH AMERICANS IN POLITICS".   CONGRESSIONAL QUARTERLY
   WEEKLY REPORT,   (JUNE 23, 1961), PP. 1042—1043.

"SPANISH AMERICANS IN POLITICS".   CONGRESSIONAL QUARTERLY
   WEEKLY REPORT,   (JUNE 23, 1961), PP. 1042—1043 (LW).

EXECUTIVE COMMITTEE.   PHOENIX, ARIZONA (SQ).

SPANISH AMERICANS: THE NEW MILITANTS.   EDITORIAL RESEARCH
   REPORTS, 1970 (SO).

SPANISH SPEAKING AMERICANS IN THE WAR: THE SOUTHWEST.
    WASHINGTON: COORDINATOR OF INTER-AMERICAN AFFAIRS,
    (1943) (SO).

"AGONY TIERRA AMARILLA" (EC*).

"CRUSADE AGAINST GRINGOS: FEDERAL   (EC*).

"FINDERS KEEPERS; ATTEMPT BY GROUP OF SPANISH-AMERICANS
    TO SEIZE LAND INNEW MEXICO". NEWSWEEK, VOL.
    68 (NOVEMBER 7, 1966), P. 40 (ED).

"MEXICAN AMERICAN LEGAL DEFENSE" (LW*).

"MEXICO UNITED STATES IMMIGRATION (EC*).

"MEXICO-UNITED STATES FARM LABOR (EC*).

"MIGRANT LABOR - HUMAN PROBLEM: (SO*).

"MIGRANT LABOR AGREEMENT WITH (EC*).

"MINORITIES: CRUSADE AGAINST GRINGOS". NEWSWEEK,
    (JANUARY 3, 1966), PP. 17-18 (SO EC).

"MOVEMENT AMONG SOUTHWESTS MEXICAN-AMERICANS" (SO*).

"POLITICAL SOCIALIZATION: ITS ROLE IN THE POLITICAL
    PROCESS". THE ANNALS OF THE AMERICAN ACADEMY
    OF POLITICAL AND SOCIAL SCIENCES, VOL. 361 (SEPTEMBER
    1965).

"RIGHTS FOR FARM WORKERS". AMERICA, VOL. 120 (APRIL 26,
    1969), PP. 492-493 (EC SI).

"SENATE UNIT AIRS MIGRANT DISPUTE". BROADCASTING, VOL.
    79 (AUGUST 3, 1970), PP. 42-43 (SI).

"TEXAS BAPTISTS WARNES RISING (EC*).

"THE MEXICAN-AMERICANS: THEIR PLIGHT AND STRUGGLES;
    RESOLUTION ON (COMMUNIST) PARTY WORK AMONG THE
    MEXICAN-AMERICAN PEOPLE". POLITICAL AFFAIRS, VOL.
    28 (JULY 1949), PP. 75-84.

"THE MEXICAN-AMERICANS: THEIR PLIGHT AND STRUGGLES;
    RESOLUTION ON (COMMUNIST) PARTY WORK AMONG THE
    MEXICAN-AMERICAN PEOPLE". POLITICAL AFFAIRS, VOL.
    28 (MAY 1949), PP. 71-80.

"THE REVOLT OF THE MEXICANS: ELECTION IN CRYSTAL CITY,
    TEXAS". TIME, VOL. 81 (APRIL 12, 1963), P. 25.

"WE'LL CRUSH ANY GRINGO WHO GETS IN OUR WAY: MEXICAN-AMERICANS
    WAGE IN AWAR OF WORDS OVER END TO VISTA".   THE
    NATIONAL CBSERVER,   (APRIL 7,   1969), P. 3 (SO).

"ZOOT-SUITS SERVICE STRIPES: (SO*).

DOCUMENTS OF THE CHICANO STRUGGLES.   NEW YORK, NEW YORK:
    PATHFINDER PRESS, INC., 1971.

MEXICAN STUDENT POSTERS: POSTERS FRCM THE UPRISING, 1968,
    LIBERTAD DE EXPRESION.   NEW YORK: STUDIES IN
    THE THIRD WORLD INC., 1971 (SO).

MEXICO (SO*).

RAZA UNIDA PARTY IS FORMED IN SOUTHWEST TEXAS.   LA CAUSA,
    LOS ANGELES.

"TEXAS CASE"   (SC*).

"ZCOT-SUIT RIOTS"   (SO*).

A MEXICAN AMERICAN MILITANCY.   NEW YORK: NEW YCRK TIMES,
    APRIL 20, 1969 (SO).

ARAGON, ROBERTC AND ARAGON, JOSE. A CHICANO VOTING RIGHTS
    ACT.   IN ED LUDWIG AND JAMES SANTIBANEZ. THE
    CHICANOS9 BALTIMORE, MARYLAND: PENGUIN BOOKS, INC.,
    1971 (SO).

ARMANDO RODRIGUEZ.   UNDERSTANDING WORKING WITH POWER   (SO*).

BANFIELD, EDWARD C. BIG CITY POLITICS; A CCMPARATIVE GUIDE
    TO THE POLITICAL SYSTEMS OF ATLANTA, BOSTON, DETROIT,
    EL PASO, LOS ANGELES, MIAMI, PHILADELPHIA, ST. LOUIS
    AND SEATTLE.   NEW YORK: RANDOM HOUSE, 1965.

BANFIELD, EDWARD C. AND WILSCN, JAMES Q. WILSON. CITY
    POLITICS.   CAMBRIDGE, MASSACHUSETTS: HARVARD
    UNIVERSITY PRESS AND THE M. I. T. PRESS,.

BARKER.   AUSTIN PAPERS (HT*).

BARKER.   LIFE STEPHEN F. AUSTIN, FCUNDER (HT*).

BARKER.   THE AUSTIN PAPERS (HT*).

BARTH, ERNEST A. L. AND ABU-LABAN, BAHA.   "POWER STRUCTURE
    AND THE NEGRO SUB-COMMUNITY".   AMERICAN SOCIOLOGICAL
    REVIEW, VOL. 24 (1959), PP. 69-76.

BARTON, MABLE EXA. THE DIPLOMATIC RELATIONS BETWEEN THE
    UNITED STATES AND MEXICO FROM 1892 TO 1900.
    UNIVERSITY OF TEXAS AT AUSTIN, MASTER'S THESIS (1935)
    (HM HUS).

BELL.   POLITICAL SHAME MEXICO   (HM*).

BEMIS, SAMUEL F.   THE LATIN AMERICAN POLICY OF THE UNITED
    STATES.   NEW YORK: NORTON, 1967.

BEMIS.   GUIDE TO DIPLOMATIC HISTORY U   (HUS*).

BERLE.   LATIN AMERICA: DIPLOMACY REALITY   (HSA*).

BIGART, HOMER.   "MEXICAN-AMERICANS STAGE PROTEST MARCH IN
    TEXAS".   THE NEW YORK TIMES, VOL. 1   (MARCH 3
    1,1969), P. 25 (SO EC).

BLAWIS, PATRICIA BELL.   TIJERINA AND THE LAND GRANTS:
    MEXICAN-AMERICANS IN STRUGGLE FOR THEIR HERITAGE.
    NEW YORK, NEW YORK:INTERNATIONAL PUBLISHERS, 1971 (HSW).

BOHN, F.   "MEXICO AND THE UNITED STATES".   CURRENT HISTORY
    MAGAZINE OF THE NEW YORK TIMES,   (SEPTEMBER, 1921).

BONGARTZ, R.   "CHICANO REBELLION: DEMAND FOR COURSES IN
    MEXICAN-AMERICAN STUDIES".   THE NATION, VOL. 208
    (MARCH 3, 1969), PP. 271-274 (SO).

BONGARTZ, ROY.   "LA RAZA IN REVOLT".   THE NATION, VOL.
    210 (JUNE 1, 1970), PP. 664-666 (SO).

BONGARTZ, ROY.   "NO MORE SOMBREROS: THE CHICANO REBELLION".
    THE NATION,   (MARCH 3, 1969), PP. 271-274 (SO).

BONGARZ, R.   "LA RAZA IN REVOLT".   THE NATION, VOL. 210
    (JUNE 1,1970), PP. 664-666 (SO).

BORUP, JERRY; BITTINGER, STANLEY; GESSNER, GEORGE;
    LAWRENCE, PATRICK.   CONTRASTING POLITICAL VALUES AND
    BEHAVIOR OF ANGLO-AMERICAN AND MEXICAN-AMERICAN
    POPULATION IN THE RIO GRANDE AREA.   LUBBOCK, TEXAS:
    RMSS CONVENTION,   (MAY 2-3, 1969) (SO).

BRATRUD, THEODORE EDWARD.   STRUCTURE AND FUNCTION OF
    MUNICIPAL GOVERNMENT IN NOGALES, ARIZONA.   ARIZONA
    STATE UNIVERSITY, MASTER'S THESIS (1968) (SO).

BRIEGEL.   HISTORY POLITICAL ORGANIZATIONS   (SO*).

BROOKS.   COMPLETE HISTORY MEXICAN WAR,   (HSW*).

BURNHILL.   "THE MEXICAN AMERICAN QUESTION"   (SO*).

BURNHILL.   "THE MEXICAN PEOPLE SOUTWEST"   (SO*).

BUSEY, J. L.   "THE POLITICAL GEOGRAPHY OF MEXICAN MIGRATION".
    COLORADO QUARTERLY, VOL. 2 (AUTUMN 1953), PP.
    181-190 (GE SI).

CALIFORNIA.   NEGROS MEXICAN—AMERICANS CALIFORNIA (EC*).

CALVO, R. C. "RIVER, NOT A WAVE".   ADULT LEADERSHIP, VOL.
    19 (SEPTEMBER 1970), PP. 70—72 (SO).

CAMEJO, ANTONIO. LA RAZA UNIDA PARTY IN TEXAS.   NEW YORK:
    PATHFINDER PRESS, INC., 1971.

CAMEJO, ANTONIO. A REPORT FROM AZTLAN: TEXAS CHICANOS
    FORGE OWN POLITICAL POWER.   NEW YORK AND SCARBOROUGH,
    ONTARIO:A MENTOR BOOK FROM NEW AMERICAN LIBRARY, 1972.

CAMEJO, ANTONIO; LOZADA, FROBEN. 1970—— THE YEAR OF THE
    CHICANO PARTY.   DENVER, COLORADO, MARCH 25—29,1970.

CARLOS.   POLITICS DEVELOPMENT RURAL MEXICO: (HM*).

CARRENO, ALBERTO MARIA. LA DIPLOMACIA EXTRAORDINARIA ENTRE
    MEXICO Y ESTADOS UNIDOS, 1786—1947.   2ND ED. MEXICO,
    JUS, 1961.

CHACON.   "OPEN LETTER TO: WOMENS INTERNATIONAL   (LMA*).

CHACON, JOSE ANDRES. THE POWER STRUCTURE: POLITICAL
    IMPLICATIONS FOR MEXICAN AMERICANS.   ALBUQUERQUE:
    SOUTHWEST COOPERATIVE EDUCATIONAL LABORATORY, 1970
    (ED).

CHANDLER.   MEXICAN AMERICAN PROTEST MOVEMENT (HT*).

CHICANO STUDIES INSTITUTES. CHICANO STUDIES: ITS
    RELATIONSHIP TO A DEVELOPING POLITICAL AWARENESS AMONG
    MIGRANTS.   CHICANO STUDIES INSTITUTES, PROGRAM
    COORDINATED BY MONTAL SYSTEMS INC.1971 (SI).

CONFERENCE ON ADULT BASIC EDUCATION.   CHICANO IS COMING
    OUT TORTILLA (SO*).

CORDASCO.   COMPARISON PERFORMANCE BILINGUAL   (HN*).

CORUNA, BERT. MEXICAN AMERICAN POLITICAL ASSOCIATION AND
    LA RAZA UNIDA PARTY: A PROGRAM FOR CHICANO POLITICAL
    ACTION FOR THE 1970'S.   NATIONAL CITY, CALIFORNIA:
    AZTEC PRINTING COMPANY, 1971.

CRUSADE FOR JUSTICE. CHICANO MORATORIUM.   DENVER,
    COLORADO: CRUSADE FOR JUSTICE.

DANTONIO.   NATIONAL IMAGES BUSINESS POLITICAL (SO*).

DANTONIO.   "INSTITUTIONAL OCCUPATIONAL REPRESENTATIONS
    (SO*).

DANTONIO.   "THE REPUTATIONAL TECHNIQUE AS (SO*).

DANTONIO.   INFLUENTIALS TWO BORDER CITIES: (SO*).

DANTONIO.   RELIGION, REVOLUTICN, REFORM   (SO*).

DAHLKE.   "RACE MINORITY RIOTS -- STUDY   (SO*).

DAVIS.   JOINT INTERVENTION UNITED STATES   (HSW*).

DAVIS.   "IMMIGRATION WESTERN HEMISPHERE"   (SI*).

DE FUNIAK.   PRINCIPLES COMMUNITY PROPERTY   (HSW*).

DE GALVEZ.   INSTRUCTIONS GOVERNING INTERIOR   (HS*).

DECASTRO.   LATIN AMERICAN RADICALISM: DOCUMENTARY   (HSA*).

DELGADO.   CHICANO MOVEMENT: SOME NCT TOO   (LMA*).

DELLON.   "FOREIGN AGRICULTURAL WORKERS   (EC*).

DELLON.   "THE ADVERSE-EFFECT POLICY AGRICULTURAL   (EC*).

DIAZ ORDAZ, GUSTAVO.   A POLITICAL HANDBOOK.   MEXICO: ,
     1964 (HM).

DICKENS, EDWIN LARRY.   THE POLITICAL ROLE OF MEXICAN-AMERICANS
     IN SAN ANTONIO, TEXAS.   LUBBOCK TEXAS: TEXAS
     TECHNICAL COLLEGE, 1969.

DICKENS, EDWIN LARRY.   THE POLITICAL ROLE OF MEXICAN-AMERICANS
     IN SAN ANTONIO, TEXAS.   ANN ARBOR, MICHIGAN:
     UNIVERSITY MICROFILMS, INC., 1971.

DONNELLEY, THOMAS C.   ROCKY MOUNTAINS POLITICS.   ALBUQUERQUE,
     NEW MEXICO: UNIVERSITY OF NEW MEXICO PRESS, 1940.

DUNNE, JOHN GREGORY.   "KING TIGER".   SATURDAY EVENING
     POST, VOL. 241   (APRIL 208   1968), P. 22 (EC).

ECKERT, JACQUELINE CLARA.   INTERNATIONAL LAW IN THE UNITED
     STATES-MEXICAN BOUNDARY RELATIONS.   UNIVERSITY OF
     TEXAS AT AUSTIN, PHD.   DISSERTATION (1939).

EL BARRIO COMMUNICATIONS PROJECT.   LA RAZA YEARBOOK.   LOS
     ANGELES: EL BARRIO COMMUNICATIONS PROJECT, 1968 (SO).

EULAU. S.   "SINARQUISMO UNITED STATES"   (SO*).

EULAU. S.   "SINARQUISMO UNITED STATES"   (SC*).

EULAU. S.   "SINARQUISMO U.S.A."   (SO*).

FAGES.   HISTORICAL, POLITICAL, NATURAL   (HC*).

FAIVRE.   CHAVEZ: ONE NEW ANSWER   (EC*).

FINCHER, ERNEST BARKSDALE. SPANISH-AMERICANS AS A
    POLITICAL FACTOR IN NEW MEXICO, 1912-1950.   NEW YORK
    UNIVERSITY, PHD. DISSERTATION (1950) (HN).

FOSTER.   OUTLINE POLITICAL HISTORY AMERICAS   (HSA*).

FREYE, HARRIET LILLIAN. A SOURCE UNIT FOR THE STUDY OF
    U. S. RELATIONS WITH LATIN AMERICA.   ARIZONA STATE
    UNIVERSITY, MASTER'S THESIS (1947).

FUCHS, LAWRENCE H. (ED.). AMERICAN ETHNIC POLICIES.   NEW
    YORK: HARPER AND ROW, 1968 (LW).

GARNETT.   "IMMEDIATE PRESSING RACE PROBLEMS (SO*).

GILL, MARIO. SINARQUISMO: SU ORIGEN, SU ESENCIA, SU
    MISSION.   MEXICO: CLUB DE LIBRO, 1944.

GLADE.   POLITICAL ECONOMY MEXICO: TWO (EC*).

GOMEZ.   "CHICANOS RESEIGED: BLOODY FIESTA" (SO*).

GOMEZ.   "KILLING RUBEN SALAZAR: NOTHING (SO*).

GONZALEZ RAMIREZ, MANUEL. LOS ELAMADOS TRATADOS DE
    BUCARELI; MEXICO Y LOS ESTADOS UNIDOS EN LA CONVENCIONES
    INTERNACIONALES DE 1923.   MEXICO, 1939.

GONZALEZ.   POLITICAL BEHAVIOR MEXICAN AMERICAN (EC*).

GOODALL, LEONARD E. URBAN POLITICS IN THE SOUTHWEST.
    TEMPE, ARIZONA: ARIZONA STATE UNIVERSITY, 1967.

GOULDNER, ALVIN W. ED. STUDIES IN LEADERSHIP.   NEW YORK:
    HARPER AND BROTHERS, PUBLISHERS, 1950.

GRAHAM.   VIOLENCE AMERICA (SO*).

GRAHAM, LAWRENCE. POLITICS IN A MEXICAN COMMUNITY.
    GAINESVILLE, FLORIDA: UNIVERSITY OF FLORIDA PRESS,
    (1968). UNIVERSITY OF FLORIDA MONOGRAPHS--SOCIAL
    SCIENCES, NUMBER 35..

GREBLER.   MEXICAN AMERICAN PEOPLE: NATIONS (SO*).

GREGG, ROBERT DANFORTH. THE INFLUENCE OF BORDER TROUBLES
    ON RELATIONS BETWEEN THE UNITED STATES AND MEXICO,
    1876-1910.   BALTIMORE: THE JOHNS HOPKINS PRESS, 1937
    (EC).

GRIEO, K. L. "ROLE OF THE MEXICAN REVOLUTION IN CONTEMPORARY
    AMERICAN POLICY".   MIDWEST QUARTERLY, VOL. 10
    (JANUARY 1969), PP. 113-129 (HM).

GRIFFITH.   "VIVA ROYBAL -- VIVA AMERICA" (SO*).

GROSSMAN, MITCHELL. MULTI-FACTIONAL POLITICS IN SAN
    ANTONIO AND BEXAR COUNTY, TEXAS. UNIVERSITY
    OF TEXAS, 1959 (SO).

GUADALUPE HIDALGO. TREATY THAT WON WEST (LW*).

GUTIERREZ DE LARA. MEXICAN PEOPLE; THEIR STRUGGLE (SO*).

GUZMAN, RALPH AND MOORE, JOAN. "THE MEXICAN AMERICANS:
    NEW WIND FROM THE SOUTHWEST". NATION, VOL. 202 (MAY
    30, 1966), PP. 645-648 (SO).

GUZMAN, RALPH. 'POLITICS AND POLICIES OF THE MEXICAN
    AMERICAN COMMUNITY.' IN EUGENE DVORIN AND ARTHUR
    MISNER, <EDS>. CALIFORNIA POLITICS AND POLICIES (SO).

GUZMAN, RALPH. "HOW EL CENTRO DID IT". FRONTIER, VOL.
    7 NO. 4 (FEBRUARY 1956), PP. 13-16 (SO).

GUZMAN, RALPH. "HOW EL CENTRO ENDED SEGRAGATION".
    FRONTIER, VOL. 7 (FEBRUARY 1956), P. 13 (SO).

GUZMAN, RALPH. "MEXICAN AMERICANS ON THE MOVE". AGENDA,
    VOL. 2 (JULY 1966), PP. 2-8 (SO).

GUZMAN, RALPH. "REASONED RADICALISM: AN ALTERNATIVE TO
    FEAR AND I(STITUTIONAL OPPRESSION". EL GRITO, VOL.
    2 NO. 4 (SUMMER 1969), PP. 39-45 (SO).

GUZMAN, RALPH. "THE HAND OF ESAU: WORDS CHANGE, PRACTICES
    REMAIN IN RACIAL COVENANTS". FRONTIER, VOL. 7 (JUNE
    1956), P. 7 (SO).

GUZMAN, RALPH. EASY CONCEPTS AND HARD REALITY: MYTHS,
    ASSUMPTIONS AND HYPOTHESES ABOUTMEXICAN AMERICANS.
    CONFERENCE OF OFFICIAL AGENCIES FOR HUMAN RIGHTS.
    PORTLAND, OREGON, 1968 (SO).

GUZMAN, RALPH. ETHICS IN FEDERALLY SUBSIDIZED RESEARCH--
    THE CASE OF THE MEXICAN AMERICAN. WASHINGTON, D.
    C.: U. S. GOVERNMENT PRINTING OFFICE, (1968) (SO).

GUZMAN, RALPH. ETHICS IN FEDERALLY SUBSIDIZED RESEARCH:
    THE CASE OF THE MEXICAN AMERICAN. UNPUBLISHED PAPER
    GIVEN AT THE CABINET COMMITTEE HEARINGS ON MEXICAN
    AMERICAN AFFAIRS. EL PASO, TEXAS, 1967 (SO).

GUZMAN, RALPH. RIGHTS WITHOUT ROOTS: A STUDY OF THE LOSS
    OF CITIZENSHIP BY NATIVE-BORN AMERICANS OF MEXICAN
    ANCESTRY. FUND FOR THE REPUBLIC, INC. AND SOUTHERN
    CALIFORNIA CHAPTER, AMERICAN CIVIL LIBERTIES UNION,
    1955 (SO).

GUZMAN, RALPH. SOCIOLOGICAL OVERVIEW OF THE MEXICAN-AMERICAN
    IN URBAN AREAS.   NUEVA VISTAS. REPORT OF THE SECOND
    ANNUAL CONFERENCE OF THE CALIFORNIA STATE DEPARTMENT
    OF EDUCATION. SACRAMENTO (SO).

GUZMAN, RALPH. THE GENTLE REVOLUTIONARIES: BROWN POWER.
    WEST MAGAZINE, LOS ANGELES TIMES, MARCH 30, 1969 (SO).

GUZMAN, RALPH. THE MEXICAN AMERICAN POPULATION: AN
    INTROSPECTIVE VIEW.   PALM SPRINGS, CALIFORNIA:
    WESTERN GOVERNMENTAL RESEARCH ASSOCIATION, AUGUST 1966
    (SO).

GUZMAN, RALPH. THE POLITICAL SOCIALIZATION OF THE
    MEXICAN-AMERICAN PEOPLE.   UNIVERSITY OF CALIFORNIA
    AT LOS ANGELES, PHD. DISSERTATION (1970) (SO).

GUZMAN, RALPH. THE POLITICAL SOCIALIZATION OF THE MEXICAN
    AMERICAN PEOPLE.   ANN ARBOR, MICHIGAN: UNIVERSITY
    MICROFILMS, 1971 (SO).

GUZMAN, RALPH. THE SOCIO-ECONOMIC POSITION OF THE
    MEXICAN-AMERICAN MIGRANT FARM WORKER.   WASHINGTON
    D. C.: NATIONAL ADVISORY COMMISSION ON RURAL POVERTY,
    (1967) (SO).

GWIN J.   "SOCIAL PROBLEMS OUR MEXICANPOPULATION"   (SO*).

GWIN.   "BACK FORTH TO MEXICO" (SC*).

GWIN.   "IMMIGRATION ALONG OUR SOUTHWEST (SO*).

GWIN.   "IMMIGRATION ALONG OUR SOUTHWEST   (SO*).

GWIN.   "MAKING FRIENDS INVADERS: MEXICAN   (SO*).

HALL, MARTIN HARDWICK. SIBLEY'S NEW MEXICO CAMPAIGN.
    AUSTIN: UNIVERSITY OF TEXAS PRESS, 1960.

HALL, MARTIN. "ROYBAL'S CANDIDACY AND WHAT IT MEANS".
    FRONTIER, VOL. 5 (JUNE 1954), PP. 5-7.

HALL, MARTIN. "400,000 MEXICAN AMERICAN VOTERS".   CHICAGO
    JEWISH FORUM, VOL. 14 (FALL 1955), PP. 19-25 (SI).

HARRINGTON, J. H. "L.A.'S STUDENT BLOWOUT".   PHI DELTA
    KAPPAN, VOL. 50 (OCTOBER 1968), PP. 74-79 (SO).

HERRERA.   THE NATIONAL CHICANO MORATORIUM (SO*).

HILL, GLADWIN. THE POLITICAL ROLE OF MEXICAN AMERICANS.
    MINORITY PROBLEMS, NEW YORK: HARPER AND ROW, 1965 (SO).

HILL, HARRY SEGNER. "THE EFFECT OF BILINGUALISM ON THE
     MEASURED INTELLIGENCE OF ELEMENTARY SCHOOL CHILDREN
     OF ITALIAN PARENTAGE". JOURNAL OF EXPERIMENTAL
     EDUCATION, VOL. 5 (SEPTEMBER 1936), PP. 75-78.

HILL. PUBLIC DOMAIN DEMOCRACY; STUDY (SO*).

HOUSEHOLDER, FRED WALTER. SOURCES OF THE TEXAS LAW
     OF MARRIED WOMEN. UNIVERSITY OF TEXAS AT AUSTIN,
     MASTER'S THESIS (1909).

HUNTER, FLOYD. COMMUNITY POWER STRUCTURE. NEW YORK:
     ANCHOR BOOKS, DOUBLEDAY AND COMPANY, INC., 1963.

HYMAN, HERBERT HIRAM. POLITICAL SOCIALIZATION: A STUDY
     IN THE PSYCHOLOGY OF POLITICAL BEHAVIOR. NEW YORK:
     FREE PRESS, 1969, 1959 (PY).

IMAZ, JOSE LUIS DE. LOS QUE MANDAN (THOSE WHO RULE).
     TRANSLATED BY CARLOS A. ASTIZ WITH MARY F. MCCARTHY.
     ALBANY, NEW YORK: STATE UNIVERSITY OF NEW YORK PRESS,
     1970.

INMAN, SAMUEL GUY. INTERVENTION IN MEXICO. NEW YORK:
     GEORGE H. DORAN CO., 1919.

JAMES, DANIEL. MEXICO AND THE AMERICANS. NEW YORK:
     PRAEGER, 1963 (EC).

JERNEGAN. AMERICAN COLONIES 1492-1750;STUDY (HS*).

JOHNSON, LYNDON B. "MEXICAN AMERICAN CONFERENCE: THE
     PRESIDENT'S REMARKS (OCTOBER 27, 1967) TO DELEGATES
     IN EL PASO". COMPILATION OF PRESIDENTIAL DOCUMENTS,
     VOL. 3 (NOVEMBER 6, 1967), PP. 1492-1493.

JOHNSON, LYNDON BAINES. "REMARKS AT MEXICAN FIESTA".
     DEPARTMENT OF STATE BULLETIN, VOL. 50 (MARCH 16,
     1964), PP. 401-403 (SO).

JOHNSON, LYNDON BAINES. A NEW FOCUS ON OPPORTUNITY FOR
     THE SPANISH SPEAKING AMERICAN; STATEMENT OF THE
     PRESIDENT. WASHINGTON, D. C.: OFFICE OF THE
     PRESIDENT, (1968) (SO).

JONES, SOLOMON JAMES. THE GOVERNMENT RIOTS OF LOS ANGELES,
     JUNE, 1943. LOS ANGELES: UNIVERSITY OF CALIFORNIA,
     1969 (SO).

JUDAH, CHARLES B. RECRUITMENT OF CANDIDATES FROM THE
     NORTHERN AND EASTERN COUNTIES OF THE NEW MEXICO HOUSE
     OF REPRESENTATIVES, 1956. ALBUQUERQUE: UNIVERSITY
     OF NEW MEXICO, (1961). DIVISION OF GOVERNMENT RESEARCH
     PUBLICATION NUMBER 59..

KAHN, SI. HOW PEOPLE GET POWER.   NEW YORK: MCGRAW HILL
    BOOK COMPANY, 1970.

KARR, K. "PROTEST: MEXICAN-AMERICAN STYLE".   MEDIA AND
    METHODS, VOL. 6 (APRIL 1970), PP. 54-56 (SO).

KELLEY, THOMAS A. "INTER-AMERICANISM BEGINS AT HOME".
    CATHOLIC DIGEST, VOL. 7 (OCTOBER 1943), PP. 18-21.

KEY, V. O. SOUTHERN POLITICS.   NEW YORK: RANDOM HOUSE,
    1949.

KEY, VALDIMER ORLANDO. SOUTHTHERN POLITICS IN STATE AND
    NATION.   NEW YORK: A. A. KNOPF, 1949.

KRUEGER, A. O. "ECONOMICS OF DISCRIMINATION".   JOURNAL
    OF POLITICS AND ECONOMICS, VOL. 71 (OCTOBER 1963),
    PP. 481-486 (EC).

LA RAZA UNICA OF MICHIGAN. LA RAZA UNIDA.   MICHIGAN.

LA RAZA UNIDA PARTY IN TEXAS. LA RAZA UNIDA PARTY
    IN TEXAS.   TEXAS.

LA RAZA UNIDA. MICHIGAN. PUBLIC RELATIONS DEPARTMENT.
    DIRECTORIO MEXICO AMERICANO.   PRODUCED BY THE PUBLIC
    RELATIONS DEPARTMENT OF LA RAZA UNIDA IN MICHIGAN..

LAHART, EDWARD. THE CAREER OF DENNIS CHAVEZ AS A MEMBER
    OF CONGRESS 1930-1934.   ALBUQUERQUE: UNIVERSITY OF
    NEW MEXICO PRESS, 1958 (HN).

LINATI, CLAUDIO. COSTUMES CIVILES, MILITAIRES ET RELIGIEUX
    DE MEXIQUE.   BRUSSELS: LITHOGRAPHIE ROYALE DE GABARD,
    1828 (RE).

LOBART, EDWARD. THE CAREER OF DENNIS CHAVEZ AS A MEMBER
    OF CONGRESS, 1930-1934.   ALBUQUERQUE, NEW MEXICO:
    UNIVERSITY OF NEW MEXICO PRESS, 1958 (HN).

LOVE, JOSEPH L. LA RAZA: MEXICAN-AMERICANS IN REBELLION.
    TRANS-ACTION: SOCIAL SCIENCE AND MODERN SOCIETY (SO
    EC).

LOVE, JOSEPH L. 'LA RAZA: MEXICAN-AMERICANS IN REBELLION.'
    INTRODUCTION BY EDWARD SIMMEN. THE CHICANO TODAY. (SO
    EC).

LOW, ALICE. POLITICAL CULTURE AND CIVIC INVOLVEMENT: A
    COMPARATIVE ANALYSIS OF IMMIGRANT ETHNIC COMMUNITIES
    IN SAN PEDROK CALIFORNIA.   UNIVERSITY OF CALIFORNIA
    AT LOS ANGELES, PHD. DISSERTATION (1971) (SI HC).

LOZADA, FROBEN; CAMEJO, ANTONIO. EL PLAN ESPIRITUAL DE
    AZTLAN.   DENVER, COLORADO, MARCH 25-29, 1970 (ED
    SO).

MACIAS, YSIDRO R. "THE CHICANO MOVEMENT". WILSON LIBRARY
     BULLETIN, VOL. 44 NO. 7 (MARCH 1970).

MACIAS, YSIDRO RAMON. EVCLUTICN OF THE MIND AND A PLAN
     FOR POLITICATL ACTION. DELIVERED AT MEXICAN-AMERICAN
     CONFERENCE, UNIVERSITY OF CALIFORNIA EXTENSION
     PROGRAM, SAN FRANCISCO, JUNE 21-22, 1969.

MACIAS, YSIDRO. THE CHICANO MOVEMENT. INTRODUCTION BY
     EDWARD SIMMEN. THE CHICANO TODAY., (SPRING 1971).
     1972.

MACK, RAYMOND DE ELMONT. CONSTITUTIONAL CENTRALISM
     IN MEXICO -- A STUDY OF THE CONSTITUTIONS OF 1836 AND
     1843. UNIVERSITY OF TEXAS AT AUSTIN, MASTER'S THESIS
     (1949).

MAHOOD, H. PRESSURE GROUPS IN AMERICAN POLITICS. NEW
     YORK: CHARLES SCRIBNER'S SONS, 1967.

MALONEY, THOMAS. FACTIONALISM AND FUTILITY: A CASE STUDY
     OF POLITICAL AND ECONOMIC REFORM IN NEW MEXICO.
     EDITED BY JUNE HELM. SEATTLE, WASHINGTON: UNIVERSITY
     OF WASHINGTON PRESS, 1968 (EC).

MANNING, WILLIAM RAY. EARLY DIPLOMATIC RELATIONS BETWEEN
     THE UNITED STATES AND MEXICO. BALTIMORE: THE JOHNS
     HOPKINS PRESS, 1916.

MARTIN. COLORADO GOVERNMENT POLITICS (HCO*).

MARTINEZ, JOHN J. "BROWN POWER CONFERENCE CENTENNIAL".
     EL GRITO, VOL. 1 NO. 2 (WINTER 1968), P. 30.

MARTINEZ, JOHN J. "CATHARSIS". EL GRITO, VOL. 1 NO.
     2 (WINTER 1968), P. 30.

MARTINEZ, JOHN R. 'LEADERSHIP AND POLITICS.' IN JULIAN
     SAMORA (ED), LA RAZA: FORGOTTEN AMERICAN.

MC CLESKEY, H. CLIFTON, AND MERRILL, BRUCE. THE POLITICAL
     BEHAVIOR OF MEXICAN-AMERICANS IN TEXAS: A PRELIMINARY
     REPORT. UNPUBLISHED PAPER PRESENTED AT THE ANNUAL
     MEETING OF THE SOUTHWESTERN SOCIAL SCIENCE ASSOCIATION:
     DALLAS, TEXAS. MARCH 28, 1970.

MC CROCKLIN. STUDY LATIN AMERICAN ATTITUDE (HSW*).

MC KEE. "COMMUNITY POWER STRATEGIES RACE (SO*).

MEISTER. "LA HUELGA BECOMES CAUSA" (EC*).

MEMMI. DOMINATED MAN (AN*).

MEMMI, ALBERT. THE COLONIZER AND THE COLONIZED. BOSTON
     MASSACHUSETTS BEACON PRESS, 1967.

MESSICK, R. G. "POLITICAL AWARENESS AMONG MEXICAN-AMERICAN
    HIGH SCHOOL STUDENTS". THE HIGH SCHOOL SCHOOL
    JOURNAL, VOL. 54 (NOVEMBER 1970), PP. 108-118 (ED).

METHUEN. ANDELE, OR MEXICAN KIOWA CAPTIVE (HM*).

MEXICAN AMERICAN POLITICAL ASSOCIATION EDUCATIONAL COUNCIL.
    THE MEXICAN AMERICAN STUDIES PROJECT. LOS ANGELES
    MEXICAN AMERICAN POLITICAL ASSOCIATION EDUCATIONAL
    COUNCIL, 1969.

MEXICO. MEXICO (EC*).

MEYER. CONCIENCIA HISTORIA NORTEAMERICANA (HM*).

MEYER. MEXICO REBEL: PASCUAL CRCZCC (HM*).

MICHIGAN. HOW BACKLOG GREW (LW*).

MID- WEST COUNCIL OF LA RAZA. MI RAZA PRIMERO. CONFERENCE
    HELD IN MUSKEGON, MICHIGAN ON JANUARY 22-23, 1972 (EC).

MIDDLETON. FORMATION TEXAS CONSTITUTION1845 (HT*).

MILL, GLADWIN. THE POLITICAL RCLE OF MEXICAN AMERICANS.
    MINORITY PROBLEMS, HARPER AND ROW, 1965 (SO).

MILLER. STUDY MEXICAN SECONDARY SCHOOLS (EC*).

MILLON, ROBERT. THE IDEOLOGY OF A PEASANT REVOLUTIONARY.
    NEW YORK: NEW WORLD PAPERBACKS, 1968 (EC).

MINOT. TREATY WITH REPUBLIC MEXICO FEBRUARY (LW*).

MONTAL SYSTEMS. MOVIMIENTO ESTUDIANTIL CHICANO (ED*).

MOORE, JOAN W. COLONIALISM: THE CASE OF THE MEXICAN
    AMERICANS. SOCIAL PROBLEMS, SPRING 1970. PP 463-472.
    ABOUT POLITICAL PARTICIPATION, INCLUDES BIBLIOGRAPHY
    (HSW).

MOORE, JOAN W. COLONIALISM: THE CASE OF THE MEXICAN
    AMERICAN.

FORNIA: A READER IN THE HISTORY CF OPPRESSION. NEW YORK:
    MACMILLAN COMPANY, 1972 (HSW).

MOORE, JOAN W. INTRODUCTICN TO MEXICAN AMERICAN PROBLEMS
    AND PROJECTS. A PROPOSAL FOR A DEPARTMENT OF CHICANO
    STUDIES, MAY 5, 1971 (HSW ED).

MOORE. LCS MEXICANOS DE LOS ESTADOSUNIDOS (SO*).

MOORE. MEXICAN AMERICAN: PROBLEMS PROSPECTS (SO*).

MOORE.   MEXICAN-AMERICANS; PROBLEMS PROSPECTS   (SO*).

MOORE.   MEXICAN-AMERICANS, PROBLEMS PROSPECTS   (SO*).

MOORE.   "MEXICAN AMERICANS: NEW WINDSOUTHWEST"   (SO*).

MOORE, W. E. "AMERICA'S MIGRATION TREATIES DURING WORLD
    WAR II".   ANNALS OF THE AMERICAN ACADEMY OF POLITICAL
    AND SOCIAL SCIENCE, VOL. 262 (MARCH 1949), PP. 31-38
    (SI EC).

MORGAN.   "TEXAS GIANT AWAKENS. GREATER (HT*).

MORLOCK, LAURA L. MEXICAN AMERICAN CIVIC LEADERSHIP IN
    A NORTHERN CITY.   MICHIGAN STATE UNIVERSITY, MASTER'S
    THESIS (1968) (SO).

MORRIS, A. P. "OF MANY THINGS: THE RIGHTS OF".   AMERICA,
    VOL. 118 (JANUARY 13,1968) (SO).

MORTON, WARD MCKINNON. FOREIGN LANDHOLDINGS IN THE MEXICAN
    AGRARIAN REVOLUTION, 1915-1927.   UNIVERSITY OF TEXAS
    AT AUSTIN, MASTER'S THESIS (1934) (EC).

MORTON, WARD MCKINNON. GOVERNMENT REGULATION OF LABOR IN
    MEXICO UNDER THE CONSTITUTION OF 1917.   UNIVERSITY
    OF TEXAS AT AUSTIN, PHD. DISSERTATION (1941) (EC).

MOZA.   "LANGUAGE DIFFERENCE POLITICAL (LA*).

MUNOZ, CARLOS. "ON THE NATURE AND CAUSE OF TENSION IN THE
    CHICANO COMMUNITY: A CRITICALANALYSIS".   AZTLAN--CHICANO
    JOURNAL OF THE SOCIAL SCIENCES AND THE ARTS, VOL. 1
    NO. 2 (FALL 1970), PP. 99-100 (SO).

MUNOZ, CARLOS. "TOWARD A CHICANO PERSPECTIVE OF POLITICAL
    ANALYSIS".   AZTLAN--CHICANO JOURNAL OF THE SOCIAL
    SCIENCES AND THE ARTS, VOL. 1 NO. 2 (FALL 1970),
    PP. 15-26 (SO).

MUNOZ, CARLOS, JR. CHICANO MILITANCY IN CALIFORNIA:
    A QUEST FOR IDENTITY AND POWER.   RACISM IN CALIFORNIA:
    A READER IN THE HISTORY OF OPPRESSION. NEW YORK, NEW
    YORK: MACMILLAN COMPANY, 1972 (SO).

MUNY, CHARLES CURTIS. "AWAKENING IN THE CORAL".
    NEW MASSES, VOL. 31 (APRIL 18, 1939), PP. 10-12 (SO).

MYRDAL.   AMERICAN DILEMMA (SO*).

NEAL, JOE WEST. STATE AND LOCAL GOVERNMENT IN NORTHEASTERN
    MEXICO: NUEVO LEON, COAHUILAAND TAMAULIPAS.
    UNIVERSITY OF TEXAS AT AUSTIN, PHD. DISSERTATION (1957).

NEAL, JOE WEST. THE POLICY OF THE UNITED STATES TOWARD
    IMMIGRATION FROM MEXICO.   UNIVERSITY OF TEXAS
    AT AUSTIN, MASTER'S THESIS (1941).

NEEDLER, MARTIN C.   LATIN AMERICAN POLITICS IN PERSPECTIVE.
    SECOND EDITION, PRINCETON: D. VAN NOSTRAND, 1968 (HSA).

NEEDLER, MARTIN C.   POLITICAL DEVELOPMENT IN LATIN AMERICA:
    INSTABILITY, VIOLENCE AND EVOLUTIONARY CHANGE.   NEW
    YORK: RANDOM HOUSE, 1968 (HSA).

NEFF.   "SOCIO-ECONOMIC STATUS INTELLIGENCE" (SO*).

NEIMAN, GILBERT. THERE IS A TYRANT IN EVERY COUNTRY.
    NEW YORK: HARCOURT, BRACE AND COMPANY, 1947.

NIEMEYER.   MEXICAN CONSTITUTIONAL CONVENTION (HM*).

NIMMO.   TEXAS POLITICAL SYSTEM (HT*).

NOVAK, MICHAEL. THEOLOGY FOR A RADICAL POLITICS.   NEW
    YORK: HERDER AND HERDER, 1969 (RE).

PADGETT, LEON VINCE. THE MEXICAN POLITICAL SYSTEM.
    BOSTON, MASSACHUSETTS: HOUGHTON-MIFFLIN COMPANY, 1966
    (HM).

PATTEE, RICHARD. "THE PUERTO RICANS".   ANNALS OF
    THE AMERICAN ACADEMY OF POLITICAL AND SOCIAL SCIENCE,
    VOL. 223 (SEPTEMBER 1942), PP. 49-54 (SO).

PENA, ALBERT. "PENA ON LA RAZA".   THE TEXAS OBSERVER,
    (OCTOBER 16, 1970).

PENA, JR., ALBERT A. POLITICS AND THE MEXICAN-AMERICAN
    IN SOUTH TEXAS.   UNPUBLISHED PAPER SUBMITTED TO DR.
    JULIAN SAMORA, 1965.

PENTONY, DE VERE. UNFINISHED REBELLIONS.   SAN FRANCISCO:
    JOSSEY-BASS, INC., 1971.

PEREZ, RUBEN. "NON-POLITICIZED POLITICAL PRISONERS".
    EL POCHO CHE, VOL. 1 (JULY 1969).

POWELL, PHILIP W. TREE OF HATE: PROPAGANDA AND PREJUDICES
    AFFECTING UNITED STATES RELATIONS WITH HISPANIC
    WORLD..   NEW YORK, NEW YORK: BASIC BOOKS, INC., 1971.

PRITCHETT.   "THE POLITICAL INFLUENCE MEXICAN (SI*).

RAAB, EARL AND LIPSET, SEYMOUR M. (EDS). FREEDOM PAMPHLETS..
    NEW YORK, N. Y. B'NAI B'RITH, 1959.

RAMOS.   SPANISH-SPEAKING LEADERSHIP TWO (SO*).

RAMPARTS.   BRACERO POLITICS: SPECIAL REPORT   (EC*).

RAUSCH, G. J., JR.   "POISON-PEN DIPLOMACY".   AMERICAS,
    VOL. 24   (JANUARY 1968), PP. 272-280 (HM).

RAY, PAUL H., (ET AL). A POLITICAL PROFILE OF LANSING,
    MICHIGAN.   INTERNAL REPORT NO. 11.   THE URBAN
    REGIONAL RESEARCH INSTITUTE. MICHIGAN STATE UNIVERSITY,
    AUGUST 18, 1966.

RENDON, ARMANDO. "HOW MUCH LONGER THE LONG ROAD".   CIVIL
    RIGHTS DIGEST, VOL. 1   NO. 2 (SUMMER 1968), PP. 34-44.

RENDON, ARMANDO. "LA RAZA: TODAY NOT MANANA".   CIVIL
    RIGHTS DIGEST, VOL. 1   (SPRING 1968).

RENDON.   CHICANO MANIFESTO   (HM*).

RICKSEEKER, CHARLES GRANT.   CIVIL DISTURBANCE IN THE
    POLITICAL PROVISION OF SONORA.   ARIZONA STATE
    UNIVERSITY, MASTER'S THESIS (1969) (SO).

RIVERA.   "CHICANOS: CULTURE, COMMUNITY   (AN*).

ROBERTS.   "AMERICAN UNTOUCHABLES: HOW MIGRANT   (SI*).

ROBERTSON, O.   MEXICO AND NON-INTERVENTION 1910-1919; THE
    POLICY, THE PRACTICE AND THE LAW.   UNIVERSITY
    OF CALIFORNIA, LOS ANGELES, PHD. DISSERTATION (1969)
    (HM).

ROCHE.   QUEST DREAM; DEVELOPMENT CIVIL   (SO*).

RODRIGUEZ, EUGENE, JR.   HENRY B. GONZALES, A POLITICAL
    PROFILE.   ST MARY'S UNIVERSITY, TEXAS, MASTER'S
    THESIS (1965) (HT).

ROEDER, SANDRA L.   THE RESTRUCTURING OF POWER IN A MEXICAN
    AMERICAN COMMUNITY.   WASHINGTON D.C. GEORGE WASHINGTON
    UNIVERSITY, (1966) (SO).

ROMANO-V.   VOICES: READINGS GRITO (AN*).

ROMANO-V.   VOICES: READINGS GRITO. (AN*).

ROMANO-V.   ESPEJO: SELECTED MEXICAN AMERICAN (AN*).

ROMERO, MATIAS.   MEXICO AND THE UNITED STATES. A STUDY
    OF SUBJECTS AFFECTING THEIR POLITICAL, COMMERCIAL,
    AND SOCIAL RELATIONS.   NEW YORK: PUTNAM, 1898 (EC
    SO).

ROMUALDI.   "HANDS ACROSS BORDER"   (EC*).

ROSENSTONE, ROBERT A. AND BOSKIN, J.   PROTEST MOVEMENTS
     OF THE NINETEEN SIXTIES.   PHILADELPHIA: AMERICAN
     ACADEMY OF POLITICAL AND SOCIAL SCIENCE, (SO).

ROYBAL, EDWARD. "PRESIDENT JOHNSON AND THE UNTOLD STORY
     OF THE MEXICAN AMERICAN COMMUNITY".   CONGRESSIONAL
     RECORD,   (JUNE   13, 1967) (SC).

ROYBAL, EDWARD. PAPERS FROM 1953-1962.   UNIVERSITY OF
     CALIFORNIA AT LOS ANGELES. SPECIAL COLLECTION LIBRARY.

RUSSELL.   "RACIAL GROUPS NEW MEXICO LEGISLATURE"   (HN*).

RUSSELL.   "STATE REGIONALISM NEW MEXICO"   (HN*).

RUSSELL.   STATE REGIONALISM NEW MEXICO   (HN*).

RYAN, FRANCES DORA. THE ELECTION LAWS OF TEXAS, 1827-1875.
     UNIVERSITY OF TEXAS AT AUSTIN, MASTER'S THESIS (1922)
     (HT).

SAN DIEGO STATE COLLEGE. CHICANOS POR LA CAUSA, '69.
     CHICANOS POR LA CAUSA, INC. (SO).

SCHWARZ, CARL EDWARD. THE MEXICAN WRIT OF AMPARO AND
     EXTRAORDINARY JUDICIAL REMEDIES AGAINST OFFICIAL ABUSE
     IN THE U. S.: A COMPARATIVE ANALYSIS.   UNIVERSITY
     OF CALIFORNIA, SANTA BARBARA, PHD. DISSERTATION (1971).

SHAPIRO, J. SALWYN. ANTICLERICALISM: CONFLICT BETWEEN
     CHURCH AND STATE IN FRANCE, ITALY AND SPAIN.   NEW
     YORK: VAN NOSTRAND REINHOLD COMPANY, 1968 (RE).

SHELTON, EDGAR GREER. POLITICAL CONDITIONS AMONG TEXAS
     MEXICANS ALONG THE RIO GRANDE.   UNIVERSITY OF TEXAS,
     MASTER'S THESIS (1946).

SHOCKLEY, JOHN STAPLES:. CHICANO REVOLT IN A TEXAS TOWN..
     LONDON, ENGLAND: NOTRE DAME PRESS, 1974 (HT).

SKOLNICK, JEROME. THE POLITICS OF PROTEST: VIOLENT ASPECTS
     OF PROTEST AND CONFRONTATION.   A STAFF REPORT TO THE
     NATIONAL COMMISSION ON THE CAUSES AND PREVENTION OF
     VIOLENCE..

SOUKUP.   PARTY FACTIONAL DIVISION TEXAS   (HT*).

SOUTHWEST COUNCIL OF FOREIGN LANGUAGE TEACHERS CONFERENCE.
     OUR BILINGUALS: SOCIAL PSYCHOLOGICAL   (SO*).

SPIESS, JAN. "FEUDALISM AND SENATOR CUTTING".   AMERICAN
     MERCURY, VOL. 33 (NOVEMBER 1934), PP. 371-374.

STEINER, STAN. 'CHICANO POWER: MILITANCE AMONG THE MEXICAN
     AMERICANS   LA RAZA. THE MEXICAN
     AMERICANS.'   INTRODUCTION BY EDWARD SIMMEN. THE
     CHICANO TODAY (SO).

STEINER, STAN. "CHICANO POWER".   NEW REPUBLIC, VOL. 162
     (JUNE 20, 1970), PP. 16-18 (SO).

STEINER, STAN. CRACKS IN THE MELTING POT: RACISM AND
     DISCRIMINATION IN AMERICAN HISTORY.   NEW YORK: HARPER
     AND ROW PUBLISHERS, 1969 (SO HSW).

STEVENS, EVELYN P. 'MEXICAN MACHISMO: POLITICS AND VALUE
     ORIENTATIONS.'   PAUL KRAMER AND ROBERT MCNICOLL,
     (EDS), LATIN AMERICAN PANORAMA (PY).

STEVENS, EVELYN P. "MEXICAN MACHISMO: POLITICS AND VALUE
     ORIENTATIONS".   WESTERN POLITICAL QUARTERLY, VOL.
     XVIII ((DECEMBER 1965)), PP. 848-857 (PY).

STOCKER.   INVISIBLE MINORITY. . . PERONO   (SI*).

STODDARD.   RISING TIDE COLOR AGAINST WHITE   (SO*).

TAYS.   REVOLUTIONARY CALIFORNIA: POLITICAL   (HC*).

THE MEXICAN- AMERICAN AMITY CONFERENCE.   "MEXICAN-AMERICAN
     AMITY CONFERENCE (SO*).

THE SACRAMENTO STATE HORNET.   CHICANO SPEAKS OUT (SO*).

THURSTON, RAYMOND LEROY.   THE COLORADO RIVER AS A FACTOR
     IN UNITED STATES-MEXICAN RELATIONS.   UNIVERSITY OF
     TEXAS AT AUSTIN, MASTER'S THESIS (1935) (HSW).

TIRADO, MIGUEL DAVID.   MEXICAN AMERICAN COMMUNITY POLITICAL
     ORGANIZATION THE KEY TO CHICANO POLITICAL POWER.
     AZTLAN--CHICANO JOURNAL OF THE SOCIAL SCIENCES AND
     THE ARTS, 1 (SO).

TOBIAS, HENRY JACK AND CHARLES E. WOODHOUSE (EDS.).
     POLITICS AND MINORITIES.   ALBUQUERQUE, NEW MEXICO:
     UNIVERSITY OF NEX MEXICO PRESS, 1967 (SO).

TOBIAS, HENRY. ETHNIC MINORITIES IN POLITICS.   ALBUQUERQUE:
     UNIVERSITY OF NEW MEXICO PRESS, 1968 (SO).

TOBIN.   "THE REVOLUTION IS NOT COMING" (SO*).

TOMASEK, ROBERT D. THE POLICICAL AND ECONOMIC IMPLICATION
     OF MEXICAN LABOR IN THE U.S. UNDER THE NON QUOTA
     SYSTE, CONTRACT LABOR PROGRAM, AND WETBACK MOVEMENT..
     ANN ARBOR, MICHIGAN: UNIVERSITY MICROFILMS, 1958 (EC).

TOMASEK, ROBERT DENNIS. THE POLITICAL AND ECONOMIC
    IMPLICATIONS OF MEXICAN LABOR IN THE UNITED STATES
    UNDER THE NON QUOTA SYSTEM, CONTRACT LABOR PROGRAM,
    AND WETBACK MOVEMENT. UNIVERSITY MICROFILMS,, 1958
    (EC).

TOMPKINS.   BAIL UNITED STATES   (B*).

TOMPKINS.   JUVENILE GANGS STREET GROUPS   (B*).

TOMPKINS.   POVERTY UNITED STATES DURINGSIXTIES   (B*).

TOMPKINS.   WHITE COLLAR CRIME   (B*).

TRESOLINI, ROCCO J.   CASES IN AMERICAN NATIONAL GOVERNMENT
    AND POLITICS.   EDITED BY ROCCO J. TRESOLINI AND
    RICHARD T. FROST. ENGLEWOOD CLIFFS, NEW JERSEY:
    PRENTICE-HALL, 1966.

U. S. MEXICAN IMMIGRATION   (LW*).

U. S. CONGRESS. SPANISH-AMERICANS IN POLITICS.   CONGRESSIONAL
    QUARTERLY WEEKLY REPORT. , (MAY 1928).

U. S. PRESIDENT. "MEXICAN-AMERICAN CONFERENCE; THE
    PRESIDENTS REMARKS (OCTOBER 28,1967) TO DELEGATES TO
    THE CONFERENCE IN EL PASO, TEXAS". WEEKLY COMPILATION
    OF PRESIDENTIAL DOCUMENTS, (NOVEMBER 6, 1967), PP.
    1492-1493.

UGALDE, ANTONIO. POWER AND CONFLICT IN A MEXICAN COMMUNITY:
    A STUDY OF POLITICAL INTEGRATION.   ALBUQUERQUE, NEW
    MEXICO: UNIVERSITY OF NEW MEXICO PRESS, 1970 (AN
    SO).

UNITED STATES.   MEXICAN AMERICAN: PAPER PRESENTED   (LW*).

UNITED STATES.   "MEXICAN AMERICAN CONFERENCE;   (EC*).

UNITED STATES.   "THE MEXICAN AMERICAN: NEW FOCUS   (EC*).

UNIV. OF TEXAS, DEPT. OF GOVERNMENT, ELECTION RESEARCH
    PROJECT COMMITTEE. TEXAS VOTES: SELECTED GENERAL
    AND SPECIAL ELECTION STATISTICS, 1944-1963.   AUSTIN,
    TEXAS: UNIVERSITY OF TEXAS, 1964 (SO).

VALDES.   SOCIOLOGICAL ANALYSIS DESCRIPTION   (SO*).

VALDES, DANIEL T. THE SPANISH-SPEAKING PEOPLE OF THE
    SOUTHWEST.   DENVER, COLORADO, (1938). BULLETIN WE-4.
    WORKS PROGRESS ADMINISTRATION PROGRAM OF EDUCATION
    AND RECREATION OF THE COLORADO STATE DEPARTMENT OF
    EDUCATION (ED SO).

VALDES, DANIEL TAPIA. A SOCIOLOGICAL ANALYSIS AND
    DESCRIPTION OF THE POLITICAL ROLE, STATUS AND VOTING
    BEHAVIOR OF AMERICANS WITH SPANISH NAMES.   UNIVERSITY
    OF COLORADO, PHD. DISSERTATION (1964) (SO).

VALDEZ, DANIEL T. LABELS IN MAJORITY-MINORITY RELATIONS.
    STATE COLLEGE, PENNSYLVANIA: UNIVERSITY PARK PRESS,
    1969 (SO).

VALDEZ, DANIEL T. THE HISPANO REVOLT; MEXICAN-AMERICANS,
    PUERTO RICANS AND SPANISH COLONIALS ON THE MOVE.
    DENVER: UNIVERSITY CF DENVER, 1969 (HS).

VANDEL.   RAZA: MEXICAN AMERICANS (SO*).

VASQUEZ, DIAMANTINA MINERVA. THE HISTORICAL DEVELOPMENT
    OF OWNERSHIP IN THE SUBSOIL RESOURCES OF MEXICO.
    UNIVERSITY OF TEXAS AT AUSTIN, MASTER'S THESIS (1946).

VIDAL, MIRTA. CHICANO LIBERATION AND REVOLUTIONARY YOUTH.
    NEW YORK: PATHFINDER PRESS, INC., (SO).

VOWELL.   POLITICS PASO, 1850-1920 (HT*).

WAGONER.   ARIZONA TERRITORY 1863-1912: (HA*).

WEEKS.   "THE LEAGUE UNITED LATIN-AMERICAN (SO*).

WEEKS.   "THE TEXAS-MEXICAN POLITICS SOUTH (HT*).

WEEKS, OLIVER DOUGLAS. TEXAS PRESIDENTIAL POLITICS
    IN 1952.   AUSTIN, TEXAS: INSTITUTE OF PUBLIC AFFAIRS,
    UNIVERSITY OF TEXAS, 1953.

WESCHLER, LOUIS F. AND GALLAGHER JOHN F. VIVA KENNEDY.
    IN ROCCO J. TRESSOLINI AND RICHARD T. FROST, EDITORS,
    CASES IN AMERICAN NATIONAL GOVERNMENT AND POLITICS,
    (MAY 2 1, 1951). 1966.

WILEY.   POLITICS PURSE STRINGS NEW MEXICOS (ED*).

WILEY.   PUBLIC SCHOOL EDUCATION NEW MEXICO (EC*).

WILGUS.   HISTORICAL ATLAS LATIN AMERICA: (HSA*).

WILKE, RAYMOND. SAN MIGUEL: A MEXICAN COLLECTIVE EJIDO.
    STANFORD: STANFORD UNIVERSITY PRESS, 1971 (HM).

WILLIAMS, DEAN L. SOME POLITICAL AND ECONOMIC ASPECTS OF
    MEXICAN IMMIGRATION INTO THE UNITED STATES SINCE 1941,
    WITH PARTICULAR REFERENCE TO THIS IMMIGRATION INTO
    THE STATE OF CALIFORNIA.   UNIVERSITY OF CALIFORNIA,
    LOS ANGELES, MASTER'S THESIS (1950) (EC SI).

WILLIAMS, ROBIN M., JR. REDUCTION OF INTERGROUP TENSIONS:
A SURVEY OF RESEARCH ON PROBLEMS OF ETHNIC, RACIAL,
AND RELIGIOUS GROUP RELATICNS. NEW YORK: SOCIAL
SCIENCE RESEARCH COUNCIL, 1947.

WINN. REVOLUTICNARY ASPECTS VALLEYFARM (SO*).

WOLFINGER. "REPUTATION REALITY STUDY COMMUNITY (SO*).

WOODS. MEXICAN ETHNIC LEADERSHIP SAN (SO*).

WRAY. CESAR CHAVEZ, DIALOGUE WITH CONGRESS (EC*).

YOUNG. MEXICAN OIL AMERICAN DIPLOMACY (HM*).

ZAMORA, ALFREDO. THE MEXICAN AMERICAN COMMUNITY AND
MEXICAN AMERICAN STUDIES. CHICANO STUDIES INSTITUTES,
(SUMMER 1970). PROGRAM COORDINATED BY MONTAL SYSTEMS.
(SO).

ZAVALA. POLITICAL PHILOSOPHY CONQUEST (HS*).

P S Y C H O L O G Y

(PY)

ABE.   PREDICTION ACADEMIC ACHIEVEMENT (ED*).

ALATIS.   BILINGUALISM LANGUAGE CONTACT: (LA*).

ALTERS.   "AMERICAN MEXICAN: SURVIVALCULTURE" (SO*).

ALTUS.   "RACIAL BILINGUAL GROUP DIFFERENCES (ED*).

ALTUS.   "THE AMERICAN MEXICAN: SURVIVAL (SO*).

ANDERSON.   NUMBER ABILITIES CONCEPTS SPANISH-SPEAKING
     (ED*).

ANDERSSON.   A NEW FOCUS BILINGUAL CHILD (ED*).

ANDERSSON.   "NEW FOCUS BILINGUAL CHILD" (ED*).

ANDERSSON.   RECRUITMENT TRAINING TEACHERS (ED*).

ANDERSSON.   BILINGUAL SCHOOLING UNITED STATES (ED*).

ANGLIN.   STUDY IMPROVEMENT SPANISH-SPEAKING (ED*).

"FACTORS AFFECTING THE INTELLIGENCE OF AMERICAN CHILDREN
     OF MEXICAN PARENTAGE.".   JOURNAL OF ABNORMAL
     AND SOCIAL PSYCHOLOGY, VOL. 46 (OCTOBER, 1951), PP.
     598-602 (ED).

"THE ENGLISH PROFICIENCY FOREIGN (ED*).

"MEXICAN AMERICAN MARKET: SURVEY (EC*).

"MEXICAN AMERICANS OPPOSE LAZY (SO*).

"NEUROSIS AND THE MEXICAN FAMILY STRUCTURE".   AMERICAN
     JOURNAL OF PSYCHIATRY, VOL. 112 (1955), PP. 411-417
     (SO).

ACQUISITION LANGUAGE BY CHILDREN (ED*).

MINORITY GROUP ADOLESCENTS IN THE UNITED STATES.
     BALTIMORE: WILLIAMS AND WILKINS, 1968 (SO).

APPEL, K. E. "ANXIETY PROBLEMS WITH CULTURAL SETTINGS".
    AMERICAN JOURNAL OF PROCTOLOGY,   (NOVEMBER 1963),
    PP. 526-529 (SO AN).

ARAIZA, YOLANDA. THE MEXICAN'S SEARCH FOR IDENTITY.   SAN
    DIEGO, CALIFORNIA, (ED).

ARAMIREZ, SANTIAGO AND PARRES, RAMON. "SOME DYNAMIC
    PATTERNS IN THE ORGANIZATION OF THE MEXICAN FAMILY".
    INTERNATIONAL JOURNAL OF SOCIAL PSYCHIATRY, VOL. 3
    (1957), PP. 18-21.

ARAMONI, A. "MACHISMO".   PSYCHOLOGY TODAY, VOL. 5 NO.
    8 (JANUARY 1972), PP. 69-72.

ARAMONI.   "PSICOANALISIS DE DINAMICA DE (AN*).

ARAMONI.   PSICOANALISIS DE DINAMICA DEUN (AN*).

ARIAS, RONALD. WE'RE SUPPOSED TO BELIEVE WE'RE INFERIOR.
    IN ED LUDWIG AND JAMES SANTIBANEZ, THE CHICANOS.
    BALTIMORE, MARYLAND; PENGUIN BOOKS, INC., 1971 (LMA).

ARLITT.   "ON NEED CAUTION ESTABLISHING (SO*).

ARTHUR.   "AN EXPERIENCE TESTING INDIAN (ED*).

ARTHUR.   "THE PREDICTIVE VALUE KUHLMANN-BINET (ED*).

ARTHUR.   ARTHUR POINT SCALE PERFORMANCE (ED*).

ARTHUR.   LEITER INTERNATIONAL PERFORMANCE (ED*).

ARTHUR.   POINT SCALE PERFORMANCE TESTS (ED*).

ATKINS.   MEASUREMENT INTELLIGENCE YOUNG (ED*).

ATKINSON.   EDUCATIONAL RETARDATION SPANISH-SPEAKING (ED*).

BARNES.   ATTITUDES MINORITY NON MINORITY (ED*).

BARZUN, JACQUES. RACE: A STUDY IN SUPERSTITION.   NEW
    YORK: HARPER AND ROW, 1965 (AN SO).

BATISTA Y CALDERON.   STUDY COUNTER-PREJUDICE MEXICAN-SPANISH
    (SO*).

BELLESTEROS.   STUDY ELEVEN YEAR OLD MEXICAN-AMERICAN (ED*).

BERNARD.   "PSYCHOLOGICAL PRINCIPLES LANGUAGE (ED*).

BERNARD.   "TEXTS CLASSROOM METHODS BILINGUAL (ED*).

BETTELHEIM.   DYNAMICS PREJUDICE (AN*).

BETTELHEIM.   SOCIAL CHANGE PREJUDICE, INCLUDING   (AN*).

BOGUE.   MODIFICATION ATTITUDES TOWARD   (SO*).

BOLDYREFF.   BY WORD MOUTH; INFORMAL ESSAYS   (ED*).

BOOTH.   NORMATIVE COMPARISON RESPONSES   (ED*).

BOUGERS, LAEL SHANNON.   A DEVELOPMENTAL STUDY OF TIME
    PERCEPTION AND TIME PERSPECTIVE IN THREE CULTURAL
    GROUPS; ANGLO AMERICAN, INDIAN AMERICAN, AND MEXICAN
    AMERICANS.   UNIVERSITY OF CALIFORNIA, LOS ANGELES,
    PHD.   DISSERTATION (1971).

BOWLES.   EFFECTIVENESS REINFORCEMENT MEANS   (ED*).

BRADISH.   ACHIEVEMENT ATTITUDES HISPANOS   (ED*).

BRANDT.   EFFECT TOKEN REINFORCEMENT WITHOUT   (ED*).

BRIDGES.   "THE RELATION INTELLIGENCE TO   (ED*).

BRIGHAM.   "INTELLIGENCE TESTS IMMIGRANT   (ED*).

BRIGHAM.   STUDY AMERICAN INTELLIGENCE   (ED*).

BRINGAS.   "THE EDUCATIONAL MISSIONARY"   (ED*).

BROGAN, DENIS W.   THE AMERICAN CHARACTER.   NEW YORK:
    KNOPF, 1944 (SO).

BRONSON.   CHANGES PERSONALITY NEEDS VALUES   (RE*).

BROOKS, RICHARD MARTIN.   THE PSYCHOLOGICAL AND CULTURAL
    BASES OF MAGICAL DISEASE BELIEFS.   UNIVERSITY
    OF ARIZONA AT TUCSON, PHD.   DISSERTATION (1964) (AN).

BROPHY.   BABY TRAIN WEST: REVEALING ENCOUNTER   (SO*).

BROWN-WRINKLE.   PITCH IMPROVEMENT ANGLO LATIN   (MU*).

BRUNER, J. S.; GOODNOW, J. J. ; AUSTIN, G. A.   A STUDY OF
    THINKING.   NEW YORK: JOHN WILEY & SONS, 1956 (SO).

BUSTRILLOS.   DECISION MAKING STYLES SELECTED   (SO*).

CABRERA.   "SCHIZOPHRENIA SOUTHWEST: MEXICAN-AMERICANS
    (ED*).

CABRERA.   AMERICAN MEXICAN-AMERICAN CULTURE   (ED*).

CABRERA.   STUDY AMERICAN MEXICAN-AMERICAN   (ED*).

CALIFORNIA STATE DEPARTMENT OF PUBLIC HEALTH.   MEXICANS
    CALIFORNIA   (ED*).

CALIFORNIA STATE DEPARTMENT OF INDUSTRIAL RELATIONS.
      PRELIMINARY REPORT SURVEY ACTIVE   (ED*).

CANAVAN, D. FIELD DEPENDENCE IN CHILDREN AS A FUNCTION
      OF GRADE, SEX, AND ETHNIC GR OUP MEMBERSHIP.   PAPER
      READ AT THE AMERICAN PSYCHOLOGICAL ASSOCIATION
      MEETING, WASHINGTON, D. C., 1969 (ED).

CAREY, JAMES EUGENE. SOME MAJOR PSYCHOLOGICAL CHARACTERISTICS
      OF SPANISH SPEAKING PEOPLE.   ARIZONA STATE UNIVERSITY,
      MASTER'S THESIS (1954).

CARLSON, FELDING S.;HENDERSON, NORMAN. "INTELLIGENCE OF
      AMERICAN CHILDREN OF MEXICAN PARENTAGE".   JOURNAL
      OF ABNORMAL AND SOCIAL PSYCHOLOGY, VOL. 45 (APRIL
      1952), PP. 544-551 (SO).

CARRILLO.   COGNITIVE IMPULSIVITY MEXICAN-AMERICAN   (ED*).

CATTEL.   "COMPARABILITY IQS OBTAINEDDIFFERENT   (ED*).

CATTELL.   CULTURE FREE INTELLIGENCE TEST   (ED*).

CATTELL.   "A CULTURE-FREE INTELLIGENCETEST   (ED*).

CATTELL.   "THE FATE NATIONAL INTELLIGENCE: (ED*).

CATTELL.   "A CULTURE-FREE INTELLIGENCETEST: (ED*).

CHAMBERS.   WILLINGNESS TO ADOPT HARD TOPLACE   (SO*).

CHANCE.   "ACCULTURATION, SELF-IDENTIFICATION   (AN*).

CHANG.   GUIDE UNDERSTANDING TEACHINGMEXICAN   (ED*).

CHAPMAN, J. CROSBY; WIGGINS, D. M. "RELATION OF FAMILY
      SIZE TO INTELLIGENCE AND SOCIO ECONOMIC STATUS OF FA
      MILY".   PEDAGOGICAL SEMINARY AND JOURNAL OF GENETIC
      PSYCHOLOGY, VOL. 32 (SEPTEMBER 1925), PP. 414-421
      (SO).

CHARLTON.   "APHASIA BILINGUAL POLYGLOT PATIENTS   (MD*).

CLARK.   MOTIVATIONAL PATTERN CULTURALLY   (SO*).

COBB.   RETARDATION ELEMENTARY SCHOOLS   (ED*).

COFFEY.   "THE ROLE CULTURAL STATUS INTELLIGENCE   (ED*).

CONNOR, LEO E. ADMINISTRATION OF SPECIAL EDUCATION
      PROGRAMS.   NEW YORK: TEACHERS COLLEGE PRESS, 1961
      (ED).

COOPER.   "PREDICTING SCHOOL ACHIEVEMENT   (ED*).

CORONA, BERT CHARLES. STUDY OF ADJUSTMENT AND INTERPERSONAL
   RELATIONS OF ADOLESCENTS OF MEXICAN DESCENT.
   UNIVERSITY OF CALIFORNIA, PHD. DISSERTATION (1955)
   (ED SO).

COX.   ANALYSIS INTELLIGENCE SUB-NORMAL (ED*).

CRAWFORD.   FORGOTTEN EGG: STUDY MENTALHEALTH (MD*).

CRAWFORD.   FORGOTTEN EGG: STUDY MENTALHEALTH (MD*).

CRUZ.   SPANISH-SPEAKING CHILDRENS EXPRESSED (ED*).

CURRIER.   "HOT-COLD SYNDROME SYMBOLIC BALANCE   (MD*).

DAER.   "AN INQUIRY INTO EFFECT BILINGUALISM (ED*).

DAILEY.   STUDY ACHIEVEMENT SPANISH RELATION (ED*).

DANIELS.   CULTURAL ASPECTS BEHAVIOR MEXICAN (AN*).

DARCY.   "A REVIEW LITERATURE EFFECTSBI-LINGUALISM (ED*).

DARCY.   "THE EFFECT BILINGUALISM UPON (ED*).

DAVENPORT.   "INTELLIGENCE QUOTIENTS MEXICAN (ED*).

DAVENPORT.   COMPARATIVE STUDY MEXICAN NON-MEXICAN (ED*).

DAVIDSON.   MEXICAN AMERICAN HIGH SCHOOLGRADUATE (ED*).

DE HOYOS.   OCCUPATIONAL EDUCATIONAL LEVELS (ED*).

DE HOYOS.   OCCUPATIONAL EDUCATIONAL LEVELS (ED*).

DE LA VEGA.   SOME FACTORS AFFECTING LEADERSHIP (ED*).

DELMET.   STUDY MENTAL SCHOLASTIC ABILITIES (ED*).

DEMOS.   "ATTITUDES MEXICAN-AMERICANSANGLO (ED*).

DEMPSEY.   CULTURE CONSERVATION TIME: COMPARISON (SO*).

DERBYSHIRE.   CHILDRENS PERCEPTIONS POLICE: (SO*).

DEUTSCH.   DISADVANTAGED CHILD LEARNINGPROCESS: (ED*).

DEUTSCH.   MINORITY GROUP CLASS STATUS AS (ED*).

DI STEFANO.   INTERPERSONAL PERCEPTIONS FIELD (ED*).

DIAZ DEL CASTILLO, BERNAL. ESTUDIOS DE PSICOLOGIA
   DEL MEXICANO.   MEXICO: EDITORIAL F. TRILLAS, 1968.

DIAZ-GUERRERO, ROGELIO. "NEUROSIS AND THE MEXICAN FAMILY
    STRUCTURE". AMERICAN JOURNAL OF PSHCHIATRY, VOL.
    112 (DEC 1955), PP. 411-417.

DITTMAR. LATIN AMERICAN STUDENTS U. S. (SO*).

DOLL, EDGAR A. "MENTAL EVALUATION CF CHILDREN WITH
    EXPRESSIVE HANDICAPS". THE AMERICAN JOURNAL
    OF ORTHOPSYCHIATRY, VOL. 21 (JAN 1951), PP. 148-154.

DRISCOLL, GERTRUDE. DRISCOLL PLAYKIT. NEW YORK,
    NEW YORK: THE PSYCHOLOGICAL CORPORATION, 1955.

DURRELL; SULLIVAN. READING CAPACITY ACHIEVEMENTTESTS
    (ED*).

DWORKIN. NATIONAL ORIGIN GHETTO EXPERIENCE (SO*).

DWORKIN. STEREOTYPES SELF-IMAGES HELD (SO*).

DWORKIN. "STEREOTYPES SELF-IMAGES HELD (SO*).

DWORKIN. POPULAR STEREOTYPES SELF-IMAGES (SO*).

EELS, KENNETH, ET. AL. INTELLIGENCE AND CULTURAL DIFFERENCES.
    CHICAGO, ILLINOIS: UNIVERSITY OF CHICAGO PRESS, 1951
    (AN ED).

EITELGEORGE. MEXICAN-AMERICAN CAUCASIAN PUPILS (ED*).

ELLIS. RELATION SOCIO-ECONOMIC STATUS (SO*).

ENRIGHT, J. B. ; JAECKLE, W. R. "PSYCHIATRIC SYMMPTOMS
    AND DIAGNOSIS IN TWO CULTURES". INTERNATIONAL
    JOURNAL OF SOCIAL PSYCHIATRY, VOL. 9 (WINTER 1963),
    P. 12 (SO).

FABREGA, HORACIO (JR) AND WALLACE, CAROLE ANN. 'VALUE
    IDENTIFICATION AND PSYCHIATRIC DISABILITY: AN ANALYSIS
    INVOLVING AMERICANS OF MEXICAN DESCENT.' IN
    NATHANIEL N. WAGNER AND MARSHA J. HAUG, CHICANOS:
    SOCIAL AND PSYCHOLOGICAL PERSPECTIVES.

FABREGA, HORACIO; SWARTZ, JON D.; WALLACE, ANN. "ETHNIC
    DIFFERENCES IN PSYCOPATHOLOGY--II. SPECIFIC DIFFERENCES
    WITH EMPHASIS ON A MEXICAN AMERICAN GROUP". JOURNAL
    OF PSYCHIATRIC RESEARCH, (DECEMBER 1968), PP. 221-235.

FISHER, GARY. "THE PERFORMANCE OF MALE PRISONERS ON THE
    MARLOWE-CROWNE SOCIAL DESIRABILITY SCALE: II DIFFERENCES
    AS A FUNCTION OF RACE AND CRIME.". JOURNAL OF
    CLINICAL PSYCHOLOGY, (OCTOBER 1967), PP. 473-475
    (SO LW).

FORBES. "BLACK PIONEERS: SPANISH SPEAKING (ED*).

FORBES.   "LA RAZA BRINGS MUCH TO SCHOOL" (ED*).

FORBES.   EDUCATION CULTURALLY DIFFERENT (ED*).

FORBES.   UNKNOWN ATHAPASCANS: IDENTIFICATION (ED*).

FORBES.   XMEXICAN-AMERICANS: HANDBOCKEDUCATORS (ED*).

FROMM.   "SOCIAL CHARACTER MEXICAN VILLAGE" (SO*).

FROMM.   SOCIAL CHARACTER MEXICAN VILLAGE: (SO*).

FUKUDA.   "A SURVEY INTELLIGENCE ENVIRONMENT (ED*).

FUNKUDA, F.   "THE INTELLIGENCE AND ENVIRONMENT OF CHILDREN".
     AMERICAN JOURNAL OF PSYCHOLOGY, VOL. 36 (1925), PP.
     124-139 (ED SO).

GAMIO.   "A COMPARISON INTELLIGENCE MEXICAN (AN*).

GAMIO.   "THE INDUSTRIAL PSYCHOLOGY IMMIGRANT (AN*).

GARRETSON.   "A STUDY CAUSES RETARDATION AMONG (ED*).

GARTH, T. R.   "THE ADMINISTRATION OF NON-LANGUAGE INTELLIGENCE
     TESTS TO MEXICANS".   JOURNAL OF ABNORMAL AND SOCIAL
     PSYCHOLOGY, VOL. 31 (APRIL 1936), PP. 53-58 (LA).

GARTH, THOMAS R.   "A COMPARISON OF MENTAL ABILITIES
     OF MIXED AND FULL BLOOD INDIANS ON A BASIS OF
     EDUCATION".   THE PSYCHOLOGICAL REVIEW, VOL. 29 (MAY
     1922), PP. 221-236.

GARTH, THOMAS R.   "A COMPARISON OF THE INTELLIGENCE
     OF MEXICAN AND MIXED AND FULL BLOOD INDIAN CHILDREN".
     PSYCHOLOGICAL REVIEW, VOL. 30 (1923), PP. 388-401.

GARTH, THOMAS R.   "THE INDUSTRIAL PSYCHOLOGY OF THE
     IMMIGRANT MEXICAN".   INDUSTRIAL PSYCHOLOGY, (MARCH
     1926), PP. 183-187 (SI).

GARTH.   "THE INTELLIGENCE MEXICAN SCHOOL (ED*).

GARTH, THOMAS R. AND CANDOR, E.   "MUSICAL TALENT OF
     MEXICANS".   AMERICAN JOURNAL OF PSYCHOLOGY, VOL. 49
     (APRIL 1937), PP. 298-301.

GARTH, THOMAS R. AND JOHNSON, HARPER D.   "THE INTELLIGENCE
     AND ACHIEVEMENT OF MEXICAN CHILDREN IN THE U. S.".
     JOURNAL OF ABNORMAL AND SOCIAL PSYCHOLOGY, VOL. 29
     (JUNE 30, 1928), PP. 222-229.

GARTH, THOMAS R. HOLCOMB, W. M. AND GOSCHE, I. "MENTAL
    FATIGUE OF MEXICAN SCHOOL CHILDREN". JOURNAL
    OF APPLIED PSYCHOLOGY, VOL. 15 (DECEMBER 1932), PP.
    675-680 (ED).

GARTH. "THE ADMINISTRATION NON-LANGUAGE (ED*).

GARTH, THOMAS, ELSON, T. H. AND MORTON, MARGARET. "THE
    INTELLIGENCE OF MEXICAN CHILDREN". SCHOOL AND
    SOCIETY, VOL. 27 (JUNE 30, 1928), PP. 791-794.

GATES, A. I. "THE CORRELATION OF ACHIEVEMENT IN SCHOOL
    SUBJECTS WITH INTELLIGENCE TESTS AND OTHER VARIABLES".
    JOURNAL OF EDUCATIONAL PSYCHOLOGY, VOL. 13 (1922),
    PP. 129-139, 223-235, 277-285.

GESCHE, IRMA. THE COLOR PREFERENCES OF ONE THOUSAND ONE
    HUNDRED AND FIFTY-TWO MEXICAN CHILDREN. UNIVERSITY
    OF TEXAS AT AUSTIN, MASTER'S THESIS (1923).

GILL. "SOME NON-INTELLECTUAL CORRELATES (ED*).

GILL. "SOME NON-INTELLECTUAL CORRELATES (ED*).

GILLIN, JOHN. "MAGICAL FRIGHT". PSYCHIATRY, VOL.
    2 (1948), PP. 387-400.

GINSBURG, SOLOMON WIENER. A PSYCHIATRIST'S VIEWS ON SOCIAL
    ISSUES. NEW YORK: COLUMBIA UNIVERSITY PRESS, 1963
    (SO).

GODDARD. "MENTAL TESTS IMMIGRANT" (SO*).

GONZALEZ PINEDA. MEXICANO: SU DINAMICA PSICOSOCIAL (SO*).

GONZALEZ PINEDA, FRANCISCO. EL MEXICANO: PSICOLOGIA DE
    SU DESTRUCTIVIDAD. MEXICO, EDITORIAL PAX.

GONZALEZ PINEDA, FRANCISCO. EL MEXICANO: SU DINAMICA
    PSICOSOCIAL. MEXICO: EDITORIAL PAX, 1959.

GOODENOUGH, FLORENCE. "RACIAL DIFFERENCES IN THE INTELLIGENCE
    OF SCHOOL CHILDREN". JOURNAL OF EXPERIMENTAL
    PSYCHOLOGY, VOL. 9 (OCTOBER 1926), PP. -388-397.

GOODENOUGH, FLORENCE. "THE RELATION OF INTELLIGENCE OF
    PRE-SCHOOL CHILDREN TO THE OCCUPATION OFTHEIR
    FATHERS". AMERICAN JOURNAL OF PSYCHOLOGY, VOL. 60
    (1928), PP. 284-302.

GOODENOUGH, FLORENCE. DRAW-A-MAN TEST. YONKERS,
    NEW YORK:WORLD BOOK, 1926.

GOULARD. STUDY INTELLIGENCE ELEVEN TWELVE (ED*).

GRAVES.   "ACCULTURATION, ACCESS, ALCOHOL   (AN*).

GRAVES.   TIME PERSPECTIVE DEFERRED GRATIFICATION   (AN*).

GROUP FOR THE ADVANCEMENT OF PSYCHIATRY.   "INTEGRATION AND
     MAL-INTEGRATION IN SPANISH-AMERICAN FAMILY PATTERNS".
     GAP REPORTS,   NO. 27 (AUGUST 1954), PP. 12-15 (SO).

GROUP FOR THE ADVANCEMENT OF PSYCHIATRY, COMMITTEE ON THE
     FAMILY.   INTEGRATION AND CONFLICT IN FAMILY BEHAVIOR.
     TOPEKA, KANSAS, 1964.

GUERRERO DIAZ, ROGELIO.   "NEUROSIS AND THE MEXICAN FAMILY
     STRUCTURE".   AMERICAN JOURNAL OF PSYCHIATRY, VOL.
     2 NO. 6 (1955), PP. 411-417.

GUTTENTAG.   GROUP COHESIVENESS, ETHNIC ORGANIZATION   (SO*).

HAGGERTY, M. E. HAGGERTY INTELLIGENCE EXAMINATION, MANUAL
     OF DIRECTIONS.   YONKERS: WORLD BOOK CO., 1929 (ED).

HAGGERTY, M. E. (ET AL).   NATIONAL INTELLIGENCE TESTS,
     MANUAL OF DIRECTIONS.   YONKERS: WORLD BOOK CO., 1924
     (ED).

HAGGERTY, M. E. AND NASH, H. B.   "MENTAL CAPACITY OF
     CHILDREN AND PATERNAL OCCUPATION".   JOURNAL OF
     EDUCATIONAL PSYCHOLOGY, VOL. 15 (1924), PP. 559-572
     (ED).

HAGWOOD, JOHN A.   THE ABILITY TO READ; ITS MEASUREMENT AND
     SOME FACTORS CONDITIONING IT.   BLOOMINGTON: INDIANA
     UNIVERSITY, (1917). INDIANA UNIVERSITY STUDIES, NO.
     34 (ED).

HANSON, EDITH JOSEPHINE. A STUDY OF INTELLIGENCE TEST
     RESULTS FOR MEXICAN CHILDREN BASED ON ENGLISH
     AND MEXICAN TEST FORMS.   UNIVERSITY OF SOUTHERN
     CALIFORNIA, MASTER'S THESIS (1931).

HARDING.   COMPARATIVE ANALYSIS RELATION   (ED*).

HAUCK, E.   ZUR DIFFERENTIELLEN PSYCHOLGIE KES INDUSTRIE
     UND LANDKINDES.   JULIUS BELTZ, LAGEUSALZA, 1929.

HAUGHT, B. F.   "MENTAL GROWTH OF THE SOUTHWESTERN INDIAN".
     THE JOURNAL OF APPLIED PSYCHOLOGY, VOL. 18 (1934),
     PP. 137-142.

HAUGHT, B. F.   "THE LANGUAGE DIFFICULTY OF SPANISH-AMERICAN
     CHILDREN".   JOURNAL OF APPLIED PSYCHOLOGY, VOL. 15
     (FEBRUARY 1931), PP. 92-95 (LA).

HELMKE, WILLARD. THE EFFECT OF ENGLISH LANGUAGE HANDICAP
     ON THE INTELLIGENCE QUOTIENTS OFSPANISH AMERICAN
     CHILDREN.   BOULDER: UNIVERSITY OF COLORADO, 1937 (ED
     LA).

HENDERSON.   "OPPORTUNITY ALIENATION PUBLIC (ED*).

HENDERSON, NORMAN B. A STUDY OF INTELLIGENCE OF CHILDREN
     OF MEXICAN AND NON-MEXICAN PARENTAGE.   MASTER'S
     OCCIDENTAL COLLEGE, 1948 (ED).

HEPNER, ETHEL MARION. SELF-CONCEPTS, VALUES, AND NEEDS
     OF MEXICAN AMERICAN UNDERACHIEVERS.   AN ARBOR,
     MICHIGAN, UNIVERSITY MICROFILMS (ED).

HERNANDEZ.   STUDY RETARDED SPANISH-SPEAKING   (ED*).

HERRIMAN.   INVESTIGATION CONCERNING EFFECT   (ED*).

HILDING.   "THE INTELLIGENCE AMERICAN CHILDREN   (ED*).

HIRSCH, NATHANIEL D. M. "A STUDY OF NATIO-RACIAL MENTAL
     DIFFERENCES".   GENETIC PSYCHOLOGY MONOGRAPHS, VOL.
     3 AND 4 (1926).

HISHIKI.   "SELF CONCEPTS SIXTH GRADE GIRLS (ED*).

HOLLAND.   "LANGUAGE BARRIER AS EDUCATIONAL   (ED*).

HOULE.   SOME SIGNIFICANT CHARACTERISTICS   (ED*).

HRDLICKA, ALES. "A STUDY OF THE INTELLIGENCE OF ANGLO-CHINESE
     CHILDREN".   EUGENICS REVIEW, VOL. 30 (1938), PP.
     109-116 (ED).

HUGHES.   COMPARATIVE STUDY INTELLIGENCE   (ED*).

HUNTER, W. S., AND SOMMER, NEIL E. "THE RELATION OF THE
     DEGREE OF INDIAN BLOOD TO SCORE ON THE OTIS INTELLIGENCE
     TEST".   JOURNAL OF COMPARATIVE PSYCHOLOGY, VOL. 11
     (1922), PP. 257-277 (ED).

HURT.   "RELIABILITY VALIDITY METROPOLITAL   (ED*).

HUSE, HOWARD R. THE PSYCHOLOGY OF FOREIGN LANGUAGE STUDY.
     CHAPEL HILL, NORTH CAROLINA: UNIVERSITY OF NORTH
     CAROLINA PRESS, 1931 (LA).

HYMAN.   POLITICAL SOCIALIZATION: STUDY (PL*).

HYMER.   STUDY SOCIAL ATTITUDES ADULTMEXICAN   (SI*).

HYMER.   STUDY SOCIAL ATTITUDES ADULTMEXICAN   (SI*).

HYMER.   STUDY SOCIAL ATTITUDES ADULTMEXICAN   (SI*).

IHRIG, MAXWELL J. A STUDY OF THE MOTIVATION OF STUDENTS
    WHO COMPLETED THE JUNIOR YEAR OF HIGH SCHOOL, AND WHO
    ARE MEMBERS OF SOCIALLY, ECONOMICALLY AND CULTURALLY
    DEPRIVED AREAS.   UNIVERSITY OF NEW MEXICO, PHD.
    DISSERTATION (1967) (ED).

INTER-AMERICAN CONGRESS OF PSYCHOLOGY. CONTRIBUCION DE
    LAS CIENCIAS PSICOLOGICAS Y DEL COMPORTAMIENTO
    AL DESAROLLO DE LOS PUEBLOS. MEMORIAS DE XI CONGRESO
    INTERAMERICANO DE PSICOLOGIA.   MEXICO, F. F.:
    UNIVERSIDAD NACIONAL AUTONOMA DE MEXICO, 1967.

JAYAGOPAL, RAJABATHER. PROBLEM SOLVING ABILITIES AND
    PSYCHOMOTOR SKILLS OF NAVAJO INDIANS, SPANISH
    AMERICANS AND ANGLOS IN JUNIOR HIGH SCHOOL.
    ANN ARBOR: UNIVERSITY OF MICHIGAN, 1971 (ED).

JOHNSON.   "A COMPARISON MENTAL AGES SCORES   (ED*).

JOHNSON, DALE L., AND SIKES, MELVIN P. "RORSCHACH AND TAT
    RESPONSES OF NEGRO, MEXICAN-AMERICAN AND ANGLO
    PSYCHIATRIC PATIENTS".   JOURNAL OF PROJECTIVE
    TECHNIQUES AND PERSONALITY ASSESSMENT,   (JUNE 1965),
    PP. 183-188 (ED).

JOHNSON, GRANVILLE B. "AN EXPERIMENTAL PROJECTION
    TECHNIQUE FOR THE ANALYSIS OF RACIAL ATTITUDES".
    THE JOURNAL OF EDUCATIONAL PSYCHOLOGY, VOL. 41 (MAY
    1950), PP. 267-278 (ED).

JOHNSON, GRANVILLE B. "BILINGUALISM AS MEASURED BY
    A REACTION-TIME TECHNIQUE AND THE RELATIONSHIP BETWEEN
    A LANGUAGE AND A NON-LANGUAGE INTELLIGENCE QUOTIENT".
    THE JOURNAL OF GENETIC PSYCHOLOGY, VOL. 82 (MARCH
    1933), PP. 3-9 (ED).

JOHNSON, GRANVILLE B. "THE ORIGIN AND DEVELOPMENT OF THE
    SPANISH ATTITUDE TOWARD THE ANGLO AND THE ANGLO
    ATTITUDE TOWARD THE SPANISH".   THE JOURNAL OF
    EDUCATIONAL PSYCHOLOGY, VOL. 41 (MAY 1950),
    PP. 428-439 (ED).

JOHNSON, GRANVILLE B., JR. "THE RELATIONSHIP EXISTING
    BETWEEN BILINGUALISM AND RACIAL ATTITUDE".   JOURNAL
    OF EDUCATIONAL PSYCHOLOGY, VOL. 42 (OCTOBER 1951),
    PP. 357-365 (ED).

JOHNSON.   "A COMPARISON VOCABULARIES ANGO-AMERICAN (ED*).

JONES, ALICE M. "A VOCABULARY STUDY OF CHILDREN IN
    A FOREIGN INDUSTRIAL COMMUNITY".   PSYCHOLOGICAL
    CLINIC, VOL. 17 (1928), PP. 13-21 (LA).

JONES.   STUDY ACCULTURATION SOCIAL ASPIRATIONS (ED*).

JONES.   ENVIRONMENTAL HANDICAP MENTAL   (ED*).

JONES, HUBERT LEDYARD.   A COMPARISON OF PHYSICAL SKILL AND
     INTELLIGENCE OF NEGRO AND SPANISH—AMERICAN BOYS OF
     JUNIOR HIGH SCHOOL AGE.   UNIVERSITY OF DENVER,
     MASTER'S THESIS (1940) (ED).

JONES.   "A CRITICAL STUDY BILINGUALISM   (ED*).

JONES.   "BILINGUALISM VERBAL INTELLIGENCE"   (ED*).

KAGAN, S., AND M. C. MADSEN.   'MEXICAN AMERICAN AND ANGLO
     AMERICAN CHILDREN OF TWO DIFFERENT AGES UNDER.'
     DEVELOPMENTAL PSYCHOLOGY.

KAMM.   TEACHING CONCEPTUAL THINKINGTO   (ED*).

KAPLAN, BERT.   "A STUDY OF RORSCHSCH RESPONSES IN FOUR
     CULTURES".   PAPERS OF THE PEABODY MUSEUM, HARVARD
     UNIVERSITY, VOL. 42   NO. 2 (1954), P. 32.

KAPLAN, J. M.   "PREDICTING MEMORY BEHAVIOR FROM COGNITIVE
     ATTITUDES TOWARD INSTABILITY".   AMERICAN PSYCHOLOGY,
     VOL. 7   (1952), P. 332.

KAPLAN, JEROME, DAVID.   TEACHING NUMBER CONSERVATION TO
     DISADVANTAGED CHILDREN.   COLUMBIA UNIVERSITY, PHD.
     DISSERTATION (1967) (ED).

KARABINUR.   "VAN ALSTYNE PICTURE VOCABULARY   (ED*).

KARNO. MARVIN.   THE ENIGMA OF ETHNICITY IN A PSYCHIATRIC
     CLINIC.   THE ENIGMA OF ETHNICITY IN A PSYCHIATRIC
     CLINIC, ARCH GEN PSYCHIATRIC.MAY, 1966.

KARNO, MARVIN AND ROBERT B. EDGERTON.   "PERCEPTION
     OF MENTAL ILLNESS IN A MEXICAN AMERICAN COMMUNITY".
     ARCHIVES OF GENERAL PSYCHIATRY,   (FEBRUARY   1969),
     PP. 233-238.

KESTON MORTON J. AND CARMINA A. JIMENEZ.   "A STUDY
     OF PERFORMANCE ON ENGLISH AND SPANISH EDITIONS OF THE
     STANFORD—BINET INTELLIGENCE TEST BY SPANISH—AMERICAN
     CHILDREN".   JOURNAL OF GENETIC PSYCHOLOGY, VOL. 85
     (1954), PP. 263-269 (ED).

KIEV.   CURANDERISMO: MEXICAN AMERICAN   (AN*).

KING, GENEVIEVE.   THE PSYCHOLOGY OF A MEXICAN COMMUNITY
     IN SAN ANTONIO, TEXAS.   UNIVERSITY OF TEXAS, MASTER'S
     THESIS (1938) (HT).

KING.   MUSICAL EXPERIENCE TO AID MEXICAN   (MU*).

KIRK, SAMUEL A., JAMES J. MCCARTHY, WINFRED D. KIRK.
    ILLINOIS TEST OF PSYCHOLINGUISTIC ABILITIES.   URBANA:
    UNIVERSITY OF ILLINOIS PRESS, 1970 (LA).

KIRTPATRICK, C. INTELLIGENCE AND IMMIGRATION.   BALTIMORE,
    WILLIAMS AND WILKINS (SI).

KITTEL. "INTELLIGENCE-TEST PERFORMANCE (ED*).

KITTELL. "BILINGUALISM LANGUAGE NON-LANGUAGE (ED*).

KLEIN, G. S., R. W. GARDNER, & H. J. SCHLESINGER.
    "TOLERANCE FOR UNREALISTIC EXPERIENCES: A STUDY OF
    THE GENERALITY OF COGNITIVE CONTROL".   BRITISH
    JOURNAL OF PSYCHOLOGY, VOL. 53 (1962), PP. 41-55.

KLINEBERG. EXPERIMENTAL STUDY OF SPEED AND OTHER FACTORS
    IN RACIAL PSYCHOLOGY.   EXPERIMENTAL STUDY OF SPEED
    AND OTHER FACTORS IN RACIAL PSYCHOLOGY, 1928.

KLINEBERG, NETTYE V. BILINGUALISM AND INTELLIGENCE IN TEN
    YEAR OLD ITALIAN GIRLS.   COLUMBIA UNIVERSITY, NEW
    YORK, MASTER'S THESIS (1932).

KLINEBERG, OTTO. RACE DIFFERENCES.   NEW YORK: HARPER AND
    BROTHERS, 1935 (SO).

KLINGER, H. "IMITATED ENGLISH CLEFT PALATE SPEECH IN A
    NORMAL SPANISH SPEAKING CHILD".   JOURNAL OF SPEECH
    AND HEARING DISORDERS, VOL. 27 (NOVEMBER 1962), PP.
    379-381.

KLITGAARD. "A GAP IS BRIDGED; SUCCESSFUL (ED*).

KNAPP. "THE EFFECTS TIME LIMITS INTELLIGENCE (ED*).

KOCH. "A STUDY TEST PERFORMANCE AMERICAN (ED*).

KOCH. COMPARATIVE STUDY PERFORMANCE (ED*).

KOENIG. "IMPROVING LANGUAGE ABILITIES (ED*).

KOLB, L. "THE INTELLIGENCE OF IMMIGRANTS AS MEASURED BY
    TESTS".   JOURNAL OF PSYCHO-ASTHENICS, VOL. 37
    (1932), PP. 393-411 (SI).

KORNHAUSER. "THE ECONOMIC STANDING PARENTS (ED*).

KORTE.   LENGTH TIME PUBLIC ASSISTANCE (SO*).

LAMB, EMILY. "RACIAL DIFFERENCES IN BIMANUAL DEXTERITY
    OF LATIN AND AMERICAN CHILDREN".   CHILD DEVELOPMENT,
    VOL. 1 (1930), PP. 204-231 (SC).

LAMBERT, W. E.; PEAL, ELIZABETH. "THE RELATION OF
    BILINGUALISM TO INTELLIGENCE". PSYCHOLOGICAL
    MONOGRAPHS: GENERAL AND APPLIED, VOL. 76 (1962), P.
    27 (ED).

LAMBERT, WALLACE. "PSYCHOLOGICAL APPROACHES TO THE STUDY
    OF LANGUAGE. PART 2". MODERN LANGUAGE JOURNAL, VOL.
    47 (1963), PP. 114-121 (ED).

LAMBERT, WALLACE: GARDNER, R. C. ATTITUDES AND MOTIVATION
    IN SECOND LANGUAGE LEARNING. ROWLEY, MASSACHUSETTS:
    NEWBURY HOUSE PUBLISHERS, INC., (ED).

LAMBERT, WALLACE: TUCKER, G. R. THE BILINGUAL EDUCATION
    OF CHILDREN. ROWLEY, MASSACHUSETTS: NEWBURY HOUSE
    PUBLISHERS, INC., (ED).

LANE, MARY B. "THE YOUNG CHILD: PRIORITIES AND POTENTIALS".
    YOUNG CHILDREN, (MARCH 1967), PP. 219-227 (ED).

LANGNER. "A TEST INTERGROUP PREJUDICEWHICH (SO*).

LARSON. "A METHOD IDENTIFYING CULTURALLY (ED*).

LASKER. RACE ATTITUDES CHILDREN (SO*).

LASKER. STUDY DEVELOPMENT RACE ATTITUDES (SO*).

LASKER. "THE QUESTION PHYSICAL SELECTION (SI*).

LEARY. "CHILDREN WHO ARE TESTED ALIEN (ED*).

LEMAN, JOHN EDWARD. AGGRESSION IN MEXICAN AMERICAN AND
    ANGLO AMERICAN DELINQUENT AND NON-DELINQUENT MALES
    AS REVEALED IN DREAMS AND THERMATIC APPERCEPTION TEST
    RESPONSES. UNIVERSITY OF ARIZONA, PHD. DISSERTATION
    (1966) (ED).

LENTZ. "RELATION I.Q. TO SIZE FAMILY" (ED*).

LEONA E. TYLER. THE PSYCHOLOGY OF HUMAN DIFFERENCES.
    NEW YORK: APPLETON, 1956 (SO).

LEOPOLD, WERNER. F. "COMPARATIVE STUDY OF MONOLINGUALS
    AND BILINGUALS IN A VERBAL TASK PERFORMANCE".
    JOURNAL OF CLINICAL PSYCHOLOGY, VOL. 17 (JANUARY
    1961), PP. 49-52.

LESSA, ORIGENES. MARTA; A SOUVENIR OF NEW YORK.
    MONOGRAPHS OF THE SOCIETY FOR RESEARCH IN CHILD
    DEVELOPMENT, (MAY 1968). 1965 (SO).

LESSER. "MENTAL ABILITIES CHILDREN DIFFERENT (ED*).

LEWIN, KURT; DEMBO, T. ; FESTINGER, L.; SEARS, P. LEVEL
    OF ASPIRATION. NEW YORK: RONALD PRESS, 1944.

LEWIS. COMPARISON ACADEMIC ACHIEVEMENT   (ED*).

LIEBERMAN.   INTONATION, PERCEPTION, LANGUAGE   (LA*).

LIVERMORE, JEAN. "INDENTIFICATION OF TEENAGE GIRLS WITH
    MEXICAN AMERICAN MINORITY".   AMERICAN JOURNAL
    OF ORTHOPSYCHIATRY, VOL. 30 (JULY 1961), PP. 630-636.

LOVE, RUTH B. SUMMARY AND RECOMMENDATIONS FOR STRENGTHENING
    COUNSELING SERVICES FOR DISADVANTAGED YOUTH.
    SACRAMENTO: CALIFORNIA STATE DEPARTMENT OF EDUCATION,
    1966 (SO ED).

LUGO.   COMPARISON DEGREES BILINGUALISM (ED*).

MANZO.   DIFFICULTIES SPANISH-SPEAKING   (ED*).

MARINA.   "THREE BASIC THEMES MEXICAN PUERTO (SO*).

MARTINEZ.   FACTORS CORRELATED WITH ETHNIC   (ED*).

MASON.   CROSS-VALIDATION STUDY PERSONALITY   (ED*).

MASON.   "CROSS-VALIDATION STUDY PERSONALITY (ED*).

MASON.   COMPARISON PERSONALITY CHARACTERISTICS (ED*).

MASON.   CASE STUDY THIRTY ADOLESCENTMEXICAN (SO*).

MASSAD.   "STIMULUS MODES LANGUAGE MEDIA; (LA*).

MC ANULTY.   "ACHIEVEMENT INTELLIGENCE TEST (ED*).

MC CAMMON.   STUDY CHILDRENS ATTITUDES TOWARD (ED*).

MC DANIEL.   RELATIONSHIPS BETWEEN SELF-CONCEPT (SO*).

MC DOWELL.   STATUS ACADEMIC CAPABILITIESACHIEVEMENT   (ED*).

MEADOW.   "SYMPTOMATIC BEHAVIOR HOSPITALIZED (MD*).

MEADOW.   "RELIGIOUS AFFILIATION PSYCHOPATHOLOGY (RE*).

MEMMI.   DOMINATED MAN (AN*).

MENDENHALL.   COMPARATIVE STUDY ACHIEVEMENT (ED*).

MERCEDES.   ARITHMETIC NORTH ELEMENTARY SCHOOL (ED*).

MERCER, JANE R. "IMPRINTS OF CULTURE ON THE PERSONALITIES
    OF CHILDREN".   CALIFORNIA MENTAL HEALTH RESEARCH
    DIGEST, (SUMMER 1967), PP. 161-162 (MD AN).

MERRYWEATHER.   STUDY COMPARATIVE ABILITY MEXICAN   (ED*).

MESSINEO, JOSEPH F. THE ENVIRONMENTAL UTILIZATION
    OF PSYCHOLINGUISTIC ABILITIES OF DISADVANTAGED SLOW
    LEARNERS IN RELATION TO THE ECOLOGY OF TEST INTELLIGENCE.
    UNPUBLISHED DOCTORS DISSERTATION UNIVERSITY OF
    ROCHESTER, 1967 (LA EC).

MICHEA, CLAUDE ANGUS. THE INTELLIGENCE OF NINE AND TEN
    YEAR OLD MEXICAN CHILDREN AS MEASURED BY THE LEITER
    INTERNATIONAL PERFORMANCE SCALE.   UNIVERSITY
    OF SOUTHERN CALIFORNIA, MASTER'S THESIS (1941).

MIGUEL, FE ALEJO. THE INFLUENCE OF BILINGUALISM ON
    PERCEPTION AND MEANING.   UCLA, (1967) (ED).

MILLER.   "LATIN AMERICAN CHILD MUSIC" (MU*).

MITCHELL.   "THE EFFECT BILINGUALISM MEASUREMENT (ED*).

MITCHELL.   EFFECT BILINGUALISM MEASUREMENT (ED*).

MONSEES, EDNA K., AND BERMAN, CAROL. "SPEECH AND LANGUAGE
    SCREENING IN A SUMMER HEAD START PROGRAM".   JOURNAL
    OF SPEECH AND HEARING DISORDERS,   (MAY 1968), PP.
    121-126 (ED).

MONTEZ.   NEED BICULTURAL PROGRAMS (ED*).

MONTEZ.   PSYCHOLOGY MEXICAN AMERICAN STUDENT   (ED*).

MONTEZ.   SOME DIFFERENCES FACTORS RELATED (ED*).

MORALES.   "JUSTICE MEXICAN AMERICAN" (LW*).

MORALES, ARMANDO. "MENTAL AND PUBLIC HEALTH ISSUES: THE
    CASE OF THE MEXICAN AMERICANS IN LOS ANGELES".   EL
    GRITO, VOL. 3 NO. 2 (WINTER 1970), PP. 3-11 (MD).

MORALES.   "POLICE DEPLOYMENT THEORIES MEXICAN (LW*).

MORALES, ARMANDO. CHICANO POLICE RIOTS.   CHICANOS: SOCIAL
    AND PSYCHOLOGICAL PERSPECTIVES. SAINT LOUIS, MISSOURI:
    THE C. V. MOSBY COMPANY, 1971 (ED SO).

MORALES, ARMANDO. DISTINGUISHING PSYCHODYNAMIC FACTORS
    FROM CULTURAL FACTORS IN THE TREATMENT OF SPANISH
    SPEAKING PATIENTS.   CHICANOS: SOCIAL AND PSYCHOLOGICAL
    PERSPECTIVES. SAINT LOUIS, MISSOURI: THE C. V. MOSBY
    COMPANY, 1971.

MORALES.   POLICE DEPLOYMENT THEORIES (LW*).

MORALES, ARMANDO. THE IMPACT OF CLASS DISCRIMINATION AND
    WHITE RACISM ON THE METNAL HEALTHOF MEXICAN AMERICANS.
    EDITED BY NATHANIEL N. WAGNER AND MARSHA J. HAUG.
    SAINT LOUIS, MISSOUR: THE C. V. MOSBY COMPANY, 1971
    (SO).

MORALES, ARMANDO. A STUDY OF RECIDIVISM OF MEXICAN
    AMERICAN JUNIOR FORESTRY CAMP GRAUDATES.   UNIVERSITY
    OF SOUTHERN CALIFORNIA, MASTER'S THESIS (1963) (ED
    SO).

MORELEON, ANGELINA C. DE. "ALGUNAS FORMAS DEL VALOR Y DE
    LA COBARDIA EN EL MEXICANO".   FILOSOFIA Y LETRAS,
    VOL. 23 (JANUARY-JUNE 1952).

MORIN, KENNETH NOAH. ATTITUDES OF TEXAS MEXICAN AMERICANS
    TOWARD MENTAL RETARDATION: A GUTTM AN FACET ANALYSIS.
    ANN ARBOR, MICH: UNIVERSITY MICROFILMS, INC., 1971
    (HT).

MORRISON, CHARLOTTE AMOS. A CCMPARISON OF THE ACHIEVEMENT
    OF MEXICAN PUPILS IN LEARNING ENGLISH INA SEGREGATED
    SCHOOL AND IN A NON-SEGREGATEC SCHOOL, 1952.
    UNIVERSITY CF OREGON, MASTER'S THESIS (1952) (ED).

MORRISON, JAMES H. HUMAN FACTORS IN SUPERVISING MINIORITY
    GROUP EMPLOYEES: CONFERENCE LEADER'S GUIDE.
    CHICAGO, ILLINOIS: PUBLIC PERSONNEL ASSOCIATION, 1970
    (SO).

MORRISSEY. "GOOD MORNING, DON PATRICIO" (SO*).

MULLIGAN. "SOCIOECONOMIC BACKGRCUND MINORITY (SO*).

MULLINS, MARTHA MERSMAN. THE PERSCNALITY CIFFERENCES
    BETWEEN UNILINGUAL AND BILINGUAL NINTH GRADESTUDENTS
    IN DEPRESSED AREAS.   UNIVERSITY OF NEW MEXICO,
    MASTER'S THESIS (1961) (ED).

MUNOZ. DIFFERENCES DROP-OUT OTHER SCHOOL (ED*).

MUNOZ. RELATION BILINGUALISM TO VERBAL (ED*).

MUNSON, JOHN. INTELLIGENCE RATINGS FOR NINETY-SEVEN
    MEXICAN CHILDREN IN ST. PAUL, MINNESOTA.   UNIVERSITY
    OF MINNESOTA, PHD. DISSERTATION (1950) (ED).

MURDOCH, KATHARINE, NADDOW, DORIS, AND BERG, NETTIE LESSER.
    A STUDY OF THE RELATION BETWEEN INTELLIGENCE AND THE
    ACQUISITION OF ENGLISH.   NATURE AND NURTURE, PART
    I, THEIR INFLUENCE UPON INTELLIGENCE, PUBLIC SCHOOL
    PUBLISHING COMPANY, BLOOMINGTON, ILLINOIS, 1928 (LAE).

MURDOCH. "A STUDY DIFFERENCES FCUND BETWEEN (AN*).

MURILLO. MEXICAN AMERICAN FAMILY (SO*).

MURPHY. APPROACHES TO CROSS CULTURALPSYCHIATRY (AN*).

NAJMI. COMPARISCN GREELEYS SPANISHAMERICAN (ED*).

NATHAN.   RELATIONSHIP ENGLISH LANGUAGE (ED*).

NICOLL.   COMPARISON PHYSICAL DEVELOPMENT   (ED*).

NICOLL.   STUDY SELF SOCIAL ADJUSTMENTPATTERNS   (ED*).

NORDVOLD, NORRIS ALTON.   SELF-ESTEEM AND ITS RELATIONSHIP
    TO MINORITY OCCUPATIONAL SUCCESS.   TEMPE: ARIZONA
    STATE UNIVERSITY, MASTER'S THESIS (1972) (EC SO).

OSGOOD, CHARLES E.   PSYCHOLINGUISTICS: A SURVEY OF THEORY
    AND RESEARCH.   BALTIMORE: WAVERLY PRESS, INC., 1954
    (LA).

PADILLA, ELIGIO R.   'THE RELATIONSHIP BETWEEN PSYCHOLOGY
    AND CHICANOS: FAILURES AND POSSIBILITIES.'   IN
    NATHANIEL N. WAGNER AND MARSHA J. HAUG (EDS),
    CHICANOS: SOCIAL AND PSYCHOLOGICAL PERSPECTIVES.

PAGE, DOROTHY.   PERFORMANCE OF SPANISH-AMERICAN CHILDREN
    ON VERBAL AND NON-VERBAL INTELLIGENCE TESTS.
    UNIVERSITY OF NEW MEXICO, MASTER'S THESIS (1931).

PAINTER.   EFFECT INSTRUCTIONAL TECHNIQUE   (ED*).

PALACE.   COMPRARATIVE DESCRIPTION ANGLO-WHITE   (SO*).

PALOMARES.   PERFORMANCE MEXICAN-AMERICAN   (ED*).

PALOMARES.   STUDY ROLE MOBILITY ACCULTURATION   (ED*).

PALOMARES.   DESEGREGATING PEOPLES MINDS   (ED*).

PARR, EUNICE P.   A COMPARATIVE STUDY OF MEXICAN AND
    AMERICAN CHILDREN IN THE SCHOOLS OF SAN ANTONIO TEXAS.
    UNIVERSITY OF CHICAGO, MASTER'S THESIS (1926) (ED).

PASAMANICK, BENJAMIN.   "THE INTELLIGENCE OF AMERICAN
    CHILDREN OF MEXICAN PARENTAGE: A DISCUSSION OF
    UNCONTROLLED VARIABLES".   JOURNAL OF ABNORMAL AND
    SOCIAL PSYCHOLOGY, VOL. 46 (OCTOBER 1951), PP.
    598-602 (SO).

PASCHAL, FRANKLIN C.   "A REPORT ON THE STANDARDIZATION OF
    THE WITMER CYLINDER TEST".   PSYCHOLOGICAL CLINIC,
    VOL. 12 (APRIL 15, 1918), PP. 54-59.

PASCHALL, FRANKLIN C., AND SULLIVAN, LOUIS R.   "RACIAL
    INFLUENCES IN THE MENTAL AND PHYSICAL DEVELOPMENT OF
    MEXICAN CHILDREN".   COMPARATIVE PSYCHOLOGY MONOGRAPHS,
    VOL. 3 NO. 14 (OCTOBER 1925).

PASCHALL, FRANKLIN C., AND SULLIVAN, LOUIS R. RACIAL
    INFLUENCES IN THE MENTAL AND PHYSICAL DEVELOPMENT OF
    MEXICAN CHILDREN. BALTIMORE: THE WILLIAMS AND
    WILKINS COMPANY, 1925.

PASOMANICK, BENJAMIN. "THE INTELLIGENCE OF AMERICAN
    CHILDREN OF MEXICAN PARENTAGE, A DISCUSSION OF THE
    UNCONTROLLED VARIABLES". JOURNAL OF ABNORMAL AND
    SOCIAL PSYCHOLOGY, VOL. 56 (1951), PP. 598-602 (SO).

PATTERSON. COMPARISON PERFORMANCES MEXICAN (SO*).

PAUL. MENTAL DISORDER SELF-REGULATING (SO*).

PEAK. SEARCH IDENTITY BY YOUNG MEXICAN-AMERICAN (AN*).

PEAL, ELIZABETH; LAMBERT, WALLACE. THE RELATION OF
    BILINGUALISM TO INTELLIGENCE. WASHINGTON, D. C.:
    AMERICAN PSYCHOLOGICAL ASSOCIATION, (1962). PSYCHOLOGICAL
    MONOGRAPHS, GENERAL AND APPLIED, VOLUME 76, NUMBER
    27.

PEAL, ELIZABETH; LAMBERT, WALLACE. THE RELATION OF
    BILINGUALISM TO INTELLIGENCE. WASHINGTON, D. C.:
    AMERICAN PSYCHOLOGICAL ASSOCIATION, 1962.

PEAL, LAMBERT. "INTELLIGENCE IN BILINGUALS RESTUDIED".
    PSYCHOLOGICAL MONOGRAPHS: GENERAL AND APPLIED, VOL.
    76 NO. 27 (1962).

PECK. "INTELLIGENCE, ETHNICITY SOCIAL (SO*).

PEEK, LEIGH, AND HODGES, AMELIA BARTHLOME. "A STUDY OF
    RACIAL DIFFERENCES IN EIDETIC IMAGERY OF PRE-SCHOOL
    CHILDREN". THE JOURNAL OF GENETIC PSYCHOLOGY, VOL.
    51 (SEPTEMBER 1937), PP. 141-161 (ED).

PEEK. RELIGIOUS SOCIAL ATTITUDES MEXICAN (SO*).

PETTIGREW, T.F. "THE MEASUREMENT AND CORRELATES OF
    CATEGORY WIDTH AS A COGNITIVE VARIABLE". JOURNAL
    OF PERSONALITY, VOL. 26 (1958), PP. 532-544 (ED).

PHILLIPS , W. "SUBCONSCIOUSNESS AND THE ACQUIREMENT OF
    A SECOND LANGUAGE". FORUM OF EDUCATION, VOL.
    8 (JUNE 1930), PP. 135-142 (EC).

PICK. "INTELLIGENCE, ETHNICITY SOCIAL (SO*).

PINTER. "THE RELATION BILINGUALISM TO (ED*).

PINTNER. "COMPARISON AMERICAN FOREIGNCHILDREN (ED*).

PINTNER. "INTELLIGENCE TESTS FOREIGN CHILDREN" (ED*).

PINTNER.   "INTELLIGENCE TESTS FOREIGN CHILDREN"   (ED*).

PINTNER.   "NON-LANGUAGE TESTS FOREIGN COUNTRIES"   (ED*).

PINTNER.   "RESULTS OBTAINED WITH NON-LANGUAGE   (ED*).

PINTNER.   "THE INFLUENCE LANGUAGE BACKGROUND   (ED*).

PINTNER.   "THE INFLUENCE LANGUAGE BACKGROUND   (ED*).

PINTNER.   INTELLIGENCE TEST; METHODS RESULTS   (ED*).

PINTNER.   MANUAL DIRECTIONS NON-LANGUAGE   (ED*).

PINTNER.   "THE MEASUREMENT PUPIL ADJUSTMENT"   (ED*).

PINTNER.   "THE RELATION BILINGUALISM TO   (ED*).

POLLACK.   SPANISH-SPEAKING STUDENTS GUIDANCE   (ED*).

POPENOE, P.   "INTELLIGENCE AND RACE".   JOURNAL OF
     HEREDITY, VOL. 13 (1922), PP. 264-269.

PORTEUS, S. D.   "RACIAL GROUP DIFFERENCES IN MENTALITY".
     TABULAE BIOLOGICAE, VOL. 18 (1937), PP. 66-75 (SO).

PORTILLA, JORGE.   FENOMENOLOGIA DEL RELAJO.   FIRST
     EDITION, MEXICO, D. F.: EDICIONES ERA, S.A., 1966.

PRESSEY.   "A COMPARISON TWO CITIES THEIR   (ED*).

PRESSEY.   "A STUDY COUNTRY CHILDREN GOOD   (ED*).

PRESSEY.   "THE INFLUENCE INADEQUATE SCHOOLING   (ED*).

PRICE.   ANALYSIS CHANGES INTELLIGENCE   (ED*).

PROWLEDGE.   TO CHANGE CHILD   (ED*).

R.   "THREE BASIC THEMES MEXICAN PUERTO   (SO*).

RAMIREZ, M.; ALEMANY, N.; HEROLD, PL L.; MACAULAY, J. AND
     RICHARDS, R.   A BICULTURALBILINGUAL FOLLOW-THROUGH
     MODEL FOR MEXICAN AMERICAN CHILDREN.   REPORT
     TO PROJECT FOLLOW-THROUGH U. S. OFFICE OF EDUCATION,
     1971 (ED).

RAMIREZ, M., AND TAYLOR, C.   SEX ROLE DETERMINANTS
     IN ATTITUDES AMONG MEXICAN AMERICAN ADOLESCENTS.
     U.S. OFFICE OF EDUCATION, BUREAU OF RESEARCH,
     DEPARTMENT OF HEALTH, EDUCATION AND WELFARE, (NOVEMBER
     1967) (AN ED).

RAMIREZ, MANUEL III.   'IDENTITY CRISIS IN THE BARRIOS.'
     IN EDWARD SIMMEN (ED), PAIN AND PROMISE: THE CHICANO
     TODAY (ED).

RAMIREZ, MANUEL III. 'IDENTITY CRISIS IN MEXICAN—AMERICAN
    ADOLESCENTS.'   IN HENRY SIOUX JOHNSON AND WILLIAM
    J. HERNANDEZ—M (EDS). EDUCATING THE MEXICAN AMERICAN
    (ED).

RAMIREZ, MANUEL III. 'MEXICAN AMERICAN CULTURAL MEMBERSHIP
    AND ADJUSTMENT TO SCHOOL.'   IN NATHANIEL N. WAGNER
    AND MARSHA J. HAUG (EDS), CHICANOS: SOCIAL AND
    PSYCHOLOGICAL PERSPECTIVES (AN).

RAMIREZ, MANUEL III. 'POTENTIAL CONTRIBUTIONS BY THE
    BEHAVIORAL SCIENCES TO EFFECTIVE PREPARATION PROGRAMS
    FOR TEACHERS OF MEXICAN AMERICAN CHILDREN.'   IN HENRY
    SIOUX JOHNSON AND WILLIAM J. HERNANDEZ—M (EDS).
    EDUCATING THE MEXICAN AMERICAN (AN).

RAMIREZ, MANUEL III. "CULTURAL DEMOCRACY: A NEW PHILOSOPHY
    FOR EDUCATING THE MEXICAN AMERICAN CHILD".   THE
    NATIONAL ELEMENTARY PRINCIPAL, VOL. 50 NO. 2 (FALL
    1971), PP. 45—46 (ED).

RAMIREZ. "IDENTIFICATION WITH MEXICANFAMILY (ED*).

RAMIREZ, MANUEL III. "IDENTIFICATION WITH MEXICAN FAMILY
    VALUES AND AUTHORITARIANISM IN MEXICAN—AMERICANS".
    JOURNAL OF SOCIAL PSYCHOLOGY,   (OCTOBER 1967), PP.
    3—11 (ED).

RAMIREZ, MANUEL III. "IDENTITY CRISIS IN THE BARRIOS".
    MUSIC EDUCATORS JOURNAL, VOL. 56 (MAY 1970), PP.
    69—70 (ED).

RAMIREZ, MANUEL III. "THE RELATIONSHIP OF ACCULTURATION
    TO EDUCATIONAL ACHIEVEMENT".   EL GRITO, VOL. 4 NO.
    4 (SUMMER 1971), PP. 21—28 (AN).

RAMIREZ, MANUEL III. POTENTIAL CONTRIBUTIONS BY THE
    BEHAVIORAL SCIENCES TO EFFECTIVE PREPARATION PROGRAMS
    FOR TEACHERS OF MEXICAN AMERICAN CHILDREN.   LAS
    CRUCES: ERIC, NEW MEXICO STATE UNIVERSITY, FEBRUARY
    1969.

RAMIREZ, SANTIAGO. EL MEXICANO: PSICOLOGIA DE SUS
    MOTIVACIONES.   MEXICO D.F. ASOCIACION PSICOANALITICA
    MEXICANA, 1960.

RAMIREZ, SANTIAGO. EL MEXICANO: PSICOLOGIA DE SUS
    MOTIVACIONES.   MEXICO: EDITORIAL PAX, 1968.

RANDALS, EDWYNA HENRIETTA. A COMPARISON OF THE INTELLIGENCE
    TEST RESULTS OF MEXICAN AND NEGRO CHILDEN IN TWO
    ELEMENTARY SCHOOLS.   UNIVERSITY OF SOUTHERN CALIFORNIA,
    MASTER'S THESIS (1929) (ED).

RAPIER. "EFFECTS VERBAL MEDITATION UPON (ED*).

RASCHAL, FRANKLIN CRESSEY; SULLIVAN, LOUIS B. RACIAL
    INFLUENCES IN THE MENTAL AND PHYSICAL DEVELOPMENT OF
    MEXICAN CHILDREN. BALTIMORE: THE WILLIAMS AND
    SILKINS COMPANY, 1925 (AN).

RAVEN, J. C. AND LEWIS, H. K. PROGRESSIVE MATRICES.   NEW
    YORK: PSYCHOLOGICAL CORPORATICN, 1951.

REAM.   STUDY SPANISH SPEAKING PUPILS (ED*).

REED.   STUDY EFFECT BALANCED READING (ED*).

REILLEY.   "MMPI SCORES MEXICAN AMERICAN (ED*).

RENNER.   SOME CHARACTERISTICS SPANISHNAME (ED*).

RICHARDS.   "ATTITUDES WHITE COLLEGE STUDENTS (SO*).

RIEBER, MORTON AND WOMACK, MARCELEETE. THE INTELLIGENCE
    OF PRESCHOOL CHILDREN AS RELATED TO ETHNIC AND
    DEMOGRAPIC VARIABLES.   IN NATHANIEL N. WAGNER, AND
    MARCHA J. HAUG (ED). SAINT LOUIS, MISSOURI: THE C.
    V. MOSBY COMPANY, 1971 (ED).

RIESTRA.   "CHANGES ATTITUCES ELEMENTARY (ED*).

RIGG.   "SOME FURTHER DATA LANGUAGE HANDICAP" (ED*).

RIGGINS.   FACTORS SOCIAL BACKGROUND WHICH (ED*).

ROBERTS.   "MINORITY SELF-IDENTIFICATION (SO*).

ROBERTS.   COMPARISON PHYSICAL STATUS, PHYSICAL (ED*).

ROBERTSON.   CCMPARATIVE STUDY PROGRESS AMERICAN (ED*).

ROBLES.   ANALYTIC DESCRIPTION PEER GROUP (ED*).

ROCA.   "PROBLEMS ADAPTING INTELLIGENCE (ED*).

ROCCO.   "THE CHICANO SOCIAL SCIENCES: (AN*).

RODRIGUEA, DARIO E. "SCME PHYSIOLOGICAL AND EDUCATIONAL
    ASPECTS OF BILINGUALISM".   AZTLAN--CHICANO JOURNAL
    OF THE SOCIAL SCIENCES AND THE ARTS, VOL. 2 NO. 1
    (SPRING 1971), PP. 79-104 (ED).

RODRIGUEZ SALA CE GOMEZGIL, MARIA LUISA.   EL ESTEREOTIPO
    DEL MEXICANO: ESTUDIO PSICOSOCIAL.   UNIVERSIDAD
    NACIONAL AUTONOMA DE MEXICO: INSTITUTO DE INVESTIGACIONES
    SOCIALES, 1965 (SO).

ROKEACH, M. "A METHOD OF STUDYING INDIVIDUAL DIFFERENCES
    IN 'NARROW MINDEDNESS'".   JOURNAL OF PERSONALITY,
    VOL. 20 (1951), PP. 219-233.

ROSENFELD, ALBERT. "MODERN MEDICINE WHERE THE CLOCK
    WALKS".   COLLIERS, VOL. 137 (FEBRUARY 3, 1956),
    PP. 24-29 (SO ED).

ROSENQUIST. "DIFFERENTIAL RESPONSES TEXAS (SO*).

RUBEL.   "LA ENVIDIA COMO PROCESO CAUSAL (AN*).

RUBEL.   "THE EPIDEMIOLOGY FOLK-ILLNESS: (AN*).

RUSSEL.   "PROBLEMS MEXICAN CHILDREN SOUTHWEST" (ED*).

RYGLE.   RAMON: LIFE AMERICAN-MEXICAN (AN*).

SAENGER, GERHART. THE SOCIAL PSYCHOLOGY OF PREJUDICE:
    ACHIEVING INTERCULTURAL UNDERSTANDING AND COOPERATION
    IN A DEMOCRACY.   NEW YORK: HARPER, 1953 (SO).

SAFFIETTI.   "BILINGUALISM BICULTURALISM" (ED*).

SAPORTA.   PSYCHOLINGUISTICS: BOOK READINGS (LA*).

SCHILLER, BELLE. "VERBAL, NUMERICAL AND SPATIAL ABILITIES
    OF YOUNG CHILDREN".   ARCHIVES OF PSYCHOLOGY, VOL.
    161 (MARCH 1934), PP. 1-69.

SCHNEIDER, VIRGINIA. ABILITIES OF MEXICAN AND WHITE.
    UNIVERSITY OF SOUTHERN CALIFORNIA, MASTER'S THESIS
    (1931) (ED).

SCHNUR.   "STUDY POSSIBLE IMPROVEMENT PROBLEM (ED*).

SCHWESINGER, G. C. HEREDITY AND ENVIRONMENT; STUDIES IN
    THE GENESIS OF PSYCHOLOGICAL CHARACTERISTICS.   NEW
    YORK: MACMILLAN, 1933.

SEIDL.   EFFECT BILINGUALISM INTELLIGENCE (ED*).

SENTER.   "WITCHES PSYCHIATRISTS" (AN*).

SENTER.   "ACCULTURATION AMONG NEW MEXICAN (AN*).

SENTER.   "THE GRAMMAR SCHOOL AS BASICACCULTURATING (AN*).

SERETA, K. E. "A COMPARATIVE STUDY OF 100 ITALIAN CHILDREN
    AT THE SIX YEAR LEVEL".   THE PSYCHOLOGICAL CLINIC,
    VOL. 16 (1924), PP. 216-231.

SERETA, K. E. "A COMPARATIVE STUDY OF 100 ITALIAN CHILDREN
    AT THE SIX-YEAR LEVEL". THE PSYCHOLOGICAL CLINIC,
    VOL. 16 (1927), PP. 216-231.

SERVEY. ANALYSIS WRITTEN LANGUAGE STRUCTURE (ED*).

SHELDON. "THE INTELLIGENCE MEXICAN CHILDREN" (ED*).

SHELDON. COMPARISON INTELLIGENCE MEXICAN (ED*).

SHIMBERG, M. "AN INVESTIGATION INTO THE VALIDITY OF NORMS
    WITH SPECIAL REFERENCE TO URBAN AND RURAL GROUPS".
    ARCHIVES OF PSYCHOLOGY, VOL. 16 (1929), PP. 1-84.

SHOTWELL, ANNA M. "PERFORMANCE RATINGS OF MEXICAN
    AND AMERICAN HIGH GRADE MENTAL DEFECTIVES". AMERICAN
    JOURNAL OF MENTAL DEFICIENCY, VOL. 49 (1945), PP.
    445-449.

SHYBUT, JOHN. DELAYED GRATIFICATION: A STUDY OF ITS
    MEASUREMENT AND ITS RELATIONSHIP TO CERTAIN BEHAVIORAL,
    PSYCHOLOGICAL AND DEMOGRAPHIC VARIABLES. UNIVERSITY
    OF COLORADO, MASTER'S THESIS (1963) (SO).

SILVERSTEIN, A. B. (ET AL). "CULTURAL FACTORS IN THE
    INTELLECTUAL FUNCTIONING OF THE MENTALLY RETARDED".
    AMERICAN JOURNAL OF MENTAL DEFICIENCY, VOL. 67
    (1962), PP. 396-401 (MD).

SILVERSTEIN. "CULTURAL FACTORS INTELLECTUAL (MD*).

SIMMONS. "THE MUTUAL IMAGES EXPECTATIONS (SO*).

SIMONIN. MUTUAL IMAGES EXPECTATIONS ANGLO-AMERICANS (SO*).

SIMPICH. MUTUAL IMMAGES EXPECTATIONS ANGLO-AMERICANS
    (SO*).

SION, ALVIN P. MENTALLY DEFICIENT MEXICAN AMERICAN
    DELINQUENT BOYS WHO MADE GOOD AFTER INSTITUTIONAL
    CARE: AN ANALYSIS OF SIX CASES. UNIVERSITY OF
    SOUTHERN CALIFORNIA, MASTER'S THESIS (1951) (ED).

SMITH. COMPARATIVE STUDY FACTS FACTORS (ED*).

SMITH. HOW TO TALK WITH PEOPLE OTHER (ED*).

SOCIETY FOR CURRICULUM STUDY. SOCIETY, PERSONALITY,
    DEVIANT (SO*).

SOFFER. SOCIO-CULTURAL CHANGES LIVESFIVE (SO*).

SOFFIETTI. "BILINGUALISM BICULTURALISM" (ED*).

SOLGUDO NAVARRO, MARIA CRISTINIA. ADJUSTMENT PROBLEMS OF
     DELINQUENT MEXICAN GIRLS. TEMPE: ARIZONA STATE
     UNIVERSITY, MASTER'S THESIS (1949) (SO).

SOMMERS, VITA S. THE IMPACT OF DUAL CULTURAL MEMBERSHIP
     ON IDENTITY. PSYCHIATRY, 27 (SO).

SOUTHWEST COUNCIL ON THE EDUCATION OF SPANISH SPEAKING
     PEOPLE. PROCEEDINGS (ED*).

SPILKA. "SOME NON-INTELLECTUAL CORRELATES (ED*).

SPOERL. "A STUDY SOME POSSIBLE FACTORS (ED*).

SPOERL. "BILINGUALITY EMOTIONAL ADJUSTMENT" (ED*).

SPRAGGIA, MARTIN. SELF-GROUP DEVALUATION AND PREJUDICE
     IN MINORITY GROUP BOYS. ANN ARBOR, MICHIGAN:
     UNIVERSITY MICROFILM, 1959 (SO).

SPRINKLE. COMPARATIVE STUDY READING INTERESTS (ED*).

ST. EDUCATIONAL ACHIEVEMENT RELATION (ED*).

STANCHFIELD. "STUDY ATTITUDINAL CHANGES MEXICAN (ED*).

STANFORD. "DONT DISCARD THOSE I.Q. TESTS" (ED*).

STARK. "THE EFFECT BILINGUALISM GENERAL (ED*).

STARKEY. SYNTHESIS INTERPRETAICN RESEARCH (ED*).

STEEN, MARGARET TROTTER. THE EFFECTS OF IMMEDIATE
     AND DELAYED REINFORCEMENT ON THE ACHIEVEMENT BEHAVIOR
     OF MEXICAN AMERICAN CHILDREN OF LOW ECONOMIC STATUS.
     STANFORD, CALIFORNIA: STANFORD UNIVERSITY, 1966 (ED
     EC).

STEIN, LISA S. "TECHNIQUES FOR PARENT DISCUSSIONS
     IN DISADVANTAGED AREAS". YOUNG CHILDREN, (MARCH
     1967), PP. 210-217 (SO).

STEIN. "THE SOCIAL DISTRIBUTION MENTAL (SO*).

STEMMLER, ANNE O. THE PSYCHOLOGICAL AND COGNITIVE ASPECTS
     OF TEACHING ENGLISH AS A SECOND LANGUAGE; SAN ANTONIO,
     TEXAS, RESEARCH PROJECT. PAPER PRESENTED AT
     THE ANNUAL MEETING OF THE AMERICAN EDUCATIONAL
     RESEARCH ASSOCIATION, FEBRUARY, 1966, CHICAGO (ED).

STENBER, JOSEPHINE. "RACIAL DIFFERENCES IN READING
     ACHIEVEMENT". THE TEXAS OUTLOOK, VOL. 24 (JANUARY
     1940), P. 32 (ED).

STEVENS. MEXICAN MACHISMO: POLITICS VALUE (PL*).

STEVENS.   "MEXICAN MACHISMO: POLITICS VALUE   (PL*).

STOCTON.   "THE DEFINITION INTELLIGENCERELATION   (ED*).

STODDARD.   MEXICAN AMERICANS   (SO*).

STOKE, STUART M AND LEHMAN, HARVEY C.   "INTELLIGENCE TEST
     SCORES OF SOCIAL AND OCCUPATIONAL GROUPS".   SCHOOL
     AND SOCIETY, VOL. 31   (MARCH 15, 1930), PP. 372-377
     (ED).

STRARD.   "A STUDY RELATION INTELLIGENCE   (ED*).

SULLIVAN.   "THE EFFECT RACE ENVIRONMENTPHYSICAL   (SI*).

SUTHERLUND.   "THE RELATIONSHIP BETWEEN 1,2   (ED*).

SWICKARD, DON L. AND SPILKA, BERNARD.   "HOSTILITY EXPRESSION
     IN SPANISH AMERICAN AND NON-SPANISH WHITE DELINQUENTS".
     JOURNAL OF CONSULTING PSYCHOLOGY, VOL. 25   (JUNE
     1961), PP. 216-220.

TATA, LORRAINE (POWERS).   A COMPARATIVE STUDY AND MEASUREMENT
     OF INNATE MUSICAL ABILITIES OF MEXICAN AND AMERICAN
     WHITE CHILDREN.   ARIZONA STATE UNIVERSITY, MASTER'S
     THESIS (1939) (MU ED).

TAYLOR, HARRY FRANKLIN.   THE MUSICAL ABILITIES OF SPANISH-AMERICAN
     CHILDREN.   DENVER UNIVERSITY, MASTER'S THESIS (1934)
     (MU   ED).

TAYLOR.   COMPARISON FIRST SECOND GENERATION   (SO*).

TAYLOR.   "RETARDATION MEXICAN CHILDREN   (ED*).

TEAGARDEN.   "CHANGE ENVIROMENT I. Q."   (ED*).

TEIMAN.   REVISED STANFORD-BINET SCALE   (ED*).

TERMAN.   CONDENSED GUIDE STANFORD REVISION   (ED*).

THOMPSON, MERRILL E., AND DOVE, CLAUDE C.   "THE RESEARCH
     QUARTERLY OF THE AMERICAN ASSOCIATION FOR HEALTH,
     PHYSICAL EDUCATION, AND RECREATION".   THE RESEARCH
     QUARTERLY OF THE AMERICAN ASSOCIATION FOR HEALTH,
     PHYSICAL EDUCATION, AND RECREATION, VOL. 13 (OCTOBER
     1942), PP. 341-346 (ED).

THOMPSON, WALLACE.   THE MEXICAN MIND: A STUDY OF NATIONAL
     PSYCHOLOGY.   BOSTON: LITTLE, BROWN, AND COMPANY, 1922
     (SO AN ED).

THOMPSON, WALLACE.   THE MEXICAN MIND: A STUDY OF NATIONAL
     PSYCHOLOGY.   NEW YORK: HARPER AND BROTHERS, 1921 (SO
     AN ED).

THOMSON.   VALIDITY STANFORD BINET TESTS (ED*).

THORNDIKE.   "THE JOURNAL EDUCATIONAL PSYCHOLOGY" (ED*).

THORNDIKE.   "JOURNAL EDUCATIONAL PSYCHOLOGY" (ED*).

TIEGS.   MANUAL CALIFORNIA ACHIEVEMENT (ED*).

TOMPLIN.   CERTAIN LANGUAGE SKILLS CHILDREN: (ED*).

TREVINO B.   "BILINGUAL EDUCATION; PSYCHOLOGICAL (ED*).

TREVINO.   "BILINGUAL INSTRUCTION PRIMARY (ED*).

TURNER, E. M.   "PERFORMANCE TESTS AS MEASURES OF GENERAL
    INTELLIGENCE".   NEW YORK SOCIETY FOR THE EXPERIMENTAL
    STUDY OF EDUCATION. CONTRIBUTIONS TO EDUCATION, VOL.
    2 (1928), PP. 59-64 (ED).

VAN VELZER.   RACE RELATION PROBLEMS 50 NORMAL (SO*).

VONTRESS.   CULTURAL DIFFERENCES: IMPLICATIONS (ED*).

WAGNER.   CHICANOS: SOCIAL PSYCHOLOGICAL (SO*).

WALLACE.   "BILINGUALISM RETARDATION" (ED*).

WALTERS.   "LANGUAGE HANDICAP STANFORD REVISION (ED*).

WANG, S. L.   "DEMONSTRATION OF THE LANGUAGE DIFFICULTY
    INVOLVED IN COMPARAING RACIAL GROUPS BY MEANS
    OF VERBAL INTELLIGENCE TESTS".   JOURNAL OF APPLIED
    PSYCHOLOGY, VOL. 10 (1926), PP. 102-106 (ED).

WANG, S. L.   "LANGUAGE DIFFICULTY IN COMPARING RACIAL
    GROUPS".   JOURNAL OF APPLIED PSYCHOLOGY,   (1926)
    (ED).

WANG, TSU LIEN.   "THE INFLUENCE OF TUITION IN THE ACQUISITION
    OF SKILL".   PSYCHOLOGICAL REVIEW MONOGRAPHS, VOL.
    34 NO. 1 (1925), P. 51.

WATTS.   LANGUAGE MENTAL DEVELOPMENT CHILDREN (ED*).

WECHSLER, DAVID.   WECHSLER INTELLIGENCE SCALE FOR CHILDREN.
    NEW YORK: THE PSYCHOLOGICAL CORPORATION, 1949.

WERNER.   PERCEPTION PREJUDICE MEXICAN-AMERICAN (SO*).

WEST.   "RACE ATTITUDES AMONG TEACHERS (SO*).

WHITE, JEAN DEMPEWOLF.   TIME ORIENTATION AS A FACTOR IN
    THE ACCULTURATION OF SOUTHWESTERN SPANISH-SPEAKING
    GROUPS.   UNIVERSITY OF TEXAS, MASTER'S THESIS (1955)
    (AN).

WHITTEN.   EXPERIMENTAL STUDY COMPARISON   (ED*).

WHORF.   RELATION HABITUAL THROUGHT BEHAVIOR   (LA*).

WHORF.   SCIENCE LINGUISTICS   (LA*).

WILHAUK.   STUDY INTER-AMERICAN TESTS RELATION   (ED*).

WILSON.   ANALYSIS ACADEMIC HOME PROBLEMS   (ED*).

WINCHESTER, GERTRUDE K.   ACHIEVEMENTS, SOCIAL CONCEPTS AND
        ATTITUDES OF THREE RACIAL GROUPS.   WHITTIER COLLEGE,
        MASTER'S THESIS (1944) (SO).

WITACRE.   SOME BODY MEASUREMENTS TEXASSCHOOL   (ED*).

WITHERS, CHARLES DINNIJES.   PROBLEMS OF MEXICAN BOYS.
        UNIVERSITY OF SOUTHERN CALIFORNIA, MASTER'S THESIS
        (1942) (ED).

WITHERSPOON.   "A COMPARISCN PROBLEMS CERTAIN   (ED*).

WOLMAN.   "CULTURAL FACTORS CREATIVITY"   (ED*).

YAMAMOTO, JOE.   CULTURAL PROBLEMS IN PSYCHIATRIC THERAPY.
        EDITED BY NATHANIEL N. WAGNER AND MARCHA J. HAUG.
        SAINT LOUIS, MISSOURI: THE C. V. MOSBY COMPANY, 1971
        (AN).

YNIGO.   MEXICAN-AMERICAN CHILDREN INTEGRATED   (ED*).

YOAKUM, C. S.   ARMY MENTAL TESTS.   NEW YORK: HENRY HOLT,
        1920.

YOUND.   MENTAL DIFFERENCES CERTAIN IMMIGRANT   (SI*).

YOUNG, ROBERT K. AND ARTHUR WEBBER.   POSITIVE AND NEGATIVE
        TRANSFER WITH BILINGUALS.   UNIVERSITY OF TEXAS,
        (1967). UNPUBLISHED MONOGRAPH..

ZINTZ.   CULTURAL ASPECTS BILINGUALISM   (ED*).

ZINTZ.   EDUCATION ACROSS CULTURES   (ED*).

R E L I G I O N

(RE)

ABEL, THEODORE. PROTESTANT HOME MISSIONS TO CATHOLIC
    IMMIGRANTS. NEW YORK: INSTITUTE OF SOCIAL AND
    RELIGIOUS SCIENCE, 1933 (SI).

AD INTERIM COMMITTEE ON LATIN AMERICAN WORK (REP).
    PRESBYTERIAN CHURCH IN THE UNITED STATES, SYNOD OF
    TEXAS, AD INTERIM COMMITTEE ON LATIN AMERICAN WORK.
    AUSTIN, TEXAS, (1952). REPORT.

ADAMS. MISSIONS NEW MEXICO, 1776: DESCRIPTION (HS*).

ADAMS. WHITE CHURCHES PLAINS: EXAMPLES (HCO*).

AHLBORN. SOLDIERS SAINTS OLD SPAIN NEW (HS*).

AHLBORN, RICHARD E. THE PENITENTE MORADAS OF ABIQUIU. S.
    WASHINGTON, D. C.. SMITHSONIAN INSTITUTION PRESS,
    (1968) (HN).

AMON, CARTER. SANTOS: AN EXHIBITION OF THE RELIGIOUS FOLK
    ART OF NEW MEXICO. FORT WORTH, TEXAS: MUSEUM
    OF WESTERN ART, 1964 (AR   AN).

ANDERSON, V. "NORTH MEETS SOUTH: AN ADVENTURE IN GOOD
    WILL". INTERNATIONAL JOURNAL OF RELIGIOUS EDUCATION,
    VOL. 22 (APRIL 1946), PP. 4-5 (SO).

ANDERSON. "NORTH MEETS SOUTH: ADVENTURE (SO*).

"ARCHBISHOP OF SANTA FE". LIFE, (DECEMBER 20, 1943)
    (HN).

"AUXILIARY BISHOPS TO BE ORDAINED". THE TIDINGS, (MARCH
    19,1971), PP. 1-5 (SO).

"CALIFORNIA'S SPANISH SPEAKING: RELIGIOUS MINISTRATION IN
    SANTA CLARA COUNTY". AMERICA, VOL. 3 (SEPTEMBER
    5, 1964), P. 222 (HC).

"CHURCHES OPPOSE BRACEROS PROGRAM". CHRISTIAN CENTURY,
    (DECEMBER 23, 1964), PP. 1580-1581 (EC).

"CHURCHMEN AND TABLE GRAPES". AMERICA, VOL. 120 (JANUARY
    4, 1969), P. 4 (EC).

"PADRES OF NEW MEXICO". NATIONAL CATHOLIC REPORTER,
    (APRIL 2, 1971).

"POVERTY SPURS ECUMENISM; MICHIGAN COUNCIL OF CHURCHES AND
    THE MICHIGAN CATHOLIC CONFERENCE COOPERATE".
    AMERICA, VOL. 112 (APRIL   10, 1965), P. 475 (SI).

"REACHING MEXICANS IN THE UNITED STATES".   MISSIONARY
    REVIEW, VOL. 50 (JANUARY   1927), PP. 50-51 (SO).

BISHOP JUAN A. AZURBE.   LOS ANGELES, CALIFORNIA, APRIL
    2, 1971.

GETTING GOD COUNTED AMONG THE MEXICANS.   ??NO INFORMATION??,
    MAY 1923 (SO).

LATIN-AMERICAN-PRESBYTERIAN CHURCHES IN TEXAS.   AUSTIN,
    TEXAS, 1952.

SYNOD'S PROGRAM COMMITTEE ON CHURCH AND SOCIETY. THE
    CHURCH'S PARTNERSHIP WITH MEXICAN AMERICANS.   AUSTIN,
    TEXAS: PRESBYTERIAN CHURCH UNITED STATES SYNOD
    OF TEXAS, (SO).

"CHURCHES AND BRACEROS" (EC*).

"MISSION CONCEPCION" (HS*).

APPLEGATE, BETTY. "LOS HERMANOS PENITENTES".   SOUTHWEST
    REVIEW, VOL. 17 (1931), PP. 100-107 (HN).

AUSTIN.   "CATHOLIC CULTURE OUR SOUTHWEST" (LI*).

AUSTIN.   "TRAIL BLOOD; ACCOUNT PENITENT (LI*).

BAIRD, JOSEPH ARMSTRONG, JR. CHURCHES OF MEXICO, 1530-1810.
    BERKELEY: UNIVERSITY OF CALIFORNIA, 1962 (HS).

BAUER, ARNOLD. "THE CHURCH AND SPANISH-AMERICAN AGRARIAN
    STRUCTURE, 1765-1865".   THE AMERICAS, VOL. 28 NO.
    1 (1971), PP. 78-98 (SO).

BAZANT.   ALIENATION CHURCH WEALTH MEXICO (HM*).

BAZANT.   DISENTAILMENT, NATIONALIZATION (HM*).

BLAKE, ROBERT N. A HISTORY OF THE CATHOLIC CHURCH IN EL
    PASO, TEXAS.   TEXAS WESTERN COLLEGE, MASTER'S THESIS
    (1948) (HT).

BOLTON.   "THE BLACK ROBES NEW SPAIN" (HS*).

BOLTON.   "THE FOUNDING MISSIONS SAN GABRIEL (HS*).

BOLTON.   "THE FOUNDING MISSION ROSARIO: (HS*).

BOLTON.   PADRE HORSEBACK: SKETCH EUSEBIO (HS*).

BOREN, CARTER E. RELIGION ON THE TEXAS FRONTIER.   SAN
     ANTONIO, TEXAS: THE NAYLOR COMPANY, 1968 (HS).

BOYD, E. SAINTS AND SAINT-MAKERS OF NEW MEXICO.   SANTA
     FE, NEW MEXICO: LABATORY OF ANTHROPOLOGY, 1946.

BOYD. "SPANISH MISSION SITES FLORIDA" (HS*).

BRADEN, CHARLES SAMUEL. RELIGIOUS ASPECTS OF THE CONQUEST
     OF MEXICO.   DURHAM, 1930. NEW YORK AND LONDON: AMS
     PRESS, INC., (HS).

BRENNER. IDOLS BEHIND ALTARS (AN*).

BRENNER. IDOLS BEHIND ALTARS (AN*).

BRONSON, LOUISE FISHER. CHANGES IN PERSONALITY NEEDS AND
     VALUES FOLLOWING CONVERSION TO PROTESTANTISM IN
     A TRADITIONALLY ROMAN CATHOLIC ETHNIC GROUP.
     UNIVERSITY OF ARIZONA, PHD. DISSERTATION (1966) (SO
     PY).

BROWN. "THE CHALLENGE MEXICAN IMMIGRATION" (SO*).

BRUGGE. NAVAJOS CATHOLIC CHURCH RECORDS (HS*).

CALLEROS, CLEOFAS; GRAHAM, MARJORIE. QUEEN OF THE
     MISSIONS: OUR LADY OF GUADALUPE.   EL PASO: AMERICAN
     PRINTING COMPANY, 1952 (HM).

CAMPA. "RELIGIOUS SPANISH FOLK-DRAMA (AN*).

CAMPA. SPANISH RELIGIOUS FOLK THEATRE (AN*).

CARRENO, ALBERTO MARIA. MISIONEROS EN MEXICO.   ED. JUS,
     MEXICO, 1961 (SO).

CHAPPELLE. LOCAL WELFARE WORK RELIGIOUSORGANIZATIONS
     (SO*).

CLEATH, R. L. "RENDERING UNTO CESAR".   CHRISTIANITY
     TODAY, VOL. 14 (JULY 3, 1970), PP. 32-33 (SO).

COLE, M. R. LOS PASTORES, AMERICAN FOLK-LORE SOCIETY.
     BOSTON AD NEW YORK: HOUGHTON, MIFFLEIN AND COMPANY,
     1907 (AN).

CONSIDINE, JOHN J., M. M. (ED). RELIGIOUS DIMENSION IN
     THE NEW LATIN AMERICA.   NOTRE DAME: FIDES PUBLISHERS,
     INC., 1966.

COPE, M. "MINISTER WHO FOLLOWS THE MIGRANTS: MIGRANT
     MINISTRY PROGRAM OF N. C. C.".   SATURDAY EVENING
     POST, VOL. 237 (JANUARY 4, 1964), PP. 34-36 (SO
     EC).

CROFOOOT, W. G., <ED>. FLYING CHIPS: LATIN-AMERICAN
    PREBYTERIANISM IN TEXAS.   AUSTIN, TEXAS: THE
    EXECUTIVE COMMITTEE OF HOME MISSIONS OF THE SYNOD OF
    THE PRESBYTERIAN CHURCH IN THE UNITED STATES, 1949
    (HT).

CURL, E. F. SOUTHWEST TEXAS METHODISM.   INTER-BOARD
    COUNCIL OF THE SOUTHWEST CONFERENCE OF THE METHODIST
    CHURCH, 1951 (HT).

DANTONIO.   RELIGION, REVOLUTION, REFORM (SO*).

DABBS.   "LOPEZS REPORT TEXAS MISSICNS (HSW*).

DABBS.   "THE TEXAS MISSIONS 1785" (HSW*).

DARLEY.   PASSIONISTS SOUTHWEST; OR, HCLY (HN*).

DASILVA, OWEN FRANCIS. MISSION MUSIC OF CALIFORNIA,
    A COLLECTION CF OLD CALIFORNIA MISSION HYMNS AND
    MASSES, TRANSCRIBED AND EDITED BY REV.OWEN DA SILVA.
    LOS ANGELES, CALIFORNIA: W.F. LEWIS, 1941 (MU).

DAWSON, JOSEPH MARTIN. "AMONG THE MEXICANS IN TEXAS".
    MISSIONARY REVIEW OF THE WORLD, VOL. 50 (OCTOBER
    1927), PP. 757-758 (SO).

DE ESPINOSA, ISIDRO FELIX. CHRONICA APOSTOLICA.
    WASHINGTCN: ACADEMY OF AMERICAN FRANCISCAN HISTORY,
    1964 (HS).

DECORME, FATHER GERARD. LAS MISIONES CEL VALLE DEL PASO.
    MS (HS).

DEFOURI, JAMES H. HISTORICAL SKETCH OF THE CATHOLIC
    CHURCH.   SAN FRANCISCO, CALIFORNIA: MC CORMICK
    BROTHERS, PRINTERS, 1887 (FS HN).

DENNY, HENRY JAMES. UNITED STATES RELIGIOUS OPINION WITH
    RESPECT TO MEXICO'S RELIGIOUS CONFLICT, 1926 AND 1927.
    CALIFCRNIA STATE COLLEGE, MASTER'S THESIS (1969) (SO).

DOLORES.   COCUMENTOS PARA HISTORIA ECLESTIASTICA (HS*).

DOMENECH.   MISSIONARY ADVENTURES TEXAS MEXICO (HT*).

DOMINGUEZ.   MISSIONS NEW MEXICO, 1776 (HN*).

DOMINGUEZ.   MISSIONS NEW MEXICO, 1776 (HN*).

DONAHUE.   AFTER KINO: JESUIT MISSIONSNORTHWESTERN (HS*).

DONAHUE.   "THE MISSIONARY ACTIVITIES FRAY (HS*).

DOYON.   CALVARY CHRIST RIO GRANDE (HS*).

DUNN.   "HISTORY NATCHITOCHES, LOUISIANA" (HS*).

DUNN.   "APACHE RELATIONS TEXAS, 1718-1750" (HS*).

DUNN.   "MISSICNARY ACTIVITIES AMONGEASTERN (HS*).

DUNN.   "THE APACHE MISSION SAN SABARIVER: (HS*).

DUNN.   "THE FOUNDING NUESTRA SENCRAREFUGION (HS*).

DUNNE.   ANDRES PEREZ DE RIBAS, PIONEER (HS*).

DUNNE.   EARLY JESUIT MISSIONS TARAHUMARA (HS*).

DUNNE.   PIONEER BLACK ROBES WEST COAST (HS*).

DUNNE.   PIONEER JESUITS NORTHERN MEXICO (HS*).

DURAN.   HISTORY INDIANS NEW SPAIN (HM*).

EDWARDS.   ROLE FAITH MISSION (HS*).

EL PASO CONGRESS.   REPORT, DEC., 1926, EDUCATION (ED*).

ELLIS, IVAN. ORIGIN AND DEVELOPMENT OF BAPTIST CHURCHES
     AND INSTITUTIONS IN SOUTHERN CALIFORNIA.   UNIVERSITY
     OF SOUTHERN CALIFORNIA, MASTER'S THESIS (1938) (HC).

EMERSON.   SOUTHWESTERN MISSIONARY CHAPLAIN: (HS*).

ENGELHARDT.   HOLY MAN SANTA CLARA (HS*).

ENGELHARDT.   MISSIONS MISSIONARIES CALIFORNIA (HS*).

ENGELHARDT.   SAN DIEGO MISSION (HS*).

ENGELHARDT.   SAN FERNANDO REY MISSION VALLEY (HS*).

ENGELHARDT.   SAN FRANCISCO OR MISSION DOLCRES (HS*).

ENGELHARDT.   SAN GABRIEL MISSION (HS*).

ENGELHARDT.   SAN JUAN CAPISTRANO MISSION (HS*).

ENGELHARDT.   SAN LUIS REY MISSION (HS*).

ENGELHARDT.   SANTA BARBARA MISSION (HS*).

ENGLEHARDT.   MISSION CONCEPCION PURISMA DE (HS*).

ENGLEHARDT.   SAN BUENAVENTURA, MISSION BYSEA (HS*).

ENGLEHARDT.   SAN JUAN CAPISTRANO MISSION (HS*).

ESPINOSA, GILBERTO. "NEW MEXICAN SANTOS".   NEW MEXICO
     QUARTERLY, VOL. 6 (1936), PP. 181-189 (HS).

ESPINOSA, JOSE EDMUNDO. SAINTS IN THE VALLEYS: CHRISTIAN
     SACRED IMAGES IN THE HISTORY, LIFE AND. ALBUQUERQUE,
     NEW MEOICO: UNIVERSITY OF NEW MEOICO PRESS, 1960 (AR).

EVANS, J. D. "DISCORD ALONG THE RIO GRANDE; TEXAS COUNCIL
     OF CHURCHES AND MEXICAN AMERICAN FARM WORKERS".
     CHRISTIAN CENTURY, VOL. 86 (MARCH 26, 1969), PP.
     397-400 (SI).

FELTER.   SOCIAL ADAPTATIONS MEXICAN CHURCHES   (SO*).

FEY, H. E. "CUT OF WORK IN TEN YEARS; N.C.C. SPONSORED
     MIGRANT MINISTRY PROGRAM".   CHRISTIAN CENTURY, VOL.
     80 (OCTOBER 9, 1963), PP. 1230-1231 (SI).

FIGUEROA.   BEZERRO GENERAL MENOLOGICO CRONOLOGICO   (HS*).

FRAZER.   GOLDEN BOUGH, STUDY MAGIC RELIGION   (AN*).

GIBSON.   EUROPEAN NAVAHO WITCHCRAFT: COMPARISON   (AN*).

GILLESPIE, REV. MSGR. PATRICK (ED.).   CATHOLIC COMMENTATOR.
     BATON ROUGE, LOUISIANA,.

HARRISON.   SURVEY ADMINISTRATIVE EDUCATIONAL   (SO*).

HAYEN, C. "STUDYING MEXICAN RELATIONS AT EL PASO".
     MISSIONARY REVIEW, VOL. 50 (APRIL 1966), PP. 110-12.

HENDERSON.   BROTHERS LIGHT: PENITENTES SOUTHWEST   (HN*).

HENDERSON.   BROTHERS LIGHT: PENITENTES SOUTHWEST   (HN*).

HOLLAND, CLIFTON L. THE RELIGIOUS DIMENSION IN SPANISH
     LOS ANGELE- A PROTESTANT CASE STUDY.   SOUTH PASADENA,
     CALIFORNIA: WILLIAM CAREY LIBRARY, 1970 (SO).

HORKA-FOLLICK, LORAYNE ANN. LOS HERMANOS PENITENTES: A
     VESTIGE OF MEDIEVALISM IN THE SOUTHWESTERN U. S..
     LOS ANGELES: WESTERNLORE PRESS, 1969 (HN).

JEFFREYS.   "SOME RULES DIRECTED CULTURECHANGE   (AN*).

JOHNSON.   TRIUNFO DE LOS SANTOS: CONSIDERATION   (HS*).

JOHNSON, J. B. "THE ALLELUJAHS: A RELIGIOUS CULT IN
     NORTHERN NEW MEXICO".   SOUTHWEST REVIEW, VOL. 22
     (JANUARY 1937), PP. 131-139 (AN).

KESSELL. JOHN. MISSION OF SORROWS: JESUIT GUEVAVI AND
     THE PIMAS, 1691-1767.   TUCSON, ARIZONA: UNIVERSITY
     OF ARIZONA PRESS, 1970 (HS).

KINCAID, EDGAR B. THE MEXICAN PASTOR.   DALLAS: THE
     SOUTHWEST PRESS, 1931 (LI).

KING.   "BISHOPS VINEYARD" (EC*).

KUBLER.   EXHIBITION RELIGIOUS FOLK ART (AR*).

KUBLER.   RELIGIOUS ARCHITECTURE NEW MEXICO (AR*).

LANDSBERGER, HENRY A. (ED.). THE CHURCH AND SOCIAL CHANGE
     IN LATIN AMERICA.   NOTRE DAME, INDIANA: UNIVERSITY
     OF NOTRE DAME PRESS, 1970 (SO).

LANGSTON.   SECULARIZATION CALIFORNIA MISSIONS (HC*).

LARA-BRAUD.   "OUR SPANISH AMERICAN NEIGHBORS; (SO*).

LARA-BRAUD.   BILINGUALISM TEXAS: EDUCATION (SO*).

LARA-BRAUD.   STATUS RELIGION AMONG MEXICAN (SO*).

LEE, JOHN D. "DIARY OF THE MORMON BATTALION MISSION".
     NEW MEXICO HISTORICAL REVIEW, VOL. 42 (1967), PP.
     165-209 (HN).

LEE, LAURENCE F. LOS HERMANOS PENITENTES.   UNIVERSITY
     OF NEW MEXICO, MASTER'S THESIS (1910) (HN).

LEUTENEGGER, B. "NEW DOCUMENTS ON FATHER JOSE MARIANO
     REYES". SOUTHWESTERN HISTORICAL QUARTERLY, VOL. 71
     NO. 4 (1968), PP. 583-602 (HS).

LEUTENEGGER, B. LIFE OF FRAY ANTONIO MARGIL, O.F.M..
     WASHINGTON, D. C.: ACADEMY OF AMERICAN FRANCISCAN
     HISTORY (HS).

LINATI.   COSTUMES CIVILES, MILITAIRESET (PL*).

LOPEZ, DANIEL R. HOW DO YOU WORK WITH THE HARD CORE
     PERSON.   LOS ANGELES: UNIVERSITY OF SOUTHERN
     CALIFORNIA, JUNE 10, 1968 (SO).

LUCEY.   "CHRISTIANIZING MEXICAN CATHOLICS" (SO*).

MAC CALLUM.   HISTORY ST. CLEMENTS CHURCH, (HT*).

MARX, W. G. "NEIGHBORS WHO MOVED IN: SPANISH-AMERICAN
     CONFERENCE ON EVANGELISM". CHRISTIANITY TODAY, VOL.
     14 (SEPTEMBER 25, 1970), PP. 60-63 (SO).

MC AVOY.   AMERICANIST HERISY ROMAN CATHOLICISM (HUS*).

MC AVOY.   HISTORY CATHOLIC CHURCH UNITED (HUS*).

MC NAMARA.   "BISHOPS, PADRES, BARRIOS" (SO*).

MEADOW, ARNOLD, AND BRONSON, LOUISE. "RELIGIOUS AFFILIATION
     AND PSYCHOPATHOLOGY IN A MEXICAN-AMERICAN POPULATION".
     JOURNAL OF ABNORMAL PSYCHOLOGY, (APRIL 1969), PP.
     177-180 (PY SO).

MILLS, GEORGE THOMPSON AND GROVE, RICHARD. LUCIFER AND
     THE CRUCIFIER; THE ENIGMA OF THE PENITENTES. DENVER:
     THE WESTERNERS INC., 1956 (AN HN).

MILLS, GEORGE THOMPSON. LUCIFER AND THE CRUCIFER;
     THE ENIGMA OF THE PENITENTES. COLORADO SPRINGS:
     TAYLOR MUSEUM, 1966 (AN HN).

MILLS, GEORGE THOMPSON. THE PEOPLE CF THE SAINTS.
     COLORADO SPRINGS: TAYLOR MUSEUM, 1967 (AN HN).

MITCHELL, JAMES ERSKINE. THE EMERGENCE OF A MEXICAN
     CHURCH: THE ASSOCIATE REFORMED PRESBYTERIAN CHURCH
     OF MEXICO.   SOUTH PASADENA, CALIFORNIA: WILLIAM CAREY
     LIBRARY, 1970 (HM).

MOYA.   SUPERSTITIONS BELIEFS AMONG SPANISH   (AN*).

NEILL, STEPHEN CHARLES. A HISTORY OF CHRISTIAN MISSIONS.
     THE PELICAN HISTORY OF THE CHURCH: 6.

NELSON.   CHURCHES IGNACIO (SO*).

NOVAK.   THEOLOGY RADICAL POLITICS (PL*).

OLIVARD.   SIXTEENTH-CENTURY METHODS SERMON (HS*).

ORTEGO, PHILIP D. RELIGIOUS THOUGHT AND PRACTICE AMONG
     MEXICAN BAPTISTS OF THE U. S., 1900-1947. UNIVERSITY
     OF SOUTHERN CALIFORNIA, PHD. DISSERTATION (1950).

ORTEGO, PHILIP D. THE REIGIOUS STATUS OF THE MEXICAN
     POPULATION OF LOS ANGELES. UNIVERSITY OF SOUTHERN
     CALIFORNIA, LOS ANGELES, MASTER'S THESIS (1932).

OWENS, SISTER M. LILIANA (ET AL). REVEREND CARLOS
     M. PINTO, S. J., APOSTLE OF EL PASO, 1892-1919.   EL
     PASO: REVISTA CATOLICA PRESS, 1951 (HT).

OXNAM.   "MEXICANS LOS ANGELES STANDPOINT (SO*).

PARISOT, P. F., AND SMITH, C. J. HISTORY OF THE CATHOLIC
     CHURCH IN THE DIOCESE OF SAN ANTONIO TEXAS, 1685-1897.
     SAN ANTONIO: CARRICO AND BOWEN, (HT).

PARKMAN.   JESUITS NORTH AMERICA (HS*).

PERRY.   PRESBYTERIAN U.S.A. EDUCATIONAL (HN*).

PHARES, ROSS.   BIBLE IN POCKET, GUN IN HAND: THE STORY OF
     FRONTIER RELIGION.   LINCOLN, NEBRASKA: UNIVERSITY
     OF NEBRASKA PRESS, 1971.

RENDON, GABINO.   HAND ON MY SHOULDER.   NEW YORK: BOARD
     OF NATIONAL MISSIONS, THE UNITED PRESBYTERIAN CHURCH
     IN THE U.S.A., 1953 (SO).

RICARD.   CONQUISTA ESPIRITUAL DE MEXICO   (HS*).

RICARD.   SPIRITUAL CONQUEST MEXICO   (HS*).

RUBEL.   "PROTESTANTISM ASSIMILATION AMONG   (AN*).

RUBEL.   "RITUAL RELATIONSHIPS OJITLAN   (AN*).

RUIZ.   CHANGE CRISIS   (SO*).

SHAPIRO.   ANTICLERICALISM: CONFLICT BETWEEN   (PL*).

STONEHOUSE, MERLIN.   JOHN WESLEY NORTH AND THE REFORM
     FRONTIER.   MINNEAPOLIS: UNIVERSITY OF MINNESOTA
     PRESS, 1965 (HSW).

STOWELL, J. S.   METHODISM'S NEW FRONTIER.   NEW YORK:
     METHODIST BOOK CONCERN, 1924 (SO).

SUMMER.   MEXICAN AMERICAN MINORITY CHURCHES   (AN*).

SUMMER.   "MEXICAN AMERICAN MINORITY CHURCHES   (AN*).

SUMNER.   "MEXICAN AMERICAN MINORITY CHURCHES   (AN*).

SWEET, WILLIAM WARREN.   RELIGION ON THE AMERICAN FRONTIER.
     NEW YORK, NEW YORK: COOPER SQUARE PUBLISHERS, INC.,
     1946 (HSW).

THOMAS.   "THE FACTOR RELIGION SELECTION   (SO*).

TOWE, EMILY.   METHODISM AND LATIN-AMERICANS IN THE UNITED
     STATES.   NEW YORK: BOARD OF MISSIONS AND CHURCH
     EXTENSION OF THE METHODIST CHURCH, 1949 (SO).

TROYER.   MEXICAN MISSIONS SOUTHWEST   (HM*).

VAIL, E. O.   "WHAT WILL IT BE? READING OR MACHISMO AND
     SOUL?".   THE CLEARING HOUSE, VOL. 45   (OCTOBER
     1970), PP. 92-96.

VERNON, WALTER N.   WILLIAM STEVENSON: RIDING PREACHER.
     DALLAS: SOUTHERN METHODIST UNIVERSITY PRESS, 1971 (HSW).

VIVAS.   "OUR SPANISH-SPEAKING U.S. CATHOLICS"   (SO*).

WAGNER, JOHN A.   THE ROLE OF THE CHRISTIAN CHURCH.   LA
    RAZA, JULIAN SAMORA (ED). NOTRE DAME: UNIVERSITY OF
    NOTRE DAME PRESS, 1969 (HS).

WAGNER, REV. JOHN.   'THE CHRISTIAN CHURCH.'   IN JULIAN
    SAMORA (ED), LA RAZA: FORGOTTEN AMERICANS (HS).

WARNER.   ARCHBISHOP LAMY, EPOCH MAKER   (HSW*).

WILDER.   "SANTOS, RELIGIOUS FOLK ART NEW   (AR*).

WILDER.   SANTOS (RELIGIOUS FOLK ART NEW   (AR*).

WOLF.   "CHURCH AND DELANO"   (EC*).

M I G R A T I O N

(SI)

ABEL. PROTESTANT HOME MISSIONS TO CATHOLIC (RE*).

ABEYTA, HECTOR. AGENCIES AND THE MIGRANT: THEORY
AND REALITY OF THE MIGRANT CONDITION. LAS CRUCES,
NEW MEXICO: ERIC, (EC).

ADAMIC. AMERICANS SPAIN MEXICO (HS*).

ADAMIC, LOUIS. FROM MANY LANDS. NEW YORK: HARPER, 1940
(SO).

ADAMIC, LOUIS. A NATION OF NATIONS. NEW YORK: HARPER,
1945 (SO).

AGUINALDO, GENERAL EMILI Y PACIS, VICENTE ALVANO. A SECOND
LOOK AT AMERICA. NEW YORK: ROBERT SPELLER & SONS,
PUBLISHERS, INC., 1957 (SO).

ALBIG, WILLIAM. "OPINIONS CONCERNING UNSKILLED MEXICAN
IMMIGRANTS". SOCIOLOGY AND SOCIAL RESEARCH, VOL.
15 (SEPT. 1930), PP. 62-72 (EC SO).

ALLEN. "MEXICAN PEON WOMEN TEXAS" (EC*).

ALLWELL, PATRICK J. MEXICAN IMMIGRATION INTO THE UNITED
STATES. UNIVERSITY OF MISSOURI, MASTER'S THESIS (1928).

ALMAZAN. "THE MEXICANS KEEP EM ROLLING" (EC*).

ALVARADO, ERNESTINE, M. "MEXICAN IMMIGRATION TO THE UNITED
STATES". NATIONAL CONFERENCE OF SOCIAL WORK,
(1920), PP. 479-80 (SO).

ALVAREZ, JOSE. "A DEMOGRAPHIC PROFILE OF THE MEXICAN
IMMIGRANT TO THE UNITED STATES, 1910-1950". JOURNAL
OF INTERNATIONAL AMERICAN STUDIES, VOL. 8 (JULY
1966), PP. 471-496 (SO AN).

AMERICAN ACADEMY OF POLITICAL AND SOCIAL SCIENCE.
"REAPPRAISING OUR IMMIGRATION (EC*).

AMERICAN FEDERATION OF LABOR. PROCEEDINGS 47TH ANNUAL
CONVENTION (EC*).

AMERICAN FEDERATION OF LABOR. "FARM WORKERS MAY FIGHT"
(EC*).

AMERICAN FRIENDS SERVICE COMMITTEE.   FARM WORKERS LAW:
     REPORT ILLEGAL (EC*).

     AMERICAN GI FORUM OF TEXAS AND TEXAS STATE FEDERATION
     OF LABOR (AFL).   WHAT PRICE WETBACKS? (EC*).

ANDERSON, HENRY PAUL. THE BRACERO PROGRAM IN CALIFORNIA,
     WITH PARTICULAR REFERENCE TO HEALTH STATUS, ATTITUDES
     AND PRACTICES.   BERKELEY, CALIFORNIA: UNIVERSITY OF
     CALIFORNIA, 1961 (EC).

ANDERSON, HENRY. FIELDS OF BONDAGE.   MARTINEZ, CALIFORNIA,
     1963 (EC).

ANDREWS.   MIGRANT AGRICULTURAL LABOR OHIO (EC*).

"FEDERAL PROGRAM PUBLIC HEALTH (MD*).

"LITTLE MEXICO IN NORTHERN CITIES".   WORLD'S WORK, VOL.
     48 (SEPTEMBER 1924), P. 466.

"WHOLL PICK STRAWBERRIES? PROBLEM (EC*).

"WILL GROWERS GET MEXICAN LABOR? (EC*).

MIGRATORY COTTON PICKERS ARIZONA (EC*).

SKETCHES OF LIFE IN THE UNITED STATES OF NORTH AMERICA AND
     TEXAS.   WACO, TEXAS: TEXIAN PRESS,.

SPANISH NAME BOOK.   UNITED STATES DEPARTMENT OF JUSTICE,
     IMMIGRATION AND NATURALIZATION SERVICE, (1963) (LW).

STANDARD OF LIVING IN AN INDIAN-MEXICAN VILLAGE AND ON A
     RECLAMATION PROJECT BY THE U. S. D. A..   SOCIAL
     RESEARCH REPORT, NO. 14, UNITED STATES DEPARTMENT OF
     AGRICULTURE, FARM SECURITY ADMINISTRATION AND BUREAU
     OF AGRICULTURAL ECONOMICS, 1938 (EC).

"TOSSED SALAD; BRACEROS" (EC*).

"ACROSS BORDER; SOUTHER CALIFORNIA (EC*).

"ACROSS THE TRACKS".   TIME, VOL. 42 (SEPT. 6, 1943),
     P. 25 (SO).

"AMERICAN FARM LABOR DISPLACES (EC*).

"ANOTHER EXTENSION; IMPORTATION (EC*).

"ASPARAGUS ASPERSIONS; DISPUTE (EC*).

"BATTLE OVER BRACEROS" (SO*).

"CARAVAN OF SORROW". LIVING AGE, VOL. 332 (SEPTEMBER
    1964), PP. 870-72 (EC).

"CHILDREN MIGRANT WORKERS POSE (ED*).

"CLASSES MEXICAN WORKERS MICHIGAN (ED*).

"CONCENTRATIONS OF FOREIGN STOCK IN THE UNITED STATES".
    CONGRESSIONAL QUARTERLY, VOL. 14 (SEPTEMBER 28,
    1956), PP. 49-55.

"EDUCATING MIGRATORY CHILDREN" (ED*).

"EXPLOITATION TENNESSEE" (EC*).

"EXPLOITATION MIGRANTS DEMANDS (EC*).

"IN THE INTEREST OF UNDERSTANDING: SOME RECENT STUDIES
    CONCERNED WITH EDUCATION OF MINORITY GROUPS".
    EDUCATION FOR VICTORY, VOL. 1 (SEPTEMBER 1943), PP.
    18-20.

"INCREASE OF MEXICAN POPULATIONS IN THE UNITED STATES, 1920
    TO 1930". MONTHLY LABOR REVIEW, VOL. 37 (JULY
    1933), PP. 46-48.

"MARCH OF MIGRANTS". LIFE, VOL. 60 (APRIL 29, 1966),
    PP. 93-94.

"MEXICAN EXODUS". NEWSWEEK, VOL. 14 NO. 5 (JULY 3 1,
    1939), P. 11.

"MEXICAN IMMIGRANTS IN EL PASO". FOREIGN LANGUAGE
    INFORMATION SERVICE, VOL. 7 (JULY 18, 1930), PP.
    44-46.

"MEXICAN IMMIGRATION". TRANSACTIONF OF THE COMMONWEALTH
    CLUB OF CALIFORNIA, VOL. 21 (MARCH 1926), PP. 1-34.

"MEXICAN INVADERS OF EL PASO". SURVEY, VOL. 36 (MARCH
    1926), PP. 380-82.

"MEXICAN JOURNEYS TO BETHLEHEM". LITERARY DIGEST, VOL.
    77 (SPRING 1959), PP. 103-4 (EC).

"MEXICAN LABOR IN THE IMPERIAL VALLEY, CALIFORNIA".
    MONTHLY LABOR REVIEW, VOL. 28 (MARCH 1929),
    PP. 59-65 (EC).

"MEXICAN MINERS GOING BACK HOME" (EC*).

"MEXICAN WETBACKS". NEWSWEEK, VOL. 32 NO. 5 (OCTOBER
    25, 1948), P. 80 (EC).

"MEXICAN LABOR COLONY AT BETHLEHEM, PENNSYLVANIA".
    MONTHLY LABOR REVIEW, VOL. 33 (JULY 3, 1969), PP.
    822-26 (EC).

"MEXICAN RIGHTS UNITED STATES"   (EC*).

"MEXICANS ASSIST: SOUTHERN PACIFIC REPORTS".   BUSINESS
     WEEK, VOL. 5   (OCTOBER   14, 1944), P. 54 (EC).

"MEXICANS ON THE JOB".   BUSINESS WEEK, VOL. 5   (JANUARY
     1, 1944), P. 82 (EC).

"MEXICO UNITED STATES IMMIGRATION   (EC*).

"MIGRANT CHILD".   OVERVIEW, VOL. 1   (OCTOBER   1960), PP.
     50-53 (ED).

"MIGRANT CHILDREN BENEFIT FROM INNOVATIVE PROJECTS".
     CATHOLIC SCHOOL JOURNAL, VOL. 67   (SEPTEMBER   1967),
     P. 84 (ED).

"MIGRANT LABOR AGREEMENT WITH   (EC*).

"MIGRANT WORKERS; IGNORANCE IS   (EC*).

"MIGRANT WORKERS PLIGHT"   (EC*).

"MIGRANT WORKERS TO BE TRAINED   (EC*).

"MIGRANTS MACHINES; BRACEROS"   (EC*).

"MIGRATORY FARM LABOR; PROBLEM   (EC*).

"MIGRATORY WORKERS UNITED STATES"   (EC*).

"MISERABLE MIGRANTS".   AMERICA, VOL. 108   (MARCH 23,
     1963), P. 386.

"MISERY ON THE MOVE".   THE ECONOMIST, VOL. 224   (DECEMBER
     30,   1967), P.   1292.

"PABLO IS A MIGRANT".   SCHOOL LIFE, VOL. 35   (JANUARY
     1953), PP. 56-58 (ED).

"POVERTY SPURS ECUMENISM; MICHIGAN   (RE*).

"PROGRAM FOR MIGRATORY LABOR".   AMERICAN CHILD, VOL. 32
     (FEBRUARY   1950), P. 1, 4.

"REPORT ON MIGRANT WORKERS".   AMERICA, VOL. 114   (MARCH
     12, 1966), P. 346.

"RESULTS ADMISSION MEXICAN LABORERS   (EC*).

"RIGHTS FARM WORKERS"   (PL*).

"ROOTS FOR THE ROOTLESS".   CHRISTIAN CENTURY, VOL. 80
     (MAY   15, 1963), PP. 635-636.

"RULES MEXICAN WORKERS AS RAILROAD (EC*).

"RURAL WORKER IN AMERICA".   MONTHLY LABOR REVIEW, VOL.
     91   (JUNE 1968), PP. 1-32 (SO   EC).

"SCHOOL GRANTS MIGRANTS" (ED*).

"SENATE UNIT AIRS MIGRANT DISPUTE" (PL*).

"STOOP LABOR".   COMMONWEAL, VOL. 81 (FEBRUARY 5,   1965),
     PP. 596-597 (EC).

"STOOP LABOR FUROR: BRACERO SYSTEM".   SCHOLASTIC TEACHER,
     VOL. 86 (MAY 6, 1965), PP. 18-19 (EC).

"STORM OVER BRACEROS".   SCHOOL AND SOCIETY, VOL. 85
     (JANUARY 1965), P. 20 (EC).

"SUMMER BRINGS MEXICANS: NATIONAL (EC*).

"THE CHURCHS PARTNERSHIP WITH (EC*).

"THE MEXICANS OF IMPERIAL VALLEY".   FOREIGN LANGUAGE
     INFORMATION SERVICE, VOL. 6 (MAY 15, 1929), PP. 85-91
     (EC).

"THE MEXICANS SAN ANTONIO: WHEN (SO*).

"UNIFORM PERSONAL HEALTH RECORD FOR MIGRANT WORKERS".
     PUBLIC HEALTH REPORTS,   (JUNE 1961), P. 533 (MD).

"WETBACK INVASION".   SCHOLASTIC, VOL. 60 (FEBRUARY 20,
     1952), P. 12 (SO   EC).

"WETBACK INVASION IN TEXAS".   NATION, VOL. 169 (AUGUST
     20, 1949), P. 168 (SO   EC).

"WETBACKS IN MIDDLE OF BORDER WAR".   BUSINESS WEEK,
     (OCTOBER 24, 1953), PP. 62-66 (EC).

"WETBACKS IN THE RIVER".   NEWSWEEK, VOL. 34 (SEPTEMBER
     12, 1949), P. 22 (EC).

"WETBACKS SWARM IN".   LIFE, VOL. 30 (MAY 2 1, 1951), PP.
     33-37 (EC).

"WETBACKS".   NEWSWEEK, VOL. 27 (MARCH 11, 1946), P. 70
     (EC).

"WETBACKS".   TIME, VOL. 57 (APRIL 9, 1951), P. 24 (EC).

"WETBACKS AND AMERICAN FARM LABOR".   NATIONAL COUNCIL OF
     CHURCHES OF CHRIST IN THE U. S. A., VOL. 32 NO. 38
     (APRIL 9, 1951) (EC).

"WETBACKS, COTTON, AND KOREA".   NATION, VOL. 172   (MAY
     5, 1951), P. 408 (EC SO).

"WITHOUT QUOTA".   SURVEY,   (MAY 15, 1924).

"WOMEN YOU'D LIKE TO KNOW: DAY CARE CENTER".   FARM
     JOURNAL, VOL. 94   (MAY 1970), PP. 60-61 (EC).

"WORKERS AND MIGRANT FIRMS".   AMERICA, VOL. 108   (JANYARY
     5, 1963), P. 4 (EC).

COMPANY THAT HELPS MIGRANTS: (EC*).

LEY DE MIGRACION DE LOS ESTADOS (EC*).

MEXICAN INVADERS RELIEVING OUR FARM LABOR SHORTAGE.
     LITERARY DIGEST, JULY 17,1920 (EC).

MEXICANS IN CALIFORNIA.   REPORT OF GOVERNOR C.C. YOUNG'S
     MEXICAN FACT-FINDING COMMITTEE. SAN FRANCISCO, (1930)
     (EC).

MEXICANS LOS ANGELES (SO*).

MEXICANS IN CALIFORNIA.   REPORT OF CALIFORNIA GOVERNOR
     C.C. YOUNG'S MEXICAN FACT COMMITTEE, 1930. SAN
     FRANCISCO: CALIFORNIA STATE PRINTING OFFICE REPRINTED
     BY R AND E RESEARCH ASSOCIATES, SAN FRANCISCO,
     CALIFORNIA, 1970 (EC).

MIGRANT LABOR ... HUMAN PROBLEM (ED*).

ORIGINS PROBLEMS TEXAS MIGRATORY (ED*).

TEXAS COMMITTEE ON MIGRANT FARM WORKERS AND THE GOOD
     NEIGHBOR COMMISSION OF TEXAS.   AUSTIN: 57TH TEXAS
     LEGISLATURE, 1962 (ED).

TEXAS COUNCIL ON MIGRANT LABOR.   TEXAS MIGRANT LABOR
     DURING 1962: OVERALL SUMMARY. MARCH 1963 (EC).

WETBACKS AND MEXICAN NATIONAL AGREEMENTS.   SAN FRANCISCO,
     (1953). THE COMMONWEALTH, VOLUME 29, NUMBER 16, PART
     2, COMMONWEALTH CLUB OF CALIFORNIA, HOTEL ST. FRANCIS.
     (EC).

WHAT PRICE WETBACKS.   AUSTIN: AMERICAN G. I. FORUM
     OF TEXAS AND TEXAS STATE FEDERATION OF LABOR, 1953
     (EC).

"AS BRACEROS LEAVE" (EC*).

"BRACEROS AND MIGRANTS" (EC*).

"BRACEROS AND MIGRANTS" (EC*).

"BRACEROS, STAY HOME"   (EC*).

"CHURCHES AND BRACEROS"   (EC*).

"MIGRATORY FARM WORKER"   (EC*).

"MIGRATORY LABOR"   (EC*).

"MIGRATORY LABOR"   (EC*).

"THE FATE OF P. L. 78"   (EC*).

"WETBACK INVASION"   (SO*).

THE MEXICAN IN LOS ANGELES, 1920.   THE MEXICAN IN
     LOS ANGELES, 1920 (SO).

THE WETBACK'S DOLLAR.   TEXAS STATE FEDERATION OF LABOR.
     (EC).

ARGOYTIA.   LOS BRACEROS   (EC*).

ARIZONA STATE COMMITTEE ON AMERICANIZATION WORK IN ARIZONA.
     PAMPHLET   (SO*).

ARIZONA STATE DEPARTMENT OF PUBLIC INSTRUCTION.   ARIZONA
     TEACHER EXCHANGE 1969   (ED*).

ARMSTRONG, JOHN M., JR.   A MEXICAN COMMUNITY: A STUDY OF
     THE CULTURAL DETERMINANTS OF MIGRATION.   YALE
     UNIVERSITY, PHD.   DISSERTATION (1949) (AN SO).

ARMSTRONG, JOHN M., JR.   A MEXICAN COMMUNITY: A STUDY OF
     THE CULTURAL DETERMINANTS OF MIGRATION.   YALE
     UNIVERSITY, PHD.   DISSERTATION (1949) (AN).

ASHBY.   ROLE MEXICAN LABOR MOVEMENT NATIONAL   (EC*).

ASTER.   TERMINATION BRACERO PROGRAM--ITS   (LW*).

ATWATER.   TABULATION FACTS CONDITIONS EXISTENT   (EC*).

BAIME.   "MIGRANT EDUCATION HAS NEW MEANING?"   (ED*).

BAKER.   "SCHOOL NURSE TO MIGRANT CHILDREN"   (MD*).

BAKER.   "BRACEROS FARM MEXICO"   (EC*).

BAMFORD.   "MEXICAN CASUAL LABOR PROBLEM   (EC*).

BAMFORD.   INDUSTRIALIZATION MEXICAN CASUAL   (EC*).

BARNES.   CALIFORNIA MIGRANT FRAM WORKER   (SO*).

BARRON.   MEXICAN PROBLEM   (SO*).

BATTEN, JAMES H. "MEXICO'S PROGRAM: AN OPPORTUNITY".
    WORLD TOMORROW, VOL. 12 (JAN 1929), PP. 36-39 (EC).

BATTEN.   "NEW FEATURES MEXICAN IMMIGRATION: (LW*).

BATTEN.   "OUR CULTURAL RELATIONS WITHMEXICO" (SO*).

BATTEN.   "THE MEXICAN IMMIGRATICN PROBLEM" (SO*).

BATTEN.   "THE MEXICAN IMMIGRATION PROBLEM" (SO*).

BATTEY.   MEXICAN SITUATION ST. PAUL (SO*).

BEGEMAN.   "WETBACKS--SLAVES TODAY" (EC*).

BENITENDI.   HANDBOOK TEACHERS MIGRANT CHILDREN (ED*).

BENJAMIN.   I AM AMERICAN, BY FAMOUS NATURALIZED (SO*).

BERARD, BERN. "DETENTION FACILITIES ALONG THE MEXICAN
    BORDER".   IMMIGRATION AND NATURALIZATION SERVICE,
    UNITED STATES DEPARTMENT OF JUSTICE, VOL. 9 NO. 3
    (SEPTEMBER 1951), PP. 32-33 (LW).

BERKSON.   THEORIES AMERICANIZATION; CRITICAL (SO*).

BEZET.   THE LATIN AMERICANS (SO*).

BLAISDELL, LOWELL L. "HARRY CHANDLER AND MEXICAN BORDER
    INTRIGUE, 1914-1917".   PACIFIC HISTORICAL REVIEW,
    (NOVEMBER 1966), PP. 385-393 (HSW).

BLANTON.   SUGGESTIONS TEACHING MIGRATORY (ED*).

BLOCH.   "FACTS ABOUT MEXICAN IMMIGRATION (SO*).

BLOCH.   REPORT MEXICAN LABOR SITUATION (EC*).

BLOCK.   FACTS ABOUT FILIPINO IMMIGRATION (EC*).

BOGARDUS.   ATTITUDES MEXICAN IMMIGRANT (SO*).

BOGARDUS.   REPATRIATION READJUSTMENT (SO*).

BOGARDUS.   "CURRENT PROBLEMS MEXICAN IMMIGRANTS" (SO*).

BOGARDUS.   MEXICAN UNITED STATES (SO*).

BOGARDUS.   MEXICAN UNITED STATES (SO*).

BOGARDUS.   "MEXICAN REPATRIATES" (SO*).

BOGARDUS.   "SECOND GENERATION MEXICANS" (SO*).

BOGARDUS.   "SECOND GENERATION MEXICANS" (SO*).

BOGARDUS.   "SECOND GENERATION MEXICANS" (SO*).

BOGARDUS.   "THE MEXICAN IMMIGRANT QUOTA" (SO*).

BOGARDUS.   "THE MEXICAN IMMIGRANT QUOTA" (SO*).

BOGARDUS.   "THE MEXICAN IMMIGRANT SEGREGATION" (SO*).

BOGARDUS.   "THE MEXICAN IMMIGRANT SEGREGATION" (SO*).

BOGARDUS.   "THE MEXICAN IMMIGRANT SEGREGATION" (SC*).

BOGARDUS.   ESSENTIALS AMERICANIZATION (SO*).

BOGARDUS.   ESSENTIALS AMERICANIZATION (SO*).

BOGARDUS.   IMMIGRATION RACE ATTITUDES (SO*).

BOGARDUS.   MEXICAN IMMIGRANT: ANNOTATEDBIBLIOGRAPHY (B*).

BOGARDUS.   RESIDENT IMMIGRANT PROBLEM (SO*).

BOGARDUS.   "MEXICAN REPATRIATES" (SO*).

BOGARDUS.   "THE MEXICAN IMMIGRANT" (SO*).

BOGARDUS.   "THE MEXICAN IMMIGRANT" (SO*).

BOGUE, DONALD JOSEPH. AN EXPLORATORY STUDY OF MIGRATION
     AND LABOR MOBILITY, USING SOCIAL SECURITY DATA.
     OXFORD, OHIO, 1950 (EC).

BRANN.   "HOUSING MIGRANT AGRICULTURAL (EC*).

BRATTEN.   "THE MEXICAN IMMIGRATION PROBLEM" (SO*).

BRESETTE.   MEXICANS UNITED STATES (SO*).

BRIGHAM.   "INTELLIGENCE TESTS IMMIGRANT (ED*).

BRODY, EUGENE B. BEHAVIOR IN NEW ENVIRONMENTS: AN
     ADAPTATION OFMIGRANT POPULATIONS.   BEVERLY HILLS:
     SAGE PUBLICATIONS, 1970 (SO).

BROOKS.   SOCIAL PROBLEMS MIGRANT FARMLABORERS (SO*).

BROWN.   "THE CHALLENGE MEXICAN IMMIGRATION" (SO*).

BROWN.   MIGRATORY COTTON PICKERS ARIZONA (EC*).

BUCHAN.   "HELPING MIGRANTS COMMUNICATE" (ED*).

BUNKER.   FIRST LOOK AT STRANGERS (SO*).

BURR.   "ALONG MIGRANT STREAM" (SC*).

BUSEY.   "THE POLITICAL GEOGRAPHY MEXICAN   (PL*).

BUSTAMANTE.   NUEVO BERNAL DIAZ O SEA HISTORIA   (HM*).

CABRANES, MANUEL.   PROGRESS REPORT ON THE PUERTO RICAN
     MIGRANTS.   NEW YORK: PUERTO RICO DEPARTMENT OF LABOR,
     1950.

CALIFORNIA COMMISSION OF IMMIGRATION AND HOUSING.
     COMMUNITY SURVEY MADE LOS ANGELES   (SO*).

CALIFORNIA COMMITTEE FOR THE STUDY OF TRANSIENT YOUTH.
     TRANSIENT YOUTH IN CALIFORNIA; A NATIONAL, STATE, AND
     LOCAL PROBLEM, REPORT AND RECOMMENDATIONS.   LOS
     ANGELES: CALIFORNIA COMMITTEE FOR THE STUDY OF
     TRANSIENT YOUTH, 1948 (ED).

CALIFORNIA GOVERNORS ADVISORY COMMITTEE ON CHILDREN AND
     YOUTH.   FAMILIES WHO FOLLOW CROPS   (EC*).

CALIFORNIA NURSES ASSOCIATION.   "LOW INCOME, LIMITED
     HEALTH CARE   (EC*).

CALIFORNIA STATE COMMISSION ON HOUSING AND IMMIGRATION.
     ANNUAL REPORTS   (SO*).

CALIFORNIA STATE DEPARTMENT OF EDUCATION.   BASIS PLAN
     ACTION IMPROVING EDUCATION   (ED*).

CALIFORNIA STATE DEPARTMENT OF JUSTICE.   GUIDE TO
     COMMUNITY RELATIONSPEACE   (EC*).

CALIFORNIA STATE DEPARTMENT OF INDUSTRIAL RELATIONS.
     NEGROES MEXICAN AMERICANS SOUTH   (EC*).

CALIFORNIA STATE DEPARTMENT OF EDUCATION.   SCHOOL HEALTH
     RECORD TRANSFER   (ED*).

CALIFORNIA STATE DIVISION OF FARM LABOR SERVICES.   STATE
     CALIFORNIA MIGRANT SERVICES   (EC*).

CALIFORNIA. GOVERNOR'S ADVISORY COMMITTEE ON CHILDREN AND
     YOUTH. SUBCO. CONFERENCE ON FAMILIES WHO FOLLOW THE
     CROPS: REPORT AND RECOMMENDATIONS. SACRAMENTO:
     SUBCOMMITTEE ON THE MIGRANT CHILD, 1967.

CALIFORNIA. GOVERNOR'S ADVISORY COMMITTEE ON CHILDREN AND
     YOUTH. SUBCOMMITTEE ON THE MIGRANT CHILD. REPORT
     AND RECOMMENDATIONS OF THE THIRD ANNUAL CONFERENCE
     ON FAMILIES WHO FOLLOW THE CROPS. SACRAMENTO:
     GOVERNOR'S ADVISORY COMMITTEE ON CHILDREN AND YOUTH,
     SUBCOMMITTEE ON THE MIGRANT CHILD, 1962.

CARNEY.   POSTWAR MEXICAN MIGRATION: 1945-1955   (HM*).

CARTER, HUGH; DOSTER, BERNICE. "RESIDENCE AND OCCUPATION
     OF NATURALIZED AMERICANS FROM MEXICO".   U. S.
     IMMIGRATION AND NATURALIZATION SERVICE MONTHLY REVIEW,
     VOL. 8 (OCTOBER 1950), PP. 47-53.

CARTER, HUGH; DOSTER, BERNICE. "SOCIAL CHARACTERISTICS
     OF ALIENS FROM THE SOUTHWEST REGISTERED FOR SELE CTIVE
     SERVICE DURING WORLD WAR II".   U. S. IMMIGRATION AND
     NATURALIZATION SERVICE MONTHLY REVIEW, VOL. 8
     (JANUARY 1951), PP. 88-94.

CARTER, HUGH; DOSTER, BERNICE. "SOCIAL CHARACTERISTICS
     OF NATURALIZED AMERICANS FROM MEXICO: AGE AND
     M ARITAL STATUS".   UNITED STATES IMMIGRATION
     AND NATURALIZATION SERVICE MONTHLY REVIEW, VOL. 8
     (SEPTEMBER 1950), PP. 35-39.

CASTILLO, M. G. "ARE THE SPANISH SPEAKING JUST ANOTHER
     IMMIGRANT GROUP?".   INTEGRATED EDUCATION, VOL. 9
     (JANUARY 1971), PP. 45-49 (ED).

CHENAULT, LAWRENCE R. THE PUERTO RICAN MIGRANT IN NEW YORK
     CITY.   NEW YORK: COLUMBIA UNIVERSITY PRESS, 1938.

CHEYNEY.   NATIONAL GOALS MIGRANT EDUCATION (ED*).

CHICANO STUDIES INSTITUTES.   CHICANO STUDIES: ITS
     RELATIONSHIP (PL*).

CHOLDIN.   MEXICAN ANERICANS TRANSITION. (EC*).

CLARK, ELMER TALMAGE. LATIN-AMERICA, U. S. A..   NEW YORK:
     JOINT DIVISION OF EDUCATION AND CULTIVATION, BOARD
     OF MISSIONS AND CHURCH EXTENSION, THE METHODIST
     CHURCH, 1942.

CLARK, ELMER TALMAGE. THE LATIN IMMIGRANT IN THE SOUTH.
     NASHVILLE, TENNESSEE: COKESBURY PRESS, 1924.

CLARK, F. D., AND LYNCH, J. THE NEW YORK VOLUNTEERS IN
     THE MEXICAN WAR.   GLORIETA, NEW MEXICO: RIO GRANDE
     PRESS, INC., (HSW).

CLARK.   "MEXICAN LABOR U. S." (EC*).

CLELAND.   ALIENS NOMADS (HC*).

CLELAND.   IRVINE RANCH (HC*).

CLINE.   "MEXICAN COMMUNITY STUDIES" (GE*).

CLISSOLD, STEPHEN. SEVEN CITIES OF CIBLOA.   NEW YORK:
     C. N. POTTER, 1962.

COBB.   RETARDATION ELEMENTARY SCHOOLS (ED*).

COHEN.   "THE FOREIGNERS OUR SCHOOLS: (ED*).

COLEMAN, JAMES S. ET AL. UPROOTED CHILDREN: THE EARLY
      LIFE OF MIGRANT FARM WORKERS.   PITTSBURGH, PENNYSLVIA:
      UNIVERSITY OF PITTSBURGH PRESS, 1970 (EC).

COLES, ROBERT AND HUGH, HARRY. "PEONAGE IN FLORIDA".
      NEW REPUBLIC, VOL. 161 (JULY 26, 1969), PP. 17-21
      (EC).

COLES, ROBERT AND HUGE, H. "THORNS ON THE YELLOW ROSE OF
      TEXAS".   THE NEW REPUBLIC, VOL. 160 (APRIL
      19, 1969), PP. 13-17 (EC).

COLES, ROBERT. "WHAT MIGRANT FARM CHILDREN LEARN".
      SATURDAY REVIEW, VOL. 48 (MAY 15, 1965) (EC).

COLKET, MEREDITH B., JR. AND BRIDGERS, FRANK E. GUIDE TO
      GENEALOGICAL RECORDS IN THE NATIONAL ARCHIVES.
      WASHINGTON, D. C.: THE NATIONAL ARCHIVES, ANTIONAL
      ARCHIVES AND RECORD SERVICE, GENERAL SERVICE ADMINISTRATION,
      (1964).

COLLINS, HENRY HILL. AMERICA'S OWN REFUGEES: OUR
      4,000,000 HOMELESS MIGRANTS.   PRINCETON, NEW JERSEY:
      PRINCETON UNIVERSITY PRESS, 1941.

COLORADO UNIVERSITY.   URBANIZATION MIGRANT (HCO*).

COLORADO.   GOVERNORS COMMITTEE MIGRANTLABOR (HCO*).

COLORADO.   REPORT GOVERNORS SURVEY COMMITTEE   (HCO*).

COLORADO.   MIGRATORY LABOR COLORADO (HCO*).

COLORADO.   MIGRANT LABOR PROBLEMS 1970S (HCO*).

COMMITTEE ON MEXICAN LABOR IN CALIFORNIA. ANNUAL REPORTS,
      1918 TO 1934.   WASHINGTON, D. C.:GOVERNMENT
      PRINTING OFFICE, (1918 TO 1934).

COMMITTEE ON MODERN LANGUAGES.   "COMMITTEE BUSINESS MEN
      TO AID (EC*).

COMMONS.   RACES IMMIGRANTS AMERICA (SO*).

COMPTON.   "GREN VALLEY ISNT SO JOLLY: (EC*).

CONANT, LORA M. THERESA AND THE DUST BOWL.   ARIZONA
      QUARTERLY, 19.

CONDE.   "SCHOOL MIGRANT CHILD" (ED*).

CONDE.   STUDENT DEBATE BRINGS SOME DEBATE (ED*).

CONDE.   MACHO PLAN WORKERS WILL INSTRUCT   (ED*).

CONWAY.   "MIGRANTS PROMISED LAND: FARM   (EC*).

CONWAY.   "MIGRANTS DIRECTIONS 67"   (EC*).

CRAWFORD, R.   "MENACE OF MEXICAN IMMIGRATION".   CURRENT
     HISTORY, VOL. 31 , PP. 902-7.

CROFT.   SOME NEW APPROACHES TO MIGRANT   (ED*).

CURRENT.   MIGRANT PROBLEMS DEMAND ATTENTION   (EC*).

DARRAH.   "A MOBILE HEALTH SERVICE MIGRANT   (MD*).

DAVIDSON, CECELIA RAGOVSKY.   "MEXICAN LABORERS IMPORTED
     INTO THE UNITED STATES".   INTERPRETER RELEASES, VOL.
     20 (OCTOBER 1943), PP. 298-300 (EC).

DAVILA.   MEXICAN MIGRATION PROBLEM (EC*).

DAVIS.   SUGAR BEET LABOR NORTHERN COLORADO   (EC*).

DAVIS, KINGSLEY; SENIOR, CLARENCE.   "IMMIGRATION FROM THE
     WESTERN HEMISPHERE".   ANNALS OF THE AMERICAN ACADEMY
     OF POLITICAL AND SOCIAL SCIENCES, VOL. 262 (MARCH
     1949), PP. 70-81 (PL).

DAWBER, MARK A.   'THE MEXICAN IMMIGRANT.'   IN OUR SHIFTING
     POPULATION, CHAPTER 11.   NEW YORK: HOME MISSIONS COUNCIL.

DEARMAN.   SOCIO-ECONOMIC STUDY LATIN-AMERICAN (SO*).

DEPENDENT AND NEGLECTED CHILDREN.   THE MEXICAN IN CALIFORNIA.
     NEW YORK: D. APPLETON CENTURY COMPANY, 1933 (EC).

DIVINE, ROBERT A.   AMERICAN IMMIGRATION POLICY, 1924-1952.
     NEW HAVEN, CONNECTICUT: YALE UNIVERSITY PRESS, 1957.

DOTSON.   "DECREASE MEXICAN POPULATION (SO*).

DOUGLASS.   MIGRANT COMMUNITY (SO*).

DUCOFF.   MIGRATORY FARM WORKERS 1949 (EC*).

EDWARDS.   "CHILDREN MIGRATORY AGRICULTURAL   (ED*).

EDWARDS.   "MIGRANT CHILDREN PUBLIC SCHOOLS--NEEDS   (ED*).

ELAC.   EMPLOYMENT MEXICAN WORKERS U. S. (EC*).

EONLEON, C. GAMIO.   "BRACEROS BRING HOME NEW WAYS".
     AMERICAS, VOL. 13 (MAY 1961), PP. 28-30.

ERICSON.   "IMPACT COMMUTERS MEXICAN-AMERICAN   (EC*).

ESQUIVEL, S. I. "THE IMMIGRANT FROM MEXICO". OUTLOOK,
    (MAY 19, 1920), PP. 125-131.

EVANS. "DISCORD ALONG RIO GRANDE; TEXAS (RE*).

FACCI. REHABILITATION MEXICAN FARM LABORERS (SO*).

FAIRCHILD. IMMIGRANT BACKGROUNDS (SO*).

FEERY. PLANNED COMMUNITY MIGRATORY FARM (EC*).

FEINGOLD. "INTELLIGENCE FIRST GENERATION (SO*).

FERIA . "WAR STATUS FILIPINO IMMIGRANTS" (SO*).

FEY. "CUT WORK TEN YEARS; N.C.C. SPONSORED (RE*).

FINNEY. COMPARATIVE STUDY RELATIVE ACHIEVEMENT (ED*).

FOERSTER. RACIAL PROBLEMS INVOLVED IMMIGRATION (SO*).

FORM. "WORK CONTACTS INTERNATIONALEVALUATIONS: (SO*).

FORM. "THE PLACE RETURNING MIGRANTS (SO*).

FRESNO. TEACHING CHILDREN WHO MOVE WITH (ED*).

FROST. "SCHOOL MIGRANT CHILD" (ED*).

FULLER. SCHOOL PROGRESS CHILDREN MIGRATORY (ED*).

FULLER. DOMESTIC IMPORTED WORKERS HARVEST (EC*).

GALLARDO, LLOYD. MEXICAN GREEN CARDERS: PRELIMINARY
    REPORT. WASHINGTON, D. C: U.S. DEPARTMENT
    OF LABOR, BUREAU OF EMPLOYMENT SECURITY, (JULY 10,
    1962) (EC).

GAMIO. "STATIC DYNAMIC VALUES INDIGENOUS (AN*).

GAMIO. MEXICAN IMMIGRANT (AN*).

GAMIO. MIGRATION PLANNING (AN*).

GAMIO. OBSERVATIONS MEXICAN IMMIGRATION (AN*).

GAMIO. PRELIMINARY SURVEY ANTECEDENTS (AN*).

GAMIO. QUANTITATIVE ESTIMATE SOURCES (AN*).

GAMIO. "MIGRATION AND PLANNING" (AN*).

GAMIO, MANUEL. THE LIFE STORY OF THE MEXICAN IMMIGRANT.
    NEW YORK, NEW YORK:DOVER PUBLICATIONS, 1971.

GARTH.   "THE INDUSTRIAL PSYCHOLOGY IMMIGRANT   (PY*).

GIVENS.   "A REPORT MIGRATORY FARM LABOR"   (EC*).

GODDARD.   "MENTAL TESTS IMMIGRANT"   (SO*).

GOLDSTEIN.   DEMOGRAPHIC BODILY CHANGES DESCENDANTS   (SO*).

GOMES, TONY.   "MIGRANT DIARY".   VISTA VOLUNTEER, VOL. 4
    (FEBRUARY 1968), PP. 3-13.

GOMEZ, R. A.   "SPANISH IMMIGRATION TO THE UNITED STATES".
    AMERICAS,   (JANUARY 13,1971), PP. 59-78.

GOOD NEIGHBOR COMMISSION OF TEXAS.   REPORT ON MIGRATORY
    FARM LABOR IN TEXAS.   AUSTIN: GOOD NEIGHBOR COMMISSION
    OF TEXAS, DECEMBER 1944 (EC).

GOODWIN.   "SPOKEN-ENGLISH LESSONS SPANISH-SPEAKING   (ED*).

GREGG.   "MEDICAL EXAMINATION VACCINATION   (MD*).

HALL.   "400,000 MEXICAN AMERICAN VOTERS"   (PL*).

HARDING.   "MIGRANT PUPILS: CHALLENGE TO   (ED*).

HARPER.   "A COMPREHENSIVE CARE PROGRAM   (MD*).

HEALY.   WANDERING WORKERS: STORY AMERICAN   (EC*).

HEFFERMAN.   "MIGRANT CHILDREN CALIFORNIASCHOOLS"   (ED*).

HENING, H. B.   DEPRIVED CHILDREN.   ALBUQUERQUE, NEW
    MEXICO: BUREAU OF IMMIGRATION OF THE TERRITORY
    OF NEWMEXICO, 1908 (HN).

HERNANDEZ ALVAREZ, JOSE.   "A DEMOGRAPHIC PROFILE OF THE
    MEXICAN IMMIGRATION TO THE UNITED STATES, 1910-1950".
    JOURNAL OF INTER-AMERICAN STUDIES,   (JULY 1966),
    PP. 471-496.

HERNANDEZ ALVAREZ, JOSE.   A DEMOGRAPHIC PROFILE OF
    THE MEXICAN IMMIGRATION TO THE UNITED STATES,
    1910-1950.   JOURNAL OF INTER-AMERICAN STUDIES, 8.

HILL, G.   TWO EVERY MINUTE ACROSS THE BORDER.   NEW YORK
    TIMES MAGAZINE,.

HILL, MERTON E.   THE DEVELOPMENT OF AN AMERICANIZATION
    PROGRAM.   UNIVERSITY OF CALIFORNIA AT BERKELEY, PHD.
    DISSERTATION (1928).

HOWSDEN.   "WHERES CAMP, MISTER?   SUMMER   (ED*).

HUFFORD, CHARLES H.   SOCIAL AND ECONOMIC EFFECTS OF THE
    MEXICAN MIGRATION INTO TEXAS.   BOULDER: UNIVERSITY
    OF COLORADO, NO DATE (EC).

HUFFORD, CHARLES HENRY.   THE SOCIAL AND ECONOMIC EFFECTS
    OF THE MEXICAN MIGRATION INTO TEXAS.   UNIVERSITY OF
    COLORADO, MASTER'S THESIS (1929) (EC).

HUMPHREY, NORMAN D.   "EDUCATION AND LANGUAGE OF DETROIT
    MEXICANS".   JOURNAL OF EDUCATIONAL SOCIOLOGY, VOL.
    17 (MAY 1944), PP. 534-542.

HUMPHREY, NORMAN D.   "EL CAMPESINO MEXICANO EN DETROIT".
    REVIEW OF MEXICAN SOCIOLOGY, VOL. 7 (1945), PP. 403-416.

HUMPHREY, NORMAN D.   "EMPLOYMENT PATTERNS OF MEXICANS IN
    DETROIT".   MONTHLY LABOR REVIEW, VOL. 61 (NOVEMBER
    1945), PP. 913-923.

HUMPHREY, NORMAN D.   "MEXICAN MIDDLETON".   COMMON GROUND,
    VOL. 6 (1946), PP. 20-28.

HUMPHREY, NORMAN D.   "MEXICAN REPATRIATION FROM MICHIGAN:
    PUBLIC ASSISTANCE IN HISTORICAL PERSPECTIVE".   SOCIAL
    SERVICE REVIEW, VOL. 15 (SEPTEMBER 1941), PP. 497-513.

HUMPHREY, NORMAN D.   "MIGRATION AND SETTLEMENT OF DETROIT
    MEXICANS".   EC GEOG, VOL. 19 (OCTOBER 1943), PP.
    358-361.

HUMPHREY, NORMAN D.   "MIGRATION AND SETTLEMENT OF DETROIT
    MEXICANS".   ECONOMIC GEOGRAPHY, VOL. 19 (OCTOBER
    1943), PP. 358-361.

HUMPHREY, NORMAN D.   "ON ASSIMILATION AND ACCULTURATION".
    PSYCHIATRY, VOL. 6 (NOVEMBER 1943), PP. 343-345.

HUMPHREY, NORMAN D.   "SOME DIETARY AND HEALTH PRACTICES
    OF DETROIT MEXICANS".   JOURNAL OF AMERICAN FOLKLORE,
    VOL. 58 (JULY 1945), PP. 255-258.

HUMPHREY, NORMAN D.   "SOME DIETARY AND HEALTH PRACTICES
    OF DETROIT MEXICANS".   JOURNAL OF AMERICAN FOLKLORE,
    VOL. 58 (1945), PP. 255-258.

HUMPHREY, NORMAN D.   "SOME MARRIAGE PROBLEMS OF DETROIT
    MEXICANS".   APPLIED ANTHROPOLOGY, VOL. 3 (DECEMBER
    1943), PP. 13-15.

HUMPHREY, NORMAN D.   "SOME MARRIAGE PROBLEMS OF DETROIT
    MEXICANS".   APPLIED ANTHROPOLGY, VOL. 3 (DECEMBER
    1943), PP. 13-15.

HUMPHREY, NORMAN D. "THE CHANGING STRUCTURE OF THE DETROIT
    MEXICAN FAMILY".   AMERICAN SOCIOLOGICAL REVIEW, VOL.
    9 (DECEMBER 1944), PP. 622-625.

HUMPHREY, NORMAN D. "THE CHANGING STRUCTURE OF THE DETROIT
    MEXICAN FAMILY: AN INDEX OF ACCULTURATION".
    AMERICAN SOCIOLOGICAL REVIEW, VOL. 9 (DECEMBER
    1944), PP. 622-626.

HUMPHREY, NORMAN D. "THE CONCEPT OF CULTURE IN SOCIAL CASE
    WORK".   SOCIOLOGY AND SOCIAL RESEARCH, VOL. 26
    (SEPTEMBER 1941), PP. 53-59.

HUMPHREY, NORMAN D. "THE CONCEPT OF CULTURE IN SOCIAL CASE
    WORK".   SSR, VOL. 26 (SEPTEMBER 1941), PP. 53-60.

HUMPHREY, NORMAN D. "THE CULTURAL BACKGROUND OF THE
    MEXICAN IMMIGRANT".   RURAL SOCIOLOGY, VOL. 13
    (1948), PP. 239-255.

HUMPHREY, NORMAN D. "THE CULTURAL BACKGROUND OF THE
    MEXICAN IMMIGRANT".   RURAL SOCIOLOGY, VOL. 13
    (SEPTEMBER 1948), PP. 239-255.

HUMPHREY, NORMAN D. "THE DETROIT MEX. IMMIGRANT &
    NATURALIZATION".   SOCIAL FORCES, VOL. 22 (MARCH
    1944), PP. 332-335.

HUMPHREY, NORMAN D. "THE DETROIT MEXICAN IMMIGRANT AND
    NATURALIZATION".   SOCIAL FORCES, VOL. 22 (MARCH
    1944), PP. 332-35.

HUMPHREY, NORMAN D. "THE EDUCATION AND LANGUAGE OF DETROIT
    MEXICANS".   JOURNAL OF EDUCATIONAL SOCIOLOGY, VOL.
    17 (MAY 1944), PP. 534-542.

HUMPHREY, NORMAN D. "THE GENERIC FOLK CULTURE OF MEXICO".
    RS, VOL. 8 (1943), PP. 364-377.

HUMPHREY, NORMAN D. "THE HOUSING AND HOUSEHOLD PRACTICES
    OF DETROIT MEXICANS".   SOCIAL FORCES, VOL. 24 (MAY
    1946), PP. 433-437.

HUMPHREY, NORMAN D. "THE HOUSING AND HOUSEHOLD PRACTICES
    OF DETROIT MEXICANS".   SOCIAL FORCES, VOL. 24
    (1946), PP. 433-437.

HUMPHREY, NORMAN D. "THE INTEGRATION OF THE DETROIT
    MEXICAN COLONY".   AMERICAN JOURNAL OF ECONOMICS AND
    SOCIOLOGY, VOL. 3 (JANUARY 1944), PP. 155-166.

HUMPHREY, NORMAN D. "THE STEREOTYPE AND THE SOCIAL TYPES
    OF MEXICAN-AMERICAN YOUTH".   JOURNAL OF SOCIAL
    PSYCHOLOGY, VOL. 22 (AUGUST 1945), PP. 69-78.

HUMPHREY, NORMAN D. "THE STEREOTYPE AND THE SOCIAL TYPES
    OF MEXICAN-AMERICAN YOUTHS". JOURNAL SOCIAL
    PSYCHOLOGY, VOL. 22 (1945), PP. 69-78.

HUMPHREYS, R. A. ECONOMIC ASPECTS OF THE FALL OF THE
    SPANISH AMERICAN EMPIRE. MEXICO, (1950). REVISTA
    DE HISTORIA DE AMERICA, NUMBER 30.

HUNT, WILLIAM ANDREW, JR. MIGRATION AND POPULATION CHANGES
    AND THEIR EDUCATIONAL IMPLICATIONS. UNIVERSITY OF
    TEXAS, MASTER'S THESIS (1941) (ED).

HYMER, EVANGELINE. A STUDY OF THE SOCIAL ATTITUDES
    OF ADULT MEXICAN IMMIGRANTS IN LOS ANGELES AND
    VICINITY. UNIVERSITY OF SOUTHERN CALIFORNIA, LOS
    ANGELES, MASTER'S THESIS (1923) (PY).

HYMER, EVANGELINE. A STUDY OF THE SOCIAL ATTITUDES
    OF ADULT MEXICAN IMMIGRANTS IN LOS ANGELES AND
    VICINITY, 1923. SAN FRANCISCO: R AND E RESEARCH
    ASSOCIATES, 1971 (PY).

HYMER, EVANGELINE. A STUDY OF THE SOCIAL ATTITUDES
    OF ADULT MEXICAN IMMIGRANTS IN LOS ANGELES AND
    VICINITY. UNIVERSITY OF SOUTHERN CALIFORNIA, (1923)
    (PY).

IDAR. WHAT PRICE WETBACKS? (EC*).

IMMIGRATION ASSOCIATION OF CALIFORNIA. ANNUAL REPORTS.
    IMMIGRATION ASSOCIATION OF CALIFORNIA.

INTERNATIONAL LABOUR OFFICE. "TEMPORARY MIGRATION
    OF MEXICAN WORKERS TO THE UNITED STATES". INTERNATIONAL
    LABOUR REVIEW, (OCTOBER 1944), PP. 519-521 (EC).

JACOBS. APPROACH TO MIGRANT BILINGUAL (ED*).

JENKS, J. W. THE IMMIGRATION PROBLEM. FUNK AND WAGNALLS,.

JEROME. MIGRATION BUSINESS CYCLES (EC*).

JOHNSTON. EDUCATION CHILDREN SPANISH SPEAKING (ED*).

JOHNSTON. EDUCATION CHILDREN SPANISH SPEAKING (ED*).

JONES, M. A. AMERICAN IMMIGRATION. CHICAGO: UNIVERSITY
    OF CHICAGO PRESS, 1961.

JORGENSON, JANET M.; WILLIAMS, DAVID E.; AND BURMA, JOHN
    H. MIGRATORY AGRICULTURAL WORKERS IN THE UNITED
    STATES. GRINNELL COLLEGE, 1960.

KARCIK, W. "WETBACK STORY". COMMONWEAL, VOL. 54 (JUNE
    13, 1951), PP. 327-329.

KARRACKER.   AGRICULTURAL SEASONAL LABORERS   (EC*).

KARRAKER.   "EDUCATION OUR RURAL SLUMS"   (ED*).

KARTMAN.   "MALARIA BLOOD SURVEY MEXICAN   (MD*).

KELLER.   "INSTRUCTING MIGRANT CHILDREN"   (ED*).

KELLEY, J. B. "THE DEPORTATION OF MEXICAN ALIENS AND ITS
     IMPACT ON FAMILY LIFE".   CATHOLIC CHARITIES REVIEW,
     VOL. 37 (OCTOBER 1954), PP. 169-171.

KELLY, PAUL M.   THE TUCSON, ARIZONA, OFFICE.   UNITED
     STATES DEPARTMENT OF JUSTICE. IMIGRATION AND NATURALIZATION
     SERVICE.

KELLY, WILLARD F. "THE WETBACK ISSUE".   THE IMMIGRATION
     AND NATURALIZATION REPORTER, VOL. 2   NO. 3 , PP. 37-39.

KIDD.   "CHANCE TO SUCCEED; PROGRAM MIGRATORY (ED*).

KIRBY.   "CHILDREN MEXICAN AMERICAN MIGRANTS: (ED*).

KIRKBRIDE, WILLIAM H. "AN ARGUMENT FOR MEXICAN IMMIGRATION".
     COMMONWEALTH CLUB, VOL. 2 NO. 12 (JUNE 1931), PP.
     11-20.

KIRTPATRICK.   INTELLIGENCE IMMIGRATION (PY*).

KLEINART, JOHN. "THE FLORIDA MIGRANT".   PHI DELTA KAPPAN,
     (OCTOBER 1967).

KLINE, HARRIET H. "BRAVO SILVESTRE".   TEXAS OUTLOOK,
     (AUGUST 1968), PP. 18-19.

KNEBEL.   "RESTRICTIVE ADMISSION STANDARDS: (EC*).

KNOX.   ECONOMIC STATUS MEXICAN IMMIGRANT   (EC*).

KOCH, WILLIAM H.   DIGNITY OF THEIR OWN; HELPING THE
     DISADVANTAGED BECOME FIRST-CLASS CITIZENS.   NEW YORK:
     FRIENDSHIP PRESS, 1966.

KOEPPLIN.   RELATIONSHIP REFORM: IMMIGRANTS (HC*).

KOLB.   "THE INTELLIGENCE IMMIGRANTSAS (PY*).

KORCIK, WILLIAM. "WETBACK STORY".   COMMONWEAL, VOL. 54
     (JUNE 13,1951), PP. 327-329.

KRAUS, MICHAEL. IMMIGRATION, THE AMERICAN MOSAIC: FROM
     PILGRIMS TO MODERN REFUGEES.   NEW YORK: VAN NOSTRAND
     REINHOLD COMPANY, 1966.

KROHN, MILDRED. "MIGRATORY HOME".   SIERRA EDUCATIONAL
     NEWS,   (NOVEMBER 1938), P. 22 (ED).

LAING.   "MIGRANT SCHOOL HELPS CHILDREN (ED*).

LANDMAN.   SOME ASPECTS ACCULTURATION MEXICAN   (AN*).

LANDOLT.   MEXICAN AMERICAN WORKERS SANANTONIO   (EC*).

LASKER, BRUNO. FILIPINO IMMIGRATION.   CHICAGO: UNIVERSITY
    OF CHICAGO PRESS, 1931.

LASKER, GABRIEL W. "THE QUESTION OF PHYSICAL SELECTION
    OF MEXICAN MIGRANTS TO THE U.S.A.".   HUMAN BIOLOGY,
    VOL. 26 (FEBRUARY 1954), PP. 52-58 (PY).

LASKER.   "AGE, ENVIRONMENT MIGRATION:FURTHER (AN*).

LATHROP.   MIGRATION INTO EAST TEXAS, 1835-1860 (HT*).

LATTINGH.   MIGRANT-BILINGUAL WORKSHOP (ED*).

LEARY, MARY E. "AS THE BRACEROS LEAVE".   REPORTER, VOL.
    32 (JANUARY 28, 1965), PP. 43-45.

LEHMANN, VAL. W. FORGOTTEN LEGIONS: SHEEP IN THE RIO
    GRANDE PLAIN OF TEXAS.   EL PASO, TEXAS: TEXAS WESTERN
    PRESS, 1969.

LEISERSON, WILLIAM M. ADJUSTING IMMIGRANT AND INDUSTRY.
    REPRINTED BY NEW YORK, NEW YORK: ARNO PRESS, 1971 (EC).

LELAND.   "MEDICAL CARE MIGRATORY WORKERS" (MD*).

LESCOHIER, DON S. "THE VITAL PROBLEM IN MEXICAN IMMIGRATION".
    NATIONAL CONFERENCE OF SOCIAL WORK,   (1927), PP. 547-54.

LETTAU, KATHRYN; SHANNON, LYLE W. "MEASURING AND ADJUSTMENT
    OF IMMIGRANT LABORERS".   THE SOUTHWESTERN SOCIAL
    SCIENCE QUARTERLY,   (SEPTEMBER 1963), PP. 139-148.

LEVENSTEIN, HARVEY. A. "AFL AND MEXICAN IMMIGRATION IN
    THE 1920'S: AN EXPERIMENT IN LABOR DIPLOMACY".
    HISPANIC AMERICAN HISTORICAL REVIEW, VOL. 48 (MAY
    1968), PP. 206-219 (HUS).

LIPSCHULTZ, ROBERT J. AMERICAN ATTITUDES TOWARD MEXICAN
    IMMIGRATION, 1924-1952.   CHICAGO, 1962.

LOCKWOOD, MYNA. BECKONING STAR.   NEW YORK: DUTTON, 1943.

LOPEZ MALO, ERNESTO. "THE IMMIGRATION OF MEXICAN LABORERS".
    CIENCIAS SOCIOLES, VOL. 5 (1964), PP. 220-227.

LOPEZ, F. "REGIONAL PROGRAM FOR MIGRAN T EDUCATION".
    PRELIMINARY STUDIES OF THE TEXAS CATHOLIC HISTORICAL
    SOCIETY, VOL. 3 NO. 6 (1940) (ED).

LOPEZ, LEO. CALIFORNIA'S PROGRAM FOR THE EDUCATION
    OF MIGRANT CHILDREN. REPORT OF THE SECOND ANNUAL
    CONFERENCE OF THE CALIFORNIA STATE DEPARTMENT
    OF EDUCATION (ED).

LOPEZ, MALO ERNESTO. "THE EMIGRATION OF MEXICAN LABORERS".
    CIENCIAS SOCIALES, VOL. 5 (OCTOBER 1954), PP. 220-227.

LORETAN. "THE APPLICATION COST-UTILITY (EC*).

LOS ANGELES COUNTY COORDINATING COUNCILS. SOME NOTES
    MEXICAN POPULATION (HC*).

LOS ANGELES DEPARTMENT OF CHARITIES. ANALYSIS MEXICAN
    REPATRIATION (HC*).

LOS ANGELESLOS ANGELES CHAMBER OF COMMERCE. MEXICAN
    REPATRIATION CALIFORNIA (HC*).

LOW. POLITICAL CULTURE CIVIC INVOLVEMENT: (PL*).

LOYD. "REMEMBERING FORGOTTEN AMERICANS" (ED*).

LUCIO. TRENDS MEXICAN ELEMENTARY EDUCATION (SO*).

LYON, RICHARD MARTIN. THE LEGAL STATUS OF AMERICAN AND
    MEXICAN MIGRATORY FARM LABOR: AN ANALYSIS OF U. S.
    FARM LABOR LEGISLATION, POLICY AND ADMINISTRATION.
    CORNELL UNIVERSITY, PHD. DISSERTATION (1954) (EC
    LW).

MACKY, ARGYLE R. PROSECUTION OF ALIEN SMUGGLERS. U. S.
    DEPARTMENT OF JUSTICE, (JULY 1951). MONTHLY REVIEW,
    VOL. 9, NO. 1, IMMIGRATION AND NATURALIZATION SERVICE.

MANGOLD. MIGRATORY CHILD WORKERS (EC*).

MARTINEZ, JOHN R. MEXICAN EMIGRATION TO THE UNITED STATES:
    1910-1930. BERKELEY: UNIVERSITY OF CALIFORNIA, 1957
    (HSW).

MARTINEZ, JOHN R. MEXICAN IMMIGRATION TO THE U.S.,
    1910-1930. SAN FRANCISCO: R & E RESEARCH ASSOCIATES,
    1971 (HSW).

MASSAGIL. BIBLIOGRAFIA SOBRE MIGRACIONDE (B*).

MASSEY, ELLIS LEONARD. MIGRATION OF THE SPANISH-SPEAKING
    PEOPLE OF HIDALGO COUNTY. UNIVERSITY OF TEXAS,
    MASTER'S THESIS (1953).

MASSEY, LEONARD ELLIS. MIGRATION OF THE SPANISH-SPEAKING
    PEOPLE OF HIDALGO COUNTY. AUSTIN: UNIVERSITY
    OF TEXAS, 1953.

MASTERS, CHARLIE. "CITIZEN MARTINEZ". ARIZONA QUARTERLY,
    VOL. 7 (AUTUM 1951), PP. 209-224.

MAXWELL, GRACE AND TAFT, REBEKAH. YOUTH PROGRAMS FOR
    MIGRANTS,"MINORITY GROUPS: SEGREGATICN AND INTEGRATION.
    NEW YORK: COLUMBIA UNIVERSITY PRESS, 1955.

MC CULLY, JOHN. "THE SPANISH-SPEAKING: NORTH FROM MEXICO".
    REPORTER, VOL. 3 (DECEMBER 26, 1950), PP. 25-28.

MC DONALD. "BASIC COMMUNICATICN PRCJECTMIGRANT (ED*).

MC ELROY. TERMINATION BRACERO PROGRAM SOME (EC*).

MC NAUGHTON. SOCIAL STUDY MEXICAN SPANISH-AMERICAN (EC*).

MC WILLIAMS, CAREY. "AMERICAS CISADVANTAGED MINORITIES:
    MEXICAN-AMERICANS". JOURNAL OF NEGRC EDUCATION, VOL.
    20 (SUMMER 1951), PP. 301-309 (HSW).

MC WILLIAMS, CAREY. "CALIFORNIA AND THE WETBACK". COMMON
    GROUND, VCL. 9-10 (SUMMER 1949), PP. 15-19 (HSW).

MC WILLIAMS, CAREY. "CALIFORNIA AND THE WETBACK". COMMON
    GROUND, VOL. 9 NO. 4 (SUMMER 1949), PP. 15-20 (HSW).

MC WILLIAMS, CAREY. "GETTING RID OF THE MEXICANS".
    AMERICAN MERCURY, VOL. 28 (SPRING 1943), PP. 322-24
    (HSW).

MC WILLIAMS, CAREY. "IS YOUR NAME GONZALEZ". NATION,
    (MARCH 15, 1947), PP. 302-304 (HSW).

MC WILLIAMS, CAREY. "LOS ANGELES: AN EMERGING PATTERN".
    COMMON GROUND, VOL. 9-10 (SPRING 1949), PP. -10 (HSW).

MC WILLIAMS, CAREY. "LOS ANGELES PACHUCO GANGS". NEW
    REPUBLIC, VCL. 108 (JANUARY 18, 1943), PP. 76-77
    (HSW).

MC WILLIAMS, CAREY. "MEXICANS TO MICHIGAN". COMMON
    GROUND, VCL. 2 NO. 1 (AUTUMN 1941), PP. 5-17 (HSW).

MC WILLIAMS, CAREY. "MIGRANTS: INQUIRY OR INQUEST?".
    NATION, VOL. 171 (SEPTEMBER 30, 1950), PP. 286-287
    (HSW).

MC WILLIAMS, CAREY. "NERVOUS LOS ANGELES". NATION, VOL.
    170 (JUNE 10, 1950), PP. 570-571 (HSW).

MC WILLIAMS, CAREY. "TEARS FOR JOSE DAVILA". NATION,
    VOL. 159 (DECEMBER 2, 1944), P. 687 (HSW).

MC WILLIAMS, CAREY. "THE FORGOTTEN MEXICAN". COMMON
    GROUND, VCL. 3 NO. 3 (SPRING 1943), PP. 65-78 (HSW).

MC WILLIAMS, CAREY. "THE LOS ANGELES ARCHIPELAGO".
    SCIENCE AND SOCIETY, VOL. 10 (1946), PP. 41-53 (HSW).

MC WILLIAMS, CAREY. "THE MEXICAN PROBLEM". COMMON
    GROUND,   NO. 3 (SPRING 1948), PP. 3-17 (HSW).

MC WILLIAMS, CAREY. "THEY SAVED THE CROPS".   INTER-AMERICAN,
    VOL. 2 (AUGUST 1943), PP. 10-14 (HSW).

MC WILLIAMS, CAREY. "THIRTY-SIX THOUSAND NEW ALIENS IN
    CALIFORNIA". PACIFIC WEEKLY,   (AUGUST 24, 1936)
    (HSW).

MC WILLIAMS, CAREY. "ZOOT-SUIT RIOTS".   NEW REPUBLIC,
    VOL. 108 (JUNE 2 1, 1943), PP. 818-820 (HSW).

MC WILLIAMS, CAREY. AL NORTE DE MEXICO: EL CONFLICTO ENTRE
    ' ANGLOS' E 'HISPANOS.'   TRANSLATED BY LYA DE
    CARDOZA. MEXICO D.F.: SIGLO XXI, 1968 (HSW).

MC WILLIAMS, CAREY. BROTHERS UNDER THE SKIN.   BOSTON:
    LITTLE BROWN AND COMPANY, 1964 (HSW).

MC WILLIAMS, CAREY. CALIFORNIA: THE GREAT EXCEPTION.
    NEW YORK: KNOPF, 1949 (HSW).

MC WILLIAMS, CAREY. CAREY MCWILLIAMS COLLECTION NUMBER
    .2.   GOVERNMENT AND PUBLIC AFFAIRS READING ROOM,
    HAINES COLLECTION, LOS ANGELES: UNIVERSITY OF
    CALIFORNIA (HSW).

MC WILLIAMS, CAREY. FACTORIES IN THE FIELD: THE STORY OF
    MIGRATORY FARM LABOR IN CALIFORNIA, 1939.   BOSTON:
    LITTLE, BROWN AND COMPANY, 1934. REPRINTED BY HAMDEN,
    CONNECTICUT: SHOE STRING, 1969 (HSW).

MC WILLIAMS, CAREY. ILL FARES THE LAND: MIGRANTS AND
    MIGRATORY LABOR IN THE UNITED STATES.   BOSTON:
    LITTLE, BROWN AND COMPANY, 1942 (HSW).

MC WILLIAMS, CAREY. MEMORANDUM ON HOUSING CONDITIONS AMONG
    MIGRATORY WORKERS IN CALIFORNIA.   PREPARED FOR
    CALIFORNIA DEPARTMENT OF INDUSTRIAL RELATIONS,
    DIVISION OF IMMIGRATION AND HOUSING. LOS ANGELES,
    MARCH 30, 1939 (HSW).

MC WILLIAMS, CAREY. NORTH FROM MEXICO: THE SPANISH-SPEAKING
    PEOPLE OF THE UNITED STATES.   NEW YORK: GREENWOOD
    PRESS, PUBLISHERS, 1968 (HSW).

MC WILLIAMS, CAREY. REPORT COVERING THE ACTIVITIES OF THE
    DIVISION OF IMMIGRATION AND HOUSING (1939-1942).
    IN THE LOS ANGELES PUBLIC LIBRARY (HSW).

MC WILLIAMS, CAREY. SOUTHERN CALIFORNIA COUNTRY, AN ISLAND
    ON THE LAND.   NEW YORK: DUELL, SLOAN AND PEARCE, 1946
    (HSW).

MC WILLIAMS, CAREY. SOUTHERN CALIFORNIA COUNTRY.   NEW
    YORK: DUELL, SLOAN & PEARCE, 1946 (HSW).

MC WILLIAMS, CAREY. TESTIMONY BEFORE L.A. COUNTY GRAND
    JURY, OCTOBER 8, 1942. RE: MEXICAN ZOOT-SUITERS..
    LOS ANGELES: RESEARCH RESOURCES STORAGE FILE,
    THE URBAN LEAGUE, (HSW).

MC WILLIAMS, CAREY. THE BORDERLANDS ARE INVADED.   EDITED
    BY MANUEL P. SERVIN. BEVERLY HILLS, CALIFORNIA:
    GLENCOE PRESS, 1970 (HSW).

MC WILLIAMS, CAREY. THE CALIFORNIA REVOLUTION.   NEW YORK:
    GROSSMAN PUBLISHER, 1968 (HSW).

MC WILLIAMS, CAREY. THE FORGOTTEN MEXICAN.   BOSTON:
    LITTLE, BROWN AND COMPANY, 1944 (HSW).

MC WILLIAMS, CAREY. 'THE LOS ANGELES RIOT OF 1943.'   IN
    ROSE T. (ED), VIOLENCE IN AMERICA (HSW).

MC WILLIAMS, CAREY. THE MEXICANS IN AMERICA.   NEW YORK:
    TEACHERS COLLEGE PRESS, 1968 (HSW).

METZLER.   FARM WORKERS SPECIALIZED SEASONAL   (EC*).

METZLER.   MIGRATORY FARMWORKERS MIDCONTINENT   (EC*).

METZLER.   "PROBLEMS CHILDREN YOUTH, EDUCATION   (EC*).

METZLER.   INCOMES MIGRATORY AGRICULTURAL   (EC*).

MEYER.   MEXICO REBEL: PASCUAL OROZCO   (HM*).

MICHIGAN A F L- C I O NEWS.   MIGRANT WORKERS: DECLARATION
    (EC*).

MICHIGAN.   REPORT RECOMMENDATIONS   (LW*).

MICHIGAN.   INFORME RECOMENDACIONES SOBRE   (LW*).

MIERA, GILBERT E. MIGRATORY LABOR IN AMERICAN AGRICULTURE.
    WASHINGTON, D. C.: U. S. GOVERNMENT OFFICE, (1951)
    (EC).

MIGRANT HEALTH PROJECT. MIGRANTS: WHERE AND WHEN:
    GEOGRAPHIC AND TEMPORAL DISTRIBUTION OF MIGRA
    NT AGRICULTURAL WORKERS AND THEIR FAMILIES IN
    WASHINGTON.   WASHINGTON, 1968 (MD).

MILLER.   MEETING NEEDS SPANISH-SPEAKING   (ED*).

MILLER.   INCOME LEVELS CONTRACT BEET WORKERS   (EC*).

MILLER, WATSON B. "ADMINISTERING OUR IMMIGRATION LAWS".
    ANNALS OF THE AMERICAN ACADEMY OF POLITICAL AND SOCIAL
    SCIENCE, VOL. 262 (MARCH 1949), PP. 178-84 (EC).

MILOR. "PROBLEM OF TRANSIENCY" (ED*).

MINNESOTA HISTORICAL SOCIETY. THE IMMIGRATION HISTORY
    NEWSLETTER. ST. PAUL, MINNESOTA,.

MITCHELL. "UNIONS TWO COUNTRIES ACT WETBACK (EC*).

MITCHELL. "WHY IMPORT FARM WORKERS" (EC*).

MOLEY, RAYMOND. "THE BRACERO BLUNDER". NEWSWEEK, VOL.
    66 (JULY 19, 1965), P. 88 (EC).

MONFROSS. FARM LABOR DIFFICULTIES CALIFORNIA (EC*).

MOORE. SOUTHWESTERN STATES DEVELOPMENTAL (HSW*).

MOORE, TRUMAN E. "SLAVES FOR RENT". ATLANTIC MONTHLY,
    VOL. 215 NO. 5 (MAY 1965), PP. 109-122 (EC).

MOORE, TRUMAN. "SLAVES FOR RENT: THE SHAME OF AMERICAN
    FARMING". THE SLAVES WE RENT. NEW YORK: RANDOM
    HOUSE, VOL. 1965 NO.   ATLANTIC
    (2 15) (EC HSW).

MOORE, TRUMAN. "SLAVES FOR RENT". LETTERS TO THE EDITOR,
    VOL. 216 NO. 2 (AUG 1965), PP. 34-35 (EC HSW).

MOORE. "AMERICAS MIGRATION TREATIES (PL*).

MORGAN. SHAME NATION: DOCUMENTED STORY (LW*).

MORIN. ORGANIZABILITY FARM LABOR UNITED (EC*).

MORRISON, ETHEL M. A HISTORY OF RECENT LEGISLATIVE
    PROPOSALS CONCERNING MEXICAN IMMIGRATIO N. UNIVERSITY
    OF SOUTHERN CALIFORNIA, MASTER'S THESIS (1929).

MOTT. "HEALTH SERVICES MIGRANT FARM (MD*).

MUNICIPAL LEAGUE OF LOS ANGELES. "THE LEAGUE'S INVESTIGATIONA
    AND ARIZONA'S DEMANDS CONCERNING MEXICAN IMMIGRATION".
    MUNICIPAL LEAGUE OF LOS ANGELES BULLETIN, VOL.
    5 (APRIL 1928), PP. 1-3.

MYERS. "MORE REPORTS CALIFORNIA FARM (EC*).

MYERS. "SPANISH-NAME PERSONS LABOR FORCE (EC*).

NATIONAL CCMMISSION ON LAW OBSERVANCE AND ENFORCEMENT.
    U. S. REPORT ON CRIME AND THE FOREIGN BORN.
    WASHINGTON, D.C., (1931). U.S. REPORT ON CRIME AND
    THE FOREIGN BORN, PUBLICATION NUMBER 10 (LW).

NATIONAL INDUSTRIAL CONFERENCE BOARD. IMMIGRATION PROBLEM
    IN THE UNITED STATES.   NATIONAL INDUSTRIAL CONFERENCE
    BOARD, 1923.

NATIONAL UNDERWRITER.   "PROGRAM DEVELOPED MOTOR VEHICLE
    (EC*).

NELSCN, EUGENE:. THE BRACERO.   BERKELEY, CALIFORNIA:
    THORP SPRINGS PRESS, 1972 (EC).

NELSON.   MIGRANT EDUCATION NEW YORK STATE   (ED*).

NEW MEXICO STATE UNIVERSITY.   MIGRANT EDUCATION, SELECTED
    BIBLIOGRAPHY   (B*).

NEWSOME, W. E. "WE OPEN DOORS FOR MIGRANT CHILDREN".
    NEA JOURNAL, VOL. 56 (APRIL 1967), PP. 27-28.

NEWTON, HORACE EDWIN. MEXICAN ILLEGAL IMMIGRATION INTO
    CALIFCRNIA, PRINCIPALLY SINCE 1945: A SOCIO-ECONOMIC
    STUDY.   CLAREMONT GRADUATE SCHOOL, 1954.

NORDYKE, L. "TEXAS CLEANS UP A MESS".   SATURDAY EVENING
    POST, VOL. 219 (JULY 27, 1946), PP. 26-27.

NORMAN, ARTHUR. "MIGRATICN TO SOUTHWEST TEXAS: PEOPLES
    AND WORDS".   SOUTHWESTERN SOCIAL SCIENCE QUARTERLY,
    VOL. 37 (SEPTEMBER 1, 1956), PP. 149-158.

NORQUEST, CARRCL. RIO GRANDE WETBACKS: MIGRANT MEXICAN
    WORKERS.   ALBUQUERQUE, NEW MEXICC: UNIVERSITY OF NEW
    MEXICO PRESS, 1971 (EC).

OKLAHOMA EMPLOYMENT SECURITY COMMISSION. A STUDY OF
    MIGRANT WORKERS IN SOUTHWEST OKLAHOMA.   OKLAHOMA
    CITY: OKLAHCMA EMPLCYMENT SECURITY COMMISSION, 1965.

OREGON.   VAMANOS PAL (SIC) NORTE   (EC*).

OSBORNE, MARIE A. S. THE EDUCATIONAL STATUS OF INTRA STATE
    MIGRANTS IN TEXAS, 1935-40.   UNIVERSITY OF TEXAS,
    MASTER'S THESIS (1954).

OVERN.   "SCHOLASTIC DIFFICULTIES CHILDREN   (ED*).

PARMAR.   "UNEMPLCYMENT OR EXILE: IS THERE (EC*).

PASCHALL, FRANKLIN C., AND SULLIVAN, LOUIS R.   RACIAL
    DIFFERENCES IN THE MENTAL AND PHYSICAL DEVELOPMENT
    OF MEXICAN CHILDREN.   BALTIMORE, MARYLAND: JOHN
    HOPKINS PRESS, 1925.

PHILADELPHIA RAILWAY.   IMMIGRATION AND THE SOUTHERN STATES.
    PHILADELPHIA RAILWAY WORLD PUBLISHING CO, 1904.

PHILLIPS.   "THE SCHOOL FOLLOWS CHILD"   (EC*).

POEK.   "SOCIAL CULTURAL FACTORS MENTAL   (MD*).

POSTELLE, Y.   "MIGRANT YOUNGSTERS: OUR FORGOTTEN CHILDREN".
    PARENTS' MAGAZINE AND BETTER FAMILY LIVING, VOL. 45
    (MAY 1970), PP. 60-63 (ED).

PRESIDENT'S COMMISSION ON MIGRATORY LABOR.   MIGRATORY LABOR
    IN AMERICAN AGRICULTURE.   WASHINGTON: GOVERNMENT
    PRINTING OFFICE, (1951).

PRESIDENT'S COMMISSION ON MIGRATORY LABOR.   REPORT OF THE
    PRESIDENTS COMMISSION ON MIGRATORY LABOR.   ??NO
    INFORMATION??, WASHINGTON: GOVERNMENT PRINTING OFFICE.

PRESS, ERNEST.   THE MEXICAN POPULATION IN LARAMIE.
    UNIVERSITY OF WYOMING, MASTER'S THESIS (1946) (HUS).

PRITCHETT, HOWARD E.   "THE POLITICAL INFLUENCE OF THE
    MEXICAN AMERICAN COMMUNITY IN THE IMPERIAL VALLEY OF
    CALIFORNIA".   NEW SCHOLAR, VOL. 1 (APRIL 1969),
    PP. 79-94 (PL).

PROPER, EMBERSON EDWARD.   COLONIAL IMMIGRATION LAWS:
    A STUDY OF THE REGULATION OF IMMIGRATION BY ENGLISH
    COLONIES IN AMERICA.   COLUMBIA UNIVERSITY. STUDIES
    IN THE SOCIAL SCIENCES, NO 31. REPRINTED BY NEW YORK,
    NEW YORK AND LONDON, GREAT BRITAIN: AMS PRESS, INC.,
    1900.

PUBLIC AFFAIRS PAMPHLETS.   NO WORK TODAY THE PLIGHT
    OF AMERICAS MIGRANTS.   NEW YORK: PUBLIC AFFAIRS
    COMMITTEE, (1953). PUBLIC AFFAIRS PAMPHLETS. NUMBER
    190 (EC).

PULLIS.   HELPING MIGRATORY MEXICAN CHILD   (ED*).

RALEY, HELEN.   "GUARDIANS OF OUR BORDER".   SUNSET, VOL.
    57 , PP. 30-31, 62.

RASKIN, A. H.   "MISFORTUNE'S CHILDREN ON THE MOVE".   NEW
    YORK TIMES MAGAZINE,   (AUGUST 6, 1961), PP. 8-9.

REUL, M. R.   "COMMUNICATING WITH THE MIGRANT".   CHILD
    WELFARE, VOL. 49 (MARCH 1970), PP. 137-145.

REYNOLDS, EVELYN DOLORES. A STUDY OF MIGRATORY FACTORS
    AFFECTING EDUCATION IN NORTH KERN COUNTY.   UNIVERSITY
    OF SOUTHERN CALIFORNIA, MASTER'S THESIS (1932) (ED).

RHOADES, ELIZABETH R. FOREIGNERS IN SOUTHERN CALIFORNIA
    DURING THE MEXICAN PERIOD.   SAN FRANCISCO, CALIFORNIA:
    R AND E RESEARCH ASSOCIATES, 1971 (HC).

RICHARDS, C. V. (ET AL). "MIGRANT TEACHER".   THE
    INSTRUCTOR, VOL. 77 (JUNE 1968), PP. 73-76 (ED).

RISCHIN, MOSES. "BEYOND THE GREAT DIVIDE: IMMIGRATION
    AND THE LAST FRONTIER".   JOURNAL OF AMERICAN HISTORY,
    (JUNE 1968), PP. 42-53 (HSW).

RIVERA.   "FORGOTTEN ONES: CHILDREN MIGRANTS" (ED*).

ROBERTS, HOLLAND. "AMERICAN UNTOUCHABLES: HOW MIGRANT
    CHILDREN ARE EXPLOITED BY THE BIG FARMERS AND
    NEGLECTED BY THE GOVERNMENT".   MAINSTREAM, VOL. 15
    (MAY 1962), PP. 29-36 (EC PL).

ROBERTS. "MEXICANS OR RUIN" (SO*).

ROBERTS. "THE DOCILE MEXICAN" (SO*).

ROBERTS. "WET AND OTHER MEXICANS" (SO*).

ROBINSON.   "THE PUBLIC HEALTH PROGRAM MEXICAN (MD*).

ROBLEDA, GOMEZ JOSE. PISCADORES Y CAMPESINOS TARACOS.
    MINISTRY OF EDUCATION, MEXICO D. F., 1943.

RODRIGUEZ-CANO, FELIPE. AN ANALYSIS OF THE MEXICAN
    AMERICAN MIGRANT LABOR FORCE IN THE STOCKBRIDGE AREA.
    EAST LANSING, MICHIGAN: DEPARTMENT OF SOCIOLOGY,
    MICHIGAN STATE UNIVERSITY, (EC).

ROJO.   "SOCIAL MALADJUSTMENT AMONG FILIPINOS (SO*).

ROSKELLEY.   BEET LABOR COLORADO (EC*).

ROUCEK.   "SOME EDUCATIONAL PROBLEMS CHILDREN (ED*).

ROUNDY, R. W. "THE MEXICAN IN OUR MIDST III".   MISSIONARY
    REVIEW OF THE WORLD, VOL. 44 (MAY 1921), PP. 371-77.

ROWELL.   "WHY MAKE MEXICO EXCEPTION" (HM*).

SALINAS, JOSE LAZARO. LA EMIGRACION DE BRACEROS.   MEXICO:
    CUAUHTEMOC, 1955.

SAMORA, JULIAN. LOS MOJADOS: THE WETBACK STORY.
    UNIVERSITY OF NOTRE DAME PRESS, 1971 (SO).

SAMPSON, O. "ELEVEN-PLUS FOR MIGRANTS; BOSTON'S EXPERIMENT".
    TIMES (LONDON) EDUCATIONAL SUPPLEMENT, VOL. 2498
    (APRIL 5, 1963), P. 723 (ED).

SANTIBANEZ, ENRIQUE. ENSAYO ACERCA DE LA IMMIGRACION
    MEXICANA EN LOS ESTADOS UNIDOS. SAN ANTONIO, TEXAS:
    THE CLEGG COMPANY, 1930.

SAVETH, EDWARD N. AMERICAN HISTORIANS AND EUROPEAN
    IMMIGRATION, 1875-1925. NEW YORK: COLUMBIA UNIVERSITY
    PRESS, 1948.

SAWYER. "WANDERER: PROFILE MIGRANT CHILD" (ED*).

SCHEFF, THOMAS J. "CHANGES IN PUBLIC AND PRIVATE LANGUAGE
    AMONG SPANISH SPEAKING MIGRANTS TO AN INDUSTRIAL
    CITY". INTERNATIONAL MIGRATION, VOL. 3 (1965), PP.
    78-86.

SCHEFF, THOMAS J.. "ACCULTURATION AND TIES TO FORMER HOME
    OF MEXICAN-AMERICANS IN AN INDUSTRIAL CITY".
    INTERNATIONAL REVIEW OF COMMUNITY DEVELOPMENT, NO.
    15-16 (1966), PP. 239-244 (AN).

SCHELBY. EDUCATION PROGRAM MIGRANT FARM (ED*).

SCHERMERHORN, R. A. 'MEXICANS AND SPANISH-SPEAKING
    AMERICANS: A MIXED CULTURE.' IN HIS THESE OUR
    PEOPLE: MINORITIES IN AMERICAN CULTURE, CHAPTER 9,
    PAGES 175-198 (AN).

SCHMIDT. AFTER BRACERO: INQUIRY INTO PROBLEMS (EC*).

SCHNUR. "STUDY POSSIBLE IMPROVEMENT PROBLEM (ED*).

SCHOLES, REV. WILLIAM E. NEXT MOVE FOR THE MIGRANTS.
    NEW YORK: FRIENDSHIP PRESS, 1966.

SCHOLES, REV. WILLIAM E. THE MIGRANT WORKER. IN LA RAZA:
    FORGOTTON AMERICANS. NOTRE DAME: UNIVERSITY OF NOTRE
    DAME PRESS, 1966.

SCHWARTZ. SEASONAL FARM LABOR UNITED STATES (EC*).

SCOTT. "ZIP TEST: QUICK LOCATOR TEST (EC*).

SCOTT, ROBIN F. "ZOOT SUIT RIOTS: A HISTORY OF THE MEXICAN
    IN LOS ANGELES". PROBE, (APRIL-JUNE 1969) (HC).

SCOTT, ROBIN F. THE SLEEPY LAGOON CASE AND THE GRAND JURY
    INVESTIGATION. EDITED BY MANUEL P. SERVIN. BEVERLY
    HILLS, CALIFORNIA: GLENCOE PRESS, 1970.

SCOTT, ROBIN F. THE URBAN MEXICAN AMERICAN IN THE
     SOUTHWEST 1932-1955. UNIVERSITY OF SOUTHERN
     CALIFORNIA, PHD. DISSERTATION (1969).

SCOTT, ROBIN F. 'THE ZOOT SUIT RICTS.' IN MANUEL
     P. SERVIN (ED), THE MEXICAN-AMERICANS: AN AWAKENING
     MINORITY (HC).

SCUGGS. "THE UNITED STATES, MEXICO WETBACKS (HSW*).

SEGALMAN. ARMY DESPAIR: MIGRANT WORKERSTREAM (ED*).

SEGALMAN, RALPH. THE IMMIGRANT POOR AND THE RESIDUAL POOR.
     PAPER PRESENTED AT THE SOUTHERN SOCIOLOGICAL ASSOCIATION
     MEETING, APRIL 5, 1966..

SEGALMAN, RALPH. THE IMMIGRANT POOR AND THE RESIDUAL POOR.
     ??NO INFORMATION??, 1966.

SHAFER. "HEALTH NEEDS SEASONAL FARMWORKERS (MD*).

SHANNON, LYLE W. "MEASURING THE ADJUSTMENT OF IMMIGRANT
     LABORERS". SOUTHWESTERN SOCIAL SCIENCE QUARTERLY,
     VOL. 44 (SEPTEMBER 1963), PP. 139-148.

SHANNON, LYLE W. "THE PREDICTION OF ECONOMIC ABSORPTION
     AND CULTURAL INTEGRATION AMONG MEXICAN AMERICANS,
     NEGROES, AND ANGLOS IN A NORTHERN INDUSTRIAL COMMUNITY".
     HUMAN ORGANIZATION, VOL. 25 (SUMMER 1966), PP. 154-162.

SHANNON, LYLE W. THE ASSIMILATION AND ACCULTURATION OF
     MIGRANTS TO URBAN AREAS. UNIVERSITY OF WISCONSIN
     URBAN PROGRAM, 1963 (AN).

SHANNON, LYLE W. THE STUDY OF MIGRANTS AS MEMBERS
     OF SOCIAL SYSTEMS. WASHINGTON: UNIVERSITY OF
     WASHINGTON PRESS, 1968 (AN).

SHANNON, LYLE W. ; KRASS, ELAINE M. "THE URBAN ADJUSTMENT
     OF IMMIGRANTS: THE RELATIONSHIP OF EDUCATION TO
     OCCUPATION AND TOTAL FAMILY INCOME". PACIFIC
     SOCIOLOGICAL REVIEW, VOL. 4 (SPRING 1963), PP. 137-142.

SHANNON, LYLE W. ; SHANNON, MAGDALINE W. THE ASSIMILATION
     OF MIGRANTS TO CITIES: ANTHROPOLOGICAL
     AND SOCIOLOGICALCONTRIBUTIONS
     6. NEW YORK: SAGE PUBLICATIONS, (1967). URBAN
     AFFAIRS ANNUAL REVIEW, CHAPTER 2.

SHANNON, LYLE; KRASS, ELAINE M. "THE ECONOMIC ABSORPTION
     OF IMMIGRANT LABORERS IN A NORTHERN INDUSTRIAL
     COMMUNITY". JOURNAL OF ECONOMICS AND SOCIOLOGY, VOL.
     23 (JANUARY 1964), PP. 65-84 (EC).

SHANNON, LYLE; KRASS, ELAINE M. THE ECONOMIC ABSORPTION
    AND CULTURAL INTEGRATION OF IMMIGRANT MEXICAN
    AMERICANS AND NEGRO WORKERS.   NATIONAL INSTITUTES
    OF HEALTH PROJECT, DEPARTMENT OF SOCIOLOGY AND
    ANTHROPOLOGY, STATE UNIVERSITY OF IOWA, 1964 (EC).

SHIELDS, VIRGINIA. ORAL EXPRESSION, REMEDIAL SPEECH AND
    ENGLISH FOR THE MIGRANT CHILD, GRADES ONE-TWELVE.
    NAPLES, FLORIDA: COLLIER COUNTY BOARD OF PUBLIC INSTRUCTION,.

SHOTWELL, LOUISA R. THE HARVESTERS--THE STORY OF THE
    MIGRANT PEOPLE.   NEW YORK: DOUBLEDAY AND COMPANY,
    INC, 1961.

SILLICORN, STANLEY A. SOUTH SANTA CLARA COUNTY MIGRANT
    TREATMENT CLINIC.   PAPER PRESENTED AT THE NATIONAL
    OUTLOCK CONFERENCE ON RURAL YOUTH, OCTOBER 23-26,
    1967, WASHINGTON, D.C..

SILVA, LUCIANO V. "CHARACTERISTICS OF MEXICAN IMMIGRATION".
    12TH ANNUAL CONFERENCE JOURNAOF THE LOS ANGELES
    COMMITTEE FOR THE PRO TECTION OF THE FOREIGN BORN,
    (1962), PP. 14-16.

SIMPICH, FREDERICH. "THE LITTLE BROWN BROTHER TREKS
    NORTH".   INDEPENDENT, VOL. 116 (SPRING 1961), PP.
    237-39.

SIMPSON. "MIGRANT CHILDREN-- FRESNO COUNTY (ED*).

SITOMER, CURTIS J. "MEXICAN-AMERICANS: A MINORITY'S
    PLIGHT".   CHRISTIAN SCIENCE MONITOR, VOL. 1
    (NOVEMBER 5, 1965), P. 3.

SKENDZEL, EDUARDO ADAM. LA COLONIA MEXICANA EN DETROIT.
    SALTILLO, COAHUILA, MEXICO, MASTER'S THESIS (1961).

SLAYDEN, JAMES. L. "BI-DIEALECTALISM: THE LINGUISTICS
    OF WHITE SUPREMACY".   ANNALS OF THE AMERICAN ACADEMY
    OF POLITICAL AND SOCIAL SCIENCE, VOL. 93 (JANUARY
    1921), PP. 121-26.

SMITH, GEORGE HARMON. WANDERERS OF THE FIELD.   NEW YORK,
    NEW YORK: JOHN DAY COMPANY, 1966.

SMITH, WILLIAM CARLSON. AMERICANS IN THE MAKING: THE
    NATURAL HISTORY OF THE ASSIMILATION OF IMMIGRANTS.
    NEW YORK: APPLETON-CENTURY, 1939.

SMITHER, HARRIET. THE DIPLOMATIC SERVICE OF ASHBEL SMITH
    OF THE REPUBLIC OF TEXAS, 1842-1845.   UNIVERSITY OF
    TEXAS AT AUSTIN, MASTER'S THESIS (1922).

SODERSTROM, JOAN. AN INVESTIGATION OF MEXICAN-AMERICAN
    MIGRANT CHILDREN POPULATION IN IDAHO AND THE EDUCATIONAL
    OPPORTUNITIES PROVIDED BY SELECTED SCHOOL DISTRICTS.
    POCATELLO: COLLEGE OF EDUCATION, IDAHO STATE UNIVERSITY,
    1967.

SOLIEN DE GONZALEZ.   "FAMILY ORGANIZATION FIVE TYPES   (EC*).

SOMMER, CHARLES G. A STUDY OF THE INCREASE IN MEXICAN
    IMMIGRATION TO THE U. S..   MEXICO CITY: UNITED STATES
    EMBASSY REPORT, 1956.

SOUTHARD.   SURVEY SCHOOL AGE CHILDREN MIGRANT   (ED*).

SOUTHARD.   PROJECT MOVE AHEAD: DEVELOPMENT   (ED*).

STARR-HUNT, JACK. "THE MEXICAN WHO WENT HOME".   LOS
    ANGELES TIMES SUNDAY MAGAZINE,   (MARCH 26,   1933),
    P. 10, 20.

STEINER, ERNEST. ON THE TRAIL OF THE IMMIGRANT.   F. H.
    REVELL COMPANY, 1906.

STEINMAN, A.; FOX, D. J. "SPECIFIC AREAS OF AGREEMENT AND
    CONFLICT IN WOMEN'S SELF-PERCEPTION AND THEIR
    PERCEPTION OF MEN'S IDEAL WOMAN IN TWO SOUTH AMERICAN
    URBAN COMMUNITIES AND AN URBAN COMMUNITY IN THE UNITED
    STATES".   JOURNAL OF MARRIAGE AND THE FAMILY, VOL.
    31 (MAY 1969), PP. 281-289 (EC).

STERN.   "CHILDREN NEGLECT: PLEA"   (ED*).

STEVENSON, EMMA REH. "THE EMIGRANT COMES HOME".   SURVEY
    GRAPHIC, VOL. 66   (MAY 1, 1931), PP. 175-177.

STEVENSON, PHILIP. "DEPORTING JESUS".   NATION, VOL. 143
    (JULY 18, 1936), PP. 67-69.

STIFF.   TEXAN EMIGRANT   (HT*).

STILWELL. "THE WETBACK TIDE"   (LI*).

STOCKER, JOSEPH-. THE INVISIBLE MINORITY. . . PERO
    NO VENCIBLES.   WASHINGTON, D. C.: NEA, DEPARTMENT
    OF RURAL EDUCATION, (1966) (EC PL).

STOWELL, J. S. "THE DANGER OF UNRESTRICTED MEXICAN
    IMMIGRATION".   CURRENT HISTORY, VOL. 28 (AUGUST
    1928), PP. 763-68.

STOWELL, J. S. THE NEAR SIDE OF THE MEXICAN QUESTION.
    NEW YORK: GEORGE H. DORAN COMPANY, 1921 (SO).

STROUT, RICHARD LEE. "A FENCE FOR THE RIO GRANDE".
    INDEPENDENT, VOL. 120 (JUNE 2, 1928), PP. 518-20.

STRUENING, E. L. ET AL. "MIGRATION AND ETHNIC MEMBERSHIP
    IN RELATICN TO SOCIAL PROBLEMS". THE AMERICAN
    BEHAVIORAL SCIENTIST, VOL. 13 (SEPTEMBER 1969), PP.
    57-87.

STURGES, VERA L. "MEXICAN IMMIGRANTS". SURVEY, VOL. 46
    (JULY 2, 1921), PP. 470-471.

STURGES, VERA L. THE PROGRESS OF ADJUSTMENT IN MEXICAN
    AND UNITED STATES LIFE. CHICAGO: UNIVERSITY
    OF CHICAGO PRESS, 1920.

SULLIVAN, LOUIS R. AND FRANKLIN, CRESSEY PASCHAL. "THE
    EFFECT OF RACE AND ENVIRONMENT ON THE PHYSICAL AND
    MENTAL DEVELOPMENT OF OUR MEXICAN IMMIGRANTS".
    PROCEEDINGS OF THE AMERICAN ANTHROPOLIGAL ASSOCIATION,
    (DECEMBER 27-28, 1923) (PY).

SUMMERS. YOU CANT MAKE IT BY BUS (ED*).

SUTTON, ELIZABETH. "THE WORLD OF THE MIGRANT CHILD".
    EDUCATION LEADERSHIP, VOL. 14 (OCTOBER 1961), P.
    223.

SUTTON, ELIZABETH. "WHEN THE MIGRANT CHILD COMES TO
    SCHOOL". THE NEA JOURNAL, VOL. 50 (OCTOBER 1961),
    PP. 32-34 (ED).

SUTTON, ELIZABETH. KNOWING AND TEACHING THE MIGRANT CHILD.
    WASHINGTON D. C.: NEA DEPARTMENT OF RURAL EDUCATION
    (ED).

SWARTZ, HARRY. SEASONAL FARM LABOR IN THE UNITED STATES.
    NEW YORK: COLUMBIA UNIVERSITY PRESS, 1945 (EC).

SWISHER, P. A. "NON-ENGLISH SPEAKING MIGRANT CHILD".
    THE INSTRUCTOR, VOL. 77 (JUNE 1968), P. 85 (ED).

TACUBER, IRENE B. "MIGRATION AND TRANSFORMATION: SPANISH
    SURNAME POPULATIONS". POPULATICN INDEX, VOL. 32
    (JANUARY 1966), PP. 3-34 (SO).

TAYLOR PAUL S. "EMPLOYMENT OF MEXICANS IN CHICAGO AND THE
    CALUMET REGION". JOURNAL OF THE AMERICAN STATISTICAL
    ASSOCIATION, VOL. 25 (JUNE 1930), PP. 206-207 (EC).

TAYLOR PAUL S. THE MEXICAN IMMIGRANT AND THE PROBLEM OF
    CRIME AND CRIMINAL JUSTICE. REPORT ON CRIME AND THE
    FOREIGN BORN, X, WASHINGTON, D. C. 1931 (EC).

TAYLOR. COMPARISON FIRST SECOND GENERATION (SO*).

TAYLOR, PAUL S. "CONTEMPORARY BACKGROUND OF CALIFORNIA
    FARM LABOR". RURAL SOCIOLOGY, VOL. 1 (1936), PP.
    401-419 (EC).

TAYLOR, PAUL S. "DROUGHT REFUGEE AND LABOR MIGRATION TO
    CALIFORNIA". MONTHLY LABOR REVIEW, VOL. 42
    (FEBRUARY 1936), PP. 312-318 (EC).

TAYLOR, PAUL S. "INCREASE OF MEXICAN LABOR IN CERTAIN
    INDUSTRIES". JOURNAL OF POLITICAL ECONOMY,
    (OCTOBER 1930).

TAYLOR, PAUL S. "MEXICANS NORTH OF THE RIO GRANDE".
    SURVEY, VOL. 66 , PP. 135-40, 197-205 (EC).

TAYLOR, PAUL S. "MIGRANT MOTHER". AMERICAN WEST, VOL.
    7 (MAY 1970), PP. 41-45 (EC).

TAYLOR, PAUL S. "MIGRATORY AGRICULTURAL WORKERS ON THE
    PACIFIC COAST". AMERICAN SOCIOLOGICAL REVIEW, VOL.
    3 (APRIL 1938), PP. 225-232 (EC).

TAYLOR, PAUL S. "MORE BARS AGAINST MEXICANS". SURVEY
    GRAPHIC, VOL. 64 (APRIL 1 1930), PP. 26-27 (EC).

TAYLOR, PAUL S. "NOTE ON STREAMS OF MEXICAN MIGRATION".
    AMERICAN JOURNAL OF SOCIOLOGY, VOL. 36 (SEPTEMBER
    1930), PP. 287-288 (EC).

TAYLOR, PAUL S. "PATTERNS OF AGRICULTURAL AND LABOR
    MIGRATION WITHIN CALIFORNIA". MONTHLY LABOR REVIEW,
    VOL. 47 (NOVEMBER 1938), PP. 980-990 (EC).

TAYLOR, PAUL S. "SOME ASPECTS OF MEXICAN IMMIGRATION".
    JOURNAL OF POLITICAL ECONOMY, VOL. 38 (OCTOBER
    1930), PP. 609-615 (EC).

TAYLOR, PAUL S. "UPRISINGS ON THE FARMS". SURVEY
    GRAPHIC, VOL. 24 (JANUARY 1935), PP. 19-22 (EC).

TAYLOR, PAUL S. CRIME AND THE FOREIGN-BORN: THE PROBLEM
    OF THE MEXICAN. WASHINGTON, D. C.: NATIONAL
    COMMISSION ON LAW OBSERVANCE AND ENFORCEMENT, (1931)
    (EC).

TAYLOR, PAUL S. MEXICAN LABOR IN THE UNITED STATES:
    BETHLEHEM, PENNSYLVANIA. BERKELEY, CALIFORNIA.
    UNIVERSITY OF CALIFORNIA PUBLICATIONS IN ECONOMICS,
    VOLUME 7, NUMBER 1, 1930. ALSO NEW YORK: ARNO PRESS,
    1971 (EC).

TAYLOR, PAUL S. MEXICAN LABOR IN THE UNITED STATES:
    IMPERIAL VALLEY. UNIVERSITY OF CALIFORNIA PUBLICATIONS
    IN ECONOMICS (EC).

TAYLOR, PAUL S. MEXICAN LABOR IN THE UNITED STATES:
    VALLEY OF THE SOUTH PLATTE, COLORADO. BERKELEY:
    UNIVERSITY OF CALIFORNIA PUBLICATIONS IN ECONOMICS,
    1929 (EC).

TAYLOR, PAUL S. MEXICAN LABOR IN THE UNITED STATES:
CHICAGO AND CALUMET REGION. BERKELEY, CALIFORNIA:
UNIVERSITY OF CALIFORNIA PUBLICATIONS IN ECONOMICS,
(1932). VOLUME 7, NUMBER 2 (EC).

TAYLOR, PAUL S. MEXICAN LABOR IN THE UNITED STATES: DIMIT
COUNTY, WINTER GARDEN DISTRICT, SOUTH TEXAS.
BERKELEY, CALIFORNIA: UNIVERSITY OF CALIFORNIA
PUBLICATIONS IN ECONOMICS, (1930). VOLUME 6 NUMBER
5 1930 (EC).

TAYLOR, PAUL S. MEXICAN LABOR IN THE UNITED STATES:
MIGRATION STATISTICS, PART I. BERKELEY, CALIFORNIA:
UNIVERSITY OF CALIFORNIA PUBLICATIONS IN ECONOMICS,
(1929). COLUMN 6, NUMBER 3 (EC).

TAYLOR, PAUL S. MEXICAN LABOR IN THE UNITED STATES:
RACIAL SCHOOL STATISTICS. UNIVERSITY OF CALIFORNIA
PUBLICATIONS IN ECON   NOMICS,
UNIVERSITY OF CALIFORNIA PRESS, 1929 (EC).

TAYLOR, PAUL S. SONGS OF THE MEXICAN MIGRATION. AUSTIN,
TEXAS: TEXAS FOLK-LORE SOCIETY, 1935 (EC).

TAYLOR, PAUL S. A SPANISH-MEXICAN PEASANT COMMUNITY.
ARANDAS IN JALISCO. BERKELEY: UNIVERSITY OF
CALIFORNIA PRESS, 1933 (EC).

TAYLOR. "INTERGROUP RELATIONS AT COSMOPOLITAN (ED*).

TEINER, ESTEINER, EDWARD ALFRED. ON THE TRAIL OF THE
IMMIGRANT. NEW YORK, CHICAGO: F. H. REVELL CO., 1906.

TETREAU, E. D. "SOCIAL ASPECTS OF ARIZONA'S FARM LABOR
PROBLEMS". SOCIOLOGY AND SOCIAL RESEARCH, VOL. 24
(JULY 1940), PP. 550-557 (EC).

TETREAU, E. D. SEASONAL LABOR ON ARIZONA IRRIGATED FARMS.
TUCSON, UNIVERSITY OF ARIZONA 1937. TUCSON:
UNIVERSITY OF ARIZONA, 1937 (EC).

TEXAS COUNCIL ON MIGRANT LABOR. MECHANIZATION AND
THE TEXAS MIGRANT. FEBRUARY 1963 (EC).

TEXAS EDUCATION AGENCY. REPORT EDUCATIONAL NEEDS MIGRANT
(ED*).

TEXAS EDUCATION AGENCY. TEXAS ADULT MIGRANT EDUCATION
(ED*).

TEXAS EDUCATION AGENCY. TEXAS PROJECT MIGRANT CHILDREN:
(ED*).

TEXAS EDUCATION AGENCY. TEXAS PROJECT EDUCATION MIGRANT
(ED*).

TEXAS EDUCATION AGENCY.   TEXAS PROJECT EDUCATION MIGRANT
    (ED*).

TEXAS GOOD NEIGHBOR COMMISSION.   TEXAS: FRIEND NEIGHBOR
    (SO*).

TEXAS MIGRANT LABOR. THE 1964 MIGRATION.   AUSTIN: GOOD
    NEIGHBOR COMMISSION OF TEXAS, 1965 (EC).

TEXAS MIGRANT LABOR:. THE 1965 MIGRATION.   AUSTIN: GOOD
    NEIGHBOR COMMISSION OF TEXAS, 1966 (EC).

TEXAS MIGRANT LABOR:. THE 1966 MIGRATION.   AUSTIN: GOOD
    NEIGHBOR COMMISSION OF TEXAS, 1967 (EC).

TEXAS STATE DEPARTMENT OF HEALTH.   LATIN-AMERICAN HEALTH
    PROBLEM (MD*).

TEXAS STATE DEPARTMENT OF HEALTH.   TEXAS STATE DEPARTMENT
    HEALTH (MD*).

TEXAS STATE EMPLOYMENT SERVICE.   ORGINS PROBLEMS TEXAS
    MIGRATORY (MD*).

TEXAS STATE EMPLOYMENT SERVICE.   ORIGINS PROBLEMS TEXAS
    MIGRATORY (EC*).

TEXAS. GOOD NEIGHBOR COMMISSION. TEXAS MIGRANT LABOR.
    ??NO INFORMATION??, 1967 (EC).

TEXAS.   PROPOSED CURRICULUM PROGRAM TEXAS   (ED*).

TEXAS: GOOD NEIGHBOR COMMISSION.   SPECIAL REPORT:
    INTER-AGENCY (SO*).

THADDEN.   MIGRATORY BEET WORKERS MICHIGAN   (EC*).

THE UNIVERSITY OF ARIZONA.   ARIZONA: ITS PEOPLE RESOURCES
    (AN*).

THOMAS.   DETERMINING EFFECTIVE EDUCATIONAL   (ED*).

THOMAS, HOWARD E., AND FLORENCE TAYLOR. MIGRANT FARM LABOR
    IN COLORADO: A STUDY OF MIGRATORY FAMILIES.   NEW
    YORK: NATIONAL CHILD LABOR COMMITTEE, 1951 (EC).

THOMPSON, ALBERT N. "THE MEXICAN IMMIGRANT WORKER
    IN SOUTHWESTERN AGRICULTURE".   AMERICAN JOURNAL OF
    ECONOMICS, VOL. 16 (OCTOBER 1956), PP. 73-81 (EC).

THOMSON.   "JOURNAL APPLIED SOCIOLCGY" (SO*).

THOMSON.   "RESTRICTION MEXICAN IMMIGRATION" (SO*).

THOMSON, CHARLES A. "WHAT OF THE BRACERO".   SURVEY, VOL.
    54 (JUNE 1, 1925), PP. 291-292 (EC).

THOMSON. "THE MAN FROM NEXT DOOR" (SO*).

THONIS, ELEANOR. A PROGRAM FOR CHILDREN WHO FOLLOW THE
    CROPS. MARYSVILLE, CALIFORNIA, SUTTER-YUBA EDUCATION
    COMMITTEE (ED).

THUNDER. "FEATURE X: SYSTEM MEXICAN CONTRACT (EC*).

TOEPEL. MIGRANT TOWN TRANSITION, MIRAGE (GE*).

TOPETE, JESUS. AVENTURAS DE UN BRACERO. MEXICO CITY:
    EDITORA GRAFIA MODERNA, S.A., 1961 (LMA).

TUBBS, LOWELL LESTER. A SURVEY OF THE PROBLEMS OF
    THE MIGRATORY MEXICANS. AUSTIN, TEXAS: UNIVERSITY
    OF TEXAS, MASTER'S THESIS (1952) (EC HSW).

TURNER, WILLIAM. "NO DICE FOR BRACEROS". RAMPARTS, VOL.
    7 (SEPTEMBER 1965), PP. 14-26 (EC).

U. S. REPORT REGIONAL CONFERENCES EDUCATION (ED*).

U. S. INFORMATION ABOUT REGISTRATION (LW*).

U. S. INFORMATION CONCERNING ENTRYMEXICAN (LW*).

U. S. PERSONS SPANISH SURNAME (LW*).

U. S. MEXICAN IMMIGRATION (LW*).

U. S. CONGRESS. CONGRESSIONAL HEARINGS. "SHOULD QUOTA LAW
    BE APPLIED TO MEXICO?". CONGRESSIONAL DIGEST, VOL.
    7 NO. 5 (MAY 1928) (EC).

U. S. INDUSTRIAL EMPLOYMENT POTENTIAL (LW*).

U. S. DOMESTIC AGRICULTURAL MIGRANTS (LW*).

U. S. SCHOOL TRANSFER RECORD SYSTEM (LW*).

U. S. ANNUAL REPORTS COMMISSIONER NATURALIZATION (LW*).

U. S. ARRANGEMENT MIGRATION TO UNITED (LW*).

U. S. MIGRATORY WORKERS: MEXICAN AGRICULTURAL (LW*).

U. S. DOMESTIC MIGRATORY FARM WORKERS: (LW*).

U. S. DOMESTIC MIGRATORY FARM-WORKERS; (LW*).

U. S. LOW-INCOME FAMILIES SPANISH-SURNAME (LW*).

U. S. INFORMATION CONCERNING ENTRYMEXICAN (LW*).

U. S. DISADVANTAGED CLASSES AMERICAN (LW*).

U. S. SOCIAL RELATIONSHIPS INSTITUTIONS (LW*).

U. S. STANDARDS LIVING RESIDENTS SEVEN (LW*).

U. S. STUDY 6,655 MIGRANT HOUSEHOLDS (LW*).

U. S. MIGRANT LABOR: HUMAN PROBLEM; (LW*).

U. S. MEXICAN MIGRATORY WORKERS SOUTH (LW*).

U. S. ORGANIZATION EFFORTS MEXICANAGRICULTURAL (LW*).

U. S. "AMERICAN JOURNAL NURSING" (LW*).

U. S. USE HEALTH AIDES MIGRANT HEALTH (LW*).

U. S. CONTINUATION MEXICAN FARM LABOR (EC*).

U. S. EXTEND MEXICAN FARM LABOR PROGRAM (EC*).

U. S. MEXICAN FARM LABOR (LW*).

U. S. HOUSE COMMITTE ON JUDICIARY. MIGRATION AND REFUGEE
    ASSISTANCE.   WASHINGTON, D. C.: U. S. GOVERNMENT
    PRINTING OFFICE, (1961).

U. S. HOUSE OF COMM ON INTERSTATE AND FOREIGN COMMERCE.
    HEALTH SERVICES FOR MIGRATORY AND SEASONAL AGRICULTURAL
    WORKERS. HEARING. 91ST CONGRESS, 1ST SESSION.
    WASHINGTON, D. C.: U. S. GOVERNMENT PRINTING OFFICE,
    (MD).

U. S. HOUSE ON IMMIGRATION AND NATURALIZATION. IMMIGRATION
    FROM LATIN AMERICA, THE WEST INDIES, AND CANADA:
    HEARINGS BEFORE SUBCOMMITTEE ON IMMIGRATION AND
    NATURALIZATION.   U. S. GOVERNMENT PRINTING OFFICE.
    JULY 12-14, 1954, (83RD CONGRESS,
    2ND SESSION ON S. 3660 AND S. 366 1).

U. S. HOUSE ON IMMIGRATION AND NATURALIZATION. SEASONAL
    AGRICULTURAL LABORERS FROM MEXICO,.   69TH CONGRESS,
    1ST SESSION, JANUARY 28-FEBRUARY 23, 1926, H. R. 6741,
    H. R. 6741, H. R. 7559; H. R. 9036, 1926. HEARING NO.
    691. WASHINGTON D.C., (1926).

U. S. HOUSE POST OFFICE AND CIVIL SERVICE COMM. MIGRANT
    FARM LABOR: A SERIOUS NATIONAL PROBLEM.   87TH
    CONGRESS, 1ST SESSION. WASHINGTON, D. C.: U.
    S. GOVERNMENT PRINTINING OFFICE, (MARCH 30, 1961)
    (EC).

U. S. HOUSE. HEARING BEFORE THE COMMITTEE ON IMMIGRATION
    AND NATURALIZATION. 69TH CONGRESS, FIRST SESSION.
    WASHINGTON, D. C.: U. S. GOVERNMENT PRI NTING OFFICE,
    (1926) (EC).

U. S. HEARINGS TEMPORARY ADMISSIONILLITERATE   (EC*).

U. S. HOUSE. IMMIGRATION AND NATURALIZATION COMMITTEE.
      HEARINGS.   HEARING BEFORE THE COMMITTEE ON IMMIGRATION
      AND NATURALIZATION, HOUSE OF REPRESENTATIVES.

U. S. IMMIGRANTS AGRICULTURE (LW*).

U. S. IMMIGRANTS INDUSTRIES (LW*).

U. S. HOUSING MIGRANT AGRICULTURALWORKERS (LW*).

U. S. MIGRANT LABOR LAW RELATIONS: (LW*).

U. S. MIGRATORY AGRICULTURAL LABOR: (LW*).

U. S. MIGRATORY AGRICULTURAL LABOR: (LW*).

U. S. RECORDS PRESIDENTS COMMISSION (LW*).

U. S. CRIME FOREIGN-BORN: PROBLEM MEXICAN (LW*).

U. S. MIGRANT EDUCATION: ADVANCED LEVEL (LW*).

U. S. MIGRANT EDUCATION: INTERMEDIATE (LW*).

U. S. MIGRANT FARM-WORKER ECONOMICOPPORTUNITY (LW*).

U. S. IMPACT COMMUTER ALIENS ALONGMEXICAN (LW*).

U. S. IMPACT COMMUTER ALIENS ALONGMEXICAN (LW*).

U. S. MIGRANT SEASONAL FARMWORKER POWERLESS (LW*).

U. S. MIGRANT SEASONAL FARMWORKER POWERLESS (LW*).

U. S. MIGRATORY FARM LABOR PROBLEMUNITED (LW*).

U. S. MIGRATORY FARM LABOR PROBLEMUNITED (LW*).

U. S. MIGRATORY FARM LABOR PROBLEMUNITED (LW*).

U. S. MIGRATORY FARM LABOR PROBLEMUNITED (LW*).

U. S. MIGRATORY FARM LABOR PROBLEMUNITED (LW*).

U. S. MIGRATORY FARM LABOR PROBLEMUNITED (LW*).

U. S. PROBLEMS MIGRANT WORKERS (LW*).

U. S. STUDY MIGRATORY LABOR (LW*).

U. S. STUDY MIGRATORY LABOR (LW*).

U. S. STUDY MIGRATORY LABOR (LW*).

U. S.   EDUCATIONAL ASSISTANCE TO MIGRANT   (LW*).

U. S.   HEARINGS BEFORE SPECIAL SUBCOMMITTEE   (LW*).

U. S.   HEARINGS BEFORE SUBCOMMITTEEMIGRATORY   (LW*).

U. S.   HEARINGS BEFORE SUB-COMMITTEE   (LW*).

U. S.   HEARINGS BEFORE SUBCOMMITTEEMIGRATORY   (LW*).

U. S.   HEARINGS BEFORE SUBCOMMITTEEMIGRATORY   (LW*).

U. S.   MIGRANT FARM WORKER AMERICA   (LW*).

U. S.   MIGRANT FARM WORKER AMERICA.   (LW*).

U. S.   MIGRANT HEALTH SOURCES   (LW*).

U. S.   MIGRANT HEALTH PROGRAM: CURRENT   (LW*).

U. S.   MIGRANT HEALTH SERVICES.   HEARINGS   (LW*).

U. S.   MIGRANT HEALTH SERVICES.   HEARINGS   (LW*).

U. S.   MIGRANT LABOR   (LW*).

U. S.   MIGRANT SEASONAL FARM WORKERPOWERLESSNESS   (LW*).

U. S.   MIGRANT SEASONAL FARMWORKER POWERLESSNESS   (LW*).

U. S.   MIGRATORY LABOR   (LW*).

U. S.   MIGRATORY FARM LABOR PROBLEMUNITED   (LW*).

U. S.   MIGRATORY FARM LABOR PROBLEMUNITED   (LW*).

U. S.   MIGRATORY FARM LABOR PROBLEMUNITED   (LW*).

U. S.   MIGRATORY FARM LABOR PROBLEMUNITED   (LW*).

U. S.   MIGRATORY LABOR BILLS   (LW*).

U. S.   MIGRATORY LABOR LEGISLATION   (LW*).

U. S.   MIGRATORY FARM LABOR PROBLEMUNITED   (LW*).

U. S.   MIGRATORY FARM LABOR PROBLEMUNITED   (LW*).

U. S.   TO CONTROL ILLEGAL MIGRATION.   (LW*).

U. S.   IMMIGRATION INTO U.S. 1820-1930   (LW*).

U. S.   MEXICAN MIGRATORY WORKERS SOUTH   (LW*).

U. S.   PECAN SHELLERS SAN ANTONIO; PROBLEM   (LW*).

ULIBARRI.   SOCIAL ATTITUDINAL CHARACTERISTICS   (ED*).

ULIBARRI.   "SOCIAL ATTITUDINAL CHARACTERISTICS   (SO*).

ULIBARRI.   SOCIAL ATTITUDINAL CHARACTERISTICS   (ED*).

ULIBARRI.   SOCIAL ATTITUDINAL CHARACTERISTICS   (SO*).

UNITED STATES CONGRESS. CONGRESSICNAL HEARINGS.
    IMMIGRATION FROM COUNTRIES OF THE WESTERN HEMISPHERE.
    ON H. R. 6455, 10955, 11687, FEBRUARY 21 TO APRIL 5,
    1928. WASHINGTON, D. C.: U. S. GOVERNMENT PRINTING
    OFFICE, (1928) (EC).

UNITED STATES CONGRESS. CONGRESSIONAL HEARINGS.
    RESTRICTICN OF WESTERN HEMISPHERE IMMIGRATION.   ON
    S. 1296, 1437, 3019, FEBRUARY 1, 27-29, MARCH 1, 5,
    1928. WASHINGTON, D. C.: U. S. GOVERNMENT PRINTING
    OFFICE, (1528) (EC).

UNITED STATES CONGRESS. CONGRESSIONAL HEARINGS. SEASONAL
    AGRICULTURAL LABORERS FROM MEXICO.   ON H. R. 6741,
    7559, 9036, JANUARY 28, 1929; FEBRUARY 3, 9, 11, 23,
    1926. WASHINGTON, D. C.: U. S. GOVERNMENT PRINTING
    OFFICE, (1926) (EC).

UNITED STATES CONGRESS.   MIGRATORY FARM LABOR PROBLEMUNITED
    (LW*).

UNITED STATES DEPARTMENT OF LABOR.   MIGRANT LABOR   (EC*).

UNITED STATES PRESIDENTS CCMMITTEE ON MIGRATORY LABOR.
    MIGRATCRY LABOR NOTES   (EC*).

UNITED STATES. DEPARTMENT OF LABOR. BUREAU CF IMMIGRATION.
    IMMIGRATION LAWS.   WASHINGTON, D. C.: BUREAU OF
    IMMIGRATION, DEPARTMENT OF LABOR, (1925).

UNITED STATES. DEPARTMENT OF THE TREASURY. BUREAU
    OF STATISTICS. IMMIGRATION IN THE UNITED STATES.
    BUREAU OF STATISTICS, DEPARTMENT CF THE TREASURY.

UNIVERSITY OF SOUTHERN CALIFORNIA. AGENCIES AND THE
    MIGRANT THEORY AND RELAITY OF THE MIGRANT CONDITION.
    LOS ANGELES, CALIFORNIA: PHILLIPS HALL OF EDUCATION,
    UNIVERSITY CF SOUTHERN CALIFCRNIA, NO DATE (EC).

VARGAS Y CAMPOS.   PROBLEMA BRACERO MEXICANO   (EC*).

WAGONER, DELMER WILLIAM. RECENT MIGRATION OF YCUNG MALES
    INTO HOUSTON, TEXAS.   UNIVERSITY OF TEXAS, MASTER'S
    THESIS (1957) (EC AN).

WALKER, HELEN W. THE CONFLICT OF CULTURES IN FIRST
     GENERATION MEXICANS IN SANTA ANA, CALIFORNIA.
     UNIVERSITY OF SOUTHERN CALIFORNIA, LOS ANGELES,
     MASTER'S THESIS (1928).

WALLIS, WILSON D. "THE MEXICAN IMMIGRANT OF CALIFORNIA".
     PACIFIC REVIEW, VOL. 2 (DECEMBER 1921), PP. 444-454
     (HC).

WALTERS, LAWRENCE L. "TRANSIENT MEXICAN AGRUCULTURAL
     LABOR".   SOUTHWEST SOCIAL SCIENCE QUARTERLY, VOL.
     22 (JUNE 1941), PP. 1-4 (EC).

WALTON, ROGER M. VERNON. A STUDY OF MIGRATORY MEXICAN
     PEA-PICKERS IN IMPERIAL VALLEY, AUGUST, 1940.
     UNIVERSITY OF SOUTHERN CALIFORNIA, MASTER'S THESIS
     (1941) (AN).

WARD, KIRKBRIDE AND HOLMES. "MEXICAN IMMIGRATION".
     TRANSACTIONS OF THE COMMONWEALTH CLUB OF CALIFORNIA,
     (MARCH 1926).

WARNSHIPS.   CRIME CRIMINAL JUSTICE AMONGMEXICANS   (LW*).

WARNSHUIS.   CRIME CRIMINAL JUSTICE AMONGMEXICANS   (LW*).

WATERS, LAWRENCE LESLIE. "TRANSIENT MEXICAN AGRICULTURAL
     LABOR".   SOUTHWESTERN SOCIAL SCIENCE QUARTERLY, VOL.
     22 (JUNE 1941), PP. 49-66 (EC).

WATSON, WALTER T. 'MEXICANS IN DALLAS.'   IN S. D. MEYERS,
     JR. NED), MEXICO AND THE UNITED STATES (SO).

WEBER, DAVID J. (ED). FOREIGNERS IN THEIR NATIVE LAND.
     ALBUQUERQUE, NEW MEXICO, UNIVERSITY OF NEW MEXICO
     PRESS, 1973.

WEBER, L. "LEARNING READINESS FOR MIGRANT CHILDREN:
     MICRO-SOCIAL LEARNING CENTER, VINELAND, NEW JERSEY".
     GRADE TEACHER, VOL. 88 (DECEMBER 1970), PP. 36-38
     (ED).

WESTERN INTERSTATE CONFERENCE ON MIGRATORY LABOR.
     PROCEEDINGS.   SAN FRANCISCO: COUNCIL OF STATE
     GOVERNMENTS, 1960 (EC).

WESTERN REGION MIGRANT HEALTH CONFERENCE.   WESTERN REGION
     MIGRANT HEALTH (EC*).

WILKERSON.   "PROGRAMS PRACTICES COMPENSATORY   (ED*).

WILLIAMS, C. S. THE NEW INTERNATIONAL MOVEMENT.
     PAN AMERICAN UNION, MAY 1924.

WILLIAMS.   SOME POLITICAL ECONOMIC ASPECTS   (PL*).

WINNIE.   PERSONS MEXICAN DESCENT UNITED   (HM*).

WITTKE, CARL F.   WE WHO BUILT AMERICA: THE SAGA OF THE
     IMMIGRANT.   REVISED EDITION. CLEVELAND: CASE WESTERN
     RESERVE UNIVERSITY PRESS, 1967 (HUS).

WITTKE, CARL F.   WE WHO BUILT AMERICA.   NEW YORK:
     PRENTICE-HALL, 1940 (HUS).

WOOD, L. D.   MANUAL FOR SUMMER WORKERS.   SAN ANTONIO,
     TEXAS: CONVENCION BAUTISTA MEXICANA DE TEXAS, 1952
     (EC).

WOOD.   "SUMMER-SCHOOL HELP MIGRANT WORKERS   (ED*).

WOOD, SAMUEL E.   "CALIFORNIA MIGRANTS".   SOCIOLOGY AND
     SOCIAL RESEARCH, VOL. 24   (JANUARY   1940), PP. 248-261.

WOODBRIDGE.   "MEXICO U. S. RACISM: HOW MEXICANS (SO*).

WRIGHT.   THEY HARVEST DESPAIR: MIGRANT   (EC*).

WRINKLE.   DESCRIPTIVE ANALYSIS MIGRANTSTUDENT   (ED*).

YINGER, JOHN MILTON AND G. E. SIMPSON.   "INTEGRATION OF
     AMERICANS OF MEXICAN, PUERTO RICAN, AND ORIENTAL
     DESCENT".   ANNALS OF THE AMERICAN ACADEMY OF
     POLITICAL AND SOCIAL SCIENCES, VOL. 304   (MRCH   1956),
     PP. 124-127 (SO   HUS).

YINGER, JOHN MILTCN.   MINORITY GROUPS IN AMERICAN SOCIETY.
     NEW YORK: MCGRAW-HILL, 1965 (SO   HUS).

YINGER, JOHN MILTON.   A MINORITY GROUP IN AMERICAN SOCIETY.
     NEW YORK: MCGRAW-HILL, 1965 (SO   HUS).

YOUND, KIMBALL.   MENTAL DIFFERENCES IN CERTAIN IMMIGRANT
     GROUPS, PSYCHOLOGICAL TESTS CF SCUTH EUROPEANS
     IN TYPICAL CALIFORNIA SCHOOLS WITH BEARING ON
     THE EDUCATIONAL POLICY AND ON THE PROBLEMS OF RACIAL
     CONTACTS IN THIS COUNTRY.   EUGENE: UNIVERSITY
     OF OREGON PRESS, 1922 (PY   ED).

YOUNG, JAN.   THE MIGRANT WORKERS AND CESAR CHAVEZ.   NEW
     YORK, NEW YORK: JULIAN MESSNER, INC., 1972 (EC).

S O C I O L O G Y

(SO)

ABERLE, SOPHIE B. THE PUEBLO INDIANS OF NEW MEXICO.
MENASHA, WISCONSIN: ANTHROPOLOGICAL ASSOCIATION, 1948
(AN).

ABRAHAM, HENRY JULIAN. FREEDOM AND THE COURT; CIVIL RIGHTS
AND LIBERTIES IN THE UNITED STATES. NEW YORK: OXFORD
UNIVERSITY PRESS, 1967 (LW).

ABRAHAM. "THE BILINGUAL CHILD, HIS PARENTS (ED*).

ACOSTA. "THE EAST L.A. 13 VS. L.A. SUPERIOR (LW*).

ACUNA. CULTURES CONFLICT, PROBLEMS MEXICAN-AMERICANS
(AN*).

ACUNA. OCCUPIED AMERICA: CHICANO STRUGGLE (AN*).

ADAIR, JOHN AND BUNKER, ROBERT. THE FIRST LOOK AT
STRANGERS. RUTGERS UNIVERSITY PRESS, 1959.

ADAIR, JOHN. THE NAVAJO AND PUEBLO SILVERSMITHS. NORMAN,
OKLAHOMA: UNIVERSITY OF OKLAHOMA PRESS, 1944 (HSW).

ADAM. "THE PIOUS FUND" (HC*).

ADAMIC. AMERICANS SPAIN MEXICO (HS*).

ADAMIC. MANY LANDS (SI*).

ADAMIC. NATION NATIONS (SI*).

ADAMIC, LOUIS. WHAT'S YOUR NAME. NEW YORK: HARPER, 1942.

ADAMS STATE COLLEGE. READINGS UNDERSTANDING SOUTHWESTERN
(AN*).

ADAMS STATE COLLEGE. READINGS UNDERSTANDING SOUTHWESTERN
(AN*).

ADAMS, RICHARD N. SOCIAL CHANGE IN LATIN AMERICA TODAY.
NEW YORK, NEW YORK: VINTAGE BOOKS, 1961.

ADLER, S. "PAPER WALLS: AMERICA AND THE REFUGE CRISIS
1938-1941". NEW REPUBLIC, VOL. 160 (FEBRUARY 15
1969), PP. 25-26.

AGUINALDO.   SECOND LOOK AT AMERICA   (SI*).

AITKINS, JAMES A. HUMAN RELATIONS IN COLORADO: A CULTURAL
    MINORITY IMPROVES ITSELF.   DENVER, COLORADO: COLORADO
    DEPARTMENT OF EDUCATION, 1961 (HCO).

ALATIS.   BILINGUALISM LANGUAGE CONTACT: (LA*).

ALBA, VICTOR. LAS IDEAS SOCIALES CONTEMPORANEAS EN MEXICO.
    MEXICO: FONDO DE CULTURA ECONCMICA, 1960.

ALBIG.   "OPINIONS CONCERNING UNSKILLED   (SI*).

ALBUQUERQUE, NEW MEXICO COMMUNITY SURVEY COMMITTEE.
    REPORT OF THE COMMUNITY SURVEY COMMITTEE.   ALBUQUERQUE:
    HEALTH, WELFARE, EDUCATION, (ED).

ALEXANDER.   KLU KLUX KLAN SOUTHWEST   (HSW*).

ALEXANDER, HARTLEY BURR. NORTH AMERICAN MYTHOLOGY.
    BOSTON: MARSHALL JONES CO, 1916.

ALFORD, HAROLD J. THE PROUD PEOPLE: THE HERITAGE
    AND CULTURE OF SPANISH-SPEAKING PEOPLE IN THE UNITED
    STATES.   NEW YORK: DAVID MCKAY COMPANY INCORPORATED,
    1972 (AN).

ALISKY, MARVIN. "THE MEXICAN-AMERICANS MAKE THEMSELVES
    HEARD".   REPORTER, VOL. 36 (FEB 9, 1967), PP. 45-48
    (PL).

ALLEN.   EDUCATIONAL OPPORTUNITIES PROGRAM   (ED*).

ALLEN.   HOW TO TALK WITH PEOPLE OTHER   (AN*).

ALLPORT, GORDON W. THE NATURE OF PREJUDICE.   CAMBRIDGE,
    MASSACHUSETTS: ADDISON-WESLEY, 1954.

ALMAGUER.   "TOWARD STUDY CHICANO COLONIALISM"   (EC*).

ALMOND.   CIVIC CULTURE   (AN*).

ALTERS, WILLIAM C. "AMERICAN MEXICAN: THE SURVIVAL OF
    A CULTURE".   JOURNAL OF SOCIAL PSYCHOLOGY,   NO. 29
    (1949), PP. 211-20 (AN PY).

ALTMAN.   MINORITY STUDENT CAMPUS: EXPECTATIONS   (ED*).

ALTUS, WILLIAM D. "THE AMERICAN MEXICAN: THE SURVIVAL
    OF A CULTURE".   JOURNAL OF SOCIAL PSYCHOLOGY, VOL.
    29 NO. 220 (MAY 1949), PP. 211-220 (AN PY).

ALVARADO.   "MEXICAN IMMIGRATION TO UNITED   (SI*).

ALVAREZ.   "A DEMOGRAPHIC PROFILE MEXICAN   (SI*).

ALVAREZ, SALVADCR. "MEXICAN—AMERICAN COMMUNITY ORGANIZATIONS".
    EL GRITO, VOL. 4 NO. 3 (SPRING 1971), PP. 68-77.

ALVAREZ, SALVADCR. MEXICAN—AMERICAN COMMUNITY ORGANIZATIONS.
    IN OCTAVIO ROMANO, VOICES: READINGS FROM ELGRITO.
    BERKELEY, CALIFORNIA: QUINTO SOL PUBLICATIONS, 1971.

ALVIDREZ. NARCOTICS DRUG USE TRENDS CALIFORNIA (LW*).

ALVIDREZ. "DRUG USE TRENDS CALIFCRNIA" (LW*).

AMARAL, J. V. "NUEVA YORK; HISPANIC CULTURE MAKES ITS
    MARK ON NEW YORK". AMERICAS, VOL. 16 (JULY 1964),
    PP. 6-11 (HS).

AMARAL. LCS GRINGOS (LMA*).

AMERICAN CHAMBER OF COMMERCE OF MEXICO. MEXICAN AMERICAN
    REVIEW. AMERICAN CHAMBER OF COMMERCE OF MEXICO,
    LUCERNE 78, MEXICO , D.F..

AMERICAN COUNCIL ON RACE RELATIONS. "MEXICAN—AMERICANS".
    AMERICAN COUNCIL ON RACE RELATIONS, NO. 7 (1949).

AMERICAN CCUNCIL CN RACE RELATIONS. DIRECTORY OF AGENCIES
    IN INTERGROUP RELATIONS; NATIONAL, REGICNAL, STATE
    AND LOCAL. CHICAGO: THE CCUNCIL, 1948.

AMERICAN CCUNCIL CN RACE RELATICNS. INTERGROUP RELATIONS
    SAN DIEGO; (ED*).

AMERICAN ETHNOLOGICAL SOCIETY. SPANISH SPEAKING PEOPLE
    UNITED (AN*).

AMERICAN PUBLIC WELFARE ASSOCIATION. PUBLIC WELFARE SURVEY
    OF SAN ANTONIO, TEXAS, A STUDY CF A LOCAL CCMMUNITY.
    CHICAGC, 1940 (HT).

AMERICANA CORPORATION. "OUR MINCRITY GROUPS: 2.
    SPANISH—SPEAKING PEOPLE". BUILDING AMERICA, VOL.
    8 NO. 5 (1943).

ANASTASI. "LANGUAGE DEVELOPMENT NONVERBAL (ED*).

ANASTASI. "SOME EFFECTS BILINGUALISM UPCN (ED*).

ANDERSON. SOCIAL CULTURAL CHARACTERISTICS (ED*).

ANDERSON, JAMES G. AND SAFAR, DWIGHT. THE INFLUENCE OF
    DIFFERENTIAL COMMUNITY PERCEPTIONS ON THE PROVISION
    OF EQUAL EDUCATIONAL CPPORTUNITIES. IN NATHANIEL
    N. WAGNER AND MARSHA J. HAUG, CHICANOS: SOCIAL AND
    PSYCHOLOGICAL PERSPECTIVES, (SUMMER 1967). 1971 (AN).

ANDERSON. "THE INFLUENCE DIFFERENTIAL COMMUNITY (ED*).

ANDERSON, JAMES G., AND JOHNSON, WILLIAM H. SOCIOCULTURAL
DETERMINANTS OF ACHIEVEMENT AMONG MEXICAN AMERICAN
STUDENTS. UNIVERSITY PARK: NEW MEXICO STATE
UNIVERSITY, 1968 (AN).

ANDERSON, NELS. MEN ON THE MOVE. CHICAGO: UNIVERSITY
OF CHICAGO PRESS, 1940.

ANDERSON. "NORTH MEETS SOUTH: ADVENTURE (RE*).

ANDERSON, V. "NORTH MEETS SOUTH: AN ADVENTURE IN
GOODWILL". INTERNATION JOURNAL OF RELIGIOUS
EDUCATION, VOL. 22 (1946), PP. 4-5 (RE).

ANDREWS. INDIANS NEW MEXICO ARIZONA (HS*).

ANDREWS, WADE H. "FAMILY COMPOSITION AND CHARACTERISTICS
OF AN ECONOMICALLY DEPRIVED CROSS-CULTURAL ROCKY
MOUNTAIN AREA". ROCKY MOUNTAIN SOCIAL SCIENCE
JOURNAL, VOL. 3 (1966), PP. 122-139 (EC).

ANDRUS. "SOCIAL LIVING CLASSES UNDERPRIVILEGED" (ED*).

"CANDOR THAT REFRESHES: COCA-COLA (EC*).

"FAMILY SERVICE ASSOCIATION OF AMERICA". SOCIAL CASEWORK
<LA CAUSA CHICANA EDITION>, VOL. 52 NO. 5 (MAY 1971).

"LABOR SOCIAL CONDITIONS MEXICANS (EC*).

"LIGHTING THE LAMP". NEWSWEEK, VOL. 58 (SEPTEMBER 4,
1961), PP. 59-60.

"LIMITATION MEXICAN FARM LABOR (EC*).

"SPANISH SURNAME WAR DEAD --VIETNAM" (PL*).

"WHO OWNS NEW MEXICO?". ECONOMIST, VOL. 244 (JULY 8,
1967), P. 113 (EC).

E SOUTHWESTERN CONFERENCE ON CULTURAL INFLUENCES ON HEALTH
SERVICES AND HOME ECONOMICS PROGRAMS. TUCSON:
UNIVERSITY OF ARIZONA, 1961 (MD).

EXECUTIVE COMMITTEE (PL*).

FARMWORKER COOKBOOK: RECIPES (EC*).

IDENTIFICATION ASSESSMENT ONGOING (ED*).

LOCAL COMMUNITY FACT BOOK FOR CHICAGO. CHICAGO COMMUNITY
INVENTORY, UNIVERSITY OF CHICAGO, 1953.

PERSONS OF SPANISH SURNAME. U.S. GOVERNMENT CENSUS
REPORT, (1960).

SOCIAL PROCESSES AND COGNITION.   WASHINGTON, D. C..

SOCIOLOGY OF THE MEXICAN AMERICAN.   FILM, 70 MINUTES, (FILM).

SPANISH AMERICANS: NEW MILITANTS   (PL*).

SPANISH SPEAKING AMERICANS WAR: (PL*).

STARVATION IN SAN ANTONIO.   IRVINE, CALIFORNIA: UNIVERSITY
     OF CALIFORNIA AT IRVINE, 1968.

STARVATION IN SAN ANTONIO.   SOCIAL WELFARE AND FACT
     FINDING COMMITTEE, 1940 (EC).

SUMMARY PROCEEDINGS TWELFTH ANNUAL   (ED*).

"VANISHING PULQUERIA"   (AN*).

THE SPANISH SPEAKING INFORMATION CENTER, HANDBOOK.   THE
     SPANISH SPEAKING INFORMATION CENTER, FLINT, MICHIGAN
     (ED).

THE STATUS OF SPANISH-SURNAMED CITIZENS IN COLORADO.
     DENVER: COLORADO COMMISSION ON SPANISH-SURNAMED
     CITIZENS, 1967 (EC   HCO).

THE VALUE OF A SINGLE HUMAN BEING.   UNIVERSITY OF
     COLORADO, 1968 (EC).

"A CHALLENGE TO BUILD A NEW SOCIETY".   THE NEW YORK TIMES,
     VOL. 1 (APRIL 20,   1969), P. 55.

"ALTHOUGH YOUR NAME MAY BE GONZALES"   (AN*).

"AMBIGUITY OF AWARDS".   CHRISTIAN CENTUREY, VOL. 87
     (NOVEMBER 4,   1970), P. 1308.

"AMERICA'S OTHER MINORITY".   THE ECONOMIST, VOL. 228
     (JUNE 8,   1968), PP. 53-54.

"AMERICAN OUTCASTS".   CHRISTIAN CENTURY, VOL. 78   (MAY
     3,   1961), P. 548.

"ANGLO-SAXONS LATIN AMERICANS   (HSW*).

"AUXILIARY BISHOPS TO BE ORDAINED"   (RE*).

"BACK TO NEIGHBORHOOD"   (ED*).

"BATTLE OVER THE BRACEROS".   BUSINESS WEEK,   (JANUARY
     9, 1965), P. 24 (SI).

"CHARITY ENDS AT HOME; PROPOSAL TO IMPROVE LIVING CONDITIONS
    IN SOUTH JE RSEY STALEMATED".   NEW REPUBLIC, VOL.
    156 (FEBRUARY 18, 1967), P. 9.

"CHICANO RIOT: UNREST IN EAST LOS ANGELES".   TIME, VOL.
    96 (SEPTEMBER 7,   1970), P. 11.

"CULTURAL AND SOCIAL COOPERATION WITH MEXICO".   BULLETIN
    OF PAN-AMERICAN UNION, WASHINGTON, D. C., VOL. 62
    (1928), PP. 176-78.

"DRUDGERY AND DESPAIR".   NEWSWEEK, VOL. 58   (OCT. 238
    1961), P. 68.

"EIGHT THOUSAND AT RITES".   ALAMO MESSENGER,   NO. 19 (MAY
    8, 1970), P. 1.

"EXCLUDED AMERICANS".   TIME, VOL. 76 (DEC. 5, 1960),
    P. 50.

"FORD FOUNDATION -- FOCUS: SOUTHWEST (ED*).

"FRITO-LAY CUTS GUN SCENES TV   (FILM*).

"HOUSE REJECTS BRACERO PROGRAM".   CHRISTIAN CENTURY, VOL.
    80 (JUNE 12, 1963), P. 766.

"IN SPANISH THEY SAY ACCION".   VISTA VOLUNTEER, VOL. 4
    (MAY 1968), PP. 22-29.

"INTER AMERICAN".   INTER-AMERICAN, VOL. 2 (MARCH 1943),
    P. 44.

"LA CAUSA CHICAN, UNA FAMILIA UNIDA".   SOCIAL CASEWORK,
    VOL. 52 NO. 5 (MAY 1971).

"LAST MINUTE NEWS: FRITO DROPS   (FILM*).

"MACHISMO RIOT FLARE-UP IN EAST LOS ANGELES'S BARRIO
    MACHISMO RIOT; FLARE-UP IN EAST LOS ANGELES'S BARRIO".
    NEWSWEEK, VOL. 77 (FEBRUARY 15, 1971), P. 34.

"MEXICAN RESIDENTS SOUTHWESTSTUDIED   (EC*).

"MEXICAN VIEW OF RACE RELATIONS".   INTER-AMERICAN, VOL.
    2 (SEPTEMBER 1943), P. 38.

"MEXICAN AMERICANS' ELGIN HASSLE OVER WHETHER AD IMPUGNS
    ZAPATA".   ADVERTISING AGE, VOL. 41   (JUNE 8, 1970),
    P. 2.

"MEXICAN AMERICANS OPPOSE 'LAZY' IMAGE".   LOS ANGELES
    TIMES, VOL. 2 (JULY 3, 1969), P. 8 (PY).

"MEXICAN-AMERICAN FRIENDSHIP".   PAN-AMERICAN MAGAZINE,
    (AUGUST 1919), PP. 24-29.

"MEXICO-UNITED STATES FARM LABOR (EC*).

"MIGRANT LABOR - A HUMAN PROBLEM: REPORT AND RECOMMENDATIONS".
     NEWSWEEK, VOL. 67 (MAY 23,   1966), PP. 32-36 (EC
     PL).

"MINORITIES: CRUSADE AGAINST (PL*).

"MINORITY GROUPS CALIFORNIA" (EC*).

"MOVEMENT AMONG THE SOUTHWEST'S MEXICAN-AMERICANS".
     NEWSWEEK, VOL. 71 (MARCH 25,   1968), P. 37 (PL).

"NEUROSIS MEXICAN FAMILY STRUCTURE" (PY*).

"NO DISCRIMINATICN".   NEW REPUBLIC, VOL. 120   (MAY   1949),
     P. 7.

"NO MEXICAN ALLCWED".   INTER-AMERICAN, VOL. 2 (SEPTEMBER
     1943), P. 8.

"NON-VIOLENCE".   LOOK,   (APRIL 1, 1969), P. 52.

"NON-WHITES TOO OFTEN IGNORED (EC*).

"NORTH OF THE BORDER".   TIME, VOL. 52 (NOVEMBER
     1, 1948), P. 38.

"OUR MEXICAN AMERICANS".   AMERICAS, VOL. 2 (OCTOBER
     1950), PP. 42-48.

"OUR SOUTHERN NEIGHBORS".   NATION,   (AUGUST 27,   1924).

"OUTCAST".   TIME, VOL. 76 (AUGUST 8,   1970), P. 66.

"PLAY FOR THE MEXICAN POPULATICN IN TOPEKA, KANSAS".
     PLAYGROUND, VOL. 13 , PP. 26-27.

"REACHING MEXICANS UNITED STATES" (RE*).

"RURAL WORKER AMERICA" (SI*).

"SAN ANTONIO BELL UNIT CRITICIZED (FILM*).

"SCHOOL BIAS TOWARD MEXICAN AMERICANS" (ED*).

"SILENT MINORITY STARTS TO SPEAK OUT".   U.S. NEWS
     AND WORLD REPORT, VOL. 69 (JULY 13, 1970), PP. 66-69.

"STUDY OF SOCIO-CULTURAL FACTORS THAT INHIBIT OR ENCOURAGE
     DELINQUENCY AMONG MEXICAN AMERICANS".   IT'S NEWS,
     VOL. 10 (FEBRUARY 1958), P. 9 (LW).

"STUDY POINTS TO ISOLATION FOR MEXICAN AMERICANS".
     NATION'S SCHOOLS, VOL. 86 (SEPTEMBER 1970), PP. 30-31.

"TEXAS CASE".   SURVEY, VOL. 83   (JANUARY   1947), P. 180
    (PL).

"THE MEXICANS OF SAN ANTONIO: WHEN DID THEY COME".   SAN
    ANTONIO EXPRESS NEWS,   (OCTOBER 24,   1965), P. 3H
    (SI).

"THE SUPPORT OF MIGRANTS: POPE PAUL'S MOTUPROPRIO".
    AMERICA, VOL. 121 (NOVEMBER 15, 1969), P. 447.

"TRYING TO RAISE THE 'CACTUS CURTAIN'".   CHRISTIAN SCIENCE
    MONITOR,   (DECEMBER 2, 1966), P. 8.

"TV: 2 FACES OF WELFARE".   THE NEW YORK TIMES, VOL. 1
    (APRIL 2 1, 1969), P. 95 (EC).

"TWENTY-EIGHT IMPORTANT MEXICANS".   COMMONWEAL, VOL. 47
    (FEBRUARY   13, 1948), PP. 436-457 (HSW).

"UNHAPPY MEXICO--OUR DUTY".   OUTLOOK, VOL. 133   (OCTOBER,
    1968), PP. 527-530 (ED LW).

"VIEWS MEXICAN WORKER HIS RETURN   (EC*).

"VIOLENCE OASIS; BRACERO PROGRAM"   (EC*).

"WELL CRUSH ANY GRINGO WHO GETS   (PL*).

"WETBACK INVASION".   CATHOLIC DIGEST, VOL. 18   (FEBRUARY
    1954), PP. 55-58 (SI).

"WETBACK INVASION TEXAS" (SI*).

"WETBACKS, COTTON, KOREA" (SI*).

"WHAT THE PEOPLE READ IN MEXICO".   AMERICAN REVIEW
    OF REVIEWS, VOL. 31 , PP. 687-88.

"ZOOT-SUIT RIOTS".   LIFE, VOL. 14 (JUNE 2 1, 1943), P.
    31 (PL).

"ZOOT-SUITS AND SERVICE STRIPES: RACE TENSION BEHIND THE
    RIOTS".   NEWSWEEK, VOL. 21 (JUNE 2 1, 1943), PP.
    35-40 (PL).

BACKGROUND FOR PLANNING.   LOS ANGELES: RESEARCH DEPARTMENT,
    WELFARE PLANNING COUNCEIL, 1963.

BACKGROUND PLANNING (HC*).

CHILDS MEDICAL RECORD (MD*).

DIRECTORY OF SPANISH-SPEAKING COMMUNITY ORGANIZATIONS.
    WASHINGTON, D. C.. 1970, (NOV 1963).

EAST LOS ANGELES BLOWOUT.   OAKLAND, CALIFORNIA: LA CAUSA
    DISTRIBUTION CENTER,.

EDUCATION DEPRESSED AREAS   (ED*).

FAR WEST SURVEYS. "A REPORT OF THE LATIN AMERICAN
    POPULATION LIVING IN LOS ANGELES, CALIFORNIA.
    PREPARED FOR RADIO STATION KALI, LOS ANGELES 1962.

FORGOTTEN EGG;   EXPLORATION INTO   (MC*).

GETTING GOD COUNTED AMONG MEXICANS   (RE*).

HUNGARUSA.   NEW YORK: BEACON PRESS, 1968.

MEXICAN AMERICAN MILITANCY   (PL*).

MEXICAN AMERICANS IN THE UNITED STATES.   WASHINGTON D.C.
    LEGISLATIVE REFERENCE SERVICE, 1964.

MEXICAN LOS ANGELES, 1920   (SI*).

MEXICAN NATIVE COSTUMES, MEXICAN   (AN*).

MEXICAN STUDENT POSTERS: POSTERS   (PL*).

MEXICANS IN THE UNITED STATES.   WASHINGTON, D. C.: PAN
    AMERICAN UNION, (SEPTEMBER   1942).

MEXICANS IN LOS ANGELES.   LOS ANGELES: CITY SURVEY
    INTERCHURCH WORLD MOVEMENT, JUNE 1920 (SI   EC).

MEXICO.   LECTURES BEFORE THE INTER-AMERICA INSTITUTE,
    CLAREMONT, CALIFORNIA, 1919 (EC   PL).

MEXICO WATCHES ASSIMILATION.   CHRISTIAN SCIENCE MONITOR,
    SEPTEMBER 29, 1965 (AN).

MEXICO.   INFORME FINAL QUE EN   (EC*).

MINORITY GROUP ADOLESCENTS UNITED   (PY*).

MINORITY GROUP ADOLESCENTS IN THE U. S..   BALTIMORE:
    WILLIAMS AND WILLIAMS, 1968 (HUS).

NATIONAL CONFERENCE CONCERNING MEXICANS AND SPANISH-AMERICANS
    IN THE UNITED STATES.   EL PASO, 1926.

PEN IS MIGHTIER.   AMERICAN JEWISH COMMITTEE, COMMUNITY
    RELATIONS SERVICE PUBLICATION, 195954.

PEOPLE OF THE CITY.   URBAN MEDIA MATERIALS,.

SYNODS PROGRAM COMMITTEE CHURCH   (RE*).

SYNOPTIC STUDIES MEXICAN CULTURE   (AN*).

TEACHING INNER-CITY SCHOOL:WHAT   (ED*).

TESTIMONY TRIAL JUAN DOMINGUEZ   (LW*).

TEXAS CHILD WELFARE SURVEY.   AUSTIN: BUREAU OF RESEARCH
     IN THE SOCIAL SCIENCES, 1938.

TEXAS MEXICAN   (LI*).

TEXAS. GOOD NEIGHBOR COMMISSION.   AUSTIN, TEXAS, 1954.

TEXAS: FRIEND AND NEIGHBOR.   AUSTIN: GOOD NEIGHBOR
     COMMISSION OF TEXAS, 1961 (AN).

"ACROSS THE TRACKS"   (SI*).

"AMERICAN DPS"   (ED*).

"AUTHENTIC PACHUCO"   (AN*).

"BAN THE BANDITO?"   (FILM*).

"CURE FOR CURANDERISMO"   (AN*).

"THE MEXICAN-AMERICAN"   (EC*).

"TIO TACO IS DEAD"   (LI*).

"WETBACK INVASION"   (SI*).

"400-WORD START"   (ED*).

THE BLACKEST WHITE MAN I KNOW; CIVIL RIGHTS LAWYER WILLIAM
     KUNSTLER IS SOUL BROTHER TO RADICALS OF MANY COLORS--THE
     ALIANZA.   LIFE 47, 4.

THE SEMINAR ON RELATIONS WITH MEXICO.   BOSTON, 1928 (AN).

ANTHONY.   "FILIPINO LABOR CENTRAL CALIFORNIA"   (EC*).

ANTILA.   UNITED STATES EDUCATIONAL POLICIES   (ED*).

APPEL.   "ANXIETY PROBLEMS WITH CULTURAL   (PY*).

ARAGON.   THEIR HERITAGE--POVERTY   (AN*).

ARAGON.   "THEIR HERITAGE--POVERTY"   (AN*).

ARAGON.   CHICANO VOTING RIGHTS ACT   (PL*).

ARCHIBEQUE, CRIZ R.   HJHJHJKJJK. ETHNIC MINORITY
    MEMBERSHIP IN THE BUILDING AND CONSTRUCTION TRADES
    UNIONS IN THE PHOENIX METROPOLITAN AREA.   TEMPE,
    ARIZONA STATE UNIVERSITY, MASTER'S THESIS (1941).

ARCINIEGA. T. A.   THE URBAN MEXICAN AMERICAN: A SOCIO-CULTURAL
    PROFILE.   LAS CRUCES, NEW MEXICO: ERIC PRESS, 1971.

ARIAS, RONALD. "THE BARRIO".   AGENDA, VOL. 2 (JULY
    1966), PP. 15-20 (AN).

ARIAS.   BARRIO (LMA*).

ARIZONA COUNCIL FOR CIVIC UNITY.   CLOSE BREACH: STUDY
    SCHOOL SEGREGATION (ED*).

ARIZONA EMPLOYMENT SERVICE.   DISTRIBUTION INDIANS, NEGROES
    (AN*).

ARIZONA STATE COMMITTEE ON AMERICANIZATION WORK IN ARIZONA.
    PAMPHLET.   PHOENIX, ARIZONA: FRIENDLY HOUSE, 192 (SI).

ARIZONA. STATE DEPARTMENT OF PUBLIC WELFARE. DIVISION
    OF RESEARCH AND STATISTICS. GENERAL ASSISTANCE
    RECIPIENTS IN ARIZONA.   PHOENIX, ARIZONA STATE
    DEPARTMENT OF PUBLIC WELFARE, DIVISION OF RESEARCH
    AND STATISTICS, (JANUARY 1951). RESEARCH MONOGRAPH
    NUMBER 8, MIMEOGRAPHED..

ARLITT, ADA HART. "ON THE NEED FOR CAUTION IN ESTABLISHING
    RACE NORMS".   THE JOURNAL OF APPLIED PSYCHOLOGY, VOL.
    5 (APRIL 1921), PP. 188-195 (PY ED).

ARMANDO RODRIGUEZ. UNDERSTANDING AND WORKING WITH
    THE POWER, STRUCTURE IN THE MEXICAN-AMERICAN COMMUNITY.
    U. S. OFFICE OF EDUCATION. WASHINGTON, D. C.: UNITED
    STATES GOVERNMENT PRINTING OFFICE, (OCTOBER, 1968)
    (PL ED).

ARMSTRONG.   REACTIONS PUERTO RICAN CHILDREN (ED*).

ARMSTRONG.   MEXICAN COMMUNITY: STUDY CULTURAL (SI*).

ARNOLD, CHARLES AUGUST.   THE FOLKLORE, MANNERS, AND CUSTOMS
    OF THE MEXICANS IN SAN ANTONIO, TEXAS.   UNIVERSITY
    OF TEXAS AT AUSTIN, MASTER'S THESIS (1928) (AN).

ARTHUR.   ARTHUR POINT SCALE PERFORMANCE (ED*).

ARTHUR.   LEITER INTERNATIONAL PERFORMANCE (ED*).

ARTHUR.   POINT SCALE PERFORMANCE TESTS (ED*).

ASHLEY-MONTAGUE.   MANS MOST DANGEROUS MYTH: FALLACY (AN*).

ASHWORTH, MAE HURLEY. WHO? SPANISH-SPEAKING AMERICANS
    IN THE U.S.A.. NEW YORK: FRIENDSHIP PRESS, 1953 (HSW).

ASTER. TERMINATION BRACERO PROGRAM--ITS (LW*).

ASTROV. AMERICAN INDIAN PROSE POETRY (LMA*).

ATENCIO. HUMAN DIMENSIONS LAND USE DISPLACEMENT (EC*).

ATKINS. CULTURAL MINORITY IMPROVES ITSELF (ED*).

ATKINSON. TEXAS INDIANS (HT*).

ATONNA. COMPARISON TRAVEL PATTERNS MEXICAN-AMERICAN (B*).

AUSTIN, ROBERT CALVIN. A COMPARATIVE ANALYSIS OF ANGLO-AMERICAN
    AND MEXICAN AMERICAN CLIENTELE SERVED BY THE TUCSON
    CHILD GUIDANCE OUTPOST CLINIC. ARIZONA STATE
    UNIVERSITY, MASTER'S THESIS (1967).

AVINS. OPEN OCCUPANCY VS. FORCED HOUSING (LW*).

AYALA DE SIFUENTES. "CONSPIRACY RIGHT TO DISSENT" (LW*).

BABCOCK. "HOUSEKEEPING IN MEXICO" (AN*).

BACA, EMILIE M. "PANCHITA". THE FAMILY, VOL. 8 (APRIL
    1927), P. 44.

BACH, MARCUS. FAITH AND MY FRIENDS. NEW YORK: WORLD
    PUBLISHERS, INC., 1951.

BAGDIGAN, BEN H. THE INVISIBLE AMERICAN. SATURDAY
    EVENING POST, DECEMBER 1963.

BAILEY, WILFRED C. "PROBLEMS IN RELOCATING THE PEOPLE OF
    ZAPATA, TEXAS". TEXAS JOURNAL OF SCIENCE, VOL. 7
    (MARCH. 1955), PP. 20-37.

BAKER. ECONOMIC ASPECTS MEXICAN MEXICAN-AMERICAN (EC*).

BAMFORD. "MEXICAN CASUAL LABOR PROBLEM (EC*).

BANDURA. ADOLESCENT AGGRESSION (LW*).

BANTON, MICHAEL (ED). THE SOCIAL ANTHROPOLOGY OF COMPLEX
    SOCIETIES. NEW YORK, NEW YORK: FREDERICK A. PREAGER,
    INC., 1966 (AN).

BARKER. "SOME ASPECTS PENETENTIAL PROCESSIONS (AN*).

BARKER. "GROWING UP BILINGUAL COMMUNITY" (LA*).

BARKER. "PACHUCO: AMERICAN-SPANISH ARGOT (LA*).

BARKER.   "SOCIAL FUNCTIONS LANGUAGE MEXICAN-AMERICAN   (LA*).

BARKER.   PACHUCO: AMERICAN-SPANISH ARGOT   (LA*).

BARKER.   SOCIAL FUNCTION LANGUAGE MEXICAN-AMERICAN   (LA*).

BARKER.   SOCIAL FUNCTIONS LANGUAGE MEXICAN-AMERICAN   (LA*).

BARKER.   "WHERE AMERICANS ARE ANGLOS"   (LI*).

BARNES.   HER MAJESTY NEVERTHELESS   (HS*).

BARNES, ROBERT F. (ET AL).   THE CALIFORNIA MIGRANT FRAM
     WORKER, HIS FAMILY AND THE RURAL COMMUNITY.   DAVIS:
     UNIVERSITY OF CALIFORNIA DEPARTMENT OF APPLIED
     BEHAVIORAL SCIENCES, 1967 (SI).

BARON.   HERE I AM. ANTHOLOGY POETRYWRITTEN   (LMA*).

BARRAZA.   HELPING MEXICAN-AMERICAN CHILDREN   (ED*).

BARRETT, DONALD N. DEMOGRAPHIC CHARACTERISTICS.   M JULIAN
     SAMORA (ED) LA, RAZA NOTRE DAME: UNIVERSITY OF NOTRE
     DAME PR ESS, 1969.

BARRETT, DONALD N. AND SAMORA, JULIAN.   THE MOVEMENT OF
     SPANISH YOUTH FROM RURAL TO URBAN SETTINGS.
     WASHINGTON, D. C.: GOVERNMENT PRINTING OFFICE, (1963).

BARRETT.   EFFECT HEADSTART EXPERIENCE DEPRIVED   (ED*).

BARRON, CLARENCE WALKER.   THE MEXICAN PROBLEM.   BOSTON
     AND NEW YORK: HOUGHTON MIFFLIN COMPANY, 1917 (SI).

BARRON, MILTON L. (ED).   MINORITIES IN A CHANGING WORLD.
     NEW YORK: ALFRED A. KNOPF, 1967.

BARRON, MILTON LEON.   AMERICAN MINORITIES; A TEXTBOOK OF
     READINGS IN INTERGROUP RELATIONS.   NEW YORK: ALFRED
     A. KNOPF, 1957.

BARUCH, DOROTHY.   THE GLASS HOUSE OF PREJUDICE.   NEW YORK:
     W. MORROW AND COMPANY, 1946.

BARZUN.   RACE: STUDY SUPERSTITION   (PY*).

BATHKE, C. S.   "ETHNIC RESPONSES TO A MODIFIED CLOTHING
     TAT".   JOURNAL OF HOME ECONOMICS, VOL. 40   (MAY
     1968), PP. 350-354.

BATISTA Y CALDERON, JUDITH.   A STUDY OF COUNTER-PREJUDICE
     IN A MEXICAN-SPANISH COMMUNITY IN THE SURROUNDINGS
     OF DES MOINES, IOWA.   DRAKE UNIVERSITY, MASTER'S
     THESIS (1948) (PY).

BATTEN.   "NEW FEATURES MEXICAN IMMIGRATION: (LW*).

BATTEN, JAMES H.   "OUR CULTURAL RELATIONS WITH MEXICO".
     PROCEEDINGS OF THE INSTITUTE OF INTERNATIONAL
     RELATIONS, VOL. 7 (1930), PP. 47-52 (SI).

BATTEN, JAMES H.   "THE MEXICAN IMMIGRATION PROBLEM".   PAN
     PACIFIC PROGRESS, VOL. 8 (1928), P. 39 (SI).

BATTEN, JAMES H.   "THE MEXICAN IMMIGRATION PROBLEM".
     PAN-PACIFIC PROGRESS, VOL. 8 , PP. 39-52 (SI).

BATTEY, VIOLA. THE MEXICAN SITUATION IN ST. PAUL.   FROM
     THE FILES ON THE INTERNATIONAL INSTITUTE, ST. PAUL,
     MINNESOTA (SI).

BAUER.   "THE CHURCH SPANISH-AMERICANAGRARIAN (RE*).

BAUER.   CONFLICTING CULTURAL VALUES BETWEEN (ED*).

BAUKEN, MANUEL. "OUR FIGHTING LOVE FOR FREEDOM: 1200
     MEMBERS OF THE FIRST FILIPINO INFANTRY TAKE OATH OF
     ALLEGIANCE WHICH MAKES THEM CITIZENS".   ASIA, VOL.
     43 (JUNE 1943), PP. 347-59.

BAUKEN, MANUEL. "WHERE IS THE HEART OF AMERICA?".   NEW
     REPUBLIC, VOL. 103 (SEPTEMBER 23, 1940), P. 410.

BAUKEN, MANUEL. "YOU CAN'T MARRY A FILIPINO". COMMONWEAL,
     VOL. 41 (MARCH 16, 1945), PP. 534-37.

BAUKEN, MANUEL. I HAVE LIVED WITH THE AMERICAN PEOPLE.
     CALDWELL, IDAHO: CAXTON PRINTERS, 1948.

BAUR.   DELINQUENCY AMONG MEXICAN BOYS (LW*).

BEAGLE, ALLAN J. GOLDSMITH, HAROLD F, AND LOOMIS, CHARLES
     P. "DEMOGRAPHIC CHARACTERISTICS OF THE UNITED
     STATES-MEXICAN BORDER".   RURAL SOCIOLOGY, VOL. 25
     (MARCH 1960), PP. 107-162 (HSW).

BEALS, RALPH. "THE MEXICAN STUDENT VIEWS THE UNITED
     STATES". ANNALS OF THE AMERICAN ACADEMY OF POLITICAL
     AND SOCIAL SCIENCE, (MARCH 1960), P. SEPTEMBER 1954
     (ED).

BEALS.   "URBANISM, URBANIZATION ACCULTURATION" (AN*).

BEALS.   ACCULTURATION (AN*).

BEALS.   NO FRONTIER TO LEARNING: MEXICAN (ED*).

BEEBE, A. A. AN ANALYSIS OF RACIAL REACTIONS OF A SELECT
    GROUP OF MEXICAN CHILDREN.   UNIVERSITY OF SOUTHERN
    CALIFORNIA, MASTER'S THESIS (1941).

BEECHER, JOHN. "TO THE REAR MARCH. 1965-1940".   RAMPARTS,
    VOL. 4 (SEPTEMBER 1965), PP. 14-32.

BEEGLE, J. ALLAN, GOLDSMITH, HAROLD, AND LOOMIS, CHARLES.
    "DEMOGRAPHIC CHARACTERISTICS OF THE UNITED STATES-MEXICAN
    BORDER".   RURAL SOCIOLOGY, VOL. 25 (MARCH 1960),
    PP. 106-162 (HSW).

BEGAY, BETTY ELLEN. A SURVEY OF LIFE EXPECTATION OF
    MEXICAN AMERICAN YOUTH FROM SEASONAL FARM LABOR
    FAMILIES.   TEMPE: ARIZONA STATE UNIVERSITY, 1968 (EC).

BELDEN ASSOCIATES.   MEXICAN-AMERICAN MARKET UNITED (EC*).

BELDEN.   LATIN-AMERICAN AUDIENCE MARKET (EC*).

BELDEN.   LATIN-AMERICAN POPULATION TEXAS: (EC*).

BELDEN.   MARKET CHARACTERISTICS SAN ANTONIO (EC*).

BELDEN.   MEXICAN-AMERICAN MARKET UNITED (EC*).

BELDEN.   RADIO LISTENING, BUYING POWER (EC*).

BELL.   MEXICAN WEST COAST LOWER CALIFORNIA (ED*).

BENDIX, REINHARD. CLASS, STATUS AND POWER; SOCIAL
    STRATIFICATION IN COMPARATIVE PERSPECTIVE.   NEW YORK:
    FREE PRESS, 1966.

BENJAMIN, ROBERT SPIERS, (ED). I AM AN AMERICAN, BY FAMOUS
    NATURALIZED AMERICANS.   FREEPORT, NEW YORK: BOOKS
    FOR LIBRARIES, INC., 1941 (SI).

BENNETT.   "FARM CRISIS, CITY CRISIS" (EC*).

BENNETT.   TARAHUMARA, INDIAN TRIBE NORTHERN (HM*).

BERKSON, ISAAC B. THEORIES OF AMERICANIZATION; A CRITICAL
    STUDY (1920).   REPRINTED BY. NEW YORK, NEW YORK: ARNO
    PRESS, 1971 (SI).

BERNAL.   COMPARATIVE CONCEPT LEARNING (ED*).

BERNAL.   "I AM MEXICAN-AMERICAN" (ED*).

BERNSTEIN.   ALTERNATIVES TO VIOLENCE; ALIENATED (LW*).

BERRY.   RACE RELATIONS; INTERACTION ETHNIC (AN*).

BETTELHEIM.   DYNAMICS PREJUDICE (AN*).

BETTELHEIM.   SOCIAL CHANGE PREJUDICE, INCLUDING (AN*).

BEZET, A. S. 'THE LATIN AMERICANS.'   IN FAIRCHILD, H.P.,
     ED.: IMMIGRATION BACKGROUNDS (SI).

BIDDICK.   "HELPING SPANISH—AMERICAN CHILDREN   (ED*).

BIDDICK.   "SPANISH AMERICAN CHILDREN RECEIVE   (ED*).

BIGART.   "MEXICAN—AMERICANS STAGE PROTEST (PL*).

BISHOPS COMMITTEE FOR THE SPANISH—SPEAKING.   PILOT PROJECT
     —— MERRIL TRUST (EC*).

BITTINGER, BEAU STANLEY. LEADERSHIP SYSTEM AND SOCIAL
     CHANGE IN A TEXAS CITY OF 100,000.   UNIVERSITY OF
     TEXAS, PHD. DISSERTATION (1967) (EC).

BLACK.   FOOD MANAGEMENT PRACTICES HEAD (MD*).

BLAIR, BERTHA, LIVELY, ANNE O. AND TRIMBLE, GLEN W.
     SPANISH—SPEAKING AMERICANS: MEXICANS AND PUERTO RICANS
     IN THE UNITED STATES.   NEW YORK: HOME MISSION
     RESEARCH UNIT, BUREAU OF RESEARCH AND SURVEY, HOME
     MISSIONS DIVISION, NATIONAL COUNCIL OF CHURCHES OF
     CHRIST IN THE UNITED STATES OF AMERICA, 1959.

BLAIR.   "WHEN NATIONALITIES MIX CLASSROOM" (ED*).

BLAIR, WILLIAM C.   "SPANISH—SPEAKING MINORITIES IN A UTAH
     MINING TOWN".   JOURNAL OF SOCIAL ISSUES, VOL. 8 NO.
     1 (1952), PP. 4—9.

BLAISDELL, LOWELL. THE DESERT REVOLUTION.   MADISON:
     UNIVERSITY OF WISCONSIN PRESS, 1962.

BLALOCK, H. M. TOWARD A THEORY OF MINORITY GROUP RELATIONS.
     NEW YORK: JOHN WILEY & SONS, 1967.

BLANCO.   "UNIDAD TRABAJO VIDA —— CINCO (EC*).

BLAZER.   SANTANA, LAST CHIEF MESCALEROS (HSW*).

BLEDSOE, THOMAS.   "RELIEF".   NEW MEXICO QUARTERLY REVIEW,
     VOL. 5 NO. 19 (AUTUMN,   1949), PP. 330—336.

BLISS, PEGGY ANN. "SIGNALS OF ANOTHER WORLD".   VISTA
     VOLUNTEER, VOL. 4 (JANUARY, 1968), PP. 3—66.

BLISS, PEGGY ANN. "THE STREETS OF LAREDO".   VISTA
     VOLUNTEER,   NO. 3 (FEBRUARY, 1967), PP. 14—18.

BLOCH, LOUIS. "FACTS ABOUT MEXICAN IMMIGRATION BEFORE AND
     SINCE THE QUOTA RESTRICTION LAWS".   JOURNAL OF THE
     AMERICAN STATISTICAL ASSOCIATION,   NO. 24 (MARCH,
     1929), PP. 50-60 (SI).

BLOOM.   "JOHNNY GRINGO AT PASS NORTH" (HSW*).

BLOOM.   "JOHNNY GRINGO NORTHERN MEXICO (HSW*).

BLOOM, LEONARD AND SHEVSKY, ESHREF. "MEXICANS IN THE
     UNITED STATES: 6 PROBLEMS IN SOCIAL DIFFERENTIATION".
     SOCIOLOGY AND SOCIAL RESEARCH, VOL. 36 (JANUARY-FEBRUARY,
     1952), PP. 150-158.

BLOOMBERG, WARNER. "THE YOUNG CHILD IN CULTURAL CHANGE".
     YOUNG CHILDREN,   (JANUARY, 1967), PP. 130-148.

BLOSSOM.   "READING PROBLEM BILINGUAL CHILD"   (ED*).

BLUMENFELD, A. A. "EFFECTS OF NEW MEXICO'S SOCIAL
     AND ECONOMIC STRUCTURE UPON GOVERNMENTAL EXPENDITURES".
     NEW MEXICO BUSINESS, VOL. 14 (AUGUST, 1961), PP.
     3-10 (EC).

BLUMENFELD, A. A. "TRENDS IN PERSONAL INCOME IN NEW MEXICO
     AND THE UNITED STATES".   NEW MEXICO BUSINESS, VOL.
     14 (OCTOBER, 1961), PP. 3-12 (EC).

BODINE.   ATTITUDES INSTITUTIONS TAOS,NEW (AN*).

BOGARDUS, EMORY S. 'ATTITUDES AND THE MEXICAN IMMIGRANT.'
     IN KIMBALL YOUNG, (ED) SOCIAL ATTITUDES, PP. 291-327
     (SI).

BOGARDUS, EMORY S. 'REPATRIATION AND READJUSTMENT.'   IN
     MANUEL P. SERVIN, THE MEXICAN-AMERICANS: AN AWAKENING
     MINORITY (SI).

BOGARDUS, EMORY S. "CHANGES IN RACIAL DISTANCES".
     INTERNATIONAL JOURNAL OF OPINION AND ATTITUDE
     RESEARCH, VOL. 1 NO. 58 (DECEMBER 1947).

BOGARDUS, EMORY S. "CONCERNING ZOOT SUIT GANGS".
     COMMUNITY COORDINATION, VOL. 11 (FEBRUARY, 1943),
     PP. 1-3.

BOGARDUS, EMORY S. "CURRENT PROBLEMS OF MEXICAN IMMIGRANTS".
     SOCIOLOGY AND SOCIAL RESEARCH, VOL. 25 (NOVEMBER,
     1940), PP. 166-174 (SI).

BOGARDUS, EMORY S. "GANGS OF MEXICAN-AMERICAN YOUTH".
     SOCIOLOGY AND SOCIAL RESEARCH, VOL. 28 (SEPTEMBER,
     1943), PP. 55-66.

BOGARDUS, EMORY S. "MEASURING CHANGE IN ETHNIC REACTIONS".
     ASR, VOL. 16 (FEBRUARY, 1951), P. 49.

BOGARDUS, EMORY S. "MEXICAN AMERICAN YOUTH AND GANGS".
    SOCIOLOGY AND SOCIAL RESEARCH, VOL. 28 (SEPTEMBER,
    1943), PP. 55-66.

BOGARDUS, EMORY S. "MEXICAN REPATRIATES".   SOCIOLOGY AND
    SOCIAL RESEARCH, VOL. 18 (NOVEMBER, 1933), PP.
    169-176 (SI).

BOGARDUS, EMORY S. "RACE REACTION BY SEXES".   SOCIOLOGY
    AND SOCIAL RESEARCH, VOL. 43 (JULY, 1959), PP. 439-443.

BOGARDUS, EMORY S. "RACIAL DISTANCE CHANGES IN THE UNITED
    STATES DURING THE PAST THIRTY YEARS".   SOCIOLOGY AND
    SOCIAL RESEARCH, VOL. 43 (NOVEMBER, 1958), PP. 127-137.

BOGARDUS, EMORY S. "RACIAL REACTIONS BY REGIONS".
    SOCIOLOGY AND SOCIAL RESEARCH, VOL. 43 (MARCH,
    1959), PP. 286-290.

BOGARDUS, EMORY S. A FORTY YEAR RACIAL DISTANCE STUDY.
    LOS ANGELES, CALIFORNIA: UNIVERSITY OF SOUTHERN
    CALIFORNIA, 1967.

BOGARDUS, EMORY S. THE MEXICAN IN THE UNITED STATES.
    LOS ANGELES: UNIVERSITY OF SOUTHERN CALIFORNIA PRESS,
    (1934). SCHOOL OF RESEARCH STUDIES, NO. 5, SOCIAL
    SCIENCE SERIES, NO. 8, UNIVERSITY OF SOUTHERN
    CALIFORNIA (SI).

BOGARDUS, EMORY S. THE MEXICAN IN THE UNITED STATES.
    NEW YORK: ARNO PRESS AND THE NEW YORK TIMES, 1970 (SI).

BOGARDUS, EMORY STEPHEN. "AMERICAN ATTITUDES TOWARD
    FILIPINOS".   SOCIOLOGY AND SOCIAL RESEARCH, VOL. 14
    (SEPTEMBER-OCTOBER 1929), PP. 56-69.

BOGARDUS, EMORY STEPHEN. "FILIPINO IMMIGRANT ATTITUDES".
    SOCIOLOGY AND SOCIAL RESEARCH, VOL. 14 (MAY-JUNE,
    1930), PP. 469-79.

BOGARDUS, EMORY STEPHEN. "MEXICAN REPATRIATES".
    SOCIOLOGY AND SOCIAL RESEARCH, VOL. 18 (AUTUMN,
    1965), PP. 169-76 (SI).

BOGARDUS, EMORY STEPHEN. "SECOND GENERATION MEXICANS".
    SOCIOLOGY AND SOCIAL RESEARCH, VOL. 13 (JANUARY,
    1929), PP. 276-283 (SI).

BOGARDUS, EMORY STEPHEN. "SECOND GENERATION MEXICANS".
    SOCIOLOGY AND SOCIAL RESEARCH, (JANUARY-FEBRUARY,
    1929), PP. 276-83 (SI).

BOGARDUS, EMORY STEPHEN. "SECOND GENERATION MEXICANS".
    SOCIOLOGY AND SOCIAL RESEARCH, VOL. 13 (AUTUMN,
    1965), PP. 276-83 (SI).

BOGARDUS, EMORY STEPHEN. "THE FILIPINO IMMIGRANT PROBLEM".
    SOCIOLOGY AND SOCIAL RESEARCH, VOL. 13 (MAY-JUNE
    1929), PP. 472-479.

BOGARDUS, EMORY STEPHEN. "THE FILIPINO PRESS IN THE UNITED
    STATES".   SOCIOLOGY AND SOCIAL RESEARCH, VOL. 28
    (JULY-AUGUST, 1933), PP. 581-85.

BOGARDUS, EMORY STEPHEN. "THE HOUSE-COURT PROBLEM".
    AMERICAN JOURNAL OF SOCIOLOGY, VOL. 22 (AUTUMN,
    1965), PP. 391-99.

BOGARDUS, EMORY STEPHEN. "THE MEXICAN IMMIGRANT".
    SOCIOLOGY AND SOCIAL RESEARCH, VOL. 12 (MARCH,
    1928), PP. 371-378 (SI).

BOGARDUS, EMORY STEPHEN. "THE MEXICAN IMMIGRANT AND THE
    QUOTA".   SOCIOLOGY AND SOCIAL RESEARCH, VOL.
    12 (MAY, 1928), PP. 371-378 (SI).

BOGARDUS, EMORY STEPHEN. "THE MEXICAN IMMIGRANT".
    JOURNAL OF APPLIED SOCIOLOGY, VOL. 11 (AUTUMN,
    1965), PP. 470-88 (SI).

BOGARDUS, EMORY STEPHEN. "THE MEXICAN IMMIGRANT AND THE
    QUOTA".   SOCIOLOGY AND SOCIAL RESEARCH, VOL.
    12 (AUTUMN, 1965), PP. 371-78 (SI).

BOGARDUS, EMORY STEPHEN. "THE MEXICAN IMMIGRANT AND
    SEGREGATION".   AMERICAN JOURNAL OF SOCIOLOGY, VOL.
    36 (AUTUMN, 1965), PP. 74-80 (SI).

BOGARDUS, EMORY STEPHEN. "THE MEXICAN IMMIGRANT AND
    SEGREGATION".   AMERICAN JOURNAL OF SOCIOLOGY,
    (JULY, 1930), PP. 74-80 (SI).

BOGARDUS, EMORY STEPHEN. "THE MEXICAN IMMIGRANT AND
    SEGREGATION".   AMERICAN JOURNAL OF SOCIOLOGY, VOL.
    13 (JULY, 1930), PP. 74-80 (SI).

BOGARDUS, EMORY STEPHEN. "WHAT RACE ARE FILIPINOS".
    SOCIOLOGY AND SOCIAL RESEARCH, VOL. 26 (JANUARY-FEBRUARY,
    1932), PP. 274-79.

BOGARDUS, EMORY STEPHEN. ESSENTIALS OF AMERICANIZATION.
    LOS ANGELES, CALIFORNIA: UNIVERSITY OF SOUTHERN
    CALIFORNIA PRESS, 1919 (SI).

BOGARDUS, EMORY STEPHEN. ESSENTIALS OF AMERICANIZATION.
    LOS ANGELES, CALIFORNIA: JESSE RAY MILLER, 1923 (SI).

BOGARDUS, EMORY STEPHEN. IMMIGRATION AND RACE ATTITUDES.
    NEW YORK, NEW YORK: D. C. HEATH AND COMPANY, 1928 (SI).

BOGARDUS. MEXICAN IMMIGRANT: ANNOTATEDBIBLIOGRAPHY (B*).

BOGARDUS, EMORY STEPHEN. RESIDENT IMMIGRANT PROBLEM.
    PROCEEDINGS OF THE INSTITUTE OF INTERNATIONAL
    RELATIONS, FIFTH SESSION, LOS ANGELES, 1930 (SI).

BOGARDUS, EMORY STEPHEN. THE NEW SOCIAL RESEARCH.   LOS
    ANGELES, CALIFORNIA: J. R. MILLER, 1926.

BOGARDUS, EMORY STEPHEN. THE SURVEY OF RACE RELATIONS ON
    THE PACIFIC COAST.   LOS ANGELES, CALIFORNIA: COUNCIL
    ON INTERNATIONAL RELATIONS, MAY 1926.

BOGEN, DAVID. "CONCERNING ZOOT SUIT GANGS".   COMMUNITY
    COORDINATION, VOL. 11 (JANUARY-FEBRUARY,   1943), PP.
    1-3.

BOGUE, DONALD J. THE POPULATION OF THE UNITED STATES.
    GLENCO: THE FREE PRESS, 1959.

BOGUE, TAYS ELIZABETH. MODIFICATION OF ATTITUDES TOWARD
    MEXICAN AMERICANS.   UNIVERSITY OF CALIFORNIA AT LOS
    ANGELES, MASTER'S THESIS (1969) (PY AN).

BOKE, RICHARD L. "ROOTS IN THE EARTH".   NEW MEXICO
    QUARTERLY REVIEW, VOL. 11 (1941), PP. 25-36.

BONGARTZ. "CHICANO REBELLION: DEMAND COURSES (PL*).

BONGARTZ. "NO MORE SOMBREROS: CHICANOREBELLION" (PL*).

BONGARTZ. "LA RAZA IN REVOLT" (PL*).

BONGARZ. "LA RAZA IN REVOLT" (PL*).

BONJEAN, CHARLES M. "COMMUNITY LEADERSHIP: A CASE STUDY
    AND CONCEPTUAL REFINEMENT".   AMERICAN JOURNAL
    OF SOCIOLOGY, VOL. 68 (MAY,   1963), PP. 672-681.

BORAH, W. R. "NEIGHBORS AND FRIENDS, A PLEA FOR JUSTICE
    TO MEXICO".   THE NATION, VOL. 124 , PP. 392-94.

BORAH, WOODROW; COOK, SHERBURNE F.   "MARRIAGE AND LEGITIMACY
    IN MEXICAN CULTURE: MEXICO AND CALIFORNIA".
    CALIFORNIA LAW REVIEW, VOL. 54 (MAY,   1966),
    PP. 946-1008 (HS).

BORREGO. SOME EDUCATIONAL ASPECTS AFFECTING (ED*).

BORTON. "REACHING CULTURALLY DEPRIVED" (AN*).

BORUP. CONTRASTING POLITICAL VALUESBEHAVIOR (PL*).

BOSSARD, JAMES H. S. "THE BILINGUAL AS A PERSON—
     LINGUISTIC IDENTIFICATION WITH STATUS".   AMERICAN
     SOCIOLOGICAL REVIEW, VOL. 23 (DECEMBER, 1945), PP.
     699-709 (LA).

BOSWICK.   "THEY SPEAK SAME LANGUAGE"   (ED*).

BOWYER, H. "SOCIAL WELFARE WORK IN RURAL MEXICO".
     BULLETIN OF PAN AMERICAN UNION,   NO. 56 , PP. 453-58.

BRADFORD.   "THE MEXICAN CHILD OUR AMERICAN (ED*).

BRADSHAW, BENJAMIN SPENCER. SOME DEMOGRAPHIC ASPECTS OF
     MARRIAGE: A COMPARATIVE STUDY OF THREE ETHNIC GROUPS.
     AUSTIN, TEXAS: UNIVERSITY OF TEXAS, MASTER'S THESIS
     (1960) (AN).

BRAGER, GEORGE, AND SPECHT, HARRY. MOBILIZING THE POOR
     FOR SOCIAL ACTION.   THE SOCIAL WELFARE FORUM.
     OFFICIAL PROCEEDINGS OF THE ANNUAL MEETING OF
     THE NATIONAL CONFERENCE ON SOCIAL WELFARE, MAY 23-25,
     1965, ATLANTIC CITY. NEW YORK: COLUMBIA UNIVERSITY
     PRESS, 1965.

BRANN.   HOUSING MIGRANT AGRICULTURALWORKERS (LW*).

BRATRUD.   STRUCTURE FUNCTION MUNICIPALGOVERNMENT (PL*).

BRATT, CHARLES. "PROFILES: LOS ANGELES".   JOURNAL
     OF EDUCATIONAL SOCIOLOGY, VOL. 19 (NOVEMBER 1945),
     PP. 179-186 (ED).

BRATTEN, JAMES H. "THE MEXICAN IMMIGRATION PROBLEM".
     PAN PACIFIC PROGRESS, VOL. 8 (1928), PP. 39-52 (SI).

BRESETTE, LINNA E. MEXICANS IN THE UNITED STATES.
     WASHINGTON: NATIONAL CATHOLIC WELFARE CONFERENCE, 1930
     (SI).

BRICKMAN.   "EL PASO WAS WIDE OPEN BORDER (ED*).

BRIDGES.   "THE RELATION INTELLIGENCE TO (ED*).

BRIEGEL, KAYE. 'THE DEVELOPMENT OF MEXICAN-AMERICAN
     ORGANIZATIONS.'   IN MANUEL P. SERVIN, AN AWAKENING
     MINORITY.

BRIEGEL, KAYE. THE HISTORY OF POLITICAL ORGANIZATIONS
     AMONG MEXICAN-AMERICANS IN LOS ANGELES SINCE THE
     SECOND WORLD WAR.   UNIVERSITY OF SOUTHERN CALIFORNIA,
     MASTER'S THESIS (1967) (PL).

BRIM, ORVILLE G. AND WHEELER, STANTON. SOCIALIZATION AFTER
     CHILDHOOD: TWO ESSAYS.   NEW YORK: JOHN WILEY AND
     SONS, 1966 (EC).

BROADBEN, ELIZABETH. THE DISTRIBUTION OF MEXICAN POPULATIONS
    IN THE UNITED STATES. UNIVERSITY OF CHICAGO,
    MASTER'S THESIS (1944) (GE).

BROADBENT, ELIZABETH. "MEXICAN POPULATION IN SOUTHWESTERN
    UNITED STATES". TEXAS GEOGRAPHIC MAGAZINE, VOL. 5
    NO. 2 (1941) (GE).

BRODY. BEHAVIOR NEW ENVIRONMENTS: ADAPTATION (SI*).

BRODY, EUGENE B. MINORITY GROUP ADOLESCENTS IN THE UNITED
    STATES. BALTIMORE: WILLIAMS AND WILKINS, 1968.

BROGAN. AMERICAN CHARACTER (PY*).

BRONSON. CHANGES PERSONALITY NEEDS VALUES (RE*).

BROOKS, MELVIN S. THE SOCIAL PROBLEMS OF MIGRANT FARM
    LABORERS. CARBONDALE, ILLINOIS: SOUTHERN ILLINOIS
    UNIVERSITY PRESS, 1960 (EC).

BROOKS, MELVIN S. THE SOCIAL PROBLEMS OF MIGRANT FARM
    LABORERS. WASHINGTON, D. C.: DEPARTMENT OF HEALTH,
    EDUCATION AND WELFARE, (1960) (EC SI).

BROOKSHIRE. "SOME NOTES INTEGRATION MEXICAN-AMERICANS
    (EC*).

BROOM, LEONARD. SOCIOLOGY. EVANSTON, ILLINOIS: ROW,
    PETERSON AND CO., 1958.

BROOM, LEONARD; SHEVSKY, ESHREF. "MEXICANS IN THE UNITED
    STATES: A PROBLEM IN SOCIAL DIFFERENTIATION".
    SOCIOLOGY AND SOCIAL RESEARCH, VOL. 36 (JANUARY-FEBRUARY
    1952), PP. 150-58.

BROOM. "SEX RACE DIFFERENCES DISCOVERED (ED*).

BROOM. "A STUDY RACE SEX DIFFERENCES (ED*).

BROPHY. FOUNDLINGS FRONTIER (HA*).

BROPHY, A. BLAKE. BABY TRAIN WEST: A REVEALING ENCOUNTER
    WITH RACIAL AND RELIGIOUS INTOLERANCE IN ARIZONA
    TERRITORY, 1904-1935. ARIZONA STATE UNIVERSITY,
    MASTER'S THESIS (1969) (HA PY).

BROWDER, WALTER G. THE PATTERN OF INTERNAL MOBILITY IN
    TEXAS: A SUBREGIONAL STUDY. AUSTIN TEXAS: UNIVERSITY
    OF TEXAS PRESS, 1944 (EC).

BROWH, F. GERALD,; MURPHY, THOMAS P. (EDITORS). EMERGING
    PATTERNS IN URBAN ADMINISTRATION. LEXINGTON,
    MASSACHUSETTS: HEATH LEXINGTON BOOKS, 1970 (EC).

BROWN.   MINORITIES, SCHOOLS POLITICS   (ED*).

BROWN, EDWIN R.   "THE CHALLENGE OF MEXICAN IMMIGRATION".
    MISSIONARY REVIEW OF THE WORLD, VOL. 49   (MARCH
    1926), PP. 192-196 (RE SI).

BROWN, FRANCIS J.   OUR RACIAL AND NATIONAL MINORITIES.
    NEW YORK, NEW YORK: PRENTICE-HALL, INC., 1945.

BROWN, FRANCIS J. AND ROUCEK, JOSEPH S.   'SPANISH AMERICANS.'
    IN ONE AMERICA.

BROWN, FRANCIS J. AND ROUCEK, JOSEPH S.   ONE AMERICA: THE
    HISTORY AND CONTRIBUTIONS AND PRESENT PROBLEMS OF OUR
    RACIAL AND NATIONAL MINORITIES.   NEW YORK: PRENTICE-HALL,
    1946 (HUS).

BROWN.   THEY SEE THEMSELVES; DOCUMENTARY   (ED*).

BROWN.   COMMUNAL INDIVIDUAL PERSONALITY   (AN*).

BROWNING, HARLEY L.; MC LEMORE, S. DALE.   "THE SPANISH
    SURNAME POPULATION OF TEXAS".   PUBLIC AFFAIRS
    COMMENT, VOL. 10 NO. 1 (JANUARY 1964).

BROWNING, HARLEY L.; MC LEMORE , S. DALE. A STATISTICAL
    PROFILE OF THE SPANISH-SURNAME POPULATION OF TEXAS.
    AUSTIN, TEXAS: POPULATION RESEARCH CENTER, UNIVERSITY
    OF TEXAS, JUNE 9, 1964.

BROZ, PERRY. "A PLACE IN THE SHADE".   ARIZONA TEACHER,
    (NOVEMBER 1961), PP. 31-33 (ED).

BRUMMET, BEATRICE G. "SOFIA LOSES HER SUNBURN".
    THE TEXAS OUTLOOK, VOL. 40 (DECEMBER 1956), PP. 14-15.

BRUNER.   "CULTURAL TRANSMISSION CULTURAL   (AN*).

BRUNER.   STUDY THINKING (PY*).

BRYAN.   "MEXICAN IMMIGRANTS UNITED STATES" (EC*).

BUCKLEY.   "DONT EAT GRAPES ALONG WITHME" (EC*).

BUCKLEY, W. F. JR. "VICTORY OF CESAR CHAVEZ".   NATIONAL
    REVIEW, VOL. 22 (SEPTEMBER 8, 1970), P. 965 (EC).

BUCKLEY, W. F.; SANCHEZ, R. V. (EDITORS).   "VIVA SANCHEZ.
    MAMA: MEXICAN-AMERICAN MINORITY AGAINST; LETTER".
    NATIONAL REVIEW, VOL. 21 (AUGUST 12, 1969),
    PP. 791-792 (EC).

BUCKNER, DELLOS URBAN. STUDY OF THE LOWER RIO GRANDE
    VALLEY AS A CULTURE AREA.   UNIVERSITY OF TEXAS AT
    AUSTIN, MASTER'S THESIS (1929).

BUECHEL.   FAMILY EXPENDITURES TWENTY-ONE   (EC*).

BUECHEL.   FAMILY EXPENDITURE PER CAPITA   (EC*).

BUECHLEY, ROBERT W. "A REPRODUCIBLE METHOD OF COUNTING
    PERSONS OF SPANISH SURNAME".   JOURNAL OF THE AMERICAN
    STATISTICAL ASSOCIATION, VOL. 56 (MARCH 1961), PP.
    88-97.

BUECHLEY.   "EXCESS LUNG CANCER MORTALITY (MD*).

BULLOUGH.   POVERTY, ETHNIC IDENTITY, HEALTH (EC*).

BUNKER, ROBERT AND ADAIR, JOHN. THE FIRST LOOK AT
    STRANGERS.   NEW BRUNSWICK, NEW JERSEY: RUTGERS
    UNIVERSITY PRESS, 1959 (SI).

BURGESS, REV. THOMAS. "ON THE AMERICAN SIDE OF THE RIO
    GRANDE".   MISSIONARY REVIEW OF THE WORLD, VOL. 50
    (SEPTEMBER 1927), PP. 689-692.

BURGUM, B. "SOCIOLOGY OF OSCAR LEWIS AS A CRITICQUE OF
    IMPERIALISM".   SCIENCE AND SOCIETY, VOL. 31 (SUMMER
    1967), PP. 323-337 (AN).

BURMA, JOHN H. 'SPANISH-SPEAKING CHILDREN.'   IN ELI
    GINZBERG, (ED) THE NATION'S CHILDREN.

BURMA, JOHN H. "INTERETHNIC MARRIAGE IN LOS ANGELES,
    1948-1959".   SOCIAL FORCES, VOL. 42 (DECEMBER
    1963), PP. 156-165.

BURMA, JOHN H. "RESEARCH NOTE ON THE MEASUREMENT OF
    INTERRACIAL MARRIAGE".   AMERICAN JOURNAL OF SOCIOLOGY,
    VOL. 57 (MAY 1952), PP. 587-589.

BURMA, JOHN H. "SPANISH-SPEAKING GROUPS IN THE UNITED
    STATES".   RURAL SOCIOLOGY, VOL. 19 (SEPTEMBER
    1954), PP. 309-310.

BURMA, JOHN H. "THE BACKGROUND OF THE CURRENT SITUATION
    FOR FILIPINO-AMERICANS".   SOCIAL FORCES, VOL. 30
    (OCTOBER 1951), PP. 42-48.

BURMA, JOHN H. "THE PRESENT STATUS OF THE SPANISH-AMERICANS
    IN NEW MEXICO".   SOCIAL FORCES, VOL. 28 (DECEMBER
    1949), PP. 133-138 (HN).

BURMA, JOHN H. MEXICAN AMERICANS IN THE UNITED STATES:
    A READER.   NEW YORK: SCHENKMAN PUBLISHING COMPANY,
    INC, 1970.

BURMA, JOHN H. SPANISH-SPEAKING GROUPS IN THE UNITED
    STATES. DURHAM, NORTH CAROLINA: DUKE UNIVERSITY
    PRESS, 1954.

BURMA, JOHN H. THE BURMA REPORT. THE BURMA REPORT
    CONCERNING RECOMMENDATIONS FOR EL RITO NORMAL SCHOOL
    (ED).

BURMA, JOHN H.; JORGENSON, JANET. "THE PUSH OF AN ELBOW;
    CIVIL RIGHTS AND OUR SPANISH-SPEAKING MINORITY".
    FRONTIER, VOL. 2 (JULY 1960), PP. 10-12 (LW).

BURMA, JOHN H.; JORGENSON, JANET
    BURMA, JOHN H. "THE PUSH OF AN ELBOW; CIVIL RIGHTS
    AND OUR SPANISH-SPEAKING MINORITY". FRONTIER, VOL.
    11 (JULY 1960), PP. 10-12 (LW).

BURMA, JOHN H.; MASUOKA, JITSUICHI; VALIEN, PRESTON (ED.).
    RACE RELATIONS: PROBLEMS AND THEORY. CHAPEL HILL:
    UNIVERSITY OF NORTH CAROLINA PRESS,.

BURNHILL, JAMES. "THE MEXICAN AMERICAN QUESTION".
    POLITICAL AFFAIRS, VOL. 32 (DECEMBER 1953),
    PP. 50-63 (PL).

BURNHILL, JAMES. "THE MEXICAN PEOPLE IN THE SOUTWEST".
    POLITICAL AFFAIRS, VOL. 32 (SEPTEMBER 1953), PP.
    43-52 (PL).

BURNSTEIN. "END SLURS MEXICAN AMERICANS" (FILM*).

BURR, ELIZABETH. "ALONG THE MIGRANT STREAM". LIBRARY
    JOURNAL, (JANUARY 15, 1966), PP. 335-336 (SI).

BURRIS, QUINCY GUY. 'LATIN AMERICANS.' IN FRANCIS J.
    BROWN AND JOSEPH SLABEY ROUCEK, (EDS) ONE AMERICA.

BURRIS, QUINCY GUY. "JUAN, A RURAL PORTRAIT". SURVEY
    GRAPHIC, VOL. 33 (DECEMBER 1944), PP. 499-503.

BURT. "MORES NURSING CARE: NURSES (MD*).

BUSTAMANTE, CHARLES J.; BUSTAMENTE, PATRICIA L. THE
    MEXICAN-AMERICAN AND THE UNITED STATES. MOUNTAIN
    VIEW: PATTY-LAR PUBLICATIONS, LTD., 1969 (HUS).

BUSTAMANTE. NUEVO BERNAL DIAZ C SEA HISTORIA (HM*).

BUSTRILLOS, M. R. DECISION MAKING STYLES OF SELECTED
    MEXICAN HOMEMAKERS. MICHIGAN STATE UNIVERSITY, PHD.
    DISSERTATION (1963) (PY).

BUTTE COUNTY SUPERINTENDENT OF SCHOOLS. ETHNIC CULTURAL
    BIBLIOGRAPHY: (B*).

BUTTER, MRS. J. W. "WOMEN OF MEXICO". MISSIONARY REVIEW,
    VOL. 39 (AUTUMN 1953), PP. 181-86 (HM).

CABRERA. RECOMMENDATICNS RELATIVE TO ORGANIZATION (ED*).

CABRERA, Y. ARTURO:. EMERGING FACES (THE MEXICAN-AMERICANS)..
    WM C. BROWN COMPANY,.

CACY, GEORGE L. REPORT. COMMISSION ON INTERNATIONAL AND
    INTERRACIAL FACTORS IN THE PROBLEM OF (EXICANS IN THE
    UNITED STATES.

CALCOTT. F. "THE MEXICAN PEON IN TEXAS
    THE MEXICAN PEON IN TEXAS". SURVEY, VOL. 6 (JUNE
    26, 1920), P. 437.

CALCOTT. F. "THE MEXICAN PEON IN TEXAS". SURVEY, VOL.
    44 (JUNE 26, 1920), PP. 437-38.

CALDERON, C. I. FOUR KEYS TO A BETTER SPEECH. TEXAS
    OUTLOOK, 48 (ED).

CALDERON, CARLOS. "FEWEST WORDS TO OPEN THE WIDEST DOORS".
    TEXAS OUTLOOK, VOL. 40 (MAY 1956), PP. 14-16 (ED).

CALDERON, CARLOS. "SEEING SOUNDS". TEXAS OUTLOOK, VOL.
    38 (OCTOBER 1954), PP. 12-13 (ED).

CALDWELL. "SEX DIFFERENCE SCHOOL ACHIEVEMENT (ED*).

CALDWELL. "TEACHER GRADES AS CRITERIA ACHIEVEMENT (ED*).

CALEF. DISTRIBUTION POPULATICN CALIFCRNIA (GE*).

CALIFORNIA ADULT ECUCATION BUREAU. S. RECOMMENDATIONS
    RELATIVE TO THE ORGANIZATION OF ACVISORY CCMMITTEES
    WHE N WORKING WITH ADULTS WITH SPANISH SURNAMES.
    SACRAMENTO, CALIFORNIA: JAMES L. TOOGOOD, 1969.

CALIFORNIA ADVISCRY COMMITTEE TO THE U. S. SEPORT
    CALIFCRNIA POLICE - MINORITY (LW*).

CALIFORNIA CITIZENS COMMITTEE ON CIVIL DISTURBANCES IN LOS
    ANGELES. REPORT RECOMMENDATIONS (LW*).

CALIFORNIA COMMISSION OF IMMIGRATICN AND HOUSING.
    A COMMUNITY SURVEY MADE IN LOS ANGELES CITY. SAN
    FRANCISCO: CALIFORNIA COMMISSION OF IMMIGRATION AND
    HOUSING, 1919 (SI).

CALIFORNIA COMMITTEE FOR THE STUDY CF TRANSIENT YOUTH.
    TRANSIENT YOUTH IN CALIFORNIA; A NATIONAL, STATE AND
    RURAL PROBLEM: REP ORT AND RECOMMENDATIONS.
    LOS ANGELES: CALIFCRNIA CCMMITTEE FOR THE STUDY OF
    TRANSIENT YOUTH, 1948.

CALIFORNIA CORRECTICNS DEPARTMENT.   CALIFORNIA PRISONERS;
    SUMMARY (LW*).

CALIFORNIA DEPARTMENT OF THE YOUTH AUTHORITY.   ANNUAL
    STATISTICAL REPORT, 1961.   SACRAMENTO, CALIFORNIA:
    CALIFORNIA DEPARTMENT OF THE YOUTH AUTHORITY, YOUTH
    AND ADULT CORRECTIONS AGENCY, 1962 (EC).

CALIFCRNIA DEPARTMENT OF THE YOUTH AUTHORITY.   CHARACTERISTICS
    OF THE CALIFORNIA YOUTH AUTHORITY PAROLE CASELOAD.
    SACRAMENTO, CALIFORNIA: CALIFORNIA DEPARTMENT OF THE
    YOUTH AUTHORITY DIVISION OF RESEARCH, JUNE 30, 1963
    (LW).

CALIFCRNIA DEPARTMENT OF THE YOUTH AUTHORITY.   EMPLOYMENT
    TRENDS AMCNG CALIFORNIA YOUTH AUTHORITY WARDS
    ON PAROLE, 1948-1962.   RESEARCH REPORT NO. 34.
    SACRAMENTO, CALIFORNIA: CALIFORNIA DEPARTMENT OF THE
    YOUTH AUTHORITY DIVISICN CF RESEARCH, JANUARY 16, 1963
    (LW).

CALIFORNIA DEPARTMENT OF INDUSTRIAL RELATIONS.   NEGROES
    MEXICAN-AMERICANS SOUTH   (EC*).

CALIFORNIA GOVERNOR C. C. YOUNG'S MEXICAN FACT-FINDING
    COMMITTEE.   MEXICANS IN CALIFORNIA.   SAN FRANCISCO,
    CALIFORNIA: R & E SESEARCH ASSOCIATES, 1970.

CALIFORNIA INTERGROUP RELATICNS BUREAU. S.   DISTRIBUTION
    RACIAL ETHNIC GROUPS   (ED*).

CALIFORNIA MINERS ASSOCIATION.   CALIFORNIA MINES MINERALS
    (EC*).

CALIFORNIA CFFICE OF THE GOVERNOR.   NEGROES MEXICAN-AMERICANS
    CALIFORNIA   (EC*).

CALIFORNIA STATE COLLEGE AT SACRAMENTC.   RESEARCH STUDY
    FELT NEEDS THREE (AN*).

CALIFORNIA STATE COMMISSICN ON HOUSING AND IMMIGRATION.
    ANNUAL REPORTS.   SACRAMENTO, CALIFORNIA: CALIFORNIA
    HOUSING AND IMMIGRATION COMMISSION, (SI).

CALIFCRNIA STATE COMMITTEE FOR THE STUDY CF TRANSIENT
    YOUTH.   TRANSIENT YOUTH IN CALIFORNIA: POLICE-MINORITY
    RELATIONS.   ??NO INFORMATION??, AUGUST 1963.

CALIFORNIA STATE DEPARTMENT OF SOCIAL WELFARE.   HEALTH,
    RELIEF, DELINQUENCYCONDITIONS   (MO*).

CALIFORNIA STATE DEPARTMENT OF CCRRECTIONS.   ANNUAL
    STATISTICAL REPORT.   SACRAMENTO, CALIFORNIA:
    CALIFORNIA YOUTH AND ADULT CORRECTIONS AGENCY,
    958-1962 (LW).

CALIFORNIA STATE DEPARTMENT OF INDUSTRIAL RELATIONS.
    CALIFORNIANS SPANISH SURNAMES: (EC*).

CALIFORNIA STATE DEPARTMENT OF CORRECTIONS.   CALIFORNIA
    PRISONERS, 1960.   SACRAMENTO, CALIFORNIA: CALIFORNIA
    STATE DEPARTMENT OF CORRECTIONS, RESEARCH DIVISION,
    ADMINISTRATIVE STATISTICS SECTION, 1961.

CALIFORNIA STATE DEPARTMENT OF EMPLOYMENT.   CHARACTERISTICS
    FARM LABOR JOB   (ED*).

CALIFORNIA STATE DEPARTMENT OF SOCIAL WELFARE.   CONTRASTS
    BETWEEN SPANISH FOLK AND ANGLO URBAN CULTURAL VALUES.
    CALIFORNIA:DEPARTMENT OF SOCIAL WELFARE, NO DATE (AN).

CALIFORNIA STATE DEPARTMENT OF SOCIAL WELFARE.   IMPLICATIONS
    OF SPANISH AMERICAN CULTURE ON FAMILY LIFE.
    CALIFORNIA: DEPARTMENT OF SOCIAL WELFARE, NO DATE.

CALIFORNIA STATE DEPARTMENT OF SOCIAL WELFARE.   IMPLICATIONS
    CULTURAL VALUESTO   (ED*).

CALIFORNIA STATE DEPARTMENT OF EMPLOYMENT.   MEXICAN
    NATIONALS CALIFORNIAAGRICULTURE   (ED*).

CALIFORNIA STATE DEPARTMENT OF INDUSTRIAL RELATIONS.
    MEXICANS CALIFORNIA   (ED*).

CALIFORNIA STATE DEPARTMENT OF EMPLOYMENT.   REPORT
    TO LEGISLATURE SPANISH-SPEAKING   (ED*).

CALIFORNIA STATE DEPARTMENT OF SOCIAL WELFARE.   THE HISTORY
    OF SPANISH-AMERICANS.   CALIFORNIA: DEPARTMENT
    OF SOCIAL WELFARE, 1963 (HSW).

CALIFORNIA STATE DIVISION OF CRIMINAL LAW AND ENFORCEMENT.
    GUIDE TO COMMUNITY RELATIONSPEACE   (LW*).

CALIFORNIA UNIVERSITY OF CALIFORNIA.   COST LIVING STUDIES:
    HOW MEXICANS   (EC*).

CALIFORNIA YOUTH AUTHORITY.   CHARACTERISTICS OF THE
    CALIFORNIA YOUTH AUTHORITY PAROLE CASELOAD.
    SACRAMENTO, CALIFORNIA: CALIFORNIA YOUTH AUTHORITY,
    1969 AND 1968 (LW).

CALIFORNIA.   DEPARTMENT OF SOCIAL WELFARE.   CULTURAL
    DIFFERENCES-TRAINING IN NON-DISCRIMINATION.
    SACRAMENTO: CALIFORNIA DEPARTMENT OF SOCIAL WELFARE,
    1965.

CALIFORNIA. GOVERNOR C. C. YOUNG'S MEXICAN FACT-FINDING
    COMMITTEE.   MEXICANS IN CALIFORNIA.   SAN FRANCISCO:
    CALIFORNIA STATE PRINTING OFFICE, 1930 (EC).

CALVO. "RIVER, NOT A WAVE" (PL*).

CAMARILLO, ALBERTO M. "CHICANO URBAN HISTORY: A STUDY OF
    COMPTON'S BARRIO, 1936-1970".   AZTLAN--CHICANO
    JOURNAL OF THE SOCIAL SCIENCES AND ARTS, VOL. 2 NO.
    2 (FALL 1972), PP. 79-106 (HSW).

CAMARILLO, ALBERTO M. "RESEARCH NOTE ON CHICANO COMMUNITY
    LEADERS: THE G. I. GENERATION".   AZTLAN--CHICANO
    JOURNAL OF THE SOCIAL SCIENCES AND THE ARTS, VOL. 2
    NO. 2 (FALL 1971), PP. 145-150.

CAMBLON, RUTH. "MEXICANS IN CHICAGO".   THE FAMILY, VOL.
    7 (NOVEMBER 1926), PP. 207-11.

CAMPBELL.   "TEACHING ABOUT CHICANO" (ED*).

CAMPBELL, DONALD T. THE GENERALITY OF AN ATTITUDE.
    UNIVERSITY OF CALIFORNIA, PHD. DISSERTATION (1947).

CARAWAY, CORINE D. A STUDY OF THE ATTITUDES OF LATIN
    AMERICAN MOTHERS TOWARD JUVENILE PROB ATION OFFICERS.
    AUSTIN: UNIVERSITY OF TEXAS, 1961.

CARDENAS, JOSE A. THE CHASM OF CONFLICTING CONCERNS.
    ADDRESS PRESENTED TO THE TEOAS UNITED COMMUNITY
    SERVICES. NOVEMBER 17, 1970.

CARILLO, ALFONSO R. "MEXICO LOOKS AT THE UNITED STATES".
    SOCIOLOGY AND SOCIAL RESEARCH, VOL. 15 (WINTER
    1971), PP. 558-61.

CARL, MAY. "OUR ANTI-SOCIAL MEXICAN CLASS".   LOS ANGELES
    COUNTY EMPLOYEE, VOL. 2 (1929), P. 12.

CARLSON, GLEN E. "COMMUNITY ORGANIZATION TURNS A CORNER".
    SOCIOLOGY AND SOCIAL RESEARCH,   (MARCH 1948), PP.
    782-786.

CARLSON.   "INTELLIGENCE AMERICAN CHILDREN (PY*).

CARLSON, LEWIS H. ; COLBERN, GEORGE A. IN THEIR PLACE:
    WHITE AMERICA DEFINES HER MINORITIES.   NEW YORK:
    JOHN WILEY & SONS, 1972.

CARLSON, OLEN E. COMMUNITY ORGANIZATION TURNS A CORNER.
    SOCIOLOGY AND SOCIAL RESEARCH, 32.

CARPENTER, C. C. MEXICANS IN CALIFORNIA: A CASE STUDY OF
    SEGREGATIONVS. NON-SEGRAGATION OF MEXICAN CHILDREN.
    UNIVERSITY OF SOUTHERN CALIFORNIA, MASTER'S THESIS
    (1934).

CARRENO.   MISIONEROS EN MEXICO (RE*).

CARRERA STAMPA, MANUEL. "COMICA TIPICA DE MMEXICO".
MEMORIAS DE LA ACADEMIA MEXICANA, VOL. 20 (1961),
PP. 21-41.

CARRILLO. IMPORTANCIA ECONOMICA SOCIALDE (EC*).

CARTER, HARLON G. "THE AIRLIFT". MONTHLY REVIEW, VOL.
9 (DECEMBER 1951), PP. 72-74.

CASAVANTES, EDWARD J. A NEW LOOK AT THE ATTRIBUTES OF THE
MEXICAN AMERICAN. ALBUQUERQUE, NEW MEXICO: SOUTHWEST
COOPERATIVE EDUCATIONAL LABRATORY, INC., MARCH 1969.

CASAVANTES, EDWARD. "PRIDE AND PREJUDICE: A MEXICAN-AMERICAN
DILEMMA". CIVIL RIGHTS DIGEST, VOL. 3 (WINTER
1970), PP. 22-27.

CASAVANTES, EDWARD. PRIDE AND PREJUDICE: A MEXICAN-AMERICAN
DILEMMA. IN NATHANIEL N. WAGNER AND MARSHA J. HAUG.
SAINT LOUIS, MISSOURI: THE C. V. MOSBY COMPANY, 1971.

CASE, FRED E.; KIRK, JAMES H. THE HOUSING STATUS OF
MINORITY FAMILIES: LOS ANGELES, 1956. LOS ANGELES:
UNIVERSITY OF CALIFORNIA. REAL ESTATE RESEARCH PROGRAM
AND THE LOS ANGELES URBAN LEAGUE, 1958.

CASO, ANTONIO. PRINCIPIOS DE ESTETICA. MEXICO: D. F.,
1925.

CASO, ANTONIO. EL PROBLEMA DE MEXICO Y LA IDEOLOGIA
NACIONAL. MEXCIO: LIBRO-MEXICO, 1955.

CASTORENA JOSE. "THE MODERN CHALLENGE TO THE CHURCH".
REGENERACION, VOL. 1 (JANUARY 1970), P. 11.

CATAPHSAN, B. T. "THE FILIPINO LABOR CYCLES IN THE U. S.".
SOCIOLOGY AND SOCIAL RESEARCH, VOL. 19 (SEPTEMBER
1934), PP. 61-63.

CATAPUSAN, B. T. "FILIPINO IMMIGRANTS AND PUBLIC RELIEF
IN THE UNITED STATES". SOCIOLOGY AND SOCIAL
RESEARCH, VOL. 23 (JULY-AUGUST 1939), PP. 546-54.

CATAPUSAN, B. T. "FILIPINO INTERMARRIAGE PROBLEMS IN THE
UNITED STATES". SOCIOLOGY AND SOCIAL RESEARCH, VOL.
19 (SEPTEMBER 1934), PP. 61-63.

CATAPUSAN, B. T. "LEISURE TIME PROBLEMS OF FILIPINO
IMMIGRANTS". SOCIOLOGY AND SOCIAL RESEARCH, VOL.
24 (JULY 1940), PP. 541-49.

CATAPUSAN, B. T. "PROBLEMS OF FILIPINO STUDENTS IN
AMERICA". SOCIOLOGY AND SOCIAL RESEARCH, VOL. 26
(NOVEMBER 1941), PP. 146-53.

CATAPUSAN, B. T. THE FILIPINO'S SOCIAL ADJUSTMENT IN THE
    UNITED STATES. UNIVERSITY OF SOUTHERN CALIFORNIA,
    PHD. DISSERTATION (1940).

CENTER FOR THE STUDY OF DEMOCRATIC INSTITUTIONS. THE
    MEXICAN AMERICANS. SANTA BARBARA, CALIFORNIA: THE
    CENTER,.

CERWIN, HERBERT. THESE ARE THE MEXICANS. NEW YORK:
    REYNAL & HITCHCOCK, 1947.

CHACON. "OPEN LETTER TO: WOMENS INTERNATIONAL (LMA*).

CHALDEK. "NURSING SERVICE MIGRANT WORKERS" (MD*).

CHAMBERS. CALIFORNIA FARM ORGANIZATIONS (EC*).

CHAMBERS, DONALD EVERARD. WILLINGNESS TO ADOPT HARD TO
    PLACE CHILDREN. WASHINGTON UNIVERSITY, PHD.
    DISSERTATION (1967) (ED PY).

CHAMBERS, R. L. "THE NEW MEXICO PATTERN". COMMON GROUND,
    VOL. 10 (SUMMER 1949), PP. 20-27 (AN).

CHANCE. "ACCULTURATION, SELF-IDENTIFICATION (AN*).

CHANDLER. MEXICAN AMERICAN PROTEST MOVEMENT (HT*).

CHAPMAN. "RELATION FAMILY SIZE TO INTELLIGENCE (PY*).

CHAPPELLE, ANGELA MARIE. LOCAL WELFARE WORK OF RELIGIOUS
    ORGANIZATIONS IN SAN ANTONIO, TEXAS. UNIVERSITY OF
    TEXAS AT AUSTIN, MASTER'S THESIS (1939) (RE).

CHASE. "MEXICANS KNOW HOW TO PLAY" (HM*).

CHASE. MEXICO, STUDY TWO AMERICAS (HM*).

CHAY. "FOR WHILE GATE WAS STUCK" (LI*).

CHAY. "I LIKE IT BETTER THAT WAY" (LMA*).

CHAY. "IN OTHER PEOPLES HOUSES" (LMA*).

CHAY. "SOMEONES UP AT MACHADOS" (LMA*).

CHAY. "THEN YOULL BE LEFT BEHIND" (LI*).

CHAY. "GRINGOS ARE FOOLS" (LMA*).

CHAY. "ITS ALL WORLD" (LMA*).

CHAY. "MARRIAGE IS DIFFERENT" (LMA*).

CHICAGO FREE WEEKLEY. "I REFUSE TO BE ABSORBED". CHICAGO
    FREE WEEKLY, VOL. 50 NO. 24 (APRIL 7, 1973), P. 3.

CHICANO TIMES.   CHICANOS: STUDENT REPORT SOCIAL   (ED*).

CHICANOS POR LA CAUSA.   "CHICANOS UNCHAINED"   (EC*).

CHRAMOSTA, SHARON.   DIRECOTRY OF COMMUNITY SERVICES IN THE
     SOUTHWEST AREA OF SAN ANTONIO, TEAS.   SAN ANTONIO:
     BISHOP'S COMMITTEE FOR THE SPANISH—SPEAKING, 1961.

CHRISTIANSEN, JOHN R.   "ESTIMATICN OF SOCIOECCNOMIC STATUS
     OF SPANISH—AMERICANS IN ATOSCOSA AND BEXAR COUNTIES,
     TEXAS".   ROCKY MOUNTAIN SOCIAL SCIENCE JOURNAL, VOL.
     2 NO. 1 (1965), PP. 215—222 (EC).

CITIZENS COMMITTEE FOR THE DEFENSE OF MEXICAN AMERICAN
     YOUTH.   SLEEPY LAGOON CASE (LW*).

CIVIL RIGHTS DIGEST.   "MEXICAN? AMERICAN?"   (LW*).

CLARK, LOIS MORGAN.   MOTIVATIONAL PATTERN IN CULTURALLY
     DISADVANTAGED FAMILIES.   TEMPE: ARIZONA STATE
     UNIVERSITY, 1965 (EC PY).

CLARK, MARGARET.   "THE SOCIAL FUNCTIONS OF MEXICAN—AMERICAN
     MEDICAL BELIEFS".   CALIFORNIA'S HEALTH, VOL. 16 (MAY
     1, 1959), PP. 153—155 (MD).

CLARK, MARGARET.   HEALTH IN THE MEXICAN CULTURE: A
     COMMUNITY STUDY.   BERKELEY: UNIVERSITY OF CALIFORNIA
     PRESS, 1951 & 1959 (MD).

CLARK, MARGARET.   SICKNESS AND HEALTH IN SAL SI PUEDES:
     MEXICAN—AMERICANS IN A CALIFORNIA COMMUNITY.
     UNIVERSITY OF CALIFCRNIA AT BERKELEY, PHD. DISSERTATION
     (1957) (MD).

CLEARY.   RECRUITMENT MINORITY PROGRAMS (LW*).

CLEATH.   "RENDERING UNTO CESAR" (RE*).

CLELAND, ROBERT GLASS.   ECONOMIC DCMINCE AND COMMUNITY
     POWER IN A MIDDLE—SIZED CITY.   MICHIGAN STATE
     UNIVERSITY, MASTER'S THESIS (1960) (AN).

CLENDENIN.   BLOCD BORDER: U. S. ARMY MEXICAN (EC*).

CLEVELAND, RICHARD.   VOAGES AND CCMMERCIAL ENTERPRISES OF
     THE SONS OF NEW ENGLAND.   NEW YORK: LEAVITT AND
     ALLEN, 1855.

CLINCHY, EVERETT R.   'EQUALITY OF OPPORTUNITY FOR LATIN—AMERICANS
     IN TEXAS: A STUDY OF THE ECONOMIC, SOCIAL, AND
     EDUCATIONAL DISCRIMINATION AGAINST LATIN—AMERICANS
     I.'   AN ARBOR: UNIVERSITY MICROFILMS (EC).

CLINE.   FARM LABOR ARIZONA SINCE TERMINATION (EC*).

CLINE, HOWARD F. "HERNANDO CORTES AND THE AZTEC INDIANS
    IN SPAIN".   THE QUARTERLY JOURNAL OF THE LIBRARY OF
    CONGRESS, VOL. 26 NO. 2 (APRIL 1969), PP. 70-90 (HS).

CLOFFORD, ROY A. THE RIO GRANDE FLOOD: A COMPARATIVE
    STUDY OF BORDER COMMUNITIES IN DISASTER.   WASHINGTON,
    D. C.: NATIONAL RESEARCH COUNCIL, NATIONAL RESEARCH
    GROUP, (1956).

COALSON.   "MEXICAN CONTRACT LABOR AMERICAN (EC*).

COAN. COMPARATIVE STUDY AMERICAN MEXICAN (ED*).

COHEN, ALBERT KIRCIDEL. DELINQUENT BOYS: THE CULTURE OF
    THE GANG.   GLENCOE, ILLINOIS:FREE PRESS, 1955.

COHEN.   HUELGA--IN STARR COUNTY TEXAS (LW*).

COHEN.   BURN BABY BURN: LOS ANGELESRACE (LW*).

COLE.   MINORITIES AMERICAN PROMISE: (ED*).

COLEMAN.   EQUALITY EDUCATIONAL OPPORTUNITY (ED*).

COLORADO UNIVERSITY.   VALUES BEHAVIOR TRI-ETHNIC COMMUNITY
    (HCO*).

COLORADO.   TIME CHANGE CHALLENGE (HCO*).

COLORADO.   A REPORT SPANISH-AMERICANS CORRECTIONAL (HCO*).

COLUMBIA UNIVERSITY. BUREAU OF APPLIED SOCIAL RESEARCH.
    THE PUERTO RICANS OF NEW YORK CITY.   NEW YORK: PUERTO
    RICO DEPARTMENT OF LABOR, 1948.

COMMISSION ON RACE AND HOUSING. WHERE SHALL WE LIVE.
    BERKELEY, UNIVERSITY OF CALIFORNIA PRESS, 1958 (EC).

COMMISSION ON SOCIAL AND ECONOMIC FACTORS. A STUDY
    OF SOCIAL AND ECONOMIC FACTORS RELATING TO SPANISH
    SPEAKING PEOPLE IN THE UNITED STATES.   A STUDY OF
    SOCIAL AND ECONOMIC FACTORS RELATING TO SPANISH
    SPEAKING PEOPLE IN THE UNITED STATES (EC).

COMMITTEE ON CULTURAL RELATIONS WITH LATIN AMERICA.   THE
    SEMINAR IN MEXICO.   NEW YORK, 1929 (AN).

COMMONS, JOHN ROGER. RACES AND IMMIGRANTS IN AMERICA.
    NEW YORK: MACMILLAN, 1920 (SI).

COMMUNITY SERVICE ORGANIZATION. EDUCATION STANDING
    COMMITTEE. GUIDELINES FOR USE BY CHAPTER EDUCATION
    COMMITTEES.   COMMUNITY SERVICE ORGANIZATION, MARCH
    23, 1957.

CONFERENCE ON ADULT BASIC EDUCATION. THE CHICANO IS COMING
    OUT OF TORTILLA FLATS, ONE WAY OR THE OTHER.
    ALBUQUERQUE: SOUTHWESTERN COOPERATIVE EDUCATION
    LABORATORY, 1968 (PL).

CONFERENCE ON EDUCATIONAL PROBLEMS OF SPECIAL CULTURAL
    GROUPS.   CULTURAL GROUPS HUMAN RELATIONS (ED*).

CONLEY, E. M. "AMERICANIZATION OF MEXICO".   AMERICAN
    REVIEW OF REVIEWS, VOL. 32 (JANUARY U, 1964), PP.
    724-25.

CONNECTICUT INTERRRACIAL COMMISSION.   INTERGROUP RELATIONS
    BIBLIOGRAPHY: (B*).

CONNELL, EARL M. THE MEXICAN POPULATION OF AUSTIN, TEXAS.
    SAN FRANCISCO, CALIFORNIA: R & E RESEARCH ASSOCIATES,
    1971 (AN).

CONNELL, EARLE MONROE. THE MEXICAN POPULATION OF AUSTIN.
    UNIVERSITY OF TEXAS, MASTER'S THESIS (1925) (AN).

COOKE.   PEOPLES SOUTHWEST (HSW*).

COON, GENE L. "PACHUCO".   COMMON GROUND, VOL. 8 (SPRING
    1948), PP. 49-52.

COOPER.   "GOOD NEIGHBORS BOXCARS" (ED*).

COOPER.   ATTITUDE CHILDREN TEACHERS TOWARD (ED*).

COOPER.   "A CONTINUING SCANDAL" (ED*).

COOPER, L. G. "AWAKENING AT SOCORRO".   TEXAS OUTLOOK,
    VOL. 50 (NOVEMBER 1966), PP. 34-35 (HN).

COPE.   "MINISTER WHO FOLLOWS MIGRANTS: (RE*).

COPP, NELSON GAGE. "WETBACKS" AND BRACEROS: MEXICAN
    MIGRANT LABORERS AND AMERICAN IMMIGRATION POLICY,
    1930-1960.   BOSTON UNIVERSITY, PHD. DISSERTATION
    (1963) (EC).

CORDOVA.   RELATIONSHIP ACCULTURATION, ACHIEVEMENT (LMA*).

CORDRY.   MEXICAN INDIAN CUSTOMS (HM*).

CORKER.   "OUR BROTHER MIGRANT" (EC*).

CORONA.   STUDY ADJUSTMENT INTERPERSONAL (PY*).

CORPIO, M. DEL. "AMERICANS AND MEXICO".   SURVEY, VOL.
    36 , PP. 642-43.

CORPUS, S. F. "SECOND GENERATION FILIPINOS IN LOS
    ANGELES".   SOCIOLOGY AND SOCIAL RESEARCH, VOL. 22
    (MAY 1938), PP. 446-51.

CORTES.   BEING AMERICAN AMERICA   (HUS*).

CORTES.   CHICANO SOCIAL BANDIT AS ROMANTIC   (HSW*).

CORTES, CARLOS E.   THE BENT CROSS. A HISTORY OF THE MEXICAN
    AMERICAN IN THE SAN BERNARDINO VALLEY.   WITH THE TEAM
    OF THE INLAND EMPIRE CHICANO COOPERATIVE HISTORY
    PROJECT (1974)..

CORTEZ, RUBEN.   ZOOT SUIT RIOTS: A HISTORY OF THE
    MEXICAN-AMERICAN IN LOS ANGELES.   PROBE.

COTHRAN.   OCCUPATIONAL PATTERNS RURAL URBAN   (EC*).

COUNCIL OF MEXICAN-AMERICAN AFFAIRS.   REPORT ON HOUSING
    DISCRIMINATION.   LOS ANGELES, MARCH 14, 1956.

COX.   ANALYSIS INTELLIGENCE SUB-NORMAL   (ED*).

COX, OLIVER CROMWELL.   CASTE, CLASS, AND RACE; A STUDY IN
    SOCIAL DYNAMICS.   GARDEN CITY, NEW YORK: DOUBLEDAY,
    1948.

CRADDOCK, GEORGE W., DAVIS, CALVIN E., AND MOOR, JEANNE
    L.   SOCIAL DISADVANTAGEMENT AND DEPENDENCY.
    LEXINGTON, MASSACHUSETTS: HEATH LEXINGTON BOOKS, 1970.

CRAIN, FOREST BURR.   THE OCCUPATIONAL DISTRIBUTION
    OF SPANISH-NAME PEOPLE IN AUSTIN, TEXAS.   UNIVERSITY
    OF TEXAS, MASTER'S THESIS (1948) (EC).

CRAIN, FOREST BURR.   A STUDY OF OCCUPATIONAL DISTRIBUTION
    OF SPANISH-NAME PEOPLE IN AUSTIN, TEXAS.   UNIVERSITY
    OF TEXAS AT AUSTIN, MASTER'S THESIS (1948).

CRAMP.   STUDY MEXICAN POPULATION IMPERIAL   (HC*).

CRASILNECK, HAROLD BERNARD.   A STUDY OF ONE HUNDRED MALE
    LATIN-AMERICAN JUVENILE DELINQUENTS IN SAN ANTONIO,
    TEXAS.   UNIVERSITY OF TEXAS, MASTER'S THESIS (1948)
    (ED).

CRAWFORD.   FORGOTTEN EGG: STUDY MENTALHEALTH   (MD*).

CRAWFORD.   FORGOTTEN EGG: STUDY MENTALHEALTH   (MD*).

CREEL.   ESTADO DE CHIHUAHUA SU HISTORIA   (HM*).

CREMONY.   LIFE AMONG APACHES   (HSW*).

CREMONY.   "THE APACHE RACE"   (HSW*).

CRISCUOLO.   COMPARISON ENRICHMENT ACCELERATION   (ED*).

CROCKER.   "A CHILD WELFARE WORKER PROGRAM   (EC*).

SOCIOLOGY   440

CROSBY, ALEXANDER. SWEATSHOPS IN THE SUN.   CONSUMERS'
    LEAGUE OF NEW YORK, 1952 (EC).

CROSBY, MURIEL <ED>. READING LADDERS FOR HUMAN RELATIONS.
    WASHINGTON: AMERICAN COUNCIL ON EDUCATION, (1963) (ED).

CROSBY, MURIEL. AN ADVENTURE IN HUMAN RELATIONS.
    CHICAGO: FOLLETT, 1965.

CUELLAR, JOSE B. "BOOK REVIEW: COMMENTS ON DELINQUENCY
    IN THREE CULTURES".   AZTLAN--CHICANO JOURNAL OF THE
    SOCIAL SCIENCES AND THE ARTS, VOL. 2 NO. 1 (SPRING
    1971), PP. 155-162.

CULBERT. "DISTRIBUTION SPANISH-AMERICAN (GE*).

CULP, ALICE B. A CASE STUDY OF THIRTY-FIVE MEXICAN
    FAMILIES WITH SPECIAL REFERENCE TO MEXICAN CHILDREN.
    UNIVERSITY OF SOUTHERN CALIFORNIA, MASTER'S THESIS
    (1927) (AN).

CULP, JOHN H. THE MEN OF GONZALEZ.   NEW YORK: WILLIAM
    SLOAN ASSOCIATES, 1960 (AN).

CUNNINGHAM.   HISTORY WOMANS CLUB 1894-1945 (HT*).

CUNNINGHAM, R. R. "NORTH AND SOUTH OF THE BORDER".
    AMERICA,   (AUGUST 17, 1957).

CUNNINGHAM, SISTER MARY, R. S. M. A DESCRIPTIVE STUDY OF
    100 FAMILIES REGISTERED AT MADONNA NEIGHBORHOOD
    CENTERS, MARCH 1962-MARCH 1963.   UNIVERSITY OF TEXAS,
    MASTER'S THESIS (1963).

CURRAN, HARRIETT EDGAR. NEW APPROACH TO HEALTH AND
    PHYSICAL EDUCATION INSTRUCTION FOR MEXICAN CHILDREN.
    SOUTHERN METHODIST UNIVERSITY, MASTER'S THESIS (1940)
    (MD ED).

CURTIN.   POVERTY, EDUCATION, KVARACEUS (ED*).

CUSHING, W. W. "THE DISTRIBUTION OF POPULATION IN MEXICO".
    GEOGRAPHICAL REVIEW, VOL. 11 , PP. 227-42.

D'ANTONIO, WILLIAM. NATIONAL IMAGES OF BUSINESS AND
    POLITICAL ELITE IN TWO-BORDER CITIES.   MICHIGAN STATE
    UNIVERSITY, PHD. DISSERTATION (1958) (EC PL).

D'ANTONIO, WILLIAM; FORM, WILLIAM H.; LOOMIS, CHARLES;
    ERICKSON, EUGENE C. "INSTITUTIONAL AND OCCUPATIONAL
    REPRESENTATIONS IN ELEVEN COMMUNITY INFLUENCE
    SYSTEMS".   AMERICAN SOCIOLOGICAL REVIEW, VOL. 26
    (JUNE 1961), PP. 440-446 (EC PL).

D'ANTONIO, WILLIAM; SAMORA JULIAN. "OCCUPATIONAL STRATIFICATION
    IN FOUR SOUTHWESTERN COMMUNITIES: A STUDY OF ETHNIC
    DIFFERENTIAL EMPLOYMENT IN HOSPITALS". SOCIAL
    FORCES, VOL. 41 (OCTOBER 1962), PP. 17-25 (EC).

D'ANTONIO, WILLIAM; ERICKSON, EUGENE C. "THE REPUTATIONAL
    TECHNIQUE AS A MEASURE OF COMMUNITY POWER: AN
    EVALUATION BASED ON COMPARATIVE AND LONGITUCINAL
    STUDIES". AMERICAN SOCIOLOGICAL REVIEW, VOL. 27
    (JUNE 1962), PP. 362-375 (EC PL).

D'ANTONIO, WILLIAM; FORM, WILLIAM H. INFLUENTIALS IN TWO
    BORDER CITIES: A STUDY IN COMMUNITY DECISION-MAKING.
    NOTRE DAME, INDIANA: UNIVERSITY CF NOTRE DAME PRESS,
    1965 (EC PL).

D'ANTONIO, WILLIAM; PIKE, F. B. RELIGION, REVOLUTION, AND
    REFORM. NEW YORK: FREDERICK A. PRAEGER, INC., 1964
    (RE PL).

D'SILVA, FABIO. "MEXICAN-AMERICANS AND VOLUTNTARY
    ASSOCIATIONS". RESEARCH REPORTS IN THE SOCIAL
    SCIENCES, VOL. 2 NO. 1 (SPRING 1968).

DA POPAVI. "INDIAN VALUES" (AN*).

DAGNALL. MEXICAN; OR LOVE LAND (AN*).

DAHLKE, H. OTTO. "RACE AND MINORITY RIOTS -- A STUDY IN
    THE TYPOLOGY OF VIOLENCE". SOCIAL FORCES, VOL. 30
    (MAY 1952), PP. 419-425 (PL).

DAL POZZO. CONSIDERATION CARPINTERIAS PROVISION (ED*).

DAUSTIN. "BETTERING INTER-AMERICAN RELATIONS (ED*).

DAVIES. "AN INVESTIGATION INTO COMPARATIVE (ED*).

DAVIES. COMPARATIVE STUDY PERFORMANCE (ED*).

DAVIS, ALLISON. SOCIAL-CLASS INFLUENCES UPON LEARNING.
    CAMBRIDGE, MASSACHUSETTS: HARVARD UNIVERSITY PRESS,
    1948 (ED).

DAVIS. PEONS (EC*).

DAVIS. REPORT ILLITERACY TEXAS (ED*).

DAVIS, ETHELYN CLARA. LITTLE MEXICO: A STUDY OF HORIZONTAL
    AND VERTICAL MOBILITY. SOUTHERN METHODIST UNIVERSITY,
    MASTER'S THESIS (1936).

DAVIS, ETHELYN CLARA. THE AMERICAN COLONY IN MEXICO CITY.
    UNIVERSITY OF MISSOURI, PHD. DISSERTATION (1942).

DAVIS.   "PERMANET BASES INTER-AMERICAN (ED*).

DAVIS, HOWARD WINGFIELD. AN ANALYSIS OF CURRENT PATTERNS
     IN HUMAN RESOURCE DEVELOPMENT IN SAN ANTONIO.   THE
     UNIVERSITY OF TEXAS AT AUSTIN, PHD. DISSERTATION
     (1966) (EC).

DAVIS.   REPORT ILLITERACY TEXAS (ED*).

DAVIS.   "VIVA LA HUELGA" (EC*).

DAWSON.   "DISADVANTAGED: EDUCATION OTHER (ED*).

DAWSON.   "AMONG MEXICANS TEXAS" (RE*).

DAY.   FORTY ACRES: CESAR CHAVEZ FARM (EC*).

DE HOYOS.   OCCUPATIONAL EDUCATIONAL LEVELS (ED*).

DE HOYOS.   OCCUPATIONAL EDUCATIONAL LEVELS (ED*).

DE HOYOS, ARTURO; DE HOYOS, GENEVIEVE. THE AMIGO SYSTEM
     AND ALIENATION OF THE WIFE IN THE CONJUGAL MEXICAN
     FAMILY.   NEW YORK, NEW YORK: WILEY, 1966.

DE LA GUERRA, DON PABLO. "EXCERPT FROM HIS SPEECH".   EL
     GRITO, VOL. 5 NO. 1 (FALL   1971), PP. 19-20 (LMA).

DE LA GUERRA, DON PABLO. "EXTRACTO DEL DISCOURSO".   EL
     GRITO, VOL. 5 NO. 1 (FALL   1971), PP. 20-21 (LMA).

DE LA ROSE.   "MINISTRY PUBLIC HEALTH WELFARE (MD*).

DE LA VEGA.   SOME FACTORS AFFECTING LEADERSHIP (ED*).

DE LAITTRE.   "THE MEXICAN AND YOU" (EC*).

DE LEON, MARCOS.   'THE HAMBURGER AND THE TACO: A CULTURAL
     REALITY.'   IN $COMMUNITY OPPORTUNITY PROGRAMS
     IN EDUCATIONS SAN DIEGO, CALIFORNIA (ED).

DE LEON, MARCOS.   'THE HAMBURGER AND THE TACO: A CULTURAL
     REALITY.'   VALLEY FORGE, PENNSYLVANIA: JUDSON PRESS
     (ED).

DE LEON, MARTHA DIAZ.   "THE RED FLOWER".   AMERICAS, VOL.
     21 NO. 3 (MARCH   1969), PP. 30-31.

DE SUAREZ, CECILIA COTA-ROBLES.   "SKIN COLOR AS A FACTOR
     OF RACIAL IDENTIFICATION AND PREFERENCE OF YOUNG
     CHICANO CHILDREN".   AZTLAN-CHICANO JOURNAL OF THE
     SOCIAL SCIENCES AND THE ARTS, VOL. 2 NO. 1 (SPRING
     1971), PP. 107-150.

DE VISSER, LOUIS ANTONINE JOHAN MARIE. ETHNIC CHARACTERISTICS
     AS FACTORS IN SOCIAL MODELING. UNIVERSITY OF
     CALIFORNIA AT SANTA BARBARA, PHD. DISSERTATION (1972).

DEAL, GERALD V. A STUDY OF THE VOCATIONAL OPPORTUNITIES
     IN POMONA VALLEY FOR MEXICAN-AMERICANS: A STUDY IN
     COUNSELING. CLAREMONT COLLEGES, MASTER'S THESIS
     (1951) (ED).

DEAN, JOHN P.; ROSEN, ALEX. A MANUAL OF INTERGROUP
     RELATIONS. CHICAGO: UNIVERSITY OF CHICAGO PRESS,
     1955.

DEARMAN, CECIL J. A SOCIO-ECONOMIC STUDY OF LATIN-AMERICAN
     FARM MIGRANTS IN TEXAS.   TEXAS A&M COLLEGE, MASTER'S
     THESIS (1947) (EC SI).

DEBOER, JOHN J. "SOME SOCIOLOGICAL FACTORS IN LANGUAGE
     DEVELOPMENT". ELEMENTARY ENGLISH, VOL. 29 (DECEMBER
     1942), PP. 482-492 (LA).

DEERING. "MUSIC AS WELDER RACES CALIFORNIA" (MU*).

DEGEREZ, T. "THREE TIMES LONELY". HORN BOOK MAGAZINE,
     VOL. 46 (FEBRUARY 1973), PP. 66-73 (ED).

DEGNAN. "MONOPOLY VINEYARDS; GRAPES WRATH (EC*).

DEHUFF. "PEOPLE OF THE SOIL" (AN*).

DEL CAMPO, PHILIP E. AN ANALYSIS OF SELECTED FACTORS IN
     THE ACCULTURATION PROCESS OF THE MEXICAN-AMERICAN
     ELEMENTARY SCHOOL CHILD. ANN ARBOR, MICHIGAN:
     UNIVERSITY MICROFILMS, INC., 1971 (ED).

DELGADO. CHICANO MOVEMENT: SOME NOT TOO (LMA*).

DELLON. "FOREIGN AGRICULTURAL WORKERS (EC*).

DELLON. "THE ADVERSE-EFFECT POLICY AGRICULTURAL   (EC*).

DELMET.   STUDY MENTAL SCHOLASTIC ABILITIES (ED*).

DEMAK.   STUDY MEANINGS SELECTED EDUCATIONAL   (ED*).

DEMAREST.   "DIFFERENCES RESULTS FIVE STANDARD (ED*).

DEMIRELES, JOVITA GONZALEZ. 'LATIN AMERICANS.'   IN BROWN,
     FRANCIS J. AND ROUCEK, JOSEPH S., EDS, OUR RACIAL AND
     NATIONAL MINORITIES; THEIR HISTORY, CONTRIBUTIONS AND
     PRESENT PROBLEMS. NEW YORK: PRENTICE-HALL, INC. (EC).

DEMOS. "ATTITUDES MEXICAN-AMERICANSANGLO (ED*).

DEMOS. "ATTITUDES MEXICAN-AMERICANSANGLO (ED*).

DEMOS.   "ATTITUDES STUDENT ETHNIC GROUPS   (ED*).

DEMPSEY, ARTHUR DUANE.   CULTURE AND THE CONSERVATION OF
    TIME: A COMPARISON OF SELECTED ETHNIC GROUPS
    IN ARIZONA.   UNIVERSITY OF ARIZONA, 1939 (PY   AN).

DENNY.   UNITED STATES RELIGIOUS OPINION   (RE*).

DENNY, JOHN W. A CENTURY OF FREEMASONRY AT EL PASO.   EL
    PASO, TEXAS: PRIVATELY PRINTED, 1956 (EC).

DENVER AREA WELFARE COUNCIL. THE SPANISH-SPEAKING
    POPULATION OF DENVER.   DENVER, COLORADO: DENVER AREA
    WELFARE COUNCIL, 1950.

DENVER UNIVERSITY NATIONAL OPINION RESEARCH CENTER. THE
    SPANISH-SPEAKING POPULATION OF DENVER.   DENVER,
    COLORADO: DENVER UNITY COUNCIL, 1946.

DEPARTAMENTO DE ESTADISTICA NACIONAL. ESTADISTICA
    NACIONAL.   MEXICO: CORREO MAYOR 31,.

DEPARTAMENTO DE LA ESTADISTICA NACIONAL. CENSO GRAL., DE
    HABITANTES.   ES DIRECCION GRAL., DE ESTADISTICA Y
    DEPARTAMENTO DE LA ESTADISTICA NACIONAL.
                       ‒
DEPARTMENT OF HEALTH, EDUCATION AND WELFARE. OFFICE OF
    THE SECRETARY MEMORANDUM: IDENTIFICACION DE DISCRIMEN
    Y DENEGACION DE SERVICIOS A BASE DE ORIGEN NACIONAL.
    WASHINGTON, D. C.: DEPARTMENT OF HEALTH, EDUCATION
    AND WELFARE, MAY 25, 1970 (ED).

DEPARTMENT OF INDUSTRIAL RELATIONS.   CALIFORNIANS SPANISH
    SURNAME (HUS*).

DERBYSHIRE, ROBERT L. 'CHILDREN'S PERCEPTIONS OF THE
    POLICE: A COMPARATIVE STUDY OF ATTITUDES AND ATTITUDE
    CHANGE.'   IN NAHANIEL N. WAGNER AND MARSHA J HAUG
    (EDS), IN CHICANOS: SOCIAL ANDPSYCHOLOGICAL PERSPECTIVES
    (AN   PY).

DERBYSHIRE, ROBERT L. "ADAPTATION OF ADOLESCENT MEXICAN
    AMERICANS TO UNITED STATES SOCIETY".   AMERICAN
    BEHAVIORAL SCIENTIST, VOL. 13 NO. 1 (SEPT-OCT 1969),
    PP. 88-103 (AN).

DES MARAIS.   ENVIRONMENTAL CULTURAL FACTORS (MD*).

DESSART, GINA. "THE BALLOON RACE".   ARIZONA QUARTERLY,
    VOL. 21 NO. 1 (SPRING 1965).

DEUTSCH.   MINORITY GROUP CLASS STATUS AS   (ED*).

DICKERSON ROY E. "SOME SUGGESTIVE PROBLEMS IN THE
    AMERICANIZATION OF MEXICANS". PEDAGOGICAL SEMINARY,
    VOL. 26 (SEPT 1919), PP. 288-297.

DITTMAR, EVA VAN. LATIN AMERICAN STUDENTS IN U. S.
    UNIVERSITIES: AN EXPLORATORY STUDY. UNIVERSITY OF
    CALIFORNIA AT LOS ANGELES, PHD. DISSERTATION (1967)
    (PY).

DOBIE. "THE MEXICAN VAQUERO TEXAS BORDER" (LI*).

DOBIE. "RANCH MEXICANS" (LI*).

DOBRIN, ARNOLD. THE NEW LIFE: LA VIDA NUEVA, AND
    THE MEXICAN AMERICANS TODAY. NEW YORK, NEW YORK:
    DODD, MEAD AND COMPANY, 1971.

DODSON, JACK ELWOOD. DIFFERENTIAL FERTILITY IN HOUSTON,
    TEXAS, 1940-1950: A STUDY OF RECENT TRENDS.
    UNIVERSITY OF TEXAS AT AUSTIN, PHD. DISSERTATION
    (1955) (AN).

DOEGE. "A DIPTHERIA EPIDEMIC RELATED (MD*).

DOHRENWEND. "TOWARD THEORY ACCULTURATION" (AN*).

DOLAN, G.K.; NEVAREZ, C. E. "FAMILY READING CIRCLES".
    CLEARING HOUSE, VOL. 41 (APRIL 1967), PP. 500-501.

DONISI, CAROL MARY. MEXICAN-AMERICAN FOOD ITEMS IN THE
    TUCSON, ARIZONA SCHOOL LUNCH PROGRAM. UNIVERSITY
    OF ARIZONA, MASTER'S THESIS (1971) (EC).

DOTSON, FLOYD. "DECREASE OF THE MEXICAN POPULATION IN THE
    U. S. ACCORDING TO THE 1950 CENSUS". MEXICAN
    SOCIOLOGICAL REVIEW, VOL. 17 (FEB 1957), P. 1955 (SI).

DOUGLAS, HELEN WALKER. THE CONFLICT OF CULTURES IN FIRST
    GENERATION MEXICANS IN SANTA ANA, CALIFORNIA.
    UNIVERSITY OF SOUTHERN CALIFORNIA, MASTER'S THESIS
    (1928) (AN).

DOUGLASS, JOSEPH H. 'MIGRANT AND THE COMMUNITY.'
    IN MINORITY GROUPS: SEGREGATION AND INTEGRATION,
    PAPERS PRESENTED AT THE 82ND ANNUAL FORUM OF THE
    NATIONAL CONFERENCE OF SOCIAL WORK, NEW YORK:
    COLUMBIA UNIVERSITY PRESS, 1955, PP. 23-36 (SI).

DROLET. "DISCUSSION PAPER PRESENTED BY (MD*).

DU BOIS. BUILD TOGETHER, AMERICANS: ADVENTURES (ED*).

DU BOIS, RACHEL DAVIS. GET TOGETHER, AMERICANS: FRIENDLY
    APPROACHES TO RACIAL AND CULTURAL CONFLICTS THROUGH
    THE NEIGHBORHOOD-HOME FESTIVAL. NEW YORK, NEWYORK:
    HARPER, 1943.

DUHL, LEONARD L., EDITOR. THE URBAN CONDITION: PEOPLE
    AND POLICY IN THE METROPOLIS. NEW YORK, NEW YORK:
    BASIC BOOKS, INC., 1963.

DUNBIER. SONORAN DESERT: ITS GEOGRAPHY (EC*).

DUNCAN. DEMOCRACYS CHILDREN: ADVENTURES (ED*).

DUNNE, JOHN GREGORY. REACH OUT RICARDO. NEW YORK, NEW
    YORK: ABELARD-SCHUMAN, LTD., 1971.

DURAN, LIVIE ISAURO; RUSSELL, BERNARD H. INTRODUCTION TO
    CHICANO STUDIES. NEW YORK, NEW YORK: THE MACMILLAN
    COMPANY, 1973.

DURHAM, JOSEPH T. "THE MELTING POT: MINORITIES SHOULD
    STRIVE FOR CULTURAL PLURALISM BUT RETAIN THEIR
    IDENTITIES". CLEARING HOUSE, (MAY 1965), PP. 547-550.

DURHAM, R. "HOUSTON'S MAYO CLINIC: COMPLICATED CHEMISTRY;
    MEXICAN-AMERICAN YOUTH ORGANIZATION". CHRISTIANITY
    TODAY, VOL. 14 (MAY 8, 1970), PP. 42-43.

DURRETT, MARY E.; HUFFMAN, WANDA. "PLAYFULNESS AND
    DIVERGENT THINKING AMONG MEXICAN-AMERICAN CHILDREN".
    JOURNAL OF HOME ECONOMICS, VOL. 60 (MAY 1968), PP.
    355-358.

DUVAL. "THE CHICANO MOVEMENT ITS BOOKS" (B*).

DWORKIN, ANTHONY GARY. 'NATIONAL ORIGIN AND GHETTO
    EXPERIENCE AS VARIABLES IN MEXICAN AMERICAN STEREOTYPY.'
    IN CHICANOS: SOCIAL AND PSYCHOLOGICAL PERSPECTIVES,
    EDITED BY NATHANIEL N. WAGNER AND MARSHA J. HAUG,
    SAINT LOUIS, MISSOURI: THE C. V. MOSBY COMPANY, 1971
    (PY).

DWORKIN, ANTHONY GARY. 'STEREOTYPES AND SELF-IMAGES HELD
    BY NATIVE-BORN AND FOREIGN-BORN MEXICAN-AMERICANS.'
    IN CHICANOS: SOCIAL AND PSYCHOLOGICAL PERSPECTIVES,
    EDITED BY NATHANIEL N. WAGNER AND MARSHA J. HAUG,
    SAINT LOUIS, MISSOURI: THE C. V. MOSBY COMPANY, 1971
    (PY).

DWORKIN, ANTHONY GARY. "STEREOTYPES AND SELF-IMAGES HELD
    BY NATIVE-BORN AND FOREIGN-BORN MEXICAN-AMERICANS".
    SOCIOLOGY AND SOCIAL RESEARCH, VOL. 49 NO. 2 (JAN
    1965), PP. 214-224 (PY).

DWORKIN, ANTHONY GARY. POPULAR STEREOTYPES AND SELF-IMAGES
    OF THE ANGLO-AMERICAN AND MEXICAN-AMERICAN.
    OCCIDENTAL COLLEGE, (1964) (PY).

EATON.   USE CAUSAL MODELS STUDY LOW INCOME (EC*).

EATON.   MEASURING DELINQUENCY; STUDYPROBATION (LW*).

EDWARDS.   SOCIAL-ECONOMIC GROUPING GAINFUL (EC*).

EDWARDS.   "SEGREGATION SPANISH-SPEAKING (ED*).

EGAN.   SOCIAL ORGANIZATION WESTERN PUEBLOS (AN*).

EL NO-V.   "SOCIAL SCIENCE, OBJECTIVITY, (AN*).

EL BARRIO COMMUNICATIONS PROJECT.   RAZA YEARBOOK (PL*).

EL PASO CONGRESS.   REPORT, DEC., 1926, EDUCATION (ED*).

ELDER, GLEN H., JR. "FAMILY STRUCTURE AND EDUCATIONAL
    ATTAINMENT: A CROSS-NATIONAL ANALYSIS".   AMERICAN
    SOCIOLOGICAL REVIEW,   NO. 30 (FEB 1965), P. 83 (ED).

ELLINGTON, KAREN B. ET AL. A COMPARATIVE ANALYSIS
    OF ATTITUDES TOWARDS MINORITY GROUP PROBLEMS: SOCIAL
    WORK STUDENTS AND ANTI POVERTY PERSONNEL.   TEMPE,
    ARIZONA: ARIZONA STATE UNIVERSITY, 1969.

ELLIOT, ROBERT S. THE HEALTH AND RELIEF PROBLEMS OF
    A GROUP OF NON-FAMILY MEXICAN MEN IN IMPERIAL COUNTY,
    CALIFORNIA.   UNIVERSITY OF SOUTHERN CALIFORNIA,
    MASTER'S THESIS (1939) (MD).

ELLIS, CHRISTINE EVANGELINE. THE RELATION OF SOCIO-ECONOMIC
    STATUS TO THE INTELLIGENCE AND SCHOOL SUCCESS
    OF MEXICAN CHILDREN.   UNIVERSITY OF TEXAS AT AUSTIN,
    MASTER'S THESIS (1932) (EC PY).

ELLIS, G. M. "BARRIERS TRAVERSED IN MICHIGAN,S TRAVERSE
    CITY".   ROTARIAN, VOL. 81 (AUG 1952), PP. 29-31.

ELLIS, HELEN H. PUBLIC WELFARE PROBLEMS IN NEW MEXICO.
    ALBUQUERQUE, NEW MEXICO: UNIVERSITY OF NEW MEXICO.
    1948, (AUG 1952) (EC).

ELLIS, JOHN M. "MORTALITY DIFFERENTIALS FOR A SPANISH-SURNAME
    POPULATION GROUP".   SOUTHWESTERN SOCIAL SCIENCE
    QUARTERLY, VOL. 39 (MAR 1959), PP. 314-321.

ELLIS, JOHN M. "SPANISH SURNAME MORTALITY DIFFERENCES IN
    SAN ANTONIO, TEXAS".   JOURNAL OF HEALTH AND HUMAN
    BEHAVIOR, VOL. 3 NO. 2 (SUMMER 1962) (EC MD).

ELLIS, JOHN M. MORTALITY IN HOUSTON TEXAS: 1949-1951: A
     STUDY OF SOCIAO-ECONOMIC DIFFERENTIALS.   UNIVERSITY
     OF TEXAS AT AUSTIN, PHD. DISSERTATION (1956) (EC).

ELLWELLS, GLADYS. FACTORS INFLUENCING THE ASSIMILATION
     OF THE MEXICAN IN TEXAS.   SOUTHERN METHODIST
     UNIVERSITY, MASTER'S THESIS (1941) (AN HT).

EMBRFEE.   BROWN AMERICA: STORY NEW RACE (HSW*).

EMCH.   THE TWO LS-LATINS, LABOR TWO (EC*).

ENCYCLOPEDIA BRITTANICA CORPORATION. MAKERS OF AMERICA--EMERGENT
     MINORITIES, 1955-1970.   ENCYCLOPEDIA BRITANNICA
     CORPORATION, 1971. <10 VOLUMES, SEE VOLUME ON MEXICANS
     IN THE UNITED STATES>.

ENDORE, S. GUY. THE SLEEPY LAGOON MYSTERY.   LOS ANGELES,
     CALIFORNIA: SLEEPY LAGOON DEFENSE COMMITTEE, 1944
     (LW).

ENGEL, MADELINE H. INEQUALITY IN AMERICA: A SOCIOLOGICAL
     PERSPECTIVE.   NEW YORK, NEW YORK: THOMAS Y. CROWELL
     COMPANY, 1971.

ENRIGHT.   "PSYCHIATRIC SYMMPTOMS DIAGNOSIS (PY*).

ENRIQUEZ .   REGIONAL CULTURAL ECONOMIC DEVELCPMENT (EC*).

ERICKSEN.   "UPRISING BARRIOS: CONCERNING (ED*).

ERICKSEN.   UPRISING BARRIOS: EDUCATINGMEXICAN-AMERICAN
     (ED*).

ERICKSEN.   "UPRISING BARRIOS" (ED*).

ERICKSON, E. H. "CONCEPT OF IDENTITY IN RACE RELATIONS:
     NOTES AND QUERIES".   DAEDALUS, VOL. 95 (WINTER
     1966), PP. 145-171.

ETHELL.   STUDY FIFTY SPANISH SPEAKINGMEXICAN (ED*).

EULAU, H. H. F. "SINARQUISMO IN THE UNITED STATES".
     INTER-AMERICAN MONTHLY, VOL. 3 (JUNE 1944), PP. 46-48
     (PL).

EULAU, H. H. F. "SINARQUISMC IN THE UNITED STATES".
     INTER-AMERICAN MONTHLY, VOL. 3 (AUGUST 1944), PP.
     47-48 (PL).

EULAU, H. H. F. "SLEEPY LAGOON CASE; COURT OF APPEAL
     REVERSES JUDGMENTS".   NEW REPUBLIC, VOL. 111 (DEC.
     11, 1944), PP. 795-796 (LW).

EULAU, HEINZ F. "SINARQUISMO IN THE U.S.A.".   MEXICAN
     LIFE, VOL. 20 (MAY 1, 1944), P. 17 (PL).

EVANS. INDIAN SAVAGE, MEXICAN BANDIT (LI*).

EVANS, KATHERINE. ONE GOOD DEED DESERVES ANOTHER.
CHICAGO, ILLINOIS: ALBERT WHITMAN COMPANY, 1964 (LJE).

EWEVER. ". . . DOWN VALLEYS WILD: EPILOGUE (EC*).

EWING, E. E. ANGLO-AMERICAN SOCIETY. CHICAGO, ILLINOIS:
RAND MC NALLY,.

EWING, E. E. LATIN AMERICAN SOCIETY. CHICAGO, ILLINOIS:
RAND MCNALLY,.

EZELL. HISPANIC ACCULTURATION GILA RIVER (HS*).

FACCI, JOSEPH A. REHABILITATION FOR MEXICAN FARM LABORERS.
MANUSCRIPT IN HAINES HALL LIBRARY, UNIVERSITY
OF CALIFORNIA, LOS ANGELES, NOVEMBER 18, 1939 (SI).

FADERMAN, LILLIAN; BRADSHAW, BARBARA. SPEAKING FOR
OURSELVES. SCOTT, FORESMAN AND COMPANY, 1969.

FAIRCHILD, HARRY PRATT. IMMIGRANT BACKGROUNDS. NEW YORK:
JOHN WILEY AND SONS, 1927 (SI).

FARMER, WILLIAM ANDREW. THE INFLUENCE OF SEGREGATION OF
MEXICAN AND AMERICAN CHILDREN UPON THE DEVELOPMENT
OF SOCIAL ATTITUDES. UNIVERSITY OF SOUTHERN
CALIFORNIA, MASTER'S THESIS (1937) (ED).

FARRELL, GRACE A. "HOMEMAKING WITH THE OTHER HALF ALONG
OUR INTERNATIONAL BORDER". JOURNAL OF HOME ECONOMICS,
VOL. 21 (DECEMBER 1951), PP. 413-18.

FARRIS, BUFORD. MEXICAN-AMERICAN CONFLICT GANGS --OBSERVATIONS
AND THEORETICAL IMPLICATIONS. SAN ANTONIO, TEXAS:
WESLEY COMMUNITY CENTER, (DECEMBER 1951). RESEARCH
AND EDUCATIONAL REPORT NUMBER 1.

FARRIS, BUFORD; BRYMER, RICHARD. "1965 - A FIVE YEAR
ENCOUNTER WITH A MEXICAN AMERICAN CONFLICT GANG:
ITSIMPLICATIONS FOR DELINQUENCY THEORY". PROCEEDINGS
OF SOUTHWESTERN SOCIOLOGICAL ASSOCIATION, VOL. 15
(DECEMBER 1951), PP. 49-55 (LW).

FARRIS, BUFORD; HALE, WILLIAM M. A METHOD AND APPROACH
TO WORKING WITH THE "MEXICAN-AMERICAN " BOY AND HIS
"GANG". WESLEY COMMUNITY CENTERS: SAN ANTONIO, TEXAS.

FAUNCE. ANALYSIS VACATIONAL AVOCATIONAL (EC*).

FAUNCE. ANALYSIS VOCATIONAL AVOCATICNAL (ED*).

FEDDER. NO LONGER DEPRIVED (ED*).

FEINGOLD, GUSTAVE H. "INTELLIGENCE CF THE FIRST GENERATION
    OF IMMIGRANT GROUPS: A STUDY AND ACRITIQUE".   THE
    JOURNAL OF EDUCATIONAL PSYCHOLCGY, VOL. 15 (FEBRUARY
    1924), PP. 65-82 (SI).

FELDER.   "EDUCATION MEXICAN-AMERICANS: (ED*).

FELDMAN.   RACIAL FACTORS AMERICAN INDUSTRY   (EC*).

FELTER, EUNICE BEALL. THE SOCIAL ADAPTATICNS OF THE
    MEXICAN CHURCHES IN THE CHICAGO AREA.   UNIVERSITY
    OF CHICAGC, MASTER'S THESIS (1941) (RE).

FERGUSSON, ERNA. MEXICAN COOKBOOK.   SANTE FE, NEW MEXICO:
    RYDAL PRESS, 1940.

FERIA , R. T. "WAR AND STATUS OF FILIPINO IMMIGRANTS".
    SOCIOLOGY AND SOCIAL RESEARCH, VOL. 31 (SEPTEMBER-OCTOBER
    1946), PP. 48-53 (SI).

FILM. HUNGER IN AMERICA.   FILM 6 MINUTES. BLACK AND
    WHITE. CAROUSEL FILMS INC. 1501 BDWY. N.Y., Y..

FISHER.   "THE PERFORMANCE MALE PRISONERS (PY*).

FISHER, IRVING. "WHAT MEXICO THINKS CF US".   SURVEY, VOL.
    36 (NOVEMBER 1964), P. 386.

FISHER, LLOYD HARRIS. THE HARVEST LABOR MARKET IN
    CALIFORNIA.   CAMBRIDGE: HARVARD UNIVERSITY PRESS,
    1953 (EC).

FISHER, LLOYD HARRIS. THE PROBLEM OF VIOLENCE: OBSERVATIONS
    ON RACE CONFLICT IN LOS ANGELES.   CHICAGO: AMERICAN
    COUNCIL ON RACE RELATIONS, 1946 (EC).

FISHER, REGINALD. "HISPANIC PEOPLE OF THE RIO GRANDE: A
    STATEMENT OF A PROGRAM OF RESEARCH BEING PLANNED IN
    THE CONSERVATION OF HUMAN RESOURCES".   EL PALACIO,
    VOL. 49 (AUGUST 1942), PP. 157-162 (EC).

FISHMAN.   "LANGUAGE MAINTENANCE LANGUAGE   (LA*).

FISHMAN.   LANGUAGE LOYALTY UNITED STATES;   (LA*).

FISHMAN.   READINGS SOCIOLOGY LANGUAGE   (LA*).

FITZPATRICK.   NEW MEXICO YOUNG PEOPLE   (ED*).

FITZPATRICK, JOSEPH P. 'THE ADJUSTMENT OF PUERTO RICANS
    TO NEW YORK CITY.'   IN MILTON L. BARRON (ED),
    MINORITIES IN A CHANGING WORLD.

FLORES.   SOCIC-ECONOMIC STATUS TREND MEXICAN   (EC*).

FOERSTER, ROBERT F. RACIAL PROBLEMS INVOLVED IN IMMIGRATION
    FROM LATIN AMERICA AND THE WEST INDIES.   WASHINGTON,
    D. C.: UL SL GOVERNMENT PRINTING OFFICE, (1925) (SI).

FOGELSON, ROBERT (ED). THE LOS ANGELES RIOTS (1969).
    REPRINTED BY, NEW YORK, NEW YORK: ARNO PRESS, 1971
    (LW).

FOGELSON, ROBERT M. THE FRAGMENTED METROPOLIS: LOS
    ANGELES 1850-1930.   CAMBRIDGE: HARVARD UNIVERSITY
    PRESS, 1967 (LW).

FOLEY.   DIVINE ECCENTRIC, LOLA MONTEZ (NP*).

FORBES.   "RACE COLOR MEXICAN-AMERICANPROBLEMS" (ED*).

FORBES.   AZTECAS NORTE: CHICANOS AZLAN (HSW*).

FORM, WILLIAM H. ; SAUER, WARREN L. COMMUNITY INFLUENTIALS
    IN A MIDDLE-SIZED CITY.   EAST LANSING, MICHIGAN:
    INSTITUTE FOR COMMUNITY DEVELOPMENT, MICHIGAN STATE
    UNIVERSITY, (1960). GENERAL BULLETIN NUMBER 5.

FORM, WILLIAM M. AND RIVERA, JULIUS. "WORK CONTACTS AND
    INTERNATIONAL EVALUATIONS: THE CASE OF A MEXICAN
    BORDER VILLAGE".   RS, VOL. 23 (MAY 1970), PP.
    286-297 (SI).

FORM, WILLIAM; D'ANTONIO, WILLIAM. "INTEGRATION AND
    CLEAVAGE AMONG COMMUNITY INFLUENTIALS IN TWO BORDER
    CITIES".   AMERICAN SOCIOLOGICAL REVIEW, VOL.
    24 (DECEMBER 1959), PP. 804-814.

FORM, WILLIAM; RIVERA, JULIUS. "THE PLACE OF RETURNING
    MIGRANTS IN A STRATIFICATION SYSTEM".   SOCIAL FORCES,
    VOL. 37 (MAY 1959), PP. 334-339 (SI).

FORSTER, ARNOLD AND EPSTEIN, BENJAMIN R. TROUBLEMAKERS:
    AN ANTI-DEFAMATION LEAGUE REPORT.   NEW YORK:
    DOUBLEDAY, 1952.

FOSHAY, ARTHUR W.; WANN, KENNETH D. CHILDREN'S SOCIAL
    VALUES: AN ACTION RESEARCH STUDY.   HORACE MANN--LINCOLN
    INSTITUTE OF SCHOOL EXPERIMENTATION, TEACHERS COLLEGE,
    COLUMBIA UNIVERSITY, NEW YORK, 1954.

FOSICK.   "EDUCATIONAL RETARDATION AMONG (ED*).

FOSTER.   "INTERPERSONAL RELATIONS PEASANT (AN*).

FOSTER.   PRIMITIVE MEXICAN ECONOMY (AN*).

FOSTER, N. "THE LEGAL STATUS OF FILIPINO INTERMARRIAGES
    IN CALIFORNIA".   SOCIOLOGY AND SOCIAL RESEARCH, VOL.
    18 (MAY-JUNE 1933), PP. 441-54 (LW).

FRAGA, FELIX AND KENNEDY, JOHN J. A STUDY OF THE RECREATIONAL
    NEEDS OF THE SENIOR LATIN-AMERICAN IN SAN ANTONIO,
    TEXAS.   SAN ANTONIO, TEXAS: OUR LADY OF THE LAKE
    COLLEGE, 1954.

FRANCESCA.   "VARIATIONS SELECTED CULTURAL   (AN*).

FRANCIS, E. K. "MULTIPLE INTERGROUP RELATIONS IN THE UPPER
    RIO GRANDE REGION".   AMERICAN SOCIOLOGICAL REVIEW,
    VOL. 21 (FEBRUARY 1956), PP. 84-87.

FRANK EVA A. "THE MEXICANS SIMPLY WON'T WORK".   NATION,
    VOL. 125 (AUGUST 17, 1927), PP. 155-57.

FRANK.   JOB TRAINING MINORITIES: INTERNAL (EC*).

FRAZIER, E. FRANKLIN. "ETHNIC AND MINORITY GROUPS
    IN WARTIME, WITH SPECIAL REFERENCE TO THE NEGRO".
    AMERICAN JOURNAL OF SOCIOLOGY, VOL. 48 (NOVEMBER
    1942), PP. 369-377.

FREYTAG, J. "SOME MEXICAN MANNERS AND CUSTOMS".   TRAVEL,
    VOL. 27 , P. 32.

FRIEDEN, BERNARD J.; MORRIS, ROBERT (EDITORS).   URBAN
    PLANNING AND SOCIAL POLICY.   NEW YORK: BASIC BOOKS,
    1968.

FRIEND.   ECONOMIC, SOCIAL DEMOGRAPHICCHARACTERISTICS (EC*).

FROMM, E. AND MACOBY, M. "SOCIAL CHARACTER IN A MEXICAN
    VILLAGE".   SATURDAY REVIEW OF LITERATURE, VOL. 53
    (DECEMBER 5, 1970), PP. 21-22 (PY).

FROMM, ERICH. SOCIAL CHARACTER IN A MEXICAN VILLAGE:
    SOCIOPSYCHOANALYTIC STUDY.   ENGLEWOOD CLIFFS, N.J.:
    PRENTICE-HALL, INC., 1970 (PY).

FROST.   DISADVANTAGED CHILD: ISSUESINNOVATIONS (ED*).

FUKUDA.   "A SURVEY INTELLIGENCE ENVIRONMENT (ED*).

FULLER, ELIZABETH. THE MEXICAN HOUSING PROBLEM IN
    LOS ANGELES.   UNIVERSITY OF SOUTHERN CALIFORNIA,
    (1920). STUDIES IN SOCIOLOGY, MONOGRAPH 17.

FULLER.   SCHOOL PROGRESS CHILDREN MIGRATORY (ED*).

FULLER, RODEN. "OCCUPATIONS OF THE MEXICAN-BORN POPULATION
    OF TEXAS, NEW MEXICO, AND ARIZONA". JOURNAL OF THE
    AMERICAN STATISTICAL ASSOCIATION, VOL. 23 (MARCH
    1928), PP. 64-74 (EC).

FUNKUDA. "THE INTELLIGENCE ENVIRONMENT (PY*).

FURNIRALL. PROPOSED PROGRAM TEACHING MEXICAN-AMERICAN
    (ED*).

GALARZA, ERNESTO ET AL. DWELLERS OF THE SUNSHINE SLUMS:
    MEXICAN AMERICAN IN THE SOUTHWEST. SANTA BARBARA:
    MCNALLY, 1969 (EC).

GALARZA. "BIG FARM STRIKE; REPORT LABOR (EC*).

GALARZA, ERNESTO. "LA MULA NO NACIO ARISCA". CENTER
    DIARY, (SEPTEMBER-OCTOBER 1966), PP. 26-33 (EC).

GALARZA, ERNESTO. "LIFE IN THE UNITED STATES FOR MEXICAN
    PEOPLE: OUT OF THE EXPERIENCE OF A MEXICAN".
    NATIONAL CONFERENCE OF SOCIAL WORK PROCEEDINGS
    OF 1929, (1929), PP. 399-404.

GALARZA, ERNESTO. "MEXICAN-AMERICANS". THE CENTER
    MAGAZINE, VOL. 4 NO. 5 (SEPTEMBER-OCTOBER 1971).

GALARZA, ERNESTO. "PROGRAM FOR ACTION". COMMON GROUND,
    VOL. 9 NO. 4 (SUMMER 1949), PP. 27-38 (EC).

GALARZA, ERNESTO. "RURAL COMMUNITY DEVELOPMENT".
    EL GRITO, VOL. 1 NO. 2 (WINTER 1968), PP. -22-27
    (EC).

GALARZA, ERNESTO. "THEY WORK FOR PENNIES". AMERICAN
    FEDERATIONIST, VOL. 59 (APRIL 1952), PP. 10-13 (EC).

GALARZA, ERNESTO. "WITHOUT BENEFIT OF LOBBY". SURVEY,
    VOL. 66 (MAY 1, 1931), P. 181 (EC).

GALARZA. BARRIO BOY (LMA*).

GALARZA. DWELLERS SUNSHINE SLUMS (EC*).

GALARZA, ERNESTO. MERCHANTS OF LABOR: THE MEXICAN BRACERO
    STORY; AN ACCOUNT OF THE MANAGEDMIGRATION OF MEXICAN
    FARM WORKERS IN CALIFORNIA, 1942-1960. SANTA
    BARBARA, CALIFORNIA: MCNALLY AND LOFTIN, 1964 (EC).

GALARZA, ERNESTO. MEXICAN ETHNIC GROUP. CALIFORNIA
    ELEMENTARY SCHOOL PRINCIPALS' ASSOCIATION, 17TH
    YEARBOOK, (1945). PP. 34-35 (EC).

GALARZA, ERNESTO. SCHOOLS FACED WITH MULTIPLICITY
     OF LEADERSHIP (SEMINAR NO. 4).   CALIFORNIA: LOS
     ANGELES CITY SCHOOLS, (1967). ADMINISTRATORS IN-DEPTH
     SEMINARS IN PROBLEMS OF DESEGREGATION AS THEY RELATE
     TO LARGE CITY SCHOOLS: SUMMARIES OF SEMINAR DISCUSSIONS.
     (ED).

GALARZA, ERNESTO. SPIDERS IN THE HOUSE AND WORKERS IN THE
     FIELD.   SANTA BARBARA: MCNALLY AND LOFT, 1969 (EC
     LMA).

GALARZA, ERNESTO; GALLEGOS, HERMAN; SAMORA JULIAN.
     MEXICAN-AMERICANS IN THE SOUTHWEST.   SANTA BARBARA:
     MCNALLY AND LOFTIN, PUBLISHERS, 1969 (EC).

GALARZA, ERNESTO; SAMORA, JULIAN. RESEARCH AND SCHOLARLY
     ACTIVITY.   CHICANO STUDIES INSTITUTES, (1970).
     PROGRAM COORDINATED BY MONTAL SYSTEMS, INC. (EC).

GALLARDO, RUDY. THE REFLECTION.   OAKLAND, NEW JERSEY:
     SCOTT, FORESMAN AND COMPANY, 1969.

GAMBLON, RUTH S. "MEXICANS IN CHICAGO".   FAMILY, VOL.
     7 (NOVEMBER 1926), PP. 207-211.

GAMIO.   "STATIC DYNAMIC VALUES INDIGENOUS (AN*).

GAMIO.   "THE INDUSTRIAL PSYCHOLOGY IMMIGRANT (AN*).

GAMIO.   "THE SEQUENCE CULTURES MEXICO" (AN*).

GAMIO.   CONSIDERACIONES SOBRE PROBLEMA (AN*).

GAMIO.   IMMIGRANTE MEXICANO, HISTORIA (AN*).

GAMIO.   MEXICAN IMMIGRANT, HIS LIFE STORY (AN*).

GAMIO.   MEXICAN IMMIGRATION TO UNITED (AN*).

GAMIO.   NUMBER, ORIGIN GEOGRAPHIC DISTRIBUTION (AN*).

GAMIO.   NUMERO, PRODEDENCIA DISTRIBUCION (AN*).

GAMIO.   OBSERVATIONS MEXICAN IMMIGRATION (AN*).

GAMIO.   PRELIMINARY SURVEY ANTECEDENTS (AN*).

GAMIO.   QUANTITATIVE ESTIMATE, SOURCES (AN*).

GAMIO.   QUANTITATIVE ESTIMATE SOURCES (AN*).

GAMIO.   "MIGRATION AND PLANNING" (AN*).

GAMIO.   "THE NEW CONQUEST" (AN*).

GANS, HERBERT J. THE URBAN VILLAGERS; GROUP AND CLASS IN
    THE LIFE OF ITALIAN—AMERICANS. NEW YORK: FREE PRESS,
    1962.

GARCIA, MRS. M. REPORT ON RELOCATION PROGRESS, AUGUST
    1961—— MAY, 1964.   STUDY MADE BY THE CASE WORK
    DIRECTOR OF THE SAN ANTONIO URBAN RENEWAL AGENCY, MAY
    13, 1964..

GARCIA, PETE. "BANDITS——OR HEROS?".   EL GRITO DEL NORTE,
    (MARCH 30,   1971), P. 13.

GARNETT, WILLIAM E. "IMMEDIATE AND PRESSING RACE PROBLEMS
    OF TEXAS".   PROCEEDINGS OF THE SOUTHWESTERN POLITICAL
    AND SOCIAL SCIENCE ASSOCIATION,   (1925), PP. 31—48.

GARNETT, WILLIAM E. "IMMEDIATE AND PRESSING RACE PROBLEMS
    OF TEXAS".   PROCEEDINGS OF THE SOUTHWESTERN POLITICAL
    AND SOCIAL SCIENCE ASSOCIATION,   (1925), PP. 31—48
    (PL).

GARRER, EARL SIMEON. PUERTO RICO UNSOLVED PROBLEM.
    ELGIN, ILL: THE ELGIN PRESS, 1945 (HUS).

GARTH, J. R. "COLOR BLINDNESS AND RACE".   ZEITSCHRIFT
    RASSENK, VOL. 4 , PP. 33—36.

GARZA, EDWARD D. LULAC: LEAGUE OF UNITED LATIN—AMERICAN
    CITIZENS.   SOUTHWEST TEXAS STATE TEACHERS COLLEGE,
    MASTER'S THESIS (1951) (ED).

GARZA, GEORGE J. "GOOD NEIGHBORS: TEXAS VERSION?".   THE
    TEXAS OUTLOOK, VOL. 27 NO. 39 (JUNE   1943) (HT).

GARZA, RAFAEL. THE CHICANO COMMUNITY IN TRANSITION.
    CHICANO STUDIES INSTITUTES, (SUMMER   1971). PROGRAM
    COORDINATED BY MONTAL SYSTEMS, INC..

GEE, MAURINE H. CHICANO, AMIGO.   WEST CALDWELL, NEW
    JERSEY: WILLIAM MORROW AND COMPANY, 1972.

GEIGEL POLANCO, VICENTE. EL DESPERTAR DE UN PUEBLO.   SAN
    JUAN, 1942.

GEORGI.   DELANO GRAPE STRIKE BOYCOTT:INROADS   (LW*).

GETTY, HARRY T. INTERETHNIC RELATIONSHIPS IN THE COMMUNITY
    OF TUCSON.   UNIVERSITY OF CHICAGO, PHD. DISSERTATION
    (1950) (HA).

GETTY, HARRY T. MEXICAN SOCIETY IN THE COMMUNITY OF
    TUCSON, ARIZONA.   TUCSON: ARIZONA STATE MUSEUM
    LIBRARY, UNIVERSITY OF ARIZONA, 1949 (HA).

GIBSON.   PROTESTANTISM LATIN AMERICANACULTURATION   (AN*).

GIBSON.   SOCIAL LIFE SAN ANTONIO (ON EVE   (HUS*).

GILBERT.   "HEALTH NEEDS MIGRANT CHILDREN   (EC*).

GILBERT, FABIOLA CABEZA DE BACA.   "NEW MEXICAN DIETS".
     JOURNAL OF HOME ECONOMICS, VOL. 34 (NOVEMBER 1942),
     PP. 668-669.

GILBERT, FABIOLA CABEZA DE BACA. WE FED THEM CACTUS.
     ALBUQUERQUE: UNIVERSITY OF NEW MEXICO, 1954 (HSW).

GILL, MARIO. NUESTROS BUENOS VECINOS (CUARTA EDICION
     AMPLIADA).   MEXICO: EDITORIAL AZTECA S.A., 1959.

GILLIN.   "ETHCS COMPONENTS MODERN LATIN-AMERICAN (AN*).

GILMORE.   "THE CONDITION POOR MEXICO, 1834" (HM*).

GILPIN.   PUEBLCS CAMERA CHRONICAL   (AR*).

GILPIN.   RIO GRANDE: RIVER DESTINY. INTERPRETATION   (AR*).

GINN, A.   MEXICANS IN BELVEDERE, CALIFORNIA: THE SOCIAL
     IMPLICATIONS.   UNIVERSITY OF SOUTHERN CALIFORNIA,
     MASTER'S THESIS (1947).

GINSBURG.   PSYCHIATRISTS VIEWS SOCIAL ISSUES   (PY*).

GINZBERG, ELI AND BRAY, DONALD W. THE UNEDUCATED.   NEW
     YORK: COLUMBIA UNIVERSITY PRESS, 1953 (ED).

GINZBERG, ELIA. THE NATION'S CHILDREN.   NEW YORK:
     COLUMBIA UNIVERSITY PRESS, 1960 (ED).

GIST, NOEL P.   "DOGMA AND DOCTRINE IN SECRET SOCIETIES".
     SOCIOLOGY AND SOCIAL RESEARCH, VOL. 23   (NOVEMBER
     1938), PP. 121-30.

GITTELSOHN.   "INFLUENCE WATER AVILABILITYSHIGELLA   (MD*).

GITTLER, JOSEPH B. ED. UNDERSTANDING MINORITY GROUPS.
     NEW YORK: JOHN WILEY AND SONS, 1956.

GLADNEY.   FOOD PRACTICES MEXICAN AMERICAN   (MD*).

GLANE, SAM. "JUVENILE GANGS IN EAST LOS ANGELES".   FOCUS,
     (SEPTEMBER 1950), PP. 136-41.

GLAZER, NATHAN AND MOYNIHAN, DANIEL PATRICK. BEYOND THE
     MELTING POT: THE NEGROES, PUERTO RICANS, JEWS,
     ITALIANS, ANDIRISH OF NEW YCRK CITY.   CAMBRIDGE,
     MASSACHUSETTS: THE M.I.T. PRESS, 1963.

GLAZER, NATHAN, AND MC ENTIRE DAVIS, EDS. STUDIES
    IN HOUSING AND MINORITY GROUPS.   BERKELEY: UNIVERSITY
    OF CALIFORNIA PRESS, 1960.

GLEASON, P. "THE MELTING POT: SYMBOL OF FUSION AND
    CONFUSION".   AMERICAN QUARTERLY, VOL. 16 (SPRING
    1964), P. 20.

GLICK.   RIGHT TO EQUAL OPPORTUNITY (EC*).

GODDARD, HENRY H. "MENTAL TESTS AND THE IMMIGRANT".
    JOURNAL OF DELINQUENCY, VOL. 2 (SEPTEMBER 1917),
    PP. 243-77 (SI PY).

GODKIN, E. L. "MEXICANIZATION".   NATION, VOL. 23 (JULY
    1963), PP. 365-66.

GOLDKIND.   COMPARISON FOLK HEALTH BELIEFS (AN*).

GOLDKIND.   FACTORS DIFFERENTIAL ACCULTURATION (AN*).

GOLDMANN, MARY ERNESTINE. A STUDY OF THE ADEQUACY
    AND ECONOMY OF SOME MEXICAN DIETARIES.   UNIVERSITY
    OF TEXAS AT AUSTIN, MASTER'S THESIS (1929).

GOLDNER, NORMAN. THE MEXICAN IN THE NORTHERN URBAN AREA:
    A COMPARISON OF TWO GENERATIONS.   UNIVERSITY
    OF MINNESOTA, MASTER'S THESIS (1959).

GOLDSCHMIDT.   "CLASS DENOMINATIONALISM RURAL (EC*).

GOLDSCHMIDT.   AS YOU SOW (EC*).

GOLDSTEIN, MARCUS SOLOMON. DEMOGRAPHIC AND BODILY CHANGES
    IN DESCENDANTS OF MEXICAN IMMIGRANTS.   AUSTIN:
    INSTITUTE OF LATIN AMERICAN STUDIES, UNIVERSITY OF
    TEXAS, 1943 (SI).

GOMEZ-QUINONES.   "PRELIMINARY REMARKS TOWARD TENTATIVE
    (HSW*).

GOMEZ-QUINONES.   SEMBRADORES RICARDO FLORES MAGON (HM*).

GOMEZ, D. F. "CHICANOS RESEIGED: THE BLOODY FIESTA".
    NATION, VOL. 212 (MARCH 15, 1971), PP. 326-328 (PL).

GOMEZ, D. F. "KILLING OF RUBEN SALAZAR: NOTHING HAS
    REALLY CHANGED IN THE BARRIO".   CHRISTIAN CENTURY,
    VOL. 88 (JANUARY 13,1971), PP. 49-52 (PL).

GONZALES CASANOVA, PABLO. SOCIOLOGIA DE LA EXPLOTACION.
    SECOND EDITION. MEXICO, D.F.: EDITORIAL SIGLO
    21, S.A., MEXICO, 1970.

GONZALES RAMIREZ, MANUEL. LA REVOLUCION SOCIAL DE MEXICO.
    MEXICO CITY, MEXICO: FONDO DE CULTURA ECONOMICA, 1960
    (HM).

GONZALES.   "MEXICAN AMERICAN CALIFORNIA"   (ED*).

GONZALES.   CHALLENGE   (ED*).

GONZALES, KATHLEEN MAY.   THE MEXICAN FAMILY IN SAN ANTONIO,
    TEXAS.   UNIVERSITY OF TEXAS AT AUSTIN, MASTER'S
    THESIS (1928).

GONZALES, KATHLEEN MAY.   THE MEXICAN FAMILY IN SAN ANTONIO,
    TEXAS.   SAN FRANCISCO, CALIFORNIA: R & E RESEARCH
    ASSOCIATES, 1971.

GONZALES, MANUEL C.   "OUR SPANIS-SPEAKING PARENT-TEACHER
    GROUPS AND THEIR PROBLEMS".   TEXAS OUTLOOK, VOL. 27
    (JUNE 1943), PP. 23-24 (ED).

GONZALES, MANUEL C.   LATIN CULTURAL CONTRIBUTIONS TO TEXAS.
    SAN ANTONIO, TEXAS: THE SAN ANTONIO ROTARY CLUB, 1944.

GONZALEZ PINEDA, FRANCISCO.   EL MEXICANO: SU DINAMICA
    PSICOSOCIAL.   MEXICO: D.F., 1969 (PY).

GONZALEZ.   "AN OUNCE PREVENTION MAY BE WORTH   (MD*).

GONZALEZ.   "FACTORS RELATING TO PROPERTY   (EC*).

GONZALEZ, ISABEL.   STEP CHILDREN OF A NATION.   AMERICAN
    COMMISSION FOR PROTECTION OF THE FOREIGN BORN, NEW,
    1947.

GONZALEZ, JOVITA.   'LATIN AMERICANS.'   IN FRANCES
    J. BROWN, AND JOSEPH ROUCEK, EDS., OUR RACIAL
    AND NATIONAL MINORITIES. THEIR HISTORY, CONTRIBUTIONS
    AND PRESENT PROBLEMS.

GONZALEZ.   "THE AMERICANS INVADE BORDERTOWNS" (HSW*).

GONZALEZ, JOVITA.   AMONG MY PEOPLE.   IN AMERICO PAREDES
    AND RAYMUND PAREDES MEXICAN-AMERICAN AUTHORS. BOSTON,
    MASSACHUSETTS: HOUGHTON MIFFLIN COMPANY, 1972 (HSW).

GONZALEZ, JOVITA.   LEAGUE OF UNITED LATIN AMERICAN
    CITIZENS: REGULATIONS AND BY-LAWS.   BROWNSVILLE,
    TEXAS: RECIO BROTHERS, 1933.

GONZALEZ, JOVITA.   SOCIAL LIFE IN CAMERON, STARR AND ZAPATA
    COUNTIES.   UNIVERSITY OF TEXAS AT AUSTIN, MASTER'S
    THESIS (1930) (HSW).

GONZALEZ, NANCIE L. SOLIEN DE.   "FAMILY ORGANIZATION IN
    FIVE TYPES OF MIGRATORY WAGE LABOR".   AMERICAN
    ANTHROPOLOGIST, VOL. 63 NO. 6 (SUMMER 1930), PP.
    1264-1280.

GONZALEZ, NANCIE L. ALIANZA FEDERAL DE MERCEDES. IN THE
    MEXICAN AMERICANS: AN AWAKENING MINORITY. EDITED BY
    MANUAL P. SERVIN. BEVERLY HILLS, CALIFORNIA: GLENCOE
    PRESS, 1970.

GONZALEZ, NANCIE L. SOLIEN DE. THE SPANIS-AMERICANS OF
    NEW MEXICO: A DISTINCTIVE HERITAGE. LOS ANGELES:
    UNIVERSITY OF CALIFORNIA, MEXICAN-AMERICAN STUDY
    PROJECT, (SEPTEMBER 1967). ADVANCE REPORT 9 (AN).

GONZALEZ. "CAREER DEVELOPMENT: LATTICE (ED*).

GONZALEZ, SIMON. EDUCATION FOR MINORITIES: THE MEXICAN
    AMERICANS. FOUNDATIONS OF EDUCATION, JOHN WILEY AND
    SONS, 1971 (AN).

GONZALO, D. F. "SOCIAL ADJUSTMENTS OF FILIPINOS IN
    AMERICA". SOCIOLOGY AND SOCIAL RESEARCH, VOL. 34
    (NOVEMBER-DECEMBER 1949), PP. 166-73.

GOOD NEIGHBOR COMMISSION OF TEXAS. COMMUNITY ORGANIZATION
    FOR INTER-AMERICAN UNDERSTANDING. AUSTIN, TEXAS:
    GOOD NEIGHBOR COMMISSION OF TEXAS.

GOOD NEIGHBOR COMMISSION OF TEXAS. MINUTES OF QUARTERLY
    MEETINGS, SEPTEMBER, 1946 , DECEMBER, 1950. GOOD
    NEIGHBOR COMMISSION OF TEXAS.

GOODMAN. RACE RACE MIXTURE AS BASIS SOCIAL (AN*).

GOODMAN. CHILDS EYE VIEWS LIFE URBANBARRIO (AN*).

GOODMAN. CHILDS EYE VIEWS LIFE URBANBARRIO (AN*).

GOODMAN. RACE AWARENESS YOUNG CHILDREN (AN*).

GOODWIN, C. C. THE COMSTOCK CLUB. SALT LAKE CITY:
    TRIBUNE JOB PRINTING, 1891.

GORDON, ALBERT ISAAC. INTERMARRIAGE: INTERFAITH, INTERRACIAL,
    INTERETHNIC. BOSTON: BEACON, 1964.

GORDON, MILTON MYRON. ASSIMILATION IN AMERICAN LIFE: THE
    ROLE OF RACE, RELIGION, AND NATIONALORIGIN.
    NEW YORK: OXFORD UNIVERSITY PRESS, 1964.

GOREE, AUDREY C. THE DISTRIBUTION OF FOOD MONEY BY TWO
    THOUSAND TEXAS FAMILIES. UNIVERSITY OF TEXAS,
    MASTER'S THESIS (1935) (EC).

GOSSETT, THOMAS F. RACE: THE HISTORY OF AN IDEA IN
    AMERICA. DALLAS: SOUTHERN METHODIST UNIVERSITY
    PRESS, 1971 (HUS).

GOTTLIEB, DAVIC (ED). AMERICA'S OTHER YOUTH: GROWING UP
    POOR. ENGLEWOOD CLIFFS, N. J.: PRENTICE-HALL, INC,
    1971.

GRAHAM, HUGH DAVIS AND GURRE, TED ROBERT. VIOLENCE
    IN AMERICA.   WASHINGTON, D. C.: U.S. GOVERNMENT
    PRINTING OFFICE, (JUNE 1969) (PL).

GRAMBS.   INTERGROUP EDUCATION; METHODS (ED*).

GRANNEBERG, A. "MAURY MAVERICK'S SAN ANTONIO".   SURVEY
    GRAPHIC, VOL. 28 (JULY 1939), PP. 420-426.

GRANT, MADISON. THE ALIEN IN OUR MIDST.   PRIVATELY PRINTED.

GRAVES.   "ACCULTURATION, ACCESS, ALCOHOL (AN*).

GRAVES.   TIME PERSPECTIVE DEFERRED GRATIFICATION (AN*).

GRAY, A. B. THE A. B. GRAY REPORT. LOS ANGELES,
    CALIFORNIA: WESTERNLORE PRESS, PUBLISHERS,.

GRAY.   "SPANISH LANGUAGE NEW MEXICO: (LA*).

GRAY, L. "ZOOT-SUIT YOUTH; OR WHAT HAPPENED TO JUAN
    GARCIA". CHILDHOOD EDUCATION, VOL. 23 (OCTOBER
    1946), PP. 67-74 (ED).

GRAY.   HISTORY AGRICULTURE SOUTHERN (AN*).

GRAYSON.   "THE EVOLUTION PRIMITIVE REBEL" (HN*).

GRAYSON.   "THE EVOLUTION PRIMITIVE REBEL" (HN*).

GREBLER, LEO. "THE NATURALIZATION OF MEXICAN IMMIGRANTS
    IN THE UNITED STATES".   INTERNATIONAL MIGRATION
    REVIEW, VOL. 1 (FALL 1966), PP. 17-32.

GREBLER, LEO. MEXICAN IMMIGRATION TO THE UNITED STATES:
    THE RECORD AND ITS IMPLICATIONS.   LOS ANGELES:
    UNIVERSITY OF CALIFORNIA, (1966). MEXICAN-AMERICAN
    STUDY PROJECT. ADVANCE REPORT 2.

GREBLER, LEO. THE MEXICAN AMERICAN PEOPLE: THE NATION'S
    SECOND LARGEST MINORITY.   NEW YORK: THE FREE PRESS,
    1970 (EC HSW ED   PL).

GREBLER, LEO. THE SCHOOLING GAP: SIGNS OF PROGRESS.
    LOS ANGELES: UNIVERSITY OF CALIFORNIA, (1967).
    MEXICAN-AMERICAN STUDY PROJECT. ADVANCE REPORT 7 (ED).

GREEN.   SOCIAL ACTION: CHILDREN MISFORTUNE (ED*).

GREER, SCOTT A. "SITUATIONAL PRESSURES AND FUNCTIONAL ROLE
    OF THE ETHNIC LABOR LEADER".   SOCIAL FORCES, VOL.
    32 (OCTOBER 1953), PP. 41-45 (EC).

GREER, SCOTT A. THE PARTICIPATION OF ETHNIC MINORITIES
    IN THE LABOR UNIONS OF LOS ANGELES COUNTY.   UNIVERSITY
    OF CALIFORNIA, LOS ANGELES, PHD. DISSERTATION (1952)
    (EC AN).

GREER, SCOTT AND BAGGISH, HENRY. CHAVEZ RAVINE: URBANIZATION
    AND OCCUPATIONAL MOBILITY IN A MEXICAN-AMERICAN
    ENCLAVE.   UNIVERSITY OF CALIFORNIA, LOS ANGELES,
    (1949). RESEARCH REPORT, DEPARTMENT OF ANTHROPOLOGY
    (EC).

GRIER.   PRIVATELY DEVELOPED INTERRACIAL   (EC*).

GRIFFITH, BEATRICE. "FINGER-TIP COATS ARE THE STYLE".
    COMMON GROUND,   (SPRING 1948), PP. 61-67.

GRIFFITH, BEATRICE. "IN THE FLOW OF TIME".   COMMON
    GROUND,   (AUTUMN 1948), PP. 13-20.

GRIFFITH, BEATRICE. "ONE WORLD KID".   COMMON GROUND,
    (WINTER 1948), PP. 13-18.

GRIFFITH, BEATRICE. "THE PACHUCO PATOIS".   COMMON GROUND,
    VOL. 7 NO. 4 (SUMMER 1947), PP. 77-84 (LA).

GRIFFITH, BEATRICE. "THE THINGS OF LIFE".   COMMON GROUND,
    VOL. 8 (SUMMER 1948), PP. 61-68.

GRIFFITH, BEATRICE. "VIVA ROYBAL -- VIVA AMERICA".
    COMMON GROUND, VOL. 10   (AUGUST 1949), PP. 61-70 (PL).

GRIFFITH, BEATRICE. "WHO ARE THE POCHUCOS".   THE PACIFIC
    SPECTATOR, VOL. 1 NO. 3 (SUMMER 1947), PP. 352-360.

GRIFFITH, BEATRICE. AMERICAN ME.   BOSTON: HOUGHTON
    MIFFLIN COMPANY, 1948.

GRIFFITH, BEATRICE. AMERICAN ME.   IN D. A. CHERNOFF, <ED>
    CALL US AMERICANS. NEW YORK: DOUBLEDAY, 1968.

GRIMES, ALAN PENDLETON. EQUALITY IN AMERICA; RELIGION,
    RACE, AND THE URBAN MAJORITY.   NEW YORK: OXFORD
    UNIVERSITY PRESS, 1964.

GROFF, PATRICK J. "CULTURALLY DEPRIVED CHILDREN: OPINIONS
    OF TEACHERS ON THE VIEWS OF REISSMAN".   EXCEPTIONAL
    CHILDREN,   (OCTOBER 1964), PP. 61-65 (ED EC).

GROSSMAN.   MULTI-FACTIONAL POLITICS SANANTONIO (PL*).

GROUP FOR THE ADVANCEMENT OF PSYCHIATRY.   "INTEGRATION
    MAL-INTEGRATIONSPANISH-AMERICAN (PY*).

GUERNSEY, J. "RISE AND SHINE: EAST OREGON PROGRAM FOR
    MIGRANT CHILDREN". AMERICAN EDUCATION, VOL.
    5 (NOVEMBER 1969), PP. 20-21.

GUERRA, IRENE. THE SOCIAL ASPIRATIONS OF A SELECTED GROUP
    OF SPANISH-NAME PEOPLE IN LAREDO, TEXAS. UNIVERSITY
    OF TEXAS, MASTER'S THESIS (1959) (ED).

GURREN, LOUISE. "FOREIGN CHILDREN LIKE TO SOUND 'AMERICAN'".
    THE INSTRUCTOR, VOL. 67 (JANUARY 1958), PP. 79-81
    (ED).

GUSEWELLE, C. W. "ROBERT MELENDEZ: RETROSPECT". THE
    TEXAS QUARTERLY, VOL. 11 (SUMMER 1968), PP. 155-167.

GUSTATSON. "RELATIONSHIP BETWEEN ETHNICGROUP (ED*).

GUTIERREZ DE LARA, L., AND PINCHON, EDGCUMB. THE MEXICAN
    PEOPLE; THEIR STRUGGLE FOR FREEDOM. GARDEN CITY,
    NEW YORK: DOUBLEDAY, PAGE AND CO., 1914 (PL EC).

GUTIERREZ. STUDY SCHOOL ATTENDANCE MIGRANT (ED*).

GUTTENTAG, MARCIA. 'GROUP COHESIVENESS, ETHNIC ORGANIZATION
    AND POVERTY.' IN NATHANIEL N. WAGNER AND MARSHA J.
    HAUG. CHICANOS. SOCIAL AND PSYCHOLOGICAL PERSPECTIVES.
    SAINT LOUIS, MISSOURI: THE C. V. MOSBY COMPANY (PY
    AN).

GUZMAN. "THE MEXICAN AMERICANS: NEW WIND (PL*).

GUZMAN. POLITICS POLICIES MEXICAN AMERICAN (PL*).

GUZMAN. "HOW CENTRO ENDED SEGRAGATION" (PL*).

GUZMAN. "MEXICAN AMERICANS MOVE" (PL*).

GUZMAN. "REASONED RADICALISM: ALTERNATIVE (PL*).

GUZMAN. "THE HAND ESAU: WORDS CHANGE, (PL*).

GUZMAN. EASY CONCEPTS HARD REALITY:MYTHS (PL*).

GUZMAN. ETHICS FEDERALLY SUBSIDIZED RESEARCH-- (PL*).

GUZMAN. ETHICS FEDERALLY SUBSIDIZED RESEARCH: (PL*).

GUZMAN. GENTLE REVOLUTIONARIES: BROWN (PL*).

GUZMAN. MEXICAN AMERICAN POPULATION:INTROSPECTIVE (PL*).

GUZMAN. POLITICAL SOCIALIZATION MEXICAN-AMERICAN (PL*).

GUZMAN. POLITICAL SOCIALIZATION MEXICAN (PL*).

GUZMAN.   RIGHTS WITHOUT ROOTS: STUDY LOSS   (PL*).

GUZMAN.   SOCIO-ECONOMIC POSITION MEXICAN-AMERICAN   (PL*).

GUZMAN.   SOCIOLOGICAL OVERVIEW MEXICAN-AMERICAN   (PL*).

GUZMAN.   "HOW EL CENTRO DID IT"   (PL*).

GWIN J. BLAINE.   "SOCIAL PROBLEMS OF OUR MEXICAN POPULATION".
    PROCEEDINGS OF THE NATIONAL CONFERENCE OF SOCIAL WORK,
    VOL. 1926   (JANUARY 1921), PP. 327-332 (PL).

GWIN, J. BLAINE.   "BACK AND FORTH TO MEXICO".   SURVEY,
    VOL. 39 , PP. 9-10 (PL).

GWIN, J. BLAINE.   "IMMIGRATION ALONG OUR SOUTHWEST BORDER".
    ANNALS OF THE AMERICAN ACADEMY OF POLITICAL AND SOCIAL
    SCIENCE, VOL. 93 , PP. 126-30 (PL).

GWIN, J. BLAINE.   "IMMIGRATION ALONG OUR SOUTHWEST BORDER".
    ANNALS OF THE AMERICAN ACADEMY OF POLITICAL AND SOCIAL
    SCIENCE, VOL. 93 (JANUARY 1921), PP. 126-130 (PL).

GWIN, J. BLAINE.   "MAKING FRIENDS OF INVADERS: MEXICAN
    REFUGEES IN ADVANCE OF THE RETURNING TROUPS".
    SURVEY, VOL. 37 , PP. 621-23 (PL).

HABER, ALAN; FERMAN, LOUIS A.; AND KORNBLUH, JOYCE
    L. POVERTY IN AMERICA: A BOOK OF READINGS.
    ANN ARBOR: UNIVERSITY OF MICHIGAN PRESS, 1968.

HACKER, D. B., (ET AL).   A STUDY OF FOOD HABITS IN
    NEW MEXICO, 1949-1952.   NEW MEXICO STATE COLLEGE:
    NEW MEXICO A & M AGRICULTURAL EXPERIMENT STATION,
    (1954). BULLETIN 384.

HADLEY.   "A CRITICAL ANALYSIS WETBACKPROBLEM"   (LW*).

HADLEY.   TIJERINA   (HSW*).

HALL, G. F.   "PROBLEMS OF SPANISH AMERICAN MINORITY AIRED
    FOR N. C. C. UNIT".   CHRISTIAN CENTURY, VOL. 86
    (NOVEMBER 19, 1969), PP. 1490-1500.

HAMBY, WILLIAM H.   "IN SEARCH OF SENORITAS".   SUNSET, VOL.
    52 (APRIL 1934), PP. 24-26.

HAMMEL, SENIE TEAQUE.   THE ASSOCIATION BETWEEN SOCIO-ECONOMIC
    STATUS AND FAMILY LIFE FOR NEGROES AND MEXICAN
    AMERICANS IN TUCSON, ARIZONA.   UNIVERSITY OF ARIZONA,
    MASTER'S THESIS (1970).

HANDLIN.   HARVARD GUIDE TO AMERICAN HISTORY   (HUS*).

HANDLIN.   "HISTORICAL PERSPECTIVES AMERICAN   (HUS*).

HANDLIN.   AMERICANS; NEW HISTORY PEOPLE   (HUS*).

HANDLIN.   BOSTONS IMMIGRANTS; STUDY ACCULTURATION   (HUS*).

HANDLIN.   CHILDREN UPROOTED   (HUS*).

HANDLIN.   RACE NATIONALITY AMERICAN LIFE   (HUS*).

HANDLIN.   THIS WAS AMERICA   (HUS*).

HANDLIN.   UPROOTED; EPIC STORY GREAT MIGRATIONS   (HUS*).

HANDMAN, MAX S. "NATIONALITY AND DELINQUENCY: THE
     MEXICANS IN TEXAS".   PROCEEDINGS OF THE NATIONAL
     CONFERENCE OF SOCIAL WORK,   (1930), PP. 133-145.

HANDMAN, MAX S. "SAN ANTONIO, THE OLD CAPITAL CITY
     OF MEXICAN LIFE AND INFLUENCE".   SURVEY, VOL. 66
     (MAY 1, 1931), PP. 163-66.

HANDMAN, MAX S. "SOCIAL PROBLEMS IN TEXAS".   SOUTHWESTERN
     POLITICAL AND SOCIAL SCIENCE QUARTERLY, VOL. 5 NO.
     3 (DECEMBER 1924).

HANDMAN, MAX S. "THE MEXICAN IMMIGRANT IN TEXAS".
     SOUTHWESTERN POLITICAL AND SOCIAL SCIENCE QUARTERLY,
     VOL. 7 NO. 1 (1926).

HANDMAN, MAX S. PRELIMINARY REPORT ON NATIONALITY
     AND DELINQUENCY: THE MEXICAN IN TEXAS.   WASHINGTON,
     D. C.: NATIONAL "OMMISSION ON LAW OBSERVANCE AND
     ENFORCEMENT, (1931).

HANDMAN, MAX S. THE MEXICAN IMMIGRANT IN TEXAS.
     SOUTHWESTERN POLITICAL AND SOCIAL SCIENCE QUARTERLY,
     7.

HANDMAN, MAX. "ECONOMIC REASONS FOR THE COMING OF
     THE MEXICAN IMMIGRANT".   AMERICAN JOURNAL OF
     SOCIOLOGY, VOL. 35 (JANUARY 1930), PP. 601-611.

HANDY, MARY OLIVIA. A HISTORY OF FORT SAM HOUSTON.
     UNIVERSITY OF TEXAS AT AUSTIN, MASTER'S THESIS (1949).

HANEY, GEORGE E. PROBLEMS AND TRENDS IN MIGRANT EDUCATION.
     SCHOOL LIFE,.

HANNA, AGNES K. "SOCIAL SERVICES ON THE MEXICAN BORDER".
     PROCEEDINGS OF THE NATIONAL CONFERENCE OF SOCIAL WORK,
     (1935), PP. 692-702.

HANNA, ALFRED JACKSON, AND HANNA, KATHRYN ABBEY. NAPOLEON
     III AND MEXICO: AMERICAN TRIUMPH OVER MONARCH.
     CHAPEL HILL: UNIVERSITY OF NORTH CAROLINA PRESS, 1971.

HANNA, P. "CULTURE AND THE INTELLECTUALS".   NATION, VOL.
     112 , PP. 585-87.

HANO, ARNOLD. "THE AWAKENING OF THE CHICANOS-- IN
     THE SCHOOLS AND BARRIOS A NEW FEELINGOF PERSONAL WORTH
     AND PRIDE HAS RISEN AMONG MEXICAN AMERICAN YOUTH.
     NOWTHEY SAY, 'BROWN IS BEAUTIFUL'".   SEVENTEEN,
     , P. MARCH 1971.

HANSEN, BEULAH L. AN EXPLORATORY STUDY OF THE NEEDS,
     CONCERNS, AND ASPIRATIONS OF MOTHERS OF THE GARDENLAND
     AND GARDEN ACRES AREAS OF SACRAMENTO.   SACRAMENTO
     STATE COLLEGE, MASTER'S THESIS (1968).

HANSEN, MARCUS LEE. THE IMMIGRANT IN AMERICAN HISTORY.
     CAMBRIDGE, MASSACHUSETTS: HARVARD UNIVERSITY PRESS,
     1940.

HANSON, EARL. LOS ANGELES COUNTY POPULATION AND HOUSING
     DATA: STATISTICAL DATA FROM 1940 CENSUS.   LOS
     ANGELES: HAYNES FOUNDATION, 1944.

HANSON.   "COMMUNICATING HEALTH ARGUMENTS (MD*).

HANSON.   "THE SYSTEMATIC LINKAGE HYPOTHESIS (MD*).

HANSON.   NURSE-PATIENT COMMUNICATION; (MD*).

HANSON.   STRUCTURE CONTENT HEALTH BELIEF (MD*).

HANSON.   NURSE-PATIENT COMMUNICATION: (MD*).

HAPGOOD, NORMAN. "PUBLIC OPINION ON MEXICO".   ANNALS OF
     THE AMERICAN ACADEMY OF POLITICAL AND SOCIAL SCIENCE,
     VOL. 132 , PP. 176-79.

HARBY, LEE C. "TEXAN TYPES AND CONTRASTS".   HARPERS
     MAGAZINE, VOL. 81 (JULY 1890), PP. 229-46.

HARDY, OSGOOD. "LOS REPATRIADOS".   POMONA COLLEGE
     MAGAZINE, VOL. 21 , PP. 71-73 (AN).

HARLEM YOUTH OPPORTUNITIES UNLIMITED, NEW YORK. YOUTH IN
     THE GHETTO: A STUDY OF THE CONSEQUENCES OF POWERLESSNESS
     AND A BLUEPRINT FOR CHANGE.   NEW YORK, 1964.

HARO.   BIBLIOGRAPHIC ESSAY (B*).

HARPER.   MAN RESOURCES MIDDLE RIO GRANDE (EC*).

HARRINGTON. "L.A.S STUDENT BLOWOUT" (PL*).

HARRINGTON, MICHAEL. THE OTHER AMERICA; POVERTY IN THE
     UNITED STATES.   NEW YORK: MACMILLAN, 1963.

HARRIS, JAMES KILBOURNE. A SOCIOLOGICAL STUDY OF A MEXICAN
    SCHOOL IN SAN ANTONIO, TEXAS. UNIVERSITY OF TEXAS
    AT AUSTIN, MASTER'S THESIS (1927) (ED).

HARRISON, DAVID C. A SURVEY OF THE ADMINISTRATIVE
    AND EDUCATIONAL POLICIES OF THE BAPTIST, METHODIST
    AND PRESBYTERIAN CHURCHES AMONG MEXICAN AMERICAN
    PEOPLE OF TEXAS. UNIVERSITY OF TEXAS, 1952 (RE).

HARVEY. "DELINQUENT MEXICAN BOY" (ED*).

HARVEY. DELINQUENT MEXICAN BOY URBANAREA (ED*).

HARVEY. SOCIO-ECONOMIC OTHER VARIATIONS (ED*).

HARWARD. HISTORY NEW MEXICO (ED*).

HAVIGHURST. SOCIAL CLASS INFLUENCES AMERICAN (ED*).

HAY. "ESCUELITA: PUBLIC HEALTH WORK (MD*).

HAYDEN, ROBERT G. "SPANISH AMERICANS OF THE SOUTHWEST".
    WELFARE IN REVIEW, VOL. 4 (APRIL 1966), PP. 14-25.

HAYNER, NORMAN S. "SOCIAL FACTORS IN ORIENTAL CRIME".
    AMERICAN JOURNAL OF SOCIOLOGY, VOL. 43 (MAY 1938),
    PP. 908-19 (AN).

HAYNER, NORMAN SYLVESTER. NEW PATTERNS IN OLD MEXICO; A
    STUDY OF TOWN AND METROPOLIS. NEW HAVEN: COLLEGE
    AND UNIVERSITY PRESS, 1966 (AN).

HAZARD, C. E. WELFARE OF FAMILIES OF SUGAR BEET LABORERS.
    WASHINGTON: UNITED STATES DEPARTMENT OF LABOR, (1939).

HEALD, J. H. "THE MEXICANS IN THE SOUTHWEST". MISSIONARY
    REVIEW OF THE WORLD, VOL. 42 (NOVEMBER 1919), PP.
    860-65.

HEER, DAVID M. "THE MARITAL STATUS OF SECOND GENERATION
    AMERICANS". AMERICAN SOCIOLOGICAL REVIEW, VOL. 26
    (APRIL 1961), PP. 233-241.

HEFFERNAN. "REPORT CONFERENCE EDUCATIONCHILDREN (ED*).

HEINS. STRICTLY GHETTO PROPERTY; STORY (ED*).

HEINS. STRICTLY GHETTO PROPERTY: STORY (ED*).

HEIZER. OTHER CALIFORNIANS: PREJUDICE (HS*).

HELLER, CELIA STOPNICA. "CHICANO IS BEAUTIFUL".
    COMMONWEAL, VOL. 91 NO. 16 (JANUARY 23, 1970), PP.
    454-458 (ED).

HELLER, CELIA STOPNICA. AMBITIONS OF MEXICAN AMERICAN
     YOUTH: GOALS AND MEANS OF MOBILITY OF HIGHSCHOOL
     SENIORS. COLUMBIA UNIVERSITY, PHD. DISSERTATION
     (1964) (ED).

HELLER, CELIA STOPNICA. BACKGROUND AND AMBITION OF MALE
     MEXICAN AMERICAN HIGH SCHOOL SENIORS IN LOS ANGELES.
     LOS ANGELES, CALIFORNIA: AMERICAN SOCIOLOGICAL
     ASSOCIATION (PAPER), 1963 (ED).

HELLER, CELIA STOPNICA. CLASS AS AN EXPLANATION OF ETHNIC
     DIFFERENCES IN MOBILITY ASPIRATIONS --.   NEW YORK,
     NEW YORK: EASTERN SOCIOLOGICAL SOCIETY, 1965 (ED).

HELLER, CELIA STOPNICA. MEXICAN AMERICAN YOUTH: FORGOTTEN
     YOUTH AT THE CROSS-ROADS.   NEW YORK: RANDOM HOUSE,
     1966 (ED).

HELLER, CELIA STOPNICA. THE PATTERN OF OFFENSES AMONG
     JUVENILES OF MEXICAN CESCENT.   PITTSBURGH: UNIVERSITY
     OF PITTSBURGH PRESS, 1961 (ED).

HELLER, CHRISTINE A. "REGIONAL PATTERNS OF DIETARY
     DEFICIENCY; SPANISH AMERICANS OF NEW MEXICO AND
     ARIZONA".   ANNALS OF THE AMERICAN ACADEMY OF
     POLITICAL AND SOCIAL SCIENCE, VOL. 225 (JULY 1970),
     P. JANUARY 1943.

HELM, JUNE (ED). SPANISH SPEAKING PECPLE IN THE UNITED
     STATES.   SEATTLE, WASHINGTON: UNIVERSITY OF WASHINGTON
     PRESS, 1968.

HENDERSON, GEORGE (ED). AMERICA'S OTHER CHILDREN.
     NORMAN, OKLAHOMA: UNIVERSITY OF OKLAHOMA PRESS, 1971.

HENDRIX.   AUDITORY DISCRIMINATION DIFFERENCES (ED*).

HENTON, J. M. "HONESTY AND COURTSHIP IN MEXICO".
     OUTLOOK, VOL. 89 , PP. 950-60 (AN).

HERNANDEZ, DELUVINA. MEXICAN AMERICAN CHALLENGE TO
     A SACRED COW.   LOS ANGELES. AZTLAN PUBLICATIONS,
     CHICANO STUDIES CENTER, UNIVERSITY OF CALIFORNIA: LOS
     ANGELES, 1970 (AN).

HERNANDEZ, DELUVINA. LA RAZA SATELLITE SYSTEM.   AZTLAN--CHICANO
     JOURNAL OF THE SOCIAL SCIENCES AND THE ARTS, 1 (AN).

HERR, SELMA ERNESTINE. THE EFFECTS OF PRE-FIRST GRADE
     TRAINING UPON READING READINESS AND READING ACHIEVEMENT
     AMONG SPANISH AMERICAN CHILDREN IN THE FIRST GRADE.
     UNIVERSITY OF TEXAS, PHD. DISSERTATION (1944) (ED).

HERRERA, ALBERT. 'THE MEXICAN AMERICAN IN TWO CULTURES.'
     IN ED LUDWIG AND JAMES SANTIBANEZ (EDS), THE CHICANOS:
     FROM CARICATURE TO SELF PORTRAIT.

HERRERA, ALBERT. 'THE NATIONAL CHICANO MORATORIUM AND THE
     DEATH OF RUBEN SALAZAR.'   IN ED LUDWIG AND JAMES
     SANTIBANEZ (EDS), THE CHICANOS: FROM CARICATURE TO
     SELF PORTRAIT (PL).

HEWES, GORDON. "MEXICANS IN SEARCH OF THE MEXICAN".
     AMERICAN JOURNAL OF ECONOMICS AND SOCIOLOGY, VOL. 13
     (JANUARY 1954), PP. 209-223.

HEWES, LAWRENCE I., AND BELL, WILLIAM Y.   INTERGROUP
     RELATIONS IN SAN DIEGO.   SAN FRANCISCO: AMERICAN
     COUNCIL ON RACE RELATIONS, 1946.

HEWES, LAWRENCE L. INTERGROUP RELATIONS IN SAN DIEGO: SOME
     ASPECTS OF COMMUNITY LIFE IN SANDIEGO WHICH PARTICULARLY
     AFFECT MINORITY GROUPS: WITH RECOMMENDATIONS FOR A
     PROGRAM OF COMMUNITY ACTION.   SAN FRANCISCO: AMERICAN
     COUNCIL FOR RACE RELATIONS, 1946.

HICKEY.   "WHEN MIGRANT CHILDREN ARRIVE (ED*).

HILL.   POLITICAL ROLE MEXICAN AMERICANS (PL*).

HILL, ROBERT TUDOR. THE PUBLIC DOMAIN AND DEMOCRACY; A
     STUDY OF SOCIAL, ECONOMIC AND POLITICAL PROBLEMS IN
     THE UNITED STATES IN RELATION TO WESTERN DEVELOPMENT.
     NEW YORK, 1910. REPRINTED BY: NEW YORK, NEW YORK AND
     LONDON, GREAT BRITAIN: AMS PRESS, INC. (EC PL).

HILLSON.   "THE REORGANIZATION SCHOOL:BRINGING (ED*).

HINMAN, GEORGE W. REPORT OF COMMISSION ON INTERNATIONAL
     AND INTERRACIAL FACTORS IN THE PROLEM OF MEXICANS IN
     THE UNITED STATES.   PHILADELPHIA: HOME MISSIONS
     COUNCIL, 1927.

HOEHLER, FRED K. (ET AL). PUBLIC WELFARE SURVEY OF SAN
     ANTONIO , TEXAS.   CHICAGO: AMERICAN PUBLIC WELFARE
     ASSOCIATION, 1940.

HOFFMAN.   REPATRIATION MEXICAN NATIONALS (EC*).

HOGUE, ALEXANDRE. "LAND OF LITTLE CHURCHES".   EL PALACIO,
     VOL. 26 (1929), PP. 204-12.

HOLLAND.   RELIGIOUS DIMENSION SPANISH LOS (RE*).

HOLLAND, WILLIAM. "CHANGE FROM WITHIN: VESPRA IN
     THE BARRIO".   VISTA VOLUNTEER, VOL. 3 (JUNE 1967),
     PP. 16-21.

HOLLENBERG, CHARLES (ED.).   ETHNIC CONFLICT IN CALIFORNIA
     HISTORY.   LOS ANGELES: TINNON-BROWN, INC., 1970 (HC).

HOLLINGSHEAD, AUGUST DE BELMONT.   SOCIAL CLASS AND MENTAL
     ILLNESS: A COMMUNITY STUDY.   NEW YORK: WILEY, 1958
     (MD).

HOLMES, B. S.   "PERILS OF THE MEXICAN INVASION".   NORTH
     AMERICAN REVIEW, VOL. 227 (MAY 1929), PP. 615-623.

HOLMES, SAMUEL J.   "AN ARGUMENT AGAINST MEXICAN IMMIGRATION".
     COMMONWEALTH CLUB, VOL. 2 NO. 12 (MAY 1929), PP.
     21-27.

HOLMES, SAMUEL J.   "PERILS OF MEXICAN INVASION".   NORTH
     AMERICAN REVIEW, VOL. 227 (MAY, 1929), PP. 615-23.

HOLTZMAN, WAYNE H.   "COMMUNITY ACTION RESEARCH--AN APPROACH
     TO SOCIAL PROBLEMS IN TEXAS CITIES".   PUBLIC AFFAIRS
     COMMENT, VOL. 6 (SEPTEMBER), PP. 1-4.

HOME MISSIONS COUNCIL.   NOTES FOR REPORT OF COMMISSION ON
     INTERNATIONAL AND INTERRACIAL FACTORS IN THE PROBLEM
     OF MEXICANS IN THE UNITED STATES.   NEW YORK, 1926.

HOME MISSIONS COUNCIL.   THE EL PASO CONFERENCE.   NEW YORK:
     HOME MISSIONS COUNCIL, 1926.

HOOVER, GLENN E.   "OUR MEXICAN IMMIGRANTS".   FOREIGN
     AFFAIRS, VOL. 8 NO. 1 (OCTOBER 1929), PP. 99-107.

HORNER, EDWARD.   A RECREATION DIRECTOR IN A MEXICAN-AMERICAN
     COMMUNITY.   UNIVERSITY OF CALIFORNIA, LOS ANGELES,
     MASTER'S THESIS (1945).

HORTON.   FOOD HABITS LIVING CONDITIONS   (MD*).

HORTON.   FOOD HABITS LIVING CONDITIONS   (MD*).

HOURWICH, ISAAC AARONOVICK.   IMMIGRATION AND LABOR: THE
     ECONOMIC ASPECTS OF EUROPEAN IMMIGRATION TO THE UNITED
     STATES.   NEW YORK, 1922, SECOND EDITION REVISED.
     REPRINTED BY: NEW YORK, NEW YORK AND LONDON, GREAT
     BRITAIN: AMS PRESS, INC., 1922.

HOUSER.   "THE TIGUA SETTLEMENT YSLETASUR"   (AN*).

HOUSING OPPORTUNITIES CENTER OF GREATER LOS ANGELES AND
     CRENSHAW NEIGHBORS.   MAINTAING AN INTEGRATED COMMUNITY.
     MAINTAINING AN INTEGRATED COMMUNITY..

HOVER, G. E.   "RESIDENT ALIEN PROBLEM OF THE SOUTHWEST".
     PROCEEDINGS OF THE INSTITUTE OF INTERNATIONAL
     RELATIONS, VOL. 4 (1929), PP. 193-194.

HOWARD, DONALD STEPHENSON. A STUDY OF THE MEXICAN,
    MEXICAN-AMERICAN AND SPANISH-AMERICAN POPULATION IN
    PUEBLO, COLORADO, 1929-1930.   UNIVERSITY OF DENVER,
    MASTER'S THESIS (1932) (ED).

HOWARD, JOHN R. AWAKENING MINORITIES: AMERICAN INDIANS,
    MEXICAN AMERICANS, PUERTO RICANS.   NEW BRUNSWICK,
    NEW JERSEY: ALDINE PUBLISHING CO, 1970.

HOWARD, JOHN R., ED. THE AWAKENING MINORITIES: AMERICAN
    INDIANS, MEXICAN-AMERICANS, AND PUERTO RICANS.
    CHICAGO, ILLINOIS: ALDINE ATHERTON, INC., 1970.

HOWARD.   ACCULTURATION SOCIAL MOBILITY   (AN*).

HOWARD.   ACCULTURATION SOCIAL MOBILITY   (AN*).

HUGHES.   RACICAL AND ETHNIC RELATIONS.   ALLYN, 1970.

HUGHES, ELIZABETH ANN.   LIVING CONDITIONS FOR SMALL-WAGE
    EARNERS IN CHICAGO.   CHICAGO: CITY OF CHICAGO,
    DEPARTMENT OF PUBLIC WELFARE, 1925 (EC).

HUGHES, EVERETT CHERRINGTON, AND HUGHES, HELEN MAC GILL.
    WHERE PEOPLES MEET: RACIAL AND ETHNIC FRONTIERS.
    GLENCOE, ILLINOIS: FREE PRESS, 1952.

HUGHES.   ENGLISH LANGUAGE FACILITY MEXICAN-AMERICAN   (ED*).

HULL.   "PROTECTIVE IMMIGRATION"   (EC*).

HUNTER, RUSSELL VERNON.   "LATIN AMERICAN ART IN THE USA".
    DESIGN, VOL. 44   (MARCH 1943), PP. 20-21.

HURLEY, R. L.   "POVERTY AND MENTAL RETARDATION".
    NEW REPUBLIC,   (JULY 27, 1968), PP. 19-20.

HURT, WESLEY.   MANZANO: A STUDY OF COMMUNITY DISORGANIZATION.
    UNIVERSITY OF NEW MEXICO, MASTER'S THESIS (1941).

HUSZAR, GEORGE BARNARD DE, COMPILER.   ANATOMY OF RACIAL
    INTOLERANCE.   NEW YORK: WILSON, 1946.

HUTCHINSON, EDWARD PRINCE.   IMMIGRANTS AND THEIR CHILDREN,
    1850-1950   1950, BY E.P.
    HUTCHINSON FOR THE SOCIAL SCIENCE RESEARCH COUNCIL
    IN COOPERATION WITH THE U.S. DEPARTMENT OF COMMERCE,
    BUREAU OF THE CENSUS..   NEW YORK: WILEY, 1956.

HUTHMACHER.   NATION NEWCOMERS: ETHNIC MINORITY   (HUS*).

ILLIWILLIAMS, CHARLES HOWARD.   A STUDY OF THE ADJUSTMENT
    OF STUDENTS FROM LATIN AMERICA AT THE UNIVERSITY OF
    TEXAS.   UNIVERSITY OF TEXAS AT AUSTIN, MASTER'S
    THESIS (1956).

INGLEHART, F. C. FACE-TO-FACE WITH THE MEXICANS. NEW
    YORK: THE MACMILLAN COMPANY, 1899.

INSTITUTE OF INTERAMERICAN PROBLEMS. ROCKY MOUNTAIN
    REGION. A SUMMARY OF THE SESSIONS ON HOUSING, HEALTH,
    NUTRITION, PUBLIC ASSISTANCE AND RECREATION. JULY,
    1943.

IRION, CLYDE. A STUDY OF NEIGHBORING IN DALLAS. SOUTHERN
    METHODIST UNIVERSITY, MASTER'S THESIS (1940).

ISSLER, A. R. "GOOD NEIGHBORS, LEND A HAND: OUR MEXICAN
    WORKERS". SURVEY GRAPHIC, VOL. 32 (OCTOBER 1943),
    PP. 289-394.

ITURRIAGA, JOSE E. 'THE CHARACTER OF THE MEXICAN.' IN
    J. L. MARTINEZ. (ED) THE MODERN MEXICO ESSAY.

ITURRIAGA, JOSE E. LA ESTRUCTURA SOCIAL Y CUTURAL
    DE MEXICO. MEXICO: FONDO DE CULTURA ECONOMICA, 1951
    (AN).

JACO. PATIENTS, PHYSICIANS ILLNESS; (MD*).

JACO. "SOCIAL FACTORS MENTAL DISORDERS (MD*).

JACO. "THE SOCIAL ISOLATION HYPOTHESIS (MD*).

JACO. SOCIAL EPIDEMIOLOGY MENTAL DISORDERS: (MD*).

JACOBS, P. THE STATE OF THE UNIONS. NEW YORK: ATHENUM,
    1963.

JACOBS, PAUL. "THE FORGOTTEN PEOPLE". THE REPORTER, VOL.
    20 (JANUARY 22, 1959), PP. 13-20.

JAVITS, JACOB K. DISCRIMINATION-- U. S. A.. NEW YORK:
    HARCOURT, BRACE, 1960.

JENKS, A. INDIAN WHITE AMALGAMATION. MINNEAPOLIS,
    MINNESOTA: UNIVERSITY OF MINNESOTA STUDIES IN
    THE SOCIAL SCIENCES, 1916.

JENSEN, JOAN MARIA. THE AMERICAN PROTECTIVE LEAGUE,
    1917-1919. UNIVERSITY OF CALIFORNIA, LOS ANGELES,
    PHD. DISSERTATION (1962) (ED).

JENSEN, MERRILL, <ED.>. REGIONALISM IN AMERICA.
    UNIVERSITY OF WISCONSIN PRESS, 1951 (HUS).

JESSEY, CORNELIA. TEACH THE ANGRY SPIRIT. NEW YORK:
    CROWN, 1949 (LI).

JESSOR. SOCIETY, PERSONALITY DEVIANTBEHAVIOR: (AN*).

JOHANSEN, SIGURD ANTHONY. "FAMILY ORGANIZATION IN SPANISH
    AMERICAN CULTURE AREA". SOCIOLOGY AND SOCIAL
    RESEARCH, VOL. 28 (NOVEMBER-DECEMBER 1943), PP. 123-131.

JOHANSEN, SIGURD ANTHONY. RURAL SOCIAL ORGANIZATION IN
    A SPANISH-AMERICAN CULTURE AREA. UNIVERSITY
    OF WISCONSIN, PHD. DISSERTATION (1941).

JOHANSEN, SIGURD ANTHONY. RURAL SOCIAL ORGANIZATION IN
    A SPANISH AMERICAN CULTURE AREA. ALBUQUERQUE:
    UNIVERSITY OF NEW MEXICO PRESS, (1948). NEW MEXICO
    PUBLICATIONS IN SOCIAL SCIENCES AND PHILOSOPHY NUMBER
    1.

JOHANSEN, SIGURD ARTHUR. RECENT POPULATION CHANGES IN NEW
    MEXICO. NEW MEXICO AGRICULTURAL EXPERIMENTAL
    STATION: NEW MEXICO STATE COLLEGE, 1941.

JOHANSEN, SIGURD. "THE SOCIAL ORGANIZATION OF SPANISH-AMERICAN
    VILLAGES". SOUTHWESTERN SOCIAL SCIENCE QUARTERLY,
    VOL. 23 (SEPTEMBER 1942), PP. 151-159.

JOHNSON, DALLAS. "THE FENCED TOLERENCE IN". SURVEY
    GRAPHIC, VOL. 36 (JULY 1947), PP. 398-99.

JOHNSON.   EDUCATING MEXICAN AMERICAN (ED*).

JOHNSON.   ETHNIC GROUP DIFFERENCES CERTAIN (ED*).

JOHNSON.   STUDY SOME ECOLOGICAL, ECONOMIC (ED*).

JOHNSON.   "REMARKS AT MEXICAN FIESTA" (PL*).

JOHNSON.   NEW FOCUS OPPORTUNITY SPANISH (PL*).

JOHNSON, RONDAL. THE AFICIONADO'S SOUTHEWESTERN COOKING.
    ALBUQUERQUE, NEW MEXICO: UNIVERSITY OF NEW MEXICO
    PRESS, 1968.

JONES, ANITA E. "MEXICAN COLONIES IN CHICAGO". SOCIAL
    SERVICE REVIEW, VOL. 2 (DECEMBER 1928), PP. 579-97.

JONES, ANITA EDGAR. CONDITIONS SURROUNDING MEXICANS IN
    CHICAGO. UNIVERSITY OF CHICAGO, MASTER'S THESIS (1928).

JONES, ROBERT C. "ETHNIC FAMILY PATTERNS: THE MEXICAN
    FAMILY IN THE UNITED STATES". AMERICAN JOURNAL OF
    SOCIOLOGY, VOL. 53 (MAY 1948), PP. 450-453 (EC).

JONES, ROBERT C. "INTEGRATION OF THE MEXICAN MINORITY IN
    THE UNITED STATES INTO DEMOCRACY". EVENTS AND TRENDS
    IN RACE RELATIONS, VOL. 4 (JANUARY 1947), PP.
    175-177 (EC).

JONES, ROBERT C. "MEXICAN AMERICAN YOUTH". SOCIOLOGY
    AND SOCIAL RESEARCH, VOL. 32 (MARCH 1948), PP.
    793-797 (EC).

JONES, ROBERT C.   "MEXICAN YOUTH IN THE UNITED STATES".
    AMERICAN TEACHER, VOL. 28 (MARCH   1944), PP. 11-15
    (EC).

JONES, ROBERT C.   "MEXICAN YOUTH IN THE UNITED STATES".
    THE TEXAS OUTLOOK, VOL. 29 (MARCH   1944), PP. 11-13
    (EC).

JONES, ROBERT C.   "THE LATIN AMERICAN PROBLEM".   SCHOOL
    AND SOCIETY, VOL. 58 (DECEMBER 4,   1943), PP. 441-443
    (EC).

JONES, ROBERT C.   COMMITTEE ON SOCIAL SERVICE COOPERATION
    OF THE PAN AMERICAN COUNCIL - HISTORY AND PURPOSE.
    CHICAGO, PAN AMERICAN COUNCIL, 1942. 2 PAGES (MIMEOGRAPHED)
    (EC).

JONES, ROBERT C.   LOS BRACEROS MEXICANOS EN LOS ESTADOS
    UNIDOS DURANTE EL PERIODO BELICO.   WASHINGTON,
    D.C.: UNION PANAMERICANA OFICINA DE INFORMACION OBRERA
    Y SOCIAL, (1946) (EC).

JONES, ROBERT C.   MEXICAN WAR WORKERS IN THE UNITED STATES:
    THE MEXICO-UNITED STATES MANPOWER RECRUITING PROGRAM,
    1942-1944.   WASHINGTON, D. C.: PAN AMERICAN UNION,
    (1945) (EC).

JONES, ROBERT C., AND WILSON, LOUIS R.   THE MEXICAN
    IN CHICAGO.   CHICAGO CHURCH FEDERATION, 1931.
    32 PAGES <PAMPHLET>. (EC).

JONES.   GOVERNMENT RIOTS LOS ANGELES,   (PL*).

JORDAN.   "RETENTION FOREIGN LANGUAGE HOME"   (ED*).

JORDAN.   NATIONALITY SCHOOL PROGRESS: (ED*).

JUAREZ.   ETHNIC GROUP IDENTITY ORIENTATIONS   (ED*).

JUSTIN.   "CULTURE CONFLICT MEXICAN AMERICAN   (ED*).

KADUSHKEN, ALFRED. CHILD WELFARE SERVICES; A SOURCEBOOK.
    NEW YORK: MACMILLAN, 1970.

KALET, ANNA. "MEXICAN CHILD WELFARE".   SURVEY, VOL. 46
    (JANUARY   1921), PP. 49-50.

KARNO, MARVIN AND MORALES, ARMANDO. "A COMMUNITY MENTAL
    HEALTH SERVICE FOR MEXICAN-AMERICANS IN A METROPOLIS."
    IN NATHANIEL N. WAGNER AND MARSHA J. HAUG, (EDS),
    CHICANOS: SOCIAL AND PSYCHOLOGICAL PERSPECTIVES.
    SANINT LOUIS, MISSOURI: THE C. V. MOSBY COMPANY (MD).

KARR.   "PROTEST: MEXICAN-AMERICAN STYLE"   (PL*).

KARRAKER, C. "RIGHT TO HAVE FUN". RECREATION , VOL. 55
(NOVEMBER 1962), P. 435.

KARRAKER, C. "TASK FOR A PEACE CORPS". CHRISTIAN
CENTURY, VOL. 80 (FEBRUARY 20, 1963), PP. 237-238.

KAUFMAN, CHARLES. FIESTA IN MANHATTAN. NEW YORK: MORROW,
1939.

KAYSAS, MELVIN R. MEXICAN AMERICAN AND CULTURAL DEPRIVATION.
CHICAGO: CHICAGO TEACHERS COLLEGE, 1964.

KEACH. EDUCATION SOCIAL CRISIS: PERSPECTIVES (ED*).

KEATING, CHARLOTTE MATTHEWS. BUILDING BRIDGES OF UNDERSTANDING.
TUCSON: PALO VERDE PUBLISHING COMPANY, 1967.

KELLER, SUZANNE ONFELD. THE URBAN NEIGHBORHOOD, A
SOCIOLOGICAL PERSPECTIVE. NEW YORK: RANDOM HOUSE,
1968.

KELLEY, E., AND OTHERS. "SEGREGATION OF MEXICAN AMERICAN
SCHOOL CHILDREN IN SOUTHERN CALIFORNIA". AMERICAN
JOURNAL OF PUBLIC HEALTH, VOL. 38 (JANUARY 1948),
PP. 30-35 (MD).

KELLY, ERNECE B. SEARCHING FOR AMERICA. TASK FORCE ON
RACISM AND BIAS, NATIONAL COUNCIL OF TEACHERS
OF ENGLISH, (FEBRUARY 1935). 1972.

KELLY, MARYNELL ATWATER <SNYDER>. A COMPARATIVE ADJUSTMENT
STUDY OF OLDER MEXICAN AMERICAN AND ANGLO WOMEN.
UNIVERSITY OF ARIZONA, MASTER'S THESIS (1966).

KENNEDY, PAUL. "CONFERENCE SIFTS U. S.—MEXICAN ISSUES".
NEW YORK TIMES, (FEBRUARY 2 1, 1965), P. 31.

KERBY. "MINORITIES OPPOSE LOS ANGELES (ED*).

KERRICK, JEAN S. PRELIMINARY REPORT--ATTITUDES OF MIGRANT
FARM POPULATION IN SANTA BARBARA COUNTY. RESEARCH
REPORT ON ATTITUDES TOWARD HEALTH, SCHOOL OF PUBLIC
HEALTH, UNIVERSITY OF CALIFORNIA, LOS ANGELES,
SEPTEMBER 8, 1964 (MD).

KIBBE, PAULINE R. "THE AMERICAN STANDARD-FOR ALL AMERICANS".
COMMON GROUND, VOL. 10 NO. 1 (AUTUMN 1949), PP. 19-28.

KIBBE, PAULINE R. THE ECONOMIC PLIGHT OF MEXICANS. NEW
YORK: APPLETON—CENTURY—CROFTS, 1953 (EC).

KIBBE, PAULINE ROCHESTER. LATIN AMERICANS IN TEXAS.
ALBUQUERQUE, NEW MEXICO: UNIVERSITY OF NEW MEXICO
PRESS, 1946.

KIENLE, JOHN EMMANUEL. HOUSING CONDITIONS AMONG THE
    MEXICAN POPULATION OF LOS ANGELES.   UNIVERSITY OF
    SOUTHERN CALIFORNIA, MASTER'S THESIS (1912).

KILLIAN, LEWIS AND CHARLES GRIGG. RACIAL CRISIS IN
    AMERICA.   ENGLEWOOD CLIFFS, NEW JERSEY: PRENTICE-HALL,
    INC., 1964.

KIMBALL.   PARENT FAMILY INFLUENCE ACADEMIC   (ED*).

KING, JOHN RANDLE. AN INQUIRY INTO THE STATUS OF MEXICAN
    SEGREGATION IN METROPOLITAN BAKERSFIELD.   CLAREMONT
    GRADUATE SCHOOL, CLAREMONT, CALIFORNIA, MASTER'S
    THESIS (1946) (HC).

KING. "AMERICAS POOR" (EC*).

KINGREA.   HISTORY FIRST TEN YEARS TEXAS   (HT*).

KIRK, GRAYSON. "FILIPINOS".   ANNALS CF THE AMERICAN
    ACADEMY OF POLITICAL AND SOCIAL SCIENCE, VOL. 223
    (SEPTEMBER 1942), PP. 45-48.

KIRK, WILLIAM. "CULTURAL CONFLICT IN MEXICAN LIFE".
    SOCIOLOGY AND SOCIAL RESEARCH, VOL. 15 (JUNE 1931),
    PP. 352-364.

KIRK, WILLIAM. "CURRENT SOCIAL MOVEMENTS IN MEXICO".
    SOCIOLOGY AND SOCIAL RESEARCH, VOL. 15 (JUNE 1931),
    PP. 403-16.

KISER. "CULTURAL PLURALISM" (AN*).

KISTLER, ROBERT. "A NEW UNIFORM FOR ANGEL".   SCOUTING,
    VOL. 59 NO. 3 (MAY-JUNE 1971), P. 36.

KLAPP, ORRIN. "MEXICAN SOCIAL TYPES".   AMERICAN JOURNAL
    OF SOCIOLOGY, VOL. 69 (JANUARY 1964), PP. 404-414.

KLINEBERG.   RACE DIFFERENCES   (PY*).

KLING, MERLE A. A MEXICAN INTEREST GROUP IN ACTION.
    ENGLEWOOD CLIFFS, NEW JERSEY, PRENTICE-HALL.

KLUCKHOHN, FLORENCE R. "CULTURAL FACTORS IN SOCIAL WORK
    PRACTICE AND EDUCATION".   SOCIAL SERVICE REVIEW, VOL.
    25 (MARCH 1951), PP. 40-45.

KNOTT.   NORTH BORDER; FOLK FESTIVALSSOUTHWEST   (AN*).

KNOWLTON.   THE NEW MEXICAN LAND WAR   (HN*).

KNOWLTON.   "AN APPROACH TO ECONOMIC SOCIAL   (EC*).

KNOWLTON.   "CAUSES LAND LOSS AMONG SPANISH   (HN*).

KNOWLTON.   "CHANGING SPANISH AMERICAN VILLAGES   (HN*).

KNOWLTON.   "PATRON—PEON PATTERN AMONG SPANISH   (HN*).

KNOWLTON.   "THE NEW MEXICAN LAND WAR"   (HN*).

KNOWLTON.   "THE SPANISH AMERICANS NEW MEXICO"   (HN*).

KNOWLTON.   "TIJERINA: HERO MILITANTS"   (HN*).

KNOWLTON.   BILINGUALISM: PROBLEM OR ASSET   (HN*).

KNOWLTON.   COMPARISON SPANISH AMERICAN MEXICAN   (HN*).

KNOWLTON.   DISCUSSION PLANNING IMPLEMENTATION   (HN*).

KNOWLTON.   IMPACT SOCIAL CHANGE UPON CERTAIN   (HN*).

KNOWLTON.   INDIAN SPANISH AMERICAN ADJUSTMENTS   (HN*).

KNOWLTON.   LAND GRANT PROBLEMS AMONG STATE   (HN*).

KNOWLTON.   PROBLEMS DIFFICULTIES PLANNING   (HN*).

KNOWLTON.   PROBLEMS PROSPECTS RURAL SPANISH   (HN*).

KNOWLTON.   RECOMMENDATIONS SOLUTION LAND   (HN*).

KNOWLTON.   SITUATION SPANISH AMERICANS NORTHERN   (HN*).

KNOWLTON.   SITUATION SPANISH AMERICANS NORTHERN   (HN*).

KNOWLTON.   SOME CONSIDERATION SITUATIONSPANISH   (HN*).

KNOWLTON.   SOME PRESENT TRENDS PROSPECTS   (HN*).

KNOWLTON.   SPANISH AMERICAN SCHOOLS 1960S   (HN*).

KNOWLTON.   INTERNATIONAL WATER LAW ALONG   (HN*).

KNOWLTON.   COMPARISON SPANISH AMERICAN MEXICAN   (HN*).

KNOWLTON.   "CHANGES STRUCTURE ROLES SPANISH   (HN*).

KNOWLTON.   "GUERRILLAS RIO ARRIBA: NEW MEXICAN   (HN*).

KNOWLTON.   "THE SPANISH AMERICANS NEW MEXICO"   (HN*).

KOMAROFF, ANTHONY L., MASUDA, MINORU AND HOLMES, THOMAS
    H. THE SOCIAL READJUSTMENT RATING SCALE: A COMPARATIVE
    STUDY OF NEGRO, MEXICAN, AND WHITE AMERICANS..
    EDITED BY NATHANIEL N. WAGNER AND MARSHA J. HAUG.
    SAINT LOUIS, MISSOURI: THE C.V. MOSBY COMPANY, 1971.

KOOB, C. A. "SNAP MINORITY".   MOMENTUM, VOL. 1 (APRIL
    1970), PP. 2—3.

KORTE, ALVIN O. <ET. AL.>. LENGTH OF TIME AND PUBLIC
    ASSISTANCE AND ACHIEVEMENT MOTIVATION OF MEXICAN
    AMERICAN MALE ADOLESCENTS.   TEMPE, ARIZONA STATE
    UNIVERSITY, 1967 (PY).

KRAMER, JUDITH R. THE AMERICAN MINORITY COMMUNITY.   NEW
    YORK, NEW YORK: THOMAS Y. CROWELL COMPANY, 1970.

KRAMER, RALPH M. PARTICIPATION OF THE POOR: COMPARATIVE
    COMMUNITY CASE STUDIES IN THE WAR ON POVERTY.
    ENGLEWOOD CLIFFS: PRENTICE-HALL, 1969.

KRASS, ELAINE M. AND OTHERS. "DIFFERENTIAL ASSOCIATION,
    CULTURAL INTEGRATION AND ECONOMIC ABSORPTION AMONG
    MEXICAN-AMERICANS AND NEGROES IN A NORTHERN INDUSTRIAL
    COMMUNITY".   SOUTHWESTERN SOCIAL SCIENCE QUARTERLY,
    VOL. 47 (DECEMBER 1966), PP. 239-252.

KRASS, ELAINE, AND LYLE SHANNON. "THE URBAN ADJUSTMENT
    OF IMMIGRANTS: THE RELATIONSHIP OF EDUCATION
    OF OCCUPATION AND TOTAL FAMILY INCOME".   PACIFIC
    SOCIOLOGICAL REVIEW,   (SPRING 1963), PP. 37-42.

KRASSOWSKI, WITOLD. NATURALIZATION AND ASSIMILATION
    PRONENESS OF CALIFORNIA IMMIGRANT POPULATIONS.
    UNIVERSITY OF CALIFORNIA, LOS ANGELES, PHD. DISSERTATION
    (1963).

KREAR.   ROLE MOTHER TONGUE AT HOME AT   (LA*).

KRESSELMAN, HAROLD B. A STUDY OF 100 MALE LATIN-AMERICAN
    JUVENILE DELINQUENTS IN SAN ANTONIO.   UNIVERSITY OF
    TEXAS, MASTER'S THESIS (1948).

KRINSKY, FRED. THE WELFARE STATE; WHO IS MY BROTHER'S
    KEEPER?.   CLAIFORNIA: GLENCOE PRESS, 1968.

KRITZER, EDITH. ST PAUL REPORT ON MEXICAN STUDY.   FROM
    THE FILES OF THE INTERNATIONAL INSTITUTE, SAINT PAUL,
    MINNESOTA, 1929 (EC).

KRUEGER.   M.A.Y.O. CAMPO   (LW*).

KURTH.   STUDY FOUR RACIAL GROUPS PASADENA   (ED*).

KVARACEUS.   AMIGO SELF-CONCEPT, IMPLICATIONS   (EC*).

LA FARGE, OLIVER. FIVE FAMILIES
    SANTA FE: THE AUTOBIOGRAPHY OF A SOUTHWESTERN TOWN.
    NEW YORK: BASIC BOOKS INC., 1959.

LA FARGE, OLIVER. THE WIND FROM THE SEA.   AUSTIN,TEXAS:
    STECK-VAUGHN COMPANY, 1967.

LADO.   RELATION SOCIAL, ECONOMIC PERSONAL   (ED*).

LAMB.   "RACIAL DIFFERENCES BIMANUALDEXTERITY (PY*).

LAMB.   MEXICAN AMERICANS: SONS SOUTHWEST (HSW*).

LAND.   SOCIAL BACKGROUND HEAD STARTPARTICIPANTS (ED*).

LANDAU. S. AMERICAN ENTERPRISE MEXICO: CASE (EC*).

LANDAZURI, ELENA. "WHY WE ARE DIFFERENT". SURVEY, VOL.
     52 (MAY 1924), PP. 159-60.

LANDES. COUNSELLING MEXICAN AMERICANS (ED*).

LANDSBERGER. CHURCH SOCIAL CHANGE LATIN AMERICA (RE*).

LANE, JOHN HART, JR. VOLUNTARY ASSOCIATIONS AMONG MEXICAN
     AMERICANS IN SAN ANTONIO, TEXAS. ANN ARBOR,
     MICHIGAN: UNIVERSITY MICROFILMS, INC., 1971.

LANE, JOHN. VCLUNTARY ASSOCIATIONS AMONG MEXICAN AMERICANS
     IN SAN ANTONIO, TEXAS. UNIVERSITY OF TEXAS AT
     AUSTIN, PHD. DISSERTATION (1968).

LANGNER, THOMAS S. "A TEST OF INTERGROUP PREJUDICE WHICH
     TAKES ACCOUNT OF INDIVIDUAL AND GROUP DIFFERENCES IN
     VALUES". JCURNAL OF ABNORMAL AND SOCIAL PSYCHOLOGY,
     VOL. 48 (OCTOBER 1953), PP. 548-554 (PY).

LANIGAN. SECOND GENERATION MEXICANS BELVEDERE (HC*).

LARA-BRAUD, J. "OUR SPANISH AMERICAN NEIGHBORS; DOMESTIC
     MISSION PROGRAMS OF U. S. PROTESTANT CHURCHES".
     CHRISTIAN CENTURY, VOL. 85 (JANUARY 10, 1968), PP.
     43-45 (RE).

LARA-BRAUD, JORGE. BILINGUALISM FOR TEXAS: EDUCATION FOR
     FRATERNITY. PREPARED AT THE REQUEST OF THE DIVISION
     OF EDUCATION OF THE TEXAS CONFERENCE OF CHURCHES. (RE
     ED).

LARA-BRAUD, JORGE. E PLURIBUS UNUM: LA RAZA. AUSTIN,
     TEXAS: SOUTHWEST INTERGROUP RELATIONS COUNCIL, INC.,
     1970.

LARA-BRAUD, JORGE. THE STATUS OF RELIGION AMONG MEXICAN
     AMERICANS. ADDRESS DELIVERED AT THE JOINT MEETING
     OF THE AMERICAN ACADEMY OF RELIGION AND THE SOCIETY
     OF BIBLICAL LITERATURE. FORT WORTH, TEXAS: SOUTHWEST
     REGION, TEXAS CHRISTINA UNIVERSITY, 1971. (RE).

LARNER, JEREMY; HOWE, IRVING. POVERTY; VIEW FROM THE LEFT.
     NEW YORK: MORROW, 1968.

LASKER, BRUNO. RACE ATTITUDES IN CHILDREN. NEW YORK:
     HOLT, 1929 (PY AN).

LASKER, BRUNO. A STUDY OF THE DEVELOPMENT OF RACE
    ATTITUDES IN CHILDREN. NEW YORK: HOLT, 1939 (PY
    AN).

LASSWELL, THOMAS E. A STUDY OF STATUS STRATIFICATION IN
    LOS ANGELES. UNIVERSITY OF SOUTHERN CALIFORNIA, PHD.
    DISSERTATION (1952).

LAURENTI. PROPERTY VALUES RACE: STUDIES (EC*).

LAZARO SALINAS, JOSE. LA EMIGRACION DE BRACEROS. MEXICO:
    CAUH TEMOC, 1955 (ED).

LEAL CARRILLO. IMPORTANCIA ECONOMICA SOCIALDE (EC*).

LEARY. RACE REGENERATION (HSW*).

LEDERE, WILLIAM J.; BURDICK, EUGENE. THE UGLY AMERICAN.
    NEW YORK: FAWCETT WORLD LIBRARY, 1960.

LEHMAN, VICTOR BOYD. A STUDY OF THE SOCIAL ADJUSTMENT OF
    THE MEXICAN-AMERICANS IN CHINO AND APROPOSED PLAN OF
    COMMUNITY ACTION UNDER SCHOOL LEADERSHIP. CLAREMONT:
    GRADUATE SCHOOL, MASTER'S THESIS (1947) (ED).

LEMERT, EDWIN M. ; ROSEBERG, JUDY. "CRIME AND PUNISHMENT
    AMONG MINORITY GROUPS IN LOS ANGELES COUNTY".
    PROCEEDINGS OF THE PACIFIC COAST SOCIOLOGICAL SOCIETY,
    (JUNE 1946), PP. 133-45.

LEMERT, EDWIN M. ; ROSEBERG, JUDY. THE ADMINISTRATION OF
    JUSTICE TO MINORITY GROUPS IN LOS ANGELES COUNTY.
    BERKELEY, CALIFORNIA: UNIVERSITY OF CALIFORNIA PRESS,
    1948 (AN).

LENERO OTERO, LUIS. INVESTIGATION DE LA FAMILIA EN MEXICO.
    INSTITUTO MEXICANO DE ESTUDIOS SOCIALES, 1968.

LEONA E. PSYCHOLOGY HUMAN DIFFERENCES (PY*).

LEONARD, OLEN E. CHANGES IN THE SPANISH SPEAKING LABOR
    FORCE OF SAGINAW COUNTY, MICHIGAN ES OF A SPANISH
    AMERICAN VILLAGE IN NEW MEXICO. MISSISSIPPI STATE
    UNIVERSITY, (SEPTEMBER 1968). REPORT 22. STATE
    COLLEGE, MISSISSIPPI: SOCIAL SCIENCE RESEARCH CENTER
    (EC).

LEONARD, OLEN E. OLDER RURAL AMERICANS: A SOCIOLOGICAL
    PERSPECTIVE. LEXINGTON: UNIVERSITY OF KENTUCKY
    PRESS, 1967 (EC).

LEONARD, OLEN E. THE ROLE OF THE LAND GRANT IN THE SOCIAL
    ORGANIZATION AND SOCIAL PROCESS. LOUISIANA STATE
    UNIVERSITY, PHD. DISSERTATION (1943) (HN).

LEONARD, OLEN E. THE ROLE OF THE LAND GRANT: THE SOCIAL
PROCESSES OF A SPANISH AMERICAN VILLAGE IN NEW MEXICO.
ALBUQUERQUE, NEW MEXICO: CALVIN HORN, PUBLISHER, INC.,
1970 (HN).

LEONARD, OLEN E.; JOHNSON, HELEN W. LOW-INCOME FAMILIES
IN THE SPANISH SURNAME POPULATION OF THE WOUTHWEST.
WASHINGTON, D. C.: ECONOMIC RESEARCH SERVICE, U.S.
DEPARTMENT OF AGRICULTURE, (APRIL 1967) (EC).

LEONARD, OLEN; LOCMIS, C. P. STANDARDS OF LIVING IN AN
INDIAN MEXICAN VILLAGE ON A RECLAMATION PROJECWHERE
BOTH BULLETS AND BALLOTS ARE DANGEROUS. WASHINGTON,
D. C.: U.S. DEPARTMENT OF AGRICULTURE, (1938).

LEONARD, OLEN; LOOMIS, C. P. THE CULTURE OF A CONTEMPORARY
RURAL COMMUNITY: EL CERRITO, NEW MEXICO. WASHINGTON:
UNITED STATES DEPARTMENT OF AGRICULTURE, (1941) (HN).

LEROY, GEORGES P. "CONTRIBUTION TO THE STUDY OF THE
'WETBACK' PROBLEM: ILLEGAL MEXICAN IMMIGRATION TO THE
UNITED STATES". POPULATION, VOL. 7 (APRIL-JUNE
1952), PP. 334-337.

LEROY, W. J. ; DINSMORE, CYRENA B. "A LETTER FROM
ENGLAND". EL GRITO, (APRIL-JUNE 1952), PP. 38-40.

LESSA. MARTA; SOUVENIR NEW YORK (PY*).

LESTER, OLIVE P. "THE WETBACK INVASION". COMMON GROUND,
VOL. 10 (AUTUMN 1949), PP. 11-19.

LEVENTMAN, SEYMOUR. MINORITY GROUP LEADERSHIP: THE
ADVANTAGES OF THE DISADVANTAGES. NEW YORK: THE
MACMILLAN CO., 1964.

LEVY. "THE CLCUDCROFT BABY SANATCRIUM" (EC*).

LEWIS, HILDA P.; LEWIS, EDWARD R. "WRITTEN LANGUAGE
PERFORMANCE OF SIXTH GRADE CHILDREN OF LOW SOCIO-ECONOMIC
STATUS FROM BILINGUAL AND FROM MONOLINGUAL BACKGROUNDS".
JOURNAL OF EXPERIMENTAL EDUCATION, VOL. 33 (SPRING
1965), PP. 337-342.

LIEBERSON, STANLEY. A SOCIETAL THEORY OF RACE AND ETHNIC
RELATIONS. EDITED BY NATHANIEL N. WAGNER AND MARSHA
J. HAUG. SANT LOUIS, MISSOURI: THE C. V. MOSBY
COMPANY, 1971.

LIN, PAUL MING-CHANG. VOLUNTARY KINSHIP AND VOLUNTARY
ASSOCIATION IN A MEXICAN AMERICAN COMMUNITY.
UNIVERSITY OF TEXAS, MASTER'S THESIS (1963) (AN).

LINTON. SOCIOCULTURAL CHARACTERISTICS (ED*).

LIPSET, S. M.; BENDIX, R. SOCIAL MOBILITY IN INDUSTRIAL
     SOCIETY.   BERKELEY: UNIVERSITY OF CALIFORNIA PRESS,
     1962.

LIPSET, S. M.; SOLARI ALDO. ELITES IN LATIN AMERICA.
     LONDON: OXFORD UNIVERSITY PRESS, 1967.

LIPSHULTZ, ROBERT J. AMERICAN ATTITUDES TOWARD MEXICAN
     IMMIGRATION ,1924-1952.   UNIVERSITY OF CHICAGO, 1962.

LITTLE, WILLSON. SPANISH SPEAKING CHILDREN IN TEXAS.
     AUSTIN, TEXAS: UNIVERSITY OF TEXAS PRESS, 1944 (HT).

LITTLE, WILLSON. SPANISH SPEAKING CHILDREN IN TEXAS.
     AUSTIN, TEXAS: UNIVERSITY OF TEXAS PRESS, 1944 (HT).

LOCKE.   WHEN PEOPLES MEET; STUDY RACE   (AN*).

LOCKE, HARVEY J.; SABAH, GEORGES; THOMAS, MARY.   INTERFAITH
     MARRIAGES.   SOCIAL PROBLEMS, 4.

LOERA.   "EDUCATION: EMERGING OPPORTUNITIES (ED*).

LOFSTEDT, CHRISTINE. THE MEXICAN POPULATION OF PASADENA,
     CALIFORNIA.   JOURNAL OF APPLIED SOCIOLOGY, 7 (HC).

LOFTIN, JAMES OTIS. MEXICAN SECONDARY EDUCATION AS
     DEVELOPED IN THE SIDNEY LANIER JUNIOR HIGH SCHOOL OF
     SAN ANTONIO,TEXAS.   TEXAS STATE TEACHERS COLLEGE,
     MASTER'S THESIS (1927) (HC).

LOHMAN, JOSEPH D. "EXPOSE, DON'T IMPOSE".   NEA JOURNAL,
     (JANUARY 1966), PP. 24-26 (ED).

LOHMAN, JOSEPH D. CULTURAL PATTERNS IN URBAN SCHOOLS.
     UNIVERSITY OF CALIFORNIA, 1967 (AN ED).

LOHMAN, JOSEPH D. A SOCIOLOGICAL APPROACH TO UNDERSTANDING
     DISADVANTAGED YOUTH.   SACRAMENTO: CALIFORNIA STATE
     DEPARTMENT OF EDUCATION, 1966.

LOMAS, CHARLES WYATT. THE AGITATOR IN AMERICAN SOCIETY.
     ENGLEWOOD CLIFFS: PRENTICE-HALL, 1968.

LOOMIS, CHARLES P. "CULTURE OF A CONTEMPORARY RURAL
     COMMUNITY".   SOCIOMETRY, VOL. 4 (FEBRUARY 1941),
     PP. 40-51.

LOOMIS, CHARLES P. "EL CERRITO, NEW MEXICO: A CHANGING
     VILLAGE".   NEW MEXICO HISTORICAL REVIEW, VOL. 33
     (JANUARY 1958), PP. 53-75.

LOOMIS, CHARLES P. "INFORMAL GROUPINGS IN A SPANISH
     AMERICAN VILLAGE".   SOCIOMENTRY, VOL. 6 (FEBRUARY
     1943), PP. 7-26.

LOOMIS, CHARLES P. "THE DEVELOPMENT OF PLANNED RURAL
    COMMUNITIES". RURAL SOCIOLOGY, VOL. 3 (DECEMBER
    1938), PP. 385-409.

LOOMIS, CHARLES P. LINKAGES OF MEXICO AND THE UNITED
    STATES. MICHIGAN AGRICULTURAL EXPERIMENT STATION:
    MICHIGAN STATE UNIVERSITY, (1966). RESEARCH BULLETIN
    14.

LOOMIS, CHARLES P. MESA, CANYON AND PUEBLO. NEW YORK:
    CENTURY COMPANY, 1925.

LOOMIS, CHARLES P. READINGS IN LATIN AMERICAN SOCIAL
    ORGANIZATION AND INSTITUTIONS. EAST LANSING:
    MICHIGAN STATE COLLEGE PRESS, 1953.

LOOMIS, CHARLES P. RELATIONS OF ANGLO-LATINO GROUPS WITH
    HOSPITALS AND COMMUNITIES. REPORT PREPARED UNDER
    THE AUSPICES OF THE UNITED STATES DEPARTMENT OF
    HEALTH, EDUCATION AND WELFARE, MICHIGAN STATE UNIVERSITY.

LOOMIS, CHARLES P. SOCIAL RELATIONSHIPS AND INSTITUTIONS
    IN SEVEN NEW RURAL COMMUNITIES. WASHINGTON, D.
    C.: UNITED STATES DEPARTMENT OF AGRICULTURE, FARM
    SECURITY ADMINISTRATION AND BUREAU OF AGRICULTURAL
    ECONOMICS, (1940).

LOOMIS, CHARLES P. SYSTEMATIC LINKAGE OF EL CERRITO.
    RURAL SOCIOLOGY, 24.

LOOMIS, CHARLES P. A COOPERATIVE HEALTH ACSSOCIATION IN
    SPANISH SPEAKING VILLAGES. AMERICAN SOCIOLOGICAL
    REVIEW, 10.

LOOMIS, CHARLES P. ; GRISHAM, GLEN. "SPANISH AMERICANS:
    THE NEW MEXICO EXPERIMENT IN VILLAGE REHABILITATION".
    APPLIED ANTHROPOLOGY, VOL. 2 NO. 3 (1943), PP. 13-37.

LOOMIS, CHARLES P.; LOOMIS, NELLIE H. SKILLED SPANISH
    AMERICAN WAR INDUSTRY WORKERS FROM NEW MEXICO.
    APPLIED ANTHROPOLOGY, 2.

LOOMIS, CHARLES P.; LEONARD, OLEN E. STANDARDS OF LIVING
    IN AN INDIAN MEXICAN VILLAGE. UNITED STATES
    DEPARTMENT OF AGRICULTURE, (1938). SOCIAL RESEARCH
    REPORT NOUMBER 14.

LOOMIS, NELLIE HOLMES. SPANISH-ANGLO ETHNIC CLEAVAGE IN
    A NEW MEXICAN HIGH SCHOOL. MICHIGAN STATE UNIVERSITY,
    PHD. DISSERTATION (1955).

LOOMIS, NOEL M. THE TEXAN-SANTA FE PIONEERS. NORMAN,
    OKLAHOMA: UNIVERSITY OF OKLAHOMA PRESS, 1958.

LOOMIS, NOEL M.; NASATIR, ABRAHAM. PEDRO VIAL AND
    THE ROADS TO SANTA FE. NORMAN: UNIVERSITY OF
    OKLAHOMA PRESS, 1967.

LOOMIS, NOEL M.; NASATIR, ABRAHAM P. PEDRO VIAL AND THE
      ROADS TO NEW SPAIN.   NORMAN, OKLAHOMA: UNIVERSITY
      OF OKLAHOMA PRESS, 1967.

LOPEZ Y RIVAS, GILBERTO. LOS CHICANOS: UNA MINORIA
      NACIONAL EXPLOTADA.   MEXICO CITY: EDITORIAL NUESTRO
      TIEMPO, 1971 (EC).

LOPEZ.   HOW DO YOU WORK WITH HARD CORE   (RE*).

LOPEZ, ENRIQUE. "OVERKILL AT THE SILVER DOLLAR; CHICANOS
      IN ANGELES".   NATION, VOL. 211 (OCTOBER 19, 1970),
      PP. 365-368.

LOPEZ, RICHARD EMILIO. ANXIETY, ACCULTURATION AND
      THE URBAN CHICANO.   BERKELEY: CALIFORNIA BOOK
      COMPANY, LTD., 1970 (AN).

LOPEZ, RONALD W. "THE EL MONTE BERRY STRIKE OF 1933".
      AZTLAN--CHICANO JOURNAL OF THE SOCIAL SCIENCES AND
      THE ARTS, VOL. 1 NO. 1 (SPRING 1970), PP. 101-114.

LOPREATA, JOSEPH. "INTERPERSONAL RELATIONS: THE PEASANT'S
      VIEW".   HUMAN ORGANIZATION, VOL. 21 NO. 1 (1962),
      PP. 21-24 (AN).

LOS ANGELES CHAMBER OF COMMERCE.   GENERAL DATA REGARDING
      MEXICAN (HC*).

LOS ANGELES CITY HEALTH DEPARTMENT.   DATA MEXICANS
      COMPILED RECORDS (HC*).

LOS ANGELES CITY PLANNING COMMISSION.   CHAVEZ RAVINE,
      COMMUNITY REDEVELOPMENT (HC*).

LOS ANGELES CITY SCHOOL DISTRICT.   MEXICAN-AMERICANS (HC*).

LOS ANGELES COUNTY BUREAU OF INSPECTIONS.   HOUSING
      SANITATION SURVEY ACTIVE (HC*).

LOS ANGELES COUNTY COORDINATING COUNCILS.   SOME NOTES
      MEXICAN POPULATION (HC*).

LOS ANGELES COUNTY COMMITTEE FOR INTERRACIAL PROGRESS.
      MINORITY GROUP EMPLOYMENT PATTERNS (HC*).

LOS ANGELES COUNTY COMMISSION ON HUMAN RELATIONS.
      POPULATION HOUSING LOS ANGELES (HC*).

LOS ANGELES COUNTY COMMISSION ON HUMAN RELATIONS.
      TRAINING PROGRAM MEXICAN AMERICANS (HC*).

LOS ANGELES COUNTY COMMISSION ON HUMAN RELATIONS.   URBAN
      REALITY: COMPARATIVE STUDY (HC*).

LOS ANGELES COUNTY DEPARTMENT OF PUBLIC SOCIAL SERVICES.
RACIAL BREAKDOWN COUNTY CITYHOUSING (HC*).

LOS ANGELES COUNTY DEPARTMENT OF PUBLIC SOCIAL SERVICES.
SELECTED GUIDE TO LITERATUREMEXICAN (HC*).

LOS ANGELES COUNTY GRAND JURY.   FINAL REPORT LOS ANGELES
COUNTY (HC*).

LOS ANGELES COUNTY GRAND JURY.   PAPERS READ MEETING HELD
OCTOBER (HC*).

LOS ANGELES COUNTY PROBATION OFFICE.   SUMMARY RECOMMENDATIONS
PROGRESS (HC*).

LOS ANGELES COUNTY TUBERCULOSIS AND HEALTH ASSOCIATION.
TUBERCULOSIS HIGH INCIDENCE AREA: (HC*).

LOS ANGELES COUNTY YOUTH COMMITTEE.   ECHO PARK STUDY:
SOCIAL ANALYSIS (HC*).

LOS ANGELES COUNTY.   HISTORY BOUNDARY COUNTRY
LOSANGELES (HC*).

LOS ANGELES COUNTY.   SURVEY MEDICAL CARE FACILITIES (HC*).

LOS ANGELES DEPARTMENT OF CHARITIES.   ANALYSIS MEXICAN
REPATRIATION (HC*).

LOS ANGELES REGION WELFARE PLANNING COUNCIL.   REPORT
SURVEY UNSPONSORED YOUTH (HC*).

LOS ANGELES, CALIFORNIA. RESEARCH DEPARTMENT, WELFARE
PLANNING COUNCIL. MEXICAN AMERICAN SURVEY PROJECT.
LOS ANGELES RESEARCH DEPARTMENT WELFARE PLANNING
COUNCIL REPORT NUMBER 75, SUMMER 1967 (EC).

LOS ANGELESLOS ANGELES CHAMBER OF COMMERCE.   MEXICAN
REPATRIATION CALIFORNIA (HC*).

LOVE.   LA RAZA: MEXICAN—AMERICANS REBELLION (PL*).

LOVE.   RAZA: MEXICAN—AMERICANS REBELLION (PL*).

LOVE.   SUMMARY RECOMMENDATIONS STRENGTHENING (PY*).

LOWE, JEANNE R.   "RACE, JOBS, AND CITIES: WHAT BUSINESS
CAN DO".   SATURDAY REVIEW, (JANUARY 11, 1969) (EC).

LOWRY.   HISTORY MISSISSIPPI, DISCOVERY (EC*).

LOYD.   "REMEMBERING FORGOTTEN AMERICANS" (ED*).

LOZADA.   PLAN ESPIRITUAL DE AZTLAN (PL*).

LOZANO.   ARE WE GOOD NEIGHBORS? (HSW*).

LUCEY, REV. ROBERT E.   "CHRISTIANIZING MEXICAN CATHOLICS".
     AMERICA, VOL. 77 (AUGUST 16, 1947), PP. 541-542 (RE).

LUCEY, REV. ROBERT E.   "JUSTICE FOR THE MEXICANS".
     COMMONWEAL, VOL. 49 (NOVEMBER 12, 1948), P. 117 (LW).

LUCEY, ROBERT E.   "MIGRATORY WORKERS".   COMMONWEAL, VOL.
     59 (JANUARY 15, 1954), PP. 370-373 (LW).

LUCIO, GABRIEL.   TRENDS IN MEXICAN ELEMENTARY EDUCATION.
     PROGRESSIVE EDUCATION, (SI   EC).

LUEVANSOS, E. D.   "MEXICAN NEIGHBORS".   HISPANIA, VOL.
     29 (AUGUST 1946), PP. 413-415 (ED).

LUGO.   VIDA DE UN RANCHERO (HC*).

LUKENS, ELEANOR.   FACTORS AFFECTING UTILIZATION OF MENTAL
     HEALTH SERVICES BY MEXICAN AMERICANS.   WORKING PAPER
     NO. 47, RESEARCH DEPARTMENT, WELFARE P6ANNING COUNCIL,
     LLOS ANGELES REGION, JUNE 1963 (MD).

LULAC.   LULAC IN ACTION: A REPORT ON THE LITTLE SCHOOL OF
     THE 400.   NEWSPAPER, 1960.

LUMMIS, CHARLES F.   THE SPANISH PIONEERS.   CHICAGO: A.
     C. MCCLURG, 1893 (AN).

LYLE, E. P., JR.   "AMERICAN INFLUENCE IN MEXICO".   WORLD'S
     WORK, VOL. 6 (SEPTEMBER 1950), PP. 38-43 (HM).

LYND.   NONVIOLENCE AMERICA: DOCUMENTARY (HUS*).

MAC CARTHY, CARRIE BELL HOOPER.   A SURVEY OF THE MEXICAN
     HARDSHIP CASES ACTIVE IN THE LOS ANGELES COUNTY
     DEPARTMENT OF CHARITIES, LOS ANGELES, CALIFORNIA.
     UNIVERSITY OF SOUTHERN CALIFORNIA, MASTER'S THESIS
     (1939).

MAC IVER, ROBERT M.   DISCRIMINATION AND NATIONAL WELFARE.
     NEW YORK: HARPER, 1949.

MAC IVER, ROBERT M.   THE MORE PERFECT UNION:A PROGRAM FOR
     THE CONTROL OF INTER-GROUP DISCRIMINATION IN THE
     UNITED STATES.   MACMILLAN, 1948.

MAC NABB, BETTY L.   "TEXAS MIGRANTS PROGRAM FROM TAX-EATERS
     TO TAX-PAYERS".   COMMUNITIES IN ACTION, VOL.
     2 (MARCH 1967), PP. 21-25.

MAC NAMARA, JOHN (ED).   "PROBLEMS OF BILINGUALISM".   THE
     JOURNAL OF SOCIAL ISSUES, VOL. 23 NO. 2 (APRIL
     1967), P. 138 (ED).

MAC NAMARA, JOHN. "THE EFFECTS OF INSTRUCTION IN A WEAKER
     LANGUAGE".   JOURNAL OF SOCIAL ISSUES, VOL. 23   NO.
     2 (1967), P. 121 (ED).

MACCOBY, MICHAEL. 'ON MEXICAN NATIONAL CHARACTER.'   IN
     NATHANIEL N. WAGNER AND MARSHA J. HAUG. CHICANOS:
     SOCIAL AND PSYCHOLOGICAL PERSPECTIVES.

MACK, RAYMOND W. OUR CHILDREN'S BURDEN; STUDIES OF
     DESEGREGATION IN INE AMERICAN COMMUNITIES.   NEW YORK:
     RANDOM HOUSE, 1968.

MACK, RAYMOND. "RIOT, REVOLT AND RESPONSIBILE ACTION".
     THE SOCIOLOGY QUARTERLY,   (SPRING), P. 147.

MACKEY, DRUZILLA R. "BOOKS WITHOUT PRINT".   SURVEY, VOL.
     68 , PP. 400-1.

MACKLIN.   CURANDERA STRUCTURAL STABILITY (AN*).

MACKLIN.   STRUCTURAL STABILITY CULTURECHANGE (AN*).

MACOBY, M. "LOVE AND AUTHORITY STUDY OF MEXICAN VILLAGERS
     LOVE AND AUTHORITY; STUDY OF MEXICAN VILLAGERS
     -".   ATLANTIC, VOL. 213 (MARCH   1964), PP. 121-126
     (LI).

MACOBY, M. "ON MEXICAN NATIONAL CHARACTER".   ANNALS OF
     THE AMERICAN ACADEMY ON POLITICAL AND SOCIAL SCIENCE,
     VOL. 370 (MARCH   1967), PP. 63-73 (LI).

MADRIL.   SOCCIAL PARTICIPATION RELATION (AN*).

MAES, ERNEST E. "THE WORLD AND PEOPLE OF CUNDIYO".   LAND
     POLICY REVISED, VOL. 4 (MARCH   1941), PP. 8-14.

MAESTAS, SIGFREDO. LIFE STYLES OF LOWER CLASS PEOPLE AND
     THEIR MOTIVATIONAL STRUCTURE.   UNIVERSITY OF
     NEW MEXICO, MASTER'S THESIS (1958).

MAISEL, ALBERT Q. "THE MEXICANS AMONG US".   READERS
     DIGEST, VOL. 68 (MARCH   1956), PP. 177-178.

MANHEIM, HENRY, AND CUMMINS, ALICE. "SELECTED MUSICAL
     TRAITS AMONG SPANISH, NEGRO, AND ANGLO-AMERICAN
     GIRLS".   SOCIOLOGY AND SOCIAL RESEARCH,   (OCTOBER
     1960), PP. 56-65.

MARCOUX.   HANDICAPS BI-LINGUAL MEXICANCHILDREN (ED*).

MARCUS.   REPLICATION STUDY ETHNIC GROUP (ED*).

MARCUS, LLOYD. 'THE TREATMENT OF MINORITIES IN SECONDARY
    SCHOOL TEXTBOOKS.'   IN MILTON L. BARRON (ED),
    MINORITIES IN A CHANGING WORLD.

MARDEN, CHARLES F., AND MEYER, GLADYS. MINORITIES
    IN AMERICAN SOCIETY.   SECOND EDITION. NEW YORK:
    AMERICAN BOOK CO., 1962.

MARDEN, CHARLES FREDERICK. MINORITIES IN AMERICAN SOCIETY.
    NEW YORK: AMERICAN BOOK COMPANY, 1952.

MARINA, R. FERNANDEZ, MALDONADO SIERRA, E. D. AND TRENT,
    R. D. "THREE BASIC THEMES IN MEXICAN AND PUERTO RICAN
    FAMILY VALUES".   JOURNAL OF SOCIAL PSYCHOLOGY, VOL.
    48 (NOVEMBER 1958), PP. 167-181 (PY).

MARQUEZ, R. SOLVING THE PROBLEMS OF CHICAGO'S POPULATION
    GROWTH.   ABRIDGED PROCEEDINGS, CITY-WIDE CONFERENCE.
    PALMER HOUSE, MAY 29, 1957..

MARSH, ELIZABETH F. DIETARY STUDIES OF FAMILIES ON RELIEF.
    UNIVERSITY OF TEXAS, MASTER'S THESIS (1935).

MARSTON, H. D. "MEXICAN TRAITS".   SURVEY, VOL. 44
    (AUGUST 2, 1920), PP. 562-64.

MARTIN, PATRICIA M. MEXICANS IN THE U. S..   NEW YORK:
    PARENTS MAGAZINE PRESS, 1971.

MARTIN, ROSCOE C. THE DEFENDANT AND CRIMINAL JUSTICE.
    AUSTIN: BUREAU OF RESEARCH IN THE SOCIAL SCIENCES,
    UNIVERSITY OF TEXAS, 1934.

MARTINEZ REYES N.   RURAL WEDDINGS   (AN*).

MARTINEZ, OSCAR. "MANIFEST MEXICANISM".   CON SAFOS, VOL.
    1 NO. 3 (MARCH 1969), PP. 34-35.

MARTINEZ, RAFAEL V. MY HOUSE IS YOUR HOUSE.   NEW YORK:
    FRIENDSHIP PRESS, JANUARY 1964.

MARTINEZ, THOMAS M. 'ADVERTISING AND RACISM: THE CASE
    OF THE MEXICAN-AMERICAN.'   IN OCTAVIO U. ROMANO-V.
    (ED), VOICES: READINGS FROM EL GRITO.

MARTINEZ, THOMAS M. 'ADVERTISING AND RACISM: THE CASE
    OF THE MEXICAN-AMERICAN.'   IN INTRODUCTION BY EDWARD
    SIMMEN. THE CHICANO TODAY.

MARTINEZ, THOMAS M. "ADVERTISING AND RACISM: THE CASE
    OF THE MEXICAN-AMERICAN".   EL GRITO, VOL. 2 NO. 4
    (SUMMER 1969), PP. 3-13.

MARTINEZ, THOMAS M. CHICANISMO.   PROGRAM COORDINATED BY
    MONTAL SYSTEMS, INC.

MARTINEZ.   "HOW ADVERTISERS PROMOTE RACISM"   (FILM*).

MARX, RICHARD. ABOUT MEXICO'S CHILDREN.   MELMONT, 1959.

MARX.   "NEIGHBORS WHO MOVED IN: SPANISH-AMERICAN   (RE*).

MASON, FLORENCE GORDON.   A CASE STUDY OF THIRTY ADOLESCENT
     MEXICAN GIRLS AND THEIR SOCIAL CONFLICTS AND ADJUSTMENT
     WITHIN THE SCHOOL.   UNIVERSITY OF SOUTHERN CALIFORNIA,
     MASTER'S THESIS (1928) (PY).

MASOUKA, JITSUICHI, AND VALIEN, PRESTON (EDS.).   RACE
     RELATIONS: PROBLEMS AND THEORY.   CHAPEL HILL:
     UNIVERSITY OF NORTH CAROLINA PRESS, 1961.

MATTHEWS, AMANDA. "SOME MEXICAN GIRLS".   OVERLAND, VOL.
     41 (AUTUM 1951), PP. 163-69.

MATTHIASON.   ACCULTURATION MEXICAN-AMERICANS   (AN*).

MATZIGKEIT.   INFLUENCE SIX MEXICAN CULTURAL   (AN*).

MAURY.   ANDERSONVILLE; CASE STUDY POVERTY (EC*).

MAUZY.   SANTA FES NATIVE MARKET (EC*).

MAVERICK, M., JR. "MARCHING FOR A GHASTLY RECOMPENSE IN
     TEXAS".   NEW REPUBLIC, VOL. 155 (SEPTEMBER 24,
     1966), P. 11.

MAYERSON, CHARLOTTE LEON, (ED).   TWO BLOCKS APART: JUAN
     GONZALES AND PETER QUINN.   NEW YORK: HOLT, RINEHART
     AND WINSTON, 1965.

MC CARY, MALLIE MUNCY. THESE MINORITIES IN OUR MIDST: WITH
     EMPHASIS ON LATIN AMERICANS IN TEXAS.   UNIVERSITY
     OF TEXAS, MASTER'S THESIS (1953) (HT).

MC CLATCHY, V. S. INCREASE IN MEXICAN POPULATION.   SAN
     FRANCISCO, (1933). BULLETIN NUMBER 316 CALIFORNIA
     JOINT IMMIGRATION C OMMITTEE.

MC CLELLAND, DAVID C. THE ACHIEVING SOCIETY.   PRINCETON:
     VAN NOSTRAND, 1961.

MC CLENAHAN, BESSIE AVERNE. THE CHANGING URBAN NEIGHBORHOOD,
     FROM NEIGHBOR TO NIGH-DWELLER: A SOCIOLOGICAL STUDY.
     LOS ANGELES: UNIVERSITY OF SOUTHERN CALIFORNIA, 1929.

MC CLENEGHAN, THOMAS J., AND GILDERSLEEVE, CHARLES R.   LAND
     USE CONTRASTS IN BORDER ECONOMY.   UNIVERSITY
     OF ARIZONA, JUNE 1964 (EC).

MC COMBS, VERNON MONROE. "RESCUING MEXICAN CHILDREN IN
     THE SOUTHWEST".   MISSIONARY REVIEW, VOL. 46 (JULY
     1923), PP. 529-32.

MC COMBS, VERNON MONROE. FROM OVER THE BORDER. NEW YORK,
    1925.

MC CONNELL, WESTON JOSEPH. SOCIAL CLEAVAGES IN TEXAS: A
    STUDY OF THE PROPOSED DIVISION OF THE STATE. NEW
    YORK: COLUMBIA UNIVERSITY, 1925.

MC DANIEL, ELIZABETH ALICE LOGAN. RELATIONSHIPS BETWEEN
    SELF-CONCEPT AND SPECIFIC VARIABLES IN A LOW INCOME
    CULTURALLY DIFFERENT POPULATION. UNIVERSITY
    OF TEXAS, PHD. DISSERTATION (1967) (PY).

MC DONAGH, EDWARD C., AND RICHARDS, EUGENE S. MEXICANS
    IN THEIR ETHNIC RELATIONS IN THE UNITED STATES. NEW
    YORK: APPLETON-CENTURY-CROFTS, 1953.

MC DONAUGH, EDWARD C. "ATTITUDES TOWARDS ETHNIC FARM
    WORKERS IN COACHELLA VALLEY". SOCIOLOGY AND SOCIAL
    RESEARCH, VOL. 40 (SEPTEMBER 1955), PP. 10-18 (EC).

MC DONAUGH, EDWARD C. "STATUS LEVELS OF THE AMERICAN
    JEWS". SOCIOLOGY AND SOCIAL RESEARCH, VOL. 32
    (JULY-AUGUST 1948), PP. 944-53.

MC DONAUGH, EDWARD C. "STATUS LEVELS OF MEXICANS".
    SOCIOLOGY AND SOCIAL RESEARCH, VOL. 35 (NOVEMBER-DECEMBER
    1950), PP. 449-59.

MC DONAUGH, EDWARD C. ETHNIC RELATIONS IN THE UNITED
    STATES. NEW YORK: APPLETON-CENTURY CROFTS, 1953.

MC DOWELL, JOHN. A STUDY OF SOCIAL AND ECONOMIC FACTORS
    RELATING TO SPANISH-SPEAKING PEOPLE IN THE UNITED
    STATES. HOME MISSIONS COUNCIL, PHILADELPHIA, 1927
    (EC).

MC DOWELL, JOHN. A STUDY OF SOCIAL AND ECONOMIC FACTORS
    RELATING TO SPANISH-SPEAKING PEOPLE IN THE UNITED
    STATES. PHILADELPHIA: HOME MISSIONS COUNCIL, 1927
    (EC).

MC DOWELL. STATUS ACADEMIC CAPABILITIESACHIEVEMENT (ED*).

MC ENTIRE, DAVIS. LEISURE ACTIVITIES OF YOUTH IN BERKELEY,
    CALIFORNIA. BERKELEY, CALIFORNIA: UNIVERSITY
    OF CALIFORNIA, 1952 (EC).

MC ENTIRE, DAVIS. RESIDENCE AND RACE; FINAL AND COMPREHENSIVE
    REPORT TO THE COMMISSION ON RACE AND HOUSING.
    BERKELEY, UNIVERSITY OF CALIFORNIA PRESS, 1960 (EC).

MC ENTIRE, DAVIS. RESIDENCE AND RACE FINAL AND COMPREHENSIVE
    REPORT TO THE COMMISSION ON RRESIDENCE AND RACE: FINAL
    AND COMPREHENSIVE REPORT TO THE COMMISSION ON ACE AND
    HOUSING. BERKELEY, CALIFORNIA: UNIVERSITY OF
    CALIFORNIA PRESS, 1960 (EC).

MC ENTIRE, DAVIS. THE LABOR FORCE IN CALIFORNIA: A STUDY
     OF CHARACTERISTICS AND TRENDS INLABOR FORCE, EMPLOYMENT,
     AND OCCUPATIONS IN CALIFORNIA, 1900-1950.   BERKELEY,
     CALIFORNIA: UNIVERSITY OF CALIFORNIA PRESS, 1952 (EC).

MC ENTIRE, DAVIS. THE LABOR FORCE IN CALIFORNIA.
     BERKELEY: UNIVERSITY OF CALIFORNIA PRESS, 1952 (EC).

MC ENTIRE, DAVIS. THE POPULATION OF CALIFORNIA: A REPORT
     OF A RESEARCH STUDY MADE BY AUTHOIZATION OF THE BOARD
     OF GOVERNORS OF THE COMMONWEALTH CLUB OF CALIFORNIA.
     SAN FRANCISCO: THE COMMONWEALTH CLUB, 1946 (EC).

MC ENTIRE, DAVIS. THE PROBLEM OF SEGREGATION.   SAN
     FRANCISCO: AMERICAN COUNCIL ON RACE RELATIONS, 1946
     (EC).

MC ENTIRE, DAVIS, AND WHETTEN, N. L. "RECENT MIGRATION
     TO THE PACIFIC COAST".   LAND POLICY REVIEW, VOL. 2
     (SEPTEMBER-OCTOBER 1939), PP. 7-17 (EC).

MC EUEN, WILLIAM. A SURVEY OF THE MEXICAN IN LOS ANGELES.
     UNIVERSITY OF SOUTHERN CALIFORNIA, LOS ANGELES,
     MASTER'S THESIS (1914).

MC GARRY.   STUDY CULTURAL PATTERNS AMONG   (AN*).

MC GARY.   THESE MINORITIES OUR MIDST: WITH   (HT*).

MC GINN, NOEL F., HARBURG, ERNEST, AND GINSBURG, GERALD
     P. "DEPENDENCY RELATIONS WITH PARENTS AND AFFILIATIVE
     RESPONSES IN MICHIGAN AND GUADALAJARA".   SOCIOMETRY,
     (SEPTEMBER 1965), PP. 305-321.

MC GINN, NOEL F., HARBURG, ERNEST, AND GINSBURG, GERALD
     P. "RESPONSES TO INTERPERSONAL CONFLICT BY MIDDLE
     CLASS MALES IN GUADALAJARA AND MICHIGAN".   AMERICAN
     ANTHROPOLOGIST,   (DECEMBER 1965), PP. 1483-1494.

MC GINNIS, JOHN H. "CITIES AND TOWNS OF THE SOUTHWEST:
     III".   SOUTHWEST REVIEW, VOL. 13 (OCTOBER 1927),
     PP. 36-47.

MC GOVNEY, D. O. "RACE DISCRIMINATION IN NATURALIZATION".
     IOWA LAW BULLETIN, VOL. 8 (1923), PP. 129-211.

MC KAIN.   "SANTA BARBARA COUNTY BETWEEN (HC*).

MC KEE, JAMES B. "COMMUNITY POWER AND STRATEGIES IN RACE
     RELATIONS: SOME CRITICAL OBSERVATONS".   SOCIAL
     PROBLEMS, VOL. 6 (1958-59), PP. 195-203 (PL).

MC KENNEY.   "THE DILEMMA SPANISH SURNAMEPEOPLE (ED*).

MC KINNON, WILLIAM, AND CENTERS, RICHARD. "AUTHORITARIANISM
    AND URBAN STRATIFICATION".   AMERICAN JOURNAL
    OF SOCIOLOGY, VOL. 61 (MAY 1956), PP. 610-620.

MC LEAN, ROBERT JACK. A COMPARATIVE STUDY OF ANGLO-AMERICAN
    AND SPANISH-NAME CHILDREN IN THE AUSTIN PUBLIC SCHOOLS
    OVER A SEVEN YEAR PERIOD.   UNIVERSITY OF TEXAS,
    MASTER'S THESIS (1950) (ED).

MC LEAN, ROBERT N. "A DYKE AGAINST MEXICANS".   NEW
    REPUBLIC, VOL. 59 (AUGUST 14, 1929), PP. 334-7 (ED).

MC LEAN, ROBERT N. "GETTING GOD COUNTED AMONG THE
    MEXICANS".   MISSIONARY REVIEW OF THE WORLD, VOL. 46
    (MAY 1923), PP. 359-63 (ED).

MC LEAN, ROBERT N. "GOODYE VINCENTE ".   SURVEY GRAPHIC,
    VOL. 46 , PP. 182-83 (ED).

MC LEAN, ROBERT N. "RUBBING SHOULDERS ON THE BORDER".
    SURVEY, VOL. 52 , PP. 184-85 (ED).

MC LEAN, ROBERT N. "TIGHTENING THE MEXICAN BORDER".
    SURVEY, VOL. 64 (APRIL 1, 1930), PP. 28-29 (ED).

MC LEAN, ROBERT N. "WHAT DO YOU KNOW ABOUT THE MEXICANS?".
    MISSIONARY REVIEW, VOL. 53 , PP. 183-87 (ED).

MC LEAN, ROBERT N. MEXICAN WORKERS IN THE UNITED STATES.
    UNIVERSITY OF CHICAGO PRESS, 1929 (ED).

MC LEAN, ROBERT N. RUBBING SHOULDERS ON THE BORDER.
    SURVEY, 52 (ED).

MC LEAN, ROBERT N. SPANISH AND MEXICANS IN COLORADO; A
    SURVEY OF THE SPANISH AMERICANS AND EXICANS IN THE
    STATE OF COLORADO.   DEPARTMENT OF CITY, IMMIGRANT
    AND INDUSTRIAL WORK, 1924 (ED).

MC LEAN, ROBERT N. THAT MEXICAN AS HE REALLY IS NORTH
    AND SOUTH OF THE RIO GRANDE.   NEW YORK: H. REVELL,
    1928 (ED).

MC LEAN, ROBERT N. THAT MEXICAN AS HE REALLY IS NORTH
    AND SOUTH OF THE RIO GRANDE, 1928.   SAN FRANCISCO:
    R AND E RESEARCH ASSOCIATES, 1971 (ED).

MC LEAN, ROBERT N. THE MEXICAN RETURNS.   NATION,
    NEW YORK, AUGUST 24, 1932 (ED).

MC LEAN, ROBERT N. THE NORTHERN MEXICAN.   NEW YORK: HOME
    MISSIONS COUNCIL, 1930 (ED).

MC LEAN, ROBERT N. THE NORTHERN MEXICAN.   SAN FRANCISCO,
    CALIFORNIA: R & E RESEARCH ASSOCIATES, 1971 (ED).

MC LEAN, ROBERT N. THE WINNING OF THE WEST.   NEW YORK:
    GEORGE PUTNAM AND SONS, 1914 (ED).

MC LEAN, ROBERT N. AND WILLIAMS, GRACE. OLD SPAIN IN NEW
    AMERICA.   COUNCIL OF WOMEN FOR HOME MISSIONS, (ED).

MC LEMORE, S. DALE. "ETHNIC ATTITUDES TOWARD HOSPITALIZATION:
    AN ILLUSTRATIVE COMPARISON OF AGLOS AND MEXICAN-AMERICANS".
    SOUTHWESTERN SOCIAL SCIENCE QUARTERLY, VOL. 43 (MARCH
    1963), PP. 341-346 (MD).

MC MICHAEL, R. N., GENNONS, RONALD B. AND MURRELL, JOE C.
    A DEMOGRAPHIC STUDY OF WEST TEXAS.   EDINBURG, TEXAS:
    PAN AMERICAN COLLEGE, 1967.

MC MILLAN, OLIVER. HOUSING DEFICIENCIES OF AGRICULTURAL
    WORKERS AND OTHER LOW INCOME GROUPS.   REPORT TO THE
    DIVISION OF HOUSING FOR THE GOVERNOR'S ADVISORY
    COMMISS ION ON HOUSING PROBLEMS, SAN FRANCISCO,
    NOVEMBER 27, 1962.

MC NAMARA PATRICK HAYES. MEXICAN AMERICANS IN LOS ANGELES
    COUNTY: A STUDY IN ACCULTURATION.   SAINT LOUIS
    UNIVERSITY, MASTER'S THESIS (1957).

MC NAMARA, PARTICK HAYES. "RUMBLES ALONG THE RIO: U.S.
    CIVIL RIGHTS COMMISSION HEARINGS IN SAN ANTOIO".
    COMMONWEAL, VOL. 89 (MARCH 14, 1969), PP. 730-732.

MC NAMARA, PATRICK HAYES. "BISHOPS, PADRES, AND THE
    BARRIOS".   COMMONWEAL, VOL. 93 (OCTOBER 30, 1970),
    PP. 116-117 (RE).

MC NAMARA, PATRICK HAYES. "MEXICAN-AMERICANS IN THE
    SOUTHWEST; MEXICAN-AMERICAN STUDY PROJECT".   AMERICA,
    VOL. 114 (MARCH 12, 1966), PP. 352-354.

MC NAUGHTON.   SOCIAL STUDY MEXICAN SPANISH-AMERICAN (EC*).

MEAD.   CULTURAL PETTERNS TECHNICAL CHANGE (AN*).

MEAD.   SPANISH AMERICANS NEW MEXICO, (AN*).

MEADOW.   "RELIGIOUS AFFILIATION PSYCHOPATHOLOGY (RE*).

MEIER.   ORAL COMMUNICATION HEALTH-DISEASE (MD*).

MEIER.   THREE ETHNIC GROUPS SOUTHWESTERN (AN*).

MEINIG.   SOUTHWEST: THREE PEOPLES GEOGRAPHICAL (HS*).

MELAS.   REVIVAL (LI*).

MEMMI.   DOMINATED MAN (AN*).

MENDIETA Y NUNEZ, LUDIO. VALOR SOCIOLOGICO DEL FOLKLORE.
    MEXICO D.F. EDICIONES DE LAW UNIVERSIDAD NACIONAL
    AUTONOMA, 1949 (AN).

MENDOZA, VICENTE T. "EL MACHISMO EN MEXICO AL TRAVES DE
    LAS CANIONES, CORRIDOS Y CANTARES".   CUADERNOS DEL
    INSTITUTO NACIONAL DE ANTROPOLOGIA, VOL. 3 (1962),
    PP. 75-86 (AN).

MERCER, JANE R. A SOCIAL AND ECONOMIC STUDY OF ETHNIC
    GROUPS IN RIVERSIDE.   PACIFIC STATE HOSPITAL RESEARCH
    DEPARTMENT, 1963 (EC).

MERCURE.   SPECIAL PROBLEMS RURAL MINORITY   (EC*).

MEREDITH.   EFFECT SOCIO-ECONOMIC BACKGROUND   (EC*).

MERMELSTEIN.   "SANDS PROJECT"   (EC*).

MEXICAN- AMERICAN PEACE COMMITTEE. THE MEXICAN AMERICAN
    LEAGUE.   THE MEXICAN-AMERICAN LEAGUE, NEW YORK, 1916.

MEXICO. DEPARTMENT OF STATE FOR FOREIGN AFFAIRS. BUREAU
    OF INTERNATIONAL NEWS SERVICE. STEVENSON, C. R. AND
    PADILLA, EZEQUIEL. THE GOOD NEIGHBOR POLICY AND
    MEXICANS IN TEXAS.   MEXICO D.F. NATIONAL AND
    INTERNATIONAL PROBLEMS, 1943 (EC HT).

MEXICO.   MEXICO (EC*).

MEXICO.   ESTUDIOS ANTROPOLOGICOS PUBLICADOS   (AN*).

MEYERS.   SPANISH-NAME PERSONS LABOR FORCE   (EC*).

MICHIGAN STATE UNIVERSITY.   MSU CHICANO COMMUNITY (B*).

MICHIGAN.   CIVIL RIGHTS COMMISSION. COMMITMENT (LW*).

MICHIGAN.   CIVIL RIGHTS COMMISSION. DIRECTIVE (LW*).

MICHIGAN.   EQUAL OPPORTUNITY HIGHER EDUCATION (LW*).

MICHIGAN.   FAIR HOUSING GUARANTEES MICHIGAN (LW*).

MICHIGAN.   FAIR HOUSING JURISDICTION MICHIGAN (LW*).

MICHIGAN.   HOW BACKLOG GREW (LW*).

MICHIGAN.   MODEL CITIES GUIDELINES (LW*).

MICHIGAN.   MODEL FAIR HOUSING ORDINANCECOUNTIES (LW*).

MICHIGAN.   PROCEDURES INVESTIGATING RESOLVING (LW*).

MICHIGAN.   RELOCATION, PUBLIC HOUSING (LW*).

MICHIGAN.   REPORT CHARACTERISTICS MICHIGANS   (LW*).

MICHIGAN.   REPORT RECOMMENDATIONS INTO STATUS   (LW*).

MICHIGAN.   TOWARD EQUALITY   (LW*).

MICHIGAN.   GARANTIAS DE IGUALES OPORTUNIDADES   (LW*).

MICHIGAN.   BILINGUE, TWO CULTURES, TWO LANGUAGES   (LW*).

MICHIGAN, ADRIAN. COMMUNITY ACTION CENTER.   AN EMPLOYMENT
     SURVEY OF LENAWEE COUNTY (EC).

MIDDAGH, JOHN. EL PASO AFTER DARK.   EL PASO: TEXAS
     WESTERN PRESS, 1958 (HT).

MIDDLETON, RUSSELL, JR. THE AGRARIAN PROGRAMS OF MEXICO,
     YUGOSLAVIA, AND ISRAEL: A STUDY IN THE SOCIOLOGY OF
     SOCIAL PLANNING.   UNIVERSITY OF TEXAS AT AUSTIN, PHD.
     DISSERTATION (1956) (HM).

MIERA. "TODAY IS FIESTA" (AN*).

MILL.   POLITICAL ROLE MEXICAN AMERICANS   (PL*).

MILLER, CURTIS R. A TYPOLOGY OF SPANISH SURNAME CENSUS
     TRACTS IN LOS ANGELES COUNTY.   UNIVERSITY OF SOUTHERN
     CALIFORNIA, MASTER'S THESIS (1960) (EC).

MILLER.   "THE MEXICAN DEPENDENCY PROBLEM"   (EC*).

MILLER.   "LATIN AMERICAN CHILD MUSIC"   (MU*).

MILLER, WALTER M. "LOWER CLASS CULTURE AS A GENERATING
     MILIEU OF GANG DELINQUENCY".   JOURNAL OF SOCIAL
     ISSUES, VOL. 14   (1958), PP. 5-19.

MILLER.   "DEVELOPING STATUS MEMBERS MINORITY   (ED*).

MILOR, J. H. "GOOD NEIGHBORLINESS BEGINS AT HOME".
     SURVEY GRAPHIC, VOL. 31   (DECEMBER 1942), P. 589.

MINER, HORACE. "THE FOLK URBAN CONTINUUM".   AMERICAN
     SOCIOLOGICAL REVIEW, VOL. 7   (OCTOBER 1952),
     PP. 529-37 (AN).

MINNESOTA.   MEXICAN MINNESOTA   (EC*).

MINNESOTA. GOVERNOR'S INTERRACIAL COMMISSION. RACE
     RELATIONS IN MINNESOTA; THE MEXICAN IN MINNESOTA.
     REPORT TO THE GOVENOR, MINNESOTA GOVENOR'S INTERRACIAL
     COMMISSION, 1948.

MINNIS, MHYRA S. "JUVENILE DELINQUENCY OFFENSES AND ETHNIC
    DELINEATION IN A SOUTHWEST COMMUNITY".   PROCEEDINGS
    OF SOUTHWESTERN SOCIOLOGICAL ASSOCIATION, VOL. 15
    (1965), PP. 69-74 (AN).

MINTZ.   "AN ANALYSIS RITUAL CO-PARENTHOOD" (AN*).

MITTLEBACK.   "ETHNIC ENDOGAMY-- CASE MEXICAN   (AN*).

MITTLEBACK.   INTERMARRIAGE MEXICAN AMERICANS   (AN*).

MONTEZ, PHILIP. RALITIES OF THE BROWN AND BLACK COMMUNITY.
    UNPUBLISHED ADDRESS GIVEN AT THE ANNUAL CONFERENCE
    OF THE NATIONAL ASSOCIATION FOR INTERGROUP RELATIONS
    ORGANIZATIONS. LOS ANGELES, CALIFORNIA, NOVEMBER 1966.

MONTGOMERY, ROBERT H. "KEGLAR HILL".   SURVEY GRAPHIC,
    VOL. 66 (MAY 1, 1931), PP. 171, 193-95.

MONTIEL, MIGUEL. "THE SOCIAL SCIENCE MYTH OF THE MEXICAN
    AMERICAN FAMILY".   EL GRITO, VOL. 3 NO. 4 (SUMMER
    1970), PP. 56-63 (AN).

MONTIEL, MIGUEL. THE SOCIAL SCIENCE MYTH OF THE MEXICAN
    AMERICAN FAMILY.   VOICES, BERKELEY, CALIFORNIA:
    QUINTO SOL PUBLICATIONS, 1971 (AN).

MONTIEL, OLVERA J., ED. YEAR BOOK OF THE LATIN-AMERICAN
    POPULATION OF TEXAS.   MEXICO CITY: MONTIEL OLVERA,
    1939.

MOORE, JOAN W. LOS MEXICANOS DE LOS ESTADOS UNIDOS Y EL
    MOVIMIENTO CHICANO.   MEXICO, D.F. FONDO DE CULTURA
    ECONOMICA, 1972 (EC PL).

MOORE, JOAN W. MEXICAN AMERICANS.   ENGLEWOOD CLIFFS, N.J.
    PRENTICE-HALL INC, 1970 (EC).

MOORE, JOAN W. MEXICAN AMERICAN: PROBLEMS AND PROSPECTS.
    MADISON: UNIVERSITY OF WISCONSIN PRESS, 1966 (EC PL).

MOORE, JOAN W. MEXICAN-AMERICANS; PROBLEMS AND PROSPECTS.
    OFFICE OF ECONOMIC OPPORTUNITY, LOS ANGELES, CALIFORNIA,
    NOVEMBER 1967 (EC PL).

MOORE, JOAN W. MEXICAN-AMERICANS, PROBLEMS AND PROSPECTS.
    WASHINGTON, D.C.: OFFICE OF ECONOMIC OPPORTUNITY,
    (1966) (EC PL).

MOORE, JOAN W. AND MITTELBACH, FRANK G. RESIDENTIAL
    SEGREGATION IN THE URBAN SOUTHWEST; A COMPARATIVE
    STUDY.   LOS ANGELES MEXICAN-AMERICAN STUDY PROJECT,
    DIVISION OF RESEARCH, GRADUATE SCHOOL OF BUSINESS
    ADMINISTRATION, UNIVERSITY OF CALIFORNIA AT LOS
    ANGELES, 1966 (EC).

MOORE, JOAN W., AND GUZMAN, RALPH. SOCIAL CLASS, ASSIMILATION
    AND ACCULTURATION. SPANISH-SPEAKING PEOPLE IN THE
    UNITED STATES: PROCEEDINGS OF THE 1968 ANNUAL SPRING
    MEETING OF THE AMERICAN ETHNOLOGICAL SOCIETY. SEATTLE,
    WASHINGTON: UNIVERSITY OF WASHINGTON PRESS, 1968 (EC
    AN).

MOORE, JOAN, AND GUZMAN, RALPH. "MEXICAN AMERICANS: NEW
    WIND FROM THE SOUTHWEST". THE NATION, VOL. 202 (MAY
    30, 1966), PP. 645-648 (EC PL).

MOORE, LUELLA. THE ADMINISTRATION OF THE SOCIAL WELFARE
    PROGRAM IN SEVERAL TYPICAL FO IGN SCHOOLS IN
    LOS ANGELES CITY. UNIVERSITY OF SOUTHERN CALIFORNIA,
    MASTER'S THESIS (1935).

MORALES. "POLICE DEPLOYMENT THEORIES MEXICAN (LW*).

MORALES. CHICANO POLICE RIOTS (PY*).

MORALES. IMPACT CLASS DISCRIMINATION WHITE (PY*).

MORALES. POLICE DEPLOYMENT THEORIES (LW*).

MORALES. STUDY RECIDIVISM MEXICAN AMERICAN (PY*).

MORALES. ANDO SANGRANDO I AM BLEEDING. (LMA*).

MORENO. VIEW MARGIN (ED*).

MORENO. PATTERN TRANSMISSION BICULTURAL (ED*).

MORENO. CANCION DE RAZA -- MEXICAN AMERICANS (ED*).

MORGAN, BELDEN. HOUSING MARKET REPORT ON MINORITY SECTOR
    OF THE LOS ANGELES METROPOLITANAREA. HOUSING MARKET
    REPORT ON MINORITY SECTOR OF THE LOS ANGELES METROPOLITAN
    AREA. LOS ANGELES AND ORANGE COUNTIES JULY 1954 (EC).

MORGAN. MONTEZUMAS DINNER: ESSAY TRIBAL (AN*).

MORGAN, PATRICIA. MEXICAN AMERICAN: A NATIONAL CONCERN.
    COMMON COUNCIL FOR AMERICAN UNITY, 20 WEST FORTIETH
    STREET, NEW YORK 18, 1959.

MORGAN. SHAME NATION: DOCUMENTED STORY (LW*).

MORGAN, PATRICIA. SHAME OF A NATION. COMMISSION
    FOR PROTECTION OF THE FOREIGN BORN, 1954.

MORIN. AMONG VALIANT, MEXICAN AMERICANS (HUS*).

MORIN, RAUL. DRAFTEES AND VOLUNTEERS. THE MEXICAN-AMERICANS:
    AN AWAKENING MINORITY. BEVERLY HILLS: GLENCOE PRESS,
    1970.

MORLOCK.   MEXICAN AMERICAN CIVIC LEADERSHIP   (PL*).

MORRIS.   "OF MANY THINGS: RIGHTS OF"   (PL*).

MORRISON.   HUMAN FACTORS SUPERVISING MINIORITY   (PY*).

MORRISSEY, P.   "GOOD MORNING, DON PATRICIO".   CATHOLIC
    WORLD, VOL. 151   (JUNE   1940), PP. 351-354 (PY).

MORTON.   MEXICAN AMERICAN SCHOOL SOCIETY   (ED*).

MULLIGAN, RAYMOND A.   "SOCIOECONOMIC BACKGROUND AND
    MINORITY ATTITUDES".   SOCIOLOGY AND SOCIAL RESEARCH,
    VOL. 45   (APRIL   1961), PP. 289-95 (EC   PY).

MULLIGAN, RAYMOND A.   NEW YORK FOUNDLINGS AT CLIFTON-MORENCI:
    SOCIAL JUSTICE IN ARIZONA TERRITORY, 1904-1905.
    BEVERLY HILLS, CALIFORNIA: GLENCOE PRESS, 1970 (AN).

MUNOZ.   "ON NATURE CAUSE TENSION CHICANO   (PL*).

MUNOZ.   "TOWARD CHICANO PERSPECTIVE POLITICAL   (PL*).

MUNOZ.   CHICANO MILITANCY CALIFORNIA: (PL*).

MUNTZ.   "AN ANALYSIS RITUAL CO-PARENTHOOD   (AN*).

MUNY.   "AWAKENING IN THE CORAL"   (PL*).

MURDOCH.   "A STUDY DIFFERENCES FOUND BETWEEN   (AN*).

MURILLO, NATHAN.   THE MEXICAN AMERICAN FAMILY.   CHICANOS:
    SOCIAL AND PSYCHOLOGICAL PERSPECTIVES. SAINT LOUIS,
    MISSOURI: THE C. V. MOSBY COMPANY, 1971 (PY).

MURO.   "COMMUNITY DEVELOPMENT"   (EC*).

MURPHY, L. F.   "EXPERIMENT IN AMERICANIZATION".   TEXAS
    OUTLOOK, VOL. 23   (NOVEMBER   1939), PP. 23-24.

MURRAY, KATHARINE MARY.   "MEXICAN COMMUNITY SERVICE".
    SOCIOLOGY AND SOCIAL RESEARCH, VOL. 17   (JULY   1933),
    PP. 545-50 (ED).

MURRAY, MARY JOHN, SISTER.   A SOCIO-CULTURAL STUDY OF 118
    MEXICAN FAMILIES LIVING IN LOW-RENT HOUSING PROJECT
    IN SAN ANTONIO.   WASHINGTON: CATHOLIC UNIVERSITY
    PRESS, 1954 (AN   EC).

MYRDAL, GUNNAR.   AN AMERICAN DILEMMA.   NEW YORK: HARPER
    AND BROTHERS PUBLISHERS, 1944 (PL).

NALL, FRANK C., AND SPEILBERG, JOSEPH. "SOCIAL AND
    CULTURAL FACTORS IN THE RESPONSES OF MEXICAN-AMERICANS
    TO MEDICAL TREATMENT". JOURNAL OF HEALTH AND SOCIAL
    BEHAVIOR, (DECEMBER 1967), PP. 299-308 (MD).

NALL, FRANK. "ROLE EXPECTATIONS: A CROSS CULTURAL STUDY".
    RURAL SOCIOLOGY, VOL. 27 (MARCH 1962), PP. 28-41.

NAMI.   STUDY FAMILY LIFE, ITS RELATION (ED*).

NATIONAL CATHOLIC WELFARE CONFERENCE. ADMINISTRATIVE
    BOARD. COMPREHENSIVE REPORT OF THE OFFICE OF
    THE BISHOP'S COMMITTEE FOR MIGRANTWORKERS.   WASHINGTON
    D.C., (EC).

NATIONAL CATHOLIC WELFARE COUNCIL. DEPARTMENT OF SOCIAL
    ACTION. THE SPANISH SPEAKING OF THE SOUTHWEST AND
    WEST.   WASHINGTON D.C., 1944.

NATIONAL CATHOLIC WELFARE CONFERENCE. DEPARTMENT OF SOCIAL
    ACTION. THE SPANISH SPEAKING OF THE SOUTHWEST AND
    WEST.   WASHINGTON: NATIONAL CATHOLIC WELFARE
    CONFERENCE, 1943.

NATIONAL CONFERENCE ON SOCIAL WELFARE. MINORITY GROUPS:
    SEGREGATION AND INTEGRATION.   NEW YORK: COLUMBIA
    UNIVERSITY PRESS, 1955.

NATIONAL CONFERENCE OF SOCIAL WORK. MINORITY GROUPS:
    SEGREGATION AND INTEGRATION.   NEW YORK: COLUMBIA
    UNIVERSITY, 1955.

NATIONAL COUNCIL FOR SOCIAL STUDIES. DEMOCRATIC HUMAN
    RELATIONS: PROMISING PRACTICES IN INTERGROUP AND
    INTERCULTURAL EDUCATION IN THE SOCIAL STUDIES.
    WASHINGTON, D. C.: NATIONAL COUNCIL FOR THE SOCIAL
    STUDIES, (1945).

NATIONAL COUNCIL FOR THE SPANISH-SPEAKING. NATIONAL
    COUNCIL FOR THE SPANISH SPEAKING. ITS NEEDS...ITS
    GOALS...ITS PROGRAMS.   RESUME OF THE VILLA CORONADO
    STUDY, 1964.

NATIONAL OPINION RESEARCH CENTER. THE SPANISH SPEAKING
    POPULATION OF DENVER--HOUSING, EMPLOYMENT, HEALTH,
    RECREATION, EDUCATION.   DENVER, COLORADO: DENVER
    UNITY COUNCIL, 1946.

NAVARRO.   CHICANO COMMUNITY (B*).

NEFF, WALTER S. "SOCIO-ECONOMIC STATUS AND INTELLIGENCE".
    THE PSYCHOLOGICAL BULLETIN, VOL. 35 (DECEMBER 1938),
    PP. 727-757 (PL EC).

NELKIN.   "RESPONSE TO MARGINALITY: CASE (B*).

NELSON, LOWRY. "SPEAKING OF TONGUES".   AMERICAN JOURNAL
    OF SOCIOLOGY, VOL. 54 (NOVEMBER 1948), PP. 202-210.

NELSON, ROBERT. THE CHURCHES IN IGNACIO.   UNIVERSITY OF
    COLORADO, JANUARY 1963 (RE).

NEUMEYER, MARTIN H. "JOINT MEETING OF THE PACIFIC
    SOCIOLOGICAL SOCIETY, SOUTHERN DIVISION, AND ALPHA
    KAPPA DELTA ON RACE RELATIONS, 1944".   SOCIOLOGY AND
    SOCIAL RESEARCH, VOL. 29 (SEPTEMBER 1944), PP. 58-62.

NEUMEYER, MARTIN H. "RACE RELAITONS CONFERENCE".
    SOCIOLOGY AND SOCIAL RESEARCH, (SEPTEMBER 1944),
    PP. 58-62.

NEW MEXICO, UNIVERSITY OF. BARELAS COMMUNITY CENTER SOCIAL
    TRAINING PROGRAM.   ALBUQUERQUE: THE UNIVERSITY OF
    NEW MEXICO BULLETIN, 1942 (ED).

NEWELL, ELIZABETH VIRGINIA. THE SOCIAL SIGNIFICANCE OF
    PADUA HILLS AS A CULTURAL AND EDUCATIONAL CENTER.
    UNIVERSITY OF SOUTHERN CALIFORNIA, MASTER'S THESIS
    (1938) (ED).

NEWMAN, KATHERINE D. THE AMERICAN EQUATION: LITERATURE
    IN A MULTI-ETHNIC CULTURE.   ROCKLEIGH, NEW JERSEY:
    ALLYN AND BACON, INC.,.

NEWMARK, MAURICE H. AND NEWMARK, MARCE R. (EDS). CENSUS
    OF THE CITY AND COUNTY OF LOS ANGELES FOR THE YEAR
    1850.   LOS ANGELES, 1929.

NIGHTINGALE.   "ON MOTIVATING DISADVANTAGEDCHILD"   (ED*).

NOLAN, H. J. "LESSON IN HOSPITALITY".   INTER-AMERICAN,
    VOL. 4 (JULY 1945), P. 37.

NORDVOLD.   SELF-ESTEEM ITS RELATIONSHIPTO (PY*).

NORRIS, FRANK. THE OCTOPUS.   NEW YORK: DOUBLEDAY, PAGE
    AND COMPANY, 1904.

NORTON, HENRY K. "MEXICAN IMPRESSIONS".   ANNALS OF THE
    AMERICAN ACADEMY OF POLITICAL AND SOCIAL SCIENCE, VOL.
    138 , PP. 74-78.

NUGENT, JOHN F. LEADERSHIP IN THE SPANISH-SPEAKING
    COMMUNITY OF LANSING, MICHIGAN.   MICHIGAN STATE
    UNIVERSITY, MASTER'S THESIS (1964).

NUTINI.   SAN BERNARDINO CONTLA; MARRIAGE (AN*).

O' BRIEN, ROBERT. "THAT NORTHERN MEXICAN".   POMONA
    COLLEGE MAGAZINE, (OCTOBER 1931), PP. 29-33 (HC).

OFFICER, JAMES EOFF. "BARRIER TO MEXICAN INTEGRATION IN
    TUCSON". KIVA, VOL. 17 (NOVEMBER-DECEMBER 1951),
    PP. 7-16.

OFFICER, JAMES EOFF. "HISTORICAL FACTORS IN INTERETHNIC
    RELATIONS IN THE COMMUNITY OF TUCSON". ARIZONIANA,
    VOL. 1 (FALL 1960), PP. 12-16.

OLIVAS, RICHARD. THE IMMIGRANT EXPERIENCE. BOSTON,
    MASSACHUSETTS: HOUGHTON MIFFLIN COMPANY, 1972.

ORNELAS, CHARLES AND GONZALEZ, MICHAEL. "THE MEXICAN
    AMERICAN PEOPLE: THE NATION'S SECOND LARGEST MINORITY".
    EL GRITO, VOL. 4 NO. 4 (SUMMER 1971), PP. 12-20 (EC
    ED HSW AN).

ORTEGO. "CABINET MEETING PASO" (ED*).

ORTEGO. "THE MEXICAN DIXON LINE: RIGHT (ED*).

ORTEGO, PHILIP D. "THE MINORITY ON THE BORDER: CABINET
    MEETING IN EL PASO". NATION, (DECEMBER 11, 1967),
    PP. 624-627 (ED).

ORTEGO. MEXICAN DIXON LINE: RIGHT SPASSAGE (ED*).

ORTEGO. "CHICAGO BLUES" (ED*).

ORTIZ, ELIZABETH LAMBERT. COMPLETE BOOK OF MEXICAN
    COOKING. NEW YORK: EVANS, 1967.

ORTIZ, MARTIN. MEXICAN AMERICANS IN THE LOS ANGELES
    REGION. LOS ANGELES, CALIFORNIA, AUGUST 1962.

ORTIZ, MARTIN. THE MEXICAN AMERICAN IN THE LOS ANGELES
    COMMUNITY. LOS ANGELES: COMMUNITY RELATIONS
    EDUCATIONAL FOUNDATION, NOVEMBER 1963.

OTERO. "MY PEOPLE" (ED*).

OXNAM, G. BROMLEY. "MEXICANS IN LOS ANGELES FROM THE
    STANDPOINT OF THE RELIGIOUS FORCES O F THE CITY".
    ANNALS OF THE AMERICAN ACADEMY OF POLITICAL AND SOCIAL
    SCIENCE, VOL. 93 (JANUARY 1921), PP. 130-33 (RE).

OXNAM, G. BROMLEY. THE MEXICAN IN LOS ANGELES: LOS ANGELES
    CITY SURVEY. INTERCHURCH WORLD MOVEMENT OF NORTH
    AMERICA, 1920.

PABLO, ANTONIO. POLITICS AND THE SPANISH WORKING CLASS
    IN APERIOD OF ECONOMIC DEVELOPMENT. UNIVERSITY OF
    CALIFORNIA, LOS ANGELES, PHD. DISSERTATION (1971).

PADFIELD, HARLAND, AND MARTIN, WILLIAM E. FARMERS, WORKERS
    AND MACHINES: TECHNOLOGICAL AND SOCIAL CHANGE IN FARM
    INDUSTRIES OF ARIZONA. UNIVERSITY OF ARIZONA PRESS,
    1965 (EC).

PAINTER, NORMAN WELLINGTON. THE ASSIMILATION OF LATIN-AMERICANS
    IN NEW ORLEANS, LOUISIANA. TULANE UNIVERSITY,
    MASTER'S THESIS (1949) (AN).

PALACE, ARTHUR LAWRENCE. A COMPRARATIVE DESCRIPTION OF
    ANGLO-WHITE AND MEXICAN-WHITE BOYS COMMITTED TO
    PACIFIC COLONY. UNIVERSITY OF SOUTHERN CALIFORNIA,
    MASTER'S THESIS (1950) (PY).

PALACIOS, ARTURO (ED). THE MEXICAN-AMERICAN DIRECTORY.
    WASHINGTON, D. C.: EXECUTIVE SYSTEMS CORPORATION, 1969.

PALFI, MARION. "MEXICAN AMERICANS". COMMON GROUND,
    (SPRING 1948), PP. 52-60.

PALMORE, ERDMAN B. 'ETHNOPHAULISMS AND ETHNOCENTRISM.'
    IN MILTON L. BARRON (ED), MINORITIES IN A CHANGING
    WORLD.

PANGER, DANIEL. "THE FORGOTTEN ONES". PROGRESSIVE, VOL.
    27 (APRIL 1963), PP. 20-23 (EC).

PANUNZIO, CONSTANTINE. "INTERMARRIAGE IN LOS ANGELES
    1924-1933". AMERICAN JOURNAL OF SOCIOLOGY, VOL. 47
    (MARCH 1942), PP. 690-701.

PARMEE, LELIA K. "PERCEPTION OF THE PERSONAL SOCIAL
    PROBLEMS BY THE STUDENTS OF DIFFERENT ETHNIC BACKGROUNDS".
    DISSERTATION ABSTRACTS, VOL. 27 (1966), P. 27A (ED).

PARSLEY, ROSA FRANCES. A STUDY OF THE EXPENDITURE FOR FOOD
    OF SOME URBAN LATIN-AMERICAN FAMILIES ON WORK RELIEF
    IN AUSTIN,TEXAS. UNIVERSITY OF TEXAS, MASTER'S
    THESIS (1935) (EC).

PARSLEY, ROSE F. FOOD EXPENDITURES IN URBAN LATIN-AMERICAN
    FAMILIES. UNIVERSITY OF TEXAS, 1935 (EC).

PARSONS, THEODORE WILLIAM. ETHNIC CLEAVAGE IN A CALIFORNIA
    SCHOOL. STANFORD UNIVERSITY, 1965 (ED).

PASAMANICK. "THE INTELLIGENCE AMERICAN CHILDREN (PY*).

PASOMANICK. "THE INTELLIGENCE AMERICAN CHILDREN (PY*).

PATRIC, GLADYS EMELIA. A STUDY OF HOUSING AND SOCIAL
    CONDITIONS IN THE ANN STREET DISTRICT OF LOS ANGELES,
    CALIFORNIA. LOS ANGELES SOCIETY FOR THE STUDY AND
    PREVENTION OF TUBERCULOSIS, 1917 (MD).

PATTEE.   "THE PUERTO RICANS"   (PL*).

PATTERSON, CHARLES J.   A COMPARISON OF PERFORMANCES
    OF MEXICAN AND AMERICAN CHILDREN IN A BI-CULTURAL
    SETTING ON MEASURES OF ABILITY,ACHIEVEMENT, AND
    ADJUSTMENT.   MICHIGAN STATE UNIVERSITY, (1960) (PY
    ED).

PAUL.   HEALTH, CULTURE COMMUNITY: CASE (MD*).

PAUL, BENJAMIN DAVID.   MENTAL DISORDER AND SELF-REGULATING
    PROCESSES IN CULTURE: A GUATEMALA ILLUSTRATION.
    MILBANK MEMORIAL FUND, INTERRELATIONS BETWEEN
    THE SOCIAL ENVIRONMENT AND PSYCHIATRIC DISORDERS. NEW
    YORK, 1953 (PY).

PAZ, FRANK X.   MEXICAN-AMERICANS IN CHICAGO.   CHICAGO:
    CHICAGO COUNCIL OF SOCIAL AGENCIES, 1948.

PEATTIE, LISA REDFIELD.   THE VIEW FROM THE BARRIO.   ANN
    ARBOR, MICHIGAN: UNIVERSITY OF MICHIGAN PRESS, 1968
    (AN).

PECK, ROBERT F.   "INTELLIGENCE, ETHNICITY AND SOCIAL ROLES
    IN ADOLESCENT SOCIETY".   SOCIOMETRY, VOL. 25 (MARCH
    1962), PP. 64-72 (PY).

PEEK, R.B.   THE RELIGIOUS AND SOCIAL ATTITUDES OF THE
    MEXICAN GIRLS OF THE CONSTITUENCY OF THE ALL NATIONS
    FOUNDATION IN LOS ANGELES.   UNIVERSITY OF SOUTHERN
    CALIFORNIA, MASTER'S THESIS (1929) (PY).

PEIFFER.   CULTURAL BACKGROUND AMERICANS (AN*).

PENALOSA, FERNANDO.   'RECENT CHANGES AMONG THE CHICANOS.'
    IN EDWARD SIMMEN (ED), PAIN AND PROMISE: THE CHICANO
    TODAY.

PENALOSA, FERNANDO.   "EDUCATION-INCOME DISCREPANCIES
    BETWEEN SECOND AND LATER-GENERATION MEXICAN-AMERICANS
    IN THE SOUTHWEST".   SOCIOLOGY AND SOCIAL RESEARCH,
    VOL. 53 (JULY 1969), PP. 448-454.

PENALOSA, FERNANDO.   "MEXICAN FAMILY ROLES".   JOURNAL OF
    MARRIAGE AND THE FAMILY, VOL. 30 (NOVEMBER 1968),
    PP. 680-688.

PENALOSA, FERNANDO.   "THE CHANGING MEXICAN-AMERICAN
    IN SOUTHERN CALIFORNIA".   SOCIAL SCIENCE REVIEW, VOL.
    51 (1967), PP. 406-415 (ED EC).

PENALOSA, FERNANDO.   "THE CHANGING MEXICAN-AMERICAN
    IN SOUTHERN CALIFORNIA".   SOCIAL SCIENCE REVIEW, VOL.
    53 (JULY 1969), PP. 448-454 (ED EC).

PENALOSA, FERNANDO. "THE CHANGING MEXICAN-AMERICAN
    IN SOUTHERN CALIFORNIA".   SOCIAL FORCES, VOL. 44
    (JUNE 1966), PP. 498-505 (ED EC).

PENALOSA, FERNANDO. "THE CHANGING MEXICAN-AMERICAN
    IN SOUTHERN CALIFORNIA".   SOCIOLOGICAL INQUIRY, VOL.
    36 (WINTER 1966), PP. 19-30 (ED EC).

PENALOSA, FERNANDO. "THE CHANGING MEXICAN-AMERICAN
    IN SOUTHERN CALIFORNIA".   PHYLON, VOL. 29 (SUMMER
    1968), PP. 119-126 (ED   EC).

PENALOSA, FERNANDO. "THE CHANGING MEXICAN-AMERICAN
    IN SOUTHERN CALIFORNIA".   SOCIOLOGY AND SOCIAL
    RESEARCH, VOL. 51 (JULY 1967), PP. 405-417.

PENALOSA, FERNANDO. "TOWARD AN OPERATIONAL DEFINITION OF
    THE MEXICAN AMERICAN".   AZTLAN--CHICANO JOURNAL OF
    THE SOCIAL SCIENCES AND THE ARTS, VOL. 1 NO.
    1 (SPRING 1970), PP. 1-12.

PENALOSA, FERNANDO. CLASS CONSCIOUSNESS AND SOCIAL
    MOBILITY IN A MEXICAN-AMERICAN COMMUNITY.   UNIVERSITY
    OF SOUTHERN CALIFORNIA, PHD. DISSERTATION (1963).

PENALOSA, FERNANDO. 'THE CHANGING MEXICAN-AMERICAN
    IN SOUTHERN CALIFORNIA.'   IN EDWARD SIMMEN (ED), PAIN
    AND PROMISE: THE CHICANO TODAY.

PENALOSA, FERNANDO; MCDONAGH, EDWARD C. 'SOCIAL MOBILITY
    IN A MEXICAN-AMERICAN COMMUNITY.'   IN NATHANIEL N.
    WAGNER AND MARSHA J. HAUG (EDS), CHICANOS: SOCIAL AND
    PSYCHOLOGICAL PERSPECTIVES.

PENALOSA, FERNANDO; MCDONAGH, EDWARD C. "EDUCATION,
    ECONOMIC STATUS AND SOCIAL-CLASS AWARENESS OF
    MEXICAN-AMERICANS".   PHYLON, VOL. 29 (SUMMER 1968),
    PP. 119-126.

PENALOSA, FERNANDO; MCDONAGH, EDWARD C. "SOCIAL MOBILITY
    IN A MEXICAN-AMRICAN COMMUNITY".   SOCIAL FORCES, VOL.
    44 (JUNE 1966), PP. 498-505.

PENROD, VESTA. CIVIL RIGHTS PROBLEMS OF MEXICAN-AMERICANS
    IN SOUTHERN CALIFORNIA.   CLAREMONT GRADUATE SCHOOL,
    CLAREMONT, CALIFORNIA, MASTER'S THESIS (1948) (LW).

PERALES, ALONSO S. EN DEFENSA DE MI RAZA.   SAN ANTONIO,
    TEXAS: ARTES GRAFICOS, 1937.

PERALES, ALONSO S. EL MEXICO AMERICANO Y POLITICA DEL SUR
    DE TEXAS.   SAN ANTONIO, TEXAS, 1931.

PERALES, ALONSO S., COMP. ARE WE GOOD NEIGHBORS?.   SAN
    ANTONIO, TEXAS: ARTES GRAFICAS, 1948.

PERRAUDIN.   ECONOMIC STATE SPANISH-AMERICAN   (EC*).

PERRY.   ECONOMIC CHARACTERISTICS TEXAS   (EC*).

PESOTTA, ROSE.   BREAD UPON THE WATERS.   NEW YORK: MEAD
     AND COMPANY, 1944.

PHILLIPS, LESTER H.   "SEGREGATION IN EDUCATION: A CALIFORNIA
     CASE STUDY".   PHYLON, VOL. 10 (FOURTH QUARTER
     1949), PP. 407-13 (ED).

PICK, ROBERT F.   "INTELLIGENCE, ETHNICITY AND SOCIAL ROLES
     IN ADOLESCENT SOCIETY".   SOCIOMETRY, VOL. 25 (JUNE
     1930), PP. 64-72 (PY).

PIERSON, G.K.   "ANALYSIS OF POPULATION CHANGES IN NEW
     MEXICO COUNTIES".   NEW MEXICO BUSINESS, VOL.
     14 (NOVEMBER 1961), PP. 2-8 (EC).

PIJOAN.   "FOOD AVAILABILITY SOCIAL FUNCTION" (MD*).

PIJOAN.   NUTRITION CERTAIN RELATED FACTORS   (MD*).

PIJOAN.   CERTAIN FACTORS INVOLVED STRUGGLE   (MD*).

PINKNEY, ALPHONSO.   "PREJUDICE TOWARD MEXICAN AND NEGRO
     AMERICANS: A COMPARISON".   PHYLON, VOL. 24 (WINTER
     1963), PP. 353-359.

PITRONE.   CHAVEZ, MAN MIGRANTS PLEA SOCIAL   (EC*).

POLIFRONI, MIO.   "INCLUDING OUR SPANISH SPEAKING NEIGHBORS".
     YOUNG CHILDREN, VOL. 20 (SUMMER 1965), PP. 351-356.

POLSBY, NELSON W.   "THE SOCIOLOGY OF COMMUNITY POWER: A
     REASSESSMENT".   SOCIAL FORCES, VOL. 37 (MARCH
     1959), PP. 232-236.

POLSBY, NELSON W.   "THREE PROBLEMS IN THE ANALYSIS
     OF COMMUNITY POWER".   AMERICAN SOCIOLOGICAL REVIEW,
     VOL. 24 (DECEMBER 1959), PP. 796-803.

PORTEUS.   "RACIAL GROUP DIFFERENCES MENTALITY" (PY*).

POST, D.   "MEXICAN-AMERICANS AND LA RAZA".   CHRISTIAN
     CENTURY, VOL. 86 (MARCH 5, 1969), PP. 325-326.

POTTER, MARGUERITE.   GRASS ROOTS DIPLOMAT.   LEO POTISHAM
     FOUNDATION, TEXAS CHRISTIAN UNIVERSITY, 1961.

PRATT.   COMPARISON SOCIAL ACHIEVEMENT   (EC*).

PRICE, JOHN A.   THE URBANIZATION OF MEXICO'S NORTHERN
     BORDER STATES.   SAN DIEGO STATE COLLEGE, 1969.

PRINCE, L. BRAFORD. RACE RELATIONS IN MINNESOTA. THE
     GOVERNOR'S, INTERRACIAL COMMISSION, SAINT PAUL, 1948.

PROIETTI, KITTI JEAN LEE, AND VALLES, MARTIN. MEXICAN
     AMERICANS: A DESCRIPTIVE STUDY OF CLIENTS AND
     NON-CLIENTS OF A COMMUNITY MENTAL HEALTH CENTER.
     ARIZONA STATE UNIVERSITY, 1970.

PROTHEROE, DONALD WESLEY. THE LANGUAGE USED BY CHILDREN
     OF CONTRASTING SOCIO-ECONOMIC GROUPS IN TASKS RELATED
     TO CONCEPT FORMATION. WAYNE STATE UNIVERSITY, PHD.
     DISSERTATION (1967) (LA   EC).

PUEBLO REGIONAL PLANNING COMMISSION. THE SOCIO-ECONOMIC
     AND PHYSICAL CHARACTERISTICS OF THE VARIOUS NEIGHBORHOODS
     IN PUEBLO. PUEBLO, COLORADO, MARCH 1965.

PUTMAN. HE SPANISH-SPEAKING PEOPLE   (ED*).

R. FERNANDEZ MARINA, E. D.; MALDONADO-SIERRA: AND TRENT,
     R. D. "THREE BASIC THEMES IN MEXICAN AND PUERTO RICAN
     FAMILY VALUES". JOURNAL OF SOCIAL PSYCHOLOGY, VOL.
     48 (NOVEMBER 1958), PP. 167-81 (PY).

RAAB, EARL (ED). AMERICAN RACE RELATIONS TODAY. GARDEN
     CITY, NEW YORK: DOUBLEDAY, 1962.

RAAB, EARL AND LIPSET, SEYMOUR MARTIN. 'THE PREJUDICED
     SOCIETY.' NATHANIEL N. WAGNER AND MARSHA J. HAUG,
     (EDS) CHICANOS: SOCIAL AND PS YCHOLOGICAL PERSPECTIVES.

RABEMAKER, JOHN A. THESE ARE AMERICANS. PALO ALTO,
     CALIFORNIA: PACIFIC BOOKS, 1951.

RADEMAKER, JOHN A. THESE ARE AMERICANS. PACIFIC BOOKS,
     1951 (HUS).

RADOMSKI. FAMILY INCOME RELATED CHARACTERISTICS (EC*).

RADTKE, T. J. "HIS NAME IS GONZALEZ". NATIONAL CATHOLIC
     MAGAZINE,   (JULY AND AUGUST 1950).

RADTKE, T. J. THE WETBACK SITUATION IN THE RIO GRANDE
     VALLEY. CORPUS CHRISTI: REPORT OF THE BISHOP'S
     COMMITTEE FOR THE SPANISH-SPEAING, AUGUST, 1950.

RAISNER, A. "NEW HORIZONS FOR THE STUDENT OF SPANISH
     SPEAKING BACKGROUND: SCIENCE SPNISH RESEARCH
     EXPERIMENT". HIGH POINTS, VOL. 48 (FALL 1966),
     PP. 19-23 (ED).

RAMIREZ. "WETBACK" CHILDREN SOUTH TEXAS (ED*).

RAMIREZ, ROBERT. 'THE WOOLEN SARAPE.' IN EDWARD SIMMEN
     (ED), PAIN AND PROMISE: THE CHICANO TODAY.

RAMOS, JUAN. SPANISH-SPEAKING LEADERSHIP IN TWO SOUTHWESTERN
    CITIES: A DESCRIPTIVE STUDY.   BRANDEIS UNIVERSITY,
    PHD. DISSERTATION (1969) (EC PL).

RAMPARTS.   BRACERO POLITICS: SPECIAL REPORT (EC*).

RAMSEY, GLENN U., AND HODGE, BEULAH. "ANGLO-LATIN PROBLEMS
    AS PERCEIVED BY PUBLIC SERVICE PERSONNEL".   SOCIAL
    FORCES, VOL. 37 (MAY 1959), PP. 339-348.

RAND, C. "PROFILES; INTERRACIAL RELATIONS BETWEEN
    MEXICANS, JAPANESE, NEGROES, WHITES IN LOS ANGELES".
    NEW YORKER, VOL. 42 (OCTOBER 15, 1966), PP. 64-66.

RANKER, JESSE E. JR. A STUDY OF JUVENILE GANGS IN
    THE HOLLENBECK AREA OF EAST LOS ANGELES.   UNIVERSITY
    OF SOUTHERN CALIFORNIA, MASTER'S THESIS (1958).

RANKIN.   MEXICAN AMERICANS MANPOWER POLICY (EC*).

RECORD, WILSON. MINORITY GROUPS AND INTERGROUP RELATIONS
    IN THE SAN FRANCISCO BAY AREA.   BERKELEY: UNIVERSITY
    OF CALIFORNIA AT BERKELEY, INSTITUTE OF GOVERNMENTAL
    STUDIES, 1963.

REDFIELD.   "ANTECEDENTS MEXICAN IMMIGRATION (AN*).

REGIL, R. AGUILAR. "PEOPLE, CLOUDS AND SKY".   SOCIOLOGY
    AND SOCIAL RESEARCH, VOL. 13 , P. 435.

REHNBERG.   ECONOMIC SOCIAL STRUCTURE COSTILLA (EC*).

REICH, JULIE M. RELOCATING THE DISPOSSESED ELDERLY: A
    STUDY OF MEXICAN AMERICANS.   UNIVERSITY OF PENNSYLVANIA,
    PHILADELPHIA INSTITUTE FOR ENVIRONMENTAL STUDIES, 1966
    (EC).

REMBAO, ALBERTO. "WHAT SHOULD BE DONE FOR JUAN GARCIA?".
    POMONA COLLEGE MAGAZINE, VOL. 17 (NOVEMBER 1970),
    PP. 145-48.

RENDON.   HAND MY SHOULDER (RE*).

RENDON, GABINO. OBJECTIVE ACCESS IN THE OPPORTUNITY
    STRUCTURE: THE ASSESSMENT OF THREE ETHNIC GROUPS WITH
    RESPECT TO QUANTIFIED SOCIAL STRUCTURAL VARIABLES.
    TRI-ETHNIC RESEARCH PROJECT, INSTITUTE OF BEHAVIORAL
    SCIENCE, UNIVERSITY OF COLORADO, (JUNE 1963). REPORT
    NUMBER 20.

RESCHENTHALER, PATRICIA. POSTWAR READJUSTMENT IN EL PASO:
    1945-1950.   EL PASO, TEXAS: TEXAS WESTERN PRESS, THE
    UNIVERSITY OF TEXAS AT EL PASO, (1968). SOUTHWESTERN
    STUDIES MONOGRAPH NUMBER 21 (ED).

REY, TONY. "TIERRA AMARILLA IS DYING".   EL GRITO, VOL.
    1 NO. 3 (SPRING 1968), PP. 10-11 (LMA).

REYES.   SURVEY PROBLEMS INVOLVED AMERICANIZATION   (AN*).

REYNOLDS.   "GIRLS AT CAMP: SPANISH AMERICAN   (LI*).

RICE.   "EDUCATION SUBCULTURAL GROUPS" (ED*).

RICE.   "INTERGROUP RELATIONS ARIZONA" (ED*).

RICE.   SOME CONTRIBUTING FACTORS DETERMINING   (ED*).

RICHARDS, EUGENE S. "ATTITUDES OF WHITE COLLEGE STUDENTS
    IN THE SOUTHWEST TOWARD ETHNIC GROUPS IN THE UNITED
    STATES".   SOCIOLOGY AND SOCIAL RESEARCH, VOL. 35
    (SEPTEMBER 1950), PP. 22-30 (PY).

RICHEY.   "EDUCATIONAL STATUS IMPORTANT (ED*).

RICKSEEKER.   CIVIL DISTURBANCE POLITICAL PROVISION   (PL*).

RIGGINS.   FACTORS SOCIAL BACKGROUND WHICH (ED*).

RISDEN, RANDALL. "STUDY OF INTERRACIAL MARRIAGES BASED
    ON DATA FOR LOS ANGELES COUNTY".   SOCIOLOGY AND
    SOCIAL RESEARCH, VOL. 39 (NOVEMBER 1954), PP. 92-95
    (AN).

RIVERA.   "CHICANOS: CULTURE, COMMUNITY (AN*).

RIVET.   "RECHERCHES ANTHROPOLOGIQUESSUR   (AN*).

ROBBINS. "ALIENATED ONES" (ED*).

ROBERTS, K. L. "MEXICANS OR RUIN".   SATURDAY EVENING
    POST, VOL. 200 (DECEMBER 1935), PP. 14-15, 142-54
    (SI EC).

ROBERTS, K. L. "THE DOCILE MEXICAN".   SATURDAY EVENING
    POST, VOL. 200 (DECEMBER 1935), PP. 39-41, 165-66
    (SI EC).

ROBERTS, K. L. "WET AND OTHER MEXICANS".   SATURDAY
    EVENING POST, VOL. 200 (DECEMBER 1935), PP. 10-11,
    137-42, 146 (SI EC).

ROBERTS, LAUNEY F. "MINORITY SELF-IDENTIFICATION THROUGH
    TEXTS: A STUDY OF PUBLICATION PROGRESS".   JOURNAL
    OF HUMAN RELATIONS,   (THIRD QUARTER, 1968),
    PP. 356-367 (PY ED).

ROBERTSON, JACK. A STUDY OF THE YOUTH NEEDS AND SERVICES
     IN DALLAS, TEXAS.   WASHINGTON, D. C.: AMERICAN
     YOUTH COMMISSION, (1938) (ED).

ROBERTSON. "ANTICIPATED ACCEPTANCE NEIGHBORHOOD (MD*).

ROBINSON, DUAN. CHANCE TO BELONG.   NEW YORK: NEW YORK
     UNIVERSITY PRESS, 1914.

ROBLES.   ANALYTIC DESCRIPTION PEER GROUP (ED*).

ROCCO.   "THE CHICANO SOCIAL SCIENCES: (AN*).

ROCHE, JOHN PEARSON. THE QUEST FOR THE DREAM; THE
     DEVELOPMENT OF CIVIL RIGHTS AND HUMAN RELATIONS IN
     MODERN AMERICA. NEW YORK: MACMILLAN, 1963 (PL).

RODRIGUEZ SALA DE GOMEZGIL.   ESTEREOTIPO MEXICANO: ESTUDIO
     (PY*).

ROEDER.   RESTRUCTURING POWER MEXICAN AMERICAN (PL*).

ROEDER, SANDRA L. A STUDY OF THE SITUATION OF MEXICAN
     AMERICANS IN THE SOUTHWEST.   WASHINGTON, D. C.:
     COMMUNITY RELATIONS SERVICE, U.S. DEPARTMENT OF
     JUSTICE,, (1967) (LW).

ROGERS.   "POVERTY BEHIND CACTUS CURTAIN" (EC*).

ROGERS.   PERCEPTION POWER STRUCTURE BY (EC*).

ROGERS.   HOUSING SITUATION MEXICANS SAN (EC*).

ROJO, T. A. "SOCIAL MALADJUSTMENT AMONG FILIPINOS IN THE
     UNITED STATES".   SOCIOLOGY AND SOCIAL RESEARCH, VOL.
     21 (MAY 1937), PP. 447-57 (SI).

ROLLINS, PHILIP ASHTON. JINGLEBOB.   NEW YORK: SCRIBNER,
     1927, 1930 (HSW LI).

ROMANO-V.   GOODBY REVOLUTION-- HELLO SLUM (AN*).

ROMANO-V.   THE ANTHROPOLOGY SOCIOLOGY MEXICAN-AMERICANS:
     (AN*).

ROMANO-V.   THE ANTRHOPOLOGY SOCIOLOGY MEXICAN-AMERICANS
     (AN*).

ROMANO-V.   VOICES: READINGS GRITO (AN*).

ROMANO-V.   VOICES: READINGS GRITO. (AN*).

ROMANO-V.   "BOARISMATIC MEDICINE, FOLK HEALING (AN*).

ROMANO-V.   "BOOK REVIEW: NORTH MEXICO" (AN*).

ROMANO-V.   "CHARISMATIC MEDICINE, FOLK HEALING (AN*).

ROMANO-V.   "GOODBY REVOLUTICN-- HELLO SLUM" (AN*).

ROMANO-V.   "GOOCBYE REVOLUTION-- HELLO SLUM" (AN*).

ROMANO-V.   "MINORITIES, HISTORY CULTURAL (AN*).

ROMANO-V.   "THE ANTHROPOLOGY SOCIOLOGY MEXICAN-AMERICANS"
     (AN*).

ROMANO-V.   "THE ANTRHOPOLOGY SOCIOLOGY MEXICAN (AN*).

ROMANO-V.   "THE CHOSEN ONE, ARCO IRIS; MISSIONARY (AN*).

ROMANO-V.   ESPEJO: SELECTED MEXICAN AMERICAN (AN*).

ROMANO-V.   PAST, PRESENT FUTURE MEXICANAMERICAN (AN*).

ROMANO-V.   "INTRODUCTORY COMMENTS" (AN*).

ROMERO.   MEXICO UNITED STATES. STUDYSUBJECTS (PL*).

ROMERO.   AMIGOS (LI*).

ROMUALDI.   "HANDS ACROSS BORDER" (EC*).

ROSALDO.   "DE MAYORIA A MINORIA" (LA*).

ROSE.   RACE PREJUDICE DISCRIMINATION: (AN*).

ROSE, ARNOLD MARSHALL. AMERICA DIVIDED: MINORITY GROUP
     RELATICNS IN THE UNITED STATES.   NEW YORK: KNOPF,
     1953.

ROSE.   AMERICA DIVIDED: MINORITY GROUP (AN*).

ROSE, ARNOLD MARSHALL. MINORITY PROBLEMS; A TEXTBOOK OF
     READINGS IN INTERGROUP RELATIONS.   NEW YORK: HARPER
     AND ROW, 1965.

ROSE.   MINORITY PROBLEMS; TEXTBOOK READINGS (AN*).

ROSE.   RACE PREJUDICE DISCRIMINATION: (AN*).

ROSE.   THEY WE; RACIAL ETHNIC RELATIONS (AN*).

ROSENFELD.   "MODERN MEDICINE WHERE CLOCKWALKS" (PY*).

ROSENQUIST, CARL M. "DIFFERENTIAL RESPONSES OF TEXAS
     CONVECTS".   AMERICAN JOURNAL OF SOCIOLOGY, VOL. 38
     (JULY 1932), PP. 10-21 (PY).

ROSENQUIST, CARL M. AND MCGARGEE, EDWIN I. DELINQUENCY
     IN THREE CULTURES.   AUSTIN: UNIVERSITY OF TEXAS
     PRESS, 1969 (AN).

ROSENQUIST, CARL M. AND BROWDER, WALTER G. FAMILY MOBILITY
    IN DALLAS, TEXAS, 1923-1938.   AUSTIN, TEXAS:
    UNIVERSITY OF TEXAS, 1942.

ROSENQUIST, CARL M. AND BROWDER, WALTER G. FAMILY MOBILITY
    IN HOUSTON, TEXAS, 1922-1938.   AUSTIN, TEXAS:
    UNIVERSITY OF TEXAS, 1942.

ROSENSTONE.   PROTEST MOVEMENTS NINETEEN SIXTIES (PL*).

ROSING, R. "WHERE OVERCROWDING AND THE OPEN PRAIRIE RUB
    ELBOWS".   SURVEY, VOL. 23 (DECEMBER 11, 1909), PP.
    362-364.

ROSKELLEY, R. W. WHEN DIFFERENT CULTURES MEET.   DENVER:
    ROCKY MOUNTAIN COUNCIL ON INTER-AMERICAN AFFAIRS, 1946
    (AN).

ROSS, FRED W. COMMUNITY ORGANIZATION IN MEXICAN AMERICAN
    COMMUNITIES.   SAN FRANCISCO, CALIFORNIA: AMERICAN
    COUNCIL ON RACE RELATIONS, 1947.

ROSS, MALCOLM. "THOSE GRINGOS".   COMMON GROUND, VOL. 8
    NO. 2 (WINTER 1948), PP. 3-13.

ROSS, WILLIAM T. SOCIAL FUNCTION OF THE MEXICAN-AMERICAN
    GODPARENT SYSTEM IN TUCSON.   UNIVERSITY OF ARIZONA,
    MASTER'S THESIS (1953) (AN).

ROWAN.   MEXICAN AMERICAN (LW*).

ROYBAL.   "PRESIDENT JOHNSON UNTOLD STORY (PL*).

ROYBAL.   MANPOWER PROGRAMMING MEXICANAMERICAN (EC*).

RUBEL.   "ANALISIS FUNCIONAL EFECTOS NEGATIVOS (AN*).

RUBEL.   "LA ENVIDIA COMO PROCESO CAUSAL (AN*).

RUBEL.   ACROSS TRACKS: MEXICAN-AMERICANS (AN*).

RUBEL.   CULTURAL LIMITATIONS SOME SOCIOLOGICAL (AN*).

RUBEL.   FAMILY PERCEPTIONS SOCIAL RELATIONS: (AN*).

RUBEL.   SOCIAL LIFE URBAN MEXICAN AMERICANS (AN*).

RUBEL.   SOME CULTURAL ANTHROPOLOGICAL (AN*).

RUBEL.   THE MYTH MELTING POT (AN*).

RUIZ.   "LATIN-AMERICAN JUVENILE DELINQUENCY (LW*).

RUIZ, REV. RALPH. CHANGE CRISIS.   SAN ANTONIO, TEXAS,
    APRIL 1971 (RE).

RUSH, LUCY (KELLEY). SOCIAL ACTIVITIES OF SOCCORRO COUNTY,
     NEW MEXICO ADOLESCENTS.   FORT COLLINS: COLORADO STATE
     UNIVERSITY, 1964 (HN).

RUSINOW, IRVING. "SPANISH AMERICANS IN NEW MEXICO".
     SURVEY GRAPHIC, VOL. 27 , PP. 95-99 (EC).

RUSINOW, IRVING. A CAMERA REPORT ON EL CERRITO, A TYPICAL
     SPANISH AMERICAN COMMUNITY IN NEW MEXICO.
     WASHINGTON, D. C.: U.S. DEPARTMENT OF AGRICULTURE,
     BUREAU OF AGRICULTURAL ECONOMICS, (1942) (EC).

RUSINOW, IRVING. A CAMERA REPORT ON EL CERRITO; A TYPICAL
     SPANISH AMERICAN COMMUNITY IN NEW MEXICO.
     WASHINGTON: U.S. GOVERNMENT PRINTING OFFICE, (1942)
     (EC).

RUSK, MARIAN TERRY. A STUDY OF DELINQUENCY AMONG URBAN
     MEXICAN-AMERICAN YOUTH.   ANN ARBOR, MICHIGAN:
     UNIVERSITY MICROFILMS, INC., 1971 (LW).

RUSSEL.   "PROBLEMS MEXICAN CHILDREN SOUTHWEST" (ED*).

RUSSELL.   "FUSING TWO CULTURES" (ED*).

RUSSELL.   "RACIAL GROUPS NEW MEXICO LEGISLATURE" (HN*).

RUSSELL.   "STATE REGIONALISM NEW MEXICO" (HN*).

RUSSELL.   STATE REGIONALISM NEW MEXICO (HN*).

RUSSMAN.   CULTURALLY DEPRIVED CHILD (AN*).

RYAN.   "THE DUBLIN MEETING WORLD FEDERATION (ED*).

SAENGER.   SOCIAL PSYCHOLOGY PREJUDICE:ACHIEVING (PY*).

SAENZ, J. LUZ. "GOOD WILL TOWARD MEN".   THE TEXAS
     OUTLOOK, VOL. 34 (DECEMBER 1950), PP. 21-22.

SAENZ, M.; PRIESTLY, H. I. SOME MEXICAN PROBLEMS.
     CHICAGO: UNIVERSITY OF CHICAGO PRESS, 1926.

SAENZ, O. L. "GOOD WILL TOWARD MEN".   TEXAS OUTLOOK, VOL.
     34 (DECEMBER 1950), PP. 21-22.

SAINT JOHN, BEREA EDITH. SPANISH-SPEAKING DELINQUENTS OF
     THE DENVER JUVENILE COURT.   UNIVERSITY OF DENVER,
     MASTER'S THESIS (1939).

SALCEDO, CONSUELO. MEXICAN AMERICAN SOCIO-CULTURAL
     PATTERNS: IMPLICATIONS FOR SOCIAL CASE WORK.
     UNIVERSITY OF SOUTHERN CALIFORNIA, MASTER'S THESIS
     (1955).

SALINAS, GUADALUPE. "MEXICAN-AMERICANS AND DESEGREGATION".
    EL GRITO, VOL. 4 NO. 4 (SUMMER 1971), PP. 59-69.

SALINAS, GUADLUPE. "MEXICAN-AMERICANS AND DESEGREGATION".
    EL GRITO, VOL. 4 NO. 4 (SUMMER 1971), PP. 36-59.

SAMORA, JULIAN (ED). LA RAZA: FORGOTTEN AMERICANS.
    UNIVERSITY OF NOTRE DAME PRESS, 1966.

SAMORA, JULIAN ; WATSON, JAMES B. "SUBORDINATE LEADERSHIP
    IN A BICULTURAL COMMUNITY: AN ANALYSIS".   AMERICAN
    SOCIOLOGICAL REVIEW, VOL. 19 (1954), PP. 413-421.

SAMORA, JULIAN AND BEEGLE, J. A. (EDS). "EDUCATION AND
    SOCIAL CHANGE IN LATIN AMERICA".   RURAL SOCIOLOGY,
    VOL. 25 NO. 1 (MARCH 1960) (MD).

SAMORA, JULIAN AND BARRETT, D. N. THE MOVEMENT OF SPANISH
    YOUTH FROM RURAL TO URBAN SETTINGS.   NATIONAL
    COMMITTEE FOR CHILDREN AND YOUTH.

SAMORA, JULIAN AND DEANE, W. N. "LANGUAGE USAGE AS
    A POSSIBLE INDEX OF ACCULTURATION".   SOCIOLOGY AND
    SOCIAL RESEARCH,   (MAY-JUNE 1956) (LA).

SAMORA, JULIAN AND D'ANTONIO, W. V. "OCCUPATIONAL
    STRATIFICATION IN FOUR SOUTHWESTERN COMMUNITIES: A
    STUDY OF ETHNIC DIFFERENTIAL EMPLOYMENT IN HOSPITALS".
    SOCIAL FORCES, VOL. 41 NO. 1 (OCTOBER 1962).

SAMORA, JULIAN AND LAMANNA, RICHARD A. MEXICAN AMERICANS
    IN A MIDWEST METROPOLIS--A STUDY OF EAST CHICAGO.
    GRADUATE SCHOOL OF BUSINESS ADMINISTRATION, LOS
    ANGELES: UNIVERSITY OF CALIFORNIA, 1967.

SAMORA, JULIAN AND LAMANNA, RICHARD A. RECENT TRENDS IN
    EDUCATIONAL STATUS OF MEXICAN-AMERICANS IN TEXAS.
    IMPROVING EDUCATIONAL OPPORTUNITIES OF THE MEXICAN-AMERICAN.
    PROCEEDINGS OF THE FIRST TEXAS CONFERENCE FOR
    THE MEXICAN-AMERICAN. SAN ANTONIO, 1967..

SAMORA, JULIAN AND SAUNDERS, LYLE. 'A MEDICAL CARE PROGRAM
    IN A COLORADO COMMUNITY.'   IN BENJAMIN PAUL (ED),
    HEALTH, CULTURE AND COMMUNITY (MD).

SAMORA, JULIAN AND WATSON, J. B. THE LANGUAGE OF FOUR-FIVE
    YEAR OLD BILINGUAL CHICANO CHILDREN.   PAPERS
    PRESENTED AT THE SOUTHWESTERN ANTHROPOLOGICAL
    ASSOCIATION CONVENTION, APRIL 18-21, 1973, SAN
    FRANCISCO, CALIFORNIA. (LA).

SAMORA, JULIAN. 'MEDICAL VOCABULARY KNOWLEDGE AMONG
    HOSPITAL PATIENTS.'   IN JAMES K. SKIPPER, JR. AND
    ROBERT C. LEONARD (EDS), REPRINTED IN: SOCIAL
    INTERACTION AND PATIENT CARE (MD).

SAMORA, JULIAN. "CONCEPTIONS OF HEALTH AND DISEASE AMONG
    SPANISH-AMERICANS". AMERICAN CATHOLIC SOCIOLOGICAL
    REVIEW, VCL. 22 (WINTER 1961), PP. 314-323.

SAMORA, JULIAN. "CONCEPTIONS OF HEALTH AND DISEASE AMONG
    SPANISH-AMERICANS". AMERICAN CATHOLIC SOCIOLOGICAL
    REVIEW, (WINTER 1961) (AN MD).

SAMORA, JULIAN. "MINORITY LEADERSHIP IN A BI-CULTURAL
    COMMUNITY: AN ANALYSIS". AMERICAN SOCIOLOGICAL
    REVIEW, (AUGUST 1954).

SAMORA. "RURAL FAMILIES URBAN SETTING: (AN*).

SAMORA, JULIAN. "THE EDUCATIONAL STATUS OF A MINORITY".
    THEORY INTO PRACTICE, VOL. 2 (JUNE 1963), PP. 144-150.

SAMORA, JULIAN. "THE SOCIAL SCIENTIST AS RESEARCHER AND
    TEACHER IN THE MEDICAL SCHOOL". JOURNAL OF HEALTH
    AND HUMAN DEHAVIOR, VOL. 1 (SPRING 1960).

SAMORA, JULIAN. "THE SOCIAL SCIENTIST AS RESEARCHER AND
    TEACHER IN THE MEDICAL SCHOOL". JOURNAL OF HEALTH
    AND HUMAN BEHAVIOR, VOL. 1 (SPRING 1960) (MD).

SAMORA, JULIAN. LOS MOJADOS: THE WETBACK STORY. NOTRE
    DAME, INDIANA: UNIVERSITY OF NOTRE DAME PRESS, 1971.

SAMORA. LOS MOJADOS: WETBACK STORY (SI*).

SAMORA, JULIAN. MINORITY LEADERSHIP IN A BICULTURAL
    COMMUNITY. ANN ARBOR: UNIVERSITY MICROFILMS.
    DOCTORAL DISSERTATION..

SAMORA, JULIAN. NATIONAL STUDY OF THE SPANISH-SPEAKING
    PEOPLE. A REPORT PREPARED FOR THE UNITED STATES
    COMMISSION ON CIVIL RIGHTS.

SAMORA, JULIAN. SOCIOLOGICAL OVERVIEW OF THE MEXICAN-AMERICAN
    IN RURAL AREAS. REPORT OF THE SECOND ANNUAL
    CONFERENCE OF THE CALIFORNIA STATE DEPARTMENT
    OF EDUCATION, 1969.

SAMORA, JULIAN. THE ACCULTURATION OF THE SPANISH-SPEAKING
    PEOPLE OF FORT COLLINS, COLORADO IN SELECTED CULTURE
    AREAS. COLORADO A AND M COLLEGE, MASTER'S THESIS
    (1947).

SAMORA, JULIAN. THE EDUCATION OF THE SPANISH-SPEAKING IN
    THE SOUTHWEST: AN ANALYSIS OF THE 1960 CENSUS
    MATERIALS. INDIANA: DEPARTMENT OF SOCIOLOGY,
    UNIVERSITY OF NOTRE DAME, 1963.

SAMORA, JULIAN. 'THE EDUCATION OF THE SPANISH-SPEAKING
IN THE SOUTHWEST: AN ANALYSIS OF THE 1960 CENSUS
MATERIALS.' IN HENRY SIOUX JOHNSON AND WILLIAM J.
HERNANDEZ-M. EDUCATING THE MEXICAN-AMERICAN.

SAMORA, JULIAN. 'THE GENERAL STATUS OF THE SPANISH
SPEAKING PEOPLE IN THE SOUTHWEST.' IN SUMMARY OF
PROCEEDINGS OF THE SOUTHWEST CONFERENCE ON SOCIAL AND
EDUCATIONAL PROBLEMS OF RURAL AND URBAN MEXICAN-AMERICAN
YOUTH.

SAMORA, JULIAN. LA RAZA: FORGOTTEN AMERICANS. NOTRE
DAME, INDIANA: UNIVERSITY OF NOTRE DAME PRESS, 1966.

SAMORA, JULIAN. 'THE SPANISH SPEAKING PEOPLE IN THE UNITED
STATES.' IN ADMINISTRATOR'S IN-DEPTH SEMINARS IN
PROBLEMS OF DESEGREGATION AS THEY RELATE TO LARGE CITY
SCHOOLS: SUMMARIES OF SEMINAR DISCUSSIONS.

SAMORA, JULIAN; BARRETT, D. N. THE MOVEMENT OF SPANISH
YOUTH FROM RURAL TO URBAN SETTINGS. NATIONAL
COMMITTEE FOR CHILDREN AND YOUTH.

SAMORA, JULIAN; BEEGLE, J. A. "EDUCATIONAL AND SOCIAL
CHANGE IN LATIN AMERICA". RURAL SOCIOLOGY, VOL. 25
NO. 1 , P. MARCH 1960.

SAMORA, JULIAN; BORDA, ORLANDO FALS; DE PINEDA, VIRGINIA.
LAS CIENCIAS SOCIALES EN LA ENSENANZA Y EN LA
INVESTIGACION. MEDICINA Y DESARROLLO ECONOMIC-LA
CONTRIBUCION DE LA EDUCACION A LA TAREA DEL DESARROLLO
ECONOMIC-SOCIAL..

SAMORA, JULIAN; D'ANTONIO, W. V. "OCCUPATIONAL STRATIFICATION
IN FOUR SOUTHWESTERN COMMUNITIES: A STUDY OF ETHNIC
DIFFERENTIAL EMPLOYMENT IN HOSPITALS". SOCIAL
FORCES, VOL. 41 NO. 1 (OCTOBER 1962).

SAMORA, JULIAN; DEANE, W. N. "LANGUAGE USAGE AS A POSSIBLE
INDEX OF ACCULTURATION". SOCIOLOGY AND SOCIAL
RESEARCH, (MAY-JUNE 1956).

SAMORA, JULIAN; GALARZA, E.; GALLEGOS, H. MEXICAN
AMERICANS IN THE SOUTHWEST. MCNALLY AND LOFTIN, 1969.

SAMORA, JULIAN; LAMANNA, RICHARD A. MEXICAN AMERICANS IN
A MIDWEST METROPOLIS: A STUDY OF EAST CHICAGO. LOS
ANGELES: UNIVERSITY OF CALIFORNIA, LOS ANGELES,
(1967). UNIVERSITY OF CALIFORNIA, LOS ANGELES MEXICAN
AMERICAN STUDY PROJECT ADVANCE REPORT NUMBER 8..

SAMORA, JULIAN; LAMANNA, RICHARD A. RECENT TRENDS
IN EDUCATIONAL STATUS OF MEXICAN AMERICANS IN TEXAS.
IMPROVING EDUCATIONAL OPPORTUNITIES OF THE MEXICAN-AMERICAN.
PROCEEDINGS OF THE FIRST TEXAS CONFERENCE FOR
THE MEXICAN-AMERICAN. SAN ANTONIO.

SAMORA, JULIAN; LARSON, RICHARD F. "RURAL FAMILIES IN AN
    URBAN SETTING: A STUDY IN PERSISTENCE AND CHANGE".
    JOURNAL OF HUMAN RELATIONS, VOL. 9 NO. 4 (AUGUST
    1961), PP. 494-503.

SAMORA, JULIAN; PLAJA, ANTONIO ORDONEZ: COHEN, LUCY M.
    "COMMUNICATION BETWEEN PHYSICIANS AND PATIENTS
    IN OUTPATIENT CLINICS; SOCIAL AND CULTURAL FACTORS".
    THE MILBANK MEMORIAL FUND QUARTERLY, VOL. 46 NO. 2
    (APRIL 1968), PP. 161-213.

SAMORA, JULIAN; SAUNDERS, L.; LARSON, R. F. "KNOWLEDGE
    ABOUT SPECIFIC DISEASES IN FOUR SELECTED SAMPLES".
    JOURNAL OF HEALTH AND HUMAN BEHAVIOR, VOL. 30 (FALL
    1962), PP. 176-184.

SAMORA, JULIAN; SAUNDERS, LYLE AND LARSON, R. F. "MEDICAL
    VOCABULARY KNOWLEDGE AMONG HOSPITAL PATIENTS".
    JOURNAL OF HEALTH AND HUMAN BEHAVIOR, VOL. 2 (SUMMER
    1961) (MD).

SAMORA, JULIAN; SAUNDERS, LYLE; LARSON, R. F. MEDICAL
    VOCABULARY KNOWLEDGE AMONG HOSPITAL PATIENTS.
    JOURNAL OF HEALTH AND HUMAN BEHAVIOR, VOLUME 2, SUMMER
    1961, PAGES 83-92 REPRINTED IN SOCIAL INTERACTION AND
    PATIENT CARE, JAMES K. SKIPPER, JR. AND ROBERT
    C. LEONARD <EDS>, J. B. LIPPINCOTT COMPANY, 1965,
    PAGES 278-291. REPRINTED IN MEDICAL CARE, READINGS
    IN THE SOCIOLOGY OF MEDICAL INSTITUTIONS, W. RICHARD
    SCOTT AND EDMUND H. VOLKART <EDS>. JOHN WILEY
    AND SONS, INC., 1966, PAGES 292-302..

SAMORA, JULIAN; SAUNDERS, LYLE. 'A MEDICAL CARE PROGRAM
    IN A COLORADO COMMUNITY.'   IN BENJAMIN PAUL (ED),
    HEALTH, CULTURE AND COMMUNITY.

SAMORA, JULIAN; WATSON, J. B. "MINORITY LEADERSHIP IN A
    BICULTURAL COMMUNITY: AN ANALYSIS".   AMERICAN
    SOCIOLOGICAL REVIEW,   (AUGUST 1954).

SAMORA, JULIAN, BORDA, ORLANDO FALS AND DE PINEDA,
    VIRGINIA. LAS CIENCIAS SOCIALES EN LA ENSENANZA Y
    EN LA INVESTIGACION.   MEDICINA Y DESARROLLO ECONOMIC-LA
    CONTRIBUCION DE LA EDUCACION A LA TAREA DEL DESARROLLO
    ECONOMIC-SOCIAL (ED).

SAMORA, JULIAN, GALARZA, E. AND GALLEGOS, H. MEXICAN-AMERICANS
    IN THE SOUTHWEST.   MCNALLY AND LOFTIN, 1969.

SAMORA, JULIAN, PLAJA, ANTONIO ORDONEZ AND COHEN, LUCY M.
    "COMMUNICATION BETWEEN PHYSICIANS AND PATIENTS
    IN OUTPATIENT CLINICS, SOCIAL AND CULTURAL FACTORS".
    THE MILBANK MEMORIAL FUND QUARTERLY, VOL. 46 NO. 2
    (APRIL 1968), PP. 161-213.

SAMORA.   "KNOWLEDGE ABOUT SPECIFIC DISEASES   (MD*).

SAN ANTONIO PUBLIC HEALTH DEPARTMENT. VITAL STATISTICS
    IN SAN ANTONIO, 1960-1964.   SAN ANTONIO, TEXAS, 1964.

SAN ANTONIO SOCIAL WELFARE ASSOCIATION, EDUCATIONAL
    COMMITTEE ON RELIEF NEEDS. 8,000 FAMILIES GO HUNGRY
    TODAY IN SAN ANTONIO.   SAN ANTONIO, TEXAS,.

SAN ANTONIO URBAN RENEWAL AGENCY. A RELOCATION HOUSING
    MARKET STUDY OF THE SAN ANTONIO STANDARD METROPOLITAN
    STATISTICAL AREA.   BEXAR COUNTY, TEXAS, OCTOBER 1963.

SAN DIEGO STATE COLLEGE.   CHICANOS POR CAUSA, 69   (PL*).

SANDOVAL, T. J. A STUDY OF SOME ASPECTS OF THE SPANISH-SPEAKING
    POPULATION IN SELECTED COMMUNITIES IN WYOMING.
    UNIVERSITY OF WYOMING, MASTER'S THESIS (1946) (EC).

SANTA BARBARA OFFICE OF THE SUPERINTENDENT OF SCHOOLS,
    COMMITTEE RESEARCH TEAMS. THE EMERGING MINORITIES
    IN AMERICA.   PREPARED BY COMMITTEE RESEARCH TEAMS,
    SANTA BARBARA, 1971.

SAPOSS, DAVID J. REPORT ON RAPID SURVEY OF RESIDENT
    LATIN-AMERICAN PROBLEMS AND RECOMMENDED PROGRAM.
    WASHINGTON, D. C.: OFFICE OF THE COORDINATOR OF
    INTER-AMERICAN AFFAIRS, APRIL 3, 1942.

SARGIS, ALBERT L. NETWORKS OF DISCORD: A STUDY OF
    THE COMMUNICATIONS SYSTEM BETWEEN SPANISH SPEAKING
    ORGANIZATIONS AND THEIR COMMUNITY.   SAN FRANCISCO
    STATE COLLEGE, MASTER'S THESIS (1966).

SATTERFIELD, DONNA MAE O. ACCULTURATION AND MARRIAGE ROLE
    PATTERNS: A COMPARATIVE STUDY OF MEXICAN-AMERICAN
    WOMEN.   UNIVERSITY OF ARIZONA, PHD. DISSERTATION
    (1966) (AN).

SAUERWEIN.   SERUM PROTEIN LIPOPROTEIN COMPONENTS   (MD*).

SAUNDERS.   MEDICAL CARE PROGRAM COLORADO   (ED*).

SAUNDERS.   SOCIOLOGICAL STUDY WETBACKS LOWER   (ED*).

SAUNDERS.   SPANISH-SPEAKING AMERICANS MEXICAN-AMERICANS
    (B*).

SAUNDERS.   SPANISH-SPEAKING POPULATION TEXAS   (ED*).

SAUNDERS.   WETBACK LOWER RIO GRANDE VALLEY   (ED*).

SAUNDERS.   READINGS UNDERSTANDING SOUTHWESTERN   (ED*).

SAUTER.   ARBOL VERDE: CULTURAL CONFLICT   (AN*).

SAXTON, LLOYD; KAUFMAN, WALTER. THE AMERICAN SCENE: SOCIAL
    PROBLEMS OF THE 70'S. BELMONT, CALIFORNIA: WADSWORTH
    PUBLISHING COMPANY, INC., 1971.

SCHAER. "A NEW LANGUAGE JOSE" (ED*).

SCHNEIDER, LOUIS; LYSGAARD, SVERE. "THE DEFERRED GRATIFICATION
    PATTERN: A PRELIMINARY STUDY". AMERICAN SOCIOLOGICAL
    REVIEW, VOL. 22 (FEBRUARY 1957), PP. 67-73.

SCHORR. "RE-CONVERTING MEXICAN AMERICANS" (ED*).

SCHRIEKE, B. 'MEXICANS AND INDIANS.' IN ALIEN AMERICANS.

SCHRIEKE, BERTHRAM JOHANNES OTTO. ALIEN AMERICANS: A STUDY
    OF RACE RELATIONS. NEW YORK: VIKING PRESS, 1936.

SCHROFF, RUTH. A STUDY OF SOCIAL DISTANCE BETWEEN MEXICAN
    PARENTS AND AMERICAN TEACHERS IN SAN BERNARDINO,
    CALIFORNIA. UNIVERSITY OF SOUTHERN CALIFORNIA,
    MASTER'S THESIS (1936) (ED).

SCHULZE, R. O.; BLOOMBERG, L. U. S. "THE DETERMINATION OF
    LOCAL POWER ELITES". AMERICAN JOURNAL OF SOCIOLOGY,
    VOL. 62 (NOVEMBER 1957), PP. 290-296.

SCHWEBEL. "LEARNING SOCIALLY DEPRIVED" (ED*).

SCHWENDINGER, JULIA; SCHWENDINGER, HERMAN. DELINQUENT
    STEREOTYPES OF PROBABLE VICTIMS. UNPUBLISHED PAPER,
    SCHOOL OF CRIMINOLOGY, UNIVERSITY OF CALIFORNIA, BERKELEY.

SCOTFORD, JOHN RYLAND. WITHIN THESE BORDERS; SPANISH
    SPEAKING PEOPLES IN THE U.S.A.. NEW YORK: FRIENDSHIP
    PRESS, 1953.

SCOTT, CARL. ETHNIC MINORITIES IN SOCIAL WORK EDUCATION.
    NEW YORK: COUNCIL ON SOCIAL WORK EDUCATION, 1971 (ED).

SCRUGGS. "TEXAS, GOOD NEIGHBOR?" (HT*).

SECKEL, JOACHIM P. EMPLOYMENT AND EMPLOYABILITY AMONG
    CALIFORNIA YOUTH AUTHORITY WARDS: A SURVEY.
    DEPARTMENT OF THE YOUTH AUTHORITY, DIVISION OF
    RESEARCH, SACRAMENTO, CALIFORNIA, (AUGUST 2 1, 1962).
    RESEARCH REPORT NUMBER 30. (EC).

SEGAL, AARON. "MEXICO AND THE MEXICAN AMERICAN". CON
    SAFOS, VOL. 2 NO. 5 (1970), PP. 16-20.

SEGAL, BERNARD E. (ED.). RACIAL AND ETHNIC RELATIONS:
    SELECTED READINGS. NEW YORK, NEW YORK: THOMAS Y.
    CROWELL COMPANY, 1966.

SENTER, DONOVAN. "ACCULTURATION AMONG NEW MEXICAN
    VILLAGERS IN COMPARISON TO ADJUSTMENT PATTERNS
    OF OTHER SPANISH SPEAKING AMERICANS". RURAL
    SOCIOLOGY, VOL. 10 (MARCH 1945), PP. 31-47 (HN).

SERRANO, RODOLFO G. BARRIO LANGUAGE--AN ANALYSIS OF POCHO
    AND PACHUCO IN A RURAL SOUTHERN CALIFORNIA COMMUNITY.
    ??NO INFORMATION??, 1973 (AN).

SERRANO, RODOLFO G. SOCIOCULTURAL INFLUENCES IN THE
    DEVELOPMENT OF MEXICAN AMERICAN LANGUAGE STYLES.
    ??NO INFORMATION??, PHD. DISSERTATION (1972) (AN).

SEXTON, P. C. SPANISH HARLEM: ANATOMY OF POVERTY. NEW
    YORK: HARPER-ROW, 1965.

SEXTON, PATRICIA CAYO. "SOCIAL CLASS AND PUPIL TURNOVER
    RATES". JOURNAL OF SOCIOLOGY, VOL. 33 (NOVEMBER
    1959), PP. 131-134.

SHAFFER, RICHARD A. "THE ANGRY CHICANOS: DEEPENING
    FRUSTRATION OF MEXICAN-AMERICANS STIRS FEARS OF
    VIOLENCE". WALL STREET JOURNAL, VOL. 175 (JUNE
    11, 1970).

SHAPIRO, HAROLD A. "HEALTH CONDITIONS IN SAN ANTONIO,
    TEXAS, 1900-1947". SOUTHWESTERN SOCIAL SCIENCE
    QUARTERLY, (DECEMBER 1953), PP. 60-76 (MD).

SHAPIRO, HAROLD A. "THE PECAN SHELLERS OF SAN ANTONIO,
    TEXAS". SOUTHWESTERN SOCIAL SCIENCE QUARTERLY, VOL.
    32 (MARCH 1952), PP. 229-243.

SHELDON, PAUL M. "MEXICAN AMERICANS IN URBAN PUBLIC
    SCHOOLS: AN EXPLORATION OF THE DROP-OUT PROBLEM".
    CALIFORNIA JOURNAL OF EDUCATIONAL RESEARCH, (JANUARY
    1961), PP. 21-26 (ED).

SHELDON, PAUL M. COMMUNITY PARTICIPATION AND THE EMERGING
    MIDDLE CLASS. N JULIAN SAMORA (ED) LA RAZA NOTRE
    DAME: UNIVERSITY OF NOTRE DAME PRESS, 1969.

SHELDON, PAUL M. MEXICAN AMERICANS IN URBAN PUBLIC HIGH
    SCHOOLS: AN EXPLORATION OF THE DROP-OUT PROBLEM.
    OCCIDENTAL COLLEGE, 1959 (ED).

SHERIF, CAROLYN W. "SELF RADIUS AND GOALS OF YOUTH
    IN DIFFERENT URBAN AREAS". SOUTHWESTERN SOCIAL
    SCIENCE QUARTERLY, VOL. 42 (DECEMBER 1961), PP. 259-267.

SHERIF, MUZAFER AND SHERIF, CAROLYN W. REFERENCE GROUPS--
    EXPLORATION INTO CONFORMITY AND DEVIATION OF ADOLESCENTS.
    NEW YORK: HARPER AND ROW, 1964.

SHEVKY, ESHREF.   YOUR NEIGHBORHOOD: A SOCIAL PROFILE OF
    LOS ANGELES.   HAYNES FOUNDATION, PAMPHLET SERIES,
    NUMBER 14, LOS ANGELES.

SHEVKY, ESHREF.   THE SOCIAL AREAS OF LOS ANGELES, ANALYSIS
    AND TYPOLOGY.   UNIVERSITY OF CALIFORNIA PRESS, 1949.

SHIBUTANI, TAMOTSU AND KWAN, KIAN M.   ETHNIC STRATIFICATION:
    A COMPARATIVE APPROACH.   NEW YORK: MACMILLAN COMPANY,
    1965 (AN).

SHONTZ, ORFA.   "THE LAND OF POCO TIEMPO: A STUDY OF MEXICAN
    FAMILY RELATIONSHIPS IN A CHANGING ENVIRONMENT".
    THE FAMILY, VOL. 8 (MAY 1927), PP. 74-79.

SHRYOCK, HENRY S.   POPULATION MOBILITY WITH IN THE U.S..
    CHICAGO: UNIVERSITY OF CHICAGO, 1964.

SHYBUT.   DELAYED GRATIFICATION: STUDYITS (PY*).

SICKELS, ALICE L.AND SICKELS, HENRY L.   THE MEXICAN
    NATIONALITY COMMUNITY IN ST PAUL IN FEBRUARY, 1935.
    ST. PAUL, MINNESOTA: INTERNATIONAL INSTITUTE, 1935.

SILVERTON, DORIS.   "MEXICAN MAIC".   MC CALLS, VOL. 98
    (OCTOBER 1970), PP. 82-83.

SIMMONS, OZZIE G.
    SIMMONS, OZZIE G. ; HANSON, ROBERT C.; WANDERER, JULES
    J.   "THE MUTUAL IMAGES AND EXPECTATIONS OF ANGLO-AMERICANS
    AND MEXICAN-AMERICNSANS".   DAEDALUS, VOL. 90 (SPRING
    1961), PP. 286-299 (PY).

SIMMONS, OZZIE G.   ANGLO-AMERICANS AND MEXICAN-AMERICANS
    IN SOUTH TEXAS: A STUDY IN DOMINANT-SUBORDINATE GROUP
    RELATIONS.   HARVARD UNIVERSITY, PHD. DISSERTATION
    (1952) (AN).

SIMMONS, OZZIE G.   'THE MUTUAL IMAGES AND EXPECTATIONS OF
    ANGLO-AMERICANS AND MEXICAN-AMERICANS.'   IN MILTON
    L. BARRON (ED), MINORITIES IN A CHANGING WORLD.

SIMONIN, LOUIS L.   THE MUTUAL IMAGES AND EXPECTATIONS OF
    ANGLO-AMERICANS AND MEXICAN-AMERICANS.   EDITED BY
    NATHANIEL N. WAGNER AND MARSHA J. HAUG., SAINT LOUIS,
    MISSOURI: THE C. V. MOSBY COMPANY (PY).

SIMPICH.   "DOWN THE RIO GRANDE" (GE*).

SIMPICH, FREDRICK.   URBANIZATION OF THE MIGRANT: PROCESSES
    AND OUTCOMES: A RESEARCH PROPOSAL.   BOULDER,
    COLORADO: INSTITUTE OF BEHAVIORAL SCIENCE, BUREAU OF
    SOCIOLOGICAL RESEARCH, JANUARY 14, 1964.

SIMPICH, FREDRICK. THE MUTUAL IMMAGES AND EXPECTATIONS
   OF ANGLO—AMERICANS AND MEXICAN AMERIANS. EDITED WITH
   AN INTRODUCTION BY EDWARD SIMMEN. NEW YORK AND
   SCARBOROUGH, ONTARIO: A MENTOR BOOK FROM NEW AMERICAN
   LIBRARY, 1972 (PY).

SIMPSON. "ALONG OUR SIDE MEXICAN BORDER" (GE*).

SIMPSON, GEORGE EATON; YINGER, J. MILTON. MEXICAN AMERICAN
   CHILDREN IN THE PUBLIC SCHOOLS. CHAPEL HILL:
   UNIVERSITY OF NORTH CAROLINA PRESS, 1937 (ED).

SIMPSON, GEORGE EATON; GINGER, J. MILTON. RACIAL AND
   CULTURAL MINORITIES; AN ANALYSIS OF PREJUDICE
   AND DISCRIMINATION. IN RACIAL AND CULTURAL MINORITIES,
   NEW YORK: HARPER AND BROTHERS.

SIMS, V. M. THE MEASUREMENT OF SOCIO—ECONOMIC STATUS.
   BLOOMINGTON, ILLINOIS: PUBLIC SCHOOL PUBLISHING
   COMPANY, 1928 (EC).

SINCOFF. STUDY RACIAL PREJUDICES STUDENTS (ED*).

SISTER MARY IMMACULATE. MEXICAN CULTURAL PATTERNS.
   SPONSORED BY THE WELFARE COUNCIL OF METROPOLITAN
   CHICAGO, OCTOBER 1957 (AN).

SIXTEENTH CENSUS OF THE UNITED STATES. POPULATION
   OF SPANISH MOTHER TONGUE: 1940. U.S. BUREAU OF
   THE CENSUS, (JUNE 1942).

SMITH, CLARA GERTRUDE. THE DEVELOPMENT OF THE MEXICAN
   PEOPLE IN THE COMMUNITY OF WATTS, CALIFORNIA.
   UNIVERSITY OF SOUTHERN CALIFORNIA, MASTER'S THESIS
   (1936) (HC).

SMITH, CLARA GERTRUDE. THE EFFECT OF THE CULTURE OF THE
   UNITED STATES UPON SOME OF THE MEXICAN IMMIGRANTS IN
   THE WATTS DISTRICT. RESEARCH REPORT, JANUARY 1931
   (HC).

SMITH, T. LYNN. THE SOCIOLOGY OF RURAL LIFE. NEW YORK:
   HARPER AND BROTHERS, 1947.

SNYDER. SOCIAL CULTURAL ASPECTS SPANISH (AN*).

SOCIETY FOR CURRICULUM STUDY. SOCIETY, PERSONALITY, AND
   DEVIANT BEHAVIOR: A STUDY OF A TRI—ETHNIC COMMUNITY.
   NEW YORK: HOLT, RINEHART AND WINSTON, 1968 (PY).

SOFFER, VIRGINIA M. SOCIO—CULTURAL CHANGES IN THE LIVES
   OF FIVE MEXICAN—AMERICAN COLLEGE GRADUATES.
   UNIVERSITY OF SOUTHERN CALIFORNIA, MASTER'S THESIS
   (1958) (PY AN).

SOLACHE, SAUL. THE IMPACT OF URBAN DEVELOPMENT IN
    THE ANTELOPE VALLEY ON ITS MEXICAN AMERICAN RESIDENTS.
    UNIVERSITY OF CALIFORNIA, LOS ANGELES, MASTER'S THESIS
    (1971) (EC).

SOLGUDO NAVARRO.   ADJUSTMENT PROBLEMS DELINQUENT   (PY*).

SOMMERS.   IMPACT DUAL CULTURAL MEMBERSHIP   (PY*).

SORENSON, ROY. RECREATION FOR EVERYBODY: A COMMUNITY PLAN
    FOR RECREATION AND YOUTH SERVICE FOR LOS ANGELES.
    REPORT OF A SURVEY CONDUCTED BY THE COMMUNITY SERVEY
    ASSOCIATED UNDER THE AUSPICES OF COMMUNITY CHEST AND
    COUNCILS, INC., FOR THE WELFARE COUNCIL OF METROPOLITAN
    LOS ANGELES, JUNE 1, 1946.

SOUTHERN METHODIST UNIVERSITY. INSTUTUTE OF PUBLIC AFFAIRS.
    MEXICO AND THE UNITED STATES: PROCEEDINGS OF
    THE FIFTH ANNUAL CONFERENCE, INSTITUTE OF PUBLIC
    AFFAIRS, AUSPICES CARNEGIE ENDOWMENT FOR INTERNATIONAL
    PEACE, DALLAS, HUNTSVILLE, WAXAHACHIE, WACO, DENTON,
    FORT WORTH.   SOUTHERN METHODIST UNIVERSITY, 1938 (EC).

SOUTHWEST COUNCIL OF LA RAZA.   FIRST ANNUAL REPORT:
    FEBRUARY (ED*).

SOUTHWEST COUNCIL OF FOREIGN LANGUAGE TEACHERS CONFERENCE,1965.
    OUR BILINGUALS: SOCIAL AND PSYCHOLOGICAL BARRIERS,
    LINGUISTIC AND PEDAGOICAL BARRIERS. REPORTS OF THE
    SECOND ANNUAL CONFERENCE.   EL PASO, 1965 (ED PL).

SOUTHWEST COUNCIL ON THE EDUCATION OF SPANISH SPEAKING
    PEOPLE.   PROCEEDINGS (ED*).

SOUTHWEST EDUCATIONAL DEVELOPMENT LABORATORY.   PROCEEDINGS:
    NATIONAL CONFERENCE (ED*).

SOUTHWEST TEXAS STATE TEACHERS COLLEGE.   BUILDING BETTER
    SCHOOL-COMMUNITY (ED*).

SOUTHWEST TEXAS STATE TEACHERS COLLEGE.   FINAL REPORT.
    PROGRAM SOUTHWEST: (ED*).

SOUTHWESTERN COOPERATIVE ECUCATIONAL LABORATORY.   CHICANO
    IS COMING OUT TORTILLA (LI*).

SOWELL, EMMIE I. A STUDY OF BOYS' CLUBS IN TEXAS WITH
    SPECIAL REFERENCE TO SAN ANTONIO.   UNIVERSITY
    OF TEXAS, MASTER'S THESIS (1940) (ED).

SPARKS, DADE. A SURVEY OF ORGANIZED LABOR IN AUSTIN.
    UNIVERSITY OF TEXAS AT AUSTIN, MASTER'S THESIS (1937).

SPAULDING.   "THE MEXICAN STRIKE AT MONTE,   (EC*).

SPENCE, ALLYN GAIVAIN. VARIABLES CONTRIBUTING TO THE
    MAINTENANCE OF THE MEXICAN AMERICAN SOCIAL STRUCTURE
    IN TUCSON. UNIVERSITY OF ARIZONA, MASTER'S THESIS
    (1968) (EC).

SPRAGGIA. SELF-GROUP DEVALUATION PREJUDICE (PY*).

STANLEY. SELECTICN CONDITION CLOTHINGLOW-INCOME (ED*).

STANLEY. TOUR SOUTH CHICAGOS MEXICANCOLONY (ED*).

STEGLICH, W. G. SURVEY OF NEEDS AND RESOURCES AMONG AGED
    MEXICAN AMERICANS. LUBBOCK, TEXAS: TEXAS TECHNOLOGICAL
    COLLEGE, 1968 (EC ED).

STEGNER, JOHN F. SOCIO-ECONOMIC BACGROUND OF ALCOHOLICS.
    FORT COLLINS: COLORADO STATE UNIVERSITY, 1970 (EC).

STEGNER. ONE NATION (LI*).

STEGNER. CNE NATION (LI*).

STEIN. "TECHNIQUES PARENT DISCUSSIONS (PY*).

STEIN, Z.; SUSSER, M. "THE SOCIAL DISTRIBUTION OF MENTAL
    RETARDATION". AMERICAN JOURNAL OF MENTAL DEFICIENCY,
    VOL. 67 (1963), PP. 811-821 (PY).

STEINER. CHICANO POWER: MILITANCE AMONG (PL*).

STEINER. CRACKS MELTING POT: RACISM CISCRIMINATION (PL*).

STEINER. "CHICANO POWER" (PL*).

STEINFIELD, MELVIN. MINORITIES, THEIR HISTORY, THEIR
    CONCERN, THEIR IMPACT. BEVERLY HILLS, CALIFORNIA:
    GLENCOE PRESS, 1970 (HUS).

STEINFIELD, MELVIN. POPULATION CHARACTERISTICS OF DALLAS
    BY CENSUS TRACTS. SOUTHERN METHODIST UNIVERSITY,
    MASTER'S THESIS (1938) (HUS).

STEINNAGLE, BILLYA. ATTITUDES TOWARDS THE STATUS AND ROLE
    OF THE OLDER PERSON IN THE MEXICANAMERICAN FAMILY.
    UNIVERSITY OF ARIZONA, MASTER'S THESIS (1967).

STENDLER. INTERGROUP EDUCATION KINDERGARTEN (ED*).

STEVENSON, C. R. AND PADILLA, EZEQUIEL. THE GOOD NEIGHBOR
    POLICY AND MEXICANS IN TEXAS. MEXICO: SECRETARIA
    DE RELACICNES EXTERIORES. BUREAU OF INTERNATIONAL NEWS
    SERVICE, (1943). NATIONAL AND INTERNATIONAL PROBLEMS
    SERIES, NUMBER 17 (HT).

STEWART, ELBERT W. THE TROUBLED LAND: SOCIAL PROBLEMS IN
    MODERN AMERICA. NEW YORK: MCGRAW-HILL BOOK COMPANY,
    1972.

STINE, J. H. "TEXAS PLAYGROUNDS INFLUENCE MEXICANS".
     PLAYGROUND, VOL. 10 (JUNE 1939), PP. 259-62.

STODDARD, CHARLES WARREN. COMPARATIVE STRUCTURES AND
     ATTITUDES ALONG THE U. S. —MEXICAN BORDER. PAPER
     PRESENTED AT THE CONFERENCE ON URBANIZATION OF THE
     UNITED STATES—MEXICAN BORDER, JUNE 15, 1968, EL PASO.
     (IN ERIC <ED 024-481) (HSW).

STODDARD, ELLWYN R. MEXICAN AMERICANS.   NEW YORK: RANDOM
     HOUSE, INC., 1973 (PY AN EC).

STODDARD, THEODORE LOTHROP. THE RISING TIDE OF COLOR
     AGAINST WHITE WORLD SUPREMACY.   NEW YORK: C.
     SCRIBNER'S SONS, 1923 (PL).

STOKER.   HA COMPARISON SYMPTOMATOLOGY (MD*).

STOLZ. "ART ABILITY MEXICAN CHILDREN" (AR*).

STONE, ROBERT. FAMILY LIFE STYLES BELOW THE POVERTY LINE.
     LEXINGTON, MASSACHUSETTS: HEATH LEXINGTON BOOKS, 1972
     (EC).

STOWELL, J. S. "A REMARKABLE CHINESE COLONY IN MEXICO".
     MISSIONARY REVIEW OF THE WORLD,   (FEBRUARY 1924).

STOWELL.   METHODISMS NEW FRONTIER (RE*).

STOWELL.   NEAR SIDE MEXICAN QUESTION (SI*).

STOWELL, J. S. A STUDY OF MEXICANS AND SPANISH AMERICANS
     IN THE UNITED STATES.   NEW YORK HOME MISSIONS
     COUNCIL, 1920.

STREGO, V. L. "PROGRESS OF ADJUSTMENT IN MEXICAN AND
     UNITED STATES LIFE".   NATIONAL CONFERENCE OF SOCIAL
     WORK, VOL. 20 , PP. 481-86.

SULLENGER, T. EARL. "THE MEXICAN POPULATION OF OMAHA".
     JOURNAL OF APPLIED SOCIOLOGY, VOL. 8 NO. 5 (MAY-JUNE
     1924), PP. 288-93.

SUTTLES, G. D. "ANATOMY OF A CHICAGO SLUM; STUDY OF
     A MULTI-ETHNIC COMMUNITY INCLUDING ITALIANS, MEXICANS,
     NEGROES, AND PUERTO RICANS".   TRANS-ACTION, VOL. 6
     (FEBRUARY 1969), PP. 16-19.

SUTTLES, G. D. THE SOCIAL ORDER OF THE SLUM: ETHNICITY
     AND TERRITORYY IN THE INNER CITY.   CHICAGO: UNIVERSITY
     OF CHICAGO PRESS, 1968.

SVOBODA.   "NEGATIVE ASPECTS EDUCATION PROGRAMS (ED*).

SWOPE, D. "LET'S MAKE DEMOCRACY WORK FOR THE LATIN
     AMERICAN CHILD".   THE TEXAS OUTLOOK, VOL. 31 (1947),
     PP. 21-22 (ED).

TACUBER.   "MIGRATION TRANSFORMATION: SPANISH (SI*).

TALBERT, ROBERT HARRIS.   SPANISH-NAME PEOPLE IN THE
    SOUTHWEST AND WEST; SOCIO-ECONOMIC CHARACTERISTICS
    OF WHITE PERSONS OF SPANISH SURNAME IN TEXAS, ARIZONA,
    CALIFORNIA, COLORADO AND NEW MEXICO.   FORT WORTH,
    TEXAS: LEO POTISHMAN FOUNDATION, TEXAS CHRISTIAN
    UNIVERSITY, 1955.

TAMBLYN.   RESEARCH ABSTRACTS RURAL EDUCATION (ED*).

TANNER, MYRTLE
    TANNER, MYRTLE L. HANDBOOK: GOOD NEIGHBOR COMMISSION
    OF TEXAS.   AUSTIN, TEXAS: GOOD NEIGHBOR COMMISSION,
    1954 (HT).

TAYLOR, JUANITA FAYE. A COMPARISON OF FIRST AND SECOND
    GENERATION MEXICAN PARENTS.   UNIVERSITY OF SOUTHERN
    CALIFORNIA, MASTER'S THESIS (1943) (PY SI).

TEEL.   "PREVENTING PREJUDICE AGAINST (ED*).

TENHOUTEN.   "EDUCATIONAL PLANS MEXICAN-AMERICAN   (ED*).

TETREAU, E. D. "THE IMPACT OF WAR ON SOME COMMUNITIES IN
    THE SOUTWEST".   AMERICAN SOCIOLOGICAL REVIEW, VOL.
    8 (JUNE   1943), PP. 249-255 (HUS).

TEXAS AGRICULTURAL EXPERIMENT STATION.   POVERTY AMONG
    SPANISH-AMERICANS (EC*).

TEXAS GOOD NEIGHBOR COMMISSION, AUSTIN. TEXAS: FRIEND
    AND NEIGHBOR.   AUSTIN, TEX: VON BOECKMAN-JONES, 1961
    (SI).

TEXAS: GOOD NEIGHBOR COMMISSION. SPECIAL REPORT:
    INTER-AGENCY TASK FORCE ON MIGRANT LABOR.   ??NO
    INFORMATION??, 1970 (SI).

THARP, ROLAND G. ET. AL.,
    THAYER, WILLIAM M. "JOURNAL OF MARRAGE AND THE
    FAMILY".   JOURNAL OF MARRIAGE AND THE FAMILY, VOL.
    30 NO. 3 (AUGUST   1968), PP. 404-412 (AN).

THE HELLER COMMITTEE FOR RESEARCH IN SOCIAL ECONOMICS OF
    THE UNIVERSITY OF CALIFORNIA AND CONSTANTINE PANUNZIO.
    HOW MEXICANS EARN AND LIVE. A STUDY OF THE INCOMES
    AND EXPENDITURES OF ONE HUNDRED MEXICAN FAMILIES IN
    SAN DIEGO, CALIFORNIA.   BERKELEY, CALIFORNIA:
    UNIVERSITY OF CALIFORNIA PRESS, (1933). PUBLICATIONS
    IN ECONOMICS. VOL. 13, NO. 1 (EC).

THE MEXICAN- AMERICAN AMITY CONFERENCE. "MEXICAN-AMERICAN
    AMITY CONFERENCE, THE".   SOUTHWESTERN POLITICAL AND
    SOCIAL SCIENCE QUARTERLY,   (SEPTEMBER 1923) (PL).

THE NATIONAL COUNCIL OF THE PROTESTANT EPISCOPAL CHURCH.
    CONFERENCE ON LATIN-AMERICAN RELATIONS IN THE
    SOUTHWESTERN UNITED STAT)>.   NEW YORK: DIVISION OF
    RACIAL MINORITIES, 1959.

THE SACRAMENTO STATE HORNET. A CHICANO SPEAKS OUT.   A
    SERIES OF 12 ARTICLES REPRINTED FROM THE SACRAMENTO
    STATE HORNET (PL).

THE UNIVERSITY OF ARIZONA.   ARIZONA: ITS PEOPLE RESOURCES
    (AN*).

THOMAS, JOHN L. "THE FACTOR OF RELIGION IN THE SELECTION
    OF MARRAGE MATES".   AMERICAN SOCIOLOGICAL REVIEW,
    VOL. 16 (AUGUST 1951), PP. 487-491 (RE).

THCMAS, PIRI. 'ALIEN TURF.'   IN LILLIAN FADERMAN
    AND BARBARA BRADSHAW (LMA).

THCMPSON, C. A. PROCEEDINGS OF THE NATIONAL CONFERENCE
    OF SOCIAL WORK.   THE UNIVERSITY OF CHICAGO PRESS,
    1929 (EC).

THCMPSON.   MEXICAN MIND: STUDY NATIONAL   (PY*).

THOMPSON.   MEXICAN MIND: STUDY NATIONAL   (PY*).

THCMPSON, WARREN S. AND P. K. WHELPTON. POPULATION TRENDS
    IN THE UNITED STATES.   NEW YORK: MCGRAW-HILL BOOK
    COMPANY, 1933.

THOMSON, CHARLES A. "COOPERATION IN WORK AMONG SPANISH-AMERICANS".
    MISSIONARY REVIEW, VOL. 41 , PP. 973-75.

THOMSON, CHARLES A. "JOURNAL OF APPLIED SOCIOLOGY".
    JOURNAL OF APPLIED SOCIOLOGY, VOL. 2 (JULY 1927),
    PP. 574-578 (SI).

THOMSON, CHARLES A. "LINKING THE TWO AMERICAS".
    MISSIONARY REVIEW, VOL. 51 , PP. 619-23.

THOMSON, CHARLES A. "MEXICANS -- AN INTERPRETATION".
    NATIONAL CONFERENCE OF SOCIAL WORK,   (1928), PP. 499-503.

THOMSON, CHARLES A. "MISSIONARY REVIEW OF THE WORLD".
    MISSIONARY REVIEW OF THE WORLD, VOL. 48 (DECEMBER
    1925), PP. 937-943 (EC).

THOMSON, CHARLES A. "RESTRICTION OF MEXICAN IMMIGRATION".
    JOURNAL OF APPLIED SOCIOLOGY, VOL. 11 , PP. 574-78
    (SI).

THOMSON, CHARLES A. "THE MAN FROM NEXT DOOR". CENTURY,
VOL. 3 , PP. 275-82 (SI).

THOMSON, CHARLES A. PROCEEDINGS OF THE NATIONAL CONFERENCE
OF SOCIAL WORK. UNIVERSITY OF CHICAGO PRESS, 1929.

THORNE, KATHLEEN, (ET AL). MINORITIES IN AMERICA. SAN
JOSE: SAN JOSE STATE COLLEGE LIBRARY, 1969.

THORP, R. G., AND OTHERS. "JOURNAL OF MARRIAGE AND THE
FAMILY". JOURNAL OF MARRIAGE AND THE FAMILY, VOL.
30 (AUGUST 1968), PP. 404-412 (AN).

THURSTON, RICHARD G. URBANIZATION AND SOCIOLOGICAL CHANGE
IN A MEXICAN-AMERICAN ENCLAVE. LOS ANGELES:
UNIVERSITY OF CALIFORNIA, PHD. DISSERTATION (1957)
(AN).

THURSTON, RICHARD G. URBANIZATION AND SOCIO-CULTURAL
CHANGE IN A MEXICAN-AMERICAN ENCLAVE. UNIVERSITY
OF CALIFORNIA, LOS ANGELES, PHD. DISSERTATION (1962)
(AN).

THURSTON, RICHARD G. URBANIZATION AND SOCIO-CULTURAL
CHANGE IN A MEXICAN-AMERICAN ENCLAVE. LOS ANGELES:
UNIVERSITY OF CALIFORNIA, PHC. DISSERTATION (1962)
(AN).

TINSLEY. BUILDING BETTER SCHOOL COMMUNITY (ED*).

TIPTON, ELIS M. "WHAT WE WANT IS ACTION: RELATIONS OF
AMERICANS AND MEXICANS IN SAN DIMAS, CALIFORNIA".
COMMON GROUND, VOL. 7 NO. 1 (AUTUMN 1946), PP. 74-81
(ED).

TIPTON. "CALIFORNIA JOURNAL ELEMENTARY (ED*).

TIRADO. MEXICAN AMERICAN COMMUNITY POLITICAL (PL*).

TOBIAS. POLITICS MINORITIES (PL*).

TOBIAS. ETHNIC MINORITIES POLITICS (PL*).

TOBIN, RICHARD L. "THE REVOLUTION IS NOT COMING".
SATURDAY REVIEW, VOL. 51 (AUGUST 17, 1968),
PP. 12-15, 61-63 (PL).

TOMPKINS. JUVENILE GANGS STREET GROUPS (B*).

TOMPKINS. POVERTY UNITED STATES DURINGSIXTIES (B*).

TOMPKINS. WHITE COLLAR CRIME (B*).

TOOGOOD, JAMES L. ADULT POPULATION DISTRIBUTION WITH
     REGARD TO SOCIAL, ECONOMIC, AND ETHNIC CHARACTERISTICS.
     SACRAMENTO, CALIFORNIA: CALIFORNIA ADULT EDUCATION
     BUREAU, 1969.

TOPPERWEIN.   JOSE MEXICAN JUMPING BEAN (EL   (LI*).

TORGERSON.   "BROWN POWER UNITY SEEN BEHIND   (ED*).

TOWE.   METHODISM LATIN-AMERICANS UNITED   (RE*).

TRAGER.   THEY LEARN WHAT THEY LIVE   (ED*).

TRASIN, WALTER. "YOU DO NOT UNDERSTAND SENOR".   CLEARING
     HOUSE, VOL. 36 (JANUARY 1962), PP. 273-275.

TREJO, ALEX T. MEXICAN AMERICAN SURVEY PROJECT. SUMMER
     YOUTH PROGRAM, VENICE, CALIFORNIA, 1967.   LOS
     ANGELES: WELFARE PLANNING COUNCIL, LOS ANGELES REGION,
     RESEARCH DEPARTMENT, 1968 (ED).

TREVINO.   MY HEART LIES SOUTH: STORY MY   (LI*).

TREVINO.   WHERE HEART IS   (LI*).

TRILLINGHAM.   "A GOOD-NEIGHBOUR POLICY LOSANGELES   (ED*).

TRIMBLE, GLEN W. DIRECTOR, HOME MISSIONS RESEARCH BUREAU
     OF RESEARCH AND SURVEY. RESPONSES TO THE BRIEF SURVEY
     OF CHURCH RELATED SPANISH-AMERICAN WORK IN THE
     CONTINENTAL UNITED STATES.   HOME MISSIONS RESEARCH
     BUREAU OF RESEARCH AND SURVEY, NATIONAL COUNCIL OF
     CHURCHES, JANUARY 10, 1960 (EC).

TROLLOPE, FRANCES. DOMESTIC MANNERS OF THE AMERICANS.
     NEW YORK: ALFRED A. KNOPF, 1949.

TUCK RUTH D. NOT WITH THE FIST: MEXICAN-AMERICANS IN A
     SOUTHWEST CITY.   NEW YORK: HARCOURT, BRACE AND
     COMPANY, 1956 (HC AN).

TUCK, RUTH D. "BEHIND THE ZOOT-SUIT RIOTS".   SURVEY
     GRAPHIC, VOL. 32 (AUGUST 1943), P. 313 (HC AN).

TUCK, RUTH D. "MEXICAN AMERICANS: A CONTRIBUTORY CULTURE".
     SACRAMENTO: CALIFORNIA ELEMENTARY SCHOOL PRINCIPALS'
     ASSOCIATION YEARBOOK, VOL. 17 (1945) (HC AN).

TUCK, RUTH D. "SPRINKLING THE GRASS ROOTS".   COMMON
     GROUND, VOL. 17 NO. 3 (SPRING 1947), PP. 80-83 (HC
     AN).

TURNER.   LOS EFECTOS DE PARTICIPACION   (HM*).

TURNER, RALPH H. AND SURACE, SAMUEL J. ZOOT-SUITERS AND
    MEXICANS: SYMBOLS IN CROWD BEHAVIOR. IN ROGER
    DANIELS AND SPENCER C. OLIN, JR. (EDS) RACISM
    IN CALIFORNIA: N READER IN THE HISTORY OF OPPRESSION.
    NEW YORK, NEW YORK: MACMILLAN COMPANY, 1972 (HC).

TURNER, RALPH. "THE SOCIOLOGY OF BEING A MEXICAN-RUSSIAN".
    EL GRITO, VOL. 1 NO. 4 (SUMMER 1968), PP. 38-40.

TURNER, RAPH H., AND SURACE, SAMUEL J. "ZOOT-SUITERS AND
    MEXICANS". AMERICAN JOURNAL OF SOCIOLOGY, VOL. 62
    (JULY 1956), PP. 14-20 (HC).

U. S.   UNITED STATES CENSUS POPULATION: (LW*).

U. S.   CHARACTERISTICS SOUTH EAST LOS (LW*).

U. S.   FIFTEENTH CENSUS UNITED STATES: (LW*).

U. S.   FIFTEENTH CENSUS UNITED STATES: (LW*).

U. S.   FIFTEENTH CENSUS UNITED STATES: (LW*).

U. S.   MOTHER TONGUE FOREIGN-BORN WHITE (LW*).

U. S.   PERSONS SPANISH SURNAME (LW*).

U. S.   PERSONS SPANISH SURNAME (1950) (LW*).

U. S.   PERSONS SPANISH SURNAME (1963) (LW*).

U. S.   PERSONS SPANISH ORIGIN UNITED (LW*).

U. S.   PERSONS SPANISH SURNAME: SOCIAL (LW*).

U. S.   POPULATION SPANISH MOTHER TONGUE (LW*).

U. S.   SIXTEENTH CENSUS UNITED STATES: (LW*).

U. S.   SIXTEENTH CENSUS UNITED STATES: (LW*).

U. S.   SPECIAL REPORT FOREIGN-BORN WHITE (LW*).

U. S.   U.S. CENSUS POPULATION: 1960, (LW*).

U. S.   U.S. CENSUS HOUSING: 1950, VOL (LW*).

U. S.   U.S. CENSUS POPULATION: 1950 (LW*).

U. S.   U.S. CENSUS POPULATION: 1950 (LW*).

U. S.   UNITED STATES CENSUS POPULATION: (LW*).

U. S.   WE MEXICAN AMERICANS (LW*).

U. S. MEXICAN IMMIGRATION (LW*).

U. S. CIVIL RIGHTS DIRECTORY (LW*).

U. S. CENSUSES 1900, 1910 1920 (LW*).

U. S. NATIVITY PARENTAGE WHITE POPULATION: (LW*).

U. S. STANDARDS LIVING INDIAN-MEXICAN (LW*).

U. S. HOUSE POST OFFICE AND CIVIL SERVICE COMM. ACCURACY
      OF 1970 CENSUS ENUMERATION AND RELATED MATTERS.
      WASHINGTON, D. C.: U. S. GOVERNMENT PRINTING OFFICE,
      (1970).

U. S. NEW FOCUS OPPORTUNITY. TESTIMONY (LW*).

U. S. PUBLIC HEALTH SURVEY SAN ANTONIO (MD*).

U. S. AVAILABILITY USEFULNESS FEDERAL (LW*).

U. S. FAIR HOUSING ACT 19679 HEARINGS (LW*).

U. S. FEDERAL MINORITY ENTERPRISE PROGRAM (LW*).

U. S. MIGRANT SEASONAL FARMWORKER POWERLESS (LW*).

U. S. MIGRANT SEASONAL FARMWORKER POWERLESS (LW*).

U. S. PROBLEMS MEXICAN AMERICAN BUSINESSMEN (LW*).

U. S. PROBLEMS MIGRANT WORKERS. HEARING (LW*).

U. S. NATIONAL NUTRITION SURVEY, PART (LW*).

U. S. PROBLEMS PROSPECTS (LW*).

U. S. AVAILABILITY USEFULNESS FEDERAL (LW*).

U. S. AVAILABILITY USEFULNESS FEDERAL (LW*).

U. S. NOT JUST SOME US (LW*).

U. S. MIGRATORY COTTON PICKERS ARIZONA (LW*).

UGALDE. POWER CONFLICT MEXICAN COMMUNITY: (PL*).

ULIBARRI, HORACIO. "SOCIAL AND ATTITUDINAL CHARACTERISTICS
      OF SPANISH-SPEAKING MIGRANT AND EX-MIGRANT WORKERS
      IN THE SOUTHWEST". SOCIOLOGY AND SOCIAL RESEARCH,
      VOL. 50 (APRIL 1966), PP. 361-370 (SI).

ULIBARRI. "TEACHER AWARENESS SOCIOCULTURAL (ED*).

ULIBARRI, HORACIO. SOCIAL AND ATTITUDINAL CHARACTERISTICS
    OF MIGRANT AND EX-MIGRANT WORKERS: NEW MEXICO,
    COLORADO, ARIZONA AND TEXAS.   LAS CRUCES, NEW MEXICO:
    ERIC CLEARINGHOUSE, (SI).

ULIBARRI.   TEACHER AWARENESS SOCIO-CULTURAL   (ED*).

ULLMAN.   ECOLOGICAL ANALYSIS SOCIAL VARIABLES   (EC*).

UNDERWOOD.   STUDY HOMES ONE HUNDRED LATIN-AMERICAN   (ED*).

UNITED STATES BUREAU OF THE CENSUS. 'WE, THE MEXICAN-AMERICANS.'
    IN EDWARD SIMMEN, THE CHICANO TODAY.

UNITED STATES PRESIDENTS COMMITTEE ON MIGRATORY LABOR.
    MIGRATORY LABOR NOTES   (EC*).

UNITED STATES. COORDINATOR OF INTER-AMERICAN AFFAIRS.
    INTER-AMERICAN ACTIVITIES IN THE UNITED STATES--SPANISH
    AND PORTUGUESE SPEAKING PEOPLE IN THE UNITED STATES.
    WASHINGTON, 1943 (HUS).

UNITED STATES. COORDINATOR OF INTER-AMERICAN AFFAIRS.
    SPANISH-SPEAKING AMERICANS IN THE WAR: THE SOUTHWEST.
    WASHINGTON, D. C.: CO-ORDINATOR OF INTER-AMERICAN
    AFFAIRS AND OFFICE OF INTER-AMERICAN AFFAIRS AND
    OFFICE OF WAR INFORMATION, (1943) (HUS).

UNITED STATES.   "MEXICAN AMERICAN CONFERENCE; (EC*).

UNITED STATES.   "THE MEXICAN AMERICAN: NEW FOCUS (EC*).

UNIV.   TEXAS VOTES: SELECTED GENERAL (PL*).

UNIVERSITY OF CALIFORNIA AT LOS ANGELES.   DIRECTORY
    ORGANIZATIONS SOUTH (EC*).

UNIVERSITY OF CALIFORNIA AT LOS ANGELES. NEW DIRECTIONS
    IN EDUCATION; ESTUDIOS FEMENILES DE LA CHICANA..
    LOS ANGELES, CALIFORNIA,.

UNIVERSITY OF DENVER. BUREAU OF BUSINESS AND SOCIAL
    RESEARCH. "HOUSING TRENDS IN DENVER, 1939-1949".
    UNIVERSITY OF DENVER REPORTS, VOL. 25 (NOVEMBER   1949).

UNIVERSITY OF NEW MEXICO.   AFFENT EDUCATIONAL COMMUNITYEXPERIMENTS
    (ED*).

UNIVERSITY OF TEXAS.   COMPARISON FAMILY INCOME EXPENDITURES
    (EC*).

UNIVERSITY OF TEXAS, BUREAU OF RESEARCH IN THE SOCIAL
    SCIENCES. POPULATION MOBILITY IN AUSTIN, TEXAS.
    AUSTIN, TEXAS: UNIVERSITY OF TEXAS PRESS, 1941.

UNIVERSITY OF TEXAS, BUREAU OF RESEARCH IN THE SOCIAL
    SCIENCES. TEXAS' CHILDREN: THE REPORT OF THE TEXAS
    CHILD WELFARE SURVEY. AUSTIN, TEXAS: UNIVERSITY OF
    TEXAS, 1938.

UPHAM. POVERTY AMONG SPANISH AMERICANS (EC*).

UTAH MIGRANT COUNCIL. SALAZAR FAMILY. SALT LAKE CITY,
    UTAH.

VACA, NICK C. "THE MEXICAN AMERICAN IN THE SOCIAL
    SCIENCES: PART I: 1936-1970". EL GRITO, VOL. 4
    NO. 1 (FALL 1970), PP. 17-51.

VACA, NICK C. "THE MEXICAN AMERICAN IN THE SOCIAL SCIENCES
    1912-1935". EL GRITO, VOL. 3 NO. 3 (SPRING 1970),
    PP. 3-24.

VACA. "THE NEGRO MOVEMENT AS ANTI-REVOLUTION" (LMA*).

VACA. MESSAGE TO PEOPLE (LMA*).

VACA, NICK C. THE PURCHASE. BERKELEY, CALIFORNIA: QUINTO
    SOL PUBLICATIONS, INC., 1969.

VALCARCEL, EMILIO DIAZ. DEMIAN SANCHEZ, G. I.. EDITED
    BY LILLIAN FADERMAN AND BARBARA BRADSHAW. OAKLAND,
    NEW JERSEY: SCOTT, FORESMAN AND COMPANY, 1969.

VALDES. "U. S. HISPANO" (EC*).

VALDES. SPANISH-SPEAKING PEOPLE SOUTHWEST (PL*).

VALDES, DANIEL T. A SOCIOLOGICAL ANALYSIS AND DESCRIPTION
    OF THE POLITICAL ROLE, STATUS AND VOTING BEHAVIOR OF
    AMERICANS WITH SPANISH NAMES. UNIVERSITY OF
    COLORADO, PHD. DISSERTATION (1964) (PL).

VALDES. SOCIOLOGICAL ANALYSIS DESCRIPTION (PL*).

VALDES, DANIEL TAPIA. A SOCIOLOGICAL ANALYSIS AND
    DESCRIPTION OF THE POLITICAL ROLE, STATUS AND VOTING
    BEHAVIOR AMERICANS WITH SPANISH NAMES. ANN ARBOR:
    UNIVERSITY MICROFILMS, 1969.

VALDEZ. CONTRAST BETWEEN SPANISH FOLK (AN*).

VALDEZ, BERNARD. CONTRASTS BETWEEN SPANISH FOLK AND ANGLO
    URBAN CULTURAL VALUES. CALIFORNIA, DEPARTMENT OF
    INSTITUTIONS, DEPARTMENT OF SOCIAL WELFARE,.

VALDEZ. IMPLICATIONS SPANISH-AMERICAN (AN*).

VALDEZ, BERNARD. IMPLICATIONS OF SPANISH AMERICAN CULTURE
    ON FAMILY LIFE.   CALIFORNIA, DEPARTMENT OF INSTITUTIONS,
    DEPARTMENT OF SOCIAL WELFARE,.

VALDEZ.   LABELS MAJORITY-MINORITY RELATIONS   (PL*).

VAN ALSTYNE.   ENVIRONMENT THREE-YEAR-OLD CHILDREN   (ED*).

VAN DEN BERGHE, PIERRE L. RACE AND ETHNICITY; ESSAYS IN
    COMPARATIVE SOCIOLOGY.   NEW YORK: BASIC BOOKS, 1970.

VAN DER EERDEN, SISTER M. LUCIA. MATERNITY CARE IN
    A SPANISH-AMERICAN COMMUNITY OF NEW MEXICO.
    WASHINGTON, D. C.: THE CATHOLIC UNIVERSITY OF AMERICA
    PRESS, 1948.

VAN VELZER, FRANCIS. RACE RELATION PROBLEMS OF 50 NORMAL
    ADOLESCENT MEXICAN-AMERICAN BOYS IN LOS ANGELES.
    UNIVERSITY OF SOUTHERN CALIFORNIA, MASTER'S THESIS
    (1936) (PY).

VANDEL, PATRICIA. LA RAZA: THE MEXICAN AMERICANS.   PALO
    ALTO, CALIFORNIA: MULTI MEDIA PRODUCTIONS, INC. IN
    COOPERATION WITH THE SOUTHWEST COUNCIL OF LA RAZA,
    PHOENIX, ARIZONA. (PL).

VANDER ZANDEN, JAMES WILFRID. AMERICAN MINORITY RELATIONS;
    THE SOCIOLOGY OF RACE AND ETHNIC GROUPS.   SECOND
    EDITION. NEW YORK: THE RONALD PRESS, 1966.

VANDER ZANDEN, JAMES WILFRID. AMERICAN MINORITY RELATIONS;
    THE SOCIOLOGY OF RACE AND ETHNIC GROUPS.   SECOND
    EDITION. NEW YORK: RONALD PRESS COMPANY, 1966.

VEGA, WILLIAM A. "POLICE AND PROFESSIONALIZATION".   EL
    GRITO, VOL. 1 NO. 4 (SUMMER 1968), PP. 18-20 (LW).

VENABLE, C. L. "CHICAGO MEXICANS MEET SYNARCHISM".
    CHRISTIAN CENTURY, VOL. 61 (OCTOBER 11, 1944), P.
    1183.

VERA, RON. "OBSERVATIONS ON THE CHICANO RELATIONSHIP TO
    MILITARY SERVICE IN LOS ANGELES COUNTY".   AZTLAN--CHICANO
    JOURNAL OF THE SOCIAL SCIENCES AND THE ARTS, VOL. 1
    NO. 2 (FALL 1970), PP. 27-37.

VERDI.   NEEDS VALUES MEXICAN AMERICANS (ED*).

VIDAL, MIRTA. CHICANAS SPEAKOUT. WOMEN: NEW VOICE OF
    LA RAZA.   NEW YORK: PATHFINDER PRESS, INC., 1971.

VIDAL.   CHICANO LIBERATION REVOLUTIONARY (PL*).

VILLAREAL.   "MEXICAN-AMERICANS UPHEAVAL" (LMA*).

VILLARREAL, EDUARDO. A STUDY OF GROUP PROCESSES IN TWO
     SMALL NATURAL GROUPS OF LATIN-AMERICANADOLESCENTS.
     UNIVERSITY OF TEXAS, MASTER'S THESIS (1962) (ED).

VILLARREAL.   "MEXICAN-AMERICANS LEADERSHIP (LMA*).

VINCENT.   "THE PROPOSED MEXICAN LABOR CODE" (EC*).

VIVAS, GUSTAVO E. "OUR SPANISH-SPEAKING U.S. CATHOLICS".
     AMERICA, VOL. 91 (MAY 15, 1954), PP. 187-188 (RE).

VOGEL.   SEASONAL LABOR SANTA BARBARACOUNTY (EC*).

VOGLER.   INFLUENCE ETHNICITY SOCIO-ECONOMIC   (ED*).

VOGT.   PEOPLE RIMROCK; STUDY VALUESFIVE (AN*).

VON ELM, SISTER THEODORE MARY. AN APPRAISAL OF PARTICIPATION
     IN THE GROUP WORK SERVICES OFFERED AT GRADALUPE
     COMMUNITY CENTER.   UNIVERSITY OF TEXAS, MASTER'S
     THESIS (1963).

WADDELL.   FROM DISSONANCE TO CONSONANCE   (AN*).

WADDELL.   DISSONANCE TO CONSONANCE BACK   (AN*).

WADDELL.   VALUE ORIENTATIONS YOUNG MEXICAN-AMERICAN   (AN*).

WAGLEY.   "A TYPOLOGY LATIN AMERICAN SUBCULTURES"   (AN*).

WAGLEY.   MINORITIES NEW WORLD: SIX CASE (AN*).

WAGLEY.   MINORITIES NEW WORLD (AN*).

WAGNER, NATHANIEL N. AND HAUG, MARSHA J. (EDS). CHICANOS:
     SOCIAL AND PSYCHOLOGICAL PERSPECTIVES.   SAINT LOUIS:
     THE C. V. MOSBY COMPANY, 1971 (PY).

WALKER.   "MEXICAN IMMIGRANTS AMERICANCITIZENSHIP"   (AN*).

WALLIS, MARIE POPE. A STUDY OF DEPENDENCY IN ONE HUNDRED
     CASES TAKEN FROM FILES OF BUREAU OFCOUNTY WELFARE.
     CATHOLIC WELFARE BUREAU, LOS ANGELES COUNTY RELIEF
     ADMINISTRATION.   UNIVERSITY OF SOUTHERN CALIFORNIA,
     MASTER'S THESIS (1935).

WALTER, PAUL ALFRED FRANCIS. POPULATION TRENDS IN
     NEW MEXICO.   ALBUQUERQUE, NEW MEXICO: UNIVERSITY OF
     NEW MEXICO, (1947). DEPARTMENT OF GOVERNMENT, DIVISION
     OF RESEARCH, PUBLICATION NUMBER 10..

WALTER.   POPULATION NEW MEXICO (HN*).

WALTER.   RACE CULTURAL RELATIONS (AN*).

WALTER.   SPANISH SPEAKING AMERICANS   (AN*).

WALTER.   STUDY ISOLATION SOCIAL CHANGE   (AN*).

WARBURTON.   WORK WELFARE AGRICULTURAL LABORERS   (EC*).

WARNER, W. L., MEEKER, M. AND EELS, K.   SOCIAL CLASS IN
     AMERICA.   CHICAGO: SCIENCE RESEARCH ASSOCIATES, 1949.

WARNER, WILLIAM LLOYD.   THE SOCIAL SYSTEMS OF AMERICAN
     ETHNIC GROUPS.   NEW HAVEN, YALE UNIVERSITY PRESS,
     LONDON, H. MILFORD, OXFORD UNIVERSITY PRESS, 1945,
     1949.

WARREN.   CULTURAL CHANGE CONTINUITY SAN   (AN*).

WATSON, JAMES B. AND SAMORA, JULIAN.   "SUBORDINATE
     LEADERSHIP IN A BICULTURAL COMMUNITY: AN ANALYSIS".
     AMERICAN SOCIOLOGICAL REVIEW, VOL. 19   (AUGUST 1954),
     P. 420 (AN).

WATSON, JAMES B. AND SAMORA, JULIAN.   "SUBORDINATE
     LEADERSHIP IN A BICULTURAL COMMUNITY: AN ANALYSIS".
     AMERICAN SOCIOLOGICAL REVIEW, VOL. 19   (AUGUST 1954),
     PP. 413-421 (AN).

WATSON, KENDRICK W.   "ZOOT SUIT, MEXICAN STYLE".
     INTERCOLLEGIAN, VOL. 61   (SEPTEMBER 1943), P. 7.

WATSON, LAWRENCE CRAIG.   GUAJIRO PERSONALITY AND URBANIZATION.
     LOS ANGELES, CALIFORNIA: LATIN AMERICAN CENTER,
     UNIVERSITY OF CALIFORNIA AT LOS ANGELES, 1968 (AN).

WATSON.   MEXICANS IN DALLAS   (SI*).

WEAVER, CHARLES NORRIS.   "ACCIDENTS AS A MEASURE OF THE
     CULTURAL ADJUSTMENT OF MEXICAN-AMERICANS".   SOCIOLOGICAL
     QUARTERLY, VOL. 2   (WINTER 1970), PP. 119-125.

WEAVER, ROBERT.   THE URBAN COMPLEX; HUMAN VALUES IN URBAN
     LIFE.   GARDEN CITY, NEW YORK: DOUBLEDAY, 1964.

WEAVER.   SOCIAL STRUCTURE CHANGE CONFLICT   (AN*).

WEEKS, OLIVER DOUGLAS.   "THE LEAGUE OF UNITED LATIN-AMERICAN
     CITIZENS: A TEXAS-MEXICAN CIVIC ORGANIZATION".
     SOUTHWESTERN POLITICAL AND SOCIAL SCIENCE QUARTERLY,
     VOL. 10   (DECEMBER 1929), PP. 257-258 (PL).

WEINBERG.   "SCHOOL IN TRANSITION"   (ED*).

WELFARE PLANNING COUNCIL, (ED) LOS ANGELES REGION. RESEARCH
     DEPARTMENT.   REPORT ON THE SURVEY OF UNSPONSORED YOUTH
     GROUPS IN THE EAST CENTRAL AREAS.   RESEARCH DEPARTMENT
     OF THE WELFARE PLANNING COUNCIL, LOS ANGELES REGION,
     JANUARY 24, 1958.

WERNER, NORMA E. AND EVANS, IDELLA M. 'PERCEPTION
    OF PREJUDICE IN MEXICAN-AMERICAN PRESCHOOL CHILDREN.'
    IN NATHANIEL N. WAGNER AND MARSHA J. HAUG (EDS),
    CHICANOS: SOCIAL AND PSYCHOLOGICAL PERSPECTIVES (PY).

WEST, GUY A. "RACE ATTITUDES AMONG TEACHERS IN THE
    SOUTHWEST".   JOURNAL OF ABNORMAL AND SOCIAL PSYCHOLOGY,
    VOL. 31 (OCTOBER-DECEMBER 1936), PP. 331-337 (PY).

WESTON.   HISTORY TREATMENT FOREING MINORITY   (HC*).

WHARBURTON, AMBER A., WOOD, HELEN AND CRANE, MARIAN. THE
    WORK AND WELFARE OF CHILDREN OF AGRICULTURAL LABORERS
    IN HIDALGO COUNTY, TEXAS.   WASHINGTON, D. C., (1943).
    PUBLICATION 298. U. S. DEPARTMENT OF LABOR, CHILDREN'S
    BUREAU. (EC).

WHARBURTON, AMBER. "CHILDREN IN THE FIELDS".   SURVEY,
    VOL. 80 (JANUARY 1944), PP. 13-15 (EC).

WHEELER, HELEN. "THE PUERTO RICAN POPULATION OF NEW YROK".
    SOCIOLOGY AND SOCIAL RESEARCH, VOL. 25 (NOVEMBER-DECEMBER
    1950), PP. 123-27.

WHEELER.   TO WEAR CITYS CROWN, BEGINNINGS (HT*).

WHEELER, THOMAS C. THE IMMIGRANT EXPERIENCE: THE ANGUISH
    OF BECOMING AMERICAN.   NEW YORK, NEW YORK: DIALDELACORTE
    PRESS, 1971 (HUS).

WHITAKER.   SUMMARY REPORT STUDY DROP-OUTS (ED*).

WHITE, ALFRED. THE APPERCEPTIVE MASS OF FOREIGNERS
    AS APPLIED TO AMERICANIZATION, THE MEXICAN GROUP,
    1923.   SAN FRANCISCO: R AND E RESEARCH ASSOCIATES,
    1971.

WHITEHEAD.   SOCIO-ECONOMIC BACKGROUND ASRELATED   (ED*).

WHITTEN.   INTERNAL DESCRIPTIVE ANALYSIS   (ED*).

WHITWELL, INEZ MARGARET. A HOMEMAKING COURSE FOR MEXICAN
    GIRLS WHO WILL BE UNABLE TO ATTEND HIGH SCHOOL.
    UNIVERSITY OF SOUTHERN CALIFORNIA, MASTER'S THESIS
    (1937) (ED).

WHITWORTH, WALLACE. SCHOOL DROP-OUTS: A COMPARISON OF
    INTEREST IN SCHOOL WITH PEER AND AUTHORITY RELATIONSHIP.
    WORDEN SCHOOL OF SOCIAL SERVICE, OUR LADY OF THE LAKE
    COLLEGE, MASTER'S THESIS (1964) (ED).

WIENS, G. QUESTIONS AND ANSWERS ON AMERICAN CITIZENSHIP.
    NEW YORK: REGENTS PUBLISHING COMPANY,.

WIGGIN.   EDUCATION NATIONALISM, HISTORICAL   (ED*).

WILLIAMS, ROBIN M.; DEAN, JOHN P. ; SUCHMAN, EDWARD A.
    STRANGERS NEXT DOOR: ETHNIC RELATIONS IN AMERICAN
    COMMUNITIES. ENGLEWOOD CLIFFS, NEW JERSEY: PRENTICE-HALL,
    1964.

WILLIAMS, STANLEY T. THE SPANISH BACKGROUND OF AMERICAN
    LITERATURE. NEW HAVEN: YALE UNIVERSITY PRESS, 1955.

WILSON. RED, BLACK, BLOND, OLIVE (AN*).

WILSON. DOMOGRAPHIC CHARACTERISTICS TEXAS (EC*).

WILSON. CERRITO: CHANGING CULTURE (EC*).

WINCHESTER. ACHIEVEMENTS, SOCIAL CONCEPTS (PY*).

WINGFIELD, CLYDE J. (ED.). URBANIZATION IN THE SOUTHWEST:
    A SYMPOSIUM. EL PASO: TEXAS WESTERN COLLEGE PRESS,
    THE UNIVERSITY OF TEXAS AT EL PASO, 1968.

WINHELD, MARK JOSEPH. PLURALISM OR ASSIMILATION?
    THE MEXICAN-AMERICAN OF TUCSON, ARIZONA. UNIVERSITY
    OF ARIZONA, MASTER'S THESIS (1969) (AN).

WINN, CARR. REVOLUTIONARY ASPECTS OF THE VALLEY FARM
    WORKERS. UNPUBLISHED PAPER PRESENTED AT THE 1970
    ANNUAL MEETING OF THE SOUTHWEST SOCIAL SCIENCE
    ASSOCIATION, DALLAS, TEXAS. 1970. (PL).

WINSLOW. MY OWN, MY NATIVE LAND (LI*).

WINTER. POOR: CULTURE POVERTY OR POVERTY (EC*).

WINTER. MEXICO HER PEOPLE TODAY (EC*).

WINTERS, ALLEN. "PEONAGE IN THE SOUTHWEST". FOURTH
    INTERNATIONAL, VOL. 14 (MAY 1953), PP. 74-78.

WINTERS, JET C. A REPORT ON THE HEALTH AND NUTRITION OF
    MEXICANS LIVING IN TEXAS. AUSTIN, TEXAS: UNIVERSITY
    OF TEXAS, BUREAU OF RESEARCH IN THE SOCIAL SCIENCES,
    (1931). STUDY NUMBER 2. (MD).

WINTON. MEXICO TODAY (LI*).

WINTON. "PROGRESS IN MEXICO" (LI*).

WISCONSIN, UNIVERSITY OF WISCONSIN. BUREAU CF AUDIO
    VISUAL INSTRUCTION. HOME IS A LONG ROAD. FILM 20
    MINUTES. BLACK AND WHITE. UNIVERSITY OF WISCONSIN,
    BUREAU OF AUDIO VISUAL INSTRUCTION MADISON, WISCONSIN..

WOLF. "CHURCH AND DELANO" (EC*).

WOLFF, KURT H. SAN CRISTOBAL, NEW MEXICO SOCIOLOGICAL
    STUDY OF A SMALL, RURAL SPANISH-ANGLO VALLEY COMMUNITY.
    UNPUBLISHED STUDY IN POSSESSION OF MR. WOLFF, SOUTHERN
    METHODIST UNIVERSITY, DALLAS, TEXAS..

WOLFINGER, RAYMOND. "REPUTATION AND REALITY IN THE STUDY
    OF COMMUNITY POWER".   AMERICAN SOCIOLOGICAL REVIEW,
    VOL. 25 (OCTOBER 1960), PP. 636-644 (PL).

WOMACK. "WHO ARE THE CHICANOS?" (AN*).

WOODBRIDGE, H. C. "MEXICO AND U. S. RACISM: HOW MEXICANS
    VIEW OUR TREATMENT OF MINORITIES".   COMMONWEALTH,
    VOL. 42 (JUNE 22, 1945), PP. 234-237 (SI).

WOODS. "CULTURAL CONDITIONING MENTAL (AN*).

WOODS, SISTER FRANCES JEROME. MEXICAN ETHNIC LEADERSHIP
    IN SAN ANTONIO, TEXAS.   WASHINGTON, D. C.: CATHOLIC
    UNIVERSITY OF AMERICA PRESS, 1949 (PL).

WOOFTER, T. J. RACES AND ETHNIC GROUPS IN AMERICAN LIFE.
    NEW YORK: MCGRAW-HILL, 1933 (AN   HUS).

WOOFTER, T. J., JR. RACES AND ETHNIC GROUPS IN AMERICAN
    LIFE.   NEW YORK: MCGRAW-HILL BOOK COMPANY, INC.,
    1933. REPRINTED BY KRAUS R RAUS REPRINT COMPANY, NEW
    YORK, 1971 (AN   HUS).

WORCESTER, DONALD E. "THE SPANISH AMERICAN PAST: ENEMY
    OF CHANGE".   JOURNAL OF INTER-AMERICAN STUDIES,
    (JANUARY 1969), PP. 66-75 (HSW).

WRIGHT . "A TALE MEXICO OR HOW TO MARRY (LI*).

WRIGHT. OCCUPATIONAL ORIENTATIONS MEXICAN (EC*).

WRIGHT, DAVID E., AND KUVLESKY, WILLIAM P. OCCUPATIONAL
    STATUS PROJECTIONS OF MEXICAN AMERICAN YOUTH RESIDING
    IN THE RIO GRANDE VALLEY.   PAPER PRESENTED AT THE
    ANNUAL MEETING OF THE SOUTHWEST SOCIOLOGICAL ASSOCIATION,
    APRIL, 1968, DALLAS. (EC EC).

WRIGHT, KATHLEEN. THE OTHER AMERICANS: MINORITIES
    IN AMERICAN HISTORY.   GREENWICH, CONNECTICUT: FAWCETT
    CREST BOOKS, 1969 (HUS).

WRZESINISKI, C. "SUMMER SCHOOL FOR MIGRANT CHILDREN;
    ENDEAVOR".   CATHOLIC SCHOOL JOURNAL, VOL. 68 (APRIL
    1968), PP. 54-55 (ED).

YBARRA. STUDY TO DETERMINE WHY SPANISH-SPEAKING (ED*).

YINGER. "INTEGRATION AMERICANS MEXICAN (SI*).

YINGER.   MINORITY GROUP AMERICAN SOCIETY (SI*).

YINGER.   MINORITY GROUPS AMERICAN SOCIETY (SI*).

YNIGO.   MEXICAN-AMERICAN CHILDREN INTEGRATED   (ED*).

YOUNG, DONALD R.   AMERICAN MINORITY PEOPLES: A STUDY IN
     RACIAL AND CULTURAL CONFLICTS IN CULTURAL ASPECTS OF
     BILINGUALISM
     EDUCATION ACROSS CULTURES.   NEW YORK: HARPER, 1932
     (AN).

YOUNG, DONALD R.   RESEARCH MEMORANDUM ON MINORITY PEOPLES
     IN THE DEPRESSION.   NEW YORK, (1937). BULLETIN NUMBER
     31. SOCIAL SCIENCE RESEARCH COUNCIL. (EC   AN).

ZAMORA.   MEXICAN AMERICAN COMMUNITY MEXICAN (PL*).

ZAMORA, TED.   SURVEY OF MEXICAN FAMILIES AND INDIVIDUALS
     SERVED BY THE NEIGHBORHOOD HOUSE.   ST. PAUL,
     MINNESOTA, APRIL 1941.

ZEIGLER.   DESEGREGATION SUPREME COURT   (LW*).

ZELENY, CAROLYN.   RELATIONS BETWEEN THE SPANISH-AMERICANS
     AND THE ANGLO-AMERICANS IN NEW MXICO: A STUDY
     OF CONFLICT AND ACCOMMODATION IN DUAL ETHNIC RELATIONSHIP.
     YALE UNIVERSITY, PHD.   DISSERTATION (1944).

ZURCHER, LOUIS A., AND MEADOW ARNOLD.   "VALUE ORIENTATION,
     ROLE CONFLICT, AND ALIENATION FROM WORK: A CROSS-CULTURAL
     STUDY".   AMERICAN SOCIOLOGICAL REVIEW, VOL. 30
     (AUGUST   1965), PP. 539-548 (AN).

ACHESON.   GEORGE WASHINTON DIAMONDS ACCOUNT   (HT*).

ADAIR, A. GARLAND,   AND CROCKETT, M. H. SR. EDS. HEROES
     OF THE ALAMO: ACCOUNTS AND DOCUMENTS OF WILLIAM B.
     TRAVIS, JAMES BOWIE, JAMES B. BONHAM AND DAVID
     CROCKETT, AND THEIR TEXAS MEMORIALS.   JERICHO, NEW
     YORK: EXPOSITION PRESS INC., 1957 (HT).

ADAMS.   BISHOP TAMARONS VISITATION NEW   (HN*).

ADAMS.   MISSIONS NEW MEXICO 1776: DESCRIPTION   (HN*).

AIMARD, GUSTAVE. THE FREEBOOTERS.   PHILADELPHIA, 1868.

AIMARD, GUSTAVE. THE GOLDEN SEEKERS.   LONDON, 1842.

ALBERT.   WESTERN AMERICA 1846-1847; ORIGINAL   (HUS*).

ANDERSON.   AMERICAN MAXIMILIANS MEXICO,   (HM*).

VISIT TO TEXAS: BEING JOURNAL   (HT*).

VISIT TO TEXAS   (HT*).

ANZA, JUAN BAUTISTA. DIARIO DE LA RUTA Y OPERACIONES QUE
     YO EL INFRASCRITO, TENIENTE CORONEL PRACTICO SEGUNDA
     VEZ, A LA CALIFORNIA SEPTENTRIONAL.   MS. ARCHIVO
     GRAL. DE LA NACION, MEX (HM HS).

ANZA, JUAN BAUTISTA. VIAJE DE SONORA A CALIFORNIA.   MS.
     ARCHIVO GRAL. DE LA NACION MEX. (HM HS).

ARLEGUI, JOSEPH. CRONICA DE LA PROVINCIA DE N. S.
     P. FRANCISCO DE ZACATECAS.   MEXICO: J. B. DE HOGAL,
     1737 (HS).

ARMIJO.   LETTER TO GENERAL KEARNY, WRITTEN   (HSW*).

ARNAZ, JOSE. RECUERDOS.   MS. BANCROFT LIBRARY,.

AUDOBON, JOHN JAMES. AUDUBON'S AMERICA, THE NARRATIVES
     AND EXPERIENCES OF JOHN JAMES AUDOBON.   BOSTON:
     JOUGHTON MIFFLIN CO., 1940 (HT HSW).

AUDUBON, JOHN W.   AUDUBON'S WESTERN JOURNALS, 1848-1850,
    BEING THE MS RECORD OF A TRIP FROM NEW YORK TO TEXAS
    AND AN OVERLANG JOURNEY THROUGH MEXICO AND ARIZONA
    TO THE GOLD-FIELDS OF CALIFORNIA.   CLEVELAND: ARTHUR
    H. CLARK COMPANY, 1906 (HSW).

AUDUBON, JOHN W.   WESTERN JOURNALS; MEXICOCALIFORNIA.
    GLORIETA, NEW MEXICO: RIO GRANDE PRESS, INC., 1969
    (HSW).

AYETA, FATHER FRANCISCO.   LETTER TO THE VICEROY, FEBRUARY
    11, 1682.   BIBLIOTECA NACIONAL DE MEXICO, PROVINCIAS
    INTERNAS, IBID., LEGAJO 2, NO. 5, UNIVERSITY OF NEW
    MEXICO TRANSCRIPT (HS).

AYETA, FATHER FRANCISCO.   LETTER TO THE VICEROY, APRIL 30,
    1682.   TEADING TEACHER (HS).

BALL.   DAYS VICTORIO   (LI*).

BALL.   MAAM JONES PECOS   (LI*).

BALL.   RUIDOSO: LAST FRONTIER   (LI*).

BANDELIER.   DIARIES, 1880-1890   (HSW*).

BANDELIER.   JOURNEY ALVAR NUNEZ CABEZA DE   (HSW*).

BARBOUR, PHILIP NORBOURNE.   JOURNALS OF THE LATE PHILIP
    NORBOURNE BARBOUR, CAPTAIN IN THE 3RD REGIMENT, UNITED
    STATES INFRANTRY, AND HIS WIFE, MARTHA ISABELLA
    HOPKINS BARBOUR, WRITTEN DURING THE WAR WITH MEXICO,
    1846.   NEW YORK: G. P. PUTNAM'S SONS, 1936 (HUS).

BARCA, CALDERON DE LA ; INGLIS, FRANCES ERSKIN.   LIFE IN
    MEXICO DURING A RESIDENCE OF TWO YEARS IN THAT
    COUNTRY.   NEW YORK: E. P DUTTON AND CO., 1931.

BARTLETT, JOHN RUSSELL.   PERSONAL NARRATIVE OF EXPLORATIONS
    AND INCIDENTS IN TEXAS, NEW MEXICO, CALIFORNIA,
    SONORA, AND CHIHUAHUA, CONNECTED WITH THE UNITED
    STATES AND MEXICAN BOUNDARY COMMISSION DURING
    THE YEARS 1850-1853.   NEW YORK: D. APPLETON CO, 1854
    (HSW).

BARTLETT, JOHN RUSSELL.   PERSONAL NARRATIVE OF EXPLORATIONS
    AND INCIDENTS IN TEXAS, NEW MEXICO, CALIFORNIA,
    SONORA, AND CHIHUAHUA, CONNECTED WITH THE UNITED
    STATES AND MEXICAN BOUNDARY COMMISSION DURING
    THE YEARS 1850, 51, '52, AND '53.   CHICAGO: RIO
    GRANDE PRESS, 1965 (HSW).

BEAN, ELLIS P. MEMOIR OF COLONEL ELLIS P. BEAN, WRITTEN
     BY HIMSELF ABOUT THE YEAR 1816.   EDITED BY W.
     P. YOAKUM. HOUSTON, TEXAS, 1930 (LI).

BEAN, ELLIS. MEMOIR. 1856.   DALLAS: BOOK CLUB OF TEXAS,
     1930 (LI).

BEAN, WALTON. BOSS RUEF'S SAN FRANCISCO.   BERKELEY:
     UNIVERSITY OF CALIFORNIA, 1952 (LI).

BEAZLEY, C. RAYMOND. VOYAGES AND TRAVELS MAINLY DURING
     THE 16TH AND 17TH CENTURIES.   WESTMINSTER: CONSTABLE
     AND CO., 1903.

BEECHER.   PLEA WEST (1835) (HSW*).

BELL.   REMINISCENCES RANGER OR EARLY (HC*).

BENAVIDES, FRAY ALONSO. BENAVIDES MEMORIAL OF 1630.
     TRANSLATED BY PETER P. FORRESTAL, (ED). WASHINGTON:
     ACADEMY OF AMERICAN FRANCISCAN HISTORY, 1954 (HS   HSW).

BENAVIDES, FRAY ALONSO. FRAY ALONSO DE BENAVIDES' REVISED
     MEMORIAL OF 1634.   FREDERICK WEBB HODGE, GEORGE P.
     HAMMOND AND AGAPITO REY, (EDS). ALBUQUERQUE: UNIVERSITY
     OF NEW MEXICO PRESS, 1945 (HS   HSW).

BENAVIDES, FRAY ALONSO. THE MEMORIAL OF FRAY ALONSO DE
     BENAVIDES, 1630..   TRANSLATED BY PETER P. FORRESTAL,
     (ED) AND ANNOTATED BY CYPRIAN J. LYNCH. WASHINGTON:
     ACADEMY OF AMERICAN FRANCISCAN HISTORY, 1954 (HS   HSW).

BENNETT, FREDERICK D. NARRATIVE OF A WHALING VOYAGE ROUND
     THE GLOBE, FROM THE YEAR 1833 TO 1836.   NEW YORK,
     NEW YORK: DA CAPO PRESS, INC., 1969 (HUS).

BERQUIN-DUVALLON. TRAVELS IN LOUISIANA AND THE FLORIDA,
     IN THE YEAR 1802.   (1806) NEW YORK, NEW YORK: DA CAPO
     PRESS, INC., 1969 (HS).

BIDWELL.   ECHOES PAST: ACCOUNT FIRST EMIGRANT (HC*).

BIDWELL.   JOURNEY TO CALIFORNIA (HC*).

BIEBER.   EXPLORING SOUTHWESTERN TRAILS (HSW*).

BIEBER.   SOUTHERN TRAILS TO CALIFORNIA (HC*).

BIGELOW.   MEMOIR LIFE PUBLIC SERVICE JOHN (HC*).

BINKLEY.   OFFICIAL CORRESPONDENCE TEXAS (HSW*).

BIXBY-SMITH, SARAH. ADOBE DAYS: LIFE ON A SHEEP RANCH IN
    EL PUEBLO DE NUESTRA SENORA DE LOS ANGELES. CEDAR
    RAPIDS, IOWA: TORCH PRESS, 1926 (HC).

BOATRIGHT. FOLK TRAVELERS: BALLADS, TALES (LI*).

BOLTON. "RECORDS MISSION NUESTRA SENORA (HS*).

BOLTON. NOTICIAS PALOU (HS*).

BORAH, WILLIAM E. PAPERS OF SENATOR WILLIAM E. BORAH.
    WASHINGTON, D. C.: LIBRARY OF CONGRESS,.

BOTELLO. ANALES SUR (HS*).

BOURNE, EDWARD GAYLORD (ED.). NARRATIVES OF THE CAREER
    OF HERNANDO DE SOTO IN THE CONQUEST OF FLORIDA AS TOLD
    BY A KNIGHT OF ELVAS. NEW YORK, NEW YORK: AMS PRESS,
    INC., 1904 (HS).

BOURNE, EULALIA. NINE MONTHS IS A YEAR. TUCSON, ARIZONA:
    UNIVERSITY OF ARIZONA PRESS, 1968.

BOWLES, SAMUEL. ACROSS THE CONTINENT. MASSACHUSETTS:
    SAMUEL BOWLES AND COMPANY, 1865 (HUS).

BRANDES, RAY (TRANS.). THE COSTANSO NARRATIVE OF THE
    PORTOLA EXPEDITION FIRST CHRONICLE OF THE SPANISH
    CONQUEST OF ALTA CALIFORNIA. NEWHALL, CALIFORNIA:
    HOGARTH PRESS, 1970 (HS).

BRECKINRIDGE, H. M. RECOLLECTIONS OF PERSONS AND PLACES
    IN THE WEST. NEW YORK, NEW YORK: DA CAPO PRESS,
    INC., 1834.

BRENIZER, LESTER C. (TRANS.). TRANSLATION OF BOOK II OF
    CERVANTES DE SALAZAR'S "CRONICA DE LA NUEVA ESPANA.
    UNIVERSITY OF TEXAS AT AUSTIN, MASTER'S THESIS (1926).

BROWNE, J. ROSS. CRUSOE'S ISLAND ... WITH SKETCHES
    OF ADVENTURE IN CALIFORNIA AND WASHOE. NEW YORK:
    HARPER AND BROTHERS, 1864 (LI).

BROWNE, J. ROSS. A TOUR THROUGH ARIZONA, 1864 OR ADVENTURES
    IN THE APACHE COUNTRY. TUCSON: ARIZONA SILHOUETTES,
    1950 (LI).

BROWNE, LINA FERGUSSON (ED.). J. ROSS BROWNE, LETTERS,
    JOURNALS, WRITINGS. ALBUQUERQUE: UNIVERSITY OF NEW
    MEXICO PRESS, 1969 (LI).

BRYANT, EDWIN. WHAT I SAW IN CALIFORNIA. NEW YORK: D.
    APPLETON AND COMPANY, 1848 (LI).

BRYANT, WILLIAM CULLEN. THE LIFE AND WORKS OF WILLIAM
    CULLEN BRYANT. NEW YORK: D. APPLETON AND COMPANY,
    1883-89 (LI).

BRYNNER.   JOURNEY WITH GENIUS: RECOLLECTIONS   (LI*).

BUCHANAN, A. RUSSELL (ED.).   "GEORGE WASHINGTON TRAHERNE:
     TEXAN COWBOY SOLDIER FROM MIER TO BUENA VISTA".
     SOUTHWESTERN HISTORICAL QUARTERLY, VOL. 58   (JULY
     1954), PP. 60-90.

BURGES, RICHARD F.   BURGES COLLECTION (NEWSPAPER CLIPPINGS,
     INTERVIEWS, MISCELLANEOUS MATERIAL IN SCRAPBOOKS).
     IN POSSESSION OF MRS. JANE BURGES PERRENOT, EL PASO,
     TEXAS..

BURTON.   LOOK WEST, 1860--ACROSS PLAINS   (HC*).

BUTTLER.   FORTY NINERS.   CHRONICLE CALIFORNIA   (HC*).

CABEZA DE VACA, ALVAR NUNEZ.   THE NARRATIVE OF ALVAR NUNEZ
     CABEZA DE VACA.   TRANSLATED BY FANNY BANDALIER.
     REPRINT, CHICAGO: RIO GRANDE PRESS, 1964 (HS).

CALVIN.   RECORD TRAVELS ARIZONA CALIFORNIA   (HS*).

CALZADA, FR. JUAN.   RESPUESTA DEL R. P. FR. JUAN CALZADA
     AL EXCELENTISIMO SENOR VIRREY, DANDOLE LAS RAZONES
     POR LAS QUE NO HAN SIDO ENTREGADAS A LAS JURISDICCIONES
     REAL, ORDINARIA Y ECLESIASTICA, LAS MISIONES DE LA
     ALTA CALIFORNIA.   ARCHIVO Y BIBLIOTECA DE LA
     SECRETARIA DE HACIENDA, COLECCION DE DOCUMENTOS
     HISTORICOS, TOMO 2, TIPOGRAFIA DE LA OFICINA IMPRESORA
     DE ESTAMPILLAS, MEXICO, 1914 (HS).

CAMPBELL, DONALD T.; LOGAN, JOHN.   AUTOBIOGRAPHY OF JOHN
     LOGAN CAMPBELL.   OAKLAND, CALIFORNIA: PRIVATELY
     PRINTED, 1940.

CASE.   THIRTY YEARS WITH MEXICANS:PEACE   (HM*).

CASTETTER.   "CAVALRY JOURNAL"   (HM*).

CLAPPE, LOUISE AMELIA KNAPP SMITH   "DAME SHIRLEY".   THE
     SHIRLEY LETTERS FROM THE CALIFORNIA MINES IN 1851-52.
     SAN FRANCISCO: THOMAS C. RUSSELL, 1922 (HC).

CLAPPE, LOUISE AMELIA KNAPP SMITH   "DAME SHIRLEY".   THE
     SHIRLEY LETTERS FROM THE CALIFORNIA MINES IN 1851-52.
     NEW YORK: ALFRED A. KNOPF, 1949 (HC).

COLDWELL, W. M.   GILLETT BOOK REVIVES PIONEER'S MEMORIES.
     EL PASO PUBLIC LIBRARY,.

CONE.   TWO YEARS CALIFORNIA   (HC*).

CONNERS.   EFFECT TEACHER BEHAVIOR VERBAL   (HUS*).

CONNOR.   SAGA TEXAS SERIES   (LI*).

COOK.   FIFTY YEARS OLD FRONTIER   (HSW*).

COOKE, EDWARD. A VOYAGE TO THE SOUTH SEA, AND ROUND THE
    WORLD, PERFORM'D IN THE YEAR 1708-1711.   NEW YORK,
    NEW YORK: DA CAPO PRESS, INC., 1969.

COPELAND, FAYETTE. KENDALL OF THE "PICAYUNE":   BEING HIS
    ADVENTURES IN NEW ORLEANS, ON THE.   NORMAN, OKLAHOMA:
    UNIVERSITY OF OKLAHOMA PRESS, 1943.

COSTANSO.   DIARIO HISTORICO DE LOS VIAJES (HS*).

CRESAP.   "EARLY CALIFORNIA AS DESCRIBED   (HC*).

CRESPI, FRAY JUAN. DIARIO DE LA PRIMERA EXPEDICION
    DE TIERRA AL DESCUBRIMIENTO DEL PUERTO DE SAN DIEGO.
    MS. ARCHIVO G. DE LA NACION (HC).

CRESPI, FRAY JUAN. DIARIO DE LA CAMINATA QUE HIZO
    LA EXPEDICION DESDE EL PUERTO DE SAN DIEGGO HASTA EL
    DE MONTERREY.   MS. ARCHIVO G. DE LA NACION.

CRESPI, FRAY JUAN. DIARIO EN LA FRAGATA NOMBRADA "SANTIAGO"
    MANDADA POR SU CAPITAN DON JUAN PEREZ A LAS COSTAS
    DEL NORTE DE MONTERREY.   MS. ARCHIVO G. DE LA NACION.

CRESPI, FRAY JUAN. FRAY JUAN CRESPI, MISSIONARY EXPLORER
    ON THE PACIFIC COAST, 1769-1774.   HUBERT EUGENE
    BOLTON. BERKELEY, CALIFORNIA; 1927. REPRINTED BY. NEW
    YORK, NEW YORK AND LONDON, GREAT BRITAIN: AMS PRESS,
    INC., (HC).

CREUTZ, HELMUT. "THE I. L. O. AND SOCIAL SECURITY
    FOR FOREIGN AND MIGRANT WORKERS".   INTERNATIONAL
    LABOR REVIEW,   (APRIL   1968), PP. 351-369 (HC).

CREVECOEUR, HECTOR ST. JEAN DE. "LETTERS FROM AN AMERICAN
    FARMER.'

CRIMMINS.   "COLONEL J. K. F. MANSFIELDS   (HT*).

CRIMMINS, COL. MARTIN L.   "COLONEL BUELL'S EXPEDITION INTO
    MEXICO IN 1880".   NEW MEXICO HISTORICAL REVIEW, VOL.
    10 (APRIL   1935), PP. 133-149 (HM).

CROCKETT.   AUTOBIOGRAPHY   (HT*).

CROCKETT.   COLONEL CROCKETTS EXPLOITS ADVENTURES   (HT*).

CROGHAN.   ARMY LIFE WESTERN FRONTIER:SELECTIONS   (HUS*).

CROIX.   TEODORO DE CROIZ NORTHERN FRONTIER   (HS*).

CRONON, E. DAVID. JOSEPHUS DANIELS IN MEXICO.   MADISON:
    UNIVERSITY OF WISCONSIN PRESS, 1960.

DABBS.   "LOPEZS REPORT TEXAS MISSIONS   (HSW*).

DABBS.   "THE TEXAS MISSIONS 1785"   (HSW*).

DALLAM.   "THE PUNITIVE EXPEDITION 1916   (HUS*).

DANA RICHARD HENRY.   TWO YEARS BEFORE MAST   (LI*).

DANIEL, JAMES MANLY.   "DIARY OF PEDRO JOSE DE LA FUENTE,
     CAPTAIN OF THE PRESIDIO OF EL PASO DELNORTE, JANUARY-JULY
     1795".   SOUTHWESTERN HISTORICAL QUARTERLY, VOL. 60
     NO. 2 , PP. 260-281 (HSW HT).

DAVIS.   WEST CAR WINDOW   (LI*).

DAVIS, ROBERT E.   DIARY OF WILLIAM BARRET TRAVIS.   WACO,
     TEXAS: TEXIAN PRESS (ND) (HT   HSW).

DAY.   AUTOBIOGRAPHY SAM HOUSTON   (HT*).

DAY.   BLACK BEANS GOOSE QUILLS, LITERATURE   (HSW*).

DE FIERRO BLANCO, ANTONIO.   THE JOURNEY OF THE FLAME: AN
     ACCOUNT OF ONE YEAR IN THE LIFE OF SENOR DON JUAN
     OBREGON.   BOSTON: HOUGHTON MIFFLIN CO.,, 1933 (HSW).

DE LUXAN, DIEGO PEREZ.   EXPEDITION INTO NEW MEXICO MADE
     BY ANTONIO DE ESPEJO, 1582-1583.   QUIVERA SOCIETY
     PUBLICATIONS. 1929. REPRINTED BY ARNO PRESS, 1971 (HUS).

DE WETTER, CHARLES SAFFORD.   "THE SMELTING WORKS AS
     REMEMBERED BY NOEL LONGUEMARE".   PASSWORD, VOL. 8
     (WINTER 1963), PP. 133-134.

DEGOLYER, E. M.   ACROSS ABORIGINAL AMERICA.   EL PASO:
     THE PERIPATETIC PRESS, 1947 (HSW).

DELANGLEZ, JEAN.   THE JOURNAL OF JEAN CAVELIER, THE ACCOUNT
     OF A SURVIVOR OF LA SALLE'S TEXAS EXPEDITION,
     1684-1688.   CHICAGO, ILLINOIS: INSTITUTE OF JESUIT
     HISTORY PUBLICATIONS, 1938 (HSW).

DELANO, ALONSO.   ACROSS THE PLAINS AND AMONG THE DIGGINS.
     CHAUBURN, CALIFORNIA: MILNER, ORTON AND MULLIGAN, 1854
     (LI).

DELANO, ALONSO.   ACROSS THE PLAINS AND AMONG THE DIGGINGS.
     NEW YORK, 1936 (LI).

DELLENBAUGH, FREDERICK S.   ROMANCE OF THE COLORADO RIVER;
     SECOND POWELL EXPEDITION.   GLORIETA, NEW MEXICO: RIO
     GRANDE PRESS, INC., (HUS).

DEMAREST, DAVID D.   DIARY.   BANCROFT LIBRARY.MS.

DESNOES, EDMUNDO. INCONSOLABLE MEMORIES. LONDON,
    ENGLAND: DEUTSCH, 1968.

DEWEESE, W. B. LETTERS FROM AN EARLY SETTLER OF TEXAS.
    WACO, TEXAS: TEXIAN PRESS, (HT).

DICK, EVERETT. TALES OF THE FRONTIER: FROM LEWIS AND CLARK
    TO THE LAST ROUNDUP. LINCOLN, NEBRASKA: UNIVERSITY
    OF NEBRASKA PRESS, 1964 (HUS).

DICK, EVERETT. TALES OF THE FRONTIER: FROM LEWIS
    AND CLARK TO THE LAST ROUNDUP. LINCOLN, NEBRASKA:
    UNIVERSITY OF NEBRASKA PRESS, 1964 (HUS).

DICK, EVERETT. VANGUARDS OF THE FRONTIER: A SOCIAL
    HISTORY OF THE NORTHERN PLAINS AND THE ROCKY MOUNTAINS
    FROM THE EARLIEST WHITE CONTACTS TO THE COMING OF THE
    HOMEMAKER. NEW YORK, NEW YORK: D. APPLETON—CENTURY
    COMPANY, 1941 (HUS).

DIFFENDERFER, MARY M. BY WAGON TRAIN FROM ST. LOUIS TO
    EL PASO IN 1865. ST. LOUIS, MISSOURI: FILES OF THE
    MISSOURI HISTORICAL SOCIETY,.

DRUMM, STELLA M., EDITOR. DOWN THE SANTA FE TRAIL AND INTO
    MEXICO: A DIARY OF SUSAN SHELBY MAGOFFIN, 1846—1847.
    NEW HAVEN, CONNECTICUT: YALE UNIVERSITY PRESS, 1965.

DU BOIS, JOHN VAN DEUSEN. CAMPAIGNS IN THE WEST, 1856—1861.
    THE JOURNALS AND LETTERS OF JOHN VAN DEUSEN DU BOIS.
    TUCSON, ARIZONA: ARIZONA PIONEERS HISTORICAL SOCIETY,
    1949 (HUS).

DUFLOT DE MOFRAS, EUGENE. EXPLORATION DU TERRITOIRE DE
    L'OREGON, DES CALIFORNIES, ET DE LA MERE VEMEILLE,
    EXECUTEE PENDANT LES ANNEES 1840—1841 ET 1842.
    PARIS, FRANCE: A. BERTRAND, 1844.

DYE. RECOLLECTION CALIFORNIA (HC*).

DYER, ALEXANDER BRYDIE. LETTER TO DR. ROBERT JOHNSTON.
    SANTA FE, NEW MEXICO, (HN).

EASTLAND, THOMAS; EASTLAND, JOSEPH. "TO CALIFORNIA THROUGH
    TEXAS AND MEXICO. THE DIARY AND LETTERS OF THOMASB.
    EASTLAND AND JOSEPH G. EASTLAND, HIS SON". CALIFORNIA
    HISTORICAL SOCIETY QUARTERLY, VOL. 18 (JUNE 1939),
    PP. 99—135 (HSW HC).

ECCLESTON, ROBERT. OVERLAND TO CALIFORNIA ON THE SOUTHWESTERN
    TRAIL, 1849. BERKELEY, CALIFORNIA: UNIVERSITY OF
    CALIFORNIA PRESS, 1950 (HC).

EDGAR, WILLIAM. "ONE WAGON TRAIN BOSS OF TEXAS". OUTING,
    VOL. 39 (JAN 1902), PP. 381—83.

EDWARDS, MARCELLUS BALL. JOURNAL OF MARCELLUS BALL
    EDWARDS. IN RALPH P BIEBER, S MARCHING WITH THE ARMY
    OF THE WEST, CALIFORNIA: ARTHUR H. CLARK COMPANY, 1936
    (HUS).

EHINGER, AUGUSTUS FREDERICK. DIARY OF HIS TRAVELS FROM
    ILLINOIS TO MEXICO AND DURING HIS SERVICE AS AMEMBER
    OF COMP. H, SECOND REGIMENT ILLINOIS VOLUNTEERS, JULY
    1846—JUNE 1847. IN THE POSSESSION OF COLONEL CHARLES
    F. WARD, ROSWELL, NEW MEXICO (HSW).

EL PASO. PASO MEXICAN REVOLUTION (HT*).

EMORY, WILLIAM H. NOTES OF A MILITARY RECONNOISSANCE.
    ALBUQUERQUE, NEW MEXICO: UNIVERSITY OF NEW MEXICO
    PRESS, 1951 (HUS).

EMORY, WILLIAM H. REPORT OF WILLIAM H. EMORY, MAJOR FIRST
    CAVALRY AND U. S. COMMISSIONER, UNITED STATES
    AND MEXICAN BOUNDARY SURVEY. 34TH CONGRESS. 1ST
    SESSION, (EX. DOC. NO. 135) (HUS).

ESCOBAR, ROMULO. "MEMORIAS DEL PASO DEL NORTE". BOLETIN
    DE LA SOCIEDAD CHIHUAHUENSE DE ESTUDIOS HISTORICOS,
    VOL. 4 (OCTOBER 20, 1946 AND NOVEMBER 20, 1946),
    PP. 61—62.

ESPINOSA Y TELLO, JOSE. BEING THE NARRATIVE OF THE VOYAGE
    MADE IN THE YEAR 1792 BY THE SCHOONERS"SUTIL"
    AND "MEXICANA" TO EXPLORE THE STRAIT OF FUCA:
    TRANSLATED FROM THE SPANISH WITH AN INTRODUCTION BY
    CECIL JANE; ILLUSTRATED...LONDON, 1930. REPRINTED
    BY: NEW YORK, NEW YORK AND LONDON, GREAT BRITAIN: AMS
    PRESS,INC., (HSA).

ESPINOSA, FRAY ISIDRO FELIX DE. CRONICA DE LOS COLEGIOS
    DE PROPAGANDA FIDE DE LA NUEVA ESPANA. WASHINGTON,
    D. C.: ACADEMY OF AMERICAN FRANCISCAN HISTORY, 1964
    (HS).

ESPINOSA. FOLK ART SPANISH NEW MEXICO (HN*).

ESPINOSA. "THE LEGEND SIERRA AZUL" (HN*).

EVANS, ALBERT S. OUR SISTER REPUBLIC; A GALA TRIP THROUGH
    TROPICAL MEXICO IN 1869—70. HARTFORD, CONNECTICUT:
    COLUMBIAN BOOK COMPANY, 1870.

EVANS, GEORGE W. B. MEXICAN GOLD TRAIL, THE JOURNAL OF
    A 49ER. SAN MARINO, CALIFORNIA: HUNTINGTON LIBRARY
    PUBLICATION, 1945 (LI).

EVANS, MRS. ROSALIE. THE ROSALIE EVANS LETTERS FROM
    MEXICO. NEW YORK, NEW YORK, 1926 (HM).

FAGES, PEDRO. EXPEDITION TO SAN FRANCISCO BAY IN 1770,
     DIARY OF PEDRO FAGES.   EDITED BY HERBERT EUGENE
     BOLTON, ACADEMY OF PACIFIC COAST HISTORY PUBLICATIONS
     II, BERKELEY 1911.

FALCONER, THOMAS. LETTERS AND NOTES ON THE TEXAN SANTA
     FE EXPEDITION, 1841-1842.   NEW YORK: DAUBER AND PINE
     BOOKSHOPS INC, 1930.

FALCONER, THOMAS. NOTES OF A JOURNEY THROUGH TEXAS AND
     NEW MEXICO IN THE YEARS 1841 AND 1842.   NEW YORK:
     DAUBER AND PINE, 1930 (LI).

FARNHAM.   TRAVELS CALIFORNIAS SCENES PACIFIC (HC*).

FERGUSON, PHILIP GOOCH. 'DIARY OF PHILIP GOOCH FERGUSON.'
     IN RALPH P. BIEBER, (ED). MARCHING WITH THE ARMY OF
     THE WEST.

FERLINGHETTI, LAWRENCE. THE MEXICAN NIGHT; TRAVEL JOURNAL.
     NEW YORK: NEW DIRECTIONS PUBLISHING CORPORATION, 1970
     (LI).

FERNANDEZ DURO.   DON DIEGO DE PENALOSA SU DESCUBRIMENTO
     (HS*).

FERNANDEZ NAVARETTE.   COLECCION DE VIAJES DESCUBRIMIENTOS
     (HS*).

FERNANDEZ-LOPEZ.   VIAJE DE DON RAMON DE SAGRA LOS (LMA*).

FERRIS, W. A. LIFE IN THE ROCKY MOUNTAINS.   DENVER: FRED
     A. ROSENSTOCK. OLD WEST PUBLISHING COMPANY, 1940 (HSW).

FIELD, STEPHEN J. PERSONAL REMINISCENCES OF EARLY DAYS
     IN CALIFORNIA WITH OTHER SKETCHES: TO WHICH IS ADDED
     THE STORY OF HIS ATTEMPTED ASSASSINATION BY A FORMER
     ASSOCIATE ON THE SUPREME BENCH OF THE STATE.   (1893)
     NEW YORK, NEW YORK: DA CAPO PRESS, INC, 1968 (HC).

FIERRO BLANCO.   JOURNEY FLAME (AN*).

FINLEY, JAMES BRADLEY. AUTOBIOGRAPHY OF REVEREND JAMES
     B. FINLEY: OR, PIONEER LIFE IN THE WEST (1853).   NEW
     YORK, NEW YORK: DA CAPO PRESS, INC., 1969 (HSW).

FISHER.   LIFE MEXICO: LETTERS FANNY CALDERON (LI*).

FITCH MARIA ANTONIAF CARRILLO, NATALIA ELIJIA.   NARRACION
     DE LA VIUDA FITCH.   MS. BANCROFT LIBRARY..

FLORES, J. J. DIARIO.   MS, IN POSSESSION OF MARIA LUISA
     FLORES.

FLORES, JOSEPH A. LIBRO MEMORIAL.   MS, IN POSSESSION OF
     MARIA LUISA FLORES.

FOIK, PAUL J. (TRANS). "CAPTAIN DON DOMINGO RAMON S DIARY
    OF HIS EXPEDITION INTO TEXAS IN 1716". PRELIMINARY
    STUDIES OF THE TEXAS CATHOLIC HISTORICAL SOCIETY, VOL.
    2 NO. 5 (1933) (HT HS).

FONT, FRAY PEDRO. DIARIO CORTO.   MS, ARCHIVO GENERAL DE
    LA NACION..

FONT, FRAY PEDRO. DIARIO QUE FORMO, EN EL VIAJE QUE HIZO
    A MONTERREY Y PUERTO DE SAN FRANCISCO MS.   MS,
    ARCHIVO GENERAL DE LA NACION..

FORRESTAL, PETER P. (TRANS.). "THE SOLIS DIARY OF 1767".
    PRELIMINARY STUDIES OF THE TEXAS CATHOLIC HISTORICAL
    SOCIETY, VOL. 1 NO. 6 (1931).

FREEMAN. ACCOUNT RED RIVER LOUISIANA, (HT*).

FREMONT, COL. JOHN CHARLES. EXPLORING EXPEDITION TO THE
    ROCKY MOUNTAINS, OREGON AND CALIFORNIA.   BUFFALO:
    GEORGE H. DERBY AND COMPANY, 1850 (LI).

FREMONT, JOHN CHARLES. MEMOIRS OF MY LIFE, INCLUDING IN
    THE NARRATIVE FIVE JOURNEYS OF WESTERN EXPLORATION
    DURING THE YEARS 1842, 1843-44, 1845-6-7, 1848-49,
    1853-4.   CHICAGO: BELFORD, CLARKE, AND COMPANY, 1887.

FUENTE, PEDRO JOSE DE LA. "DIARY OF PEDRO JOSE DE
    LA FUENTE, CAPTAIN OF THE PRESIDIO OF EL PASO
    DELNORTE, JANUARY—JULY, 1765".   SOUTHWESTERN
    HISTORICAL QUARTERLY, VOL. 60 (OCTOBER 1956), PP.
    260-81 (HT).

GALLEGOS, HERNAN. "RELACION".   NEW MEXICO HISTORICAL
    REVIEW, VOL. 2 (OCTOBER 1927), PP. 334-362 (HN).

GARCES.   TRAIL SPANISH PIONEER; DIARYITENARY (HS*).

GARCES.   DIARIO DE ENTRADA QUE SE PRACTICA (HS*).

GARDNER.   HIDDEN HEART BAJA (HS*).

GERSTACKER, FRIEDRICK. WILD SPORTS IN THE FAR WEST.
    PHILADELPHIA: LIPPINCOTT, 1876 (HSW).

GILPATRICK, W. WANDERING IN MEXICO.   LONDON, 1912.

GLASGOW, BRIG. GEN. WILLIAM J. CONVERSATIONS.   CONVERSATIONS
    AT EL PASO, TEXAS (LI).

GODAY.   WHEN I WAS GIRL MEXICO (LI*).

GONZALEZ DE MENDOZA, JUAN. 'A BRIEF RELATION OF TWO
   NOTABLE VOYAGES, THE FIRST MADE BY FRIER AUGUSTIN RUYZ
   ...; THE SECOND BY ANTONIO DE ESPEJO ... TAKEN OUT
   OF THE HISTORYOF CHINA WRITTEN BY FRIER JUAN GONZALES
   DE MENDOCA.'   IN THE VOYAGES, TRAFFIQUES AND
   DISCOVERIES OF FOREIGN VOYAGERS...BY RICHARD HAKLUYT,
   VOLUME 10.

GORDON.   INHERIT EARTH; STORIES MEXICAN   (LI*).

GORDON.   INHERIT EARTH; STORIES MEXICAN   (LI*).

GRANT, ULYSSES SIMPSON.   PERSONAL MEMOIRS OF U. S. GRANT.
   NEW YORK: THE CENTURY COMPANY, 1895.

GREEN, THOMAS JEFFERSON.   JOURNAL OF THE TEXIAN EXPEDITION
   AGAINST MIER.   AUSTIN: THE STECK COMPANY, 1935.

GREEN, THOMAS JEFFERSON.   JOURNAL OF THE EXPEDITION AGAINST
   MIER: WITH REFLECTIONS UPON THE PRESENT POLITICAL
   AND PROBABLE FUTURE RELATIONS OF TEXAS, MEXICO AND
   THE UNITED STATES.   NEW YORK: HARPER, 1845 (HSW HT).

GREGG, JOSIAH.   COMMERCE OF THE PRAIRIES OR THE JOURNAL
   OF A SANTA FE TRADER DURING EIGHT EXPEDITIONS ACROSS
   THE GREAT WESTERN PRAIRIES AND A RESIDENCE OF NEARLY
   NINE YEARS IN NORTHERN MEXICO.   PHILADELPHIA: J. W.
   MOORE, 1851 (HSW).

GREGG, JOSIAH.   DIARY AND LETTERS OF JOSIAH GREGG:
   SOUTHWESTERN ENTERPRISES, 1840-1847.   EDITED
   BY MAURICE GARLAND FULTON, WITH AN INTRODUCTION BY
   PAUL HORGAN. NORMAN: UNIVERSITY OF OKLAHOMA PRESS,
   1941 (HSW).

GREGG, JOSIAH.   DIARY AND LETTERS OF JOSIAH GREGG:
   EXCURSIONS IN MEXICO AND CALIFORNIA,1847-1850.
   EDITED BY MAURICE GARLAND FULTON, WITH AN INTRODUCTION
   BY PAUL HORGAN. NORMAN: UNIVERSITY OF OKLAHOMA PRESS,
   1944 (HSW).

GREGG, JOSIAH.   THE COMMERCE OF THE PRAIRIES.   EDITED BY
   MILO MILTON QUAIFE. LINCOLN, NEBRASKA: UNIVERSITY OF
   NEBRASKA PRESS, 1967 (HSW).

GREGG, JOSIAH.   THE COMMERCE OF THE PRAIRIES, THE JOURNAL
   OF A SANTA FE TRADER.   REPRINT FROM THE EDITION OF
   1844. DALLAS: SOUTHWEST PRESS, 1933 (HSW).

GREGG, KATE L., ED.   THE ROAD TO SANTA FE.   ALBUQUERQUE,
   NEW MEXICO: UNIVERSITY OF NEW MEXICO PRESS, 1968.

GUTIERREZ CE LARA, JOSE BERNARDC. "CIARY...1811–1812".
     ELIZABETH H. WEST (TRANS) AMERICAN HISTORICAL REVIEW,
     VOL. 5 NO. 34 (HS).

HAINES, FRANCIS D., JR., (ED). THE SNAKE COUNTRY EXPEDITION
     OF 1830–1831. NORMAN OKLAHOMA: UNIVERSITY OF
     OKLAHOMA PRESS, 1971.

HAKLUYT, RICHARD. THE VOYAGES, TRAFFIQUES AND DISCOVERIES
     OF FOREIGN VOYAGERS... IN THE "NAVIGATIONS" BY RICHARD
     HAKLUYT (ED ERNEST RHYS). (VOLUME 2 OF THE PRINCIPAL
     VOYAGES).. NEW YORK: E. P. DUTTON & CO., 1928.

HALE.   TWENTY FOUR YEARS COWBOY RANCHMAN   (HT*).

HALL, JAMES. NOTES ON THE WESTERN STATES: CONTAINING
     DESCRIPTIVE SKETCHES OF THEIR SCIL, CLIMATES,
     RESOURCES AND SCENERY.   (1838) NEW YORK, NEW YORK:
     DA CAPO PRESS, INC., 1969.

HALL, JAMES. THE WEST: ITS COMMERCE AND NAVIGATION.
     (1848). NEW YORK, NEW YORK: DA CAPO PRESS, INC., 1969.

HAMILTON.   EARLY CAY OIL TALES MEXICO (HM*).

HAMMOND.   NARRATIVES CORONADO EXPEDITION   (HSW*).

HASTINGS, LANSFORD W. THE IMIGRANT'S GUIDE TO OREGON AND
     CALIFCRNIA.   NEW YORK, NEW YORK: DA CAPO PRESS, INC.,
     1969.

HASTINGS, MONTANA. CLASSIFICACION Y ESTUDIO ESTADISTICO
     DE 3,719 ALUMNOS, DE LAS ESCUELAS S.   MEXICO CITY:
     PUBLICATIONS OF THE SECRETARY OF PUBLIC EDUCATION,
     1929 (LI).

HATCHER.   "LETTERS EARLY AMERICAN TRAVELER--MARY (HT*).

HITCHCOCK, ETHAN ALLEN. FIFTY YEARS IN CAMP AND FIELD.
     DIARY OF MAJOR GENERAL ETHAN ALLEN HITCHCOCK, U. S.
     A.. EDITED BY W. A. CROFFUT, NEW YORK: G. P.
     PUTNAM'S SONS, 1909.

HOFFMAN, FRITZ L. DIARY OF THE ALARCON EXPEDITION INTO
     TEXAS, 1718–1719, FRAY FRANCISCO CELIZ.   ALBUQUERQUE,
     NEW MEXICO: QUIVIRA SOCIETY, 1935 (HT).

HOFFMAN, FRITZ LEC (TRANS AND ED). DIARY OF THE ALARCON
     EXPEDITION INTO TEXAS, 1718–1719.   THE QUIVIRA
     SOCIETY, LOS ANGELES; REPRINTED IN 1967 BY ARNO PRESS,
     NEW YORK,.

HOLLEY, MARY AUSTIN. LETTERS OF AN EARLY AMERICAN
     TRAVELER.   EDITED BY MATTIE AUSTIN HATCHER. DALLAS:
     SOUTHWEST PRESS, 1933.

HOLLEY, MARY AUSTIN. TEXAS.   BALTIMORE: ARMSTRONG AND
    PLASKITT, 1833, REPRINT LEXINGTON, KENTUCKY: CLARKE,
    1836, REPRINT AUSTIN: STECK, 1935 (HT).

HOLLEY, MARY AUSTIN. THE TEXAS DIARY, 1835—1838.   AUSTIN:
    THE UNIVERSITY OF TEXAS PRESS, 1965.

HORN.   LIFE TOM HORN, GOVERNMENT SCOUT (HSW*).

HOWBERT, IRVING J. MEMORIES OF A LIFETIME IN THE PIKE'S
    PEAK REGION.   GLORIETA, NEW MEXICO: RIO GRANDE PRESS,
    INC.,.

HOWE.   LIFE LETTERS GEORGE BANCROFT (HSW*).

HUGHES, GEORGE W. MEMOIR DESCRIPTIVE OF THE MARCH OF A
    DIVISION OF THE UNITED STATES ARMY UNDER THE COMMAND
    OF BRIGADIER GENERAL JOHN E. WOOL, FROM SAN ANTONIO
    DEBEXAR, IN TEXAS, TO SALTILLO, IN MEXICO.   SENATE
    EXECUTIVE DOCUMENT 32, 31ST CONGRESS, 1ST SESSION.
    WASHINGTON, (1850) (HT).

HUGHES, GEORGE W. REPORT OF THE SECRETARY OF WAR,
    COMMUNICATING A MAP.   SENATE EXECUTIVE DOCUMENT 32,
    31ST CONGRESS, 1ST SESSION.

HUGHES, JOHN TAYLOR. DONIPAHAN'S EXPEDITION AND THE
    CONQUEST OF NEW MEXICO AND CALIFORNIA.   TOPEKA,
    KANSAS: THE AUTHOR, 1907 (HSW).

JAMES, THOMAS. THREE YEARS AMONG THE INDIANS AND MEXICANS.
    WATERLOO, ILLINOIS, 1846. REPRINTED SAINT LOUIS:
    MISSOURI HISTORICAL SOCIETY, 1916.

JAMES, THOMAS. THREE YEARS AMONG THE INDIANS AND MEXICANS.
    NEW YORK: CITADEL PRESS, 1966.

JEFFERSON, THOMAS. TRAVELS IN THE CALIFORNIA AND SCENES
    IN THE PACIFIC OCEAN.   CALIFORNIA CENTENNIAL
    EDITIONS, 1947 (LI HC).

KEMP. MAURY. FROM THE MEMOIRS OF MAURY KEMP.   TYPESCRIPT,
    EL PASO PUBLIC LIBRARY.

KENDALL, G. WILKENS. SANTA FE EXPEDITIONS.   LONDON: WILLY
    AND PUTNAM, 1844 (HN).

KENDALL, GEORGE WILKINS. NARRATIVE OF AN EXPEDITION ACROSS
    THE GREAT SOUTHWESTERN PRAIRIES, FROM TEXAS TO SANTA
    FE.   LONDON. HENRY WASHBURN, 1847. NEW YORK. HARPER
    & BROTHERS 1844. ANN ARBOR: UNIVERSITY MICROFILM, 1966.

KENDALL, GEORGE WILKINS. NARRATIVE OF THE TEXAS SANTA FE
    EXPEDITION.   CHICAGO: LAKESIDE PRESS, 1929.

KENDALL, GOERGE WILKINS. NARRATIVE OF THE TEXAS SANTA FE
     EXPEDITION.   LONDON: HENRY WASHBOURNE, 1847.

KENLY, JOHN REESE. MEMOIRS OF A MARYLAND VOLUNTEER, WAR
     WITH MEXICO, IN THE YEARS 1846-7-8.   PHILADELPHIA:
     J. B. LIPPINCOTT AND CO., 1873 (HSW).

KIRKHAM, STANTON DAVIS.   MEXICAN TRAILS; A RECORD OF TRAVEL
     IN MEXICO, 1904-07, AND A GLIMPSE AT THE LIFE OF THE
     MEXICAN INDIAN.   NEW YORK: PUTNAM, 1909.

KLUCKHOHN, CLYDE. TO THE FOOT OF THE RAINBOW.   GLORIETA,
     NEW MEXICO: RIO GRANDE PRESS, INC., 1967 (HSW).

KOHLBERG, ERNST. LETTERS, 1875-1877.   TRANSLATED FROM
     THE GERMAN. ORIGINAL DOCUMENTS. EL PASO PUBLIC
     LIBRARY. <EXCERPTS QUOTED BY PERMISSION OF EL PASO
     PUBLIC LIBRARY.> (HT).

KOHLBERG, WALTER. A TRANSLATION OF THE LETTERS WRITTEN
     BY ERNEST KOHLBERG, 1875, 1876, 187.   MS IN POSSESSION
     OF MRS. LEONARD GOODMAN (HT).

KRESS, MARGARET KENNEY. "DIARY OF A VISIT OF INSPECTION
     TO THE TEXAS MISSIONS MADE BY FRAY GASPARJOSE DE SOLIS
     IN THE YEAR 1767-1768".   SOUTHWESTERN HISTORICAL
     QUARTERLY, VOL. 35 NO. 1 (1931), PP. 28-76 (HS).

LA RENAUDIERE, PHILLIPE FRANCOIS DE.   MEXICQUE ET GUATEMALA.
     PARIS: FIRNIM DIDOT, 1843 (HM).

LAFORA, NICOLAS DE.   RELACION DE UN VIAJE QUE HIZO A LOS
     PRESIDIOS INTERNOS SITUADOS EN LA FRONTERA DE
     LA AMERICA SEPTENTRIONAL.   MEXICO: EDITORIAL PEDRO
     ROBLEDO, 1939.

LANCE, CHARLES H.; CARROLL, L. RILEY. THE SOUTHWESTERN
     JOURNALS OF ADOLPH F. BANDELIER, 1883-1884.
     ALBUQUERQUE, NEW MEXICO: UNIVERSITY OF NEW MEXICO
     PRESS, 1970 (HSW).

LANE, FRANKLIN KNIGHT. LETTERS OF FRANKLIN K. LANE,
     PERSONAL AND POLITICAL.   EDITED BY ANNE WINTERMUTE
     LANE AND LOUISE HERRICK VAIL. BOSTON: HOUGHTON MIFFLIN
     COMPANY, 1922.

LANGE, CHARLES H. ; RILEY, CARROL. THE SOUTHWESTERN
     JOURNALS OF ADOLPH F. BANDELIER, 1880-1882.
     ALBUQUERQUE, NEW MEXICO: UNIVERSITY OF NEW MEXICO
     PRESS, (HSW).

LANSING, ROBERT. WAR MEMOIRS.   INDIANAPOLIS: BOBBS-MERRILL
     COMPANY, 1935.

LAPEROUSE GALAUP, JEAN FRANCOIS DE. A VOYAGE AROUND THE
     WORLD.   TRANSLATION J. JOHNSON, LONDON, 1798.

LARKIN, THOMAS OLIVER. PRIVATE AND OFFICIAL CORRESPONDENCE.
    MS. BANCROFT LIBRARY.

LEAKEY, JOHN. THE WEST THAT WAS: FROM TEXAS TO MONTANA.
    DALLAS: SOUTHERN METHODIST UNIVERSITY PRESS, 1958 (HSW).

LEAKEY, JOHN; YOST, NELLIE SNYDER. THE WEST THAT WAS: FROM
    TEXAS TO MONTANA. LINCOLN, NEBRASKA: UNIVERSITY OF
    NEBRASKA PRESS, 1965 (HSW).

LECLERCQ, JULES JOSEPH. VOYAGE AU MEXIQUE, DE NEW YORK
    A VERA-CRUZ, EN SUIVANT LES ROUTE DE TERRE. PARIS:
    HACHETTE, 1885.

LEE, ROBERT E. RECOLLECTIONS AND LETTERS OF GENERAL ROBERT
    E. LEE. NEW YORK: DOUBLEDAY PAGE, 1904.

LINVINGSTON-LITTLE, D. E. THE MEXICAN WAR DIARY OF THOMAS
    D. TENNERY. NORMAN: UNIVERSITY OK OKLAHOMA PRESS,
    1970.

LOOK, GEORGE. REMINISCENCES. COPY IN POSSESSION
    OF WYNDHAM K. WHITE (LI).

LOPEZ DE GOMARA, FRANCISCO. GENERAL HISTORIE OF THE WEST
    INDIES. LONDON: J. M. DENT, 1928 (HS).

LORD, WALTER (ED). THE FREMANTLE DIARY: BEING THE JOURNAL
    OF LIEUTENANT COLONEL ARTHUR JAMES LYON FREMANTLE,
    COLDSTREAM GUARDS, ON HIS THREE MONTHS IN THE SOUTHERN
    STATES. BOSTON: LITTLE, BROWN, 1959 (HSW).

MAGOFFIN, SUSAN (SHELBY). DOWN THE SANTA FE TRAIL AND INTO
    MEXICO; THE DIARY OF SUSAN SHELBY MAGOFONN, 1846-1847..
    EDITED BY STELLA M. DRUMM. NEW HAVEN, YALE UNIVERSITY
    PRESS, 1962.

MARCY, COL. RANDOLPH B. 30 YEARS OF ARMY LIFE ON THE
    BORDER. NEW YORK: HARPER, 1866.

MARCY, COL. RANDOLPH B. THE PRAIRIES TRAVELER. WIALIAMSTON,
    MASSACHUSETTS: CORNER HOUSE, 1968.

MARR, COLONEL JAMES. "IN THE OLD DAYS". EL PASO HEARLD,
    (FEBRUARY 2 1, MARCH7, 1943).

MARSHALL, THOMAS MAITLAND. "ST. VRAIN'S EXPEDITION TO THE
    GILA IN 1846". SOUTHWESTERN HISTORICAL QUARTERLY,
    VOL. 19 (JANUARY 1916), PP. 251-260.

MARTIN. "FROM TEXAS TO CALIFORNIA 1849: (HT*).

MARTIN. "FROM TEXAS TO CALIFORNIA 1849: (HT*).

MARTIN. "FROM TEXAS TO CALIFORNIA 1849: (HT*).

MARTIN, THOMAS S. NARRATIVE OF FREMONT'S EXPEDITION,
    1845-1847.   MS. BANCROFT. LIBRARY,.

MAVERICK, MARY ANN. MEMOIRS.   SAN ANTONIO, ALAMO PRINTING
    CO.

MAYER, WILLIAM. EARLY TRAVELERS IN MEXICO, 1534-1816.
    MEXICO, 1961.

MC CONNELL, H. H. FIVE YEARS A CAVALRYMAN.   JACKSBORO,
    TEXAS: J.N. ROGERS, 1889 (LI).

MC KEE.   NARRATIVE SURRENDER COMMAND U   (HN*).

MC NARY, JAMES GRAHAM. THIS IS MY LIFE.   ALBUQUERQUE:
    UNIVERSITY OF NEW MEXICO PRESS, 1956.

MENDOZA, DIEGO HURTADO DE. ALGUNAS CARTAS DE DON DIEGO
    HURTADO DE MENDOZA.   NEW YORK, NEW YORK AND LONDON,
    GREAT BRITAIN: AMS PRESS INC,.

MERIWETHER, DAVID. MY LIFE IN THE MAOUNTAINS AND ON THE
    PLAINS.   NORMAN: UNIVERSITY OF OKLAHOMA PRESS, 1965
    (HSW).

MERRIAM.   WAY OUT WEST: RECOLLECTIONSTALES   (LI*).

MILLER.   WEST ALFRED JACOB MILLER (1837)   (AR*).

MILLER, E. T. "THE CONNECTION OF PENALOSA WITH THE
    LA SALLE EXPEDITION".   QUARTERLY OF THE TEXAS STATE
    HISTORICAL ASSOCIATION, VOL. 5 NO. 2 (1901),
    PP. 97-112 (HS HT).

MONTLEZUN, BARON DE. VOYAGE FAIT DANS LE ANNEES 1816 ET
    1817, DE NEW YORCK A LA NOUVELLE-ORLEANS ET DE
    L'ORENOQUE AU MISSISSIPPI ...(1818).   CAMBRIDGE:
    HARVARD UNIVERSITY PRESS, 1949 (HUS).

MONTOYA.   NEW MEXICO 1602. JUAN DE MONTOYAS   (HS*).

MORALES- CARRICN ARTURO. THE EXPEDITION OF FRANCISCO
    XAVIER MINA.   UNIVERSITY OF TEXAS, MASTER'S THESIS
    (1936) (HSW).

MOREAU DE SAINT- MERY, MEDERIC LOUIS ELIE. VOYAGE
    AUX ETATS-UNIS DE L'AMERIQUE, 1793-1798.   CAMBRIDGE:
    HARVARD UNIVERSITY PRESS, 1949 (HUS).

MOREHEAD, CHARLES R. PERSONAL RECOLLECTIONS OF CHARLES
    R. MOREHEAD.   DONIPHAN'S EXPEDITION. KANSAS CITY,
    MISSOURI: BRYANT AND DOUGLAS BOOK AND STATIONERY
    COMPANY, 1907 (HUS).

NEIHARDT.   SPLENDID WAYFARING: EXPLOITSADVENTURES   (HSW*).

NUTTALL, THOMAS. A JOURNAL OF TRAVEL INTO THE ARKANSAS
TERRITORY DURING THE YEAR 1819. PHILADELPHIA: T.
H. PALMER, 1821. REPRINT, GLENDALE, CALIFORNIA: CLARK,
1905.

OBER, FREDERICK ALBION. TRAVELS IN MEXICO AND LIFE AMONG
THE MEXICANS. BOSTON: ESTES AND LAURIAT, 1884.

OLIVA, LEO E. SOLDIERS ON THE SANTA FE TRAIL. NORMAN,
OKLAHOMA: UNIVERSITY OF OKLAHOMA PRESS, 1967.

OLMSTED, FREDERICK LAW. A JOURNEY THROUGH TEXAS: OR, A
SADDLE TRIP ON THE SOUTH-WESTERN FRONTIERWITH
A STATISTICAL APPENDIX. NEW YORK: DIX, EDWARDS AND
COMPANY, 1857.

OLMSTED, R. R. (ED). SCENES OF WONDER AND CURIOSITY FROM
HUTCHINGS CALIFORNIA MAGAZINE1856-1861. BERKELEY:
HOWELL-NORTH, 1962.

ORTEGA, JOSE FRANCISCO. PERSONAL REMINISCENCES.
MS. BANCROFT LIBRARY.

OTERO. MY LIFE FRONTIER (HN*).

PARKMAN, FRANCIS. THE JOURNALS OF FRANCIS PARKMAN. NEW
YORK: HARPER AND BROTHERS, 1947.

PARKMAN, FRANCIS. THE OREGON TRAIL. PHILADELPHIA: JOHN
C. WINSTON COMPANY, 1931.

PATTIE, JAMES C. PERSONAL NARRATIVE OF JAMES O. PATTIE
OF KENTUCKY. CLEVELAND: ARTHUR H. CLARK COMPANY,
1905.

PATTIE, JAMES C. THE PERSONAL NARRATIVE OF JAMES O. PATTIE
OF KENTUCKY. CHICAGO: LAKESIDE PRESS, 1930.

PEON. COMO VIVEN LOS MEXICANOS EN LOS (LI*).

PERKINS, WILLIAM. THREE YEARS IN CALIFORNIA: JOURNAL OF
LIFE AT SONORA, 1849-1852. BERKELEY, CALIFORNIA:
UNIVERSITY OF CALIFORNIA PRESS, 1964.

PERKINS, WILLIAM. WILLIAM PERKINS' JOURNAL. BERKELEY
AND LOS ANGELES: UNIVERSITY OF CALIFORNIA PRESS, 1964.

PERKINS, WILLIAM. EL CAMPO DE LOS SONORAENSES. BUENOS
AIRES, 1937.

PERSHING, JOHN JOSEPH. LETTERS (UNPUBLISHED) 1915-1917.
PRIVATE COLLECTION, WASHINGTON, D.C..

PERSHING, JOHN JOSEPH. MY EXPERIENCES IN THE WORLD WAR.
NEW YORK: FREDERICK H. STOKES COMPANY, 1931.

PICCOLO, S.J., PADRE FRANCISCO MARIA. INFORME DEL ESTADO
    DE LA NUEVA CRISTIANDAD.   MADRID, 1962.

PIKE, ZEBULCN MONTEGOMERY. EXPLCRATORY TRAVELS THROUGH
    THE WESTERN TERRITORIES OF NORTH AMERICA, COMPRISING
    A VOYAGE FROM ST. LOUIS, ON THE MISSISSIPPI, TO THE
    SOURCE OF THAT RIVER, AND A JCURNEY THROUGH THE
    INTERIOR OF LOUISIANA, AND THE NORTHEASTERN PROVINCES
    OF NEW SPAIN. PERFORMED IN THE YEARS OF 1805, 1806,
    807, BY ORDER OF THE GOVERNMENT OF THE UNITED STATES.
    DENVER: H. LAWRENCE AND COMPANY, 1889.

PIKE, ZEBULON MONTEGOMERY. THE EXPEDITIONS OF ZEBULON
    MONTGOMERY PIKE DURING THE YEARS 1805-6-7.   EDITED
    BY ELLIOTT COUES. NEW YORK: FRANCIS P. HARPER, 1895.

PIKE, ZEBULCN MONTEGOMERY.   THE SOUTHWESTERN EXPEDITION
    OF ZEBULON M PIKE.   CHICAGO: R. R. DONNELLEY
    AND SONS, 1925.

PIKE, ZEBULON.   AN ACCOUNT OF EXPEDITIONS TO THE SOURCES
    OF THE MISSISSIPPI AND THROUGH THE EASTERN PARTS OF
    LOUISIANA TO THE SOURCES OF THE ARKANSAS, KANSAS, LA
    PLATTE, AND PIERRE JUAN RIVERS; PERFORMED BY ORDER
    OF THE GOVERNMENT OF THE UNITED STATES DURING
    THE YEARS 1805, 1806, 1807 AND A TOUR THROUGH
    THE INTERIOR PARTS CF NEW SPAIN WHEN CONDUCTED THROUGH
    THESE PROVINCES BY ORDER OF THE CAPTAIN GENERAL IN
    THE YEAR 1807.   PHILADELPHIA, 1810.

PORTOLA, GASPAR DE. DIARY OF GASPAR DE PORTOLA DURING THE
    CALIFORNIA EXPEDITION OF 1760-1770.   DONAL EUGENE
    SMITH (ED), ACADEMY OF PACIFIC COAST HISTORY,
    PUBLICATICN I. BERKELEY, 1909.

POWELL, H. M. T.   THE SANTA FE TRAIL TO CALIFCRNIA,
    1849-1852. THE JOURNAL AND DRAWINGS H.M.T. POWELL..
    SAN FRANCISCO, 1931. REPRINTEC BY NEW YORK, NEW YORK
    AND LONDON, GREATBRITAIN: AMS PRESS, INC, 1931.

POWELL, J. W.   EXPLORATIONS OF THE COLORADO RIVER AND ITS
    CANYONS.   NEW YORK: DOVER PUBLICATIONS, 1895.
    CHICAGO, ILLINOIS: UNIVERSITY OF CHICAGO PRESS, 1957.

POWELL, JOHN WESLEY.   DOWN THE COLORACO: CIARY CF THE FIRST
    TRIP THROUGH THE GRAND CANYON.   NEW YORK, NEW YORK:
    E. P. DUTTON AND COMPANY, INC, 1969.

PRICE, THOMAS W.   BRIEF NOTES TAKEN ON A TRIP TO THE CITY
    OF MEXICO IN 1878.   PRIVATELY PRINTED, 1878.

PURCHAS, SAMUEL.   PURCHAS: HIS PILGRIMAGE (1625).
    GLASGCW: MACLEHOSE, 1906.

QUAIFE, MILO MILTON <ED.>. THE JOURNALS OF CAPTAIN
MERIWETHER LEWIS AND SERGEANT JOHN ORDWAY KEPT ON THE
EXPEDITION OF WESTERN EXPLORATION, 1803-1806.
MADISON, WISCONSIN: THE SOCIETY PRESS, 1916, 1965 (HSW).

REID, JOHN C. REID'S TRAMP; OR A JOURNAL OF THE INCIDENTS
OF TEN MONTHS TRAVEL THROUGH TEXAS, NEW MEXICO,
ARIZONA, SONORA, AND CALIFORNIA. REPRINT, AUSTIN,
TEXAS: THE STECK COMPANY, 1935 (HSW).

RICHARDSON, WILLIAM H. "JOURNAL OF WILLIAM H. RICHARDSON".
MISSOURI HISTORICAL REVIEW, VOL. 22 (OCTOBER
1927-JULY 1928), PP. 193-236, 331-360, 511-542.

RICHIE, ED. CONVERSATIONS. EAGLE PASS, TEXAS,.

ROBINSON, JACOB S. A JOURNAL OF THE SANTA FE EXPEDITION
UNDER COLONEL DONIPHAN: NARRATIVES OF THE TRANS-MISSISSIPPI
FRONTIERS (1848). PORTSMOUTH JOURNAL PRESS, 1848.
REPRINT, PRINCETON: PRINCETON UNIVERSITY PRESS, 1932
(HSW).

ROBLES, VITO ALESSIO (ED). DIARIO Y DERROTERO DE LO
CAMINADO, VISTA Y OBSERVADO, EN LA VISITA QUE HIZO
A LOS PRESIDIOS DE LA NUEVA ESPANA SEPTENTRIONAL EL
BRIGADIER PEDRO DE RIVERA CON UNA INTRODUCCION Y NOTAS
POR VITO ALESSIO ROBLES. MEXICO: TALLER AUTOGRAPHIA,
1946 (HS).

RODRIGUEZ, J. M. RODRIGUEZ MEMOIRS OF EARLY TEXAS. SAN
ANTONIO, TEXAS: STANDARD PRINTING COMPANY, 1961 (HT).

ROMERO, J. M. MEMORIAS. MS. BANCROFT LIBRARY.

RONQUILLO, E. W. NOTES ON "RIO GRANDE DRY" IN 1851 AND
1863. WRITTEN AUGUST 23, 1877. ORIGINAL DOCUMENT.
SAN MARINO, HENRY E. HUNTINGTON LIBRARY. (EXCERPTS
QUOTED BY PERMISSION OF THE HUNTINGTON LIBRARY.).

ROSS, PATRICIA. "VILLAGE O F MANY BLESSINGS". TRAVEL,
(FEBRERO 1935), PP. 25-37.

RUSSELL, JOHN BARTLETT. PERSONAL NARRATIVE. NUEVA YORK,
1954.

RYAN, WILLIAM. PERSONAL ADVENTURES IN UPPER AND LOWER
CALIFORNIA. LONDON, 1850.

SAGE, RUFUS B. LETTERS AND PAPERS 1836-1837. GLENDALE:
THE ARTHUR H. CLARK COLLECTION, 1956.

SANCHEZ, JOSE MARIA. "A TRIP TO TEXAS IN 1828".
SOUTHWESTERN HISTORICAL QUARTERLY, VOL. 29 NO.
4 (1926), PP. 249-288 (HT).

SANCHEZ, JOSE MARIA. VIAJE A TEXAS -- EN 1828-1829, DIARIO
   DEL TENIENTE D. JOSE MARIA SANCHEZ, MIEMBRO DE
   LA COMISICN DE LIMITES. MEXICO: PAPELES HISTORICOS,
   1939 (HT).

SCHARMANN, HERMANN B. OVERLAND JOURNEY TO CALIFORNIA, FROM
   THE PAGES OF A PIONEER'S DIARY. FREEPORT, NEW YORK:
   BOOKS FOR LIBRARIES, INC., 1918.

SCHROEDER. COLONY MOVE: GASPAR CASTANO DE (HS*).

SCOTT, GENERAL WINFIELD. MEMOIRS. SHELDON, 1864.

SCOTT, HUGH LENNOX. PAPERS OF MAJOR GENERAL HUGH L. SCOTT.
   MS. WASHINGTON. THE LIBRARY OF CONGRESS.

SCOTT, HUGH LENNOX. SOME MEMORIES OF A SOLDIER.
   NEW YORK: THE CENTURY COMPANY, 1928.

SERRA, FRAY JUNIPERO. DIARIO DE LORETO A SAN DIEGO 1769.
   ORIGINAL EN ARCHIVO GENERAL DE LA NACION. (HC).

SERRA, FRAY JUNIPERO. JUNIPERO SERRA TO VICEROY BUCARELI,1772.
   LESLEY BYRD SIMPSON (TRANS AND ED). NOTICIAS. SANTA
   BARBARA HISTORICAL SOCIETY, 1961.

SERRA, FRAY JUNIPERO. WRITINGS OF JUNIPERO SERRA. EDITED
   BY ANTOINE TIBESAR. WASHINGTON, ACADEMY OF AMERICAN
   FRANCISCAN HISTORY, 1955-66..

SESPINOSA. "FIRST EXPEDITION VARGAS INTO (HN*).

SHALER, WILLIAM. JOURNAL OF A VOYAGE BETWEEN CHINA AND
   THE NORTHWESTERN COAST OF AMERICA, MADE IN 1804.
   CLAREMONT, CALIFORNIA: SAUNDERS STUDIO PRESS, 1935.

SHERIDAN, PHILIP H. PERSONAL MEMOIRS. NEW YORK: CHARLES
   L. WEBSTER COMPANY, 1888.

SILGREAVES, LORENZC. EXPEDITION DOWN THE ZUNI AND COLORADO
   RIVERS. GLORIETA, NEW MEXICO: RIO GRANDE PRESS, INC.,.

SIMPSON, R. E. ALONG OLD TRAILS OF NEW MEXICO AND ARIZONA.
   BOSTON: HOUGHTON, 1929 (HN).

SMITH, GEORGE WINSTON:JUDAH, CHARLES (EDS.). CHRONICLES
   OF THE GRINGOS: THE U. S. ARMY IN THE MEXICAN WAR,
   1846-1848. ALBUQUERQUE, NEW MEXICO: UNIVERSITY OF
   NEW MEXICO PRESS, 1968 (HSW).

SOLIS, FRAY GASPAR JOSE DE. "DIARY OF A VISIT OF INSPECTION
   OF THE TEXAS MISSIONS MADE BY FRAY GASPARJOSE DE SOLIS
   IN THE YEAR 1767-1768". SOUTHWESTERN HISTORICAL
   QUARTERLY, VOL. 35 NO. 1 (1931), PP. 28-76 (HT).

SOLIS, FRAY GASPAR JOSE DE. "THE SOLIS DIARY OF 1767".
PRELIMINARY STUDIES OF THE TEXAS CATHOLIC HISTORICAL
SOCIETY, VOL. 1 NO. 6 (1931) (HT).

STEELE, JAMES W. FRONTIER ARMY SKETCHES. ALBUQUERQUE,
NEW MEXICO: UNIVERSITY OF NEW MEXICO PRESS, (LI).

STEELE, JAMES W. OLD CALIFORNIA DAYS. CHICAGO: W. B.
CONLY CO., 1893 (LI).

STEPHENS. INCIDENTS TRAVEL YUCATAN (AN*).

STONE, MARTHA. AT THE SIGN OF MIDNIGHT: THE CONCHEROS
DANCES OF MEXICO. TUCSON, ARIZONA: UNIVERSITY OF
ARIZONA PRESS, (LI).

STRONG, GEORGE TEMPLETON. THE DIARY OF GEORGE TEMPLETON
STRONG. NEW YORK: THE MACMILLAN COMPANY, 1952.

STUART, EVANS R. TRANSLATION FROM THE SPANISH OF THE
ACCOUNT BY THE PILOT FERREL OF THE VOYAGE OF CABRILLO
ALONG THE WEST COAST OF NORTH AMERICA, IN 1542, WITH
INTRODUCTORY NOTES BY H. W. HENSAW. WASHINGTON, 1879
(HS).

STUART, ROBERT. ON THE OREGON TRAIL: ROBERT STUART'S
JOURNEY OF DISCOVERY (1812-1813). NORMAN, OKLAHOMA:
UNIVERSITY OF OKLAHOMA PRESS, 1953 (HUS).

SUMMERHAYES, MARTHA. 'VANISHED ARIZONA; RECOLLECTIONS OF
ARMY LIFE 187090.' PHILADELPHIA, LIPPINCOTT 1908;
SALEM, MASSACHUSETTS: THE SALEM PRESS COMPANY: 1911;
CHICAGO: LAKESIDE PRESS (HA).

SUMPTER, JESSE. LIFE OF JESSE SUMPTER, OLDEST CITIZEN OF
EAGLE PASS, TEXAS, COMMENCED TOBE WRITTEN DOWN MAY
30, 1902. TAKEN DOWN BY HARRY WARREN. FINISHED JUNE
14, 1906. ORIGINAL DOCUMENT. TYPESCRIPT. EAGLE PASS,
TEXAS, PRIVATE COLLECTION. (HT).

SWETT. PUBLIC EDUCATION CALIFORNIA: (ED*).

TAMAYO, JORGE L. EPISTOLARIO DE BENITO JUAREZ; SELECCION,
PROLOGO Y NOTAS DE JORGE L. TAMAYO. MEXICO. MEXICO:
FONDO DE CULTURA ECONOMICA, 1957 (HM).

TAYLOR. EXPLORATION LOWER CALIFORNIA (HC*).

TAYLOR. ELDORADO, OR ADVENTURES PATHEMPIRE (HC*).

THOMPSON, CORONEL WILLIAM. REMINISCENCES OF A PIONEER.
SAN FRANCISCO, 1912.

THOMPSON, WADDY. RECOLLECTIONS OF MEXICO. NEW YORK:
WILEY AND PUTNAM, 1846 (LI).

THOREAU. S.   WRITINGS HENRY DAVIC THOREAU   (LI*).

THWAITES.   ANALYTICAL INDEX TO SERIES   (HSW*).

THWAITES.   ANDRE MICHAUXS TRAVELS INTOKENTUCKY   (HSW*).

THWAITES.   BRACKENRIDGES JOURNAL UP MISSOURI   (HSW*).

THWAITES.   BRADBURYS TRAVELS INTERIOR AMERICA   (HSW*).

THWAITES.   BUTTRICKS VOYAGES, 1812-19.EVENSS   (HSW*).

THWAITES.   COMPRISING SERIES ORIGINAL PAINTINGS   (HSW*).

THWAITES.   CUMINGS TOUR TO WESTERN COUNTRY   (HSW*).

THWAITES.   EARLY WESTERN TRAVELS, 1748-1846   (HSW*).

THWAITES.   FARNHAMS TRAVELS GREAT WESTERN   (HSW*).

THWAITES.   FAUXS MEMORABLE DAYS AMERICA   (HSW*).

THWAITES.   FAUXS MEMORABLE DAYS AMERICA: (HSW*).

THWAITES.   FLAGGS FAR WEST, 1836-37: PART   (HSW*).

THWAITES.   FLAGGS FAR WEST: PART II. DE   (HSW*).

THWAITES.   FLINTS LETTERS AMERICA, 1818-20   (HSW*).

THWAITES.   GREGGS COMMERCE PRAIRIES: PART   (HSW*).

THWAITES.   HULMES JOURNAL, 1818-19. FLOWERS   (HSW*).

THWAITES.   JAMESS ACCOUNTS S. H. LONGS   (HSW*).

THWAITES.   JOHN LONGS JOURNAL, 1768-1782   (HSW*).

THWAITES.   JOURNALS OF: CONRAD WEISER, 1748   (HSW*).

THWAITES.   MAXIMILIAN, PRINCE WIEDS, TRAVEL   (HSW*).

THWAITES.   NUTTALLS TRAVELS INTO ARKANSAS   (HSW*).

THWAITES.   OGDENS LETTERS WEST, 1821-23   (HSW*).

THWAITES.   PALMERS JOURNAL TRAVELS OVER   (HSW*).

THWAITES.   PATTIES PERSONAL NARRATIVE,1824-30   (HSW*).

THWAITES.   ROSSS ADVENTURES FIRST SETTLERS   (HSW*).

THWAITES.   WYETHS OREGON, OR SHORT HISTORY   (HSW*).

TIERNEY, LUKE, PARSONS, WILLIAM B (ET AL). PIKE'S PEAK
    GOLD RUSH GUIDEBOOKS OF 1859. EDITED BY LEROY R.
    HAFEN. GLENDALE: ARTHUR H. CLARKE COMPANY, 1941 (HSW
    HC).

TURNER, HENRY SMITH. THE ORIGINAL JOURNALS OF HENRY SMITH
    TURNER. DWIGHT L. CLARKE. NORMAN, OKLAHOMA:
    UNIVERSITY OF OKLAHOMA PRESS, 1966 (HSW).

TURRELL, CHARLES B. CALIFORNIA NOTES. SAN FRANCISCO,
    1876.

TYSON. DIARY OF A PHYSICIAN IN CALIFORNIA. ??NO
    INFORMATION??, (HC).

VALDES, DOROTEA. REMINISCENCIAS. MANUSCRIPT. BANCROFT
    LIBRARY..

VALLEJO. REMINISCENCIAS HISTORICAS DECALIFORNIA (HC*).

VARGAS ZAPATA LUJAN PONCE DE LEON. FIRST EXPEDITION
    VARGAS INTONEW (HS*).

VIGNE, GODFREY THOMAS. TRAVELS IN MEXICO, SOUTH AMERICA,
    ETC., ETC.. LONDON: W. H. ALLEN, 1863.

WALLACE, LEW. AN AUTOBIOGRAPHY. NEW YORK: HARPER AND
    BROTHERS, 1906.

WALLIS, MRS. JONNIE LOCKHART. SIXTY YEARS ON THE BRAZOS--THE
    LIFE AND LETTERS OF DR. JOHN WASHINGTON LOCKHART,
    1824-1900. (1930). REPRINTED BY NEW YORK, NEW YORK:
    ARNO PRESS, 1971 (HT).

WALSH, THOMAS J. PAPERS OF SENATOR THOMAS J. WALSH..
    MSS. WASHINGTON, THE LIBRARY OF CONGRESS..

WHIPPLE , LT. A. W. PATHFINDER IN THE SOUTHWEST:
    THE ININERARY OF LIEUTENANT A.W. WHIPPLE DURING HIS
    EXPLORATIONS FOR A RAILWAY ROUTE FROM FORT SMITH TO
    LOS ANGELES IN THE YEARS 1853-1854. NORMAN,
    OKLAHOMA: UNIVERSITY OF OKLAHOMA PRESS, 1941 (HSW).

WHITLOCK, BRAND. JOURNAL. NEW YORK: APPLETON-CENTURY
    COMPANY, 1936.

WILSON, IRIS HIGBIE. NOTICIAS DE NUTKA: AN ACCOUNT OF
    NOOTKA SOUND IN 1792. SEATTLE: UNIVERSITY OF
    WASHINGTON PRESS, 1970 (HS).

WINSHIP. JOURNEY CORONADO, 1540-1542,CITY (HS*).

WISE. LOS GRINGOS (HC*).

WISE. LOS GRINGOS (HC*).

WISE.   LOS GRINGOS OR INSIDE VIEW MEXICO (HC*).

WISLIZENUS, A. MEMOIR OF A TOUR THROUGH NORHTERN MEXICO,
     CONNECTED WITH COLONEL DONIPHAN'S EXPEDITION, 1846—47.
     WASHINGTON: TIPPIN AND STREEPEN, PRINTERS, (1848).
     30TH CONGRESS, 1ST SESSION. SENATE MISCELLANEOUS
     NUMBER 26. (HM).

WISTER, OWEN. OWEN WISTER OUT WEST, HIS JOURNALS AND
     LETTERS.   UNIVERSITY OF CHICAGO PRESS, 1958 (HSW).

WROTH.   "THE FRONTIER PRESICIOS NEW SPAIN: (HS*).

YLARREQUI SALAZAR.   DATOS DE LOS TRABAJOS ASTRONOMICOS
     (HM*).

ZARATE SALMERON (PADRE).   RELACIONES DE TODAS LAS COSAS
     (HS*).

AARONS, ALFRED C. B
AARONS, ALFRED C., GORDON, BARBARA Y. AND STEWART, WILLIAM A. (ED) ED
    LA
ABBOTT, E. C. (TEDDY BLUE), AND SMITH, HELENA HUNTINGTON LI
ABBOTT, W. L. EC
ABE, CLIFFORD ED PY
ABEL, ANNIE LOUISE)ED. HUS
ABEL, LIONEL LI
ABEL, THEODORE RE SI
ABELARDO LMA
ABELS, ROBERT HUS
ABERLE, SOPHIE B. AN SC
ABERNETHY, FRANCIS E. HT LI
ABEYTA, HECTOR EC SI
ABRAHAM, HENRY JULIAN LW SO
ABRAHAM, WILLARD ED SO
ABRAMS, WILLARD ED
ABREU GOMEZ, ERMILIO HM
ABUDU, ASSIBI O. EC HC
ACHESON, SAM AND OH CONNELL, JULIE, A.H. HT TJ
ACHESON, SAM H. HT LI
ACHESON, SAM H.,)ET AL.,EDS HT LI
ACHESON, SAM,)ET AL AT LI
ACKERMAN, R. E. ED HN
ACOSTA, M. ED
ACOSTA, OSCAR ZETA LW SO
ACOSTA, OSCAR ZETA LMA
ACOSTA, ROBERT TORRES ED
ACOSTA, ROBERTO HM HSW
ACUNA, RUDOLPH AN HM HSW LJE PL SO
AD INTERIM COMMITTEE ON LATIN AMERICAN WORK (REP) RE
ADAIR, A. GARLAND, AND CROCKETT, M. H. SR. EDS. HT TJ
ADAIR, DOUG EC PL
ADAIR, JOHN HSW SO
ADAIR, JOHN AND BUNKER, ROBERT SO
ADAM, V. G. HC SO
ADAMIC, LOUIS HS SI SO
ADAMS STATE COLLEGE B
ADAMS STATE COLLEGE. CENTER FOR CULTURAL STUDIES B ED HCO
ADAMS STATE COLLEGE. THE CENTER FOR CULTURAL STUDIES AN
    SO
ADAMS STATE COLLEGE. POTTS, ALFRED, ET AL (EDITORS) B
ADAMS STATE COLLEGE, CENTER FOR CULTURAL STUDIES AN SO
ADAMS, ANDY LI
ADAMS, ELEANOR B.)ED. AND TRANS. HN TJ
ADAMS, ELEANOR B., AND FRAY ANGELICO CHAVEZ HN TJ
ADAMS, ELEANOR B., AND SCHOLES, FRANCE V. B LMA
ADAMS, ELEANOR BURNHAM AND FRAY ANGELICO CHAVEZ HN HS RE
ADAMS, EMMA H. LI
ADAMS, HENRY HUS PL
ADAMS, JOHN, AND JOHN QUINCY HUS PL
ADAMS, RAMON B LI
ADAMS, RAMON F. B LI
ADAMS, RICHARD N. SO
ADAMS, ROBERT H. HCO RE

ASTER, RICHARD FREDERICK JR. LW SI SO
ASTIGARRAGA, L. M. LJE
ASTROV, MARGOT LI
ASTROV, MARGOT)ED LMA SO
ATENCIO, TOMAS C. EC SO
ATHEARN, ROBERT G. EC HSW
ATHERTON, GERTRUDE HC LI
ATKIN, RONALD HM
ATKIND, ELIZABETH H. LJE
ATKINS, E. LAE
ATKINS, JAMES A. AN ED SO
ATKINS, RUTH ELLEN ED SO
ATKINSON, MARY JOURDAN HT SO
ATKINSON, ROSA M. ED PY
ATL AN AR
ATONNA, PETER B SO
ATUNEZ Y ACEVEDO, RAFAEL ED
ATWATER, ERNESTA E. EC SI
ATWATER, JAMES D. AND RUIZ, RAMON EDUARDO HM
ATWOOD, E. BAGBY LA
AUDIO VISUAL DEPARTMENT, BOARD OF NATIONAL MISSIONS,
     UNITED PRESBYTERIAN FILM
AUDOBON, JOHN JAMES HSW HT TJ
AUDUBON, JOHN W. HSW TJ
AUERBACH, JEROLD EC LW
AUSTIN, MARY AR ED HS LI RE
AUSTIN, MATTIE ALICE HT LW
AUSTIN, ROBERT CALVIN SO
AUSTIN, STEPHEN F. HSW HT
AVEDANO, FAUSTO LMA
AVERETT, WALTER. HS LA
AVILA, MANUEL AN HM
AVINS, ALFRED LW SO
AYALA DE SIFUENTES, LORETTA LW SO
AYER, GEORGE W. ED LA
AYERS, ATLEE BERNARD AR HM
AYETA, FATHER FRANCISCO HS TJ
AZUELA, MARIANO HM LI LMA
B'NAI B'RITH B
BABBITT, IRVING LI
BABCOCK, CORA C AN SO
BABCOCK, EDNA E., HELEN KWAPIL, AND EDITH ANN BACH (EDS) LJS
BABIN, PATRICK B
BACA AN MD
BACA, EMILIE M. SO
BACA, FIDEL GARCIA ED
BACH, MARCUS SO
BACKUS, BERTHA RHODES EC LA
BADAL, ALDEN W. ED
BADGER, JOSEPH E. LI
BAERRESEN, DONALD EC HM HSW
BAEZ, JOAN LMA
BAEZ, SERGIO MADERO LJS
BAGDIGAN, BEN H. SO
BAHR, J. ED
BAILEY JESSIE BROMILOW HN HS

BENAVIDES, ILMA MARIANA HT
BENDER, A. B. HSW HT
BENDIX, REINHARD SO
BENEDICT, RUTH AN
BENES, RONALD J. HS
BENITENDI, WILMA LEE, (ET AL) ED SI
BENITEZ, FERNANDO HM HS
BENJAMIN, ROBERT SPIERS, (ED) SI SO
BENNETT, CATHERINE ED
BENNETT, CHARLES E. HS
BENNETT, FAY EC SO
BENNETT, FREDERICK D HUS TJ
BENNETT, JAMES A. HN HUS
BENNETT, WENDELL C. HM SO
BENSON, NETTIE LEE, (ED) HM HS
BENTLEY, HAROLD W. LA
BENTLEY, HAROLD W. AND SAVAGE, H. J. LA
BENTON, THOMAS HART LI
BENTON, WILLIAM (ED) LJS
BERARD, BERN LW SI
BERDINE, I. HC HM HS
BERE, MAY ED
BERERTER, CARL AND ENGELMANN, SIEGFRIED ED
BERESFORD, MARTHA HM
BERGER, JOHN A. HC HS
BERGER, JOSEF LI
BERGER, MAX ED HT
BERGER, MORROE LW
BERISTAIN DE SOUZA, DR. DON JOSE MARIANO B HSA
BERKSON, ISAAC B. SI SO
BERLANDIER, JEAN LUIS HT
BERLE, ADOLF AUGUSTUS HSA PL
BERLIN, IRVING N. ED
BERLITZ SCHOOLS OF LANGUAGES OF AMERICA LJS
BERLITZ, C. AND STRUMPEN-DARRIE, ROBERT (EDS) LJS
BERMAN, J. J. AND HIGHTOWER, J. EC
BERMAN, MARK L. ED
BERNAL, E. M., JR. ED SO
BERNAL, IGNACIO AR HM
BERNAL, IGNACIO AND SOUSTELLE, JACQUE AR HM
BERNAL, IGNACIO. B
BERNAL, J. J. ED SO
BERNAL, JOSEPH ED
BERNAL, RAFAEL AN
BERNALILLO COUNTY, NEW MEXICO. BOARD OF EDUCATION ED HN
BERNARD, W. ED PY
BERNE, ERIC AN
BERNEY, T. D. AND COOPER, R. L. LA
BERNEY, TOMI EISENBERG, ANNE B
BERNHARDT, GEORGE MARCELLUS EC
BERNSTEIN, HARRY EC
BERNSTEIN, MARVIN DAVID EC
BERNSTEIN, SAUL LW SO
BERQUIN-DUVALLON HS TJ
BERREY, LESTER V. AND VANDEN BARK, MELVIN LA

BRADFORD, H. F. ED SO
BRADING, D. A. HM
BRADISH, DAMARIS ED PY
BRADSHAW, BENJAMIN SPENCER AN SO
BRADY, A. M. B
BRADY; DONALD V. AT
BRAGER, GEORGE, AND SPECHT, HARRY SO
BRAMBILA, ALBERTO M. PELAYO LA
BRAMELD, THEODORE ED
BRANCH, DOUGLAS LI
BRAND, DONALD D. EC GE HS
BRANDENBERGER, WILLIAM SAMUEL HT
BRANDENBURG, FRANK RALPH HM
BRANDES, RAY HS
BRANDES, RAY (TRANS.) HS TJ
BRANDT, LARRY JACOB ED PY
BRANIGAN, JOHN ED
BRANLEY, FRANKLYN LJS
BRANLEY, FRANKLYN M. LJS
BRANN, RICHARD R. EC LW SI SO
BRANTLEY, HAROLD ED
BRANTLEY, HAROLD C. ED
BRASE, CHARLES LCUNG HSW
BRATRUD, THEODORE EDWARD PL SO
BRATT, CHARLES ED SO
BRATTEN, JAMES H. SI SO
BRAULT, G. J. ED LAF
BRAUND, ROBERT A. (ET AL) ED
BRAUNSHAUSEN, NICOLAS ED
BRAYER, HERBERTO HS LW
BREBNER, JOHN BARTLET HS
BRECKENRIDGE, W. M. LI
BRECKINRIDGE, H. M. TJ
BREITHAUPT, THELMA LI
BREMER, LAVILLE. HS
BREND, RUTH M. LA
BRENGELMAN, FREDERICK H. AND MANNING, JOHN C. LA
BRENIZER, LESTER C. (TRANS.) TJ
BRENNER, ANITA AN HM HS LJE RE
BRESETTE, LINNA E. SI SO
BRESWICK, WILLIAM NEALE EC
BRETT, DOROTHY LI
BREWER, J. MASON LI
BREWER, SAMUEL AARON, JR. ED HSA
BREWSTER, MELA SEDILLO AN AT
BREYMANN, WALTER N. HM
BRIARCLIFF MANOR B
BRIARCLIFF, REINDORP B
BRICKMAN, WILLIAM (ED.) ED SO
BRIDGERS, W. W. HSW HT
BRIDGES, CLARENCE ALLAN HSW HT
BRIDGES, CLARENCE ALLEN HSW
BRIDGES, J. W. AND COLER, L. E. ED PY SO
BRIDGES, WILLIAM LJS
BRIEGEL, KAYE PL SO

CALEF, WESLEY CARR GE SO
CALEXICO UNITED SCHOOL DISTRICT ED LAE
CALHOUN, ROBERT ERRCL AR
CALI, FRANCOIS AR
CALIFORNIA ADULT EDUCATION BUREAU SO
CALIFORNIA ADVISORY COMMITTEE TO THE U. S. COMMISSION OF CIVIL RIGHTS HC
     LW SO
CALIFORNIA APPRENTICESHIP STANDARDS DIVISION ED HC
CALIFORNIA CITIZENS' COMMITTEE ON CIVIL DISTURBANCES IN LOS ANGELES LW
     SO
CALIFORNIA COMMISSION CF IMMIGRATION AND HOUSING SI SO
CALIFORNIA COMMITTEE FOR THE STUDY OF TRANSIENT YOUTH ED   SI SO
CALIFORNIA COMMITTEE TO SURVEY THE AGRICULTURAL LABOR RESOURCES
       OF SAN J EC
CALIFORNIA CORRECTIONS DEPARTMENT LW SO
CALIFORNIA CRIMINAL LAW ANC ENFORCEMENT DIVISION LW
CALIFORNIA CRIMINAL STATISTICS BUREAU LW
CALIFORNIA DEPARTMENT OF HEALTH, BUREAU OF OCCUPATIONAL HEALTH EC
     LW MD
CALIFORNIA DEPARTMENT OF INDUSTRIAL RELATIONS EC HC SO
CALIFORNIA DEPARTMENT OF PUBLIC HEALTH MD
CALIFORNIA DEPARTMENT OF THE YOUTH AUTHORITY EC LW SC
CALIFORNIA ECONOMIC OPPORTUNITY OFFICE EC
CALIFORNIA ELEMENTARY AND SECONDARY EDUCATICN BUREAU HC
CALIFORNIA ELEMENTARY SCHOOL PRINCIPAL'S ASSOCIATION ED
CALIFORNIA FEDERATION FOR CIVIC UNITY EC MD
CALIFORNIA GOVERNOR EC
CALIFORNIA GOVERNOR C. C. YOUNG'S MEXICAN FACT FINDING COMMITTEE EC   LW
CALIFORNIA GOVERNOR C. C. YOUNG'S MEXICAN FACT-FINDING CCMMITTEE EC
     HC SO
CALIFORNIA GOVERNOR'S ADVISORY COMMITTEE ON CHILDREN AND YOUTH EC   SI
CALIFORNIA GOVERNOR'S COMMITTEE TO SURVEY THE AGRICULTURAL LABOR
        RESOURC EC
CALIFORNIA GOVERNOR'S COMMITTEE TO SURVEY THE AGRICULTURAL
        RESOURCES OF EC
CALIFORNIA GOVERNOR'S CONFERENCE ON FARM WORKERS' HOUSING EC
CALIFORNIA GOVERNOR'S OFFICE, SELECTED CALIFORNIA NEWSPAPER
        PUBLISHERS, EC
CALIFORNIA HISTORICAL SOCIETY HC
CALIFORNIA INTERGROUP RELATIONS BUREAU ED SO
CALIFORNIA LIBRARY ASSOCIATION B
CALIFORNIA MINER'S ASSOCIATION EC SO
CALIFORNIA NURSES ASSOCIATION EC SI
CALIFORNIA OFFICE OF THE GOVERNOR EC SO
CALIFORNIA STATE ADVISORY COMMITTEE ON CIVIL RIGHTS ED LW
CALIFORNIA STATE ADVISORY COMMITTEE TO THE UNITED STATES COMMISSION
        ON C ED
CALIFORNIA STATE BOARD OF FORESTRY EC
CALIFORNIA STATE COLLEGE B
CALIFORNIA STATE COLLEGE AT LOS ANGELES B
CALIFORNIA STATE COLLEGE AT SACRAMENTO AN SO
CALIFORNIA STATE COLLEGE AT SACRAMENTO. LIBRARY B
CALIFORNIA STATE COLLEGE, FRESNO B
CALIFORNIA STATE COLLEGE, HAYWARD B
CALIFORNIA STATE COLLEGE, LONG BEACH B
CALIFORNIA STATE COLLEGE, LOS ANGELES B
CALIFORNIA STATE COLLEGE, SAN BERNADINO B

CALIFORNIA STATE COLLEGE, SAN BERNARDINO B
CALIFORNIA STATE COLLEGE, SAN FERNANDO VALLEY B
CALIFORNIA STATE COLLEGE, SAN JOSE B
CALIFORNIA STATE COMMISSION ON FAIR EMPLOYMENT PRACTICES EC
CALIFORNIA STATE COMMISSION ON HOUSING AND IMMIGRATION SI SO
CALIFORNIA STATE COMMITTEE FOR THE STUDY OF TRANSIENT YOUTH SO
CALIFORNIA STATE DEPARTMENT OF CORRECTIONS LW SO
CALIFORNIA STATE DEPARTMENT OF EDUCATION B ED HC MD SI
CALIFORNIA STATE DEPARTMENT OF EDUCATION. MEXICAN AMERICAN
      EDUCATION RE ED
CALIFORNIA STATE DEPARTMENT OF EDUCATION. DIVISION OF IMMIGRANT
      EDUCATIO ED
CALIFORNIA STATE DEPARTMENT OF EDUCATION. MEXICAN-AMERICAN
      EDUCATION RE ED
CALIFORNIA STATE DEPARTMENT OF EMPLOYMENT ED HC HSW SO
CALIFORNIA STATE DEPARTMENT OF INDUSTRIAL RALATIONS EC
CALIFORNIA STATE DEPARTMENT OF INDUSTRIAL RELATIONS EC ED
      HC PY SI SO
CALIFORNIA STATE DEPARTMENT OF INDUSTRIAL RELATIONS,
      OF IMMIGRATION AND EC
CALIFORNIA STATE DEPARTMENT OF JUSTICE EC LW SI
CALIFORNIA STATE DEPARTMENT OF PUBLIC HEALTH. BUREAU OF CHILD HYGIENE EC
CALIFORNIA STATE DEPARTMENT OF PUBLIC HEALTH, BUREAU OF CHILD HYGIENE EC
CALIFORNIA STATE DEPARTMENT OF SOCIAL WELFARE AN ED HSW MD SO
CALIFORNIA STATE DIVISION OF CRIMINAL LAW AND ENFORCEMENT LW SO
CALIFORNIA STATE DIVISION OF FARM LABOR SERVICES EC SI
CALIFORNIA STATE FAIR EMPLOYMENT PRACTICES DIVISION EC
CALIFORNIA STATE LAW LIBRARY B LW
CALIFORNIA STATE LEGISLATURE. JOINT COMMITTEE ON AGRICULTURE
      AND LIVEST EC
CALIFORNIA STATE LEGISLATURE. JOINT COMMITTEE ON HIGHER EDUCATION ED
CALIFORNIA STATE LEGISLATURE. SENATE COMMITTEE ON EDUCATION ED
CALIFORNIA STATE LEGISLATURE. SENATE FACTFINDING SUBCOMMITTEE
      ON UN-AME EC LW
CALIFORNIA STATE LEGISLATURE. ASSEMBLY EC ED
CALIFORNIA STATE LEGISLATURE. ASSEMBLY COMMITTEE ON AGRICULTURE EC
CALIFORNIA STATE LEGISLATURE. COMMITTEE ON AGRICULTURE EC
CALIFORNIA STATE LIBRARY B
CALIFORNIA STATE MINERALOGIST GE HC
CALIFORNIA STATE MINING BUREAU GE
CALIFORNIA STATE OFFICE OF ECONOMIC OPPORTUNITY EC
CALIFORNIA STATE OFFICE OF MINERALOGY GE
CALIFORNIA STATE OFFICE OF PLANNING EC
CALIFORNIA STATE POLYTECHNIC COLLEGE B
CALIFORNIA STATE POLYTECHNIC COLLEGE, SAN LUIS OBISPO B
CALIFORNIA STATE RELIEF ADMINISTRATION EC
CALIFORNIA STATE RELIEF ADMINSTRATION EC
CALIFORNIA UNIVERSITY AT LOS ANGELES B
CALIFORNIA UNIVERSITY AT SANTA BARBARA B
CALIFORNIA UNIVERSITY OF CALIFORNIA, BERKELEY. HELLER COMMITTEE
      FOR RES EC SO
CALIFORNIA UNIVERSITY, BERKELEY B
CALIFORNIA YOUTH AUTHORITY LW SO
CALIFORNIA. DEPARTMENT OF SOCIAL WELFARE SC
CALIFORNIA. GOVERNOR EC PL
CALIFORNIA. GOVERNOR C. C. YOUNG'S MEXICAN FACT COMMITTEE EC
CALIFORNIA. GOVERNOR'S ADVISORY COMMITTEE ON CHILDREN AND YOUTH.
      SUBCO SI

COLORADO DEPARTMENT OF EDUCATION B
COLORADO MIGRANT COUNCIL B
COLORADO MIGRANT COUNCIL PRESS B
COLORADO UNIVERSITY. INSTITUTE OF BEHAVIORAL SCIENCES HCO
      SI SO
COLORADO. COLORADO MIGRANT COUNCIL B ED HCO
COLORADO. GOVERNOR'S SURVEY COMMITTEE EC HCO SI
COLORADO. LEGISLATIVE COUNCIL EC HCO SI
COLORADO. MIGRANT EDUCATION RESEARCH PROJECT EC ED HCO
COLORADO. STATE CIVIL RIGHTS COMMISSION HCO LW SO
COLCRADO. STATE DEPARTMENT OF EMPLOYMENT ED HCO
COLORADO. STATE DEPARTMENT OF INSTITUTIONS HCO LW SO
COLTHARP, LURLINE H. LA
COLTHARP, MARY L. LA
COLTON, RAY C. HUS
COLTON, WALTER HC HUS
COLUMBIA UNIVERSITY B
COLUMBIA UNIVERSITY. BUREAU OF APPLIED SOCIAL RESEARCH SO
COLUMBUS, CHRISTOPHER HS
COLVIN, STEPHEN S. AND ALLEN, RICHARD D. ED LA
COLYER, VINCENT HUS
COMAN, KATHARINE EC HSW
COMANDANCIA DE LA SEGUNDA ZONA MILITAR HM
COMAS, JUAN AN HM
COMERCIO EC
COMFIRT, WILL LEVINGTON LI
COMMAGER, HENRY STEEL HUS
COMMISSION FOR MEXICAN AMERICAN AFFAIRS. CULTURAL DISTRIBUTION CENTER B
COMMISSION ON RACE AND HOUSING EC SO
COMMISSION ON SOCIAL AND ECONOMIC FACTORS EC SO
COMMISSIONER OF INDIAN AFFAIRSCOMMISSIONER-GENERAL
        OF IMMIGRATIONANONYMO HUS
COMMITTEE ON CULTURAL RELATIONS WITH LATIN AMERICA AN SO
COMMITTEE ON MEXICAN LABOR IN CALIFORNIA SI
COMMITTEE ON MODERN LANGUAGES. AMERICAN COUNCIL ON EDUCATION EC
        SI
COMMITTEE ON STUDIES FOR THE GOLDEN ANNIVERSARY WHITE HOUSE
        CONFERENCE F ED
COMMITTEE ON TEACHING ENGLISH TO SPEAKERS OF OTHER LANGUAGES B
COMMONS, JOHN ROGER SI SO
COMMUNITY SERVICE ORGANIZATION. EDUCATION STANDING COMMITTEE SO
COMPTON, NEVILLE EC SI
CON SAFOS NP
CONANT, JAMES BRYANT ED
CONANT, LORA M. SI
CONCHEFF, B. ED LJE
CONDE, C. ED SI
CONDE, CARLOS ED SI
CONDE, CARLOS D. (ED) B
CONDIE, MARGUERITE S. ED
CONDIT, ELEANOR DALY ED
CONDRON, STUART HARKINS HT
CONE, MARY HC TJ
CONFERENCE INTERNATIONALE SUR LE BILINGUISME, LUXEMBURG ED
CONFERENCE ON ADULT BASIC EDUCATION PL SO
CONFERENCE ON EDUCATIONAL PROBLEMS IN THE SOUTHWEST EC
CONFERENCE ON EDUCATIONAL PROBLEMS OF SPECIAL CULTURAL GROUPS ED

COON, GENE L. SO
COON, MARY W. ED
COON, RUBY IRENE ED LAF
COOPER, ELIZABETH K. EC SO
COOPER, JAMES FENIMORE LI
COOPER, JAMES FENIMORE, LI
COOPER, JAMES G. ED LA PY
COOPER, L. G. HN SC
COOPER, LEE LJS
COOPER, LEE P. LJS
COOPER, R. L. ED LA
COOPERATIVE CHILDREN'S BCCK CENTER B
COOPERATIVE PROGRAM FOR EDUCATIONAL OPPORTUNITY ED
COPE, M. EC RE SO
COPE, MALENA LJE
COPELAND, FAYETTE TJ
COPELAND, LLE ILA AND DOVELL, J. E. HS
COPENHAVER, CHRISTINA BOELKE, JOANNE B
COPP, NELSON GAGE EC SO
CORAJE NP
CORAL WAY ELEMENTARY SCHOOL, DADE COUNTY PUBLIC SCHOOLS, MIAMI,
       FLORIDA ED
CORBETT, WILLIAM HSW
CORBIN, RICHARD AND MURIEL CROSBY, ET ED LA
CORBUSIER HA
CORCORAN, LILLIAN HAGUE EC HT
CORDASCO, F. M. ED
CORDASCO, FRANK M. ED HN PL
CORDOVA, ALFRED G. AND JUDAH, CHARLES ED
CORDOVA, FERNANDO A. EC LMA SO
CORDOVA, IGNACIO R. ED
CORDRY, DONALD AND CORDRY, DOROTHY HM SO
CORKER, JEANNE L. EC SO
CORLE, EDWIN HS HSW LI
CORMACK, JOSEPH M. AND BARKER, FREDERICK F. EC LW
CORNELIUS, JOHN SCOTT LI
CORNELL, E. L. AND COXE, W. W. ED
CORNELL, EARL MONROE ED
CORNER, WILLIAM HT
CORNISH, BEATRICE QUIJADA HT
CORNWELL, MARY BELPRE, PURA B
CORNYN, JOHN H. HN
COROMINAS, JUAN LA
CORONA, BERT PL
CORONA, BERT CHARLES ED PY SO
CORONADO MAGAZINE NP
CORONEL, P. ED
CORPIO, M. DEL. SO
CORPUS, S. F. SO
CORTES, HERNAN HSW
CORTES, HERNANDO HS
CORTES, CARLOS E. AN EC HC HSW HT HUS LI LMA SO
CORTES, CARLOS E. AND CAMPBELL, R. ALEX HSW
CORTES, CARLOS E. CASTANEDA, ALFREDO RAMIREZ,
       MANUEL III AND BARRERA, ED MSH
CORTES, CARLOS E. GREEN, ALAN JOSEPH, JAMES AND GINSBERG, ARLIN HSW

EWING, RUSSELL C. HM
EWING, T. W. HCO
EWTON, RALPH W. JR. AND ORNSTEIN, JACOB (EDS) LA
EYRING, EDWARD ED LA
EZELL, PAUL H. HS SC
FABREGA, HORACIO (JR) AND WALLACE, CAROLE ANN. PY
FABREGA, HORACIO SWARTZ, JON D. WALLACE, ANN PY
FACCI, JOSEPH A SI SO
FACTS ON FILE, INC. B
FADERMAN, LILLIAN BRADSHAW, BARBARA SO
FAGES, PEDRO HC PL TJ
FAGG, JOHN E. HSA
FAIRBANKS, G LA
FAIRCHILD, HARRY PRATT SI SO
FAIVRE, LYNN EC PL
FALCONER, THOMAS LI TJ
FALLOWS, MARJORIE EC
FALTIS, J. ED
FANTINI, ALBINO EDWARD MD
FARABEE, ETHEL SADIE HM
FARBER, LT. COLONEL JAMES HT LI
FARENHOLT, MARY K. EC LW MD
FARGO, GEORGE ALBERT ED
FARIAS, MARIA J LA
FARMER, GEORGE L. ED
FARMER, WILLIAM ANDREW ED SO
FARNHAM, CARRIE EVANGELINE HS
FARNHAM, J. T. HC HS
FARNHAM, THOMAS JEFFERSON. HC TJ
FARNUM, MABEL HS
FARQUHAR, FRANCES P., ED. AN HC LI
FARRELL, GRACE A. SO
FARRIS, BUFORD SO
FARRIS, BUFORD BRYMER, RICHARD LW SO
FARRIS, BUFORD HALE, WILLIAM M. SO
FARRIS, FRANCES BRAMLETTE HT
FATOUT, PAUL LA
FAULK , ODIE HS HT
FAULK, ODIE B. B HA HM HS HSW HT
FAULK, ODIE B. BRINKERLOFF, SIDNEY B. HS HSW
FAULK, ODIE B. , ECITOR HCO HS
FAULKNER, EDWARD H. HUS
FAULKNER, HAROLD UNDERWOOD TYLER, KEPNER HUS
FAUNCE, HILDA LI
FAUNCE, LEO WORTHINGTON EC ED SO
FAY, ELIOT GILBERT LI
FEDDER, RUTH EC ED SO
FEDERATION OF EMPLOYMENT AND GUIDANCE SERVICE B
FEDERICO, HELEN LJS
FEELY, J. T. ED
FEERY, ALLISON B. EC SI
FEHRENBACH, T. R. HT
FEHRENBACHER, DON E. HC HSW
FEHRENBACHER, DON E. TUTOROW, NORMAN E. HC
FEINGOLD, GUSTAVE H. SI SO

GAINES, JOHN S. ED HSW
GALARZA, ERNESTO EC ED LJS LMA SO
GALARZA, ERNESTO ET AL EC SO
GALARZA, ERNESTO GALLEGOS, HERMAN SAMORA JULIAN EC SO
GALARZA, ERNESTO SAMORA, JULIAN EC SO
GALBRAITH, CLARE KEARNEY ED
GALINDO, J. EUSEBIO HC
GALLAGHER, F. M. (TRANS.) HN
GALLARDO, LLOYD EC SI
GALLARDO, RUDY SO
GALLEGLY, JOSEPH LI
GALLEGOS, ALBERTO LMA
GALLEGOS, HERNAN HN TJ
GALLEN, A. A. LI
GALLENKAMP, CHARLES HM
GALLOS, EDWARDO L. (EDITOR) HM
GALVAN, R. A. LA
GALVAN, ROBERT A. LA
GALVEZ, BERNARDO DE. HS
GALVIN, SEAN (TRANS.   ED.) HS
GAMBLE, LEO M. ED
GAMBLON, RUTH S. SO
GAMBOA, ERASMO HUS
GAMBRELL, HERBERT AND VIRGINIA HT
GAMBRELL, HERBERT P. HT LI
GAMBRELL, HERBERT, (ED.) HT
GAMBRELL, HERBERT, EDITOR HT
GAMEZ, GEORGE LOPEZ ED
GAMEZ, LUIS EZEQUIEL LA
GAMIO, MANUEL AN HM PY SI SO
GAMIO, MANUEL AND OTHERS AN HM
GANAWAY, LOOMIS MORTON HN
GANILH, ANTHONY HSW LI
GANITH, ANTHONY HSW LI
GANNON, MICHAEL V. HS
GANS, HERBERT J. SC
GANTT, FRED, JR. DAWSON, IRVING G. HAGARD, LUTHER G., JR. (EDITORS) HT
GARAZA, GEORGE J. HT
GARBER, PAUL NEFF HSW
GARCIA BACA, FIDEL ED
GARCIA ICAZBALCETA LA
GARCIA LOYA, DIEGO HM
GARCIA Y CUBAS, ANTONIO GE HM
GARCIA, ANGELA BARAJAS ED
GARCIA, ERNEST FELIX LA
GARCIA, ERNEST J. ED
GARCIA, MARIO T. LMA
GARCIA, MRS. M. SO
GARCIA, RICHARD LMA
GARCIA, ROGELIA O. HS HT
GARCES, FRANCISCO TOMAS HERMENGILDO HS TJ
GARCES, FRAY FRANCISCO HS TJ
GARCIA CUBAS, ANTONIC B GE
GARCIA NIETO, JOSE LJS
GARCIA RUIZ, RAMON LJS

GILBERT, ARNOLD, AND O' ROURKE, PAUL F. EC MD
GILBERT, ARNOLD, AND SCHLOESSER, PATRICIA EC MD SO
GILBERT, EDMUND W. HSW
GILBERT, ENNIS H. ED
GILBERT, FABIOLA CABEZA DE BACA HSW SO
GILBERT, N. LJE
GILBERT, W. H. B
GILES, GEOFFREY JAMES HS
GILL, LOIS J. AND SPILKA, B. ED PY
GILL, MARIO PL SO
GILL, T. J. AND SPILKA, B. ED PY
GILL, WAYNE FILM
GILLESPIE, REV. MSGR. PATRICK (ED.) RE
GILLETT, JAMES B. HT
GILLETTE, GEORGE CURTISS EC
GILLIN, JOHN AN HSA PY SO
GILLINGHAM, ROBERT C. HC
GILLIS, EVERETT A. LI
GILLMOR, FRANCES HM HN LI
GILLMORE, GLADYS HC
GILLMORE, KENNETH O. EC
GILMAN, HARRY EC
GILMORE, J. V. ED
GILMORE, N. RAY HM SO
GILMORE, N. RAY, AND GILMORE, GLADYS W. EC HC
GILPATRICK, W. TJ
GILPIN, LAURA AR SO
GILSTRAP, ROBERT LI
GILTNER, MARY ANNETTE ED
GINBURG, RUTH ED
GINN, A. SO
GINN, JAMES M. HS
GINSBURG, RUTH ED LAF
GINSBURG, SOLOMON WIENER PY SO
GINZBERG, ELI AND BRAY, DONALD W. ED SO
GINZBERG, ELIA ED SO
GIST, NOEL P. SO
GITTELSOHN, A. M., HEMPHILL, E. C., HOLLISTER, A. C. AND BECK, M. D. MD
    SO
GITTINGER, ROY HSW
GITTLER, JOSEPH B. ED. SC
GIVENS, R. A. EC SI
GLADE, WILLIAM PATTON, JR. EC
GLADE, WILLIAM PATTON, JR. AND ANDERSON, C. W. EC PL
GLADNEY, VIRGINIA M. MD SO
GLADWIN, HAROLD S. HSW
GLANE, SAM SO
GLASGOW, BRIG. GEN. WILLIAM J. LI TJ
GLASS, JUDITH CHANIN EC
GLASS, NELLIE MAY ED
GLASSCOCK, C. B. HSW
GLASSCOCK, WILLIAM DONLEY ED HS
GLAZER, NATHAN AND MOYNIHAN, DANIEL PATRICK SO
GLAZER, NATHAN, AND MC ENTIRE DAVIS, EDS SO
GLEASON, DUNCAN GE HC

HUFFORD, CHARLES H. EC SI
HUFFORD, CHARLES HENRY EC SI
HUGHES SO
HUGHES, ANNE E. HS
HUGHES, ELIZABETH ANN EC SO
HUGHES, EVERETT CHERRINGTON, AND HUGHES, HELEN MAC GILL SO
HUGHES, GEORGE W. HT TJ
HUGHES, JOHN F. ET AL ED
HUGHES, JOHN TAYLOR HSW TJ
HUGHES, LOIS S. ED PY
HUGHES, MARIE ED
HUGHES, MARIE AND SANCHEZ, GEORGE ED
HUGHES, MARIE M. AND PALM, REUBEN R. ED
HUGHES, MARIE MORRISON ED LA SO
HUGHES, VERNON HT
HUGHES, W. J. HSW
HUGHEY, A. H. ED
HULET, CLAUDE B
HULL, HARRY E. EC SO
HUMBOLT, ALEXANDER, FREIHERR VON HS
HUME, MARTIN A. HS
HUMPHREY, NORMAN D. SI
HUMPHREYS, R. A. SI
HUNDLEY, NORRIS CECIL HSW
HUNDLEY, NORRIS, JR. HSW
HUNLEY, JOSEPHINE KELLER HT
HUNNICUTT, HELEN MARGARET HM
HUNT, AURORA HUS
HUNT, R. D., AND SANCHEZ, NELLIE V. HC
HUNT, ROCKWELL DENNIS HC
HUNT, WILLIAM ANDREW, JR. ED SI
HUNTER, FLOYD PL
HUNTER, JOHN MARVIN, EC HT LI
HUNTER, RUSSELL VERNON SO
HUNTER, STANLEY M. AR
HUNTER, VICKIE AND HAMMA, ELIZABETH LJE
HUNTER, W. S., AND SOMMER, NEIL E. ED PY
HUNTINGTON LIBRARY B
HUNTINGTON, ELLSWORTH HSA HUS
HUNTLEY, HENRY V. HC
HUPB, LORETTA B. LJS
HURLEY, R. L. SO
HURT, M., JR., AND MISHRA, S. P. ED PY
HURT, WESLEY SO
HURTA, J. CONRAD ED
HUSE HC
HUSE, HOWARD R. LA PY
HUSER, C. W. ED HT
HUSTON, CLEBURNE HT
HUSZAR, GEORGE BARNARD DE, COMPILER SO
HUTCHINS, THOMAS HS
HUTCHINS, WELLS A. HS
HUTCHINSON, CECIL ALAN HS HSA
HUTCHINSON, CORNELIA ED
HUTCHINSON, EDWARD PRINCE SO

LANE, JOHN HART, JR. SO
LANE, LYDIA SPENCER HSW
LANE, MARY B. ED PY
LANG, MARGARET H. HSW LW
LANGE, CHARLES H. HN
LANGE, CHARLES H.   RILEY, CARROL HSW TJ
LANGE, DALE B
LANGFORD, GERALD LI
LANGFORD, WALTER M. LMA
LANGHAM, LOUCILLE GRACE ED MD
LANGLEY, WILLARD ED
LANGNER, THOMAS S. PY SO
LANGSTON, KATHRYN LEE HC RE
LANIER, SIDNEY HT
LANIGAN, MARY C. HC SO
LANNING, FRANK ROBBINS, RUSSELL ED
LANNING, JOHN TATE HS
LANSFORD, WILLIAM DOUGLAS HM LI
LANSING, ROBERT TJ
LANSTROM, BJOUR HS
LAPEROUSE GALAUP, JEAN FRANCOIS DE TJ
LARA-BRAUD, J. RE SO
LARA-BRAUD, JORGE ED RE SO
LAREW, LEONOR A. ED LA
LARKIN, MARGARET LI
LARKIN, THOMAS OLIVER TJ
LARNER, JEREMY HOWE, IRVING SO
LAROUSSE LJS
LARRALDE, CARLOS LMA
LARRALDE, ELSA HM
LARREY, MARTIN GERMIN LMA
LARROYO, FRANCISCO AN
LARSON, OLAF L. HS
LARSON, RICHARD OLSON, JAMES L. ED PY
LARSON, ROBERT W. HN
LASKER, BRUNO AN PY SI SO
LASKER, GABRIEL W. PY SI
LASKER, GABRIEL W.   EVANS, F. G. AN SI
LASSWELL, MARY HT
LASSWELL, THOMAS E. SO
LATHAM, JEAN LEE HT
LATHROP, BARNES F. HT SI
LATTINGH, LUCILE H. (ED.) ED SI
LAUER, JAMES HENRY HS
LAUGHLIN, RUTH HN
LAUMBACH, VERNA HS
LAURENTI, LUIGI EC SO
LAURITZEN, JONREED HS
LAUT, A. C. EC
LAUT, AGNES HSW LI
LAVELL, C. B. ET AL B
LAVELL, C. G. ,ET AL B SO
LAVELL, FRANCIS HN
LAVENDAR, DAVID HSW
LAW, WILLIAM ED

LEWIS, JON EC ED
LEWIS, LLOYD ED
LEWIS, MACMILLAN HUS
LEWIS, MADALYNNE AN AT
LEWIS, OSCAR AN HC
LEWIS, RICHARD   WILSON, JANE (EDS.) HN
LEWIS, WILLIAM FRANCIS 3RD HSA
LEWITON, MINA LJE
LEXAN, JOAN LJE
LEY, WILLY LJS
LEY, WILLY. LJS
LIBRARY OF CONGRESS B
LIBRARY SERVICE TO THE EDUCATIONALLY DISADVANTAGED B
LICHTER, S. O. , ET AL. ED
LIDDLE, GORDON PHILIP ED
LIEBERMAN, MARK HM
LIEBERMAN, PHILIP LA PY
LIEBERSON, STANLEY SO
LIEUWEN, EDWIN HM HSA
LIN, PAUL MING-CHANG AN SO
LINATI, CLAUDIO PL RE
LINK, WILLIAM R. ED
LINN, GEORGE BYRON LA
LINTHICUM, JOHN BUREN ED
LINTON, THOMAS HARVEY ED SO
LINVINGSTON-LITTLE, D. E. TJ
LIPMAN, JEAN AR
LIPPARD, GEORGE LMA
LIPSCHULTZ, ROBERT J. SI
LIPSET, S. M.   BENDIX, R. SO
LIPSET, S. M.   SOLARI ALDO SO
LIPSHULTZ, ROBERT J SO
LIRA, MIGUEL N., AND ZAMORA, VALENTIN (EDS) LJS
LISS, SHELDON B. HT
LISTER, FLORENCE HM
LITTLE, LAWRENCE B
LITTLE, WILLSON HT SO
LIVERMORE, HAROLD V. HS
LIVERMORE, JEAN PY
LIVSEY, ROSEMARY EARNSHAW ED
LLOYD, EVERETT LI
LLOYD, ROBIN EC
LOBART, EDWARD HN PL
LOBDELL, HELEN BERNICE HN
LOBSENZ, NORMAN M. LJS
LOCKE, ALAIN LE ROY   STERN, BERNHARD J. (EDS.) AN SO
LOCKE, HARVEY J. SABAH, GEORGES THOMAS, MARY SO
LOCKE, RAYMOND FRIDAY HSW
LOCKWOOD, FRANK C. HA
LOCKWOOD, MYNA LJE SI
LOERA, FRANCISCO LOERA, ROMERO LOERA, JOSE ALVAREZ, MARIO ED
      SO
LOEVINGER, J. ED
LOFSTEDT, ANNA C. ED
LOFSTEDT, CHRISTINE HC SO

LORETAN, JOSEPH O. HSW
LORETAN, JOSEPH O. , ET AL EC SI
LORGE, I. ARSENIAN , S. ED
LORGE, IRVING DIAMOND, LORRAINE KRUGLOV ED
LOS ANGELES CHAMBER OF COMMERCE, RESEARCH DEPARTMENT EC HC
      SO
LOS ANGELES CITY HEALTH DEPARTMENT HC MD SO
LOS ANGELES CITY PLANNING COMMISSION EC HC SO
LOS ANGELES CITY SCHOOL DISTRICT B ED HC SO
LOS ANGELES CITY SCHOOLS ED HC LAE
LOS ANGELES COMMITTEE ON SCHOLARSHIPS EC ED HC
LOS ANGELES COUNTY BOARD OF EDUCATION B
LOS ANGELES COUNTY BUREAU OF INSPECTIONS HC MD SO
LOS ANGELES COUNTY COMMISSION ON HUMAN RELATIONS EC ED HC
      SO
LOS ANGELES COUNTY COMMITTEE FOR INTERRACIAL PROGRESS HC
      MD SO
LOS ANGELES COUNTY COORDINATING COUNCILS, INFORMATION DIVISION HC
      SI SO
LOS ANGELES COUNTY DEPARTMENT OF PUBLIC SOCIAL SERVICES EC
      HC SO
LOS ANGELES COUNTY GRAND JURY HC LW SO
LOS ANGELES COUNTY PROBATION OFFICE HC SO
LOS ANGELES COUNTY TUBERCULOSIS AND HEALTH ASSOCIATION HC
      MD SO
LOS ANGELES COUNTY YOUTH COMMITTEE HC SO
LOS ANGELES COUNTY, CALIFORNIA EC ED HC
LOS ANGELES COUNTY, CALIFORNIA. BOARD OF EDUCATION AN AT
      ED MU
LOS ANGELES COUNTY, CALIFORNIA, COUNTY SURVEYOR GE HC SO
LOS ANGELES COUNTY, CALIFORNIA, HUMAN RELATIONS COMMISSION HC
      LW SO
LOS ANGELES COUNTY, CALIFORNIA, SUPERINTENDENT OF SCHOOLS ED
      HC
LOS ANGELES DEPARTMENT OF CHARITIES HC SI SO
LOS ANGELES PUBLIC LIBRARY B
LOS ANGELES REGION WELFARE PLANNING COUNCIL HC SO
LOS ANGELES STAR HC NP
LOS ANGELES SUPERINTENDENT OF SCHOOLS OFFICE B ED HC
LOS ANGELES TIMES HC NP
LOS ANGELES TIMES EDUCATION SERVICES DEPARTMENT B
LOS ANGELES, CALIFORNIA. RESEARCH DEPARTMENT,
      WELFARE PLANNING COUNCIL EC SO
LOS ANGELESLOS ANGELES CHAMBER OF COMMERCE EC HC SI SO
LOS CUATRO LMA
LOS ESTADOS UNIDOS B
LOTT, V. N. FENWICK, V. M. EC HT
LOUVAIN, ROBERT. LJS
LOVE, CLARA M. EC HSW
LOVE, JOHNNIE ANDREW EC HM
LOVE, JOSEPH L. EC PL SO
LOVE, RUTH B. ED PY SC
LOVECRAFT, H. P. LI LMA
LOVELACE, MAUD HART HSW LI
LOW, ALICE HC LJS PL SI

MAGOFFIN, SUSAN (SHELBY) TJ
MAHAKIAN, CHARLES ED
MAHLER, THEODOR LMA
MAHON, EMMIE GIDDINGS W., AND KIELMAN, CHESTER V. HSW
MAHON, EMMIE WHEATLEY HSW
MAHON, EMMIE WHEATLY HSW
MAHONEY, MARY K. ED
MAHOOD, H. PL
MAIDD, PETER   MC COY, JOHN B
MAILTAND, SHERIDAN T., AND KNEBEL, STANLEY M. EC
MAISEL, ALBERT Q. SO
MAISEL, JAY MAX HM
MAISSIN, EUGENE HM HT
MAJOR, MABEL AND SMITH, REBECCA W., EDS. LI
MAJOR, MABEL SMITH, REBECCA PEARCE, T. M. B
MAJOR, MABEL, AND PEARCE, T. M. (EDS) LI
MAJOR, MABEL, SMITH, REBECCA W. AND PEARCE, T. M. LI
MALAGON-BARCELO, JAVIER HS LW
MALARET, AUGUSTO LA
MALDONADO, JESUS LMA ED
MALHERBE, E. G. ED
MALKOC, ANNA MARIA B
MALLERY, RICHARD D. LA
MALLOY, WILLIAM M. LW
MALONEY, THOMAS EC PL
MALONEY, THOMAS J. EC HN
MALSTEAD, ROGER HENRY LAE
MALTBY, WILLIAM S. HS
MAMIS, NANCY WILCOX, PRESTON B
MAMORU, STANLEY LA
MANAGERS, D. H. EC ED
MANCILLAS, STELLA LMA
MANCISIDOR, JOSE HM
MANFREDINI, JAMES MANFRED HS
MANGAN, FRANK HT
MANGELS, ANNA LA
MANGOLD, GEORGE B. AND HILL, LILLIAN B. EC SI
MANHEIM, HENRY AND CUMMINS, ALICE MU
MANHEIM, HENRY, AND CUMMINS, ALICE SO
MANJE CAPITAN, JUAN MATEO HM
MANLY, WILLIAM LEWIS HC
MANN, C. LA
MANN, EDWARD B. HN
MANN, VIRGINIA R. MD
MANNING, JOHN C. ED LAE
MANNING, WILLIAM RAY PL
MANNIX, DANIEL P. AND COWLEY, MALCOLM EC
MANSELL, MABEL JEANETTE LI
MANUEL, H. T. AND RATHER, A. ED
MANUEL, HERSCHEL T. ED
MANUEL, HERSCHEL T. AND HUGHES, LOIS ED
MANUEL, HERSCHEL T. AND WRIGHT C. E. ED
MANZO, RICARDO ED PY
MARIN, LUIS MUNOZ LMA
MARANON, GREGORIO LI

MEYER, MICHAEL C. HM PL SI
MEYER, SAMUEL L. AND CULLEN, ARTHUR J. ED
MEYERS, FREDERIC EC HT SO
MEYERSON, M. D. ED
MEZA LEON HC HM
MICHAEL, ALICE B
MICHEA, CLAUDE ANGUS PY
MICHEL, JOSEPH AN ED LAF LJS
MICHIGAN *A*F*L-*C*I*O NEWS EC SI
MICHIGAN STATE UNIVERSITY. LIBRARY B ED
MICHIGAN STATE UNIVERSITY. OFFICE OF THE VICE PRESIDENT
      FOR UNIVERSITY B EC SO
MICHIGAN UNIVERSITY INSTITUTE OF LABORATORIES AND INDUSTRIAL RELATIONS B
MICHIGAN. CIVIL RIGHTS COMMISSION EC ED LW PL SI SO
MICHIGAN. CIVIL RIGHTS COMMISSION. RESEARCH DIVISION LW
      SO
MICHIGAN. STATE BOARD OF EDUCATION ED LW
MICHIGAN. UNIVERSITY OF MICHIGAN B ED
MICHIGAN. CIVIL RIGHTS COMMISSION, COMISION DE DERECHOS CIVILES EC
      LW SO
MICHIGAN. COMISION DE DERECHOS CIVILES EC LW SI
MICHIGAN. PONTIAC SCHOOL DISTRICT EC LW SO
MICHIGAN, ADRIAN EC SO
MICKEY, BARBARA B
MID- WEST COUNCIL OF LA RAZA EC PL
MIDDAGH, JOHN HT SO
MIDDLETON, ANNIE LAURA HT PL
MIDDLETON, P. H. HM
MIDDLETON, RUSSELL, JR. HM SO
MIDWEST EDUCATORS' CONFERENCE AGAINST DISCRIMINATION ED LW
MIERA, GILBERT E. AN EC SI SO
MIGRANT EDUCATION CENTER B
MIGRANT HEALTH PROJECT MD SI
MIGUEL, FE ALEJO ED PY
MIKESELL, MARVIN W. GE HC
MILES, BERYL. AN HM
MILL, GLADWIN PL SO
MILLARES, CARLO B
MILLER, ALFRED JACOB AR TJ
MILLER, BONNIE BELLE ED SI
MILLER, CURTIS R. EC SO
MILLER, E. AND BUTTERBAUGH, W. F. ED
MILLER, E. T. HS HT TJ
MILLER, EDMUND THORNTON EC HT
MILLER, ELAINE KAY AN LMA
MILLER, FRANK EC SI
MILLER, GARY ALAN EC PL
MILLER, HELEN STRASHEIM, LORRAINE B
MILLER, HERMAN P. EC HUS
MILLER, JOAQUIN AN LI MU
MILLER, M. R. TANQUIST AN HS
MILLER, MARGARET B
MILLER, MICHAEL V. EC
MILLER, R. R. EC SO
MILLER, W. MU PY SO

MONROY PADILLA, NATALIC LJS
MONSEES, EDNA K., AND BERMAN, CAROL ED PY
MONTAGUE, ASHLEY AN
MONTAL SYSTEMS, INCORPORATED ED PL
MONTEBELLO, GEORGE BALLARD, LOWELL B
MONTEIRO, PALMYRA V. M. B GE
MONTELORES STUDIES CENTER STAFF B
MONTEVERDE, MILDRED AR
MONTEZ, PHILIP ED PY
MONTEZ, PHILIP, ET AL EC
MONTGOMERY, ELIZABETH RIDER HS
MONTGOMERY, ROBERT H. SO
MONTGOMERY, VAIDA STEWART, ED. LI
MONTGOMERY, WHITNEY LI
MONTHLY LABOR REVIEW EC
MONTIEL, MIGUEL AN SO
MONTIEL, OLVERA J., ED. SO
MONTLEZUN, BARON DE HUS TJ
MONTOYA, ANASTASIO ED
MONTOYA, JOSE LMA
MONTOYA, JUAN DE HN HS TJ
MOODY, ALAN LI
MOODY, RALPH LJE
MOONEY, GERTRUDE AN AR ED
MOONEY, HARRY JOHN, JR. LI
MOORE, CONRAD TAYLOR GE HSW
MOORE, DANIEL G. LI
MOORE, ERNEST B
MOORE, ETHEL AND CHAUNCEY O. AN HSW MU
MOORE, FARAONE ED MD
MOORE, HAROLD E., AND SCHUFLETOWSKI, CHARLES ED HSW SI
MOORE, HARRY T. LI
MOORE, HARRY T., ED. LI
MOORE, J. PRESTON HS HUS
MOORE, JOAN B
MOORE, JOAN W. EC ED HSW PL SO
MOORE, JOAN W. AND MITTELBACH, FRANK G. EC SO
MOORE, JOAN W., AND GUZMAN, RALPH AN EC SO
MOORE, JOAN, AND GUZMAN, RALPH EC PL SO
MOORE, JOHN BASSETT HM HSW HUS
MOORE, LUELLA SO
MOORE, MARILYN ED
MOORE, MILBURN R. MU
MOORE, RICHARD ROY WOODS HSW
MOORE, TRUMAN EC HSW SI
MOORE, TRUMAN E. EC SI
MOORE, VERA LEE ED
MOORE, W. E. EC PL SI
MOORE, WILMAN HARPER HT
MOORHEAD, MAX L. HM HN HS HSW
MOQUIN, WAYNE, AND VAN DOREN, CHARLES, EDS. HSW
MORA, JOSEPH JACINTO HC HSW
MORA, RICARDO LMA
MORALES JIMENEZ, ALBERTO B
MORALES- CARRION ARTURO HSW TJ

MORALES, ARMANDO ED LW MD PY SO
MORALES, DIONICIO EC ED HC
MORALES, DR. ARMANDC. LMA SO
MORALES, FRANCISCO C. LJS
MORALES, HENRY ED
MORALES, PADRON, FRANCISCO HS
MORALES, RAFAEL LJS
MORAN, AGNES B. EC LAE
MORAN, MATTIE BELLE SAUER ED LA
MOREAU DE SAINT- MERY, MEDERIC LOUIS ELIE HUS TJ
MOREFIELD, RICHARD F. HC
MOREHART, MARTHA JUNE HSW LI
MOREHEAD, CHARLES R. HUS TJ
MORELEON, ANGELINA C. DE. PY
MORENO, BERTHA LMA
MORENO, CARLOS LMA
MORENO, DANIEL B HM
MORENO, E. ED SO
MORENO, EDWARD ED SO
MORENO, EDWARD V. AN ED SO
MORENO, PABLO C. HM
MORENO, PHILLIP HECTCR AR ED
MORENO, RAQUEL LMA
MORENO, STEVE LMA
MOREY, ELIZABETH MAY HS
MORFI, AUGUSTIN HT
MORFI, FRAY JUAN AGUSTIN HS HT
MORGAN, BELDEN EC SC
MORGAN, DALE L HAMMCND, GEORGE P. B
MORGAN, DALE LOWELL HSW
MORGAN, H. WAYNE HUS
MORGAN, LEWIS HENRY AN SO
MORGAN, NEIL HSW
MORGAN, PATRICIA LW SI SO
MORGAN, THOMAS B. HT PL
MORIN, ALEXANDER EC SI
MORIN, KENNETH NOAH HT PY
MORIN, RAUL HUS SO
MORISSEY, RICHARD S. HSW
MORLOCK, LAURA L. PL SC
MORNER, MAGNUS AN
MORRELL, ELAINE LEWIS ED HT
MORRELL, WILLIAM PARKER HC
MORRILL, D. B. ED
MORRILL, SIBLEY S. HT
MORRIS, A. P. PL SO
MORRIS, ANN AXTELL HSW LI
MORRIS, EARL HALSTEAD AR HSW
MORRIS, EFFIE B
MORRIS, JOHN W. HSW
MORRIS, RICHARD B. HSW
MORRIS, WRIGHT LI
MORRISEY, RICHARD J. EC HS
MORRISON, CHARLOTTE AMOS ED PY
MORRISON, ETHEL M. SI

MORRISON, JAMES H. PY SO
MORRISSEY, P. PY SO
MORROW, JUDITH B
MORROW, WILLIAM W. HM HS
MORSE, FREDERIC C. EC HT
MORSE, H. GE HC
MORTON, F. R. ED LA
MORTON, JOHN A. EC SO
MORTON, OHLAND HM HSW HT
MORTON, ROBERT LEE, AND OTHERS LJS
MORTON, WARD MCKINNON EC PL
MOSELEY, ELIZABETH R. HT LI
MOSELY, EDWARD, ED. AN HSW
MOSES, BERNARD HS HSA
MOSES, MONTROSE J. AR AT FILM
MOSK, SANFORD A. EC HM
MOTOGAMA, E. C. ED
MOTOLINIA, TORIBIO HS
MOTT, FREDERICK D. MD SI
MOULTON, WILLIAM G. LA
MOUSTAFA, A. TAHER, AND WEISS, GERTRUDE EC MD
MOUTON, REV. RICHARD(EDS.) NP
MOWAT, OLIVE M. LA
MOYA, BENJAMIN S. AN RE
MOYERS, ROBERT ARTHUR ED HN
MOYLAN, SISTER MARY PRUDENCE, B. V. M. LI LMA
MOZA, H. LA PL
MUCKLEROY, ANNA HT
MUGICA, PEDRO DE LA
MUIR, JOHN HC
MULKY, CARL MD
MULLIGAN, RAYMOND A. AN EC PY SO
MULLIN, ROBERT N. HN HT
MULLINS, MARTHA MERSMAN ED PY
MULS, ERNEST E. EC
MULTI-ETHNIC MEDIA SELECTED BIBLIOGRAPHIES B
MULTI-ETHNIC RESOURCES B
MULTI-MEDIA PRODUCTIONS FILM
MULTI-MEDIA PRODUCTIONS, INC. FILM
MULVANEY, I. ED
MUMEY, NOLIE HSW LI
MUNICIPAL LEAGUE OF LOS ANGELES SI
MUNK, JOSEPH A. B
MUNOZ COTA, JOSE HM
MUNOZ, CARLOS PL SO
MUNOZ, CARLOS, JR. PL SO
MUNOZ, HENRY, JR. EC
MUNOZ, MAURILIO HN
MUNOZ, RAFAEL FELIPE HM HSW
MUNOZ, ROSALIO FLORIAN EC PY
MUNRO, F. HSW
MUNSON, JOHN ED PY
MUNTZ, SIDNEY W. AND WOLF, ERIC R. AN SO
MUNY, CHARLES CURTIS PL SC
MURBARGER, NELL AN HSW
MURDOCH, KATHARINE, NACCOW, DORIS, AND BERG, NETTIE LESSER LAE

NATIONAL CAPITAL SESQUICENTENNIAL COMMISSION AR
NATIONAL CATHOLIC WELFARE CONFERENCE. ADMINISTRATIVE BOARD EC SO
NATIONAL CATHOLIC WELFARE CONFERENCE. DEPARTMENT OF SOCIAL ACTION SO
NATIONAL CATHOLIC WELFARE COUNCIL. DEPARTMENT OF SOCIAL ACTION SO
NATIONAL CHILD LABOR COMMITTEE EC
NATIONAL CLEARINGHOUSE FOR MENTAL HEALTH INFORMATION B
NATIONAL COMMISSION ON LAW OBSERVANCE AND ENFORCEMENT LW SI
NATIONAL COMMISSION ON PROFESSIONAL RIGHTS AND RESPONSIBILITIES
     OF N E A ED
NATIONAL COMMITTEE ON EMPLOYMENT OF YOUTH B
NATIONAL COMMITTEE ON THE EDUCATION OF MIGRANT CHILDREN B
NATIONAL CONFERENCE OF CHRISTIANS AND JEWS B
NATIONAL CONFERENCE OF SOCIAL WORK SO
NATIONAL CONFERENCE ON EDUCATIONAL OPPORTUNITIES FOR
     MEXICAN AMERICANS ED
NATIONAL CONFERENCE ON SOCIAL WELFARE B SO
NATIONAL CONSORTIA FOR BILINGUAL EDUCATION B
NATIONAL CONVENTION OF EDUCATIONAL OPPORTUNITIES FOR
     MEXICAN AMERICANS ED
NATIONAL COUNCIL FOR SOCIAL STUDIES SO
NATIONAL COUNCIL FOR THE SPANISH-SPEAKING SO
NATIONAL COUNCIL OF TEACHERS OF ENGLISH. TASK FORCE ON TEACHING
     ENGLISH ED
NATIONAL COUNCIL ON NATURALIZATION AND CITIZENSHIP B ED
NATIONAL COUNCIL ON NATURALIZATION AND CITIZENSHIP COMMITTEE
     ON EDUCATIO B
NATIONAL EDUCATION ASSOCIATION B ED
NATIONAL EDUCATION ASSOCIATION OF THE U. S. DEPARTMENT OF
     SUPERVISORS A ED
NATIONAL EDUCATION ASSOCIATION OF THE U.S. ED
NATIONAL FARM WORKERS ASSOCIATION EC
NATIONAL INDUSTRIAL CONFERENCE BOARD SI
NATIONAL OPINION RESEARCH CENTER SO
NATIONAL UNDERWRITER EC SI
NAVA, JULIAN HSW
NAVARRO GARCIA, LUIS LMA
NAVARRO TOMAS, TOMAS LA
NAVARRO Y NORIEGA, FERNANDO HS
NAVARRO, ELISEO B SO
NAVARRO, J. L. LMA
NEAL, ARMINTA AR
NEAL, DOROTHY JENSEN LI
NEAL, ELMA ED
NEAL, JOE WEST PL
NEAR, ARTHUR WARD HS
NEEDLER, MARTIN C. HSA PL
NEFF, WALTER S. EC PL SO
NEHLS, EDWARD (ED) LI
NEIGHBORS, KENNETH HT
NEIGHBOURS, KENNETH FRANKLIN HT
NEIHARDT, JOHN G. HSW TJ
NEIL, PALMER MEREDITH EC
NEILL, STEPHEN CHARLES RE
NEIMAN, GILBERT PL
NELKIN, D. B SO
NELSON, A. B. HSW HT
NELSON, EASTIN, AND MEYERS, FREDERIC EC
NELSON, EDNA DEU PREE B HC
NELSON, EUGENE EC

PASSOW, A. HARRY ED
PAST, RAY (ET AL) ED
PASTOR, ANGELE, AND OTHERS LJS
PASTOR, ANGELES LJS
PATRIC, GLADYS EMELIA MD SO
PATRICK, REMBERT W PATRICK, ELEANOR B FISACKERLY, HESTER G. HS
PATTEE, RICHARD PL SO
PATTEN, LEWIS B. HSW
PATTEN, RODERICK B. HSW
PATTERSON, CHARLES J. ED PY SO
PATTERSON, JOHN CLARKE HM
PATTERSON, PAUL LI
PATTERSON, R. E. EC HT
PATTERSON, WILLIAM R. AND JOYCE, EUGENIA ED
PATTIE, JAMES O. TJ
PATTON , F. H. LW
PAUL BLACKWOOD (ED). LJS
PAUL BURNFORD FILM PRODUCTIONS ED
PAUL, BENJAMIN DAVID MD PY SO
PAUL, G. F. HS LI
PAUL, RODMAN W. HC HSW
PAULIN, ARTHURO D. GE HC HM
PAXSON, FREDERIC LOGAN HSW
PAYERAS, P. MARIANO HS
PAYNE, LEONIDAS W. HT
PAYNE, R. ED
PAYNE, VIOLA M. LI
PAYNE, WILLIAM EC LW
PAZ, FRANK X. SO
PAZ, OCTAVIO LMA
PEAK, GEORGE JOSEPH ED
PEAK, HORACE AN PY
PEAL, ELIZABETH LAMBERT, WALLACE PY
PEAL, LAMBERT PY
PEARCE, T. M. HN LA LI LMA
PEARCE, T. M. (ED) AN HN
PEARCE, T. M. MAJOR, MABEL, AND SMITH, REBECCA W. HSW LI
PEARCE, T. M., AND COOK, JIM HSW LI
PEARCE, T. M., AND THOMASON, A. P. (EDS) HSW LI
PEARCE, T.M. LA
PEARCE, T.M. HENDON, TELFAIR HSW LI
PEARCE, THOMAS M. HSW LA LI
PEARCE, W.M. HN
PEARSON, JIM BERRY HN
PEATTIE, LISA REDFIELD AN SO
PEAVEY, JOHN R. LI
PEAVY, CHARLES D. HT
PEAVY, CHARLES D., AND SIRINGO, CHARLES A. LI
PECK, ANNE MERRIMAN LJE
PECK, BARBARA PAULA EC
PECK, LEIGH ED LJE
PECK, ROBERT F. PY SC
PEDTK, DOROTHY, ET AL B
PEDTKE, DOROTHY A., (ET AL) B LAE
PEEK, LEIGH, AND HODGES, AMELIA BARTHLOME ED PY

PRESLEY, JAMES WRIGHT HS HUS
PRESS, ERNEST HUS SI
PRESSEY, S. L. ED PY
PRESSEY, S.L. ED PY
PRESTWOOD, NADINE H. HT
PREUSS, K. T. HSA
PRICE, ANNE BROYLES HM HUS
PRICE, GLENN W. HM HUS
PRICE, GRADY DANIEL HUS
PRICE, JAMES DAVID ED PY
PRICE, JOAN LJE
PRICE, JOHN A. AN SO
PRICE, THOMAS W. TJ
PRICHARD, MICHAEL B
PRICHARD, MICHAEL THOMAS ED
PRIDA, RAMON HUS
PRIDGEN, MRS. VELMA HILL HT
PRIESTLEY, H. I. HM
PRIESTLEY, HERBERT I. HM
PRIESTLEY, HERBERT INGRAM HS
PRIESTLY, HERBERT INGRAM B
PRIETO, MARIANA LJE LJS
PRIETO, MARIANA B. LJS
PRINCE, L. B. HN
PRINCE, L. BRAFORD SO
PRINCE, LE BARON BRADFORD HN
PRINCE, RUTH G. ED
PRINGLE, HENRY F. HUS
PRITCHARD, NANCY B
PRITCHARD, W. T. HN
PRITCHETT, HOWARD E. PL SI
PROBERT, ALAN HSW
PROBST, PIERRE LJS
PROCTER, BEN H. HT
PROCTOR, BEN H. LW
PROGRESSIVE EDUCATION ASSOCIATION, THE REPORTS AND RECORDS COMMITTEE ED
PROIETTI, KITTI JEAN LEE, AND VALLES, MARTIN SO
PROPER, EMBERSON EDWARD SI
PROTHEROE, DONALD WESLEY EC LA SO
PROVOST, F. LI
PROWLEDGE, FRED ED PY
PRUTER, KARL HS
PRYOR, GUY C. ED
PUBLIC AFFAIRS FILM
PUBLIC AFFAIRS INFORMATION SERVICE B
PUBLIC AFFAIRS PAMPHLETS EC SI
PUCKETT, FIDELIA M. HN
PUEBLO REGIONAL PLANNING COMMISSION SO
PUERTO RICAN STUDY, LANGUAGE GUIDE SERIES LAE
PUERTO RICO DEPARTMENT OF EDUCATION ED
PULLIS, JESSICA K. ED SI
PULSE, INC. EC
PURCELL, JOANNE BURLINGAME HS
PURCHAS, SAMUEL TJ
PURWIN, L. ED

ROBERTS, HELEN, M. AN HS
ROBERTS, HOLLAND EC PL SI
ROBERTS, HOLLAND D. AND KAULFERS, WALTER V. ED LA
ROBERTS, K. L. EC SI SC
ROBERTS, LAUNEY F. ED PY SC
ROBERTS, MARTA LI
ROBERTS, MARY LAKE ED
ROBERTS, MARY MARSHALL ED PY
ROBERTS, NEIL ALDEN ED LA
ROBERTS, WARREN LI
ROBERTSON, CLYDE REEVES ED PY
ROBERTSON, DONALD AR HS
ROBERTSON, FRANK DELBERT HS
ROBERTSON, JACK ED SC
ROBERTSON, JAMES A. (TRANS AND ED) HS HUS
ROBERTSON, JAMES ALEXANDER (ED) HS HUS
ROBERTSON, LEON S. MD SC
ROBERTSON, O. HM PL
ROBERTSON, WILLIAM SPENCE HM
ROBINSON, ALFRED HC
ROBINSON, BENELLE H. LJE
ROBINSON, BENNELLE LJE
ROBINSON, CECIL B HM HS HSW HT LI
ROBINSON, DUAN SO
ROBINSON, DUNCAN W. HT
ROBINSON, FAYETTE HM
ROBINSON, G. C. HT LI
ROBINSON, H. GE HSA
ROBINSON, JACOB S. HSW TJ
ROBINSON, NORMA J. MD SI
ROBINSON, P. F. ED
ROBINSON, WILLIAM WILCCX HC HS
ROBLEDA, GOMEZ JOSE SI
ROBLES, ERNEST A. ED PY SC
ROBLES, MIGUEL A. HM
ROBLES, VITO ALESSIO (ED) HS TJ
ROCA, PABLO ED PY
ROCCO, RAYMOND A. AN PY SO
ROCHA, JOSE G. B
ROCHE, JOHN PEARSON PL SO
ROCQ. MARGARET MILLER (ED) B HC
ROCQ, MARGARET B
RODARI, GIANNI LJS
RODEE, NONA ED
RODMAN, SELDEN HS
RODRIGUEA, DARIO E. ED PY
RODRIGUEZ MARIN, F. AN HS
RODRIGUEZ MONDRAGON, FILEMON HC HS
RODRIGUEZ SALA DE GOMEZGIL, MARIA LUISA PY SO
RODRIGUEZ-PACHECO, OSVALDO EC ED
RODRIGUEZ, ARMANDO EC
RODRIGUEZ, ARMANDO M. ED
RODRIGUEZ, DAVID AND LELEVIER, BENJAMIN ED HSW
RODRIGUEZ, DAVID L. ED HSW
RODRIGUEZ, EUGENE, JR. HT PL

ROOSEVELT, THEODORE HSW LI
ROOT, FRANK AND CONNELLEY, WM. HC HUS
ROOTS, FLOY EULA ED
ROQUERMORE, LOIS ED
ROSALDO, RENATO LA LMA SO
ROSALES, ARTURO LMA
ROSALES, FRANCISCO ED
ROSALES, JOHN A. ED
ROSBACH, EDITH VIRGINIA HUNTER HS HSW
ROSE, ARNOLD M. (ED) AN SO
ROSE, ARNOLD MARSHALL AN SO
ROSE, ARNOLD MARSHALL, AND ROSE, CAROLINE (EDS) AN SO
ROSE, FRED D. B
ROSE, PETER ISAAC AN SO
ROSEN, CARL AND ORTEGO, PHILIP B
ROSEN, CARL L. ED LA LAE
ROSEN, CARL L. AND ORTEGO, PHILIP D. ED LAE
ROSEN, CARL ORTEGO, PHILIP B
ROSEN, EVELYN R. HSW
ROSENAU, FRED S. AN ED
ROSENBLAT, ANGEL AN
ROSENBLATT, JOAN BARBOZA SHUFRO AN MD
ROSENFELD, ALBERT ED PY SO
ROSENQUIST, CARL M. PY SO
ROSENQUIST, CARL M. AND BROWDER, WALTER G. SO
ROSENQUIST, CARL M. AND MCGARGEE, EDWIN I. AN SO
ROSENQUIST, CARL M. AND MEGARGEE, EDWIN I. AN
ROSENSTONE, ROBERT A. AND BOSKIN, J. PL SO
ROSENTHAL JACOBSON, L. B
ROSING, R. SO
ROSKELLEY, R. W. AN EC SI SO
ROSS, EDWARD A. HM
ROSS, FRED W. SO
ROSS, J. C. EC ED
ROSS, MALCOLM SO
ROSS, MARY HS HSW
ROSS, MARY AND BOLTON, HERBERT EUGENE HS HUS
ROSS, PATRICIA TJ
ROSS, PATRICIA E. LJS
ROSS, STANLEY B
ROSS, STANLEY ROBERT HM
ROSS, VICTORIA LYNN ED LAE
ROSS, WILLIAM T. AN SO
ROTUNDA, DOMINIC P. SMITH, WILLARD M. AND WRIGHT, EVALINE UHL LAE
ROUCEK, J. S. ED SI
ROUNDY, R. W. SI
ROURKE, CONSTANCE HUS LI
ROUSE, LURA NELSON ED
ROUSSEAU, MANUEL ESTRADA B
ROWAN, BOB KENDALL, ELLIS, AND STROUD, MARY ED
ROWAN, HELEN EC LI LW SO
ROWELL, CHESTER H. HM SI
ROY, ADDIE MAY HT
ROY, MARY MARGUERITE HSW HT HUS
ROYBAL, EDWARD PL SO

SAENZ, AARON HM
SAENZ, ALFREDO N. ED
SAENZ, GERARDO LMA
SAENZ, J. LUZ SO
SAENZ, M. PRIESTLY, H. I. SO
SAENZ, MOISES EC
SAENZ, O. L. SO
SAENZ, PILAR ED
SAER, D. J. ED
SAER, H. ED
SAER, HYELLA ED
SAFFIETTI, JAMES P. ED PY
SAGAR, KEITH LI
SAGE, RUFUS B. TJ
SAHAGUN, BERNARDINO DE HS
SAINT JOHN, BEREA EDITH SO
SAKOLSKI, AARON M. HSW
SALADINI, VICTOR EC
SALAS, FLOYD AN
SALAS, RUBIO HN
SALAZ, RUBEN DARIO LMA
SALAZAR ROVIROSA, ALFONSO GE
SALAZAR, HERMENCIA CORELLA ED
SALAZAR, JOHN H. HSA
SALAZAR, RUBEN LMA
SALCEDO, CONSUELO SC
SALINAS, GUADALUPE SC
SALINAS, GUADLUPE SO
SALINAS, JOSE LAZARO SI
SALINAS, LUIS OMAR LMA
SALINAS, LUIS OMAR AND FADERMAN, LILLIAN (EDS). LMA
SALINAS, OMAR LMA
SALINAS, RICARDO LMA
SALINAS, RODOLFO LMA
SALPOINTE, JEAN BAPTISTE HN
SAMANIEGO, LA FONTAINE, IRIARTE, AND OTHERS LJS
SAMISH, ARTHUR H. THOMAS, BOB HC
SAMORA, JULIAN AN ED MD SI SO
SAMORA, JULIAN (ED) SO
SAMORA, JULIAN WATSON, JAMES B. SO
SAMORA, JULIAN AND BARRETT, D. N. SO
SAMORA, JULIAN AND BEEGLE, J. A. (EDS) MD SO
SAMORA, JULIAN AND D'ANTONIO, W. V. SO
SAMORA, JULIAN AND DEANE, W. N. LA SO
SAMORA, JULIAN AND LAMANNA, RICHARD A. SO
SAMORA, JULIAN AND SAUNDERS, LYLE MD SO
SAMORA, JULIAN AND WATSON, J. B. LA SO
SAMORA, JULIAN BARRETT, D. N. SO
SAMORA, JULIAN BEEGLE, J. A. SO
SAMORA, JULIAN BORDA, ORLANDO FALS DE PINEDA, VIRGINIA SO
SAMORA, JULIAN D'ANTONIO, W. V. SO
SAMORA, JULIAN DEANE, W. N. SO
SAMORA, JULIAN GALARZA, E. GALLEGOS, H. SO
SAMORA, JULIAN LAMANNA, RICHARD A. SO
SAMORA, JULIAN LARSON, RICHARD F. SO
SAMORA, JULIAN PLAJA, ANTONIO ORDONEZ COHEN, LUCY M. SO

SAMORA, JULIAN SAUNDERS, L. LARSON, R. F. SO
SAMORA, JULIAN SAUNDERS, LYLE SO
SAMORA, JULIAN SAUNDERS, LYLE AND LARSON, R. F. MD SO
SAMORA, JULIAN SAUNDERS, LYLE LARSON, R. F. SO
SAMORA, JULIAN WATSON, J. B. SO
SAMORA, JULIAN, BORDA, ORLANDO FALS AND DE PINEDA, VIRGINIA ED
    SO
SAMORA, JULIAN, GALARZA, E. AND GALLEGOS, H. SO
SAMORA, JULIAN, PLAJA, ANTONIO ORDONEZ AND COHEN, LUCY M. SO
SAMORA, JULIAN, SAUNDERS, L. AND LARSON, R. F. MD SO
SAMPSON, O. ED SI
SAN ANTONIO CITY PLANNING DEPARTMENT EC
SAN ANTONIO HOUSING AUTHORITY EC
SAN ANTONIO INDEPENDENT SCHOOL DISTRICT ED
SAN ANTONIO PUBLIC HEALTH DEPARTMENT SO
SAN ANTONIO SOCIAL WELFARE ASSOCIATION, EDUCATIONAL
        COMMITTEE ON RELIEF SO
SAN ANTONIO URBAN RENEWAL AGENCY SO
SAN BERNARDINO AND RIVERSIDE COUNTIES B
SAN DIEGO CITY SCHOOL DISTRICT B
SAN DIEGO CITY SCHOOLS B ED
SAN DIEGO PUBLIC LIBRARY B
SAN DIEGO SCHOOLS B ED
SAN DIEGO STATE COLLEGE PL SO
SAN DIEGO STATE COLLEGE LIBRARY B
SAN DIEGO, CALIFORNIA, CITY SCHOOLS AN EC ED HSW SO
SAN FERNANDO STATE COLLEGE B
SAN FERNANDO VALLEY STATE COLLEGE B
SAN FRANCISCO BOARD OF SUPERVISORS HC
SAN FRANCISCO UNIFIED SCHOOL DISTRICT ED
SAN JOAQUIN COUNTY LIBRARY B
SAN JOSE EXPERIMENTAL SCHOOL ED LAE
SAN JOSE TRAINING SCHOOL ED
SAN JOSE UNIFIED SCHOOL DISTRICT ED
SAN JOSE, CALIFORNIA. SAN JOSE UNIFIED SCHOOL DISTRICT LMA
SAN MATEO COUNTY OFFICE OF EDUCATION ED
SANCHEZ ALONSO, BENITO B HS
SANCHEZ BARBA, MARIO HERNANDEZ HS
SANCHEZ LAMEGO, MIGUEL A. HT
SANCHEZ NAVARRO HT
SANCHEZ-NAVARRO, CARLOS HT
SANCHEZ, A. M. ED
SANCHEZ, ARMAND EC
SANCHEZ, ARMAND J. EC
SANCHEZ, DR. GEORGE I. (ED) B EC ED
SANCHEZ, FRANK ED
SANCHEZ, GEORGE I. ED HM
SANCHEZ, GEORGE I. AND PUTNAM, HOWARD B
SANCHEZ, GEORGE I. PUTMAN, HOWARD ED
SANCHEZ, GEORGE I., AND SAUNDERS, LYLE ED
SANCHEZ, GEORGE I SAUNDERS, LYLE ED
SANCHEZ, GEORGE I98 AND EASTLACK, CHARLES L. ED
SANCHEZ, JOSE MARIA HT TJ
SANCHEZ, L.G.G. ED
SANCHEZ, LIONEL ED
SANCHEZ, LUISA G. G. SANCHEZ, GEORGE I. ED

SONNICHSEN. C. L. B
SONNICHSEN, C. L. B
SONNICHSEN, CHARLES LELAND HSW LI
SONNICHSEN, CHARLES LELAND MC KINNEY, M. G. HSW LI
SONQUIST, HANNE D. AND KAMII, CONSTANCE K. HSW LI
SORENSEN, VIRGINIA LI
SORENSON, ROY SO
SORVIG, RALPH HS LA
SOSIN, JACK M. HSW
SOUKUP, JAMES RUDOLPH MC CLESKY, CLIFRON HOOLOWAY, HARRY HT
      PL
SOUSTELLE, JACQUES HM
SOUTHARD, J. K. ED SI
SOUTHARD, J. K. ET AL ED SI
SOUTHERN COLORADO STATE COLLEGE B
SOUTHERN METHODIST UNIVERSITY. INSTUTUTE OF PUBLIC AFFAIRS EC
      SO
SOUTHWEST COUNCIL OF FOREIGN LANGUAGE TEACHERS ED
SOUTHWEST COUNCIL OF FOREIGN LANGUAGE TEACHERS CONFERENCE,1965 ED
      PL SO
SOUTHWEST COUNCIL OF LA RAZA B ED FILM SO
SOUTHWEST COUNCIL ON THE EDUCATION OF SPANISH SPEAKING PEOPLE ED
      PY SO
SOUTHWEST COUNCIL ON THE EDUCATION OF SPANISH-SPEAKING PEOPLE ED
SOUTHWEST EDUCATIONAL DEVELOPMENT LABORATORY ED SO
SOUTHWEST NETWORK, STUDY COMMISSION ON UNDERGRADUATE EDUCATION
      AND THE E ED
SOUTHWEST TEXAS STATE TEACHERS COLLEGE AR ED HUS SO
SOUTHWEST TEXAS STATE TEACHERS COLLEGE (SOUTHWEST TEXAS STATE
      UNIVERSITY ED
SOUTHWESTERN COOPERATIVE ECUCATIONAL LABORATORY AN B ED LI
      SO
SOUTHWESTERN COOPERATIVE ECUCATIONAL LABORATORY, INC. ED
SOUTHWESTERN COUNCIL OF LA RAZA B
SOWELL, EMMIE I ED SO
SPALDING, N. ED
SPAR, JEROME LJS
SPARKS, DADE SO
SPARKS, EARLE SYLVESTER HC HS
SPAULDING, CHARLES B. EC SO
SPELL, JEFFERSON REA ED LAF
SPELL, LOTA M. B ED HS HSA HSW
SPELL, MRS. LOTA MAY HARRIGAN ED HS MU
SPENCE, A. G., ET A. ED
SPENCE, ALLYN GAIVAIN EC SO
SPENCE, CLARK C. EC HSW
SPENCE, LEWIS HM
SPERRY, ARMSTRONG LI LJE
SPICER, EDWARD AN HA HSW HUS
SPICER, EDWARD B. AN HS
SPICER, EDWARD H. AN HS HSW
SPICER, EDWARD HOLLAND (ED.) EC
SPIELBERG, JOSEPH AN MD
SPIESS, JAN PL
SPILKA, BERNARD GILL, LOIS ED PY
SPIRO, MELFORD AN
SPLAWN, MARY RUTH GE HSW HT

SPLEVACK, YETLA LJE
SPOERL, D. T. ED PY
SPOLSKY, BERNARD ED LA
SPRADLIN, T. RICHARD LMA
SPRAGGIA, MARTIN PY SO
SPRAGUE, JOHN T. HS HUS
SPRAGUE, MARSHALL HSW
SPRAGUE, WILLIAM FORREST HM
SPRATLING, WILLIAM PHILIP LI
SPRATT, JOHN S. EC HT
SPRINKLE, EUNICE CAROLINE ED PY
ST. JOHN, C. W. ED PY
STABB, MARTIN S. HM
STACY, MAY H. LI
STAHORN, CARRIE A. HSW
STAMBAUGH, J. LEE   STAMBAUGH, LILLIAN J. HT
STAMBAUGH, JACOB LEE EC HT
STAMPS, PEARL PAULINE HC
STANCHFIELD, J. M.   HOVEY, B. ED PY
STANDEFER, HARMON BISHOP EC
STANDERFORD, BETWY LAE
STANEK, MURIEL LJE LJS
STANFORD UNIVERSITY B
STANFORD, M. R. ED PY
STANLEY, F. ED
STANLEY, GRACE C. EC ED SO
STANLEY, MEMOREE SUE OSBORN LA
STANLEY, OMA GE HA
STANLEY, RAMOND WALLACE ED SO
STANTON, ROBERT BREWSTER LI
STARK, RICHARD B. AN HN HS
STARK, W. A. ED PY
STARKEY, R. J. ED PY
STARNES, GARY BERT HS HT
STARR-HUNT, JACK SI
STARR, F. HM
STARR, FREDERICK HM
STAVENHAGEN, RODOLFO EC
STEAKLEY, DAN LEWIS HT
STECK, FRANCIS B
STECK, FRANCIS BORGIA HS HT
STECKMESSER, KENT LADD LI
STEELE, JAMES W. LI TJ
STEEN, MARGARET TROTTER EC ED PY
STEEN, RALPH W. (ED.) HT
STEEN, RALPH W.   DONECKER, FRANCES HT
STEGLICH, W. G. EC ED SO
STEGNER, JOHN F. EC SO
STEGNER, WALLACE E. LI SO
STEIGER, A. LA
STEIN, LISA S. PY SO
STEIN, Z.   SUSSER, M. PY SO
STEINBECK, JOHN LI
STEINER, EDWARD ALFRED LI
STEINER, ERNEST SI

TORRES, JOSE ACOSTA LMA
TORRES, LUCY LMA
TORRES, LUIS LLORENS LMA
TORRES, RIOSECO, ARTURC HSA LMA
TORRES, SALVADOR RCBERTO AR LMA
TOSCANO, SALVADCR AR HM
TOULMIN, HARRY A. HM HUS
TOULOUSE, JOSEPH H. HS HT
TOULOUSE, JOSEPH H., JR. AN B HN HS
TOUSSAINT, MANUEL AR HS
TOWE, EMILY RE SC
TOWNE, CHARLES WAYLAND HSW
TOWNSEND, E. E. HT
TOWSEND, E. E. HT
TOZZER, ALFRED M. HM
TRAGER, H. AND YARROW, M. R. ED SO
TRASIN, WALTER SC
TRASK, DAVID F. B
TRASK, DAVID MOYER, MICHAEL C. AND TRASK, ROGER R. (EDS) B
        HSA HUS
TRAVEN, B. LI
TREADWELL, EDWARD EC HSW
TREFF, S. L. ED
TREJO, A.D. B
TREJO, ALEX T. ED SC
TREJO, ARNULFO B
TREJO, ARNULFO D. EC LMA
TREMAYNE, FRANK G. HC HM
TRENNERT, ROBERT ANTHONY HUS
TRENT, ELWOOD SANFCRD AR
TRESOLINI, ROCCO J. PL
TREUTLEIN, THEODORE E. HC
TREUTLEIN, THEODORE E. (TRANS AND ED) HS HSW
TREVINO B. G. ED PY
TREVINO, B. G. ED PY
TREVINO, ELIZABETH LI SO
TREVINO, ELIZABETH BCRTCN DE LI SO
TRILLINGHAM, CLINTON CONROY AND HUGHES, MARIE M. ED SO
TRIMBLE, GLEN W. DIRECTOR, HOME MISSIONS RESEARCH
        BUREAU OF RESEARCH AND EC SO
TROIKE, RUDOLPH C. E LAE
TROLLOPE, FRANCES SC
TROWBRIDGE, EDWARD D. HM
TROXEL, O. C. HUS
TROYER, MRS. L. HM RE
TRUJILLC, LUIS M. LA
TRUJILLO, MARCELA L. EC
TRUJILLO, MARCELLA EC
TRUJILLO, RAFAEL HM HS
TSUZAKI, STANLEY M. LA
TUBBS, LOWELL LESTER. EC HSW SI
TUCK RUTH D. AN HC SO
TUCK, RUTH D. AN HC SO
TUCKER, DOLORES AN MU
TUCKER, MARY B

WITHDRAWAL